CHILTON'S
Car Care
Guide

1992 EDITION

A Chek-Chart Publication

H.M. Gousha

2001 The Alameda, P.O. Box 49006
San Jose, CA 95161-9006
Simon & Schuster

I

ACKNOWLEDGEMENTS

In producing this Guide, Chek-Chart has relied on the cooperation and assistance of the manufacturers whose products are included in the text. Without the help of the many marketing, engineering, service, and publications departments involved, this work would not have been possible.

At Chek-Chart Publications, the following individuals contributed to this work: Robert W. Colver, Editor; William J. Turney, Arnold Czarnecki, Tom Sullivan, Cathy Godwin, Researcher/Writers; John Badenhop, Gerald McEwan, F. J. Zienty, Graphic Artists; Daniel Doornbos, Production Manager; Lucille Dietrich, Virginia McConnell, Production Assistants; Maria Glidden, Diane Maurice, Typographers; Ramona Torres, Production Coordinator. The entire project was under the direction of Roger Fennema, Executive Editor.

The publisher has made every reasonable effort to insure that the material in this book is as accurate and up-to-date as possible. However, neither Chek-Chart nor any of its related companies can be held responsible for mistakes or omissions, or for changes in procedures or specifications by equipment manufacturers or suppliers.

Read This First!

The *Car Care Guide* is designed to provide essential service information for all domestic cars, light trucks, and most imports. It is a complete directory of service and maintenance specifications that you, the technician, will need to properly care for your customers' vehicles in accordance with vehicle manufacturers' service recommendations. The *Car Care Guide* can be one of the most useful tools available, providing you take a few minutes to learn how to use it. This brief introduction to the *Guide* will show you:

- How to locate information
- How the *Guide* is arranged
- How to use the *Guide* to sell service.

How to Locate Information

The key to finding information in this *Guide* lies in the two-part index. You will notice that shaded tabs are visible on the edge of each page when you close the book. These tabs correspond to the index page at the front of the book. Lubrication and preventative maintenance information in the first half of this book are keyed to the grey tabs, and underhood service information and specifications in the second half of this book are keyed to the black tabs, all arranged alphabetically by vehicle manufacturer.

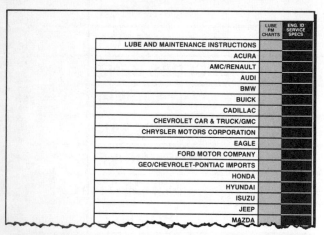

As an alternative, you can use another index located on pages VI through VII. This index is an alphabetical listing by model and year, with corresponding page numbers for lubrication charts and underhood service charts.

MODEL/YEAR		SERVICE DIAGRAMS	LUBE PM	ENG. ID TUNE-UP
Fleetwood	1983-92	37-38	39-42	55
Fox	1987-92	228-229	231	221
FX	1987-88	217-219	222	212
Galant	1985-92	167-168	170-172	159
Geo	1989-92	126-127	128-131	122
GL (Subaru)	1983-89	214	215-216	207

How the Guide Is Arranged

So that you can quickly find the information you need, your *Car Care Guide* is divided into three sections:

- **Lubrication and Maintenance Information**, which includes lube and maintenance instructions, lubrication diagrams and specifications, and preventative maintenance schedules
- **Capacities; Tire and Wheel Data; Tables**, which includes cooling and air conditioning system capacities, cooling system air bleed locations, wheel and tire specifications, and wheel-nut torque values
- **Underhood Service Information**, which includes underhood service instructions, diagrams, and specifications.

Lubrication and Maintenance Information

The first section of the *Car Care Guide*, which is keyed with the grey index tabs, contains information you need to lubricate and maintain customers' vehicles according to the vehicle manufacturers' specifications. This section begins with general service instructions, including:

- Crankcase Service
- Engine Systems
- Emission Controls
- Drivetrain Service
- Chassis Service
- Wheel Bearing Service
- Brakes and Tires
- Air Conditioning.

Following these instructions are Lubrication and Preventative Maintenance (Lube/PM) charts for domestic cars, light trucks, and popular imports. Chassis and engine diagrams show service lubrication points. Tables on the pages following these diagrams list lubricant capacities and recommendations, which are abbreviated on the charts. Use the "Key To Lubricants" to determine what the abbreviations mean. For example, HB stands for Hydraulic Brake Fluid, SAE J1703 or DOT-3 or -4, as indicated on the Key.

An important feature of the Lube/PM charts is the factory maintenance schedule for each vehicle. These charts list the services required at specific time or mileage intervals by the manufacturers. A table containing lubrication information for less popular imports completes the lubrication section of your *Guide*.

TURBOCHARGED ENGINES
EVERY 3 MO/3 MI—5 KM
Crankcase . . . . change oil

Oil filter . . . . replace
Initial service, then every other oil change

EVERY 6 MONTHS
Brake master cylinder . . . . check level **HB**

Clutch free pedal travel . . . . . check/adjust
Front wheel drive models, every 5 mi (8 km)

Power steering reservoir . . check level **PS**

Capacities; Tire and Wheel Data; Tables

Following the lubrication section are tables listing cooling and air conditioning system capacities, cooling system air bleed locations, and tire pressures, sizes, and wheel-nut torques for domestic cars, light trucks and vans, and popular imports.

Underhood Service Information

The last section of the *Guide*, which is keyed to the black tabs, includes the specifications and instructions you need to perform underhood service on 1983-92 domestic cars, light trucks, and most imports. This section begins with instructions related to the underhood service specifications. Refer to these guidelines whenever how-to questions arise:

- General Information
- Electrical and Ignition Systems
- Fuel Systems
- Engine Mechanical
- Engine Computer Systems.

Following these instructions are Underhood Service Specifications, which are arranged alphabetically by vehicle manufacturer. Information in this section includes: engine identification information, cylinder numbering, firing order, and timing mark diagrams, followed by specifications necessary to perform underhood service.

Using the specification tables

To use the specification tables properly, you must determine which engine is in the vehicle you are servicing. Turn to the appropriate manufacturer's section, and locate the Engine Identification table. Use the vehicle identification number (VIN) on the vehicle and our table to identify the following:

- Model year of the car
- Engine code location
- Engine code
- Engine displacement, type of fuel system, and horsepower.

Once you know exactly which engine you are working on, using the diagrams and charts is simple. Following the engine codes are diagrams showing cylinder numbering sequences, firing order, and timing marks for each engine

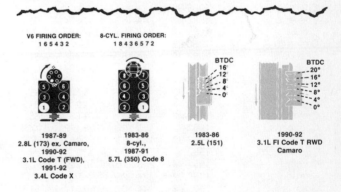

listed. Then complete specifications and notes required to test and diagnose engine electrical, ignition, fuel, mechanical, and computer systems are listed.

How to Use the Guide to Sell Service

Your *Car Care Guide* can help increase profits every time you service a car because it provides you and your customer with the manufacturer's recommended services and service intervals required to properly maintain a vehicle. Many customers will simply get an annual tune-up and lube job, or they will bring in their cars for service when they "think" it is time. Others will wait until the vehicle is not operating properly before having it serviced. Very few customers consistently have their cars serviced according to the factory recommendations.

You can do your customers a favor by using the *Car Care Guide* to point out the factory-recommended services. For the customer it is better service — for you it is greater profit. Once you make a habit of using the *Guide* in this way, you will find it easy to sell more service because the *Guide* will do it for you. The 1992 *Car Care Guide* is the best tool you have to increase the quality and profitability of your business.

MODEL/YEAR		SERVICE DIAGRAMS	LUBE PM	ENG. ID TUNE-UP	MODEL/YEAR		SERVICE DIAGRAMS	LUBE PM	ENG. ID TUNE-UP
Monaco	1990-92	100	101	97	Stanza	1983-92	172-175	176-178	167
Monte Carlo	1983-88	44-46	47-51	61	Starion	1983-89	162-163	165-168	159
MR2	1985-92	213-215	217-219	212	Starlet	1983-84	213-215	216-217	212
Mustang	1983-92	103-105	106-112	100	Stealth	1991-92	77-78	83	85
MX-3	1992	150-152	155	148	Stellar	1985-87	135	136	135
MX-6	1988-92	150-152	155	148	Sterling	1987-89	—	234	—
M3	1987-92	27	29	42	Storm	1990-92	126-127	129	122
M5	1987-92	27	29	42	Stylus	1990-92	139-140	142	139
M6	1987-89	27	29	42	Summit	1989-92	100	102	97
M30	1990-92	—	233	—	Sunbird	1983-92	194-196	201-205	189
					Sunburst	1985-87	126-127	128	122
New Yorker	1983-92	69-70	71-76	77	Sundance	1987-92	69-70	75-76	77
Ninety-Eight	1983-92	182-184	185-190	177	Supra	1983-92	213-215	216-219	212
Nova	1985-88	126-127	128	122	SVX	1992	—	212	106
NX	1991-92	176-179	182	167	Swift	1989-92	—	234	—
NSX	1991-92	—	233	—					
					Talon	1990-92	100	102	97
Omega	1983-85	182-184	185-187	177	Taurus	1986-92	103-105	109-112	100
Omni	1983-90	69-70	71-76	77	TC by Maserati	1989-91	69-70	76	77
Optima	1989-91	194-196	205	189	Tempest	1988-89	194-196	201	189
					Tempo	1984-92	103-105	107-112	100
Parisienne	1983-86	194-196	201-205	189	Tercel	1983-92	213-215	216-219	212
Park Avenue	1983-92	30-32	33-36	46	Thunderbird	1983-92	103-105	106-112	100
Passat	1989-92	224-225	227	221	Topaz	1984-92	103-105	109-112	100
Phoenix	1983-84	194-196	197-199	189	Toronado	1983-92	182-184	185-190	177
Pony	1984-87	135	136	135	Town Car	1983-92	103-105	106-112	100
Precidia	1992	150-152	155	148	Town & Country	1983-92	69-70	71-76	77
Precis	1987-92	167-168	171-172	159	Tracer	1987-92	103-105	110-112	100
Prelude	1983-91	132	133-134	128	Trans AM	1983-92	194-196	201-205	189
Premier	1988-92	100	101-102	97	Tredia	1983-88	163-164	165-167	159
Previa	1991-92	213-215	219	148	Troféo	1989-92	182-184	190	177
Prizm	1989-92	126-127	130	122	Turismo	1983-87	69-70	71-75	77
Probe	1989-92	103-105	111-112	100					
Protegé	1990-92	150-152	155	148	Vigor	1992	17	18	28
Pulsar	1983-90	176-179	180-185	167	V8 Quattro	1989-92	24	26	36
Quantum	1983-88	224-225	227-228	221	XJ6	1983-92	—	233	—
Quattro	1983-87	24	25	36	XT Coupe	1985-91	210	212	207
Q45	1990-92	—	233	—	XT6	1985-91	210	212	207
Rabbit	1983-84	224-225	227-228	221	Zephyr	1983	103-105	106	110
Reatta	1988-91	30-32	36	46					
Regal	1983-92	30-32	33-36	46	80, 80 Quattro	1988-92	24	25-26	36
Reliant	1983-89	69-70	71-76	77	88 Royale	1990-92	182-184	190	177
Riviera	1983-92	30-32	33-36	46	90, 90 Quattro	1988-91	24	25-26	36
Roadmaster	1991-92	30-32	36	46	100, 100 Quattro	1989-92	24	26	36
Rodeo	1991-92	139-140	144	139	190 Series	1984-92	159	160-161	155
RX-7	1983-91	150-152	153	148	200, 200 Quattro	1989-91	24	26	36
					200SX	1983-88	172-175	176-177	167
Sable	1986-92	103-105	110-112	100	210	1983	172-175	176	167
Sapporo	1983	77-78	79	85	240 Series (M.B.)	1983	159	160	155
Scirocco	1983-89	224-225	227	221	240 Series (Volvo)	1983-92	229	230-232	226
Scorpio	1988-89	113	113	100	240SX	1989-92	172-175	181	167
Scoupe	1991-92	135	138	135	260 Series (M.B.)	1987-89	159	160	155
SC 300	1992	—	233	—	280ZX (Nissan)	1983	172-175	176	167
SC 400	1992	—	233	—	300 Series (M.B.)	1983-92	159	160-161	155
Sentra	1983-92	172-175	176-178	167	300ZX (Nissan)	1984-92	172-175	180-181	167
Serenia	1992	150-152	155	148	318i	1983-92	27	29	42
Seville	1983-92	37-38	39-42	55	320i	1983	27	28	42
Shadow	1987-92	69-70	75-76	77	323	1986-92	150-152	154-155	148
Skyhawk	1983-89	30-32	33-36	46	325e, 325i	1984-92	27	29	42
Skylark	1983-92	30-32	33-36	46	350 SD, SDL	1991	159	160	155
Somerset Regal	1985-87	30-32	35-36	46	380 Series	1983-85	159	160	155
Sonata	1989-92	135	137-138	135	400	1983-92	159	160	155
Spectrum	1985-89	126-127	128-129	122	405	1989-92	191	193	185
Spider	1983-90	—	233	—	420 Series	1986-91	159	160-161	155
Spirit (AMC)	1983	19	20	31	500 Series (M.B.)	1984-92	159	160-161	155
Spirit (Dodge)	1989-92	69-70	76	77	504	1983-84	191	192	185
Sports Coupe (SC)	1992	213	213	206	505	1983-92	191	192-193	185
Sports Sedan (SL, SL1)	1992	213	213	206	524td, 525, 528e	1983-92	27	28-29	42
					533i, 535i	1983-92	27	29	42
Sports Touring Sedan (SL2)	1992	213	213	206	560 Series	1986-91	159	160-161	155
Sprint	1985-89	126-127	128-129	122	600	1983-88	69-70	71-76	177

Introduction

WARRANTY SERVICE REQUIREMENTS

Most automakers warrant their new models for a specific mileage or period of time from the date of delivery. Some items, such as tires and batteries, are not usually covered by the vehicle warranty, but instead are covered under separate warranties provided by the component manufacturers. The length of the basic vehicle warranty coverage varies from one automaker to the next. Some manufacturers offer extended protection on certain components, and others offer longer warranty coverage at an extra charge. Federal law requires, however, that the emission control systems and related components of all passenger cars and light-duty trucks be warranted for 5 years or 50,000 miles (80,000 km) whichever comes first. According to the 1990 Clean Air Act, this warranty period will be modified at a later time.

To keep warranties in effect, all manufacturers require vehicle owners to service their vehicles at specific intervals. The service charts in this manual detail the services required to protect both the basic vehicle warranty and the emission control system warranty. Follow the instructions on each manufacturer's maintenance chart to determine the services required to maintain the warranty. Always give customers an itemized work order for their records showing the date and mileage that the required services were performed.

Contents

CRANKCASE SERVICE

ENGINE OILS

Engine oil is identified in two ways: by the American Petroleum Institute (API) Service Classification and by the Society of Automotive Engineers (SAE) Viscosity Number. Manufacturers' recommendations for both are shown on the service charts.

API SERVICE CLASSIFICATIONS

The API Service Classifications rate engine oils on their ability to lubricate, resist oxidation, prevent high- and low-temperature engine deposits, and protect the engine from rust and corrosion. The Service Classifications are two-letter codes beginning with either an "S" or a "C." The "S" prefix designates oils formulated for gasoline engine service. The "C" prefix designates oils formulated for diesel engine service.

There are a total of seven "S" classifications (SA through SG) and seven "C" classifications (CA through CF-4). However, only seven of the fourteen classifications are used in modern gasoline and diesel engines:

API Service SF

SF-rated oils are recommended for gasoline engines in passenger cars and some trucks made in 1980 and later. Oils developed for this type of service resist oxidation and wear better than oils with the obsolete SE classification. SF-rated oils also protect against engine deposits, rust, and corrosion. Oils meeting API Service Classification SF may be used where SE, SD, or SC oils are recommended.

API Service SG

SG-rated oils are recommended for gasoline engines in many passenger cars and trucks made in 1989 and later. Oils developed for SG service provide protection against oxidation, rust, corrosion, and engine deposits formed by high temperatures better than oils with the SE or SF Service Classifications. You may substitute SG-rated oil for SF- or SE-rated oils.

API Service CC

CC-rated oils are recommended for some naturally aspirated, turbocharged, or supercharged diesel engines operated in moderate or severe conditions, and some heavy-duty gasoline engines. This type of oil was introduced in 1961, and protects against deposits formed by high temperatures and bearing corrosion in diesel engines. It also protects against rust, corrosion, and low-temperature deposits in gasoline engines.

API Service CD

CD-rated oils are recommended for some naturally aspirated, turbocharged, or supercharged diesel engines where highly effective control of wear and deposits is important. It is also recommended when using fuels of a wide quality range, including high sulfur fuels. This type of oil was introduced in 1955, and protects against bearing corrosion and deposits formed by high temperatures in diesel engines.

API Service CD-II

CD-II rated oils offer the same protection as CD-rated oils, with additional protective properties for use in heavy-duty two-stroke diesel engines. Vehicles requiring this type of oil are not covered in this manual.

API Service CE

CE-rated oils are recommended for turbocharged or supercharged heavy-duty diesel engines made in 1983 and later. This oil is specially designed for vehicles that are operated under both low-speed/high-load and high-speed/high-load conditions. You may substitute CE-rated oil for CC- or CD-rated oils.

API Service CF-4

CF-4 oils provide improved performance over CE oils in control of oil consumption and piston deposits. These oils are designed for high-speed, four-stroke diesel engines, particularly those used in heavy-duty, on-highway trucks. Introduced late in 1990, CF-4 oils are required in some vehicles to meet 1991 EPA emission regulations, and may be used where CC, CD, or CE oils are specified. Vehicles requiring this type of oil are not covered in this manual.

Some oils are identified with dual API Service Classifications separated by a slash, for example, SG/CC, SG/CD, SF/CC, or SF/CD. These oils meet the requirements of both Service Classifications, and you can use them in any engine that calls for one or the other. Many manufacturers specify oils that meet both "S" and "C" Service Classifications. This is particularly true for heavy-duty and turbocharged engines. If the manufacturer recommends an oil with a dual Service Classification, do not use an oil that meets only a single classification, as this may void the engine warranty.

SAE VISCOSITY GRADES

The SAE Viscosity Grade is a number that corresponds to an oil's resistance to flow. Typical oil Viscosity Grade numbers are 5W, 10W, 15W, 20W, 20, 30, 40, and 50. If the Viscosity Grade number is low, the oil is thin and flows easily. If the number is high, the oil is thick and has a greater resistance to flow. A "W" after the viscosity grade indicates that the oil viscosity is measured at low temperatures and is intended for use in cold weather.

Oil viscosity is greatly affected by temperature. When an oil is cold, its viscosity increases, and it does not flow easily. If you use a high-viscosity oil in low temperature conditions, heavily loaded engine parts will not receive oil until the engine warms and the oil thins. When an oil is hot, it thins out and flows easily. If you use a low-viscosity oil in an engine that runs at extremely high temperatures, the oil film between critical engine parts will thin and may break down. This allows moving parts to touch, resulting in rapid wear and possible engine damage.

In the past, manufacturers recommended single-grade oils. However, you must change single-grade oils with respect to the changing seasonal temperatures. Low-viscosity oils are required in winter, while high-viscosity oils are needed in summer. Today, single-grade oils are recommended primarily for heavy-duty and diesel engines.

Modern oils have dual Viscosity Grade numbers separated by a dash, such as 5W-30, 10W-30, 15W-40, or 20W-50. These multigrade oils meet the low- and high-temperature specifications for both viscosities of oil indicated. Additives called "viscosity index improvers" cause oils to flow well at low temperatures, yet still resist thinning at high temperatures. In most cases, you can use multigrade oils in passenger vehicles throughout the year.

Most automakers do not recommend using low-viscosity multigrade (nor single-grade) oils for sustained high-speed driving, trailer towing, or other circumstances where the engine is placed under constant, heavy load. Check the service charts for the recommended grade of oil you should use for various temperatures and driving conditions.

ENERGY CONSERVING OILS

In addition to Service Classification and Viscosity Grade, some oils are designated as Energy Conserving or Energy Conserving II by the API. These oils are specially formulated to reduce internal engine friction, and thus improve fuel economy by 1.5 or 2.7 percent respectively. Energy Conserving oils usually have friction-reducing additives and a relatively low viscosity.

ENGINE OIL IDENTIFICATION

The API uses the Engine Service Classification Symbol, or "doughnut", on oil containers to help you identify oil types. The API Service Classification is in the upper half of the symbol, the SAE Viscosity Grade is in the center of the symbol, and the words "Energy Conserving" or "Energy Conserving II" are in the lower half of the symbol if the oil is formulated to meet "Energy Conserving" requirements. Always make sure that the oil quality information on the API "doughnut" meets the vehicle manufacturer's specifications. For some vehicles, you will need special oil that has requirements beyond the API oil classifications. Always check the manufacturer's specifications.

CRANKCASE OIL LEVEL CHECK

Check the crankcase oil level with the engine off and the vehicle on level ground. After shutting off a hot engine, wait at least one minute before you check the oil. This allows the oil to drain back into the pan. Some vehicles require more time for the fluid to drain into the oil pan, so check the service charts. Remove the crankcase dipstick, and wipe it clean with a lint-free cloth. Reinsert the dipstick fully into its tube. Then remove it and check that the oil level is between the LOW or ADD mark and the MAX or FULL mark.

CAUTION: Read the crankcase dipstick markings carefully. If you overfill the engine, the oil will foam, resulting in reduced lubrication and other problems.

If the oil level is below the LOW or ADD mark, add enough oil to raise the level above that mark. On most cars, the distance between the ADD and FULL marks is equivalent to approximately one quart (0.95 liter) of oil. When checking or changing the oil, you do not have to fill the crankcase all the way up to the FULL mark. If the oil level is above ADD, the engine will be adequately lubricated.

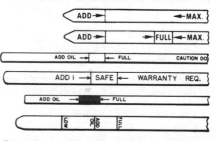

Read dipsticks carefully because the markings can vary from manufacturer to manufacturer.

On Ford engines built between 1984 and mid-1987, do not fill the crankcase oil higher than the MAX mark on the dipstick. The MAX mark is a tolerance limit that corresponds to approximately 1/2 quart (0.47 liter) above the proper engine oil level. When the crankcase is correctly filled with the quantity of oil indicated on the service charts, the level will register below the MAX line.

Some Ford vehicles built through 1985 have a SAFE range indication on the dipstick. For these vehicles, do not fill above the SAFE range.

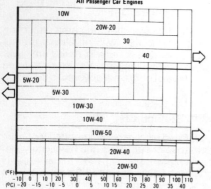

OIL VISCOSITY RECOMMENDATIONS
All Passenger Car Engines

This chart shows oil viscosity recommendations based on ambient temperature.

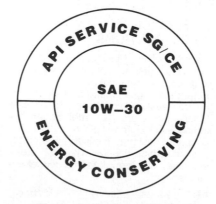

The API engine service classification symbol, or "doughnut", has the information needed to identify engine oils.

On Ford engines built from mid-1987 through 1988, when the crankcase is correctly filled with the quantity of oil indicated on the service charts, the oil level may be up to, but must be no higher than 1/8″ (4.2 mm) above the FULL line.

On Ford engines built from 1989 through 1991, the crankcase oil level may be up to but must be no higher than the ''F'' in the word ''FULL'' on the dipstick.

CRANKCASE OIL DRAIN AND REFILL

The service charts show manufacturers' recommended oil change intervals for normal driving conditions. The crankcase capacities are shown in liters and quarts. Most of the crankcase capacities listed do not include an oil filter change, so check the notes on the service charts. If you do change the filter, you may need to add additional oil. Under severe service, such as trailer towing or continual stop-and-go driving, manufacturers recommend more frequent oil changes. These recommendations are also shown on the service charts.

To change the crankcase oil, locate the crankcase drain plug, and position the drain pan under it. Always check the service charts because some vehicles have more than one drain plug. Many Ford V-8 engines have two crankcase drain plugs. Some imported vehicles have a remote oil reservoir that must be drained as well.

Select the proper wrench or socket to fit the drain plug. Not all drain plugs have a normal hex head. Some require a large Allen wrench or other special tool. Never use an adjustable wrench, pipe wrench, or locking pliers to remove a drain plug unless the drain plug is so damaged that you cannot remove it any other way. In this case, make sure you have a new, replacement drain plug before removing the old one.

Remove the drain plug by unscrewing it. As the plug nears the end of its travel, turn it slowly until it comes loose. Then catch it in the wrench or socket as it is removed. If the oil drain pan is equipped with a screen, allow the drain plug to drop into the pan, first making sure that the screen is not torn or missing. You can remove the plug from the pan after the oil has finished draining. Wipe the plug clean with a shop towel and set it aside.

CAUTION: As you remove the crankcase drain plug, beware of extremely hot oil that can splash out. Take care not to get burned. Be sure to clean your hands with soap and water because used engine oil contains harmful chemicals.

After the oil has drained, install a new drain plug gasket and the oil drain plug. Torque it to manufacturer's specifications. Crankcase oil capacities are listed on the service charts. Some capacities include the amount of oil required when changing the filter, but most do not. Read the notes on the service charts to check

this. When changing both the oil and filter, fill the crankcase with the amount of oil specified, start the engine to circulate the oil, then shut off the engine and check the oil level on the dipstick. Add oil as necessary to raise the level to between the ADD and FULL marks.

Some vehicles are equipped with a remote reservoir that holds reserve oil. Oil from the reserve reservoir is pumped to the engine if the oil level is low. Be sure to refill a remote oil reservoir with the manufacturer's recommended lubricant.

OIL FILTER SERVICE

Replace the engine oil filter at the intervals shown on the service charts. Most late-model cars and light trucks use a spin-on oil filter, although a few vehicles still use the older cartridge-type filters.

To replace a spin-on oil filter, remove it with a strap-type or cap-type oil filter wrench. If the filter is mounted base down, punch a hole in the top of the filter body, and allow the oil in the filter to drain into the pan. This will reduce spills when you remove the filter.

Before you install the new filter, compare its gasket mating surface with the one on the old filter. The new filter's gasket must make full contact with the sealing surface

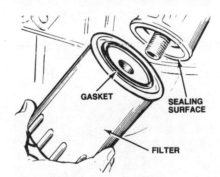

Clean the sealing surface on the engine block, and lubricate the filter gasket before installing the filter.

on the engine. Wipe the engine sealing surface clean, and lubricate the gasket on the new filter with fresh oil. Spin the filter on by hand until the gasket lightly contacts the sealing surface. Then tighten the filter 1/2 to 3/4 turn, or as instructed by the vehicle manufacturer.

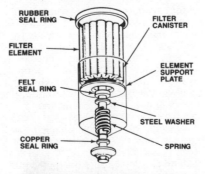

Replace the filter element in a typical cartridge-type oil filter.

To replace a cartridge-type oil filter, unscrew the bolt or bolts that secure the filter canister, and separate the canister from the engine. Remove and discard the filter element, wash out the canister with clean solvent, and blow it dry. Inspect sealing rings and washers inside the canister. They should be in good condition. Replace the O-ring seal where the canister mounts to the engine. Reassemble the canister with a new filter element, mount it on the engine, and tighten the securing bolt or bolts to the manufacturer's specifications.

After changing either type of oil filter, torque the crankcase drain plug in place, refill the engine with oil, start the engine, and check for leaks at the base of the filter. Check the oil level and add additional oil if necessary.

ENGINE SYSTEMS

ACCESSORY DRIVE BELT SERVICE

Inspect and adjust the accessory drive belts at the intervals recommended on the service charts. Inspect and replace belts that are cracked, frayed, separating, brittle, contaminated with grease or oil, glazed, or excessively worn.

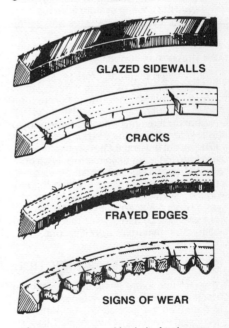

GLAZED SIDEWALLS

CRACKS

FRAYED EDGES

SIGNS OF WEAR

Inspect accessory drive belts for damage, using the illustration as a guide.

If the belts are in good condition, or if you have installed a new belt, check and adjust belt tension using a strand tension gauge. If the vehicle has a flat serpentine belt, use a tension gauge designed for that type of belt. A loose belt slips under load, and a belt that is too tight wears out quickly and damages accessory bearings. Belt tensions differ depending on whether they are new or used. Correct specifications for both are found in the

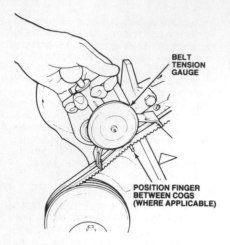

Use a tension gauge like the one illustrated to check accessory belt tension.

"Underhood Service" section of this manual.

COOLING SYSTEM SERVICE

ENGINE COOLANT

All car manufacturers recommend ethylene glycol antifreeze because it prevents engine freeze-up in winter, raises the boiling point of the coolant in summer, and protects the cooling system from rust and corrosion. In modern vehicles with aluminum cooling system components, you must use a quality coolant that contains the proper anti-corrosion additives.

Most vehicle manufacturers recommend a 50/50 mixture of coolant and water, which provides antifreeze protection down to approximately –30°F (–34°C). Higher antifreeze concentrations, up to 67 percent, lower the freezing point even further, but beyond 67 percent antifreeze, the freezing point rises sharply. High concentrations of coolant additives also will cause the coolant to gel, which inhibits cooling system effectiveness. Always top up a cooling system with a 50/50 mixture of water and coolant, which meets the vehicle manufacturer's specifications.

COOLING SYSTEM INSPECTION

Check the coolant level, and inspect the cooling system at the intervals recommended on the service charts. Almost all late-model vehicles have sealed cooling systems with coolant recovery reservoirs made of translucent plastic. In these systems, check the coolant level at the reservoir, not at the radiator.

CAUTION: Do not remove the radiator cap on a hot engine because the cooling system may be pressurized up to 20 psi (138kPa). If the cap is removed, boiling coolant will gush out, causing serious burns.

To check the coolant level in a sealed system, look at the reservoir and make sure the level is between the HOT and COLD

marks. When the engine is at operating temperature, the coolant level should be

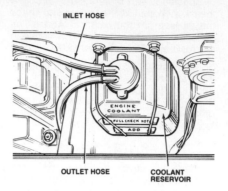

A coolant recovery reservoir is used on almost all late-model vehicle cooling systems.

at or near the HOT mark. If not, top up the reservoir with a 50/50 mixture of water and antifreeze. Do not overfill the reservoir, and do not fill it to the HOT mark when the engine is cold. This will cause the reservoir to overflow as the coolant heats up and expands.

CAUTION: The coolant reservoir on some cars is attached to the windshield washer fluid reservoir. Do not confuse these reservoirs by mixing washer fluid with engine coolant, or vice versa.

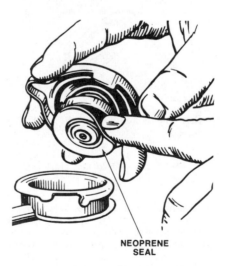

Inspect the radiator cap seal for brittleness.

Inspect the cooling system whenever you check the coolant level. Check the fan belt as instructed in the "Accessory Drive Belt" section of this manual. Inspect all radiator, bypass, and heater hoses. Replace any hoses that are cracked, brittle, swollen, or have exterior damage. Squeeze the hoses with your hand, and replace any that feel soft or spongy. Inspect the radiator for leaks around the tank seams and core fins. Check the radiator cap, and replace it if it does not fit tightly on the filler neck or if the seal is not soft and pliable. Be sure the replacement radiator cap is rated for the correct pressure.

COOLING SYSTEM FLUSH AND REFILL

Coolant additives deteriorate with age, so be sure to replace coolant and flush the radiator at the intervals recommended on the service charts. Unless the cooling system is obviously rusty, corroded, or contaminated, a fresh-water flush is usually adequate. On heavily contaminated systems, you may have to use a power flush or chemical cleaner. Do not use chemical cleaners unless absolutely necessary. If you do, follow the product manufacturer's instructions carefully.

To flush a cooling system with fresh water, remove the thermostat, and open the radiator and engine block drain plugs. On late-model cars that do not have drain plugs, loosen the lower radiator hose so that it leaks. Place a water hose in the radiator filler neck, and adjust the flow rate to keep the water level at the top of the radiator while water drains from it. Put the heater controls in the full hot position. Then start the engine and allow it to idle. Flush the system for ten minutes or until all traces of the old coolant are gone.

To refill the system, premix antifreeze and water in a 50/50 blend. See the "Cooling System Capacities" section of this manual for the amount you should add. Reinstall the thermostat, and with the heater controls in the full hot position, fill the radiator to the top of the filler neck. Add coolant mix to the COLD mark on the reservoir. Some cars have special bleeder valves that you must open while filling the system to release trapped air. See the "Cooling System Air Bleed Chart" for special instructions on filling and bleeding cooling systems.

Install the radiator cap to the first notch. Then start the engine, and allow it to idle until it reaches operating temperature. When the thermostat opens and coolant circulates throughout the system, stop the engine, remove the radiator cap, and top up the radiator with coolant as needed. Reinstall the radiator cap and tighten it fully. Then fill the recovery reservoir to the HOT mark with coolant.

POWER STEERING SERVICE

POWER STEERING FLUID

Power steering fluid is hydraulic oil that is designed to be compatible with rubber hoses and seals in the power steering system. It resists thinning and breakdown at high temperatures, and usually contains an additive to maintain good flow at temperatures as low as –20° to 40°F (–29° to 4°C).

Some automakers recommend special power steering fluids, although others specify Automatic Transmission Fluid (ATF). Always use the type of fluid recommended by the vehicle manufacturer, as shown on the service charts. Never mix different types of fluid, and never use brake fluid in place of power steering fluid or ATF. These fluids have entirely different properties, and each will destroy the rubber seals and hoses if used in the wrong system.

POWER STEERING FLUID LEVEL CHECK

Check the fluid level in the power steering fluid reservoir at the intervals listed on the service charts. Generally, you should check the level with the fluid warm, the engine off, and the front wheels straight ahead. Some dipsticks are graduated with HOT and COLD level markings.

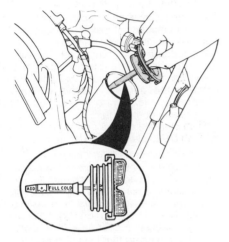

Check the power steering fluid level at the reservoir with a dipstick.

If the fluid level is very low, you may have to add new fluid and bleed trapped air from the system. To bleed trapped air, start the engine, and turn the steering wheel from lock to lock several times. When the steering feels consistent, stop the engine and recheck the fluid level. Add more fluid if necessary.

AIR FILTER SERVICE

A dirty or damaged air filter restricts intake airflow, affecting engine performance and life. Replace the air filter at the intervals listed on the service charts. In dusty conditions, filters are contaminated with dirt and debris rather quickly, so you should replace them frequently. Also, replace an air filter if the filter element does not seal properly with the air cleaner housing, or if there are holes or tears in the filter paper.

AIR FILTER INSPECTION

Automotive and light-truck engines use several types of disposable filters. Filters are mounted either on top of the carburetor or throttle body, or are mounted elsewhere in the air intake system. To inspect a filter, remove it from the air cleaner housing. Clamps or wingnuts usually hold the housing cover in place. Remove the cover and filter element.

Inspect the filter for physical damage. Shine a light through the filter to locate holes or tears in the filter paper. If the paper was originally white, and is now gray or brown, you should replace it. Some filters contain a layer of activated charcoal to reduce emissions, and appear gray in color even when new. If in doubt, compare the new filter to the replacement filter. Flex a flat filter, and check for material trapped between the pleats.

THERMOSTATICALLY CONTROLLED AIR CLEANERS

A thermostatically controlled air cleaner supplies warm air to the carburetor or throttle body during engine warmup. When servicing the air cleaner, be careful not to damage the temperature sensor or vacuum motor on the thermostatic control unit. Fuel injected systems using a mass airflow sensor do not use temperature control.

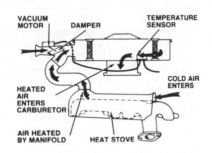

Do not damage the temperature sensor or vacuum motor on the thermostatic control unit when changing the air filter.

FUEL FILTER SERVICE

Replace fuel filters at the intervals listed on the service charts. Fuel filters remove contaminants from gasoline or diesel fuel as it passes into the carburetor or injection system. If you do not replace fuel filters periodically, contaminants will clog them, restricting fuel flow. The two most common types of fuel filters are carburetor inlet filters and inline filters.

To change a carburetor inlet fuel filter, remove the fuel line at the carburetor. Unscrew the inlet fitting and remove the gaskets, filter, and spring. Clean debris from the carburetor inlet, and insert the spring and new filter element. Using new gaskets, install and tighten the inlet fitting. Reconnect the fuel line to the carburetor.

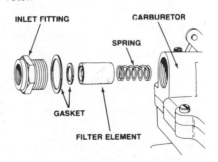

Replace the filter element in a typical carburetor inlet filter.

To change an inline filter on a carbureted engine, remove the clamps at each end and pull the hoses from the filter fittings. Install the new filter in the fuel line with the arrow or other symbol pointing in the direction of fuel flow. Do not push too hard on the thin metal or plastic filter case because it can buckle or crack, causing internal filter damage and a possible fuel leak. Tighten the clamps once the filter is in position.

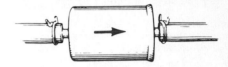

Hose clamps secure an inline fuel filter to the fuel lines in a carbureted engine.

Most fuel injection systems maintain pressure in the fuel lines even when the engine is off. To prevent fuel from spraying when you remove the filter, follow the vehicle manufacturer's instructions to bleed off pressure. Some inline fuel filters on fuel-injection systems have threaded fittings at the fuel lines. Use flare nut wrenches to remove and reinstall these filters. If you use regular open-end wrenches, you may distort the fittings, possibly resulting in fuel leaks.

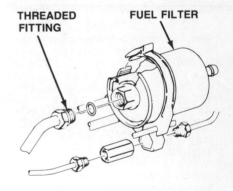

Threaded fittings secure the fuel filter to the high-pressure fuel lines in a fuel-injected engine.

CAUTION: If fuel is sprayed on a hot engine, it poses a serious fire hazard. Be sure to bleed pressure from the fuel line before loosening clamps or fittings.

EMISSION CONTROLS

The service charts in this book contain the required emission control services and service intervals. Specifications and adjustment instructions are provided in the "Underhood Service" section. Always check published emission control and tune-up data against the emission decal or label on the vehicle. If differences exist, use the specifications from the decal or label.

CRANKCASE EMISSION CONTROLS

The Positive Crankcase Ventilation (PCV) system draws filtered air into the crankcase through a hose from the air cleaner, and then meters crankcase fumes into the intake system through a PCV valve. The PCV valve is usually installed in a valve cover, in a PCV system hose, or in the intake manifold. It is connected by a hose to the intake manifold or the base of the carburetor or throttle body.

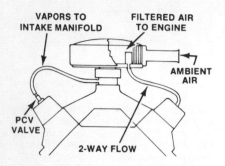

This is a typical closed PCV system.

Clean or replace the PCV valve at the intervals listed on the service charts. At the same time, inspect PCV hoses for cracks, deterioration, and clogging. Use special oil-resistant hose that is designed for PCV systems if you must replace defective hoses. Do not use heater hose.

Some PCV systems have a separate air filter or flame arrestor in the crankcase air inlet line. Clean or replace the filter or flame arrestor at the intervals listed on the service charts. The filter or flame arrestor might be a wire mesh or screen located in the air cleaner where the PCV line attaches, or it may be a separate element installed in the line at the valve cover. Be sure to service it regularly for proper PCV operation.

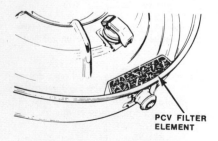

Some PCV filters or flame arrestors are located in the air cleaner housing.

PCV systems on diesel engines may have an oil filler breather cap, a flow control valve, and ventilation filters on the valve covers that connect to a flow control valve on the air intake crossover. Replace the breather cap and flow control valve, and inspect all other PCV system components at the intervals listed on the service charts.

EVAPORATIVE EMISSION CONTROLS

The evaporative emission control system traps any vapors released from the fuel in the gas tank. The vapors are routed to the engine so they can be burned. The typical system consists of a non-vented fuel tank cap with vacuum and pressure relief valves, a vapor-liquid separator, a vapor storage canister, a purge control valve, and several hoses that connect these components to the fuel tank and intake manifold.

Inspect evaporative emission control system hoses for deterioration and loose connections. Periodically clean the filter in the vapor storage canister of some systems, or replace them as required. See the service charts for required evaporative emission control system service.

EXHAUST EMISSION CONTROLS

Engine exhaust accounts for about 62 percent of a vehicle's hydrocarbon (HC) emissions, and is the sole source for carbon monoxide (CO) and oxides of nitrogen (NO_x) emissions. Manufacturers have made various modifications to basic engine designs to control these exhaust emissions, and several add-on devices are used as well. Service operations and intervals for exhaust emission control devices are listed on the service charts.

AIR INJECTION SYSTEMS

Most air injection systems use a belt-driven air pump to supply air to the exhaust ports in the cylinder head or to the exhaust manifold. The air mixes with the hot exhaust and promotes further burning of HC and oxidizing of CO to CO_2. The system also includes distribution manifolds and hoses, check valves, and either a gulp valve or a diverter valve to suppress backfires.

Another type of air injection system, called pulse-air injection, uses low pressure pulses in the exhaust manifold to draw fresh air into the system. This design is much simpler than systems using an air pump, and consists of an air distribution manifold, and one or more pulse-air valves.

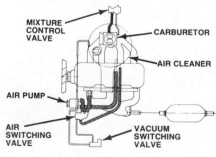

Some air injection systems use a belt-driven air pump.

Inspect and service air injection components at the intervals listed on the service charts. Perform the following services as needed. Check the air pump drive belt tension and condition. If the pump has an external filter, clean or replace it as required. Inspect hoses for loose connections, cracking, or burning. With the engine running at fast idle, disconnect the hose at the pump side of the check valve and check for airflow. Check for exhaust gases leaking back through a check valve. This is often indicated by a burned hose. Test the backfire suppressor valve according to the manufacturer's instructions.

Clean or replace air injector nozzles if they are clogged with exhaust deposits. Replace defective valves and hoses. You can overhaul an air pump, but usually they are replaced if they malfunction. Never oil a noisy air pump, as this will damage the pump's internal components.

EXHAUST GAS RECIRCULATION (EGR)

Exhaust gas recirculation systems control NO_x emissions by recycling a small amount of exhaust gas back into the intake system. This dilutes the incoming air-fuel mixture and lowers combustion temperatures. Maximum EGR is required during cruising or moderate acceleration. EGR is not needed at idle or during high-speed operation at wide-open throttle.

The most common type of EGR system uses a spring-loaded, vacuum-actuated poppet valve to control the amount of exhaust entering the intake system. The EGR valve is usually mounted on the intake manifold or on a plate under the carburetor or throttle body. It is connected to the intake and exhaust systems by passages in the manifolds or by external tubing. The EGR valve is held closed by a spring and is opened by a vacuum signal. Depending on the system design, the vacuum signal is controlled by any number of vacuum amplifiers, temperature override switches, computer-controlled solenoids, or exhaust backpressure transducers.

To maintain an EGR system, inspect passages for carbon buildup, inspect hoses for deterioration, verify the proper vacuum signals to the EGR valve, and check the valve for proper operation. The required maintenance operations and intervals are listed on the service charts.

To check EGR valve operation, accelerate the engine to 1500 to 2000 rpm, and watch the valve stem. The stem should move, indicating valve operation. You can also check valve operation by running the engine at a fast idle and removing the vacuum line from the valve. If the valve is working correctly, it should close and engine speed should increase 100 to 150 rpm.

In almost all cases, if the EGR valve is clogged, you should replace it. Some EGR valves can be cleaned. Remove it from the engine, and scrape or brush off deposits. You can clean some valves in a spark plug sandblaster. Others can be cleaned with power brushes, or by simply tapping the valve with a plastic hammer. Follow the manufacturer's recommendations.

CATALYTIC CONVERTERS

Beginning in 1975, most cars sold in North America were equipped with two-way catalytic converters. These converters contain a catalyst (platinum or palladium) that promotes an oxidizing reaction, changing HC and CO to water and carbon dioxide (CO_2). The air injection systems on many engines aid converters in oxidizing HC and CO.

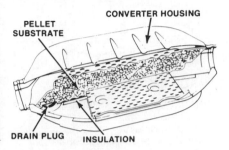

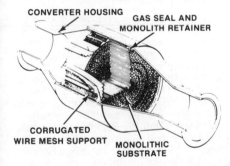

A catalytic converter may be filled with pellets (top), or may have a solid, monolithic substrate (bottom).

Some 1978 and 1979 cars and most 1980 and later cars have three-way or oxidation/reduction converters. These converters contain a second catalytic material, usually rhodium, to chemically reduce NO_x to free nitrogen (N_2) and oxygen (O_2). They still oxidize HC and CO.

All converter-equipped cars must use unleaded fuel because the catalyst is poisoned and destroyed by the lead additives used in leaded gasoline. To prevent the use of leaded fuel in these cars, unleaded gas pump nozzles and fuel tank filler necks in cars with catalytic converters are smaller in diameter than those that use leaded fuels. Federal law prohibits pumping leaded gas into any car that requires unleaded fuel, except in genuine emergencies.

Federal law also requires that catalytic converters last a minimum of 50,000 miles (80,000 km). No service should be necessary during this period. At a later time, these warranty periods may be revised. In the past, the catalyst in pellet-type converters could be removed and

replaced with fresh material. Now, you must replace both the pellet-type and monolithic converter when damaged or when their life-span is exhausted.

EXHAUST OXYGEN SENSORS

Cars with three-way catalytic converters use an oxygen sensor in the exhaust manifold to achieve proper catalytic converter operation. The sensor measures the amount of oxygen in the engine exhaust and generates an electric signal used to precisely control the air-fuel ratio. An oxygen sensor is a very sensitive type of battery. Never touch the body of the sensor and the output wire at the same time with tools or jumper leads or you will short out and damage the sensor.

On some vehicles, you must replace the oxygen sensor at scheduled intervals. Sensor replacement intervals, when required, are listed on the service charts. When you replace an oxygen sensor, coat the threads with an anti-seize compound specially formulated for this purpose. Some sensors come with a compound coating already on the threads.

Check the fluid levels in transmissions and other drivetrain components at the intervals listed on the service charts. Always use the proper lubricant (shown on the charts) when topping up or changing fluid. The most common lubricants used in transmissions and other drivetrain components are specially formulated automatic transmission fluids and gear oils. However, some manual transmissions use engine oil.

AUTOMATIC TRANSMISSION FLUID (ATF)

Although ATF is used in some manual transmissions, its primary application is in automatic transmissions. Manufacturers specify one of two basic ATF types: those that are friction modified, and those that are not. The differences between friction modified and unmodified fluids are chemically complex, but the essential factor is that friction modified fluids contain additives that make them more slippery under certain operating conditions.

DEXRON®-II, used in most modern automatic transmissions, and MERCON® used in most late-model Ford transmissions, are friction modified fluids. If you use an unmodified fluid in a transmission that requires friction modified fluid, harsh shift action will be the most noticeable result. Although this will be objectionable to the customer, it will probably not cause any long-term damage.

Type F fluid, used in all Ford automatic transmissions through 1976 and more recent automatics from other manufacturers, is an unmodified fluid. If you use a

friction-modified fluid in a transmission requiring unmodified fluid, slow shift action and increased slippage will result. Over time, increased heat and wear will cause premature transmission failure.

Several manufacturers require special automatic transmission fluids to accommodate particular transmission designs. In some cases, the recommended fluid for a transmission changes from one model year to the next because of internal modifications. Always consult the service charts to obtain the proper fluid type for the transmission you are servicing.

GEAR OILS

Gear oils are used in many transmissions and other drivetrain components. As with motor oils, both the API and SAE have established rating systems for gear oils. The API Service Classifications run from GL-1 through GL-5. The most common gear oils for late-model cars and light trucks are GL-4 and GL-5. They contain Extreme Pressure (EP) additives, which lubricate the hypoid final drive gears. To avoid synchronizer damage, some transmissions use a special GL-4 with non-reactive EP additives. Some manufacturers use special gear oils that are not classified under the API system. These are designated HP, EP, and GLS on the service charts. See the Key to Lubricants for a description of the these gear oils.

The SAE Viscosity Grades for gear oils are similar to those for engine oils. Some examples are 75W, 80W, 80, 90, and 140. Although higher numbers are assigned to gear oils, the oils are not necessarily higher in viscosity than engine oils. As with engine oils, gear oil viscosity grades are measured at both high and low temperatures, and are available in multigrade designations such as 75W-90 and 80W-90.

Special gear oil is often required for limited-slip differentials. Some vehicle manufacturers recommend that you mix an additive with the gear oil. If this is required, you will find the information on the service charts.

MANUAL TRANSMISSION FLUID LEVEL CHECK

Place the vehicle on a hoist, and locate the check/fill plug, as shown on the chassis diagram. Do not remove any other fasteners from the outside of the transmission as this may dislodge internal parts, requiring transmission removal and repair. Clean the area around the check/fill plug, and remove the plug using the appropriate wrench.

To check the transmission fluid level, insert your fingertip or a bent piece of wire into the check/fill opening. In most transmissions, the fluid level must be even with the lower edge of the opening. If the level is low, top up the transmission to the lower edge of the check/fill opening using the recommended lubricant. Reinstall the plug.

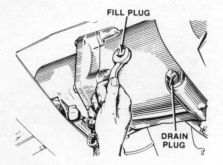

Check the manual transmission fluid level at the fill plug.

On some manual transmissions, the proper fluid level is not at the lower edge of the check/fill opening, but rather at a specified level below the lower edge of the opening. In at least one transmission, the proper fluid level is above the lower edge of the check/fill opening, which prevents checking the level in a conventional manner. Special instructions for checking the transmission oil are listed on the service charts.

Many FWD (and rear-engine RWD) cars combine the transmission and final drive into a single unit called a transaxle. In a manual transaxle, usually the same fluid lubricates both the transmission and the final drive, and one check/fill plug is used to service the fluid level for both. A few manual transaxles have two check/fill plugs — one for the transmission and one for the final drive. Always refer to the service charts for the proper lubricants in these applications. Refill capacities for manual transmissions are listed on the service charts.

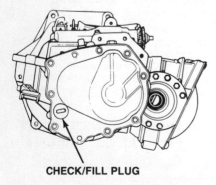

CHECK/FILL PLUG

This Chrysler transaxle, used from 1986 to the present, has a rubber fill plug located on the driver's side of the unit.

CLUTCH FLUID LEVEL CHECK

On vehicles with a hydraulic clutch, check and top up the clutch fluid level at the intervals recommended by the automaker. Before checking the fluid level, wipe the

top and sides of the reservoir to prevent clutch fluid contamination when you remove the reservoir top. Fill the reservoir to the FULL mark with the manufacturer's recommended clutch fluid. Do not overfill the reservoir because, on some vehicles, the extra space in the reservoir accepts fluid that is displaced as the clutch wears. If the clutch fluid level is extremely low, check the system for leaks.

If you repair the clutch, bleed trapped air according to the manufacturer's instructions. Do not reuse clutch fluid that is bled from the system, as it is likely to be contaminated with moisture.

AUTOMATIC TRANSMISSION SERVICE

The most common automatic transmission services are checking and topping up the fluid level. However, some automatic transmissions require periodic fluid changes, along with filter cleaning or replacement. All of the vehicle manufacturers' required services and recommended intervals are listed on the service charts.

FLUID LEVEL CHECK

Most manufacturers specify that you check the automatic transmission fluid with the vehicle on a level surface and the transmission at normal operating temperature. Some manufacturers suggest that you apply the parking and service brakes and, with the engine idling, move the transmission selector lever through all gear ranges. Place the lever in either PARK or NEUTRAL, as specified on the service chart. Remove the transmission dipstick, wipe it clean with a lint-free cloth, and reinsert it, making sure it is fully seated. Remove the dipstick again, and check that the level is between the ADD and FULL marks on the blade.

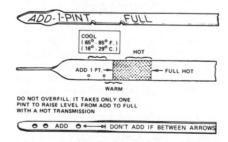

Automatic transmission dipstick markings may vary between manufacturers.

If the fluid level is low, add the required amount of the correct fluid through the dipstick tube. Generally, the distance between the ADD and FULL marks on the dipstick is equal to about one pint (0.47 liter) of fluid. Never overfill an automatic transmission, as this will cause fluid loss, foaming, and erratic shift action.

Many FWD (and rear-engine RWD) cars combine the transmission and final drive into a single unit called a transaxle. In an automatic transaxle, the same fluid *might*

be used to lubricate both the transmission and the final drive. For many of these transaxles, you must add and check the fluid level for both components at the transaxle dipstick tube. Other automatic transaxles have a separate housing and check/fill plug for the final drive gears. In this type of transaxle, you must service the two units separately, sometimes with different lubricants, adding transmission fluid at the dipstick tube and final drive lubricant at the check/fill plug. Always refer to the service charts for the proper lubricants in these applications.

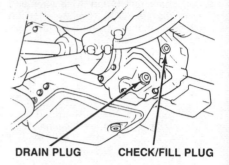

DRAIN PLUG   **CHECK/FILL PLUG**

The final drive used with many Toyota engines is lubricated at a separate check/fill plug.

DRAINING THE AUTOMATIC TRANSMISSION

Some car manufacturers recommend periodic automatic transmission fluid changes, particularly when the vehicle is used in severe service conditions. You can find recommended change intervals, along with any special draining instructions, on the service charts. Drain the fluid at normal operating temperature with the engine off. Remove the transmission pan, and catch the fluid in a drain pan. Clean the pan gasket surfaces and the transmission case before reinstalling the pan and a new gasket.

TRANSMISSION FILTERS

All automatic transmissions have a filter on the fluid pickup in the sump, and some

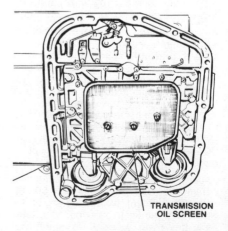

TRANSMISSION OIL SCREEN

This is a typical position for the filter or screen in an automatic transmission.

manufacturers call for periodic filter replacement. Transmission filters are either paper, fine-mesh wire screens, or spin-on filters similar to engine oil filters. Remove and inspect the filter whenever the fluid is changed. Be careful when doing this, as the filter might retain other components in the valve body. Replace paper filters, and clean screens with fresh solvent, drying them with compressed air. If the screen has any holes or is so dirty that you cannot clean it easily, replace it.

FILLING THE TRANSMISSION

Fill the transmission with the type of fluid specified on the service chart. Use the amount of fluid indicated for "Initial Refill", "Service Refill", or "Refill". The refill capacities take into account the amount of fluid retained by the transmission once it is drained. The "Total Fill" capacity is for a dry, newly rebuilt unit. Do not over-fill. After you add the transmission fluid, apply the parking and service brakes. Then start the engine and allow it to idle for about two minutes. Move the selector lever through all gear positions if specified by the manufacturer, and return it to PARK or NEUTRAL, as specified on the service chart. Check the fluid level and add fluid as needed to top up the level to, but not above, the ADD mark on the dipstick. Allow the engine and transmission to reach operating temperature. Then recheck the fluid level. If required, add fluid to bring the level to the FULL mark on the dipstick. Check the drain plugs, pan gasket, and dipstick tube for leaks.

DIFFERENTIAL FLUID LEVEL CHECK

Many FWD (and rear-engine RWD) cars combine the transmission and final drive in a single unit called a transaxle. You can find information on manual transaxles in the section titled "Manual Transmission Fluid Level Check". Information on automatic transaxles is located in the section titled "Automatic Transmission Service".

The differential is used on front-engine RWD vehicles, and is located at the rear axle. To check the fluid level, place the vehicle on a hoist, and clean the area around the check/fill plug. Remove the plug using the appropriate wrench, and

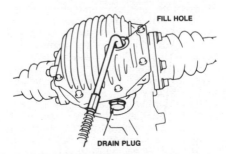

FILL HOLE

DRAIN PLUG

This illustrates topping up the oil level in a differential.

check the differential fluid level by inserting your fingertip or a bent piece of wire into the opening. In most applications, the fluid level should be even with the lower edge of the check/fill opening. On a few vehicles, the proper fluid level is a specified distance below the lower edge of the opening. This information is called out on the service charts. If the fluid level is low, top up the differential using the recommended lubricant, and reinstall the plug.

TRANSFER CASE FLUID LEVEL CHECK

A transfer case is used on 4WD vehicles to transmit power to the front and rear axles. The transfer case is usually positioned behind the transmission, although on some vehicles it may be beside the transmission. Place the vehicle on a hoist, and clean the area around the check/fill plug. Remove the plug, and check the fluid level by inserting your finger or a bent piece of wire into the opening. The fluid level should be level with or a short distance below the opening, as specified by the manufacturer. If the level is low, add the appropriate lubricant, as described in the service charts.

CHASSIS SERVICE

All chassis lubrication services and intervals are listed on the service charts. See the chassis diagrams to locate lubrication points. Manufacturer's recommended lubricants are listed on each vehicle's service chart.

VEHICLE HOISTING

Recommended lift points for vehicles are shown as black squares (■) on the chassis diagrams. Position the lift adapters carefully to distribute the vehicle weight evenly. When lifting a vehicle, raise the hoist slowly until it just contacts the chassis. Then double-check the lift adapters to be sure they are secure and that the vehicle does not shift when you raise it. Make sure that the lift does not hit brake lines, wiring harnesses, or exhaust system components.

CAUTION: Take special care when removing wheels, brake drums, the fuel tank, or other components at the rear of FWD vehicles. Because most of the powertrain weight on these vehicles is located above (or in front of) the front axle centerline, any significant reduction in weight at the rear may cause the car to tip forward on the hoist.

CHASSIS AND WHEEL BEARING GREASE

All greases are made from oils and a thickening agent to ensure that the lubricant clings to the surfaces where it is needed. Manufacturers frequently speci-

fy different types of greases for the chassis and wheel bearings. Some greases meet the specifications for both and are called multi-purpose greases. Greases may be classified in two ways: by their National Lubricating Grease Institute (NLGI) number, and by the type of thickening agent used.

The NLGI number designates the viscosity or consistency of a grease — the higher the number, the thicker the grease. The NLGI number is only a means of comparison. It is not a measure of quality or performance. Typically, wheel bearing greases and most chassis greases have an NLGI #2 consistency number.

Greases are thickened with soaps made of calcium, sodium, lithium, or aluminum. The type and amount of soap determines the melting point, appearance, texture, and water resistance of a grease. Most manufacturers today recommend grease made with a lithium-based thickener because these greases have a fairly high melting point and offer good water resistance.

A new NLGI grease classification system was introduced in 1990, and you may see the new designators on grease containers. Under the new system, greases must pass performance tests and are given designators, as in the API service classifications for oils. Greases passing all requirements in one or more of the categories display the approved NLGI designator on the package. The classifications are "GC" for wheel bearing grease, "LB" for chassis grease, and "GC-LB" for greases that can be used on both wheel bearings and chassis components.

NATIONAL LUBRICATING GREASE INSTITUTE

NLGI

AUTOMOTIVE
WHEEL BEARING & CHASSIS
LUBRICANT

GC-LB

This label reflects the NLGI grease classification system that was introduced in 1990.

Greases also contain additives that improve their performance, such as molybdenum disulfide or "moly", which improves the anti-wear and anti-seize properties of a grease. To increase the load-carrying ability under extreme pressure, EP additives are sometimes used.

Never mix different types of greases. When you lubricate chassis fittings or repack wheel bearings, use greases that meet the vehicle manufacturer's specifications.

CHASSIS LUBRICATION

Standard grease fittings are used on many suspension and steering joints that require lubrication. However, some have metal or plastic plugs that you must remove before lubricating the joints. With the vehicle raised on a hoist, locate the lubrication points using the vehicle's chassis diagram as a guide. Wipe each fitting or plug with a clean cloth to remove dirt and contaminated grease. Remove the plugs and install fittings in their place. Although some manufacturers recommend that the plugs be replaced after lubrication is complete, it is faster and more beneficial to the customer to simply leave the fittings in place so the car will be ready for the next lubrication service. Then apply grease as described below.

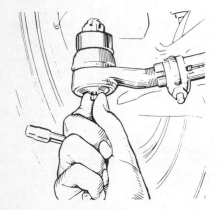

Some joints have plugs that you must remove prior to lubrication.

APPLYING GREASE

Two types of grease fittings are used on cars and light trucks: those with a protruding nipple, and those with a slightly dished face. Nipple fittings are the most common, and are typically found on suspension components. Dished fittings are more rare, and are used on some driveshaft universal joints and in other locations where space is limited.

To grease a nipple-type fitting, press the gun straight onto the nipple and hold it firmly in place. Apply the grease slowly to prevent damage to seals. If the joint has a sealed boot, apply lubricant slowly until the boot begins to bulge. If the joint has a non-sealed boot, apply the lubricant until the old grease is forced from the seal. Wipe off excess grease from the fitting after you have lubricated it.

To prevent "grease lock" on an idler arm, push up and pull down on the arm while applying grease. When lubricating front suspension ball joints, be sure the grease reaches all friction surfaces by moving the wheel from side to side while applying the lubricant. When applying grease to weight-carrying ball joints, remove the load from the joints to improve lubricant flow. During cold weather, allow ball joints to warm to at least 10°F (–12°C) before greasing them.

To lubricate grease fittings with a flat dished face, press the special needle-type nozzle of the grease gun against the center of the fitting, and maintain a constant pressure while applying grease to the joint. Joints with this type of fitting are usually unsealed, so apply grease slowly until the old grease is expelled. Wipe off excess grease from the fitting after you finish lubricating it.

DRIVESHAFT LUBRICATION

You do not have to lubricate most late-model driveshaft universal joints. However, inspect the joints regularly, and replace them if you find leaks or damage. Some universal joints are lubricated through grease fittings. Refer to the service charts for the type of lubricant and service intervals for these driveshaft joints. Apply small amounts of grease slowly and at low pressure. A few light trucks have universal joints without fittings, but you must service them periodically. At the intervals indicated on the service charts, remove and disassemble these joints, and repack them with grease.

On most late-model cars, the driveshaft spline is enclosed in the transmission housing and lubricated by the transmission fluid. When the spline is located between the front and rear universal joints, lubricate it separately. If the spline has a fitting, apply lubricant until it appears around the splines or at the vent hole on the end of the shaft. If you find a grease plug, remove it, install a fitting, and apply grease. In this case, be sure to remove the fitting and replace the plug to prevent an imbalance in the driveshaft. You must disassemble a driveshaft spline if it does not have a fitting or plug. Coat the spline with the recommended lubricant, and reassemble.

On some RWD passenger cars and 4WD vehicles, double Cardan U-joints are used to couple the front and rear sections of the driveshaft. Some require periodic lubrication through a dished grease fitting near the middle of the joint. Apply grease at low pressure. Lubricant types and service intervals are listed on the service charts.

The CV joints on FWD axles operate under very high loads and use unique greases. These joints usually do not require periodic lubrication. If the CV joint's protective rubber boot is damaged, you may have to repack the CV joint with grease or replace the entire joint. Use only the lubricant recommended by the vehicle manufacturer.

This section covers service of tapered roller wheel bearings that are used on the front wheels of RWD vehicles, and the rear wheels of FWD vehicles. Refer to the

service charts for lubrication intervals, types of lubricants, and adjustment specifications.

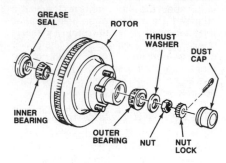

You must disassemble the wheel to replace the wheel bearings.

The rear wheel bearings on most RWD vehicles are either lubricated by the final drive gear oil, or are sealed assemblies, and require no periodic service. The front wheel bearings on most FWD vehicles are sealed assemblies that also require no periodic maintenance.

BEARING REMOVAL WITH DRUM BRAKES

Remove the wheel cover, spindle dust cap, cotter pin, nut lock (if used), retaining nut, and thrust washer. Rock the wheel slightly to loosen the outer bearing. Remove the bearing and place it in clean solvent.

Lift the wheel hub from the spindle. Avoid dragging the inner bearing across the spindle. Remove the inner bearing and seal by tapping lightly with a mallet and dowel or seal driver, which you must insert through the hub. Discard the grease seal and place the inner bearing in clean solvent. Unless the bearings are damaged and must be replaced, do not attempt to remove bearing races from the hub.

BEARING REMOVAL WITH DISC BRAKES

With disc brakes, remove the brake caliper before the hub and rotor to access the bearing. You do not have to disconnect the hydraulic fluid line from the caliper.

Remove the caliper mounting bolts, clips, or pins. If you are disassembling a fixed brake caliper with shims, be sure to mark them so you can reinstall the shims in the same locations. Siphon some fluid from the appropriate chamber of the master cylinder reservoir. Then lever the caliper pistons slightly into their bores, or compress the piston into the caliper housing with a large C-clamp. Lift the caliper from the rotor, and hang it from a convenient point on the suspension or body with a piece of wire or cable to support it. Do not allow the caliper to hang from the brake hose.

Once the caliper is clear of the rotor, remove the hub and bearings using the same methods described for vehicles with drum brakes.

BEARING CLEANING AND LUBRICATION

Wash the wheel bearings in solvent with a brush, and inspect them for scratches, pitting, discoloration, loose or damaged cages, and uneven wear. Replace defective bearings and their matching races. Carefully dry the bearings with compressed air. Then wrap them in a clean, lint-free cloth until you are ready to repack them. Dirt will wear the bearings prematurely.

Wipe old grease from the bearing races and spindle with a clean, lint-free cloth. For drum brakes, vacuum brake dust and dirt from the brake drum using a vacuum equipped with a high-efficiency particulate filter.

CAUTION: Do not clean the brake drum with compressed air. Many brake lining compounds contain asbestos, and inhaling brake dust is a serious health hazard.

Repack the bearings using the type of grease specified on the service chart. Use a bearing packer if possible, as it effectively distributes lubricant to the bearing cages. If you pack the bearings by hand, be sure to thoroughly work the grease into the cages and rollers. Apply a thin coat of grease to the races in the hub, the hub cavity, and the spindle. Do not fill the hub cavity with grease.

BEARING INSTALLATION AND ADJUSTMENT

Install the inner bearing and a new grease seal in the hub. Seat the seal with a drift, and put a light coat of grease on the sealing lip. Place the hub on the spindle, being careful not to hit the inner bearing. Install the outer bearing and thrust washer. Tighten the retaining nut just enough to seat the outer bearing and hold the wheel on the spindle.

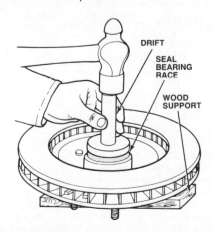

DRIFT

SEAL
BEARING
RACE

WOOD
SUPPORT

Use a drift to install a wheel bearing seal.

Tapered roller bearings operate best with a slight amount of endplay. Each manufacturer's specifications are given on the service charts. There are several methods of adjusting wheel bearings for the correct endplay. The three most common are summarized below.

After adjusting the bearing, be sure to secure it. On most cars, the wheel bearing adjustment setting is maintained by a cotter pin that passes through a slotted retaining nut, or nut lock, and a hole in the spindle. Always install new cotter pins when adjusting bearings. Some cars have retaining nuts that are staked in place after the bearings are adjusted. This is done by driving a portion of the end of the nut into a slot on the spindle. Whenever you remove one of these nuts, you must replace it with a new one. Use a rounded chisel to stake the nut because a sharp one will cut the metal instead of bending it.

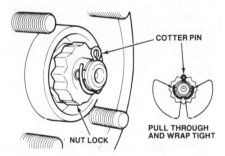

COTTER PIN

PULL THROUGH
AND WRAP TIGHT

NUT LOCK

Install a nut lock and cotter pin to keep the bearing adjusted.

HAND METHOD

Spin the wheel by hand and tighten the retaining nut hand-tight to seat the bearing. Back off the nut $1/4$ to $1/2$ turn, and then re-tighten it until it is finger tight. If a nut lock is used, position it over the retaining nut so that its slots align with a spindle hole. If the nut itself is slotted, back it off $1/12$ to $1/6$ turn to align the slots with a spindle hole. Install a new cotter pin.

TORQUE WRENCH METHOD

Spin the wheel by hand and tighten the retaining nut with a torque wrench to the specified value. Depending on the vehicle manufacturer's instructions, either back off the nut the specified amount and install a new cotter pin, or back off the nut, re-tighten it to the second specified torque, and install a new cotter pin. If a nut lock is used, position it over the retaining nut before you install the cotter pin.

DIAL INDICATOR METHOD

Spin the wheel and tighten the retaining nut to seat the bearing. Back off the nut the specified amount and mount a dial indicator on the wheel. Place the tip of the indicator probe against the end of the spindle and zero the dial indicator. Slide the wheel in and out on the spindle and observe the dial indicator reading. Tight-

en or loosen the retaining nut as necessary to align the slots with the spindle hole and to adjust bearing endplay to within the manufacturer's limits specified on the service charts.

BRAKES AND TIRES

Proper brake operation and good tire condition are critical to vehicle safety. Conduct a thorough inspection of the brakes, tires, and wheels regularly to determine any service needs. The intervals for these inspections are listed on the service charts.

BRAKE INSPECTION

In order to accurately diagnose and effectively correct any brake system problems, make the following checks as part of a brake inspection procedure. Follow the vehicle manufacturer's recommended procedures for complete brake service.

- Check tire pressure before diagnosing brake problems.
- Check the brake pedal for excessive noise, friction, sponginess, or side-to-side movement. There should be good pedal reserve travel, and the pedal should not drop under steady pressure.
- Make sure the brake lights come on with each pedal application, and go off as the pedal is released. Be sure the brake warning light on the instrument panel illuminates only when the parking brake is on.
- Inspect the master cylinder for leaks and other damage. Be sure vent holes in the reservoir cover are open. Fluid should be at the proper level and should not show signs of contamination.
- Check brake lines and hoses for bulges, cracks, or other signs of deterioration.
- Pad and shoe lining wear should not exceed the minimum thicknesses given on the service charts. Check for cracking, glazing, and contamination with grease or brake fluid.
- Inspect drums and rotors for cracks, scoring, and other distortion or damage.

BRAKE FLUIDS

Brake fluid transmits the force that applies the brakes to stop the car. If the brake fluid level is low or if air enters the hydraulic system, partial or complete brake failure will result. The same is true if inferior fluid, or fluid of the wrong type, is used. Always use brake fluid that meets the vehicle manufacturer's specifications.

There are two ways of identifying brake fluids: by their type and by their Department of Transportation (DOT) grade number. Brake fluids can be made of three different materials: polyglycol, silicone, and Hydraulic System Mineral Oil

(HSMO). The fluid type identifies the basic ingredient in the fluid. There are also three DOT grades of fluid: DOT 3, DOT 4, and DOT 5. The DOT grade numbers are performance standards established by the government. The higher the number, the more stringent the standard.

Polyglycol brake fluid is the most common type. All current polyglycol fluids are DOT 3 or DOT 4 grade. Most domestic automakers specify polyglycol DOT 3 fluids. Ford Motor Company cars use a heavy-duty DOT 3 fluid with an extra high boiling point. Many import automakers specify DOT 4 polyglycol fluid.

CAUTION: Polyglycol brake fluid is a strong solvent that dissolves paint on contact. This type of fluid also has a strong natural attraction for water, which reduces its boiling point. Avoid spillage, and always store unused polyglycol brake fluid in a tightly sealed container.

Silicone brake fluids are the only type that meet all of the DOT 5 specifications. Silicone fluid has an extremely high boiling point, is not a solvent, and does not absorb moisture. Despite this, silicone fluid is not used as original equipment in mass production cars at this time. Silicone fluid is compatible with polyglycol fluid, but the two types do not actually blend together. For this reason, do not mix silicone and polyglycol brake fluids.

BRAKE FLUID LEVEL CHECK

Check the brake fluid level in the master cylinder reservoir at the intervals shown on the service charts. Also check the fluid level before and after performing brake work.

CONVENTIONAL BRAKE SYSTEM

Brake fluid reservoirs can be made of plastic or cast in metal as an integral part of the master cylinder. Most translucent plastic reservoirs have marks molded into them that indicate high and low fluid levels. To check the level, simply look

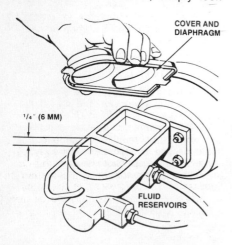

In some vehicles, you must remove the cover on the master cylinder to check the fluid level.

through the reservoir. Some cars have opaque plastic reservoirs that are filled to a mark or plastic ring located inside the reservoir. To check the fluid level in these master cylinders, remove the reservoir cover, or filler caps, to expose the markings.

On a master cylinder with an integral metal reservoir, remove the cover to check the fluid level. With this type of reservoir, the maximum level is designed to be $^1/_4$ inch (6 mm) from the top. To check the brake fluid level, wipe the fluid reservoir and cover clean. Then remove the cover by releasing the wire bail with a screwdriver.

POWERMASTER BRAKE SYSTEM

The GM Powermaster brake booster combines a master cylinder and hydraulic power booster into a single assembly. The Powermaster fluid reservoir is divided into three chambers. The two smaller chambers on the outside of the reservoir serve the master cylinder. The single large chamber on the inside of the reservoir serves the power booster.

Before you remove the reservoir cover to check the fluid levels, discharge the booster accumulator by pumping the brake pedal with the ignition off until the pedal feel becomes noticeably harder. Remove the reservoir cover and adjust the fluid levels so they are between the maximum and minimum level markings cast into the walls of the chambers. Because the booster chamber is open to the atmosphere, never transfer fluid from the large reservoir into either of the smaller ones.

ANTI-LOCK BRAKE SYSTEMS

The method of checking the brake fluid level on a car equipped with an anti-lock braking system varies with the vehicle manufacturer.

To check the brake fluid level in the Ford/Teves anti-lock braking system, turn the ignition switch on and pump the brake pedal until the hydraulic pump motor begins to run. When the pump stops, the accumulator is fully charged. Check that the fluid level is even with the MAX mark cast into the reservoir body.

To check the brake fluid level in the GM/Teves system, turn the ignition switch off and pump the brake pedal a minimum of 25 times until the pedal feel becomes noticeably different. When this occurs, the accumulator is discharged. Check that the fluid level is even with the FULL mark on the reservoir body. Open the reservoir and refill to the mark if the fluid is low.

To check the brake fluid level in the Chrysler/Bosch or Bendix system, turn the ignition switch off and pump the brake pedal. For the Bosch system, pump the pedal at least 25 times, and for the Bendix system, pump the brake pedal at least 40 times. When the brake pedal pressure becomes noticeably different, the accu-

mulator is discharged. Check that the fluid level is even with the filter/screen in the reservoir body. Open the reservoir and refill to just below the filter/screen if the fluid is low.

For many imports, check the brake fluid in an anti-lock braking system in the same way you would check a conventional system, but consult the manufacturer's service manual for details. For Volkswagens with anti-lock brakes, check the fluid level as you would a Chrysler/Bosch system.

PARKING BRAKE CABLE LUBRICATION

Lubricate the parking brake as required to maintain ease of operation. Apply a thin film of water resistant grease to the exposed portions of the cable assemblies, pivot points, and cable guides. Check and adjust parking brake application at the equalizer lock nut if needed. If the vehicle is equipped with a vacuum-release parking brake, inspect the vacuum hose, power unit, pawls, springs, and cable.

TIRE ROTATION

To help prolong tire life, the automotive industry recommends that you rotate tires at 5000 to 8000 mile (8000 to 12,800 km) intervals. Always recheck the tire pressures after rotation to maintain proper front-to-rear balance. The tire industry cautions that when tires of different types are used on front and rear axles, they should be rotated on the same axle. Also, certain high-performance tires are designed to turn in one direction, and you must rotate them from front to rear on the same side only. Do not rotate studded snow tires.

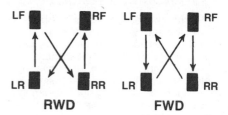

Tire rotation procedures may vary depending on the type of tires used on the vehicle, and whether the vehicle is front- or rear-wheel drive.

WHEEL-NUT TORQUE

Roadside tire and wheel changing is one of the few car services performed by the owner. Be sure to tighten the nuts evenly in a criss-cross pattern, and avoid installing the nuts so tightly that the owner cannot remove them with a hand wrench.

Changes in wheel design and use of downsized disc brakes have made proper nut tightening very important in order to avoid distortion of the wheel, hub, and brake rotor. To prevent such damage, use the wheel-nut installation torques provided by the vehicle manufacturer. Wheel-nut torques are located at the back of the "Tires" section in the center of this manual.

AIR CONDITIONING

The air conditioning (AC) system cools and dehumidifies passenger compartment air. This is done by evaporating refrigerant within a finned radiator, called an evaporator. As the refrigerant evaporates, it absorbs heat from air passing into the passenger compartment, and causes moisture to condense out of the air onto the cool evaporator surface.

Most AC systems combine the air conditioner and heater into one unit. This is referred to as the "re-heat" system because the air is first cooled and dehumidified, and then warmed to the desired temperature. Several cable- or vacuum-operated doors direct inside or outside air through or around the evaporator or heater core, then out the floor, dash, or defroster outlets, as selected by the operator. Models with Automatic Temperature Control (ATC) use several sensors, vacuum motors, and switches to make these adjustments automatically. In many respects, ATC systems are similar to manually controlled systems.

Energy to operate the air conditioner comes from the engine, which drives the compressor with a belt. The compressor uses the engine's mechanical energy to pressurize the refrigerant. The refrigerant used in automobiles is dichlorodifluoromethane, or Refrigerant-12, "R-12" for short. R-12 boils at –21°F (–29°C), is nontoxic, noncorrosive, colorless, odorless, soluble in oil, and easy to handle, making it ideal for use in automotive air conditioning systems. Because R-12 is believed to contribute to ozone degradation, it is being replaced. Some vehicle manufacturers will be using HFC-134a rather than R-12 in the near future.

BASIC AC SYSTEMS

The following sections describe a basic TXV (thermostatic expansion valve) AC system, and several variations on the basic system, all of which are used today. The diagrams illustrate refrigerant flow only, and are not intended to show actual component locations on the car.

TXV SYSTEM

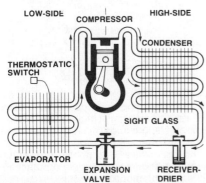

The R-12 leaves the compressor as a hot, high-pressure gas. It flows to the condenser, where it is cooled by passing ambient air and condensed into a warm, high-pressure liquid. It then flows to the receiver-drier, where excess R-12 is stored and a desiccant removes moisture that would otherwise freeze and block components or cause corrosion. On some systems, a sight glass allows the technician to observe the passing R-12.

The liquid R-12 leaves the receiver-drier and passes through the liquid line to the expansion valve. At the expansion valve, pressure is removed from the R-12, turning it into a low pressure, low temperature liquid/gaseous mixture. Heat from the air passing over the evaporator is absorbed by the refrigerant, which causes the passing air to cool. Cool air enters the passenger compartment. The R-12 leaves the evaporator as a low-pressure gas that returns to the compressor and repeats the cycle. A pressure or temperature switch, usually at the evaporator, signals the compressor to turn on. This type of system is used on late-model Honda, Nissan, and Toyota vehicles.

STV SYSTEM

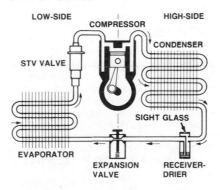

This system is a variation of the basic TXV AC system. The temperature of the evaporator is controlled by a suction throttling valve (STV) to prevent freezing. The STV regulates evaporator pressure to prevent evaporator freeze up. This system is used on some late-model Nissan vehicles with automatic temperature control.

FIXED ORIFICE TUBE SYSTEM

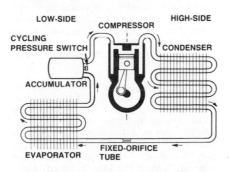

In this type of system, the accumulator performs the same function as the receiver-drier in other systems, but is located

between the evaporator outlet and compressor inlet, acting as a receiver for any liquid refrigerant until it vaporizes. A pressure-sensitive switch on the accumulator housing cycles the compressor clutch to maintain the correct evaporator pressure. A fixed orifice tube is used in place of an expansion valve. This system does not use a sight glass. The fixed orifice tube system used on late-model Ford vehicles is called the Fixed-Orifice Tube Cycling Clutch system (FOTCC). In GM vehicles it is called the Cycling-Clutch Orifice Tube system (CCOT).

COMBINATION VALVE SYSTEMS

Combination valves combine the functions of a TXV, an STV, or a variety of other components into a single assembly. Chrysler uses an H-valve, which looks like a block mounted near the evaporator. Ford used a mini-combination valve on air conditioning systems in the early 1980s. The Ford combination valve also is mounted near the evaporator.

OTHER COMPONENTS

In addition to the major system components, there may be one or more additional controls that affect system operation. To protect against excessively high pressures (475 psi or 3300 kPa and above) a safety relief valve may be installed near the compressor outlet. Some systems have a high-pressure cutoff switch that de-energizes the compressor clutch until high-side pressure returns to normal.

Many systems have a low-pressure cut-out switch that de-energizes the compressor clutch when low-side pressures are too low, preventing compressor damage in the event of refrigerant loss. On some cars, an ambient switch prevents operation of the compressor below a certain temperature, usually about 32°F (0°C). Other switches are used to interrupt compressor operation during periods of high engine load such as wide-open throttle, heavy power steering use, or overheating.

COMPRESSOR LUBRICATION

All AC systems circulate a small amount of refrigerant oil with the R-12 to lubricate the compressor. Check the oil level by removing an inspection plug on the compressor after discharging the system or isolating the compressor, or check the oil by draining and measuring the oil from the compressor. Oil may be lost from the system by large leaks and during component replacement.

When the condenser, receiver-drier, or accumulator is replaced, add 1 ounce (30 ml) of oil. When you replace an evaporator, add about 2 or 3 ounces (60 or 90 ml) of extra oil. A new compressor usually comes with the correct amount of oil in it, but some manufacturers recommend that you drain this oil and add fresh oil before installation. Always check the manufacturer's instructions for oil replacement because AC systems can vary slightly among manufacturers. Use only special refrigerant oil. Do not overfill or underfill, as poor performance or damage can result.

AIR CONDITIONING CHECKS

Air conditioning troubleshooting requires diagnosing problems in four systems:

- The electrical system, including the compressor clutch, switches, blower motor, and their controls
- The air distribution system, including the ducts, doors, cables, vacuum motors, and their controls
- The heating system, including the heater core, heater control valve, temperature blend door, and their controls
- The refrigeration system and its components.

A complete diagnostic procedure of all systems is beyond the scope of this manual, but general instructions are covered here.

SYSTEM INSPECTION

Before testing the system with a manifold gauge set, check the following items:

- Electrical wiring must be intact without worn insulation or broken wires. Connectors must be clean and tight.
- Vacuum lines must not be cracked, broken, or deteriorated. Vacuum motors must be connected and operating correctly.
- Refrigeration lines must be intact and not visibly leaking.
- Compressor drive belts must be in good condition and properly tensioned. The compressor seal must not be leaking.
- All components must be properly mounted.
- The condenser fins must be free of obstructions.

With the system operating:

- All controls must function properly.
- High-side refrigeration lines must be warm or hot, and low-side lines must be cool.

SYSTEM TESTS

Connect the manifold gauge set to the service valves, run the engine, and turn on the air conditioning system. Operate the system for 5 to 10 minutes with the engine speed at fast idle, the car doors and windows open, the air conditioner on MAX, and the blower speed on HIGH.

Check the sight glass (if present) for the following indications:

A clear sight glass indicates that the system is properly charged, is over-charged, or is completely discharged. Verify the condition by using the manifold gauge set to test the system pressures.

Foam or bubbles in the sight glass indicate that the refrigerant charge is low, or air is in the system. Occasional bubbles when the compressor clutch cycles are normal in some systems.

Oil streaks in the sight glass indicate that too much refrigerant oil is circulating. This symptom is often seen when the system has a low refrigerant charge.

A clouded or gray sight glass indicates that the desiccant in the receiver-drier has broken down and is circulating in the system.

LEAK TESTS

Refrigerant leaks cause about 80 percent of air conditioner failures. Leaks may be the result of loose fittings, or damaged or deteriorated hoses, seals, and O-rings. Test for leaks when you see low readings on the test gauges, foam, bubbles or oil streaks in the sight glass, and during routine service. With the engine and air conditioning system off, the test gauges should show at least 60 to 80 psi (415 to 550 kPa).

LEAK DETECTION

A large leak in the AC system will produce visible oil residue on hoses, connections, or seals. The residue eventually picks up dirt and appears greasy. If the system looses oil, check the compressor oil level before evacuating and recharging the system. Cans of R-12 with dyed oil are available to help spot leaks. The dye in the refrigerant will be seen at leaking points. This method is not recommended by some vehicle manufacturers, however, and may void the warranty, so be sure to check the vehicle manufacturer's recommendations before using R-12 with dye.

The best way to locate smaller refrigerant leaks is with an electronic leak detector. Most detectors sound and show a light when a leak is found. Always calibrate and use the detector according to the directions. Because electronic testers are very sensitive, R-12 in the air may set them off before the leak is found. Allow ample fresh air to circulate around the car, and use the detector probe to locate leaks around fittings and seals.

OTHER CHECKS

In addition to other repairs, replace the receiver-drier, the desiccant, or the accumulator whenever:

- There is evidence of moisture in the system, indicated by dark, thick refrigerant oil or internal corrosion of metal parts.
- The expansion valve, STV valve, or orifice tube is replaced because of corrosion or freezing.
- The system has been left open for a long time because of a major leak or damage.
- The receiver-drier inlet or outlet lines are cool or frosted while the system is operating.
- The accumulator contains more than 5 ounces (150 ml) of oil, indicating a clogged oil bleed.
- The sight glass is clouded, indicating desiccant is circulating in the system.
- All the R-12 has been lost from the system.

AC SYSTEM REPAIRS

Before opening any AC system connections for repair, turn off the engine and evacuate R-12 from the system. Open fittings slowly in case there is residual pressure. On Ford models with garter-spring couplings, use a special tool to separate the lines.

When reassembling fittings, carefully in-

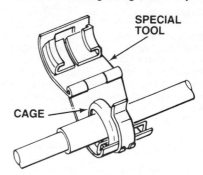

spect O-rings, and replace them as necessary. Ford garter-spring couplings require special O-rings. Lubricate O-rings with refrigerant oil before assembly. Use two tubing wrenches to tighten fittings. Take care not to overtighten the connections.

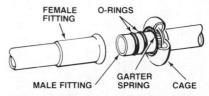

After discharging and opening a system for service, you must thoroughly evacuate and sometimes flush it before recharging the system. After recharging, check for leaks as described in preceding sections, and test system performance in all operating modes.

NORMAL GAUGE READINGS

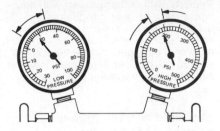

The exact operating pressures for AC systems vary with the specific application. The following charts provide some examples of typical system operating pressures.

LOW-SIDE PRESSURES

Although there may be slight differences in gauge readings depending on the manufacturer's system layout, the following low pressure gauge readings are common at about 70°F (21°C).

TXV systems:

   20-30 psi (140-200 kPa)

Cycling clutch, orifice tube systems:

Cycle off:	10-15 psi (69-105 kPa)
Cycle on:	35-40 psi (240-275 kPa)
Cycle range:	20-30 psi (140-210 kPa)

HIGH-SIDE PRESSURES

High-side pressures may also vary slightly from system to system. Ambient temperature and humidity effect high-side gauge readings, as shown on the following chart. When taking high-side pressure readings, consider the ambient temperature and humidity, and how they effect gauge readings.

Ambient Temperature		High Pressure Gauge Reading	
°F*	°C*	psi**	kPa**
60	16	95-115	650-790
65	18	105-125	725-860
70	21	115-135	790-930
75	24	130-150	900-1035
80	27	150-170	1035-1170
85	29	165-185	1140-1275
90	32	175-195	1210-1345
95	35	185-205	1275-1415
100	38	210-230	1450-1590
105	41	230-250	1590-1725
110	43	250-270	1725-1865
115	46	265-285	1830-1965
120	49	280-310	1930-2140

 * Ambient temperatures taken two inches in front of condenser.

** Gauge readings increase with relative humidity. The above readings are with a fully charged system, engine at fast idle, and a large fan creating airflow through the condenser.

ABNORMAL GAUGE READINGS AND SYSTEM SERVICE

The following section contains gauge readings and other symptoms that indicate problems in the air conditioning system.

Low-side low, high-side low

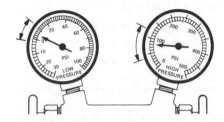

Condition 1

Low-side: Low, below 15 psi (105 kPa).

High-side: Low, below 175 psi (1210 kPa) at 90°F (32°C).

Sight Glass: Stream of bubbles.

Evaporator Discharge Air: Only slightly cool.

Diagnosis: Low refrigerant charge, possible leaks.

Remedy: Locate and repair leaks. Check compressor oil level. Evacuate and recharge.

Condition 2

Low-side: Very low, well below 15 psi (105 kPa).

High-side: Very low, well below 175 psi (1210 kPa) at 90°F (32°C).

Sight Glass: No bubbles, no liquid R-12 noticeable.

Evaporator Discharge Air: Warm.

Diagnosis: Refrigerant charge excessively low. Possibly serious leaks.

Remedy: Add partial R-12 charge. Locate and repair leaks. Check compressor oil level. Evacuate and recharge.

Condition 3

Low-side: Very low, 0 psi (0 kPa) or a vacuum.

High-side: Low, below 175 psi (1210 kPa) at 90°F (32°C).

Evaporator Discharge Air: Only slightly cool.

Expansion Valve: Inlet is cool, possibly frosted, or sweating heavily.

Diagnosis: Expansion valve stuck closed or screen clogged.

Remedy: If expansion valve inlet is cool, test valve operation by alternately cooling and warming it. If valve operation is satisfactory, clean contact surfaces of sensing bulb and evaporator outlet pipe. Reinstall bulb. If valve operation is unsatisfactory, replace valve. If expansion valve inlet is

frosted or sweating, clean or replace valve screen. Evacuate and recharge.

Condition 4

Low-side: Very low, well below 15 psi (105 kPa).

High-side: Low, below 175 psi (1210 kPa) at 90°F (32°C). May read normal to high if restriction is immediately downstream of service valve.

Evaporator Discharge Air: Only slightly cool.

Liquid Line: Cool, possibly frosted or sweating heavily.

Receiver-Drier: Possibly frosted or sweating heavily.

Diagnosis: Restriction in receiver-drier or liquid line.

Remedy: Replace receiver-drier, liquid line, or other defective parts. Evacuate and recharge.

Low-side high, high-side normal

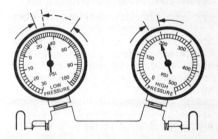

Condition 5

Low-side: Compressor cycles off higher than normal, around 24-28 psi (165-190 kPa), when it should cycle off at 10-15 psi (69-105 kPa). Compressor cycles on close to normal at 35-40 psi (240-275 kPa). Reduced cycle range of 6-8 psi (40-55 kPa).

High-side: Normal.

Compressor: Turns on and off too rapidly.

Diagnosis: Defective thermostatic switch.

Remedy: Replace switch.

Condition 6

Low-side: Compressor cycles off higher than normal at 26-29 psi (180-200 kPa) when it should cycle off at 10-15 psi (69-105 kPa). Compressor cycles on higher than normal at 50-55 psi (345-380 kPa) when it should cycle on at 35-40 psi (240-275 kPa). Cycle range normal at 20-30 psi (140-210 kPa).

High-side: Normal.

Evaporator Discharge Air: Warms excessively when compressor off.

Diagnosis: Misadjusted thermostatic switch or defective pressure-sensing switch.

Remedy: Adjust or replace switch.

Low-side high, high-side high

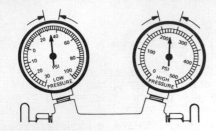

Condition 7

Low-side: High, well above 30 psi (205 kPa).

High-side: High, well above 195 psi (1345 kPa) at 90°F (32°C).

Sight Glass: Possibly occasional bubbles.

Evaporator Discharge Air: Warm.

Liquid Line: Very Hot.

Diagnosis: Condenser malfunction or overcharge.

Remedy: Check compressor drive belt. Check condenser mounting and check for obstructions and reduced airflow. Check engine cooling system performance, including clutch-type fan. If problem is not corrected, discharge system to low-charge condition (bubbles in sight glass). Recharge to normal pressures, then add 1/4 to 1/2 pound (0.11 to 0.22 kg) additional R-12. If recharging does not correct problem, remove, inspect, and clean or replace condenser. Evacuate and recharge.

Condition 8

Low-side: High, above 30 psi (205 kPa).

High-side: High, above 195 psi (1345 kPa) at 90°F (32°C).

Sight Glass: Occasional bubbles.

Evaporator Discharge Air: Warm or only slightly cool.

Diagnosis: Large amount of air in system, possibly moisture in system.

Remedy: Replace receiver-drier or accumulator. Evacuate and recharge.

Condition 9

Low-side: High, above 30 psi (205 kPa).

High-side: High, above 195 psi (1345 kPa) at 90°F (32°C).

Evaporator Discharge Air: Warm.

Evaporator: Heavy sweating.

Suction Line: Heavy sweating.

Diagnosis: Expansion valve stuck open or temperature-sensing bulb inoperative.

Remedy: Test expansion valve by alternately cooling and warming it. If valve operation is satisfactory, clean contact surfaces of sensing bulb and evaporator outlet pipe. Reinstall bulb. If valve operation is unsatisfactory, replace valve. Evacuate and recharge.

Low-side high, high-side low

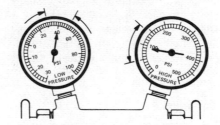

Condition 10

Low-side: High, above 30 psi (205 kPa).

High-side: Low, well below 175 psi (1210 kPa) at 90°F (32°C).

Sight Glass: Clear.

Evaporator Discharge Air: Warm or only slightly cool.

Diagnosis: Malfunctioning compressor.

Remedy: Isolate compressor with stem-type service valves or discharge system. Inspect and repair compressor. Check compressor oil level. Measure oil in accumulator, if equipped. If more than 5 ounces (150 ml), oil bleed is plugged. Replace accumulator. Evacuate and recharge.

Low-side normal, high-side normal, poor cooling

Condition 11

Low-side: Normal but constant. Does not indicate cycling or modulation.

High-side: Normal but may be slightly higher or lower than 175 psi (1210 kPa) at 90°F (32°C).

Sight Glass: Possibly occasional bubbles.

Evaporator Discharge Air: Only slightly cool.

Diagnosis: Some air or moisture in system.

Remedy: Test for leaks and repair as necessary. Replace receiver-drier or accumulator. Check compressor oil level. Evacuate and recharge.

Condition 12

Low-side: Normal, but may drop to vacuum due to water freezing in system.

High-side: Normal, but will drop if low-side drops.

Sight Glass: Possibly tiny bubbles.

Evaporator Discharge Air: Cold, but becomes warm when low-side pressure drops into vacuum.

Diagnosis: Excessive moisture in system.

Remedy: Replace receiver-drier or accumulator. Evacuate and recharge.

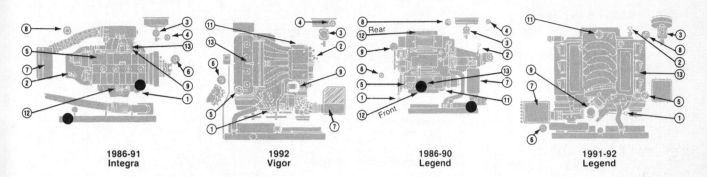

HOOD RELEASE: Inside

1986-91
Integra

1992
Vigor

1986-90
Legend

1991-92
Legend

① Crankcase dipstick
② Transmission dipstick
③ Brake fluid reservoir
④ Clutch fluid reservoir
⑤ Oil fill cap
⑥ Power steering reservoir
⑦ Air filter
⑧ Fuel filter
⑨ Oil filter
⑩ PCV filter
⑪ EGR valve
⑫ Oxygen sensor
⑬ PCV valve

0 FITTINGS
0 PLUGS

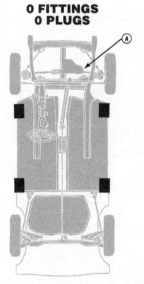

1986-91
Integra

0 FITTINGS
0 PLUGS

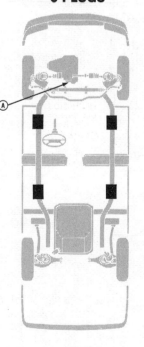

1992
Vigor

0 FITTINGS
0 PLUGS

1986-90
Legend

0 FITTINGS
0 PLUGS

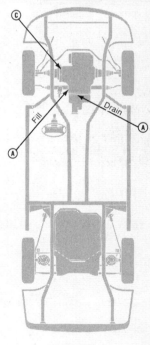

1991-92
Legend

● Cooling system **drain**

■ Lift adapter position

Ⓐ Manual transmission/transaxle,
drain & fill

Ⓑ Transfer case, NOT USED

Ⓒ Transaxle, final drive, drain & fill

Ⓓ Differential, NOT USED

SERVICE AT TIME OR MILEAGE—WHICHEVER OCCURS FIRST

AAIPM1   AAIPM1

Perform the following maintenance services at the intervals indicated to keep both the vehicle and emission warranties in effect.

MI—MILES IN THOUSANDS
KM—KILOMETERS IN THOUSANDS

EVERY 6 MO/7.5 MI—12 KM
Brake pads .... inspect

Crankcase .... change oil

Clutch release arm .... check freeplay
1990-91

Oil filter .... replace

EVERY 7.5 MI—12 KM
Tires .... rotate

EVERY 12 MO/15 MI—24 KM
Air conditioner filter, Vigor .... replace

Brake system .... inspect
Inspect calipers, hoses, lines
Check thickness of rotors

Exhaust system .... inspect

Front wheel alignment ..... inspect/adjust

Suspension mounting bolts ...... inspect

Clutch pedal travel .... check

Power steering .... check level PS
Inspect power steering system

Valve clearance, ex. Legend ...... adjust

AT FIRST 15 MO/15 MI—24 KM;
THEN EVERY 30 MO/30 MI—48 KM
Parking brake adjustment .... check

Steering system .... inspect

EVERY 24 MO/30 MI—48 KM
Anti-lock brake system .... inspect

Brake fluid .... replace HB

Final drive,
   1991-92 Legend ..... change lubricant

Fuel lines & connections .... inspect

Transaxle, automatic .... change lubricant

Transaxle, manual ...... change lubricant

Air cleaner element .... replace

Cooling system
   1986-88 .... replace coolant EC
Inspect hoses & connections
Initial service at 36 mo/45 mi (72 km)

Drive belt(s) .... inspect/adjust

Spark plugs ex. 1991-92 Legend .. replace

1989-92, AT 36 MO/45 MI—72 KM;
THEN AT 60 MO/75 MI—120 KM;
THEN EVERY 24 MO/30 MI—48 KM
Cooling system .... change coolant

EVERY 48 MO/60 MI—96 KM
Anti-lock brake system high
   pressure hose .... replace

Catalytic converter heat shield .... inspect

Crankcase emission control
   system .... inspect
Check PCV valve & blowby filter

Distributor cap & rotor .... inspect
Inspect ignition wires

EGR system, ex. Integra .... inspect

Evaporative control system ..... inspect

Fuel filter .... replace
Check fuel hoses

Idle speed & CO .... inspect
Check 1986-87 fast idle system

Ignition timing & control system ... inspect

Secondary air supply, Legend .... inspect

EVERY 72 MO/60 MI—96 KM
Spark plugs, 1991-92 Legend .... replace

1990 LEGEND, 1991-92 ALL,
EVERY 72 MO/90 MI—144 KM
Timing belt .... replace

Water pump .... inspect

SEVERE SERVICE
Brake discs, caliper and pads—Inspect every 6 mo/7.5 mi (12 km)

Crankcase—Change oil & filter every: 1986-90, 3 mo/3 mi (5 km); 1991, 3 mo/3.75 mi (6 km)

Power steering system—Inspect every 6 mo/7.5 mi (12 km)

Transmission & 1991-92 Legend final drive—Change fluid or lubricant every 12 mo/15 mi (24 km) when towing a trailer

KEY TO LUBRICANTS

AF	DEXRON®-II Automatic Transmission Fluid
EC	Ethylene Glycol Coolant
GL-4	Gear Oil, API Service GL-4
GL-5	Gear Oil, API Service GL-5
HB	Hydraulic Brake Fluid, DOT 3 or 4
PS	Power Steering Fluid Honda Part No. 08208-99961
SG	Motor Oil, API Service SG

CRANKCASE .... SG

CAPACITY, Refill:	Liters	Qt
Integra: 1986-87	3.0	3.2
1988-91	3.3	3.5
Legend: 1986-90	4.0	4.2
1991-92	4.5	4.8
Vigor	4.0	4.2

Capacity shown does not include filter. When replacing filter, additional oil may be needed

1986-87
Above 14°F (–10°C) 20W-40, 20W-50
Above –4°F (–20°C) 10W-40
–4° to 90°F (–20° to 32°C) 10W-30
Below 32°F (0°C) 5W-30
Below 14°F (–10°C) 5W-20
1988-92
Above 20°F (–7°C) 10W-30
All temperatures 5W-30*
* Preferred

TRANSAXLE, Automatic .... AF

CAPACITY, Initial Refill*:	Liters	Qt
Integra: 1986-89	2.4	2.5
1990-91	3.0	3.2
Legend	3.2	3.4
Vigor	2.5	2.6

* With engine at operating temperature, shift transmission through all gears. Turn engine off and check fluid level within one minute

TRANSAXLE, Manual .... SG
Above 15°F (–10°C), 30; above –5°F (–20°C), 20W-40
All temperatures 10W-30, 10W-40

CAPACITY, Refill:	Liters	Pt
Integra: 1986-89	2.3	4.8
1990-91	2.1	4.4
Legend	2.2	4.6
Vigor	1.8	3.8

FINAL DRIVE
1991-92 Legend, Vigor GL-4, GL-5
Above 0°F (–18°C), 90; below 0°F (–18°C), 80W, 80W-90

CAPACITY, Refill:	Liters	Pt
All w/MT & AT	1.0	2.2

SERVICE LOCATIONS — ENGINE AND CHASSIS

HOOD RELEASE: Front or inside

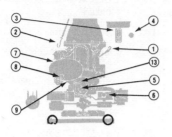

1983
2.5L (151) GM

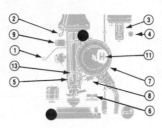

1983-84
2.5L (150) AMC

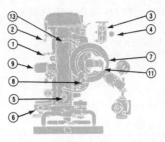

1983-88
4.2L (258)

① Crankcase dipstick
② Transmission dipstick
③ Brake fluid reservoir
④ Clutch fluid reservoir
⑤ Oil fill cap
⑥ Power steering reservoir
⑦ Air filter
⑧ Fuel filter
⑨ Oil filter
⑩ PCV filter
⑪ EGR valve
⑫ Oxygen sensor
⑬ PCV valve

4-8 PLUGS

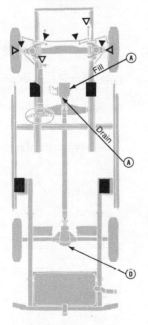

Concord, Spirit

9 PLUGS 6-7 FITTINGS

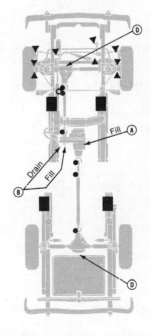

Eagle

LIFTING CAUTION
— Never lift car with bumper jack —

■ Lift adapter position
▲ Plug △ Plug, some models
● Cooling system drain
● Fitting ○ Fitting, some models
○ Cooling system drain, some models

Ⓐ Manual transmission/transaxle, drain & fill
Ⓑ Transfer case, drain & fill
Ⓒ Automatic transaxle final drive, NOT USED
Ⓓ Differential, drain & fill

AMERICAN MOTORS
1983 Concord, Eagle, Spirit

MI—MILES IN THOUSANDS
KM—KILOMETERS IN THOUSANDS

FIRST 5 MI—8 KM
Carb. to manifold bolts . . . . torque
4-cyl. only

Drive belts . . . . inspect/adjust

Idle speeds . . . . check/adjust

AT FIRST 5 MO/5 MI—8 KM; THEN EVERY 7.5 MO/7.5 MI—12 KM
Brake caliper . . . . lubricate **BL**
Disc brake abutment surface

Crankcase . . . . change oil

Differential . . . . check level

Exhaust system . . . . inspect

Propeller shaft splines . . . . lubricate **LB**

Steering linkage
  Eagle only . . . . **5 plugs** lubricate **LB**
Inspect seals & components; lubricate ball joints

Transfer case . . . . check level

Transmission, manual
  ex. Eagle . . . . check level

Battery . . . . check level

Brake & clutch
  master cylinders . . . . . . check level **HBH**

Cooling system . . . . check level

Oil filter . . . . replace
All Calif. 4-cyl. with automatic transmission, initial service, then every 15 mi (24 km)

Power steering reservoir . . . .check level **PS**

Steering gear, manual . . . . . check level **LB**

Transmission, automatic . . . . . . check level
Fluid warm, engine idling, shift through all positions, leave in NEUTRAL

EVERY 12 MONTHS
Cooling system . . . . change coolant **EC**
Initially at 20 mo/20 mi (32 km)

AT FIRST 12.5 MO/12.5 MI—20 KM; THEN EVERY 15 MO/15 MI—24 KM
Brake system . . . . check
Replace disc pads when lining is thickness of metal shoe. Lubricate caliper abutment surfaces. Inspect & lubricate where necessary

Clutch ex. Eagle . . . . adjust
Inspect & lubricate linkage

Fuel system . . . . inspect
Ex. Spirit, Concord
Check cap, tank, lines, hoses & connections

Ignition coil & wires Eagle . . . . inspect
4-cyl. Calif. models

Steering & suspension . . . . check

Steering linkage ex. Eagle . . . . lubricate **LB**
Inspect seals & components; lubricate ball joints

Carburetor . . . . inspect
Check & adjust idle speeds & mixture. Check choke for free movement

Fuel filter . . . . replace

Vacuum fittings, hoses & connections
  Eagle . . . . inspect

Body . . . . lubricate

EAGLE, EVERY 27.5 MO/27.5 MI—44 KM
Transmission, auto. . . . . change fluid

Differential . . . . change lubricant

Trans. manual . . . . change lubricant

Transfer case . . . . change lubricant

EVERY 30 MO/30 MI—48 KM
Differential, ex. Eagle . . . . change lubricant

Front wheel bearings
  ex. Eagle . . . . clean/repack **GC**
Torque 25 ft lb, back off nut 1/3 turn, retorque to 6 in. lb finger tight

Transmission, manual
  ex. Eagle . . . . change lubricant

Air cleaner element . . . . replace

Air injection system,
  ex. Eagle . . . . inspect/clean

Carburetor . . . . inspect
Check & adjust idle speed & mixture. Check choke for free movement

Charcoal canister filter,
  ex. Eagle . . . . replace

Distributor advance . . . . check

Distributor cap & rotor . . . . inspect

Drive belts . . . . inspect/adjust
Recommended service is every 42.5 mo/42.5 mi (68 km)

EGR system, ex. Eagle . . . . check
Inspect hoses and connections

Fuel system, ex. Eagle . . . . inspect
Check cap, tank, lines, hoses, and connections

Ignition coil & wires . . . . inspect
Concord & Spirit

Ignition timing . . . . check

Oxygen sensor . . . . replace/reset
Concord and Spirit all; Eagle Calif. 4-cyl.

PCV filter . . . . clean
All Calif. 4-cyl. with automatic transmission, replace

PCV valve . . . . replace
Inspect hoses & connections

Spark plugs . . . . replace

TAC system . . . . inspect

Vacuum fittings, hoses &
  connections . . . . inspect

SEVERE SERVICE
Crankcase—Change oil: Eagle, every 2.5 mi (4 km)

Transmission, automatic—Except Eagle, adjust bands, change fluid & filter every 30 mo/30 mi (48 km)

Air cleaner element—Replace at 15 mi (24 km)

KEY TO LUBRICANTS

AF	DEXRON®-II Automatic Transmission Fluid
BL	Brake Lubricant
EC	Ethylene Glycol Coolant Mix 50/50 with water
EP	Extreme Pressure Gear Lubricant
GC	Wheel Bearing Grease, NLGI Category GC
GL-5	Gear Oil, API Service GL-5
GL-5 ★	Special Lubricant for Twin-Grip Differential
HBH	Hydraulic Brake Fluid, Extra Heavy-Duty
LB	Chassis Grease, NLGI Category LB
PS	Power Steering Fluid
SF	Motor Oil, API Service SF
SG	Motor Oil, API Service SG

CRANKCASE . . . . SG

CAPACITY, Refill:	Liters	Qt
4-cyl.	2.3	2.5
6-cyl.	3.8	4.0

Capacity shown is without filter. When replacing filter, additional oil may be needed

Above 40°F (4°C)	20W-40, 20W-50
Above 0°F (−18°C)	10W-30, 10W-40
Below 60°F (16°C)	5W-30

TRANSMISSION, Automatic . . . . AF

CAPACITY, Initial Refill*:	Liters	Qt
All models	3.8	4.0

*With the engine at operating temperature, shift transmission through all gears. Check fluid level in PARK and add fluid as needed
For Adjustment Specifications, see Service Instr.

TRANSMISSION, Manual
T-4, T-5		EP†
Others 80W-90, 85W-90 **GL-5**		

†75W-90 **GL-5** may be used for top-up only

CAPACITY, Refill:	Liters	Pt
3-speed	1.4	3.0
4-speed SR4	1.6	3.3
T4 Spirit, Concord	1.9	4.0
T4 Eagle	1.7	3.5
5-speed Eagle	1.9	4.0
Spirit, Concord	2.1	4.5

TRANSFER CASE . . . . AF

CAPACITY, Refill:	Liters	Pt
All models	2.8	6.0

DIFFERENTIAL
With Trailer Tow Pkg.	80W-140 **GL-5**
Standard	85W-90 **GL-5**
Twin-Grip, Trac-Lok	85W-90 **GL-5 ★**

CAPACITY, Refill:	Liters	Pt
All ex. Eagle front	1.4	3.0
Eagle front	1.2	2.5

TWIN-GRIP IDENTIFICATION:
Sticker located in cargo compartment near spare tire

SERVICE AT TIME OR MILEAGE—WHICHEVER OCCURS FIRST

AMPM6　　　　　　　　　　　　　　　　　　　　AMPM6

W　SERVICE TO MAINTAIN EMISSION WARRANTY

MI—MILES IN THOUSANDS
KM—KILOMETERS IN THOUSANDS

1984-85, AT FIRST 5 MI—8 KM
1986-88, AT FIRST 5 MO/5 MI—8 KM
Engine idle speed . . . . adjust

Carburetor mounting bolts . . . . torque

1984, FIRST 5 MO/5 MI—8 KM;
THEN EVERY 7.5 MO/7.5 MI—12 KM
1985, EVERY 7.5 MI—12 KM
1986-88, EVERY 7.5 MO/7.5 MI—12 KM
W Crankcase . . . . change oil

Differentials . . . . check level

W Exhaust system . . . . inspect

W Oil filter . . . . replace

Propeller shaft . . . . lubricate **LB**
Splines & cardan "U" joints

Steering linkage . . . . lubricate **LB**
Inspect seals & components; lubricate ball joints

Transfer case . . . . check level

Transmission, manual . . . . check level

Battery . . . . check
Also check tie downs, connections, case, voltage

Brake & clutch
　master cylinders . . . . . . check level **HBH**

W Cooling system . . . . check level **EC**

W Drive belts . . . . check/adjust
V-belts only

Power steering reservoir . . . check level **PS**

Transmission, automatic . . . . . . check level
Fluid warm, engine idling, shift through all positions, leave in NEUTRAL

Tires . . . . check

1984, FIRST 12.5 MO/12.5 MI—20 KM;
THEN EVERY 15 MO/15 MI—24 KM
1985-88, EVERY 30 MO/30 MI—48 KM
Brake system . . . . check
Replace disc pads when lining is thickness of metal shoe. Lubricate caliper abutment surfaces. Inspect & lubricate where necessary. Check parking brake operation, wheel cylinders, lines & master cylinder

W Fuel system . . . . inspect
Check cap, tank, lines, hoses & connections

Steering & suspension . . . . check

W Fuel filter . . . . replace

Body . . . . lubricate

1984, EVERY 20 MO/20 MI—24 KM
1985, EVERY 22.5 MI—30 KM
1986-88, EVERY 22 MO/22.5 MI—30 KM
W Cooling system . . . . change coolant **EC**
Flush and service system

EVERY 30 MO/30 MI—48 KM
Clutch adjustment . . . . check

Differentials . . . . change lubricant

Transfer case . . . . change lubricant

Transmission, automatic . . . . . change fluid

Transmission, manual . . change lubricant

W Air cleaner element . . . . replace

W Carburetor choke . . . . clean
Check for free movement

Distributor advance . . . . check

Distributor cap & rotor . . . . inspect

W Drive belts . . . . inspect/adjust

W PCV filter . . . . clean
Ex. 1985 Calif. models

W PCV valve . . . . replace
Ex. 1985 Federal models
Inspect hoses & connections

W Spark plugs . . . . replace

W TAC system . . . . inspect

Vacuum fittings, hoses &
　connections . . . . inspect

1985-88 EVERY 52 MO/52.5 MI—84.5 KM
W Air valve . . . . check
1985-86

W Carburetor WOT switch
　& Sole-vac . . . . check
1985-86

W Charcoal canister & filter . . . . replace

W Distributor cap & rotor . . . . replace

W Drive belts . . . . replace

W Emission control
　devices (all) . . . . check
1985-88

W Emission system vacuum hoses . . . replace

W Fuel filler cap . . . . replace

W Ignition wires . . . . replace

W Ignition timing & idle speeds . . . . . . check

W Oxygen sensor . . . . replace

1987-88 EVERY 60 MO/60 MI
Battery . . . . replace

SEVERE SERVICE
Crankcase—Change oil & oil filter every 3.5 mo/3.75 mi (6 km)

Air cleaner element—Replace at 15 mi (24 km)

Transfer case, differentials, transmission—Change lubricants every 15 mo/15 mi (24 km)

KEY TO LUBRICANTS

AF　　DEXRON®-II Automatic Transmission Fluid

CC　　Motor Oil, API Service CC

EC　　Ethylene Glycol Coolant
　　　Mix 50/50 with water

EP　　Extreme Pressure Gear Lubricant

GL-5　Gear Oil, API Service GL-5

HBH　Hydraulic Brake Fluid, Extra Heavy-Duty

LB　　Chassis Grease, NLGI Category LB

MA　　MERCON® Automatic Transmission Fluid

PS　　Power Steering Fluid

SF　　Motor Oil, API Service SF

SG　　Motor Oil, API Service SG

CRANKCASE . . . . **SG**
CAPACITY, Refill:　　　　　Liters　　Qt
4-cyl. . . . . 3.3　　3.5
6-cyl. . . . . 3.8　　4.0
Capacity shown is without filter. When replacing filter, additional oil may be needed
Above 30°F (−1°C) 20W-40, 20W-50
Above 0°F (−18°C) 10W-30, 10W-40
Below 60°F (16°C) 5W-30

TRANSMISSION, Automatic
1984-86 . . . . **AF†**
1987-88 . . . . **MA**
† **MA** can be used for top-off
CAPACITY, Initial Refill*:　　Liters　　Qt
All models . . . . 3.8　　4.0
*With the engine at operating temperature, shift transmission through all gears. Check fluid level in PARK and add fluid as needed

TRANSMISSION, Manual . . . . **EP†**
CAPACITY, Refill:　　　　　Liters　　Pt
4-speed . . . . 1.7　　3.5
5-speed . . . . 1.9　　4.0
†When specified lube is not available: 1984, 75W-90 **GL-5** may be used for top-up only
1985-88, 85W-90 **GL-5** may be used for top-up only

TRANSFER CASE
Models 119 & 129 . . . . **MA**
Others . . . . **AF†**
† **MA** can be used for top-off
CAPACITY, Refill:　　　　　Liters　　Pt
1984-85 . . . . 2.8　　6.0
1986-88 . . . . 3.3　　7.0

DIFFERENTIALS
With Trailer Tow Pkg. 80W-140 **GL-5**
Trac-Lok 1988 . . . . 80W-140 **GL-5**
Add 4 oz. part #8983 100 003
Standard 75W-90 **GL-5**
CAPACITY, Refill:　　　　　Liters　　Pt
Rear . . . . 1.4　　3.0
Front . . . . 1.2　　2.5

AMC/RENAULT
1983-87 Alliance, Encore, GTA

SERVICE LOCATIONS — ENGINE AND CHASSIS

HOOD RELEASE: Inside

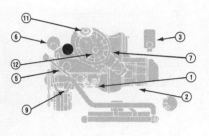

1983-87
1397cc Alliance, Encore

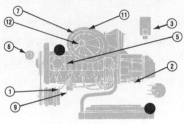

1985-87
1721cc Alliance, Encore

① Crankcase dipstick
② Transmission dipstick
③ Brake fluid reservoir
④ Clutch fluid reservoir
⑤ Oil fill cap
⑥ Power steering reservoir
⑦ Air filter
⑧ Fuel filter
⑨ Oil filter
⑩ PCV filter
⑪ EGR valve
⑫ Oxygen sensor
⑬ PCV valve

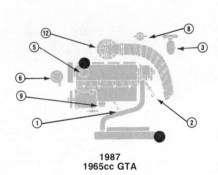

1987
1965cc GTA

● Cooling system drain

0 FITTINGS
0 PLUGS

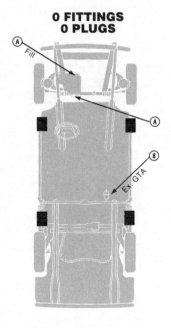

1983-87
Alliance, Encore, GTA

Ⓐ Manual transmission/transaxle,
   drain & fill
Ⓑ Transfer case, NOT USED
Ⓒ Automatic transaxle final drive,
   NOT USED
Ⓓ Differential, NOT USED

CAUTION: On front wheel drive vehicles the center of gravity is further forward than on rear wheel drive vehicles. When removing major components from the rear of the vehicle while it is on a hoist, the vehicle must be supported in a manner to prevent it from tipping forward.

■ Lift adapter position

SERVICE AT TIME OR MILEAGE—WHICHEVER OCCURS FIRST

RTIPM2   RTIPM2

W   SERVICE TO MAINTAIN EMISSION WARRANTY

MI—MILES IN THOUSANDS
KM—KILOMETERS IN THOUSANDS

1985-87, AT FIRST 7.5 MI—12 KM;
THEN EVERY 15 MI—24 KM
Drive belts . . . . check/adjust
1.4L eng.

1986-87,
EVERY 7.5 MO/7.5 MI—12 KM
1983-85,
EVERY 6 MO/7.5 MI—12 KM
W Crankcase . . . . change oil

W Oil filter . . . . replace
At first oil change, then at every other oil change

Transaxle, automatic . . . . check level
Engine at slow idle in PARK
For cold fluid (preferred method), use dipstick side
marked "COLD". For hot fluid, use dipstick side
marked "HOT"

Transaxle, manual . . . . check level

Suspension & suspension
   rubber boots . . . . inspect

Tires . . . . inspect
Check pressure & wear

Battery . . . . clean terminals
Check voltage. Inspect case & tiedowns

Brake fluid reservoir . . . . . . check level **HB**

Cooling system . . . . check level **EC**

Drive belts . . . . check/adjust
Ex. 1.4L Alliance, 1.7L, 2.0L

Power steering reservoir . . check level **PS**

1983,
EVERY 12 MO/15 MI—24 KM
1984-87, EVERY 15 MO/15 MI—24 KM
Exhaust system . . . . inspect

Front brake pads . . . . inspect

Air conditioning . . . . check operation

Body . . . . lubricate 10W **MO**
Door hinges & latches as needed. Inspect wiring &
hose routings

1983, EVERY 24 MO/30 MI—48 KM
1984-87,
EVERY 30 MO/30 MI—48 KM
Cooling system . . . . . . change coolant **EC**
1984, initial service then at start of every winter season

Hoses & connectors . . . . . . inspect/tighten
Check vacuum hoses, and cooling, fuel, brake, and
power steering systems

Transaxle, automatic . . . . change fluid
Clean/change filter

Transaxle, manual . . . . . . change lubricant

Rear brakes . . . . inspect
Also adjust parking brake

Brake hoses . . . . inspect

Steering rods & ball joints . . . . . . inspect

W Air cleaner element . . . . replace

Clutch free play . . . . adjust

Drive belts . . . . check/adjust
1.7L & 2.0L eng.

W Spark plugs . . . . replace

KEY TO LUBRICANTS

AF	DEXRON®-II Automatic Transmission Fluid
CC	Motor Oil, API Service CC
EC	Ethylene Glycol Coolant Mix 50/50 with water
GL-5	Gear Oil, API Service GL-5
HB	Hydraulic Brake Fluid, DOT 3
MO	Motor Oil
PS	Power Steering Fluid AMC/Jeep power steering fluid
SG	Motor Oil, API Service SG

CRANKCASE . . . . **SG**
CAPACITY, Refill: Liters   Qt
Includes filter:
1983 . . . .   3.0   3.3
1983* 3.8   4.0
1984-87 1.4L 3.8   4.0
1985-86 1.7L 5.2   5.5
1987 1.7L, 2.0L 4.7   5.0
* Built March 1983 & later. Identified by a yellow sticker on
   the cylinder head cover
Above 30°F (–1°C) 20W-40, 20W-50
Above 0°F (–18°C) 10W-30, 10W-40
Below 60°F (16°C) 5W-30

TRANSAXLE, Automatic . . . . **AF**
CAPACITY, Initial Refill*:   Liters   Qt
All models 2.4   2.5
* With the engine at operating temperature, shift transmis-
   sion through all gears. Check fluid level in PARK and add
   fluid as needed
When refilling transmission, add one bottle of anti-foam
additive Part No. 8983 100 034 to transmission
Caution: This transmission is extremely sensitive to over-
fill or underfill conditions

TRANSAXLE, Manual 75W-90 **GL-5**
CAPACITY, Refill: Liters   Pt
4-speed 3.2   6.8
5-speed 3.4   7.2
To drain, remove bottom plug

SERVICE LOCATIONS — ENGINE AND CHASSIS

AIIDP-1

HOOD RELEASE: Inside

AIIDP-1

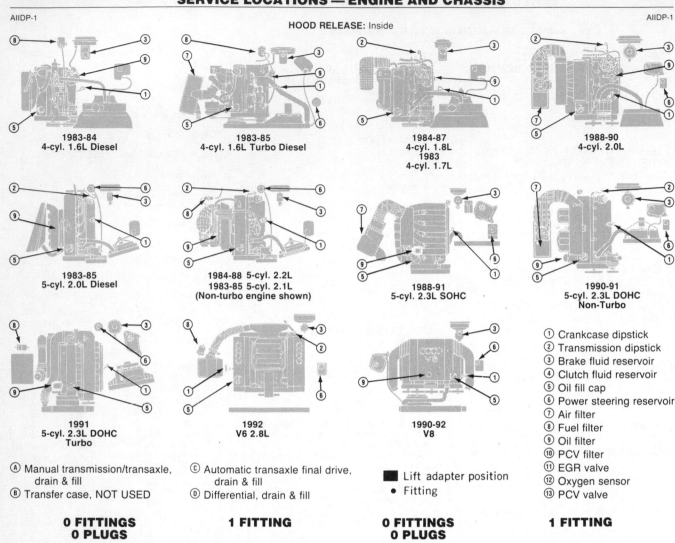

1983-84
4-cyl. 1.6L Diesel

1983-85
4-cyl. 1.6L Turbo Diesel

1984-87
4-cyl. 1.8L
1983
4-cyl. 1.7L

1988-90
4-cyl. 2.0L

1983-85
5-cyl. 2.0L Diesel

1984-88 5-cyl. 2.2L
1983-85 5-cyl. 2.1L
(Non-turbo engine shown)

1988-91
5-cyl. 2.3L SOHC

1990-91
5-cyl. 2.3L DOHC
Non-Turbo

1991
5-cyl. 2.3L DOHC
Turbo

1992
V6 2.8L

1990-92
V8

① Crankcase dipstick
② Transmission dipstick
③ Brake fluid reservoir
④ Clutch fluid reservoir
⑤ Oil fill cap
⑥ Power steering reservoir
⑦ Air filter
⑧ Fuel filter
⑨ Oil filter
⑩ PCV filter
⑪ EGR valve
⑫ Oxygen sensor
⑬ PCV valve

Ⓐ Manual transmission/transaxle, drain & fill
Ⓑ Transfer case, NOT USED
Ⓒ Automatic transaxle final drive, drain & fill
Ⓓ Differential, drain & fill

■ Lift adapter position
• Fitting

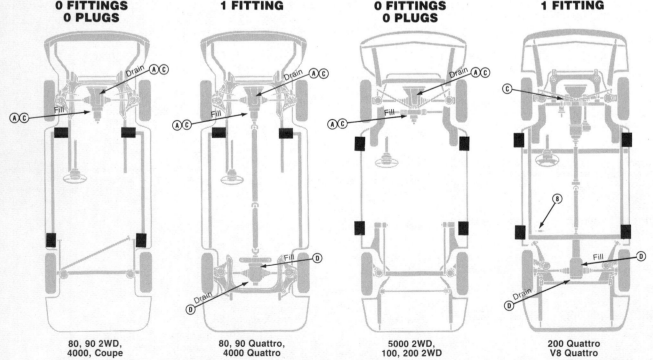

**0 FITTINGS
0 PLUGS**

1 FITTING

**0 FITTINGS
0 PLUGS**

1 FITTING

80, 90 2WD,
4000, Coupe

80, 90 Quattro,
4000 Quattro

5000 2WD,
100, 200 2WD

200 Quattro
V8 Quattro

CAUTION: On front wheel drive vehicles the center of gravity is further forward than on rear wheel drive vehicles. When removing major components from the rear of the vehicle while it is on a hoist, the vehicle must be supported in a manner to prevent it from tipping forward.

SERVICE AT TIME OR MILEAGE—WHICHEVER OCCURS FIRST

AllPM2   Perform the following maintenance services at the intervals indicated to keep the vehicle warranties in effect   AllPM2

W SERVICE TO MAINTAIN EMISSION WARRANTY

MI—MILES IN THOUSANDS
KM—KILOMETERS IN THOUSANDS

1983-85 TURBO DIESEL,
1984-88 GAS TURBO,
EVERY 6 MO/5 MI—8 KM
ALL OTHER ENGINES,
EVERY 6 MO/7.5 MI—12 KM

W Cooling system .... check level **EC**

W Crankcase .... change oil

W Crankcase oil filter .... replace
At initial service only

Diesel fuel filter .... drain water

W Turbocharger oil filter .... replace
At initial service only

EVERY 12 MO/15 MI—24 KM
Brake system .... Inspect/adjust
Check for damage & leaks, check pad thickness, check
& adjust pedal travel, check pressure regulator, adjust
hand brake

Drive shaft boots .... inspect

W Exhaust system .... inspect

Front suspension .... inspect
Check ball joint & tie rod dust seals, check tie rods,
check drive axle boots

W Fuel filter .... replace
5000 gasoline engine only
Not required for Calif. warranty

Final drive, automatic .... check level

Transaxle, automatic .... check level

Transaxle, manual .... check level

Wheels & tires .... inspect

W Air filter element .... clean
Not required for Calif. warranty

Brake master cylinder .... check level **HB**

Compression .... check

W Crankcase oil filter .... replace

W PCV system .... inspect
Diesel engine only

W Idle speed, ex. Turbo .... check/adjust
Not required for Calif. warranty

W Mini fuel filter screen .. remove/replace
1984-87 4000S, Coupe, 4000 Quattro: Remove hollow
bolt with screen from inlet side of fuel distributor, install
new bolt without screen (Part No. N0210712, 4-cyl.;
049133245, 5-cyl.)

Power steering .... check level
With Central Hydraulic System, **SLF**
Without Central Hydraulic System, **AF**

W Spark plugs .... replace
1983 All ex. Turbo
1984-86 Coupe & 5000S only
Not required for Calif. warranty

W Turbocharger .... inspect

W Turbocharger oil filter .... replace

Valve clearance .... check/adjust
1983 all engines, 1984-85 Diesel engines & Quattro
Coupe only

Windshield washers .... fill

Clutch free play .... check/adjust

Door hinges .... lubricate **MO**

W Fuel tank & lines .... inspect

Sunroof rails .... clean/lubricate **SLS**

EVERY 24 MONTHS
Brakes .... change fluid **HB**
Check operation of warning light switch

EVERY 24 MO/30 MI—48 KM
Automatic Transmission .. change fluid **AF**
Clean pan & strainer, replace gasket

Front axle .... inspect
Check ball joint & tie rod dust seals, check tie rods

Propshaft, Quattro 4WD .... lubricate **LM**

W Air filter element .... replace

W Diesel fuel filter .... replace
Not required for Calif. warranty

W Drive belts .... check/adjust
Recommended replacement on Diesels

W Oxygen sensor .... replace
Reset mileage counter

W Spark plugs .... replace

W Tank fuel filter .... replace
4000 & Coupe only
Not required for Calif. warranty

KEY TO LUBRICANTS
See other Audi chart

CRANKCASE
Diesel engines .... **SG/CD**
Gasoline engines .... **SG**

CAPACITY, Refill:

	Liters	Qt
Diesel engines:		
1983 4000	3.3	3.5
1983-85 5000	4.7	5.0
4-cyl. gasoline engines:		
1983-87 4000	2.8	3.0
1988 80, 90	2.5	2.6
5-cyl. gasoline engines:		
1983 4000, Coupe	4.0	4.2
1983 5000 ex. Turbo	4.3	4.5
1983 5000 Turbo	3.5	3.7
1983-85 Quattro Coupe	3.8	4.0
1984-87 Coupe	3.3	3.5
1984-88 5000	4.3	4.5
1988 80, 90	3.5	3.7

Capacity shown is without filter. When replacing filter, additional oil may be needed

1983-87

68° to 104°F (20° to 40°C)	40
32° to 86°F (0° to 30°C)	30
14° to 86°F (–10° to 30°C)	20W-40, 20W-50
14° to 50°F (–10° to 10°C)	20W-20
5° to 86°F (–15° to 30°C)	15W-40, 15W-50
–4° to 50°F (–20° to 10°C)	10W-30, 10W-40*
–22° to 14°F (–30° to –10°C)	5W-20†

*10W-40 not recommended for 1986-87 models
†5W-20 not recommended for Diesel engines

1988

Above 68° F (20°C)	40
32° to 86°F (0° to 30°C)	30
Above 14°F (–10°C)	20W 40, 20W-50
14° to 50°F (–10° to 10°C)	20W-20
Below 25°F (–4°C)	10W
Above 5°F (–15°C)	15W-40, 15W-50
0° to 60°F (–18° to 16°C)	10W-30, 10W-40
Below 14°F (–10°C)	5W-20, 5W-30

TRANSMISSION, Automatic .... **AF**
Does not include final drive

CAPACITY, Refill:

	Liters	Qt
1983 5000	3.0	3.2
1983-87 4000	3.0	3.2
1983-88 5000	3.3	3.5
1988 80, 90	3.0	3.2

Add specified quantity. With engine at operating temperature, shift transmission through all gears. Check level in PARK and add fluid as needed

TRANSAXLE, Manual
1983-86 .... 80W-90 **GL-4**
1987-88 .... 75W-90 **GL-4**†
†Synthetic gear oil, Audi Part No. G050 000

CAPACITY, Refill:

	Liters	Pt
FWD Models:		
80, 90	2.4	5.0
4000 4-cyl. 4-speed	1.7	3.6
4000 4-cyl. 5-speed	2.0	4.2
4000 5-cyl.	2.4	5.0
5000	2.6	5.4
Quattro Models:		
80, 90	2.8	6.0
4000, from 8-12-84	2.2	4.6
To 8-13-84	3.2	6.8
5000, from 7-15-85	2.2	4.6
To 7-16-85	3.1	6.6
Turbo Coupe	3.6	7.6

FINAL DRIVE, Auto. Trans 90 **GL-5**

CAPACITY, Refill:

	Liters	Pt
1983 5000	1.0	2.2
1983-87 4000	0.9	2.0
1984-88 5000	0.9	2.0
1988 80, 90	0.8	1.6

REAR DIFFERENTIAL 90 **GL-5**

CAPACITY, Refill:

	Liters	Pt
80, 90, 4000	0.8	1.6
5000	1.7	3.6
Turbo Quattro Coupe	2.2	4.6

AUDI
1989-92 All Models

CHEK-CHART

AllPM3   Perform the following maintenance services at the intervals indicated to keep the vehicle warranties in effect   AllPM3
W   SERVICE TO MAINTAIN EMISSION WARRANTY

MI—MILES IN THOUSANDS
KM—KILOMETERS IN THOUSANDS

EVERY 7.5 MI—12 KM
Brake master cylinder
1990 . . . . check level **HB**

Cooling system 1990 . . . . . check level **EC**

Hydraulic system/power steering
1989-90 . . . . check level **SLF**

W Crankcase . . . . change oil

W Crankcase oil filter . . . . replace
At initial service only

Windshield washers . . . . fill

Automatic shift
lock 1990-91 . . . . check

EVERY 12 MO/15 MI—24 KM
Brake system . . . . inspect/adjust
Check for damage & leaks, check pad thickness, check
& adjust pedal travel, check pressure regulator, adjust
hand brake

Drive shaft boots . . . . inspect

W Exhaust system . . . . inspect

Final drive, automatic . . . . check level

Transaxle, automatic . . . . check level
Level check not required for V8 Quattro

Transaxle, manual . . . . check level

Wheels & tires . . . . inspect

Battery . . . . check level

Brake master cylinder . . . . check level **HB**

Cooling system . . . . check level **EC**

W Crankcase oil filter . . . . replace

Hydraulic system/
power steering . . . . check level **SLF**

W Idle speed, ex. Turbo . . . check/adjust
Not required for Calif. warranty

On-Board diagnostic system . . check/clear

Electrical equipment . . . . inspect

Sunroof rails . . . . clean/lubricate **SLS**

EVERY 24 MONTHS
Brakes . . . . change fluid **HB**
Check operation of warning light switch

EVERY 24 MO/30 MI—48 KM
Automatic Transmission . . change fluid **AF**
Clean pan & strainer, replace gasket

Front axle . . . . inspect
Check ball joint & tie rod dust seals, check tie rods

Propshaft, Quattro 4WD . . . . lubricate **LM**

W Air filter element . . . . replace

W Drive belts . . . . check/adjust

W Spark plugs . . . . replace

W Timing belt, V8 . . . . check/adjust

EVERY 60 MI—96 KM
Oxygen sensor . . . . replace

1991 EVERY 24 MO/90 MI—144 KM
Engine coolant, V8 . . . . replace **EC**

1990 EVERY 90 MI—144 KM
Timing belt, V8 . . . . replace

SEVERE SERVICE
Crankcase—Change oil and filter at half of
recommended interval

Air Filter—Replace at 12 mo/15 mi (24 km)

KEY TO LUBRICANTS

AF	DEXRON®-II Automatic Transmission Fluid
CD	Motor Oil, API Service CD
EC	Ethylene Glycol Coolant Mix with water to desired freeze protection
GL-4	Gear Oil, API Service GL-4
GL-5	Gear Oil, API Service GL-5
HB	Hydraulic Brake Fluid, DOT 4
LM	Lithium Grease
MO	Motor Oil
SG	Motor Oil, API Service SG
SLF	Special Lubricant—Fluid Audi Part No. G002 000
SLS	Silicone Lubricant-Spray

CRANKCASE . . . . SG

CAPACITY, Refill	Liters	Qt
4-cyl. 2.0L:		
1989-90 80, 90	2.5	2.6
5-cyl. 2.2L, 2.3L:		
1989-91 80, 90	3.0	3.2
1989-91 100, 200	4.0	4.2
1990-91 Coupe Quattro . . .	4.0	4.2
V6 2.8L:		
1992 100	5.0*	5.3*
V8 3.6L:		
1990-91 V8 Quattro	8.0*	8.5*
V8 4.2L:		
1992 V8 Quattro	8.0*	8.5*

Capacity shown is without filter. When replacing filter, additional oil may be needed
*Capacity shown includes filter, add specified amount,
  run engine to operating temperature. Recheck level and
  correct as necessary

Above 68°F (20°C)	40
32° to 86°F (0° to 30°C)	30
Above 14°F (−10°C)	20W-40, 20W-50
14° to 50°F (−10° to 10°C)	20W-20
Below 25°F (−4°C)	10W
Above 5°F (−15°C)	15W-40, 15W-50
0° to 60°F (−18° to 16°C)	10W-30, 10W-40
Below 14°F (−10°C)	5W-20*, 5W-30

*5W-20 not recommended for 1992 models

TRANSMISSION, Automatic . . . . AF
Does not include final drive

CAPACITY, Refill	Liters	Qt
80, 90	3.0	3.2
100, 200	3.0	3.2
V8 Quattro	3.8†	4.0†

Add specified quantity. With engine at operating temperature, shift transmission through all gears. Check fluid level
in PARK and add fluid as needed
†Vehicle is not equipped with a transmission dipstick, special tools and procedure required, see manufacturer's
  service literature

TRANSAXLE, Manual . . . 75W-90 GL-4†
†Synthetic Gear Oil, Audi Part No. G005 000

CAPACITY, Refill:	Liters	Pt
Coupe, 80, 90, 100 2WD . .	2.4	5.0
Coupe, 90, 100 4WD	2.9	6.0
200 2WD	2.6	5.4
200 4WD To 9-13-88	2.2	4.6
From 9-12-88	2.6	5.4

FINAL DRIVE, Auto. Trans.
1989-91		90W **GL-5**
1992	75W-90 **GL-4†**

†Synthetic Gear Oil, Audi Part No. G005 000

CAPACITY, Refill:	Liters	Pt
80, 90	0.8	1.6
100, 200	1.0	2.2
V8 Quattro	0.5	1.0

REAR DIFFERENTIAL 90W GL-5
CAPACITY, Refill:	Liters	Pt
Coupe, 90	0.8	1.6
100, 200, V8 Quattro	1.7	3.6

SERVICE LOCATIONS — ENGINE AND CHASSIS

BWIDP-1   BWIDP-1

HOOD RELEASE: Inside

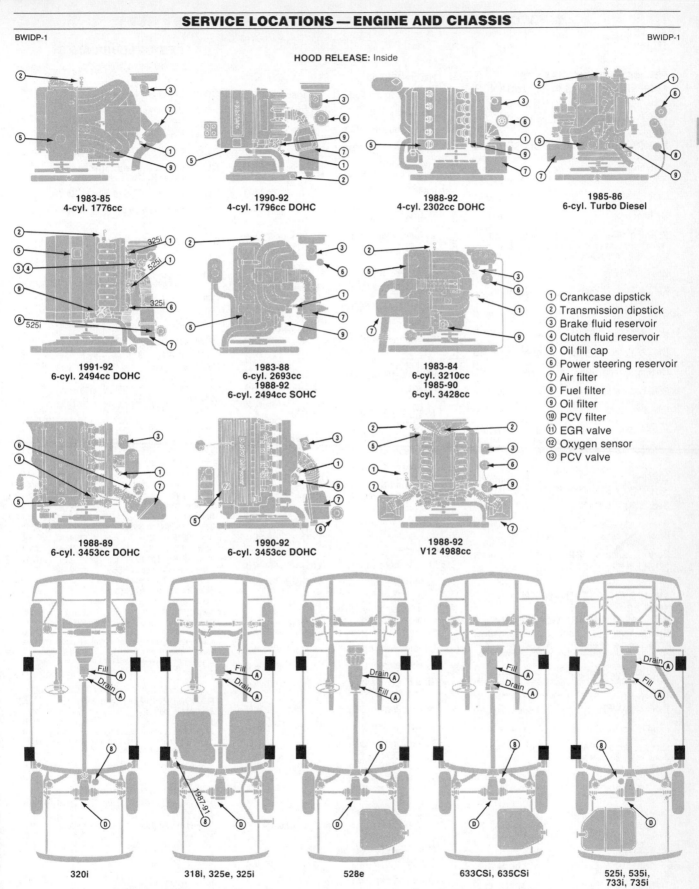

1983-85
4-cyl. 1776cc

1990-92
4-cyl. 1796cc DOHC

1988-92
4-cyl. 2302cc DOHC

1985-86
6-cyl. Turbo Diesel

1991-92
6-cyl. 2494cc DOHC

1983-88
6-cyl. 2693cc
1988-92
6-cyl. 2494cc SOHC

1983-84
6-cyl. 3210cc
1985-90
6-cyl. 3428cc

① Crankcase dipstick
② Transmission dipstick
③ Brake fluid reservoir
④ Clutch fluid reservoir
⑤ Oil fill cap
⑥ Power steering reservoir
⑦ Air filter
⑧ Fuel filter
⑨ Oil filter
⑩ PCV filter
⑪ EGR valve
⑫ Oxygen sensor
⑬ PCV valve

1988-89
6-cyl. 3453cc DOHC

1990-92
6-cyl. 3453cc DOHC

1988-92
V12 4988cc

320i

318i, 325e, 325i

528e

633CSi, 635CSi

525i, 535i,
733i, 735i

■ Lift adapter
position

Ⓐ Manual transmission/transaxle,
drain & fill

Ⓑ Transfer case, 325iX only

Ⓒ Automatic transaxle final drive,
NOT USED

Ⓓ Differential, drain & fill

Copyright 1992 by H.M. Gousha, a division of Simon & Schuster

BMW
1983 320i, 1985-86 524td Turbo Diesel

MI—MILES IN THOUSANDS
KM—KILOMETERS IN THOUSANDS

1983, EVERY 7.5 MI—12 KM
1985-86,
INDICATED LUBRICATION SERVICE
Brakes 1985-86 .... inspect
Check thickness of pads & rotors, check condition of hoses, lines & fittings, check operation of hand brake

Crankcase .... change oil

Oil filter .... replace

Steering 1985-86 .... inspect/adjust
Check tightness of steering box, joint disc & threaded connections. Adjust free play

Wheels & tires .... inspect

Air conditioner 1983 .... check charge

Battery 1983 .... check level

Brake master cylinder .... check level **HB**

Clutch master cylinder .... check level **HB**

Cooling system 1983 ...... inspect/fill **EC**

Fuel separator, diesel .... drain trap

Idle & mixture 1983 .... check/adjust

Power steering .... check level **AF**
On models with Hydro Boost, pump brake pedal several times to discharge accumulator before checking level

Lighting .... inspect
Check all lighting, aim headlights as necessary

Seat belts .... inspect

Windshield wipers .... inspect
Check condition of blades, aim washers, fill

Service indicator, 524td .... reset
Special tool required

1983, EVERY 15 MI—24 KM
1985-86,
INDICATED INSPECTION SERVICE I
Brakes 1983 .... inspect
Check thickness of pads & rotors, check condition of hoses, lines & fittings, check operation of hand brake

Drive shaft & axles 1983 .... inspect
Inspect flexible couplings & constant velocity joint boots

Exhaust system .... inspect/tighten

Final drive .... check level

Hand brake 1985-86 ...... inspect/adjust
Check shoes & cables for wear, adjust & lube

Steering 1983 .... inspect/adjust
Check tightness of steering box, joint disc & threaded connections. Adjust free play

Transmission, automatic
1985-86 ....change fluid **AF**
Replace strainer & gasket, do not repeat at interval II

Transmission, automatic
1983 .... check level

Transmission, manual ..... check level

Air conditioner .... check/tighten
Tighten compressor mounts, check operation & charge

Battery 1985-86 .... check/fill

Cooling system 1985-86 ... inspect/fill **EC**

Drive belts 1983 .... check/adjust

Engine mounts 1983 ..... inspect/tighten

Engine preheat system, diesel ..... check

Fuel injection .... inspect
Check & tighten hoses, lines & fittings

Ignition points 1983 .... replace

Intake manifold 1983 .... inspect
Check hoses & tighten

Oxygen sensor 1983 .... check operation

Throttle linkage .... lubricate **LM**

Valve clearance .... check/adjust

Door locks & hinges . tighten/lubricate **MO**

Hood & trunk catches ...... lubricate **LM**

Sunroof .... lubricate

Service indicator, 524td .... reset
Special tool required

EVERY 12 MONTHS
Brakes .... change fluid **HB**

1983, EVERY 30 MI—48 KM
1985-86,
INDICATED INSPECTION SERVICE II
Clutch .... inspect

Drive belts 1985-86 .... check/adjust

Drive shaft & axles 1985-86 ...... inspect
Inspect flexible couplings & constant velocity joint boots

Final drive .... change lubricant

Fuel filter .... replace
Not required for Calif. warranty

Front wheel bearings ... check/adjust **WB**

Hand brake 1983 .... inspect/adjust
Check shoes & cables for wear, adjust & lube

Transmission, automatic
1983 ....change fluid **AF**
Replace strainer & gasket, do not repeat at interval II

Transmission, manual ... change lubricant

Air filter element .... replace

Glow plugs, diesel .... replace
At every second interval

Injection timing, diesel ...... check/adjust

Oxygen sensor .... replace

Spark plugs 1983 .... replace

Timing belt, diesel .... check/adjust

Service indicator, 524td .... reset
Special tool required

EVERY 48 MONTHS
Cooling system ...... replace coolant **EC**

1983, EVERY 60 MI—100 KM
Distributor cap & rotor .... inspect

Ignition timing, 320i .... check/adjust

Ignition wires .... inspect

Power steering filter .... replace

KEY TO LUBRICANTS

AF	DEXRON®-II Automatic Transmission Fluid	
CD	Motor Oil API Service CD	
EC	Ethylene Glycol Coolant Mix 50% with water	
GL-4	Gear Oil, API Service GL-4	
GL-5	Gear Oil, API Service GL-5	
GLS	Gear Lubricant, Special Mobil SHC 630, synthetic lubricant	
HB	Hydraulic Brake Fluid, DOT 4	
LM	Lithium Multipurpose Grease	
MO	Motor Oil	
SF	Motor Oil, API Service SF	
SG	Motor Oil, API Service SG	
SLF	Special Lubricant, Fluid BMW Part No. 81 22 9 407 549	
WB	Wheel Bearing Grease	

CRANKCASE
Gasoline engines .... **SF**
Diesel engines .... **SF/CD**
Gasoline engines:
68° to 122°F (20° to 50°C) 40
32° to 86°F (0° to 30°C) 30
14° to 122°F (–10° to 50°C) 20W-50
–4° to 104°F (–20° to 40°C) 15W-50
–4° to 86°F (–20° to 30°C) 15W-40
–4° to 50°F (–20° to 10°C) 20
–22° to 68°F (–30° to 20°C) 10W-50
–22° to 50°F (–30° to 10°C) 10W-40
–22° to 41°F (–30° to 5°C) 10W-30
–40° to 23°F (–40° to –5°C) 5W-30
–40° to 14°F (–40° to –10°C) 5W-20
Diesel engines:
Above 68°F (20°C) 40
32° to 86°F (0° to 30°C) 30
Above 32°F (0°C) 20W-40, 20W-50
Above 23°F (–5°C) 15W-40, 15W-50
14° to 68°F (–10° to 20°C) 20W-20
5° to 86°F (–15° to 30°C) 10W-40, 10W-50
5° to 50°F (–15° to 10°C) 10W-30
–4° to 32°F (–20° to 0°C) 10
Below 14°F (–10°C) 5W-20, 5W-30

CAPACITY, Refill:	Liters	Qt
1983 320i	3.8	4.0
1985-86 524td	4.5	4.8

Capacity shown is without filter. When replacing filter, additional oil may be needed
Additional oil may be needed if oil cooler is drained

TRANSMISSION, Automatic .... AF

CAPACITY, Refill:	Liters	Qt
All	2.0	2.1

Add specified quantity. With engine at operating temperature, shift transmission through all gears. Check level in PARK and add fluid as needed

TRANSMISSION, Manual
1983 .... 80W **GL-4**
1985-86 .... **AF**

CAPACITY, Refill:	Liters	Pt
1983 320i	1.4	3.0
1985-86 524td	1.6	3.4

DIFFERENTIAL 90 GL-5

CAPACITY, Refill:	Liters	Pt
1983 318i	0.9	1.9
1985-86 524td	1.7	3.6

SERVICE AT TIME OR MILEAGE—WHICHEVER OCCURS FIRST

BWIPM2   BWIPM2
Perform the following maintenance services at the intervals indicated to keep the vehicle warranties in effect

W   **SERVICE TO MAINTAIN EMISSION WARRANTY**

MI—MILES IN THOUSANDS
KM—KILOMETERS IN THOUSANDS

1992 INDICATED ENGINE OIL SERVICE

W Crankcase . . . . change oil

W Oil filter . . . . replace

Service indicator . . . . reset
Special tool required

Final drive, 325i . . . . change lubricant
At first service interval only

1983-91 INDICATED LUBRICATION SERVICE
1992 INDICATED INSPECTION SERVICE I

Brakes . . . . inspect
Check thickness of pads & rotors, check condition of hoses, lines & fittings, check operation of hand brake

W Crankcase 1983-91 . . . . change oil

W Oil filter 1983-91 . . . . replace

Steering . . . . inspect/adjust
Check tightness of steering box, joint disc & threaded connections. Adjust free play

Wheels & tires . . . . inspect

Brake master cylinder . . . . check level **HB**

Clutch master cylinder . . . . check level **HB**

W Drive belts 1983-88 . . . . inspect/adjust
Ex. V12 engine, required for warranty at inspection service II only

Lighting . . . . inspect
Check all lighting, aim headlights as necessary

Power steering . . . . check level **AF**
Ex. models with self-leveling suspension
On models with Hydro Boost, pump brake pedal several times to discharge accumulator before checking level

Power steering w/self
leveling suspension . . . check level **SLF**

Seat belts . . . . inspect

Windshield wipers . . . . inspect
Check condition of blades, aim washers, fill

Service indicator 1983-91 . . . . reset
Special tool required

1983-90, EVERY 12 MONTHS
Brakes . . . . change fluid **HB**

INDICATED INSPECTION SERVICE I

Exhaust system . . . . inspect/tighten

Final drive . . . . check level

W Fuel filter 1983-88 . . . . replace
Required for warranty at inspection service II
Not required for Calif. warranty

Hand brake . . . . inspect/adjust
Check shoes & cables for wear, adjust & lube

Suspension . . . . inspect
Check condition of axle joints, tie rods & linkage

Transmission,
automatic 1983-91 . . . . change fluid **AF**
Replace strainer & gasket, do not repeat at inspection service II

Transmission . . . . check level

Air conditioner . . . . check/tighten
Tighten compressor mounts, check operation & charge

Battery . . . . check/fill

Cooling system . . . . inspect/fill **EC**

Engine diagnostic system
1989-92 . . . . access codes

W Engine idle & mixture
1983-88 . . . . check/adjust
Calif. only

Fuel injectors 1987-91 . . . . clean
Clean carbon from intake valves as necessary

Microfilter, interior air . . . . replace
Does not apply to all models

Throttle linkage . . . . lubricate **LM**

W Valve clearance . . . . check/adjust
Ex. 1.8L DOHC, 2.5L DOHC & V12 engines

Door, hood, trunk
hinges . . . . tighten/lubricate **MO**

Door, hood, trunk latches . . . lubricate **LM**

Fuel tank, lines, cap . . . . inspect
Clean filter screen on fuel pickup

Sunroof . . . . lubricate

Service indicator . . . . reset
Special tool required

EVERY 24 MONTHS
Brakes 1991-92 . . . . change fluid **HB**

Cooling system . . . . . . replace coolant **EC**

INDICATED INSPECTION SERVICE II

Clutch . . . . inspect

Drive shaft & axles . . . . inspect
Inspect flexible couplings & constant velocity joint boots

Final drive . . . . change lubricant
Includes front differential on 325ix

W Fuel filter 1989-92 . . . . replace
Not required for Calif. warranty

Front wheel bearings
1983-90 . . . . check/adjust **WB**

Transfer case, 325ix . . . . change lubricant

Transmission,
automatic 1992 . . . . change fluid **AF**

Transmission, manual . . . change lubricant
Ex. 325e & 528e

W Air filter element . . . . replace

Air intake dust separators, 850i . . . . clean

Automatic skid & traction
control filter . . . . replace
1991 735i, 750iL & 850i if equipped

W Drive belts 1989-92 . . . . inspect/adjust
Replace belts on 1991 M5. Not required for Calif. warranty

W Spark plugs . . . . replace

Timing belt, 2.5L, 2.7L . . . . . inspect/adjust
Replace belt every second service

Service indicator . . . . reset
Special tool required

EVERY 36 MONTHS
Air bag system . . . . inspect
Visually check system components

1983-88, EVERY 30 MI—48 KM
W Oxygen sensor . . . . replace

1989-92, EVERY 50 MI—80 KM
W Oxygen sensor . . . . replace

KEY TO LUBRICANTS
See other BMW chart

CRANKCASE . . . . **SF, SG**
DOHC engines:
All temperatures 15W-40, 15W-50
SOHC engines:

Temperature	Grade
68° to 122°F (20° to 50°C)	40
32° to 86°F (0° to 30°C)	30
14° to 122°F (−10° to 50°C)	20W-50
−4° to 104°F (−20° to 40°C)	15W-50
−4° to 86°F (−20° to 30°C)	15W-40
−4° to 50°F (−20° to 10°C)	20
−22° to 68°F (−30° to 20°C)	10W-50
−22° to 50°F (−30° to 10°C)	10W-40
−22° to 41°F (−30° to 5°C)	10W-30
−40° to 23°F (−40° to −5°C)	5W-30
−40° to 14°F (−40° to −10°C)	5W-20

CAPACITY, Refill:	Liters	Qt
1983-84 533i, 633CSi, 733i	5.0	5.3
1983-85 318i	3.8	4.0
1983-88 325e, 528e	4.0	4.2
1985-90 535i, 635CSi, 735i	5.0	5.3
1988-90 M3	4.0	4.2
1988-90 M5, M6	5.0	5.3
1988-91 325i	4.0	4.2
1988-92 750iL	6.5	6.8
1988-92 525i	4.0	4.2
1990-92 318i	4.3	4.5
1991-92 535i, M5, 735i	5.0	5.3
1991-92 850i	6.5	6.8
1992 325i	5.8	6.0

Capacity shown is without filter. When replacing filter, additional oil may be needed
Additional oil may be needed if oil cooler is drained

TRANSMISSION, Automatic . . . . **AF**

CAPACITY, Refill:	Liters	Qt
1983-87 All	2.0	2.1
1988-90 All	3.0	3.2
1991-92 325i, 525i, 535i	3.0	3.2
1991-92 735i	3.0	3.2
1991-92 750iL	3.5	3.7
1991-92 850i	3.5	3.7

Add specified quantity. With engine at operating temperature, shift transmission through all gears. Check level in PARK and add fluid as needed

TRANSMISSION, Manual
Inspect for color coded fluid identification label, usually affixed to passenger side of the transmission bellhousing. Verify fluid installed before topping up or refilling transmission

GREEN LABEL♦ . . . . **GLS**
RED LABEL♦ . . . . **AF**
NO LABEL† **80W GL-4**
♦ Units that are factory filled with **AF** or **GLS** are fitted with 17mm external hex head drain and fill plugs
† Units that are factory filled with **GL-4** are fitted with 17mm internal hex (Allen) head drain and fill plugs

CAPACITY, Refill:	Liters	Pt
1983-84 533i, 633CSi, 733i	1.6	3.4
1983-85 318i	1.2	2.5
1983-88 528e	1.6	3.4
1985-87 535i, 635CSi, 735i	1.6	3.4
1987-90 M5	1.3	2.7
1988-89 635CSi, M6	1.3	2.7
1988-90 325i, 525i, 535i	1.3	2.7
1988-91 M3	1.2	2.5
1988-92 735i	1.3	2.7
1991-92 525i	1.0	2.2
1991-92 325i, 535i, M5	1.3	2.7
1991-92 850i	2.3	4.8

TRANSFER CASE . . . . **AF**

CAPACITY, Refill:	Liters	Pt
325ix	0.5	1.0

DIFFERENTIAL **90 GL-5**

CAPACITY, Refill:	Liters	Pt
Rear:		
1983-84 533i, 633CSi, 733i	1.7	3.6
1983-85 318i	0.9	1.9
1983-88 325, 325e, 528e	1.7	3.6
1985-90 635CSi, M6	1.9	4.0
1985-92 535i, M5, 735i	1.9	4.0
1988-92 750iL	1.9	4.0
1988-92 M3, 325i, 525i	1.7	3.6
1990-92 318i	0.9	1.9
1991-92 850i	1.9	4.0
Front:		
1988-90 325ix	0.7	1.4

SERVICE LOCATIONS — ENGINE AND CHASSIS

HOOD RELEASE: Inside

① Crankcase dipstick
② Transmission dipstick
③ Brake fluid reservoir
④ Clutch fluid reservoir
⑤ Oil fill cap
⑥ Power steering reservoir
⑦ Air filter
⑧ Fuel filter
⑨ Oil filter
⑩ PCV filter
⑪ EGR valve
⑫ Oxygen sensor
⑬ PCV valve

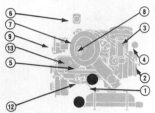

**1983-86
1.8L (112) 2V,
2.0L (122)
Code G, P, B**

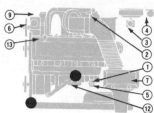

**1987-89
2.0L (122) Code 1**

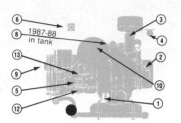

**1983-86
1.8L (112) FI, Code O
1987-88
2.0L (122) OHC Code K**

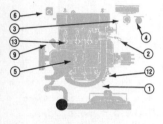

**1983-86
1.8L (112) Turbo, Code J
1987
2.0L (122) Turbo Code M**

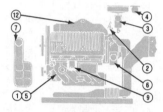

**1992
2.3L Code 3
Skylark**

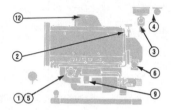

**1988-91
2.3L 16 valve Code D
Skylark**

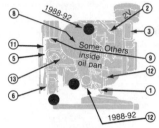

**1983-92
2.5L (151)
(2V shown)
Code 5, R, U
Air induction
system varies.**

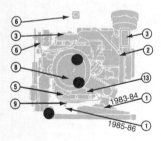

**1983-86
2.8L (173) 2V Code X, Z**

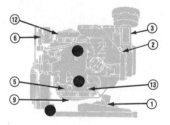

**1985-86
2.8L (173) FI
Code W**

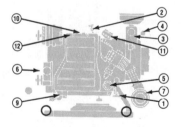

**1987-89
2.8L (173) Code W
1989-92
3.1L Code T Regal**

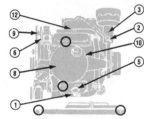

**1983-84
3.0L (181) 2V
Code E**

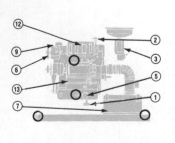

**1985-88
3.0L (181) FI
Code L**

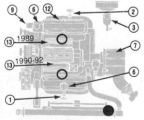

**1989-92
3.3L Code N
Century, Skylark**

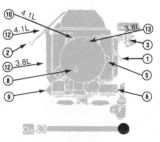

**1983-87
3.8L (231), 2V
4.1L (252)
Code A, 4**

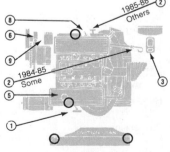

**1984-88
3.8L (231) FI Code 3
1986 3.8L FI Code B**

● Cooling system drain   ○ Cooling system drain, some models

SERVICE LOCATIONS — ENGINE AND CHASSIS

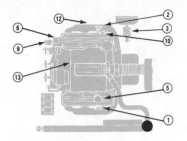

1988-91 3.8L (231) Code C
Electra, LeSabre, Reatta, Riviera

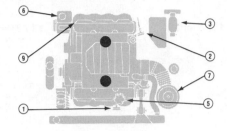

1990-92 3.8L Code L
Electra, Reatta, Regal, Riviera

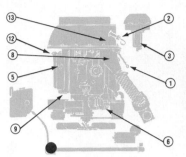

1983 3.8L (231)
Turbocharged
Code 3

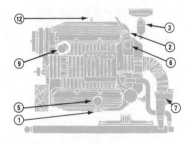

1992
3.8L Code 1
Supercharged
Park Avenue Ultra

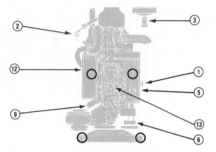

1984-85
3.8L (231) Turbo
Code 9

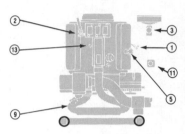

1986-88
3.8L (231) Turbo
Code 7

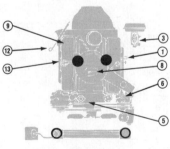

1983-90
5.0L (307)

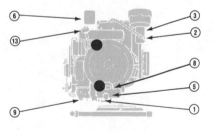

1983-85
4.3L (262)
Diesel
Code T

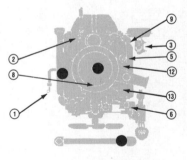

1983-87
4.4L (267), 5.0L (305)

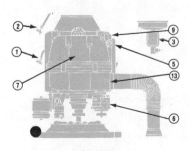

1991-92
5.0L Code E
5.7L Code 7
Roadmaster

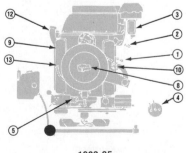

1983-85
5.0L (307)

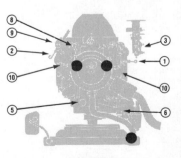

1983-85
5.7L (350) Diesel
Code N

● Cooling system drain   ○ Cooling system drain, some models

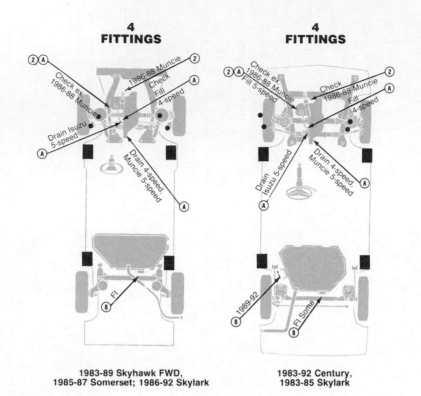

4 FITTINGS

4 FITTINGS

1983-89 Skyhawk FWD,
1985-87 Somerset; 1986-92 Skylark

1983-92 Century,
1983-85 Skylark

0-4 FITTINGS

11 FITTINGS

4 FITTINGS

11 FITTINGS

8 FITTINGS

1988-92 Regal

1983-85 Riviera

1986-92 Riviera,
1988-91 Reatta

1983-90 Estate Wagon,
1983-84 Electra,
1983-85 LeSabre,
1983-87 Regal,
1991-92 Roadmaster

1985-91 Electra FWD,
1986-92 LeSabre FWD

■ Lift adapter position
△ Plug, some models
• Fitting

Ⓐ Manual transmission/transaxle, drain & fill
Ⓑ Transfer case, NOT USED

Ⓒ Automatic transaxle final drive, drain & fill
Ⓓ Differential, drain & fill

② Transmission dipstick
⑧ Fuel filter

CAUTION: On front wheel drive vehicles the center of gravity is further forward than on rear wheel drive vehicles. When removing major components from the rear of the vehicle while it is on a hoist, the vehicle must be supported in a manner to prevent it from tipping forward.

SERVICE AT TIME OR MILEAGE—WHICHEVER OCCURS FIRST

BKPM9   BKPM9

MI—MILES IN THOUSANDS
KM—KILOMETERS IN THOUSANDS

EVERY 6 MONTHS
Brake master cylinder . . . . . check level **HB**

Clutch pedal free travel . . . . . check/adjust
Front wheel drive models, every 5 mi (8 km)

Power steering reservoir . . . . check level **PS**

Transaxle or trans., auto. . . . . . check level

FIRST 7.5 MI—12 KM
Carburetor mounting bolts . . . . torque

Engine idle speed . . . . adjust
Gasoline eng. without Idle Speed or Idle Air Control

Diff., Limited-Slip . . . . change lubricant

Tires . . . . rotate
Radial tires, every 15 mi (24 km) after initial service.
Check brake pads. Lug nut torque, ft lb: Riviera, 140;
other front wheel drive, 100; LeSabre & Electra station
wagons, 100; all others, 80 ex. 90 with aluminum
wheels

GASOLINE, FIRST 7.5 MI—12 KM; THEN EVERY 24 MO/30 MI—48 KM DIESEL, FIRST 5 MI—8 KM; THEN EVERY 30 MI—48 KM
Choke & hoses, gasoline . . . . . check/clean

Engine idle speed, Diesel . . . . adjust

GASOLINE, EVERY 12 MO/7.5 MI—12 KM DIESEL, EVERY 12 MO/5 MI—8 KM
Crankcase . . . . change oil

Differential . . . . check level

Exhaust pressure regulator valve &
  hoses, 6-cyl. Diesel . . . . inspect/test
After initial inspection, check again at 15 mi (24 km) &
every 15 mi (24 km) thereafter

Exhaust system . . . . inspect

Front suspension &
  steering linkage . . . . **4-11 fittings LB**

Oil filter . . . . replace
Turbocharged, at every oil change; all others at first oil
change, then at 12 mo/15 mi (24 km) intervals only

Parking brake cables & guides . . . . coat **LB**
Check adjustment

Shift linkage . . . . coat **LB**
With floor shift, coat contact faces

Suspension & steering . . . . inspect
Also inspect front drive axle boots and seals

Transmission/transaxle . . . . check level

Drive belts . . . . inspect/adjust

Throttle linkage . . . . inspect
Check for damage or binding

Body . . . . lubricate

EVERY 12 MONTHS
Cooling system . . . . .inspect & tighten hoses
Wash radiator filler neck & cap; pressure test system.
Clean exterior of radiator core and air conditioning con-
denser

EVERY 12 MO/15 MI—24 KM
Crankcase ventilation system,
  Diesel . . . . inspect
Clean filters in each valve cover, pipes & tubes

EVERY 24 MO/30 MI—48 KM
Cooling system . . . . change coolant **EC**
Flush system

EVERY 36 MO/30 MI—48 KM
Air cleaner element . . . . replace
Ex. Diesel & 2.0L

EGR system . . . . clean/inspect

EVERY 30 MI—48 KM
Clutch cross shaft . . . . **1 plug LB**

Front wheel bearings ex.
  front wheel drive . . . . . . clean/repack **GC**
Service at mileage interval or at each brake reline,
whichever comes first. Tighten spindle nut to 12 ft lb
while turning wheel. Back off 1/2 turn & retighten finger
tight. End play, .001″-.005″

Fuel tank, cap & lines, ex. Diesel . . . inspect

Air cleaner element, Diesel . . . . . replace

Fuel filter, Diesel . . . . replace

Ignition timing . . . . adjust
Inspect distributor cap, clean or replace

Ignition wires . . . . inspect/clean

Injection pump timing, Diesel . . . . . . adjust

PCV valve ex. Diesel . . . . inspect
Blow out or replace hoses

Spark plugs . . . . replace

Vacuum advance system
  & hoses . . . . inspect
As equipped

EVERY 50 MI—80 KM
Air cleaner element, 2.0L . . . . replace

EVERY 100 MI—160 KM
Transaxle or trans., auto. . . . . change fluid
Clean sump screen or replace filter

SEVERE SERVICE
Crankcase—Change oil: Gasoline, every 3
mo/3 mi (4.8 km); Diesel, every 3 mo/2.5 mi
(4 km). Change filter at each oil change

Front wheel bearings—Repack every 15 mi
(24 km)

Transaxle or transmission, automatic—
Change fluid & filter or clean screen
every 15 mi (24 km)

Differential—Change lubricant every 7.5 mi
(12 km) when towing a trailer

KEY TO LUBRICANTS

AF	DEXRON®-IIE Automatic Transmission Fluid
CD	Motor Oil, API Service CD
EC	Ethylene Glycol Coolant Mix with water to –34°F (–37°C) protection
GC	Wheel Bearing Grease, NLGI Category GC
GL-5	Gear Oil, API Service GL-5
GL-5★	Special Lubricant for Limited-Slip Differential
GLS	Gear Lubricant, Special 4-speed, GM Part No. 1052931 5-speed, GM Part No. 12345349
HB	Hydraulic Brake Fluid, DOT 3
LB	Chassis Grease, NLGI Category LB
PS	Power Steering Fluid
SG	Motor Oil, API Service SG Use Energy Conserving-II Oils

CRANKCASE
Diesel engine . . . . **SG/CD**
Gasoline engine . . . . **SG**

CAPACITY, Refill	Liters	Qt
Diesel, including filter		
6-cyl.	5.6	6.0
8-cyl.	6.6	7.0
Gasoline		
4-cyl. 1.8L & 2.5L	2.8	3.0
Others	3.8	4.0

Gasoline capacity shown is without filter. When replacing
filter, additional oil may be needed

Diesel Engine:
Above 32°F (0°C) . . . . 30♦
0° to 60°F (–18° to 16°C) 15W-40
Below 60°F (16°C) 10W-30

Gasoline Engine:
Above 40°F (4°C) 30
Above 20°F (–7°C) 20W-20, 20W-40, 20W-50
Above 10°F (–12°C) 15W-40
Above 0°F (–18°C) 10W-30*
Below 60°F (16°C) . . . . 5W-30†

† 5W-30 may be used up to 100°F (38°C) in 4-cyl. & 2.8L
V-6 engines

♦30 is preferred above 32°F (0°C), especially for continuous duty driving

* 10W-30 preferred above 0°F (–18°C)

TRANSMISSION/TRANSAXLE,
  Automatic . . . . **AF**

CAPACITY, Initial Refill*	Liters	Qt
Front wheel drive		
ex. Riviera	3.8	4.0
Riviera†	3.0	3.3
200 Transmission	3.3	3.5
700-R4 Transmission	4.7	5.0
Others	2.8	3.0

* With the engine at operating temperature, shift transmission
through all gears. Let engine slow idle in PARK for 3 minutes
or more. Check fluid level and add fluid as needed
†Differential serviced separately

TRANSAXLE, Manual
4-speed . . . . **AF**
5-speed . . . . **GLS**

CAPACITY, Refill:	Liters	Pt
4-speed	2.8	6.0
5-speed	2.5	5.4

DIFFERENTIAL/FINAL DRIVE
Standard & Riviera . . . 80W, 80W-90* **GL-5**
Limited-Slip . . . . . 80W, 80W-90* **GL-5★**
* For vehicles normally operated in Canada, 80W only

CAPACITY, Refill:	Liters	Pt
Regal	1.7	3.5
Riviera	1.6	3.3
LeSabre, Electra:		
7¹/₂″ ring gear	1.7	3.5
8¹/₂″, 8³/₄″ ring gear	2.0	4.3

LIMITED-SLIP IDENTIFICATION:
Tag under rear cover-attaching bolt

SERVICE AT TIME OR MILEAGE—WHICHEVER OCCURS FIRST

BKPM10   BKPM10

MI—MILES IN THOUSANDS
KM—KILOMETERS IN THOUSANDS

1.8L TURBO, EVERY 3 MO/3 MI—5 KM
Crankcase .... change oil
Oil filter .... replace
Initial service, then every other oil change

EVERY 6 MONTHS
Brake master cylinder ..... check level **HB**
Clutch pedal free travel ..... check/adjust
Front wheel drive models, every 5 mi (8 km)
Power steering reservoir ... check level **PS**

FIRST 7.5 MI—12 KM
Carburetor or T.B.I. mounting
  bolts .... torque
Engine idle speed .... adjust
Gasoline eng. without Idle Speed or Idle Air Control
Diff., Limited-Slip .... change lubricant
Tires .... rotate
Radial tires, every 15 mi (24 km) after initial service.
Check brake linings. Lug nut torque, ft lb: 1985 LeSabre & Electra wagon w/3/4″ bolts & steel wheels, 80; w/ aluminum wheels, 90; all others, 100. 1984 Riviera & other front wheel drive, 100; LeSabre & Electra station wagons, 100; all others, 80 ex. 90 with aluminum wheels

GASOLINE, FIRST 7.5 MI—12 KM; THEN EVERY 24 MO/30 MI—50 KM
Choke & hoses .... check/clean

DIESEL FIRST 5 MI—8 KM; THEN EVERY 30 MI—48 KM
Engine idle speed .... adjust

GASOLINE, EVERY 12 MO/7.5 MI—12 KM DIESEL, EVERY 12 MO/5 MI—8 KM
Brake system .... inspect
Check hydraulic system for leaks. Inspect linings
Crankcase ex. 1.8L Turbo ..... change oil
Differential .... check level
Exhaust pressure regulator valve &
  hoses, Diesel .... inspect/test
After initial inspection, check again at 15 mi (24 km) & every 15 mi (24 km) thereafter
Exhaust system .... inspect
Suspension &
  steering linkage .... 4-11 fittings **LB**
Oil filter ex. 1.8L Turbo .... replace
3.8L turbocharged, 6- & 8-cyl. diesel, at every oil change; all others at first oil change, then at every 12 mo/15mi (24 km)
Parking brake cables & guides .... coat **LB**
Check adjustment
Shift linkage .... coat **LB**
With floor shift, coat contact faces
Suspension & steering .... inspect
Also inspect front drive axle boots and seals
Transaxle or transmission ..... check level
Drive belts .... inspect/adjust
Throttle linkage .... inspect
Check for damage or binding
Water separator .... drain
As equipped
Body .... lubricate

EVERY 12 MONTHS
Cooling system .... inspect & tighten hoses
Wash radiator filler neck & cap; pressure test system. Clean exterior of radiator core and air conditioning condenser. Inspect coolant, service as required

EVERY 12 MO/15 MI—24 KM
Crankcase ventilation system,
  Diesel .... inspect
Clean filters in each valve cover, pipes & tubes

EVERY 24 MO/30 MI—50 KM
Cooling system ...... change coolant **EC**
Flush system
Vacuum/Air pump belts ..... inspect/adjust
Replace as needed

EVERY 36 MO/30 MI—50 KM
Air cleaner element .... replace
Ex. Diesel & 2.0L
EGR system .... clean/inspect

EVERY 30 MI—50 KM
Clutch cross shaft .... **1 plug LB**
Rear wheel drive only
Front wheel bearings ex.
  front wheel drive ..... clean/repack **GC**
Service at mileage interval or at each brake reline, whichever comes first. Tighten spindle nut to 12 ft lb while turning wheel. Back off 1/2 turn & retighten finger tight. End play, .001″-.005″
Fuel tank, cap & lines, ex. Diesel ..... inspect
Air cleaner element, Diesel .... replace
Distributor cap .... inspect
Fuel filter, Diesel .... replace
Ignition timing .... adjust
Inspect distributor cap, clean or replace
Ignition wires .... inspect/clean
Injection pump timing, Diesel ...... adjust
PCV valve ex. Diesel .... inspect
Blow out or replace hoses
Spark plugs .... replace
Thermostatic air cleaner .... inspect
Vacuum advance system
  & hoses .... inspect
As equipped

EVERY 50 MI—80 KM
Air cleaner element, 2.0L .... replace

EVERY 100 MI—160 KM
Transaxle or trans., auto. .... change fluid
Clean sump screen or replace filter

SEVERE SERVICE
Carburetor or T.B.I.—Torque mounting bolts & adjust idle speed at 6 mi (10 km), also inspect carburetor choke & hoses

Crankcase—Change oil: Gasoline, every 3 mo/3 mi (5 km); Diesel, every 3 mo/2.5 mi (4 km). Change filter at each oil change

Front suspension & steering linkage— Lubricate every: Gasoline, 6 mo/6 mi (10 km); Diesel, 6 mo/5 mi (8 km)

Front wheel bearings—Repack every 15 mi (24 km) or at each brake service, whichever comes first

Transaxle or transmission, automatic— Change fluid & filter or clean screen every 15 mi (24 km)

Differential—Change lubricant every 7.5 mi (12 km) when towing a trailer

KEY TO LUBRICANTS

AF	DEXRON®-IIE Automatic Transmission Fluid
CD	Motor Oil, API Service CD
EC	Ethylene Glycol Coolant Mix with water to –34°F (–37°C) protection
GC	Wheel Bearing Grease, NLGI Category GC
GL-5	Gear Oil, API Service GL-5
GL-5 ★	Special Lubricant for Limited-Slip Differential
GLS	Gear Lubricant, Special 4-speed, GM Part No. 1052931 5-speed, GM Part No. 12345349
HB	Hydraulic Brake Fluid, DOT 3
LB	Chassis Grease, NLGI Category LB
PS	Power Steering Fluid
SG	Motor Oil, API Service SG Use Energy Conserving-II oils

CRANKCASE
Diesel engine .... **SG/CD**
Gasoline engine .... **SG**

CAPACITY, Refill:	Liters	Qt
Diesel, including filter		
6-cyl.	5.6	6.0
8-cyl.	6.6	7.0
Gasoline		
4-cyl. 2.5L	2.8	3.0
Others	3.8	4.0

Gasoline, capacity shown is without filter. When replacing filter, additional oil may be needed

Diesel Engine:
Above 32°F (0°C) .... 30♦
0° to 60°F (–18° to 16°C) 15W-40
Below 60°F (16°C) 10W-40
Gasoline Engine:
Above 40°F (4°C) 30
Above 20°F (–7°C) 20W-20
Above 10°F (–12°C) 15W-40
Above 0°F (–18°C) 10W-30
Below 60°F (16°C) .... 5W-30†
♦30 is preferred above 32°F (0°C), especially for continuous duty driving
† 5W-30 may be used up to 100°F (38°C) in 4-cyl. & 2.8L V6 engines

TRANSMISSION/TRANSAXLE,
Automatic .... **AF**

CAPACITY, Initial Refill*:	Liters	Qt
125 Transmission	3.8	4.0
Riviera†	3.0	3.3
200 Transmission	3.3	3.5
250 Transmission	3.8	4.0
440 Transmission	5.8	6.0
Others	2.8	3.0

* With the engine at operating temperature, shift transmission through all gears. Let engine slow idle in PARK for 3 minutes or more. Check fluid level and add fluid as needed
†Differential serviced separately

TRANSAXLE, Manual .... **GLS**

CAPACITY, Refill:	Liters	Pt
4-speed	2.8	6.0
5-speed	2.5	5.4

DIFFERENTIAL/FINAL DRIVE
Standard & Riviera ... 80W, 80W-90* **GL-5**
Limited-Slip ...... 80W, 80W-90* **GL-5 ★**
* For vehicles normally operated in Canada, 80W only

CAPACITY, Refill:	Liters	Pt
Regal	1.7	3.5
Riviera	1.6	3.3
LeSabre, Electra RWD:		
7 1/2″ ring gear	1.7	3.5
8 1/2″, 8 3/4″ ring gear	2.0	4.3

LIMITED-SLIP IDENTIFICATION:
Tag under rear cover-attaching bolt

SERVICE AT TIME OR MILEAGE—WHICHEVER OCCURS FIRST

BKPM11   BKPM11

MI—MILES IN THOUSANDS
KM—KILOMETERS IN THOUSANDS

1.8L TURBO
EVERY 3 MO/3 MI—5 KM
Crankcase .... change oil

Oil filter .... replace
Initial service, then every other oil change

EVERY 6 MONTHS
Brake master cylinder .... check level **HB**

Clutch .... check/adjust
Front wheel drive models, every 5 mi (8 km)

Power steering reservoir .. check level **PS**

FIRST 7.5 MI—12 KM
Carburetor or T.B.I. mounting
    bolts .... torque

Engine idle speed .... adjust
Without Idle Speed or Idle Air Control

Diff., Limited-Slip .... change lubricant
One time service only

Tires .... rotate
Radial tires, every 15 mi (24 km) after initial service.
Check brake linings. Lug nut torque, ft lb: LeSabre &
Electra wagon w/3/4" bolts and steel wheels, 80;
w/aluminum wheels, 90; all others, 100

FIRST 7.5 MI—12 KM;
THEN EVERY 24 MO/30 MI—50 KM
Choke & hoses .... check/clean

EVERY 12 MO/7.5 MI—12 KM
Brake system .... inspect
Check hydraulic system for leaks. Inspect linings

Crankcase ex. 1.8L Turbo ..... change oil

Differential .... check level

Exhaust system .... inspect

Suspension &
    steering linkage ...... **4-11 fittings LB**

Oil filter ex. 1.8L Turbo ...... replace
3.8L turbocharged, at every oil change; all others at
first oil change, then at every other oil change only

Parking brake cables & guides ... coat **LB**
Check adjustment

Shift linkage .... coat **LB**
With floor shift, coat contact faces

Suspension & steering .... inspect
Also inspect front drive axle boots and seals

Transaxle or transmission .... check level

Drive belts .... inspect/adjust

Throttle linkage .... inspect
Check for damage or binding

Body .... lubricate

EVERY 12 MONTHS
Cooling
    system........inspect & tighten hoses
Wash radiator filler neck & cap; pressure test system.
Clean exterior of radiator core and air conditioning con-
denser. Inspect coolant, service as required

EVERY 24 MO/30 MI—50 KM
Cooling system ...... change coolant **EC**
Flush system

Vacuum/Air pump belts .... inspect/adjust
Replace as needed

EVERY 36 MO/30 MI—50 KM
Air cleaner element .... replace

EGR system .... clean/inspect

EVERY 30 MI—50 KM
Clutch cross shaft .... **1 plug LB**

Front wheel bearings ex.
    front wheel drive ..... clean/repack **GC**
Service at mileage interval or at each brake reline,
whichever comes first. Tighten spindle nut to 12 ft lb
while turning wheel. Back off 1/2 turn & retighten finger
tight. End play, .001"-.005"

Fuel tank, cap & lines .... inspect

Distributor cap .... inspect

Ignition timing .... adjust
Inspect distributor cap, clean or replace

Ignition wires .... inspect/clean

PCV valve .... inspect
Blow out or replace hoses

Spark plugs .... replace

Thermostatic air cleaner .... inspect

Vacuum advance system
    & hoses .... inspect
As equipped

EVERY 50 MI—80 KM
Air cleaner element, 2.0L .... replace

EVERY 100 MI—160 KM
Transaxle or trans., auto. .... change fluid
Clean sump screen or replace filter

SEVERE SERVICE
Carburetor or T.B.I.—Torque mounting
bolts & adjust idle speed at 6 mi (10 km).
Inspect carburetor choke & hoses at 6 mi (10
km) then every 30 mi (50 km)

Crankcase—Change oil and oil filter every 3
mo/3 mi (5 km)

Front suspension & steering linkage—
Lubricate every 6 mo/6 mi (10 km)

Front wheel bearings RWD—Repack every
15 mi (24 km) or at each brake service,
whichever comes first

Transaxle or transmission, automatic—
Change fluid & filter or clean screen every
15 mi (24 km)

Differential—Change lubricant every 7.5 mi
(12 km) when towing a trailer

KEY TO LUBRICANTS
AF   DEXRON®-IIE Automatic Transmission
       Fluid
EC   Ethylene Glycol Coolant
       Mix with water to –34°F (–37°C) protection
GC   Wheel Bearing Grease NLGI Category
       GC
GL-5   Gear Oil, API Service GL-5
GL-5★   Special Lubricant for Limited-Slip
       Differential
GLS   Gear Lubricant, Special
       4-speed, GM Part No. 1052931
       5-speed, GM Part No. 12345349
HB   Hydraulic Brake Fluid, DOT 3
LB   Chassis Grease, NLGI Category LB
PS   Power Steering Fluid
SG   Motor Oil, API Service SG
       Use Energy Conserving-II oils

CRANKCASE .... SG

CAPACITY, Refill:	Liters	Qt
4-cyl. 2.5L	2.8	3.0
Others	3.8	4.0

Capacity shown is without filter. When replacing filter, additional oil may be needed

1.8L Turbo:
Above 40°F (4°C) 30
Below 40°F (4°C) 10W-30
Other 4-cyl. & 2.8L V6:
Above 40°F (4°C) 30
Above 0°F (–18°C) 10W-30
All temperatures .... 5W-30♦
All others:
Above 40°F (4°C) 30
Above 20°F (–7°C) 20W-20
Above 10°F (–12°C) 15W-40
Above 0°F (–18°C) .... 10W-30♦
Below 60°F (16°C) 5W-30
♦Preferred

TRANSMISSION/TRANSAXLE,
Automatic .... AF

CAPACITY, Initial Refill*:	Liters	Qt
125 Transmission	3.8	4.0
200 Transmission	3.3	3.5
440 Transmission	5.8	6.0
Others	2.8	3.0

* With the engine at operating temperature, shift transmission
through all gears. Let engine slow idle in PARK for 3 minutes
or more. Check fluid level and add fluid as needed

TRANSAXLE, Manual .... GLS

CAPACITY, Refill:	Liters	Pt
4-speed	2.8	6.0
5-speed:		
7-bolt alum. end cap	2.5	5.4
9-bolt steel end cap	1.9	4.0

DIFFERENTIAL
Standard 80W, 80W-90* **GL-5**
Limited-Slip ...... 80W, 80W-90* **GL-5★**

CAPACITY, Refill:	Liters	Pt
7 1/2" ring gear	1.7	3.5
8 1/2", 8 3/4" ring gear	2.0	4.3

* For vehicles normally operated in Canada, 80W only
LIMITED-SLIP IDENTIFICATION:
Tag under rear cover-attaching bolt

SERVICE AT TIME OR MILEAGE—WHICHEVER OCCURS FIRST

BKPM12   BKPM12

Perform the following maintenance services at the intervals indicated to keep the vehicle warranties in effect.

W SERVICE TO MAINTAIN EMISSION WARRANTY

MI—MILES IN THOUSANDS
KM—KILOMETERS IN THOUSANDS

2.0L TURBO
EVERY 3 MO/3 MI—5 KM

W Crankcase . . . . change oil

W Oil filter . . . . replace
Initial service, then every other oil change

EVERY 6 MONTHS
Brake master cylinder . . . . check level **HB**

Clutch master cylinder . . . . check level **HB**

Power steering reservoir . . check level **PS**

FIRST 7.5 MI—12 KM
W Carburetor or T.B.I. mounting
bolts except 2.3L engine . . . . . torque

W Engine idle speed . . . . adjust
Without Idle Speed or Idle Air Control

Diff., Limited-Slip . . . . change lubricant
As equipped

Tires . . . . inspect/rotate
Initial service, then every 15 mi (24 km). Check brake linings

FIRST 7.5 MI—12 KM;
THEN EVERY 24 MO/30 MI—50 KM
W Choke & hoses . . . . check/clean

EVERY 12 MO/7.5 MI—12 KM
Brake system . . . . inspect
Check hydraulic system for leaks. Inspect linings

W Crankcase ex. 2.0L Turbo . . change oil

W Oil filter ex. 2.0L Turbo . . . . replace
3.8L turbocharged, at every oil change; all others at first oil change, then at every other oil change, but at least every 12 months

Differential . . . . check level

W Exhaust system . . . . inspect

Suspension &
steering linkage . . . . . . **4-11 fittings LB**

Parking brake cable guides . . . . . . coat **LB**
Check adjustment

Shift linkage . . . . coat **LB**
With floor shift, coat contact faces

Suspension & steering . . . . inspect
Also inspect front drive axle boots and seals

Transaxle or transmission . . . . check level

W Drive belts . . . . inspect/adjust

W Throttle linkage . . . . inspect
Check for damage or binding

Body . . . . lubricate

EVERY 12 MONTHS
W Cooling
system . . . . . inspect & tighten hoses
Wash radiator filler neck & cap; pressure test system. Clean exterior of radiator core and air conditioning condenser. Inspect coolant, service as required

EVERY 24 MO/30 MI—50 KM
W Cooling system . . . . change coolant **EC**
Flush system

W Drive belts . . . . inspect/adjust

EVERY 36 MO/30 MI—50 KM
W Air cleaner element . . . . replace

Crankcase inlet air filter . . . . replace
As equipped

W EGR system . . . . clean/inspect
1987-90 engine codes H, K, M, R, U, Y, 1, 7

W Fuel tank, cap & lines . . . . inspect

EVERY 30 MI—50 KM
Front wheel bearings ex.
front wheel drive . . . . . clean/repack **GC**
Service at mileage interval or at each brake reline, whichever comes first. Tighten spindle nut to 12 ft lb while turning wheel. Back off nut & retighten finger tight. End play, .001"-.005". Loosen nut just enough that hole in spindle lines up with slot in nut. (Not more than 1/2 flat.)

EGR system . . . . clean/inspect
1991-92 engine codes E, R, U, 7

W Distributor cap . . . . inspect
Except distributorless ignition

W Ignition timing . . . . adjust
Inspect distributor cap, clean or replace.
Except distributorless ignition

W Ignition wires . . . . inspect/clean
As equipped

W PCV valve . . . . replace
Blow out or replace hoses

W Spark plugs . . . . replace

W Thermostatic air cleaner . . . . . . inspect

W Vacuum advance system
& hoses . . . . inspect
As equipped

EVERY 100 MI—160 KM
Transaxle or trans., auto. . . . . change fluid
Clean sump screen or replace filter

SEVERE SERVICE
W Carburetor or T.B.I. except 2.3L engine—
Torque mounting bolts & adjust idle speed at 6 mi (10 km). Inspect carburetor choke & hoses at 6 mi (10 km) then every 30 mi (50 km)

W Crankcase—Change oil and oil filter every 3 mo/3 mi (5 km)

Suspension & steering linkage—Lubricate every oil change

Front wheel bearings RWD—Repack every 15 mi (24 km) or at each brake service, whichever comes first

Tires—inspect/rotate at 6 mi (10 km), then every 15 mi (24 km)

Transaxle or transmission, automatic—Change fluid & filter or clean screen every 15 mi (24 km)

Differential—Change lubricant every 7.5 mi (12 km) when towing a trailer

KEY TO LUBRICANTS

AF	DEXRON®-IIE Automatic Transmission Fluid
EC	Ethylene Glycol Coolant
Mix with water to –34°F (–37°C) protection
GC	Wheel Bearing Grease,
NLGI Category GC
GL-5	Gear Oil, API Service GL-5
GL-5 ★	Special Lubricant for Limited-Slip Differential
GLS	Gear Lubricant, Special
HB	Hydraulic Brake Fluid, DOT 3
LB	Chassis Grease, NLGI Category LB
PS	Power Steering Fluid
SG	Motor Oil, API Service SG

CRANKCASE . . . . SG
CAPACITY, Refill:

	Liters	Qt
1987 4-cyl. 2.5L Somerset, Skylark
w/Auto. Trans., Century .	2.8	3.0
1987 Others, 1988-92	3.8	4.0

Capacity shown is without filter. When replacing filter, additional oil may be needed

2.0L Turbo:
Above 40°F (4°C) . . . . 30★
All temperatures . . . . 10W-30♦
1987-88 3.0L V6, 3.8L V6;
1990 3.8L V6 Code L;
1991-92 3.3L V6, 3.8L V6:
Above 40°F (4°C) . . . . 30★
Above 0°F (–18°C) . . . . .10W-30♦
Below 60°F (16°C) 5W-30
1987-92
All others:
Above 40°F (4°C) . . . . 30★
Above 0°F (–18°C) 10W-30
All temperatures . . . . 5W-30♦
♦Preferred
★Use only if other specified grades are unavailable

TRANSMISSION/TRANSAXLE,
Automatic . . . . AF
CAPACITY, Initial Refill*:

	Liters	Qt
125 (3T40)	3.8	4.0
200 C	3.3	3.5
440-T40 (4T60), 4T60E . . .	5.8	6.0
700-R4 (4L60)	4.7	5.0
Others	2.8	3.0

* With the engine at operating temperature, shift transmission through all gears. Let engine slow idle in PARK for 3 minutes or more. Check fluid level and add fluid as needed

TRANSAXLE, Manual . . . . GLS
CAPACITY, Refill:

	Liters	Pt
5-speed Isuzu†	2.6	5.4
5-speed Muncie‡	1.9	4.0

†Has a 7-bolt aluminum end cap
‡Has a 9-bolt steel end cap

DIFFERENTIAL
Standard 80W-90* **GL-5**
Limited-Slip . . . . 80W-90* **GL-5 ★**
*For vehicles normally operated in Canada, 80W only
CAPACITY, Refill:

	Liters	Pt
7½" ring gear	1.7	3.5
8½", 8¾" ring gear	2.0	4.3

LIMITED-SLIP IDENTIFICATION:
Tag under rear cover-attaching bolt

CHEK-CHART

SERVICE LOCATIONS — ENGINE AND CHASSIS

CCDP-1   CCDP-1

HOOD RELEASE: Inside

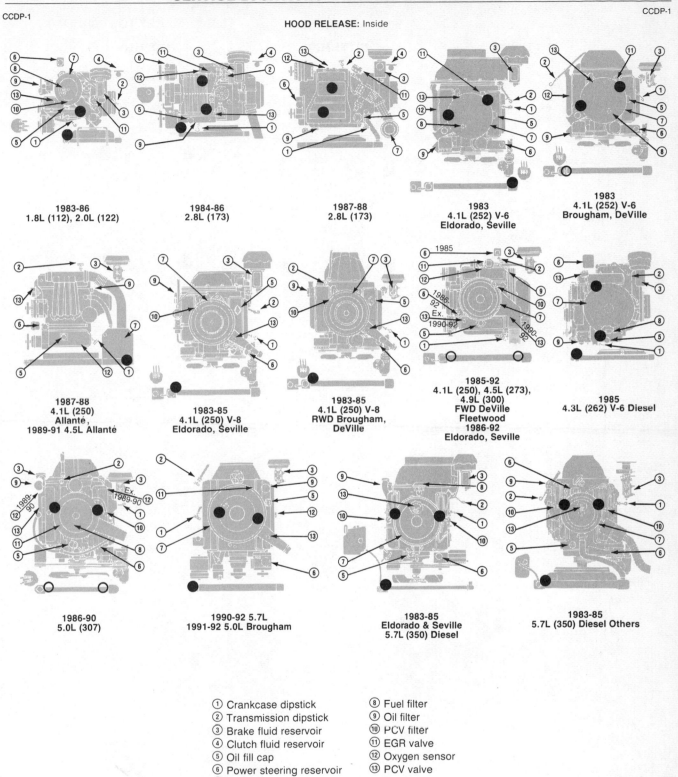

1983-86
1.8L (112), 2.0L (122)

1984-86
2.8L (173)

1987-88
2.8L (173)

1983
4.1L (252) V-6
Eldorado, Seville

1983
4.1L (252) V-6
Brougham, DeVille

1987-88
4.1L (250)
Allanté,
1989-91 4.5L Allanté

1983-85
4.1L (250) V-8
Eldorado, Seville

1983-85
4.1L (250) V-8
RWD Brougham,
DeVille

1985-92
4.1L (250), 4.5L (273),
4.9L (300)
FWD DeVille
Fleetwood
1986-92
Eldorado, Seville

1985
4.3L (262) V-6 Diesel

1986-90
5.0L (307)

1990-92 5.7L
1991-92 5.0L Brougham

1983-85
Eldorado & Seville
5.7L (350) Diesel

1983-85
5.7L (350) Diesel Others

① Crankcase dipstick
② Transmission dipstick
③ Brake fluid reservoir
④ Clutch fluid reservoir
⑤ Oil fill cap
⑥ Power steering reservoir
⑦ Air filter
⑧ Fuel filter
⑨ Oil filter
⑩ PCV filter
⑪ EGR valve
⑫ Oxygen sensor
⑬ PCV valve

● Cooling system drain   ○ Cooling system drain, some models

CADILLAC
1983-92 All Models

SERVICE LOCATIONS — ENGINE AND CHASSIS

11 FITTINGS

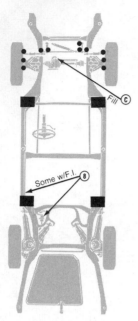

Fill Ⓒ

Some w/F.I. ⑧

1983-85 Eldorado, Seville

4 FITTINGS

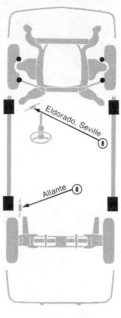

Eldorado, Seville ⑧

Allanté ⑧

1986-92 Eldorado, Seville
1987-92 Allanté

4 FITTINGS

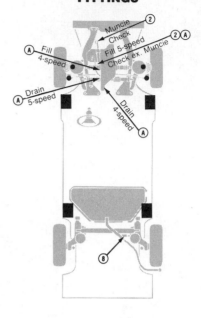

Muncie ②
Check
Fill 5-speed
Ⓐ Fill 4-speed
Check ex. Muncie ②Ⓐ
Ⓐ Drain 5-speed
Drain 4-speed Ⓐ
⑧

1983-88 Cimarron

6-8 FITTINGS

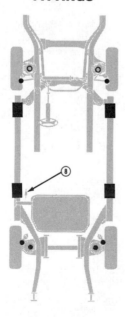

⑧

1985-92 FWD DeVille, Fleetwood

11 FITTINGS

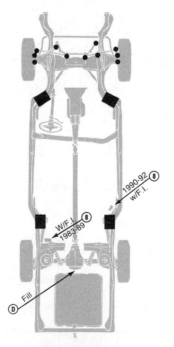

1990-92 w/F.I. ⑧
W/F.I. 1983-89 ⑧
Ⓓ Fill

LIFTING CAUTION
Do not use frame contact hoist on Commercial or 75 Series. Do not use bumper jack on Commercial

All RWD

CAUTION: On front wheel drive vehicles the center of gravity is further forward than on rear wheel drive vehicles. When removing major components from the rear of the vehicle while it is on a hoist, the vehicle must be supported in a manner to prevent it from tipping forward.

■ Lift adapter position
• Fitting ○ Fitting, some models

Ⓐ Manual transmission/transaxle, drain & fill
Ⓑ Transfer case, NOT USED

Ⓒ Automatic transaxle final drive, drain & fill
Ⓓ Differential, drain & fill

② Transmission dipstick
⑧ Fuel filter

SERVICE AT TIME OR MILEAGE—WHICHEVER OCCURS FIRST

CCPM7   CCPM7

MI—MILES IN THOUSANDS
KM—KILOMETERS IN THOUSANDS

FIRST 6 MO/7.5 MI—12 KM
Throttle body mounting . . . . torque
At mileage interval only

EVERY 12 MO/7.5 MI—12 KM
Crankcase . . . . change oil

Final Drive/Differential . . . . check level
Inspect front axle boots and seals

Front suspension &
   steering linkage . . . . . . **4-11 fittings LB**
Inspect steering linkage & suspension

Limited-Slip differential . . change lubricant
At 7.5 mi (12 km)

Parking brake cables & guides . . . coat **LB**

Tires . . . . rotate
At first 7.5 mi (12 km); then every 15 mi (24 km). Check disc brake pads; replace when 1/8″ thick. Lug nut torque, 100 ft lb. Torque wire wheels at first 500 mi (800 km)
Check drum brake lining & parking brake adjustment

Brake master cylinder . . . . check level **HB**
Inspect brake hoses & lines every 12 mo/10 mi (16 km)

Cooling system . . . . check level **EC**

Exhaust system . . . . inspect

Oil filter . . . . replace
At first oil change, then every other but at least every 12 mo

Power steering reservoir . . check level **PS**
Inspect hoses & lines every 6 mo/10 mi (16 km)

Transaxle/trans., automatic . . . check level
Every 6 mo
At operating temperature, engine idling, in PARK. Check for leaks. Lubricate linkage with **MO**

Body . . . . lubricate
Every 6 mo
Flush underbody every spring

EVERY 12 MO/15 MI—24 KM
Cooling
   system . . . . inspect & tighten hoses
Wash radiator filler neck & cap; pressure test system. Clean exterior of radiator core & air conditioning condenser

EVERY 24 MO/30 MI—48 KM
Cooling system . . . . . . change coolant **EC**
Flush system

EVERY 30 MI—48 KM
Front wheel bearings ex. Cimarron,
   Eldorado & Seville . . . . clean/repack **GC**
Or at time of front brake relining. Torque, 12 ft lb. Back off to 0; tighten nut finger tight & replace cotter pin

Air cleaner element . . . . replace
Every 36 mo. Replace PCV filter element

Air cleaner valve . . . . check
Every 12 mo

EGR system . . . . check/clean
Every 36 mo/30 mi (48 km)

Fuel cap, tank, lines . . . . inspect

Ignition timing . . . . check/adjust
Inspect distributor cap & rotor, clean or replace

PCV valve & hoses . . . . inspect

Spark plugs . . . . replace

Spark plug wires . . . . inspect

EVERY 100 MI—160 KM
Transaxle/transmission,
   automatic . . . . change fluid
Replace sump filter

SEVERE SERVICE
Crankcase — Change oil & filter every 3 mo/3 mi (4.8 km)

Final Drive/Differential ex. 4-cyl. w/manual transmission—Change lubricant every 7.5 mi (12 km)

Front wheel bearings ex. Cimarron, Eldorado & Seville—Clean/repack with **GC** every 15 mi (24 km)

Transaxle or transmission, automatic—Change fluid every 15 mi (24 km). Clean sump or replace filter

KEY TO LUBRICANTS

AF	DEXRON®-IIE Automatic Transmission Fluid
CC	Motor Oil, API Service CC
CD	Motor Oil, API Service CD
EC	Ethylene Glycol Coolant Mix 50% to 75% with water
GC	Wheel Bearing Grease, NLGI Category GC
GL-5	Gear Oil, API Service GL-5
GL-5★	Special Lubricant for Limited-Slip Differential
GLS	Gear Lubricant, Special
HB	Hydraulic Brake Fluid, DOT 3
LB	Chassis Grease, NLGI Category LB
MO	Motor Oil
PS	Power Steering Fluid
SF	Motor Oil, API Service SF
SG	Motor Oil, API Service SG

CRANKCASE . . . SG, SF, SF/CC, SF/CD

CAPACITY, Refill:	Liters	Qt
Eldorado, Seville w/4.1L eng.	4.7	5.0
Others	3.8	4.0

Capacity shown is without filter. When replacing filter, additional oil may be needed

Above 40°F (4°C)	30
Above 20°F (−7°C) . . . 20W-20, 20W-40, 20W-50	
Above 10°F (−12°C)	15W-40
Above 0°F (−18°C)	10W-30*
Below 60°F (16°C)	5W-30†

* 10W-30 is preferred above 0°F (−18°C)
†5W-30 may be used up to 100°F (38°C) in 4-cyl. engines

TRANSMISSION/TRANSAXLE,
Automatic . . . . **AF**

CAPACITY, Initial Refill*:	Liters	Qt
700-R4 Trans.	4.7	5.0
325 Trans.†	3.3	3.5
Others ex. 4-cyl. engine . . .	5.0	5.3
4-cyl. eng.	3.8	4.0

* With the engine at operating temperature, shift transmission through all gears. Let engine slow idle in PARK for three minutes. Check fluid level and add fluid as needed
†Differential serviced separately

TRANSAXLE, Manual
4-speed . . . . **AF**
5-speed . . . . **GLS**

CAPACITY, Refill:	Liters	Pt
4-speed	2.8	6.0
5-speed	2.6	5.4

DIFFERENTIAL/FINAL DRIVE
Standard & Eldorado,
   Seville 80W, 80W-90* **GL-5**
Limited-Slip . . . . 90 **GL-5★**
*For vehicles normally operated in Canada, 80W only

CAPACITY, Refill:	Liters	Pt
Eldorado, Seville	1.5	3.2
RWD w/7½″ ring gear† . . .	1.7	3.5
Others	2.0	4.3

†Identified by an F as the third character

LIMITED-SLIP IDENTIFICATION:
Fourth character is R or 4 of identification number stamped on axle tube near differential

CADILLAC
1983 All Diesel Models

CCPM8   CCPM8

MI—MILES IN THOUSANDS
KM—KILOMETERS IN THOUSANDS

FIRST 5 MI—8 KM
Engine idle speeds .... check/adjust

EVERY 12 MO/5 MI—8 KM
Crankcase .... change oil

Final Drive/Differential .... check level
Inspect front axle boots and seals

Front suspension &
  steering linkage ...... **4-11 fittings LB**
At mileage interval only
Inspect steering linkage & suspension

Limited-Slip differential .. change lubricant
One time service. All models at 7.5 mi (12 km)

Parking brake cables & guides ... coat **LB**

Tires .... rotate
Radial tires: At first 7.5 mi (12 km); then every 15 mi (24 km). Check disc brake pads; replace when 1/8″ thick. Lug nut torque, 100 ft lb. Torque wire wheels at first 500 mi (800 km)
Check drum brake lining & parking brake adjustment

Brake master cylinder .... check level **HB**

Cooling system .... check level **EC**

Drive belts .... inspect/adjust
Every 6 mo

Exhaust system .... inspect

Oil filter .... replace

Power steering reservoir .. check level **PS**

Transaxle/trans., automatic ... check level
Every 6 mo
At operating temperature, engine idling, in PARK. Check for leaks. Lubricate linkage with **MO**

Body .... lubricate
Every 6 mo
Flush underbody every spring

EVERY 12 MO/15 MI—24 KM
Cooling
  system .... inspect & tighten hoses
Wash radiator filler neck & cap; pressure test system. Clean exterior of radiator core & air conditioning condenser

Crankcase ventilation system ...... clean
Filters & breather cap-valve units in each valve cover

Throttle linkage .... check

EVERY 24 MO/30 MI—48 KM
Cooling system ...... change coolant **EC**
Flush system

EVERY 30 MI—48 KM
Front wheel bearings ex. Cimarron,
  Eldorado & Seville .... clean/repack **GC**
Or at time of front brake relining. Torque, 12 ft lb. Back off to 0; tighten nut finger tight & replace cotter pin

Air cleaner element .... replace

Engine idle speed .... check/adjust

Fuel filter .... replace

Fuel injection pump
  timing .... check/adjust

EVERY 100 MI—160 KM
Transaxle/transmission,
  automatic .... change fluid
Replace sump filter

SEVERE SERVICE
Crankcase—Change oil every 3 mo/2.5 mi (4 km)

Final Drive/Differential w/manual transmission—Change lubricant every 5 mi (8 km)

Front wheel bearings ex. Eldorado & Seville—Clean/repack with **GC** every 15 mi (24 km)

Transaxle or transmission, automatic—Change fluid every 15 mi (24 km). Clean sump or replace filter

KEY TO LUBRICANTS

AF	DEXRON®-IIE Automatic Transmission Fluid
CC	Motor Oil, API Service CC
CD	Motor Oil, API Service CD
EC	Ethylene Glycol Coolant Mix 50% to 75% with water
GC	Wheel Bearing Grease, NLGI Category GC
GL-5	Gear Oil, API Service GL-5
GL-5★	Special Lubricant for Limited-Slip Differential
HB	Hydraulic Brake Fluid, DOT 3
LB	Chassis Grease, NLGI Category LB
MO	Motor Oil
PS	Power Steering Fluid
SF	Motor Oil, API Service SF

CRANKCASE .... **SF/CC, SF/CD**

CAPACITY, Refill:	Liters	Qt
All (includes filter)	6.6	7.0
Above 32°F (0°C)		30*
0° to 60°F (−18° to 16°C)		15W-40
Below 60°F (16°C)		10W-30

*30 is preferred above 32°F (0°C), especially for continuous duty driving

TRANSMISSION/TRANSAXLE,
  Automatic .... **AF**

CAPACITY, Initial Refill*:	Liters	Qt
200 Trans.	5.0	5.3
325 Trans.†	3.3	3.5

*With the engine at operating temperature, shift transmission through all gears. Let engine slow idle in PARK for three minutes. Check fluid level and add fluid as needed
†Differential serviced separately

DIFFERENTIAL/FINAL DRIVE
Standard & Eldorado,
  Seville 80W, 80W-90* **GL-5**
Limited-Slip .... 90 **GL-5★**
*For vehicles normally operated in Canada, 80W only

CAPACITY, Refill:	Liters	Pt
Eldorado, Seville	1.5	3.2
RWD w/7½″ ring gear† ..	1.7	3.5
Others	2.0	4.3

†Identified by an F as the third character
LIMITED-SLIP IDENTIFICATION:
Fourth character is R or 4 of identification number stamped on axle tube near differential

SERVICE AT TIME OR MILEAGE—WHICHEVER OCCURS FIRST

CCPM10   CCPM10

MI—MILES IN THOUSANDS
KM—KILOMETERS IN THOUSANDS

FIRST 5 MI—8 KM
Engine idle speed ....check/adjust

Exhaust pressure
   regulator valve 1985 ....inspect

EVERY 6 MONTHS
Power steering reservoir .. check level **PS**

Brake master cylinder .... check level **HB**

Cooling system ....check level **EC**
At each fuel stop

EVERY 12 MO/5 MI—8 KM
Crankcase ....change oil
Drain water separator

Final Drive/Differential .... check level
Inspect front drive axle boots & seals

Front suspension &
   steering linkage .... **11 fittings LB**
At mileage interval only
Inspect steering linkage & suspension

Parking brake cables & guides ... coat **LB**
At mileage interval only

Tires ....rotate
At first 5 mi (8 km), then every 15 mi (24 km). Check
disc brake pads; replace when 1/8″ thick. Check drum
brake lining & parking brake adjustment. Inspect brake
hoses & lines. Lug nut torque, 100 ft lb. Torque wire
wheels at first 500 mi (800 km)

Transmission
   shift linkage ....lubricate **MO**

Drive belts ....inspect/adjust

Exhaust system ....inspect

Oil filter ....replace

Transmission, automatic ..... check level
At operating temperature, engine idling, in PARK.
Check for leaks. Lubricate linkage with **MO**

Body hinges ....lubricate **MO**
Flush underbody every spring

EVERY 12 MO/15 MI—24 KM
Cooling
   system ....inspect & tighten hoses
Every 12 months only. Wash radiator filler neck & cap;
pressure test system. Clean exterior of radiator core &
air conditioning condenser

Crankcase ventilation system ......clean
Filters & breather cap-valve units in each valve cover

Exhaust pressure
   regulator valve 1985 ....inspect
At mileage interval only

EVERY 24 MO/30 MI—48 KM
Cooling system ......change coolant **EC**
Flush system

Front wheel bearings, rear
   wheel drive cars ..... clean/repack **GC**
Or at time of front brake relining. Torque, 12 ft lb. Back
off to 0; tighten nut finger tight & replace cotter pin

Air cleaner element ....replace

Engine idle speed ....check/adjust

Fuel filter ....replace

Fuel injection pump
   timing ....check/adjust

EVERY 100 MI—160 KM
Transmission, automatic .... change fluid
Replace sump filter

SEVERE SERVICE
Crankcase—Change oil & filter every
3 mo/2.5 mi (4 km). Drain water separator

Final Drive/Differential—Change lubricant
every 5 mi (8 km) when towing a trailer

Front suspension & steering linkage, parking brake cables & guides, transmission linkage & body hinges—Lubricate every 6 mo/
5 mi (8 km)

Front wheel bearings, rear wheel drive
cars—Clean/repack with **GC** every 15 mi
(24 km)

Transmission, automatic—Change fluid
every 15 mi (24 km). Clean sump or replace
filter

KEY TO LUBRICANTS

AF	DEXRON®-IIE Automatic Transmission Fluid
CC	Motor Oil, API Service CC
CD	Motor Oil, API Service CD
EC	Ethylene Glycol Coolant Mix 50% to 75% with water
GC	Wheel Bearing Grease, NLGI Category GC
GL-5	Gear Oil, API Service GL-5
GL-5★	Special Lubricant for Limited-Slip Differentials
HB	Hydraulic Brake Fluid, DOT 3
LB	Chassis Grease, NLGI Category LB
MO	Motor Oil
PS	Power Steering Fluid
SF	Motor Oil, API Service SF

CRANKCASE .... SF/CC, SF/CD

CAPACITY, Refill:	Liters	Qt
Including filter		
4.3L	5.7	6.0
5.7L	6.5	7.0
Above 32°F (0°C)		30*
0° to 60°F (−18° to 16°C)		15W-40
Below 60°F (16°C)		10W-30

*30 is preferred above 32°F (0°C), especially for continu-
ous duty driving

TRANSMISSION/TRANSAXLE,
   Automatic .... **AF**

CAPACITY, Initial Refill*:	Liters	Qt
FWD DeVille, Fleetwood ..	5.5	5.8
325 Trans.†	3.3	3.5
All other models	5.0	5.3

*With the engine at operating temperature, shift transmis-
sion through all gears. Let engine slow idle in PARK for
three minutes. Check fluid level and add fluid as needed
†Differential serviced separately

DIFFERENTIAL/FINAL DRIVE
Eldorado, Seville & All RWD Only
Standard & Eldorado,
   Seville 80W, 80W-90* **GL-5**
Limited-Slip ...... 80W, 80W-90 **GL-5★**
*For vehicles normally operated in Canada, 80W only

CAPACITY, Refill:	Liters	Pt
Eldorado, Seville	1.5	3.2
All RWD	2.0	4.3

CHEK-CHART

SERVICE AT TIME OR MILEAGE—WHICHEVER OCCURS FIRST

CCPM9   CCPM9
Perform the following maintenance services at the intervals indicated to keep the vehicle warranties in effect.

W SERVICE TO MAINTAIN EMISSION WARRANTY

MI—MILES IN THOUSANDS
KM—KILOMETERS IN THOUSANDS

FIRST 7.5 MI—12.5 KM

W Choke & hoses ex. FI . . . . . check/clean

W Engine idle speeds ex. FI . . check/adjust

W Carburetor or throttle
   body mounting . . . . torque

EVERY 6 MONTHS

Power steering reservoir . . check level **PS**

Brake master cylinder . . . . check level **HB**
Also Cimarron hydraulic clutch

Cooling system . . . . check level **EC**
At each fuel stop

EVERY 12 MO/7.5 MI—12.5 KM

W Crankcase . . . . change oil
Check level at each fuel stop

Final Drive/Differential . . . . check level
Ex. models with transverse engine

Front suspension &
   steering linkage . . . . . . **4-11 fittings LB**
Inspect steering linkage & suspension, also inspect
front drive axle boots & seals

Parking brake cables & guides . . . coat **LB**
1989-90, only lubricate cable adjuster

Tires . . . . rotate
At first 7.5 mi (12 km); then every 15 mi (24 km). Check
disc brake pads; replace when 1/8″ thick. Inspect brake
hoses & lines, check drum brake lining & parking brake
adjustment. Lug nut torque, 100 ft lb. Torque wire
wheels at first 500 mi (800 km)

Transmission/transaxle
   shift linkage . . . . lubricate **MO**

Drive belts ex. 1990 . . . . inspect/adjust

W Exhaust system . . . . inspect

W Oil filter . . . . replace
At first oil change, then every other but at least every
12 mo

Transaxle/transmission . . . . . . check level
At operating temperature, engine idling, in PARK.
Check for leaks

Body hinges . . . . lubricate **MO**
Flush underbody every spring

EVERY 12 MONTHS

W Cooling
   system . . . . . inspect & tighten hoses
Wash radiator filler neck & cap; pressure test system.
Clean exterior of radiator core & air conditioning condenser

EVERY 24 MO/30 MI—50 KM

W Cooling system . . . . change coolant **EC**
Flush system

W Drive belts . . . . inspect/adjust
1984-89 AIR pump & vacuum pump only

EVERY 30 MI—50 KM

Front wheel bearings, rear
   wheel drive cars . . . . . clean/repack **GC**
Or at time of front brake relining. Torque, 12 ft lb. Back
off to 0; tighten nut finger tight & replace cotter pin

W Air cleaner valve . . . . check

W Choke & hoses ex. FI . . . . check

W Fuel cap, tank, lines . . . . inspect

W Ignition timing . . . . check/adjust
1984 clean/inspect distributor cap & rotor, clean or replace

W PCV valve & hoses . . . . inspect

W Spark plugs . . . . replace

W Spark plug wires . . . . clean/inspect

   Vacuum hoses 1985 . . . . check

EVERY 36 MO/30 MI—50 KM

W Air cleaner element . . . . replace
Ex. 2.0L eng.

W A.I.R. filter 1987-90 . . . . replace

W EGR system . . . . check/clean
Not required for 1986 Brougham, 1987-88 Cimarron

W PCV filter . . . . replace
Ex. 2.0L eng.

EVERY 50 MI—80 KM

W Air cleaner & PCV
   filter element 4-cyl. . . . . replace

EVERY 100 MI—160 KM

Transaxle/transmission,
   automatic . . . . change fluid
Replace sump filter

SEVERE SERVICE

W Carburetor or TBI—Torque mounting
bolts. Adjust idle speed (ex. with FI) at
first 6 mi (10 km), also check carburetor
choke & hoses

Crankcase—Change oil & filter every 3 mo/
3 mi (5 km)

Final Drive/Differential—Change lubricant
(ex. models with transverse engine) every
7.5 mi (12.5 km) when towing a trailer

Front suspension & steering linkage, parking brake cables & guides, transmission or
transaxle shift linkage, body hinges—
Lubricate every 6 mo/6 mi (10 km)

Front wheel bearings, rear wheel drive
cars—Clean/repack with **GC** every 15 mi (25
km)

Tires—Rotate at first 6 mi (10 km)

Transaxle or transmission, automatic—
Change fluid & filter every 15 mi (24 km).
Clean sump or replace filter

KEY TO LUBRICANTS

AF	DEXRON®-IIE Automatic Transmission Fluid
EC	Ethylene Glycol Coolant Mix 50% to 75% with water
GC	Wheel Bearing Grease, NLGI Category GC
GL-5	Gear Oil, API Service GL-5
GL-5★	Special Lubricant for Limited-Slip Differentials
GLS	Gear Lubricant, Special
HB	Hydraulic Brake Fluid, DOT 3
LB	Chassis Grease, NLGI Category LB
MO	Motor Oil
PS	Power Steering Fluid
SG	Motor Oil, API Service SG
WB	Wheel Bearing Grease

CRANKCASE . . . . SG

CAPACITY, Refill:	Liters	Qt
4.1L, 4.5L Allanté	5.7	6.0
All other FWD 4.1L, 4.5L, 4.9L eng.	4.7	5.0
Others	3.8	4.0

Capacity shown is without filter. When replacing filter,
additional oil may be needed

Above 40°F (4°C)	30
Above 20°F (–7°C) 1984-86	20W-20
Above 10°F (–12°C) 1984-86	15W-40
Above 0°F (–18°C)	10W-30†
Below 100°F (38°C) Cimarron & 1988-89 5.0L	5W-30*
Below 60°F (16°C) ex. Cimarron & 1988-89 5.0L	5W-30

*Preferred in Cimarron & 1989 5.0L
† Preferred ex. Cimarron & 1989 5.0L

TRANSMISSION/TRANSAXLE, Automatic . . . . AF

CAPACITY, Initial Refill*:	Liters	Qt
Allanté	7.6	8.0
Cimarron	3.8	4.0
1986-90 Eldorado, Seville & 1985-90 FWD DeVille, Fleetwood	6.2	6.5
Others†	5.0	5.3

*With the engine at operating temperature, shift transmis-
sion through all gears. Let engine slow idle in PARK for at
least 3 minutes. Check fluid level and add fluid as needed
†1984-85 Eldorado, Seville differential serviced separately

TRANSAXLE, Manual . . . . GLS

CAPACITY, Refill:	Liters	Pt
4-speed	2.8	6.0
5-speed Isuzu†	2.6	5.4
5-speed Muncie‡	1.9	4.0

†Has 7-bolt aluminum end cap
‡Has 9-bolt steel end cap

DIFFERENTIAL/FINAL DRIVE
1984-85 Eldorado, Seville & All RWD Only
Standard & Eldorado,
   Seville 80W, 80W-90* **GL-5**
Limited-Slip . . . . . . 80W, 80W-90 **GL-5★**
*For vehicles normally operated in Canada, 80W only

CAPACITY, Refill:	Liters	Pt
Eldorado, Seville	1.5	3.2
1989-90 RWD w/2.73 & 2.93:1 ratio	1.7	3.5
All other RWD	2.0	4.3

CADILLAC
1991-92 All Gasoline Models

SERVICE AT TIME OR MILEAGE—WHICHEVER OCCURS FIRST

Perform the following maintenance services at the intervals indicated to keep the vehicle warranties in effect.

W   SERVICE TO MAINTAIN EMISSION WARRANTY

MI—MILES IN THOUSANDS
KM—KILOMETERS IN THOUSANDS

EVERY 6 MONTHS
Power steering reservoir . . check level **PS**

Brake master cylinder . . . . check level **HB**

Cooling system . . . . check level **EC**
At each fuel stop

EVERY 12 MO/7.5 MI—12.5 KM
W Crankcase . . . . change oil
Check level at each fuel stop

RWD differential . . . . check level

Front suspension &
    steering linkage . . . . . . **4-11 fittings LB**
Inspect steering linkage & suspension, also inspect
front drive axle boots & seals

Parking brake cables & guides . . . coat **LB**

Tires . . . . rotate
At first 7.5 mi (12 km); then every 15 mi (24 km). Check
disc brake pads; replace when 1/8″ thick. Inspect brake
hoses & lines, check drum brake lining & parking brake
adjustment. Lug nut torque, 100 ft lb. Torque wire
wheels at first 500 mi (800 km)

Transmission/transaxle
    shift linkage . . . . lubricate **MO**

W Exhaust system . . . . inspect

W Oil filter . . . . replace
At first oil change, then every other but at least every
12 mo

Transaxle/transmission . . . . . . check level
Check for leaks

Body hinges . . . . lubricate **MO**
Flush underbody every spring

EVERY 12 MONTHS
W Cooling
    system . . . . . inspect & tighten hoses
Wash radiator filler neck & cap; pressure test system.
Clean exterior of radiator core & air conditioning con-
denser

EVERY 24 MO/30 MI—50 KM
W Cooling system . . . . change coolant **EC**
Flush system

EVERY 30 MI—50 KM
Front wheel bearings, rear
    wheel drive cars . . . . . clean/repack **GC**
Or at time of front brake relining. Torque, 12 ft lb. Back
off to 0; tighten nut finger tight & replace cotter pin

W Fuel cap, tank, lines . . . . inspect

W Ignition timing . . . . check/adjust

W PCV valve & hoses 1991 . . . . . . inspect

W Spark plugs . . . . replace
1991 all, 1992 Brougham

W Spark plug wires . . . . clean/inspect

EVERY 36 MO/30 MI—50 KM
W Air cleaner element . . . . replace

W A.I.R. filter . . . . replace

W EGR system . . . . check/clean

W PCV filter . . . . replace

EVERY 100 MI—160 KM
Spark plugs, 1992 ex.
    Brougham . . . . replace

Transaxle/transmission,
    automatic . . . . change fluid
Replace sump filter

SEVERE SERVICE
Crankcase—Change oil & filter every 3 mo/
3 mi (5 km)

RWD differential—Change lubricant every
7.5 mi (12.5 km) when towing a trailer

Front suspension & steering linkage, parking brake cables & guides, transmission or
transaxle shift linkage, body hinges—
Lubricate every 6 mo/6 mi (10 km)

Front wheel bearings, rear wheel drive
cars—Clean/repack with **GC** every 15 mi (25
km)

Tires—Rotate at first 6 mi (10 km)

Transaxle or transmission, automatic—
Change fluid & filter every 15 mi (24 km).
Clean sump or replace filter

KEY TO LUBRICANTS

AF	DEXRON®-IIE Automatic Transmission Fluid
EC	Ethylene Glycol Coolant Mix 50% to 75% with water
GC	Wheel Bearing Grease, NLGI Category GC
GL-5	Gear Oil, API Service GL-5
GL-5★	Special Lubricant for Limited-Slip Differentials
GLS	Gear Lubricant, Special
HB	Hydraulic Brake Fluid, DOT 3
LB	Chassis Grease, NLGI Category LB
MO	Motor Oil
PS	Power Steering Fluid
SG	Motor Oil, API Service SG

CRANKCASE . . . . SG

CAPACITY, Refill:	Liters	Qt
Allanté	5.7	6.0
All other FWD	4.7	5.0
RWD	3.8	4.0

Capacity shown is without filter. When replacing filter,
additional oil may be needed

Above 40°F (4°C) 30
Above 0°F (–18°C) . . . . 10W-30†
Below 60°F (16°C) 5W-30
† Preferred

TRANSMISSION/TRANSAXLE,
    Automatic . . . . AF

CAPACITY, Initial Refill*:	Liters	Qt
Allanté	6.2	6.5
Other FWD	5.7	6.0
Brougham	4.7	5.0

*With the engine at operating temperature, shift transmis-
sion through all gears. Let engine slow idle in PARK for at
least 3 minutes. Check fluid level and add fluid as needed

DIFFERENTIAL
Standard 80W-90* **GL-5**
Limited-Slip . . . . 80W-90* **GL-5★**
*For vehicles normally operated in Canada, 80W

CAPACITY, Refill:	Liters	Pt
RWD	2.0	4.3

CHEK-CHART

SERVICE LOCATIONS — ENGINE AND CHASSIS

CTDP-1   CTDP-1

HOOD RELEASE: Inside

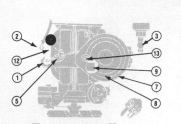

1983-87
1.6L (98)
Code C

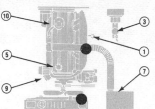

1983-86
1.8L (111) Diesel
Code D

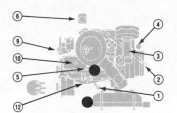

1983-86
1.8L (112) Code G,
2.0L (122) Code B, P

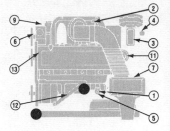

1987-91
2.0L (122) Code 1
2.2L Code G
Cavalier, Corsica, Beretta

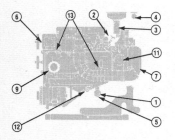

1992
2.2L Code 4
Cavalier, Corsica, Beretta

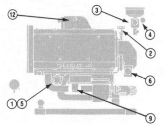

1990-92
2.3L Code A
Corsica, Beretta

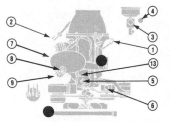

1983-86 2.5L (151)
Code V, 2, F
Camaro

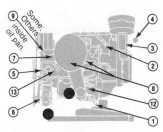

1983-92
2.5L (151)
Code 2, 5, R
Air induction
system varies.

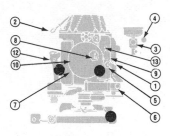

1983-84
2.8L 2V Code 1
Camaro

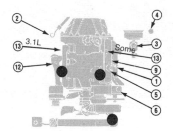

1985-92
2.8L (173) FI Code S
3.1L FI Code T
Camaro

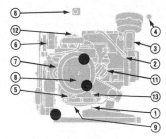

1983-86
2.8L (173) 2V
Code X, Z
Citation, Celebrity

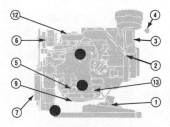

1985-86
2.8L (173) FI
Cavalier, Celebrity, Citation
Code W

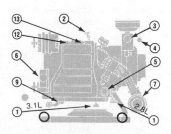

1987-92
2.8L (173) Code W
3.1L Code T
1990-92 Cavalier, Celebrity,
Corsica, Beretta, Lumina

① Crankcase dipstick
② Transmission dipstick
③ Brake fluid reservoir
④ Clutch fluid reservoir
⑤ Oil fill cap
⑥ Power steering reservoir
⑦ Air filter
⑧ Fuel filter
⑨ Oil filter
⑩ PCV filter
⑪ EGR valve
⑫ Oxygen sensor
⑬ PCV valve

SERVICE LOCATIONS — ENGINE AND CHASSIS

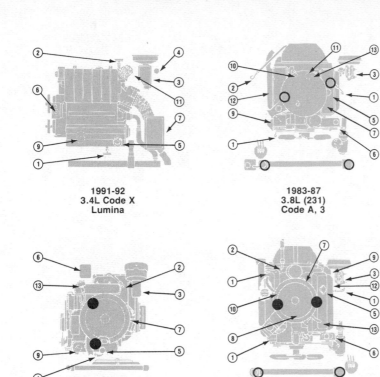

1991-92
3.4L Code X
Lumina

1983-87
3.8L (231)
Code A, 3

1983-84
3.8L (229)
Code K, 9

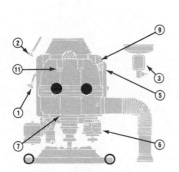

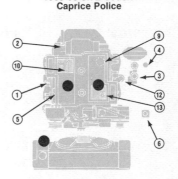

1983-85
4.3L (262) V-6 Diesel
Code T

1983-88
4.3L (262) Code Z;
5.0L (305) 4V Code G, H;
5.7L (350) Code 6

1988-91 5.0L (305) FI Code E
Camaro, Caprice
1989-90 5.7L Code 7
Caprice Police

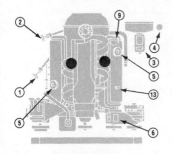

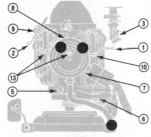

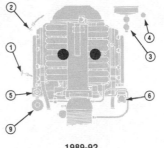

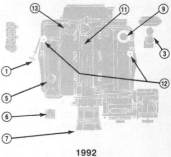

1991 5.0L Code E
5.7L Code 7 Caprice

1986-90
5.0L (307) Code Y

1983-84
5.0L (305) FI Camaro
5.7L (350) Corvette

1985-92
5.0L (305) FI Camaro
5.7L (350) Code 8
Camaro, Corvette

1983-85
5.7L (350) Diesel
Code N

1989-92
5.7L Code J
Corvette

1992
5.7L Code P
Corvette

● Cooling system drain   ○ Cooling system drain, some models

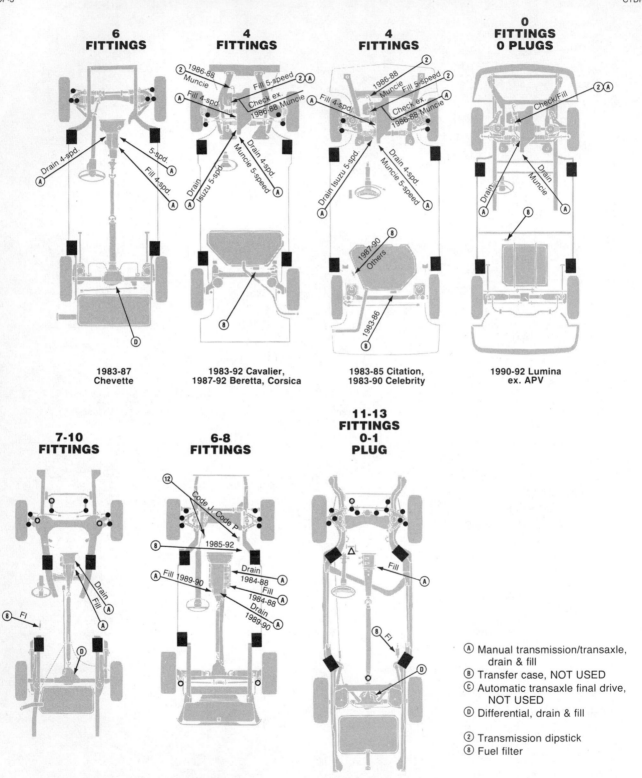

CAUTION: On front wheel drive vehicles the center of gravity is further forward than on rear wheel drive vehicles. When removing major components from the rear of the vehicle while it is on a hoist, the vehicle must be supported in a manner to prevent it from tipping forward.

■ Lift adapter position   △ Plug, some models   ● Fitting   ○ Fitting, some models

Copyright 1992 by H.M. Gousha, a division of Simon & Schuster

CHEK-CHART

SERVICE AT TIME OR MILEAGE—WHICHEVER OCCURS FIRST

CTPM7   CTPM7

MI—MILES IN THOUSANDS
KM—KILOMETERS IN THOUSANDS

4-CYL. DIESEL
EVERY 12 MO/3.75 MI—6 KM
Crankcase . . . . change oil

Oil filter . . . . replace
After initial service, replace every 12 mo or 7.5 mi (12 km)

Engine idle speed . . . . adjust
After initial service, adjust only every 30 mi (48 km)

EVERY 6 MONTHS
Brake master cylinder . . . . . check level **HB**

Clutch free pedal travel . . . . check/adjust
Front wheel drive models, every 5 mi (8 km)

Power steering reservoir . . . check level **PS**

Transaxle or trans., auto. . . . check level

FIRST 7.5 MI—12 KM
Carburetor mounting bolts . . . . torque

Engine idle speed, gasoline . . . . adjust
Ex. engines with Idle Speed or Idle Air Control

Diff., Limited-Slip . . . . change lubricant
One time service only

Transmission, manual,
  4-cyl. Diesel . . . . change lubricant
Service every 30 mi (48 km) thereafter

GASOLINE: FIRST 7.5 MI—12 KM; THEN EVERY 24 MO/30 MI—48 KM
6-, 8-CYL. DIESEL: FIRST 5 MI—8 KM; THEN EVERY 30 MI—48 KM
Choke & hoses, ex. Diesel . . . . check/clean

Engine idle speed, Diesel . . . . adjust

GASOLINE, EVERY 12 MO/7.5—12 KM
DIESEL, EVERY 5 MI—8 KM
Crankcase ex. 4-cyl. Diesel . . . . change oil

Differential . . . . check level

Exhaust pressure regulator valve &
  hoses, 6-cyl. Diesel . . . . inspect/test
After initial inspection, check again at 15 mi (24 km) & every 15 mi (24 km) thereafter

Exhaust system . . . . inspect

Front suspension &
  steering linkage . . . . . . **4-11 fittings LB**

Oil filter, ex. 4-cyl. Diesel . . . . replace
6-, 8-cyl. Diesel, at every oil change; all others at first oil change, then at 12 mo/15 mi (24 km) intervals only

Parking brake cables & guides . . . . coat **LB**
Check adjustment

Shift linkage . . . . coat **LB**
With floor shift, coat contact faces

Suspension & steering . . . . inspect
Also inspect drive axle boots and seals

Tires . . . . rotate
Radial tires, every 15 mi (24 km) after initial service. Check brake pads. Lug nut torque, ft lb: Chevette, 70; all front wheel drive & Impala or Caprice wagons, 100; all others, 80 ex. 90 with aluminum wheels

Transaxle or transmission . . . . check level
Ex. 4-cyl. Diesel

Drive belts . . . . inspect/adjust

Throttle linkage . . . . inspect
Check for damage or binding

Body . . . . lubricate

EVERY 12 MONTHS
Cooling system . . . . inspect & tighten hoses
Wash radiator filler neck and cap; pressure test system. Clean exterior of radiator core and air conditioning condenser

EVERY 12 MO/15 MI—24 KM
Crankcase ventilation system,
  6-, 8-cyl. Diesel . . . . inspect
Clean filters in each valve cover, pipes & tubes

EVERY 15 MI—24 KM
Valve clearance,
  4-cyl. Diesel . . . . check/adjust

EVERY 24 MO/30 MI—48 KM
Cooling system . . . . change coolant **EC**
Flush system

EVERY 36 MO/30 MI—48 KM
Air cleaner element . . . . replace
Ex. Diesel, 1.6L & 2.0L

EGR system . . . . clean/inspect

EVERY 30 MI—48 KM
Clutch cross shaft . . . . **1 plug LB**

Front wheel bearings ex. front
  wheel drive . . . . clean/repack **GC**
Service at mileage interval or at each brake reline, whichever comes first. Tighten spindle nut to 12 ft lb while turning wheel. Back off 1/2 turn & retighten finger tight. End play, .001″-.005″

Rear wheel inner bearings,
  Corvette . . . . repack **GC**
Service every 30 mi (48 km) or at each brake reline

Fuel cap, tank, and lines, ex. Diesel inspect

Air cleaner element, Diesel . . . . replace

Fuel filter, Diesel . . . . replace

Ignition timing . . . . adjust
Inspect distributor cap, clean or replace

Ignition wires . . . . inspect/clean

Injection pump timing,
  Diesel . . . . check/adjust

PCV valve ex. Diesel . . . . inspect
Blow out or replace hoses

Spark plugs . . . . replace

Vacuum advance
  system & hoses . . . . inspect
As equipped

EVERY 50 MI—80 KM
Air cleaner element, 1.6L, 2.0L . . . . replace

EVERY 100 MI—160 KM
Transaxle or trans., auto. . . . . change fluid
Clean sump screen or replace filter

SEVERE SERVICE
Crankcase—Change oil: Gasoline, every 3 mo/3 mi (4.8 km); Diesel: 4-cyl., every 3 mo/ 2 mi (3.2 km); 6- & 8-cyl., every 3 mo/2.5 mi (4 km). Change filter at each oil change

Front wheel bearings—Repack every 15 mi (24 km)

Transaxle or transmission, automatic—Change fluid & filter or clean screen every 15 mi (24 km)

Differential, 4-cyl. Diesel—Change lubricant every 7.5 mi (12 km) when towing a trailer

KEY TO LUBRICANTS

AF	DEXRON®-IIE Automatic Transmission Fluid
CD	Motor Oil, API Service CD
EC	Ethylene Glycol Coolant
	Mix with water to –34°F (–37°C) protection
GC	Wheel Bearing Grease, NLGI Category GC
GLS	Gear Lubricant, Special
	G.M. Part No. 12345349
GL-5	Gear Oil, API Service GL-5
GL-5★	Special Lubricant for Limited-Slip Differential
HB	Hydraulic Brake Fluid, DOT 3
LB	Chassis Grease, NLGI Category LB
PS	Power Steering Fluid
SG	Motor Oil, API Service SG
	Use Energy Conserving-II oils

CRANKCASE
Diesel engine . . . . **SG/CD**
Gasoline engine . . . . **SG**

CAPACITY, Refill:	Liters	Qt
Diesel, including filter		
4-, 6-cyl.	5.8	6.0
8-cyl.	6.6	7.0
Gasoline: 2.5L (151) eng.	2.8	3.0
Others	3.8	4.0

Gasoline capacity shown is without filter. When replacing filter, additional oil may be needed

Diesel Engine:
4-cyl.
Above 32°F (0°C) . . . . 30♦
Above 15°F (–10°C) 15W-40
All temperatures 10W-30
6-, 8-cyl.
Above 32°F (0°C) . . . . 30♦
0° to 60°F (–18° to 16°C) 15W-40
Below 60°F (16°C) 10W-30
Gasoline Engine:
Above 40°F (4°C) 30
Above 20°F (–7°C) 20W-20, 20W-40, 20W-50
Above 10°F (–12°C) 15W-40
Above 0°F (–18°C) 10W-30*
Below 60°F (16°C) . . . . 5W-30△
△5W-30 may be used up to 100°F (38°C) in 4-cyl. & 2.8L V-6 engines
♦30 is preferred above 32°F (0°C), especially for continuous duty driving
*10W-30 is preferred above 0°F (–18°C)

TRANSMISSION/TRANSAXLE,
Automatic . . . . **AF**

CAPACITY, Initial Refill*:	Liters	Qt
Front wheel drive	3.8	4.0
180 Transmission	2.8	3.0
200 Transmission	3.3	3.5
350 Transmission	2.8	3.0
700-R4 Transmission	4.7	5.0

*With the engine at operating temperature, shift transmission through all gears. Let engine slow idle in PARK for 3 minutes or more. Check fluid level and add fluid as needed

TRANSMISSION/TRANSAXLE, Manual
FWD: 4-speed . . . . **AF**
  5-speed . . . . **GLS**
RWD: 4-speed **80W, 80W-90*** **GL-5**
  5-speed Camaro, Chevette Gasoline . **AF**
  5-speed 4-cyl. Diesel . . . . . . **5W-30 SG**
*For vehicles normally operated in Canada, 80W only

CAPACITY, Refill	Liters	Pt
FWD: 4-speed	2.8	6.0
5-speed	2.6	5.4
RWD: Chevette 4-speed	1.7	3.5
5-speed, gasoline	1.9	4.0
5-speed, diesel	1.5	3.1
Camaro 5-speed	1.7	3.5
Others	1.7	3.5

DIFFERENTIAL
Standard **80W, 80W-90*** **GL-5**
Limited-Slip . . . . . . **80W, 80W-90*** **GL-5★**
*For vehicles normally operated in Canada, 80W only

CAPACITY, Refill:	Liters	Pt
Chevette	0.8	1.7
Corvette	1.8	3.8
Impala, Caprice wagon		
or w/code L engine	1.9	4.3
Others	1.5	3.1

LIMITED-SLIP IDENTIFICATION:
Tag under rear cover-attaching bolt

Copyright 1992 by H.M. Gousha, a division of Simon & Schuster

CHEVROLET
1984-85 All Models
Includes Chevrolet El Camino, GMC Caballero

CTPM8 CTPM8

KEY TO LUBRICANTS
See other Chevrolet charts

MI—MILES IN THOUSANDS
KM—KILOMETERS IN THOUSANDS

4-CYL. DIESEL
EVERY 12 MO/3.75 MI—6 KM
Crankcase . . . . change oil
Oil filter . . . . replace
After initial service, replace every 12 mo or 7.5 mi (12 km)
Engine idle speed . . . . adjust
After initial service, adjust only every 30 mi (48 km)

EVERY 6 MONTHS
Brake master cylinder . . . . . check level **HB**
Clutch free pedal travel . . . . . check/adjust
Front wheel drive models, every 5 mi (8 km)
Power steering reservoir . . . check level **PS**

FIRST 7.5 MI—12 KM
Carburetor or T.B.I. mounting
  bolts . . . . torque
Engine idle speed, gasoline . . . . adjust
Ex. engines with Idle Speed or Idle Air Control
Diff., Limited-Slip . . . . change lubricant
One time service only
Tires . . . . rotate
Radial tires, every 15 mi (24 km) after initial service.
Check brake linings. Lug nut torque, ft lb: Chevette, 80;
all front wheel drive, Corvette, Impala or Caprice Wagons, 100; all others, 80 ex. with aluminum wheels, 90
Transmission, manual,
  4-cyl. Diesel . . . . change lubricant
Service every 30 mi (48 km) thereafter

GASOLINE: FIRST 7.5 MI—12 KM; THEN EVERY 24 MO/30 MI—50 KM
Choke & hoses . . . . check/clean

6-, 8-CYL. DIESEL: FIRST 5 MI—8 KM; THEN EVERY 30 MI—50 KM
Engine idle speed . . . . adjust

GASOLINE, EVERY 12 MO/7.5 MI—12 KM
DIESEL, EVERY 12 MO/5 MI—8 KM
Crankcase ex. 4-cyl. Diesel . . . . change oil
Brake system . . . . inspect
Check hydraulic system for leaks. Inspect brake linings
Differential . . . . check level
Exhaust pressure regulator valve &
  hoses, Diesel . . . . inspect/test
After initial inspection, check again at 15 mi (24 km) &
every 15 mi (24 km) thereafter
Exhaust system . . . . inspect
Front suspension &
  steering linkage . . . . . . 4-11 fittings **LB**
Oil filter, ex. 4-cyl. Diesel . . . . replace
6-, 8-cyl. Diesel, at every oil change; all others at first oil
change, then every other oil change or 12 mo
Parking brake cables & guides . . . . coat **LB**
Check adjustment
Shift linkage . . . . coat **LB**
With floor shift, coat contact faces
Suspension & steering . . . . inspect
Also inspect drive axle boots and seals
Transaxle or transmission . . . . . check level
Ex. 4-cyl. Diesel
Drive belts . . . . inspect/adjust
Throttle linkage . . . . inspect
Check for damage or binding
Water separator . . . . drain
As equipped
Body . . . . lubricate

EVERY 12 MONTHS
Cooling system . . . inspect & tighten hoses
Wash radiator filler neck and cap; pressure test system. Clean exterior of radiator core and air conditioning
condenser. Inspect coolant and service as needed

EVERY 12 MO/15 MI—24 KM
Crankcase ventilation system,
  6-, 8-cyl. Diesel . . . . inspect
Clean filters in each valve cover, pipes, & tubes

EVERY 15 MI—24 KM
Valve clearance,
  4-cyl. Diesel . . . . check/adjust

EVERY 24 MO/30 MI—50 KM
Cooling system . . . . . . change coolant **EC**
Flush system
Vacuum/Air pump belts . . . . inspect/adjust
Replace as needed

EVERY 36 MO/30 MI—50 KM
Air cleaner element . . . . replace
Ex. Diesel, 1.6L & 2.0L
EGR system . . . . clean/inspect

EVERY 30 MI—50 KM
Clutch cross shaft . . . . **1 plug LB**
Front wheel bearings ex. front
  wheel drive . . . . clean/repack **GC**
Service at mileage interval or at each brake reline,
whichever comes first. Tighten spindle nut to 12 ft lb
while turning wheel. Back off 1/2 turn & retighten finger
tight. End play, .001"-.005"
Fuel cap, tank, and
  lines, ex. Diesel . . . . inspect
Transmission, manual,
  OD unit . . . . replace fluid
Corvette only
Air cleaner element, Diesel . . . . replace
Distributor cap . . . . inspect
Fuel filter, Diesel . . . . replace
Idle speed, 4-cyl. Diesel . . . . adjust
Ignition timing . . . . adjust
Inspect distributor cap, clean or replace
Ignition wires . . . . inspect/clean
Injection pump timing,
  Diesel . . . . check/adjust
PCV valve ex. Diesel . . . . inspect
Blow out or replace hoses
Spark plugs . . . . replace
Thermostatic air cleaner . . . . inspect
Vacuum advance
  system & hoses . . . . inspect
As equipped

EVERY 50 MI—80 KM
Air cleaner element, 1.6L, 2.0L . . . . replace

EVERY 100 MI—160 KM
Transaxle or trans., auto. . . . . change fluid
Clean sump screen or replace filter

SEVERE SERVICE
Carburetor or T.B.I.—Torque mounting
bolts & adjust idle speed at 6 mi (10 km),
also inspect carburetor choke & hoses
Crankcase—Change oil: Gasoline, every 3
mo/3 mi (5 km); Diesel: 4-cyl., every 3 mo/2
mi (3.2 km); 6- & 8-cyl., every 3 mo/2.5 mi (4
km). Change filter at each oil change
Front suspension & steering linkage—
Lubricate every: Gasoline, 6 mo/6 mi (10
km); Diesel, every 6 mo/5 mi (8 km)
Front wheel bearings—Repack every 15 mi
(24 km) or every brake service, whichever
comes first
Transaxle or transmission, automatic—
Change fluid & filter or clean screen every
15 mi (24 km)
Differential, 4-cyl. Diesel—Change lubricant
every 5 mi (8 km) when towing a trailer

CRANKCASE
Diesel engine . . . . **SG/CD**
Gasoline engine . . . . **SG**

CAPACITY, Refill:	Liters	Qt
Diesel, including filter		
4-, 6-cyl.	5.8	6.0
8-cyl.	6.6	7.0
Gasoline,		
2.5L (151) eng.	2.8	3.0
Others	3.8	4.0

Gasoline, capacity shown is without filter. When replacing
filter, additional oil may be needed

Diesel Engine:
4-cyl.
Above 32°F (0°C) . . . . 30♦
Above 15°F (−10°C) 15W-40
Below 100°F (38°C) 10W-30
6-, 8-cyl.
Above 32°F (0°C) . . . . 30♦
0° to 60°F (−8° to 16°C) 15W-40
Below 60°F (16°C) 10W-30
Gasoline Engine:
Above 40°F (4°C) 30
Above 20°F (−7°C) 20W-20
Above 10°F (−12°C) 15W-40
Above 0°F (−18°C) 10W-30
Below 60°F (16°C) . . . . 5W-30†
♦30 is preferred above 32°F (0°C), especially for continuous duty driving
†5W-30 may be used up to 100°F (38°C) in 4-cyl. & 2.8L 6-cyl. engines

TRANSMISSION/TRANSAXLE,
Automatic . . . . **AF**

CAPACITY, Initial Refill*:	Liters	Qt
125 Transmission	3.8	4.0
180 Transmission	2.8	3.0
200 Transmission	3.3	3.5
200-4R Transmission	4.8	5.0
250 Transmission	3.8	4.0
350 Transmission	2.8	3.0
440 Transmission	6.0	6.3
700-R4 Transmission	4.7	5.0

* With the engine at operating temperature, shift transmission
through all gears. Let engine slow idle in PARK for 3 minutes
or more. Check fluid level and add fluid as needed

TRANSMISSION/TRANSAXLE, Manual
FWD . . . . **GLS**
RWD: 4-speed Camaro . . . . **AF**
  4-speed others 80W, 80W-90* **GL-5**
  5-speed 4-cyl. Diesel . . . . 5W-30 **SG**
  5-speed, others . . . . **AF**
  Corvette OD unit . . . . **AF**
* For vehicles normally operated in Canada, 80W only

CAPACITY, Refill:	Liters	Pt
FWD: 4-speed	2.8	6.0
5-speed	2.6	5.5
RWD: Corvette	1.0	2.2
OD unit	1.6	3.6
Chevette 4-speed	1.7	3.5
5-speed, gasoline	1.9	4.0
5-speed, diesel	1.5	3.1
Camaro 5-speed	1.7	3.5
Others	1.7	3.5

DIFFERENTIAL
Standard 80W, 80W-90* **GL-5**
Limited-Slip . . . . . . 80W, 80W-90* **GL-5★**
* For vehicles normally operated in Canada, 80W only

CAPACITY, Refill:	Liters	Pt
Chevette	0.8	1.7
Corvette	1.5	3.2
Impala, Caprice wagon		
or w/code L engine	1.9	4.3
Others	1.5	3.1

LIMITED-SLIP IDENTIFICATION:
Tag under rear cover-attaching bolt

SERVICE AT TIME OR MILEAGE—WHICHEVER OCCURS FIRST

CTPM9   CTPM9

MI—MILES IN THOUSANDS
KM—KILOMETERS IN THOUSANDS

DIESEL
EVERY 12 MO/3.75 MI—6 KM
Crankcase . . . . change oil

Oil filter . . . . replace
After first two services, replace every 12 mo or 7.5 mi (12 km)

Engine idle speed . . . . adjust
After initial service, adjust only every 30 mi (48 km)

EVERY 6 MONTHS
Brake master cylinder . . . . check level **HB**

Clutch free pedal travel . . . . check/adjust
Front wheel drive models, every 5 mi (8 km)

Power steering reservoir . . check level **PS**

FIRST 7.5 MI—12 KM
Carburetor or T.B.I. mounting
  bolts . . . . torque

Crankcase ex. Diesel . . . . change oil
Change oil filter

Engine idle speed, gasoline . . . . adjust
Ex. engines with Idle Speed or Idle Air Control

Diff., Limited-Slip . . . . change lubricant
One time service only

Transmission, manual,
  Diesel . . . . change lubricant
Service every 30 mi (48 km) thereafter

GASOLINE,
EVERY 12 MO/7.5 MI—12 KM
DIESEL,
EVERY 12 MO/3.75 MI—6 KM
Crankcase ex. Diesel . . . . change oil

Oil filter, ex. Diesel . . . . replace

Brake system . . . . inspect
Check hydraulic system for leaks. Inspect brake linings

Differential . . . . check level

Exhaust pressure regulator valve &
  hoses, Diesel . . . . inspect/test
After initial inspection, check again at 15 mi (24 km) & every 15 mi (24 km) thereafter

Exhaust system . . . . inspect

Front suspension &
  steering linkage . . . . . . **4-11 fittings LB**

Parking brake cables & guides . . . coat **LB**
Check adjustment

Shift linkage . . . . coat **LB**
With floor shift, coat contact faces

Suspension & steering . . . . inspect
Also inspect drive axle boots and seals

Tires . . . . rotate
Radial tires, every 15 mi (24 km) after initial service. Check brake linings. Lug nut torque, ft lb: Chevette, 80; all front wheel drive, Corvette or Caprice w/13/16" lug nuts, 100; all others, 80 ex. with aluminum wheels, 90

Transaxle or transmission . . . . check level
Ex. Diesel

Drive belts . . . . inspect/adjust

Throttle linkage . . . . inspect
Check for damage or binding

Water separator . . . . drain
As equipped

Body . . . . lubricate

EVERY 12 MONTHS
Cooling
  system . . . . inspect & tighten hoses
Wash radiator filler neck and cap; pressure test system. Clean exterior of radiator core and air conditioning condenser. Inspect coolant and service as needed

EVERY 15 MI—24 KM
Valve clearance, Diesel . . . . . check/adjust

EVERY 24 MO/30 MI—50 KM
Cooling system . . . . . . change coolant **EC**
Flush system

Choke & hoses . . . . check/clean

Vacuum/Air pump belts . . . . inspect/adjust
Replace as needed

EVERY 36 MO/30 MI—50 KM
Air cleaner element . . . . replace
Ex. Diesel, 1.6L & 2.0L

EGR system . . . . clean/inspect

EVERY 30 MI—50 KM
Clutch cross shaft . . . . **1 plug LB**

Front wheel bearings ex. front wheel
  drive & Corvette . . . . . . clean/repack **GC**
Service at mileage interval or at each brake reline, whichever comes first. Tighten spindle nut to 12 ft lb while turning wheel. Back off 1/2 turn & retighten finger tight. End play, .001"-.005"

Fuel cap, tank, and lines,
  ex. Diesel . . . . inspect

Transmission, manual Corvette
  OD unit . . . . replace fluid

Air cleaner element, Diesel . . . . . . replace

Distributor cap . . . . inspect

Fuel filter, Diesel . . . . replace

Idle speed, Diesel . . . . adjust

Ignition timing . . . . adjust
Inspect distribution cap, clean or replace

Ignition wires . . . . inspect/clean

PCV valve ex. Diesel . . . . inspect
Blow out or replace hoses

Spark plugs . . . . replace

Thermostatic air cleaner . . . . inspect

Vacuum advance system &
  hoses . . . . inspect
As equipped

EVERY 50 MI—80 KM
Air cleaner element, 1.6L, 2.0L . . . . replace

EVERY 100 MI—160 KM
Transaxle or trans., auto. . . . . change fluid
Clean sump screen or replace filter

SEVERE SERVICE
Carburetor or T.B.I.—Torque mounting bolts & adjust idle speed at 6 mi (10 km), also inspect carburetor choke & hoses

Crankcase—Change oil: Gasoline, every 3 mo/3 mi (5 km); Diesel: every 3 mo/2 mi (3.2 km). Change filter at each oil change

Differential, Diesel—Change lubricant every 5 mi (8 km) when towing a trailer

Differential, Gasoline—Change lubricant every 7.5 mi (12 km)

Front suspension & steering linkage— Lubricate every: Gasoline, 6 mo/6 mi (10 km); Diesel every 12 mo/6 mi (9.6 km)

Front wheel bearings, RWD ex. Corvette— Repack every 15 mi (24 km) or every brake service, whichever comes first

Transaxle or transmission, automatic— Change fluid & filter or clean screen every 15 mi (24 km)

KEY TO LUBRICANTS
See other Chevrolet charts

CRANKCASE
Diesel engine . . . . SG/CD
Gasoline engine . . . . SG

CAPACITY, Refill:	Liters	Qt
Diesel, including filter	5.8	6.0
Gasoline, 2.5L (151)	2.8	3.0
Others	3.8	4.0

* Preferred
Gasoline, capacity shown is without filter. When replacing filter, additional oil may be needed

Diesel Engine:
Above 32°F (0°C) 30
Above 15°F (−10°C) 15W-40
Below 100°F (38°C) 10W-30*

Gasoline Engine:
5.0L (307)
Above 40°F (4°C) 30
Above 20°F (−7°C) 20W-20
Above 10°F (−12°C) 15W-40
Above 0°F (−18°C) 10W-30*
Below 60°F (16°C) 5W-30

Others:
Above 40°F (4°C) 30
Above 0°F (−18°C) 10W-30
All temperatures 5W-30*
* Preferred

TRANSMISSION,
TRANSAXLE, Automatic . . . . AF

CAPACITY, Initial Refill*:	Liters	Qt
125 Transmission	3.8	4.0
180 Transmission	3.3	3.5
200 Transmission	3.3	3.5
200-4R Transmission	4.8	5.0
440 Transmission	6.0	6.3
700-R4 Transmission	4.7	5.0

* With the engine at operating temperature, shift transmission through all gears. Let engine slow idle in PARK for 3 minutes or more. Check fluid level and add fluid as needed

TRANSMISSION/TRANSAXLE, Manual
FWD . . . . **GLS**
RWD: 4-speed 80W, 80W-90* **GL-5**
* For vehicles normally operated in Canada, 80W only
5-speed Diesel . . . . **GLS†**
†GM Part No. 1052931
5-speed others . . . . **AF**
Corvette OD unit . . . . **AF**

CAPACITY, Refill:	Liters	Pt
FWD: 4-speed	2.8	6.0
5-speed Isuzu†	2.5	5.4
5-speed Muncie‡,		
Celebrity	1.9	4.0
5-speed Muncie‡ others . .	2.1	4.4
RWD: Corvette	1.0	2.2
OD unit	1.6	3.3
Chevette 4-speed	1.7	3.5
5-speed, gasoline	2.0	4.2
5-speed, Diesel	1.6	3.4
Camaro	1.7	3.5

† Has 7-bolt aluminum end cap
‡ Has 9-bolt steel end cap

DIFFERENTIAL
Standard 80W, 80W-90* **GL-5**
Limited-Slip . . . . . 80W, 80W-90* **GL-5★**

CAPACITY, Refill:	Liters	Pt
Chevette	0.8	1.7
Camaro	1.5	3.2
Caprice, Monte Carlo, El Camino		
8½" ring gear	1.9	4.3
Others	1.7	3.5

* For vehicles normally operated in Canada, 80W only
LIMITED-SLIP IDENTIFICATION:
Tag under rear cover-attaching bolt

CHEVROLET
1987 All Models Except Nova, Spectrum, Sprint
Includes Chevrolet El Camino, GMC Caballero

SERVICE AT TIME OR MILEAGE—WHICHEVER OCCURS FIRST

CTPM10   CTPM10

Perform the following maintenance services at the intervals indicated to keep the vehicle warranties in effect.
W   SERVICE TO MAINTAIN EMISSION WARRANTY

MI—MILES IN THOUSANDS
KM—KILOMETERS IN THOUSANDS

EVERY 6 MONTHS

Brake master cylinder . . . . check level **HB**

Clutch master cylinder . . . . check level **HB**

Power steering reservoir . . check level **PS**

FIRST 7.5 MI—12 KM

W Carburetor or T.B.I. mounting
   bolts . . . . torque

Choke & hoses . . . . check/clean
As equipped

Crankcase . . . . change oil
Change oil filter

W Engine idle speed . . . . adjust
Ex. engines with Idle Speed or Idle Air Control

Diff., Limited-Slip . . . . change lubricant
One time service only

Tires . . . . rotate
Initial service, then every 15 mi (24 km) after initial service. Check brake linings

EVERY 12 MO/7.5 MI—12 KM

W Crankcase . . . . change oil

W Oil filter . . . . replace
At first oil change, then every other or 12 months

Brake system . . . . inspect
Check hydraulic system for leaks. Inspect brake linings

Differential . . . . check level

Exhaust system . . . . inspect

Suspension &
   steering linkage . . . . . . **0-11 fittings LB**

Parking brake cable guides . . . . . . coat **LB**
Check adjustment

Shift linkage . . . . coat **LB**
With floor shift, coat contact faces

Suspension & steering . . . . inspect
Also inspect drive axle boots and seals

Transaxle or transmission . . . . check level

W Drive belts . . . . inspect/adjust

W Throttle linkage . . . . inspect
Check for damage or binding

Body . . . . lubricate

EVERY 12 MONTHS

W Cooling
   system . . . . . inspect & tighten hoses
Wash radiator filler neck and cap; pressure test system. Clean exterior of radiator core and air conditioning
condenser. Inspect coolant and service as needed

EVERY 24 MO/30 MI—50 KM

W Cooling system . . . . change coolant **EC**
Flush system

EVERY 36 MO/30 MI—50 KM

W Air cleaner element . . . . replace
Ex. 1.6L & 2.0L

W EGR system . . . . clean/inspect
Engine vin codes C, G, H, R, Y, 1, 6

Crankcase inlet air filter . . . . replace
As equipped

W Fuel cap, tank, and lines . . . . . . inspect

EVERY 30 MI—50 KM

Front wheel bearings ex. front wheel
   drive & Corvette . . . . . . clean/repack **GC**
Service at mileage interval or at each brake reline,
whichever comes first. Tighten spindle nut to 12 ft lb
while turning wheel. Back off nut & retighten finger
tight. Loosen nut just enough that hole in spindle lines
up with slot in nut (not more than 1/2 flat). End play,
.001"-.005"

Transmission, manual Corvette
   OD unit . . . . replace fluid

W Clutch cross shaft lever . . . . **LB**
Lubricate

W Distributor cap . . . . inspect
Except distributorless ignition

W Ignition timing . . . . adjust
Except distributorless ignition

W Ignition wires . . . . inspect/clean

W PCV valve . . . . replace
Blow out or replace hoses

W Spark plugs . . . . replace

W Thermostatic air cleaner . . . . . . inspect

W Vacuum advance system &
   hoses . . . . inspect
As equipped

EVERY 50 MI—80 KM

W Air cleaner element . . . . replace
1.6L, 2.0L

EVERY 100 MI—160 KM

Transaxle or trans., auto. . . . . change fluid
Clean sump screen or replace filter

SEVERE SERVICE

W Carburetor or T.B.I.—Torque mounting
bolts & adjust idle speed at 6 mi (10 km),
also inspect carburetor choke & hoses

W Crankcase—Change oil: Every 3 mo/3 mi
(5 km); Change filter at each oil change

Differential—Change lubricant every 7.5 mi
(12 km)

Front suspension & steering linkage—
Lubricate every oil change

Front wheel bearings, RWD ex. Corvette—
Repack every 15 mi (24 km) or every brake
service, whichever comes first

Tires—Rotate first 6 mi (9 km), then every 15
mi (24 km)

Transaxle or transmission, automatic—
Change fluid & filter or clean screen every
15 mi (24 km)

KEY TO LUBRICANTS

AF	DEXRON®-IIE Automatic Transmission Fluid
EC	Ethylene Glycol Coolant Mix with water to –34°F (–37°C) protection
GC	Wheel Bearing Grease, NLGI Category GC
GLS	Gear Lubricant, Special FWD, G.M. Part No. 12345349 Camaro, G.M. Part No. 1052931
GL-5	Gear Oil, API Service GL-5
GL-5 ★	Special Lubricant for Limited-Slip Differential
HB	Hydraulic Brake Fluid, DOT 3
LB	Chassis Grease, NLGI Category LB
PS	Power Steering Fluid
SG	Motor Oil, API Service SG Use Energy Conserving-II oils

CRANKCASE . . . . SG

CAPACITY, Refill:	Liters	Qt
2.5L (151)	2.8	3.0
Others	3.8	4.0

Capacity shown is without filter. When replacing filter, additional oil may be needed

3.8L:
Above 40°F (4°C) . . . . 30†
Above 0°F (–18°C) 10W-30*
Below 60°F (16°C) 5W-30

Others:
Above 40°F (4°C) . . . . 30†
Above 0°F (–18°C) 10W-30
All temperatures 5W-30*

* Preferred
†Use only if other specified grades are unavailable

TRANSMISSION/TRANSAXLE,

Automatic . . . . AF

CAPACITY, Initial Refill*:	Liters	Qt
125 (3T40)	3.8	4.0
180 (3L30)	3.3	3.5
200C	3.3	3.5
200-4R	4.8	5.0
440-T4 (4T60)	6.0	6.3
700-R4 (4L60)	4.7	5.0

* With the engine at operating temperature, shift transmission through all gears. Let engine slow idle in PARK for 3
minutes or more. Check fluid level and add fluid as needed

TRANSMISSION/TRANSAXLE, Manual
FWD . . . . **GLS**
RWD: 4-speed 80W, 80W-90* **GL-5**
5-speed Camaro . . . . **GLS†**
5-speed, others . . . . **AF**
Corvette OD unit . . . . **AF**

* For vehicles normally operated in Canada, 80W only

CAPACITY, Refill:	Liters	Pt
FWD: 4-speed	2.8	6.0
5-speed Isuzu†	2.5	5.4
5-speed Muncie‡:		
Celebrity	1.9	4.0
Others	2.1	5.0
RWD: Corvette	1.0	2.2
OD unit	1.6	3.3
Chevette 4-speed	3.1	6.6
5-speed	2.0	4.2
Camaro	3.1	6.6

† Has 7-bolt aluminum end cap
‡ Has 9-bolt steel end cap

DIFFERENTIAL
Standard 80W-90* **GL-5**
Limited-Slip . . . . 80W-90* **GL-5 ★**

* For vehicles normally operated in Canada, 80W only

CAPACITY, Refill:	Liters	Pt
Chevette	0.8	1.7
Camaro	1.7	3.6
Caprice, Monte Carlo, El Camino		
8 1/2" ring gear	1.9	4.3
Corvette	1.7	3.5

LIMITED-SLIP IDENTIFICATION:
Tag under rear cover-attaching bolt

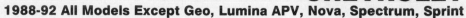

SERVICE AT TIME OR MILEAGE—WHICHEVER OCCURS FIRST

CTPM11　　　　　　　　　　　　　　　　　　　　　CTPM11

Perform the following maintenance services at the intervals indicated to keep the vehicle warranties in effect.

W　SERVICE TO MAINTAIN EMISSION WARRANTY

MI—MILES IN THOUSANDS
KM—KILOMETERS IN THOUSANDS

EVERY 6 MONTHS
Brake master cylinder . . . . check level **HB**

Clutch master cylinder . . . . check level **HB**

Power steering reservoir . . check level **PS**

FIRST 7.5 MI—12 KM
W Carburetor or T.B.I. mounting
　　bolts . . . . torque

Choke & hoses . . . . check/clean
As equipped

Crankcase . . . . change oil
Change oil filter

W Engine idle speed . . . . adjust
Ex. engines with Idle Speed or Idle Air Control

Diff., Limited-Slip . . . . . . change lubricant
One time service only

Tires . . . . rotate
Initial service, then every 15 mi (24 km) after initial service. Check brake linings

EVERY 12 MO/7.5 MI—12 KM
W Crankcase . . . . change oil

W Oil filter . . . . replace
At first oil change, then every other or 12 months

Brake system . . . . inspect
Check hydraulic system for leaks. Inspect brake linings

Differential . . . . check level

W Exhaust system . . . . inspect

Suspension &
　steering linkage . . . . . . **0-11 fittings LB**

Parking brake cable guides . . . . . . coat **LB**
Check adjustment

Shift linkage . . . . coat **LB**
With floor shift, coat contact faces

Suspension & steering . . . . inspect
Also inspect drive axle boots and seals

Transaxle or transmission . . . . check level

W Drive belts . . . . inspect/adjust

W Throttle linkage . . . . inspect
Check for damage or binding

Body . . . . lubricate

EVERY 12 MONTHS
W Cooling
　　system . . . . . inspect & tighten hoses
Wash radiator filler neck and cap; pressure test system. Clean exterior of radiator core and air conditioning condenser. Inspect coolant and service as needed

EVERY 24 MO/30 MI—50 KM
W Cooling system . . . . change coolant **EC**
Flush system

Choke & hoses . . . . check/clean
As equipped

W Drive belts . . . . inspect/adjust

EVERY 36 MO/30 MI—50 KM
W Air cleaner element 1988-92 . . . replace
Ex. 2.0L

EGR system . . . . clean/inspect
1988-90 engine vin codes
E, G, H, J, R, Y, 1, 7

W Crankcase inlet air filter . . . . . . replace
As equipped

Fuel cap, tank, and lines . . . . inspect

EVERY 30 MI—50 KM
Front wheel bearings ex. front wheel
　　drive & Corvette . . . . . . clean/repack **GC**
Service at mileage interval or at each brake reline, whichever comes first. Tighten spindle nut to 12 ft lb while turning wheel. Back off nut & retighten finger tight. Loosen nut just enough that hole in spindle lines up with slot in nut (not more than 1/2 flat). End play, .001"-.005"

Transmission, manual Corvette
　　OD unit 1988 . . . . replace fluid

Air cleaner element . . . . replace
1991-92

EGR system . . . . clean/inspect
1991-92 engine vin codes E, G, R, Z, 4, 7, 8

W Distributor cap . . . . inspect
Except distributorless ignition

W Ignition timing . . . . adjust
Except distributorless ignition

W Ignition wires . . . . inspect/clean
Some models

W PCV valve . . . . replace
Some models blow out or replace hoses

W Spark plugs . . . . replace

W Thermostatic air cleaner . . . . . . inspect
1988-91 some models

EVERY 60 MI—100 KM
PCV system . . . . inspect
1992 some models

FIRST 60 MI—100 KM;
THEN EVERY 15 MI—25 KM
Camshaft timing belt . . . . inspect
3.4L Code X engine

EVERY 100 MI—160 KM
Transaxle or trans., auto. . . . . change fluid
Clean sump screen or replace filter

SEVERE SERVICE
W Carburetor or T.B.I., except 2.3L—
Torque mounting bolts & adjust idle speed at 6 mi (10 km), also inspect carburetor choke & hoses

W Crankcase—Change oil: Every 3 mo/3 mi (5 km); Change filter at each oil change

Differential—Change lubricant every 7.5 mi (12 km)

Front suspension & steering linkage—Lubricate every oil change

Front wheel bearings, RWD ex. Corvette—Repack every 15 mi (24 km) or every brake service, whichever comes first

Tires—Rotate first 6 mi (9 km), then every 15 mi (24 km)

Transaxle or transmission, automatic—Change fluid & filter or clean screen every 15 mi (24 km)

KEY TO LUBRICANTS

AF	DEXRON®-IIE Automatic Transmission Fluid
EC	Ethylene Glycol Coolant Mix with water to –34°F (–37°C) protection
GC	Wheel Bearing Grease, NLGI Category GC
GLS	Gear Lubricant, Special
GL-5	Gear Oil, API Service GL-5
GL-5 ★	Special Lubricant for Limited-Slip Differential
HB	Hydraulic Brake Fluid, DOT 3
LB	Chassis Grease, NLGI Cateogry LB
PS	Power Steering Fluid
SG	Motor Oil, API Service SG

CRANKCASE . . . . **SG††**
††Corvette Code P, engine oil must also meet GM spec. 4718M. Oil meeting this spec. may also be identifed as synthetic

CAPACITY, Refill:

	Liters	Qt
1990-92 Corvette Code J . .	7.1	7.6
1991-92 3.4L Code X	4.7	5.0
Others	3.8	4.0

Capacity shown is without filter. When replacing filter, additional oil may be needed

1992 Corvette Code P:
All temperatures 5W-30**
Corvette 5.7L Code J:
Above 40°F (4°C) . . . . 30†
Above 0°F (–18°C) 10W-30*
Below 60°F (16°C) 5W-30
Others:
Above 40°F (4°C) . . . . 30†
Above 0°F (–18°C) 10W-30
All temperatures 5W-30*
* Preferred
* * Must meet GM spec. 4718M.
†Use only if other specified grades are unavailable

TRANSMISSION/TRANSAXLE,
　Automatic . . . . **AF**

CAPACITY, Initial Refill*:	Liters	Qt
125 (3T40)	3.8	4.0
180 (3L30)	3.3	3.5
200C	3.3	3.5
200-4R	4.8	5.0
440-T4 (4T60)	5.7	6.0
700-R4 (4L60)	4.7	5.0
4T60E	7.6	7.4

* With the engine at operating temperature, shift transmission through all gears. Let engine slow idle in PARK for 3 minutes or more. Check fluid level and add fluid as needed

TRANSMISSION/TRANSAXLE, Manual
FWD . . . . **GLS**
RWD: 1988 Corvette . . 80W, 80W-90 **GL-5**
　　OD unit . . . . **AF**
　1989-92 Corvette . . . . **GLS**
　Camaro . . . . **AF**
* For vehicles normally operated in Canada, 80W only

CAPACITY, Refill:	Liters	Pt
FWD: 4-speed	2.8	6.0
5-speed Isuzu†	2.5	5.4
5-speed Muncie‡, 　Celebrity	1.9	4.0
5-speed Muncie‡ others . .	2.1	5.0
RWD: Corvette 1988	1.0	2.2
OD unit	1.6	3.3
Corvette 1989-92	2.1	4.4
Camaro	2.8	6.0

† Has 7-bolt aluminum end cap
‡ Has 9-bolt steel end cap

DIFFERENTIAL
Standard 80W-90* **GL-5**
Limited-Slip . . . . 80W-90* **GL-5 ★**
* For vehicles normally operated in Canada, 80W only

CAPACITY, Refill:	Liters	Pt
Camaro	1.7	3.6
Caprice, Monte Carlo 　8½" ring gear	1.9	4.3
Corvette	1.7	3.5

LIMITED-SLIP IDENTIFICATION:
Tag under rear cover-attaching bolt

CHEVROLET/GMC TRUCKS
1983-92 All Models
Includes Chevrolet Lumina APV, Oldsmobile Bravada and Silhouette, Pontiac Trans Sport

SERVICE LOCATIONS — ENGINE AND CHASSIS

CTTDP-1   CTTDP-1

1983-85
1.9L (119)

1983-85
2.0L (122)

1984-85
2.2L Diesel

1985-92
2.5L (151)
Some   Some
Van only   Van only

1983-92
2.8L (173)
S Series
Calif.
Ex. Calif.
1983-85
1986-92

1990-92
3.1L FI Code D
Lumina APV, Silhouette, Trans Sport

1992
3.8L Code L
Lumina APV, Silhouette, Trans Sport

1983-84
4.1L (250) Blazer, Jimmy

1983-85 4.1L (250) Code D
1983-89 4.8L (292) Code T

1992
4.3L HO CPI
S Series, Astro, Safari

1985-86 4.3L 4V Code N
1986-92 4.3L FI Code Z
Air induction system varies.
FI
Ex. 4WD
S series
4V
Ex. FI
Van
Van only
4WD series

5.0L (305), 5.7L (350), 6.6L (400) C, K, R, V Blazer, Jimmy
Ex. FI

5.0L (305) G Series
5.7L (350) P Series
Some. Others on body
1983-86
1987-92

1983-92
6.2L (379) Diesel

7.4L (454) (4V shown)
Suburban, 1992
Pickups, some
Suburban ex. 1992
Some
1991-92
1988-92
1988-92 Van
1988-92 Van
1 Van
1989-92

① Crankcase dipstick
② Transmission dipstick
③ Brake fluid reservoir
④ Clutch fluid reservoir
⑤ Oil fill cap
⑥ Power steering reservoir
⑦ Air filter
⑧ Fuel filter
⑨ Oil filter
⑩ PCV filter
⑪ EGR valve
⑫ Oxygen sensor
⑬ PCV valve

● Cooling system drain   ○ Cooling system drain, some models

CHEVROLET/GMC TRUCKS
1983-92 All Models
Includes Chevrolet Lumina APV, Oldsmobile Bravada and Silhouette, Pontiac Trans Sport

SERVICE LOCATIONS — ENGINE AND CHASSIS

CTTDP-2   CTTDP-2

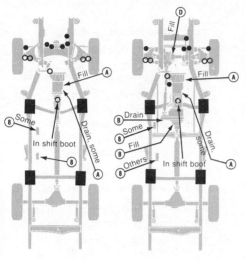

2-WHEEL DRIVE

S10, S15

4-WHEEL DRIVE

S10, S15
1991-92 Bravada

2-WHEEL DRIVE

1985-92
Astro, Safari

**1990-92
Lumina APV,
Silhouette,
Trans Sport**

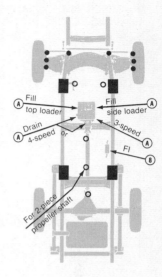

2-WHEEL DRIVE

Blazer, Jimmy
1983-86
C-10, -20, -30
-1500, -2500, -3500
1987-88
R-10, -20, -30
1989-91
R-1100, -2500, -3500

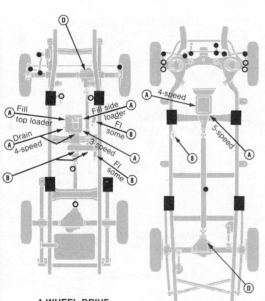

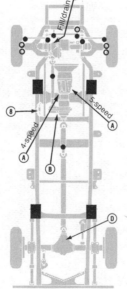

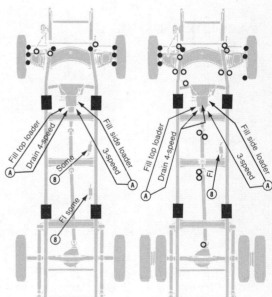

4-WHEEL DRIVE

Blazer, Jimmy
1983-86
K-10, -20, -30
-1500, -2500. -3500
1987-88
V-10, -20, -30,
-1500, -2500, -3500
1989-91
V1500, -2500, -3500

1988-92
C-1500, -2500, -3500
1992
Blazer, Yukon,
Suburban

1988-92
K-1500, -2500, -3500
1992
Blazer, Yukon,
Suburban

SINGLE REAR WHEELS

Others

DUAL REAR WHEELS

Others

■ Lift adapter position

● Fitting   ○ Fitting, some models

Ⓐ Manual transmission/transaxle,
   drain & fill

Ⓑ Transfer case, drain & fill

Ⓒ Automatic transaxle final drive,
   NOT USED

Ⓓ Differential, drain & fill

⑧ Fuel filter

CHEVROLET/GMC TRUCKS
1983 All Diesel Models

CHEK-CHART

MI—MILES IN THOUSANDS
KM—KILOMETERS IN THOUSANDS

FIRST 5 MI—8 KM
Engine idle speed . . . . adjust

EVERY 12 MO/5 MI—8 KM
Crankcase . . . . change oil

Oil filter . . . . replace

FIRST 5 MI—8 KM; THEN EVERY 15 MI—24 KM
Exhaust system . . . . inspect
Exhaust pressure regulator valve, check operation

EVERY 6 MO
Brake master cylinder . . . . check level **HB**

Clutch pedal free play . . . . . . check/adjust

Power steering or brake
  Hydro-Boost reservoir . . . check level **PS**

Transmission, auto. . . . . check level

EVERY 12 MO/5 MI—8 KM
Fittings ex. CV joint . . . . lubricate **LB**

Parking brake cables &
  guides . . . . coat **LB**

Shift linkage . . . . coat **LB**

Battery . . . . check level

Cooling system . . . . check level **EC**

Crankcase oil fill tubes, filters
  & breather caps . . . . clean

Transmission, manual . . . . . . check level

Body . . . . lubricate
Flush underbody every spring

EVERY 12 MO/10 MI—16 KM
Brakes & power steering . . . inspect hoses
Check disc brake pads for wear

Suspension & steering . . . . inspect

Air intake system . . . . inspect
Service only every 10 mi (16 km)

Drive belts . . . . inspect/adjust

Thermostatically controlled
  fan . . . . check operation

Underhood shields &
  insulation . . . . check condition
Service only every 10 mi (16 km)

EVERY 12 MO/12 MI—19.2 KM
Cooling
  system . . . . inspect & tighten hoses
Wash radiator filler neck & cap; pressure test system.
Clean exterior of radiator core

EVERY 12 MO/15 MI—24 KM
Drum brake lining . . . . inspect
Replace shoes when linings are 1/32" thick. Check parking brake adjustment

Crankcase vent. system . . . . inspect
Inspect rubber fittings, hoses & regulator every 30 mi (48 km)

Throttle linkage . . . . inspect
Check for damage or binding

EVERY 30 MI—48 KM
Front wheel bearings
  2WD . . . . clean/repack **GC**
Tighten spindle nut to 12 ft lb, back off 1/4-1/2 turn; hand tighten & loosen 1/12-1/8 turn. End play, .001"-.005". Service whenever brakes are relined.

Front wheel bearings
  4WD . . . . clean/repack **GC**
Tighten inner adjusting nut to 50 ft lb; back off & re-tighten to 35 ft lb while hub is turning. Back off up to 3/8 turn; install lockwasher; install outer lock nut; tighten to ft lb: K-30, -3500, 65; all others, 160-205. End play, .001"-.010". Service whenever brakes are relined

EVERY 15 MI—24 KM
Exhaust pressure regulator
  valve . . . . check operation

Fuel filter . . . . replace

EVERY 24 MO/24 MI—38.4 KM
Cooling system . . . . . . change coolant **EC**
Flush system, inspect hoses. Replace hoses if checked, swollen or rotted, and change coolant every 24 mo/30 mi (48 km)

EVERY 30 MI—48 KM
Air cleaner element . . . . replace

Engine idle speed . . . . adjust

Steering gear,
  manual . . . . check for leaks **LS**

EVERY 100 MI—160 KM
Transmission, automatic . . . . change fluid

SEVERE SERVICE
Crankcase—Change oil every 3 mo/2.5 mi (4 km). Change oil filter at every oil change

Differential—Change lubricant every 5 mi (8 km)

Fittings—Lubricate every 2 mo/2.5 mi (4 km)

Transmission, automatic—Change fluid every 15 mi (24 km)

KEY TO LUBRICANTS

AF	DEXRON®-IIE Automatic Transmission Fluid
CD	Motor Oil, API Service CD
CE	Motor Oil, API Service CE
EC	Ethylene Glycol Coolant Mix with water to –34°F (–37°C) protection
GC	Wheel Bearing Grease, NLGI Category GC
GL-5	Gear Oil, API Service GL-5
GL-5 ★	Special Lubricant for Locking or Limited-Slip Differentials
HB	Hydraulic Brake Fluid, DOT 3
LB	Chassis Grease, NLGI Category LB
LS	Steering Gear Lubricant
PS	Power Steering Fluid
SG	Motor Oil, API Service SG Use Energy Conserving-II oils

CRANKCASE . . . . **SG/CE**

CAPACITY, Refill:	Liters	Qt
All models, including filter . .	6.6	7.0
Above 32°F (0°C)		30*
0° to 60°F (–18° to 16°C)		15W-40
Below 60°F (16°C)		10W-30

* 30 is preferred above 32°F (0°C), especially for continuous duty driving

TRANSMISSION, Automatic . . . . **AF**

CAPACITY, Initial Refill*:	Liters	Qt
Turbo Hydra-Matic 400	3.3	3.5

*With the engine at operating temperature, shift transmission through all gears. Let engine slow idle in PARK for 3 minutes or more. Check fluid level and add fluid as needed

TRANSMISSION, Manual
4-speed (Side Load) . . . . **AF**
4-speed (Top Load),
  3-speed 80W, 80W-90* **GL-5**
*For vehicles normally operated in Canada, 80W only

CAPACITY, Refill:	Liters	Pt
3-speed	1.5	3.3
4-speed	4.0	8.2

TRANSFER CASE . . . . **AF**

CAPACITY, Refill:	Liters	Pt
K-30, K-3500; NP205	2.4†	5.0†
Others, NP208	4.8	10.0

†Fill to one inch of fill plug

DIFFERENTIAL
Locking/
  Limited-Slip . . . . . 80W, 80W-90 **GL-5 ★**
Others 80W, 80W-90* **GL-5**
*For vehicles normally operated in Canada, 80W only

CAPACITY, Refill:	Liters	Pt
Front:		
K-30, K-3500	2.8	6.0
All others	2.4	5.0
Rear:		
8 1/2" ring gear	2.0	4.2
9 1/2" ring gear	2.6	5.5
Dana 9 3/4" ring gear . . .	2.8	6.0
10 1/2" ring gear	2.6	5.5
Rockwell 12" ring gear . .	6.6	14.0

SERVICE AT TIME OR MILEAGE—WHICHEVER OCCURS FIRST

CTTPM11   CTTPM11

MI—MILES IN THOUSANDS
KM—KILOMETERS IN THOUSANDS

FIRST 4 MO/6 MI—9.6 KM; THEN EVERY 12 MO/12 MI—19.2 KM
Engine idle speed . . . . adjust

Idle stop solenoid . . . . check

EVERY 4 MO/6 MI—9.6 KM
Brakes & power
   steering . . . . inspect hoses/pads
Inspect drum brake lining, check parking brake

Crankcase . . . . change oil

Differential, front & rear . . . . . check level
Locking differential, change lubricant after first 6 mi (9.6 km)

Engine drive belts . . . . inspect/adjust

Exhaust system . . . . inspect

Fittings
   ex. CV joint . . . . lubricate **LB**

Oil filter . . . . replace
At first oil change, then every 4 mo/12 mi (19.2 km)

Parking brake cables & guides . . . coat **LB**

Shift linkage . . . . coat **LB**
With floor shift, coat lever contact faces

Suspension & steering . . . . inspect

Throttle linkage . . . . inspect
Check for damage or binding

Transfer case . . . . check level
Check vent hose

Transmission, manual . . . . check level

Universal CV joint, 4WD . . . . . . **fitting LB**

Battery . . . . check level

Body . . . . lubricate
Flush underbody every spring

EVERY 6 MONTHS
Brake master cylinder . . . . check level **HB**

Clutch pedal free travel . . . . . check/adjust

Power steering reservoir . . check level **PS**

Transmission, automatic . . . . check level

EVERY 12 MO/12 MI—19.2 KM
Front wheel bearings,
   2WD . . . . clean/repack **GC**
Tighten spindle nut to 12 ft lb, back off 1/4-1/2 turn, hand tighten & loosen 1/12-1/6 turn. End play, .001″-.005″. Service whenever brakes are relined

Front wheel bearings
   4WD . . . . clean/repack **GC**
Tighten inner adjusting nut to 50 ft lb; back off & re-tighten to 35 ft lb while hub is turning. Back off up to 3/8 turn; install lockwasher; install outer lock nut, tighten to 160-205 ft lb. End play, .001″-.010″. Service whenever brakes are relined

Air cleaner . . . . inspect/test

Carb. to manifold bolts . . . . torque

Cooling system . . . . change coolant **EC**
Flush system, inspect hoses

Fuel filter in carb. inlet . . . . replace

Manifold heat valve . . . . check **MH**

PCV system . . . . check

Thermostatically controlled fan . . . . . test

Throttle return control system
   & hoses . . . . check/inspect

EVERY 12 MI/19.2 KM
Air cleaner element . . . . replace

Air intake system . . . . check for leaks

Eng. shield & insulation . . . . inspect

Drive belts . . . . replace/adjust
Air pump only

Ignition timing . . . . adjust
Inspect distributor cap; clean or replace

Ignition wires . . . . clean/inspect

Spark plugs . . . . replace

EVERY 24 MO/24 MI—38.4 KM
Choke & hoses . . . . check/clean
Check vacuum break

EFE system . . . . check **MH**

Fuel cap, tank & lines . . . . inspect

ECS canister & hoses . . . . inspect

Idle mixture 6-cyl. 292 eng. . . . . . adjust

Vacuum advance system
   & hoses . . . . inspect

EVERY 24 MI—38.4 KM
Differential . . . . change lubricant

Transmission, automatic . . . . change fluid
Clean sump screen or replace filter

PCV valve & filter . . . . replace
Blow out or replace system hoses

EVERY 36 MI—57.6 KM
Clutch cross shaft . . . . **0-1 fitting LB**

EVERY 48 MO/48 MI—76.8 KM
Engine governor . . . . inspect/test

SEVERE SERVICE
Crankcase—Change oil every 2 mo/3 mi (4.8 km). Change filter every oil change

Differential(s)—Change lubricant every 12 mi (19.2 km); locking differential every 6 mi (9.6 km)

Fittings—Lubricate every 3 mo/3 mi (4.8 km)

Transmission, automatic—Change fluid every 12 mi (19.2 km)

KEY TO LUBRICANTS

AF	DEXRON®-IIE Automatic Transmission Fluid
EC	Ethylene Glycol Coolant Mix with water to −34°F (−37°C) protection
GC	Wheel Bearing Grease, NLGI Category GC
GL-5	Gear Oil, API Service GL-5
GL-5★	Special Lubricant for Locking Differential
HB	Hydraulic Brake Fluid, DOT 3
LB	Chassis Grease, NLGI Category LB
MH	Manifold Heat Valve Solvent
PS	Power Steering Fluid
SG	Motor Oil, API Service SG Use Energy Conserving-II oils

CRANKCASE . . . . SG

CAPACITY, Refill:	Liters	Qt
6-cyl. 292 eng.	4.7	5.0
8-cyl. 454 ex. K-30, -3500 .	5.7	6.0
K-30, -3500	4.7	5.0
Others	3.8	4.0

Capacity shown is without filter. When replacing filter, additional oil may be needed

Above 40°F (4°C)	30
Above 20°F (−7°C) . . .	20W-20, 20W-40, 20W-50
Above 10°F (−12°C)	15W-40
Above 0°F (−18°C)	10W-30*
Below 60°F (16°C)	5W-30

*10W-30 preferred above 0°F (−18°C)

TRANSMISSION, Automatic . . . . AF

CAPACITY, Initial Refill*:	Liters	Qt
Hydra-Matic 200C	3.3	3.5
Hydra-Matic 350	2.8	3.0
Hydra-Matic 400	3.3	3.5
Hydra-Matic 700-R4	4.7	5.0

*With the engine at operating temperature, shift transmission through all gears. Let engine slow idle in PARK for 3 minutes or more. Check fluid level and add fluid as needed

TRANSMISSION, Manual
4-speed (Side Load) . . . . **AF**
4-speed (Top Load),
   3-speed 80W, 80W-90* **GL-5**
*For vehicles normally operated in Canada, 80W only

CAPACITY, Refill:	Liters	Pt
3-speed	1.4	3.0
4-speed	4.0	8.2

TRANSFER CASE . . . . AF

CAPACITY, Refill:	Liters	Pt
K-30, -3500; NP205	2.4†	5.0†
Others, NP208	4.8	10.0

† Fill to one inch of fill plug

DIFFERENTIAL
Locking . . . . **GL-5★**
Others 80W, 80W-90* **GL-5**
*For vehicles normally operated in Canada, 80W only

CAPACITY, Refill:	Liters	Pt
Front:		
K-20, -2500	2.4	5.0
K-30, -3500	2.8	6.0
Blazer, Jimmy	2.4	5.0
Rear:		
8½″ ring gear	2.0	4.2
9½″ ring gear	2.6	5.5
Dana 9¾″ ring gear . . .	2.8	6.0
10½″ ring gear:		
Chev.	2.6	5.5
Dana	3.4	7.2
Rockwell 12″ ring gear . .	6.6	14.0

CHEVROLET/GMC TRUCKS
1983 All Unleaded Gasoline Models

CTTPM12   CTTPM12

MI—MILES IN THOUSANDS
KM—KILOMETERS IN THOUSANDS

FIRST 6 MO/7.5 MI—12 KM; THEN AT 30 MI—48 KM

Carb. to manifold bolts . . . . torque
Ex. 1.9L (119) 4-cyl.

Choke & hoses . . . . check/clean
Also service at 45 mi (72 km). Check hoses & vacuum break

EFE system . . . . check **MH**

Engine idle speed . . . . adjust

Vacuum advance system
    ex. Calif. . . . . inspect
Also service at 45 mi (72 km)

EVERY 12 MO/7.5 MI—12 KM

Brakes & power
    steering . . . . inspect hoses/pads
Inspect drum brake lining, check parking brake

Crankcase . . . . change oil

Differential, front & rear . . . . . . check level
Locking differential, change lubricant after first 7.5 mi (12 km)

Engine drive belts . . . . inspect/adjust

Exhaust system . . . . inspect

Fittings
    ex. CV joint . . . . lubricate **LB**
C-20, -2500; G-30, -3500; P-20, -2500, lubricate every 4 mo/6 mi (9.6 km)

Oil filter . . . . replace
At first oil change, then every 12 mo/15 mi (24 km)

Parking brake cables & guides . . . coat **LB**

Shift linkage . . . . coat **LB**
With floor shift, coat lever contact faces

Suspension & steering . . . . inspect

Throttle linkage . . . . inspect
Check for damage or binding

Transfer case . . . . check level
Check vent hose

Transmission, manual . . . . check level

Universal CV joint, 4WD . . . . fitting **LB**

Battery . . . . check level

Cooling system . . . . check level **EC**

Body . . . . lubricate
Flush underbody every spring

EVERY 6 MONTHS

Brake master cylinder . . . . check level **HB**

Clutch pedal free travel . . . . . check/adjust

Power steering reservoir . . check level **PS**

Transmission, automatic . . . . . check level

EVERY 12 MONTHS

Air cleaner . . . . inspect/test

EVERY 12 MO/15 MI-24 KM

Fuel cap, tank & lines . . . . inspect

Cooling system . . . . inspect, tighten hoses
Wash radiator filler neck & cap; pressure test system.
Clean exterior of radiator core & air conditioning condenser

Drive belts . . . . inspect/adjust
Vacuum or air pump only

Ignition wires . . . . clean/inspect
Every 15 mi (24 km) only ex. Calif. models, every 30 mi (48 km)

PCV system . . . . check
Service every 15 mi (24 km) only

EVERY 15 MI—24 KM

Engine valves . . . . adjust
1.9L (119) 4-cyl. only

Fuel filter in carb. inlet . . . . replace
Ex. Calif. models

Ignition wires . . . . inspect/clean
Calif. models, only every 30 mi (48 km)

EVERY 30 MI—48 KM

Clutch cross shaft . . . . **0-1 fitting LB**

Front wheel bearings,
    2WD . . . . clean/repack **GC**
Tighten spindle nut to 12 ft lb, back off 1/4-1/2 turn, hand tighten & loosen 1/12-1/6 turn. End play, .001"-.005". Service whenever brakes are relined

Front wheel bearings
    4WD . . . . clean/repack **GC**
Tighten inner adjusting nut to 50 ft lb; back off & re-tighten to 35 ft lb while hub is turning. Back off up to 3/8 turn; install lockwasher; install outer lock nut, tighten to 160-205 ft lb. End play, .001"-.010". Service whenever brakes are relined

Air cleaner element . . . . replace

ECS canister & hoses ex. Calif. . . . inspect

Eng. shield & insulation . . . . inspect

Idle stop solenoid . . . . inspect/test

Ignition timing . . . . adjust
Inspect distributor cap; clean or replace

PCV valve & filter . . . . replace

Spark plugs . . . . replace

Vacuum advance system . . . . inspect

EVERY 24 MO/30 MI—48 KM

Cooling system . . . . . . change coolant **EC**
Flush system; inspect hoses

EVERY 100 MI—160 KM

Transmission, automatic . . . . change fluid
Clean sump screen

SEVERE SERVICE

Crankcase—Change oil every 3 mo/3 mi (4.8 km). Change filter every oil change

Differential(s)—Change lubricant every 7.5 mi (12 km)

Front wheel bearings—Repack every 15 mi (24 km) or whenever brakes are relined

Transmission, automatic—Change fluid every 15 mi (24 km)

KEY TO LUBRICANTS

AF	DEXRON®-IIE Automatic Transmission Fluid
EC	Ethylene Glycol Coolant Mix with water to –34°F (–37°C) protection
GC	Wheel Bearing Grease, NLGI Category GC
GL-5	Gear Oil, API Service GL-5
GL-5★	Special Lubricant for Locking Differential
HB	Hydraulic Brake Fluid, DOT 3
LB	Chassis Grease, NLGI Category LB
MH	Manifold Heat Valve Solvent
PS	Power Steering Fluid
SG	Motor Oil, API Service SG Use Energy Conserving-II oils

CRANKCASE . . . . SG

CAPACITY, Refill:	Liters	Qt
6-cyl. 292 eng.	4.7	5.0
Others	3.8	4.0

Capacity shown is without filter. When replacing filter, additional oil may be needed

Above 40°F (4°C)	30
Above 20°F (–7°C) 20W-20, 20W-40, 20W-50	
Above 10°F (–12°C) 15W-40	
Above 0°F (–18°C) 10W-30*	
Below 60°F (16°C) . . . . 5W-30†	

† 5W-30 preferred in 4-cyl. & 2.8L V-6 engines up to 100°F (38°C)
* 10W-30 preferred above 0°F (–18°C)

TRANSMISSION, Automatic . . . . AF

CAPACITY, Initial Refill*:	Liters	Qt
Hydra-Matic 200C	3.3	3.5
Hydra-Matic 350	2.8	3.0
Hydra-Matic 400	3.3	3.5
Hydra-Matic 700-R4	4.7	5.0

*With the engine at operating temperature, shift transmission through all gears. Let engine slow idle in PARK for 3 minutes or more. Check fluid level and add fluid as needed

TRANSMISSION, Manual

S10, S15 . . . . **AF♦**
Others:
  3-speed 80W, 80W-90* **GL-5**
  4-speed (Side Load) . . . . **AF**
  4-speed (Top Load) . . 80W, 80W-90* **GL-5**
*For vehicles normally operated in Canada, 80W only
♦S10 5-speed (RPO MM5) models, with V.I.N. breakpoints:

       D0100042 thru D0142325,
       D2100011 thru D2161259,
       D8100001 thru D8143461,
and S15 5-speed (RPO MM5) models, with V.I.N. breakpoints:

       D0500002 thru D0513078,
       D2500003 thru D2512501,
       D8500050 thru D8507851,
use a special fluid, GM Part No. 1052951

CAPACITY, Refill: S10, S15:	Liters	Pt
4-speed (Top Load)	3.0	6.3
4-speed (Sectional Case) . .	2.3	4.8
5-speed	2.0	4.2
Others:		
3-speed	1.4	3.0
4-speed	3.8	8.0

TRANSFER CASE . . . . AF

CAPACITY, Refill:	Liters	Pt
K-30, -3500; NP205	2.4†	5.0†
Others, NP208	4.8	10.0

†Fill to within one inch of plug hole

DIFFERENTIAL

Locking . . . . **GL-5★**
Others 80W, 80W-90* **GL-5**
*For vehicles normally operated in Canada, 80W only

CAPACITY, Refill: Front:	Liters	Pt
S series	1.2	2.6
Others	2.4	5.0
Rear:		
S series, 7 1/2" ring gear .	†	†
8 1/2" ring gear	2.0	4.2
9 1/2" ring gear	2.6	5.5
Dana 9 3/4" ring gear . . .	2.8	6.0
10 1/2" ring gear:		
Chev.	2.6	5.5
Dana	3.4	7.2

† Fill to 3/8" (9.5 mm) of fill plug hole

CHEVROLET/GMC TRUCKS
1984-85 All Leaded Gasoline Models

SERVICE AT TIME OR MILEAGE—WHICHEVER OCCURS FIRST

CTTPM13   CTTPM13

MI—MILES IN THOUSANDS
KM—KILOMETERS IN THOUSANDS

FIRST 4 MO/6 MI—9.6 KM;
THEN EVERY 12 MO/12 MI—19.2 KM
Engine idle speed . . . . adjust
Idle stop solenoid . . . . check

FIRST 6 MI—9.6 KM
Locking differential . . . . . change lubricant

EVERY 4 MO/6 MI—9.6 KM
Brakes & power
  steering . . . . inspect hoses/pads
Inspect drum brake lining, check parking brake

Crankcase . . . . change oil

Standard differentials . . . . check level

Engine drive belts . . . . inspect/adjust

Exhaust system . . . . inspect

Fittings ex. CV joint . . . . lubricate **LB**
C-20, -2500; G-30, -3500

Oil filter . . . . replace
At first oil change, then every 4 mo/12 mi (19.2 km)

Parking brake cables & guides . . . coat **LB**

Shift linkage . . . . coat **LB**
With floor shift, coat lever contact faces

Suspension & steering . . . . inspect

Throttle linkage . . . . inspect
Check for damage or binding

Tires & wheels . . . . inspect
Check tires for abnormal wear & wheels for damage

Transfer case . . . . check level
Check vent hose

Transmission,
  automatic 1984 . . . . check level

Transmission, manual . . . . check level

Universal CV joint . . . . **fitting LB**
Lubricate splines/yokes & U-joints

Battery, 1984 . . . . check level

Body . . . . lubricate
Flush underbody every spring

EVERY 6 MONTHS
Brake master cylinder . . . . check level **HB**
Clutch pedal free travel . . . . . check/adjust
Power steering reservoir . . check level **PS**

EVERY 12 MO/12 MI—19.2 KM
Fittings . . . . **LB**
Ex. C-20, -2500; G-30, -3500

Front wheel bearings,
  2WD . . . . clean/repack **GC**
Tighten spindle nut to 12 ft lb, back off 1/4-1/2 turn, hand tighten & loosen 1/12-1/6 turn. End play, .001"-.005". Service whenever brakes are relined

Front wheel bearings,
  4WD . . . . clean/repack **GC**
Tighten inner adjusting nut to 50 ft lb; back off & re-tighten to 35 ft lb while hub is turning. Back off up to 3/8 turn; install lockwasher; install outer lock nut, tighten to 160-205 ft lb. End play, .001"-.010". Service whenever brakes are relined

Carb. to manifold bolts . . . . torque

Fuel filter in carb. inlet . . . . replace

Manifold heat valve . . . . check **MH**

PCV system . . . . check

Thermostatically controlled
  air cleaner . . . . inspect/test

Thermostatically controlled fan . . . . . . test

Throttle return control system
  hoses . . . . check/inspect

EVERY 12 MI—19.2 KM
Air cleaner element . . . . replace

Air intake system . . . . check for leaks

Cooling system . . . . . . change coolant **EC**
Flush system, inspect hoses

Eng. shield & insulation . . . . inspect

Drive belts . . . . replace/adjust
Air pump only

Ignition timing . . . . adjust
Inspect distributor cap; clean or replace

Ignition wires . . . . clean/inspect

Spark plugs . . . . replace

EVERY 24 MO/24 MI—38.4 KM
Choke & hoses . . . . check/clean
Check vacuum break

EFE system . . . . check **MH**

Fuel cap, tank & lines . . . . inspect

ECS canister & hoses . . . . inspect

Idle mixture 6-cyl. 292 eng. . . . . . . adjust

Vacuum advance sys., hoses . . . . . inspect

EVERY 24 MI—38.4 KM
Standard diff.(s) . . . . change lubricant

Transmission, automatic . . . . change fluid
Clean sump screen or replace filter

PCV valve & filter . . . . replace
Blow out or replace system hoses. 1.9L engine, clean PCV orifice

EVERY 36 MI—57.6 KM
Clutch cross shaft . . . . **0-1 fitting LB**

EVERY 36 MO/36 MI—60 KM
EGR system . . . . check/clean

EVERY 48 MO/48 MI—76.8 KM
Engine governor . . . . inspect/test

1985 EVERY 100 MI—160 KM
Transmission, automatic . . . . change fluid
Clean sump screen

SEVERE SERVICE
Crankcase—Change oil every 2 mo/3 mi (4.8 km). Change filter every oil change

Standard diff.(s)—Change lubricant every 12 mi (19.2 km). Locking diff.(s) every 6 mi (9.6 km)

Fittings—Lubricate every 3 mo/3 mi (4.8 km)

Transmission, automatic—Change fluid: 1984, every 12 mi (19.2 km); 1985, every 15 mi (24 km)

KEY TO LUBRICANTS

AF	DEXRON®-IIE Automatic Transmission Fluid
EC	Ethylene Glycol Coolant Mix with water –34°F (–37°C) protection
GC	Wheel Bearing Grease, NLGI Category GC
GL-5	Gear Oil, API Service GL-5
GL-5★	Special Lubricant for Locking Differential GM Part No. 1052271 or 1052272 (Canada 992867)
HB	Hydraulic Brake Fluid, DOT 3
LB	Chassis Grease, NLGI Category LB
MH	Manifold Heat Valve Solvent
PS	Power Steering Fluid GM Part No. 1050017; Canada 992646
SG	Motor Oil, API Service SG Use Energy Conserving-II oils

CRANKCASE . . . . SG

CAPACITY, Refill:	Liters	Qt
6-cyl. 292 eng.	4.7	5.0
8-cyl. 454 eng.		
K30/K35 models	4.8	5.0
8-cyl. 454 eng.		
other models	5.7	6.0
Others	3.8	4.0

Capacity shown is without filter. When replacing filter, additional capacity may be needed

Above 40°F (4°C) 30
Above 20°F (–7°C) 20W-20
Above 10°F (–12°C) 15W-40
Above 0°F (–18°C) 10W-30*
Below 60°F (16°C) 5W-30

* Preferred

TRANSMISSION, Automatic . . . . AF

CAPACITY, Initial Refill*:	Liters	Qt
Hydra-Matic 350	3.3	3.5
Hydra-Matic 400	4.1	4.3
Hydra-Matic 700-R4	4.7	5.0

* With the engine at operating temperature, shift transmission through all gears. Let engine slow idle in PARK for 3 minutes or more. Check fluid level and add fluid as needed

TRANSMISSION, Manual
4-speed (Side Load) . . . . **AF**
3-, 4-speed
  (Top Load) 80W, 80W-90* **GL-5**
* For vehicles normally operated in Canada, 80W only

CAPACITY, Refill:	Liters	Pt
3-speed	1.4	3.0
4-speed (Top Load)	4.0	8.4
4-speed (Side Load)	4.0	8.4

TRANSFER CASE . . . . AF

CAPACITY, Refill:	Liters	Pt
K30, -3500; NP205	2.4†	5.0†
Others, NP208	4.8	10.0

†Fill to one inch of fill plug hole

DIFFERENTIAL
Locking . . . . 80W, 80W-90* **GL-5★†**
Others 80W, 80W-90* **GL-5**
* For vehicles normally operated in Canada, 80W only
† May use GL-5 for top-up only

CAPACITY:	Liters	Pt
Blazer, Jimmy front	2.4	5.0
Others:		
Front:		
K-20, -2500	1.9	4.0
K30, -3500	2.8	6.0
Rear:		
Chev. 8½" ring gear	2.0	4.2
Chev. 9½" ring gear	2.6	5.5
Chev. 10½" ring gear	2.6	5.4
Dana 9¾" ring gear	2.8	6.0
Dana 10½" ring gear	3.4	7.2
Rockwell 12" ring gear . .	6.6	14.0

CHEVROLET/GMC TRUCKS
1984-85 All Unleaded Gasoline Models

MI—MILES IN THOUSANDS
KM—KILOMETERS IN THOUSANDS

FIRST 6 MO/7.5 MI—12 KM; THEN AT 30 MI—48 KM

Carb. or TBI manifold bolts . . . . torque
Ex. 1.9L engine

Choke & hoses . . . . check/clean
1984, also service at 45 mi (72 km); 1985, at 30 mi (48 km). Check hoses & vacuum break

EFE system . . . . check **MH**
Ex. 1.9L engine

Engine idle speed . . . . adjust
Initial service, then at 45 mi (75 km)

Vacuum advance system
ex. Calif. . . . . inspect
Also service at 45 mi (72 km)

FIRST 7.5 MI—12 KM

Locking differential . . . . . change lubricant

EVERY 12 MO/7.5 MI—12 KM

Brakes & power
steering . . . . inspect hoses/pads
Inspect drum brake lining, check parking brake

Crankcase . . . . change oil

Standard differentials . . . . check level

Engine drive belts . . . . inspect/adjust

Exhaust system . . . . inspect

Oil filter . . . . replace
At first oil change, then every 12 mo/15 mi (24 km)

Parking brake cables & guides . . . coat **LB**

Shift linkage . . . . coat **LB**
With floor shift, coat lever contact faces

Suspension & steering . . . . inspect

Throttle linkage . . . . inspect
Check for damage or binding

Tires & wheels . . . . inspect
Check tires for abnormal wear & wheels for damage

Transfer case . . . . check level
Check vent hose

Transmission, automatic . . . . . check level

Transmission, manual . . . . check level

Universal CV joint . . . . **fitting LB**
Lubricate splines/yokes & U-joints

Battery, 1984 . . . . check level

Cooling system . . . . check level **EC**

Body . . . . lubricate
Flush underbody every spring

EVERY 6 MONTHS

Brake master cylinder . . . . check level **HB**

Clutch pedal free travel . . . . . check/adjust

Power steering reservoir . . check level **PS**

EVERY 12 MONTHS

Air cleaner . . . . inspect/test

EVERY 12 MO/15 MI—24 KM

Fittings . . . . **LB**

Fuel cap, tank & lines . . . . inspect

Cooling system . . . . . inspect/tighten hoses
Wash radiator filler neck & cap; pressure test system. Clean exterior of radiator core & air conditioning condenser

Drive belts . . . . inspect/adjust
Vacuum or air pump only

Ignition wires . . . . clean/inspect
Every 15 mi (24 km) only ex. Calif. models, every 30 mi (48 km)

PCV system . . . . check
Service every 15 mi (24 km) only

EVERY 30 MI—48 KM

Air cleaner element . . . . replace

Eng. shield & insulation . . . . inspect

Idle stop solenoid . . . . inspect/test

Ignition timing . . . . adjust
Inspect distributor cap; clean or replace

Spark plugs . . . . replace

Vacuum advance Calif. . . . . check

EVERY 30 MI—48 KM

Front wheel bearings,
2WD . . . . clean/repack **GC**
Tighten spindle nut to 12 ft lb, back off 1/4-1/2 turn, hand tighten & loosen 1/12-1/6 turn. End play, .001"-.005". Service whenever brakes are relined

Front wheel bearings,
4WD . . . . clean/repack **GC**
Tighten inner adjusting nut to 50 ft lb; back off & re-tighten to 35 ft lb while hub is turning. Back off up to 3/8 turn; install lockwasher; install outer lock nut, tighten to 160-205 ft lb. End play, .001"-.010". Service whenever brakes are relined

EVERY 15 MI—24 KM

Engine valves 1.9L eng. . . . . adjust

Distributor . . . . inspect
California models, inspect every 30 mi (48 km)

Fuel filter in carb. inlet ex. Calif. . . replace

Ignition wires . . . . inspect/clean
Calif. models, only every 30 mi (48 km)

EVERY 24 MO/30 MI—48 KM

Cooling system . . . . . . change coolant **EC**
Flush system; inspect hoses

EVERY 30 MI—48 KM

ECS canister & hoses
ex. Calif. . . . . inspect

PCV valve & filter . . . . replace
Blow out or replace system hoses. 1.9L engine, clean PCV orifice

EVERY 30 MI—48 KM

Clutch cross shaft . . . . **0-1 fitting LB**

EVERY 36 MO/36 MI—60 KM

EGR system . . . . check/clean

EVERY 100 MI—160 KM

Transmission, automatic . . . . change fluid
Clean sump screen

SEVERE SERVICE

Crankcase—Change oil every 3 mo/3 mi (4.8 km). Change filter every oil change

Standard diff.(s)—Change lubricant every 7.5 mi (12 km). Locking diff.(s) every 7.5 mi (12 km)

Fittings—Lubricate every 3 mo/3 mi (4.8 km)

Front wheel bearings—Repack every 15 mi (24 km) or whenever brakes are relined

Transmission, automatic—Change fluid every 15 mi (24 km)

KEY TO LUBRICANTS

AF DEXRON®-IIE Automatic Transmission Fluid

EC Ethylene Glycol Coolant
Mix with water –34°F (–37°C) protection

GC Wheel Bearing Grease, NLGI Category GC

GL-5 Gear Oil, API Service GL-5

GL-5★ Special Lubricant for Locking Differential
GM Part No. 1052271 or 1052272; Canada, 992667

HB Hydraulic Brake Fluid, DOT 3

LB Chassis Grease, NLGI Category LB

MH Manifold Heat Valve Solvent

PS Power Steering Fluid
GM Part No. 1050017; Canada, 992646

SG Motor Oil, API Service SG
Use Energy Conserving-II oils

CRANKCASE . . . . SG

CAPACITY, Refill:	Liters	Qt
4-cyl. 1.9L	3.8	4.0
4-cyl. 2.5L	2.8	3.0
6-cyl. 4.3L	3.8	4.0
6-cyl. 292 eng.	4.7	5.0
Others	3.8	4.0

Capacity shown is without filter. When replacing filter, additional oil may be needed

Above 40°F (4°C)	30
Above 20°F (–7°C)	20W-20
Above 10°F (–12°C)	15W-40
Above 0°F (–18°C)	10W-30†
Below 60°F (16°C)	5W-30*

* 5W-30 preferred up to 100°F (38°C) in 1.9L, 2.0L, 2.5L & 2.8L engines
†10W-30 preferred for 292 6-cyl., 4.3L V-6, all V-8

TRANSMISSION, Automatic . . . . AF

CAPACITY, Initial Refill*:	Liters	Qt
Hydra-Matic 350	3.3	3.5
Hydra-Matic 400	4.1	4.3
Hydra-Matic 700-R4	4.7	5.0

* With the engine at operating temperature, shift transmission through all gears. Let engine slow idle in PARK for 3 minutes or more. Check fluid level and add fluid as needed

TRANSMISSION, Manual

Astro, Safari: 4-speed . 80W, 80W-90* **GL-5**
5-speed . . . . **AF**
S10, S15 . . . . **AF**
Others:
4-speed (Side Load) . . . . **AF**
3-, 4-speed
(Top Load) 80W, 80W-90* **GL-5**

*For vehicles normally operated in Canada, 80W only

CAPACITY, Refill:	Liters	Pt
3-speed	1.4	3.0
S10, S15, Astro, Safari:		
4-speed (Top Load)	2.0	4.2
4-speed (Sectional Case)	2.3	4.8
5-speed	2.0	4.4
Others:		
4-speed (Top Load)	4.0	8.4
4-speed (Side Load)	4.0	8.4

TRANSFER CASE . . . . AF

CAPACITY, Refill:	Liters	Pt
K30, -3500; NP205	2.4†	5.0†
Others, NP208	4.8	10.0

†Fill to one inch of fill plug hole

DIFFERENTIAL

Locking . . . . 80W, 80W-90* **GL-5★♦**
Others 80W, 80W-90* **GL-5**
*For vehicles normally operated in Canada, 80W only
♦May use **GL-5** for top-up only

CAPACITY, Refill:	Liters	Pt
Blazer, Jimmy front	2.4	5.0
Others:		
Front:		
K10, -20, -1500, -2500	1.9	4.0
K30, -3500	2.8	6.0
S10, -15	1.2	2.6
Rear:		
Chev. 8½″ ring gear	2.0	4.2
Chev. 9½″ ring gear	2.6	5.5
Chev. 10½″ ring gear	2.6	5.4
Dana 9¾″ ring gear	2.8	6.0
Dana 10½″ ring gear	3.4	7.2
Rockwell 12″ ring gear	6.6	14.0

SERVICE AT TIME OR MILEAGE—WHICHEVER OCCURS FIRST

CTTPM18   CTTPM18

MI—MILES IN THOUSANDS
KM—KILOMETERS IN THOUSANDS

FIRST 12 MO/7.5 MI—12.5 KM
Differential, locking ..... change lubricant

EVERY 12 MO/7.5 MI—12 KM
Brakes & power
 steering .... inspect hoses/pads
Inspect drum brake lining, check parking brake

Crankcase .... change oil

Oil filter .... replace
At first oil change, then every 15 mi (24 km), but at least
every 12 mo

Differential, front & rear ...... check level

Exhaust system .... inspect

Fittings .... lubricate **LB**

Parking brake cable guides ...... coat **LB**

Propeller shaft .... **LB**
Lubricate U-joints/splines

Shift linkage .... coat **LB**
With floor shift, coat lever contact faces

Suspension & steering .... inspect

Throttle linkage .... inspect
Check for damage or binding

Tires .... check/rotate
Initially, then every 15 mi (25 km)

Transfer case .... check level
Check vent hose

Transmission, automatic ..... check level

Universal CV joint, 4WD ...... **fitting LB**

Cooling system .... check level **EC**

Body .... lubricate
Flush underbody every spring

EVERY 6 MONTHS
Brake master cylinder .... check level **HB**

Clutch pedal free travel ..... check/adjust

Power steering reservoir .. check level **PS**

EVERY 12 MO/15 MI—24 KM
Cooling system .... inspect, tighten hoses
Wash radiator filler neck & cap; pressure test system.
Clean exterior of radiator core & air conditioning con-
denser. Service coolant as needed

EVERY 30 MI — 48 KM
Clutch fork ball stud .... lubricate **GC**
Some, lubricate sparingly

Front wheel bearings,
 2WD .... clean/repack **GC**
Tighten spindle nut to 12 ft lb while turning wheel forward. Adjust spindle nut to "just loose" position by
hand. Back off until the hole in spindle aligns with slot.
Do not back off more than 1/4 turn.

Fuel filter .... replace

Fuel tank, cap & lines .... inspect

Air cleaner element .... replace

ECS canister & hoses ex. Calif..... inspect

EFE system .... check

EGR system .... inspect

Engine drive belts .... inspect/adjust

Eng. shield & insulation .... inspect

Ignition timing .... check
Inspect distributor cap & ign. wires; clean or replace

PCV system .... inspect
Replace filter

Spark plugs .... replace

Spark plug wires .... inspect

Transmission, automatic . change fluid **AF**
Replace filter

Transmission, manual ... change fluid **AF**
4-speed Isuzu with one piece bell housing transmission
case

EVERY 24 MO/30 MI—48 KM
Cooling system ...... change coolant **EC**
Flush system; inspect hoses

EVERY 60 MI—100 KM
Idle speed .... adjust
Except engine codes E, R, Z

SEVERE SERVICE
Crankcase—Change oil and filter every 3 mi
(5 km). Also lubricate chassis

Differential(s)—Check lubricant every 3 mi
(5 km). Change fluid at least every 15 mi (24
km)

Front wheel bearings, 2WD only—Repack
every 15 mi (24 km) or whenever brakes are
relined

Fuel filter and spark plugs—Replace every
30 mi (50 km)

Fuel tank, cap, and lines—Inspect

Tires—Inspect, rotate at 6 mi (10 km), then
every 15 mi (25 km)

Transmission, automatic—Change fluid and
filter every 15 mi (24 km)

KEY TO LUBRICANTS

AF	DEXRON®-IIE Automatic Transmission Fluid
CE	Motor Oil, API Service CE
EC	Ethylene Glycol Coolant GM Spec. No. 6038-M
GC	Wheel Bearing Grease, NLGI Category GC
GL-5	Gear Oil, API Service GL-5
HB	Hydraulic Brake Fluid, DOT 3
LB	Chassis Grease, NLGI Category LB
PS	Power Steering Fluid GM Part No. 1050017; Canada, 992646
SG	Motor Oil, API Service SG

CRANKCASE .... SG, SG/CE

CAPACITY, Refill:	Liters	Qt
4-cyl. 2.5L	2.8	3.0
Others	3.8	4.0

Capacity shown is without filter. When replacing filter, additional oil may be needed

Above 40°F (4°C)	30
Above 20°F (−7°C)	20W-20
Above 10°F (−12°C)	15W-40
Above 0°F (−18°C)	10W-30*
Below 100°F (38°C)	5W-30†

† Preferred ex. V6 4.3L
* Preferred V6 4.3L

TRANSMISSION, Automatic .... AF

CAPACITY, Initial Refill*:	Liters	Qt
180C 3L30	2.8	3.0
700-R4 4L60	4.7	5.0

*With the engine at operating temperature, shift transmis-
 sion through all gears. Check fluid level in PARK and add
 fluid as needed

TRANSMISSION, Manual

Astro, Safari:
4-speed 80W, 80W-90*	**GL-5**
5-speed	**AF**
S-Series All	**AF**

*Vehicles normally operated in Canada, 80W only

CAPACITY, Initial Fill:	Liters	Pt
Astro, Safari:		
4-speed	1.2	2.6
5-speed	2.0	4.4
S-Series:		
4-speed Isuzu w/one piece bell housing trans. case	2.3	4.9
4-speed w/top load	2.0	4.2
5-speed	2.0	4.4

TRANSFER CASE .... AF

CAPACITY, Refill:	Liters	Pt
NP207	2.2	4.6
NP231	1.0	2.2

DIFFERENTIAL
Standard & locking .. 80W, 80W-90* **GL-5**
*For vehicles normally operated in Canada, 80W only

CAPACITY, Refill:	Liters	Pt
Front	1.2	2.6
Rear	1.9†	3.9†

† Fill to within 3/8" (9.5 mm) of fill plug hole

CHEK-CHART

SERVICE AT TIME OR MILEAGE—WHICHEVER OCCURS FIRST

CTTPM16   CTTPM16

Perform the following maintenance services at the intervals indicated to keep the vehicle warranties in effect

W   SERVICE TO MAINTAIN EMISSION WARRANTY

MI—MILES IN THOUSANDS
KM—KILOMETERS IN THOUSANDS

FIRST 6 MO/6 MI—10 KM
Locking differential . . . . . change lubricant
Initial service, then every other oil change

W Choke & hoses . . . . inspect
W Carb. mounting bolt torque . . . . . check
W Engine idle speeds . . . . adjust
W Idle stop solenoid . . . . check
W Vacuum advance system . . . . . . inspect

EVERY 6 MO/6 MI—10 KM
Brakes & power
   steering . . . . inspect hoses/pads
Inspect drum brake lining, check parking brake

W Crankcase . . . . change oil
W Standard differentials . . . . . check level
Engine drive belts . . . . inspect/adjust
W Exhaust system . . . . inspect
W Fittings
   ex. CV joint . . . . lubricate **LB**
W Oil filter . . . . replace
At first oil change, then every other

Parking brake cable guides . . . . . . coat **LB**
Shift linkage . . . . coat **LB**
With floor shift, coat lever contact faces

Suspension & steering . . . . inspect
Throttle linkage . . . . inspect
Check for damage or binding

Transfer case . . . . check level
Check vent hose

W Transmission, manual . . . . . check level
Universal CV joint, 4WD . . . . . . **fitting LB**
Body . . . . lubricate
Flush underbody every spring

EVERY 6 MONTHS
Brake master cylinder . . . . check level **HB**
Clutch pedal free travel . . . . . check/adjust
Power steering or hydro-boost
   reservoir . . . . check level **PS**
Transmission, automatic . . . . . check level

EVERY 7.5 MI—12 KM
Tires 1987 . . . . inspect/rotate

EVERY 12 MO/12 MI—19.2 KM
W Accessory drive belts . . . . inspect
W Idle speed . . . . check
W Thermostatically controlled fan . . . . test
W Throttle return control system
   & hoses . . . . check/inspect

EVERY 12 MI/19.2 KM
W Eng. shield & insulation . . . . inspect
W Manifold heat valve . . . . . . check **MH**
W Spark plugs . . . . replace

EVERY 24 MO/24 MI—38.4 KM
W Front wheel bearings,
   2WD . . . . clean/repack **GC**
Tighten spindle nut to 12 ft lb, back off 1/4-1/2 turn, hand tighten & loosen 1/12-1/6 turn. End play, .001"-.005". Service whenever brakes are relined

W Front wheel bearings
   4WD . . . . clean/repack **GC**
Tighten inner adjusting nut to 50 ft lb; back off & re-tighten to 35 ft lb while hub is turning. Back off up to 3/8 turn; install lockwasher; install outer lock nut, tighten to 160-205 ft lb. End play, .001"-.010". Service whenever brakes are relined

W Air cleaner . . . . inspect/test
W Air intake system . . . . . . check for leaks
W Carb. to manifold bolts . . . . torque
W Choke & hoses . . . . check/clean
Check vacuum break

Cooling system . . . . . . change coolant **EC**
Flush system, inspect hoses

W EFE system . . . . check **MH**
W EGR system . . . . check
W Fuel cap, tank & lines . . . . inspect
W Fuel filter in carb. inlet . . . . replace
W ECS canister & hoses . . . . inspect
W Idle mixture 6-cyl. 292 eng. . . . . . adjust
California only
W Ignition timing . . . . adjust
Inspect distributor cap; clean or replace
W PCV system . . . . check
W Vacuum advance system
   & hoses . . . . inspect

EVERY 24 MI—38.4 KM
W Standard differential . . change lubricant
W Transmission, automatic . . change fluid
Replace filter
W PCV valve & filter . . . . replace
Blow out or replace system hoses

EVERY 30 MI—50 KM
Clutch cross shaft . . . . 0-1 fitting **LB**
Clutch fork ball stud . . . . lubricate **GC**
1987 some models, lubricate sparingly

EVERY 48 MO/48 MI—76.8 KM
Engine governor . . . . inspect/test

EVERY 60 MI—100 KM
Idle mixture 6-cyl. . . . . adjust
Ignition wires . . . . clean/inspect

SEVERE SERVICE
W Crankcase—Change oil every 3 mi (5 km). Change filter every oil change
W Differential(s)—Change lubricant every 3 mi (5 km)
EFE system—Check at 3 mi (5 km), then at 12 mi (19.2 km), then at every 12 mi (19.2 km)
W Engine idle speeds & carb. mounting bolt torque—Check/adjust every 12 mi (19.2 km)
W Fittings—Lubricate every 3 mi (5 km)
Front wheel bearings—Repack every 12 mi (19.2 km)
W Fuel filter—Replace every 12 mi (19.2 km)
Tires 1987—Inspect & rotate every 6 mi (10 km)
W Transmission, automatic—Change fluid and filter every 12 mi (19.2 km)

KEY TO LUBRICANTS

AF	DEXRON®-IIE Automatic Transmission Fluid
EC	Ethylene Glycol Coolant Mix with water to –34°F (–37°C) protection
GC	Wheel Bearing Grease, NLGI Category GC
GL-5	Gear Oil, API Service GL-5
GL-5 ★	Special Lubricant for Locking Differential GM Part No. 1052271 or 1052272; Canada, 992867
HB	Hydraulic Brake Fluid, DOT 3
LB	Chassis Grease, NLGI Category LB
MH	Manifold Heat Valve Solvent
PS	Power Steering Fluid GM Part No. 1050017; Canada 992646
SG	Motor Oil, API Service SG Use Energy Conserving-II Oils

CRANKCASE . . . . SG

CAPACITY, Refill:	Liters	Qt
6-cyl. 292 eng.	4.7	5.0
8-cyl. 350	3.8	4.0
8-cyl. 454	4.8*	5.0*
8-cyl. 454	5.7	6.0

*1986 K30, -35 pickup only
Capacity shown is without filter. When replacing filter, additional oil may be needed

1986
Above 40°F (4°C) 30
Above 20°F (–7°C) 20W-20
Above 10°F (–12°C) 15W-40
Above 0°F (–18°C) 10W-30*
Below 60°F (16°C) 5W-30

1987
Above 40°F (4°C) 30
Above 0°F (–18°C) 10W-30*
Below 60°F (16°C) 5W-30
*Preferred

TRANSMISSION, Automatic . . . . AF

CAPACITY, Initial Refill*:	Liters	Qt
Hydra-Matic 350	3.3	3.5
Hydra-Matic 400	4.1	4.3
Hydra-Matic 700-R4	4.7	5.0

*With the engine at operating temperature, shift transmission through all gears. Let engine slow idle in PARK for 3 minutes or more. Check fluid level and add fluid as needed

TRANSMISSION, Manual
4-speed (Side Load) . . . . **AF**
4-speed (Top Load),
   3-speed 80W, 80W-90* **GL-5**
*For vehicles normally operated in Canada, 80W only

CAPACITY, Refill:	Liters	Pt
3-speed	1.4	3.0
4-speed	4.0	8.4

TRANSFER CASE . . . . AF

CAPACITY, Refill:	Liters	Pt
K, V-30, -3500	2.4*	5.0*
Others	4.8	10.0

*Fill to one inch (25 mm) of fill plug

DIFFERENTIAL
Locking . . . . **GL-5 ★**
Others 80W, 80W-90* **GL-5**
*For vehicles normally operated in Canada, 80W only

CAPACITY, Refill:	Liters	Pt
Front	2.8	6.0
Rear:		
Chev. 8 1/2" ring gear	2.0	4.2
Chev. 9 1/2" ring gear	2.6	5.5
Dana 9 3/4" ring gear	2.8	6.0
Dana 10 1/2" ring gear	3.4	7.2
Rockwell 12" ring gear	6.6	14.0

CHEVROLET/GMC TRUCKS
1986-87 C, G, K, P, R, V Series
Unleaded Gasoline Models

SERVICE AT TIME OR MILEAGE—WHICHEVER OCCURS FIRST

CTTPM17   CTTPM17
Perform the following maintenance services at the intervals indicated to keep the vehicle warranties in effect

W   SERVICE TO MAINTAIN EMISSION WARRANTY

MI—MILES IN THOUSANDS
KM—KILOMETERS IN THOUSANDS

FIRST 6 MO/7.5 MI—12.5 KM
Carb. to manifold bolts 1986 ..... torque

Choke & hoses 1986 .... check/clean
Check hoses & vacuum break

W EFE system .... check **MH**

Engine idle speed 1986 .... adjust

Vacuum advance system 1986 ... inspect

EVERY 7.5 MI—12 KM
Brakes & power
   steering .... inspect hoses/pads
Inspect drum brake lining, check parking brake

W Crankcase .... change oil

W Differential, front & rear .... check level
Locking differential, change lubricant after first 7.5 mi
(12 km)

Engine drive belts .... inspect/adjust

W Exhaust system .... inspect

W Fittings
   ex. CV joint .... lubricate **LB**

W Oil filter .... replace
At first oil change, then every 15 mi (24 km)

W Choke & hoses .... check/clean

Parking brake cable guides ...... coat **LB**

Shift linkage .... coat **LB**
With floor shift, coat lever contact faces

W Suspension & steering .... inspect

Throttle linkage .... inspect
Check for damage or binding

Tires .... check/rotate
1986 at first service, then every other oil change
1987 at every oil change

Transfer case .... check level
Check vent hose

W Transmission, automatic ... check level

W Transmission, manual
   4-speed (Side Load) .... change fluid
First service, then every 30 mi (48 km)

Universal CV joint, 4WD .... fitting **LB**

W Cooling system .... check level **EC**

Body .... lubricate
Flush underbody every spring

EVERY 6 MONTHS
Brake master cylinder .... check level **HB**

Clutch pedal free travel ..... check/adjust

Power steering or hydro-boost
   reservoir .... check level **PS**

EVERY 12 MONTHS
Air cleaner .... inspect/test

Idle speed control device 1987 .... check

EFE system .... check

EVERY 12 MO/15 MI—24 KM
W Cooling system .... inspect, tighten hoses
Wash radiator filler neck & cap; pressure test system.
Clean exterior or radiator core & air conditioning condenser. Service coolant as needed

Drive belts 1986 .... inspect/adjust
Vacuum or air pump only

W PCV system .... check
Service every 15 mi (24 km) only

EVERY 30 MI—48 KM
Clutch cross shaft .... 0-1 fitting **LB**

Clutch fork ball stud
   1987 .... lubricate **GC**
Some models — lubricate sparingly

W Front wheel bearings,
   2WD .... clean/repack **GC**
Tighten spindle nut to 12 ft lb, back off 1/4-1/2 turn, hand tighten & loosen 1/12-1/6 turn. End play, .001″-.005″. Service whenever brakes are relined

W Front wheel bearings
   4WD .... clean/repack **GC**
Tighten inner adjusting nut to 50 ft lb, back off & re-tighten to 35 ft lb while hub is turning. Back off up to 3/8 turn; install lockwasher; install outer lock nut, tighten to 160-205 ft lb. End play, .001″-.010″. Service whenever brakes are relined

Transmission, automatic .... change fluid
Replace filter

W Fuel tank, cap & lines .... inspect

W Air cleaner element .... replace

W ECS canister & hoses
   ex. Calif. .... inspect

W EGR system .... inspect

W Fuel filter .... replace

W Idle stop solenoid .... inspect/test

W Ignition timing .... adjust
Inspect distributor cap & ign. wires; clean or replace

W PCV valve & filter .... replace

W Spark plugs .... replace

W Thermostatic air cleaner ...... inspect

W Vacuum advance system ...... inspect
Service every 15 mi (24 km) thereafter

EVERY 24 MO/30 MI—48 KM
W Cooling system .... change coolant **EC**
Flush system; inspect hoses

EVERY 60 MI—100 KM
Carb. to manifold bolts .... torque

Engine idle speed .... check/adjust

EVRV 1987 .... inspect

SEVERE SERVICE
W Crankcase—Change oil and filter every 3 mi (5 km). Also lubricate chassis

W Differential(s)—Change lubricant every 7.5 mi (12 km)

Front wheel bearings—Repack every 15 mi (24 km) or whenever brakes are relined

W Transmission, automatic—Change fluid and filter every 15 mi (24 km)

Tires 1987—Inspect & rotate every 6 mi (10 km)

KEY TO LUBRICANTS

AF	DEXRON®-IIE Automatic Transmission Fluid
EC	Ethylene Glycol Coolant Mix with water to –34°F (–37°C) protection
GC	Wheel Bearing Grease, NLGI Category GC
GL-5	Gear Oil, API Service GL-5
GL-5★	Special Lubricant for Locking Differential GM Part No. 1052271 or 1052272; Canada, 992867
HB	Hydraulic Brake Fluid, DOT 3
LB	Chassis Grease, NLGI Category LB
MH	Manifold Heat Valve Solvent
PS	Power Steering Fluid GM Part No. 1050017; Canada, 992646
SG	Motor Oil, API Service SG Use Energy Conserving-II Oils

CRANKCASE .... SG

CAPACITY, Refill:	Liters	Qt
V8 7.4L (454)	4.8	5.0
All others	3.8	4.0

Capacity shown is without filter. When replacing filter, additional oil may be needed

1986:
Above 40°F (4°C)	30
Above 20°F (–7°C)	20W-20
Above 10°F (–12°C)	15W-40
Above 0°F (–18°C)	10W-30*
Below 60°F (16°C)	5W-30

1987:
Above 40°F (4°C)	30
Above 0°F (–18°C)	10W-30*
Below 60°F (16°C)	5W-30

*Preferred

TRANSMISSION, Automatic .... AF

CAPACITY, Initial Refill*:	Liters	Qt
Hydra-Matic 350	3.3	3.5
Hydra-Matic 400	4.1	4.3
Hydra-Matic 700-R4	4.7	5.0

*With the engine at operating temperature, shift transmission through all gears. Let engine slow idle in PARK for 3 minutes or more. Check fluid level and add fluid as needed

TRANSMISSION, Manual
3-speed,
   4-speed (Top Load) 80W, 80W-90* **GL-5**
*For vehicles normally operated in Canada, 80W only
4-speed (Side Load) .... **AF**

CAPACITY, Refill:	Liters	Pt
3-speed	1.4	3.0
4-speed	4.0	8.4

TRANSFER CASE .... AF

CAPACITY, Refill:	Liters	Pt
30, -35 series	2.4*	5.0*
Others	4.8	10.0

*Fill to one inch (25 mm) of fill plug

DIFFERENTIAL
Locking .... **GL-5★**
Others 80W, 80W-90* **GL-5**
*For vehicles normally operated in Canada, 80W only

CAPACITY, Refill:	Liters	Pt
Front	1.9	4.0
Rear:		
Chev. 8½″ ring gear ...	2.0	4.2
Chev. 9½″ ring gear ...	2.6	5.5
Dana 9¾″ ring gear ...	2.8	6.0
10½″ ring gear		
Chev.	2.6	5.5
Dana	3.4	7.2
Rockwell 12″ ring gear	6.6	14.0

CHEVROLET/GMC TRUCKS
1984-87 All Diesel Models

CTTPM14   CTTPM14

Perform the following maintenance services at the intervals indicated to keep the vehicle warranties in effect

W   SERVICE TO MAINTAIN EMISSION WARRANTY

MI—MILES IN THOUSANDS
KM—KILOMETERS IN THOUSANDS

FIRST 5 MI—8 KM
Locking diffs. 6.2L . . . . . . change lubricant

W Exhaust pressure regulator
6.2L . . . . inspect

W Engine idle speed 6.2L . . . check/adjust

FIRST 7.5 MI—12 KM
Locking diff. 2.2L . . . . change lubricant

W Engine idle speed 2.2L . . . check/adjust

EVERY 7.5 MI—12 KM
Differentials 2.2L . . . . check level
Tires 1987 . . . . inspect/rotate

EVERY 6 MONTHS
Brake master cylinder . . . . check level **HB**

Power steering or brake
Hydro-Boost reservoir . . . check level **PS**

Clutch pedal free play . . . . . . check/adjust

2.2L, EVERY 12 MO/7.5 MI—12 KM
1984-86 6.2L,
EVERY 12 MO/5 MI—8 KM
1987, EVERY 5 MI—8 KM
Brake system . . . . inspect
Check hydraulic system & hoses for leaks, cracks & general condition. Check parking brake adjustment

Chassis . . . . lubricate **LB**

Differentials 6.2L . . . . check level

W Crankcase . . . . change oil

W Oil filter . . . . replace

Exhaust system . . . . inspect

Four-wheel drive . . . . inspect
Check transfer case & axle fluid levels. Lubricate U-joints with **CV**, splines/yokes & steering linkage with **LB**

Steering & suspension . . . . inspect

Transmission, auto. 6.2L . . . . . check level

Transmission, manual . . . . . check level

Transmission, manual
W/OD . . . . lubricate shifter **LB**
Sideloaded transmissions with grease fitting

Drive belts 1986 . . . . inspect/adjust
Replace as needed

Throttle linkage . . . . inspect

Tires 1984-86 . . . . inspect
Check pressure & condition. Rotate & check every 15 mi (24 km) thereafter

EVERY 10 MI—16 KM
W Differentials 6.2L . . . . . change lubricant
Locking axles in vehicles of 8600 lb GVW & above

W Air intake system . . . . inspect

W Thermostatically controlled
fan . . . . check operation

W Under hood shields &
insulation . . . . check condition

EVERY 12 MONTHS
Parking brake . . . . check
Check operation

W Cooling system .inspect & tighten hoses
Wash radiator filler neck & cap; pressure test system. Clean exterior of radiator core

FIRST 12 MO/15 MI—24 KM;
THEN EVERY 30 MI—48 KM
W Crankcase ventilation
system 6.2L . . . . inspect
Inspect rubber fittings, hoses & regulator

EVERY 12 MO/15 MI—24 KM
W Drive belts 2.2L . . . . inspect/adjust
Replace as needed

EVERY 15 MI—24 KM
W Exhaust pressure regulator
valve 6.2L . . . . check operation

PCV system . . . . inspect

W Valves 2.2L . . . . adjust

EVERY 24 MO/24 MI—38.4 KM
Cooling system . . . . . . change coolant **EC**
Flush system, inspect hoses. Replace hoses if checked, swollen or rotted

Transmission, auto. 6.2L . . . . change fluid
Vehicles over 8600 lb GVW

EVERY 25 MI—40 KM
Standard diffs. . . . . change lubricant
Of 8600 lb GVW & above

EVERY 30 MI—48 KM
Clutch cross shaft . . . . lubricate **LB**

W Front wheel bearings
6.2L 2WD . . . . clean/repack **GC**
Tighten spindle nut to 12 ft lb, back off 1/4-1/2 turn; hand tighten & loosen 1/12-1/8 turn. End play, .001″-.005″. Service whenever brakes are relined

W Front wheel bearings
6.2L 4WD . . . . clean/repack **GC**
Tighten inner adjusting nut to 50 ft lb; back off & re-tighten to 35 ft lb while hub is turning. Back off up to 3/8 turn; install lockwasher; install outer lock nut; tighten to ft lb: K-30, -3500, 65; all others, 160-205. End play, .001″-.010″. Service whenever brakes are relined

W Air cleaner element . . . . replace

W Engine idle speed . . . . adjust

Transmission, auto. 6.2L . . . . change fluid
Vehicles under 8600 lb GVW

EVERY 60 MI—96 KM
W CDRV system 1987 . . . . check

Drive belts 1987 . . . . inspect

EVERY 100 MI—160 KM
Transmission, auto. 6.2L . . . . change fluid
1984-85

SEVERE SERVICE
W Crankcase—Change oil & filter every:
2.2L, 3 mo/3 mi (5 km); 6.2L, 3 mo/2.5 mi (4 km)

Differential—Change lubricant every: 1984-85 6.2L standard under 8600 lb GVW, & all locking, 5 mi (8 km); standard of 8600 lb GVW & above, 10 mi (16 km); 2.2L, 7.5 mi (12 km). 1986-87, every oil change

Engine idle speed, 2.2L—Adjust at 6 mi (9.6 km)

W Fittings—Lubricate every: 2.2L, 3 mo/6 mi (9.6 km); 6.2L, 3 mo/2.5 mi (4 km)

Tires 1987—Inspect & rotate every 6 mi (10 km)

W Transmission, automatic—6.2L change fluid every: Models over 8600 lb GVW, 12 mi (20 km); Models under 8600 lb GVW, 15 mi (24 km)

W Wheel bearings—Repack every 15 mi (24 km)

KEY TO LUBRICANTS

AF	DEXRON®-IIE Automatic Transmission Fluid
CE	Motor Oil, API Service CE
EC	Ethylene Glycol Coolant Mix with water to −34°F (−37°C) protection
GC	Wheel Bearing Grease, NLGI Category GC
GL-5	Gear Oil, API Service GL-5
GL-5★	Special Lubricant for Locking Differential GM Part No. 1052271 or 1052272; Canada, 992867
HB	Hydraulic Brake Fluid, DOT 3
LB	Chassis Grease, NLGI Category LB
PS	Power Steering Fluid GM Part No. 1050017; Canada, 992646
SG	Motor Oil, API Service SG

CRANKCASE . . . . **SG/CE**

CAPACITY, Refill:	Liters	Qt
2.2L (w/o filter) 1984	5.7	6.0
2.2L (w/o filter) 1985	5.2	5.5
6.2L (Includes filter)	6.6	7.0

2.2L 1984-85
Above 32°F (0°C) 30
Above 15°F (−9°C) 15W-40
Below 100°F (38°C) 10W-30*
6.2L
Above 32°F (0°C) 30*
Above 0°F (−18°C) 15W-40
Below 60°F (16°C) 10W-30
*Preferred

TRANSMISSION, Automatic . . . . **AF**

CAPACITY, Initial Refill*:	Liters	Qt
Turbo Hydra-Matic 350 . . .	3.3	3.5
Turbo Hydra-Matic 400 . . .	4.1	4.3
Turbo Hydra-Matic 700-R4 .	4.7	5.0

*With the engine at operating temperature, shift transmission through all gears. Let engine slow idle in PARK for 3 minutes or more. Check fluid level and add fluid as needed

TRANSMISSION, Manual
2.2L . . . . **AF**
6.2L 4-speed O.D. (Side Load) . . . . **AF**
Others . . . . 80W, 80W-90† **GL-5**
†For vehicles normally operated in Canada, 80W only

CAPACITY, Refill:	Liters	Pt
2.2L all	2.0	4.2
6.2L 3-speed	1.5	3.2
6.2L 4-speed	4.0	8.4

TRANSFER CASE . . . . **AF**

CAPACITY, Refill:	Liters	Pt
30/3500 series	2.4	5.0
Others	4.8	10.0

DIFFERENTIAL
Locking . . . . **GL-5★**
Standard 80W, 80W-90* **GL-5**
*For vehicles normally operated in Canada, 80W only

CAPACITY, Refill:	Liters	Pt
Front:		
K, V-10, -1500, -20, -2500	1.9	4.0
K, V-30, -3500	2.8	6.0
All others	2.4	5.0
Rear:		
Chev. 8½″ ring gear . . .	2.0	4.2
Chev. 9½″ ring gear . . .	2.6	5.5
Chev. 10½″ ring gear . . .	2.6	5.4
Dana 9¾″ ring gear . . .	2.8	6.0
Dana 10½″ ring gear . . .	3.4	7.2
Rockwell 12″ ring gear . .	6.6	14.0

SERVICE AT TIME OR MILEAGE—WHICHEVER OCCURS FIRST

CTTPM24   CTTPM24

Perform the following maintenance services at the intervals indicated to keep the vehicle warranties in effect

W   SERVICE TO MAINTAIN EMISSION WARRANTY

MI—MILES IN THOUSANDS
KM—KILOMETERS IN THOUSANDS

SYCLONE, TYPHOON, EVERY 3 MO/2.5 MI—4 KM
W Crankcase . . . . oil change
Change oil filter at each oil change

Chassis . . . . lubricate **LB**

SYCLONE, TYPHOON, FIRST 6 MI—10 KM
Tires . . . . check/rotate
Initially, then every 15 mi (25 km) or as necessary

EVERY 6 MONTHS
Brake master cylinder . . . . check level **HB**

Clutch pedal free travel . . . . . check/adjust

Power steering reservoir . . check level **PS**

FIRST 12 MO/7.5 MI—12.5 KM
Throttle body mounting bolts . . . . . . torque
4.3L engine code Z

Differential, rear locking . change lubricant

Tires . . . . check/rotate
Initially, then every 15 mi (25 km) or as necessary

EVERY 12 MO/7.5 MI—12 KM
Brakes & power
   steering . . . . inspect hoses/pads
Inspect drum brake lining, check parking brake

W Crankcase . . . . change oil

W Oil filter . . . . replace
At first oil change, then every 15 mi (24 km), but at least every 12 mo

Differential, front & rear . . . . . . check level

Exhaust system . . . . inspect

Fittings . . . . lubricate **LB**

Parking brake cable guides . . . . . . coat **LB**

Propeller shaft . . . . **LB**
Lubricate U-joints/splines ex. Bravada

Shift linkage . . . . coat **LB**
With floor shift, coat lever contact faces

Suspension & steering . . . . inspect

Throttle linkage . . . . inspect
Check for damage or binding

Transfer case . . . . check level
Check vent hose

Transmission, automatic . . . . . check level

Universal CV joint, 4WD . . . . fitting **LB**

Double cardan joint . . . . lubricate **LB**
Syclone, Typhoon

W Cooling system . . . . check level **EC**

Body . . . . lubricate
Flush underbody every spring

EVERY 12 MO/15 MI—24 KM
W Cooling system . . inspect, tighten hoses
Wash radiator filler neck & cap; pressure test system. Clean exterior of radiator core & air conditioning condenser. Service coolant as needed

EVERY 30 MI — 48 KM
Clutch fork ball stud . . . . lubricate **GC**
Some, lubricate sparingly

W Fuel filter 1992 . . . . replace

W Fuel tank, cap & lines 1992 . . . . inspect

W Spark plug wires 1992 . . . . replace

W Engine drive belts . . . . inspect

Front wheel bearings,
   2WD . . . . clean/repack **GC**
Tighten spindle nut to 12 ft lb while turning wheel forward. Adjust spindle nut to "just loose" position by hand. Back off until the hole in spindle aligns with slot. Do not back off more than 1/4 turn.

W Air cleaner element . . . . replace

W ECS canister & hoses ex. Calif. . .inspect

EFE system . . . . check

W EGR system . . . . inspect

Eng. shield & insulation . . . . inspect

W Spark plugs . . . . replace

Thermostatically controlled
   air cleaner 1987-88 . . . . inspect

Transmission, automatic . change fluid **AF**
Replace filter

Transmission, manual . . . change fluid **AF**
1987 4-speed Isuzu with one piece bell housing transmission case

EVERY 24 MO/30 MI—48 KM
Cooling system . . . . . . change coolant **EC**
Flush system; inspect hoses

Charge air
   cooling system . . . . . change coolant **EC**
Syclone, Typhoon only

EVERY 60 MI—100 KM
W EVRV system . . . . check

W Fuel filter 1987-91 . . . . replace

W PCV system . . . . check
Some models

W Fuel tank, cap, lines 1987-91 . . . inspect

W Ignition timing . . . . check

W Spark plug wires 1987-91 . . . . . inspect

W Engine drive belts 1987-91 . . . . inspect

SEVERE SERVICE
Crankcase—Change oil and filter every 3 mi (5 km). Also lubricate chassis

Differential—Check lubricant every 3 mi (5 km). Change fluid at least every 15 mi (24 km)

Front wheel bearings, 2WD only—Repack every 15 mi (24 km) or whenever brakes are relined

W Fuel filter and spark plugs—Replace every 30 mi (50 km)

W Fuel tank, cap, and lines—Inspect

Tires—Inspect, rotate at 6 mi (10 km), then every 15 mi (25 km)

Transfer case—Change fluid every 30 mi (50 km)

Transmission, automatic—Change fluid and filter every 15 mi (24 km)

KEY TO LUBRICANTS

AF   DEXRON®-IIE Automatic Transmission Fluid

CE   Motor Oil, API Service CE

EC   Ethylene Glycol Coolant
      GM Spec. No. 6038-M

GC   Wheel Bearing Grease, NLGI Category GC

GL-5   Gear Oil, API Service GL-5

HB   Hydraulic Brake Fluid, DOT 3

LB   Chassis Grease, NLGI Category LB

PS   Power Steering Fluid
      GM Part No. 1050017; Canada, 992646

SG   Motor Oil, API Service SG

CRANKCASE . . . . SG, SG/CE
Note: 1992 Syclone, Typhoon oil must be Mobil 1 synthetic or equivalent

CAPACITY, Refill:	Liters	Qt
4-cyl. 2.5L	2.8	3.0
Others	3.8	4.0

Capacity shown is without filter. When replacing filter, additional oil may be needed

1987-88:
Above 40°F (4°C) . . . . 30‡
Above 0°F (−18°C) 10W-30*
Below 60°F (16°C) 5W-30

**1987-88 others,
1988-92 except Syclone, Typhoon:**
Above 40°F (4°C) . . . . 30‡
Above 0°F (−18°C) 10W-30
All temperatures 5W-30*

1992 Syclone, Typhoon:
All temperatures 10W-30
† Preferred
‡ May be used when other recomended viscosities are unavailable

TRANSMISSION, Automatic . . . . AF

CAPACITY, Initial Refill*:	Liters	Qt
180C 3L30	2.8	3.0
700-R4 4L60	4.7	5.0

*With the engine at operating temperature, shift transmission through all gears. Check fluid level in PARK and add fluid as needed

TRANSMISSION, Manual . . . . AF

CAPACITY, Initial Fill:	Liters	Pt
Astro, Safari		
4-speed 1987	2.3	4.9
5-speed	2.0	4.4
S-Series:		
4-speed Isuzu w/one piece		
bell housing		
trans. case 1987	2.3	4.9
4-speed w/top load	2.0	4.2
5-speed	2.0	4.4

TRANSFER CASE . . . . AF

CAPACITY, Refill:	Liters	Pt
NP207	2.2	4.6
NP231, NP233	1.0	2.2
BW4472 (Full Time)	1.5	3.2

DIFFERENTIAL
Standard & locking . . 80W, 80W-90* **GL-5**
*For vehicles normally operated in Canada, 80W only

CAPACITY, Refill:	Liters	Pt
Front, Astro, Safari,		
Bravada	1.7	3.5
Front S-series	1.2	2.6
Rear, Bravada	1.7	3.5
Rear, others	1.9†	3.9†

† Fill to within 3/8" (9.5 mm) of fill plug hole

CHEVROLET/GMC TRUCKS
1988-89 C, G, K, P, R, V Series
All Heavy Duty Gasoline Models

CHEK-CHART

SERVICE AT TIME OR MILEAGE—WHICHEVER OCCURS FIRST

CTTPM19   CTTPM19

Perform the following maintenance services at the intervals indicated to keep the vehicle warranties in effect

W SERVICE TO MAINTAIN EMISSION WARRANTY

Includes: 1988, all carburetted models; 1989, C & K Series with 5.7L, 7.4L engines and over 8500 GVWR. R & V Series with 5.7L, 7.4L 4V engines and over 8500 GVWR. G Series with 5.7L engine and over 10,000 GVWR; and all P Series

MI—MILES IN THOUSANDS
KM—KILOMETERS IN THOUSANDS

FIRST 6 MO/24 MI — 40 KM
W Engine idle speed . . . . adjust
Ex. engines with idle control

EVERY 6 MONTHS
Brake master cylinder . . . . check level **HB**

Clutch pedal free travel . . . . . check/adjust

Power steering or hydro-boost
reservoir . . . . check level **PS**

Transmission, automatic . . . . check level
At operating temperature, engine idling in PARK

EVERY 7.5 MI—12 KM
Tires . . . . inspect/rotate

FIRST 12 MO/7.5 MI—12.5 KM
Locking differential . . . . . change lubricant

W Choke & hoses . . . . inspect
As equipped

W Idle stop solenoid . . . . check
Ex. engines with idle control

W Vacuum advance system . . . . . inspect
As equipped

EVERY 12 MO/6 MI—10 KM
Brakes & power
steering . . . . inspect hoses/pads
Inspect drum brake lining, check parking brake

W Crankcase . . . . change oil

W Oil filter . . . . replace
At first oil change, then every other, but at least every 12 mo

Standard differentials . . . . check level

Engine drive belts . . . . inspect/adjust

Exhaust system . . . . inspect

Parking brake cable guides . . . . . . coat **LB**

Shift linkage . . . . coat **LB**
With floor shift, coat lever contact faces

Front suspension & steering . lubricate **LB**

Throttle linkage . . . . inspect
Check for damage or binding

Transfer case . . . . check level
Check vent hose

Transmission, manual . . . . check level

Propeller shaft . . . . lubricate **LB**
Lubricate U-joints/splines

Universal CV joint, 4WD . . . . . . **fitting LB**

Body . . . . lubricate
Flush underbody every spring

EVERY 12 MO/12 MI—19.2 KM
W Accessory drive belts . . . . inspect

W Thermostatically controlled fan . . . . test

W Throttle return control system
& hoses . . . . check/inspect

EVERY 12 MI/19.2 KM
Eng. shield & insulation . . . . . . inspect

W Manifold heat valve . . . . check **MH**

W Spark plugs . . . . replace
Engines using leaded fuel

EVERY 24 MO/24 MI—38.4 KM
Front wheel bearings,
2WD . . . . clean/repack **GC**
Tighten spindle nut to 12 ft lb, while turning wheel forward. Adjust spindle nut to "just loose" position by hand. Back spindle nut until hole in spindle aligns with slot. Do not back off more than 1/4 turn

---

W Air intake system . . . . . . check for leaks

W Carb. to manifold bolts . . . . torque

W Choke & hoses . . . . check/clean
Check vacuum break

Cooling system . . . . . change coolant **EC**
Flush system, inspect hoses

W EFE system . . . . check **MH**

W EGR system . . . . check

W Fuel cap, tank & lines . . . . inspect

W Fuel filter in carb. inlet . . . . . . replace

W ECS canister & hoses . . . . inspect

W Idle mixture 6-cyl. 292 eng. . . . . . adjust
California only

W Ignition timing some models . . . . adjust
Inspect distributor cap and rotor; clean or replace

EVERY 24 MI—38.4 KM
Standard differential . . . . change lubricant

Transmission, automatic . . . . change fluid
Replace filter

W PCV valve & filter . . . . replace
Blow out or replace system hoses

W Idle speed . . . . adjust

EVERY 30 MI—50 KM
Clutch cross shaft . . . . **0-1 fitting LB**

W Air cleaner
and PCV filter . . . . replace

Clutch fork ball stud . . . . lubricate **GC**
Some models — lubricate sparingly

W PCV system . . . . check

W Vacuum advance system
& hoses . . . . inspect

W Spark plugs . . . . replace
Engines using unleaded fuel

EVERY 48 MO/48 MI—76.8 KM
Engine governor . . . . inspect/test

EVERY 60 MI—100 KM
Idle mixture 6-cyl. . . . . adjust

Ignition wires . . . . clean/inspect

W PCV system . . . . inspect

SEVERE SERVICE
W Crankcase—Change oil every 3 mi (5 km). Change filter every oil change

Differential—Check lubricant every 3 mi (5 km). Change fluid at least every 15 mi (24 km)

EFE system—Check at 3 mi (5 km), then at 12 mi (19.2 km), then at every 12 mi (19.2 km)

W Engine idle speed—Check/adjust every 12 mi (19.2 km)

Fittings—Lubricate every 3 mi (5 km)

Front wheel bearings—Repack every 12 mi (19.2 km)

W Fuel filter—Replace every 12 mi (19.2 km)

Tires—Inspect & rotate first 6 mi (10 km) then every 15 mi (24 km)

Transmission, automatic—Change fluid and filter every 12 mi (19.2 km)

KEY TO LUBRICANTS
See other Chevrolet/GMC Truck charts

CRANKCASE . . . . SG

CAPACITY, Refill:	Liters	Qt
6-cyl. 292 eng.	4.7	5.0
6-cyl. 4.3L	3.8	4.0
8-cyl. 350	3.8	4.0
8-cyl. 454 4V ex. 1988 V30/35	5.7	6.0
8-cyl. 454 others	4.8	5.0

Capacity shown is without filter. When replacing filter, additional oil may be needed

Above 40°F (4°C) . . . . 30†
Above 0°F (−18°C) 10W-30*
Below 60°F (16°C) 5W-30
*Preferred
†May be used when other recommended viscosities are unavailable

TRANSMISSION, Automatic . . . . AF

CAPACITY, Initial Refill*:	Liters	Qt
400 (3L80)	4.1	4.3
700-R4 (4L60)	4.7	5.0

*With the engine at operating temperature, shift transmission through all gears. Let engine slow idle in PARK for 3 minutes or more. Check fluid level and add fluid as needed

TRANSMISSION, Manual
4-speed:
Top shift, iron case . . . . **GLS**
GM Part No. 12345577
Side shift, side load . . . . **AF**
Top shift, aluminum case, 1988 . . . **GLS**
GM Part No. 1052931

CAPACITY, Refill:	Liters	Pt
4-speed:		
Top shift, iron case	4.0	8.4
Side shift, side load	4.0	8.4
Top shift, aluminum case	1.8	3.8

TRANSFER CASE . . . . AF

CAPACITY, Refill:	Liters	Pt
NP205	2.4*	5.0*
NP208	4.8	10.8
NP231	1.2	2.5
NP241	2.1	4.5
BW1370	1.5	3.1

To identify, see tag on case
*Fill to one inch (25 mm) of fill plug

DIFFERENTIAL
Conventional
& locking 80W, 80W-90* **GL-5**
*For vehicles normally operated in Canada, 80W only

CAPACITY, Refill:	Liters	Pt
Front:		
K-30/35	2.1	4.6
V-30/35	2.8	6.0
Rear:		
Chev. 8½" ring gear . . .	2.0	4.2
Chev. 9½" ring gear . . .	2.6	5.5
Dana 9¾" ring gear . . .	2.8	6.0
Dana 10½" ring gear . . .	3.4	7.2
Rockwell 12" ring gear . .	6.6	14.0

SERVICE AT TIME OR MILEAGE—WHICHEVER OCCURS FIRST

CTTPM20

Perform the following maintenance services at the intervals indicated to keep the vehicle warranties in effect

W SERVICE TO MAINTAIN EMISSION WARRANTY

1988, All TBI engines. 1989: All 2.5L, 2.8L, 4.3L, 5.0L; 5.7L under 8501 GVWR ex. G-Van 5.7L under 10001 GVWR G-Van; 7.4L TBI. 1990-91: All 2.5L, 2.8L, 5.0L; 4.3L ex. P-model; 5.7L (ex. G 31303, and P-model) under 8501 GVWR, 7.4L 454 SuperSport. 1992 4.3L ex. P-Model; 5.0L, 5.7L under 8501 GVWR, 7.4L SuperSport.

MI—MILES IN THOUSANDS
KM—KILOMETERS IN THOUSANDS

EVERY 6 MONTHS
Brake master cylinder . . . . . check level **HB**

Clutch pedal free travel . . . . . . check/adjust

Power steering or hydro-boost
  reservoir . . . . check level **PS**

FIRST 12 MO/7.5 MI—12.5 KM
Differential, locking . . . . change fluid

EVERY 12 MO/7.5 MI—12 KM
Brakes & power
  steering . . . . inspect hoses/pads
Inspect drum brake lining, check parking brake

W Crankcase . . . . change oil

W Oil filter . . . . replace
At first oil change, then every other oil change

W Differential, front & rear . . . . . check level

W Exhaust system . . . . inspect

W Choke & hoses . . . . check/clean
1988-90 some

Parking brake cable guides . . . . . . coat **LB**

Propeller shaft . . . . lubricate **LB**
Lubricate U-joints & splines

Shift linkage . . . . coat **LB**
With floor shift, coat lever contact faces

W Front suspension &
  steering . . . . lubricate **LB**

Throttle linkage . . . . inspect
Check for damage or binding

Tires . . . . check/rotate
1988-89 every 7.5 mi (24 km)
1990-92 initially, then every 15 mi (24 km)

Transfer case . . . . check level
Check vent hose

W Transmission, automatic . . . . check level

Universal CV joint, 4WD . . . . . . **fitting LB**

W Cooling system . . . . check level **EC**

Body . . . . lubricate
Flush underbody every spring

EVERY 12 MO/15 MI—24 KM
W Cooling system . . inspect, tighten hoses
Wash radiator filler neck & cap; pressure test system.
Clean exterior or radiator core & air conditioning condenser. Service coolant as needed

EVERY 24 MI—40 KM
Transmission,
  automatic . . . . change filter & fluid **AF**
Trucks over 8600 GVWR

EVERY 30 MI—48 KM
Clutch cross shaft . . . . 0-1 fitting **LB**

Clutch fork ball stud . . . . lubricate **GC**
Some models — lubricate sparingly

W Front wheel bearings,
  2WD . . . . clean/repack **GC**
Tighten spindle nut to 12 ft lb while turning wheel forward by hand. Adjust spindle nut to ''just loose'' position by hand. Then back off spindle nut until hole in spindle aligns with slot in nut. Do not back off nut more than 1/4 turn

Transmission,
  automatic . . . . . . change filter & fluid **AF**
Trucks over 8600 GVWR

W Air cleaner element . . . . replace

W ECS canister & hoses
  ex. Calif. . . . . inspect

W EGR system . . . . inspect

W Spark plugs . . . . replace

W Vacuum advance system . . . . . . inspect
Service every 15 mi (24 km) thereafter

EVERY 24 MO/30 MI—48 KM
W Cooling system . . . . . change coolant **EC**
Flush system; inspect hoses

EVERY 60 MI—100 KM
W Engine drive belts . . . . inspect/adjust

W Engine idle speed . . . . check/adjust
1988-90

W Engine timing . . . . check
Some. Inspect cap & rotor

EVRV . . . . inspect

W Fuel filter . . . . replace

W Fuel tank, cap & lines . . . . inspect

W PCV system . . . . inspect
1989-91

SEVERE SERVICE
W Crankcase—Change oil and filter every 3 mi (5 km). Also lubricate chassis

W Differential—Check lubricant every 3 mi (5 km). Change lubricant fluid at least every 15 mi (24 km)

Front wheel bearings—Repack every 15 mi (24 km) or whenever brakes are relined

W Fuel filter—Replace every 30 mi (50 km)

W Fuel tank, cap & lines—Inspect every 30 mi (50 km)

W Transmission, automatic—Change fluid every 15 mi (24 km)

Tires & Brake systems—Inspect & rotate tires first 6 mi (10 km) then every 15 mi (24 km)

KEY TO LUBRICANTS
See other Chevrolet/GMC Truck charts

CRANKCASE . . . . SG

CAPACITY, Refill:	Liters	Qt
7.4L 4V ex. 1988 V30/35 . .	5.7	6.0
7.4L others 1988-90	4.8	5.0
7.4L 1991-92	5.7	6.0
All others	3.8	4.0

Capacity shown is without filter. When replacing filter, additional oil may be needed

7.4L:
Above 40°F (4°C) . . . . 30†
Above 0°F (–18°C) . . . . 10W-30 *
Below 60°F (16°C) 5W-30

Others:
Above 40°F (4°C) . . . . 30†
Above 0°F (–18°C) 10W-30
All temperatures . . . . 5W-30 *
* Preferred
†May be used only when other recommended viscosities are not available

TRANSMISSION, Automatic . . . . AF

CAPACITY, Initial Refill*:	Liters	Qt
400 (3L80)	4.1	4.3
475 (3L80-HD)	4.1	4.3
700-R4 (4L60), 4L80E	4.7	5.0

* With the engine at operating temperature, shift transmission through all gears. Let engine slow idle in PARK for 3 minutes or more. Check fluid level and add fluid as needed

TRANSMISSION, Manual
4-speed:
Top shift, iron case, 1988-91 . . . . . **GLS**
GM Part No. 12345577
Side shift, side load, 1988-89 . . . . . . **AF**
Top shift, aluminum case, 1988 . . . **GLS**
GM Part No. 1052931
5-speed: Sectional case . . . . **GLS**
GM Part No. 12345349, 1988-92; or
GM Part No. 1052931, 1988-91
Top shift, iron case, 1991-92 . . . . . **GLS**
GM Part No. 12345871

CAPACITY, Refill:	Liters	Pt
4-speed:		
Top shift, iron case	4.0	8.4
Side shift, side load	4.0	8.4
Top shift, aluminum case . .	1.8	3.8
5-speed: Sectional case . . .	1.9	4.0
Top shift, iron case	3.8	8.0

* Approximate, fill to level of fill plug

TRANSFER CASE (4 × 4) . . . . AF

CAPACITY, Refill:	Liters	Pt
NP205	2.4*	5.0*
NP208	4.8	10.0
NP231	1.0	2.2
NP241	2.1	4.5
BW1370, 4401	1.5	3.1
BW4470	3.1	6.5

To identify, see tag on case
* Fill to within one inch (25 mm) of fill plug

DIFFERENTIAL
Conventional &
  locking 80W, 80W-90* **GL-5**
* For vehicles normally operated in Canada, 80W only

CAPACITY, Refill:		
	Liters	Pt
Front:		
K-10/15, -20/25 1988-92 .	1.7	3.6
K-30/35 1988-92	2.1	4.6
V-10/15, -20/25 1988-89 .	1.9	4.0
V-30/35 1988-89	2.8	6.0
V-10/15, -20/25 1990-91 .	1.7	3.6
V-30/35, 1990-91	2.1	4.6
Rear:		
Chev. 8¹/₂″ ring gear . . .	2.0	4.2
Chev. 9¹/₂″ ring gear . . .	2.6	5.5
Dana 9³/₄″ ring gear . . .	2.6	5.5
10¹/₂″ ring gear:		
Chev.	3.4	7.2
Dana	2.6	5.5
Rockwell 12″ ring gear . .	6.6	14.0

CHEVROLET/GMC TRUCKS
1988-92 All Diesel Models

SERVICE AT TIME OR MILEAGE—WHICHEVER OCCURS FIRST

CTTPM21   CTTPM21

Perform the following maintenance services at the intervals indicated to keep the vehicle warranties in effect

W SERVICE TO MAINTAIN EMISSION WARRANTY

MI—MILES IN THOUSANDS
KM—KILOMETERS IN THOUSANDS

FIRST 12 MO/5 MI—8 KM
Locking differentials . . . . change lubricant

FIRST 5 MI—8 KM
W Engine idle speed . . . . check/adjust

FIRST 25 MI — 40 KM
EGR system 6.2L w/light
   duty emissions . . . . check
Then at 45 mi (72 km), 60 mi (96 km), then every 15 mi (40 km)

EVERY 7.5 MI—12 KM
Tires . . . . inspect/rotate
Then every 15 mi (25 km)

EVERY 6 MONTHS
Brake master cylinder . . . . check level **HB**
1988-89

Power steering . . . . check level **PS**
1988-89

Clutch system . . . . check/adjust

1988, EVERY 5 MI—8 KM
1989-92, EVERY 12 MO/5 MI—8 KM
Brake system . . . . inspect
Pads, drum linings, hoses

Brake master cylinders . . . check level **HB**
1990-92

Power steering . . . . check level **PS**
1990-92

Differentials . . . . check level

W Crankcase . . . . change oil

W Oil filter . . . . replace

Exhaust system . . . . inspect

Four-wheel drive . . . . inspect
Check transfer case & axle fluid levels

Propeller shaft(s) . . . . lubricate **LB**
Lubricate U-joints & splines

Parking brake cable guides . . lubricate **LB**

Front suspension & steering . lubricate **LB**

Transmission, automatic . . . . . check level

Transmission, manual . . . . . . check level

Transmission, manual
  W/OD . . . . lubricate shifter **LB**
Sideloaded transmission with grease fitting

Throttle linkage . . . . inspect

EVERY 10 MI—16 KM
Air intake system . . . . inspect

Underhood shields &
  insulation . . . . check condition

EVERY 12 MO/10 MI—16 KM
Thermostatically controlled
  fan . . . . check operation

EVERY 12 MONTHS
Parking brake . . . . check
Check operation

W Cooling
  system . . . . inspect & tighten hoses
Wash radiator filler neck & cap; pressure test system.
Clean exterior of radiator core

EVERY 15 MI—24 KM
W Air cleaner element . . . . replace
6.2L code J, 6.5L code F

EVERY 30 MO/24 MI—40 KM
W Cooling system . . . . change coolant **EC**
Flush system, inspect hoses. Replace hoses if checked, swollen or rotted

EVERY 24 MI—40 KM
Transmission, automatic . . . . change fluid
Models over 8600 lb GVW

EVERY 25 MI—40 KM
Standard diffs. . . . . change lubricant
Of 8600 lb GVW & above

EVERY 30 MI—48 KM
Clutch crankshaft . . . . lubricate **LB**
If present

Clutch fork ball stud . . . . **GC**
Some

Front wheel bearings
  6.2L 2WD . . . . clean/repack **GC**
Tighten spindle nut to 12 ft lb while turning wheel forward. Adjust spindle nut to "just loose" position by hand. Back off nut until hole in spindle aligns with slot. Do not back off more than 1/4 turn

W Air cleaner element
  code C eng. . . . . replace

W Crankcase ventilation
  system . . . . inspect
Inspect rubber fittings, hoses & regulator

W Engine idle speed . . . . adjust

W Fuel filter . . . . replace

Transmission, automatic . . . . change fluid
Vehicles under 8600 lb GVW

EVERY 60 MI — 96 KM
W Exhaust pressure regulator
  valve . . . . check operation

W CDRV system . . . . check

Drive belts . . . . inspect/adjust
Replace as needed

SEVERE SERVICE
W Crankcase—Change oil & filter every 3 mo/2.5 mi (4 km)

Chassis — Lubricate every 2.5 mi (4 km)

Differential—Change lubricant every 15 mi (24 km); more often for heavy-duty or off-road service

W Fittings—Lubricate every 3 mo/2.5 mi (4 km)

Tires—Inspect & rotate first 6 mi (10 km) then every 15 mi (25 km)

Transmission, automatic—Change fluid every: Models over 8600 lb GVW, 12 mi (20 km); Models under 8600 lb GVW, 15 mi (24 km)

Wheel bearings—Repack every 15 mi (24 km)

KEY TO LUBRICANTS
See other Chevrolet/GMC Truck charts

CRANKCASE . . . . SG/CE

CAPACITY, Refill*:	Liters	Qt
6.2L, 6.5L	6.6	7.0

*Includes filter

1988-89
Above 32°F (0°C) 30*
Above 0°F (–18°C) 15W-40
Below 60°F (16°C) 10W-30
1990-92
Above 0°F (–18°C) 15W-40*
Above 32°F (0°C) 30
Below 60°F (16°C) 10W-30
*Preferred

TRANSMISSION, Automatic . . . . AF

CAPACITY, Initial Refill*:	Liters	Qt
350	3.3	3.5
400 (3L80)	4.1	4.3
700-R4 (4L60), 4L80E	4.7	5.0

* Add specified quantity. With the engine at operating temperature, shift transmission through all gears. Let engine slow idle in PARK for 3 minutes or more. Check fluid level and add fluid as needed

TRANSMISSION, Manual
4-speed:
  Top shift, iron case 1988-91 . . . . . . **GLS**
  GM Part No. 12345577
  Side shift, side load 1988-89 . . . . **AF**
5-speed:
  Top shift, iron case 1991-92 . . . . . . **GLS**
  GM Part No. 12345871

CAPACITY, Refill:	Liters	Pt
4-speed:		
Top shift, iron case	4.0	8.4
Side shift, side load	4.0	8.4
5-speed:		
Top shift, iron case	3.8	8.0

TRANSFER CASE . . . . AF

CAPACITY, Refill:	Liters	Pt
NP205	2.4*	5.0*
NP208	4.8	10.0
NP241	2.1	4.5
BW1370, 4401	1.5	3.1
BW4470	3.1	6.5

To identify, see tag on case
*Fill to within one inch (25 mm) below fill plug

DIFFERENTIAL
Standard & locking . . 80W, 80W-90* **GL-5**
*For vehicles normally operated in Canada, 80W only

CAPACITY, Refill:	Liters	Pt
Front:		
K-10/15, -20/25, 1988-92	1.7	3.6
K-30/35, 1988-92	2.1	4.6
V-10/15, -20/25, 1988-89	1.9	4.0
V-30/35, 1988-89	2.8	6.0
V-10/15-20/25, 1990-91	1.7	3.6
V-30/35, 1990-91	2.1	4.6
Rear:		
Chev. 8½" ring gear	2.0	4.2
Chev. 9½" ring gear	2.6	5.5
Chev. 10½" ring gear	3.4	7.2
Dana 9¾" ring gear	2.6	5.5
Dana 10½" ring gear	2.6	5.5
Rockwell 12" ring gear	6.6	14.0

SERVICE AT TIME OR MILEAGE—WHICHEVER OCCURS FIRST

CTTPM23   CTTPM23

Perform the following maintenance services at the intervals indicated to keep the vehicle warranties in effect

W   SERVICE TO MAINTAIN EMISSION WARRANTY

1990, 4.3L P-models, all models with 5.7L, over 8500 GVWR, 7.4L all except 454 Super Sport; 1991, 4.3L P-models, 5.7 P-models, high cube, and cutaway van, 4.3L in models over 9500 GVWR, 5.7L in models over 8500 GVWR, 7.4L all except 454 Super Sport

MI—MILES IN THOUSANDS
KM—KILOMETERS IN THOUSANDS

FIRST 6 MO
W Engine idle speed . . . . adjust
1990-91

EVERY 6 MONTHS
Brake master cylinder . . . . check level **HB**

Clutch pedal free travel . . . . . check/adjust

Power steering or hydro-boost
    reservoir . . . . check level **PS**

Transmission, automatic . . . . . check level
At operating temperature, engine idling in PARK

EVERY 7.5 MI—12 KM
Tires . . . . inspect/rotate
Initial service, 15 mi (24 km)

FIRST 12 MO/7.5 MI—12.5 KM
Locking differential . . . . . change lubricant

EVERY 12 MO/6 MI—10 KM
Brakes & power
    steering . . . . inspect hoses/pads
Inspect drum brake lining, check parking brake

W Crankcase . . . . change oil

W Oil filter . . . . replace
At first oil change, then every other, but at least every 12 mo.

W Standard differentials . . . . . check level

Engine drive belts . . . . inspect/adjust

W Exhaust system . . . . inspect

Parking brake cable guides . . . . . . coat **LB**

Shift linkage . . . . coat **LB**
With floor shift, coat lever contact faces

Front suspension & steering . lubricate **LB**

Throttle linkage . . . . inspect
Check for damage or binding

Transfer case . . . . check level
Check vent hose

W Transmission, manual . . . . . check level

Propeller shaft . . . . lubricate **LB**
Lubricate U-joints/splines

Universal CV joint, 4WD . . . . **fitting LB**

Body . . . . lubricate
Flush underbody every spring

EVERY 12 MO/12 MI—19.2 KM
W Accessory drive belts . . . . inspect

W Thermostatically controlled fan . . . . test

W Throttle return control system
    & hoses . . . . check/inspect

EVERY 12 MI/19.2 KM
Eng. shield & insulation . . . . inspect

W Manifold heat valve . . . . check **MH**

W Spark plugs . . . . replace
1990 engines using leaded fuel

EVERY 24 MO/24 MI—38.4 KM
W Front wheel bearings,
     2WD . . . . clean/repack **GC**
Tighten spindle nut to 12 ft lb, while turning wheel forward. Adjust spindle nut to ''just loose'' position by hand. Back spindle nut until hole in spindle aligns with slot. Do not back off more than 1/4 turn

W Air intake system . . . . . . check for leaks

Cooling system . . . . . change coolant **EC**
Flush system, inspect hoses

W EGR system . . . . check
1990

W Fuel cap, tank & lines . . . . inspect

W Fuel filter . . . . replace

W ECS canister & hoses . . . . inspect

W Ignition timing, some models . . . . adjust
Inspect distributor cap and rotor; clean or replace

EVERY 24 MI—38.4 KM
Standard differential . . . . change lubricant

Transmission, automatic . . . . change fluid
Replace filter

W PCV valve & filter . . . . replace

W Engine idle speed . . . . adjust
1990-91

EVERY 27 MI—45 KM
W Spark plugs . . . . replace
1991-92

EVERY 30 MI—50 KM
Clutch cross shaft . . . . **0-1 fitting LB**

W Air cleaner
    and PCV filter . . . . replace

Clutch fork ball stud . . . . lubricate **GC**
Some models — lubricate sparingly

EVERY 48 MO/48 MI—76.8 KM
Engine governor . . . . inspect/test

EVERY 60 MI—100 KM
W Ignition wires . . . . clean/inspect

W EGR system . . . . inspect
1991-92

SEVERE SERVICE
W Crankcase—Change oil every 3 mi (5 km). Change filter every oil change

W Differential—Check lubricant every 3 mi (5 km). Change fluid at least every 15 mi (24 km)

EFE system—Check at 3 mi (5 km), then at 12 mi (19.2 km), then at every 12 mi (19.2 km)

W Fittings—Lubricate every 3 mi (5 km)

Front wheel bearings—Repack every 12 mi (19.2 km)

W Fuel filter—Replace every 12 mi (19.2 km)

Tires—Inspect & rotate first 6 mi (10 km) then every 15 mi (24 km)

W Transmission, automatic—Change fluid and filter every 12 mi (19.2 km)

KEY TO LUBRICANTS
See other Chevrolet/GMC Truck charts

CRANKCASE . . . . SG

CAPACITY, Refill:	Liters	Qt
6-cyl. 4.3L	3.8	4.0
8-cyl. 5.7L	3.8	4.0
8-cyl. 7.4L: 1990	4.8	5.0
1991-92	5.8	6.0

Capacity shown is without filter. When replacing filter, additional oil may be needed

Above 40°F (4°C) . . . . 30†
Above 0°F (–18°C) 10W-30*
Below 60°F (16°C) 5W-30
* Preferred
†May be used when other recommended viscosities are unavailable

TRANSMISSION, Automatic . . . . AF

CAPACITY, Initial Refill*:	Liters	Qt
350	3.3	3.5
400 (3L80)	4.1	4.3
475 (3L80-HD)	4.1	4.3
700-R4 (4L60), 4L80E	4.7	5.0

*With the engine at operating temperature, shift transmission through all gears. Let engine slow idle in PARK for 3 minutes or more. Check fluid level and add fluid as needed

TRANSMISSION, Manual
4-speed:
    Top shift, iron case, 1990-91 . . . . . **GLS**
GM Part No. 12345577
5-speed: Sectional case . . . . **GLS**
GM Part No. 12345349, 1988-92; or
GM Part No. 1052931, 1988-91
    Top shift iron case, 1991-92 . . . . . . **GLS**
GM Part No. 12345871

CAPACITY, Refill:	Liters	Pt
4-speed:		
Top shift, iron case	4.0	8.4
5-speed: Sectional case . . .	1.9*	4.0*
Top shift iron case	3.8	8.0

* Approximate, fill to level of fill plug

TRANSFER CASE . . . . AF

CAPACITY, Refill:	Liters	Pt
NP205	2.4*	5.0*
NP241	2.1	4.5
BW1370, 4401	1.5	3.1
BW4470	3.1	6.5

To identify, see tag on case
* Fill to one inch (25 mm) of fill plug

DIFFERENTIAL
Conventional
    & locking 80W, 80W-90* **GL-5**
*For vehicles normally operated in Canada, 80W only

CAPACITY, Refill:	Liters	Pt
Front	2.1	4.6
Rear:		
Chev. 8½" ring gear . . .	2.0	4.2
Chev. 9½" ring gear . . .	2.6	5.5
Dana 9¾" ring gear . . .	2.8	6.0
Dana 10½" ring gear . .	3.4	7.2
Rockwell 12" ring gear . .	6.6	14.0

SERVICE AT TIME OR MILEAGE—WHICHEVER OCCURS FIRST

CTTPM22 CTTPM22

Perform the following maintenance services at the intervals indicated to keep the vehicle warranties in effect

W   SERVICE TO MAINTAIN EMISSION WARRANTY

MI—MILES IN THOUSANDS
KM—KILOMETERS IN THOUSANDS

FIRST 7.5 MI—12.5 KM
W T.B.I. mounting bolts/nuts . . . . . . torque
3.1L engine code D

EVERY 6 MONTHS
Brake master cylinder . . . . check level **HB**

Brakes & power
   steering . . . . inspect hoses/pads
Check parking brake

Exhaust system . . . . inspect

Power steering reservoir . . check level **PS**

EVERY 12 MO/7.5 MI—12 KM
W Crankcase . . . . change oil

W Oil filter . . . . replace
At first oil change, then every other, but at least every
12 mo

Exhaust system . . . . inspect

Front suspension . . . . **4 fittings LB**

Parking brake cable guides . . . . . . coat **LB**
Do not lubricate brake cables

Brake systems . . . . inspect

Shift linkage . . . . lubricate **MO**

Suspension & steering . . . . inspect

Throttle linkage . . . . inspect
Check with cold engine

Front drive axle boots . . . . inspect

Tires . . . . check/rotate
Initial service, then every 15 mi (24 km)

Transaxle, automatic . . . . check level

W Cooling system . . . . . . check level **EC**

Body . . . . lubricate
Flush underbody every spring

EVERY 12 MO/15 MI—24 KM
W Cooling system . . inspect, tighten hoses
Wash radiator filler neck & cap; pressure test system.
Clean exterior of radiator core & air conditioning con-
denser. Service coolant as needed

EVERY 30 MI — 48 KM
W Fuel tank, cap & lines . . . . inspect

W Fuel filter . . . . replace
1990-91

W Crankcase air filter . . . . replace

W Ignition timing 1992 3.1L . . . . check
Inspect distributor cap & spark plug wires

EGR system . . . . inspect
3.1L engine code D

W Spark plugs . . . . replace

W Spark plug wires . . . . inspect
1992

Thermostatically controlled
   air cleaner . . . . inspect
3.1L engine code D

EVERY 24 MO/30 MI—48 KM
W Cooling system . . . . change coolant **EC**
Flush system; inspect hoses

W Engine drive belts . . . . inspect
1992

EVERY 30 MO/30 MI — 50 KM
W Air cleaner element . . . . replace

EVERY 60 MI—100 KM
EVRV system . . . . check
3.1L engine code D

W Engine drive belts . . . . . . inspect/adjust
1990-91

W Ignition timing 1990-91 3.1L . . . . . check
Inspect distributor cap & ign. wires; clean or replace

W PCV system . . . . check

Spark plug wires . . . . inspect
1990-91

EVERY 100 MI — 160 KM
Transaxle, automatic . . . . change fluid
Replace filter

SEVERE SERVICE
W Crankcase—Change oil and filter every 3
mo/3 mi (5 km)

Chassis—Lubricate every 12 mo/3 mi (5 km)

W Transaxle, automatic—Change fluid and
filter every 15 mi (24 km)

KEY TO LUBRICANTS

AF	DEXRON®-IIE Automatic Transmission Fluid
EC	Ethylene Glycol Coolant Mix with water to –34°F (–37°C) protection
HB	Hydraulic Brake Fluid, DOT 3
LB	Chassis Grease, NLGI Category LB
MO	Motor Oil
PS	Power Steering Fluid GM Part No. 1050017; Canada, 992646
SG	Motor Oil, API Service SG

CRANKCASE . . . . **SG**
CAPACITY, Refill: Liters   Qt
All 3.8   4.0
Capacity shown is without filter. When replacing filter, ad-
ditional oil may be needed
3.1L VIN code D
Above 40°F (4°C) . . . . 30‡
Above 0°F (–18°C) 10W-30
All temperatures 5W-30*
3.8L VIN code D
Above 40°F (4°C) . . . . 30‡
Above 0°F (–18°C) 10W-30*
Below 60°F (16°C) 5W-30
*Preferred
‡May be used when other recommended viscosities are
unavailable

TRANSMISSION/TRANSAXLE,
   Automatic . . . . **AF**
CAPACITY, Initial Refill*:   Liters   Qt
3T40 (3-speed) 3.8   4.0
4T60-E (4-speed) 5.7   6.0
*With the engine at operating temperature, shift transmis-
sion through all gears. Let engine slow idle in PARK for 3
minutes or more. Check fluid level and add fluid as needed

CHRYSLER, DODGE, PLYMOUTH
1983-92 All Models Including FWD Vans
Except Challenger, Colt, Conquest, Sapporo, Vista; 1990-92 Laser, Stealth

SERVICE LOCATIONS — ENGINE AND CHASSIS

HOOD RELEASE: Inside

① Crankcase dipstick
② Transmission dipstick
③ Brake fluid reservoir
④ Clutch fluid reservoir
⑤ Oil fill cap
⑥ Power steering reservoir
⑦ Air filter
⑧ Fuel filter
⑨ Oil filter
⑩ PCV filter
⑪ EGR valve
⑫ Oxygen sensor
⑬ PCV valve

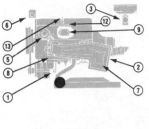

**1983-86
1.6L (97)**

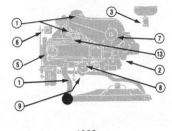

**1983
1.7L (105)**

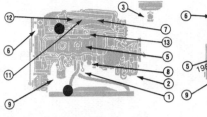

**1983-87
2.2L (135) 2V**

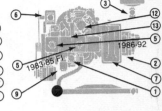

**1983-92
2.2L (135) FI**

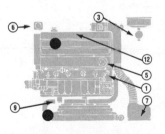

1989-92 2.2L 16V Turbo

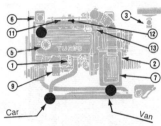

**1984-92
2.2L (135) & 2.5L Turbo
ex. 16V**

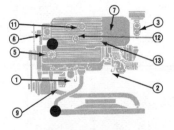

**1986-92
2.5L (153) FI**

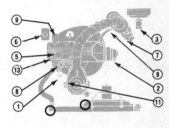

**1983-87
2.6L (156)**

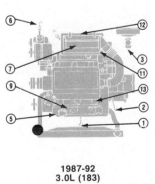

**1987-92
3.0L (183)**

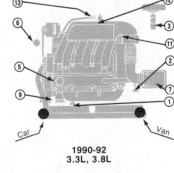

**1990-92
3.3L, 3.8L**

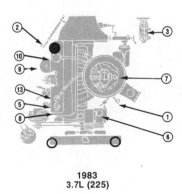

**1983
3.7L (225)**

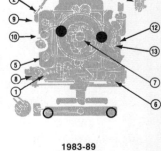

**1983-89
5.2L (318)**

● Cooling system drain   ○ Cooling system drain, some models

CHRYSLER, DODGE, PLYMOUTH
1983-92 All Models Including FWD Vans
Except Challenger, Colt, Conquest, Sapporo, Vista; 1990-92 Laser, Stealth

SERVICE LOCATIONS — ENGINE AND CHASSIS

CRDP-2

CRDP-2

2-4 FITTINGS

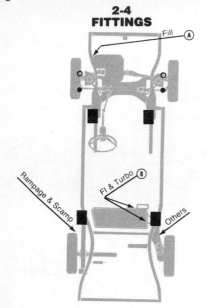

Dodge: Omni, 024,
FWD Charger, De Tomaso, Rampage
Plymouth: Horizon,
Scamp, Turismo

4 FITTINGS

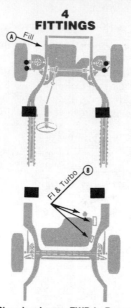

Chrysler: Laser, FWD LeBaron,
Limousine, E Class, Maserati TC,
FWD New Yorker
Dodge: Aries, 400, 600, Daytona,
Dynasty, Lancer, Shadow, Spirit
Plymouth: Acclaim, Reliant,
FWD Caravelle, Sundance
FWD Imperial

2-4 FITTINGS

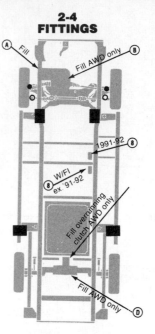

Mini Ram Van,
Caravan, Voyager
1990-92 Chrysler
Town & Country

**0 FITTINGS
0 PLUGS**

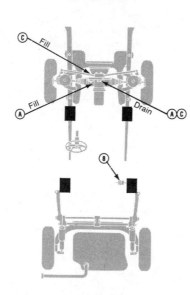

1990-92
Dodge Monaco

9-10 FITTINGS

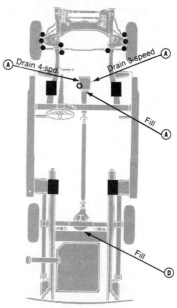

Chrysler: Imperial (1983),
Cordoba (1983),
RWD New Yorker, 5th Ave.,
Newport (1984-89)
Dodge: Diplomat, Mirada
Plymouth:
RWD Caravelle Salon,
Gran Fury

Ⓐ Manual transmission/transaxle,
   drain & fill
Ⓑ Transfer case, drain & fill
Ⓒ Automatic transaxle final drive,
   drain & fill
Ⓓ Differential, drain & fill

⑧ Fuel filter

■ Lift adapter position   • Fitting   ○ Fitting, some models

CAUTION: On front wheel drive vehicles the center of gravity is further forward than on rear wheel drive vehicles. When removing major components from the rear of the vehicle while it is on a hoist, the vehicle must be supported in a manner to prevent it from tipping forward.

CHRYSLER, DODGE, PLYMOUTH
1983 All Models
Except Challenger, Colt, Sapporo

SERVICE AT TIME OR MILEAGE—WHICHEVER OCCURS FIRST

CRPM6   CRPM6

MI—MILES IN THOUSANDS
KM—KILOMETERS IN THOUSANDS

EVERY 12 MO/7.5 MI—12 KM
Brake hoses . . . . check

Crankcase . . . . change oil

Differential . . . . check for leaks

Front suspension &
   steering linkage . . . . . . inspect seals **BJ**

Oil filter . . . . replace
If mileage is less than 7.5 mi (12 km) each 12 mo, replace every oil change; otherwise replace every 24 mo/
15 mi (24 km)

Universal joints . . . . inspect
Replace leaking or damaged joints

Brake master cylinder . . . . check level **HB**
Fill to bottom of split ring

Carburetor, 4-cyl. . . . . clean **PC**
Canadian cars only

Cooling system . . . . check **EC**
Every 12 mo only

Power steering reservoir . . check level **PS**

Steering gear, manual . . check leaks **GL-5**

Transmission, automatic . . . . . check level
Fluid warm, engine idling, 4-cyl. in PARK, others in
NEUTRAL

Body . . . . lubricate

EVERY 15 MI—24 KM
Drive belts . . . . inspect/adjust
Check air pump belts, required for California warranty
every 30 mi (48 km)

EGR system . . . . check
Canadian leaded fuel cars only

Spark plugs . . . . replace
Vehicles w/o catalytic converter only

Valve clearance . . . . check
1.6L, 1.7L, & 2.6L engines only; one time service required for 1.7L engine

EVERY 30 MI—48 KM
Brake linings . . . . inspect
4-cyl., every 22.5 mi (36 km). Replace disc pads when
1/32" thick

Wheel bearings:
   Front ex. 4-cyl.;
    rear 4-cyl. . . . . inspect **WB**
4-cyl., every 22.5 mi (36 km). Clean & repack whenever
brake drums or rotors are removed. To adjust, torque
20-25 ft lb; back off nut to 0 (no preload); finger tighten
nut & install lock nut with pin. End play, .001"-.003"

Air cleaner element . . . . replace
2.6L engines only, others every 52.5 mi (84 km)

Carburetor choke shaft, fast idle cam
   & pivot pin . . . . clean **PC**

Fuel filter 2.2L FI . . . . replace

Spark plugs . . . . replace
Vehicles with catalytic converter only

EVERY 36 MO/30 MI—48 KM
Front suspension & steering
   linkage . . . . **4-9 fittings BJ**
Fill until grease flows out. Do not rupture seals

FIRST 36 MO/52.5 MI—84 KM;
THEN EVERY 24 MO/30 MI—48 KM
Cooling system . . . . . . change coolant **EC**
Flush system

EVERY 52.5 MI—84 KM
Crankcase inlet air cleaner . . . . . . clean/oil
Located in air cleaner or on valve cover

SERVICE AS REQUIRED
Clutch cable 4-cyl. . . . . lubricate **LM**

Tires . . . . inspect/rotate
Lug nut torque, ft lb: 4-cyl., 80; others, 90

Transmission linkage 4-cyl. . . lubricate **LM**
With manual transmission, remove shift unit & replace
grommets, bushings & clip when lubricating

Fuel filter . . . . replace

Fuel vapor canister element . . . . . . replace

PCV valve . . . . replace

SEVERE SERVICE
Crankcase—Change oil every 3 mo/3 mi
(4.8 km). Replace filter every second oil
change

Differential ex. 4-cyl.—Change lubricant
every 36 mi (57.6 km)

Front suspension ball joints—4-cyl., inspect
every 3 mo/3 mi (4.8 km); others, lubricate
every 18 mo/15 mi (24 km)

Front wheel bearings ex. 4-cyl.—Clean and
repack every 9 mi (14 km) or whenever
brake rotors are removed

Manual transaxle—Change fluid & clean
pan magnet every 15 mi (24 km)

Steering linkage—Lubricate every 18 mo/15
mi (24 km)

Rear wheel bearings 4-cyl.—Clean/repack
every 9 mi (14 km), or whenever rear brake
drums are removed

Transmission, automatic—Change fluid
every 15 mi (24 km). Replace filter & adjust
bands at each drain

Universal joints—Inspect every 3 mo/3 mi
(4.8 km)

Air cleaner element—Inspect every 15 mi
(24 km)

KEY TO LUBRICANTS

AF	DEXRON®-II ATF
AP	MOPAR ATF-PLUS
BJ	Suspension Lubricant Chrysler Part No. 4318062; Canada, 2456029
EC	Ethylene Glycol Coolant Mix 50% to 70% with water
GL-4	Gear Oil, API Service GL-4
GL-5	Gear Oil, API Service GL-5
GL-5 ★	Special Lubricant for Sure-Grip Differential Chrysler Part No. 4318059 plus 4 oz. Part No. 4318060
HB	Hydraulic Brake Fluid, DOT 3
LM	Lithium Grease, EP No. 2
PC	Carburetor Cleaner
PS	Power Steering Fluid Chrysler Part No. 4318055; Canada, 2062024
SF	Motor Oil, API Service SF
SG	Motor Oil, API Service SG
WB	Wheel Bearing Grease

CRANKCASE . . . . SF, SG

CAPACITY, Refill:	Liters	Qt
1.6L engine	2.8	3.0
2.6L engine	4.3	4.5
Others	3.8	4.0

Capacity shown is without filter. When replacing filter, additional oil may be needed
Above 20°F (−7°C) 20W-40, 20W-50, 30
20° to 80°F (−7° to 27°C) 20W-20
Above 10°F (−12°C) 15W-40
Above 0°F (−18°C) . . . 10W-30, 10W-40, 10W-50
Below 60°F (16°C) 5W-30, 5W-40
5.2L-4V engines used for maximum performance service:
40, 30, or 20W-40, 20W-50 providing cold starting is satisfactory

TRANSMISSION, Automatic . . . AF†, AP

CAPACITY, Initial Refill*:	Liters	Qt
All	3.8	4.0

*With the engine at operating temperature, shift transmis-
sion through all gears. Check fluid level in PARK and add
fluid as needed
†RWD with lock-up torque converter, if shudder or excess
slippage occurs, use **AP**

TRANSAXLE, Manual
A-460 4-speed, A-465 5-speed . . . **AF, AP**
A-460 transmission is in Omni & Horizon cars when starter
motor is on the firewall side of the engine
A-412 4-speed **GL-4**
Above −10°F (−23°C), 90, 80W-90, 85W-90; −30°
to −10°F (−34° to −23°C), 80W, 80W-90, 85W-90;
below −30°F (−34°C), 75W

CAPACITY, Refill:	Liters	Pt
Omni, Horizon		
w/A-412 trans.	1.4	3.0
Other 4-cyl.		
w/A-460 trans.	1.9	3.8
w/A-465 trans.	2.1	4.6

DIFFERENTIAL
Standard **GL-5**
Sure-Grip . . . . 90 **GL-5 ★**
Above −10°F (−23°C), 90, 80W-90, 85W-90; −30°
to −10°F (−34° to −23°C), 80W, 80W-90; below
−30°F (−34°C), 75W

CAPACITY, Refill:	Liters	Pt
7¼" ring gear w/2½" dia. axle tube†	1.2	2.5
Others w/3" & 3½" dia. axle tubes†	2.1	4.5

†Measured adjacent to differential

SERVICE AT TIME OR MILEAGE—WHICHEVER OCCURS FIRST

CRPM7   CRPM7

MI—MILES IN THOUSANDS
KM—KILOMETERS IN THOUSANDS

TURBO ENGINE, EVERY 6 MO/7.5 MI—12 KM
Crankcase .... change oil
Oil filter .... replace

EVERY 12 MO/7.5 MI—12 KM
Brake hoses .... check

Crankcase .... change oil
Ex. turbo eng.

Differential .... check for leaks
4-cyl., check manual transaxle fluid level

Front suspension &
steering linkage ...... inspect seals **BJ**

Oil filter .... replace
Ex. turbo eng. If mileage is less than 7.5 mi (12 km)
each 12 mo, replace every oil change; otherwise replace every 24 mo/15 mi (24 km)

Universal joints .... inspect
Replace leaking or damaged joints

Brake master cylinder .... check level **HB**
Fill to bottom of split ring

Carburetor or throttle
body .... spray solvent **PC**
4-cyl. Canadian vehicles only. Use aerosol only in Turbo engines

Cooling system .... check **EC**
Every 12 mo only

Power steering reservoir .. check level **PS**

Steering gear, manual .. check leaks **GL-5**

Transmission, automatic ..... check level
Fluid warm, engine idling, 4-cyl. in PARK, others in
NEUTRAL

Body .... lubricate

EVERY 15 MI—24 KM
Drive belts .... inspect/adjust
Check air pump belts, required for California warranty
every 30 mi (48 km)

EGR system .... check
Canadian leaded fuel cars only

Spark plugs .... replace
Vehicles w/o catalytic converter only

Valve clearance .... check
1.6L & 2.6L eng. only

EVERY 30 MI—48 KM
Brake linings .... inspect
4-cyl., every 22.5 mi (36 km). Replace disc pads when
1/32″ above rivet head or backing plate

Wheel bearings:
Front ex. 4-cyl.;
rear 4-cyl. .... inspect **WB**
4-cyl. every 22.5 mi (36 km). Clean and repack whenever brake drums or rotors are removed. To adjust,
torque 20-25 ft lb; back off nut 1/4 turn then finger tight-
en nut & install lock nut with pin. End play, .001″-.003″

Air cleaner element .... replace
2.6L eng. only

Carburetor choke shaft, fast idle cam
& pivot pin .... clean **PC**

Spark plugs .... replace
Vehicles with catalytic converter only

EVERY 36 MO/30 MI—48 KM
Front suspension & steering
linkage .... 4-9 fittings **BJ**
Fill until grease flows out. Do not rupture seals

FIRST 36 MO/52.5 MI—84 KM; THEN EVERY 24 MO/30 MI—48 KM
Cooling system ...... change coolant **EC**
Flush system

EVERY 52.5 MI—84 KM
Air cleaner element .... replace
1.6L & 2.6L eng. only

Crankcase inlet air cleaner ...... clean/oil
Located in air cleaner or on valve cover

Fuel filter .... replace
Fuel injection & turbocharged engines

SERVICE AS REQUIRED
Clutch cable 4-cyl. .... lubricate **LM**

Tires .... inspect/rotate
Lug nut torque, ft lb; 4-cyl., 95; others, 85

Transmission linkage 4-cyl. .. lubricate **LM**
With manual transmission, remove shift unit & replace
grommets, bushings & clip when lubricating

Fuel filter .... replace

Fuel vapor canister element ...... replace

PCV valve .... replace

SEVERE SERVICE
Brake linings—Inspect every 9 mi (14 km)

Crankcase—Change oil every 3 mo/3 mi
(4.8 km). Replace filter every second oil
change ex. with turbocharger at every oil
change

Differential ex. 4-cyl.—Change lubricant
every 36 mi (57.6 km)

Front suspension ball joints—4-cyl., inspect
every 3 mo/3 mi (4.8 km); others, lubricate
every 18 mo/15 mi (24 km)

Front wheel bearings ex. 4-cyl.—Clean and
repack every 9 mi (14 km) or whenever
brake rotors are removed

Manual transaxle—Change fluid & clean
pan magnet every 15 mi (24 km)

Steering linkage—Lubricate every 18 mo/15
mi (24 km)

Rear wheel bearings 4-cyl.—Clean or repack every 9 mi (14 km), or whenever rear
brake drums are removed

Transmission, automatic—Change fluid
every 15 mi (24 km). Replace filter & adjust
bands at each drain

Universal joints—Inspect every 3 mo/3 mi
(4.8 km)

Air cleaner element—Inspect every 15 mi
(24 km)

KEY TO LUBRICANTS

AF	DEXRON®-II ATF
AP	MOPAR ATF-PLUS®
BJ	Suspension Lubricant Chrysler Part No. 4318062; Canada, 2456029
CC	Motor Oil, API Service CC
CD	Motor Oil, API Service CD
EC	Ethylene Glycol Coolant Mix 50% to 70% with water
GL-5	Gear Oil, API Service GL-5
GL-5★	Special Lubricant for Sure-Grip Differential Chrysler Part No. 4318059 plus 4 oz. Part No. 4318060
HB	Hydraulic Brake Fluid, DOT 3
LM	Lithium Grease, EP No. 2
PC	Carburetor Cleaner
PS	Power Steering Fluid Chrysler Part No. 4318055; Canada, 2062024
SF	Motor Oil, API Service SF
SG	Motor Oil, API Service SG
WB	Wheel Bearing Grease

CRANKCASE
Turbo
engine .. **SG, SF/CC, SF/CD*, SG/CD***
Others .. **SF, SG, SF/CC, SF/CD, SG/CD**

CAPACITY, Refill:	Liters	Qt
1.6L engine	2.8	3.0
2.2L Turbo engine	4.8	5.0
2.6L engine	4.3	4.5
Others	3.8	4.0

*Preferred
Capacity shown is without filter. When replacing filter, additional oil may be needed

Above 20°F (–7°C) ... 10W-30, 10W-40, 10W-50, 15W-40, 20W-40, 20W-50, 30	
20° to 80°F (–7° to 27°C) 20W-20	
Above 10°F (–12°C) 15W-40	
Above 0°F (–18°C) ... 10W-30, 10W-40, 10W-50	
Below 60°F (16°C) 5W-30, 5W-40	

5.2L-4V engines used for maximum performance service:
40, 30, or 20W-40, 20W-50 providing cold starting is satisfactory

TRANSMISSION, Automatic ... **AF†, AP**

CAPACITY, Initial Refill*:	Liters	Qt
All	3.8	4.0

*With the engine at operating temperature, shift transmis-
sion through all gears. Check fluid level in PARK and add
fluid as needed
†RWD with lock-up torque converter, if shudder or excess
slippage occurs, use **AP**

TRANSAXLE, Manual .... **AF, AP**

CAPACITY, Refill:	Liters	Pt
4-speed	1.8	4.0
5-speed	2.1	4.6

DIFFERENTIAL
Standard **GL-5**
Sure-Grip .... 90 **GL-5★**
Above –10°F (–23°C), 90, 80W-90, 85W-90; –30°
to –10°F (–34° to –23°C), 80W, 80W-90; below
–30°F (–34°C), 75W

CAPACITY, Refill:	Liters	Pt
7¼″ ring gear w/2½″ dia. axle tube†	1.2	2.5
8¼″ ring gear w/3″ dia. axle tube†	2.1	4.5

†Measured adjacent to differential

CHEK-CHART

CHRYSLER, DODGE, PLYMOUTH
1985 All Models Including FWD Vans
Except Colt, Conquest, Vista

MI—MILES IN THOUSANDS
KM—KILOMETERS IN THOUSANDS

TURBO ENGINE,
EVERY 6 MO/7.5 MI—12 KM
Crankcase . . . . change oil
Oil filter . . . . replace

EVERY 12 MO/7.5 MI—12 KM
Brake hoses . . . . check
Crankcase . . . . change oil
Ex. turbo eng.
Differential . . . . check for leaks
4-cyl., check manual transaxle fluid level
Front suspension &
  steering linkage . . . . . . inspect seals BJ
Oil filter . . . . replace
Ex. turbo eng. If mileage is less than 7.5 mi (12 km)
each 12 mo, replace every oil change; otherwise re-
place every 24 mo/15 mi (24 km)
Universal joints . . . . inspect
Replace leaking or damaged joints
Brake master cylinder . . . . check level HB
Fill to bottom of split ring
Carburetor or throttle
  body . . . . spray solvent PC
4-cyl. Canadian vehicles only. Use aerosol only in Tur-
bo engines
Cooling system . . . . check EC
Every 12 mo only
Power steering reservoir . . check level PS
Steering gear, manual . . check leaks GL-5
Transmission, automatic . . . . . check level
Fluid warm, engine idling, 4-cyl. in PARK, others in
NEUTRAL
Body . . . . lubricate

EVERY 15 MI—24 KM
Drive belts . . . . inspect/adjust
Check air pump belts, required for California warranty
every 30 mi (48 km)
EGR system . . . . check
Canadian leaded fuel cars only
Spark plugs . . . . replace
Vehicles w/o catalytic converter only
Valve clearance . . . . check
1.6L & 2.6L eng. only. FWD Vans, initial service then
every 45 mi (72 km)

EVERY 30 MI—48 KM
Brake linings . . . . inspect
4-cyl., every 22.5 mi (36 km). Replace disc pads when
1/32" above rivet head or backing plate
Wheel bearings:
  Front ex. 4-cyl.;
  rear 4-cyl. . . . . inspect WB
4-cyl., every 22.5 mi (36 km). Clean and repack whenever brake drums or rotors are removed. To adjust,
torque 20-25 ft lb; back off nut 1/4 turn then finger tight-
en nut & install lock nut with pin. End play, .001"-.003"
Air cleaner element . . . . replace
2.2L FWD Vans & all with 2.6L eng. only
Carburetor choke shaft, fast idle cam
  & pivot pin . . . . clean PC
Also check FWD Van carburetor choke heat source
Spark plugs . . . . replace
Vehicles with catalytic converter only

EVERY 36 MO/30 MI—48 KM
Front suspension & steering
  linkage . . . . 4-9 fittings BJ
Fill until grease flows out. Do not rupture seals

FIRST 36 MO/52.5 MI—84 KM;
THEN EVERY 24 MO/30 MI—48 KM
Cooling system . . . . change coolant EC
Flush system

FWD VANS
EVERY 52.5 MI—84 KM
Air injection system . . . . inspect
Fuel tank cap . . . . inspect
Fuel vapor canister(s) . . . . replace
Idle speed . . . . check/adjust
Oxygen sensor . . . . replace
PCV valve . . . . replace
Vacuum & fuel hoses . . . . inspect
Vacuum operated
  emission components . . . . inspect

ALL MODELS
EVERY 52.5 MI—84 KM
Air cleaner element . . . . replace
1.6L & 2.6L eng. only
Crankcase inlet air cleaner . . . . . clean/oil
Located in air cleaner or on valve cover
Fuel filter . . . . replace
Fuel injection & turbocharged engines

FWD VANS
EVERY 60 MI—96 KM
Ignition cables, distributor
  cap & rotor . . . . replace
Check distributor
Ignition timing . . . . check/adjust
Also check 2.2L cam timing

SERVICE AS REQUIRED
Clutch cable 4-cyl. . . . . lubricate LM
Tires . . . . inspect/rotate
Lug nut torque, ft lb; 4-cyl., 95; others, 85
Transmission linkage 4-cyl. . . lubricate LM
With manual transmission, remove shift unit & replace
grommets, bushings & clip when lubricating
Fuel filter . . . . replace
Fuel vapor canister element . . . . . replace
PCV valve . . . . replace

SEVERE SERVICE
Brake linings—Inspect every 9 mi (14 km)
Crankcase—Change oil: Highway, police,
taxi, limousine, all without turbo engine,
every 6 mo/5 mi (8 km); all others, every 3
mo/3 mi (4.8 km). Replace filter every second oil change ex. with turbocharger at
every oil change
Differential ex. 4-cyl.—Change lubricant
every 36 mi (57.6 km)
Front suspension ball joints—4-cyl., inspect
every 3 mo/3 mi (4.8 km); others, lubricate
every 18 mo/15 mi (24 km)
Front wheel bearings ex. 4-cyl.—Clean and
repack every 9 mi (14 km) or whenever
brake rotors are removed
Manual transaxle—Change fluid & clean
pan magnet every 15 mi (24 km)
Steering linkage—Lubricate every 18 mo/15
mi (24 km)
Rear wheel bearings 4-cyl.—Clean or repack every 9 mi (14 km), or whenever rear
brake drums are removed
Transmission, automatic—Change fluid
every 15 mi (24 km). Replace filter & adjust
bands at each drain
Universal joints—Inspect every 3 mo/3 mi
(4.8 km)
Air cleaner element—Inspect every 15 mi
(24 km)

KEY TO LUBRICANTS

AF	DEXRON®-II ATF
AP	MOPAR ATF-PLUS®
BJ	Suspension Lubricant Chrysler Part No. 4318062; Canada, 2456029
CC	Motor Oil, API Service CC
CD	Motor Oil, API Service CD
EC	Ethylene Glycol Coolant Mix 50% to 70% with water
GL-5	Gear oil, API Service GL-5
GL-5★	Special Lubricant for Sure-Grip Differential Chrysler Part No. 4318059 plus 4 oz. Part No. 4318060
HB	Hydraulic Brake Fluid, DOT 3
LM	Lithium Grease, EP No. 2
PC	Carburetor Cleaner
PS	Power Steering Fluid Chrysler Part No. 4318055; Canada, 2062024
SF	Motor Oil, API Service SF
SG	Motor Oil, API Service SG
WB	Wheel Bearing Grease

CRANKCASE
Turbo
  engine . . SG, SF/CC, SF/CD*, SG/CD*
Others . . SF, SG, SF/CC, SF/CD, SG/CD
*Preferred

CAPACITY, Refill:	Liters	Qt
1.6L engine	2.8	3.0
2.2L Turbo engine	4.8	5.0
2.6L engine	4.3	4.5
Others	3.8	4.0

Capacity shown is without filter. When replacing filter, additional oil may be needed
Above 20°F (−7°C) . . 10W-30, 10W-40, 10W-50,
                15W-40, 20W-40, 20W-50, 30
20° to 80°F (−7° to 27°C) 20W-20
Above 10°F (−12°C) 15W-40
Above 0°F (−18°C) . . . 10W-30, 10W-40, 10W-50
Below 16°F (16°C) 5W-30*, 5W-40
Below 90°F (32°C)† 5W-30*, 5W-40
†5.2L-2V engines only
*5W-30 is preferred in 5.2L-2V engines
5.2L-4V engines used for maximum performance service:
40, 30, or 20W-40, 20W-50 providing cold starting is satisfactory

TRANSMISSION, Automatic . . . AF†, AP
CAPACITY, Initial Refill*: Liters Qt
All 3.8   4.0
*With the engine at operating temperature, shift transmis-
sion through all gears. Check fluid level in PARK and add
fluid as needed
†RWD with lock-up torque converter, if shudder or excess
slippage occurs, use AP

TRANSAXLE, Manual . . . . AF, AP
CAPACITY, Refill:	Liters	Pt
4-speed	1.8	4.0
5-speed	2.1	4.6

DIFFERENTIAL
Standard GL-5
Sure-Grip . . . . 90 GL-5★
Above −10°F (−23°C), 90, 80W-90, 85W-90; −30°
to −10°F (−34° to −23°C), 80W, 80W-90; below
−30°F (−34°C), 75W

CAPACITY, Refill:	Liters	Pt
7¼" ring gear w/2½" dia. axle tube†	1.2	2.5
8¼" ring gear w/3" dia. axle tube†	2.1	4.5

†Measured adjacent to differential

CHRYSLER, DODGE, PLYMOUTH
1986 All Models Including FWD Vans
Except Colt, Conquest, Raider, Vista

SERVICE AT TIME OR MILEAGE—WHICHEVER OCCURS FIRST

CRPM9   CRPM9

MI—MILES IN THOUSANDS
KM—KILOMETERS IN THOUSANDS

TURBO ENGINE,
EVERY 6 MO/7.5 MI—12 KM
Crankcase . . . . change oil
Oil filter . . . . replace

EVERY 12 MO/7.5 MI—12 KM
Brake hoses . . . . check
Crankcase . . . . change oil
Ex. turbo eng.
Differential . . . . check for leaks
FWD, check manual transaxle fluid level
Exhaust manifold heat valve . . . spray **MH**
Front suspension &
  steering linkage . . . . . . inspect seals **BJ**
Oil filter . . . . replace
Ex. turbo eng. If mileage is less than 7.5 mi (12 km)
each 12 mo, replace every oil change; otherwise re-
place every 24 mo/15 mi (24 km)
Universal joints & boots . . . . inspect
Replace leaking or damaged joints
Brake master cylinder . . . . check level **HB**
Fill to bottom of split ring
Cooling system . . . . check **EC**
Every 12 mo only
Power steering reservoir . . check level **PS**
Steering gear, manual . . check leaks **GL-5**
Transmission, automatic . . . . . check level
Body . . . . lubricate

EVERY 15 MI—24 KM
Drive belts . . . . inspect/adjust
Check air pump belts, required for California warranty
every 30 mi (48 km)
EGR system . . . . check
Canadian leaded fuel Vans with 2.6L engine only
Spark plugs . . . . replace
Vehicles w/o catalytic converter only
Valve clearance . . . . check
1.6L & 2.6L eng. only. FWD Vans, initial service then
every 45 mi (72 km)

EVERY 22.5 MI—36 KM
Brake linings . . . . inspect
Replace disc pads when 1/32″ above rivet head or
backing plate
Wheel bearings:
  Front for RWD
  Rear for FWD . . . . inspect **LM**
Clean and repack whenever brake drums or rotors are
removed. To adjust, torque 20-25 ft lb; back off nut 1/4
turn then finger tighten nut & install lock nut with pin.
End play, .001″-.003″

EVERY 30 MI—48 KM
Air cleaner element . . . . replace
FWD Vans only
Carburetor choke shaft, fast idle cam
  & pivot pin . . . . clean **PC**
Check FWD Van choke and exhaust heat source every
24 mo/30 mi (48 km)
Spark plugs . . . . replace
Vehicles with catalytic converter only

EVERY 36 MO/30 MI—48 KM
Front suspension & steering
  linkage . . . . 4-9 fittings **BJ**
Fill until grease flows out. Do not rupture seals

FIRST 36 MO/52.5 MI—84 KM;
THEN EVERY 24 MO/30 MI—48 KM
Cooling system . . . . . . change coolant **EC**
Flush system

FWD VANS
EVERY 52.5 MI—84 KM
Air injection system . . . . inspect
Fuel tank cap . . . . inspect
Fuel vapor canister(s) . . . . replace
Idle mixture, propane . . . . . . check/adjust
Oxygen sensor . . . . replace
At mileage or every 60 mo
PCV valve . . . . replace
At mileage or every 60 mo
Vacuum & fuel hoses . . . . inspect
At mileage or every 24 mo
Vacuum operated
  emission components . . . . inspect

ALL MODELS
EVERY 52.5 MI—84 KM
Crankcase inlet air cleaner . . . . . . clean/oil
Located in air cleaner or on valve cover
Fuel filter . . . . replace
Fuel injection & turbocharged engines

FWD VANS
EVERY 60 MI—96 KM
Ignition cables, distributor
  cap & rotor . . . . replace
Check distributor
Ignition timing . . . . check/adjust

SERVICE AS REQUIRED
Clutch cable FWD . . . . lubricate **LM**
Tires . . . . inspect/rotate
Lug nut torque, ft lb; FWD, 95; others, 85
Transmission linkage FWD . . lubricate **LM**
With manual transmission, remove shift unit & replace
grommets, bushings & clip when lubricating
Fuel filter . . . . replace
Fuel vapor canister element . . . . . . replace
PCV valve . . . . replace

SEVERE SERVICE
Brake lining—Inspect every 9 mi (14 km)
Crankcase—Change oil: Highway, police,
taxi, limousine, all without turbo engine &
when not operating at sustained high speed
driving when above 90°F (32°C), every 6
mo/5 mi (8 km); all others, every 3 mo/3 mi
(4.8 km). Replace filter every second oil
change ex. with turbocharger at every oil
change
Rear differential—Change lubricant every
36 mi (57.6 km)
Front suspension ball joints—FWD, inspect
every 3 mo/3 mi (4.8 km); others, lubricate
every 18 mo/15 mi (24 km)
Front wheel bearings ex. FWD—Clean and
repack every 9 mi (14 km) or whenever
brake rotors are removed
Manual transaxle—Change fluid & clean
pan magnet every 15 mi (24 km)
Steering linkage—Lubricate every 18 mo/15
mi (24 km)
Rear wheel bearings FWD—Clean and repack every 9 mi (14 km), or whenever rear
brake drums are removed
Transmission, automatic—Change fluid
every 15 mi (24 km). Replace filter & adjust
bands at each drain
Universal joints—Inspect every 3 mo/3 mi
(4.8 km)
Air cleaner element—Inspect every 15 mi
(24 km)

KEY TO LUBRICANTS

AF	DEXRON®-II ATF
AP	MOPAR ATF-PLUS®
BJ	Suspension Lubricant Chrysler Part No. 4318062; Canada, 2456029
CC	Motor Oil, API Service CC
CD	Motor Oil, API Service CD
EC	Ethylene Glycol Coolant Mix 50% to 70% with water
GL-5	Gear Oil, API Service GL-5
GL-5★	Special Lubricant for Sure-Grip Differential Chrysler Part No. 4318059 plus 4 oz. Part No. 4318060
HB	Hydraulic Brake Fluid, DOT 3
LM	Lithium Grease, EP No. 2
MH	Manifold Heat Valve Solvent
PC	Carburetor Cleaner
PS	Power Steering Fluid Chrysler Part No. 4318055; Canada, 2062024
SF	Motor Oil, API Service SF
SG	Motor Oil, API Service SG

CRANKCASE
All models . **SG, SF/CC, SF/CD*, SG/CD***
* Preferred with Turbo engine

CAPACITY, Refill:	Liters	Qt
1.6L engine	2.8	3.0
2.2L Turbo engine	4.8	5.0
2.6L engine	4.3	4.5
Others	3.8	4.0

Capacity shown is without filter. When replacing filter, additional oil may be needed
Above 20°F (–7°C) . . 10W-30, 10W-40, 10W-50,
                     15W-40, 20W-40, 20W-50, 30
20° to 80°F (–7° to 27°C) 20W-20
Above 10°F (–12°C) 15W-40
Above 0°F (–18°C) . . . 10W-30, 10W-40, 10W-50
Below 100°F (38°C) 5W-30*, 5W-40
* Not recommended in 4-cyl. Vans, Turbo, or 1.6L above
60°F (16°C) or in 5.2L-4V engines at any temperature
5.2L-4V engines used for maximum performance service:
40, 30, or 20W-40, 20W-50 providing cold starting is satisfactory

TRANSMISSION/TRANSAXLE,
  Automatic . . . . **AF†, AP**

CAPACITY, Initial Refill*:	Liters	Qt
All	3.8	4.0

* With the engine at operating temperature, shift transmission through all gears. Check fluid level in PARK and add
fluid as needed
†RWD with lock-up torque converter, if shudder or excess
slippage occurs, use **AP**

TRANSAXLE, Manual . . . . **AF, AP**

CAPACITY, Refill:	Liters	Pt
4-speed A460	1.8	4.0
5-speed A525	2.1	4.6

REAR DIFFERENTIAL
Standard **GL-5**
Sure-Grip . . . . **90 GL-5★**
Above –10°F (–23°C), 90, 80W-90, 85W-90; –30°
to –10°F (–34° to –23°C), 80W, 80W-90, 85W-90;
below –30°F (–34°C), 75W

CAPACITY, Refill:	Liters	Pt
7¼″ ring gear w/2½″ dia. axle tube†	1.2	2.5
8¼″ ring gear w/3″ dia. axle tube†	2.1	4.5

† Measured adjacent to differential

CHRYSLER, DODGE, PLYMOUTH
1987 All Models Including FWD Vans
Except Colt, Conquest, Raider, Vista

SERVICE AT TIME OR MILEAGE—WHICHEVER OCCURS FIRST

CRPM10   Dodge Monaco, see Eagle/Renault   CRPM10
W   SERVICE TO MAINTAIN EMISSION WARRANTY

MI—MILES IN THOUSANDS
KM—KILOMETERS IN THOUSANDS

TURBO ENGINE, EVERY 6 MO/7.5 MI—12 KM

Crankcase . . . . change oil
Every 3 mo/3 mi (4.8 km) if SF/CD or SG/CD oil is not used

Oil filter . . . . replace
Every other oil change

EVERY 12 MO/7.5 MI—12 KM

Brake hoses . . . . check

Crankcase ex. Turbo . . . . change oil

Differential . . . . check for leaks
FWD, check manual transaxle fluid level

Exhaust manifold heat valve . . . spray **MH**

Front suspension &
  steering linkage . . . . . . inspect seals **BJ**

Oil filter ex. Turbo . . . . replace
Every other oil change ex. if mileage is less than 7.5 mi (12 km) each 12 mo, replace every oil change

Universal joints & boots . . . . inspect
Replace leaking or damaged joints

Brake master cylinder . . . . check level **HB**
Fill to bottom of split ring

Cooling system . . . . check **EC**
Every 12 mo only ex. vans at mileage

Power steering reservoir . . check level **PS**

Steering gear, manual . . check leaks **GL-5**

Transmission, automatic . . . . . check level

Body . . . . lubricate

EVERY 15 MI—24 KM

W Drive belts . . . . inspect/adjust
Check air pump belts, required for California warranty every 30 mi (48 km)

W EGR system . . . . check
Canadian leaded fuel Vans with 2.6L engine only

EVERY 22.5 MI—36 KM

Brake linings . . . . inspect
Replace disc pads when 1/32" above rivet head or backing plate

Wheel bearings:
  Front for RWD
  Rear for FWD . . . . inspect **LM**
Clean and repack whenever brake drums or rotors are removed. To adjust, torque 20-25 ft lb; back off nut 1/4 turn then finger tighten nut & install lock nut with pin. End play, .001"-.003"

W Valve clearance . . . . check
2.6L eng. only. Initial service then every 45 mi (72 km)

EVERY 30 MI—48 KM

W Air cleaner element . . . . replace
FWD Vans only

W Carburetor choke shaft, fast idle cam
  & pivot pin . . . . clean **PC**
Check FWD Van choke heat source every 24 mo/30 mi (48 km)

W PCV filter 2.2L, 2.5L . . . . replace
FWD Vans only

W Spark plugs . . . . replace

EVERY 36 MO/30 MI—48 KM

Front suspension & steering
  linkage . . . . 4-9 fittings **BJ**
Fill until grease flows out. Do not rupture seals

FIRST 36 MO/52.5 MI—84 KM; THEN EVERY 24 MO/30 MI—48 KM

Cooling system . . . . . . change coolant **EC**
Flush system

FWD VANS: EVERY 52.5 MI—84 KM

EGR valve & tube . . . . replace
At mileage or every 60 mo or when indicated by emissions maintenance reminder light if equipped. Also clean passages

Idle mixture, propane . . . . check/adjust

Oxygen sensor . . . . replace
Every 82.5 mi (132 km) or when indicated by emissions maintenance reminder light if equipped

PCV valve . . . . replace
At mileage or every 60 mo

Vacuum operated
  emission components . . . . inspect
Replace for Vans at 60 mi (96 km)

ALL MODELS EVERY 52.5 MI—84 KM

Crankcase inlet air cleaner . . . . . . clean/oil
Located in air cleaner or on valve cover

FWD VANS: EVERY 60 MI—96 KM

Ignition cables . . . . replace

Distributor cap & rotor . . . . replace
Check distributor

Ignition timing . . . . check/adjust

SERVICE AS REQUIRED

Clutch cable FWD . . . . lubricate **LM**

Tires . . . . inspect/rotate
Lug nut torque, ft lb; FWD, 95; others, 85

Transmission linkage FWD . . lubricate **LM**
With manual transmission, remove shift unit & replace grommets, bushings & clip when lubricating

Fuel filter . . . . replace

Fuel vapor canister element . . . . . replace

PCV valve . . . . replace

SEVERE SERVICE

Brake lining—Inspect every 9 mi (14 km)

Crankcase—Change oil: Highway, police, taxi, limousine, all without turbo engine & when not operating at sustained high speed driving when above 90°F (32°C), every 6 mo/5 mi (8 km); all others, every 3 mo/3 mi (4.8 km). Replace filter every second oil change ex. with turbocharger at every oil change

Rear differential—Change lubricant every 36 mi (57.6 km)

Front suspension ball joints—FWD, inspect every 3 mo/3 mi (4.8 km); others, lubricate every 18 mo/15 mi (24 km)

Front wheel bearings ex. FWD—Clean and repack every 9 mi (14 km) or whenever brake rotors are removed

Manual transaxle—Change fluid & clean pan magnet every 15 mi (24 km)

Steering linkage—Lubricate every 18 mo/15 mi (24 km)

Rear wheel bearings FWD—Clean or re-pack every 9 mi (14 km), or whenever rear brake drums are removed

Transmission, automatic—Change fluid every 15 mi (24 km). Replace filter & adjust bands at each drain

Universal joints—Inspect every 3 mo/3 mi (4.8 km)

Air cleaner element—Inspect every 15 mi (24 km)

KEY TO LUBRICANTS

AF	DEXRON®-II ATF
AP	MOPAR ATF-PLUS®
BJ	Suspension Lubricant Chrysler Part No. 4318062; Canada, 2456029
CD	Motor Oil, API Service CD
EC	Ethylene Glycol Coolant Mix 50% to 70% with water
GL-5	Gear Oil, API Service GL-5
GL-5★	Special Lubricant for Sure-Grip Differential Chrysler Part No. 4318059 plus 4 oz. Part No. 4318060
HB	Hydraulic Brake Fluid, DOT 3
LM	Lithium Grease, EP No. 2
MH	Manifold Heat Valve Solvent
PC	Carburetor Cleaner
PS	Power Steering Fluid Chrysler Part No. 4318055; Canada, 2062024
SF	Motor Oil, API Service SF
SG	Motor Oil, API Service SG

CRANKCASE . . . . SG, SG/CD*
*Preferred with Turbo engine

CAPACITY, Refill:	Liters	Qt
2.6L engine	4.3	4.5
Others	3.8	4.0

Capacity shown is without filter. When replacing filter, additional oil may be needed

Above 20°F (−7°C) 10W-30, 10W-40,
     10W-50, 15W-40, 20W-40, 20W-50, 30
20° to 80°F (−7° to 27°C) 20W-20
Above 10°F (−12°C) 15W-40
Above 0°F (−18°C) . . . 10W-30, 10W-40, 10W-50
Below 100°F (38°C) 5W-30*, 5W-40
*Not recommended in Turbo or 4-cyl. Vans; above 60°F (16°C); or in all 5.2L-4V engines at any temperature
5.2L-4V engines used for maximum performance service: 40, 30, or 20W-40, 20W-50 providing cold starting is satisfactory

TRANSMISSION/TRANSAXLE,
Automatic . . . . AF, AP†

CAPACITY, Initial Refill*:	Liters	Qt
All	3.8	4.0

*With the engine at operating temperature, shift transmission through all gears. Check fluid level in PARK and add fluid as needed
†RWD with lock-up torque converter, if shudder or excess slippage occurs, use **AP**

TRANSAXLE,
Manual . . . . 5W-30 SG/CD, SG

CAPACITY, Refill:	Liters	Pt
4-speed A460	1.8	4.0
5-speed A525	2.1	4.6
5-speed A520, A555	2.3	4.8

REAR DIFFERENTIAL

Standard **GL-5**
Sure-Grip . . . . 90 **GL-5★**
Above −10°F (−23°C), 90, 80W-90, 85W-90; −30° to −10°F (−34° to −23°C), 80W, 80W-90, 85W-90; below −30°F (−34°C), 75W

CAPACITY, Refill:	Liters	Pt
7¼" ring gear w/2½" dia. axle tube†	1.2	2.5
8¼" ring gear w/3" dia. axle tube†	2.1	4.5

† Measured adjacent to differential

SERVICE AT TIME OR MILEAGE—WHICHEVER OCCURS FIRST

CRPM11   CRPM11

Dodge Monaco, see Eagle/Renault
W SERVICE TO MAINTAIN EMISSION WARRANTY

MI—MILES IN THOUSANDS
KM—KILOMETERS IN THOUSANDS

TURBO ENGINE & ALL 1991-92, EVERY 6 MO/7.5 MI—12 KM
Crankcase . . . . change oil
1988-90 every 3 mo/3 mi (4.8 km) if following oil is not
used: 1988, SF/CD or SG/CD; 1989-90, SG/CD
Oil filter . . . . replace
Every other oil change

EVERY 12 MO/7.5 MI—12 KM
Brake hoses . . . . check

Crankcase ex. Turbo eng.
1988-90 . . . . change oil
Differential . . . . check for leaks
FWD, check manual transaxle fluid level
Exhaust manifold heat valve . . . spray **MH**
Front suspension &
  steering linkage . . . . . . inspect seals **BJ**
Oil filter ex. Turbo eng.
1988-90 . . . . replace
Every other oil change ex. if mileage is less than 7.5 mi
(12 km) each 12 mo, replace every oil change
Universal joints & boots . . . . inspect
Replace leaking or damaged joints
Brake master cylinder . . . . check level **HB**
Fill to bottom of split ring
Cooling system . . . . check **EC**
Every 12 mo only ex. vans at mileage
Power steering reservoir . . check level **PS**
Steering gear, manual . . check leaks **GL-5**
Transmission, automatic . . . . . check level
Body . . . . lubricate

EVERY 15 MI—24 KM
W Drive belts . . . . inspect/adjust
Do not adjust auto-tension type. Check air pump belts,
required for California warranty every 30 mi (48 km)

EVERY 22.5 MI—36 KM
Brake linings . . . . inspect
Replace disc pads when 1/32″ above rivet head or
backing plate
Wheel bearings:
  Front for RWD
  Rear for FWD . . . . inspect **LM**
Clean and repack whenever brake drums or rotors are
removed. To adjust, torque 20-25 ft lb; back off nut 1/4
turn then finger tighten nut & install lock nut with pin.
End play, .001″-.003″

1991-92 EVERY 30 MO/30 MI—48 KM
W Air cleaner element ex. vans . . . replace

EVERY 30 MI—48 KM
W Air cleaner element . . . . replace
FWD Vans only
W Carburetor choke shaft, fast idle cam
  & pivot pin . . . . clean **PC**
Check FWD Van choke heat source every 24 mo/30 mi
(48 km)
W PCV filter 2.2L, 2.5L . . . . replace
FWD Vans only
W Spark plugs . . . . replace

EVERY 36 MO/30 MI—48 KM
Front suspension & steering
  linkage . . . . 4-9 fittings **BJ**
Fill until grease flows out. Do not rupture seals

FIRST 36 MO/52.5 MI—84 KM; THEN EVERY 24 MO/30 MI—48 KM
Cooling system . . . . . . change coolant **EC**
Flush system

FWD VANS: EVERY 52.5 MI—84 KM
EGR valve & tube 1988-91 . . . . replace
At mileage or every 60 mo or when indicated by emis-
sions maintenance reminder light if equipped. Also
clean passages every 60 mi (96 km)
Oxygen sensor . . . . replace
Every 82.5 mi (132 km) or when indicated by emissions
maintenance reminder light if equipped
Vacuum operated
  emission components . . . . inspect
Replace for Vans at 60 mi (96 km)

ALL MODELS EVERY 52.5 MI—84 KM
Crankcase inlet air cleaner . . . . . clean/oil
Located in air cleaner or on valve cover
3.0L, 3.3L Van every 60 mi (96 km)

FWD VANS: EVERY 60 MI—96 KM
Drive belts 1990-92 . . . . replace
Replace 1991-92 Serpentine belts only when needed
Ignition cables . . . . replace
Distributor cap & rotor ex.
  3.3L, 3.8L . . . . replace
Check distributor
Ignition timing ex. 3.3L, 3.8L . check/adjust
PCV valve . . . . replace
When indicated by emissions maintenance reminder
light if equipped
Timing belt 3.0L eng. . . . . . check/replace
Thereafter every 30 mi (48 km)

SERVICE AS REQUIRED
Clutch cable FWD . . . . lubricate **LM**
Tires . . . . inspect/rotate
Lug nut torque, ft lb; FWD, 95; others, 85
Transmission linkage FWD . . lubricate **LM**
With manual transmission, remove shift unit & replace
grommets, bushings & clip when lubricating
Fuel filter . . . . replace
Fuel vapor canister element . . . . . . replace
PCV valve . . . . replace

SEVERE SERVICE
Brake lining—Inspect every 9 mi (14 km)
Crankcase—Change oil: Highway, police,
taxi, limousine, all without turbo engine &
when not operating at sustained high speed
driving when above 90°F (32°C), every 6
mo/5 mi (8 km); all others, every 3 mo/3 mi
(4.8 km). Replace filter every second oil
change ex. with 1988-90 turbocharger at
every oil change
Rear differential 1988-89—Change lubricant every 36 mi (57.6 km)
Front suspension ball joints—FWD, inspect
every 3 mo/3 mi (4.8 km); others, lubricate
every 18 mo/15 mi (24 km)
Front wheel bearings ex. FWD—Clean and
repack every 9 mi (14 km) or whenever
brake rotors are removed
4WD power transfer unit—Change fluid
every 12 mi (29 km)
4WD overrunning clutch and rear carrier—
Change fluid every 22.5 mi (36 km)
Steering linkage—Lubricate every 18 mo/15
mi (24 km)
Rear wheel bearings FWD—Clean or repack every 9 mi (14 km), or whenever rear
brake drums are removed
Transmission, automatic—Change fluid
every 15 mi (24 km). Replace filter & adjust
bands at each drain
Universal joints—Inspect every 3 mo/3 mi
(4.8 km)
Air cleaner element—Inspect every 15 mi
(24 km)

KEY TO LUBRICANTS
See other Chrysler charts

CRANKCASE . . . . SG, SG/CD*
*Preferred with Turbo engine. SG/CD required for 1991-
92 Turbo eng.

CAPACITY, Refill:	Liters	Qt
All	3.8	4.0

Capacity shown is without filter. When replacing filter, additional oil may be needed

1988-89
Above 20°F (–7°C) 10W-30, 15W-40, 30
20° to 80°F (–7° to 27°C) . . . . 20W-20†
Above 10°F (–12°C) 15W-40
Above 0°F (–18°C) 10W-30
Below 100°F (38°C) 5W-30*
*Not recommended in Turbo or 4-cyl. Vans; 1987-88,
above 60°F (16°C); 1989, above 32°F (0°C) or in all 5.2L-
4V engines at any temperature
5.2L-4V engines used for maximum performance service:
40, 30, or 20W-40, 20W-50 providing cold starting is satisfactory

1990-92
All eng. above 0°F (–18°C) 10W-30*
2.5L Van & Turbo below 32°F (0°C) . . . . 5W-30†
Non-Turbo ex. 2.5L Van
  below 100°F (38°C) 5W-30
*Preferred in all Turbo & 2.5L Van
†Preferred in all non-Turbo ex. 2.5L Van

TRANSMISSION/TRANSAXLE, Automatic
1988 . . . . AF, AP†
1989-92 . . . . AP•

CAPACITY, Initial Refill*:	Liters	Qt
All	3.8	4.0

*With the engine at operating temperature, shift transmis-
sion through all gears. Check fluid level in PARK and add
fluid as needed
†RWD with lock-up torque coverter if shudder or excess
slipage occurs, use AP
•May use AF only when AP is not available

TRANSAXLE, Manual
1989-90 Horizon, Omni . . . . AF, AP
1989-91 ex. Horizon,
  Omni . . . . 5W-30 SG, SG/CD
1988 . . . . 5W-30 SF/CC, SF/CD,
                              SG/CD, SG

CAPACITY, Refill:	Liters	Pt
5-speed A525	2.1	4.6
5-speed A520, A523, A543, A555, A568, A569	2.3	4.8

REAR DIFFERENTIAL, 1988-89
Standard GL-5
Sure-Grip . . . . 90 GL-5★
Above –10°F (–23°C), 90, 80W-90, 85W-90; –30°
to –10°F (–34° to –23°C), 80W, 80W-90, 85W-90;
below –30°F (–34°C), 75W

CAPACITY, Refill:	Liters	Pt
7¼″ ring gear w/2½″ dia. axle tube†	1.2	2.5
8¼″ ring gear w/3″ dia. axle tube†	2.1	4.5

† Measured adjacent to differential

4WD MINI VAN, 1991-92
Power Transfer Unit &
  Rear Carrier Assembly . . . 80W-90GL-5
Overrunning Clutch . . . . AP

CAPACITY, Refill:	Liters	Pt
Power Transfer Unit	1.15	2.4
Rear Carrier	1.9	4.0
Overrrunning Clutch	0.4	0.8

CHRYSLER, DODGE, PLYMOUTH
**1983-92 Challenger, Colt, Conquest, Raider, Ram 50,
Sapporo, Vista; 1990-92 Laser, Stealth**

SERVICE LOCATIONS — ENGINE AND CHASSIS

CRIDP-1

CRIDP-1

HOOD RELEASE: Inside

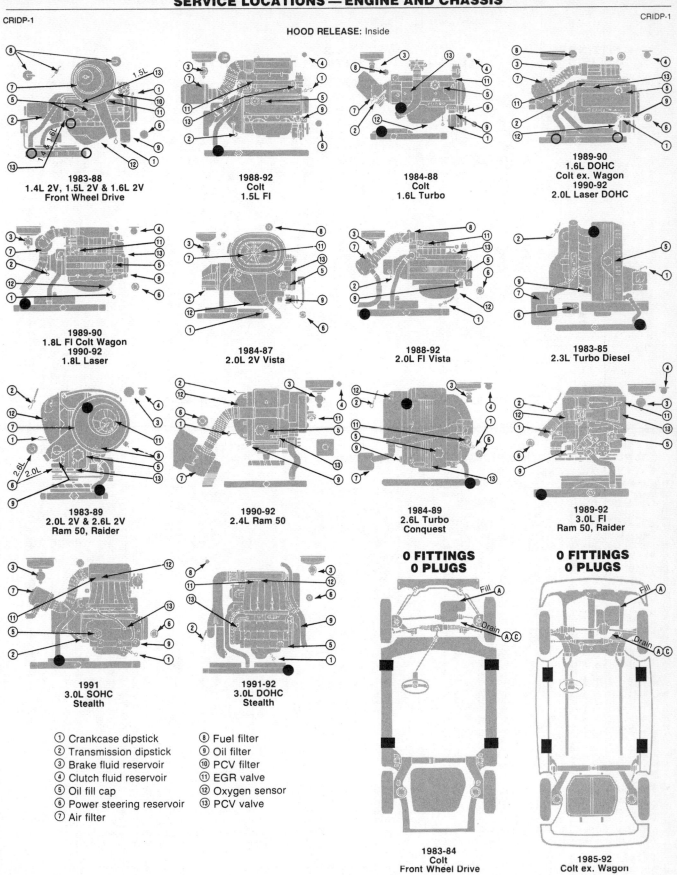

**1983-88
1.4L 2V, 1.5L 2V & 1.6L 2V
Front Wheel Drive**

**1988-92
Colt
1.5L FI**

**1984-88
Colt
1.6L Turbo**

**1989-90
1.6L DOHC
Colt ex. Wagon
1990-92
2.0L Laser DOHC**

**1989-90
1.8L FI Colt Wagon
1990-92
1.8L Laser**

**1984-87
2.0L 2V Vista**

**1988-92
2.0L FI Vista**

**1983-85
2.3L Turbo Diesel**

**1983-89
2.0L 2V & 2.6L 2V
Ram 50, Raider**

**1990-92
2.4L Ram 50**

**1984-89
2.6L Turbo
Conquest**

**1989-92
3.0L FI
Ram 50, Raider**

**1991
3.0L SOHC
Stealth**

**1991-92
3.0L DOHC
Stealth**

**0 FITTINGS
0 PLUGS**

Fill Ⓐ

Drain Ⓐ Ⓒ

**1983-84
Colt
Front Wheel Drive**

**0 FITTINGS
0 PLUGS**

Fill Ⓐ

Drain Ⓐ Ⓒ

**1985-92
Colt ex. Wagon**

① Crankcase dipstick
② Transmission dipstick
③ Brake fluid reservoir
④ Clutch fluid reservoir
⑤ Oil fill cap
⑥ Power steering reservoir
⑦ Air filter
⑧ Fuel filter
⑨ Oil filter
⑩ PCV filter
⑪ EGR valve
⑫ Oxygen sensor
⑬ PCV valve

● Cooling system drain   ○ Cooling system drain, some models   ■ Lift adapter position

CHRYSLER, DODGE, PLYMOUTH
1983-92 Challenger, Colt, Conquest, Raider, Ram 50, Sapporo, Vista; 1990-92 Laser, Stealth

CHEK-CHART

SERVICE LOCATIONS — ENGINE AND CHASSIS

CRIDP-2   CRIDP-2

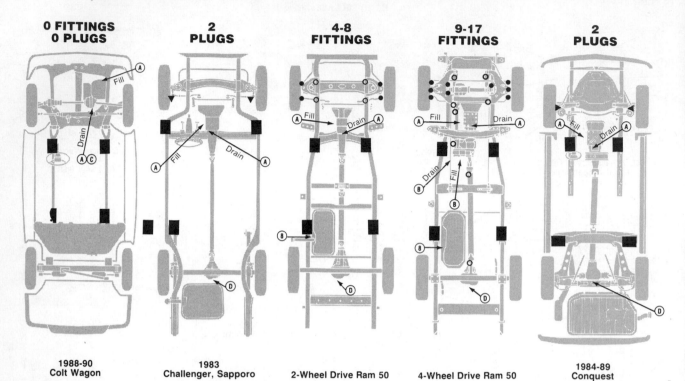

0 FITTINGS 0 PLUGS	**2 PLUGS**	**4-8 FITTINGS**	**9-17 FITTINGS**	**2 PLUGS**
1988-90 Colt Wagon	1983 Challenger, Sapporo	2-Wheel Drive Ram 50	4-Wheel Drive Ram 50	1984-89 Conquest

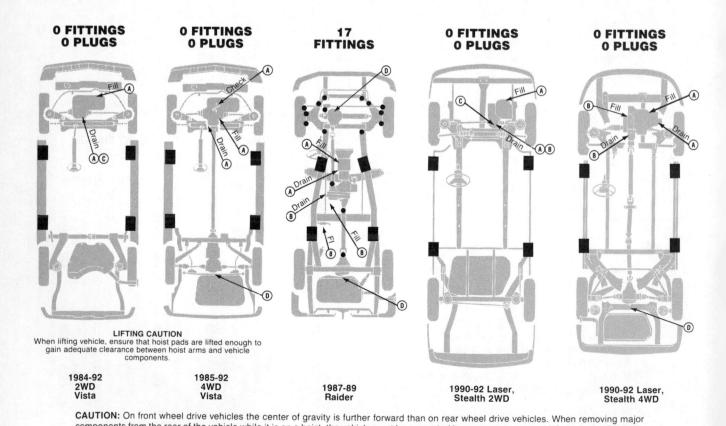

0 FITTINGS 0 PLUGS	**0 FITTINGS 0 PLUGS**	**17 FITTINGS**	**0 FITTINGS 0 PLUGS**	**0 FITTINGS 0 PLUGS**

LIFTING CAUTION
When lifting vehicle, ensure that hoist pads are lifted enough to gain adequate clearance between hoist arms and vehicle components.

1984-92 2WD Vista	1985-92 4WD Vista	1987-89 Raider	1990-92 Laser, Stealth 2WD	1990-92 Laser, Stealth 4WD

CAUTION: On front wheel drive vehicles the center of gravity is further forward than on rear wheel drive vehicles. When removing major components from the rear of the vehicle while it is on a hoist, the vehicle must be supported in a manner to prevent it from tipping forward.

■ Lift adapter position   ▲ Plug   Ⓐ Manual transmission/transaxle,   Ⓒ Automatic transaxle final drive,
● Fitting   ○ Fitting, some models   drain & fill   drain & fill
                                           Ⓑ Transfer case, drain & fill   Ⓓ Differential, drain & fill

SERVICE AT TIME OR MILEAGE—WHICHEVER OCCURS FIRST

CRIPM3   CRIPM3

MI—MILES IN THOUSANDS
KM—KILOMETERS IN THOUSANDS

TURBO ENGINES
EVERY 6 MO/3 MI—4.8 KM
Crankcase .... change oil

Oil filter .... replace
At second oil change, then every other

EVERY 12 MO/7.5 MI—12 KM
Crankcase .... change oil
Ex. turbo engine

Exhaust system .... inspect

Oil filter .... replace
Ex. turbo engine. At second oil change, then every other oil change

Power steering .... check level **AF**
Check for leaks & condition of belts

Steering gear,
  manual .... check level 90 **GL-5**
Remove lower right bolt of cover & fill through fill hole to 3/4″ (w/4-bolt cover) or 7/8″ (w/3-bolt cover) from top of bolt hole. Check steering wheel free play

Transmission, automatic ..... check level

Body 1983 .... lubricate

EVERY 12 MO/15 MI—24 KM
Cooling system .... inspect
Every 12 mo only

Crankcase emission system .... clean
1983 FWD Canadian only

Engine compartment rubber &
  plastic components .... inspect

EVERY 15 MI—24 KM
Disc & drum brake lining & hoses . inspect
Wheel cylinders, inspect every 30 mi (48 km)

Tires 1983 .... check/rotate

Distributor points & condenser ... replace
FWD Canada only. Inspect cap, rotor & lubricate distributor cam wick & breaker shaft **MO**

Drive belts .... inspect/adjust
1984, initial service, then every 30 mi (48 km)

EGR valve Canada .... check/clean

Idle speed & mixture .... check/adjust
Canadian gasoline only

Ignition timing & dwell ...... check/adjust
Canada only

Spark plugs .... replace
Canada only

Valve clearance .... inspect/adjust

EVERY 24 MO/30 MI—48 KM
Coolant .... drain/flush/refill **EC**

EVERY 30 MI—48 KM
Ball joint, steering linkage seals &
  FWD steering &
  drive shaft boots .... inspect

Differential .... check level
Replace lubricant in limited slip differentials

Front wheel bearings
  ex. FWD .... clean/repack **WB**
Inspect for leaks. Inspect & repack whenever rotors are removed

Rear wheel bearings
  FWD .... clean/repack **WB**
Inspect for leaks. Repack whenever drums are removed

Transaxle, automatic FWD .. change fluid
Change filter & adjust bands

Transmission, manual .... check level

Air cleaner filter
  ex. carbon element .... replace

Choke & linkage .... clean **PC**

Drive belts .... replace

Evaporative control canister ...... replace
Canadian engines only. 1984 U.S. engines every 5 yr/ 50 mi (80 km)

Spark plugs .... replace
U.S. only

EVERY 4 YEARS
Brakes .... change fluid **HB**
Also change hydraulic clutch fluid

EVERY 5 YR/50 MI—80 KM
Crankcase emission system .... clean

Evaporative control system ...... inspect

Fuel filter .... replace
Check fuel system cap, tank, lines & connections

Fuel, water, & fuel vapor hoses
  ex. Canada .... check/replace
Not required for Calif. warranty ex. water hoses

Hot air control valve .... check
FWD Canada. Inside carburetor air cleaner snorkel

Ignition timing .... check/adjust
U.S. only

Ignition wires .... check/replace

Oxygen sensor........... check/replace

Vacuum hoses .... check
Secondary air hoses & crankcase ventilation hoses. Ex. Canada

SEVERE SERVICE
Air cleaner filter—Replace more frequently

Crankcase—Change oil every 3 mo/3 mi (4.8 km) & filter at second oil change, then all every other oil change

Transmission, automatic, rear wheel drive— Change fluid, filter, & adjust bands every 30 mi (48 km)

Transmission, manual—Change lubricant every 30 mi (48 km)

Spark plugs—Replace every 15 mi (24 km)

KEY TO LUBRICANTS
AF	DEXRON®-II ATF
AP	MOPAR ATF-PLUS®
CD	Motor Oil, API Service CD
EC	Ethylene Glycol Coolant
	Mix 50% to 70% with water
GL-4	Gear Oil, API Service GL-4
GL-5	Gear Oil, API Service GL-5
GL-5★	Special Lubricant for Limited-Slip Differentials
HB	Hydraulic Brake Fluid, DOT 3
MO	Motor Oil
PC	Carburetor Cleaner
SE	Motor Oil, API Service SE
SF	Motor Oil, API Service SF
SG	Motor Oil, API Service SG
WB	Wheel Bearing Grease

CRANKCASE
Gasoline engine .... **SE, SF, SG**
Diesel engine .... **CD**

CAPACITY, Refill:	Liters	Qt
1.4L	3.0	3.1
1.6L	3.5	3.7
2.0L, 2.6L	3.8	4.0
2.0L	3.5	3.7

Capacity shown is without filter. When replacing filter, additional oil may be needed
Above 32°F (0°C) 20W-20, 20W-40, 20W-50
Above −10°F (−23°C) . 10W-30, 10W-40, 10W-50
Below 60°F (16°C) 5W-20*, 5W-30, 5W-40
*Not recommended for sustained high-speed driving

TRANSMISSION/TRANSAXLE,
  Automatic .... **AF, AP**

CAPACITY, Initial Refill*:	Liters	Qt
Front wheel drive	4.0	4.2
Rear wheel drive	3.8	4.0

*With the engine at operating temperature, shift transmission through all gears. Check fluid level in NEUTRAL and add fluid as needed

TRANSMISSION/TRANSAXLE,
  Manual 80W, 75W-85W **GL-4**

CAPACITY, Refill:	Liters	Pt
All FWD	2.3	4.8
RWD: 4-speed	2.1	4.4
5-speed	2.3	4.8

DIFFERENTIAL
Limited-Slip .... **GL-5★**
Other **GL-5**
Above −10°F (−23°C), 90, 85W-90, 80W-90; −30° to −10°F (−34° to −23°C), 80W, 80W-90; below −30°F (−34°C), 75W

CAPACITY, Refill:	Liters	Pt
Ex. truck	1.3	2.8
Truck	1.5	3.2

LIMITED-SLIP IDENTIFICATION:
Lift rear of vehicle, turn one wheel and the other will turn in the same direction

DODGE/PLYMOUTH
1985 Colt, Conquest, Vista

SERVICE AT TIME OR MILEAGE—WHICHEVER OCCURS FIRST

CRIPM4   CRIPM4

MI—MILES IN THOUSANDS
KM—KILOMETERS IN THOUSANDS

TURBO ENGINES
EVERY 6 MO/3 MI—4.8 KM
Crankcase . . . . change oil

Oil filter . . . . replace
At second oil change, then every other

EVERY 12 MO/7.5 MI—12 KM
Crankcase ex. turbo . . . . change oil

Oil filter ex. turbo . . . . replace
Every second oil change, but at least every 12 months

EVERY 12 MO/15 MI—24 KM
Brake system . . . . inspect
Check brake lining, hoses & lines, wheel & master cylinders, brake fluid

Exhaust system . . . . inspect

Cooling system . . . . inspect
Service as required

Power steering fluid . . . . check **AF**
Also check hoses

EVERY 15 MI—24 KM
Limited-Slip differential . . . . change oil

Drive belts . . . . inspect/adjust
Water pump & alternator only

Idle speed, Gasoline . . . . check/adjust
Initial service for throttle positioner, then every 50 mi (80 km)

Valve clearance . . . . inspect/adjust
Adjust jet valve only on 2.0L & 2.6L engines

EVERY 24 MO/30 MI—48 KM
Ball joint, steering linkage seals &
  FWD steering &
  drive shaft boots . . . . inspect

Front wheel bearings,
  FWD . . . . clean/repack **WB**
Inspect for leaks. Inspect & repack whenever rotors are removed

Rear wheel bearings,
  RWD . . . . clean/repack **WB**
Inspect for leaks. Repack whenever drums are removed

Coolant . . . . drain/flush/refill **EC**

EVERY 30 MI—48 KM
Differential . . . . check level

Transaxle, automatic FWD . . change fluid
Change filter & adjust bands

Transmission/Transaxle,
  manual . . . . check level

Air cleaner filter . . . . replace

Choke & linkage . . . . clean **PC**

Drive belts . . . . replace
Water pump & alternator only

Spark plugs . . . . replace

AT FIRST 4 YR/60 MI—96 KM;
THEN EVERY 12 MO/15 MI—24 KM
Air conditioning system . . . . inspect

Power steering belt . . . . check

EVERY 4 YR/60 MI—96 KM
Brakes . . . . change fluid **HB**

EVERY 5 YR/50 MI—80 KM
Carburetor mounting, 4 × 4 Vista . . . check

Crankcase emission
  system . . . . check/clean

EGR valve, 4 × 4 Vista . . . . replace
Clean sub-EGR valve

Evaporative control system . . . . . . inspect
Replace canister

Fuel filter . . . . replace
Check fuel system, tank, lines & connections

Fuel, water, & fuel
  vapor hoses . . . . check/replace
Replace fuel cap on 4 × 4 Vista

Hot air control valve, 4 × 4 Vista . . . . check
Ex. Calif. Inside carburetor air cleaner snorkel

Ignition timing . . . . check/adjust

Ignition wires . . . . check/replace

Secondary air system,
  4 × 4 Vista . . . . inspect
Ex. Calif.

Turbocharger oil & air
  intake hoses . . . . replace

Oxygen sensor . . . . check/replace

Vacuum hoses . . . . replace
Secondary air hoses & crankcase ventilation hoses

Vacuum control system solenoid
  valve air filter, 4 × 4 Vista . . . . . . replace

EVERY 60 MI—96 KM
Timing belts . . . . replace
Ex. 2.6L engine

SEVERE SERVICE
Air cleaner filter, PCV system & brake
system—Service more frequently

Crankcase—Change oil every 3 mo/3 mi
(4.8 km) & filter every second oil change

Transmission, automatic, rear wheel drive—
Change fluid, filter, & adjust bands every 30
mi (48 km)

Vista 4 × 4 manual transmission—Change
lubricant every 30 mi (48 km)

Spark plugs—Replace every 15 mi (24
km)

KEY TO LUBRICANTS

AF	DEXRON®-II ATF
AP	MOPAR ATF-PLUS®
CC	Motor Oil, API Service CC
CD	Motor Oil, API Service CD
EC	Ethylene Glycol Coolant Mix 50% to 70% with water
GL-4	Gear Oil, API Service GL-4
GL-5	Gear Oil, API Service GL-5
GL-5★	Special Lubricant for Limited-Slip Differentials
HB	Hydraulic Brake Fluid, DOT 3
PC	Carburetor Cleaner
SF	Motor Oil, API Service SF
SG	Motor Oil, API Service SG
WB	Wheel Bearing Grease

CRANKCASE . . . . **SF, SF/CC, SG**

CAPACITY, Refill:	Liters	Qt
1.5L	2.5	2.7
1.6L Turbo	3.0	3.2
2.0L	3.5	3.7
2.6L	4.3	4.6

Capacity shown is without filter. When replacing filter, additional oil may be needed

Turbo Models
Above 32°F (0°C) 20W-20, 20W-40
Above −10°F (−23°C) 10W-30
Below 60°F (16°C) 5W-30

All Other Models
Above 32°F (0°C) 20W-20, 20W-40, 20W-50
Above −10°F (−23°C) . 10W-30, 10W-40, 10W-50
Below 60°F (16°C) . . . . . 5W-20★, 5W-30, 5W-40
★Not recommended for sustained high-speed driving

TRANSMISSION/TRANSAXLE,
  Automatic . . . . **AF, AP**

CAPACITY, Initial Refill★:	Liters	Qt
Front wheel drive & 4 × 4 Vista	4.0	4.2
Conquest	5.0	5.3

★With the engine at operating temperature, shift transmission through all gears. Check fluid level in NEUTRAL and add fluid as needed

TRANSMISSION/TRANSAXLE, Manual
FWD 75W-85W **GL-4**
RWD 80W, 75W-85W **GL-4**

CAPACITY, Refill:	Liters	Pt
Colt	2.1	4.4
w/turbo	2.3	4.8
Vista 2WD	2.3	4.8
4WD	2.1	4.4
Conquest	2.3	4.8

TRANSFER CASE . 80W, 75W-85W **GL-4**

CAPACITY, Refill:	Liters	Pt
Vista	0.7	1.5

DIFFERENTIAL
Limited-Slip . . . . **GL-5★**
Other **GL-5**
Above −10°F (−23°C), 90, 85W-90, 80W-90; −30°
to −10°F (−34° to −23°C), 80W, 80W-90; below
−30°F (−34°C), 75W

CAPACITY, Refill:	Liters	Pt
All ex. Limited-Slip Vista	1.3	2.8
Limited-Slip Vista	0.8	1.7

LIMITED-SLIP IDENTIFICATION:
Lift rear of vehicle, turn one wheel and the other will turn in the same direction

SERVICE AT TIME OR MILEAGE—WHICHEVER OCCURS FIRST

CRIPM5   CRIPM5

MI—MILES IN THOUSANDS
KM—KILOMETERS IN THOUSANDS

TURBO ENGINES, EVERY 6 MO/3 MI—4.8 KM
Crankcase .... change oil

Oil filter .... replace
Every second oil change

EVERY 12 MO/7.5 MI—12 KM
Crankcase ex. turbo .... change oil

Oil filter ex. turbo .... replace
At every second change, but at least every 12 months

EVERY 12 MO/15 MI—24 KM
Brake system .... inspect
Check linings, hoses & lines, wheel & master cylinders, brake fluid

Exhaust system .... inspect

Clutch fluid, Conquest .... check **HB**

Cooling system .... inspect
Service as required

Power steering fluid .... check **AF**
Also check hoses

EVERY 15 MI—24 KM
Limited-Slip differential .... change oil

Drive belts .... inspect/adjust
Water pump & alternator only

Idle speed .... check/adjust
Required w/carburetor only

Throttle position system .... check
Initial service, then every 50 mi (80 km)

Valve clearance .... inspect/adjust
Adjust jet valve only on 2.0L & 2.6L engines

EVERY 24 MO/30 MI—48 KM
Ball joint, steering linkage seals &
  FWD steering &
  drive shaft boots .... inspect

Front wheel bearings
  RWD .... clean/repack **WB**
Inspect for leaks. Inspect & repack whenever rotors are removed

Rear wheel bearings
  FWD .... clean/repack **WB**
Inspect for leaks. Repack whenever drums are removed

Coolant .... drain/flush/refill **EC**

EVERY 30 MI—48 KM
Differential .... check level

Transaxle, automatic FWD .. change fluid
Change filter & adjust bands

Transmission/Transaxle,
  manual .... check level

Air cleaner filter .... replace

Choke & linkage .... clean **PC**
Required w/carburetor only

Drive belts .... replace
Water pump & alternator only

Spark plugs .... replace

AT FIRST 4 YR/60 MI—96 KM; THEN EVERY 12 MO/15 MI—24 KM
Air conditioning system .... inspect

Power steering belt .... check

EVERY 4 YR/60 MI—96 KM
Brakes .... change fluid **HB**
Also change hydraulic clutch fluid

EVERY 5 YR/50 MI—80 KM
Carburetor mounting, Vista .... check

Crankcase emission
  system .... check/clean

Distributor cap, rotor & advance
  system 4WD Vista .... check
Ex. California

EGR valve, 4WD Vista .... replace
Clean sub-EGR valve

Evaporative canister .... replace

Evaporative control system ...... inspect

Fuel filter .... replace
Check fuel system tank, lines & connections

Fuel, water, & fuel
  vapor hoses .... check/replace
Replace fuel cap on 4WD Vista

Hot air control valve,
  4WD Vista .... check
Ex. Calif. Inside carburetor air cleaner snorkel

Ignition timing .... check/adjust

Ignition wires .... check/replace

Secondary air system,
  4WD Vista .... inspect
Ex. California

Turbocharger air intake
  & oil hoses .... replace

Oxygen sensor .... check/replace

Vacuum hoses .... replace
Secondary air hoses & crankcase ventilation hoses

Vacuum control system solenoid
  valve air filter, 4WD Vista ...... replace
Ex. California

EVERY 60 MI—96 KM
Timing belts .... replace
Ex. 2.6L engine

SEVERE SERVICE
Air cleaner filter, PCV system & brake system—Service more frequently

Crankcase—Change oil every 3 mo/3 mi (4.8 km) & filter every second oil change

Transmission, automatic, rear wheel drive— Change fluid, filter, & adjust bands every 30 mi (48 km)

Transfer case, 4WD Vista manual transmission—Change lubricant every 30 mi (48 km)

Spark plugs—Replace every 15 mi (24 km)

KEY TO LUBRICANTS

AF	DEXRON®-II ATF
AP	MOPAR ATF-PLUS®
CC	Motor Oil, API Service CC
EC	Ethylene Glycol Coolant Mix 50% to 70% with water
GL-4	Gear Oil, API Service GL-4
GL-5	Gear Oil, API Service GL-5
GL-5★	Special Lubricant for Limited-Slip Differentials
HB	Hydraulic Brake Fluid, DOT 3
PC	Carburetor Cleaner
SF	Motor Oil, API Service SF
SG	Motor Oil, API Service SG
WB	Wheel Bearing Grease

CRANKCASE .... SF, SF/CC, SG

CAPACITY, Refill:	Liters	Qt
1.5L	3.0	3.2
1.6L Turbo	3.6	3.8
2.0L	3.5	3.7
2.6L	4.3	4.6

Capacity shown is without filter. When replacing filter, additional oil may be needed
Turbo Models
Above 32°F (0°C) 20W-20, 20W-40
Above −10°F (−23°C) 10W-30
Below 60°F (16°C) 5W-30
All Other Models
Above 32°F (0°C) 20W-20, 20W-40, 20W-50
Above −10°F (−23°C) . 10W-30, 10W-40, 10W-50
Below 60°F (16°C) 5W-20*, 5W-30, 5W-40
*Not recommended for sustained high-speed driving

TRANSMISSION/TRANSAXLE, Automatic .... AF, AP

CAPACITY, Initial Refill*:	Liters	Qt
Conquest	5.0	5.3
Others	4.0	4.2

*With the engine at operating temperature, shift transmission through all gears. Check fluid level in NEUTRAL and add fluid as needed

TRANSMISSION/TRANSAXLE, Manual
FWD 75W-85W **GL-4**
RWD 80W, 75W-85W **GL-4**

CAPACITY, Refill:	Liters	Pt
Colt	2.1	4.4
w/turbo	2.3	4.8
Vista 2WD	2.3	4.8
4WD	2.1	4.4
Conquest	2.3	4.8

TRANSFER CASE 80W, 75W-85W GL-4

CAPACITY, Refill:	Liters	Pt
Vista 4WD	0.7	1.5

DIFFERENTIAL
Limited-Slip .... **GL-5★**
Standard **GL-4, GL-5**
Above −10°F (−23°C), 90, 85W-90, 80W-90; −30° to −10°F (−34° to −23°C), 80W, 80W-90; below −30°F (−34°C), 75W

CAPACITY, Refill:	Liters	Pt
All ex. Limited-Slip		
4WD Vista	1.3	2.8
Limited-Slip 4WD Vista	0.8	1.7

LIMITED-SLIP IDENTIFICATION:
Lift rear of vehicle, turn one wheel and the other will turn in the same direction

CHRYSLER/DODGE/PLYMOUTH
1987-88 Colt, Conquest, Vista

SERVICE AT TIME OR MILEAGE—WHICHEVER OCCURS FIRST

CRIPM10 CRIPM10

W SERVICE TO MAINTAIN EMISSION WARRANTY

MI—MILES IN THOUSANDS
KM—KILOMETERS IN THOUSANDS

TURBO ENGINES:
EVERY 6 MO/3 MI—4.8 KM

W Crankcase .... change oil

W Oil filter .... replace
Every second oil change

EVERY 12 MO/7.5 MI—12 KM

W Crankcase ex. turbo .... change oil

W Oil filter ex. turbo .... replace
At every second change, but at least every 12 months

EVERY 12 MO/15 MI—24 KM

Brake hoses .... check
Check rear drum linings & wheel cylinders every 24 mo/
15 mi (24 km)

Disc brake pads .... inspect

Cooling system .... inspect
Service as required

Power steering fluid .... check **AF**
Also check hoses

Transaxle, automatic .... check level

EVERY 15 MI—24 KM

Limited-Slip differential
1987 .... change oil

W Idle speed .... check/adjust
Required w/carburetor only

W Valve clearance .... inspect/adjust
Adjust only when specifications are on emission label

EVERY 24 MO/30 MI—48 KM

Ball joint, steering linkage seals &
FWD steering &
drive shaft boots .... inspect

Front wheel bearings
RWD .... clean/repack **WB**
Inspect for leaks. Inspect & repack whenever rotors are
removed

Rear wheel bearings
FWD .... clean/repack **WB**
Inspect for leaks. Repack whenever drums are re-
moved

Coolant .... drain/flush/refill **EC**

EVERY 30 MI—48 KM

Differential .... check level
Limited-Slip, change oil

Transaxle, automatic FWD .. change fluid
Change filter & adjust bands

Transmission/Transaxle,
manual .... check level

W Air cleaner filter .... replace

W Choke & linkage .... clean **PC**

W Drive belts .... replace
Water pump & alternator only. Not required for 1988
emission warranty

W Spark plugs .... replace

EVERY 4 YR/60 MI—96 KM

Brakes .... change fluid **HB**
Also change hydraulic clutch fluid

EVERY 5 YR/50 MI—80 KM

Carburetor or throttle body
mounting, 1987 4WD Vista ...... check

W Distributor cap, rotor & advance
system 1987 4WD Vista .... check
Ex. California

EGR valve, 4WD .... replace
Clean 1987 sub-EGR valve

W Fuel filter .... replace

W Fuel lines, connections, fill cap
& tank .... check

W Fuel, water, & fuel
vapor hoses .... check/replace
Replace fuel cap

EVERY 5 YR/60 MI—96 KM

W Crankcase emission
system .... check/clean

W Evaporative control system ...... inspect

W Ignition wires .... check/replace

W Secondary air system &
hot intake air control valve
1987 4WD ex. Calif. .... inspect

W Turbocharger air intake &
oil hoses .... replace

W Vacuum hoses .... replace

W Vacuum control system solenoid
valve air filter Vista
4WD ex. Calif. .... replace

EVERY 60 MI—96 KM

Timing belts .... replace
Also replace the balancer belt when equipped

EVERY 80 MI—128 KM

W Oxygen sensor .... check/replace

EVERY 100 MI—160 KM

W Evaporative canister, 4WD .... replace

SEVERE SERVICE

W Air cleaner filter, PCV system & brake
system—Service more frequently

W Crankcase—Change oil every 3 mo/3 mi
(4.8 km) & filter every second oil change

Transmission, automatic, rear wheel drive—
Change fluid, filter, & adjust bands every 30
mi (48 km)

Transfer case, 4WD Vista manual
transaxle—Change lubricant every 30 mi
(48 km)

W Spark plugs—Replace every 15 mi (24 km)

KEY TO LUBRICANTS

AF	DEXRON®-II Automatic Transmission Fluid
AP	MOPAR ATF-PLUS®
CC	Motor Oil, API Service CC
EC	Ethylene Glycol Coolant Mix 50% to 70% with water
GL-4	Gear Oil, API Service GL-4
GL-5	Gear Oil, API Service GL-5
GL-5★	Special Lubricant for Limited-Slip Differentials
HB	Hydraulic Brake Fluid, DOT 3
PC	Carburetor Cleaner
SF	Motor Oil, API Service SF
SG	Motor Oil, API Service SG
WB	Wheel Bearing Grease

CRANKCASE .... SF, SF/CC, SG

CAPACITY, Refill:	Liters	Qt
1.5L	3.0	3.2
1.6L Turbo	3.6	3.8
2.0L	3.5	3.7
2.6L	4.3	4.6

Capacity shown is without filter or oil cooler. When replacing filter, additional oil may be needed

Turbo Models
Above 32°F (0°C) 20W-20, 20W-40
Above −10°F (−23°C) 10W-30
Below 60°F (16°C) 5W-30
All Other Models
Above 32°F (0°C) 20W-20, 20W-40, 20W-50
Above −10°F (−23°C) 10W-30,
10W-40, 10W-50
Below 60°F (16°C) 5W-20*, 5W-30, 5W-40
* Not recommended for sustained high-speed driving

TRANSMISSION/TRANSAXLE,
Automatic .... AF, AP

CAPACITY, Initial Refill*:	Liters	Qt
Conquest	5.0	5.3
Others	4.0	4.2

* With the engine at operating temperature, shift transmission through all gears. Check fluid level in NEUTRAL and
add fluid as needed

TRANSMISSION/TRANSAXLE, Manual
FWD 75W-85W **GL-4**
RWD 80W, 75W-85W **GL-4**

CAPACITY, Refill:	Liters	Pt
Colt	1.8	3.7
Vista 2WD	2.5	5.3
Vista 4WD	2.1	4.4
Conquest	2.3	4.8

TRANSFER
CASE 80W, 75W-85W GL-4

CAPACITY, Refill:	Liters	Pt
Vista 4WD	0.7	1.5

DIFFERENTIAL
Limited-Slip .... **GL-5★**
Standard **GL-5**
Above −10°F (−23°C), 90, 85W-90, 80W-90; −30°
to −10°F (−34° to −23°C), 80W, 80W-90; below
−30°F (−34°C), 75W

CAPACITY, Refill:	Liters	Pt
Conquest	1.3	2.8
Vista 4WD	0.8	1.7

LIMITED-SLIP IDENTIFICATION:
Lift rear of vehicle, turn one wheel and the other will turn in
the same direction

SERVICE AT TIME OR MILEAGE—WHICHEVER OCCURS FIRST

CRIPM11   CRIPM11

W SERVICE TO MAINTAIN EMISSION WARRANTY

MI—MILES IN THOUSANDS
KM—KILOMETERS IN THOUSANDS

TURBO ENGINES:
EVERY 6 MO/5 MI—8 KM
Crankcase . . . . change oil

Oil filter . . . . replace
Every second oil change

EVERY 12 MO/7.5 MI—12 KM
Crankcase ex. turbo . . . . change oil

Oil filter ex. turbo . . . . replace
At every second change, but at least every 12 months

EVERY 12 MO/15 MI—24 KM
Brake hoses . . . . check

Disc brake pads . . . . inspect

Drive shaft boots . . . . inspect

Power steering fluid . . . . check **AF**

Transaxle, automatic . . . . check level

EVERY 15 MI—24 KM
W Valve clearance . . . . inspect/adjust
Adjust only when specifications are on emission label

EVERY 24 MO/30 MI—48 KM
Ball joint, steering linkage seals &
   FWD steering . . . . inspect

Drive shaft joints 1989
   Vista 4WD . . . . lubricate **LM**

Front wheel bearings
   RWD . . . . clean/repack **WB**
Inspect for leaks. Inspect & repack whenever rotors are removed

Rear drum brake lining
   & wheel cylinders . . . . inspect

Rear wheel bearings
   FWD . . . . clean/repack **WB**
Inspect for leaks. Repack whenever drums are removed

Coolant . . . . drain/flush/refill **EC**

Fuel hoses, 1991-92 . . . . inspect

EVERY 30 MI—48 KM
Differential . . . . check level
Limited-Slip, change oil

Transaxle, automatic FWD . . change fluid
Change filter & adjust bands

Transmission/Transaxle,
   manual . . . . check level

W Air cleaner filter . . . . replace

W Drive belts . . . . replace
Water pump & alternator only. Not required for 1989-90 emission warranty

W Spark plugs . . . . replace
Ex. Stealth DOHC

EVERY 5 YR/50 MI—80 KM
EGR valve, 4WD ex. Stealth . . . . . replace

W Fuel lines, connections, fill cap
   & tank . . . . check

W Fuel, water, & fuel
   vapor hoses . . . . check/replace

EVERY 5 YR/60 MI—96 KM
W Crankcase emission
   system . . . . check/clean
4WD only ex. Stealth

W Evaporative control system . . . . . inspect
4WD only ex. Stealth

W Ignition wires . . . . check/replace
4WD only ex. Stealth

W Vacuum hoses . . . . replace
4WD only ex. Stealth

W Vacuum control system solenoid
   valve air filter 1989 Vista
   4WD ex. Calif. . . . . replace

EVERY 60 MI—96 KM
Spark plugs . . . . replace
Stealth DOHC only

Timing belts . . . . replace
Also replace the balancer belt when equipped

EVERY 80 MI—128 KM
W Oxygen sensor . . . . check/replace

EVERY 100 MI—160 KM
W Evaporative canister . . . . replace

SEVERE SERVICE
W Air cleaner filter, PCV system & brake
system—Service more frequently

W Crankcase—Change oil every 3 mo/3 mi
(4.8 km) & filter every second oil change

Transmission, automatic, rear wheel drive—
Change fluid, filter, & adjust bands every 30
mi (48 km)

Transfer case, 4WD Vista & 4WD Colt manual transaxle—Change lubricant every 30
mi (48 km)

W Spark plugs—Replace every 15 mi (24 km)

KEY TO LUBRICANTS

AF	DEXRON®-II Automatic Transmission Fluid
AP	MOPAR ATF-PLUS®
CD	Motor Oil, API Service CD
EC	Ethylene Glycol Coolant Mix 50% to 70% with water
GL-4	Gear Oil, API Service GL-4
GL-5	Gear Oil, API Service GL-5
GL-5★	Special Lubricant for Limited-Slip Differentials
HB	Hydraulic Brake Fluid, DOT 3
LM	Lithium Grease, EP No. 2
PC	Carburetor Cleaner
SG	Motor Oil, API Service SG
WB	Wheel Bearing Grease

CRANKCASE . . . . SG, SG/CD

CAPACITY, Refill:	Liters	Qt
1.5L Colt	3.0	3.2
1.6L	4.0	4.2
1.8L, 2.0L ex. DOHC, 2.4L	3.5	3.8
2.0L DOHC	4.0	4.2
2.6L	4.3	4.6
3.0L	4.0	4.2

Capacity shown is without filter or oil cooler. When replacing filter, additional oil may be needed
Turbo Models
Above 32°F (0°C) 20W-20, 20W-40
Above –10°F (–23°C) 10W-30
Below 60°F (16°C) 5W-30
All Other Models
Above 32°F (0°C) . . . 20W-20, 20W-40, 20W-50
Above –10°F (–23°C) 10W-30,
10W-40, 10W-50
Below 60°F (16°C) 5W-20*, 5W-30, 5W-40
*Not recommended for sustained high-speed driving

TRANSMISSION/TRANSAXLE,
   Automatic
1989 . . . . **AF, AP**
1990-92 . . . . **AP**

CAPACITY, Initial Refill*:	Liters	Qt
Conquest	5.0	5.3
Stealth	4.5	4.8
Others	4.0	4.2

*With the engine at operating temperature, shift transmission through all gears. Check fluid level in NEUTRAL and add fluid as needed

TRANSMISSION/TRANSAXLE, Manual
RWD 80W, 75W-85W **GL-4**
FWD: 1989-91 . . . . 75W-85W **GL-4**
   1992 . . . . 75W-85W, 75W-90 **GL-4**

CAPACITY, Refill:	Liters	Pt
5-speed RWD	2.3	4.8
Colt ex. wagon: 4-speed	1.7	3.6
5-speed	1.8	3.8
Turbo	2.1	4.4
Colt wagon: 1.5L	1.8	3.8
1.8L	2.2	4.6
Vista: 1989-91 2WD	2.5	5.2
4WD	2.1	4.4
1992: 1.8L	1.8	3.8
2.4L	2.3	4.8
Laser	1.8	3.8
Turbo	2.2	4.6
Stealth: 2WD	2.3	4.8
4WD	2.4	5.0

TRANSFER
   CASE 80W, 75W-85W **GL-4**

CAPACITY, Refill:	Liters	Pt
Vista 4WD 1989-91	0.7	1.5
Vista 4WD 1992	0.6	1.2
Colt 4WD	0.5	1.1
Stealth 4WD	0.3	0.6

DIFFERENTIAL
Limited-Slip . . . . **GL-5★**
Standard **GL-5**
Above –10°F (–23°C), 90, 85W-90, 80W-90; –30°
to –10°F (–34° to –23°C), 80W, 80W-90; below
–30°F (–34°C), 75W

CAPACITY, Refill:	Liters	Pt
Conquest	1.3	2.8
Vista 4WD: 1989-91	0.8	1.7
1992	0.7	1.5
Colt, Stealth	1.1	2.3

LIMITED-SLIP IDENTIFICATION:
Lift rear of vehicle, turn one wheel and the other will turn in
the same direction

DODGE/PLYMOUTH
1983-84 Ram 50

CRIPM6   CRIPM6

MI—MILES IN THOUSANDS
KM—KILOMETERS IN THOUSANDS

DIESEL ENGINES
EVERY 6 MO/3 MI—4.8 KM
Crankcase . . . . change oil

Oil filter . . . . replace
At second oil change, then every other

EVERY 12 MO/7.5 MI—12 KM
Crankcase . . . . change oil
Ex. diesel engine

Exhaust system . . . . inspect

Oil filter . . . . replace
Ex. diesel engine. At second oil change, then every other oil change

Power steering . . . . check level **AF**
Check for leaks & condition of belts

Steering gear,
  manual . . . . check level 90 **GL-5**
Remove lower right bolt of cover & fill through fill hole to 3/4″ (w/4-bolt cover) or 7/8″ (w/3-bolt cover) from top of bolt hole. Check steering wheel free play

Transmission, automatic . . . . . check level

Body 1983 . . . . lubricate

EVERY 12 MO/15 MI—24 KM
Cooling system . . . . inspect
Every 12 mo only

Engine compartment rubber &
  plastic components . . . . inspect

EVERY 15 MI—24 KM
Disc & drum brake lining & hoses . inspect
Wheel cylinders, inspect every 30 mi (48 km)

Tires 1983 . . . . check/rotate

Upper control arm
  bushings . . . . lubricate **WB**
Lug nut torque, ft lb: Steel wheels, 51-58; aluminum wheels, 58-73

Drive belts . . . . inspect/adjust
1984, initial service, then every 30 mi (48 km)

EGR valve Canada . . . . check/clean

Idle speed & mixture . . . . check/adjust
Canadian gasoline only

Ignition timing . . . . check/adjust
Canada only. Check ignition wires

Spark plugs . . . . replace
Canada only

Valve clearance . . . . inspect/adjust

EVERY 24 MO/30 MI—48 KM
Coolant . . . . drain/flush/refill **EC**

Hydraulic clutch, Diesel . . change fluid **HB**
Every 4 years

Vacuum pump oil hoses, Diesel . . . inspect

EVERY 30 MI—48 KM
Differential . . . . check level
Replace lubricant in limited-slip differentials

Front wheel bearings . . . clean/repack **WB**
Inspect for leaks. Inspect & repack whenever rotors are removed

Transmission, manual . . . . check level
Also check transfer case

Air cleaner filter
  ex. carbon element . . . . replace

Choke & linkage . . . . clean **PC**

Drive belts . . . . replace

Evaporative control canister . . . . . . replace
Canadian engines only. 1984 U.S. engines every 5 yr/ 50 mi (80 km)

Fuel filter, Diesel . . . . replace

Spark plugs . . . . replace
U.S. only

Turbocharger air intake
  hoses, Diesel . . . . replace

EVERY 4 YEARS
Brakes . . . . change fluid **HB**
Also change hydraulic clutch fluid

EVERY 5 YR/50 MI—80 KM
Crankcase emission system,
  Gasoline . . . . clean

Evaporative control system . . . . . . inspect

Fuel filter, Gasoline . . . . replace
Check fuel system cap, tank, lines & connections

Fuel, water, & fuel vapor hoses
  ex. Canada . . . . check/replace
Not required for Calif. warranty ex. water hoses

Ignition timing . . . . check/adjust
U.S. only

Ignition wires . . . . check/replace

Timing & balancer belts, Diesel . . . .replace

Turbocharger oil & air intake hoses
  ex. Diesel . . . . replace

Oxygen sensor . . . . .check/replace

Vacuum hoses . . . . check
Secondary air hoses & crankcase ventilation hoses. Ex. Canada

SEVERE SERVICE
Air cleaner filter—Replace more frequently

Crankcase—Change oil: Gasoline, every 3 mo/3 mi (4.8 km) & filter at second oil change, then all every other oil change. Diesel, change oil every 2 mo/2 mi (3.2 km) & filter every other oil change

Transmission, automatic—Change fluid, filter, & adjust bands every 30 mi (48 km)

Transmission, manual & Transfer case—Change lubricant every 30 mi (48 km)

Spark plugs—Replace every 15 mi (24 km)

Upper control arm bushings, Pickup—Lubricate every 7.5 mi (12 km)

KEY TO LUBRICANTS

AF	DEXRON®-II ATF
AP	MOPAR ATF-PLUS®
CD	Motor Oil, API Service CD
EC	Ethylene Glycol Coolant Mix 50% to 70% with water
GL-4	Gear Oil, API Service GL-4
GL-5	Gear Oil, API Service GL-5
GL-5 ★	Special Lubricant for Limited-Slip Differentials
HB	Hydraulic Brake Fluid, DOT 3
MO	Motor Oil
PC	Carburetor Cleaner
SE	Motor Oil, API Service SE
SF	Motor Oil, API Service SF
SG	Motor Oil, API Service SG
WB	Wheel Bearing Grease

CRANKCASE
Gasoline engine . . . . **SE, SF, SG**
Diesel engine . . . . **CD**

CAPACITY, Refill:	Liters	Qt
2-wheel drive:		
2.0L	3.5	3.7
2.3L diesel	5.0	5.3
2.6L	4.5	4.7
4-wheel drive:		
2.0L	4.5	4.7
2.3L	5.5	5.8
2.6L	5.3	5.6

Capacity shown is without filter. When replacing filter, additional oil may be needed
Gasoline engines:
Above 32°F (0°C) 20W-20, 20W-40, 20W-50
Above −10°F (−23°C) . 10W-30, 10W-40, 10W-50
Below 60°F (16°C) 5W-20*, 5W-30, 5W-40
*Not recommended for sustained high-speed driving
Diesel engines:
32° to 104°F (0° to 40°C) 30
Above 14°F (−10°C) 20W-40
Above 5°F (−15°C) 15W-40
−4° to 104°F (−20° to 40°C) 10W-30
Below 50°F (10°C) 5W-30

TRANSMISSION,
Automatic . . . . **AF, AP**

CAPACITY, Initial Refill*:	Liters	Qt
All	3.8	4.0

*With the engine at operating temperature, shift transmission through all gears. Check fluid level in NEUTRAL and add fluid as needed

TRANSMISSION,
Manual 80W, 75W-85W **GL-4**

CAPACITY, Refill:	Liters	Pt
4-speed RWD	2.1	4.4
5-speed RWD	2.3	4.8

TRANSFER
CASE 80W, 75W-85W **GL-4**

CAPACITY, Refill:	Liters	Pt
All models	2.2	4.6

DIFFERENTIAL
Limited-Slip . . . . **GL-5 ★**
Other **GL-5**
Above −10°F (−23°C), 90, 85W-90, 80W-90; −30° to −10°F (−34° to −23°C), 80W, 80W-90; below −30°F (−34°C), 75W

CAPACITY, Refill:	Liters	Pt
Front	1.1	2.3
Rear	1.5	3.2

LIMITED-SLIP IDENTIFICATION:
Lift rear of vehicle, turn one wheel and the other will turn in the same direction

SERVICE AT TIME OR MILEAGE—WHICHEVER OCCURS FIRST

CRIPM7   CRIPM7

MI—MILES IN THOUSANDS
KM—KILOMETERS IN THOUSANDS

CALIF. DIESEL
EVERY 6 MO/3 MI—4.8 KM

Crankcase .... change oil

Oil filter .... replace
At second oil change, then every other

FEDERAL DIESEL
EVERY 5 MI—8 KM

Crankcase .... change oil

Oil filter .... replace
At second oil change, then every other

GASOLINE,
EVERY 12 MO/7.5 MI—12 KM

Crankcase .... change oil

Oil filter .... replace
Every second oil change, but at least every 12 months

EVERY 12 MO/15 MI—24 KM
Brake system .... inspect
Check brake lining, hoses & lines, wheel & master cylinders, brake fluid

Exhaust system .... inspect

Cooling system .... inspect
Service as required

Power steering fluid .... check **AF**
Also check hoses

Upper control arm &
ball joints .... lubricate **WB**

EVERY 15 MI—24 KM
Limited-Slip differential .... change oil

Drive belts .... inspect/adjust
Water pump & alternator only

Idle speed, Gasoline .... check/adjust
Initial service for throttle positioner, then every 50 mi (80 km)

Valve clearance .... inspect/adjust
Adjust jet valve only on 2.0L & 2.6L engines

EVERY 24 MO/30 MI—48 KM
Front wheel bearings ... clean/repack **WB**
Inspect for leaks. Inspect & repack whenever rotors are removed

Coolant .... drain/flush/refill **EC**

Drive shaft joints .... lubricate **WB**

Fuel filter, Diesel .... replace

Hydraulic clutch, Diesel .. change fluid **HB**
Every 4 years

Turbocharger air intake & vacuum
pump oil hoses, Diesel .... replace

EVERY 30 MI—48 KM
Differential .... check level

Transmission, automatic .... change fluid
4WD only

Air cleaner filter .... replace

Choke & linkage .... clean **PC**

Drive belts .... replace
Water pump & alternator only

Idle speed, Diesel .... check/adjust

Spark plugs .... replace

AT FIRST 4 YR/60 MI—96 KM;
THEN EVERY 12 MO/15 MI—24 KM
Air conditioning system .... inspect

Power steering belt .... check

EVERY 4 YR/60 MI—96 KM
Brakes .... change fluid **HB**

EVERY 5 YR/50 MI—80 KM
Carburetor mounting .... check

Crankcase emission system,
Gasoline .... check/clean

Distributor .... check
Ex. California

EGR valve .... replace
Clean sub-EGR valve

Evaporative control system ..... inspect
Replace canister

Fuel filter, Gasoline .... replace
Check fuel system, tank, lines & connections

Fuel, water, & fuel
vapor hoses .... check/replace
Replace fuel cap

Fuel system, Diesel ..... check for leaks

Hot air control valve .... check
Ex. Calif. Inside carburetor air cleaner snorkel

Ignition timing .... check/adjust

Ignition wires .... check/replace

PCV hoses, Diesel .... replace

Secondary air system .... inspect
Ex. California

Timing, Diesel .... replace
At mileage interval only

Oxygen sensor .... check/replace

Vacuum hoses .... replace
Secondary air hoses & crankcase ventilation hoses

Vacuum control system solenoid
valve air filter .... replace

EVERY 60 MI—96 KM
Timing belts .... replace
Ex. Diesel & 2.6L engine

SEVERE SERVICE
Air cleaner filter, PCV system & brake
system—Service more frequently

Crankcase—Change oil every 3 mo/3 mi
(4.8 km) & filter every second oil change.
Diesel, change oil every 2 mo/2 mi (3.2 km)
& filter every other oil change

Transmission, automatic—Change fluid, filter, & adjust bands every 30 mi (48 km)

Transfer case, manual transmission—
Change lubricant every 30 mi (48 km)

Spark plugs—Replace every 15 mi (24 km)

Upper control arm bushings—Lubricate
every 7.5 mi (12 km)

KEY TO LUBRICANTS

AF	DEXRON®-II ATF
AP	MOPAR ATF-PLUS®
CC	Motor Oil, API Service CC
CD	Motor Oil, API Service CD
EC	Ethylene Glycol Coolant Mix 50% to 70% with water
GL-4	Gear Oil, API Service GL-4
GL-5	Gear Oil, API Service GL-5
GL-5★	Special Lubricant for Limited-Slip Differentials
HB	Hydraulic Brake Fluid, DOT 3
PC	Carburetor Cleaner
SF	Motor Oil, API Service SF
SG	Motor Oil, API Service SG
WB	Wheel Bearing Grease

CRANKCASE
Gasoline engine .... SF, SF/CC, SG
Diesel engine .... CD

CAPACITY, Refill:	Liters	Qt
2.0L	3.5	3.7
2.6L 2-wheel drive:		
2.3L diesel	5.0	5.3
2.6L	4.5	4.8
4-wheel drive:		
2.3L diesel	5.5	5.8
2.6L	5.3	5.6

Capacity shown is without filter. When replacing filter, additional oil may be needed

Gasoline engines:
Above 32°F (0°C) 20W-20, 20W-40, 20W-50
Above −10°F (−23°C) . 10W-30, 10W-40, 10W-50
Below 60°F (16°C) 5W-20*, 5W-30, 5W-40
* Not recommended for sustained high-speed driving
Diesel engines:
32° to 104°F (0° to 40°C) 30
Above 14°F (−10°C) 20W-40
Above 5°F (−15°C) 15W-40
−4° to 104°F (−20° to 40°C) 10W-30
Below 50°F (10°C) 5W-30

TRANSMISSION, Automatic .... AF, AP
CAPACITY, Initial Refill*:	Liters	Qt
All	3.8	4.0

* With the engine at operating temperature, shift transmission through all gears. Check fluid level in NEUTRAL and add fluid as needed

TRANSMISSION,
Manual 80W, 75W-85W, **GL-4**
CAPACITY, Refill:	Liters	Pt
4-speed	2.1	4.4
5-speed	2.3	4.8

TRANSFER CASE . 80W, 75W-85W **GL-4**
CAPACITY, Refill:	Liters	Pt
All models	2.2	4.6

DIFFERENTIAL
Limited-Slip .... **GL-5★**
Other **GL-4, GL-5**
Above −10°F (−23°C), 90, 85W-90, 80W-90; −30° to −10°F (−34° to −23°C), 80W, 80W-90; below −30°F (−34°C), 75W
CAPACITY, Refill:	Liters	Pt
Front	1.1	2.3
Rear:		
All ex. Limited-Slip Truck	1.3	2.8
Limited-Slip Truck	1.5	3.2

LIMITED-SLIP IDENTIFICATION:
Lift rear of vehicle, turn one wheel and the other will turn in the same direction

DODGE/PLYMOUTH
1986 Ram 50

CRIPM8

CRIPM8

MI — MILES IN THOUSANDS
KM — KILOMETERS IN THOUSANDS

EVERY 12 MO/7.5 MI — 12 KM
Crankcase .... change oil

Oil filter .... replace
At every second change, but at least every 12 months

EVERY 12 MO/15 MI — 24 KM
Brake system .... inspect
Check linings, hoses & lines, wheel & master cylinders, brake fluid

Exhaust system .... inspect

Cooling system .... inspect
Service as required

Power steering fluid .... check **AF**
Also check hoses

Upper control &
    ball joints .... lubricate **WB**

EVERY 15 MI — 24 KM
Limited-Slip differential .... change oil

Drive belts .... inspect/adjust
Water pump & alternator only

Idle speed .... check/adjust
Required w/carburetor only

Throttle position system .... check
Initial service, then every 50 mi (80 km)

Valve clearance .... inspect/adjust
Adjust jet valve only on 2.0L & 2.6L engines

EVERY 24 MO/30 MI — 48 KM
Front wheel bearings ... clean/repack **WB**
Inspect for leaks. Inspect & repack whenever rotors are removed

Coolant .... drain/flush/refill **EC**

Drive shaft joints .... lubricate **WB**

EVERY 30 MI — 48 KM
Differential .... check level

Transmission, automatic .... change fluid
4WD only

Transmission, manual .... check level
Also check Ram 50 transfer case

Air cleaner filter .... replace

Choke & linkage .... clean **PC**
Required w/carburetor only

Drive belts .... replace
Water pump & alternator only

Spark plugs .... replace

AT FIRST 4 YR/60 MI — 96 KM;
THEN EVERY 12 MO/15 MI — 24 KM
Air conditioning system .... inspect

Power steering belt .... check

EVERY 4 YR/60 MI — 96 KM
Brakes .... change fluid **HB**
Also change hydraulic clutch fluid

EVERY 5 YR/50 MI — 80 KM
Crankcase emission
    system .... check/clean

Distributor cap, rotor &
    advance system .... check
Ex. California

EGR valve .... replace
Clean sub-EGR valve

Evaporative canister .... replace

Evaporative control system ...... inspect

Fuel filter .... replace
Check fuel system tank, lines & connections

Fuel, water, & fuel
    vapor hoses .... check/replace
Replace fuel cap

Hot air control valve .... check
Ex. Calif. Inside carburetor air cleaner snorkel

Ignition timing .... check/adjust

Ignition wires .... check/replace

Secondary air system .... inspect
Ex. California

Oxygen sensor .... check/replace
Ex. California

Vacuum hoses .... replace
Secondary air hoses & crankcase ventilation hoses

Vacuum control system solenoid
    valve air filter .... replace
Ex. California

EVERY 60 MI — 96 KM
Timing belts .... replace
Ex. 2.6L engine

SEVERE SERVICE
Air cleaner filter, PCV system & brake system — Service more frequently

Crankcase — Change oil every 3 mo/3 mi (4.8 km) & filter every second oil change

Transmission, automatic — Change fluid, filter, & adjust bands every 30 mi (48 km)

Transfer case, manual transmission — Change lubricant every 30 mi (48 km)

Spark plugs — Replace every 15 mi (24 km)

Upper control arm bushings — Lubricate every 7.5 mi (12 km)

KEY TO LUBRICANTS

AF	DEXRON®-II ATF
AP	MOPAR ATF-PLUS®
CC	Motor Oil, API Service CC
CD	Motor Oil, API Service CD
EC	Ethylene Glycol Coolant Mix 50% to 70% with water
GL-4	Gear Oil, API Service GL-4
GL-5	Gear Oil, API Service GL-5
GL-5★	Special Lubricant for Limited-Slip Differentials
HB	Hydraulic Brake Fluid, DOT 3
PC	Carburetor Cleaner
SF	Motor Oil, API Service SF
SG	Motor Oil, API Service SG
WB	Wheel Bearing Grease

CRANKCASE .... SF, SF/CC, SG

CAPACITY, Refill:	Liters	Qt
2.0L	3.5	3.7
2.6L:		
2WD	4.5	4.8
4WD	5.3	5.6

Capacity shown is without filter. When replacing filter, additional oil may be needed
Above 32°F (0°C) 20W-20, 20W-40, 20W-50
Above −10°F (−23°C) . 10W-30, 10W-40, 10W-50
Below 60°F (16°C) 5W-20*, 5W-30, 5W-40
*Not recommended for sustained high-speed driving

TRANSMISSION, Automatic .... AF, AP

CAPACITY, Initial Refill*:	Liters	Qt
All models	3.8	4.0

*With the engine at operating temperature, shift transmission through all gears. Check fluid level in NEUTRAL and add fluid as needed

TRANSMISSION,
    Manual 80W, 75W-85W **GL-4**

CAPACITY, Refill:	Liters	Pt
4-speed	2.1	4.4
5-speed	2.3	4.8

TRANSFER
    CASE 80W, 75W-85W **GL-4**

CAPACITY, Refill:	Liters	Pt
All models	2.2	4.6

DIFFERENTIAL
Limited-Slip .... **GL-5★**
Standard **GL-4, GL-5**
Above −10°F (−23°C), 90, 85W-90, 80W-90; −30°
to −10°F (−34° to −23°C), 80W, 80W-90; below
−30°F (−34°C), 75W

CAPACITY, Refill:	Liters	Pt
Front	1.1	2.3
Rear:		
Ex. Limited-Slip	1.3	2.8
Limited-Slip	1.5	3.2

LIMITED-SLIP IDENTIFICATION:
Lift rear of vehicle, turn one wheel and the other will turn in the same direction

SERVICE AT TIME OR MILEAGE—WHICHEVER OCCURS FIRST

CRIPM9   **W SERVICE TO MAINTAIN EMISSION WARRANTY**   CRIPM9

**MI — MILES IN THOUSANDS
KM — KILOMETERS IN THOUSANDS**

EVERY 12 MO/7.5 MI — 12 KM
W Crankcase . . . . change oil

W Oil filter . . . . replace
At every second change, but at least every 12 months

EVERY 12 MO/15 MI — 24 KM
Automatic transmission . . . . . . check level

Brake hoses . . . . check
Check rear linings & wheel cylinders every 24 mo/15 mi (24 km)

Cooling system . . . . inspect
Service as required

Power steering fluid . . . . check **AF**
Service as required. Also check hoses

Suspension joints
   w/fittings . . . . lubricate **LM**
Also inspect 1989-91 drive shaft boots

EVERY 15 MI — 24 KM
Limited-Slip differential
   1987 . . . . change oil

W Idle speed . . . . check/adjust
Not required for California

W Valve clearance . . . . inspect/adjust
Required when specifications are on emission label. Adjust jet valve only on 2.0L & 2.6L engines

EVERY 24 MO/30 MI — 48 KM
Front wheel bearings . . . clean/repack **WB**
Inspect for leaks. Inspect & repack whenever rotors are removed

Coolant . . . . drain/flush/refill **EC**

Drive shaft joints . . . . lubricate **LM**

Suspension joints
   w/o fittings . . . . inspect

EVERY 30 MI — 48 KM
Differential . . . . check level
1988-89 Limited-Slip, change oil

Transmission, automatic . . . . change fluid
4WD only. Also change Raider transfer case fluid

Transmission, manual . . . . . . check level
Also check Raider transfer case

W Air cleaner filter . . . . replace

W Carburetor choke & linkage . . . . clean **PC**

W Drive belts . . . . replace
Water pump & alternator only. Not required for 1988-91 emission warranty

W Spark plugs . . . . replace

EVERY 4 YR/60 MI — 96 KM
Brakes 1987-88 . . . . change fluid **HB**
Also change hydraulic clutch fluid

EVERY 5 YR/50 MI — 80 KM
Carburetor mounting
   1987-88 ex. California . . . . check
At mileage only. 1988 Pickup every 60 mi (96 km)

EGR valve ex. Calif. & 3.0L . . . . . . replace
Clean 1987 Raider sub-EGR valve

W Evaporative canister . . . . replace
1988-89 every 100 mi (160 km)

W Fuel filter . . . . replace

W Fuel lines, connections, fill cap
   & tank . . . . check

W Fuel, water, & fuel
   vapor hoses . . . . check/replace
Replace fuel cap

W Oxygen sensor
   ex. 1989 Calif. . . . . check/replace
Calif. every 80 mi (128 km)

EVERY 5 YR/60 MI—96 KM
W Crankcase emission
   system . . . . check/clean
1989 every 80 mi (128 km)

W Distributor cap, rotor & advance
   system ex. California . . . . check

W Evaporative control system
   ex. 1989 Calif. . . . . inspect

W Hot intake air control valve
   ex. Calif. check

W Ignition wires
   ex. 1989 Calif. . . . . check/replace

W Secondary air system 1987-88
   ex. Calif. . . . . inspect

W Vacuum hoses . . . . replace
Secondary air hoses & crankcase ventilation hoses

W Vacuum control system solenoid
   valve air filter ex. Calif. . . . . replace

EVERY 60 MI — 96 KM
Timing belts . . . . replace
Ex. 2.6L engine

SEVERE SERVICE
W Air cleaner filter, PCV system & brake system — Service more frequently

W Crankcase — Change oil every 3 mo/3 mi (4.8 km) & filter every second oil change

Transmission, automatic — Change fluid, filter, & adjust bands every 30 mi (48 km)

Transfer case, manual transmission — Change lubricant every 30 mi (48 km)

W Spark plugs — Replace every 15 mi (24 km)

KEY TO LUBRICANTS

AF	DEXRON®-II Automatic Transmission Fluid
AP	MOPAR ATF-PLUS®
CD	Motor Oil, API Service CD
EC	Ethylene Glycol Coolant Mix 50% to 70% with water
GL-4	Gear Oil, API Service GL-4
GL-5	Gear Oil, API Service GL-5
GL-5★	Special Lubricant for Limited-Slip Differentials
HB	Hydraulic Brake Fluid, DOT 3
LM	Lithium Grease, EP No. 2
PC	Carburetor Cleaner
SG	Motor Oil, API Service SG
WB	Wheel Bearing Grease

CRANKCASE . . . . SG, SG/CD
CAPACITY, Refill:	Liters	Qt
2.0L: 1987-88	3.5	3.7
1989	3.9	4.0
2.6L:		
1987 2WD	4.5	4.8
1988 2WD	3.8	4.0
1989 Pickup: 4WD	4.5	4.7
2WD	3.8	4.0
1987-88 4WD Pickup . .	5.3	5.6
1987-89 4WD Raider . .	4.5	4.8
3.0L 1989 Raider	4.3	4.5

Capacity shown is without filter. When replacing filter, additional oil may be needed
Above 32°F (0°C) 20W-20, 20W-40, 20W-50
Above –10°F (–23°C) . 10W-30, 10W-40, 10W-50
Below 60°F (16°C) 5W-20*, 5W-30, 5W-40
*Not recommended for sustained high-speed driving

TRANSMISSION, Automatic . . . . AF, AP
CAPACITY, Initial Refill*:	Liters	Qt
All models	5.0	5.3

*With the engine at operating temperature, shift transmission through all gears. Check fluid level in NEUTRAL and add fluid as needed

TRANSMISSION,
Manual 80W, 75W-85W **GL-4**
CAPACITY, Refill:	Liters	Pt
5-speed	2.3	4.8

TRANSFER
CASE 80W, 75W-85W **GL-4**
CAPACITY, Refill:	Liters	Pt
All models	2.2	4.6

DIFFERENTIAL
Limited-Slip . . . . **GL-5★**
Standard **GL-4, GL-5**
Above –10°F (–23°C), 90, 85W-90, 80W-90; –30° to –10°F (–34° to –23°C), 80W, 80W-90; below –30°F (–34°C), 75W

CAPACITY, Refill:	Liters	Pt
Front	1.1	2.3
Rear, Pickup:		
1987 ex. Limited-Slip . .	1.3	2.8
1987 Limited-Slip	1.5	3.2
1988-89 All	1.5	3.2
Rear, Raider:		
w/2.6L eng.	1.8	3.8
w/3.0L eng.	2.6	5.5

LIMITED-SLIP IDENTIFICATION:
Lift rear of vehicle, turn one wheel and the other will turn in the same direction

DODGE/PLYMOUTH
1990-92 Ram 50

SERVICE AT TIME OR MILEAGE—WHICHEVER OCCURS FIRST

CRIPM12   **W SERVICE TO MAINTAIN EMISSION WARRANTY**   CRIPM12

MI — MILES IN THOUSANDS
KM — KILOMETERS IN THOUSANDS

EVERY 12 MO/7.5 MI — 12 KM
Crankcase . . . . change oil

Oil filter . . . . replace
At every second change, but at least every 12 months

EVERY 12 MO/15 MI — 24 KM
Automatic transmission . . . . . . check level

Brake hoses & pads . . . . check
Check rear linings & wheel cylinders every 24 mo/15 mi (24 km)

Drive shaft boots . . . . inspect

Power steering fluid . . . . check **AF**
Service as required. Also check hoses

Suspension joints
w/fittings 1990-91 . . . . lubricate **LM**
Also inspect drive shaft boots

EVERY 24 MO/30 MI — 48 KM
Front wheel bearings
1990 . . . . clean/repack **WB**
Inspect for leaks. Inspect & repack whenever rotors are removed

Coolant . . . . drain/flush/refill **EC**

Drive shaft joints . . . . lubricate **LM**

W Fuel hoses 1991-92 . . . . check

Suspension joints
w/fittings, 1992 . . . . lubricate **LM**

Suspension joints
w/o fittings . . . . inspect

EVERY 30 MI — 48 KM
Differential . . . . check level
Limited-Slip, change oil

Transmission, automatic . . . . change fluid
4WD only. Also change transfer case fluid

Transmission, manual . . . . . . check level

W Air cleaner filter . . . . replace

Drive belts . . . . replace
Water pump & alternator only.

W Spark plugs . . . . replace

EVERY 5 YR/50 MI — 80 KM
EGR valve ex. Calif. & 3.0L . . . . . . replace

W Evaporative canister . . . . replace
Every 100 mi (160 km)

W Fuel lines, connections, fill cap
& tank . . . . check

W Fuel, water, & fuel
vapor hoses 1990 . . . . check/replace

W Oxygen sensor . . . . check/replace
Every 80 mi (128 km)

EVERY 5 YR/60 MI—96 KM
W Crankcase emission
system . . . . check/clean
Every 80 mi (128 km)

W Distributor cap, rotor & advance
system ex. 1990-91 Calif. . . . . check

W Evaporative control system
ex. Calif. . . . . inspect

W Hot intake air control valve
ex. Calif. 1990-91 . . . . check

W Ignition wires
ex. Calif. . . . . check/replace

W Vacuum hoses 1990-91 . . . . replace
Secondary air hoses & crankcase ventilation hoses

EVERY 60 MI — 96 KM
Timing belts . . . . replace

EVERY 100 MI — 160 KM
Evaporative canister . . . . replace

SEVERE SERVICE
W Air cleaner filter, PCV system & brake
system — Service more frequently

W Crankcase — Change oil every 3 mo/3 mi
(4.8 km) & filter every second oil change

Transmission, automatic — Change fluid, filter, & adjust bands every 30 mi (48 km)

Transfer case, manual transmission —
Change lubricant every 30 mi (48 km)

W Spark plugs — Replace every 15 mi (24 km)

KEY TO LUBRICANTS
AF	DEXRON®-II Automatic Transmission Fluid
AP	MOPAR ATF-PLUS®
CD	Motor Oil, API Service CD
EC	Ethylene Glycol Coolant Mix 50% to 70% with water
GL-4	Gear Oil, API Service GL-4
GL-5	Gear Oil, API Service GL-5
GL-5★	Special Lubricant for Limited-Slip Differentials
HB	Hydraulic Brake Fluid, DOT 3
LM	Lithium Grease, EP No. 2
PC	Carburetor Cleaner
SG	Motor Oil, API Service SG
WB	Wheel Bearing Grease

CRANKCASE . . . . SG, SG/CD
CAPACITY, Refill:	Liters	Qt
2.4L	3.5	3.7
3.0L	4.3	4.5

Capacity shown is without filter. When replacing filter, additional oil may be needed
Above 32°F (0°C) 20W-20, 20W-40, 20W-50
Above −10°F (−23°C) . 10W-30, 10W-40, 10W-50
Below 60°F (16°C) 5W-20*, 5W-30, 5W-40
*Not recommended for sustained high-speed driving

TRANSMISSION, Automatic . . . . AP
CAPACITY, Initial Refill*:	Liters	Qt
All models	5.0	5.3

*With the engine at operating temperature, shift transmission through all gears. Check fluid level in NEUTRAL and add fluid as needed

TRANSMISSION,
Manual . 80W, 75W-85W, 75W-90 **GL-4**
CAPACITY, Refill:	Liters	Pt
5-speed	2.3	4.8

TRANSFER
CASE . . 80W, 75W-85W, 75W-90 **GL-4**
CAPACITY, Refill:	Liters	Pt
All models	2.2	4.6

DIFFERENTIAL
Limited-Slip . . . . **GL-5★**
Standard **GL-4, GL-5**
Above −10°F (−23°C), 90, 85W-90, 80W-90; −30° to −10°F (−34° to −23°C), 80W, 80W-90; below −30°F (−34°C), 75W
CAPACITY, Refill:	Liters	Pt
Front: 2.4L	1.1	2.3
3.0L	2.6	5.5
Rear: 2.4L	1.5	3.2
3.0L	2.6	5.5

LIMITED-SLIP IDENTIFICATION:
Lift rear of vehicle, turn one wheel and the other will turn in the same direction

SERVICE LOCATIONS — ENGINE AND CHASSIS

DETDP-1   DETDP-1

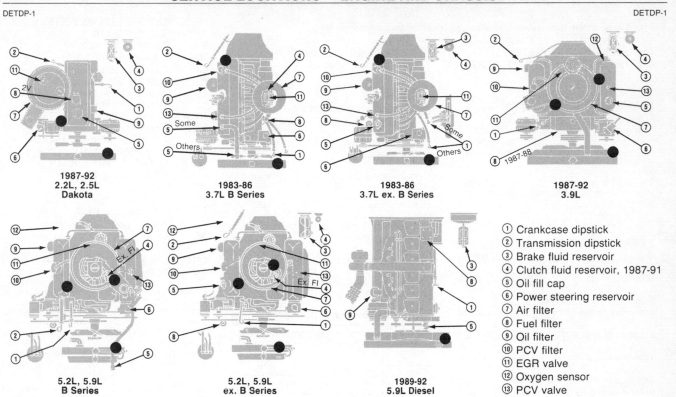

1987-92 2.2L, 2.5L Dakota

1983-86 3.7L B Series

1983-86 3.7L ex. B Series

1987-92 3.9L

5.2L, 5.9L B Series

5.2L, 5.9L ex. B Series

1989-92 5.9L Diesel

① Crankcase dipstick
② Transmission dipstick
③ Brake fluid reservoir
④ Clutch fluid reservoir, 1987-91
⑤ Oil fill cap
⑥ Power steering reservoir
⑦ Air filter
⑧ Fuel filter
⑨ Oil filter
⑩ PCV filter
⑪ EGR valve
⑫ Oxygen sensor
⑬ PCV valve

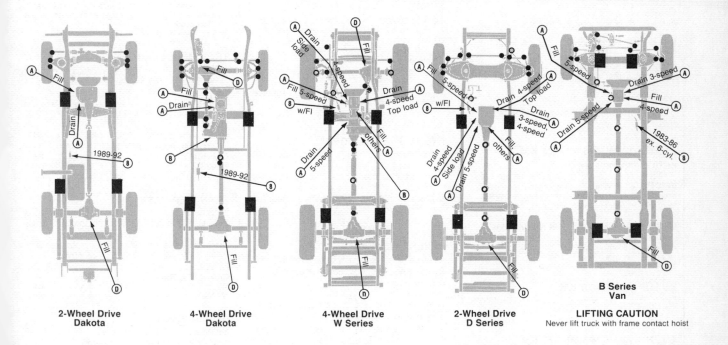

2-Wheel Drive Dakota

4-Wheel Drive Dakota

4-Wheel Drive W Series

2-Wheel Drive D Series

B Series Van

LIFTING CAUTION
Never lift truck with frame contact hoist

● Cooling system drain   ■ Lift adapter position
• Fitting   ○ Fitting, some models

Ⓐ Manual transmission/transaxle, drain & fill
Ⓑ Transfer case, drain & fill
Ⓒ Automatic transaxle final drive, NOT USED
Ⓓ Differential, drain & fill

CHEK-CHART

SERVICE AT TIME OR MILEAGE—WHICHEVER OCCURS FIRST

DETPM9   DETPM9

8,500 & under GVWR. GVWR is found on Safety Certification Label on left door lock pillar

MI—MILES IN THOUSANDS
KM—KILOMETERS IN THOUSANDS

EVERY 6 MO/7.5 MI—12 KM
Fittings (4 × 4):
   Steering linkage . . . . lubricate **BJ**
   Others . . . . lubricate **LM**
Includes front wheel bearings; remove wheels to reach fitting

Transfer case linkage . . . . lubricate
NP205 lubricate with **MO**; NP208 lubricate with **LM**
Service as required

EVERY 12 MO/7.5 MI—12 KM
Crankcase . . . . change oil

Differential . . . . check for leaks

Suspension ball joints, seals,
   U-joints (sealed) (4 × 2) . . . . inspect

Transfer case (4 × 4) . . . . check level

Transmission, manual . . . . check level

Wheel nuts, steering linkage &
   spring clip nuts . . . . torque

Brake master cylinder . . . . check level **HB**

Oil filter . . . . replace
At every other oil change or at least every 12 mo

Power steering reservoir . . check level **PS**

Transmission, automatic . . . . . check level
Fluid warm, engine idling, in NEUTRAL

Body & brake
   actuating mechanisms . . . . lubricate **MO**

EVERY 12 MO/15 MI—24 KM
Front wheel bearings
   (4 × 4) . . . . inspect **LM**
Ex. 44F-BJ & 60F front differentials. At mileage interval only. Also clean & repack front spindle needle bearings as required & when replacing disc pads

Carburetor choke shaft, fast idle cam
   & pivots . . . . clean **PC**
Every 12 mo/30 mi (48 km)

EVERY 12 MI—19 KM
Tires . . . . rotate

EVERY 12 MO/48 MI—77 KM
Rear wheel bearings . . . . inspect **LM**
Models with Spicer Dana 60 or 70 series differential only. Repack as required. Repack all models whenever axles are removed or brakes are serviced

EVERY 15 MI—24 KM
Drive belts . . . . inspect/adjust

Spark plugs . . . . replace
Without catalytic converter

EVERY 24 MO/22.5 MI—36 KM
Fittings & wheel stops
   (4 × 2) . . . . lubricate **LM**
Ex. front suspension ball joints & steering linkage

Front suspension ball joints &
   steering linkage (4 × 2) . . . . lubricate **BJ**

Parking brake ratio
   lever pivot . . . . lubricate **LM**

Transmission linkage . . . . **fitting LM**
OD only, while in reverse, engine off

EVERY 22.5 MI—36 KM
Brake linings . . . . inspect

Front spindle needle bearings
   (4 × 4) . . . . inspect **LM**
With 44F-BJ & 60F front differentials, lubricate as required & when replacing disc pads

Front wheel bearings (4 × 2) . . . inspect **LM**
Also inspect at brake inspection or servicing; lubricate rear wheel bearings whenever axles are removed. Clean/repack front wheel bearings when replacing disc pads

Transmission, automatic . . . . change fluid
Every 37.5 mi (60 km). Not required for Ram Wagon or Voyager. Replace filter & adjust bands

EVERY 30 MI—48 KM
Cooling system . . . . . . change coolant **EC**
At first 36 mo/52.5 mi (84 km), then every 24 mo/30 mi (48 km)

Air cleaner element . . . . replace
Only required for Calif. 6-cyl. eng.

Spark plugs . . . . replace
Vehicles with catalytic converter

EVERY 37.5 MI—60 KM
Transfer case . . . . change lubricant

Transmission, manual . . . change lubricant

Crankcase inlet air cleaner . . . . . . clean/oil
Every 52.5 mi (84 km)

SEVERE SERVICE
Crankcase—Drain every 3 mo/3 mi (4.8 km). Every 50 hours for 4-wheel drive used for off-road driving

Drive line fittings—Lubricate every 3 mo/3 mi (4.8 km) ex. 4-wheel drive, every 1 mi (1.6 km), includes front wheel bearing inspection for off-road use. Lubricate daily if operating in water

Suspension ball joints—Lubricate every engine oil change

Transmission, automatic—Change fluid every 12 mi (19 km) or every 12 mo when plowing snow. Replace filter & adjust bands

Transmission, manual—Change lubricant every 18 mi (29 km)

KEY TO LUBRICANTS

AF	DEXRON®-II ATF
AP	MOPAR ATF-PLUS®
BJ	Suspension Lubricant
CC	Motor Oil, API Service CC
CD	Motor Oil, API Service CD
EC	Ethylene Glycol Coolant Mix with water to desired freeze protection
GL-5	Gear Oil, API Service GL-5
GL-5★	Special Lubricant for Anti-Spin, Limited-Slip, Powr-Loc, Sure-Grip or Trac-Loc Differential
HB	Hydraulic Brake Fluid, DOT 3
LM	Lithium Grease, EP No. 2
MO	Motor Oil
PC	Carburetor Cleaner
PS	Power Steering Fluid
SF	Motor Oil, API Service SF
SG	Motor Oil, API Service SG

CRANKCASE . . . SF, SF/CC, SG, SG/CD

CAPACITY, Refill:	Liters	Qt
All	4.7	5.0

Capacity shown is without filter. When replacing filter, additional oil may be needed

Above 20°F (–7°C) . . 10W-30, 10W-40, 10W-50, 15W-40, 20W-40, 20W-50, 30
20° to 80°F (–7° to 27°C) 20W-20
Above 10°F (–12°C) 15W-40
Above 0°F (–18°C) . . . 10W-30, 10W-40, 10W-50
Below 60°F (16°C) 5W-30, 5W-40

TRANSMISSION, Automatic . . . . **AF, AP**

CAPACITY, Initial Refill*:	Liters	Qt
All models w/o torque converter drain . .	3.8	4.0

*With the engine at operating temperature, shift transmission through all gears. Check fluid level in PARK and add fluid as needed
To drain, remove oil pan

TRANSMISSION, Manual
A833 OD . . . . **AF, AP**
75W, 75W-80, 80W-90, 85W-90, 90 **GL-5** may be used
NP435 . . . . **GL-5, SF, SG**
SF, SG: Above 32°F (0°C), 50; below 32°F (0°C), 30
GL-5: Above 90°F (32°C), 140; above –10°F (–23°C), 90; below –10°F (–23°C), 80W

CAPACITY, Refill:	Liters	Pt
NP435	3.3	7.0
A833 OD	3.5	7.5

TRANSFER CASE
NP205 . . . . **GL-5, SF, SG**
SF, SG: Above 32°F (0°C), 50; below 32°F (0°C), 30
GL-5: Above 90°F (32°C), 140; above –10°F (–23°C), 90; below –10°F (–23°C), 80W
NP208 . . . . **AF, AP**

CAPACITY, Refill:	Liters	Pt
NP205	2.1	4.5
NP208	2.8	6.0

DIFFERENTIAL
Standard **GL-5**
Anti-Spin, Limited-Slip, Powr-Loc,
   Sure-Grip, Trac-Loc . . . . . . 90 **GL-5★**
Above 90°F (32°C), 140, 80W-140, 85W-140; above –10°F (–23°C), 90, 80W-90, 80W-140, 85W-140; below 10°F (–23°C), 75W, 80W, 75W-90, 80W-140

CAPACITY, Refill:	Liters	Pt
Front: 4-wheel drive		
ex. Spicer 60F	1.7	3.5
Spicer 60F	3.1	6.5
Rear: Spicer 60, 60 HD . . .	2.8	6.0
Spicer 70	3.1	6.5
Others	2.1	4.5

DODGE/PLYMOUTH TRUCKS
1983 All Heavy Duty Emissions Models

SERVICE AT TIME OR MILEAGE—WHICHEVER OCCURS FIRST

DETPM10

DETPM10

Over 8,500 GVWR. GVWR is found on Safety Certification Label on left door lock pillar

**MI—MILES IN THOUSANDS
KM—KILOMETERS IN THOUSANDS**

EVERY 6 MO/6 MI—9.6 KM
Fittings (4 x 4):
  Steering linkage .... lubricate **BJ**
  Others .... lubricate **LM**
Includes front wheel bearings: remove wheels to reach fitting

Transfer case linkage .... lubricate
NP205 lubricate with **MO**; NP208 lubricate with **LM**
Service as required

EVERY 12 MO/6 MI—9.6 KM
Crankcase .... change oil

Differential .... check for leaks

Suspension ball joints, seals,
  U-joints (sealed) (4 x 2) .... inspect

Transfer case (4 x 4) .... check level

Transmission, manual .... check level

Wheel nuts, steering linkage &
  spring clip nuts .... torque

Brake master cylinder .... check level **HB**

Oil filter .... replace
At every other oil change or at least every 12 mo

Power steering reservoir .. check level **PS**
Hydroboost **PS** fluid required for B-350 school bus

Transmission, automatic ..... check level
Fluid warm, engine idling, in NEUTRAL

Body & brake
  actuating mechanisms .... lubricate **MO**

EVERY 12 MO/12 MI—19 KM
Front wheel bearings
  (4 x 4) .... inspect **LM**
Ex. 44F-BJ & 60F front differentials. At mileage interval only. Also clean & repack front spindle needle bearings as required & when replacing disc pads

Carburetor choke shaft, fast idle cam
  & pivots .... clean **PC**

Crankcase inlet air cleaner ...... clean/oil

EVERY 12 MI—19 KM
Tires .... rotate

Air cleaner paper element .... clean

EGR system .... check
Vehicles without catalytic converter

PCV system .... check

EVERY 12 MO/48 MI—77 KM
Rear wheel bearings .... inspect **LM**
Models with Spicer Dana 60 or 70 series differential only. Repack as required. Repack all models whenever axles are removed or brakes are serviced

EVERY 18 MI—29 KM
Automatic choke .... check

Drive belts .... inspect/adjust

Emission & fuel hoses .... inspect

Engine operation .... check
Curb idle speed & ignition timing

Fuel filter .... replace

Ignition cables, distributor cap
  & rotor .... check

Manifold heat valve .... lubricate **MH**

Spark plugs .... replace

EVERY 24 MO/24 MI—38 KM
Fittings & wheel stops
  (4 x 2) .... lubricate **LM**
Ex. front suspension ball joints & steering linkage

Front suspension ball joints &
  steering linkage (4 x 2) .... lubricate **BJ**

Parking brake ratio
  lever pivot .... lubricate **LM**

Transmission linkage .... **fitting LM**
OD only, while in reverse, engine off

EVERY 24 MI—38 KM
Brake linings .... inspect

Front spindle needle bearings
  (4 x 4) .... inspect **LM**
With 44F-BJ & 60F front differentials, lubricate as required & when replacing disc pads

Front wheel bearings (4 x 2) ... inspect **LM**
Also inspect at brake inspection or servicing; lubricate rear wheel bearings whenever axles are removed. Clean/repack front wheel bearings when replacing disc pads

Transmission, automatic .... change fluid
Every 37.5 mi (60 km). Not required for Ram Wagon or Voyager. Replace filter & adjust bands

Cooling system ...... change coolant **EC**
At first 36 mo/48 mi (77 km), then every 24 mo/30 mi (48 km)

Air cleaner element .... replace

PCV valve .... replace

EVERY 36 MI—58 KM
Transfer case .... change lubricant

Transmission, manual ... change lubricant

SEVERE SERVICE
Crankcase—Drain every 3 mo/3 mi (4.8 km). Every 50 hours for 4-wheel drive used for off-road driving

Drive line fittings—Lubricate every 3 mo/3 mi (4.8 km) ex. 4-wheel drive, every 1 mi (1.6 km), includes front wheel bearing inspection for off-road use. Lubricate daily if operating in water

Suspension ball joints—Lubricate every engine oil change

Transmission, automatic—Change fluid every 12 mi (19 km) or every 12 mo when plowing snow. Replace filter & adjust bands

Transmission, manual—Change lubricant every 18 mi (29 km)

KEY TO LUBRICANTS

AF	DEXRON®-II ATF
AP	MOPAR ATF-PLUS®
BJ	Suspension Lubricant
CC	Motor Oil, API Service CC
CD	Motor Oil, API Service CD
EC	Ethylene Glycol Coolant
	Mix with water to desired freeze protection
GL-5	Gear Oil, API Service GL-5
GL-5★	Special Lubricant for Anti-Spin, Limited-Slip, Powr-Loc, Sure-Grip or Trac-Loc Differential
HB	Hydraulic Brake Fluid, DOT 3
LM	Lithium Grease, EP No. 2
MH	Manifold Heat Valve Solvent
MO	Motor Oil
PC	Carburetor Cleaner
PS	Power Steering Fluid
SF	Motor Oil, API Service SF
SG	Motor Oil, API Service SG

CRANKCASE ... SF, SF/CC, SG, SG/CD

CAPACITY, Refill:	Liters	Qt
All models	4.7	5.0

Capacity shown is without filter. When replacing filter, additional oil may be needed
Above 20°F (–7°C) .. 10W-30, 10W-40, 10W-50, 15W-40, 20W-40, 20W-50, 30
20° to 80°F (–7° to 27°C) 20W-20
Above 10°F (–12°C) 15W-40
Above 0°F (–18°C) ... 10W-30, 10W-40, 10W-50
Below 60°F (16°C) ... 5W-30, 5W-40

TRANSMISSION, Automatic .... AF, AP

CAPACITY, Initial Refill*:	Liters	Qt
All models w/o torque converter drain ..	3.8	4.0

*With the engine at operating temperature, shift transmission through all gears. Check fluid level in PARK and add fluid as needed

TRANSMISSION, Manual
A833 OD .... AF, AP
75W, 75W-80, 80W-90, 85W-90, 90 GL-5 may be used
NP435 .... GL-5, SF, SG
SF, SG: Above 32°F (0°C), 50; below 32°F (0°C), 30
GL-5: Above 90°F (32°C), 140; above –10°F (–23°C), 90; below –10°F (–23°C), 80W

CAPACITY, Refill:	Liters	Pt
NP435	3.3	7.0
A833 OD	3.5	7.5

TRANSFER CASE
NP205 .... GL-5, SF, SG
SF, SG: Above 32°F (0°C), 50; below 32°F (0°C), 30
GL-5: Above 90°F (32°C), 140; above –10°F (–23°C), 90; below –10°F (–23°C), 80W
NP208 .... AF, AP

CAPACITY, Refill:	Liters	Pt
NP205	2.1	4.5
NP208	2.8	6.0

DIFFERENTIAL
Standard GL-5
Anti-Spin, Limited-Slip, Powr-Loc,
  Sure-Grip, Trac-Loc .... 90 **GL-5★**
Above 90°F (32°C), 140, 80W-140, 85W-140; above –10°F (–23°C), 90, 80W-90, 80W-140, 85W-140; below 10°F (–23°C), 75W, 80W, 75W-90, 80W-140

CAPACITY, Refill:	Liters	Pt
Front: 4-wheel drive ex. Spicer 60F	1.7	3.5
Spicer 60F	3.1	6.5
Rear: Spicer 60, 60 HD ..	2.8	6.0
Spicer 70	3.1	6.5
Others	2.1	4.5

DODGE TRUCKS
1984 All Rear Wheel & 4-Wheel
Light Duty Emissions Models Except Ram 50

SERVICE AT TIME OR MILEAGE—WHICHEVER OCCURS FIRST

DETPM11   DETPM11

8,500 & under GVWR. GVWR is found on Safety Certification Label on left door lock pillar. See 1984 passenger car chart for front wheel drive vans & pickups

MI—MILES IN THOUSANDS
KM—KILOMETERS IN THOUSANDS

EVERY 6 MO/7.5 MI—12 KM
Fittings (4 × 4):
  Steering linkage .... lubricate **BJ**
  Others .... lubricate **LM**
Includes front wheel bearings; remove wheels to reach fitting

Transfer case linkage .... lubricate
NP205 lubricate with **MO**
NP208 lubricate with **LM**. Service as required

EVERY 12 MO/7.5 MI—12 KM
Crankcase .... change oil

Differential .... check for leaks

Suspension ball joints, seals,
  U-joints (sealed) (4 × 2) .... inspect

Transfer case (4 × 4) .... check level

Transmission, manual .... check level

Wheel nuts, steering linkage &
  spring clip nuts .... torque

Brake master cylinder .... check level **HB**

Oil filter .... replace
At every other oil change or at least every 12 mo

Power steering reservoir .. check level **PS**

Transmission, automatic ..... check level
Fluid warm, engine idling, in NEUTRAL

Body & brake
  actuating mechanisms .... lubricate **MO**

EVERY 12 MO/15 MI—24 KM
Front wheel bearings
  (4 × 4) .... inspect **LM**
Ex. 44F-BJ & 60F front differentials. At mileage interval only. Also clean & repack front spindle needle bearings as required & when replacing disc pads

EVERY 12 MO/30 MI—48 KM
Carburetor choke shaft, fast idle cam
  & pivots .... clean **PC**

EVERY 12 MI—19 KM
Tires .... rotate

EVERY 12 MO/48 MI—77 KM
Rear wheel bearings .... inspect **LM**
Models with Spicer Dana 60 or 70 series differential only. Repack as required. All models: whenever axles are removed or brakes are serviced, repack

EVERY 15 MI—24 KM
Drive belts .... inspect/adjust

Spark plugs .... replace
Models without catalytic converter

EVERY 24 MO/22.5 MI—36 KM
Fittings & wheel stops
  (4 × 2) .... lubricate **LM**
Ex. front suspension ball joints & steering linkage

Front suspension ball joints &
  steering linkage (4 × 2) .... lubricate **BJ**

Parking brake ratio
  lever pivot .... lubricate **LM**

Transmission linkage .... fitting **LM**
OD only, while in reverse, engine off

EVERY 22.5 MI—36 KM
Brake linings .... inspect

Front spindle needle bearings
  (4 × 4) .... inspect **LM**
With 44F-BJ & 60F front differentials, lubricate as required & when replacing disc pads

Front wheel bearings (4 × 2) ... inspect **LM**
Also inspect at brake inspection or servicing; lubricate rear wheel bearings whenever axles are removed. Clean/repack front wheel bearings when replacing disc pads

EVERY 30 MI—48 KM
Cooling system ...... change coolant **EC**
Also flush system at first 36 mo/52.5 mi (84 km), then every 24 mo/30 mi (48 km)

Air cleaner element .... replace
Required for all Calif. engs. & some 6-cyl. with computerized carburetor control

Spark plugs .... replace
Models with catalytic converter

EVERY 37.5 MI—60 KM
Transfer case .... change lubricant

Transmission, automatic .... change fluid
Not required for Ram Wagon. Replace filter & adjust bands

Transmission, manual ... change lubricant

Crankcase inlet air cleaner ..... clean/oil
Every 52.5 mi (84 km)

SEVERE SERVICE
Crankcase—Drain every 3 mo/3 mi (4.8 km). Every 50 hours for 4-wheel drive used for off-road driving

Drive line fittings—Lubricate every 3 mo/3 mi (4.8 km) ex. 4-wheel drive, every 1 mi (1.6 km), includes front wheel bearing inspection for off-road use. Lubricate daily if operating in water

Suspension ball joints—Lubricate every engine oil change

Transmission, automatic—Change fluid every 12 mi (19 km) or every 12 mo when plowing snow. Replace filter & adjust bands

Transmission, manual—Change lubricant every 18 mi (29 km)

KEY TO LUBRICANTS
AF	DEXRON®-II ATF
AP	MOPAR ATF-PLUS®
BJ	Suspension Lubricant
CC	Motor Oil, API Service CC
CD	Motor Oil, API Service CD
EC	Ethylene Glycol Coolant
	Mix with water to desired freeze protection
GL-5	Gear Oil, API Service GL-5
GL-5★	Special Lubricant for Anti-Spin, Limited-Slip, Powr-Loc, Sure-Grip or Trac-Loc Differential
HB	Hydraulic Brake Fluid, DOT 3
LM	Lithium Grease, EP No. 2
MO	Motor Oil
PC	Carburetor Cleaner
PS	Power Steering Fluid
SF	Motor Oil, API Service SF
SG	Motor Oil, API Service SG

CRANKCASE ... SF, SF/CC, SG, SG/CD
CAPACITY, Refill:	Liters	Qt
All models	4.7	5.0

Capacity shown is without filter. When replacing filter, additional oil may be needed
Above 20°F (–7°C) .. 10W-30, 10W-40, 10W-50,
              15W-40, 20W-40, 20W-50, 30
20° to 80°F (–7° to 27°C) 20W-20
Above 10°F (–12°C) 15W-40
Above 0°F (–18°C) .. 10W-30, 10W-40, 10W-50
Below 60°F (16°C) 5W-30, 5W-40

TRANSMISSION, Automatic .... AF, AP
CAPACITY, Initial Refill*:	Liters	Qt
All models w/o torque converter drain ..	3.8	4.0

*With the engine at operating temperature, shift transmission through all gears. Check fluid level in PARK and add fluid as needed

TRANSMISSION, Manual
A833 OD .... **AF, AP**
75W, 75W-80, 80W-90, 85W-90, 90 **GL-5** may be used
NP435 .... **GL-5, SF, SG**
SF, SG: Above 32°F (0°C), 50; below 32°F (0°C), 30
GL-5: Above 90°F (32°C), 140; above –10°F (–23°C), 90; below –10°F (–23°C), 80W

CAPACITY, Refill:	Liters	Pt
NP435	3.3	7.0
A833 OD	3.5	7.5

TRANSFER CASE
NP205 .... **GL-5, SF, SG**
SF, SG: Above 32°F (0°C), 50; below 32°F (0°C), 30
GL-5: Above 90°F (32°C), 140; above –10°F (–23°C), 90; below –10°F (–23°C), 80W
NP208 .... **AF, AP**

CAPACITY, Refill:	Liters	Pt
NP205	2.1	4.5
NP208	2.8	6.0

DIFFERENTIAL
Standard **GL-5**
Anti-Spin, Limited-Slip, Powr-Loc,
  Sure-Grip, Trac-Loc .... **GL-5★**
Above 90°F (32°C), 140, 80W-140, 85W-140; above –10°F (–23°C), 90, 80W-90, 80W-140, 85W-140; below –10°F (–23°C), 75W, 80W, 75W-90, 80W-140

CAPACITY, Refill:	Liters	Pt
Front: 4-wheel drive		
Spicer 60F	3.1	6.5
Others	1.7	3.5
Rear: Spicer 60, 60 HD ...	2.8	6.0
Spicer 70	3.1	6.5
Others	2.1	4.5

DODGE TRUCKS
1984 All Heavy Duty Emissions Models

SERVICE AT TIME OR MILEAGE—WHICHEVER OCCURS FIRST

DETPM12   DETPM12

Over 8,500 GVWR. GVWR is found on Safety Certification Label on left door lock pillar

MI—MILES IN THOUSANDS
KM—KILOMETERS IN THOUSANDS

EVERY 6 MO/6 MI—9.6 KM
Fittings (4 × 4):
Steering linkage .... lubricate **BJ**
Others .... lubricate **LM**
Includes front wheel bearings; remove wheels to reach fitting

Transfer case linkage .... lubricate
NP205 lubricate with **MO**; NP208 lubricate with **LM**
Service as required

EVERY 12 MO/6 MI—9.6 KM
Crankcase .... change oil

Differential .... check for leaks

Suspension ball joints, seals,
U-joints (sealed) (4 × 2) .... inspect

Transfer case (4 × 4) .... check level

Transmission, manual .... check level

Wheel nuts, steering linkage &
spring clip nuts .... torque

Brake master cylinder .... check level **HB**

Oil filter .... replace
At every other oil change or at least every 12 mo

Power steering reservoir .. check level **PS**

Transmission, automatic ..... check level
Fluid warm, engine idling, in NEUTRAL

Body & brake
actuating mechanisms .... lubricate **MO**

EVERY 12 MO/12 MI—19 KM
Front wheel bearings
(4 × 4) .... inspect **LM**
Ex. 44F-BJ & 60F front differentials. At mileage interval only. Also clean & repack front spindle needle bearings as required & when replacing disc pads

Carburetor choke shaft, fast idle cam
& pivots .... clean **PC**

Crankcase inlet air cleaner ...... clean/oil

EVERY 12 MI—19 KM
Tires .... rotate

Air cleaner paper element .... clean

EGR system .... check
Clean passages also
Vehicles without catalytic converter

PCV valve & system .... check

EVERY 12 MO/48 MI—77 KM
Rear wheel bearings .... inspect **LM**
Models with Spicer Dana 60 or 70 series differential only. Repack as required. All models: whenever axles are removed or brakes are serviced, repack

EVERY 18 MI—29 KM
Automatic choke .... check

Drive belts .... inspect/adjust

Emission & fuel hoses .... inspect

Engine operation .... check
Curb idle speed & ignition timing

Fuel filter .... replace

Ignition cables, distributor cap
& rotor .... check

Manifold heat valve .... lubricate **MH**

Spark plugs .... replace

EVERY 24 MO/24 MI—38 KM
Fittings & wheel stops
(4 × 2) .... lubricate **LM**
Ex. front suspension ball joints & steering linkage

Front suspension ball joints &
steering linkage (4 × 2) .... lubricate **BJ**

Parking brake ratio
lever pivot .... lubricate **LM**

Transmission linkage .... **fitting LM**
OD only, while reverse, engine off

EVERY 24 MI—38 KM
Brake linings .... inspect

Front spindle needle bearings
(4 × 4) .... inspect **LM**
With 44F-BJ & 60F front differentials, lubricate as required & when replacing disc pads

Front wheel bearings (4 × 2) ... inspect **LM**
Also inspect at brake inspection or servicing; lubricate rear wheel bearings whenever axles are removed. Clean/repack front wheel bearings when replacing disc pads

Transmission, automatic .... change fluid
Not required for Ram Wagon. Replace filter & adjust bands

Cooling system ...... change coolant **EC**
Flush system also at first 36 mo/48 mi (77 km), then every 24 mo/30 mi (48 km)

Air cleaner element .... replace

PCV valve .... replace

EVERY 36 MI—58 KM
Transfer case .... change lubricant

Transmission, manual ... change lubricant

SEVERE SERVICE
Crankcase—Drain every 3 mo/3 mi (4.8 km). Every 50 hours for 4-wheel drive used for off-road driving

Drive line fittings—Lubricate every 3 mo/3 mi (4.8 km) ex. 4-wheel drive, every 1 mi (1.6 km), includes front wheel bearing inspection for off-road use. Lubricate daily if operating in water

Suspension ball joints—Lubricate every engine oil change

Transmission, automatic—Change fluid every 12 mi (19 km) or every 12 mo when plowing snow. Replace filter & adjust bands

Transmission, manual—Change lubricant every 18 mi (29 km)

KEY TO LUBRICANTS
AF	DEXRON®-II ATF
AP	MOPAR ATF-PLUS®
BJ	Suspension Lubricant
CC	Motor Oil, API Service CC
CD	Motor Oil, API Service CD
EC	Ethylene Glycol Coolant
	Mix with water to desired freeze protection
GL-5	Gear Oil, API Service GL-5
GL-5★	Special Lubricant for Anti-Spin, Limited-Slip, Powr-Loc, Sure-Grip or Trac-Loc Differential
HB	Hydraulic Brake Fluid, DOT 3
LM	Lithium Grease, EP No. 2
MH	Manifold Heat Valve Solvent
MO	Motor Oil
PC	Carburetor Cleaner
PS	Power Steering Fluid
SF	Motor Oil, API Service SF
SG	Motor Oil, API Service SG

CRANKCASE ... SF, SF/CC, SG, SG/CD
CAPACITY, Refill:	Liters	Qt
All models	4.7	5.0

Capacity shown is without filter. When replacing filter, additional oil may be needed

Above 20°F (−7°C) ..	10W-30, 10W-40, 10W-50, 15W-40, 20W-40, 20W-50, 30
20° to 80°F (−7° to 27°C)	20W-20
Above 10°F (−12°C)	15W-40
Above 0°F (−18°C) ...	10W-30, 10W-40, 10W-50
Below 60°F (16°C)	5W-30, 5W-40

TRANSMISSION, Automatic .... AF, AP
CAPACITY, Initial Refill*:	Liters	Qt
All models w/o torque converter drain ..	3.8	4.0

*With the engine at operating temperature, shift transmission through all gears. Check fluid level in PARK and add fluid as needed

TRANSMISSION, Manual
A833 OD .... **AF, AP**
75W, 75W-80, 80W-90, 85W-90, 90 **GL-5** may be used
NP435 .... **GL-5, SF, SG**
SF, SG: Above 32°F (0°C), 50; below 32°F (0°C), 30
GL-5: Above 90°F (32°C), 140; above −10°F (−23°C), 90; below −10°F (−23°C), 80W

CAPACITY, Refill:	Liters	Pt
NP435	3.3	7.0
A833 OD	3.5	7.5

TRANSFER CASE
NP205 .... **GL-5, SF, SG**
SF, SG: Above 32°F (0°C), 50; below 32°F (0°C), 30
GL-5: Above 90°F (32°C), 140; above −10°F (−23°C), 90; below −10°F (−23°C), 80W
NP208 .... **AF, AP**

CAPACITY, Refill:	Liters	Pt
NP205	2.1	4.5
NP208	2.8	6.0

DIFFERENTIAL
Standard **GL-5**
Anti-Spin, Limited-Slip, Powr-Loc,
Sure-Grip, Trac-Loc ...... **GL-5★**
Above 90°F (32°C), 140, 80W-140, 85W-140; above −10°F (−23°C), 90, 80W-90, 80W-140, 85W-140; below −10°F (−23°C), 75W, 80W, 75W-90, 80W-140

CAPACITY, Refill:	Liters	Pt
Front: 4-wheel drive		
Spicer 60F	3.1	6.5
Others	1.7	3.5
Rear: Spicer 60, 60 HD ...	2.8	6.0
Spicer 70	3.1	6.5
Others	2.1	4.5

SERVICE AT TIME OR MILEAGE—WHICHEVER OCCURS FIRST

DETPM14   **W**   **SERVICE TO MAINTAIN EMISSION WARRANTY**   DETPM14

8,500 & under GVWR is found on Safety Certification Label on left door lock pillar. See passenger car charts for front wheel drive vans

MI—MILES IN THOUSANDS
KM—KILOMETERS IN THOUSANDS

EVERY 6 MO/7.5 MI—12 KM
Fittings (4 × 4):

Steering linkage .... lubricate **BJ**

Others .... lubricate **LM**
Includes front wheel bearings ex. Dakota; remove wheels to reach fitting if equipped

Transfer case linkage .... lubricate
NP205 lubricate with **MO**
NP207, NP208 lubricate with **LM**. Service as required

EVERY 12 MO/7.5 MI—12 KM
W Crankcase .... change oil

Differential ...... check for leaks

W Engine coolant, hoses
& clamps 1987 .... check
Every 12 months only

Suspension ball joints, seals,
U-joints (sealed) (4 × 2) .... inspect

Transfer case (4 × 4) .... check level

Transmission, manual ..... check level

Brake master cylinder .... check level **HB**

W Oil filter .... replace
At every other oil change or at least every 12 mo

Power steering reservoir .. check level **PS**

Transmission, automatic .... check level
Fluid warm, engine idling, in NEUTRAL

Body & brake
actuating mechanisms .... lubricate **MO**

EVERY 12 MO/15 MI—24 KM
Front wheel bearings
(4 × 4) ex. Dakota .... inspect **LM**
Ex. 44F-BJ & 60F front differentials. At mileage interval only. Also clean & repack front spindle needle bearings as required & when replacing disc pads

EVERY 12 MO/30 MI—48 KM
W Carburetor choke shaft, fast idle cam
& pivots .... clean **PC**

EVERY 12 MI—19 KM
Tires .... rotate

EVERY 12 MO/48 MI—77 KM
Rear wheel bearings .... inspect **LM**
Repack as required or whenever axles are removed or Dana axle brakes are serviced, repack

EVERY 15 MI—24 KM
W Drive belts .... inspect/adjust
Not required for Calif. warranty

Spark plugs 1985-86 .... replace
Models without catalytic converter

EVERY 24 MO/22.5 MI—36 KM
Fittings & wheel stops (4 × 2)
1985-86 .... lubricate **LM**
Ex. front suspension ball joints & steering linkage

Front suspension ball joints &
steering linkage (4 × 2) .... lubricate **BJ**

Parking brake ratio
lever pivot .... lubricate **LM**

Transmission linkage .... **fitting LM**
OD only, while in reverse, engine off

EVERY 22.5 MI—36 KM
Brake linings .... inspect

Front spindle needle bearings
(4 × 4) ex. Dakota .... inspect **LM**
With 44F-BJ & 60F front differentials, lubricate as required & when replacing disc pads

Front wheel bearings (4 × 2) ... inspect **LM**
Also inspect at brake inspection or servicing; lubricate rear wheel bearings whenever axles are removed. Clean/repack front wheel bearings when replacing disc pads ex. Dakota, clean/repack when brake rotors are resurfaced

EVERY 30 MI—48 KM
Cooling system ...... change coolant **EC**
Also flush system at first 36 mo/52.5 mi (84 km), then every 24 mo/30 mi (48 km). Required for 1987 emission warranty

W Air cleaner element .... replace
Clean air filter wrapper if equipped

W Choke heat source .... check
Electrical/Coolant source ex. 1987 Dakota coolant. Exhaust source: 1985 at mileage, 1986 every 24 mo or mileage, 1987 every 24 mo/52.5 mi (84 km)
Not required for Calif. warranty

W Drive belts ....inspect/adjust

W PCV filter 1987 .... replace
If equipped

W Spark plugs .... replace
Models with catalytic converter

EVERY 37.5 MI—60 KM
Transfer case .... change lubricant

Transmission, automatic .... change fluid
Not required for Ram Wagon. Replace filter & adjust bands

Transmission, manual ... change lubricant

EVERY 52.5 MI—84 KM
Air injection system 1985-86 ...... check

Crankcase inlet air cleaner
ex. 4-cyl. .... clean/oil

EGR valve .... check
Or every 60 months for 1986-87. Clean passages. 1987 replace EGR valve & tube

Fuel filter .... replace

Fuel tank cap 1985-86 .... inspect

Fuel vapor canister(s) 1985-86 .... replace

Idle speed .... check
Vehicles w/carburetor only

Manifold heat valve 1986-87
if equipped .... check/lubricate **MH**

Oxygen sensor .... replace
Or every 60 months for 1986

PCV valve .... replace
Or every 60 months for 1986-87

Vacuum & fuel rubber hoses ...... check

Vacuum operated
emission components .... inspect
1987 replace

EVERY 60 MI—96 KM
Ignition cables, distributor cap
& rotor .... replace
Also inspect distributor 1985-86

Ignition timing .... check

SEVERE SERVICE
W Crankcase—Drain every 3 mo/3 mi (4.8 km). Every 50 hours for 4-wheel drive used for off-road driving

Drive line fittings—Lubricate every 3 mo/3 mi (4.8 km). Inspect 4-wheel drive front wheel bearings every 1 mi (1.6 km) for off road use. Lubricate daily if operating in water

Suspension ball joints—Lubricate every engine oil change

Transmission, automatic—Change fluid every 12 mi (19 km) or every 12 mo when plowing snow. Replace filter & adjust bands

Transmission, manual—Change lubricant every 18 mi (29 km)

KEY TO LUBRICANTS

AF	DEXRON®-II ATF
AP	MOPAR ATF-PLUS®
BJ	Suspension Lubricant
CC	Motor Oil, API Service CC
CD	Motor Oil, API Service CD
EC	Ethylene Glycol Coolant
	Mix with water to desired freeze protection
GL-5	Gear Oil, API Service GL-5
GL-5★	Special Lubricant for Anti-Spin, Limited-Slip, Powr-Loc, Sure-Grip or Trac Loc Differential
HB	Hydraulic Brake Fluid, DOT 3
LM	Lithium Grease, EP No. 2
MH	Manifold Heat Valve Solvent
MO	Motor Oil
PC	Carburetor Cleaner
PS	Power Steering Fluid
SF	Motor Oil, API Service SF
SG	Motor Oil, API Service SG

CRANKCASE ...... SF/CC, SF/CD, SG

CAPACITY, Refill:	Liters	Qt
4-cyl.	3.8	4.0
All others	4.7	5.0

Capacity shown is without filter. When replacing filter, additional oil may be needed

Above 20°F (–7°C) .. 10W-30, 10W-40, 10W-50, 15W-40, 20W-40, 20W-50, 30
20° to 80°F (–7° to 27°C) 20W-20
Above 10°F (–12°C) 15W-40
Above 0°F (–18°C) 10W-30, 10W-40, 10W-50
Below 60°F (16°C) 5W-30, 5W-40

TRANSMISSION, Automatic ... AF†, AP

CAPACITY, Initial Refill*:	Liters	Qt
All models	3.8	4.0

*With the engine at operating temperature, shift transmission through all gears. Check fluid level in PARK and add fluid as needed
†1986 and later may use AF only when AP is not available

TRANSMISSION, Manual

A833 OD .... **AF, AP**
75W, 75W-80, 80W-90, 85W-90, 90 **GL-5** may be used
NP435 ...... **GL-5, SF/CC, SF/CD, SG**
SF/CC, SF/CD, SG: Above 32°F (0°C), 50; below 32°F (0°C), 30
GL-5: Above 90°F (32°C), 140; above –10°F (–23°C), 90; below –10°F (–23°C), 80W
NP2500 ..... **10W-30 SF/CC, SF/CD, SG**
Below 30°F (–1°C), may use **AF**

CAPACITY, Refill:	Liters	Pt
NP435	3.3	7.0
NP2500	1.9	4.0
A833 OD	3.5	7.5

TRANSFER CASE

NP205 ...... **GL-5, SF/CC, SF/CD, SG**
SF/CC, SF/CD, SG: Above 32°F (0°C), 50; below 32°F (0°C), 30
GL-5: Above 90°F (32°C), 140; above –10°F (–23°C), 90; below –10°F (–23°C), 80W
NP207, NP208 .... **AF, AP**

CAPACITY, Refill:	Liters	Pt
NP205, NP207	2.1	4.5
NP208	2.8	6.0

DIFFERENTIAL

Standard **GL-5**
Anti-Spin, Limited-Slip, Powr-Loc,
Sure-Grip, Trac-Loc .... **GL-5★**
Above 90°F (32°C), 140; above –10°F (–23°C), 90, 80W-90, 80W-140, 85W-140; below –10°F (–23°C), 75W, 80W, 75W-90, 80W-140

CAPACITY, Refill:	Liters	Pt
Front: 4-wheel drive		
Dakota	1.2	2.6
Spicer 60F axle	3.1	6.5
Others	2.7	5.6
Rear: 7¼" ring gear with 2½" dia. axle housing adjacent to differential	1.2	2.5
Spicer 60, 60 HD	2.8	6.0
Spicer 70	3.3	7.0
Others	2.1	4.5

SERVICE AT TIME OR MILEAGE—WHICHEVER OCCURS FIRST

DETPM15   **W SERVICE TO MAINTAIN EMISSION WARRANTY**   DETPM15

Over 8,500 GVWR. GVWR is found on Safety Certification Label on left door lock pillar. Follow (I) for Calif. or single air pump vehicles; (II) for dual air pump vehicles ex. Calif. when noted below.

MI—MILES IN THOUSANDS
KM—KILOMETERS IN THOUSANDS

EVERY 6 MO/6 MI—9.6 KM

Fittings (4 × 4):
Steering linkage .... lubricate **BJ**
Others .... lubricate **LM**
Includes front wheel bearings; remove wheels to reach fitting if equipped
Transfer case linkage .... lubricate
NP205 lubricate with **MO**
NP208 lubricate with **LM**. Service as required

EVERY 12 MO/6 MI—9.6 KM

w Crankcase .... change oil
Differential .... check for leaks
Suspension ball joints, seals,
  U-joints (sealed) (4 × 2) .... inspect
Transfer case (4 × 4) .... check level
Transmission, manual .... check level
Wheel nuts, steering linkage &
  spring clip nuts .... torque
Brake master cylinder .... check level **HB**
w Oil filter .... replace
At every other oil change or at least every 12 mo
Power steering reservoir .. check level **PS**
NOTE: 1987 CB & MB 350 require Hydroboost Power Steering Fluid Part No. 4318056 or equivalent
Transmission, automatic .... check level
Fluid warm, engine idling, in NEUTRAL
Body & brake
  actuating mechanisms .... lubricate **MO**

EVERY 12 MO/12 MI—19 KM

Front wheel bearings
  (4 × 4) .... inspect **LM**
Ex. 44F-BJ & 60F front differentials. At mileage interval only. Also clean & repack front spindle needle bearings as required & when replacing disc pads
w Carburetor choke shaft, fast idle cam
  & pivots ex. 1987 (II) ...... clean **PC**
Check choke heat source at mileage only
w Crankcase inlet air cleaner ... clean/oil

EVERY 12 MI—19 KM

Tires .... rotate
w Air cleaner element &
  wrapper ex. 1987 (II) .... clean
w Carburetor choke, vacuum kick & fast idle
  cam ex. 1987 (II) ...... check/adjust
w EGR system (I) ex. Calif. .... check
Clean passages also
w PCV valve & system (I) .... check

EVERY 12 MO/48 MI—77 KM

Rear wheel bearings .... inspect **LM**
Repack as required or whenever axles are removed or Dana axle brakes are serviced, repack

EVERY 18 MI—29 KM

w Drive belts .... inspect/adjust
Not required for Calif. emissions warranty w/1987 (II)
w Emission & fuel hoses (I) ...... inspect
Engine operation (I) 1985 .... check
Curb idle speed & ignition timing
Fuel filter 1985-86 .... replace
w Ignition cables (I) .... check
Manifold heat valve
  ex. 1987 (II) .... lubricate **MH**
w Spark plugs ex. 1987 (II) .... replace

1985-86 EVERY 24 MO/24 MI—38 KM

Fittings & wheel stops (4 × 2) ..lubricate **LM**
Ex. front suspension ball joints & steering linkage
Front suspension ball joints &
  steering linkage (4 × 2) .... lubricate **BJ**
Parking brake ratio
  lever pivot .... lubricate **LM**
Transmission linkage .... fitting **LM**
OD only, while in reverse, engine off

EVERY 24 MI—38 KM

w Air pump filter 1987 (II) .... replace
Brake linings .... inspect
Front spindle needle bearings
  (4 × 4) .... inspect **LM**
With 44F-BJ & 60F front differentials, lubricate as required & when replacing disc pads
Front wheel bearings (4 × 2) ... inspect **LM**
Also inspect at brake inspection or servicing; lubricate rear wheel bearings whenever axles are removed. Clean/repack front wheel bearings when replacing disc pads
Transmission, automatic .... change fluid
Not required for Ram Wagon. Replace filter & adjust bands
Cooling system ...... change coolant **EC**
Flush system also at first 36 mo/48 mi (77 km), then every 24 mo/30 mi (48 km).
w Engine operation (I) 1986-87 .... check
Curb idle speed & ignition timing
w Air cleaner element .... replace
Clean wrapper for 1987 (II)
w PCV valve (I) .... replace

EVERY 30 MI—48 KM

w Carburetor choke shaft, fast
  idle cam & pivots 1987 (II) .. clean **PC**
Check choke heat source
w Spark plugs 1987 (II) .... replace

EVERY 36 MI—58 KM

w Drive belts 1987 (II) ..... inspect/adjust
Transfer case .... change lubricant
Transmission, manual ... change lubricant

(II) EVERY 54 MI—85 KM

Air injection system .... check
Fuel tank cap 1985-86 .... inspect
Fuel vapor canister(s) 1985-86 .... replace
Ignition cables, distributor cap
  & rotor 1985-86 .... replace
Also inspect distributor
Ignition timing 1985-86 ..... check/adjust
Manifold heat valve .... lubricate **MH**
PCV valve 1985-87 .... replace
Propane idle 1986-87 ...... check/adjust
Vacuum operated emission
  components .... check
Inspect & replace as necessary

EVERY 60 MI—96 KM

Ignition cables, distributor cap
  & rotor 1987 (II) .... replace
Ignition timing 1987 (II) .... check/adjust

EVERY 78 MI—125 KM

Alternator brushes 1987 (II) ...... replace

SERVICE AS REQUIRED

w Fuel filter 1987 .... replace

SEVERE SERVICE

w Crankcase—Drain every 3 mo/3 mi (4.8 km). Every 50 hours for 4-wheel drive used for off-road driving
Drive line fittings—Lubricate every 3 mo/3 mi (4.8 km) ex. W-350 4-wheel drive, every 1 mi (1.6 km), includes front wheel bearing inspection for off-road use. Lubricate daily if operating in water
Suspension ball joints—Lubricate every engine oil change
Transmission, automatic—Change fluid every 12 mi (19 km) or every 12 mo when plowing snow. Replace filter & adjust bands
Transmission, manual—Change lubricant every 18 mi (29 km)

KEY TO LUBRICANTS

AF	DEXRON®-II ATF
AP	MOPAR ATF-PLUS®
BJ	Suspension Lubricant
CC	Motor Oil, API Service CC
CD	Motor Oil, API Service CD
EC	Ethylene Glycol Coolant
	Mix with water to desired freeze protection
GL-5	Gear Oil, API Service GL-5
GL-5★	Special Lubricant for Anti-Spin, Limited-Slip, Powr-Loc, Sure-Grip or Trac-Loc Differential
HB	Hydraulic Brake Fluid, DOT 3
LM	Lithium Grease, EP No. 2
MH	Manifold Heat Valve Solvent
MO	Motor Oil
PC	Carburetor Cleaner
PS	Power Steering Fluid
SF	Motor Oil, API Service SF
SG	Motor Oil, API Service SG

CRANKCASE ...... SF/CC, SF/CD, SG

CAPACITY, Refill:	Liters	Qt
All	4.7	5.0

Capacity shown is without filter. When replacing filter, additional oil may be needed

Above 20°F (–7°C) ... 10W-30, 10W-40, 10W-50, 15W-40, 20W-40, 20W-50, 30
20° to 80°F (–7° to 27°C) 20W-20
Above 10°F (–12°C) 15W-40
Above 0°F (–18°C) ... 10W-30, 10W-40, 10W-50
Below 60°F (16°C) 5W-30, 5W-40

TRANSMISSION, Automatic ... AF†, AP

CAPACITY, Initial Refill*:	Liters	Qt
All models w/o torque converter drain ...	3.8	4.0

*With the engine at operating temperature, shift transmission through all gears. Check fluid level in PARK and add fluid as needed
†1986 and later may use **AF** only when **AP** is not available

TRANSMISSION, Manual

A833 OD .... **AF, AP**
75W, 75W-80, 80W-90, 85W-90, 90 **GL-5** may be used
NP435 .... **GL-5, SF/CC, SF/CD, SG**
SF/CC, SF/CD, SG: Above 32°F (0°C), 50; below 32°F (0°C), 30
GL-5: Above 90°F (32°C), 140; above –10°F (–23°C), 90; below –10°F (–23°C), 80W

CAPACITY, Refill:	Liters	Pt
NP435	3.3	7.0
A833 OD	3.5	7.5

TRANSFER CASE

NP205 .... **GL-5, SF/CC, SF/CD, SG**
SF/CC, SF/CD, SG: Above 32°F (0°C), 50; below 32°F (0°C), 30
GL-5: Above 90°F (32°C), 140; above –10°F (–23°C), 90; below –10°F (–23°C), 80W
NP208 .... **AF, AP**

CAPACITY, Refill:	Liters	Pt
NP205	2.1	4.5
NP208	2.8	6.0

DIFFERENTIAL

Standard **GL-5**
Anti-Spin, Limited-Slip, Powr-Loc,
  Sure-Grip, Trac-Loc .... **GL-5★**
Above 90°F (32°C), 140, 80W-140, 85W-140; above –10°F (–23°C), 90, 80W-90, 80W-140, 85W-140; below –10°F (–23°C), 75W, 80W, 75W-90, 80W-140

CAPACITY, Refill:	Liters	Pt
Front: 4-wheel drive		
Spicer 60F	3.1	6.5
Others	2.7	5.6
Rear: Spicer 60, 60 HD ...	2.8	6.0
Spicer 70	3.3	7.0
Others	2.1	4.5

CHEK-CHART

SERVICE AT TIME OR MILEAGE—WHICHEVER OCCURS FIRST

DETPM17   **W**   **SERVICE TO MAINTAIN EMISSION WARRANTY**   DETPM17

Over 8,500 GVWR. GVWR is found on Safety Cert. Label on left door lock pillar. Follow (I) for Calif. or single air pump vehicles; (II) for dual air pump vehicles ex. Calif. when noted below. All GVWR series Vans & Wagons except Canada & Calif. models use light duty schedule found on previous page.

MI—MILES IN THOUSANDS
KM—KILOMETERS IN THOUSANDS

EVERY 6 MO/6 MI—9.6 KM
Fittings (4 × 4):

Steering linkage . . . . lubricate **BJ**

Others . . . . lubricate **LM**
Includes front wheel bearings; remove wheels to reach fitting if equipped

EVERY 12 MO/6 MI—9.6 KM
Crankcase . . . . change oil

Differential . . . . check for leaks

Engine coolant, hoses, clamps (II) . inspect
Every 12 months only

Suspension ball joints, seals,
U-joints (sealed) (4 × 2) . . . . inspect

Transfer case (4 × 4) . . . . check level

Transmission, manual . . . . . . check level

Wheel nuts, steering linkage &
spring clip nuts . . . . torque

Brake master cylinder . . . . check level **HB**

Oil filter . . . . replace
At every other oil change or at least every 12 mo

Power steering reservoir . . check level **PS**
CB & MB 350 require Hydroboost Power Steering Fluid

Transmission, automatic . . . . check level
Fluid warm, engine idling, in NEUTRAL

Body & brake
actuating mechanisms . . . . lubricate

EVERY 12 MO/12 MI—19 KM
Front wheel bearings
(4 × 4) . . . . inspect **LM**
Ex. 44F-BJ & 60F front differentials. At mileage interval only. Also clean & repack front spindle needle bearings as required & when replacing disc pads

W Carburetor choke shaft, fast idle cam
& pivots (I) . . . . clean **PC**
Check choke heat source at mileage only

W Crankcase inlet air cleaner
(II) . . . . clean/oil

EVERY 12 MI—19 KM
Tires . . . . rotate

W Air cleaner element &
wrapper (I) . . . . clean

W Carburetor choke, vacuum kick & fast idle
cam (I) . . . . check/adjust

W PCV valve & system (I) . . . . check

EVERY 12 MO/48 MI—77 KM
Rear wheel bearings . . . . . . inspect **LM**
Repack as required or whenever axles are removed or Dana axle brakes are serviced, repack

EVERY 18 MI—29 KM
Air filter . . . . clean

W Drive belts . . . . inspect/adjust

W Emission & fuel hose (I) . . . . inspect

W Engine operation (I) . . . . check
Curb idle speed & ignition timing

W Ignition cables (I) . . . . check

W Manifold heat valve (I) . . . . lubricate **MH**

W Spark plugs (I) . . . . replace

EVERY 24 MI—38 KM
W Air cleaner element . . . . replace
Also clean wrapper for (II)

W Air pump filter (II) . . . . replace

Brake linings . . . . inspect

Front spindle needle bearings
(4 × 4) . . . . inspect **LM**
With 44F-BJ & 60F front differentials, lubricate as required & when replacing disc pads

Front wheel bearings (4 × 2) . . . inspect **LM**
Also inspect at brake inspection or servicing; lubricate rear wheel bearings whenever axles are removed. Clean/repack front wheel bearings when replacing disc pads

Transmission, automatic . . . . change fluid
Not required for Ram Wagon. Replace filter & adjust bands

Cooling system . . . . . . change coolant **EC**
Flush system also at first 36 mo/48 mi (77 km), then every 24 mo/30 mi (48 km)

Crankcase inlet air cleaner (II) . . . clean/oil

W PCV valve (I) . . . . replace

EVERY 30 MI—48 KM
W Carburetor choke shaft, fast
idle cam & pivots (II) . . . . . . clean **PC**
Check choke heat source

W Spark plugs (II) . . . . replace

EVERY 36 MI—58 KM
Transfer case . . . . change lubricant

Transmission,
manual, gasoline . . . . . change lubricant

(II) EVERY 54 MI—85 KM
Air injection system . . . . check

Manifold heat valve . . . . lubricate **MH**

Propane idle . . . . check/adjust

EVERY 60 MI—96 KM
Ignition cable, distributor cap
& rotor (II) . . . . replace

Ignition timing (II) . . . . check/adjust

PCV valve ex. (I) . . . . replace
Or as indicated by emissions maintenance light

Vacuum operated emission components,
ex. (I) . . . . replace
Or as indicated by emissions maintenance light

EVERY 78 MI—125 KM
Alternator brushes (II) . . . . replace

SERVICE AS REQUIRED
W Fuel filter . . . . replace

Transfer case linkage . . . . lubricate
NP205, **MO**; NP208 & NP241 **LM**

SEVERE SERVICE
Crankcase—Drain every 3 mo/3 mi (4.8 km). Every 50 hours for 4-wheel drive used for off-road driving

Drive line fittings—Lubricate every 3 mo/3 mi (4.8 km) ex. W-350 4-wheel drive, every 1 mi (1.6 km), includes front wheel bearing inspection for off-road use. Lubricate daily if operating in water

Suspension ball joints—Lubricate every engine oil change

Transmission, automatic—Change fluid every 12 mi (19 km) or every 12 mo when plowing snow. Replace filter & adjust bands

Transmission, manual, change lubricant every 18 mi (29 km)

KEY TO LUBRICANTS

AF	DEXRON®-II ATF
AP	MOPAR ATF-PLUS®
BJ	Suspension Lubricant
CC	Motor Oil, API Service CC
CD	Motor Oil, API Service CD
EC	Ethylene Glycol Coolant
	Mix with water to desired freeze protection
GL-5	Gear Oil, API Service GL-5
GL-5★	Special Lubricant for Anti-Spin, Limited-Slip, Powr-Loc, Sure-Grip or Trac-Loc Differential
HB	Hydraulic Brake Fluid, DOT 3
LM	Lithium Grease, EP No. 2
MH	Manifold Heat Valve Solvent
MO	Motor Oil
PC	Carburetor Cleaner
PS	Power Steering Fluid
SF	Motor Oil, API Service SF
SG	Motor Oil, API Service SG

CRANKCASE . . . . SF/CC, SF/CD, SG, SG/CD

CAPACITY, Refill:	Liters	Qt
All	3.8	4.0

Capacity shown is without filter. When replacing filter, additional oil may be needed

Above 20°F (–7°C)	10W-30, 15W-40, 30
Above 10°F (–12°C)	15W-40
Above 0°F (–18°C)	10W-30
Below 60°F (16°C)	5W-30

TRANSMISSION, Automatic . . . . . . AP†

CAPACITY, Initial Refill*:	Liters	Qt
All models	3.8	4.0

*With the engine at operating temperature, shift transmission through all gears. Check fluid level in PARK and add fluid as needed

†May use **AF** only when **AP** is not available

TRANSMISSION, Manual
A833 OD . . . . **AF, AP**
75W, 75W-80, 80W-90, 85W-90, 90 **GL-5** may be used

NP435: **GL-5, SF/CC, SF/CD, SG, SG/CD**
SF/CC, SF/CD, SG, SG/CD: Above 32°F (0°C), 50; below 32°F (0°C), 30
GL-5: Above 90°F (32°C), 140; above –10°F (–23°C), 90; below –10°F (–23°C), 80W

CAPACITY, Refill:	Liters	Pt
NP435	3.3	7.0
A833 OD	3.5	7.5

TRANSFER CASE
NP205: **GL-5, SF/CC, SF/CD, SG, SG/CD**
SF/CC, SF/CD, SG, SG/CD: Above 32°F (0°C), 50; below 32°F (0°C), 30
GL-5: Above 90°F (32°C), 140; above –10°F (–23°C), 90; below –10°F (–23°C), 80W

NP207, 208, 241 . . . . **AF**

CAPACITY, Refill:	Liters	Pt
NP205, NP207	2.1	4.5
NP208	2.8	6.0
NP241	2.2	4.6

DIFFERENTIAL
Standard & all Dana/Spicer **GL-5**
Anti-Spin, Limited-Slip, Powr-Loc,
Sure-Grip, Trac-Loc
ex. Dana/Spicer . . . . **GL-5★**
Above 90°F (32°C), 140, 80W-140, 85W-140; above –10°F (–23°C), 90, 80W-90, 80W-140, 85W-140; below –10°F (–23°C), 75W, 80W, 75W-90, 80W-140

CAPACITY, Refill:	Liters	Pt
Front: 4-wheel drive		
Spicer 60F	3.1	6.5
Others	2.7	5.6
Rear: Dana 60, 60 HD	2.8	6.0
Dana 70	3.3	7.0
Others	2.1	4.5

DODGE TRUCKS
1988-92 All Rear Wheel & 4-Wheel
Light Duty Gasoline Emission Models Except Raider & Ram 50

SERVICE AT TIME OR MILEAGE—WHICHEVER OCCURS FIRST

DETPM16   **W   SERVICE TO MAINTAIN EMISSION WARRANTY**   DETPM16

8,500 & under GVWR & all GVWR for B-Series Vans & Wagons except 1988 Canada & Calif. models. GVWR is found on Safety Certification Label on left door lock pillar. 1989-92: models with emission & hose routing label on underside of the hood. See passenger car charts for front wheel drive vans

MI—MILES IN THOUSANDS
KM—KILOMETERS IN THOUSANDS

EVERY 6 MO/7.5 MI—12 KM
Crankcase 1991-92 . . . . change oil
Replace oil filter at every other oil change but at least every 12 mo

Fittings 4WD,
   Steering linkage . . . . lubricate **BJ**

   Others . . . . lubricate **LM**
Includes front wheel bearings ex. Dakota; remove wheels to reach fitting if equipped

Transfer case linkage . . . . lubricate
NP205 lubricate with **MO**
NP207, NP208, NP241 lubricate with **LM**. Service as required

EVERY 12 MO/7.5 MI—12 KM
W Crankcase 1988-90 . . . . change oil
Replace oil filter at every other oil change but at least every 12 mo

Differential . . . . check for leaks

W Engine coolant, hoses
   & clamps . . . . check
Every 12 months only

Suspension ball joints, seals,
   U-joints (sealed) 2WD . . . . inspect

Transfer case . . . . check level

Transmission, manual . . . . check level

Brake master cylinder . . . . check level **HB**

Power steering reservoir . . check level **PS**

Transmission, automatic . . . . check level
Fluid warm, engine idling, in NEUTRAL

Body & brake
   actuating mechanisms . . . . lubricate **MO**

EVERY 12 MO/15 MI—24 KM
Brake booster bellcrank
   pivot B-350 series . . . . . . lubricate **MO**

W Drive belts . . . . inspect/adjust
Not required for Calif. warranty

Front wheel bearings
   4WD ex. Dakota . . . . inspect **LM**
At mileage interval only or when replacing disk pads. With 44F-BJ & 60F front differentials, clean & repack needle bearings

Steering linkage 1991-92 . . . . lubricate **BJ**

EVERY 12 MO/30 MI—48 KM
W Carburetor choke shaft, fast idle cam
   & pivots 1988 . . . . clean **PC**

EVERY 12 MI—19 KM
Tires . . . . rotate

EVERY 12 MO/48 MI—77 KM
Rear wheel bearings . . . . . . inspect **LM**
Repack as required or whenever axles are removed or Dana axle brakes are serviced, repack

EVERY 24 MO/22.5 MI—36 KM
Front suspension ball joints & 1988-90
   steering linkage 2WD . . . . lubricate **BJ**

Parking brake ratio
   lever pivot . . . . lubricate **LM**

Transmission linkage . . . . **fitting LM**
OD only, while in reverse, engine off

EVERY 22.5 MI—36 KM
Brake linings . . . . inspect

Front wheel bearings 2WD . . . . inspect **LM**
Also inspect at brake inspection or servicing; lubricate rear wheel bearings whenever axles are removed. Clean/repack front wheel bearings when replacing disc pads ex. Dakota, clean/repack when brake rotors are resurfaced

EVERY 30 MI—48 KM
Cooling system . . . . . . change coolant **EC**
Also flush system at first 36 mo/52.5 mi (84 km), then every 24 mo/30 mi (48 km)

W Air cleaner element . . . . replace
Clean air filter wrapper if equipped

W Drive belts . . . . inspect/adjust

W PCV filter . . . . replace
If equipped

W Spark plugs . . . . replace

EVERY 37.5 MI—60 KM
Transfer case . . . . change lubricant

Transmission, automatic . . . . change fluid
Not required for Ram Wagon. Replace filter & adjust bands

Transmission, manual . . . change lubricant

EVERY 52.5 MI—84 KM
Fuel filter . . . . replace

Vacuum & fuel rubber hoses . . . . . . check

EVERY 60 MI—96 KM
W Choke heat source 1988 . . . . check
Not required for Calif. warranty

Crankcase inlet air cleaner
   ex. 4-cyl . . . . clean/oil

Drive belts (V-Type) 1990-91 . . . . . replace

EGR Valve & Tube . . . . replace
Clean passages

Idle speed . . . . adjust
Vehicles w/carburetor only

Ignition cables, distributor cap
   & rotor . . . . replace

Ignition timing . . . . check

Manifold heat valve
   if equipped . . . . check/lubricate **MH**

Oxygen sensor . . . . replace

PCV valve . . . . replace

Vacuum operated emission
   components . . . . replace

SEVERE SERVICE
W Crankcase—Drain every 3 mo/3 mi (4.8 km). Every 50 hours for 4-wheel drive used for off-road driving

Differential 1990-92 — Change lubricant every 12 mo/12 mi (19 km)

Drive line fittings—Lubricate every 3 mo/3 mi (4.8 km). Inspect 4-wheel drive front wheel bearings every 1 mi (1.6 km) for off road use. Lubricate daily if operating in water

Suspension ball joints—Lubricate every engine oil change

Transmission, automatic—Change fluid every 12 mi/12 mo (19 km) when plowing snow. Replace filter & adjust bands

Transmission, manual—Change lubricant every 18 mi (29 km)

KEY TO LUBRICANTS

AF	DEXRON®-II ATF
AP	MOPAR ATF-PLUS®
BJ	Suspension Lubricant
CD	Motor Oil, API Service CD
EC	Ethylene Glycol Coolant
	Mix with water to desired freeze protection
GL-4	Gear Oil, API Service GL-4
GL-5	Gear Oil, API Service GL-5
GL-5★	Special Lubricant for Anti-Spin, Limited-Slip, Powr-Loc, Sure-Grip or Trac-Loc Differential
HB	Hydraulic Brake Fluid, DOT 3
LM	Lithium Grease, EP No. 2
MH	Manifold Heat Valve Solvent
MO	Motor Oil
PC	Carburetor Cleaner
PS	Power Steering Fluid
SG	Motor Oil, API Service SG

CRANKCASE . . . . SG, SG/CD

CAPACITY, Refill:	Liters	Qt
All	3.8	4.0

Capacity shown is without filter. When replacing filter, additional oil may be needed
Above 20°F (−7°C) 1988-89 10W-30, 15W-40, 30
Above 10°F (−12°C) 1988-89 . . . . 15W-40
Above 0°F (−18°C) 10W-30
Below 60°F (16°C) 1988 . . . . 5W-30
Below 32°F (0°C) 1989-91 . . . . 5W-30

TRANSMISSION, Automatic . . . . . . AP†

CAPACITY, Initial Refill*:	Liters	Qt
All models	3.8	4.0

*With the engine at operating temperature, shift transmission through all gears. Check fluid level in NEUTRAL and add fluid as needed
†May use AF only when AP is not available

TRANSMISSION, Manual
AX-15 . . . . 75W-90 **GL-5**
A833 OD . . . . **AF, AP**
75W, 75W-80, 80W-90, 85W-90, 90 **GL-5** may also be used
NP435 . . . . **GL-5, SG, SG/CD**
SG, SG/CD: Above 32°F (0°C), 50; below 32°F (0°C), 30
GL-5: Above 90°F (32°C), 140; above −10°F (−23°C), 90; below −10°F (−23°C), 80W
NP2500 . . . . 10W-30 **SG, SG/CD**
Use **AP** below 32°F (0°C) to improve shift efforts
NV4500 . . . . 75W-90 **GL-4***
* Synthetic

CAPACITY, Refill:	Liters	Pt
NP435	3.3	7.0
NP2500	1.9	4.0
AX-15	3.1	6.6
NV4500	4.9	10.4
A833 OD	3.5	7.5

TRANSFER CASE
NP205 . . . . **GL-5, SG, SG/CD**
SG, SG/CD: Above 32°F (0°C), 50; below 32°F (0°C), 30
GL-5: Above 90°F (32°C), 140; above −10°F (−23°C), 90; below −10°F (−23°C), 80W
NP207, 208, 231, 241 . . . . **AF, AP**

CAPACITY, Refill:	Liters	Pt
NP205, NP207	2.1	4.5
NP208	2.8	6.0
NP231: 1988-91	1.2	2.5
1992	1.0	2.2
NP241	2.2	4.6

DIFFERENTIAL
Above 90°F (32°C), 140, 80W-140, 85W-140; above −10°F (−23°C), 90, 80W-90, 80W-140, 85W-140; below −10°F (−23°C), 75W, 80W, 75W-90, 80W-140
Standard & all Dana, Spicer **GL-5**
Anti-Spin, Limited-Slip, Powr-Loc,
   Sure-Grip, Trac-Loc
   ex. Dana, Spicer . . . . **GL-5★**

CAPACITY, Refill:	Liters	Pt
Front: 4-wheel drive		
Dakota	1.2	2.6
Spicer 60F axle	3.1	6.5
Others	2.7	5.6
Rear		
Dana 60, 60 HD	1.4	3.0
Dana 70	2.8	6.0
	3.3	7.0
	2.1	4.5

ANTI-SPIN, LIMITED-SLIP, POWR-LOC,
SURE-GRIP OR TRAC-LOC IDENTIFICATION:
Lift both rear wheels off ground, turn one wheel & other will rotate in same direction

SERVICE AT TIME OR MILEAGE—WHICHEVER OCCURS FIRST

DETPM19   **W SERVICE TO MAINTAIN EMISSION WARRANTY**   DETPM19

Heavy duty models have emission control label on the air cleaner and hose routing label on underside of the hood.

MI—MILES IN THOUSANDS
KM—KILOMETERS IN THOUSANDS

EVERY 6 MO/6 MI—9.6 KM
Crankcase 1991-92 . . . . change oil

Fittings & 1991-92 2WD, 4WD;
Steering linkage . . . . lubricate **BJ**

Others . . . . lubricate **LM**
Includes front wheel bearings; remove wheels to reach fitting if equipped

EVERY 12 MO/6 MI—9.6 KM
Crankcase 1989-90 . . . . change oil
Change oil filter every other oil change but at least every 12 mo

Differential . . . . check for leaks

Engine coolant, hoses, clamps . . . inspect
1989, every 12 months only. 1990-92, at mileage interval only

Suspension ball joints, seals,
U-joints (sealed) 2WD . . . . inspect

Transfer case . . . . check level

Transmission, manual . . . . . check level

Wheel nuts, steering linkage &
spring clip nuts . . . . torque

Brake master cylinder . . . . check level **HB**

Power steering reservoir . . check level **PS**
CB & MB 350 require Hydroboost Power Steering Fluid **PS ★**

Transmission, automatic . . . . . check level
Fluid warm, engine idling, in NEUTRAL

Body & brake
actuating mechanisms . . . . lubricate

EVERY 12 MO/12 MI—19 KM
Front wheel bearings
4WD . . . . inspect **LM**
At mileage interval only or when replacing disk pads. With 44F-BJ & 60F front differentials, clean & repack front spindle needle bearings

W Crankcase inlet air cleaner . . . clean/oil

EVERY 12 MI—19 KM
Tires . . . . rotate

EVERY 12 MO/48 MI—77 KM
Rear wheel bearings . . . . inspect **LM**
Repack as required or whenever axles are removed or Dana axle brakes are serviced, repack

EVERY 18 MI—29 KM
Air filter . . . . clean

W Drive belts . . . . inspect/adjust

EVERY 24 MI—38 KM
Air cleaner element . . . . replace

W Air pump filter . . . . replace

Brake linings . . . . inspect

Front wheel bearings 2WD . . . . inspect **LM**
Also inspect at brake inspection or servicing; lubricate rear wheel bearings whenever axles are removed. Clean/repack front wheel bearings when replacing disc pads

Transmission, automatic . . . . change fluid
Not required for Ram Wagon. Replace filter & adjust bands

Cooling system . . . . . . change coolant **EC**
Flush system also at first 36 mo/48 mi (77 km), then every 24 mo/30 mi (48 km)

Crankcase inlet air cleaner . . . . . clean/oil

EVERY 30 MI—48 KM
W Spark plugs . . . . replace

EVERY 36 MI—58 KM
Transfer case . . . . change lubricant

Transmission,
manual, gasoline . . . . . change lubricant

EVERY 54 MI—85 KM
Drive belts, V type 1989-91 . . . . . . replace

EVERY 60 MI—96 KM
EGR valve gasoline . . . . replace
Also clean passages. Or as indicated by emissions maintenance light

Ignition cables, distributor cap
& rotor . . . . replace

Ignition timing . . . . check/adjust

PCV valve . . . . replace
Or as indicated by emissions maintenance light

Vacuum operated
emission components . . . . replace
Or as indicated by emissions maintenance light

Manifold heat valve . . . . lubricate **MH**

EVERY 78 MI — 125 KM
Alternator brushes, 1989 . . . . replace

EVERY 82.5 MI—132 KM
Oxygen sensor . . . . replace
Or as indicated by emissions maintenance light

SERVICE AS REQUIRED
W Drive belts 1992 . . . . replace

W Fuel filter . . . . replace

Transfer case linkage . . . . lubricate
NP205, **MO**; NP208 & NP241, **LM**

SEVERE SERVICE
Crankcase—Drain every 3 mo/3 mi (4.8 km). Every 50 hours for 4-wheel drive used for off-road driving

Differential 1990-92—Change lubricant every 12 mo/12 mi (19 km)

Drive line fittings—Lubricate every 3 mo/3 mi (4.8 km) ex. W-350, every 1 mi (1.6 km), includes front wheel bearing inspection for off-road use. Lubricate daily if operating in water

Suspension ball joints—Lubricate every engine oil change

Transmission, automatic—Change fluid every 12 mo/12 mi (19 km) when plowing snow. Replace filter & adjust bands

Transmission, manual—Change lubricant every 18 mi (29 km)

KEY TO LUBRICANTS
See other Dodge/Plymouth Truck charts

CRANKCASE . . . . **SG, SG/CD**

CAPACITY, Refill:	Liters	Qt
All	3.8	4.0

Capacity shown is without filter. When replacing filter, additional oil may be needed
Above 20°F (–7°C), 1989 . . 10W-30, 15W-40, 30
Above 10°F (–12°C), 1989 . . . . 15W-40
Above 0°F (–18°C) 10W-30
Below 32°F (0°C) 5W-30

TRANSMISSION, Automatic . . . . . . **AP†**

CAPACITY, Initial Refill*:	Liters	Qt
All models	3.8	4.0

*With the engine at operating temperature, shift transmission through all gears. Check fluid level in NEUTRAL and add fluid as needed
†May use **AF** only when **AP** is not available

TRANSMISSION, Manual
AX-15 . . . . 75W-90 **GL-5**
A833 OD . . . . **AF, AP**
75W, 75W-80, 80W-90, 85W-90, 90 **GL-5** may be used
NP435 . . . . **GL-5, SG, SG/CD**
SF/CC, SF/CD, SG, SG/CD: Above 32°F (0°C), 50; below 32°F (0°C), 30
GL-5: Above 90°F (32°C), 140; above –10°F (–23°C), 90; below –10°F (–23°C), 80W
NV4500 . . . . 75W-90 **GL-4***
*Synthetic

CAPACITY, Refill:	Liters	Pt
NP435	3.3	7.0
AX-15	3.1	6.6
NV4500	4.9	10.4
A833 OD	3.5	7.5

TRANSFER CASE
NP205: . . . . **GL-5, SG, SG/CD**
SG, SG/CD: Above 32°F (0°C), 50; below 32°F (0°C), 30
GL-5: Above 90°F (32°C), 140; above –10°F (–23°C), 90; below –10°F (–23°C), 80W
NP207, 208, 241 . . . . **AF, AP**

CAPACITY, Refill:	Liters	Pt
NP205, NP207	2.1	4.5
NP208	2.8	6.0
NP241	2.2	4.6

DIFFERENTIAL
Above 90°F (32°C), 140, 80W-140, 85W-140; above –10°F (–23°C), 90, 80W-90, 80W-140, 85W-140; below –10°F (–23°C), 75W, 80W, 75W-90, 80W-140
Standard & all Dana/Spicer **GL-5**
Anti-Spin, Limited-Slip, Powr-Loc,
Sure-Grip, Trac-Loc
ex. Dana/Spicer . . . . **GL-5 ★**

CAPACITY, Refill:	Liters	Pt
Front: 4-wheel drive		
Spicer 60F	3.1	6.5
Others	2.7	5.6
Rear: Dana 60, 60 HD	2.8	6.0
Dana 70	3.3	7.0
Others	2.1	4.5

SERVICE AT TIME OR MILEAGE—WHICHEVER OCCURS FIRST

DETPM18   W   **SERVICE TO MAINTAIN EMISSION WARRANTY**   DETPM18

MI—MILES IN THOUSANDS
KM—KILOMETERS IN THOUSANDS

EVERY 6 MO/6 MI—9.6 KM
W Air filter . . . . clean/inspect
Also inspect air inlet pipe

Fittings 4WD;
  Steering linkage . . . . lubricate **BJ**

Others . . . . lubricate **LM**
Includes front wheel bearings; remove wheels to reach fitting if equipped

Crankcase . . . . change oil & filter

EVERY 12 MO/6 MI—9.6 KM
Differential(s) . . . . check for leaks

Suspension ball joints, seals,
  U-joints (sealed) 4WD . . . . inspect

Transfer case . . . . check level

Transmission, manual . . . . check level

Wheel nuts, steering linkage &
  spring clip nuts . . . . torque

Brake master cylinder . . . . check level **HB**

Power steering reservoir . . check level **PS**

Transmission, automatic . . . . . check level
Fluid warm, engine idling, in NEUTRAL

Body & brake
  actuating mechanisms . . . . lubricate

EVERY 12 MO/12 MI—19 KM
Drive belts . . . . inspect/adjust

Engine coolant, hoses & clamps . . inspect

Front wheel bearings
  4WD . . . . inspect **LM**
At mileage interval only or when replacing disk pads. With 44F-B5 & 60F front differentials, clean & repack front spindle needle bearings.

Fuel filter . . . . replace

Transmission, automatic . . . . change fluid
Replace filter & adjust bands

EVERY 12 MI—19 KM
Air filter, Calif. . . . . replace

Tires . . . . rotate

EVERY 12 MO/48 MI—77 KM
Rear wheel bearings . . . . inspect **LM**
Repack as required or whenever axles are removed or Dana axle brakes are serviced, repack

EVERY 18 MI—29 KM
Injection pump timing &
  idle speed . . . . check/adjust

EVERY 24 MI—38 KM
Air filter . . . . replace

Brake linings . . . . inspect

Fan hub . . . . inspect

Front wheel bearings 2WD . . . . inspect **LM**
Also inspect at brake inspection or servicing; lubricate rear wheel bearings whenever axles are removed. Clean/repack front wheel bearings when replacing disc pads

Cooling system . . . . . . change coolant **EC**
Flush system also at first 36 mo/48 mi (77 km), then every 24 mo/30 mi (48 km)

Underhood plastic &
  rubber components . . . . inspect

Valve clearance . . . . check/adjust

Engine vibration dampener . . . . . . inspect

EVERY 36 MI—58 KM
Transfer case . . . . change lubricant

Transmission,
  manual, gasoline . . . . . change lubricant

EVERY 60 MI—96 KM
Vacuum operated
  emission components . . . . replace
Or as indicated by emissions maintenance light

EVERY 78 MI—125 KM
Alternator brushes, 1989 . . . . replace

SERVICE AS REQUIRED
W Fuel filter . . . . replace

Transfer case linkage . . . . lubricate
NP205, **MO**

SEVERE SERVICE
Crankcase—Change oil and filter every 3 mo/3 mi (4.8 km)

Differential 1990-92—Change lubricant every 12 mo/12 mi (19 km)

Drive line fittings—Lubricate every 3 mo/3 mi (4.8 km) ex. W-350, every 1 mi (1.6 km), includes front wheel bearing inspection for off-road use. Lubricate daily if operating in water

Suspension ball joints—Lubricate every engine oil change

Transmission, manual—Change lubricant every 18 mi (29 km)

KEY TO LUBRICANTS

AF	DEXRON®-II ATF
AP	MOPAR ATF-PLUS®
BJ	Suspension Lubricant
CD	Motor Oil, API Service CD
CE	Motor Oil, API Service CE
EC	Ethylene Glycol Coolant Mix with water to desired freeze protection
GL-5	Gear Oil, API Service GL-5
HB	Hydraulic Brake Fluid, DOT 3
LM	Lithium Grease, EP No. 2
MO	Motor Oil
SG	Motor Oil, API Service SG

CRANKCASE . . . . CE, SG/CE

CAPACITY, Refill:	Liters	Qt
5.9L	10.4	11.0

Capacity shown is without filter. When replacing filter, fill it with oil before installing. Run engine and check dipstick, additional oil may be needed
Above 10°F (–12°C) 15W-40
0° to 10°F (–18° to –12°C) 10W-30
–10° to 0°F (–23° to –18°C) 10W-30*
Below 0°F (–18°C) . . . . 5W-30 synthetic
*With block heater

TRANSMISSION, Automatic . . . . . . AP†

CAPACITY, Initial Refill*:	Liters	Qt
All models	3.8	4.0

*With the engine at operating temperature, shift transmission through all gears. Check fluid level in NEUTRAL and add fluid as needed
†May use AF only when AP is not available

TRANSMISSION,
Manual . . . . 5W-30 SG, SG/CD

CAPACITY, Refill:	Liters	Pt
Getrag G-360	3.3	7.0

TRANSFER CASE
NP205 . . . . **GL-5, SG, SG/CD**
SG, SG/CD: Above 32°F (0°C), 50; below 32°F (0°C), 30
GL-5: Above 90°F (32°C), 140; above –10°F (–23°C), 90; below –10°F (–23°C), 80W

CAPACITY, Refill:	Liters	Pt
NP205	2.1	4.5

DIFFERENTIAL
Above 90°F (32°C), 140, 80W-140, 85W-140; above –10°F (–23°C), 90, 80W-90, 80W-140, 85W-140; below –10°F (–23°C), 75W, 80W, 75W-90, 80W-140
Standard & all Dana/Spicer **GL-5**
Anti-Spin, Limited-Slip, Powr-Loc,
  Sure-Grip, Trac-Loc
  ex. Dana/Spicer . . . . **GL-5★**

CAPACITY, Refill:	Liters	Pt
Front: Spicer 60F	3.1	6.5
Others	2.7	5.6
Rear: Dana 60, 60 HD	2.8	6.0
Dana 70	3.3	7.0
Others	2.1	4.5

SERVICE LOCATIONS — ENGINE AND CHASSIS

EEIDP-1

EEIDP-1

HOOD RELEASE: Inside

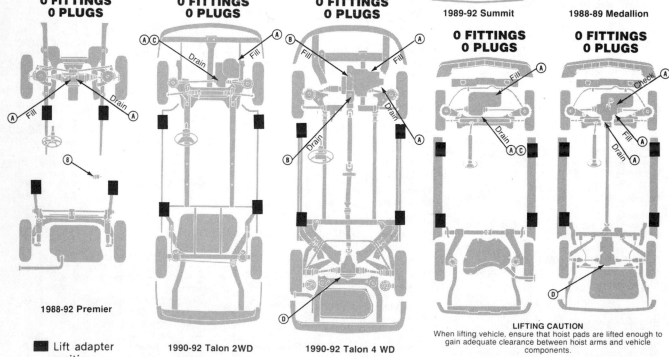

**1989-92
1.5L Summit**

**1989-90
1.6L DOHC Summit
1990-92
2.0L DOHC Talon**

**1988-89
2.2L Medallion**

**1988-89
2.5L Premier**

**1988-92
3.0L Premier**

① Crankcase dipstick
② Transmission dipstick
③ Brake fluid reservoir
④ Clutch fluid reservoir
⑤ Oil fill cap
⑥ Power steering reservoir
⑦ Air filter
⑧ Fuel filter
⑨ Oil filter
⑩ PCV filter
⑪ EGR valve
⑫ Oxygen sensor
⑬ PCV valve

● Cooling system drain   ○ Cooling system drain, some models

Ⓐ Manual transmission/transaxle, drain & fill
Ⓑ Transfer case, drain & fill
Ⓒ Automatic transaxle final drive, drain & fill
Ⓓ Differential, drain & fill

**0 FITTINGS
0 PLUGS**

**0 FITTINGS
0 PLUGS**

**0 FITTINGS
0 PLUGS**

**0 FITTINGS
0 PLUGS**

**0 FITTINGS
0 PLUGS**

**0 FITTINGS
0 PLUGS**

**0 FITTINGS
0 PLUGS**

1989-92 Summit

1988-89 Medallion

1988-92 Premier

■ Lift adapter position

1990-92 Talon 2WD

1990-92 Talon 4 WD

LIFTING CAUTION
When lifting vehicle, ensure that hoist pads are lifted enough to gain adequate clearance between hoist arms and vehicle components.

**1992 Summit Wagon
2WD**

**1992 Summit Wagon
4WD**

CAUTION: On front wheel drive vehicles the center of gravity is further forward than on rear wheel drive vehicles. When removing major components from the rear of the vehicle while it is on a hoist, the vehicle must be supported in a manner to prevent it from tipping forward.

SERVICE AT TIME OR MILEAGE—WHICHEVER OCCURS FIRST

EEIPM1 EEIPM1

W SERVICE TO MAINTAIN EMISSION WARRANTY

**MI—MILES IN THOUSANDS
KM—KILOMETERS IN THOUSANDS**

**1988-90,
EVERY 7.5 MO/7.5 MI—12 KM
1991,
EVERY 12 MO/7.5 MI—12 KM
1992,
EVERY 6 MO/7.5 MI—12 KM**

W Crankcase . . . . change oil

W Oil filter . . . . replace
Premier, Monaco, every oil change. Medallion at first
oil change, then every other

Exhaust system . . . . inspect

Transaxle, automatic . . . . check level
With engine at operating temperature and at slow idle,
move shift lever through all gear ranges, then check
fluid level when lever is in PARK. Use dipstick side
marked hot. Add fluid as needed
For cold fluid (preferred method), use dipstick side
marked ''COLD'' (60°-100°F [16°-38°C])

Hoses & connectors . . . . . . inspect/tighten
Check vacuum hoses, and cooling, fuel, brake, and
power steering systems

Drive belts . . . . inspect
Medallion 2.2L eng.

Drive shaft boots . . . . inspect

Transaxle, manual . . . . check level

Suspension, steering, & axle
    shaft boots . . . . inspect

Tires . . . . inspect
Check pressure & wear

Battery . . . . clean terminals
Check voltage, fluid level. Inspect case & tiedowns

Brake fluid reservoir . . . . . . check level **HB**

Brake and fuel hoses . . . . check

Clutch, Medallion . . . . adjust
Pull up clutch (against the stop) to activate self adjuster

Hydraulic clutch . . . . check level **HB**

Cooling system . . . . check level **EC**

Power steering reservoir . . check level **PS**

EVERY 12 MO
Cooling system . . . . inspect

EVERY 15 MO/15 MI—24 KM
W Drive belts 3.0L eng. . . . . inspect

Evaporative system . . . . inspect

**1988-90, EVERY 15 MI—24 KM
1991-92, EVERY 22 MI—36 KM**
Brake linings . . . . inspect
Parking brake . . . . check/adjust

EVERY 22.5 MO/22.5 MI—36 KM
Rear wheel bearings . inspect/lubricate **GC**

**1988-90,
EVERY 22.5 MI—36 KM
1991-92, EVERY 30 MI—48 KM**
W Spark plugs . . . . replace

**1988-90,
EVERY 22.5 MO/22.5 MI—36 KM
1991-92,
EVERY 36 MO/30 MI—48 KM**
Ball joints & tie rod ends . inspect/lube **LB**

EVERY 30 MO/30 MI—48 KM
Cooling system . . . . . . change coolant **EC**
Initial service, then at the beginning of each winter sea-
son

Body . . . . lubricate 10W **MO**
Door hinges & latches as needed. Inspect wiring &
hose routings

W Fuel filter . . . . replace

Ignition system . . . . inspect
Distributor cap, rotor, wires

Transaxle, automatic . . . . change fluid
Clean/change filter

Transaxle, manual . . . . . . change lubricant

W Air cleaner element . . . . replace

Valves 2.2L eng. . . . . adjust

SEVERE SERVICE
Crankcase — Change oil every 3 mo/3 mi
(4.8 km); change oil filter at first, then every
other oil change.
Universal joints & ball joints — inspect every
oil change

Tie rod ends — Lubricate every 18 mo/15 mi
(24 km)
Brake linings, and rear wheel bearings —
Inspect every 9 mi (14.4 km)

Engine air filter — Inspect every 15 mi (24
km)

Automatic transaxle — Change fluid, filter,
and adjust bands every 15 mi (24 km)

KEY TO LUBRICANTS

AF DEXRON®-II Automatic Transmission
Fluid

CD Motor Oil, API Service CD

EC Ethylene Glycol Coolant
With ALUGARD 340-2™. Mix 50/50 with distilled
water

GC Wheel Bearing Grease,
NLGI Category GC

GLS Gear Lubricant, Special
Mopar Part No. 82200945

GL-5 Gear Oil, API Service GL-5

HB Hydraulic Brake Fluid, DOT 3

LB Chassis Grease, NLGI Category LB

MA MERCON® Automatic Transmission
Fluid

MO Motor Oil

PS Power Steering Fluid
Jeep/Eagle: Premier, 8982 200 946; Medallion,
8993342

SG Motor Oil, API Service SG

CRANKCASE
Medallion . . . . **SG**
Premier, Monaco . . . . **SG, SG/CD**

CAPACITY, Refill:	Liters	Qt
Includes filter:		
2.2L Medallion	5.0	5.3
2.5L Premier	4.7	5.0
3.0L Premier, Monaco . .	5.7	6.0

1988-89
Above 30°F (−1°C) 20W-40, 20W-50
Above 0°F (−18°C) 10W-30
Below 60°F (16°C) 5W-30
1990-92
Above 0°F (−18°C) 10W-30
Below 60°F (16°C) 5W-30*
* Preferred when temperatures consistently fall below
10°F (−12°C)

TRANSAXLE, Automatic
Premier final drive serviced separately
Medallion 1988 . . . . **AF**
Medallion 1989; Premier, Monaco . . . . **MA**

CAPACITY, Initial Refill*:	Liters	Qt
Medallion	2.5	2.7
Premier, Monaco	2.6	2.8

* With the engine at operating temperature, shift transmission through all gears. Check fluid level in PARK and add
fluid as needed

TRANSAXLE, Manual 75W-90 **GL-5**

CAPACITY, Refill:	Liters	Pt
Medallion	2.3	5.0
Premier	3.4	7.0

FINAL DRIVE
Premier, Monaco w/Auto. Trans. . . . . **GLS**

CAPACITY, Refill:	Liters	Pt
4-cyl. Premier	0.9	1.8
6-cyl. Premier, Monaco . .	0.7	1.3

EEIPM2

SERVICE AT TIME OR MILEAGE—WHICHEVER OCCURS FIRST

EEIPM2

W SERVICE TO MAINTAIN EMISSION WARRANTY

MI—MILES IN THOUSANDS
KM—KILOMETERS IN THOUSANDS

TURBO ENGINES:
EVERY 6 MO/5 MI—8 KM
Crankcase .... change oil

Oil filter .... replace
Every second oil change

EVERY 12 MO/7.5 MI—12 KM
Crankcase ex. turbo .... change oil

Oil filter ex. turbo .... replace
At every second change, but at least every 12 months

EVERY 12 MO/15 MI—24 KM
Brake hoses .... check
Check rear drum linings & wheel cylinders every 24 mo/
15 mi (24 km)

Disc brake pads .... inspect

Drive shaft boots .... inspect

Power steering fluid .... check AP
May use AF when AP is not available. Also check
hoses

Transaxle, automatic .... check level

EVERY 15 MI—24 KM
W Valve clearance .... inspect/replace
Adjust only when specifications are on emission label

EVERY 24 MO/30 MI—48 KM
Ball joint, steering linkage seals &
    FWD steering .... inspect

Drum brake linings .... inspect
Ex. Talon

Exhaust system .... check

W Fuel hoses 1991-92 .... check

Rear wheel bearings
    Summit .... clean/repack GC
Inspect for leaks. Repack whenever drums are removed

Coolant .... drain/flush/refill EC

EVERY 30 MI—48 KM
Differential, Limited-Slip ..... change fluid

Differential .... check level
Ex. Limited-Slip

Drive belts .... inspect

Transaxle, automatic .... change fluid
Change filter & adjust bands

Transaxle, manual .... check level

W Air cleaner filter .... replace

W Spark plugs .... replace

EVERY 5 YR/50 MI—80 KM
W Evaporative canister .... replace
4WD only

W Fuel lines, connections, fill cap
    & tank .... check

W Fuel, water, & fuel
    vapor hoses 1989-90 .... check/replace

EVERY 5 YR/60 MI—96 KM
W Crankcase emission
    system .... check/clean
4WD only

EVERY 60 MI—96 KM
Timing belts .... replace
Also replace the balancer belt when equipped

SEVERE SERVICE
W Air cleaner filter, PCV system disc brake
pads, drum brake linings—Service more frequently

W Crankcase—Change oil every 3 mo/3 mi
(4.8 km) & filter every second oil change

W Spark plugs—Replace every 15 mi (24 km)

KEY TO LUBRICANTS

AF	DEXRON®-II Automatic Transmission Fluid
AP	MOPAR ATF-PLUS®
CD	Motor Oil, API Service CD
EC	Ethylene Glycol Coolant
	Mix 50% to 70% with water
GC	Wheel Bearing Grease
GL-4	Gear Oil, API Service GL-4
GL-5	Gear Oil, API Service GL-5
GL-5 ★	Special Lubricant for Limited-Slip Differentials
HB	Hydraulic Brake Fluid, DOT 3
SG	Motor Oil, API Service SG

CRANKCASE .... SG, SG/CD

CAPACITY, Refill:	Liters	Qt
1.5L	3.0	3.2
1.8L, 2.4L	3.5	3.7
2.0L	4.0	4.2

Capacity shown is without filter or oil cooler. When replacing filter, additional oil may be needed

Turbo Models
Above 32°F (0°C) 20W-20, 20W-40
Above −10°F (−23°C) 10W-30
Below 60°F (16°C) 5W-30

All Other Models
Above 32°F (0°C) 20W-20, 20W-40, 20W-50
Above −10°F (−23°C) 10W-30,
                                10W-40, 10W-50
Below 60°F (16°C) 5W-20*, 5W-30, 5W-40
* Not recommended for sustained high-speed driving

TRANSAXLE/Automatic .... AP†
†May use AF when AP is not available

CAPACITY, Initial Refill*:	Liters	Qt
All	4.0	4.2

* With the engine at operating temperature, shift transmission through all gears. Check fluid level in PARK and add
fluid as needed

TRANSAXLE/Manual
1989-91 .... 75W-85W **GL-4**
1992 .... 75W-85W, 75W-90 **GL-4**

CAPACITY, Refill:	Liters	Pt
Summit & Talon		
FWD non-Turbo	1.8	3.7
Talon 4WD Turbo	2.2	4.6
Talon 4WD, Summit Wagon AWD	2.3	4.9
Summit Wagon 1.8L FWD	1.8	3.8
Summit Wagon 2.4L FWD	2.3	4.8

TRANSFER CASE
1989-91 .... 80W, 75W-85W **GL-4**
1992 .... 75W-85W, 75W-90 **GL-4**

CAPACITY, Refill:	Liters	Pt
Talon 4WD, Summit Wagon AWD	0.6	1.3

DIFFERENTIAL **GL-5**
All 4WD
Above −10°F (−23°C), 90, 85W-90, 80W-90; −30°
to −10°F (−34° to −23°C), 80W, 80W-90; below
−30°F (−34°C), 75W

CAPACITY, Refill:	Liters	Pt
All models	0.7	1.5

LIMITED-SLIP IDENTIFICATION:
Lift rear of vehicle, turn one wheel and the other will turn in
the same direction

SERVICE LOCATIONS — ENGINE AND CHASSIS

HOOD RELEASE: Inside, except some Fairmont, Zephyr front

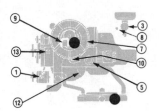

1988-89
1.3L (81) 2V
Festiva

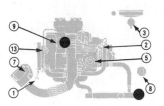

1989-92
1.3L FI
Festiva

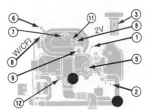

1.6L (98) 2V,
1.9L (113) 2V, CFI
Escort, Lynx, EXP, LN7

① Crankcase dipstick
② Transmission dipstick
③ Brake fluid reservoir
④ Clutch fluid reservoir
⑤ Oil fill cap
⑥ Power steering reservoir
⑦ Air filter
⑧ Fuel filter
⑨ Oil filter
⑩ PCV filter
⑪ EGR valve
⑫ Oxygen sensor
⑬ PCV valve

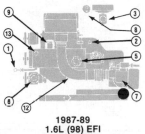

1987-89
1.6L (98) EFI
Tracer

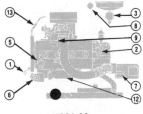

1991-92
1.6L ex. Turbo
Capri

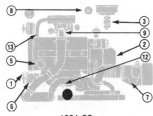

1991-92
1.6L Turbo
Capri

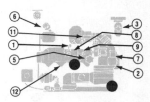

1983-85
1.6L (98) EFI
Escort, Lynx, EXP, LN7

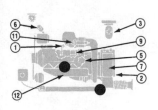

1984-85
1.6L (98) Turbo
Escort, Lynx, EXP

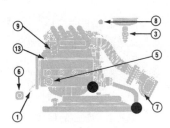

1991-92
1.8L DOHC
Tracer

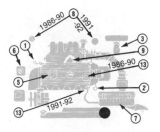

1986-92
1.9L (116) EFI
Escort, Lynx, EXP, Tracer

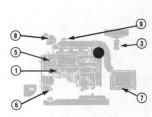

1984-87
2.0L (122) Diesel
Escort, Lynx, Tempo, Topaz

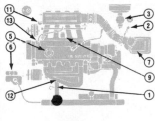

1989-92
2.2L EFI
Probe

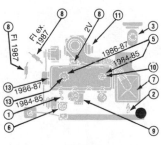

1984-87
2.3L (140) Tempo, Topaz

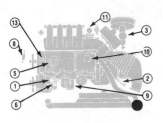

1988-92
2.3L (140) Tempo, Topaz

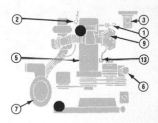

1983-88
2.3L (140) Turbo

● Cooling system drain

SERVICE LOCATIONS — ENGINE AND CHASSIS

FDDP-2   FDDP-2

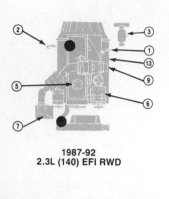

1987-92
2.3L (140) EFI RWD

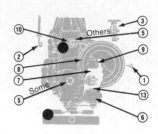

1983-86
2.3L (140) 1V

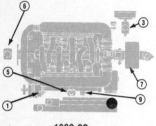

1984-85
2.4L (146) Diesel
Mark VII, Continental

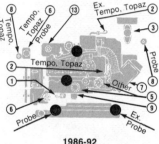

1986-91
2.5L (153)
Taurus, Sable

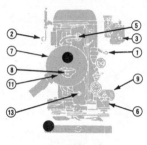

1989-92
3.0L DOHC-SHO
Taurus

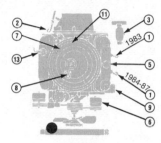

1986-92
3.0L (183) ex. DOHC-SHO

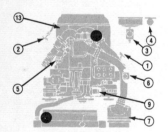

1983
3.3L (200)

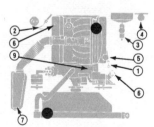

1983-87
3.8L (232) RWD

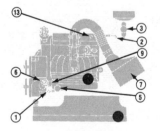

1989-92
3.8L Supercharged
Thunderbird, Cougar

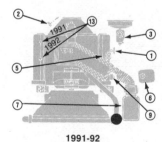

1988-92 3.8L (232) RWD
ex. Supercharged
Thunderbird, Cougar

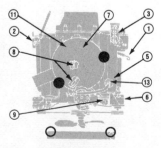

1988-92
3.8L (232) FWD
Taurus, Sable

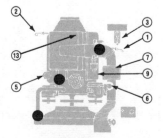

1991-92
4.6L
Town Car

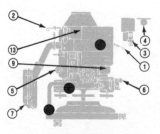

1983-85
4.2L (255), 5.0L (302)
1983-91
5.8L (351)

1986-92
5.0L (302) Lincoln
Town Car, Crown Victoria,
Grand Marquis

1986-92 5.0L (302)
All Others

● Cooling system drain   ○ Cooling system drain, some models

SERVICE LOCATIONS — ENGINE AND CHASSIS

0 FITTINGS 0 PLUGS

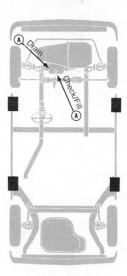

1988-92 Festiva

0 FITTINGS 0 PLUGS

1991-92 Capri, Escort
1987-92 Tracer

0 FITTINGS 0 PLUGS

1989-92 Probe

0 FITTINGS 0 PLUGS

1983-90 Escort, Lynx, EXP, LN7
1983-92 2WD Tempo, Topaz

0 FITTINGS 0 PLUGS

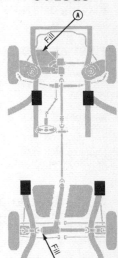

Tempo, Topaz 4WD

2 FITTINGS, POLICE 0 FITTINGS, OTHERS 0 PLUGS

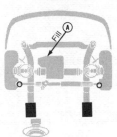

Sable, Taurus, 1988-92 Continental

0-2 FITTINGS 0-2 PLUGS

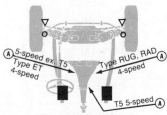

AIR SUSPENSION
Turn air suspension off
(switch located in trunk on left side)
before jacking or hoisting vehicle

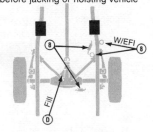

Fairmont, Zephyr (1983);
Capri (1983-86); Mustang;
Thunderbird & Cougar XR-7 (1983-88),
LTD & Marquis (1983-86),
Continental (1983-87), Mark VII

0-4 FITTINGS 0-5 PLUGS

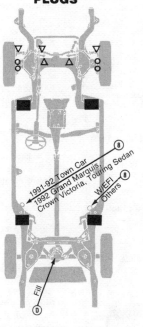

Crown Victoria & Grand Marquis,
Lincoln Town Car, Mark VI

0 FITTINGS 0 PLUGS

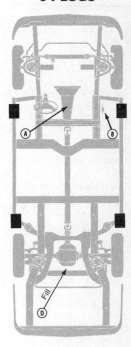

1989-92 Thunderbird, Cougar

LIFTING CAUTION Never lift car with bumper jack

CAUTION: On front wheel drive vehicles the center of gravity is further forward than on rear wheel drive vehicles. When removing major components from the rear of the vehicle while it is on a hoist, the vehicle must be supported in a manner to prevent it from tipping forward.

- ■ Lift adapter position
- △ Plug, some models
- ○ Fitting, some models
- Ⓐ Manual transmission/transaxle, drain & fill
- Ⓑ Transfer case, NOT USED
- Ⓒ Automatic transaxle final drive, NOT USED
- Ⓓ Differential, drain & fill
- Ⓔ Fuel filter

FORD, LINCOLN, MERCURY
1983 All Models

Follow (A) maintenance schedule for Canada when noted below when (A) is found on engine emission decal

MI—MILES IN THOUSANDS
KM—KILOMETERS IN THOUSANDS

FIRST 7.5 MO/7.5 MI—12 KM
Drive belts . . . . inspect/adjust
(A) schedule required for 4-cyl. only
Not required for Calif. warranty or single wide serpentine belt

Idle speeds . . . . check/adjust
3.3L engine only

Manifold heat valve . . . check/lubricate **MH**
Ex. Calif. Some, 3.8L, 4.2L & 5.0L eng. only

4-CYL. TURBO ENGINE,
EVERY 12 MO/5 MI—8 KM
OTHERS, EVERY 12 MO/7.5 MI—12 KM
Crankcase . . . . change oil

Oil filter . . . . replace
All ex. 2.3L, 3.3L and (A) schedule at first oil change, then every other, except replace at scheduled oil change if 12 mo or more since replacement

EVERY 12 MONTHS
Cooling system . . . . inspect

4-CYL. TURBO ENGINE,
EVERY 15 MI—24 KM
Spark plugs . . . . replace
Ex. Calif.

EVERY 30 MI—48 KM
Brake system . . . . inspect
Inspect hoses & replace lining when less than 1/32" thick or within 1/32" of any rivet head ex. disc pads, 1/8" thick

Front suspension . . 0-2 fittings/plugs **LM**

Front wheel bearings . . . . inspect **LM**
Ex. with front wheel drive. Torque 17-25 ft lb; back off nut 1/2 turn, retighten to 10-15 in. lb

Steering linkage . . . . 0-5 plugs **LL**

Air cleaner element . . . . replace

Brake master cyl. . . . . . check level **HBH**

Choke system . . . . check
(A) schedule every 22.5 mi (36 km). Clean & lubricate

Crankcase filter . . . . replace
Located in air cleaner housing. 2.3L non-Turbo & 8-cyl. eng., every 52.5 mi (84 km). Not required for 1.6L EFI eng.

Drive belts ex.
4-cyl. (A) . . . . inspect/adjust
8-cyl. (A) schedule every 22.5 mi (36 km). Not required for single wide serpentine belt

Idle speeds ex. 1.6L eng.
& 4-cyl. Turbo . . . . check/adjust
Not required for Calif. warranty

Manifold heat
valve . . . . check/lubricate **MH**
At this interval, then every 15 mi (72 km). Ex. Calif. Some 3.8L, 4.2L & 5.0L only

Spark plugs . . . . replace
All ex. 4-cyl. 49 state Turbo eng. (A) schedule, every 22.5 mi (36 km)

1.6L 4-CYL. & 3.8L V-6,
EVERY 36 MO/30 MI—48 KM
2.3L TURBO ENGINE,
EVERY 36 MO/50 MI—80 KM
OTHERS,
EVERY 36 MO/52.5 MI—84 KM
Cooling system . . . . . . change coolant **EC**

Cooling system hoses &
clamps . . . . inspect

EVERY 60 MI—96 KM
Engine timing belt 1.6L eng. . . . . . replace
Only required when replace "Timing Belt" decal is on eng.

SERVICE AS REQUIRED
Rear wheel bearings . . . . inspect **LM**
With front wheel drive. When replacing rear brake linings. Torque 17-25 ft lb; back off 1/2 turn, retighten to 10-15 in. lb

Steering mechanism . . . . inspect

Tires . . . . rotate/balance
Lug nut torque, 80-105 ft lb

Transmission linkage . . . . . . lubricate **LM**

Crankcase air filter . . . . replace
Located in air cleaner housing. As required after 50 mi (80 km)

Distributor wick under rotor . . . . . 10W **SG**

PCV filter . . . . replace

Power steering reservoir . . check level **FA**

Body hinges . . . . lubricate **MO**

Fluid leaks on pavement . . . . check

SEVERE SERVICE
In addition to normal service
Crankcase—Change oil every 3 mo/3 mi (4.8 km); change filter every other oil change ex. 4-cyl. Turbo, change filter at every oil change

Differential (Traction-Lok)—Drain every 7.5 mi (12 km)

Transmission, automatic—Change lubricant every 30 mi (48 km)

Spark plugs—Check, clean & regap every 6 mi (9.6 km) ex. 4-cyl. Turbo, every 3 mi (4.8 km)

KEY TO LUBRICANTS

EC	Ethylene Glycol Coolant Mix 50/50 with water or at least to −20°F (−29°C) protection
EP	Extreme Pressure Gear Lubricant Ford Part No. D8DZ-19C547-A
FA	Automatic Transmission Fluid, Type F
HBH	Hydraulic Brake Fluid, Extra Heavy-Duty
HP	Hypoid Gear Oil Ford Part No. E0AZ-19580A
HP★	Hypoid Gear Oil for Traction-Lok Differential Ford Part No. E0AZ-19580A
LL	Steering Linkage Lubricant
LM	Lithium Grease, with Polyethylene & Molybdenum Disulfide
MA	MERCON® Automatic Transmission Fluid
MH	Manifold Heat Valve Solvent
MO	Motor Oil
SG	Motor Oil, API Service SG

CRANKCASE . . . . SG
CAPACITY, Refill:

	Liters	Qt
All	3.8	4.0

Some 8-cyl. engines have 2 oil drain plugs
Capacity is without filter. When replacing filter, additional oil may be needed

SINGLE VISCOSITY
Above 40°F (4°C) 30
MULTI-VISCOSITY
Below 100°F (38°C) 5W-30**
Above 0°F (−18°C) 10W-30*, 10W-40*
Above 10°F (−12°C) 15W-40
Above 20°F (−7°C) 20W-40, 20W-50
* Preferred viscosity above 0°F (−18°C) in all engines except 1.6L & 2.3L Tempo, Topaz
** Preferred viscosity below 100°F (38°C) in 1.6L & 2.3L Tempo, Topaz. All others, recommended for 60°F (16°C)

TRANSMISSION/TRANSAXLE,
Automatic . . . . MA
CAPACITY, Initial Refill*:

	Liters	Qt
FWD (Total Fill)	9.2	9.8
RWD	2.8	3.0

*With the engine at operating temperature, shift transmission through all gears. Check fluid level in PARK and add fluid as needed

TRANSMISSION/TRANSAXLE, Manual
FWD . . . . **MA** or **FA**
RWD: T5 5-speed . . . . **MA**
Others . . . . 80W **EP**
CAPACITY, Refill:

	Liters	Pt
FWD: 4-speed	2.3	5.0
5-speed	2.9	6.2
RWD: 4-speed		
RAD & SR4 models	1.7	3.5
w/OD	2.1	4.5
Others	1.3	2.8
5-speed OD	1.8	3.7

Transmission model indicated on upper left area tag on extension housing

DIFFERENTIAL
Standard . . . . 90 **HP**
Traction-Lok . . . . 90 **HP★**
CAPACITY, Refill:

Differential Type:	Liters	Pt
WGG	1.2	2.5
WGY	1.9	4.0
WFZ	1.8	3.7
Others	1.7	3.5

Type indicated on upper left area of differential tag
TRACTION-LOK IDENTIFICATION:
Axle model indicated by a letter C, D, E, R or Z on plate at driver's door

FORD, LINCOLN, MERCURY
1984 All Gasoline Models

SERVICE AT TIME OR MILEAGE—WHICHEVER OCCURS FIRST

FDPM15   FDPM15

MI—MILES IN THOUSANDS
KM—KILOMETERS IN THOUSANDS

EVERY MONTH
Cooling system . . . . check level **EC**

EVERY 6 MONTHS
Drive belts . . . . inspect

Radiator, heater & AC hoses . . . . . inspect

4-CYL. TURBO ENGINE, FIRST 5 MI—8 KM OTHERS, FIRST 7.5 MI—12 KM
Tires . . . . rotate
Thunderbird & Cougar only. Initial interval then every 15 mi (24 km)

Drive belts . . . . inspect/adjust
Not required for Calif. warranty or Mustang/Capri w/5.0L eng.

Manifold heat
valve . . . . check/lubricate **MH**
Some models only. Not required for Calif. warranty

EVERY 12 MONTHS
Brake master cyl. . . . . . check level **HBH**

Cooling system . . . . inspect

Power steering reservoir . . check level **FA**

Transmission controls
& linkage . . . . lubricate **LM**

Body hinges . . . . lubricate **MO**

4-CYL. TURBO ENGINE, EVERY 12 MO/5 MI—8 KM OTHERS, EVERY 12 MO/7.5 MI—12 KM
Crankcase . . . . change oil

Oil filter . . . . replace
2.3L eng. ex. H.S.C. & all Turbocharged, replace at every oil change. All others, at first oil change, then every other

EVERY 15 MI—24 KM
Spark plugs . . . . replace
1.6L EFI non-Turbo when used for over 70 mph continuous duty driving. Not required for Calif. warranty

EVERY 30 MI—48 KM
Brake system . . . . inspect
Inspect hoses & replace lining when less than 1/32" thick or within 1/32" of any rivet head ex. disc pads, 1/8" thick

Front suspension . . 0-2 fittings/plugs **LM**

Front wheel bearings . . . . inspect **LM**
Ex. with front wheel drive. Torque 17-25 ft lb; back off nut 1/2 turn, retighten to 10-15 in. lb

Steering linkage . . . . 0-5 plugs **LL**

Air cleaner element . . . . replace

Choke System . . . . clean/check
Not required for 1.6L & 3.8L EFI or Turbo engines

Crankcase filter . . . . replace
2.3L non-Turbo & 8-cyl. eng., every 52.5 mi (84 km). Not required for 1.6L EFI non-Turbo eng.

Drive belts . . . . inspect/adjust
Not required for Mustang/Capri w/5.0L eng.

Manifold heat
valve . . . . check/lubricate **MH**
At this interval, then every 15 mi (72 km). Some models only. Not required for Calif. warranty

Spark plugs . . . . replace
Ex. 2.3L Turbo

4-CYL. EX. TURBO & 3.8L V-6, EVERY 36 MO/30 MI—48 KM TURBO ENGINE, EVERY 36 MO/50 MI—80 KM 8-CYL., EVERY 36 MO/52.5 MI—84 KM
Cooling system . . . . . . change coolant **EC**

Cooling system hoses &
clamps . . . . inspect

SERVICE AS REQUIRED
Rear wheel bearings . . . . inspect **LM**
With front wheel drive. When replacing rear brake linings. Torque 17-25 ft lb; back off 1/2 turn, retighten to 10-15 in. lb

Steering mechanism . . . . inspect

Tires . . . . rotate/balance
Lug nut torque, 80-105 ft lb

Fluid leaks on pavement . . . . check

SEVERE SERVICE
In addition to normal service
Crankcase—Change oil every 3 mo/3 mi (4.8 km); change filter every other oil change

Transmission/Transaxle, automatic—Change lubricant every 30 mi (48 km)

Spark plugs—Check, clean & regap every 6 mi (9.6 km)

KEY TO LUBRICANTS

EC	Ethylene Glycol Coolant Mix 50/50 with water or at least to –20°F (–29°C) protection
EP	Extreme Pressure Gear Lubricant Ford Part No. D8DZ-19C547A
FA	Automatic Transmission Fluid, Type F
HBH	Hydraulic Brake Fluid, Extra Heavy-Duty
HP	Hypoid Gear Oil Ford Part No. E0AZ-19580A
HP★	Hypoid Gear Oil for Traction-Lok Differential Ford Part No. E0AZ-19580A
LL	Steering Linkage Lubricant
LM	Lithium Grease, with Polyethylene & Molybdenum Disulfide
MA	MERCON® Automatic Transmission Fluid
MH	Manifold Heat Valve Solvent
MO	Motor Oil
SG	Motor Oil, API Service SG

CRANKCASE . . . . SG

CAPACITY, Refill:	Liters	Qt
1.6L	3.3	3.5
2.3L Turbo	4.3	4.5
Others	3.8	4.0

Some 8-cyl. engines have 2 oil drain plugs
Capacity shown is without filter. When replacing filter, additional oil may be needed

SINGLE VISCOSITY
Above 40°F (4°C) 30
MULTI-VISCOSITY
Below 100°F (38°C) . . . . 5W-30★★
Above 0°F (–18°C) . . . . 10W-30★, 10W-40★
Above 10°F (–12°C) 15W-40
Above 20°F (–7°C) 20W-40, 20W-50
★ Preferred viscosity above 0°F (–18°C) in all engines except Tempo, Topaz & 1.6L
★★ Preferred viscosity below 100°F (38°C) in Tempo, Topaz & 1.6L
All others, recommended for below 60°F (16°C)

TRANSMISSION/TRANSAXLE, Automatic . . . . MA

CAPACITY, Initial Refill★:	Liters	Qt
Tempo, Topaz (Total Fill) . .	7.9	8.3
Escort, Lynx, EXP	9.2	9.8
RWD	2.8	3.0

★RWD, with the engine at operating temperature, shift transmission through all gears. Check fluid level in PARK and add fluid as needed

TRANSMISSION/TRANSAXLE, Manual
FWD . . . . **MA** or **FA**
RWD: 4-speed . . . . 80W **EP**
     5-speed . . . . **MA**

CAPACITY, Refill:	Liters	Pt
FWD: 4-speed	2.5	5.2
5-speed	2.9	6.2
RWD: 4-speed	1.3	2.8
5-speed	2.4	5.0

DIFFERENTIAL
Standard . . . . 90 **HP**
Traction-Lok . . . . 90 **HP★**

CAPACITY, Refill:	Liters	Pt
Crown Victoria, Town Car, Grand Marquis	1.8	3.7
Others	1.5	3.2

TRACTION-LOK IDENTIFICATION:
Axle model indicated by a letter C, D, E, M, R, W or Z on plate at driver's door

SERVICE AT TIME OR MILEAGE—WHICHEVER OCCURS FIRST

FDPM17   FDPM17

MI—MILES IN THOUSANDS
KM—KILOMETERS IN THOUSANDS

EVERY MONTH
Cooling system . . . . check level **EC**

EVERY 6 MONTHS
Accessory drive belts . . . . inspect

Radiator, heater & AC hoses . . . . . inspect

TURBO ENGINE, FIRST 5 MI—8 KM
OTHERS, FIRST 7.5 MI—12 KM
Accessory drive belts . . . . . . inspect/adjust
Not required for Calif. warranty

Manifold heat
  valve . . . . check/lubricate **MH**
Some models only. Not required for Calif. warranty

EVERY 12 MONTHS
Brake master cyl. . . . . . check level **HBH**

Cooling system . . . . inspect

Power steering reservoir . . check level **FA**

Transmission controls
  & linkage . . . . lubricate **LM**

Body hinges . . . . lubricate **MO**

TURBO ENGINE, EVERY 5 MI—8 KM
OTHERS,
EVERY 12 MO/7.5 MI—12 KM
Crankcase . . . . change oil

Oil filter . . . . replace
2.3L eng. ex. H.S.C. & all Turbocharged, replace at
every oil change. All others, at first oil change, then
every other

EVERY 15 MI—24 KM
Air cleaner element . . . . replace
5.0L HO eng. only

Spark plugs . . . . replace
Turbo eng. only. Not required for Calif. warranty

EVERY 30 MI—48 KM
Front suspension . . **0-2 fittings/plugs LM**

Steering linkage . . . . **0-5 plugs LL**

Air cleaner element . . . . replace

Choke system . . . . clean/check
Not required for 1.6L EFI or Turbo engines

Crankcase emission filter . . . . replace
1.6L & 3.8L eng. only

Crankcase oil separator filter . . . . . replace
1.6L Turbo eng. only

Accessory drive belts . . . . . . inspect/adjust

Manifold heat
  valve . . . . check/lubricate **MH**
At this interval, then every 15 mi (24 km). Some models
only. Not required for Calif. warranty

Spark plugs . . . . replace

Vacuum spark delay valve . . . . . . replace
1.6L with idle speed control. Not required for Calif. warranty

EVERY 36 MO/30 MI—48 KM
Cooling system . . . . . . change coolant **EC**

EVERY 52.5 MI—84 KM
Crankcase emission filter . . . . replace
Except 1.6L & 3.8L engines

EVERY 60 MI—96 KM
EGR vacuum solenoid filter . . . . . . replace
3.8L eng. only

SERVICE AS REQUIRED
Brake system . . . . inspect
Inspect hoses & replace lining when less than 1/32"
thick or within 1/32" of any rivet head ex. disc pads, 1/8"
thick

Front wheel bearings . . . . inspect **LM**
Ex. with front wheel drive. Torque 17-25 ft lb; back off
nut 1/2 turn, retighten to 10-12 in. lb

Rear wheel bearings . . . . inspect **LM**
With front wheel drive. When replacing rear brake linings. Torque 17-25 ft lb; back off 1/2 turn, retighten to
10-12 in. lb

Steering mechanism . . . . inspect

Tires . . . . rotate/balance
Lug nut torque, 80-105 ft lb

Fluid leaks on pavement . . . . check

SEVERE SERVICE
In addition to normal service
Crankcase—Change oil & filter every 3 mo/
3 mi (4.8 km)

Transmission/Transaxle, automatic—
Change lubricant every 30 mi (48 km)

Steering linkage—When equipped with
plugs or fittings lubricate every 15 mi (24 km)

Air cleaner element—Replace as required

Accessory drive belts—Inspect/adjust at
first 3 mi (4.8 km)

Crankcase emission filter—Replace every
30 mi (48 km)

Cooling system hoses & clamps—Check
every 36 mo/30 mi (48 km)

EGR vacuum solenoid filter 3.8L eng.—
Replace every 30 mi (48 km)

Manifold heat valve—Check/lubricate at
first 6 mi (9.6 km)

Spark plugs—Check, clean & regap every 6
mi (9.6 km)

KEY TO LUBRICANTS

EC	Ethylene Glycol Coolant Mix 50/50 with water or at least to –20°F (–29°C) protection
EP	Extreme Pressure Gear Lubricant Ford Part No. D8DZ-19C547-A
FA	Automatic Transmission Fluid, Type F
HBH	Hydraulic Brake Fluid, Extra Heavy-Duty
HP	Hypoid Gear Oil Ford Part No. E0AZ-19580A
HP★	Hypoid Gear Oil for Traction-Lok Differentials Ford Part No. E0AZ-19580A
LL	Steering Linkage Lubricant
LM	Lithium Grease, with Polyethylene & Molybdenum Disulfide
MA	MERCON® Automatic Transmission Fluid
MH	Manifold Heat Valve Solvent
MO	Motor Oil
SG	Motor Oil, API Service SG

CRANKCASE . . . . SG

CAPACITY, Refill:	Liters	Qt
1.6L	3.3	3.5
2.3L (inc. filter)	4.7	5.0
Others	3.8	4.0

8-cyl. engines have 2 oil drain plugs. Add 0.45 liter (0.5 qt)
for police oil cooler
Capacity shown is without filter. When replacing filter, additional oil may be needed

SINGLE VISCOSITY
Above 40°F (4°C) 30
MULTI-VISCOSITY
Below 100°F (38°C) . . . . 5W-30★★
Above 0°F (–18°C) . . . . 10W-30★, 10W-40★
Above 10°F (–12°C) 15W-40
Above 20°F (–7°C) 20W-40, 20W-50
★ Preferred viscosity above 0°F (–18°C) in all engines ex-
cept Tempo, Topaz & 1.6L
★★ Preferred viscosity below 100°F (38°C) in Tempo, To-
paz & 1.6L. All Others, recommended for below 60°F
(16°C)

TRANSMISSION/TRANSAXLE,
Automatic . . . . **MA**

CAPACITY, Initial Refill★:	Liters	Qt
FWD (Total Fill)	7.9	8.3
RWD	2.8	3.0

★ RWD, with the engine at operating temperature, shift
transmission through all gears. Check fluid level in PARK
and add fluid as needed

TRANSMISSION/TRANSAXLE, Manual
FWD . . . . **MA** or **FA**
RWD: 4-speed . . . . 80W **EP**
  5-speed . . . . **MA**

CAPACITY, Refill:	Liters	Pt
FWD: 4-speed	2.5	5.2
5-speed	2.9	6.2
RWD: 4-speed	1.3	2.8
5-speed	2.4	5.0

DIFFERENTIAL
Standard . . . . 90 **HP**
Traction-Lok . . . . 90 **HP★**

CAPACITY, Refill:	Liters	Pt
Crown Victoria, Town Car, Grand Marquis	1.8	3.7
Others	1.5	3.2

SERVICE AT TIME OR MILEAGE—WHICHEVER OCCURS FIRST

FDPM16   FDPM16

Perform the following maintenance services at the intervals indicated to keep the vehicle warranties in effect

W   SERVICE TO MAINTAIN EMISSION WARRANTY

MI—MILES IN THOUSANDS
KM—KILOMETERS IN THOUSANDS

EVERY MONTH
Cooling system . . . . check level **EC**

EVERY 6 MONTHS
Accessory drive belts . . . . inspect

Radiator heater & AC hoses . . . . . . inspect

2.4L, FIRST 5 MI—8 KM
Accessory drive belts . . . . . . inspect/adjust
Not required for Calif. warranty

W Valve clearance . . . . adjust

EVERY 12 MONTHS
Brake master cyl. . . . . . . check level **HBH**

W Cooling system . . . . inspect

Power steering reservoir . . check level **FA**

Transmission controls
  & linkage . . . . lubricate **LM**

Body hinges . . . . lubricate **MO**

2.4L, EVERY 5 MI—8 KM
2.0L, EVERY 7 MO/7.5 MI—12 KM
W Crankcase . . . . change oil

W Oil filter . . . . replace
2.4L, at every oil change; 2.0L at first oil change, then
every other except bypass filter

W Water separator . . . . drain
Replace filter element as required

2.0L, EVERY 15 MI—24 KM
W Crankcase bypass oil filter . . . . replace

W Valve clearance . . . . adjust
1987 inspect, adjust if necessary

EVERY 30 MI—48 KM
Front suspension . . 0-2 fittings/plugs **LM**

Steering linkage . . . . 0-2 plugs **LL**

Transmission, automatic . . . . change fluid
2.4L eng. only

W Air cleaner element . . . . replace

W Accessory drive belts . . . . inspect
2.0L eng. only

W Fuel filter element . . . . replace
2.4L eng. only

W Idle speed . . . . check/adjust

W Injection pump
   dynamic timing 2.4L . . . check/adjust

EVERY 36 MO/30 MI—48 KM
W Cooling system . . . . change coolant **EC**

W Cooling system clamps
   & hoses . . . . inspect

2.4L, EVERY 60 MI—96 KM
Fuel injectors . . . . check

Glow plugs . . . . replace

Timing belt . . . . replace

2.0L, EVERY 100 MI—160 KM
Cam & fuel injection
   pump drive belts . . . . replace

SERVICE AS REQUIRED
Brake system . . . . inspect
Inspect hoses and replace linings when less than 1/32″
thick or within 1/32″ of any rivet head ex. disc pads, 1/8″
thick

Front wheel bearings . . . . inspect **LM**
Ex. front wheel drive. Torque 17-25 ft lb; back off nut 1/2
turn, retighten to 10-12 in. lb

Rear wheel bearings . . . . inspect **LM**
With front wheel drive. When replacing rear brake linings. Torque 17-25 ft lb; back off 1/2 turn, retighten to
10-12 in. lb

Steering mechanism . . . . inspect

Tires . . . . rotate/balance
Lug nut torque, 80-105 lb

Fluid leaks on pavement . . . . check

SEVERE SERVICE
In addition to normal service
W Crankcase—Change oil & filter every 3
mo/3 mi (4.8 km); change 2.0L bypass
filter every 6 mi (9.6 km)

Steering linkage—When equipped with
plugs or fittings, lubricate every 15 mi (24
km)

Transmission/Transaxle, automatic—
Change lubricant every 30 mi (48 km)

W Air cleaner element—Replace as required

KEY TO LUBRICANTS

CC	Motor Oil, API Service CC
CD	Motor Oil, API Service CD
EC	Ethylene Glycol Coolant Mix 50/50 with water or at least to –20°F (–29°C) protection
FA	Automatic Transmission Fluid, Type F
HBH	Hydraulic Brake Fluid, Extra Heavy-Duty
HP	Hypoid Gear Oil Ford Part No. E0AZ-19580A
LL	Steering Linkage Lubricant
LM	Lithium Grease, with Polyethylene & Molybdenum Disulfide
MA	MERCON® Automatic Transmission Fluid
MO	Motor Oil
SF	Motor Oil, API Service SF
SG	Motor Oil, API Service SG

CRANKCASE
2.0L . . . . . **SF/CC, SF/CD, SG/CC, SG/CD**
2.4L . . . . **SF/CD, SG/CD**

CAPACITY, Refill:	Liters	Qt
2.0L	6.8*	7.2*
2.4L	6.2†	6.5†

* Includes primary and bypass oil filters
†Includes oil filter

SINGLE VISCOSITY
2.0L engines
40° to 100°F (4° to 38°C) 30
2.4L engines
14° to 68°F (–10° to 20°C) 20W-20
40° to 86°F (4° to 30°C) 30
Above 68°F (20°C) 40

MULTI-VISCOSITY
2.0L engines
Below 60°F (16°C) 5W-30
0° to 100°F (–18° to 38°C) 10W-30*
Above 10°F (–12°C) 15W-40
Above 20°F (–7°C) 20W-40, 20W-50
2.4L engines
–22° to 86°F (–30° to 30°C) 5W-30
0° to 86°F (–18° to 30°C) 10W-30
Above 20°F (–7°C) 15W-40
* Preferred

TRANSMISSION, Automatic . . . . MA
CAPACITY, Total Fill:	Liters	Qt
Mark VII, Continental	7.6	8.0

TRANSAXLE, Manual . . . . FA or MA
CAPACITY, Refill:	Liters	Pt
4-speed	2.5	5.2
5-speed	2.9	6.2

DIFFERENTIAL . . . . 90 HP
CAPACITY, Refill:	Liters	Pt
Mark VII, Continental	1.5	3.2

SERVICE AT TIME OR MILEAGE—WHICHEVER OCCURS FIRST

FDPM18   FDPM18

Perform the following maintenance services at the intervals indicated to keep the vehicle warranties in effect

W   SERVICE TO MAINTAIN EMISSION WARRANTY

MI—MILES IN THOUSANDS
KM—KILOMETERS IN THOUSANDS

EVERY MONTH
Cooling system . . . . check level **EC**

EVERY 6 MONTHS
Accessory drive belts . . . . inspect

Radiator, heater & AC hoses . . . . . inspect

FIRST 7.5 MI—12 KM
W Manifold heat
valve . . . . .check/lubricate **MH**
5.8L eng. only. Not required for Calif. warranty

EVERY 12 MONTHS
Brake master cyl. . . . . . . check level **HBH**

W Cooling system . . . . inspect
Also 1987, hoses and clamps

Power steering reservoir . . check level **FA**

Transmission/Transaxle controls
& linkage . . . . lubricate **LM**

Body hinges . . . . lubricate **MO**

1986 TURBO ENGINE, EVERY 5 MI—8 KM
1986 OTHERS, EVERY 12 MO/7.5 MI—12 KM
1987 TURBO ENGINE, EVERY 6 MO/5 MI—8 KM
1987 OTHERS, EVERY 6 MO/7.5 MI—12 KM
W Crankcase . . . . change oil

W Oil filter . . . . replace
All 1986 2.3L eng. ex. Tempo, Topaz, & all 1987, replace at every oil change. All other 1986, at first oil change, then every other

EVERY 15 MI—24 KM
Air cleaner element 1986 . . . . replace
5.0L HO eng. only

W Spark plugs . . . . replace
Turbo eng. only. Not required for Calif. warranty

EVERY 30 MI—48 KM
Front suspension . . 0-4 fittings/plugs **LM**

Steering linkage . . . . 0-5 plugs **LM**
1986 may use **LL**

W Air cleaner element . . . . replace

W Choke system . . . . clean/check
Not required for EFI or Turbo engines

W Crankcase emission filter . . . . . replace
Not required for 3.0L engine

W Accessory drive belts . . . . . inspect/adjust

W Manifold heat
valve . . . . check/lubricate **MH**
At this interval, then every 15 mi (72 km). Some models only. Not required for Calif. warranty

W Spark plugs . . . . replace

Vacuum spark delay valve
1986 . . . . replace
1.9L 2V with idle speed control. Not required for Calif. warranty

EVERY 36 MO/30 MI—48 KM
W Cooling system . . . . change coolant **EC**

EVERY 60 MI—96 KM
EGR vacuum solenoid filter . . . . . . replace
3.8L eng. only

SERVICE AS REQUIRED
Brake system . . . . inspect
Inspect hoses & replace lining when less than 1/32" thick or within 1/32" of any rivet head ex. disc pads, 1/8" thick

Front wheel bearings . . . . inspect **LM**
Ex. with front wheel drive. Torque 17-25 ft lb; back off nut 1/2 turn, retighten to 10-12 in. lb

Rear wheel bearings . . . . inspect **LM**
With front wheel drive ex. with 4WD Tempo, Topaz. When replacing rear brake linings. Torque 17-25 ft lb; back off 1/2 turn, retighten to 10-12 in. lb

Steering mechanism . . . . inspect

Tires . . . . rotate/balance
Lug nut torque, 80-105 ft lb

Fluid leaks on pavement . . . . check

SEVERE SERVICE
In addition to normal service
W Crankcase—Change oil & filter every 3 mo/3 mi (4.8 km)

Transmission/Transaxle, automatic—Change lubricant every 30 mi (48 km)

Steering linkage Crown Victoria & Grand Marquis—When equipped with plugs or fittings lubricate every 15 mi (24 km)

W Air cleaner element—Replace as required

W Accessory drive belts—1986, inspect/adjust at first 3 mi (4.8 km)

W Cooling system hoses & clamps 1986—Check every 36 mo/30 mi (48 km)

W EGR vacuum solenoid filter 3.8L eng.—Replace every 30 mi (48 km)

W Manifold heat valve—Check/lubricate at first 6 mi (9.6 km)

W Spark plugs—Check, clean & regap every 6 mi (9.6 km)

KEY TO LUBRICANTS
EC Ethylene Glycol Coolant
Mix 50/50 with water or at least to –20°F (–29°C) protection
EP Extreme Pressure Gear Lubricant
Ford Part No. D8DZ-19C547-A
FA Automatic Transmission Fluid, Type F
HBH Hydraulic Brake Fluid, Extra Heavy-Duty
HP Hypoid Gear Oil
Ford Part No. E0AZ-19580A
HP★ Hypoid Gear Oil for Traction-Lok Differential
Ford Part No. E0AZ-19580A
LM Lithium Grease, with Polyethylene & Molybdenum Disulfide
MA MERCON® Automatic Transmission Fluid
MH Manifold Heat Valve Solvent
MO Motor Oil
SG Motor Oil, API Service SG

CRANKCASE . . . . **SG**

CAPACITY, Refill:	Liters	Qt
1.9L	3.3	3.5
2.3L, 2.5L (inc. filter)	4.7	5.0
3.0L (inc. filter)	4.2	4.5
Others	3.8	4.0

8-cyl. engines have 2 oil drain plugs. Add 0.45 liter (0.5 qt) for police oil cooler
Capacity is without filter. When replacing filter, additional oil may be needed
SINGLE VISCOSITY
Above 40°F (4°C) 30
MULTI-VISCOSITY
Below 100°F (38°C) . . . . 5W-30★★
Above 0°F (–18°C) . . . . 10W-30★, 10W-40★
Above 10°F (–12°C) 15W-40
Above 20°F (–7°C) 20W-40, 20W-50
★Preferred viscosity above 0°F (–18°C) except Tempo, Topaz, Escort, Lynx, EXP, Taurus, Sable
★★Preferred viscosity below 100°F (38°C) in Tempo, Topaz, Escort, Lynx, EXP, Taurus, Sable. All others recommended for below 60°F (16°C)

TRANSMISSION/TRANSAXLE,
Automatic . . . . **MA**

CAPACITY, Initial Refill★:	Liters	Qt
FWD: AXOD	12.5	13.1
4WD Tempo, Topaz	9.5	10.0
Others	7.9	8.3
RWD	2.8	3.0

★RWD, with the engine at operating temperature, shift transmission through all gears. Check fluid level in PARK and add fluid as needed

TRANSMISSION/TRANSAXLE, Manual
FWD . . . . **MA** or **FA**
RWD: 4-speed . . . . 80W **EP**
5-speed . . . . **MA**

CAPACITY, Refill:	Liters	Pt
FWD	2.9	6.2
RWD: 4-speed	1.3	2.8
5-speed	2.4	5.0

DIFFERENTIAL
Standard . . . . 90 **HP**
Tempo, Topaz 4WD . . . . 90 **HP★**
Traction-Lok . . . . 90 **HP★**

CAPACITY, Refill:	Liters	Pt
1987 Continental, Mark VII & Mustang w/Limited-Slip 8.8" ring gear	2.2	4.5
4WD Tempo, Topaz	0.6	1.3
All others RWD	1.7	3.7

FORD, LINCOLN, MERCURY
1988-90 All Models Except Merkur

SERVICE AT TIME OR MILEAGE—WHICHEVER OCCURS FIRST

FDPM19   FDPM19

Perform the following maintenance services at the interval indicated to keep the vehicle warranties in effect

W   SERVICE TO MAINTAIN EMISSION WARRANTY

MI — MILES IN THOUSANDS
KM — KILOMETERS IN THOUSANDS

EVERY MONTH
Cooling system . . . . check level **EC**

EVERY 6 MONTHS
Accessory drive belts . . . . inspect
Festiva, Tracer only

Radiator, heater & AC hoses . . . . . inspect

FIRST 7.5 MI — 12 KM
Tires . . . . rotate
At this interval, then every 15 mi (24 km)

EVERY 12 MONTHS
Brake master cyl. . . . . . . check level **HBH**

W Cooling system . . . . inspect
Also hoses and clamps

Power steering reservoir . . check level **FA**

Transmission/Transaxle controls
    & linkage . . . . lubricate **LM**

Transmission/Transaxle,
    manual . . . . check level

Body hinges . . . . lubricate **MO**

TURBO & SUPERCHARGED ENGINE, EVERY 6 MO/5 MI — 8 KM OTHERS, EVERY 6 MO/7.5 MI — 12 KM
W Crankcase oil & filter . . . . replace
Or when indicated by vehicle maintenance monitor, whichever occurs first

EVERY 15 MI — 24 KM
Front suspension &
    steering linkage . . . . . . fittings/plugs **LM**
RWD only

Steering & brake system
    Festiva, Tracer . . . . inspect

W Valve clearance 1.3L 2V . . . . adjust

W Idle speed 1.3L 2V . . . . check

Choke linkage &
    shaft 1.3L 2V . . . . clean/inspect

PCV valve 5.0L . . . . replace
Replace 1990 crankcase ventilation filter

Spark plugs . . . . replace
Turbo eng. only

EVERY 24 MO/24 MI — 38.4 KM
Battery fluid
    1990 3.0L SHO . . . . check level

EVERY 30 MI — 48 KM
Brake system . . . . inspect
Inspect hoses & replace lining when 1/32″ from rivet head ex. disc pads when 1/8″ thick

Front suspension . . 0-4 fittings/plugs **LM**
1.3L, 1.6L eng. inspect ball joints, driveshaft boots & fuel lines

W Air cleaner element . . . . replace

W Choke system . . . . clean/check
Not required for EFI engines

W Crankcase emission filter . . . . . replace
Not required for 1.3L, 1.6L, 3.0L engine

W Accessory drive belts . . . inspect/adjust

W Fuel filter 1.3L 2V . . . . replace

W Spark plugs (ex. platinum) . . . . . replace

Supercharger fluid
    1990 3.8L . . . . check level

Wheel bearings . . . . . . inspect/repack **LM**
Non-driving wheels only. Not required for Festiva, Tracer, Probe

EVERY 36 MO/30 MI — 48 KM
W Cooling system . . . . change coolant **EC**

EVERY 45 MI — 72 KM
Transaxle, Festiva, Tracer . . . . . . inspect
Change rod boots

EVERY 60 MI — 96 KM
Fuel filter 1.3L, 1.6L,
    2.2L & Probe 3.0L . . . . replace

Spark plugs (platinum) . . . . replace

Timing belt 1.3L, 1.6L, 2.2L . . . . . . replace

Wheel bearings Festiva, Tracer
    front & rear . . . . lubricate **LM**

SERVICE AS REQUIRED
Steering mechanism . . . . inspect

Tires . . . . rotate/balance
Lug nut torque, 80-105 ft lb

Fluid leaks on pavement . . . . check

SEVERE SERVICE
In addition to normal service

W Crankcase — Change oil & filter every 3 mo/3 mi (4.8 km)

Transmission/Transaxle, automatic — Change lubricant every 30 mi (48 km)

W Air cleaner element — Replace as required

W Spark plugs 1988 3.0L eng. — Replace every 30 mi (48 km)

Tires 1989-90 — Rotate at first 6 mi (9.6 km), then every 15 mi (24 km)

KEY TO LUBRICANTS

EC   Ethylene Glycol Coolant
Mix 50/50 with water or at least to –20°F (–29°C) protection

FA   Automatic Transmission Fluid, Type F

HBH   Hydraulic Brake Fluid, Extra Heavy-Duty

HP   Hypoid Gear Oil
Ford Part No. E0AZ-19580A

HP★   Hypoid Gear Oil for Traction-Lok Differential
Ford Part No. E0AZ-19580A

LM   Lithium Grease, with Polyethylene & Molybdenum Disulfide

MA   MERCON® Automatic Transmission Fluid

MO   Motor Oil

SG   Motor Oil, API Service SG

CRANKCASE . . . . SG

CAPACITY, Refill:	Liters	Qt
1.3L	3.0	3.2
1.6L (incl. filter)	3.3	3.5
1.9L	3.3	3.5
2.2L	3.9	4.1
2.3L, 2.5L, 3.0L SHO (incl. filter)	4.7	5.0
3.0L ex. SHO & Probe, 3.8L FWD (incl. filter) . . .	4.3	4.5
3.0L Probe, 3.8L RWD, 5.0L, 5.8L	3.8	4.0

8-cyl. engines have 2 oil drain plugs. Add 0.45 liter (0.5 qt) for Police oil cooler
Capacity shown is without filter. When replacing filter, additional oil may be needed

Below 100°F (38°C) 5W-30**
Below 32°F (0°C) 1988 1.3L, 1.6L 5W-30
Above 0°F (–18°C) 10W-30*
Above 0°F (–18°C) 1988 . . . . 10W-40*
*Preferred in 8-cyl., 1.3L, 1.6L, 2.3L Turbo
**Preferred in 1.9L, 2.3L (non-Turbo), 2.5L, 3.0L, 3.8L. Approved only below 60°F (16°C) for 5.0L & 5.8L, 1989-90 1.3L & 1.6L

TRANSMISSION/TRANSAXLE,
Automatic . . . . MA

CAPACITY, Total Fill:	Liters	Qt
AXOD, AXODE	12.2	12.8
4WD Tempo, Topaz	9.5	10.0
Taurus ex. O.D.	7.4	8.0
Festiva	2.8*	3.0*
Tracer	5.7	6.0
Others, FWD	7.9	8.3
All RWD	2.8*	3.0*

*Initial Refill: With the engine at operating temperature, shift transmission through all gears. Check fluid level in PARK and add fluid as needed

TRANSMISSION/TRANSAXLE,
Manual . . . . MA*
*Tracer built prior to Jan. 7, 1987 use **FA**. Thereafter use **MA**

CAPACITY, Refill:	Liters	Pt
Festiva	2.5	5.2
Probe ex. Turbo	3.4	7.2
Probe w/Turbo	3.7	7.8
1988-89 Tracer	3.2	6.8
All others, FWD	2.9	6.2
Mustang	2.6	5.5
Thunderbird, Cougar	3.0	6.4

DIFFERENTIAL
Standard . . . . 90 **HP**
Tempo, Topaz 4WD . . . . 90 **HP★**
Traction-Lok . . . . 90 **HP★**

CAPACITY, Refill:	Liters	Pt
7.5″ ring gear: 1989-90		
Thunderbird/Cougar	1.4	3.0
Others	1.5	3.25
8.8″ ring gear: 1989-90		
Thunderbird/Cougar	1.5	3.25
Others	1.8	3.75
Tempo, Topaz 4WD	0.6	1.3

SERVICE AT TIME OR MILEAGE—WHICHEVER OCCURS FIRST

FDPM20   FDPM20

Perform the following maintenance services at the intervals indicated to keep the vehicle warranties in effect

W   SERVICE TO MAINTAIN EMISSION WARRANTY

MI — MILES IN THOUSANDS
KM — KILOMETERS IN THOUSANDS

EVERY MONTH
Cooling system . . . . check level **EC**

EVERY 6 MONTHS
Accessory drive belts . . . . inspect
Festiva only

Radiator, heater & AC hoses . . . . . inspect

EVERY 12 MONTHS
Brake master cyl. . . . . . . check level **HBH**

W Cooling system . . . . inspect
Also hoses and clamps

Power steering reservoir . . check level **FA**

Transmission/Transaxle controls
& linkage . . . . lubricate **LM**

Transmission/Transaxle,
manual . . . . check level

Body hinges . . . . lubricate **MO**

SUPERCHARGED ENGINE,
EVERY 6 MO/5 MI — 8 KM
OTHERS,
EVERY 6 MO/7.5 MI — 12 KM
W Crankcase oil & filter . . . . replace
Or when indicated by vehicle maintenance monitor,
whichever occurs first

EVERY 15 MI — 24 KM
Brake system, 1992 Capri
& Probe . . . . inspect
Inspect hoses and replace lining when 1/32" from rivet
head ex. disc pads when 1/8" thick

Front suspension &
steering linkage . . . . . . fittings/plugs **LM**
RWD only

Steering & brake system
Festiva . . . . inspect

PCV valve (if equipped) . . . . replace
Replace crankcase ventilation filter

EVERY 24 MO/24 MI — 38.4 KM
Battery fluid 3.0L SHO . . . . . . check level

EVERY 30 MI — 48 KM
Brake system ex. 1992 Capri
& Probe . . . . inspect
Inspect hoses & replace lining when 1/32" from rivet
head ex. disc pads when 1/8" thick

Front suspension . . 0-4 fittings/plugs **LM**
1.3L, 1.6L, 1.8L, 1.9L eng. inspect ball joints, driveshaft
boots & fuel lines

W Air cleaner element . . . . replace

W Crankcase emission filter . . . . . replace
Not required for 1.3L, 1.6L, 1.8L, 3.0L engine

W Accessory drive belts . . . inspect/adjust

W Spark plugs (ex. platinum) . . . . . replace

Supercharger fluid 3.8L . . . . . . check level

Wheel bearings . . . . . . inspect/repack **LM**
Non-driving wheels only. Not required for Festiva,
Probe, Thunderbird, Cougar, Town Car, Continental

EVERY 36 MO/30 MI — 48 KM
W Cooling system . . . . change coolant **EC**

EVERY 60 MI — 96 KM
Fuel filter 1.3L, 1.6L,
2.2L & Probe 3.0L . . . . replace

Spark plugs (platinum) . . . . replace

Timing belt
1.3L, 1.6L, 1.8L, 2.2L . . . . replace

SERVICE AS REQUIRED
Steering mechanism . . . . inspect

Tires . . . . rotate/balance
Lug nut torque, 80-105 ft lb

Fluid leaks on pavement . . . . check

SEVERE SERVICE
In addition to normal service

W Crankcase — Change oil & filter every 3
mo/3 mi (4.8 km)

Transmission/Transaxle, automatic —
Change lubricant every 30 mi (48 km)

W Air cleaner element — Replace as required

Tires — Rotate at first 6 mi (9.6 km), then
every 15 mi (24 km)

KEY TO LUBRICANTS
See other Ford, Lincoln, Mercury charts

CRANKCASE		SG
CAPACITY, Refill:	**Liters**	**Qt**
1.3L	3.0	3.2
1.6L	3.0	3.2
1.8L	3.6	3.8
1.9L	3.3	3.5
2.2L	3.9	4.1
2.3L RWD, 2.5L, 3.0L SHO, 4.6L (incl. filter)	4.7	5.0
2.3L FWD, 3.0L ex. SHO & Probe, 3.8L FWD (incl. filter)	4.3	4.5
3.0L Probe, 3.8L RWD, 5.0L, 5.8L	3.8	4.0

5.0L, 5.8L engines have 2 oil drain plugs. Add 0.45 liter
(0.5 qt) for Police oil cooler
Capacity shown is without filter. When replacing filter, additional oil may be needed

1991:
Below 100°F (38°C), ex. 2.2L,
5.0L, 5.8L 5W-30**
Below 60°F (16°C), 2.2L, 5.0L, 5.8L 5W-30
Above 0°F (–18°C), ex. 1.8L 10W-30*
Above –13°F (–25°C), 1.8L 10W-30
1992 1.8L, 2.2L, 5.0L:
Above 0°F (–18°C) . . . . 10W-30†
Below 60°F (16°C) . . . . 5W-30††
1992 Others:
Above 0°F (–18°C) 10W-30
All temperatures . . . . 5W-30†
*Preferred for 2.2L, 5.0L, 5.8L engines
**Preferred ex. 1.8L, 5.0L, 5.8L engines
†Preferred
††Preferred below 0°F (–18°C)

TRANSMISSION/TRANSAXLE,		
Automatic		**MA**
CAPACITY, Total Fill:	**Liters**	**Qt**
AXOD, AXODE	12.2	12.8
4WD Tempo, Topaz	9.5	10.0
Taurus ex. O.D.	7.4	8.0
Festiva	2.8*	3.0*
Capri	5.7	6.0
Probe	6.8	7.2
Escort & Tracer	5.8	6.1
Others, FWD	7.9	8.3
All RWD	2.8*	3.0*

*Initial Refill: With the engine at operating temperature,
shift transmission through all gears. Check fluid level in
PARK and add fluid as needed

TRANSMISSION/TRANSAXLE,		
Manual		**MA**
CAPACITY, Refill:	**Liters**	**Pt**
Festiva	2.5	5.2
Probe ex. Turbo	3.4	7.2
Probe w/Turbo	3.7	7.8
Capri	3.2	6.8
Escort & Tracer	2.7	5.6
Mustang	2.6	5.5
Thunderbird, Cougar	3.0	6.4
All others, FWD	2.9	6.2

DIFFERENTIAL		
Standard		90 **HP**
Tempo, Topaz 4WD		90 **HP** ★
Traction-Lok		90 **HP** ★
CAPACITY, Refill:	**Liters**	**Pt**
7.5" ring gear:		
Thunderbird/Cougar	1.4	3.0
Others	1.5	3.25
8.8" ring gear:		
Thunderbird/Cougar	1.5	3.25
Others	1.8	3.75
Tempo, Topaz 4WD	0.6	1.3

SERVICE AT TIME OR MILEAGE—WHICHEVER OCCURS FIRST

FDIPM3

HOOD RELEASE: Inside

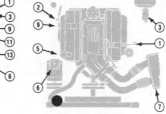

1985-89
4-cyl. 2.3L (140) Turbo

1988-89
V6 2.9L (179)

FDIPM3

0-4 FITTINGS
1985 only

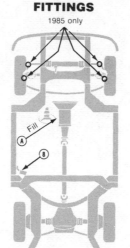

Fill

1985-89 XR4TI
1988-89 Scorpio

LIFTING CAUTION
Never lift car with bumper jack

① Crankcase dipstick
② Transmission dipstick
③ Brake fluid reservoir
④ Clutch fluid reservoir
⑤ Oil fill cap
⑥ Power steering reservoir
⑦ Air filter
⑧ Fuel filter
⑨ Oil filter
⑩ PCV filter
⑪ EGR valve
⑫ Oxygen sensor
⑬ PCV valve

Ⓐ Manual transmission/transaxle, drain & fill
Ⓑ Transfer case, NOT USED
Ⓒ Automatic transaxle final drive, NOT USED
Ⓓ Differential, drain & fill

■ Lift adapter position
○ Fitting, some models
● Cooling system drain

KEY TO LUBRICANTS

AF DEXRON®-II Automatic Transmission Fluid

EC Ethylene Glycol Coolant
Mix 50/50 with water or at least to –20°F (–29°C) protection

FA Automatic Transmission Fluid, Type F

GLS Gear Lubricant, Special
Ford Spec. No. ESD-M2C175-A

HBH Hydraulic Brake Fluid, Extra Heavy-Duty

HP★ Hypoid Gear Oil for Traction-Lok Differential

LL Steering Linkage Lubricant

LM Lithium Grease, with Polyethylene

MA MERCON® Automatic Transmission Fluid

MO Motor Oil

SG Motor Oil, API Service SG

Perform the following maintenance services at the intervals indicated to keep the vehicle warranties in effect

W SERVICE TO MAINTAIN EMISSION WARRANTY

MI — MILES IN THOUSANDS
KM — KILOMETERS IN THOUSANDS

EVERY MONTH
Automatic transmission fluid . . . . check level
Cooling system . . . . check level **EC**

EVERY 6 MONTHS
Accessory drive belts . . . . inspect
Radiator, heater & AC hoses . . . . . inspect

EVERY 5 MI — 8 KM
W Accessory drive
belts 4-cyl. . . . . inspect/adjust
Not required for Calif. or 1988 warranty
Tires 1989 . . . . rotate
At first 5 mi (8 km) then every 15 mi (24 km)

EVERY 12 MONTHS
Brake master cyl. . . . . . check level **HBH**
W Cooling system . . . . inspect
Power steering reservoir . . . . . check level
1985-87, **FA**
1988-89, **MA**
Transmission controls
& linkage . . . . lubricate **LM**
Body hinges & locks . . . . . . lubricate **MO**

1985-86, EVERY 12 MO/5 MI — 8 KM
1987-89, 4-CYL.,
EVERY 6 MO/5 MI — 8 KM
1988-89 V6,
EVERY 6 MO/7.5 MI — 12 KM
W Crankcase . . . . change oil
W Oil filter . . . . replace

EVERY 15 MI — 24 KM
W Accessory drive
belts V6 . . . . inspect/adjust
W Spark plugs . . . . replace
Not required for Calif. or 1988 warranty

EVERY 30 MI — 48 KM
Brake linings 1988-89 . . . . inspect

Front suspension 1985 . . . **0-2 fittings LM**
Front wheel bearings
1988-89 . . . . inspect/repack **LM**
W Fuel filter 1988-89 . . . . replace
Steering linkage 1985 . . . . **0-2 fittings LL**
W Air cleaner element . . . . replace
W Accessory drive belts . . . . . . inspect/adjust
W Crankcase emission
filter V6 . . . . replace
W Spark plugs 1988 . . . . replace

EVERY 36 MO/30 MI — 48 KM
W Cooling system . . . . . . change coolant **EC**

1988-89, EVERY 60 MI — 96 KM
PCV valve . . . . replace

SERVICE AS REQUIRED
Brake system . . . . inspect
Inspect hoses & replace lining when less than 1/32″ thick or within 1/32″ of any rivet head ex. disc pads, 1/8″ thick
Steering mechanism . . . . inspect
Tires . . . . rotate/balance
Lug nut torque, 80-105 ft lb.
Fluid leaks on pavement . . . . check

SEVERE SERVICE
In addition to normal service
W Crankcase — Change oil & filter every 3 mo/3 mi (4.8 km)
Transmission, automatic — Change lubricant: V6, at first 6 mi (9.6 km); then all, every 30 mi (48 km)
W Air cleaner element — Replace as required
W Accessory drive belts — Inspect/adjust: 1985-87, at first 3 mi (4.8 km); 1988, every 15 mi (24 km)
W Cooling system hoses & clamps — Check every 36 mo/30 mi (48 km)
W Spark plugs — Ex. 1988 4-cyl., check, clean & regap every 6 mi (9.6 km)

CRANKCASE . . . . **SG**

CAPACITY, Refill:	Liters	Qt
Includes filter		
All models	4.7	5.0

1985-87
Below 60°F (16°C) 5W-30
Above 0°F (–18°C) 10W-30*, 10W-40*
Above 10°F (–12°C) 15W-40
Above 20°F (–7°C) 20W-40, 20W-50
Above 40°F (4°C) 30
1988-89
Below 60°F (16°C) 5W-30
Above 0°F (–18°C) 10W-30*
Above 0°F (–18°C) 1988 . . . . 10W-40*
*Preferred viscosity above 0°F (–18°C) in all engines

TRANSMISSION, Automatic . . . . **MA**
1985-87, may use **AF**

CAPACITY, Total Fill:	Liters	Qt
XR4Ti	7.6	8.0
Scorpio	8.7	9.3

Total or dry fill shown, use less fluid when refilling

TRANSMISSION, Manual . . . . **GLS**

CAPACITY, Refill:	Liters	Pt
5-speed	1.3	2.6

DIFFERENTIAL . . . . **90 HP★**

CAPACITY, Refill:	Liters	Pt
1985	1.5	3.2
1986-89	1.3	2.7

SERVICE LOCATIONS — ENGINE AND CHASSIS

FDTDP-1   FDTDP-1

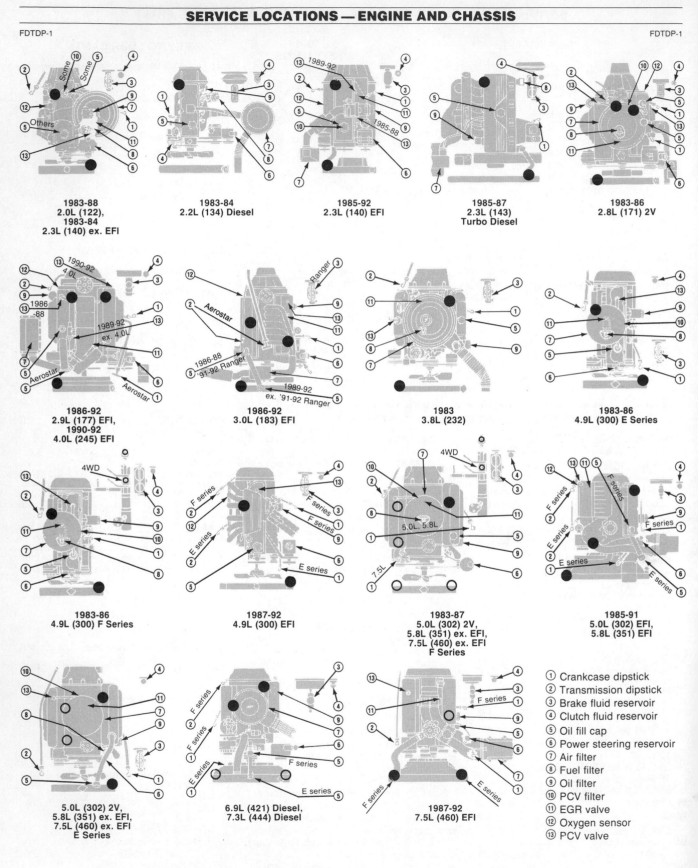

1983-88
2.0L (122),
1983-84
2.3L (140) ex. EFI

1983-84
2.2L (134) Diesel

1985-92
2.3L (140) EFI

1985-87
2.3L (143)
Turbo Diesel

1983-86
2.8L (171) 2V

1986-92
2.9L (177) EFI,
1990-92
4.0L (245) EFI

1986-92
3.0L (183) EFI

1983
3.8L (232)

1983-86
4.9L (300) E Series

1983-86
4.9L (300) F Series

1987-92
4.9L (300) EFI

1983-87
5.0L (302) 2V,
5.8L (351) ex. EFI,
7.5L (460) ex. EFI
F Series

1985-91
5.0L (302) EFI,
5.8L (351) EFI

5.0L (302) 2V,
5.8L (351) ex. EFI,
7.5L (460) ex. EFI
E Series

6.9L (421) Diesel,
7.3L (444) Diesel

1987-92
7.5L (460) EFI

① Crankcase dipstick
② Transmission dipstick
③ Brake fluid reservoir
④ Clutch fluid reservoir
⑤ Oil fill cap
⑥ Power steering reservoir
⑦ Air filter
⑧ Fuel filter
⑨ Oil filter
⑩ PCV filter
⑪ EGR valve
⑫ Oxygen sensor
⑬ PCV valve

● Cooling system drain   ○ Cooling system drain, some models

SERVICE LOCATIONS — ENGINE AND CHASSIS

FDTDP-2   FDTDP-2

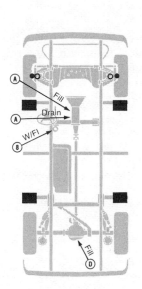

Aerostar
2-Wheel Drive

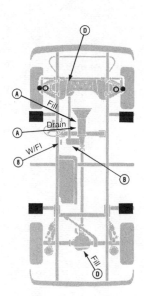

Aerostar
4-Wheel Drive

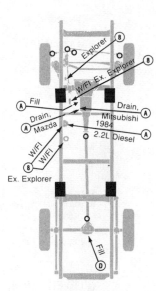

Ranger, Bronco II, Explorer
2-Wheel Drive

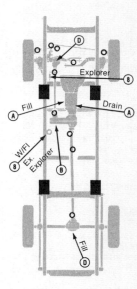

Ranger, Bronco II, Explorer
4-Wheel Drive

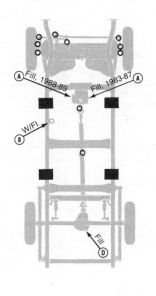

E Series
(Econoline)

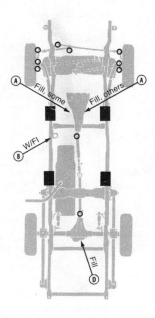

F Series
2-Wheel Drive

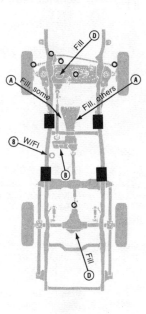

Bronco, F-150
4-Wheel Drive

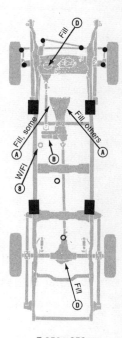

F-250, -350
4-Wheel Drive

■ Lift adapter position
● Fitting   ○ Fitting, some models

Ⓐ Manual transmission/transaxle,
   drain & fill
Ⓑ Transfer case, drain & fill

Ⓒ Automatic transaxle final drive,
   NOT USED
Ⓓ Differential, drain & fill

⑧ Fuel filter

FORD TRUCKS
1983 All Leaded Gasoline Models

CHEK-CHART

SERVICE AT TIME OR MILEAGE—WHICHEVER OCCURS FIRST

FDTPM13   FDTPM13

Follow (E) for all models ex. Canadian 5.0 & 5.8L engines; (L) for Canadian models with 5.0 & 5.8L engines

MI—MILES IN THOUSANDS
KM—KILOMETERS IN THOUSANDS

(L) FIRST 6 MO/6 MI—9.6 KM
THEN EVERY 12 MO/15 MI—24 KM
Initial timing . . . . check

(E) EVERY 12 MO/5 MI—8 KM
(L) EVERY 12 MO/6 MI—9.6 KM
Automatic transmission external
   controls . . . . lubricate **LM**
At mileage interval only

Crankcase . . . . change oil

Fittings . . . . lubricate **LM**
At mileage only

Oil filter . . . . replace
(L) at first oil change, then every other, or at least every 12 mo

Wheel lug nuts . . . . torque
At mileage only

EVERY 12 MONTHS
Cooling system . . . . inspect **EC**
Hoses, clamps. Replace coolant if necessary

EVERY 15 MI—24 KM
Air cleaner temp. control (L) . . . . check

Choke linkage . . . . clean

Crankcase breather cap (L) . . . . clean

Drive belts . . . . inspect/adjust

Fuel filter (E) . . . . replace
First 15 mo/15 mi (24 km), then every 30 mo/30 mi (48 km)

PCV system (L) . . . . check

Spark plugs . . . . replace

EVERY 30 MO/30 MI—48 KM
Brake system . . . . inspect
Lubricate disc brake caliper rails **BL**. Check all brake lines & lining

Front hubs 4 × 4 . . . . inspect **LS**
With automatic hub locks, inspect lubricant in drag sleeve; special lubricant required

Front wheel bearings . . . . inspect **LM**
4 × 2: Torque to 22-25 ft lb, back off nut 1/8 turn. End play .001″-.010″. 4 × 4: F-150 & Bronco, torque adjusting nut to 50 ft lb, back off 1/8 turn, install lockwasher, torque outer lock nut to 150 ft lb. End play .001″-.006″. F-250, -350, torque adjusting nut to 50 ft lb, back off, torque to 31-39 ft lb, back off 135-150 degrees, install lockwasher, torque outer lock nut to 65 ft lb, bend tabs. End play .001″-.009″

Rear wheel bearings, Dana axle . . . . . . **LM**
Clean & repack. Necessary to remove axle shafts

Air cleaner element . . . . replace

Brake master cylinder . . . check level **HBH**

Clutch reservoir . . . . check level **HBH**

Crankcase filter . . . . replace

Fuel vapor system (L) . . . . inspect

Manifold heat valve,
   inline 4.9L . . . . lubricate **MH**
Then every 15 mi (24 km)

PCV valve . . . . replace
(L) also clean PCV system hoses & tubes

Transfer case front
   output slip shaft . . . . lubricate **LM**

(E) EVERY 36 MO/40 MI—64 KM
(L) EVERY 36 MO/42 MI—67.2 KM
Cooling system . . . . . . change coolant **EC**

SERVICE AS REQUIRED
Parking brake linkage
   pivots & clevices . . . . lubricate **LM**

Manual steering gear . . . . . check level **LS**

Power steering . . . . check level **FA**

Body . . . . lubricate

Fluid leaks on pavement . . . . inspect

SEVERE SERVICE
Crankcase—Change oil every 3 mo/3 mi (4.8 km); change oil filter every 6 mo/6 mi (9.6 km)

Differentials, transfer case & all transmissions—Check level daily when operating in water (if water has entered, change lubricant)

Front wheel bearing lubricant, 4 × 4 front spindle needle bearing & hub lock lubricant, disc & drum brake components—Inspect every 1 mi (1.6 km) or daily if operating in mud or water

Fittings, front hub bearings & Dana rear wheel bearings—Lubricate every 1 mi (1.6 km) or daily when operating in mud or water

Transmission, automatic—Change fluid every 30 mi (48 km)

Spark plugs—Check, clean & regap every 6 mi (9.6 km)

KEY TO LUBRICANTS

BL	Self-adjusting Brake Lubricant
EC	Ethylene Glycol Coolant Mix 50/50 with water to at least −20°F (−29°C) protection
EP	Extreme Pressure Gear Lubricant Ford Part No. D8DZ-19C547-A
FA	Automatic Transmission Fluid, Type F
HBH	Hydraulic Brake Fluid, Extra Heavy-Duty
HP	Hypoid Gear Oil Ford Part No. E0AZ-19580-A
HP★	Hypoid Gear Oil for Limited-Slip or Traction-Lok Differential
LM	Lithium Grease, with Polyethylene
LS	Steering Gear Lubricant
MA	MERCON® Automatic Transmission Fluid
MH	Manifold Heat Valve Solvent
SG	Motor Oil, API Service SG

CRANKCASE . . . . SG
CAPACITY, Refill:

	Liters	Qt
All	4.7	5.0

Capacity shown is without filter. When replacing filter, additional oil may be needed
SINGLE VISCOSITY
Above 40°F (4°C) 30
MULTI-VISCOSITY
Below 60°F (16°C) 5W-30
Above 0°F (−18°C) 10W-30, 10W-40
Above 10°F (−12°C) 15W-40
Above 20°F (−7°C) 20W-40, 20W-50

TRANSMISSION, Automatic . . . . MA
CAPACITY, Initial Refill*:

	Liters	Qt
C-6	4.7	5.0
Others	2.8	3.0

* With the engine at operating temperature, shift transmission through all gears. Check fluid level in PARK and add fluid as needed

TRANSMISSION, Manual . . . . . . 80W EP
CAPACITY, Refill:

	Liters	Pt
3-speed	1.7	3.5
4-speed ex. OD	3.3	7.0
W/OD	2.1	4.5

TRANSFER CASE . . . . MA
CAPACITY, Refill:

	Liters	Pt
NP208	3.3	7.0
Warner 1345	3.0	6.5

DIFFERENTIAL
Standard . . . . 90 **HP**
Limited-Slip . . . . 90 **HP★**

CAPACITY, Refill:	Liters	Pt
Front:		
Dana 44	1.7	3.8
Dana 50	1.9	4.0
Rear:		
Ford	2.6	5.5
Dana 60 & 61	2.8	6.0
Dana 70 HD	3.5	7.4
Dana 70	3.1	6.5

LIMITED-SLIP OR TRACTION-LOK
   IDENTIFICATION:
Letter & number on plate on door lock pillar

SERVICE AT TIME OR MILEAGE—WHICHEVER OCCURS FIRST

FDTPM14   FDTPM14

Follow (B) for E-, F-100, -150 2-wheel drive inline 6-cyl. (A) for all others

MI—MILES IN THOUSANDS
KM—KILOMETERS IN THOUSANDS

(B) FIRST 5 MI—8 KM
(A) FIRST 7.5 MI—12 KM;
THEN EVERY 12 MO/15 MI—24 KM
Curb & fast idle speeds Ranger .... check
Then every 30 mi (48 km)

Drive belts .... check
(B) at first 10 mi (16 km)
Not required for Calif. warranty

Exhaust heat control valve
(A) 5.0L .... check/lubricate **MH**
Not required for Calif. warranty

Intake manifold heat valve
(A) 5.0L .... check
Not required for Calif. warranty

(A) EVERY 12 MO/7.5 MI—12 KM
(B) EVERY 12 MO/10 MI—16 KM
Automatic transmission external
controls ex. Ranger ...... lubricate **LM**
At mileage interval only

Crankcase .... change oil

Fittings .... lubricate **LM**
At mileage only

Oil filter .... replace

Wheel lug nuts .... torque
At mileage only

EVERY 12 MONTHS
Cooling system .... inspect **EC**
Hoses, clamps. Replace coolant if necessary

EVERY 30 MI—48 KM
Choke linkage .... clean

Drive belts .... inspect/adjust

Spark plugs .... replace

EVERY 30 MO/30 MI—48 KM
Brake system .... inspect
Lubricate disc brake caliper rails **BL**. Check all brake lines & lining

Front hubs 4×4 .... inspect **LS**
With automatic hub locks, inspect lubricant in drag sleeve; special lubricant required

Front wheel bearings .... inspect **LM**
4×2 ex. Ranger: Torque to 22-25 ft lb, back off nut 1/8 turn. End play .001″-.010″. Ranger 4×2: Torque to 17-25 ft lb, back off 1/2 turn then torque to 10-15 in. lb. 4×4 ex. Ranger: F-150 & Bronco, torque adjusting nut to 50 ft lb, back off 1/8 turn, install lockwasher, torque to 31-39 ft lb, back off 135-150 degrees, install lockwasher, torque outer locknut to 65 ft lb, bend tabs. End play .001″-.009″. Ranger: Torque adjusting nut to 35 ft lb, back off 1/4 turn. With manual locking hubs, torque outer lock nut to 150 ft lb; with automatic locking hubs, torque adjusting nut to 16 in. lb. Install snap ring and hub assembly. End play .001″-.003″

Rear wheel bearings, Dana axle ..... **LM**
Clean & repack. Necessary to remove axle shafts

Air cleaner element .... replace

Brake master cylinder ... check level **HBH**

Clutch reservoir .... check level **HBH**

Crankcase filter .... replace

Manifold heat valve,
inline 4.9L & 5.0L .... lubricate **MH**
Then every 15 mi (24 km). Also check 5.0L intake manifold heat valve. Not required for Calif. warranty with 4.9L & 5.0L engines

Transfer case front
output slip shaft .... lubricate **LM**

(B) EVERY 36 MO/50 MI—80 KM
(A) EVERY 36 MO/52.5 MI—84 KM
Cooling system ...... change coolant **EC**
3.8L V-6 every 36 mo/30 mi (48 km)

SERVICE AS REQUIRED
Parking brake linkage
pivots & clevices .... lubricate **LM**

Manual steering gear ..... check level **LS**

Power steering .... check level **FA**

Body .... lubricate

Fluid leaks on pavement .... inspect

SEVERE SERVICE
Crankcase—Change oil every 3 mo/3 mi (4.8 km); change oil filter every 6 mo/6 mi (9.6 km)

Differentials, transfer case & all transmissions—Check level daily when operating in water (if water has entered, change lubricant)

Front wheel bearing lubricant, 4×4 front spindle needle bearing & hub lock lubricant, disc & drum brake components—Inspect every 1 mi (1.6 km) or daily if operating in mud or water

Fittings, front hub bearings & Dana rear wheel bearings—Lubricate every 1 mi (1.6 km) or daily when operating in mud or water

Transmission, automatic—Change fluid every 30 mi (48 km)

Spark plugs—Check, clean & regap every 6 mi (9.6 km)

KEY TO LUBRICANTS
BL	Self-adjusting Brake Lubricant
EC	Ethylene Glycol Coolant
	Mix 50/50 with water or at least to −20°F (−29°C) protection
EP	Extreme Pressure Gear Lubricant
	Ford Part No. D8DZ-19C547-A
FA	Automatic Transmission Fluid, Type F
HBH	Hydraulic Brake Fluid, Extra Heavy-Duty
HP	Hypoid Gear Oil
	Ford Part No. E0AZ-19580-A
HP★	Hypoid Gear Oil for Limited-Slip or Traction-Lok Differential
LM	Lithium Grease, with Polyethylene
LS	Steering Gear Lubricant
MA	MERCON® Automatic Transmission Fluid
MH	Manifold Heat Valve Solvent
SG	Motor Oil, API Service SG

CRANKCASE .... SG
CAPACITY, Refill:	Liters	Qt
2.0L	4.2	4.5
2.3L	5.2	5.5
2.8L	3.8	4.0
Others	4.7	5.0

Capacity shown is without filter. When replacing filter, additional oil may be needed

SINGLE VISCOSITY
Above 40°F (4°C) 30
MULTI-VISCOSITY
Below 60°F (16°C) 5W-30
Above 0°F (−18°C) 10W-30, 10W-40
Above 10°F (−12°C) 15W-40
Above 20°F (−7°C) ... 20W-40, 20W-50

TRANSMISSION, Automatic .... MA
CAPACITY, Initial Refill*:	Liters	Qt
C-6	4.7	5.0
Others	2.8	3.0

*With the engine at operating temperature, shift transmission through all gears. Check fluid level in PARK and add fluid as needed

TRANSMISSION, Manual ...... 80W EP
CAPACITY, Refill:	Liters	Pt
3-speed	1.7	3.5
4-speed Ranger	1.4	3.0
5-speed Ranger	1.7	3.6
Other 4-speed ex. OD	3.3	7.0
W/OD	2.1	4.5

TRANSFER CASE .... MA
CAPACITY, Refill:	Liters	Pt
NP208	3.3	7.0
Warner 1345	3.0	6.5
Warner 1350 Ranger	1.4	3.0

DIFFERENTIAL
Standard .... 90 **HP**
Limited-Slip .... 90 **HP★**
CAPACITY, Refill:	Liters	Pt
Front:		
Dana 28 Ranger	0.5	1.0
Dana 44	1.7	3.6
Dana 50	1.8	3.8
Rear:		
Ranger w/8-bolt cover	1.4	3.0
Ranger w/7.5″ ring gear	1.9†	4.0†
Ranger w/Trak-Lok	2.8†	6.0†
Ford 8.8″, 9.0″ ring gear	2.6	5.5
Dana 60 & 61	2.8	6.0
Dana 70 HD	3.5	7
Dana 70	3.0	3.0

†Fill no higher than 1/4″-9/16″ below fill plug

LIMITED-SLIP OR TRACTION-LOK IDENTIFICATION:
Letter & number on plate on door lock pillar

CHEK-CHART

SERVICE AT TIME OR MILEAGE—WHICHEVER OCCURS FIRST

FDTPM16 FDTPM16

Follow (L) schedule for Canadian models with 5.0 & 5.8L engines; (E) for all others

MI—MILES IN THOUSANDS
KM—KILOMETERS IN THOUSANDS

(L) FIRST 6 MO/6 MI—9.6 KM
Initial timing . . . . check

(E) EVERY 12 MO/5 MI—8 KM
(L) EVERY 12 MO/6 MI—9.6 KM
Automatic transmission external
   controls . . . . lubricate **LM**
At mileage interval only

Crankcase . . . . change oil

Fittings . . . . lubricate **LM**
At mileage only

Oil filter . . . . replace
(L) at first oil change, then every other, or at least every
12 mo

Wheel lug nuts . . . . torque
At mileage only

EVERY 12 MONTHS
Cooling system . . . . inspect **EC**
Hoses, clamps. Replace coolant if necessary

EVERY 15 MI—24 KM
Air cleaner temp. control (L) . . . . check

Crankcase breather cap (L) . . . . clean

Drive belts . . . . inspect/adjust

Fuel filter (E) . . . . replace
At first 15 mo/15 mi (24 km), then every 30 mo/30 mi (48
km)

PCV system (L) . . . . check

Spark plugs . . . . replace

EVERY 30 MO/30 MI—48 KM
Brake system . . . . inspect
Lubricate disc brake caliper rails **BL**. Check all brake
lines & lining

Front hubs 4 × 4 . . . . inspect **LS**
With automatic hub locks, inspect lubricant in drag
sleeve; special lubricant required

Front wheel bearings . . . . inspect **LM**
4 × 2: Torque to 22-25 ft lb, back off nut 1/8 turn. End
play .001"-.010". 4 × 4: F-150 & Bronco: Torque adjusting nut to 50 ft lb, back off 1/8 turn, install lockwasher,
torque outer lock nut to 150 ft lb. End play .001"-.006".
F-250, -350: Torque adjusting nut to 50 ft lb, back off,
torque to 31-39 ft lb, back off 135-150 degrees, install
lockwasher, torque outer lock nut to 65 ft lb, bend tabs.
End play .001"-.009"

Rear wheel bearings, Dana axle . . . . . . **LM**
Clean & repack. Necessary to remove axle shafts

Air cleaner element . . . . replace

Brake master cylinder . . . check level **HBH**

Clutch reservoir . . . . check level **HBH**

Crankcase filter . . . . replace

Fuel vapor system (L) . . . . inspect

Manifold heat valve 4.9L . . . . lubricate **MH**
Then every 15 mi (24 km). Not required for Calif. warranty with (B) engines

PCV valve . . . . replace
(L) also clean PCV system hoses & tubes

Transfer case front
   output slip shaft . . . . lubricate **LM**

(E) EVERY 36 MO/40 MI—64 KM
(L) EVERY 36 MO/45 MI—72 KM
Cooling system . . . . . . change coolant **EC**

SERVICE AS REQUIRED
Parking brake linkage
   pivots & clevices . . . . lubricate **LM**

Manual steering gear . . . . . check level **LS**

Power steering . . . . check level **FA**

Body . . . . lubricate

Fluid leaks on pavement . . . . inspect

SEVERE SERVICE
Crankcase—Change oil every 3 mo/3 mi
(4.8 km); change oil filter every 6 mo/6 mi
(9.6 km)

Differentials, transfer case & all
transmissions—Check level daily when operating in water (if water has entered,
change lubricant)

Front wheel bearing lubricant, 4 × 4 front
spindle needle bearing & hub lock lubricant,
disc & drum brake components—Inspect
every 1 mi (1.6 km) or daily if operating in
mud or water

Fittings, front hub bearings & Dana rear
wheel bearings—Lubricate every 1 mi (1.6
km) or daily when operating in mud or water

Transmission, automatic—Change fluid every 30 mi (48 km)

Spark plugs—Check, clean & regap every 6
mi (9.6 km)

KEY TO LUBRICANTS

BL	Self-adjusting Brake Lubricant
EC	Ethylene Glycol Coolant Mix 50/50 with water at least to –20°F (–29°C) protection
EP	Extreme Pressure Gear Lubricant Ford Part No. D8DZ-19C547-A
FA	Automatic Transmission Fluid, Type F
HBH	Hydraulic Brake Fluid, Extra Heavy-Duty
HP	Hypoid Gear Oil Ford Part No. E0AZ-19580-A
HP ★	Hypoid Gear Oil for Limited-Slip or Traction-Lok Differential
LM	Lithium Grease, with Polyethylene
LS	Steering Gear Lubricant
MA	MERCON® Automatic Transmission Fluid
MH	Manifold Heat Valve Solvent
SG	Motor Oil, API Service SG

CRANKCASE . . . . SG

CAPACITY, Refill:	Liters	Qt
All models	4.7	5.0

Capacity shown is without filter. When replacing filter, additional oil may be needed

SINGLE VISCOSITY
Above 40°F (4°C) 30
MULTI-VISCOSITY
Below 60°F (16°C) 5W-30
Above 0°F (–18°C) 10W-30, 10W-40
Above 10°F (–12°C) 15W-40
Above 20°F (–7°C) 20W-40, 20W-50

TRANSMISSION, Automatic . . . . MA

CAPACITY, Initial Refill*:	Liters	Qt
C-6	4.7	5.0
Others	2.8	3.0

* With the engine at operating temperature, shift transmission through all gears. Check fluid level in PARK and add
fluid as needed

TRANSMISSION, Manual . . . . . . 80W EP

CAPACITY, Refill:	Liters	Pt
3-speed	1.7	3.5
4-speed	3.3	7.0
W/OD	2.1	4.5

TRANSFER CASE . . . . MA

CAPACITY, Refill:	Liters	Pt
NP208	4.3	9.0
Warner 1345	3.0	6.5

DIFFERENTIAL
Standard . . . . 90 **HP**
Limited-Slip . . . . 90 **HP ★**

CAPACITY, Refill:	Liters	Pt
Front:		
Dana 44	1.7	3.8
Dana 50	1.9	4.0
Rear:		
Ford w/8.8", 9.0" ring gear	2.6	5.5
Dana 60 & 61	2.8	6.0
Dana 70 HD	3.5	7.4
Dana 70	3.1	6.5

LIMITED-SLIP OR TRACTION-LOK
  IDENTIFICATION:
Letter & number on plate on door lock pillar

SERVICE AT TIME OR MILEAGE—WHICHEVER OCCURS FIRST

FDTPM17   FDTPM17

Follow (A) schedule for E-, F-150 2-wheel drive inline 6-cyl.; (B) for all others

MI—MILES IN THOUSANDS
KM—KILOMETERS IN THOUSANDS

(A) FIRST 5 MI—8 KM
(B) FIRST 7.5 MI—12 KM; THEN EVERY 12 MO/15 MI—24 KM
Drive belts . . . . check
(A) at first 10 mi (16 km)
Not required for Calif. warranty

Exhaust heat control valve
(B) 5.0L . . . . check/lubricate **MH**
Not required for Calif. warranty

Intake manifold heat valve
(B) 5.0L . . . . check
Not required for Calif. warranty

Valve clearance 2.8L eng. . . . . adjust

(B) EVERY 12 MO/7.5 MI—12 KM
(A) EVERY 12 MO/10 MI—16 KM
Automatic transmission external
controls ex. Ranger . . . . . . lubricate **LM**
At mileage interval only

Crankcase . . . . change oil

Fittings . . . . lubricate **LM**
At mileage only

Oil filter . . . . replace

Wheel lug nuts . . . . torque
At mileage only

EVERY 12 MONTHS
Cooling system . . . . inspect **EC**
Hoses, clamps. Replace coolant if necessary

EVERY 30 MI—48 KM
Drive belts . . . . inspect/adjust

Spark plugs . . . . replace

Valve clearance
2.8L eng. . . . . check/adjust

EVERY 30 MO/30 MI—48 KM
Brake system . . . . inspect
Lubricate disc brake caliper rails **BL**. Check all brake lines & lining

Front hubs 4×4 . . . . inspect **LS**
With automatic hub locks, inspect lubricant in drag sleeve; special lubricant required

Front wheel bearings . . . . inspect **LM**
4 × 2 ex. Ranger: Torque to 22-25 ft lb, back off nut 1/8 turn. End play .001″-.010″. Ranger 4 × 2: Torque to 17-25 ft lb, back off 1/2 turn then torque to 10-15 in. lb. 4 × 4 ex. Ranger: F-150 & Bronco: Torque adjusting nut to 50 ft lb, back off 1/4 turn, install lockwasher, torque outer lock nut to 150 ft lb. End play .001″-.006″. F-250, -350: Torque adjusting nut to 50 ft lb, back off, torque to 31-39 ft lb, back off 135-150 degrees, install lockwasher, torque outer lock nut to 65 ft lb, bend tabs. End play .001″-.009″. 4 × 4 Ranger: Torque adjusting nut to 35 ft lb, back off 1/4 turn. With manual locking hubs, torque outer lock nut to 150 ft lb; with automatic locking hubs, torque adjusting nut to 16 in. lb. Install snap ring and hub assembly. End play .001″-.003″

Rear wheel bearings, Dana axle . . . . . **LM**
Clean & repack. Necessary to remove axle shafts

Air cleaner element . . . . replace

Brake master cylinder . . . check level **HBH**

Clutch reservoir . . . . check level **HBH**

Crankcase filter . . . . replace

Manifold heat valve,
4.9L & (B) 5.0L . . . . lubricate **MH**
Then every 15 mi (24 km). Also check (B) 5.0L intake manifold heat valve. Not required for Calif. warranty with (B) 4.9L & (B) 5.0L engines

Transfer case front
output slip shaft . . . . lubricate **LM**

(A) EVERY 36 MO/50 MI—80 KM
(B) EVERY 36 MO/52.5 MI—84 KM
Cooling system . . . . . . change coolant **EC**

SERVICE AS REQUIRED
Parking brake linkage
pivots & clevices . . . . lubricate **LM**

Manual steering gear . . . . . check level **LS**

Power steering . . . . check level **FA**

Body . . . . lubricate

Fluid leaks on pavement . . . . inspect

SEVERE SERVICE
Crankcase—Change oil every 3 mo/3 mi (4.8 km); change oil filter every 6 mo/6 mi (9.6 km)

Differentials, transfer case & all transmissions—Check level daily when operating in water (if water has entered, change lubricant)

Front wheel bearing lubricant, 4×4 front spindle needle bearing & hub lock lubricant, disc & drum brake components—Inspect every 1 mi (1.6 km) or daily if operating in mud or water

Fittings, front hub bearings & Dana rear wheel bearings—Lubricate every 1 mi (1.6 km) or daily when operating in mud or water

Transmission, automatic—Change fluid every 30 mi (48 km)

Spark plugs—Check, clean & regap every 6 mi (9.6 km)

KEY TO LUBRICANTS
BL	Self-adjusting Brake Lubricant
EC	Ethylene Glycol Coolant
	Mix 50/50 with water or at least to –20°F (–29°C) protection
EP	Extreme Pressure Gear Lubricant
	Ford Part No. D8DZ-19C547-A
FA	Automatic Transmission Fluid, Type F
HBH	Hydraulic Brake Fluid, Extra Heavy-Duty
HP	Hypoid Gear Oil
	Ford Part No. E0AZ-19580-A
HP★	Hypoid Gear Oil for Limited-Slip or Traction-Lok Differential
LM	Lithium Grease, with Polyethylene
LS	Steering Gear Lubricant
MA	MERCON® Automatic Transmission Fluid
MH	Manifold Heat Valve Solvent
SG	Motor Oil, API Service SG

CRANKCASE . . . . SG
CAPACITY, Refill:	Liters	Qt
2.0L & 2.8L	3.8	4.0
Others	4.7	5.0

Capacity shown is without filter. When replacing filter, additional oil may be needed

SINGLE VISCOSITY
Above 40°F (4°C) 30
MULTI-VISCOSITY
Below 60°F (16°C) 5W-30
Above 0°F (–18°C) 10W-30, 10W-40
Above 10°F (–12°C) 15W-40
Above 20°F (–7°C) 20W-40, 20W-50

TRANSMISSION, Automatic . . . . . . MA
CAPACITY, Initial Refill*:	Liters	Qt
C-6	4.7	5.0
Others	2.8	3.0

*With the engine at operating temperature, shift transmission through all gears. Check fluid level in PARK and add fluid as needed

TRANSMISSION, Manual . . . . . . 80W EP
CAPACITY, Refill:	Liters	Pt
3-speed	1.7	3.5
4-speed Ranger, Bronco II .	1.4	3.0
5-speed Ranger, Bronco II .	1.7	3.6
Other 4-speed ex. OD	3.3	7.0
W/OD	2.1	4.5

TRANSFER CASE . . . . MA
CAPACITY, Refill:	Liters	Pt
NP208	4.3	9.0
Warner 1345	3.0	6.5
Warner 1350 Ranger, Bronco II	1.4	3.0

DIFFERENTIAL
Standard . . . . 90 **HP**
Limited-Slip . . . . 90 **HP★**
CAPACITY, Refill:	Liters	Pt
Front:		
Dana 28 Ranger, Bronco II .	0.5	1.0
Dana 44	1.7	3.8
Dana 50	1.9	4.0
Rear:		
Ranger w/8-bolt cover	1.6	3.3
Ranger w/7.5″ ring gear . .	2.4†	5.0†
Ranger w/8.8″ ring gear . .	2.6†	5.5†
Bronco II	2.6†	5.5†
Ford w/8.8″, 9.0″ ring gear	2.6	5.5
Dana 60 & 61	2.8	6.0
Dana 70 HD	3.5	7.4
Dana 70	3.1	6.5

†Fill no higher than 1/4″- 9/16″ below fill plug

LIMITED-SLIP OR TRACTION-LOK IDENTIFICATION:
Letter & number on plate on door lock pillar

SERVICE AT TIME OR MILEAGE—WHICHEVER OCCURS FIRST

FDTPM19   FDTPM19

Perform the following maintenance services at the intervals indicated to keep the vehicle warranties in effect.

W SERVICE TO MAINTAIN EMISSION WARRANTY

MI—MILES IN THOUSANDS
KM—KILOMETERS IN THOUSANDS

FIRST 7.5 MI—12 KM
Drive belts 1985 . . . . check

W Exhaust manifold heat
   valve . . . . check/lubricate **MH**
Not required for Calif. warranty

W Intake manifold heat valve . . . . . . check
5.8L 4V & 1986 5.0L engines only. Not required for Calif. warranty

Valve clearance
   1985-86 2.8L eng. . . . . . . check/adjust

1985-86, EVERY 12 MO/7.5 MI—12 KM
1987, EVERY 6 MO/7.5 MI—12 KM
Automatic transmission
   external controls . . . . . lubricate **LM**
At mileage interval only

Clutch release lever
   pivot 1987 . . . . lubricate **LM**

W Crankcase . . . . change oil

Fittings . . . . lubricate **LM**
At mileage only

W Oil filter . . . . replace

Transmission linkage 1985-86 . . . lubricate
3-speed manual only. Inspect & adjust column linkage.
At mileage interval only

Wheel lug nuts . . . . torque
At mileage only

EVERY 12 MONTHS
W Cooling system . . . . inspect **EC**
Hoses, clamps. Replace coolant if necessary

EVERY 15 MI—24 KM
W Air cleaner element . . . . replace
5.8L 4V eng.

Disc brake caliper slide rails
   ex. 1985-86 Aerostar, Bronco II,
   Ranger . . . . lubricate **BL**

EVERY 30 MI—48 KM
Brake system . . . . inspect
Lubricate disc brake caliper slide rails **BL**. Check all
brake lines & lining

Front hubs 4 × 4 . . . . inspect **LS**
Inspect spindle needle & thrust bearings **LM**. With automatic hub locks, inspect lubricant in drag sleeve; special lubricant required

Front wheel
   bearings . . . . inspect/lubricate **LM**

W Air cleaner element . . . . replace

Brake master cylinder . . . check level **HBH**

W Carburetor hang-on devices . . . . inspect
Clean choke linkages & external controls ex. FI

Clutch reservoir . . . . check level **HBH**

W Crankcase filter . . . . replace
Ex. 2.3L, 2.9L, 3.0L

Drive belts . . . . inspect/adjust

W Exhaust manifold
   heat valve . . . . lubricate **MH**
If equipped

W Intake manifold heat valve . . . . . . check
5.8L 4V & 1986 5.0L engines only. Not required for
Calif. warranty

W Spark plugs . . . . replace

Throttle ball stud . . . . lubricate **LM**

Transfer case front output
   & axle shafts . . . . lubricate **LM**

Valve clearance
   2.8L eng. 1985-86 . . . . . . check/adjust

EVERY 36 MO/30 MI—48 KM
W Cooling system . . . . change coolant **EC**

EVERY 60 MI—96 KM
Transfer case . . . . change fluid

Idle speed control air bypass valve
   5.0L EFI, 1987 4.9L . . . . clean

EGR valve . . . . replace

EGR vacuum solenoids . . . . replace

Exhaust valve
   position sensor . . . . replace
On electronic EGR valve

Ignition wires . . . . replace

Injector tips 1985-86 . . . . clean/check
EFI engs. 2.3L, 2.9L & 5.0L

Oxygen sensor . . . . replace

PCV valve . . . . replace

Thermactor hoses & clamps ex. 2.9L,
   1987 2.3L & 3.0L . . . . check

SERVICE AS REQUIRED
Parking brake linkage
   pivots & clevices . . . . lubricate **LM**

Manual steering gear . . . . . check level **LS**

Power steering . . . . check level **FA**

Body . . . . lubricate

Fluid leaks on pavement . . . . inspect

SEVERE SERVICE
W Crankcase—Change oil & filter every 3
mo/3 mi (4.8 km)

Differentials, transfer case & all transmissions—Check level daily when operating
in water (if water has entered, change lubricant)

W EGR solenoid filter all 1985-86; 1987
Aerostar, Bronco II, Ranger—Replace
every 30 mi (48 km) when operating on
dusty roads

Front wheel bearing lubricant, 4 × 4 front
spindle needle bearing & hub lock lubricant,
disc & drum brake components—Inspect
every 1 mi (1.6 km) or daily if operating in
mud or water

Fittings, front hub bearings & disc brake caliper slide rails—Lubricate every 1 mi (1.6
km) or daily when operating in mud or water

Transmission, automatic—Change fluid
every 30 mi (48 km). Lubricate external controls every 1 mi (1.6 km)

W Spark plugs—Check, clean & regap
every 6 mi (9.6 km)

KEY TO LUBRICANTS
See other Ford Truck charts

CRANKCASE . . . . SG

CAPACITY, Refill:	Liters	Qt
1985 2.3L w/steel pan	4.7	5.0
2.3L w/aluminum pan	3.8	4.0
All other 2.0L, 2.3L, 2.8L, 2.9L, 3.0L	3.8	4.0
Others	4.7	5.0

Capacity shown is without filter. When replacing filter, additional oil may be needed

SINGLE VISCOSITY
Above 40°F (4°C)	30

MULTI-VISCOSITY
Below 100°F (38°C) 3.0L	5W-30*
Below 60°F (16°C)	5W-30
Above 0°F (–18°C)	10W-30†, 10W-40†
Above 10°F (–12°C)	15W-40
Above 20°F (–7°C)	20W-40, 20W-50

* Preferred
† Preferred ex. 3.0L eng.

TRANSMISSION, Automatic . . . . . . MA

CAPACITY, Initial Refill*:	Liters	Qt
C-6	4.7	5.0
Others	2.8	3.0

* With the engine at operating temperature, shift transmission through all gears. Check fluid level in PARK and add
fluid as needed

TRANSMISSION, Manual
1987 F-Series w/5-speed . . . . **MA**
Others . . . . **80W EP**

CAPACITY, Refill:	Liters	Pt
3-speed	1.7	3.5
4-speed Ranger, Bronco II	1.4	3.0
Other 4-speed ex. OD	3.3	7.0
W/OD	2.1	4.5
1985-86 5-speed OD (Mazda) Aerostar, Ranger, Bronco II	1.7	3.6
1987 5-speed OD (Mazda) Aerostar, Ranger, Bronco II	2.8	5.9
5-speed OD (Mitsubishi) Ranger, Bronco II	2.3	4.8
Other 5-speed OD	3.5	7.4

TRANSFER CASE . . . . **MA**

CAPACITY, Refill:	Liters	Pt
NP208	4.3	9.0
Warner 1345	3.0	6.5
Warner 1350 Ranger, Bronco II	1.4	3.0

DIFFERENTIAL
Standard . . . . 90 **HP**
Limited-Slip . . . . 90 **HP ★**

CAPACITY, Refill:	Liters	Pt
Front:		
Dana 28 Ranger, Bronco II	0.5	1.0
Dana 44	1.7	3.8
Dana 50	1.9	4.0
Dana 60	2.8	6.0
Rear:		
Aerostar ex. Dana	1.7†	3.5†
Aerostar w/Dana	1.2	2.5
Bronco II	2.6†	5.5†
Ranger w/7.5″ ring gear	2.4†	5.0†
Ranger w/8.8″ ring gear	2.6†	5.5†
Other Ford		
w/8.8″, 9.0″ ring gear*	2.6	5.5
w/10¼″ ring gear*	3.1	6.5
Dana 60 & 61	2.8	6.0
Dana 70 HD	3.5	7.4
Dana 70	3.1	6.5

* 8.8″ & 10¼″ have removable cover, 9.0″ does not
†Fill no higher than ¼″- 9/16″ below fill plug

**LIMITED-SLIP OR TRACTION-LOK
IDENTIFICATION:**
Label on door lock pillar has letter and number

SERVICE AT TIME OR MILEAGE—WHICHEVER OCCURS FIRST

FDTPM15   FDTPM15

Perform the following maintenance services at the intervals indicated to keep the vehicle warranties in effect.

W   **SERVICE TO MAINTAIN EMISSION WARRANTY**
Follow (D) for all 8-cyl. models; (D1) for all 4-cyl. models when noted below

MI—MILES IN THOUSANDS
KM—KILOMETERS IN THOUSANDS

EVERY MONTH
- **W** Cooling system 1986-87 . . . check level

(D) FIRST 5 MI—8 KM; THEN EVERY 15 MI—24 KM
- **W** Automatic transmission vacuum regulator . . . . . . check/adjust
- **W** Curb idle speed . . . . check
- **W** Idle return spring & throttle . . . . . check

EVERY 6 MO/5 MI—8 KM
- Automatic transmission external controls (D) . . . . lubricate **LM**
  At mileage only
- **W** Bypass oil filter (D1) ex. Turbo . . . . replace
  Every 6 mo/10 mi (16 km)
- Clutch lever pivots 1987 (D) . . . . lubricate **LM**
  At mileage only
- **W** Crankcase . . . . change oil
- Driveshaft joints (D1) . . . . lubricate **LM**
  When equipped with fittings
- Fittings (D) . . . . lubricate **LM**
  At mileage only
- **W** Oil filter . . . . replace
- **W** Fuel filter at left frame . . . . change
  1986-87 2.3L only
- **W** Fuel/water separator . . . . drain
  At mileage only
  More frequently if dash light illuminates
- Steering linkage . . . . lubricate **LM**
  When equipped with fittings
- Wheel lug nuts . . . . torque

EVERY 12 MONTHS
- **W** Cooling system . . . . inspect **EC**
  Hoses, clamps. Replace coolant if necessary

EVERY 15 MI—24 KM
- Disc brake caliper slide rails 1985-87 . . . . lubricate **BL**
  1986-87 (D) inspect disc brake system
  1987 (D) inspect drum brake lining, lines & hoses
- Drive belts 1983-85 . . . . inspect/adjust
- **W** Fuel filter (D) . . . . replace
- **W** Valve clearance (D1) . . . . adjust

EVERY 30 MI—48 KM
- Brake system . . . . inspect
  Lubricate disc brake caliper rails **BL**. Check all brake lines & lining
- **W** Drive belts 1986-87 . . . . . . inspect/adjust
- Fittings (D1) . . . . lubricate **LM**
- Front hubs 4 x 4 (D) . . . . clean/repack **LM**
  With automatic hub locks, inspect lubricant in drag sleeve; special lubricant required. Inspect 1985-86 spindle needle & thrust bearings
- Fuel filter (D1) . . . . replace
  Located in engine compartment

Front wheel bearings
- 4-cyl. 1983-84 . . . . inspect **LM**
- 8-cyl. & 1985-87 4-cyl. . . . . . . clean/repack **LM**

Rear wheel bearings, Dana axle (D) . . . **LM**
1983-84 only. Clean & repack. Necessary to remove axle shafts

- **W** Air cleaner element . . . . replace
- **W** Air induction system & hoses . . . inspect
  Also inspect turbo inlet hose
- Brake master cylinder . . . check level **HBH**
- Clutch reservoir . . . . check level **HBH**
- **W** Idle speed (D1) Turbo, 1986-87 . . . . check/adjust
- Power steering . . . . check level **FA**
- **W** Throttle ball stud 1985-87 . . lubricate **LM**

EVERY 36 MO/50 MI—80 KM
- **W** Cooling system . . . . change coolant **EC**
  1987 every 36 mo/30 mi (48 km)
- **W** Timing belts (D1) Turbo . . . . replace
  At mileage interval only. Also replace balance shaft belt

EVERY 60 MI—96 KM
- Transfer case 1985-87 . . . . . . change fluid

SERVICE AS REQUIRED
- Parking brake linkage pivots & clevices . . . . lubricate **LM**
- Manual steering gear . . . . . check level **LS**
- Power steering . . . . check level **FA**
- Body . . . . lubricate
- Fluid leaks on pavement . . . . inspect

SEVERE SERVICE
- **W** Crankcase—4-cyl. engine ex. Turbo: Change oil & primary filter every 3 mo/3 mi (4.8 km); change oil bypass filter every 6 mo/6 mi (9.6 km). 4-cyl. Turbo engine: Change oil every 2 mo/2 mi (3.2 km); change oil filter every other oil change. 8-cyl. engine: Change oil & filter every 3 mo/2.5 mi (4 km) except filter with extensive idling only, change filter every other oil change
- Differentials, transfer case & all transmissions—Check level daily when operating in water (if water has entered, change lubricant)
- Front wheel bearing lubricant, 4 x 4 front spindle needle bearing & hub lock lubricant, disc & drum brake components—Inspect every 1 mi (1.6 km) or daily if operating in mud or water
- Fittings, front hub bearings & 1983-84 Dana rear wheel bearings—Lubricate every 1 mi (1.6 km) or daily when operating in mud or water
- Transmission, automatic—Change fluid every 30 mi (48 km)
- **W** Air cleaner element—4-cyl. engine, replace every 3 mo/3 mi (4.8 km)

KEY TO LUBRICANTS
See other Ford Truck charts

CRANKCASE . . SF/CC*, SF/CD, SG/CE
* Recommended for 2.2L 4-cyl. only

CAPACITY, Refill:	Liters	Qt
4-cyl.*	6.6	7.0
8-cyl.*	9.3	10.0

* Includes filter

4-cyl. Engine ex. Turbo
SINGLE VISCOSITY
- 0° to 60°F (−18° to 16°C) 10W
- 20° to 90°F (−7° to 32°C) 20W-20
- 40° to 90°F (4° to 38°C) 30
- Above 50°F (10°C) 40

MULTI-VISCOSITY
- Below 60°F (16°C) . . . . .5W-30†
- 0° to 100°F (−18° to 38°C) 10W-30
- Above 0°F (−18°C) 15W-40
- 20° to 100°F (−7° to 38°C) . . 20W-40, 20W-50

4-cyl. Turbo Engine
- Below 50°F (10°C) . . . . .5W-30†
- Above 35°F (2°C) 30
- Above 14°F (−10°C) 20W-40
- Above 5°F (−15°C) 15W-40
- Above −5°F (−21°C) 10W-30

8-cyl. Engine
- Above 32°F (0°C) 30
- Above 10°F (−12°C) 20W-40
- Above 0°F (−18°C) 15W-40
- Below 90°F (32°C) 10W-30

† Recommended for improved low temperature starting below 0°F (−18°C)

TRANSMISSION, Automatic . . . . MA

CAPACITY, Initial Refill*:	Liters	Qt
C-6	4.7	5.0
Others	2.8	3.0

* With the engine at operating temperature, shift transmission through all gears. Check fluid level in PARK and add fluid as needed

TRANSMISSION, Manual
1987 F-Series w/5-speed . . . . **MA**
Others . . . . **80W EP**

CAPACITY, Refill:	Liters	Pt
3-speed	1.7	3.5
4-speed Ranger, Bronco II . . .	1.4	3.0
Other 4-speed ex. OD	3.3	7.0
W/OD	2.1	4.5
1985-86 5-speed OD (Mazda)	1.7	3.6
1987 5-speed OD (Mazda)	2.8	5.9
5-speed OD (Mitsubishi)	2.3	4.8
Other 5-speed OD	3.5	7.4

TRANSFER CASE . . . . MA

CAPACITY, Refill:	Liters	Pt
NP208	4.3	9.0
Warner 1345	3.0	6.5
Warner 1350	1.4	3.0
Warner 1356	1.9	4.0

DIFFERENTIAL
Standard . . . . 90 **HP**
Limited-Slip . . . . 90 **HP ★**

CAPACITY, Refill:	Liters	Pt
Front:		
Dana 28 Bronco II, Ranger	0.5	1.0
Dana 44	1.7	3.8
Dana 50	1.9	4.0
Dana 60	2.8	6.0
Rear:		
Bronco II	2.6†	5.5†
Ranger w/7.5″ ring gear . .	2.4†	5.0†
Ranger w/8.8″ ring gear . .	2.6†	5.5†
Ford w/8.8″, 9.0″ ring gear* . .	2.6	5.5
w/10¼″ ring gear*	3.1	6.5
Dana 60 & 61	2.8	6.0
Dana 70 HD	3.5	7.4
Dana 70	3.1	6.5

* 8.8″ & 10¼″ have removable rear cover, 9.0″ does not
†Fill no higher than 1/4″- 9/16″ below fill plug

LIMITED-SLIP OR TRACTION-LOK IDENTIFICATION
Label on door lock pillar shows letter & number

SERVICE AT TIME OR MILEAGE—WHICHEVER OCCURS FIRST

FDTPM18   FDTPM18

Perform the following maintenance services at the intervals indicated to keep the vehicle warranties in effect.

W   SERVICE TO MAINTAIN EMISSION WARRANTY

Follow (L) schedule for 1985-86 Canadian 4.9L engines; (E) for 1985 E- & F-250, -350 models with 1984 model year on emission decal; (G) for 1987 4.9L EFI & 7.5L EFI w/unleaded fuel; (F) for all others when noted below

MI—MILES IN THOUSANDS
KM—KILOMETERS IN THOUSANDS

DAILY

W Air filter restriction
   indicator (E) . . . . check
Replace element when indicator shows red

1985-86 (F) FIRST 5 MI—8 KM
1985-86 (L) FIRST 6 MO/6 MI—9.6 KM
Initial timing (L) . . . . check
Idle speeds 4.9L (F) . . . . check/adjust
Throttle decel control 4.9L (F) . . . . . check

1987 (F) (G)
EVERY 6 MO/5 MI—8 KM
OTHER (E) (F)
EVERY 12 MO/5 MI—8 KM
(L) EVERY 12 MO/6 MI—9.6 KM
Air cleaner, oil bath
   (E) (F) ex. 1987 . . . . clean/oil
At mileage only

Automatic transmission external
   controls . . . . lubricate LM
At mileage interval only

Clutch release lever
   1987 . . . . lubricate LM
At mileage only

W Crankcase . . . . change oil
Fittings . . . . lubricate LM
At mileage only

W Oil filter . . . . replace
1985 (L) at first oil change, then every other, or at least every 12 mo

Transmission linkage 1985-86 . . . lubricate
Manual 3-speed only. Check & adjust column linkage

Wheel lug nuts . . . . torque
At mileage only

EVERY 12 MONTHS

W Cooling system . . . . inspect EC
Hoses, clamps. Replace coolant if necessary

EVERY 15 MI—24 KM

W Air cleaner temp. control (L) . . . . . check
W Choke linkage (L) (E) . . . . . clean/check
Also check air valve (L)

Disc brake system 1986-87 . . . . . . inspect
Lubricate caliper slide rails BL

W Drive belts . . . . inspect/adjust
W Fuel filter (E) (F) . . . . replace
At first 15 mi (24 km), then every 30 mi (48 km)

Idle speeds 4.9L (F)
   1985-86 . . . . check/adjust
Also check decel control system

W PCV system (L) . . . . check
Also check hoses & tubes

W Spark plugs ex. (G) . . . . replace

EVERY 30 MI—48 KM
Brake system . . . . inspect
Lubricate disc brake caliper slide rails BL. Check all brake lines & lining

Front hubs 4 × 4 . . . . inspect LS
Inspect spindle needle bearings LM. With automatic hub locks, inspect lubricant in drag sleeve; special lubricant required

Front wheel
   bearings . . . . inspect/lubricate LM

W Air cleaner element . . . . replace
Except models w/restriction indicator

Brake master cylinder
   1985-86 . . . . check level HBH
Clutch reservoir . . . . check level HBH
W Crankcase filter . . . . replace
W Fuel vapor system (L) . . . . inspect
W Exhaust manifold heat valve
   (E) (F) if equipped . . . . . lubricate MH
W Spark plugs (G) . . . . replace
Transfer case front output
   & axle slip shafts . . . . lubricate LM
Throttle ball stud . . . . lubricate LM

(E) EVERY 36 MO/40 MI—64 KM
(F) (G) (L) EVERY 36 MO/30 MI—48 KM
W Cooling system . . . . change coolant EC

EVERY 50 MI—80 KM
W PCV valve (F) . . . . replace

EVERY 60 MI—96 KM
Transfer case . . . . change fluid
Carburetor hang-on devices (F) . . . inspect
Clean choke & external controls

EGR valve (F) (G) . . . . replace
Exhaust valve position
   sensor (G) 1987 . . . . replace
Idle speed control air
   bypass valve (G) . . . . clean
Ignition wires (F) (G) . . . . replace
Oxygen sensor (G) 1987 . . . . replace
PCV valve (G) . . . . replace
Thermactor hoses & clamps
   (F) (G) . . . . check

SERVICE AS REQUIRED
Parking brake linkage
   pivots & clevices . . . . lubricate LM
Manual steering gear . . . . . check level LS
Power steering . . . . check level FA
Body . . . . lubricate
Fluid leaks on pavement . . . . inspect

SEVERE SERVICE
W Crankcase—Change oil & filter every 3 mo/3 mi (4.8 km)

1985-86 EGR solenoid filter—Replace every 30 mi (48 km) when operating on dusty roads

Differentials, transfer case & all transmissions—Check level daily when operating in water (if water has entered, change lubricant)

Front wheel bearing lubricant, 4 × 4 front spindle needle bearing & hub lock lubricant, disc & drum brake components—Inspect every 1 mi (1.6 km) or daily if operating in mud or water

Fittings, front hub bearings & disc brake caliper slide rails—Lubricate every 1 mi (1.6 km) or daily when operating in mud or water

Transmission, automatic—Change fluid every 30 mi (48 km). Lubricate external controls every 1 mi (1.6 km)

W Spark plugs—Check, clean & regap every 6 mi (9.6 km)

KEY TO LUBRICANTS

BL	Self-adjusting Brake Lubricant
EC	Ethylene Glycol Coolant
	Mix 50/50 with water at least to −20°F (−29°C) protection
EP	Extreme Pressure Gear Lubricant
FA	Automatic Transmission Fluid, Type F
HBH	Hydraulic Brake Fluid, Extra Heavy-Duty
HP	Hypoid Gear Oil
HP★	Hypoid Gear Oil for Limited-Slip or Traction-Lok Differential
LM	Lithium Grease, with Polyethylene
LS	Steering Gear Lubricant
MA	MERCON® Automatic Transmission Fluid
MH	Manifold Heat Valve Solvent
SG	Motor Oil, API Service SG

CRANKCASE . . . . SG

CAPACITY, Refill:

	Liters	Qt
All models:	4.7	5.0

Capacity shown is without filter. When replacing filter, additional oil may be needed

Above 40°F (4°C)	30
Below 60°F (16°C)	5W-30
Above 0°F (−18°C)	10W-30*, 10W-40*
Above 10°F (−12°C)	15W-40
Above 20°F (−7°C)	20W-40, 20W-50

*Preferred

TRANSMISSION, Automatic . . . . MA

CAPACITY, Initial Refill*:

	Liters	Qt
C-6	4.7	5.0
Others	2.8	3.0

*With the engine at operating temperature, shift transmission through all gears. Check fluid level in PARK and add fluid as needed

TRANSMISSION, Manual

1987 5-speed . . . . MA
All others . . . . 80W EP

CAPACITY, Refill:

	Liters	Pt
3-speed	1.7	3.5
4-speed ex. OD	3.3	7.0
W/OD	2.1	4.5
5-speed	3.5	7.4

TRANSFER CASE . . . . MA

CAPACITY, Refill:

	Liters	Pt
NP208	4.3	9.0
Warner 1345	3.0	6.5
Warner 1356	1.9	4.0

DIFFERENTIAL

Standard . . . . 90 HP
Limited-Slip . . . . 90 HP★

CAPACITY, Refill:

	Liters	Pt
Front:		
Dana 44	1.7	3.8
Dana 50	1.9	4.0
Dana 60	2.8	6.0
Rear:		
Ford w/8.8″, 9.0″ ring gear*	2.6	5.5
10¼″ ring gear*	3.1	6.5
Dana 60 & 61	2.8	6.0
Dana 70 HD	3.5	7.4
Dana 70	3.1	6.5

*8.8″ & 10¼″ have removable cover, 9.0″ does not

LIMITED-SLIP OR TRACTION-LOK IDENTIFICATION:
Label on door lock pillar shows letter and number

SERVICE AT TIME OR MILEAGE—WHICHEVER OCCURS FIRST

FDTPM20   FDTPM20

Perform the following maintenance services at the intervals indicated to keep the vehicle warranties in effect.

W SERVICE TO MAINTAIN EMISSION WARRANTY

MI—MILES IN THOUSANDS
KM—KILOMETERS IN THOUSANDS

EVERY 6 MO/7.5 MI—12 KM
Automatic transmission
   external controls . . . . lubricate **LM**
At mileage interval only. 1992, also check fluid level

Clutch reservoir . . . . check level **HBH**

W Crankcase . . . . change oil

Fittings . . . . lubricate **LM**
At mileage only

W Oil filter . . . . replace

Power steering . . . . check level **FA**

Tires . . . . rotate
At mileage, then every 15 mi (24 km) after initial service

Wheel lug nuts . . . . torque
At mileage only

EVERY 12 MONTHS
Body . . . . lubricate **SLS**

W Cooling system . . . . inspect **EC**
Hoses, clamps. Replace coolant if necessary

Transmission, Transfer case
   & differential(s) . . . . check level

EVERY 15 MI—24 KM
Disc brake caliper
   slide rails . . . . lubricate **BL**
Also lubricate 1992 knuckle top & bottom inner pad slots. Inspect disc brake system

Drum brake system 1991-92 . . . . . inspect
Also check hoses & lines

Transfer case linkage . . . . lubricate **LM**
Shift lever pivot bolt & control rod connecting pins. F-series only

EVERY 36 MO/30 MI—48 KM
W Cooling
   system . . . . change coolant **EC**

EVERY 30 MI—48 KM
Brake system . . . . inspect
Lubricate disc brake caliper slide rails **BL**. Check all brake lines & lining

Front hubs 4 × 4 . . . . inspect **LS**
Inspect spindle needle & thrust bearings **LM**. With automatic hub locks, inspect lubricant in drag sleeve; special lubricant required

Front wheel
   bearings . . . . inspect/lubricate **LM**

W Air cleaner element . . . . replace

Brake master cylinder . . . check level **HBH**

W Carburetor hang-on
   devices 2.0L . . . . inspect
Clean choke linkages & external controls ex. FI

W Crankcase emission filter . . . . replace
Ex. 2.3L, 2.9L, 1988-89 3.0L, Ranger 4.0L. Also known as crankcase ventilation filter for 1992

Drive belts 1988-89 . . . . . . inspect/adjust

W Spark plugs (ex. platinum) . . . . replace

Throttle ball stud . . . . lubricate **LM**

Transfer case front output
   & axle shafts . . . . lubricate **LM**

EVERY 60 MI—96 KM
Transfer case . . . . change fluid

Drive belts 1990-92 . . . . . . inspect/adjust
Ex. 2.9L, 3.0L, 4.0L

Idle speed control air bypass valve
   (if equipped) 1988-91 . . . . . check/clean

EGR valve 2.0L . . . . replace

Ignition wires 1988-91 . . . . replace

Manual transmission . . . . change oil

PCV valve . . . . replace

Spark plugs (platinum) . . . . replace

Thermactor hoses & clamps ex.
   2.3L, 2.9L & 3.0L . . . . check

Throttle body 1990-91 . . . . . . check/clean

1991-92 EVERY 100 MI—160 KM
Differential (rear) . . . . change lubricant

SERVICE AS REQUIRED
Parking brake linkage
   pivots & clevices . . . . lubricate **LM**

Manual steering gear . . . . . check level **LS**

Fluid leaks on pavement . . . . inspect

SEVERE SERVICE
W Crankcase—Change oil & filter every 3 mo/3 mi (4.8 km)

Differentials, transfer case & all transmissions—Check level daily when operating in water (if water has entered, change lubricant)

W EGR solenoid filter, 1988 2.3L eng.— Replace every 30 mi (48 km) when operating on dusty roads

Front wheel bearing lubricant, 4 × 4 front spindle needle bearing & hub lock lubricant, disc & drum brake components—Inspect every 1 mi (1.6 km) or daily if operating in mud or water

Fittings, front hub bearings & disc brake caliper slide rails—Lubricate every 1 mi (1.6 km) or daily when operating in mud or water

Transmission, automatic—Change fluid every 30 mi (48 km). Lubricate external controls every 1 mi (1.6 km)

W Spark plugs 1988-91—Check, clean & regap: Aerostar every 30 mi (48 km); others, every 15 mi (24 km)

DIFFERENTIAL
Aerostar, front . . . . **MA**
1992 F150, F250, front . . . . **GLS**
1990-92 Bronco II, Explorer, Ranger,
   front* . . . . **GLS**
All others:
   Standard . . . . 90 **HP**
   Limited-Slip . . . . 90 **HP ★**

CAPACITY, Refill:	Liters	Pt
Front:		
Dana 28 Ranger, Bronco II	0.5	1.0
Dana 28-2 Aerostar	1.0	2.2
Dana 35 Ranger, Bronco II,		
Explorer	1.7	3.5
Dana 44	1.7	3.6
Dana 50	1.8	3.8
Dana 60	2.8	5.8
Rear:		
Aerostar w/Ford 7.5″ ring		
gear	1.7†	3.5†

KEY TO LUBRICANTS
See other Ford Truck charts

CRANKCASE . . . . **SG**

CAPACITY, Refill:	Liters	Qt
1992 3.0L	3.3	3.5
2.3L, 2.9L, 4.0L,		
1988-91 3.0L	3.8	4.0
Others	4.7	5.0

Capacity shown is without filter. When replacing filter, additional oil may be needed

Below 100°F (38°C)
  1988-91 2.3L, 3.0L 5W-30*
All Temp. 1992 2.3L, 2.9L, 3.0L, 4.0L . . 5W-30*
Below 60°F (16°C), all other eng. 5W-30
Above 0°F (–18°C) . . . . 10W-30†
Above 0°F (–18°C) 1988 . . . . 10W-40
Above 10°F (–12°C) 1988 . . . . 15W-40
* Preferred for 2.3L, 3.0L; 1992 2.9L, 4.0L
†Preferred for all eng. ex. 2.3L, 3.0L; 1992 2.9L, 4.0L

TRANSMISSION, Automatic . . . . **MA**

CAPACITY, Initial Refill*:	Liters	Qt
C-6 (shallow pan)	4.7	5.0
C-6 (deep pan)	5.6	6.0
Others	2.8	3.0

* With the engine at operating temperature, shift transmission through all gears. Check fluid level in PARK and add fluid as needed

TRANSMISSION, Manual
4-speed . . . . 80W **EP**
5-speed Mitsubishi* . . . . 80W **EP**
5-speed, All others . . . . **MA**
* Used in some Ranger & Bronco II 4WD and identified by drain plug located in middle of pan

CAPACITY, Refill:	Liters	Pt
5-speed (Mazda)		
R1, R2 Aerostar, Ranger,		
Bronco II, Explorer	2.6	5.6
Bronco, Econoline,		
F-series	3.6	7.6
5-speed S5-42 ZF		
Bronco, Econoline,		
F-series	3.2	6.8
5-speed (Mitsubishi)		
Ranger, Bronco II	2.3	4.8
4-speed ex. OD	3.3	7.0
W/OD	2.1	4.5

TRANSFER CASE . . . . **MA**
1988 Bronco II 2WD Warner 1359 gearbox does not contain any fluid lubricant. Do not attempt to service

CAPACITY, Refill:	Liters	Pt
Warner 1345	3.0	6.5
Warner 1350 Ranger,		
Bronco II	1.4	3.0
Warner 1354 Ranger,		
Bronco II, Explorer	1.2	2.5
Warner 1356	1.9	4.0
Spicer TC28 Aerostar	2.1	4.5

CAPACITY, Refill:	Liters	Pt
Aerostar w/Ford 8.8″ ring		
gear	2.5†	5.3†
Aerostar w/Dana	1.2	2.5
Bronco II	2.6	5.5
Ranger w/7.5″ ring gear	2.4†	5.0†
Ranger w/8.8″ ring gear	2.6†	5.5†
Other Ford		
w/8.8″ ring gear**	2.6	5.5
w/10¼″ ring gear**	3.1	6.5
Dana 60 & 61 ex. 60-IU	2.8	6.0
Dana 60-IU	3.0	6.3
Dana 70 ex. HD	3.1	6.5
70 HD	3.5	7.4
Dana 80	3.9	8.3

* With Auto-locking Hubs
* * 8.8″ & 10¼″ have removable cover
† Fill no higher than ¼″ to 9/16″ below fill plug

LIMITED-SLIP OR TRACTION-LOK
IDENTIFICATION:
Label on door lock pillar has letter and number

FORD TRUCKS
1988-92 All Diesel Models

SERVICE AT TIME OR MILEAGE—WHICHEVER OCCURS FIRST

Perform the following maintenance services at the intervals indicated to keep the vehicle warranties in effect.

W SERVICE TO MAINTAIN EMISSION WARRANTY

MI—MILES IN THOUSANDS
KM—KILOMETERS IN THOUSANDS

EVERY MONTH
W Cooling system .... check level

FIRST 5 MI—8 KM; THEN EVERY 15 MI—24 KM
W Automatic transmission vacuum
   regulator 1988 .... check/adjust

W Curb idle speed .... check

W Fuel injector pump .... inspect
   Clean & lubricate face cam

W Idle return spring & throttle ..... check

   Tires, 1989-92 .... rotate

EVERY 6 MO/5 MI—8 KM
Automatic transmission external
   controls .... lubricate **LM**
At mileage only

Clutch lever pivots .... lubricate **LM**
At mileage only

Clutch reservoir .... check level **HBH**
At mileage only

W Crankcase .... change oil

Fittings .... lubricate **LM**
At mileage only

W Oil filter .... replace

Power steering .... check level **FA**

W Fuel/water separator .... drain
At mileage only
More frequently if dash light illuminates

Steering linkage .... lubricate **LM**
When equipped with fittings

Wheel lug nuts .... torque

EVERY 12 MONTHS
Body .... lubricate **SLS**

W Cooling system .... inspect **EC**
Hoses, clamps. Replace coolant if necessary

Transmission, transfer case
   & differential .... check level

EVERY 15 MI—24 KM
Disc brake caliper slide rails &
   1992 knuckle top & bottom
   inner pad slots .... lubricate **BL**
Inspect brake system lining, lines & hoses

Parking brake fluid
   F-Super Duty .... check level **MA**
Unit located behind transmission

EVERY 36 MO/30 MI—48 KM
W Cooling
   system .... change coolant **EC**

EVERY 30 MI—48 KM
Brake system .... inspect
Lubricate disc brake caliper rails **BL**. Check all brake
lines & lining

W Drive belts .... inspect/adjust

Front hubs 4×4 .... clean/repack **LM**
With automatic hub locks, inspect lubricant in drag
sleeve; special lubricant required

Front wheel bearings ... clean/repack **LM**

W Air cleaner element .... replace

W Air induction system & hoses ... inspect

Brake master cylinder ... check level **HBH**

W Throttle ball stud .... lubricate **LM**

EVERY 60 MI—96 KM
Manual transmission .... change oil

Transfer case .... change fluid

Fuel filter .... replace

1991-92 EVERY 100 MI—160 KM
Differential (rear) .... change lubricant

SERVICE AS REQUIRED
Parking brake linkage
   pivots & clevices .... lubricate **LM**

Manual steering gear ..... check level **LS**

Fluid leaks on pavement .... inspect

SEVERE SERVICE
W Crankcase—Change oil & filter every 3
mo/2.5 mi (4 km)

Differentials, transfer case & all transmissions—Check level daily when operating in water (if water has entered, change lubricant)

Differential—Rear F-Super Duty, change lubricant every 30 mi (48 km). For extended trailer towing above 70°F (21°C) and extended wide open throttle above 45 mph change lubricant every 3 mo/3 mi (4.8 km). Where 75W-140 synthetic gear oil, Spec. No. M2C192-A is used, no scheduled drain interval

Front wheel bearing lubricant, 4×4 front spindle needle bearing & hub lock lubricant, disc & drum brake components—Inspect every 1 mi (1.6 km) or daily if operating in mud or water

Fittings & front hub bearings, clutch release lever pivot & disc brake caliper slide rails—Lubricate every 1 mi (1.6 km) or daily when operating in mud or water

Transmission, automatic—Change fluid every 30 mi (48 km)

Transmission, manual 1989-92 HD M50D (S5-42-ZF)—Change fluid every 30 mi (48 km)

KEY TO LUBRICANTS
BL	Self-adjusting Brake Lubricant
CE	Motor Oil, API Service CE
EC	Ethylene Glycol Coolant Mix 50/50 with water at least to −20°F (−29°C) protection
EP	Extreme Pressure Gear Lubricant
FA	Automatic Transmission Fluid, Type F
GLS	4×4 Gear Oil (75W Synthetic) Ford Part No. F1TZ-19580-A
HBH	Hydraulic Brake Fluid, Extra Heavy-Duty
HP	Hypoid Gear Oil
HP★	Hypoid Gear Oil for Limited-Slip or Traction-Lok Differential
LM	Lithium Grease, with Polyethylene
LS	Steering Gear Lubricant
MA	MERCON® Automatic Transmission Fluid
SG	Motor Oil, API Service SG
SLS	Special Lubricant—Spray Ford Part No. D7AZ-19584-A

CRANKCASE .... SG/CE
CAPACITY, Refill:	Liters	Qt
All models (incl. filter)	9.3	10.0
Above 32°F (0°C)		30*
Above 10°F (−12°C) 1988		20W-40
Above 0°F (−18°C)		15W-40
Below 90°F (32°C)		10W-30†

* Preferred above 32°F (0°C)
†Preferred below 32°F (0°C)

TRANSMISSION, Automatic .... MA
CAPACITY, Initial Refill*:	Liters	Qt
C-6	4.7	5.0

* With the engine at operating temperature, shift transmission through all gears. Check fluid level in PARK and add fluid as needed

TRANSMISSION, Manual
4-speed .... 80W **EP**
5-speed OD .... **MA**
CAPACITY, Refill:	Liters	Pt
5-speed OD (Mazda trans.) R2	3.6	7.6
5-speed OD S5-42 ZF	3.2	6.8
5-speed OD (Mitsubishi trans.)	2.3	4.8
Other 5-speed OD	3.5	7.4
4-speed ex. OD	3.3	7.0
W/OD	2.1	4.5

TRANSFER CASE .... MA
CAPACITY, Refill:	Liters	Pt
Warner 1345	3.0	6.5
Warner 1356	1.9	4.0

DIFFERENTIAL
1992 F250, front* .... **GLS**
All others:
  Standard .... 90 **HP**
  Limited-Slip .... 90 **HP★**
* With Dana axle only
CAPACITY, Refill:	Liters	Pt
Front:		
Dana 44	1.7	3.6
Dana 50	1.8	3.8
Dana 60	2.8	6.0
Rear:		
Ford w/8.8″ ring gear* ...	2.6	5.5
w/10¼″ ring gear*	3.1	6.5
Dana 60 & 61 ex. 60-IU ...	2.8	6.0
Dana 60-IU	3.0	6.3
Dana 70 ex. HD	3.1	6.5
70 HD	3.5	7.4
Dana 80	3.9	8.3

*8.8″ & 10¼″ have removable rear cover

LIMITED-SLIP OR TRACTION-LOK IDENTIFICATION
Label on door lock pillar shows letter & number

SERVICE AT TIME OR MILEAGE—WHICHEVER OCCURS FIRST

FDTPM22   FDTPM22

Perform the following maintenance services at the intervals indicated to keep the vehicle warranties in effect.

W SERVICE TO MAINTAIN EMISSION WARRANTY

MI—MILES IN THOUSANDS
KM—KILOMETERS IN THOUSANDS

EVERY 6 MO/5 MI—8 KM
Automatic transmission external
   controls . . . . lubricate **LM**
At mileage interval only. Also check fluid level 1992

Clutch release lever
   7.5L F-series . . . . lubricate **LM**

Clutch reservoir . . . . check level **HBH**
At mileage only

W Crankcase . . . . change oil

Fittings . . . . lubricate **LM**
At mileage only

W Oil filter . . . . replace

Power steering . . . . check level **FA**

Tires . . . . rotate
At mileage, then every 15 mi (24 km) after initial service

Wheel lug nuts . . . . torque
At mileage only

EVERY 12 MONTHS
Body . . . . lubricate **SLS**

W Cooling system . . . . inspect **EC**
Hoses, clamps. Replace coolant if necessary

Transmission, transfer case
   & differential . . . . check level

EVERY 15 MI—24 KM
Disc brake system . . . . inspect
Lubricate caliper slide rails & 1992 knuckle top & bottom inner pad slots **BL**

Drum brake system 1991-92 . . . . . inspect
Also check hoses & lines

Drive belts . . . . inspect/adjust

Parking brake fluid 1990-92
   F-Super Duty . . . . check level **MA**
Unit located behind transmission

Transfer case linkage . . . . lubricate **LM**
Shift lever pivot bolt & control rod connecting pins

EVERY 36 MO/30 MI—48 KM
W Cooling
   system . . . . change coolant **EC**

EVERY 30 MI—48 KM
Brake system . . . . inspect
Lubricate disc brake caliper slide rails **BL**. Check all brake lines & lining

Front hubs 4×4 . . . . inspect **LS**
Inspect spindle needle bearings **LM**. With automatic hub locks, inspect lubricant in drag sleeve; special lubricant required

Front wheel
   bearings . . . . inspect/lubricate **LM**

W Air cleaner element . . . . replace

W Crankcase emission filter . . . . . . replace
Also known as crankcase ventilation filter for 1992

Parking brake fluid 1988-89
   F-super duty . . . . check level **MA**
Unit located behind transmission

W Spark plugs . . . . replace

Transfer case front output
   & axle slip shafts . . . . lubricate **LM**

Throttle ball stud . . . . lubricate **LM**
Also 1992 kickdown cable ball studs

EVERY 60 MI—96 KM
Transfer case . . . . change fluid

Idle speed control air
   bypass valve . . . . clean

Ignition wires . . . . replace

Manual transmission . . . . change oil

PCV valve . . . . replace

Thermactor hoses & clamps . . . . check

Throttle body 1990 . . . . check/clean

1991-92 EVERY 100 MI—160 KM
Differential (rear) . . . . . . change lubricant

SERVICE AS REQUIRED
Parking brake linkage
   pivots & clevices . . . . lubricate **LM**

Manual steering gear . . . . . check level **LS**

Fluid leaks on pavement . . . . inspect

SEVERE SERVICE
W Crankcase—Change oil & filter every 3 mo/3 mi (4.8 km)

Differentials, transfer case & all transmissions—Check level daily when operating in water (if water has entered, change lubricant)

Differential—Rear F-Super Duty, change lubricant every 30 mi (48 km). For extended trailer towing above 70°F (21°C) and extended wide open throttle above 45 mph change lubricant every 3 mo/3 mi (4.8 km). Where 75W-140 synthetic gear oil, Spec. No. M2C192-A is used, no scheduled drain interval

Front wheel bearing lubricant, 4×4 front spindle needle bearing & hub lock lubricant, disc & drum brake components—Inspect every 1 mi (1.6 km) or daily if operating in mud or water

Fittings, front hub bearings, clutch release lever pivot 7.5L engine & disc brake caliper slide rails—Lubricate every 1 mi (1.6 km) or daily when operating in mud or water

Transmission, automatic—Change fluid every 30 mi (48 km). Lubricate external controls every 1 mi (1.6 km)

Transmission, manual 1989-92 HD M50D (S5-42 SF)—Change fluid every 30 mi (48 km)

W Spark plugs 1988-91—Check, clean & re-gap: every 15 mi (24 km)

KEY TO LUBRICANTS

BL	Self-adjusting Brake Lubricant
EC	Ethylene Glycol Coolant Mix 50/50 with water at least to –20°F (–29°C) protection
EP	Extreme Pressure Gear Lubricant Ford Part No. D8DZ-10C547-A
FA	Automatic Transmission Fluid, Type F
GLS	4×4 Gear Oil (75W Synthetic) Ford Part No. F1TZ-19580-A
HBH	Hydraulic Brake Fluid, Extra Heavy-Duty
HP	Hypoid Gear Oil Ford Part No. EOAZ-19580-A
HP★	Hypoid Gear Oil for Limited-Slip or Traction-Lok Differential
LM	Lithium Grease, with Polyethylene
LS	Steering Gear Lubricant
MA	MERCON® Automatic Transmission Fluid
MH	Manifold Heat Valve Solvent
SG	Motor Oil, API Service SG
SLS	Special Lubricant—Spray Ford Part No. D7AZ-19584-A

CRANKCASE . . . . SG
CAPACITY, Refill:	Liters	Qt
All models	4.7	5.0

Capacity shown is without filter. When replacing filter, additional oil may be needed
Below 60°F (16°C) 5W-30
Above 0°F (–18°C) 10W-30*
Above 0°F (–18°C) 1988 . . . . 10W-40
Above 10°F (–12°C) 1988-90 . . . . . . 15W-40
*Preferred

TRANSMISSION, Automatic . . . . MA
CAPACITY, Initial Refill*:	Liters	Qt
C-6 (deep pan)	5.6	6.0
C-6 (shallow pan)	4.7	5.0
Others	2.8	3.0

*With the engine at operating temperature shift transmission through all gears. Check fluid level in PARK and add fluid as needed

TRANSMISSION, Manual
4-speed . . . . 80W **EP**
5-speed OD . . . . **MA**
CAPACITY, Refill:	Liters	Pt
4-speed ex. OD	3.3	7.0
W/OD	2.1	4.5
5-speed OD (Mazda) R2	2.6	5.6
5-speed OD S5-42 ZF	3.2	6.8

TRANSFER CASE . . . . MA
CAPACITY, Refill:	Liters	Pt
Warner 1345	3.0	6.5
Warner 1356	1.9	4.0

DIFFERENTIAL
1992 F250, front* . . . . **GLS**
All others:
   Standard . . . . 90 **HP**
   Limited-Slip . . . . 90 **HP★**
*With Dana axle only
CAPACITY, Refill:	Liters	Pt
Front:		
Dana 44	1.7	3.6
Dana 50	1.8	3.8
Dana 60	2.8	6.0
Rear:		
Ford w/8.8″ ring gear*	2.6	5.5
w/10¹⁄₄″ ring gear*	3.1	6.5
Dana 60 & 61 ex. 60-IU	2.8	6.0
Dana 60-IU	3.0	6.3
Dana 70 ex. HD	3.1	6.5
70 HD	3.5	7.4
Dana 80	3.9	8.3

*8.8″ & 10¹⁄₄″ have removable cover
LIMITED-SLIP OR TRACTION-LOK IDENTIFICATION:
Label on door lock pillar shows letter and number

HOOD RELEASE: Inside

① Crankcase dipstick
② Transmission dipstick
③ Brake fluid reservoir
④ Clutch fluid reservoir
⑤ Oil fill cap
⑥ Power steering reservoir
⑦ Air filter
⑧ Fuel filter
⑨ Oil filter
⑩ PCV filter
⑪ EGR valve
⑫ Oxygen sensor
⑬ PCV valve

1984-88
Sprint, Firefly 2V

1989-92
Metro, Sprint, Firefly

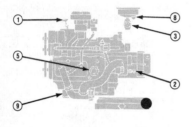

1987-91
Sprint Turbo
Firefly Turbo

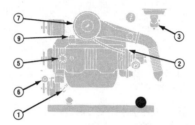

1985-89
Spectrum, Sunburst 2V

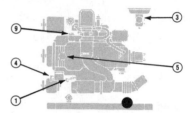

1987-88
Spectrum Turbo
Sunburst Turbo

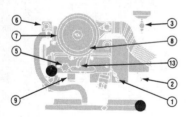

1985-88
1.6L Nova ex. Twin Cam

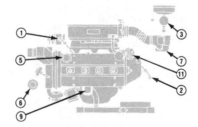

1988 1.6L Nova Twin Cam
1989-92 1.6L Prizm Code 5

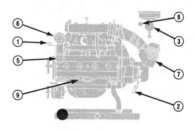

1989-92 1.6L Prizm
Code 6

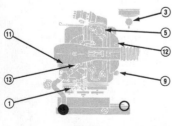

1989-92
1.6L Tracker

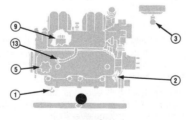

1990-92
1.6L SOHC Code 6
Storm

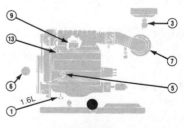

1990-92
1.6L DOHC Code 5
1.8L DOHC Code 8
Storm

● Cooling system drain   ○ Cooling system drain, some models

SERVICE LOCATIONS — ENGINE AND CHASSIS

0 FITTINGS
0 PLUGS

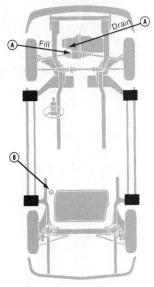

1989-92
Metro, Sprint, Firefly

0 FITTINGS
0 PLUGS

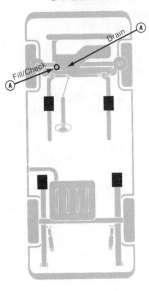

1985-88
Sprint, Firefly

0 FITTINGS
0 PLUGS

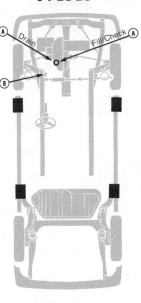

1985-87 Sunburst
1985-89 Spectrum
1990-92 Storm

0 FITTINGS
0 PLUGS

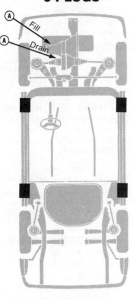

1985-88 Nova
1989-92 Prizm

0 FITTINGS
0 PLUGS

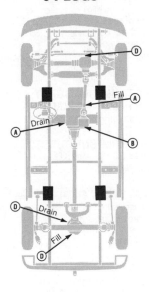

1989-92 Tracker

Ⓐ Manual transmission/transaxle, drain & fill

Ⓑ Transfer case, drain & fill

Ⓒ Automatic transaxle final drive, NOT USED

Ⓓ Differential, drain & fill

⑧ Fuel filter

CAUTION: On front wheel drive vehicles the center of gravity is further forward than on rear wheel drive vehicles. When removing major components from the rear of the vehicle while it is on a hoist, the vehicle must be supported in a manner to prevent it from tipping forward.

■ Lift adapter position

CHEVROLET - PONTIAC
1985-88 Sprint, Firefly, Spectrum, Sunburst, Nova

SERVICE AT TIME OR MILEAGE—WHICHEVER OCCURS FIRST

CTIPM2   CTIPM2

W   SERVICE TO MAINTAIN EMISSION WARRANTY

MI—MILES IN THOUSANDS
KM—KILOMETERS IN THOUSANDS

SPECTRUM, SUNBURST TURBO, EVERY 6 MO/3 MI—5 KM
- W   Crankcase . . . . change oil
- W   Oil filter . . . . replace
  Replace every other oil change

SPRINT, FIREFLY TURBO, EVERY 12 MO/5 MI—8 KM
- W   Crankcase . . . . change oil
  Change filter at each oil change

SPRINT, FIREFLY, AT FIRST 7.5 MI—12.5 KM; THEN EVERY 15 MI—25 KM
- Tires . . . . rotate
- W   Engine idle speed . . . . check/adjust

NOVA, FIRST 10 MI—16 KM
- Engine idle speed . . . . check/adjust
  1988 only

EVERY 6 MONTHS/OIL CHANGE
- Clutch & brake fluid . . . . check level **HB**
- Clutch pedal freeplay . . . . check/adjust
- Power steering fluid . . . . check level
  Nova, **AF**; Spectrum, Sunburst, **PS**

SPECTRUM, SUNBURST, AT FIRST 7.5 MI—12.5 KM; THEN EVERY 30 MI—50 KM
- Manual transaxle . . . . change lubricant

NOVA, EVERY 12 MO/10 MI—16.7 KM ALL OTHERS, EVERY 12 MO/7.5 MI—12.5 KM
- Brake system . . . . inspect
  Check parking brake adjustment
- Tires, Nova . . . . rotate
- W   Crankcase . . . . change oil
  Sprint ex. Turbo, Firefly, Nova: change filter at each oil change
  Spectrum, Sunburst ex. Turbo: change filter at first oil change, then every other
- Chassis ex. Nova . . . . lubricate **LM**
  Lubricate transaxle shift linkage, hood latch, door latch & hinges, parking brake cable guides & underbody contact points
- W   Exhaust system . . . . inspect
- Steering & suspension . . . . inspect
  Check boots, seals, & all components
- Transaxle . . . . check level
- W   Drive belts . . . . check/adjust
- W   Throttle linkage . . . . inspect

EVERY SPRING
- Underbody . . . . flush

SPRINT, EVERY 12 MO/15 MI—25 KM
- W   Fuel tank, cap & lines . . . . inspect

EVERY 15 MI—25 KM
- Transaxle, manual . . . . change lubricant
  Sprint, Firefly only
- W   Cooling system . . . . inspect
- Idle speed,
  1985-86 Nova . . . . check/adjust

Throttle position system
  1985-86 Nova . . . . adjust
- W   Valves ex. 1987-88 Nova . . . . . . adjust
- Fuel tank, cap, lines . . . . inspect
  Spectrum, Sunburst only

NOVA, EVERY 20 MI—32 KM
- Chassis . . . . lubricate **LM**

SPECTRUM, SUNBURST, EVERY 24 MO/22.5 MI—37.5 KM
- Power steering fluid . . . . change **PS**

SPRINT, FIREFLY, EVERY 24 MO/30 MI—50 KM
- W   Air cleaner . . . . replace element
- W   Carburetor choke . . . . inspect
- W   Fuel cut solenoid . . . . inspect
- W   Fuel filter . . . . replace
- W   PCV system . . . . inspect
- W   Pulse air system . . . . inspect
- W   Spark plug wires . . . . check
  Also check distributor cap & rotor

EVERY 30 MI—50 KM
- Rear wheel bearings . . . . repack **LM**
- Transaxle, automatic . . . . change fluid
  Spectrum, Sunburst only
- W   Air cleaner . . . . replace element
  Spectrum, Sunburst, Nova only
- W   Choke system . . . . inspect
  Sprint, Firefly, Spectrum, Sunburst, 1985-86 Nova
- W   Cooling system . . . . . change coolant **EC**
- W   Drive belts . . . . check/adjust
- W   Oxygen sensor . . . . inspect
  Sprint, Firefly only. Check indicator light to assure proper system function
- W   Spark plugs ex.
  1985-86, 88 Nova . . . . replace
  Spark plug wires,
  1985-86 Nova . . . . clean/check
- W   Valves 1987 Nova . . . . adjust

SPECTRUM, SUNBURST, EVERY 45 MI—75 KM
- Power steering hoses . . . . replace

SPECTRUM, SUNBURST, EVERY 60 MI—96 KM
- Timing belt . . . . replace

NOVA, EVERY 60 MI—96 KM
- Vapor canister . . . . inspect
- Fuel cap gasket . . . . replace
- Spark plugs, 1988 . . . . replace
- Valves, 1988 . . . . adjust

SEVERE SERVICE
- W   Air cleaner element—Sprint, Firefly, replace as needed, Nova every 3 mo/5 mi (8 km)
- W   Crankcase—Ex. Nova, change oil & filter every 3 mo/3 mi (5 km). Nova, change oil & filter every 6 mo/5 mi (8 km)
- Chassis—Lubricate every 6 mo/6 mi (10 km)
- Transaxle—Ex. 1987-88 Nova, change fluid every 15 mi (25 km)
- Transaxle—1987-88 Nova, change fluid every 20 mi (33 km)
- Timing belt—Nova, replace every 60 mi (96 km)

KEY TO LUBRICANTS

AF	DEXRON®-II Automatic Transmission Fluid
EC	Ethylene Glycol Coolant Mix with water to –34°F (–37°C) protection
GLS	Special Gear Lubricant
GL-5	Gear Oil, API Service GL-5
HB	Hydraulic Brake Fluid, DOT 3
LM	Lithium Grease, EP
PS	Power Steering Fluid GM Part No. 1052884
SG	Motor Oil, API Service SG

CRANKCASE . . . . SG

CAPACITY, Refill:	Liters	Qt
Sprint, Firefly (includes filter)	3.5	3.7
Spectrum, Sunburst	2.8	3.0
Nova 2V	3.0	3.2
Nova FI	3.4	3.6

Ex. Sprint, Firefly, capacity shown is without filter. When replacing filter, additional oil may be needed

1985 ex. Nova
- Above 40°F (4°C) 30
- Above 20°F (–7°C) 20W-20
- Above 10°F (–12°C) 15W-40
- Above 0°F (–18°C) 10W-30
- Below 100°F (38°C) 5W-30*

1985-88 Nova
- Above 10°F (–12°C) . . . . 15W-40, 20W-40†, 20W-50†
- Above 0°F (–18°C) . . . . . . 10W-30*, 10W-50†
- Below 50°F (10°C) 5W-30

1988 Spectrum Turbo
- Above 40°F (4°C) . . . . 30●
- Above 0°F (–18°C) 10W-30*
- Below 60°F (16°C) 5W-30

1988 Sprint, Firefly Turbo
- Above 40°F (4°C) . . . . 30●
- All temperatures 10W-30*

1986-88 Others
- Above 40°F (4°C) 30
- Above 0°F (–18°C) 10W-30
- All temperatures 5W-30*

* Preferred
† Not recommended for 1985-87 models
● May be used only if other recommended viscosities are not available

TRANSAXLE, Automatic . . . . AF

CAPACITY, Initial Refill*:	Liters	Qt
Spectrum, Sunburst♦	6.0	6.3
Sprint, Firefly	1.5	1.6
Nova 3-speed†	2.3	2.4
4-speed††	3.1	3.3

* With the engine at operating temperature, shift transmission through all gears. Check fluid level in PARK and add fluid as needed
†Differential serviced separately
††Has overdrive switch on selector lever
♦Total or dry fill shown, use less fluid when refilling

TRANSAXLE, Manual
Sprint, Firefly . . . .**GLS**
Spectrum,
 Sunburst . . . . 5W-30 **SG**
Nova 75W-90*, 80W-90 **GL-5**
* Vehicles operated in Canada, 80W

CAPACITY, Refill:	Liters	Pt
Sprint, Firefly	2.3	4.8
Spectrum, Sunburst:		
1985-87	2.8	5.8
1988	1.9	4.0
Nova	2.6	5.4

DIFFERENTIAL
Nova 3-speed w/AT . . . . **AF**

CAPACITY, Refill:	Liters	Pt
Nova	1.4	3.0

SERVICE AT TIME OR MILEAGE—WHICHEVER OCCURS FIRST

GOIPM1   GOIPM1

Perform the following maintenance services at the intervals specified to keep the vehicle warranties in effect.

W SERVICE TO MAINTAIN EMISSION WARRANTY

MI—MILES IN THOUSANDS
KM—KILOMETERS IN THOUSANDS

SPRINT & FIREFLY TURBO, EVERY 12 MO/5 MI—8 KM
W Crankcase . . . . change oil
Change filter at each oil change

SPECTRUM, FIRST 5 MI—8 KM
Engine idle speed . . . . adjust

FIRST 7.5 MI—12.5 KM; THEN EVERY 15 MI—25 KM
Tires . . . . inspect, rotate

W Engine idle speed . . . . check/adjust
1989 Metro, Sprint, Firefly

METRO, SPRINT, FIREFLY, EVERY 7.5 MO/7.5 MI—12.5 KM SPECTRUM, STORM, EVERY 12 MO/7.5 MI—12.5 KM
Crankcase ex. Turbo . . . change oil & filter
Spectrum, Storm: change oil filter at first oil change, then every other but at least every 12 months

Chassis . . . . lubricate LM
Lubricate transaxle shift linkage, hood latch, door latch & hinges, parking brake cable guides & underbody contact points

Clutch bushing & linkage . . . . lubricate
Spectrum, Storm

Transaxle . . . . check level

W Exhaust system . . . . inspect

Steering & suspension . . . . inspect
Check boots, seals, & all components

W Drive belts . . . . check/adjust

W Throttle linkage . . . . inspect

EVERY SPRING
Underbody . . . . flush

EVERY 12 MO/15 MI—25 KM
W Fuel tank, cap & lines . . . . inspect

Brake System . . . . inspect HB

EVERY 15 MI—25 KM
Transaxle, manual . . . . . . change lubricant
1989 Metro, Sprint, Firefly only

W Cooling system . . . . inspect

W Idle speed . . . . check/adjust
1989 Metro, Sprint, Firefly

W Valves . . . . adjust
1989 Spectrum 1.5L
1990-92 Storm 1.6L Code 6

SPECTRUM, STORM, EVERY 24 MO/22.5 MI—37.5 KM
Power steering fluid . . . . change PS

EVERY 24 MO/30 MI—50 KM
W Air cleaner . . . . replace element

W Carburetor choke . . . . inspect
1989 Metro, Sprint, Firefly

W Drive belts . . . . inspect/adjust

W Fuel cut solenoid . . . . inspect
1989 Metro, Sprint, Firefly

W Fuel filter . . . . replace
1989 Metro, Sprint, Firefly

W PCV system . . . . inspect
1989 Metro, Sprint, Firefly

W Pulse air system . . . . inspect
1989 Metro, Sprint, Firefly

W Spark plug wires . . . . check
1989 Metro, Sprint, Firefly. Also check distributor cap & rotor

EVERY 30 MI—50 KM
Rear wheel bearings . . . . repack LM
1989 Spectrum

Transaxle, automatic . . . . . . change fluid
Spectrum, Storm only

Transaxle, manual . . . . . change lubricant
Spectrum, Storm only

W Choke system . . . . inspect
1989 Spectrum

W Cooling system . . . . change coolant EC

W Oxygen sensor . . . . inspect
1989 Metro, Sprint, Firefly. Check indicator light to assure proper system function

PCV valve & hoses . . . . inspect
Spectrum, Storm

W Spark plugs . . . . replace

EVERY 45 MO/45 MI—75 KM
Power steering hoses . . . . replace
Spectrum, Storm

Transaxle oil hoses . . . . replace
1991-92 Metro

EVERY 60 MI—96 KM
Spark plug wires . . . . replace
1990-92 Metro, Sprint, Firefly

Timing belt, Spectrum, Storm . . . . replace

W Valves . . . . adjust
1990-91 Storm 1.6L Code 5

EVERY 100 MI—166 KM
Automatic transmission . . . . . change fluid

SEVERE SERVICE
W Air cleaner element—Metro, Sprint, Firefly, replace as needed

W Crankcase—Metro, Sprint, Firefly, change oil & filter every 3 mo/3 mi (5 km); Spectrum, Storm, change oil every 3 mo/3 mi (5 km). Change oil filter at first oil change, then every other

Chassis—Lubricate every 6 mo/6 mi (10 km)

Transaxle, manual, Metro—Change fluid every 12 mo/12 mi (20 km)

Transaxle, automatic—Change fluid every 15 mi (25 km)

KEY TO LUBRICANTS

AF	DEXRON®-IIE Automatic Transmission Fluid
EC	Ethylene Glycol Coolant Mix with water to –34°F (–37°C) protection
GLS	Special Gear Lubricant GM Part No. 12345349
GL-5	Gear Oil, API Service GL-5
HB	Hydraulic Brake Fluid, DOT 3
LM	Lithium Grease with EP
PS	Power Steering Fluid GM Part No. 1052884
SG	Motor Oil, API Service SG

CRANKCASE . . . . SG

CAPACITY, Refill:	Liters	Qt
Metro, Firefly, Sprint (incl. filter)	3.5	3.7
Spectrum	2.8	3.0
Storm: SOHC	3.0	3.2
DOHC	3.8	4.0

Capacity shown is without filter. When replacing filter, additional oil may be needed

Firefly & Sprint Turbo:
Above 40°F (4°C) 1989 . . . . 30†
All temperatures 10W-30*
Others:
Above 40°F (4°C) . . . . 30†
Above 0°F (–18°C) 10W-30**
All temperatures ex. Storm DOHC 5W-30*
Below 60°F (16°C), Storm DOHC 5W-30
Below 0°F (–18°C) 5W-30**
†May be used only if other recommended viscosities are not available
* Preferred
* * Preferred for Storm Codes 5 (DOHC), & 8 (DOHC)

TRANSAXLE, Automatic . . . . AF

CAPACITY, Initial Refill*:	Liters	Qt
Metro, Sprint, Firefly	1.5	1.6
Spectrum	6.0†	6.3†
Storm	3.0	3.2

* With the engine at operating temperature, shift transmission through all gears. Let engine slow idle in PARK for 3 minutes or more. Check fluid level and add fluid as needed
†Total or dry fill shown

TRANSAXLE, Manual . . . . GLS

CAPACITY, Refill:	Liters	Pt
Metro, Sprint, Firefly	2.4	5.0
Spectrum, Storm	1.9	4.0

GEO
1989-92 Prizm

CHEK-CHART

Perform the following maintenance services at the interval indicated to keep the vehicle warranties in effect.

W SERVICE TO MAINTAIN EMISSION WARRANTY

MI—MILES IN THOUSANDS
KM—KILOMETERS IN THOUSANDS

W FIRST 7.5 MI—12.5 KM,
THEN EVERY 36 MO/30 MI—50 KM
Engine idle speed . . . . check/adjust

EVERY 6 MONTHS/OIL CHANGE
Clutch & brake fluid . . . . . . check level **HB**

Power steering fluid . . . . . . check level **AF**

1989,
EVERY 12 MO/10 MI—16.7 KM
1990-92,
EVERY 12 MO/7.5 MI—12.5 KM
Brake system . . . . inspect
Inspect hoses & lines for damage/wear.
Inspect friction surfaces for wear or cracks. Check for leaks. Check parking brake adjustment

W Crankcase . . . . change oil
Change oil filter at each oil change

Tires . . . . inspect/rotate

W Exhaust system . . . . inspect

Steering & suspension . . . . inspect
Check boots, seals, & all components

Transaxle . . . . check level

W Drive belts . . . . check/adjust

W Throttle linkage . . . . inspect

EVERY SPRING
Underbody . . . . flush

EVERY 15 MI—25 KM
Chassis . . . . lubricate **LM**
Lubricate transaxle shift linkage, hood latch, door latch & hinges, parking brake cable guides & underbody contact points

W Cooling system . . . . inspect

EVERY 30 MI—50 KM
W Spark plugs VIN Code 6 . . . . . . replace

W Air cleaner VIN Code 6 . . . . replace

EVERY 36 MO/30 MI—50 KM
W Air cleaner VIN Code 5 . . . . replace

Fuel lines & connections . . . . inspect

Exhaust system . . . . inspect

FIRST 36 MO/45 MI—75 KM;
THEN EVERY 24 MO/30 MI—50 KM
W Cooling system . . . . change coolant **EC**

EVERY 72 MO/60 MI—100 KM
W Spark plugs VIN Code 5 . . . . . . replace

Timing belt . . . . replace
At mileage interval only

W Vapor canister . . . . inspect

Valve clearance . . . . check/adjust
At mileage interval only

W Fuel cap gasket . . . . replace

EVERY 100 MI—166 KM
Automatic transmission . . . . . change fluid

SEVERE SERVICE
W Air cleaner element—Every 3 mo/5 mi (8 km)

Chassis—Lubricate every 7.5 mi (12.5 km)

W Crankcase—Change oil & filter every 6 mo/3.75 mi (6.2 km)

Transaxle, manual & automatic; AT differential—Change fluid every 15 mi (25 km)

KEY TO LUBRICANTS

AF	DEXRON®-IIE Automatic Transmission Fluid
EC	Ethylene Glycol Coolant Mix with water to –34°F (–37°C) protection
GL-5	Gear Oil, API Service GL-5
HB	Hydraulic Brake Fluid, DOT 3
LM	Lithium Grease with EP
SG	Motor Oil, API Service SG

CRANKCASE . . . . **SG**

CAPACITY, Refill:	Liters	Qt
Code 5	3.4	3.6
Code 6	3.0	3.2

Capacity shown is without filter. When replacing filter, additional oil may be needed

1989-90
Above 40°F (4°C) . . . . 30†
Above 0°F (–18°C) 10W-30
All temperatures 5W-30*
1991-92
Above 0°F (–18°C) 10W-30*
Below 50°F (10°C) 5W-30
†May be used only if other recommended viscosities are not available
*Preferred

TRANSAXLE, Automatic . . . . **AF**
3-speed differential serviced separately

CAPACITY, Initial Refill*:	Liters	Qt
3-speed	2.3	2.4
4-speed	3.1	3.3

*With the engine at operating temperature, shift transmission through all gears. Let engine slow idle in PARK for 3 minutes or more. Check fluid level and add fluid as needed

TRANSAXLE,
Manual 75W-90 **GL-4, GL-5**

CAPACITY, Refill:	Liters	Pt
All	2.3	4.8

DIFFERENTIAL
3-speed AT . . . . **AF**

CAPACITY, Refill:	Liters	Pt
All	1.4	3.0

SERVICE AT TIME OR MILEAGE—WHICHEVER OCCURS FIRST

GOIPM2   GOIPM2

Perform the following maintenance services at the interval indicated to keep the vehicle warranties in effect.

W SERVICE TO MAINTAIN EMISSION WARRANTY

MI—MILES IN THOUSANDS
KM—KILOMETERS IN THOUSANDS

FIRST 7.5 MI—12.5 KM
Manual transmission, differentials & transfer case . . . . change fluid

Tires . . . . rotate

EVERY 7.5 MO/7.5 MI — 12.5 KM
Clutch & brake fluid . . . . . . check level **HB**

Clutch pedal freeplay . . . . check/adjust

W Crankcase . . . . change oil
Change filter every oil change

Locking front hubs . . . . inspect

Steering & suspension . . . . inspect

Power steering fluid,
   1990-92 . . . . check level **AF**

Transmission & transfer case . check level

EVERY 12 MO/7.5 MI—12.5 KM
Brake system . . . . inspect
Check parking brake adjustment

Chassis . . . . lubricate **LM**
Lubricate transaxle shift linkage, hood latch, door latch & hinges, parking brake cable guides & underbody contact points

W Exhaust system . . . . inspect

Steering & suspension . . . . inspect
Check boots, seals, & all components

W Drive belts . . . . check/adjust

W Throttle linkage . . . . inspect

EVERY SPRING
Underbody . . . . flush

EVERY 15 MI—25 KM
Brake system . . . . inspect

Tires . . . . rotate

W Cooling system, 1989 . . . . inspect

W Idle speed . . . . check/adjust

W Valve clearance . . . . adjust

EVERY 15 MO/15 MI—24 KM
Propellor shaft & U-joints . . . . inspect

Wheel bearings . . . . inspect

EVERY 24 MO/24 MI — 40 KM
W Cooling system, 1990 .change coolant **EC**

EVERY 30 MI—50 KM
Transmission, manual & transfer case . . . . change fluid

W Air cleaner . . . . replace element

W Cooling system . . . . change coolant **EC**

W Drive belts . . . . check/adjust

Fuel tank, cap & lines . . . . inspect

W PCV filter . . . . replace
If equipped

Timing belt . . . . inspect/adjust

W Spark plugs . . . . replace

EVERY 50 MI—83 KM
Automatic transmission cooler hoses . . . . replace

W EGR system . . . . inspect

W PCV valve . . . . replace

EVERY 60 MI—96 KM
W Distributor cap & ignition wires . . . . replace

W Drive belts . . . . replace

W Emission hoses . . . . replace

Fuel cap . . . . replace

Ignition timing . . . . check/adjust

Wiring harness . . . . inspect

EVERY 80 MI—133 KM
W Oxygen sensor . . . . replace

EVERY 100 MI—166 KM
Automatic transmission . . . . . change fluid

W Catalytic converter . . . . inspect

W ECM sensors . . . . inspect

W Fuel injectors, 1990-92 . . . . inspect

W Vapor canister . . . . replace

SEVERE SERVICE
W Crankcase—Change oil & filter every 3 mo/3 mi (5 km)

Chassis—Lubricate every 6 mo/6 mi (10 km)

Transmission, transfer case & differentials—Change lubricant every 15 mo/15 mi (12.5 km)

KEY TO LUBRICANTS

AF   DEXRON®-IIE Automatic Transmission Fluid

EC   Ethylene Glycol Coolant
Mix with water to –34°F (–37°C) protection

GL-4   Gear Oil, API Service GL-4

GL-5   Gear Oil, API Service GL-5

HB   Hydraulic Brake Fluid, DOT 3

LM   Lithium Grease with EP

SG   Motor Oil, API Service SG
Use Energy Conserving-II oils

CRANKCASE . . . . **SG**

CAPACITY, Refill:	Liters	Qt
All (incl. filter)	4.0	4.2
Above 40°F (4°C)		30
Above 0°F (–18°C)		10W-30
All temperatures		5W-30*

*Preferred

TRANSMISSION, Automatic . . . . **AF**

CAPACITY, Initial Refill*:	Liters	Qt
All	2.8	3.0

*With the engine at operating temperature, shift transmission through all gears. Let engine slow idle in PARK for 3 minutes or more. Check fluid level and add fluid as needed

TRANSMISSION, Manual . . **75W-90 GL-5**

CAPACITY, Refill:	Liters	Pt
All	1.5	3.2

TRANSFER CASE **75W-90 GL-5**

CAPACITY, Refill:	Liters	Pt
All	1.7	3.6

DIFFERENTIAL **75W-90 GL-5**

CAPACITY, Refill:	Liters	Pt
Front	1.0	2.1
Rear	2.2	4.6

HONDA
1983-92 Civic, CRX, Accord, Prelude

SERVICE LOCATIONS — ENGINE AND CHASSIS

HOOD RELEASE: Inside

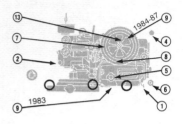

1983-89
All 2V & 3V engines

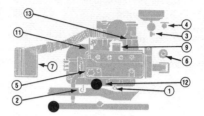

1988-91
1488cc ex. HF

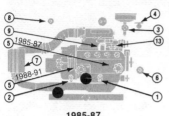

1985-87
Civic, CRX
1488cc FI;
1988-91
Civic, CRX
1488cc HF, 1590cc MFI

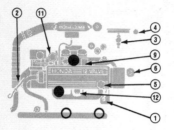

1984-89
Accord, Prelude
1830cc 2 × IV,
1830cc FI,
1958cc 2 × IV,
1955cc FI

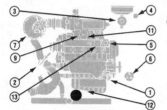

1990-91
Prelude
2056cc

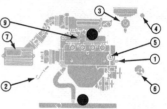

1990-92
Accord, Prelude
2156cc

① Crankcase dipstick
② Transmission dipstick
③ Brake fluid reservoir,
④ Clutch fluid reservoir
   Some models only
⑤ Oil fill cap
⑥ Power steering reservoir
⑦ Air filter
⑧ Fuel filter
⑨ Oil filter
⑩ PCV filter
⑪ EGR valve
⑫ Oxygen sensor
⑬ PCV valve

0 FITTINGS
0 PLUGS

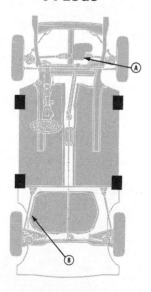

All ex. 4WD Wagon

0 FITTINGS
0 PLUGS

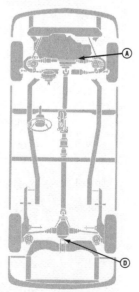

4WD Wagon

■ Lift adapter position
○ Cooling system drain, some models
● Cooling system drain

Ⓐ Manual transmission/transaxle,
   drain & fill
Ⓑ Transfer case, NOT USED
Ⓒ Automatic transaxle final drive,
   NOT USED
Ⓓ Differential, drain & fill

SERVICE AT TIME OR MILEAGE—WHICHEVER OCCURS FIRST

HAIPM2   HAIPM2

MI—MILES IN THOUSANDS
KM—KILOMETERS IN THOUSANDS

EVERY 7.5 MI—12 KM
Crankcase . . . . change oil

Front brake pads & yoke or caliper slide
  performance . . . . inspect

Oil filter . . . . replace

Clutch pedal travel . . . . check
Accord, Prelude check fluid level, **HB**

Power steering . . . . inspect **PS**

EVERY 15 MO/15 MI—24 KM
Brake hoses, lines, fluid . . . . inspect

Front wheel alignment . . . . . inspect/adjust

Muffler & suspension
  mounting bolts . . . . inspect

Power steering . . . . inspect **PS**

Throttle opener & control valve
  1983 . . . . inspect

Valve clearance . . . . adjust

FIRST 15 MO/15 MI—24 KM;
THEN EVERY 30 MO/30 MI—48 KM
Transaxle, automatic . . . . change fluid

Cooling system . . . . check level

EVERY 30 MO/30 MI—48 KM
Brake fluid . . . . replace **HB**
Inspect rear brakes & parking brake

Cooling system . . . . . change coolant **EC**
Inspect hoses & connections. 1983-85, initial service at
45 mi (72 km)

Front suspension & steering . . . . . inspect
2-wheel steering only

Fuel tank, lines & connections . . . . inspect

Transaxle, manual . . . . . . change lubricant

Air cleaner element . . . . replace

Choke mechanism . . . . clean

Drive belt(s) . . . . inspect/adjust

Spark plugs . . . . replace

EVERY 60 MI—96 KM
Catalytic converter heat shield
  auto. trans., 1983-84 . . . . inspect

Wheel bearings . . . . inspect
1983 rear, lubricate

Choke ex. FI . . . . inspect

Crankcase emission control
  system . . . . inspect
Check PCV valve & blowby filter

Distributor cap & rotor . . . . inspect

EGR system . . . . inspect

Evaporative control system . . . . . . inspect
Ex. FI

Fuel filter(s) . . . . replace
Check fuel hoses. Replace hoses on carburetted engines

Idle speed & CO . . . . inspect
Check idle control system

Ignition timing, control system,
  wiring . . . . inspect

Intake air temp. control ex. FI . . . . inspect

Secondary air supply . . . . inspect
Carburetted engines only

Speed sensor 1983 . . . . inspect

Throttle control unit . . . . inspect
Carburetted engines only

SEVERE SERVICE
Crankcase—Change oil & filter every 3 mo/
3 mi (5 km)

KEY TO LUBRICANTS
AF	DEXRON®-II Automatic Transmission Fluid
EC	Ethylene Glycol Coolant
GL-5	Gear Oil, API Service GL-5
HB	Hydraulic Brake Fluid, DOT 3 or 4
LM	Lithium Grease, with Moly
MO	Motor Oil
PS	Power Steering Fluid
SE	Motor Oil, API Service SE
SF	Motor Oil, API Service SF

CRANKCASE . . . . **SF**

CAPACITY, Refill:	Liters	Qt
All models	3.0	3.2

Capacity shown is without filter. When replacing filter, additional oil may be needed
Above 14°F (−10°C)	20W-40, 20W-50
Above −4°F (−20°C)	10W-40
−4° to 90°F (−20° to 32°C)	10W-30
Below 32°F (0°C)	5W-30
Below 14°F (−10°C)	5W-20

TRANSAXLE, Automatic . . . . **AF**

CAPACITY, Refill*:	Liters	Qt
1983 Civic	2.5	2.6
1983-85 Accord	2.8	3.0
Prelude	2.8	3.0
1984-85 Civic, CRX	2.4	2.5

*With the engine at operating temperature, shift transmis-
sion through all gears. Turn engine off and check fluid
level within 1 minute

TRANSAXLE, Manual . . . . **SE, SF**
Above 20°F (−7°C)	30
Above 0°F (−18°C)	20W-40
All temperatures	10W-30, 10W-40

CAPACITY, Refill:	Liters	Pt
4-speed	2.3	4.8
5-speed:		
Accord, Prelude	2.4	5.0
Civic: 1983	2.5	5.2
1984-85	2.3	4.8

DIFFERENTIAL **GL-5**
4WD Wagon:
Above 41°F (5°C)	90
Below 41°F (5°C)	80

CAPACITY, Refill:	Liters	Pt
1985 4WD Civic wagon . . .	1.0	2.2

HONDA
1986-92 Civic, CRX, Accord, Prelude

Perform the following maintenance services at the intervals indicated to keep both the vehicle and emission warranties in effect.

MI—MILES IN THOUSANDS
KM—KILOMETERS IN THOUSANDS

EVERY 6 MO/7.5 MI—12 KM
Clutch freeplay . . . . check/adjust

Crankcase . . . . change oil

Front brake pads & yoke or caliper slide
   performance . . . . inspect

Oil filter . . . . replace

Power steering . . . . inspect **PS**

EVERY 12 MO/15 MI—24 KM
Brake discs, hoses, lines, fluid . . . . inspect
1990-92, inspect rear disc brakes

Exhaust system . . . . inspect

Front wheel alignment . . . . . inspect/adjust

Suspension
   mounting bolts . . . . inspect

Clutch pedal travel 1986-87 . . . . check

Power steering . . . . inspect **PS**

Steering & suspension . . . . inspect
4-wheel steering only

Valve clearance . . . . adjust

EVERY 24 MO/30 MI—48 KM
Anti-lock brake
   system operation . . . . inspect

Brake fluid . . . . replace **HB**
Inspect rear drum brakes & parking brake lever free-play

Cooling system . . . . . . change coolant **EC**
Inspect hoses & connections. Initial service at 36 mo/45 mi (72 km)

Drive belt(s) . . . . inspect/adjust

Front suspension & steering . . . . . . inspect
2-wheel steering only. Initial service at 12 mo/15 mi (24 km)

Fuel tank, lines & connections . . . . inspect

Rear differential, 4WD . . change lubricant
1991, initial service at 36 mo/45 mi (72 km)

Transaxle, automatic . . . . change fluid

Transaxle, manual . . . . . change lubricant

Air cleaner element . . . . replace

Choke mechanism ex. FI . . . . clean

Spark plugs . . . . replace

EVERY 48 MO/60 MI—96 KM
Wheel bearings . . . . inspect

Anti-lock brake system
   high pressure hose . . . . .replace

Choke ex. FI . . . . inspect

Crankcase emission control system inspect
Check PCV valve & blowby filter

Distributor cap & rotor . . . . inspect

EGR system . . . . inspect

Evaporative control system . . . . . inspect

Fuel filter(s) . . . . replace
Check fuel hoses. Replace rubber hoses

Idle speed & CO . . . . inspect
Check idle control system

Ignition timing, control system,
   wiring . . . . inspect

Intake air temp. control ex. FI . . . . inspect
1988 Prelude, 1986-87 All

Secondary air supply 1986-89 . . . . inspect
Carburetted engines only

Throttle control . . . . inspect
Carburetted engines only

1990-92, EVERY 72 MO/90 MI— 144 KM
Timing belt . . . . replace
Also replace 1992 Prelude balancer belt

Water pump . . . . inspect

SEVERE SERVICE
Clutch freeplay—Check every 3 mo/3.75 mi (6 km)
Crankcase—Change oil & filter every: 1986-89, 3 mo/3 mi (5 km); 1990-92, 3 mo/3.75 mi (6 km)
Front & rear brakes, clutch pedal travel & power steering system—Inspect every 6 mo/7 mi (12 km)
Power steering system—inspect every 6 mo/7.5 mi (12 km)
Transaxles, automatic & manual—1988-92 Accord, Prelude, change fluid or lubricant every 12 mo/15 mi (24 km) when towing a trailer

---

KEY TO LUBRICANTS

AF	DEXRON®-II Automatic Transmission Fluid
EC	Ethylene Glycol Coolant
GL-5	Gear Oil, API Service GL-5
HB	Hydraulic Brake Fluid, DOT 3 or 4
PS	Power Steering Fluid Honda Part No. 08208-99961
SG	Motor Oil, API Service SG Use Energy Conserving-II oils

CRANKCASE . . . . SG

CAPACITY, Refill:	Liters	Qt
1988-91 Prelude	3.4	3.6
1992 Prelude: SOHC	3.5	3.7
DOHC	4.0	4.2
1990-92 Accord	3.5	3.7
1992 Civic (incl. filter)	3.3	3.5
1986-91 Others	3.0	3.2

Capacity shown is without filter. When replacing filter, additional oil may be needed
1986-87
Above 14°F (−10°C) 20W-40, 20W-50
Above −4°F (−20°C) 10W-40
−4° to 90°F (−20° to 32°C) 10W-30
Below 32°F (0°C) 5W-30
Below 14°F (−10°C) 5W-20
1988-92
Above 20°F (−7°C) 10W-30
All temperatures . . . . 5W-30 *
* Preferred

TRANSAXLE, Automatic . . . . AF

CAPACITY, Refill*:	Liters	Qt
Prelude: 1986-91	2.8	3.0
1992	2.4	2.5
Civic, CRX: 2WD: 1986-91 .	2.4	2.5
1992	2.7	2.9
4WD: 1986-90	2.7	2.9
1991	3.2	3.4
Accord: 1986-89	3.0	3.2
1990-92	2.4	2.5

* With the engine at operating temperature, shift transmission through all gears. Turn engine off and check fluid level within 1 minute

TRANSAXLE, Manual . . . . SG
Above 20°F (−7°C) 30
Above 0°F (−18°C) 20W-40
All temperatures . . . . 10W-30 *, 10W-40*
* Preferred

CAPACITY, Refill:	Liters	Pt
1986-87: 4-speed	2.3	4.8
5-speed:		
Accord, Prelude	2.4	5.0
Civic	2.3	4.8
1988-92: Civic, CRX, 2WD	1.8	3.8
4WD	2.3	4.8
Prelude	1.9	4.0
Accord, 1988-89	2.3	4.8
Accord, 1990-92	1.9	4.0

DIFFERENTIAL GL-5
Above 41°F (5°C) 90
Below 41°F (5°C) 80

CAPACITY, Refill:	Liters	Pt
4WD Civic wagon: 1986-87	1.0	2.2
1988-91	0.6	1.2

SERVICE LOCATIONS — ENGINE AND CHASSIS

HIIDP-1   HIIDP-1

HOOD RELEASE: Inside

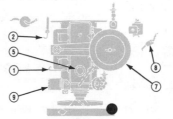

1986-89
1468cc
Excel

1990-91
1468cc FI
Excel, Scoupe

1984-87
1439cc, 1597cc
Pony, Stellar

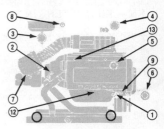

1992
1597cc DOHC
Elantra

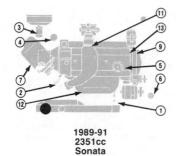

1989-91
2351cc
Sonata

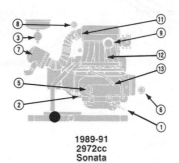

1989-91
2972cc
Sonata

① Crankcase dipstick
② Transmission dipstick
③ Brake fluid reservoir
④ Clutch fluid reservoir
⑤ Oil fill cap
⑥ Power steering reservoir
⑦ Air filter
⑧ Fuel filter
⑨ Oil filter
⑩ PCV filter
⑪ EGR valve
⑫ Oxygen sensor
⑬ PCV valve

0 FITTINGS
0 PLUGS

0 FITTINGS
0 PLUGS

0 FITTINGS
0 PLUGS

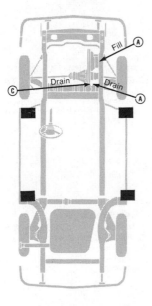

1986-92
Excel, Scoupe

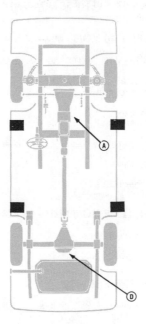

1984-87
Pony, Stellar

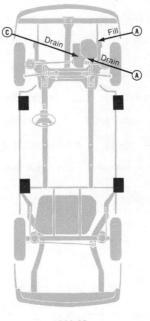

1989-92
Elantra, Sonata

■ Lift adapter position   ● Cooling system drain
○ Cooling system drain, some models

Ⓐ Manual transmission/transaxle, drain & fill
Ⓑ Transfer case, NOT USED

Ⓒ Automatic transaxle final drive, drain & fill
Ⓓ Differential, drain & fill

HYUNDAI
1984-87 Pony, 1985-87 Stellar

SERVICE AT TIME OR MILEAGE—WHICHEVER OCCURS FIRST

HIIPM1

MI — MILES IN THOUSANDS
KM — KILOMETERS IN THOUSANDS

EVERY 6 MO/7.5 MI — 12 KM
Front brakes .... inspect
Calipers, rotors, replace pads when lining is .040 in. thick or less. Check parking brake adjustment

Wheel nut torque .... check

Air cleaner element .... inspect
1987 Stellar

Cooling system .... inspect
1987 Stellar

Crankcase .... change oil

Drive belts .... inspect

EGR system .... inspect
Ex. 1987 Stellar

Fuel filter & lines .... inspect

Oil filter .... replace

Spark plugs .... inspect
Ex. 1987 Stellar

EVERY 12 MO/15 MI — 24 KM
Brake line & hoses .... inspect

Brake master cylinder .... check level **HB**

Chassis nuts & bolts .... check torque
1987 Stellar

Drive shaft U-joints .... inspect

Exhaust system .... inspect

Parking brake .... check/adjust

Rear brakes .... inspect
Inspect drums, replace lining when .040 in. or less

Rear differential .... check level

Steering & suspension .... inspect

Steering gearbox .... check level 90 **GL-4**

Transmission, manual ...... check level
1987 Stellar

Wheel alignment .... check/adjust

Air cleaner element .... replace

Cooling system .... inspect

Evaporative emission
control system .... inspect

Idle speed .... check/adjust
Also adjust idle mixture & choke

Ignition timing & wires ...... check/adjust
Also inspect points & condenser

Power steering .... check level **AF**
Check pump belt and hoses

Thermo valve .... check

Transmission, automatic ..... check level

Vacuum hoses & connections .... inspect
Ex. 1987 Stellar

Valve clearance .... adjust

EVERY 18 MO/22.5 MI — 36 KM
Spark plug wires .... replace
Ex. 1987 Stellar

EVERY 24 MO/30 MI — 48 KM
Wheel bearings .... inspect

Rear differential .... change fluid

Transmission, manual &
automatic .... change fluid

Steering gearbox ... change fluid 90 **GL-4**

Air cleaner element .... replace
1987 Stellar

Brake fluid .... change **HB**

Cooling system ...... change coolant **EC**

Drive belt .... replace
1987 Stellar alternator only

Fuel filter .... replace
1987 Stellar

Spark plugs .... replace

Timing belt .... inspect
1987 Stellar

Vacuum & vent hoses .... inspect
1987 Stellar

1986-87, EVERY 36 MO/45 MI — 72 KM
Cooling system ...... replace coolant **EC**

EVERY 40 MO/50 MI — 80 KM
EGR system, 1987 .... inspect

Evaporative emission
control system .... inspect

Fuel filter .... replace
Ex. 1987 Stellar

Ignition timing .... check/adjust

PCV valve .... inspect

Rubber hoses .... replace
Vacuum, air pump, PCV

EVERY 48 MO/60 MI — 96 KM
Carbon canister .... inspect

Timing belt .... replace
1987 Stellar

SEVERE SERVICE
Brake fluid — 1987, change every 12 mo/15 mi (24 km)

Crankcase — Change oil & filter every 3 mo/6 mi (12 km)

Steering, suspension, driveshafts, & boots — Inspect more frequently

Transmission, manual & automatic — Change fluid every 12 mo/15 mi (24 km)

KEY TO LUBRICANTS

AF	DEXRON®-II Automatic Transmission Fluid
CC	Motor Oil, API Service CC
EC	Ethylene Glycol Coolant
GL-4	Gear Oil, API Service GL-4
GL-5	Gear Oil, API Service GL-5
HB	Hydraulic Brake Fluid, DOT 3
LM	Lithium Grease, EP
SF	Motor Oil, API Service SF

CRANKCASE .... SF, SF/CC

CAPACITY, Refill:	Liters	Qt
All models	3.5	3.7

Capacity shown is without filter. When replacing filter, additional oil may be needed

1987
Above 32°F (0°C) ... 20W-20, 20W-40, 20W-50
Above −8°F (−22°C) .. 10W-30, 10W-40, 10W-50
Below 60°F (16°C) 5W-20, 5W-30, 5W-40

1984-86
60° to 86°F (16° to 30°C) 30
32° to 60°F (0° to 16°C) 20
14° to 60°F (−10° to 16°C) 20W-20
0° to 32°F (−18° to 0°C) 10W
−4° to 115°F (−20° to 45°C) ... 10W-30, 10W-40
−40° to 86°F (−40° to 30°C) 5W-30

TRANSMISSION, Automatic .... **AF**

CAPACITY, Refill*:	Liters	Qt
All models	4.0	4.2

*With the engine at operating temperature, shift transmission through all gears. Check fluid level in PARK and add fluid as needed

TRANSMISSION,
Manual .. 75W-90, 80W-90 **GL-4, GL-5**

CAPACITY, Refill:	Liters	Pt
Pony: 4-speed	1.7	3.6
5-speed	2.0	4.2
Stellar	2.0	4.2

DIFFERENTIAL 90 **GL-5**
Below 14°F (−10°C), 75W-90

CAPACITY, Refill:	Liters	Pt
Pony	1.1	2.4
Stellar	1.0	2.2

SERVICE AT TIME OR MILEAGE—WHICHEVER OCCURS FIRST

HIIPM2   HIIPM2

Perform the following maintenance services at the intervals indicated to keep both the vehicle and emission warranties in effect.

MI—MILES IN THOUSANDS
KM—KILOMETERS IN THOUSANDS

EVERY 6 MO/7.5 MI—12 KM
Driveshaft & steering
  boots, Canada . . . . inspect

Front brakes . . . . inspect
Calipers, rotors, replace pads when lining is .040 in.
thick or less. Canada, inspect parking brake

Air cleaner element, Canada . . . . . inspect

Choke, Canada . . . . inspect

Cooling system, Canada . . . . inspect

Crankcase . . . . change oil

Fuel filter & lines, Canada . . . . inspect

Transmission, manual,
  Canada . . . . check level

Oil filter . . . . replace

Vacuum hoses, Canada . . . . inspect

EVERY 12 MO/15 MI—24 KM
Brake lines & hoses . . . . inspect
U.S., check fluid level

Drive shafts & CV boots, U.S. . . . . inspect

Exhaust system . . . . inspect

Rear brakes . . . . inspect
Inspect drums, replace lining when .040 in. or less.
Also check parking brake adjustment

Steering and suspension system . . inspect

Brake master cylinder . . . . check level **HB**

Cooling system, U.S. . . . . inspect

Cooling system,
  Canada . . . . replace coolant **EC**
Flush system

Drive belts . . . . inspect

Idle speed . . . . check/adjust

Power steering . . . . check level **AF**

Spark plugs, Canada . . . . inspect

Throttle positioner . . . . inspect
Initial service only

Trans., automatic, Canada . . . check level

Valve clearance, 4-cyl. . . . . adjust
Sonata jet valve only

EVERY 24 MO/30 MI—48 KM
Rear wheel
  bearings . . . . inspect/lubricate **LM**

Transmission, manual &
  automatic . . . . change fluid

Air cleaner element . . . . replace

Brake fluid, U.S. . . . . replace **HB**
Canada, inspect level

Choke, U.S. . . . . inspect

Cooling system, U.S. . . . replace coolant **EC**
Flush system

Drive belt . . . . replace
Alternator only

EGR system, Canada . . . . inspect

Fuel filter & lines, U.S. . . . . inspect

Spark plugs . . . . replace

Timing belt, Canada . . . . inspect

EVERY 40 MO/50 MI—80 KM
Brake fluid, Canada . . . . replace

Carbon canister . . . . replace

EGR system, U.S. . . . . inspect

Evaporative emission
  control system . . . . inspect

Fuel filter . . . . replace

Fuel & vapor hoses . . . . replace

Ignition timing . . . . check/adjust
Excel only

Ignition wires, Excel . . . . replace

Oxygen sensor . . . . replace

PCV valve . . . . inspect

Vacuum hoses . . . . replace

Throttle positioner . . . . inspect

EVERY 48 MO/60 MI—96 KM
Timing belt . . . . replace

SEVERE SERVICE
Air cleaner element & U.S. PCV system—
Inspect/replace more frequently

Brake fluid, transmission lubricant,
Canada—Replace every 12 mo/15 mi (24 km)

Crankcase—Change oil & filter every 3 mo/3 mi (4.8 km)

Exhaust system, Canada—Inspect every 6 mo/7.5 mi (12 km)

Brake pads & linings—Inspect more often

Spark plugs, U.S.—Replace every 18 mo/24 mi (40 km)

Steering, suspension, driveshafts, & boots, U.S.—Inspect every 6 mo/7.5 mi (12 km)

KEY TO LUBRICANTS

AF	DEXRON®-II ATF
AP	HYUNDAI ATF Automatic Transmission Fluid or MOPAR ATF-PLUS
CD	Motor Oil, API Service CD
EC	Ethylene Glycol Coolant
GL-4	Gear Oil, API Service GL-4
HB	Hydraulic Brake Fluid, DOT 3
LM	Lithium Grease, EP
SG	Motor Oil, API Service SG

CRANKCASE . . . . **SG**

CAPACITY, Refill:	Liters	Qt
Excel	3.0	3.2
Sonata: 4-cyl.	3.5	3.7
V6	3.7	3.9

Capacity shown is without filter. When replacing filter, additional oil may be needed
Above 32°F (0°C) 20W-20, 20W-40, 20W-50
Above −10°F (−23°C) . 10W-30, 10W-40, 10W-50
Below 60°F (16°C) 5W-20*, 5W-30, 5W-40
* Not recommended for sustained high speed driving

TRANSAXLE, Automatic
1986 . . . . **AF, AP**
1987-89 . . . . **AP**

CAPACITY, Refill*:	Liters	Qt
All models	4.0	4.2

* With the engine at operating temperature, shift transmission through all gears. Check fluid level in NEUTRAL and add fluid as needed

TRANSAXLE,
Manual . . **75W-85W, 75W-90 GL-4, GL-5**

CAPACITY, Refill:	Liters	Pt
Excel	2.1	4.4
Sonata	2.5	5.4

HYUNDAI
1990-92 Elantra, Excel, Scoupe, Sonata

HIIPM3   HIIPM3

Perform the following maintenance services at the intervals indicated to keep both the vehicle and emission warranties in effect.

MI—MILES IN THOUSANDS
KM—KILOMETERS IN THOUSANDS

U.S., AT FIRST & SECOND 5 MO/7.5 MI—12 KM;
THEN EVERY 10 MO/7.5 MI—12 KM
CANADA,
EVERY 6 MO/7.5 MI—12 KM
Crankcase . . . . change oil

Oil filter . . . . replace

U.S.,
AT FIRST 10 MO/15 MI—24 KM;
THEN EVERY 20 MO/15 MI—24 KM
CANADA, EVERY 15 MI—24 KM
Brake lines & hoses . . . . inspect

Drive shafts & CV boots . . . . inspect

Front brakes . . . . Inspect
Calipers, rotors, replace pads when lining is .040 in. thick or less

Power steering reservoir . . check level **AF**

Power steering system 1990 . . . . . inspect

Brake master cylinder . . . . check level **HB**

Cooling system 1990 . . . . inspect

Fuel lines & connections 1990 . . . . inspect

Power steering . . . . check level **AF**

Transmission, automatic . . . . . check level

Valve clearance, 4-cyl. . . . . adjust
Sonata 2.4L jet valve only

U.S., EVERY 30 MO/30 MI—48 KM
CANADA, EVERY 30 MI—48 KM
Exhaust system . . . . inspect

Rear brakes . . . . inspect
Inspect drums, replace lining when .040 in. or less. Also check parking brake adjustment

Steering and suspension system . . inspect

Rear wheel bearings . . . . inspect

Transaxle, automatic . . . . change fluid

Transaxle, manual . . . . check level

Air cleaner element . . . . replace

Brake fluid . . . . replace **HB**
Canada, at least every 24 mo

Cooling system . . . . . . replace coolant **EC**
Flush system. Canada, at least every 24 mo.

Drive belts . . . . inspect

Spark plugs . . . . replace
Ex. 1992 V6

Timing belt, 1990 . . . . inspect

U.S., EVERY 60 MO/52.5 MI—84 KM
CANADA, EVERY 52.5 MI—84 KM
Carbon canister 1990 . . . . replace

EGR system 1990 . . . . inspect

Fuel filter . . . . replace

Fuel & vapor hoses . . . . inspect
1990 All, 1991 Canada only, replace

Fuel tank cap . . . . inspect
1990 All, 1991 Canada only, replace

Ignition timing . . . . check/adjust
1990 Excel only

Oxygen sensor 1990 . . . . replace

PCV valve 1990 . . . . inspect

Vacuum hoses . . . . inspect
1990 All, 1991 Canada only, replace

U.S., EVERY 70 MO/60 MI—96 KM
CANADA, EVERY 60 MI—96 KM
Ignition wires 1990 . . . . inspect

Drive belt 1990 . . . . replace
Alt. & PS only

Spark plugs . . . . replace
1992 V6

Timing belt . . . . replace

SEVERE SERVICE
Air cleaner element—Inspect/replace more frequently

Crankcase—Change oil & filter every 3 mo/3 mi (4.8 km)

Brake system—Inspect more often

Spark plugs—Replace every 18 mo/24 mi (40 km)

Steering, suspension, driveshafts, & boots—Inspect every 6 mo/7.5 mi (12 km)

KEY TO LUBRICANTS

AF	DEXRON®-II ATF
AP	Hyundai ATF Automatic Transmission Fluid or MOPAR ATF-PLUS
CD	Motor Oil, API Service CD
EC	Ethylene Glycol Coolant
GL-4	Gear Oil, API Service GL-4
HB	Hydraulic Brake Fluid, DOT 3
LM	Lithium Grease, EP
SG	Motor Oil, API Service SG

CRANKCASE . . . . **SG, SG/CD**

CAPACITY, Refill:	Liters	Qt
Excel, Scoupe	3.0	3.2
Elantra	4.0	4.2
Sonata: 2.0L	3.3	3.5
2.4L	3.5	3.7
3.0L	3.7	3.9

Capacity shown is without filter. When replacing filter, additional oil may be needed
Above 32°F (0°C) 20W-20, 20W-40, 20W-50
Above −10°F (−23°C) . 10W-30, 10W-40, 10W-50
Below 60°F (16°C) 5W-20*, 5W-30, 5W-40
*Not recommended for sustained high speed driving

TRANSAXLE, Automatic . . . . **AP**

CAPACITY, Refill*:	Liters	Qt
All models	4.0	4.2

*With the engine at operating temperature, shift transmission through all gears. Check fluid level in NEUTRAL and add fluid as needed

TRANSAXLE,
Manual . . 75W-85W, 75W-90 **GL-4, GL-5**

CAPACITY, Refill:	Liters	Pt
Excel, Scoupe:		
4-speed	1.7	3.6
5-speed	1.8	3.8
Elantra	1.8	3.8
Sonata: 1989-91	2.5	5.4
1992	1.8	3.8

SERVICE LOCATIONS — ENGINE AND CHASSIS

HOOD RELEASE: Inside

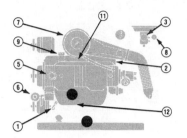

1985-89
I-Mark
1471cc 2V

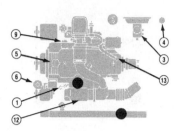

1987-89
I-Mark
1471cc Turbo

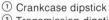

① Crankcase dipstick
② Transmission dipstick
③ Brake fluid reservoir
④ Clutch fluid reservoir
⑤ Oil fill cap
⑥ Power steering reservoir
⑦ Air filter
⑧ Fuel filter
⑨ Oil filter
⑩ PCV filter
⑪ EGR valve
⑫ Oxygen sensor
⑬ PCV valve

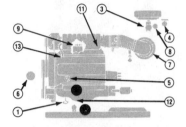

1989-92
I-Mark, Stylus, Impulse FWD
1588cc DOHC,
1809cc DOHC

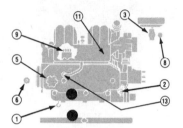

1990-92
Stylus, Impulse
1588cc SOHC

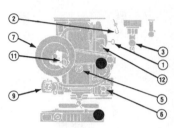

1983-87
I-Mark, Pickup, Trooper
1817cc Gas,
1949cc 2V

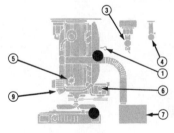

1983-85
I-Mark
1817cc
Diesel

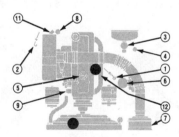

1983-87
Impulse
1949cc FI

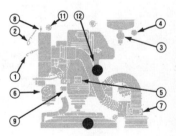

1985-89
Impulse
1994cc Turbo

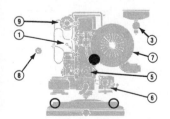

1983-87
Pickup, Trooper
2238cc Diesel

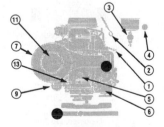

1986-92
Amigo, Pickup, Trooper
2256cc 2V

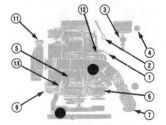

1988-92
Amigo, Pickup, Trooper,
Impulse, Rodeo
2256cc FI,
2559cc

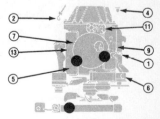

1989-92
Pickup, Trooper, Rodeo
V6 2.8L, 3.1L

● Cooling system drain   ○ Cooling system drain, some models

SERVICE LOCATIONS — ENGINE AND CHASSIS

0 FITTINGS
0 PLUGS

0 FITTINGS
0 PLUGS

0 FITTINGS
0 PLUGS

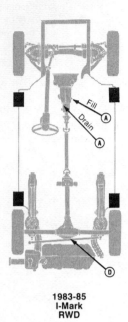

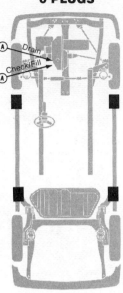

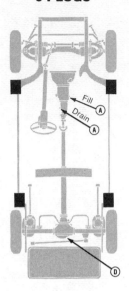

1983-85
I-Mark
RWD

1985-89
I-Mark
FWD
1990-92
Stylus, Impulse FWD

1983-89
Impulse

7-10 FITTINGS, 1983-87

8-9 FITTINGS, 1983-87
1-2 FITTINGS, 1988-92

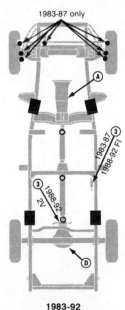

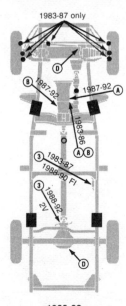

1983-92
2WD Amigo,
Pickup, Rodeo

1983-92
4WD Amigo, Pickup
Trooper, Rodeo

ⓐ Manual transmission/transaxle,
drain & fill

ⓑ Transfer case, drain & fill

ⓒ Automatic transaxle final drive,
NOT USED

ⓓ Differential, drain & fill

■ Lift adapter position   • Fitting   o Fitting, some models

SERVICE AT TIME OR MILEAGE—WHICHEVER OCCURS FIRST

IUIPM1   IUIPM1

Perform the following maintenance services at the intervals indicated to keep both the vehicle and emission warranties in effect.

MI — MILES IN THOUSANDS
KM — KILOMETERS IN THOUSANDS

1983 DIESEL,
EVERY 12 MO/3.75 MI — 6 KM
1984-85 DIESEL,
GASOLINE,
EVERY 12 MO/7.5 MI — 12 KM
Crankcase . . . . change oil

Oil filter . . . . replace
Gasoline, at first oil change, then every other. Diesel, every oil change

EVERY 12 MONTHS
Air conditioning system . . . . inspect

AT FIRST 7.5 MI — 12 KM;
THEN EVERY 30 MI — 48 KM
Rear differential . . . . change lubricant

Transmission, transaxle
  manual . . . . change lubricant
Initial service for RWD only

EVERY 12 MO/7.5 MI — 12 KM
Body . . . . lubricate
Hinges **MO**, automatic transmission shift linkage & clutch pivot points **MO**, clutch fork joint & cross shaft **LM**, parking brake cables **LM**

Brake line & hoses . . . . inspect
Impulse, check hydraulic clutch lines & hoses

Front disc brake pads . . . . inspect
RWD cars only. Replace when lining is .067 in. or less

Exhaust system . . . . inspect
RWD cars only

Propeller shaft flange bolts . . . . torque
18-20 ft-lbs

Rear axle . . . . check level

Steering & suspension . . . lube fittings **LM**
All RWD cars only, also inspect front end components

Transmission, manual . . . . . . check level

Brake master cyl. . . . . check level **HB**

Clutch fluid . . . . check level **HB**

Coolant . . . . check level **EC**

Fluid leaks under vehicle . . . . check

Power steering reservoir . . check level **AF**
Also check system hoses

Tires & wheels . . . . inspect
Check for wear, vibrations, air pressure

Transmission, automatic . . . . . check level

Body . . . . flush
Wash under car every spring

EVERY 15 MI — 24 KM
Engine idle speed, Gasoline . . . . . adjust
RWD I-Mark ex. Calif.

Valve clearance . . . . check/adjust
SOHC engines only

EVERY 12 MO/15 MI — 24 KM
Fuel tank, cap & lines . . . . inspect

Rear drum brakes . . . . inspect
RWD cars only. Replace shoes when lining is .039 in. or less. Check all other hardware & parking brake adjustment

Brake & clutch pedals . . . . . . lubricate **MO**
Also check clutch adjustment

Brake fluid, Impulse . . . . change **HB**

Cooling system . . . . inspect
Pressure test system & inspect cap. Check condition of all hoses & tighten hose clamps

Cruise control, Impulse . . . inspect system

Throttle linkage . . . . check

EVERY 22.5 MI — 36 KM
Power steering fluid . . . . change **AF**
FWD I-Mark, Impulse only

EVERY 30 MI — 48 KM
Wheel bearings . . . . repack **WB**
Front on RWD cars, rear on FWD cars

Transmission, transaxle
  automatic . . . . change fluid
1988-89 Impulse, initial service at 15 mi (24km)

Air cleaner element . . . . replace

Engine idle speed, Diesel . . . . adjust

Fuel filter, Diesel . . . . replace

Spark plugs . . . . replace

EVERY 24 MO/30 MI — 48 KM
Cooling system . . . . . . replace coolant **EC**
Flush system

Carb. choke & hoses . . . . inspect
I-Mark 2V only

Drive belts . . . . inspect

EVERY 45 MI — 72 KM
Power steering hoses . . . . change
FWD I-Mark only

EVERY 60 MI — 96 KM
Timing belt . . . . replace
1988-89 only

Valve clearance . . . . check/adjust
DOHC engine only

SEVERE SERVICE
Crankcase — Change oil every 3 mo/3 mi (4.8 km). Change oil filter every other oil change

Brake pads & linings — Inspect more often

Transmission, automatic — Change fluid & filter every 15 mi (24 km)

KEY TO LUBRICANTS
See other Isuzu Charts

CRANKCASE
Gasoline:
  1987-89 . . . . SF, SF/CC, SF/CD
  1983-86 . . . . SE, SE/CC, SF
Diesel . . . . . . SE/CC, SF/CC, SF/CD

CAPACITY, Refill:	Liters	Qt
1471cc	2.8	3.0
1588cc DOHC	3.8	4.0
1817cc Gasoline, 1949cc, 1994cc, 2254cc	3.2	3.4
1817cc Diesel	5.2	5.5

Gasoline engines, capacity shown is without filter. When replacing filter, additional oil may be needed
Diesel engine, capacity includes oil filter

1987-89:
I-Mark:
Above 40°F (5°C) 30
Above 10°F (–12°C) . . 15W-40, 20W-40, 20W-50
Above 0°F (–18°C) 10W-30
Below 60°F (16°C), Turbo & DOHC 5W-30
All temperatures, ex. Turbo, DOHC 5W-30
Impulse
Above 77°F (25°C) 40, 50
Above 5°F (–15°C) . . . 15W-40, 20W-40, 20W-50
32° to 100°F (0° to 38°C) 30
5° to 60°F (–15° to 16°C) 20W
–13° to 100°F (–25° to 38°C) 10W-30
–13° to 32°F (–25° to 0°C) 10W
Below 100°F (38°C) 5W-30
1983-86:
Above 40°F (5°C) 30
Above 20°F (–7°C) . . 20W-20, 20W-40, 20W-50†
Above 0°F (–18°C) . . . . 10W-30, 10W-40†
0° to 60°F (–18° to 15°C) 10W
Below 60°F (15°C) 5W-30
Below 20°F (–7°C) 5W-20
†10W-40, 20W-50 not recommended for 1986 models
Diesel:
Above 75°F (24°C) 40
Above 32°F (0°C) 30
Above 10°F (–14°C) . . 15W-40, 20W-40, 20W-50
Below 85°F (30°C) 10W-30
Below 10°F (–14°C) . . . . 5W-30†
†Not recommended for sustained high speed driving

TRANSMISSION/TRANSAXLE,
  Automatic . . . . **AF**

CAPACITY, Initial Refill*:	Liters	Qt
All models	2.0	2.1

* With the engine at operating temperature, shift transmission through all gears. Check fluid level in PARK and add fluid as needed

TRANSMISSION/TRANSAXLE, Manual
I-Mark FWD . . . . 5W-30 **SF**
In areas where temperature is consistently over 90°F (32°C), 15W-40, 20W-40, 20W-50
Impulse RWD . . . . **SF**
Above 90°F (32°C), 40; 0° to 90°F (–18° to 32°C), 30; below 50°F (10°C), 10W-30; all temperatures, 5W-30†
†Preferred
I-Mark RWD . . . . **SF**
1983
Above 50°F (10°C), 40; 0° to 90°F (–18° to 32°C), 30; below 50°F (10°C), 10W-30
1984-85
Above 90°F (32°C), 40; below 90°F (32°C), 5W-30

CAPACITY, Refill:	Liters	Pt
1985-87 I-Mark FWD	2.8	5.6
1988-89 I-Mark	1.9	4.0
RWD: 4-speed	1.3	2.6
5-speed	1.6	3.3

DIFFERENTIAL, RWD Models
Standard **GL-5**
Limited-Slip . . . . **GL-5★**
Above 50°F (10°C), 140; 0° to 90°F (–18° to 32°C), 90; below 50°F (10°C), 80

CAPACITY, Refill:	Liters	Pt
1988-89 All	1.5	3.2
1984-86 ex. Turbo	1.0	2.2
1984-86 Turbo	1.5	3.2
1983	1.3	2.7

ISUZU
1990-92 Impulse, Stylus

Perform the following maintenance services at the intervals indicated to keep both the vehicle and emission warranties in effect.

MI — MILES IN THOUSANDS
KM — KILOMETERS IN THOUSANDS

TURBO,
EVERY 6 MO/5 MI — 8 KM
OTHERS,
EVERY 12 MO/7.5 MI — 12 KM
Crankcase . . . . change oil

Oil filter . . . . replace
At first oil change, then every other

EVERY 12 MO/7.5 MI — 12 KM
Body . . . . lubricate
Hinges **MO**, transaxle shift linkage & clutch pivot points
MO, clutch fork joint & cross shaft **LM**, parking brake
cables **LM**

Rear axle . . . . check level

Transmission, manual . . . . check level

Brake master cylinder . . . . check level **HB**

Coolant . . . . check level **EC**

Fluid leaks under vehicle . . . . check

Power steering reservoir . . check level **AF**
Also check system hoses

Tires & wheels . . . . inspect
Check for wear, vibrations, air pressure

Transmission, automatic . . . . . check level

Body . . . . flush
Wash under car every spring

EVERY 15 MI — 24 KM
Valve clearance . . . . check/adjust
SOHC engines only

EVERY 12 MO/15 MI — 24 KM
Fuel tank, cap & lines . . . . inspect

Cooling system . . . . inspect
Pressure test system & inspect cap. Check condition of
all hoses & tighten hose clamps

EVERY 24 MO/22.5 MI — 36 KM
Power steering fluid . . . . change **AF**

EVERY 30 MI — 48 KM
Transaxle, automatic . . . . change fluid

Transaxle, manual . . . . . . change lubricant

Transfer case, 4WD . . . . change lubricant

Propellor shaft, 4WD . . check/lubricate **LM**
Tighten flange bolts to 26 ft-lbs (35 Nm)

Rear axle, 4WD . . . . change lubricant

Air cleaner element . . . . replace

Spark plugs . . . . replace

EVERY 24 MO/30 MI — 48 KM
Cooling system . . . . . . replace coolant **EC**
Flush system

Drive belts . . . . inspect

EVERY 60 MI — 96 KM
Timing belt . . . . replace

Valve clearance . . . . check/adjust
1990-91 DOHC engine only

SEVERE SERVICE
Crankcase—Change oil every 3 mo/3 mi
(4.8 km). Change oil filter every other oil
change

Brake pads & linings — Inspect more often

Air cleaner element — Change more frequently

Transmission, automatic — Change fluid &
filter every 15 mi (24 km)

KEY TO LUBRICANTS

AF	DEXRON®-II Automatic Transmission Fluid
CD	Motor Oil, API Service CD
EC	Ethylene Glycol Coolant
GL-5	Gear Oil, API Service GL-5
HB	Hydraulic Brake Fluid DOT 3
LM	Lithium Multipurpose Grease
SF	Motor Oil, API Service SF
SG	Motor Oil, API Service SG

CRANKCASE . . . . **SG, SG/CD**

CAPACITY, Refill:	Liters	Qt
1588cc SOHC	3.0	3.2
1588cc, 1809cc DOHC . .	3.8	4.0

Capacity shown is without filter. When replacing filter, additional oil may be needed
Above 40°F (5°C) 30
Above 10°F (−12°C) . . 15W-40, 20W-40, 20W-50
Above 0°F (−18°C) 10W-30
Below 60°F (16°C), DOHC 5W-30
All temperatures, ex. DOHC 5W-30

TRANSAXLE, Automatic . . . . **AF**

CAPACITY, Total Refill†:	Liters	Qt
All models	3.0	3.2

†Total (dry) fill shown. Use less fluid when refilling

TRANSAXLE, Manual . . . . **5W-30 SF**
In areas where temperature is consistently over 90°F
(32°C), 15W-40, 20W-40, 20W-50

CAPACITY, Refill:	Liters	Pt
All	1.9	4.0

TRANSFER CASE **80W-90 GL-5**

CAPACITY, Refill:	Liters	Pt
Impulse 4WD	1.3	2.8

REAR DIFFERENTIAL **GL-5**
Above 50°F (10°C) 140
0° to 90°F (−18° to 32°C) 90
Below 50°F (10°C) 80

CAPACITY, Refill:	Liters	Pt
Impulse 4WD	0.7	1.4

SERVICE AT TIME OR MILEAGE—WHICHEVER OCCURS FIRST

IUIPM2   IUIPM2

Perform the following maintenance services at the intervals indicated to keep both the vehicle and emission warranties in effect.

MI — MILES IN THOUSANDS
KM — KILOMETERS IN THOUSANDS

**1983 DIESEL,
EVERY 12 MO/3.75 MI — 6 KM
1984-87 DIESEL,
1983-87 GASOLINE,
EVERY 12 MO/7.5 MI — 12 KM**

Crankcase . . . . change oil

Oil filter . . . . replace
Gasoline, at first oil change, then every other. Diesel, every oil change

EVERY 12 MONTHS
Air conditioning system . . . . inspect

AT FIRST 7.5 MI — 12 KM;
THEN EVERY 30 MI — 48 KM
Front & rear
    differentials . . . . change lubricant

Transmission, manual, transfer
    case . . . . change lubricant

EVERY 7.5 MI — 12 KM
Accelerator linkage . . . . lubricate **MO**

Tires . . . . rotate

EVERY 12 MO/7.5 MI — 12 KM
Body . . . . lubricate
Hinges **MO**, automatic transmission shift linkage & clutch pivot points **MO**, clutch fork joint & cross shaft **LM**, parking brake cables **LM**

Brake line & hoses . . . . inspect

Front disc brake pads . . . . inspect
Replace when lining is .067 in. or less

Exhaust system . . . . inspect

Propeller shaft flange bolts . . . . torque
18-20 ft-lbs

Rear axle . . . . check level

Steering & suspension . . . lube fittings **LM**
Also inspect front end components

Transmission, manual . . . . check level

Brake master cyl. . . . . check level **HB**

Clutch fluid . . . . check level **HB**
When equipped with hydraulic clutch

Coolant . . . . check level **EC**

Fluid leaks under vehicle . . . . check

Power steering reservoir . . check level **AF**
Also check system hoses

Tires & wheels . . . . inspect
Check for wear, vibration, air pressure

Transmission, automatic . . . . . check level

Water separator, Diesel . . . . drain

EVERY 15 MI — 24 KM
Engine idle speed, Gasoline . . . . . . adjust
Ex. California

Valve clearance . . . . check/adjust

EVERY 12 MO/15 MI — 24 KM
Fuel tank, cap & lines . . . . inspect

Rear drum brakes . . . . inspect
Replace shoes when lining is .039 in. or less. Check all other hardware & parking brake adjustment

Brake & clutch pedals . . . . . . lubricate **MO**
Also check freeplay

Steering gearbox . . . . . . check level **GL-5**

4WD universal joints
    & slip yokes . . . . lubricate Moly **LM**

Cooling system . . . . inspect
Pressure test system & inspect cap. Check condition of all hoses & tighten hose clamps

Cruise control, Impulse . . . inspect system

Drive belts . . . . inspect
Diesel eng.

Throttle linkage . . . . check

EVERY 22.5 MI — 36 KM
Power steering fluid . . . . change **AF**
1983-85

EVERY 30 MI — 48 KM
Clutch lines & hoses . . . . inspect

Front wheel bearings . . . . repack **WB**

Transfer case, w/AT . . . . inspect fluid

Transmission, automatic . . . . change fluid

Air cleaner element . . . . replace

Air cleaner housing . . . . inspect
Ex. California

Engine idle speed, Diesel . . . . adjust

Fuel filter . . . . replace
Ex. California

Ignition wires . . . . inspect

Power steering fluid . . . . change **AF**
1986-87

Spark plugs . . . . replace

Steering gearbox . . change lubricant **GL-5**

EVERY 24 MO/30 MI — 48 KM
Air pump . . . . inspect

Cooling system . . . . . . replace coolant **EC**
Flush system

Carb. choke & hoses . . . . inspect

Distributor advance . . . . check

Drive belts . . . . inspect
Gasoline eng.

EGR system . . . . inspect

Ignition timing . . . . check/adjust
1986-87

PCV valve & hose . . . . clean

Steering gearbox . . . . check/adjust
1986-87

EVERY 45 MI — 72 KM
Power steering hoses . . . . change

EVERY 60 MI — 96 KM
Timing belt . . . . replace
1986-87 2.3L

SEVERE SERVICE
Crankcase—Change oil every 3 mo/3 mi (4.8 km). Change oil filter every other oil change

Brake pads & linings—Inspect more often

Transmission, automatic—Change fluid & filter every 15 mi (24 km)

KEY TO LUBRICANTS
AF	DEXRON®-II Automatic Transmission Fluid
CC	Motor Oil, API Service CC
CD	Motor Oil, API Service CD
EC	Ethylene Glycol Coolant
GL-5	Gear Oil, API Service GL-5
GL-5★	Special Lubricant for Limited-Slip Differential
HB	Hydraulic Brake Fluid, DOT 3 or 4
LM	Lithium Grease
MO	Motor Oil
SE	Motor Oil, API Service SE
SF	Motor Oil, API Service SF
WB	Wheel Bearing Grease

CRANKCASE
Gasoline . . . . **SE, SE/CC, SF**
Diesel:
Non-Turbo . . . . **SE/CC, SF/CC, SF/CD**
Turbo . . . . **SE/CC, SF/CC, SE/CD, SF/CD, CD†**

†SE/CD, SF/CD, CD are preferred

CAPACITY, Refill:	Liters	Qt
1817cc, 1949cc	3.2	3.4
2254cc	3.8	4.0
Diesel	5.7	6.0

Gasoline engines, capacity shown is without filter. When replacing filter, additional oil may be needed
Diesel engines, capacity includes oil filter

Gasoline engines:
Above 40°F (5°C) 30
Above 20°F (−7°C) . . 20W-20, 20W-40, 20W-50†
Above 0°F (−18°C) . . . . . . 10W-30, 10W-40†
0° to 60°F (−18° to 15°C) 10W
Below 60°F (15°C) 5W-30
Below 20°F (−7°C) 5W-20
†10W-40, 20W-50 not recommended for 1986-87 models

Diesel engines:
Above 75°F (24°C) 40
Above 32°F (0°C) 30
Above 10°F (−14°C) . . 15W-40, 20W-40, 20W-50
Below 85°F (30°C) 10W-30
Below 10°F (−14°C) . . . . 5W-30†

†Not recommended for sustained high speed driving

TRANSMISSION, Automatic . . . . **AF**
CAPACITY, Initial Refill*:	Liters	Qt
All	2.0	2.1

*With the engine at operating temperature, shift transmission through all gears. Check fluid level in PARK and add fluid as needed

TRANSMISSION, Manual &
MT Transfer Case . . . . **SF**
1985-87:
Above 90°F (32°C), 40; all temperatures, 5W-30†
1983-84:
Above 50°F (10°C), 40; 0° to 90°F (−18° to 32°C), 30; below 50°F (10°C), 10W-30
†Preferred

CAPACITY, Refill:	Liters	Pt
2WD: 4-speed	1.3	2.6
5-speed	1.6	3.3
4WD: 1986-87	4.5	9.7
1983-85	2.4	5.2

DIFFERENTIAL **GL-5**
Above 50°F (10°C), 140; 0° to 90°F (−18° to 32°C), 90; below 50°F (10°C), 80W-90
CAPACITY, Refill:	Liters	Pt
Front	0.8	1.7
Rear	1.4	2.9

ISUZU
1988-92 Amigo, Pickup, Rodeo, Trooper

Perform the following maintenance services at the intervals indicated to keep both the vehicle and emission warranties in effect.

MI — MILES IN THOUSANDS
KM — KILOMETERS IN THOUSANDS

AT FIRST 7.5 MI — 12 KM; THEN AT 60 MI — 96 KM; THEN EVERY 15 MI — 24 KM
Engine idle speed . . . . adjust
Ex. 2.8L

EVERY 7.5 MI — 12 KM
Rear axle . . . . check level
Rodeo, Pickup w/V6 only

Throttle body
   mounting bolts, 2.8L, 3.1L . . . . . . torque

Tires . . . . rotate

EVERY 6 MO/7.5 MI — 12 KM
Accelerator linkage . . . . lubricate **MO**

Body . . . . lubricate
Hinges **MO**, automatic transmission shift linkage & clutch pivot points **MO**, clutch fork joint & cross shaft **LM**, parking brake cables **LM**

Ball joints, Trooper . . . . lubricate **LM**

Front & rear
   propeller shafts . . . . lubricate
Sliding yokes, **LM**; U-joints, Moly **LM**

EVERY 12 MO/7.5 MI — 12 KM
Brake line & hoses . . . . inspect

Propeller shaft flange bolts . . . . . . torque
20-25 ft-lbs (30-34 Nm)

Suspension & steering . . . . inspect
1990-92 Amigo, Pickup only

Crankcase . . . . change oil

Oil filter . . . . replace
At first oil change, then every other

Exhaust system . . . . inspect

Automatic transmission . . . . . . check level

Battery fluid level, ex. 2.8L, 3.1L . . . check

Brake master cyl. . . . . check level **HB**

Clutch fluid . . . . check level **HB**
When equipped with hydraulic clutch

Coolant . . . . check level **EC**

Fluid leaks under vehicle . . . . check

Starter safety switch . . . . check

Tires & wheels . . . . inspect
Check for wear, vibration, air pressure

AT FIRST 15 MI — 24 KM; THEN AT 30 MI — 48 KM; THEN EVERY 30 MI — 48 KM
Differentials, front
   & rear . . . . change lubricant
Except Saginaw rear axle

Manual transmission . . . . change lubricant

Transfer case . . . . change lubricant
Ex. 4-cyl. w/AT

EVERY 15 MI — 24 KM
Valve clearance . . . . check/adjust
4-cyl. only

EVERY 12 MO/15 MI — 24 KM
Front disc pads . . . . inspect
Replace when lining is .039 in. or less. Also check parking brake

Brake & clutch pedals . . . . . . lubricate **MO**
Also check freeplay

Cooling system . . . . inspect
Pressure test system & inspect cap. Check condition of all hoses & tighten hose clamps

Cruise control . . . . inspect system

Throttle linkage . . . . check

EVERY 30 MI — 48 KM
Front wheel bearings . . . . repack **WB**

Air cleaner element . . . . replace
Also replace V6 crankcase filter

Air cleaner housing 2.8L, 3.1L . . . . inspect

Cooling system . . . . . . replace coolant **EC**
Flush system

Carb. choke & hoses . . . . inspect

Ignition wires 2.8L, 3.1L . . . . inspect

Power steering fluid . . . . change **AF**

Spark plugs . . . . replace

EVERY 12 MO/30 MI — 48 KM
Automatic transmission & transfer case,
   4WD w/AT ex. 2.8L, 3.1L . . . check level

Clutch lines & hose . . . . inspect
Models with hydraulic clutch only

EVERY 24 MO/30 MI — 48 KM
Drive belts . . . . inspect

Steering gearbox . . . . check/adjust

EVERY 60 MI — 96 KM
Fuel tank, cap & lines . . . . inspect

Ignition timing 2.8L, 3.1L . . . . check/adjust

PCV system 2.8L, 3.1L . . . . inspect

Timing belt . . . . replace

Radiator core & AC condenser . . . . . clean

Spark plug wires . . . . inspect
1990-92 only

EVERY 90 MI — 144 KM
Oxygen sensor . . . . replace

SEVERE SERVICE
Crankcase — Change oil every: 4-cyl., 3 mo/ 3.75 mi (6 km); V6, 3 mo/3 mi (4.8 km). All engines, change oil filter every other oil change

Differential, Saginaw — Change lubricant every 15 mi (24 km)

Transmission, automatic — Change fluid & filter every 20 mi (32 km)

Transfer case, 4-cyl. w/AT — Change fluid every 20 mi (32 km)

KEY TO LUBRICANTS

AF	DEXRON®-II Automatic Transmission Fluid
EC	Ethylene Glycol Coolant
GL-5	Gear Oil, API Service GL-5
HB	Hydraulic Brake Fluid, DOT 3 or 4
LM	Lithium Multipurpose Grease With Moly where noted
MO	Motor Oil
SF	Motor Oil, API Service SF
SG	Motor Oil, API Service SG
WB	Wheel Bearing Grease

CRANKCASE . . . . SG

CAPACITY, Refill:	Liters	Qt
2.3L: 1988-91	3.6	3.8
1992	3.2	3.4
2.6L: 1988-90	4.5	4.8
1991-92	3.9	4.1
2.8L, 3.1L	3.8	4.0
3.2L	5.0	5.3

Capacity shown is without filter. When replacing filter, additional oil may be needed

Above 40°F (5°C)	30
Above 20°F (−7°C)	20W-20, 20W-40
Above 0°F (−18°C)	10W-30*
0° to 60°F (−18° to 15°C)	10W
Below 60°F (15°C)	5W-30
Below 20°F (−7°C)	5W-20

* Preferred

TRANSMISSION, Automatic . . . . AF

CAPACITY, Initial Refill*:	Liters	Qt
2WD	2.5	2.6
4WD	4.5	4.8

*With the engine at operating temperature, shift transmission through all gears. Check fluid level in PARK and add fluid as needed

TRANSMISSION, Manual

B.W. T-5 . . . . AF	
All others . . . . SF	

Above 90°F (32°C), 40; All temperatures, 5W-30†
†Preferred

CAPACITY, Refill:	Liters	Pt
B.W. T-5	2.3	4.8
Others: 2.3L	1.5	3.2
2.6L, 2.8L, 3.1L, 3.2L	3.0	6.2

TRANSFER CASE

W/Manual Transmission . . . . SF
Above 90°F (32°C), 40; all temperatures, 5W-30

W/Automatic Transmission: 4-cyl. . . . . . AF

   V6 . . . . SF
Above 90°F (32°C), 40; all temperatures, 5W-30

CAPACITY, Refill:	Liters	Pt
Man. trans.	1.5	3.2
Auto. trans.: 4-cyl.	0.8	1.6
V6	1.5	3.2

DIFFERENTIAL

1990-92 W/Saginaw
   rear axle 80W-90 **GL-5**
All others **GL-5**
Above 50°F (10°C), 140; 0° to 90°F (−18° to 32°C), 90; below 50°F (10°C), 80W-90

CAPACITY, Refill:	Liters	Pt
Front	1.5	3.2
Rear: 2.3L	1.5	3.2
2.6L, 2.8L, 3.1L, 3.2L	1.8	3.8
All w/Saginaw axle	1.9	4.0

Saginaw axle has removable rear cover without fill plug

SERVICE LOCATIONS — ENGINE AND CHASSIS

HOOD RELEASE: Front; CJ models, also release side latches

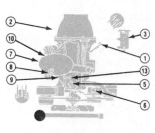

1983
2.5L (151) GM

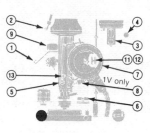

1984-86
2.5L (150) AMC 1V

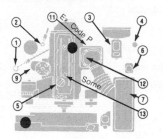

1986-92
2.5L (150) FI

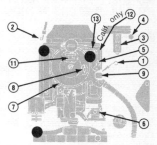

1984-86
2.8L (173)

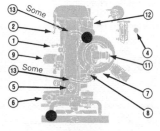

1983-90
4.2L (258)

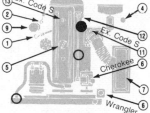

1988-92
4.0L (242)

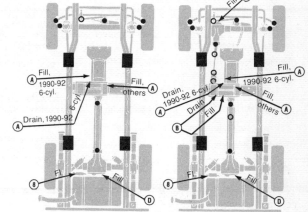

1985-92
Cherokee 2WD

1984-92 Cherokee 4WD,
Wagoneer

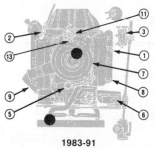

1983-91
8-cyl.

① Crankcase dipstick
② Transmission dipstick
③ Brake fluid reservoir
④ Clutch fluid reservoir
⑤ Oil fill cap
⑥ Power steering reservoir
⑦ Air filter
⑧ Fuel filter
⑨ Oil filter
⑩ PCV filter
⑪ EGR valve
⑫ Oxygen sensor
⑬ PCV valve

Ⓐ Manual transmission/transaxle, drain & fill
Ⓑ Transfer case, drain & fill

Ⓒ Automatic transaxle final drive, NOT USED
Ⓓ Differential, drain & fill

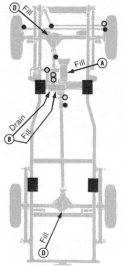

1983
Cherokee, Wagoneer,
J-Series Truck;
1984-91
Grand Wagoneer,
1984-88
J-Series Truck

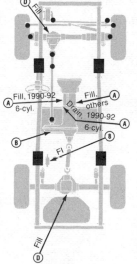

1987-92
Wrangler

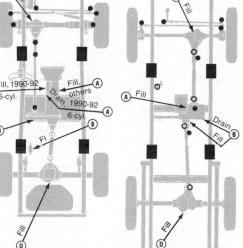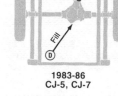

1983-86
CJ-5, CJ-7

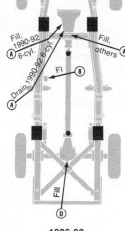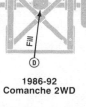

1986-92
Comanche 2WD

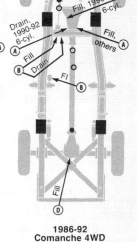

1986-92
Comanche 4WD

● Cooling system drain
■ Lift adapter position
● Fitting

○ Cooling system drain, some models
○ Fitting, some models

SERVICE AT TIME OR MILEAGE—WHICHEVER OCCURS FIRST

JPPM3   JPPM3

MI—MILES IN THOUSANDS
KM—KILOMETERS IN THOUSANDS

FIRST 5 MO/5 MI—8 KM

Carb. mounting bolts 4-cyl. . . . .check/adjust

Drive belts . . . . inspect/adjust

Idle speed ex. 8-cyl. . . . . check/adjust

FIRST 5 MO/5 MI—8 KM;
THEN EVERY 7.5 MO/7.5 MI—12 KM

Crankcase . . . . change oil
When most trips are under 6 miles (9.6 kilometers), change every 2.5 mi (4 km)

Exhaust system . . . . inspect
Check catalytic converter for damage

Oil filter . . . . replace
4-cyl. Calif., initial service then every 15 mo/15 mi (24 km)

Battery . . . . check level
Check battery condition every fall

Brake master cylinder . . . . .check level **HBH**

Clutch fluid reservoir
   4-cyl. . . . . check level **HBH**

Cooling system . . . . check level

Power steering reservoir . . . check level **PS**

Trans., automatic . . . . check level

FIRST 5 MO/5 MI—8 KM;
THEN EVERY 7.5 MO/7.5 MI—12 KM
SEVERE DRIVING, ONCE
BETWEEN SCHEDULED
SERVICE

Clutch lever & linkage CJ . . . . . . **fitting LM**

Differentials, front & rear . . . . . check level

Steering linkage CJ . . . . **4 fittings LM**

Transmission, manual &
   transfer case . . . . check level

U-joints & splines CJ . . . . **fitting LM**
Double cardan joint requires special adapter

Steering gear, manual . . . . . check level **LM**

4-CYL., FIRST 7.5 MO/7.5 MI—12 KM

Distributor advance mechanism . . . inspect

Vacuum hoses & connections . . . . . . check

EVERY 12 MONTHS

Cooling system . . . . . . change coolant **EC**
Initially at 12.5 mo/12.5 mi (20 km)

AT FIRST 12.5 MO/12.5 MI—20 KM;
THEN EVERY 15 MO/15 MI—24 KM

Fuel filter . . . . replace

Fuel system . . . . inspect
Ex. 8-cyl. filler cap, tank, lines & connections

Drive belts 4-cyl. . . . . inspect/adjust

FIRST 12.5 MO/12.5 MI—20 KM;
THEN EVERY 15 MO/15 MI—24 KM
SEVERE DRIVING,
FIRST 5 MO/5 MI—8 KM;
THEN EVERY 7.5 MO/7.5 MI—12 KM

Brakes . . . . inspect

Chassis . . . . inspect

Clutch lever & linkage ex. CJ . . . . **LM**

U-joints & splines ex. CJ . . . . . . **fitting LM**

Steering linkage ex. CJ . . . . . **4 fittings LM**

Body . . . . lubricate

EVERY 30 MO/30 MI—48 KM
SEVERE DRIVING,
EVERY 12.5 MO/12.5 MI—20 KM

Transmission, automatic . . . . . change fluid
Install new filter & O-ring seal

EVERY 27 MO/27 MI—44 KM
SEVERE DRIVING, ONCE
BETWEEN SCHEDULED SERVICE

Front wheel bearings . . . . clean/repack **WB**
While rotating wheel, torque inner locknut to 50 ft lb, back off 1/6 turn. CJ models, install lockwasher, torque outer locknut to 50 ft lb, bend lip of tabbed washer over locknut. Other models, align lockwasher hole with peg on inner locknut. Tighten outer locknut to 50 ft lb minimum

Hubs, front locking . . . . lubricate **LM**

EVERY 30 MO/30 MI—48 KM

Fuel system 8-cyl. . . . . check
Filler cap, tank, lines & connections

Trans., manual . . . . .change lubricant

Transfer case . . . . change lubricant

Air cleaner element . . . . replace
Replace once in between scheduled changes if driving under predominately dusty conditions

AIR system hoses 8-cyl. . . . . inspect

AI or Air Guard hose, PCV &
   vacuum hoses & connections . . . . check

Choke linkage . . . . lubricate

Distributor cap & rotor . . . . . . clean/inspect

Idle speeds . . . . check/adjust

Ignition timing . . . . check

Manifold heat valve V8 . . . . check **MH**

Oil fill cap 8-cyl. filter type . . . . clean

Oxygen sensor 4-cyl. Calif. . . . . . . replace
Reset maintenance signal

PCV system . . . . check
Valve replacement recommended. Replace filter on 4-cyl. Calif., clean others. 8-cyl., filter in oil fill cap. Service filters once between scheduled changes if driving under predominately dusty conditions

Spark plugs . . . . replace

TAC system . . . . inspect

Vacuum hoses, connections . . . . . . inspect

EVERY 30 MO/30 MI—48 KM
SEVERE DRIVING,
EVERY 15 MO/15 MI—24 KM

Differentials front & rear . . change lubricant
Severe driving, service only every 30 mo/30 mi (48 km)

EVERY 45 MO/45 MI—72 KM

Distributor advance mechanism
   4-cyl. ex. Calif. . . . . inspect

KEY TO LUBRICANTS

AF	DEXRON®-II Automatic Transmission Fluid
CE	Motor Oil, API Service CE
EC	Ethylene Glycol Coolant Mix with water to −34°F (−37°C) protection
EP	Extreme Pressure Gear Lubricant
GL-5	Gear Oil, API Service GL-5
GL-5★	Special Lubricant for Trac-Lok Differential
HBH	Hydraulic Brake Fluid, Extra Heavy Duty
LM	Lithium Grease, EP
MH	Manifold Heat Valve Solvent
PS	Power Steering Fluid
SG	Motor Oil, API Service SG
WB	Wheel Bearing Lubricant

CRANKCASE . . . . SG

CAPACITY, Refill:	Liters	Qt
4-cyl.	2.3	2.5
6-cyl.	4.7	5.0
8-cyl.	3.8	4.0

Capacity shown is without filter. When replacing filter, additional oil may be needed

Above 30°F (−1°C)	20W-40, 20W-50
Above 0°F (−18°C)	10W-30, 10W-40
Below 60°F (16°C)	5W-30

TRANSMISSION, Automatic . . . . AF

CAPACITY, Refill*:	Liters	Qt
All models	4.0	4.3

*With the engine at operating temperature, shift transmission through all gears. Check fluid level in NEUTRAL and add fluid as needed
To drain, remove oil pan

TRANSMISSION, Manual

T4, T5, T176	**EP†**
Others	80W-90, 85W-90 **GL-5**

†SAE 85W-90 **GL-5** may be used for top-up only, and only when specified lubricant is not available

CAPACITY, Refill:	Liters	Pt
4-speed:		
T4	1.8	3.9
T18	3.1	6.5
SR4	1.4	3.0
T176	1.7	3.5
5-speed:		
T5	2.1	4.5

TRANSFER CASE

Model 208	**AF**
Model 229 Selec-Trac	**AF**
Model 300	85W-90 **GL-5**

CAPACITY, Refill:	Liters	Pt
Model 208, 229S-T	2.8	6.0
Model 300	1.9	4.0

*Model 300 used in CJ, models 208 & 229 used in all others

DIFFERENTIAL

Front: Selec-Trac	75W-90	**GL-5**
Others	85W-90	**GL-5**
Rear: Standard	85W-90	**GL-5**
Trac-Lok	85W-90	**GL-5★**

CAPACITY, Refill:	Liters	Pt
Front: CJ	1.2	2.5
All w/Selec-Trac	2.1	4.5
Others	1.4	3.0
Rear: All ex. J-20	2.3	4.8
J-20	2.8	6.0

TRAC-LOK IDENTIFICATION:
Metal tag attached to rear cover stamped with "Use Limited-Slip Diff. Lube only"

SERVICE AT TIME OR MILEAGE—WHICHEVER OCCURS FIRST

JPPM4   **W SERVICE TO MAINTAIN EMISSION WARRANTY**   JPPM4

MI—MILES IN THOUSANDS
KM—KILOMETERS IN THOUSANDS
DIESEL: FIRST 1 MO/1 MI—1.6 KM
W Cylinder head bolts . . . . torque
Torque to 70-77 ft lbs
W Valve clearance . . . . adjust
GASOLINE: FIRST 5 MO/5 MI—8 KM
W Carburetor mounting bolts . . . . torque
W Idle speeds . . . . check/adjust
GASOLINE:
1984, FIRST 5 MO/5 MI—8 KM;
THEN EVERY 7.5 MO/7.5 MI—12 KM
1985-87,
EVERY 7.5 MO/7.5 MI—12 KM
DIESEL:
1985-87 EVERY 5 MO/5 MI—8 KM
W Crankcase . . . . change oil
Exhaust system . . . . inspect
W Oil filter . . . . replace
Propeller shafts
  CJ/Wrangler . . . . lubricate **LM**
U-joint & splines or yokes
Steering & gear, manual . . check level **LM**
Steering linkage
  CJ/Wrangler . . . . lubricate **LM**
Inspect seals & components. Lubricate ball joints
Transfer case . . . . check level
Differentials . . . . check level
Transmission, manual . . . . . . check level
Battery . . . . check level
Clean terminals, check tiedowns, & voltage
Brake master cylinder . . . check level **HBH**
Clutch fluid reservoir . . . . check level **HBH**
W Cooling system . . . . check level **EC**
W Drive belts, gasoline . . . . check/adjust
Then at 30 mi (48 km), then every 15 mi (24 km)
Drive belts, diesel . . . . check/adjust
Then at 15 mi (24 km), then every 15 mi (24 km)
Power steering reservoir . . check level **PS**
Tires . . . . check
Transmission, automatic . . . . check level
Fluid warm, engine idling, shift lever in all positions, leave in PARK
DIESEL:
1985-87,
EVERY 15 MO/15 MI—24 KM
Cooling system . . . . change coolant
Initial service at 25 mi (40 km)
W Fuel filter . . . . replace
Drive belts, Diesel . . . . check/adjust
1984,
FIRST 12.5 MO/12.5 MI—20 KM;
THEN EVERY 15 MO/15 MI—24 KM
1985-87,
EVERY 30 MO/30 MI—48 KM
Brakes . . . . inspect
Front & rear brake linings, master cylinder, calipers, wheel cylinders. Check general condition of system
Chassis . . . . inspect
Steering gear & linkage, springs, shocks, tires; check overall steering & suspension condition
W Fuel filter . . . . replace
W Fuel system . . . . inspect
Ex. 1985 Federal models. Check filler cap, tank, lines, hoses & connections
Body . . . . lubricate
Hinges, door latches, slides, locks

Parking brake & clutch pedal
  freeplay . . . . check/adjust
1984, FIRST 20 MO/20 MI—32 KM
1985-87, EVERY 22.5 MI—36 KM
Cooling system . . . . . . change coolant **EC**
1984, EVERY 27 MO/27.5 MI—44 KM
1985-87, EVERY 30 MI—48 KM
Front wheel bearings . . . clean/repack **WB**
Replace spindle oil & bearing seals. While rotating wheel, torque inner locknut to 50 ft lb, back off 1/6 turn. CJ models, install lockwasher, torque outer locknut to 50 ft lb, bend lip of tabbed washer over locknut. Other models, align lockwasher hole with peg on inner locknut. Tighten outer locknut to 50 ft lb minimum
Hubs, front locking . . . . lubricate **LM**
EVERY 30 MO/30 MI—48 KM
Differentials, front & rear . . . . change fluid
Trans., automatic . . . . . . change fluid/filter
Transmission, manual . . . change lubricant
Transfer case . . . . change lubricant
W Air cleaner element . . . . replace
W Charcoal canister inlet filter . . . . . replace
W Choke system . . . . clean
Clutch system . . . . inspect
Distributor cap & rotor . . . . inspect
EFE system,
  1985 6-cyl. ex. Calif. . . . . check
W Idle speeds, Diesel 1987 . . . . check/adjust
W Ignition timing . . . . check
For applicable engines, see underhood specifications
W Ignition wires . . . . check
V6 engines ex. California
Manifold heat valve 8-cyl. . . . . check **MH**
W PCV system . . . . check
Ex. 1985 Federal 4- & 8-cyl. models. Replace valve, clean or replace filter
W Spark plugs . . . . replace
TAC system . . . . inspect
Distributor advance . . . . check
Vacuum hoses, connections . . . inspect
Valve clearance diesel only . . . adjust
GASOLINE:
EVERY 52 MO/52.5 MI—84.5 KM
W Drive belts . . . . replace
W Vacuum hoses . . . . replace
(emission system)
W Ignition wires . . . . replace
W Distributor cap & rotor . . . . replace
W Fuel filler cap . . . . replace
W Charcoal canister & filter . . . . . . replace
W Oxygen sensor . . . . replace
DIESEL:
EVERY 55 MO/55 MI—88 KM
W Injection pump timing belt . . . . . . inspect
W Crankcase vent system . . . . inspect
W Reference pressure regulator . . . . . check
DIESEL:
EVERY 110 MO/110 MI—116 KM
W Injection pump timing belt . . . . . . replace
SEVERE SERVICE
Perform scheduled maintenance twice as frequently

KEY TO LUBRICANTS
See other Jeep charts

CRANKCASE
Gasoline engine . . . . SG
Diesel engine . . . . SG/CE

CAPACITY, Refill:	Liters	Qt
2.1L Diesel	4.7	5.0
4-cyl. & 2.8L V6	3.8	4.0
6-cyl.	4.7	5.0
8-cyl.	3.8	4.0

Capacity shown is without filter. When replacing filter, additional oil may be needed
Gasoline Engine:
Above 30°F (−1°C) 20W-40, 20W-50
Above 0°F (−18°C) 10W-30, 10W-40
Below 60°F (16°C) 5W-30
Diesel Engine:
Above 30°F (−1°C) 20W-40, 20W-50
Above 20°F (−7°C) 15W-40
−10° to 100°F (−23° to 38°C) 10W-30
Below 50°F (10°C) 5W-30

TRANSMISSION, Automatic . . . . AF
CAPACITY, Initial Refill*:	Liters	Qt
All models	3.8	4.0

*With the engine at operating temperature, shift transmission through all gears. Check fluid level in PARK (1987 Cherokee, Comanche, Wagoneer) or NEUTRAL (all others) and add fluid as needed

TRANSMISSION, Manual
AX4 & AX5**
  (Sectional Case*) 75W-90 GL-5
B.A.10** (5 speed) 75W-90 GL-5
T4 & T5 (Top-load) . . . . **EP†**
T176 Jeep Truck, Grand Wagoneer . . **EP†**
*Case has cast iron & aluminum sections
** B.A.10 has I.D. plate on passenger side of transmission front case. AX5 has I.D. code stamped next to drain plug
†85W-90 GL-5 may be used for top-up only, and only when specified lubricant is not available

CAPACITY, Refill:	Liters	Pt
AX4 2WD	3.7	7.8
AX4 4WD	3.5	7.4
AX5 2WD	3.5	7.4
AX5 4WD	3.3	7.0
B.A.10/5 2WD	2.0	4.2
B.A.10/5 4WD	1.6	3.5
T4	1.8	3.9
T5	2.1	4.5
T176	1.7	3.5

TRANSFER CASE
Model 300 . . . . EP
Others . . . . AF

CAPACITY, Refill:	Liters	Pt
CJ, Model 300	1.9	4.0
Cherokee, Wagoneer, Comanche:		
1984-86 Model 207	2.1	4.5
Model 228	3.3	7.0
1987 Model 231	1.1	2.2
Model 242	1.2	2.5
Wrangler, Model 207	2.1	4.5
Grand Wagoneer:		
J series truck:		
Model 208	2.8	6.0
Model 229	2.8	6.0

DIFFERENTIAL
Standard 75W-90 GL-5
Trac-Lok, rear . . . . 75W-90 GL-5★
Trailer Tow Pkg. 80W-140 GL-5

CAPACITY, Refill:	Liters	Pt
Front: CJ, Wagoneer, Cherokee,		
Comanche,		
Wrangler, YJ	1.2	2.5
Others w/o Selec-Trac	1.4	3.0
Others w/Selec-Trac	2.1	4.5
Rear: Comanche:		
7⁹⁄₁₆″ ring gear	1.2	2.5
8⁷⁄₈″ ring gear	2.3	4.8
Cherokee, Wagoneer	1.2	2.5
CJ, Grand Wagoneer,		
J10	2.3	4.8
J20	2.8	6.0

TRAC-LOK IDENTIFICATION:
Metal tag attached to rear cover stamped with "Use Limited-Slip Diff. Lube only"

SERVICE AT TIME OR MILEAGE—WHICHEVER OCCURS FIRST

JPPM5   JPPM5

W   SERVICE TO MAINTAIN EMISSION WARRANTY

MI—MILES IN THOUSANDS
KM—KILOMETERS IN THOUSANDS

FIRST 5 MO/5 MI—8 KM
W Idle speeds . . . . check/adjust
Wrangler & YJ 6-cyl., Grand Wagoneer

EVERY 7.5 MO/7.5 MI—12 KM
W Crankcase . . . . change oil
Change oil filter every oil change

W Exhaust system . . . . inspect
California only

Propeller shafts . . . . lubricate **LB**
U-joint & splines or yokes

Steering & gear, manual . . check level **LB**

Steering linkage
  Wrangler, YJ . . . . lubricate **LB**
Inspect seals & components. Lubricate ball joints

Transfer case . . . . check level

Transmission, manual . . . . . . check level

Battery . . . . check level
Clean terminals, check tiedowns, & voltage

Brake master cylinder . . . check level **HBH**

Clutch fluid reservoir . . . . check level **HBH**

Cooling system . . . . check level **EC**

Power steering reservoir . . check level **PS**

Tires . . . . check

Transmission, automatic . . . . . check level
Grand Wagoneer, Wrangler, YJ, check in neutral; others, check in park

EVERY 15 MO/15 MI — 24 KM
W Drive belts . . . . inspect, adjust
Wrangler & YJ, Grand Wagoneer

EVERY 22.5 MI — 36 KM
Cooling system . . . . . . change coolant **EC**

EVERY 30 MO/30 MI—48 KM
Brakes . . . . inspect
Front & rear brake linings, master cylinder, calipers, wheel cylinders. Check general condition of system

Chassis . . . . inspect
Steering gear & linkage, springs, shocks, tires; check overall steering & suspension condition

Differentials, front & rear . . . . change fluid

Front wheel bearing
  2WD . . . . check/repack **LB**

W Fuel filter . . . . replace

W Fuel system . . . . inspect
Check filler cap, tank, lines, hoses & connections

Trans., automatic . . . . . . change fluid/filter

Transmission, manual . . . change lubricant

Transfer case . . . . change lubricant

W Air cleaner element . . . . replace

W Choke system . . . . clean

Clutch system . . . . inspect

Distributor cap & rotor . . . . inspect

W Drive belts . . . . inspect/adjust
Comanche, Cherokee, Wagoneer

Idle speeds . . . . check/adjust
Wrangler & YJ 6-cyl., Grand Wagoneer
California only

W Ignition timing . . . . check
For applicable engines, see underhood specifications

W Manifold heat valve 8-cyl. . . . lubricate **MH**

W PCV filter . . . . clean/oil
Wrangler & YJ, Grand Wagoneer

Parking brake & clutch pedal
  freeplay . . . . check/adjust

W Spark plugs . . . . replace

TAC system . . . . inspect

Distributor advance . . . . check

Vacuum hoses, connections . . . inspect

Body . . . . lubricate
Hinges, door latches, slides, locks

EVERY 52 MO/52.5 MI—84.5 KM
W Drive belts . . . . replace

W Vacuum hoses . . . . replace
(emission system)

W Ignition wires . . . . replace

W Distributor cap & rotor . . . . replace

EVERY 82 MO/82.5 MI—133 KM
W PCV valve . . . . replace
Wrangler & YJ, Grand Wagoneer

W Fuel filter cap . . . . replace

W Oxygen sensor . . . . replace
Ex. V8

W Idle speeds . . . . check/adjust
Wrangler & YJ 6-cyl., Grand Wagoneer

SEVERE SERVICE
Perform scheduled maintenance twice as frequently

KEY TO LUBRICANTS

AF   DEXRON®-II Automatic Transmission
      Fluid
AP   ATF-PLUS® Automatic Transmission
      Fluid
CD   Motor Oil, API Service CD
EC   Ethylene Glycol Coolant
      Mix with water to −34°F (−37°C) protection
EP   Extreme Pressure Gear Lubricant
GC   Wheel Bearing Grease,
      NLGI Category GC
GL-5   Gear Oil, API Service GL-5
GLS   Gear Lubricant, Special
HBH   Hydraulic Brake Fluid, Extra
      Heavy Duty
LB   Chassis Grease, NLGI Category LB
MA   MERCON® Automatic Transmission
      Fluid
MH   Manifold Heat Valve Solvent
PS   Power Steering Fluid
SG   Motor Oil, API Service SG

CRANKCASE . . . . SG, SG/CD

CAPACITY, Refill:	Liters	Qt
4-cyl., 8-cyl.	3.8	4.0
6-cyl.	4.7	5.0

Capacity shown is without filter. When replacing filter, additional oil may be needed
Above 30°F (−1°C) 20W-40, 20W-50
Above 0°F (−18°C) 10W-30, 10W-40
Below 60°F (16°C) 5W-30

TRANSMISSION, Automatic
727, 999 . . . . **AP†**
AW-4 . . . . **MA††**
†MA, AF may be used for top off only
††AF may be used for top off only

CAPACITY, Initial Refill*:	Liters	Qt
All models	3.8	4.0

* With the engine at operating temperature, shift transmission through all gears. Check fluid level in PARK (Comanche, Cherokee, Wagoneer) or NEUTRAL (All others) and add fluid as needed

TRANSMISSION, Manual . . 75W-90 GL-5

CAPACITY, Refill:	Liters	Pt
AX4 2WD*	3.7	7.8
AX4 4WD*	3.5	7.4
AX5 2WD*	3.5	7.4
AX5 4WD*	3.3	7.0
B.A.10/5 2WD**	2.5	5.2
B.A.10/5 4WD**	2.3	4.9

* Case has cast iron & aluminum sections
** B.A.10 has I.D. plate on passenger side of transmission front case. AX5 has I.D. code stamped next to drain plug

TRANSFER CASE . . . . MA, AF

CAPACITY, Refill:	Liters	Pt
Model 229 Grand		
Wagoneer	2.8	6.0
Model 231: Wrangler, YJ .	1.5	3.3
Cherokee, Comanche,		
Wagoneer	1.0	2.2
Model 242 Cherokee,		
Wagoneer	1.4	3.0

DIFFERENTIAL
Comanche, Grand Wagoneer
  Wrangler, YJ 75W-90 **GL-5**
  With trailer tow pkg. . . . 80W-140 **GL-5**
Cherokee 75W-90 **GL-5**
  With Class III hitch . . . . 80W-140 **GLS***
* Mopar synthetic gear oil
* All with Limited-Slip differential, add one container Mopar Trac-Loc additive

CAPACITY	Liters	Pt
Grand Wagoneer	1.8	3.8
Comanche w/Metric		
Ton Pkg.	1.4	3.0
Others	1.2	2.5

SERVICE AT TIME OR MILEAGE—WHICHEVER OCCURS FIRST

JPPM6   JPPM6

W   SERVICE TO MAINTAIN EMISSION WARRANTY

MI—MILES IN THOUSANDS
KM—KILOMETERS IN THOUSANDS

FIRST 5 MO/5 MI—8 KM

W Carburetor mounting bolts . . . . torque
As equipped

W Idle speeds . . . . check/adjust
Wrangler, YJ, Grand Wagoneer

PCV valve . . . . check
Grand Wagoneer, Wrangler, YJ

EVERY 7.5 MO/7.5 MI—12 KM

W Crankcase . . . . change oil
Change oil filter at each oil change

Exhaust system . . . . inspect

Battery . . . . clean/inspect
Check electrolyte level ex. maintenance free type

Brake master cylinder . . . check level **HBH**

Clutch fluid reservoir . . . . check level **HBH**

W Cooling system . . . . check level **EC**
Inspect hoses, tighten clamps, check radiator cap

Power steering reservoir . . check level **PS**

Propeller shafts . . . . lubricate **GC-LB**
U-joint & splines or yokes; inspect seals

Steering & gear,
    manual . . . . check level **GC-LB**

Steering linkage,
    ball joints . . . . lubricate **GC-LB**

Transfer case, differentials . . . check level

Transmission, manual . . . . . . check level

Tires . . . . check

Transmission, automatic . . . . check level

EVERY 15 MI—24 KM

Air filter . . . . replace
California Grand Wagoneer

Drive belts . . . . inspect/adjust
Grand Wagoneer

Idle speed . . . . check/adjust
Initial service for Calif. only

FIRST 36 MO/22.5 MI—36 KM;
THEN EVERY 24 MO OR
EVERY 22.5 MI—36 KM

Cooling system . . . . . . replace coolant **EC**
Grand Wagoneer only

CALIF. GRAND WAGONEER
FIRST 30 MI—48 KM

Distributor cap & rotor . . . . replace

Ignition timing . . . . check/adjust

Vacuum hoses . . . . inspect

EVERY 30 MI—48 KM

Brakes . . . . inspect
Front & rear brake linings, master cylinder, calipers,
wheel cylinders. Check general condition of system

Chassis . . . . inspect
Steering gear & linkage, springs, shocks, tires; check
overall steering & suspension condition

Differentials, front & rear . . . . change fluid

Front wheel bearing . check/repack **GC-LB**
Grand Wagoneer, 2WD Cherokee, 2WD Comanche

W Fuel filter . . . . replace
1990-91

W Fuel system . . . . inspect
Check filler cap, tank, lines, hoses & connections

Trans., automatic . . . . . . change fluid/filter

Transmission, manual . . . change lubricant

Transfer case . . . . change lubricant

W Air cleaner element . . . . replace

W Choke system . . . . clean
As equipped

Clutch system . . . . inspect

Distributor cap & rotor . . . . inspect

W Drive belts . . . . inspect/adjust
Ex. Grand Wagoneer

Idle speeds . . . . check/adjust

Ignition timing . . . . check
Calif. Grand Wagoneer

Manifold heat valve 8-cyl. . . . . . check **MH**

Parking brake & clutch pedal
    freeplay . . . . check/adjust

PCV filter . . . . clean/oil
Grand Wagoneer, Wrangler, YJ

PCV hoses . . . . replace
Calif. Grand Wagoneer

W Spark plugs . . . . replace

TAC system . . . . inspect
Calif. Grand Wagoneer

Distributor advance . . . . check
Calif. Grand Wagoneer

Vacuum hoses, connections . . . . . inspect

Body . . . . lubricate
Hinges, door latches, slides, locks

FIRST 36 MO/52.5 MI—84.5 KM;
THEN EVERY 24 MO/30 MI—48 KM

W Cooling system . . . . . . change coolant **EC**
All ex. Grand Wagoneer

GRAND WAGONEER,
EVERY 52 MO/52.5 MI—84.5 KM

W Drive belts . . . . replace
    Idle speed . . . . check/adjust

W Ignition timing . . . . check

Vacuum hoses . . . . replace
(emission system)

W Ignition wires . . . . replace

W Distributor cap & rotor . . . . replace

EVERY 60 MI — 96 KM

Battery . . . . replace

W Distributor cap & rotor . . . . replace
Ex. Grand Wagoneer

W Drive belts . . . . replace
Ex. Grand Wagoneer

W Fuel filter . . . . replace
1992

W Ignition wires . . . . replace
Ex. Grand Wagoneer

Vacuum hoses . . . . replace
Ex. Grand Wagoneer

EVERY 82.5 MI—133 KM

W Oxygen sensor . . . . replace

PCV valve . . . . replace
Ex. Wrangler, YJ

SEVERE SERVICE

Crankcase — Change oil & filter every 3 mo/
3 mi (4.8km)

Perform other scheduled maintenance twice
as frequently

KEY TO LUBRICANTS

AF	DEXRON®-II Automatic Transmission Fluid
AP	ATF-PLUS® Automatic Transmission Fluid
CD	Motor Oil, API Service CD
CE	Motor Oil, API Service CE
EC	Ethylene Glycol Coolant Mix with water to –34°F (–37°C) protection
GC	Wheel Bearing Grease, NLGI Category GC
GL-5	Gear Oil, API Service GL-5
GL-5★	Special Lubricant for Trac-Lok Differential
GLS	Gear Lubricant, Special
HBH	Hydraulic Brake Fluid, Extra Heavy Duty
LB	Chassis Grease, NLGI Category LB
MA	MERCON® Automatic Transmission Fluid
MH	Manifold Heat Valve Solvent
PS	Power Steering Fluid
SG	Motor Oil, API Service SG
WB	Wheel Bearing Lubricant

CRANKCASE . . . . . . SG, SG/CD, SG/CE

CAPACITY, Refill:	Liters	Qt
4-cyl.	3.8	4.0
6-cyl.	5.7	6.0
8-cyl.	4.7	5.0

Capacity shown includes filter
Above 0°F (–18°C) 10W-30
Below 60°F (16°C) 5W-30

TRANSMISSION, Automatic

32RH (1992 Wrangler) . . . . **AP†**
727, 999 . . . . **AP†**
AW-4 . . . . **MA†**
†AF may be used for top off only

CAPACITY, Initial Refill*:	Liters	Qt
AW4, 727	4.0	4.3
999, 32RH	3.8	4.0

*With the engine at operating temperature, shift transmission through all gears. Check fluid level in PARK (Comanche, Cherokee, Wagoneer) or NEUTRAL (All others) and add fluid as needed

TRANSMISSION, Manual . . 75W-90 GL-5

CAPACITY, Refill:	Liters	Pt
AX4 2WD	3.7	7.8
AX4 4WD	3.5	7.4
AX5 2WD	3.5	7.4
AX5 4WD	3.3	7.0
AX15 2WD	3.2	6.7
AX15 4WD	3.2	6.8

AX4, AX5 transmissions have drain on bottom of case.
AX15 transmission has drain on passenger side of case

TRANSFER CASE . . . . MA, AF

CAPACITY, Refill:	Liters	Pt
Model 229 Grand Wagoneer	2.8	6.0
Model 231: Wrangler, YJ . Cherokee, Comanche, Wagoneer	1.5	3.3
	1.0	2.2
Model 242 Cherokee, Wagoneer	1.4	3.0

DIFFERENTIAL

Comanche, Grand Wagoneer,
    Wrangler, YJ 75W-90 **GL-5**
    With trailer tow pkg. 80W-140 **GL-5**
Cherokee 75W-90 **GL-5**
    With Class III hitch . . . . 80W-140 **GLS***
*Mopar synthetic gear oil
All with Limited-Slip differential, add one container Mopar
Trac-Loc additive

CAPACITY	Liters	Pt
Grand Wagoneer	1.8	3.8
Comanche w/Metric Ton Pkg.	1.4	3.0
Wagoneer, Cherokee 8¼″ axle*	2.0	4.4
Others	1.2	2.5

*3″ axle shaft tube diameter

SERVICE LOCATIONS — ENGINE AND CHASSIS

MAIDP-1   MAIDP-1

HOOD RELEASE: Inside

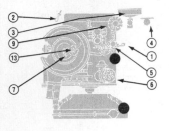

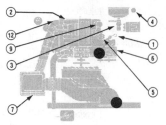

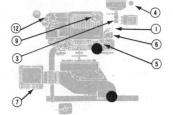

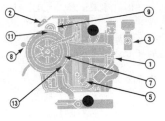

1983-85
RX-7
1146cc 4V

1985-91
RX-7
1308cc FI ex.
Turbo

1987-91
RX-7
1308cc Turbo

1983
GLC Wagon
1490cc

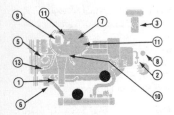

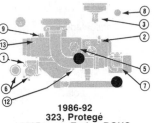

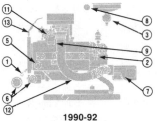

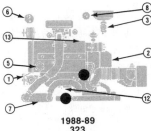

1983-85
GLC FWD
1490cc

1986-92
323, Protegé
1597cc ex. Turbo, DOHC

1990-92
323, Protegé
1597cc DOHC

1988-89
323
1597cc Turbo

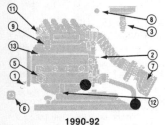

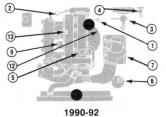

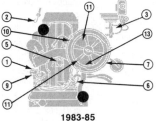

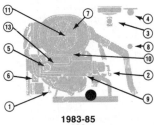

1990-92
323, Protegé
1839cc DOHC

1990-92
MX-5 Miata
1597cc DOHC

1983-85
B2000
1970cc

1983-85
626
1998cc 2V

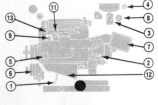

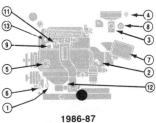

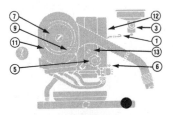

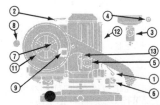

1986-87
626
1998cc FI

1986-87
626
1998cc Turbo

1986-87
B2000
1998cc

1987-92
B2200
2184cc 2V

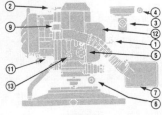

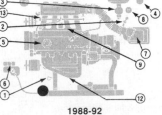

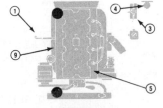

1990-92
B2200
2184cc FI

1988-92
626, MX6
2184cc

1983-84
2209cc, B2200
Diesel

① Crankcase dipstick
② Transmission dipstick
③ Brake fluid reservoir
④ Clutch fluid reservoir
⑤ Oil fill cap
⑥ Power steering reservoir
⑦ Air filter
⑧ Fuel filter
⑨ Oil filter
⑩ PCV filter
⑪ EGR valve
⑫ Oxygen sensor
⑬ PCV valve

● Cooling system drain

SERVICE LOCATIONS — ENGINE AND CHASSIS

MAIDP-2

MAIDP-2

HOOD RELEASE: Inside

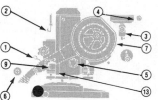

1987-88
B2600
2555cc

1989-92
B2600, MPV
2606cc

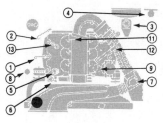

1988-92
929, MPV
2954cc

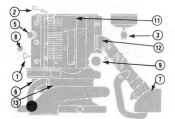

1990-91
929
2954cc DOHC

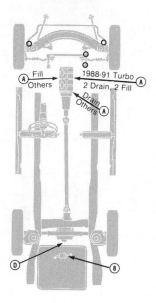

1-4
FITTINGS

1988-91 Turbo
2 Drain, 2 Fill

Fill
Others

Drain
Others

1983-91
RX-7

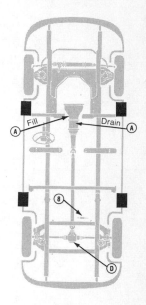

0 FITTINGS
0 PLUGS

Fill   Drain

1990-92
MX-5 Miata

● Cooling system drain
■ Lift adapter position
○ Fitting, some models
▲ Plug

Ⓐ Manual transmission/transaxle,
   drain & fill
Ⓑ Transfer case, drain & fill
Ⓒ Automatic transaxle final drive,
   NOT USED
Ⓓ Differential, drain & fill

Ⓢ Fuel filter

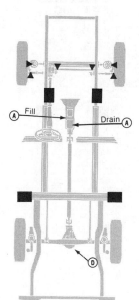

6
PLUGS

Fill   Drain

1983
GLC Wagon

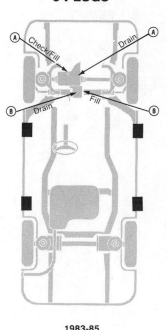

0 FITTINGS
0 PLUGS

Check/Fill   Drain

Drain   Fill

1983-85
FWD GLC,
1986-92
323, Protegé, MX-3

CAUTION: On front wheel drive vehicles the center of gravity is further forward than on rear wheel drive vehicles. When removing major components from the rear of the vehicle while it is on a hoist, the vehicle must be supported in a manner to prevent it from tipping forward.

SERVICE LOCATIONS — ENGINE AND CHASSIS

MAIDP-3   MAIDP-3

0 FITTINGS
0 PLUGS

1983-92
626 MX-6

0 FITTINGS
0 PLUGS

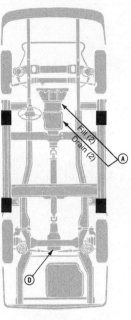

1988-91
929

0 FITTINGS
0 PLUGS

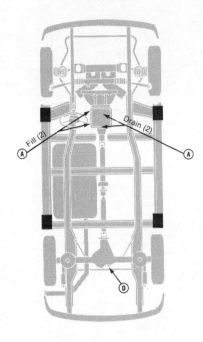

1989-92 MPV

8-10
PLUGS

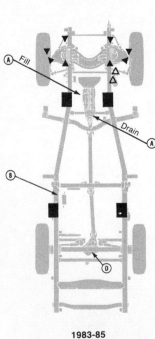

1983-85
Pickup

0 FITTINGS
4 PLUGS

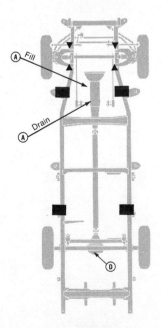

1986-92
2WD Pickup

5-7 FITTINGS
4 PLUGS

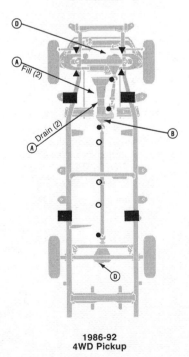

1986-92
4WD Pickup

CAUTION: On front wheel drive vehicles the center of gravity is further forward than on rear wheel drive vehicles. When removing major components from the rear of the vehicle while it is on a hoist, the vehicle must be supported in a manner to prevent it from tipping forward.

■ Lift adapter position   ▲ Plug   △ Plug, some models   ● Fitting   ○ Fitting, some models

SERVICE AT TIME OR MILEAGE—WHICHEVER OCCURS FIRST

MAIPM1   MAIPM1

Perform the following maintenance services at the intervals indicated to keep both the vehicle and emission warranties in effect.

MI — MILES IN THOUSANDS
KM — KILOMETERS IN THOUSANDS

TURBO, EVERY 5 MO/5 MI — 8 KM
Crankcase .... change oil

Oil filter .... replace

EVERY 7.5 MO/7.5 MI — 12 KM
Crankcase ex. Turbo .... change oil
Change oil filter every other oil change

Differential 1983 .... check level
Replace lubricant at initial service

Disc brake pads 1983-88 .... inspect
Replace pads when shoe & lining is 5/16″ thick

Transmission, manual ...... check level
1983

Brake & clutch pedal free play ..... check
1983

Brake & clutch
reservoirs .... check level **HB**

Parking brake .... check
1983

Power steering reservoir .. check level **FA**
From 8/86, **AF** may be used

Transmission, automatic ..... check level

1988-91, EVERY 12 MO
AC system .... inspect

EVERY 15 MO/15 MI — 24 KM
Brake system 1983-86 .... inspect
Check fluid hoses, connections & parking brake

Driveshaft boots 1986-88 .... inspect

Choke system .... spray clean
1984-85 Federal 4-bbl. only

Cooling system hoses .... inspect

Clutch 1984-87 .... inspect
Clutch fluid & freeplay

Engine oil level
warning system .... inspect

Idle speed 1984-91 .... check/adjust
Check dashpot & throttle opener with AC for binding

Spark plugs 1984-91 .... inspect

Steering gear 1983-88 .. check level **GL-4**

Steering wheel freeplay 1983-85 ... check

Body & chassis nuts,
bolts 1983-88 .... torque

EVERY 30 MO/30 MI — 48 KM
Brake fluid .... replace **HB**
Check power brake unit & hoses

Brake system 1989-91 .... inspect

Differential 1983-87 ..... change lubricant

Driveshaft boots 1989-91 .... inspect

Exhaust system heat shields ..... inspect

Front wheel bearings .... **LM**
Adjust preload to .9-2.2 lb (.4-1 kg) on spring scale attached to wheel bolt

Idler arm 1983-86 .... **1-2 fittings LM**
As equipped with fittings

Lower arm ball joints ..... **0-2 fittings LM**
As equipped with fittings

Steering linkage & suspension .... inspect

Toe control hub and control
link 1986-91 .... inspect

Trans., manual 1983-87 . change lubricant

Air cleaner element .... replace

Cooling level warning
system .... inspect

Cooling system ...... change coolant **EC**

Drive belts .... inspect/adjust
Ex. air pump

Fuel filter 1984-88 .... replace

Fuel lines .... inspect

Spark plugs .... replace

Body & chassis nuts,
bolts, 1989-91 .... torque

1988-91,
EVERY 60 MO/60 MI — 96 KM
Differential .... change lubricant

Fuel filter .... replace

Transmission, manual ... change lubricant

SERVICE AS REQUIRED
Starting assist
system .... inspect seasonally
To replenish fluid, add a mixture of 90% **EC** and 10% water to system reservoir

SEVERE SERVICE
Brake fluid 1983-87 — With extensive brake use or in humid climates, change fluid annually

Crankcase — Change oil & filter: 1988-91 ex. Turbo, 5 mo/5 mi (8 km); 1988-91 Turbo, 3 mo/3 mi (5 km); 1983-87, more frequently

Differential 1989-91 — Change lubricant every 30 mo/30 mi (48 km)

Transmission, manual 1989-91—Change lubricant every 30 mo/30 mi (48 km)

Air cleaner element — Inspect & change more frequently in very dusty or sandy areas

KEY TO LUBRICANTS

AF	Automatic Transmission Fluid DEXRON®-II
EC	Ethylene Glycol Coolant
FA	Automatic Transmission Fluid, Type F
GL-4	Gear Oil, API Service GL-4
GL-5	Gear Oil, API Service GL-5
GL-5★	Special Lubricant for Limited-Slip Differential
HB	Hydraulic Brake Fluid, DOT 3 or 4
LM	Lithium Grease, with Moly
SG	Motor Oil, API Service SG

CRANKCASE .... **SG**

CAPACITY, Refill:	Liters	Qt
RX-7 4V	4.2	4.4
RX-7 FI	4.4	4.7

Capacity shown is without filter. When replacing filter, additional oil may be needed

1983-90:
Above 15°F (–9°C) 20W-40, 20W-50
Above –15°F (–26°C) 10W-40, 10W-50
–15° to 85°F (–26° to 29°C) 10W-30
Below 32°F (0°C) 5W-30
Below 0°F (–18°C), 1983-85 .... 5W-20
1991:
Above: –15°F (–25°C) 10W-30
Below 32°F (0°C) 5W-30

TRANSMISSION, Automatic
1986 models, refer to lubricant specifications label under hood to determine proper lubricant

1983-5/86 .... **FA**
6/1986-90 .... **AF**

CAPACITY, Initial*:	Liters	Qt
1983-85	6.2†	6.6†
1986-91	4.0*	4.2*

†Total (dry) fill shown, use less fluid when refilling
*With the engine at operating temperature, shift transmission through all gears. Check fluid level in PARK and add fluid as needed

TRANSMISSION, Manual
1983-85 .... 80W-90 **GL-4, GL-5**
Above 0°F (–18°C), 90; below 0°F (–18°C), 80W
1986-91 .... 75W-90 **GL-4, GL-5**
Above 50°F (10°), may use 80W-90

CAPACITY, Refill:	Liters	Pt
1983-85	1.7	3.6
1986-88	2.0	4.2
Turbo	2.5	5.2
1989-91	2.5	5.2

DIFFERENTIAL
Standard **GL-5**
Above 0°F (–18°C), 90; below 0°F (–18°C), 80W
Limited-Slip .... 90 **GL-5★**

CAPACITY, Refill:	Liters	Pt
1983-85 Standard	1.2	2.5
Limited-Slip	1.6	3.4
1986-91	1.3	2.8
Turbo	1.4	3.0

SERVICE AT TIME OR MILEAGE—WHICHEVER OCCURS FIRST

MAIPM2   MAIPM2

Perform the following maintenance services at the intervals indicated to keep both the vehicle and emission warranties in effect.

MI — MILES IN THOUSANDS
KM — KILOMETERS IN THOUSANDS

TURBO ENGINES,
EVERY 5 MO/5 MI — 8 KM
Crankcase .... change oil

Oil filter .... replace

EVERY 7.5 MO/7.5 MI — 12 KM
Crankcase, gasoline .... change oil
Ex. Turbo

Differential .... check level
1983, check fluid at initial service, then every 30 mi (48 km)

Disc brake pads .... inspect
Replace pads when shoe & lining is 7mm thick. Inspect parking brake

Driveshaft boots .... inspect

Oil filter .... replace
Replace 2.0L diesel oil bypass filter every other oil change

Power steering fluid,
    1983 .... check level **FA**

Rack seal boots .... inspect
1984-87

Transaxle, manual 1983 ..... check level
Replace fluid at initial service only

Brake & clutch pedal freeplay ..... check
Check parking brake

Brake & clutch reservoirs . check level **HB**
1983

Oil bypass filter, Diesel .... replace

Steering wheel free play 1983 ..... check

Transaxle, auto. 1983 .... check level

EVERY 15 MO/15 MI — 24 KM
Brake system .... inspect
Power brake unit, linings, hoses & connections

Body & chassis nuts & bolts ...... torque

Power steering fluid &
    lines 1984-87 .... inspect
1987 All, **AF**; 1986 626, **AF**; Others, **FA**

Cooling system .... inspect
Change 2.0L diesel engine coolant

Choke system 1984-86 .... inspect

Idle speed & mixture .... check/adjust
Ex. diesel

Spark plugs .... replace
1984-87, inspect

Steering
    gear ...... check level/inspect 90 **GL-4**

Valve clearance .... adjust

EVERY 30 MO/30 MI — 48 KM
Ball joints .... inspect

Brake system .... change fluid **HB**
Check 2.0L diesel engine clutch fluid reservoir
1986-87, check parking brake & brake & clutch pedal freeplay

Cooling system ...... change coolant **EC**
Ex. diesel

Exhaust system heat shield
    ex. diesel .... inspect

Rear wheel bearings .... lubricate **LM**
FWD GLC, 323, 626

Steering system .... inspect

Transaxle, automatic 1984-87 . check level

Transmission, manual ... change lubricant
RWD only

Air cleaner element .... replace

Drive belts .... inspect/adjust

Emission control system .... inspect
Canister & evaporative check & cut valve

Fuel filter 1984-87 .... replace
Inspect 1986-87 fuel lines

Idle speed .... check/adjust
2.0L diesel engine

Spark plugs .... replace

EVERY 60 MO/60 MI — 96 KM
Timing belt .... replace
1983-85 626 gasoline, 1986-87 all

SEVERE SERVICE
Brake fluid — With extensive brake use or in humid climates, change fluid annually

Crankcase — Change oil & filter more frequently

Air cleaner element — Inspect & change more frequently in very dusty or sandy areas

KEY TO LUBRICANTS

AF	Automatic Transmission Fluid, DEXRON®-II
CC	Motor Oil, API Service CC
CD	Motor Oil, API Service CD
EC	Ethylene Glycol Coolant
FA	Automatic Transmission Fluid, Type F
GL-4	Gear Oil, API Service GL-4
GL-5	Gear Oil, API Service GL-5
HB	Hydraulic Brake Fluid, DOT 3 or 4
LM	Lithium Grease, with Moly
SF	Motor Oil, API Service SF
SG	Motor Oil, API Service SG

CRANKCASE
Gasoline engine .... **SF, SG**
Diesel engine .... **CC, CD**

CAPACITY, Refill:	Liters	Qt
GLC	3.0	3.2
323	3.4	3.6
626	3.9	4.1
Diesel engine	5.0	5.3

Capacity shown is without filter. When replacing filter, additional oil may be needed

Gasoline engines:

Above 85°F (29°C)	40
Above −9°F (−9°C)	20W-40, 20W-50
Above −15°F (−25°C)	10W-40, 10W-50
32° to 105°F (0° to 39°C)	30
15° to 65°F (−9° to 20°C)	20W-20
−15° to 85°F (−25° to 29°C)	10W-30
Below 32°F (0°C)	5W-30
Below −5°F (−20°C)	5W-20

Diesel engines:

Above 104°F (40°C)	40
32° to 104°F (0° to 40°C)	30
14° to 77°F (−10° to 25°C)	20W-20
−13° to 86°F (−25° to 30°C)	10W-30
Below −4°F (−20°C)	5W-30

TRANSMISSION/TRANSAXLE,
Automatic
1985-86 models, refer to lubricant specifications label under hood to determine proper fluid

1983-5/86 323, GLC	**FA**
5/1986-87 323	**AF**
1983-1/85 626	**FA**
2/1985-87 626	**AF**

CAPACITY†:	Liters	Qt
GLC RWD	5.7	6.0
All FWD	5.7	6.0

†Total (dry) fill shown, use less fluid when refilling

TRANSMISSION/TRANSAXLE, Manual
Refer to Lubricant Specifications label under hood to determine proper fluid
Verify fluid installed before topping-up or refilling transaxle

1987 323, 626 ...... **AF, FA, GL-4, GL-5**
    Above 0°F (−18°C), 80W-90, 90
    Below 0°F (−18°C), **AF, FA**
1985-86 GLC, 323, 626 .. **FA, GL-4, GL-5**
    Above 0°F (−18°C), 80W-90, 90
    Below 0°F (−18°C), **FA**
1983-84 GLC, 626 ...... **FA, GL-4, GL-5**
    Above 0°F (−18°C), 80W-90, 90
    Below 0°F (−18°C), 80W (1983-84 GLC)
    Below 64°F (18°C), **FA**

CAPACITY, Total Refill:	Liters	Pt
GLC, 323	3.2	6.8
GLC wagon: 4-speed ...	1.3	2.7
5-speed	1.7	3.6
626 ex. Turbo	3.4	7.2
626 Turbo	3.7	7.8

DIFFERENTIAL **GL-5**
Above 0°F (−18°C), 90; below 0°F (−18°C), 80W

CAPACITY, Refill:	Liters	Pt
1983 GLC wagon	0.8	1.7

SERVICE AT TIME OR MILEAGE—WHICHEVER OCCURS FIRST

MAIPM4   MAIPM4

Perform the following maintenance services at the intervals indicated to keep both the vehicle and emission warranties in effect.

MI—MILES IN THOUSANDS
KM—KILOMETERS IN THOUSANDS

TURBO ENGINES, EVERY 5 MO/5 MI—8 KM
Crankcase . . . . change oil

Oil filter . . . . replace

EVERY 6 MONTHS
Transmission, automatic . . . . . check level

Power steering fluid
   reservoir . . . . check level **AF**

EVERY 7.5 MO/7.5 MI—12 KM
Body . . . . lubricate
Hinges, locks

Crankcase, gasoline . . . . change oil
Ex. Turbo

Oil filter . . . . replace

EVERY 12 MONTHS
Air conditioning system . . . . inspect

EVERY 15 MO/15 MI—24 KM
Disc brakes 1988 . . . . inspect
Power brake unit, linings, hoses & connections

Clutch 1988 . . . . check freeplay

Cooling system 1988-89 . . . . inspect

EVERY 30 MO/30 MI—48 KM
Body & chassis nuts & bolts . . . . . . torque

Brake system 1989-92 . . . . inspect
Check linings, hoses & lines, connections

Clutch 1989-92 . . . . check freeplay

Cooling system . . . . . . change coolant **EC**
1990-92, also inspect system

Drum brakes 1988 . . . . inspect

Driveshaft boots . . . . inspect

Exhaust system heat shield . . . . . . inspect

Steering & suspension system . . . . inspect
Front & 4-wheel steering rear. Replace solenoid valve oil filter on 4-wheel steering models

Air cleaner element . . . . replace

Drive belts . . . . inspect/adjust

Fuel lines . . . . inspect

Idle speed . . . . check/adjust

Spark plugs . . . . replace

EVERY 60 MO/60 MI—96 KM
Manual transmission . . . . change lubricant
Miata, 929 only

Transfer case oil . . . . change lubricant
323, Protegé 4WD

Rear axle . . . . change lubricant

Fuel filter . . . . replace

Timing belt . . . . replace
At mileage interval only

SEVERE SERVICE
Air cleaner element & cooling system —
Inspect every 15 mo/15 mi (24 km)

Crankcase — Change oil & filter: ex. Turbo, 5 mo/5 mi (8 km); Turbo, 3 mo/3 mi (5 km)

Disc brakes 1989-92—Inspect every 15 mo/ 15 mi (24 km)

Manual transmission (RWD), transfer case, rear axle—Change lubricant every 30 mo/30 mi (48 km)

KEY TO LUBRICANTS
See other Mazda charts

CRANKCASE . . . . SG

CAPACITY, Refill:	Liters	Qt
323, MX-3, Precidia:		
4-cyl.	3.0	3.2
Turbo	3.2	3.4
V6	3.7	3.9
Protegé	3.6	3.8
Miata	3.2	3.4
626, MX-6	3.9	4.1
929, Serenia	4.5	4.8

Capacity shown is without filter. When replacing filter, additional oil may be needed

1988-90:
Above 85°F (29°C) 40
Above 15°F (–9°C) 20W-40, 20W-50
Above –15°F (–25°C) 10W-40, 10W-50
32° to 105°F (0° to 39°C) 30
15° to 65°F (–9° to 20°C) 20W-20
–15° to 85°F (–25° to 29°C) 10W-30
Below 32°F (0°C) 5W-30
Below –5°F (–20°C) 5W-20

1991-92:
Above –15°F (–25°C) 10W-30
Below 32°F (0°C) 5W-30

TRANSMISSION/TRANSAXLE, Automatic . . . . AF

CAPACITY, Total Fill:	Liters	Qt
323, Protegé	6.3	6.7
MX-3, Precidia: 4-cyl. . . .	6.3	6.7
V6	5.8	6.1
626, MX-6	6.8	7.2
Miata, 929, Serenia*	4.0	4.2

*Initial refill shown. With engine at operating temperature, shift transmission through all gears. Check fluid level in PARK and add fluid as needed

TRANSMISSION/TRANSAXLE, Manual
Refer to lubricant specifications label under hood to determine proper fluid
Verify fluid installed before topping-up or refilling transaxle

323, Protegé:
1991-92: 2WD SOHC 75W-90 **GL-4**
     DOHC . . . . **AF, FA**
Above 0°F (–18°C), 80W-90 **GL-4**
  4WD . . . . 75W-90 **GL-4, AF**
1990:
  SOHC . . . . **AF, FA**, 75W-90 **GL-4, GL-5**
Above 0°F (–18°C), 80W-90 **GL-4, GL-5**
  DOHC . . . . **AF, FA**
Above 0°F (–18°C), 80W-90 **GL-4, GL-5**
1988-89: 2WD . . . . **AF, FA**
May also use 80W-90, 90 **GL-4, GL-5**
  4WD . . . . **AF**
MX-3, Precidia 75W-90 **GL-4, GL-5**
May also use 80W-90 **GL-4, GL-5** above 0°F (–18°C); or **AF** below 0°F (–18°C)
626: 1991-92 . . . . **AF**, 75W-90 **GL-4, GL-5**
Above 0°F (–18°C), 80W-90, 90 **GL-4, GL-5**
  1988-90 . . . . **AF**
Above 0°F (–18°C), 80W-90, 90 **GL-4, GL-5**
Miata, 929, Serenia . 75W-90 **GL-4, GL-5**
Above 50°F (10°C), 80W-90

CAPACITY, Total Refill:	Liters	Pt
323, Protegé:		
1990-92: SOHC	2.7	5.6
DOHC	3.4	7.1
1988-89:		
2WD ex. Turbo	3.2	6.8
4WD	3.6	7.6
Turbo	3.4	7.1
MX-3, Precidia	2.7	5.6
Miata	2.0	4.2
626, MX-6, ex. Turbo . . .	3.4	7.2
Turbo	3.7	7.8
929, Serenia	2.5	5.2

TRANSFER CASE
323, Protegé **GL-5**
Above 0°F (–18°C), 90; below 0°F (–18°C), 80W
All others **GL-4, GL-5**
All temperatures, 75W-90; above 50°F (10°), 80W-90

CAPACITY, Refill:	Liters	Pt
323, Protegé 4WD	0.5	1.1

DIFFERENTIAL **GL-5**
Above 0°F (–18°C), 90; below 0°F (–18°C), 80W

CAPACITY, Refill:	Liters	Pt
323, Protegé 4WD, Miata	0.7	1.4
929, Serenia	1.3	2.8

MAZDA
1983-87 B2000, 2200 Diesel Pickups

MAIPM3   MAIPM3

Perform the following maintenance services at the intervals indicated to keep both the vehicle and emission warranties in effect.

MI — MILES IN THOUSANDS
KM — KILOMETERS IN THOUSANDS

FIRST 2 MI — 3 KM
Crankcase . . . . change oil

Oil filter . . . . replace

Idle speed . . . . check/adjust

DIESEL,
EVERY 3.75 MO/3.75 MI — 6 KM
Crankcase . . . . change oil
Replace filter

Sedimentor . . . . drain water

EVERY 7.5 MO/7.5 MI — 12 KM
Crankcase, gasoline . . . . change oil

Differential . . . . check level
1983-84, check fluid at initial service, then every 30 mi (48 km)

Disc brake pads . . . . inspect
Replace pads when shoe & lining is 7mm thick. Inspect parking brake

Oil filter . . . . replace

Power steering fluid . . . . . . check level **FA**

Transmission, manual
   1983 . . . . check level

Brake & clutch pedal free play . . . . . check
Check parking brake

Brake & clutch reservoirs . check level **HB**

Oil bypass filter, Diesel . . . . replace

Steering wheel free play 1983 . . . . . check

Transmission, automatic . . . . . check level
Initial service, then every 30 mi (48 km)

EVERY 15 MO/15 MI — 24 KM
Brake system . . . . inspect
Power brake unit, linings, hoses & connections

Body & chassis nuts & bolts . . . . . . torque

Power steering lines 1984-87 . . . . . inspect
Check steering system components

Cooling system . . . . inspect

Choke system 1984-87 . . . . inspect

Idle speed & mixture . . . . . . check/adjust
Ex. diesel. 1986-87, inspect idle switch

Steering
   gear . . . . . . check level/inspect 90 **GL-4**

Seat belts & retractors, 1984-87 . . inspect

Valve clearance . . . . adjust
1983-86

EVERY 30 MO/30 MI — 48 KM
Ball joints . . . . inspect
1983-84 B2000, lubricate, **LM**

Brake system . . . . change fluid **HB**
1986-87, check parking brake & clutch pedal freeplay

Cooling system . . . . . . change coolant **EC**
Ex. diesel

Driveshaft boots, 4WD . . . . inspect

Exhaust system heat shield
   1983-85 ex. diesel . . . . inspect

Steering . . . . lubricate **LM**
Wheel bearings; upper arm shaft & idler arm when equipped with fittings

Transfer case & 4WD auto.
   transmission . . . . change fluid
Also lubricate 4WD propeller shaft

Transmission, manual
   1983-86 . . . . change lubricant

Air cleaner element . . . . replace

Drive belts . . . . inspect/adjust

Emission control system . . . . inspect
Canister & evaporative check & cut valve

Engine bolts ex. 1983-85 . . . . adjust
Intake & exhaust manifold & cylinder head

Fuel filter 1984-87 . . . . replace
Inspect 1986-87 fuel lines

Spark plugs . . . . replace

EVERY 4 YEARS
Transmission, automatic,
   rubber hoses . . . . replace

Transmission, manual . . . change lubricant

EVERY 60 MO/60 MI — 96 KM
Ignition timing . . . . adjust
1986-87

O2 sensor, PCV & EGR valve . . . . replace
1986-87

Timing belt . . . . replace
1986-87

SEVERE SERVICE
Brake fluid — With extensive brake use or in humid climates, change fluid annually

Crankcase — Change oil & filter more frequently

Air cleaner element — Inspect & change more frequently in very dusty or sandy areas

KEY TO LUBRICANTS

AF	Automatic Transmission Fluid, DEXRON®-II
CC	Motor Oil, API Service CC
CD	Motor Oil, API Service CD
EC	Ethylene Glycol Coolant
FA	Automatic Transmission Fluid, Type F
GL-4	Gear Oil, API Service GL-4
GL-5	Gear Oil, API Service GL-5
HB	Hydraulic Brake Fluid, DOT 3 or 4
LM	Lithium Grease, with Moly
SF	Motor Oil, API Service SF
SG	Motor Oil, API Service SG

CRANKCASE
Gasoline engine . . . . **SF, SG**
Diesel engine . . . . **CC, CD**

CAPACITY, Refill:	Liters	Qt
2.0L	3.6	3.8
2.2L Diesel	5.0	5.3

Capacity shown is without filter. When replacing filter, additional oil may be needed

Gasoline engines:
Above 85°F (29°C)	40
Above 15°F (–9°C)	20W-40, 20W-50
Above –15°F (–25°C)	10W-40, 10W-50
32° to 105°F (0° to 39°C)	30
15° to 65°F (–9° to 20°C)	20W-20
–15° to 85°F (–25° to 29°C)	10W-30
Below 32°F (0°C)	5W-30
Below –5°F (–20°C)	5W-20

Diesel engines:
Above 104°F (40°C)	40
32° to 104°F (0° to 40°C)	30
14° to 77°F (–10° to 25°C)	20W-20
–13° to 86°F (–25° to 30°C)	10W-30
Below –4°F (–20°C)	5W-30

TRANSMISSION, Automatic
1984-85 . . . . **FA**
1986-87 . . . . **AF**

CAPACITY, Refill*:	Liters	Qt
All	4.0	4.2

*With the engine at operating temperature, shift transmission through all gears. Check fluid level in PARK and add fluid as needed

TRANSMISSION, Manual . . . GL-4, GL-5
Above 0°F (–18°C), 90; below 0°F (–18°C), 80W; all temperatures: 80W-90

CAPACITY, Refill:	Liters	Pt
B2000, 2200 Diesel:		
4-speed	1.4	3.0
5-speed	1.7	3.6

DIFFERENTIAL **GL-5**
Above 0°F (–18°C), 90; below 0°F (–18°C), 80W

CAPACITY, Refill:	Liters	Pt
All models	1.3	2.8

SERVICE AT TIME OR MILEAGE—WHICHEVER OCCURS FIRST

MAIPM5   MAIPM5

Perform the following maintenance services at the intervals indicated to keep both the vehicle and emission warranties in effect.

MI — MILES IN THOUSANDS
KM — KILOMETERS IN THOUSANDS

EVERY 6 MONTHS
Brake & clutch reservoirs . check level **HB**

Power steering reservoir .. check level **AF**

Transmission, automatic ..... check level

EVERY 7.5 MO/7.5 MI — 12 KM
Crankcase .... change oil

Oil filter .... replace

EVERY 12 MONTHS
Air conditioning system .... inspect

EVERY 15 MO/15 MI — 24 KM
Brake system .... inspect
Power brake unit, linings, hoses & connections

Body & chassis nuts & bolts ...... torque

Propeller shaft, 4WD .... lubricate **LM**

Choke, 2.2L .... spray clean

Cooling system .... inspect

Drive belt, 2.6L .... inspect

Idle speed .... check/adjust
Also inspect idle switch

Steering
gear ...... check level/inspect 90 **GL-4**
Also inspect steering linkage

Spark plugs .... inspect

Valve clearance .... adjust
2.6L jet valve

EVERY 30 MO/30 MI — 48 KM
Ball joints .... inspect

Brake system .... change fluid **HB**

Cooling system ...... change coolant **EC**

Differentials .... change lubricant

Driveshaft boots, 4WD .... inspect

Exhaust system heat shields ..... inspect

Steering .... lubricate **LM**
Wheel bearings; upper arm shaft

Transmission, manual ... change lubricant

Transfer case & 4WD auto.
transmission .... change fluid
Also lubricate 4WD propeller shaft

Air cleaner element .... replace

Choke, 2.6L .... spray clean

Drive belts .... inspect/adjust
2.6L engine, replace

Fuel filter, 2.2L .... replace

Fuel lines .... inspect

Spark plugs .... replace

2.6L, EVERY 50 MO/50 MI — 80 KM
Distributor spark advance/timing ... check

Ignition wires .... replace

Intake temp. control system ...... inspect

PCV valve .... inspect

Throttle position system .... inspect

EVERY 60 MO/60 MI — 96 KM
EGR valve .... replace

Emission systems vacuum hoses . replace

Fuel filter, 2.6L .... replace

High altitude compensator filter ... replace

Ignition timing 2.2L .... check/adjust

PCV valve, 2.2L .... inspect

Timing belt, 2.2L .... replace

EVERY 80 MI — 128 KM
Oxygen sensor .... replace

SEVERE SERVICE
Crankcase — Change oil & filter every 5 mo/ 5 mi — (8 km)

Air cleaner element — Inspect & change more frequently

KEY TO LUBRICANTS

AF	Automatic Transmission Fluid, DEXRON®-II
CC	Motor Oil, API Service CC
CD	Motor Oil, API Service CD
EC	Ethylene Glycol Coolant
FA	Automatic Transmission Fluid, Type F
GL-4	Gear Oil, API Service GL-4
GL-5	Gear Oil, API Service GL-5
HB	Hydraulic Brake Fluid, DOT 3 or 4
LM	Lithium Grease, with Moly
SF	Motor Oil, API Service SF
SG	Motor Oil, API Service SG

CRANKCASE .... SF, SG

CAPACITY, Refill:	Liters	Qt
2.2L	3.9	4.1
2.6L: 2WD	3.8	4.0
4WD	4.5	4.8

Capacity shown is without filter. When replacing filter, additional oil may be needed

Above 85°F (29°C)	40
Above 15°F (–9°C)	20W-40, 20W-50
Above –15°F (–25°C)	10W-40, 10W-50
32° to 105°F (0° to 39°C)	30
15° to 65°F (–9° to 20°C)	20W-20
–15° to 85°F (–25° to 29°C)	10W-30
Below 32°F (0°C)	5W-30
Below –5°F (–20°C)	5W-20

TRANSMISSION, Automatic .... AF

CAPACITY, Initial Refill*:	Liters	Qt
All	4.0	4.2

*With the engine at operating temperature, shift transmission through all gears. Check fluid level in PARK and add fluid as needed

TRANSMISSION, Manual ... GL-4, GL-5
B2200:
Above 0°F (–18°C), 90; below 0°F (–18°C), 80W; all temperatures: 80W-90
B2600:
Above 0°F (–18°C), 80, 80W-90; below 0°F (–18°C), 75W-80; all temperatures, 75W-90

CAPACITY, Refill:	Liters	Pt
B2200: 4-speed	1.7	3.6
5-speed	2.0	4.2
B2600: 2WD	2.8	6.0
4WD	3.2	6.8

TRANSFER CASE GL-4
Above 0°F (–18°C), 80, 80W-90; below 0°F (–18°C), 75W; all temperatures, 75W-80

CAPACITY, Refill:	Liters	Pt
4WD	2.0	4.2

DIFFERENTIAL GL-5
Above 0°F (–18°C), 90; below 0°F (–18°C), 80W

CAPACITY, Refill:	Liters	Pt
B2200	1.3	2.8
B2600: Front	1.2	2.6
Rear, 2WD	1.3	2.8
Rear, 4WD	1.7	3.6

MAZDA
1989-92 B2200, 2600 Pickups; 1989-91 MPV
Navajo — See Ford Trucks, Explorer

SERVICE AT TIME OR MILEAGE—WHICHEVER OCCURS FIRST

MAIPM6   MAIPM6

Perform the following maintenance services at the intervals indicated to keep both the vehicle and emission warranties in effect.

MI — MILES IN THOUSANDS
KM — KILOMETERS IN THOUSANDS

EVERY 6 MONTHS
Brake & clutch fluid
  master cylinder .... check level **HB**

Power steering reservoir .. check level **AF**

Transmission, automatic ..... check level

EVERY 7.5 MO/7.5 MI — 12 KM
Crankcase .... change oil

Oil filter .... replace

EVERY 12 MONTHS
Air conditioning system .... inspect

EVERY 15 MO/15 MI — 24 KM
Propeller shaft, 4WD .... lubricate **LM**

Choke, B2200 .... clean/inspect

Cooling system .... inspect

Idle speed .... check/adjust
B2200 also inspect idle switch
Initial service for B2600, MPV

Seat belts & retractors .... inspect

Valve clearance .... adjust

EVERY 30 MO/30 MI — 48 KM
Body & chassis nuts & bolts ...... torque

Brake system .... change fluid **HB**

Brake system .... inspect

Cooling system ...... change coolant **EC**

Driveshaft boots, 4WD .... inspect

Steering & suspension,
  ex. MPV .... lubricate **LM**
Wheel bearings; upper arm shaft

Steering gearbox oil ...... check 90 **GL-4**

Steering & suspension system .... inspect

Air cleaner element .... replace

Drive belts .... inspect/adjust

Fuel filter B2200 .... replace

Fuel lines & hoses .... inspect

Idle speed, B2600, MPV .... check/adjust
Initial service at 15 mo/15 mi (24 km)

Spark plugs .... replace

EVERY 60 MO/60 MI — 96 KM
Differentials .... change lubricant

Transfer case .... change lubricant

Transmission, automatic .... change fluid

Transmission, manual ... change lubricant

EGR valve, B2200 .... replace
At mileage interval only

Emission systems vacuum hoses . replace
B2200, B2600

Fuel filter, B2600, MPV .... replace

High altitude
  compensator air filter .... replace

Ignition timing .... check/adjust

PCV valve .... inspect

Timing belt, B2200, MPV V6 ..... replace
At mileage interval only

EVERY 80 MI — 128 KM
Emission systems vacuum hoses .. replace
MPV

Oxygen sensor .... replace

SEVERE SERVICE
Crankcase — Change oil & filter 5 mo/5 mi (8 km)

Air cleaner element — Inspect & change more frequently

Front disc brakes — Inspect every 15 mo/15 mi (24 km)

Transmissions, transfer case, differentials — Change fluid or lubricant every 30 mo/30 mi (48 km)

KEY TO LUBRICANTS

AF	Automatic Transmission Fluid, DEXRON®-II
CC	Motor Oil, API Service CC
CD	Motor Oil, API Service CD
EC	Ethylene Glycol Coolant
FA	Automatic Transmission Fluid, Type F
GL-4	Gear Oil, API Service GL-4
GL-5	Gear Oil, API Service GL-5
HB	Hydraulic Brake Fluid, DOT 3 or 4
LM	Lithium Grease, with Moly
SG	Motor Oil, API Service SG

CRANKCASE .... SG
CAPACITY, Refill:	Liters	Qt
2.2L	3.9	4.1
2.6L, 3.0L	4.5	4.8

Capacity shown is without filter. When replacing filter, additional oil may be needed

1989-90:
Above 85°F (29°C) 40
Above 15°F (–9°C) 20W-40, 20W-50
Above –15°F (–25°C) 10W-40, 10W-50
32° to 105°F (0° to 39°C) 30
15° to 65°F (–9° to 20°C) 20W-20
–15° to 85°F (–25° to 29°C) 10W-30
Below 32°F (0°C) 5W-30
Below –5°F (–20°C) 5W-20
1991-92:
Above –15°F (–25°C) 10W-30
Below 32°F (0°C) 5W-30

TRANSMISSION, Automatic .... AF
CAPACITY, Initial Refill*:	Liters	Qt
All	4.0	4.2

* With the engine at operating temperature, shift transmission through all gears. Check fluid level in PARK and add fluid as needed

TRANSMISSION, Manual ... GL-4, GL-5
All temperatures, 75W-90; above 50°F (10°C), 80W-90
CAPACITY, Refill:	Liters	Pt
B2200: 4-speed	1.7	3.6
5-speed	2.0	4.2
B2600: 2WD	2.8	6.0
4WD	3.2	6.8
MPV	2.5	5.2

TRANSFER CASE GL-4, GL-5
All temperatures, 75W-90; above 32°F (0°C), 80W-90
CAPACITY, Refill:	Liters	Pt
B2600	2.0	4.2
MPV	1.5	3.2

DIFFERENTIAL GL-5
Above 0°F (–18°C), 90; below 0°F (–18°C), 80W
CAPACITY, Refill:	Liters	Pt
B2200	1.2	2.6
B2600: Front	1.5	3.2
Rear: 2WD	1.3	2.8
4WD	1.7	3.6
MPV: Front	1.7	3.6
Rear	1.5	3.2

SERVICE LOCATIONS — ENGINE AND CHASSIS

MZIDP-1   HOOD RELEASE: Inside   MZIDP-1

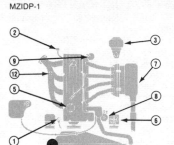

4-cyl. 2.2L Diesel
1984-85 190D

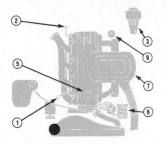

4-cyl. 2.3L
1984-88, 1991-92 190E

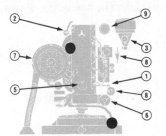

4-cyl. 2.4L Diesel
1983 240D

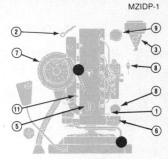

5-cyl. 3.0L Turbo Diesel
1983-85 300 CD, SD, TD

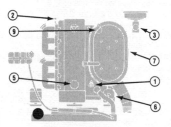

6-cyl. 2.6L, 3.0L Gas
1986-92 300E
1987-89 260E
1987-92 190 2.6L

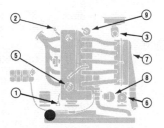

5-cyl. 2.5L Diesel
1986-89, 1991 190D

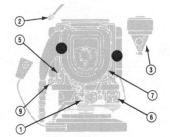

V8 3.8L, 4.2L
5.0L, 5.6L
1982-89 All w/V8
1990-91 420SEL, 560SEC, SEL

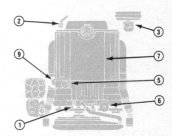

1990-92
V8 5.0L DOHC

0 FITTINGS
0 PLUGS

0 FITTINGS
0 PLUGS

0 FITTINGS
0 PLUGS

0 FITTINGS
0 PLUGS

0 FITTINGS
0 PLUGS

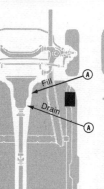

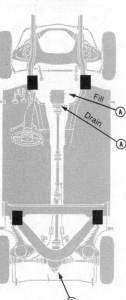

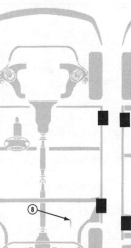

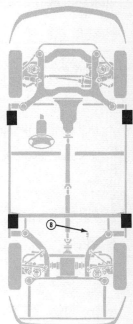

1984-92 201 Chassis:
190E, 190D;
1986-92 124 Chassis:
260E, 300D, 300CE, 300E,
300TD, 300TE, 400E, 500E

1983-89 107 Chassis:
380SL, 560SL

1983-85 123 Chassis:
240D, 300D, 300CD, 300TD;
1983-91 126 Chassis:
300SD, 300SDL, 300SE, 300SEL,
380SE, 380SEC, 380SEL, 420SEL,
500SEC, 500SEL, 560SEC, 560SEL

1990-92 129 Chassis;
300SL, 500SL

1992 140 Chassis;
300SE, 400SE,
500SEL, 600SEL

① Crankcase dipstick
② Transmission dipstick
③ Brake fluid reservoir
④ Clutch fluid reservoir
⑤ Oil fill cap
⑥ Power steering reservoir
⑦ Air filter
⑧ Fuel filter
⑨ Oil filter

⑩ PCV filter
⑪ EGR valve
⑫ Oxygen sensor
⑬ PCV valve
⑭ Hydropneumatic
   suspension reservoir

Ⓐ Manual transmission/transaxle,
   drain & fill
Ⓑ Transfer case, NOT USED
Ⓒ Automatic transaxle final drive,
   NOT USED
Ⓓ Differential, drain & fill

■ Lift adapter position
● Cooling system drain

MERCEDES-BENZ
1983-89, 1991-92 All Diesel Models

CHEK-CHART

SERVICE AT TIME OR MILEAGE—WHICHEVER OCCURS FIRST

MZIPM1   MZIPM1

W SERVICE TO MAINTAIN EMISSION WARRANTY

MI—MILES IN THOUSANDS
KM—KILOMETERS IN THOUSANDS

1992 300SD, EVERY 7.5 MI—12 KM
ALL OTHERS, EVERY 5 MI—8 KM

W Crankcase . . . . change oil
At least once a year if year-round multigrade oil is used.
Otherwise, at least every spring & fall

W Oil filter . . . . replace
At least once a year if year-round multigrade oil is used.
Otherwise, at least every spring & fall

W Transmission,
    manual 1983-89 . . . . change lubricant
One time service only

W Engine control
    linkage . . . . inspect/lubricate **SLF**

Battery 1983-89 . . . . check level

EVERY 24 MO/15 MI—24 KM
Brake system . . . . inspect
Clean brake discs & pads, road test system. Adjust
parking brake at first interval only

Differential . . . . check level

Front axle, steering
    linkage & boots . . . . inspect

Steering . . . . check free play
Inspect linkage & retorque mounting bolts

Tires & wheels . . . . inspect
Dismount to inspect, rotate if necessary

W Transmission, manual . . . . . check level

W Air filter element 1983-89 . inspect/clean

Brake & clutch reservoir . . check level **HB**

Battery . . . . check level

W Cooling system . . . . check level **EC**
Check degree of antifreeze protection

Drive belts . . . . inspect/adjust

W Fuel system . . . . inspect
Check fuel tank, lines

Injection timing 1991-92 . . . . check/adjust
At first service interval only

Level control 300TD . . . . . check level **SLF**

Power steering reservoir . . check level **PS**
Inspect condition of lines & hoses

W Transmission, automatic . . . check level

Valve clearance 1983-85 . . . . adjust
Ex. 4-cyl. 2.2L

Windshield washers . . . . fill

Body . . . . lubricate **CL**

Air conditioner . . . . inspect
Check operation and Freon® charge

Electrical equipment . . . . inspect

Seat belts . . . . inspect

Tape deck head . . . . clean

EVERY 30 MI—48 KM
Propeller shaft . . . . check flex discs

W Transmission, automatic . . change fluid
Replace internal filter

W Air filter element . . . . replace

Clutch plate 1983-86 . . . . check wear

W Fuel filter . . . . replace

W Fuel prefilter . . . . inspect/replace

W Injection pump timing
    1983-89 . . . . check/adjust
One time service only

W Idle speed 1983-89 . . . . . . check/adjust

W Idle control knob 240D . . . check/adjust

Parking brake cables . . . . inspect
Check for free operation of cables

Air recirculation filter . . . . replace
1992 300SD only

1983-85, EVERY 12 MO
1986-89, EVERY 24 MO
1991-92, EVERY 24 MO
Preferably in the spring
Brake system . . . . change fluid **HB**

Body water drains . . . . clean

Chassis & body . . . . inspect
Check for damage & corrosion

Sunroof rails . . . . lubricate **LM**

EVERY 36 MO
W Engine coolant . . . . replace **EC**

SEVERE SERVICE
Crankcase—Change oil & filter, every 2.5 mi
(4 km)

Transmission, automatic—Change fluid
every 15 mi (24 km)

Air filter element—Clean/replace, every 15
mi (24 km) or as needed

Tires—Inspect every 7.5 mi (12 km)

KEY TO LUBRICANTS♦

AF	DEXRON®-II Automatic Transmission Fluid
CC	Motor Oil, API Service CC
CD	Motor Oil, API Service CD
EC	Ethylene Glycol Coolant Mix with water to desired freeze protection
GLS	Gear Lubricant, Special Mercedes-Benz Part No. 900 26 03 15
GL-5	Gear Oil, API Service GL-5
GL-5★	Special Lubricant for Limited-Slip Differential Mercedes-Benz Part No. 000 583 09 04
HB	Hydraulic Brake Fluid, Extra Heavy-Duty DOT 4
LM	Lithium Multipurpose Grease
PS	Power Steering Fluid Mercedes-Benz Part No. 000 989 88 03
SF	Motor Oil, API Service SF
SLF	Special Lubricant—Fluid Mercedes-Benz Part No. 000 989 91 03 10

♦Note: Use only Mercedes-Benz approved fluids

CRANKCASE . . . . SF/CC, SF/CD

CAPACITY, Refill*:	Liters	Qt
4-cyl.: 1983-84 2.4L	6.5	6.9
1984 2.2L	6.0	6.3
1985 2.2L	6.5	6.9
5-cyl.: 1983 3.0L ex. Turbo	6.5	6.9
1983-84 3.0L Turbo	7.5	7.9
1985 3.0L Turbo	8.0	8.5
1986-89 2.5L	7.0	7.4
1991 2.5L	7.5	7.9
1992 2.5L	7.0	7.4
6-cyl.: 1986-87 3.0L, all . . .	8.0	8.5
1991 3.5L	8.0	8.5

*All capacities shown include filter. On models with oil cooler, additional oil may be needed when cooler is drained

1983-89, 1991:
Above 86°F (30°C) 40
Above 32°F (0°C) 30, 20W-40, 20W-50
32° to 77°F (0° to 25°C) 1982-85 . . . 20W-30
Above 5°F (–15°C) 15W-40, 15W-50
23° to 68°F (–5° to 20°C) 1982-85 . . . . . 20W-20
Above –4°F (–20°C) 10W-40, 10W-50
–4° to 50°F (–20° to 10°C) 10W*, 10W-30
Below 14°F (–10°C) 5W-20, 5W-30
*240D only

1992:
All temperatures 5W-50
Above 32°F (0°C) 30, 20W-40, 20W-50
Above 5°F (–15°C) 15W-40, 15W-50
Above –4°F (–20°C) 10W-40
Below 50°F (10°C) 10W-30
Below 14°F (–10°C) 5W-30

TRANSMISSION, Automatic . . . . . . AF

CAPACITY, Initial Refill*:	Liters	Qt
1983 240D, 300 Series		
w/o Turbo	4.8	5.1
1983-85 300 Series		
w/Turbo	6.2	6.5
1984-89 190D	5.5	5.8
1986-87 300 Series	6.2	6.5
1991-92 300D	5.5	5.8
1991 350SD, 350SDL	6.2	6.6
1992 300SD	7.1	7.5

*Add specified quantity. With engine at operating temperature, shift transmission through all gears. Check fluid level in PARK and add fluid as needed

TRANSMISSION, Manual . . . . GLS

CAPACITY, Refill:	Liters	Pt
1983	1.3	2.8
1984-87	1.5	3.2

DIFFERENTIAL
Standard 85W-90, 90 **GL-5**
Limited-Slip . . . . 90 **GL-5★**

CAPACITY, Refill:	Liters	Pt
190 Series	0.7	1.4
240D, 1983-87 300 Series . .	1.1	2.4
1991 300SD, SDL	1.3	2.8
1991-92 300D	1.1	2.4

LIMITED-SLIP IDENTIFICATION:
Metal plate on rear of differential, near fill plug

SERVICE AT TIME OR MILEAGE—WHICHEVER OCCURS FIRST

MZIPM2   MZIPM2

W   SERVICE TO MAINTAIN WARRANTY

MI—MILES IN THOUSANDS
KM—KILOMETERS IN THOUSANDS

EVERY 7.5 MI—12 KM

W Crankcase . . . . change oil
At least once a year if year-round multigrade oil is used.
Otherwise, at least every spring & fall

W Oil filter . . . . replace
At least once a year if year-round multigrade oil is used.
Otherwise, at least every spring & fall

W Transmission,
   manual . . . . change lubricant
One time service only (1984-87)

W Engine control
   linkage . . . . inspect/lubricate **SLF**
At least twice a year

   Rear engine mount . . . . check/adjust
4MATIC models only, at first interval only

   Battery 1983-90 . . . . check level

EVERY 24 MO/15 MI—24 KM

   Brake system . . . . inspect
Clean brake discs & pads, road test system. Adjust
parking brake ex. 140 chassis, at initial service only

   Clutch control . . . . inspect

   Differential . . . . check level
1990-91 4MATIC models, check front differential level

   Front axle, steering
   linkage & boots . . . . inspect

   Steering . . . . check free play
1983-91, retorque mounting bolts

   Tires & wheels . . . . inspect
Dismount to inspect, rotate and correct pressure if necessary

W Transmission, manual . . . . . check level

   Transfer case . . . . check level
1990-92 4MATIC models

   Brake & clutch reservoir . . check level **HB**

   Battery 1991-92 . . . . check level

W Cooling system . . . . check level **EC**
Check degree of antifreeze protection

   Drive belts . . . . inspect/adjust

W Spark plugs 1983-86 . . . . replace
Not required for Calif. emissions warranty

   Spark plugs 1987-92 . . . . inspect
Replace as necessary

W Fuel system . . . . inspect
Check fuel tank, lines

   Level control . . . . check level **SLF**

   Power steering reservoir . . check level **PS**
Inspect condition of lines & hoses

W Transmission, automatic . . . check level

W Valve clearance . . . . adjust
1986-87 190E-16 only

   Windshield washers . . . . check/fill

   Body . . . . lubricate **CL**

   Climate control system . . . . inspect
Check operation and Freon® charge

   Convertible top 1990-92 . . . . inspect
Check level of hydraulic system, check operation of
locking lug

   Electrical equipment . . . . inspect

   Heating & ventilation filter . . . . . . replace
1990-92 300SL, 500SL only

   Seat belts . . . . inspect

   Tape deck head . . . . clean

EVERY 30 MI—48 KM

   Propeller shaft . . . . check flex discs

   Steering gear 1992 . . . . tighten
Retorque mounting bolts

W Transmission, automatic . . change fluid
Replace internal filter

W Air filter element . . . . replace
Replace air pump filter element if equipped

   Clutch disc . . . . check wear

   Parking brake cables . . . . inspect
Check for free operation of cables

   Oxygen sensor 1983-85 . . . . replace
One time service only

W Spark plugs . . . . replace
Calif. 1983-86, all models 1987-92

   Air recirculation filter . . . . replace
1992 140 chassis only

EVERY 60 MI—96 KM

W Fuel filter . . . . replace

W Oxygen sensor 1986-90 . . . . replace
One time service only

1983-85, EVERY 12 MO
1986-92, EVERY 24 MO
Preferably in the spring

   Brake system . . . . change fluid **HB**

   Body water drains . . . . clean

   Chassis & body . . . . inspect
Check for damage & corrosion

   Sunroof rails . . . . lubricate **LM**

EVERY 36 MO

W Engine coolant . . . . replace **EC**

SEVERE SERVICE

   Crankcase—Change oil & filter every 3.75
mi (6 km)

   Tires—Inspect every 7.5 mi (12 km)

   Transmission, automatic—Change fluid
every 15 mi (24 km)

   Air filter element—Clean/replace every 15
mi (24 km) or as needed

KEY TO LUBRICANTS
See other Mercedes-Benz chart

CRANKCASE . . . . SF/CC, SF/CD		
CAPACITY, Refill*:	Liters	Qt
4-cyl.:		
1984-88, 1991-92 190E . . .	5.0	5.3
6-cyl.:		
1986-89 3.0L	6.0	6.3
1987-91 2.6L	6.0	6.3
1990-92 3.0L SOHC ex.		
4MATIC	6.0	6.3
1990-92 3.0L SOHC		
4MATIC	6.5	6.9
1990-92 3.0L DOHC	7.5	7.9
8-cyl.:		
All models	8.0	8.5
12-cyl.:		
1992 600SEL	10.00	10.6

*All capacities shown include filter. On models with oil
cooler, additional oil may be needed when cooler is
drained

1983-91
Above 86°F (30°C), 1983-89	40
Above 32°F (0°C), 1983-89	30
Above 32°F (0°C) 20W-40, 20W-50	
Above 5°F (−15°C) 15W-40, 15W-50	
Above −4°F (−20°C) 10W-40, 10W-50	
−4° to 50°F (−20° to 10°C) 10W-30	
Below 14°F (−10°C) 5W-20, 5W-30	

1992:
All temperatures 5W-50	
Above 32°F (0°C) 20W-40, 20W-50	
Above 5°F (−15°C) 15W-40, 15W-50	
Above −4°F (−20°C) 10W-40	
−4° to 50°F (−20° to 10°C) 10W-30	
Below 14°F (−10°C) 5W-30	

TRANSMISSION, Automatic . . . . AF		
CAPACITY, Initial Refill*:	Liters	Qt
1983-85 190E	5.5	5.8
1983-92 All w/V8 engine . .	7.7	8.1
1986-92 190E, 260E, 300E		
2.6L	6.0	6.3
1986-92 300 Series ex. SL,		
2.6L	6.2	6.6
1990-92 300SL	6.0	6.3
1992 600SEL	7.7	8.1

* Add specified quantity. With engine at operating temperature, shift transmission through all gears. Check fluid
level in PARK and add oil as needed

TRANSMISSION, Manual . . . . GLS		
CAPACITY, Refill*:	Liters	Pt
1984-92 All ex. 300SL . . .	1.5	3.2
1990-92 300SL	1.6	3.4

TRANSFER CASE . . . . AF		
CAPACITY, Refill:	Liters	Pt
1990-92 300E 4MATIC	0.7	1.4

REAR DIFFERENTIAL
Standard 85W-90, 90 **GL-5**	
Limited-Slip . . . . 90 **GL-5★**	

CAPACITY, Refill*:	Liters	Pt
1983-91 All w/V8 engine . .	1.3	2.8
1984-89 190E	0.7	1.4
1986-92 300 Series ex. SL	1.1	2.3
1987-90 260E	1.1	2.3
1990-92 190E	1.1	2.3
1990-92 300SL	1.3	2.8

FRONT DIFFERENTIAL 85W-90, 90 **GL-5**
CAPACITY, Refill*:	Liters	Pt
1990-92 300E 4MATIC	1.0	2.2

LIMITED-SLIP IDENTIFICATION:
Metal plate on rear of differential, near fill plug

SERVICE LOCATIONS — ENGINE AND CHASSIS

HOOD RELEASE: Inside

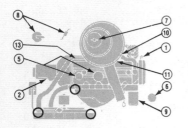
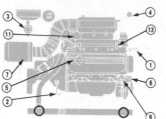
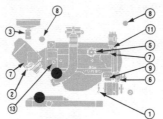

① Crankcase dipstick
② Transmission dipstick
③ Brake fluid reservoir
④ Clutch fluid reservoir
⑤ Oil fill cap
⑥ Power steering reservoir
⑦ Air filter
⑧ Fuel filter
⑨ Oil filter
⑩ PCV filter
⑪ EGR valve
⑫ Oxygen sensor
⑬ PCV valve

1985-89
1468cc 2V,
Mirage, Precis

1989-92
1468cc FI
Mirage, Precis

1983-88
1597cc, 1795cc Turbo
Tredia, Cordia, Mirage

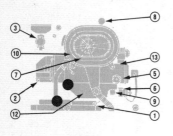
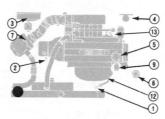
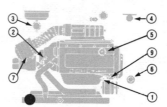
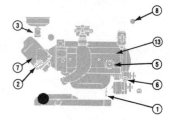

1983-88
1997cc
Tredia, Cordia

1989-92
1755cc, 1997cc SOHC
Galant, Eclipse

1989-92
1597cc DOHC Turbo,
1997cc DOHC
Galant, Eclipse, Mirage

1984-87
2350cc
Galant

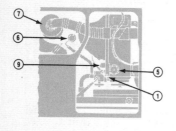
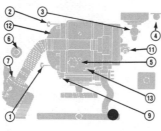
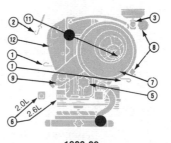
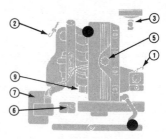

1987-90
2350cc
Van

1990-92
2350cc
Pickup

1983-89
1997cc, 2555cc
Pickup, Montero

1983-85
2346cc Diesel
Pickup

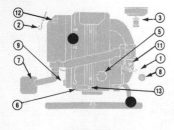
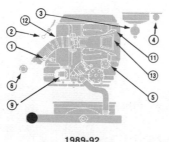
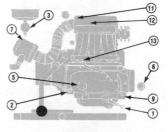
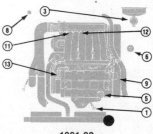

1983-89
2555cc Turbo
Conquest

1989-92
2972cc
Montero, Pickup

1988-92
2972cc SOHC
Sigma, 3000GT

1991-92
2972cc DOHC
3000GT

● Cooling system drain   ○ Cooling system drain, some models

SERVICE LOCATIONS — ENGINE AND CHASSIS

0 FITTINGS
0 PLUGS

1985-92 Mirage
1987-92 Precis

0 FITTINGS
0 PLUGS

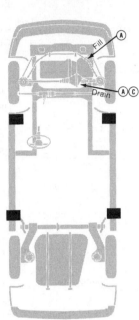

1983-88
Tredia, Cordia

0 FITTINGS
0 PLUGS

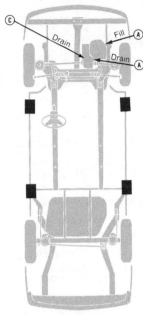

1984-92 Galant
1988-91 Sigma
1990-92 Eclipse
1991-92 3000GT

4-7 FITTINGS
0-4 PLUGS

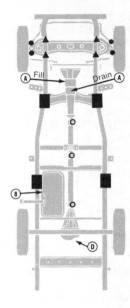

1983-92
2-Wheel Drive Pickup

8-17 FITTINGS

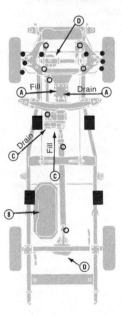

1983-92
4-Wheel Drive Pickup

17 FITTINGS

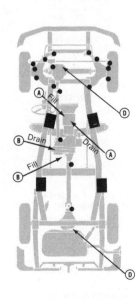

1984-91
Montero

2 PLUGS

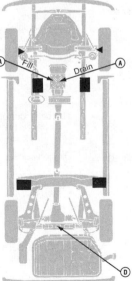

1983-89
Starion

2 FITTINGS
2 PLUGS

1987-90
Van

■ Lift adapter position
▲ Plug △ Plug, some models
● Fitting ○ Fitting, some models

Ⓐ Manual transmission/transaxle, drain & fill
Ⓑ Transfer case, drain & fill

Ⓒ Automatic transaxle final drive, drain & fill
Ⓓ Differential, drain & fill
Ⓑ Fuel filter

MITSUBISHI
1983 Cordia, Tredia, Starion

MI — MILES IN THOUSANDS
KM — KILOMETERS IN THOUSANDS

TURBO ENGINE, EVERY 6 MO/3 MI — 4.8 KM
Crankcase .... change oil

Oil filter .... replace
Every other oil change

EVERY 12 MO/7.5 MI — 12 KM
Crankcase .... change oil
Ex. Turbo engine

Exhaust system .... inspect

Oil filter .... replace
Ex. Turbo engine. Every other oil change

Power steering .... check level **AF**
Check for leaks & condition of belts & boots

Steering gear .... check free play

Transmission, automatic ..... check level

EVERY 12 MONTHS
Cooling system .... inspect

EVERY 15 MI — 24 KM
Brake hoses .... inspect

Disc brake pads .... inspect

Limited-Slip differential ...... change fluid

Drive belts .... inspect/adjust
Initial service, then every 30 mi (48 km)

Valve clearance .... inspect/adjust

EVERY 24 MO/30 MI — 48 KM
Coolant .... drain/flush/refill **EC**

EVERY 30 MI — 48 KM
Ball joint, steering linkage seals &
FWD steering &
drive shaft boots .... inspect

Differential .... check level
Ex. Limited-Slip

Front wheel bearings
ex. FWD .... clean/repack **LM**
Inspect for leaks. Inspect & repack whenever rotors are
removed

Rear brakes .... inspect
Check brake shoes & wheel cylinders

Rear wheel bearings
FWD .... clean/repack **LM**
Inspect for leaks. Repack whenever drums are re-
moved

Transaxle, automatic FWD .. change fluid
Change filter & adjust bands

Transmission, manual ...... check level

Air cleaner filter .... replace

Brake master cylinder .... check level **HB**

Choke & linkage .... clean **PC**

Drive belts .... replace

Spark plugs .... replace

EVERY 48 MONTHS
Brakes .... change fluid **HB**
Also change hydraulic clutch fluid

EVERY 60 MO/50 MI — 80 KM
Crankcase emission system .... clean

Evaporative control system ...... inspect
Replace canisters

Fuel filter .... replace
Check fuel system cap, tank, lines & connections

Fuel, water, &
fuel vapor hoses .... check/replace

Ignition timing .... check/adjust

Ignition wires .... check/replace

Turbocharger oil &
air intake hoses .... replace

Oxygen sensor .... check/replace

Vacuum hoses .... check
Secondary air hoses & crankcase ventilation hoses

SEVERE SERVICE
Air cleaner filter — Replace more frequently

Brake shoes & pads — Inspect more frequently

Crankcase — Change every 3 mo/3 mi (4.8
km) & filter at every other oil change

Spark plugs — Replace every 15 mi (24 km)

KEY TO LUBRICANTS

AF	DEXRON®-II Automatic Transmission Fluid
AP	Mitsubishi Plus ATF
EC	Ethylene Glycol Coolant Mix 50% to 70% with water
GL-4	Gear Oil, API Service GL-4
GL-5	Gear Oil, API Service GL-5
GL-5★	Special Lubricant for Limited-Slip Differentials Mitsubishi Part No. 8149630EX
LM	Lithium Grease, EP
HB	Hydraulic Brake Fluid, DOT 3
PC	Carburetor Cleaner
SE	Motor Oil, API Service SE
SF	Motor Oil, API Service SF

CRANKCASE .... SE, SF

CAPACITY, Refill:	Liters	Qt
1.8L, 2.0L	3.5	3.7
2.6L	3.8	4.0

Capacity shown is without filter. When replacing filter, ad-
ditional oil may be needed
Above 32°F (0°C) 20W-20, 20W-40, 20W-50
Above −10°F (−23°C) . 10W-30, 10W-40, 10W-50
Below 60°F (16°C) 5W-20*, 5W-30, 5W-40
*Not recommended for sustained high-speed driving

TRANSMISSION/TRANSAXLE, Automatic .... AF, AP

CAPACITY, Initial Refill*:	Liters	Qt
All models	4.0	4.2

*With the engine at operating temperature, shift transmis-
sion through all gears. Check fluid level in NEUTRAL and
add fluid as needed

TRANSMISSION/TRANSAXLE, Manual
FWD 80W, 75W-85W **GL-4**
RWD 80W, 75W-85W **GL-4**

CAPACITY, Refill:	Liters	Pt
FWD: W/o Turbo	2.1	4.6
W/Turbo	2.3	4.8
RWD: 4-speed	2.1	4.4
5-speed	2.3	4.8

DIFFERENTIAL
Limited-Slip .... **GL-5★**
Standard **GL-5**
Above −10°F (−23°C), 90, 85W-90; −30°
to −10°F (−34° to −23°C), 80W, 80W-90; below
−30°F (−34°C), 75W

CAPACITY, Refill:	Liters	Pt
All models	1.3	2.8

SERVICE AT TIME OR MILEAGE—WHICHEVER OCCURS FIRST

MIIPM2A

MIIPM2A

MI — MILES IN THOUSANDS
KM — KILOMETERS IN THOUSANDS

TURBO ENGINE, EVERY 6 MO/3 MI — 4.8 KM
Crankcase .... change oil

Oil filter .... replace
Every other oil change

EVERY 12 MO/7.5 MI — 12 KM
Crankcase .... change oil
Ex. Turbo engine

Exhaust system .... inspect

Oil filter .... replace
Ex. Turbo engine. Every other oil change

Power steering .... check level **AF**
Check for leaks & condition of belts & boots

Steering gear .... check free play

Transmission, automatic ..... check level

EVERY 12 MONTHS
Cooling system .... inspect

EVERY 15 MI — 24 KM
Brake hoses .... inspect

Disc brake pads .... inspect

Limited-Slip differential ...... change fluid

Drive belts .... inspect/adjust
Initial service, then every 30 mi (48 km)

Valve clearance .... inspect/adjust

EVERY 24 MO/30 MI — 48 KM
Coolant .... drain/flush/refill **EC**

EVERY 30 MI — 48 KM
Ball joint, steering linkage seals & FWD steering & drive shaft boots .... inspect

Differential .... check level
Ex. Limited-Slip

Front wheel bearings
  ex. FWD .... clean/repack **LM**
Inspect for leaks. Inspect & repack whenever rotors are removed

Rear brakes .... inspect
Check brake shoes & wheel cylinders

Rear wheel bearings
  FWD .... clean/repack **LM**
Inspect for leaks. Repack whenever drums are removed

Transaxle, automatic FWD .. change fluid
Change filter & adjust bands

Transmission, manual .... check level

Air cleaner filter .... replace

Brake master cylinder .... check level **HB**

Choke & linkage .... clean **PC**

Drive belts .... replace

Spark plugs .... replace

EVERY 48 MONTHS
Brakes .... change fluid **HB**
Also change hydraulic clutch fluid

EVERY 60 MO/50 MI — 80 KM
Crankcase emission system .... clean

Evaporative control system ...... inspect
Replace canisters

Fuel filter .... replace
Check fuel system cap, tank, lines & connections

Fuel, water, & fuel vapor hoses .... check/replace

Ignition timing .... check/adjust

Ignition wires .... check/replace

Turbocharger oil & air intake hoses .... replace

Oxygen sensor .... check/replace

Vacuum hoses .... check
Secondary air hoses & crankcase ventilation hoses

SEVERE SERVICE
Air cleaner filter — Replace more frequently

Brake shoes & pads — Inspect more frequently

Crankcase — Change every 3 mo/3 mi (4.8 km) & filter at every other oil change

Spark plugs — Replace every 15 mi (24 km)

KEY TO LUBRICANTS

AF	DEXRON®-II Automatic Transmission Fluid
AP	Mitsubishi Plus ATF
EC	Ethylene Glycol Coolant Mix 50% to 70% with water
GL-4	Gear Oil, API Service GL-4
GL-5	Gear Oil, API Service GL-5
GL-5★	Special Lubricant for Limited-Slip Differentials Mitsubishi Part No. 8149630EX
LM	Lithium Grease, EP
HB	Hydraulic Brake Fluid, DOT 3
PC	Carburetor Cleaner
SE	Motor Oil, API Service SE
SF	Motor Oil, API Service SF

CRANKCASE .... SE, SF

CAPACITY, Refill:	Liters	Qt
1.8L, 2.0L	3.5	3.7
2.6L	3.8	4.0

Capacity shown is without filter. When replacing filter, additional oil may be needed
Above 32°F (0°C) 20W-20, 20W-40, 20W-50
Above –10°F (–23°C) . 10W-30, 10W-40, 10W-50
Below 60°F (16°C) 5W-20*, 5W-30, 5W-40
*Not recommended for sustained high-speed driving

TRANSMISSION/TRANSAXLE, Automatic .... AF, AP

CAPACITY, Initial Refill*:	Liters	Qt
All models	4.0	4.2

*With the engine at operating temperature, shift transmission through all gears. Check fluid level in NEUTRAL and add fluid as needed

TRANSMISSION/TRANSAXLE, Manual
FWD 80W, 75W-85W **GL-4**
RWD 80W, 75W-85W **GL-4**

CAPACITY, Refill:	Liters	Pt
FWD: W/o Turbo	2.1	4.6
W/Turbo	2.3	4.8
RWD: 4-speed	2.1	4.4
5-speed	2.3	4.8

DIFFERENTIAL
Limited-Slip .... **GL-5★**
Standard **GL-5**
Above –10°F (–23°C), 90, 85W-90, 80W-90; –30° to –10°F (–34° to –23°C), 80W, 80W-90; below –30°F (–34°C), 75W

CAPACITY, Refill:	Liters	Pt
All models	1.3	2.8

MITSUBISHI

1985-86 Cordia, Galant, Mirage, Starion, Tredia

MIIPM4   MIIPM4

MI — MILES IN THOUSANDS
KM — KILOMETERS IN THOUSANDS

TURBO ENGINES,
EVERY 6 MO/3 MI — 4.8 KM
Crankcase . . . . change oil

Oil filter . . . . replace
At second oil change, then every other

EVERY 12 MO/7.5 MI — 12 KM
Crankcase ex. Turbo . . . . change oil

Oil filter ex. Turbo . . . . replace
Every second oil change, but at least every 12 months

EVERY 12 MO/15 MI — 24 KM
Brake system . . . . inspect
Check brake lining, hoses & lines, wheel & master cylinders, brake fluid

Exhaust system . . . . inspect

Cooling system . . . . inspect
Service as required

Power steering fluid . . . . check **AF**
Also check hoses

EVERY 15 MI — 24 KM
Limited-Slip differential . . . . change oil

Drive belts . . . . inspect/adjust

Idle speed . . . . check/adjust
Initial service for throttle positioner 50 mi (80 km)

Valve clearance . . . . inspect/adjust
Adjust jet valve only on models with hydraulic lifters

EVERY 24 MO/30 MI — 48 KM
Ball joint, steering linkage seals &
  FWD steering &
  drive shaft boots . . . . inspect

Front wheel bearings
  RWD cars . . . . clean/repack **LM**
Inspect for leaks. Inspect & repack whenever rotors are removed

Rear wheel bearings FWD cars, ex.
  w/disc brakes . . . . clean/repack **LM**
Inspect for leaks. Repack whenever drums are removed

Coolant . . . . drain/flush/refill **EC**

EVERY 30 MI — 48 KM
Differential, RWD or 4WD . . . . check level

Transaxle, automatic FWD . . change fluid
Change filter & adjust bands

Transmission/Transaxle,
  manual . . . . check level
Also check 4WD transfer case fluid level

Air cleaner filter . . . . replace

Choke & linkage . . . . clean **PC**

Drive belt . . . . replace
Water pump & alternator only

Spark plugs . . . . replace

AT FIRST 48 MO/60 MI — 96 KM;
THEN EVERY 12 MO/15 MI — 24 KM
Air conditioning system . . . . inspect

Power steering belt . . . . check

EVERY 48 MO/60 MI — 96 KM
Brakes . . . . change fluid **HB**
Also change clutch fluid, as equipped

EVERY 60 MO/50 MI — 80 KM
Crankcase emission
  system . . . . check/clean **PC**

Evaporative control system . . . . . . inspect
Replace canister

Fuel filter . . . . replace
Check fuel system, tank, lines & connections

Fuel, water, & fuel
  vapor hoses . . . . check/replace

Ignition timing . . . . check/adjust

Ignition wires . . . . check/replace

Throttle positioner . . . . check/adjust

Turbocharger oil & air
  intake hoses . . . . replace

Oxygen sensor . . . . check/replace

Vacuum hoses . . . . replace
Secondary air hoses & crankcase ventilation hoses

EVERY 60 MI — 96 KM
Timing belt . . . . replace

SEVERE SERVICE
Air cleaner filter, PCV system & brake
system — Service more frequently

Crankcase — Change oil every 3 mo/3 mi
(4.8 km) & filter every second oil change

Transmission, automatic, rear wheel
drive — Change fluid, filter, & adjust bands
every 30 mi (48 km)

Spark plugs — Replace every 15 mi (24 km)

KEY TO LUBRICANTS

AF	DEXRON®-II Automatic Transmission Fluid
AP	Mitsubishi Plus ATF
CC	Motor Oil, API Service CC
EC	Ethylene Glycol Coolant Mix 50% to 70% with water
GL-4	Gear Oil, API Service GL-4
GL-5	Gear Oil, API Service GL-5
GL-5★	Special Lubricant for Limited-Slip Differentials Mitsubishi Part No. 8149630EX
HB	Hydraulic Brake Fluid, DOT 3
LM	Lithium Grease, EP
PC	Carburetor Cleaner
SF	Motor Oil, API Service SF

CRANKCASE . . . . SF, SF/CC

CAPACITY, Refill:	Liters	Qt
1.5L	3.0	3.2
1.6L Turbo	3.5	3.7
1.8L, 2.0L, 2.3L	3.5	3.7
2.6L	3.8	4.0

Capacity shown is without filter. When replacing filter, additional oil may be needed

Turbo Models
Above 32°F (0°C) 20W-20, 20W-40
Above −10°F (−23°C) 10W-30
Below 60°F (16°C) . . . . 5W-30†
†Preferred below 60°F (16°C) when temperatures drop below −10°F (−23°C)

All Other Models
Above 32°F (0°C) 20W-20, 20W-40, 20W-50
Above −10°F (−23°C) . 10W-30, 10W-40, 10W-50
Below 60°F (16°C) 5W-20*, 5W-30, 5W-40
*Not recommended for sustained high-speed driving

TRANSMISSION/TRANSAXLE,
Automatic . . . . AF, AP

CAPACITY, Initial Refill*:	Liters	Qt
Front wheel drive	4.0	4.2
Starion	3.8	4.0

*With the engine at operating temperature, shift transmission through all gears. Check fluid level in NEUTRAL and add fluid as needed

TRANSMISSION/TRANSAXLE, Manual
Starion 80W, 75W-85W, **GL-4**
Others 75W-85W **GL-4**

CAPACITY, Refill:	Liters	Pt
Mirage	2.1	4.4
W/Turbo	2.3	4.8
Cordia, Tredia	2.3	4.8
Galant	2.5	5.2
Starion	2.3	4.8

DIFFERENTIAL
Limited-Slip . . . . **GL-5★**
Standard **GL-5**
Above −10°F (−23°C), 90, 85W-90, 80W-90; −30° to −10°F (−34° to −23°C), 80W, 80W-90; below −30°F (−34°C), 75W

CAPACITY, Refill:	Liters	Pt
Starion	1.3	2.8

SERVICE AT TIME OR MILEAGE—WHICHEVER OCCURS FIRST

MIIPM5   MIIPM5

W   SERVICE TO MAINTAIN EMISSION WARRANTY

MI — MILES IN THOUSANDS
KM — KILOMETERS IN THOUSANDS

TURBO ENGINES
EVERY 6 MO/3 MI — 4.8 KM
Crankcase .... change oil

Oil filter .... replace
At second oil change, then every other

EVERY 12 MO/7.5 MI — 12 KM
Crankcase ex. Turbo .... change oil

Oil filter ex. Turbo .... replace
Every second oil change, but at least every 12 months

EVERY 12 MO/15 MI — 24 KM
Disc brake pads .... inspect
Also check brake hoses

Exhaust system .... inspect

Cooling system .... inspect
Service as required

Power steering fluid .... check **AF**
Also check hoses

EVERY 15 MI — 24 KM
Limited-Slip differential .... change oil

W Idle speed 4-cyl. .... check/adjust

W Valve clearance .... inspect/adjust

EVERY 24 MO/30 MI — 48 KM
Ball joint, steering linkage seals &
    FWD steering &
    drive shaft boots .... inspect

Drum brakes .... inspect
Linings, wheel cylinders

Front wheel bearings
    RWD cars .... clean/repack **LM**
Inspect for leaks. Inspect & repack whenever rotors are removed

Rear wheel bearings FWD cars, ex.
    w/disc brakes .... clean/repack **LM**
Inspect for leaks. Repack whenever drums are removed

Coolant .... drain/flush/refill **EC**

EVERY 30 MI — 48 KM
Differential, RWD or 4WD .... check level

Transaxle, automatic FWD .. change fluid
Change filter & adjust bands

Transmission/Transaxle,
    manual .... check level
Also check 4WD transfer case fluid level

W Air cleaner filter .... replace

W Choke & linkage .... clean **PC**

Drive belt .... replace
Water pump & alternator only

W Spark plugs .... replace

EVERY 60 MO/50 MI — 80 KM
W Crankcase emission
    system .... check/clean **PC**

W Evaporative control
    system .... inspect
Replace canister

W Fuel filter .... replace

W Fuel system .... inspect
Tank, lines, connections, cap

W Fuel, water, & fuel
    vapor hoses .... check/replace

W Ignition wires .... check/replace

W Turbocharger oil & air
    intake hoses .... replace

W Oxygen sensor .... check/replace

W Vacuum hoses .... replace
Secondary air hoses & crankcase ventilation hoses

EVERY 60 MI — 96 KM
Timing & balancer belt .... replace
As equipped

SEVERE SERVICE
W Air cleaner filter, PCV system & brake
system — Service more frequently

Crankcase—Change oil every 3 mo/3 mi
(4.8 km) & filter every second oil change

Transmission, automatic, rear wheel
drive — Change fluid, filter, & adjust bands
every 30 mi (48 km)

W Spark plugs — Replace every 15 mi (24 km)

KEY TO LUBRICANTS
AF   DEXRON®-II Automatic Transmission Fluid
AP   Mitsubishi Plus ATF
CD   Motor Oil, API Service CD
EC   Ethylene Glycol Coolant
         Mix 50% to 70% with water
GL-4 Gear Oil, API Service GL-4
GL-5 Gear Oil, API Service GL-5
GL-5★ Special Lubricant for Limited-Slip Differentials
         Mitsubishi Part No. 8149630EX
LM   Lithium Grease, EP
PC   Carburetor Cleaner
SG   Motor Oil, API Service SG

CRANKCASE .... SG, SG/CD

CAPACITY, Refill:	Liters	Qt
1.5L	3.0	3.2
1.6L Turbo	3.7	3.9
1.8L, 2.0L, 2.3L ..	3.5	3.7
2.6L	4.3	4.6
3.0L	4.0	4.2

Capacity shown is without filter. When replacing filter, additional oil may be needed

Turbo Models
Above 32°F (0°C) 20W-20, 20W-40
Above −10°F (−23°C) 10W-30
Below 60°F (16°C) .... 5W-30†
†Preferred below 60°F (16°C) when temperatures drop below −10°F (−23°C)

All Other Models
Above 32°F (0°C) 20W-20, 20W-40, 20W-50
Above −10°F (−23°C) . 10W-30, 10W-40, 10W-50
Below 60°F (16°C) 5W-20*, 5W-30, 5W-40
* Not recommended for sustained high-speed driving

TRANSMISSION/TRANSAXLE,
    Automatic .... **AF, AP**

CAPACITY, Initial Refill*:	Liters	Qt
Front wheel drive	4.0	4.2
Starion	5.0	5.3

* With the engine at operating temperature, shift transmission through all gears. Check fluid level in NEUTRAL and add fluid as needed

TRANSMISSION/TRANSAXLE, Manual
Starion 80W, 75W-85W, **GL-4**
Others 75W-85W, **GL-4**

CAPACITY, Refill:	Liters	Pt
Mirage: 4-speed	1.7	3.6
5-speed	1.8	3.8
Cordia, Tredia	2.3	4.8
Galant, Sigma	2.5	5.2
Starion	2.3	4.8

DIFFERENTIAL
Limited-Slip .... **GL-5★**
Standard **GL-5**
Above −10°F (−23°C), 90, 85W-90, 80W-90; −30° to 10°F (−34° to 23°C), 80W, 80W-90; below −30°F (−34°C), 75W

CAPACITY, Refill:	Liters	Pt
Starion	1.3	2.8

MITSUBISHI
1989-92 Eclipse, Expo, Galant, Mirage, Sigma, Starion, 3000GT
Precis—See Hyundai Excel

SERVICE AT TIME OR MILEAGE—WHICHEVER OCCURS FIRST

W   SERVICE TO MAINTAIN EMISSION WARRANTY

MI — MILES IN THOUSANDS
KM — KILOMETERS IN THOUSANDS

TURBO ENGINES
EVERY 6 MO/5 MI — 8 KM
Crankcase . . . . change oil

Oil filter . . . . replace
At second oil change, then every other

EVERY 12 MO/7.5 MI — 12 KM
Crankcase ex. Turbo . . . . change oil

Oil filter ex. Turbo . . . . replace
Every second oil change, but at least every 12 months

EVERY 12 MO/15 MI — 24 KM
Disc brake pads . . . . inspect
Also check brake hoses

Power steering fluid . . . . check **AF**
Also check hoses

Transaxle, automatic . . . . check level

EVERY 15 MI — 24 KM
Limited-Slip differential . . . . change oil
Starion only

W Valve clearance . . . . inspect/adjust
1.5L only. Others, as equipped, adjust jet valve only on
models with hydraulic lifters

EVERY 24 MO/30 MI — 48 KM
Ball joint, steering linkage seals &
FWD steering &
drive shaft boots . . . . inspect

Drum brakes . . . . inspect
Linings, wheel cylinders

Exhaust system . . . . inspect

Front wheel bearings
RWD cars . . . . clean/repack **LM**
Inspect for leaks. Inspect & repack whenever rotors are
removed

Coolant . . . . drain/flush/refill **EC**

W Fuel hoses 1991 . . . . inspect

EVERY 30 MI — 48 KM
Differential, RWD or 4WD . . . . check level
With Limited-Slip, change lubricant

Transaxle, automatic FWD . . change fluid
Change filter & adjust bands

Transmission/Transaxle,
manual . . . . check level
Also check 4WD transfer case fluid level

W Air cleaner filter . . . . replace

W Choke & linkage . . . . clean **PC**

Drive belt . . . . inspect
Water pump & alternator only

W Spark plugs . . . . replace
Ex. 3.0L DOHC

EVERY 60 MO/50 MI — 80 KM
W Fuel system . . . . inspect
Tank, lines, connections, cap

W Fuel, water, & fuel
vapor hoses 1989-90 . . . . check/replace

EVERY 60 MI — 96 KM
W Spark plugs . . . . replace
3.0L DOHC

Timing & balancer belt . . . . replace
As equipped

EVERY 120 MO
SRS air bag system . . . . inspect

SEVERE SERVICE
W Air cleaner filter, PCV system & brake
system — Service more frequently

Crankcase — Change oil every 3 mo/3 mi
(4.8 km) & filter every second oil change

Spark plugs — Replace every 15 mi (24 km)

Transmission, automatic, rear wheel
drive — Change fluid, filter, & adjust bands
every 30 mi (48 km)

KEY TO LUBRICANTS

AF	DEXRON®-II Automatic Transmission Fluid
AP	Mitsubishi Plus ATF
CD	Motor Oil, API Service CD
EC	Ethylene Glycol Coolant Mix 50% to 70% with water
GL-4	Gear Oil, API Service GL-4
GL-5	Gear Oil, API Service GL-5
GL-5★	Special Lubricant for Limited-Slip Differentials Mitsubishi Part No. 8149630EX
HB	Hydraulic Brake Fluid, DOT 3 or DOT 4
LM	Lithium Grease, EP
PC	Carburetor Cleaner
SG	Motor Oil, API Service SG

CRANKCASE . . . . SG, SG/CD

CAPACITY, Refill:	Liters	Qt
1.5L	3.0	3.2
1.6L	4.0	4.2
1.8L, 2.0L SOHC, 2.4L . .	3.5	3.7
2.0L DOHC	4.0	4.2
2.6L	4.3	4.6
3.0L	4.0	4.2

Capacity shown is without filter. When replacing filter, additional oil may be needed

Turbo Models
Above 32°F (0°C) 20W-20, 20W-40
Above −10°F (−23°C) 10W-30
Below 60°F (16°C) . . . . 5W-30†
†Preferred below 60°F (16°C) when temperatures drop below −10°F (−23°C)

All Other Models
Above 32°F (0°C) 20W-20, 20W-40, 20W-50
Above −10°F (−23°C) . 10W-30, 10W-40, 10W-30
Below 60°F (16°C) 5W-20*, 5W-30, 5W-40
* Not recommended for sustained high-speed driving

TRANSMISSION/TRANSAXLE,
Automatic . . . . AP

CAPACITY, Initial Refill*:	Liters	Qt
Starion	5.0	5.3
3000GT, Diamante	4.5	4.8
All others	4.0	4.2

* With the engine at operating temperature, shift transmission through all gears. Check fluid level in NEUTRAL and add fluid as needed

TRANSMISSION/TRANSAXLE, Manual
Starion 80W, 75W-85W, **GL-4**
Others, 1989-91 . . . . 75W-85W **GL-4**
1992 . . . . 75W-90, 75W-85W **GL-4**

CAPACITY, Refill:	Liters	Pt
Mirage: 4-speed	1.7	3.6
5-speed	1.8	3.8
Sigma	2.5	5.2
Galant, Eclipse: SOHC . .	1.8	3.8
DOHC	2.3	4.8
3000GT: 2WD	2.3	4.8
4WD	2.4	5.0
Expo: FWD, 1.8L	1.8	3.8
2.4L	2.3	4.8
4WD	2.3	4.8
Starion	2.3	4.8

TRANSFER CASE
1989-91 . . . . . . 75W-85W **GL-4, GL-5**
1992 . . . . . . 75W-90, 75W-85W **GL-4, GL-5**

CAPACITY, Refill:	Liters	Pt
4WD Galant, Eclipse, Expo	0.6	1.2
4WD 3000GT	0.3*	0.6*

* Fill no higher than 1/2 inch (13 mm) below fill hole

DIFFERENTIAL
Limited-Slip . . . . **GL-5★**
Standard **GL-5**
Above −10°F (−23°C), 90, 85W-90, 80W-90; −30° to −10°F (−34° to −23°C), 80W, 80W-90; below −30°F (−34°C), 75W

CAPACITY, Refill:	Liters	Pt
Starion	1.3	2.8
4WD Galant, Eclipse, Expo	0.7	1.5
4WD 3000GT	1.1	2.3

SERVICE AT TIME OR MILEAGE—WHICHEVER OCCURS FIRST

MIIPM1   MIIPM1

MI — MILES IN THOUSANDS
KM — KILOMETERS IN THOUSANDS

DIESEL ENGINE, EVERY 6 MO/3 MI — 4.8 KM
Crankcase . . . . change oil

Oil filter . . . . replace
Every other oil change

EVERY 12 MO/7.5 MI — 12 KM
Crankcase . . . . change oil
Ex. Diesel engine

Exhaust system . . . . inspect

Oil filter . . . . replace
Ex. Diesel engine. Every other oil change

Power steering . . . . check level **AF**
Check for leaks & condition of belts & boots

Steering gear,
  manual . . . . check level 90 **GL-4**
Remove lower right bolt of cover & fill through fill hole to 3/4″ (w/4-bolt cover) or 7/8″ (w/3-bolt cover) from top of bolt hole. Check steering wheel free play

Transmission, automatic . . . . . check level

EVERY 12 MONTHS
Cooling system . . . . inspect

EVERY 15 MI — 24 KM
Brake hoses . . . . inspect

Disc brake pads . . . . inspect

Limited-Slip differential . . change lubricant

Upper control arm bushings . lubricate **LM**

Drive belts . . . . inspect/adjust
Initial service, then every 30 mi (48 km)

Valve clearance . . . . inspect/adjust

EVERY 24 MO/30 MI — 48 KM
Coolant . . . . drain/flush/refill **EC**

EVERY 30 MI — 48 KM
Steering & front suspension . . . . . . inspect

Differential(s) . . . . check level

Front wheel bearings . . . clean/repack **LM**
Inspect for leaks. Inspect & repack whenever rotors are removed

Rear brakes . . . . inspect
Check brake shoes & wheel cylinders

Transmission, 4WD . . . . change fluid
Change filter & adjust bands

Transfer case . . . . check level

Transmission, manual . . . . check level

Air cleaner filter . . . . replace

Brake master cylinder . . . check level **HB**

Choke & linkage . . . . clean **PC**

Drive belts . . . . replace

Fuel filter, Diesel . . . . replace

Idle speed, Diesel . . . . check/adjust

Spark plugs . . . . replace

Turbocharger air intake hoses,
  Diesel . . . . replace

Vacuum pump oil hoses,
  Diesel . . . . inspect/replace

EVERY 48 MO
Brakes . . . . change fluid **HB**
Also change hydraulic clutch fluid, as equipped

EVERY 60 MO/50 MI — 80 KM
Crankcase emission system . . . . clean

Evaporative control system . . . . . . inspect
Replace canisters

Fuel filter, Gasoline . . . . replace
Check fuel system cap, tank, lines & connections

Fuel, water, & fuel
  vapor hoses . . . . check/replace

Ignition timing . . . . check/adjust

Ignition wires . . . . check/replace

Turbocharger oil &
  air intake hoses . . . . replace

Oxygen sensor . . . . check/replace

Timing & balancer belts, Diesel . . . replace

Turbocharger oil hoses, Diesel . . . replace

Vacuum hoses . . . . check
Secondary air hoses & crankcase ventilation hoses

SEVERE SERVICE
Air cleaner filter — Replace more frequently

Brake shoes & pads — Inspect more frequently

Crankcase — Change every, Gasoline, 3 mo/3 mi (4.8 km) & filter at every other oil change. Diesel, 2 mo/2 mi (3.2 km) & filter at every other oil change

4WD manual transmission & transfer case — Change lubricant every 30 mi (48 km)

Spark plugs — Replace every 15 mi (24 km)

KEY TO LUBRICANTS

AF	DEXRON®-II Automatic Transmission Fluid
AP	Mitsubishi Plus ATF
CC	Motor Oil, API Service CC
CD	Motor Oil, API Service CD
EC	Ethylene Glycol Coolant Mix 50% to 70% with water
GL-4	Gear Oil, API Service GL-4
GL-5	Gear Oil, API Service GL-5
GL-5★	Special Lubricant for Limited-Slip Differentials Mitsubishi Part No. 8149630EX
HB	Hydraulic Brake Fluid, DOT 3
LM	Lithium Grease, EP
PC	Carburetor Cleaner
SE	Motor Oil, API Service SE
SF	Motor Oil, API Service SF

CRANKCASE
Gasoline engine . . . . **SE, SF**
Diesel engine . . . . **CD**

CAPACITY, Refill*:	Liters	Qt
2WD: 2.0L	3.5	3.7
2.3L Diesel	4.5	4.7
2.6L	3.8	4.0
4WD: 2.0L	4.5	4.7
2.3L Diesel	5.4	5.6
2.6	5.5	5.7

* Capacity shown is without filter. When replacing filter, additional oil may be needed

Gasoline engines:
Above 32°F (0°C) 20W-20, 20W-40, 20W-50
Above −10°F (−23°C) . 10W-30, 10W-40, 10W-50
Below 60°F (16°C) 5W-20*, 5W-30, 5W-40
Diesel engines:
Above 14°F (−10°C) 20W-40
Above 5°F (−15°C) 15W-40
32° to 104°F (0° to 40°C) 30
−4° to 104°F (−2° to 40°C) 10W-30
Below 50°F (10°C) 5W-30

TRANSMISSION, Automatic . . . . **AF, AP**
CAPACITY, Initial Refill*:	Liters	Qt
All models	3.8	4.0

* With the engine at operating temperature, shift transmission through all gears. Check fluid level in NEUTRAL and add fluid as needed

TRANSMISSION,
Manual 80W, 75W-85W **GL-4**
CAPACITY, Refill:	Liters	Pt
4-speed: 2WD	2.1	4.4
4WD	2.2	4.6
5-speed: 2WD	2.3	4.8
4WD	2.2	4.6

TRANSFER
CASE 80W, 75W-85W **GL-4**
CAPACITY, Refill:	Liters	Pt
All models	2.2	4.6

DIFFERENTIALS
Limited-Slip . . . . **GL-5★**
Standard **GL-4, GL-5**
Above −10°F (−23°C), 90, 85W-90, 80W-90; −30° to −10°F (−34° to −23°C), 80W, 80W-90; below −30°F (−34°C), 75W
CAPACITY, Refill:	Liters	Pt
Front	1.1	2.3
Rear: Pickup	1.5	3.2
Montero	1.8	3.8

SERVICE AT TIME OR MILEAGE—WHICHEVER OCCURS FIRST

MIIPM3   **W**   SERVICE TO MAINTAIN EMISSION WARRANTY   MIIPM3

MI — MILES IN THOUSANDS
KM — KILOMETERS IN THOUSANDS

1985, CALIF. DIESEL & TURBO ENGINES EVERY 6 MO/3 MI — 4.8 KM
Crankcase . . . . change oil
Oil filter . . . . replace
At second oil change, then every other

1985, FEDERAL DIESEL EVERY 6 MO/5 MI — 8 KM
Crankcase . . . . change oil
Oil filter . . . . replace
At second oil change, then every other

GASOLINE, EVERY 12 MO/7.5 MI — 12 KM
Crankcase . . . . change oil
Oil filter . . . . replace
Every second oil change, but at least every 12 months

EVERY 12 MO/15 MI — 24 KM
Brake system . . . . inspect
Check brake lining, hoses & lines, wheel & master cylinders, brake fluid

Exhaust system . . . . inspect

Upper control arm &
  ball joints . . . . lubricate **LM**
With fittings only

Cooling system . . . . inspect
Service as required

Power steering fluid . . . . check **AF**
Also check hoses

Transmission, automatic . . . . . check level

EVERY 15 MI — 24 KM
Limited-Slip differential . . . . change oil
1985-87

W Drive belts . . . . inspect/adjust
Water pump & alternator only

W Idle speed, 2V Gasoline . . . . check/adjust
1985-86, initial service for throttle positioner

W Valve clearance 4-cyl. . . . . . inspect/adjust
Gasoline, jet valve only

EVERY 24 MO/30 MI — 48 KM
Ball joint, steering linkage seals &
  drive shaft boots . . . . inspect

Drive shaft joints . . . . lubricate **LM**

Front wheel bearings
  ex. FWD . . . . clean/repack **LM**
Inspect for leaks. Inspect & repack whenever rotors are removed

Coolant . . . . drain/flush/refill **EC**

W Fuel filter, Diesel . . . . replace

Turbocharger air intake & vacuum
  pump oil hoses, Diesel . . . . replace

EVERY 30 MI — 48 KM
Differential(s) . . . . check level

Limited-Slip differential . . . . change oil
1988-89

Transmission, manual & transfer
  case . . . . check level

W Air cleaner filter . . . . replace

W Choke & linkage . . . . clean **PC**

Drive belts . . . . replace
Water pump & alternator only

W Idle speed, Diesel . . . . check/adjust

W Spark plugs . . . . replace

AT FIRST 48 MO/60 MI — 96 KM; THEN EVERY 12 MO/15 MI — 24 KM
Air conditioning system . . . . inspect

Power steering belt . . . . check
1985-86

EVERY 48 MO/60 MI — 96 KM
Brakes . . . . change fluid **HB**

Hydraulic clutch, Diesel . . change fluid **HB**

EVERY 60 MO/50 MI — 80 KM
Carburetor mounting . . . . check

W Crankcase emission system,
  Gasoline . . . . check/clean **PC**

W Distributor . . . . check

  EGR valve 4-cyl. . . . . replace
Clean sub-EGR valve

W Evaporative control system . . . . . inspect
1985-87, replace canister

W Fuel filter, Gasoline . . . . replace
Check fuel system, tank, lines & connections

W Fuel, water, & fuel
  vapor hoses . . . . check/replace

W Fuel system, Diesel . . . . . . check for leaks

W Hot air control valve . . . . check
Ex. FI, inside carburetor air cleaner snorkel

  Ignition timing . . . . check/adjust
1985-86

W Ignition wires . . . . check/replace

W PCV hoses, Diesel . . . . replace

W Secondary air system . . . . inspect
Ex. Van

W Timing belt, Diesel . . . . replace

  Throttle position sensor . . . . . check/adjust
1985-86

W Oxygen sensor . . . . check/replace

W Vacuum control system solenoid
  valve air filter . . . . replace

EVERY 60 MI — 96 KM
Timing belt . . . . replace

EVERY 100 MI — 160 KM
Canister . . . . replace
1988-89

SEVERE SERVICE
W Air cleaner filter, PCV system & brake
  system — Service more frequently

W Crankcase — Change oil every 3 mo/3 mi
(4.8 km) & filter every second oil change.
Diesel, change oil every 2 mo/2 mi (3.2 km)
& filter every other oil change

  Transmission, automatic — Change fluid, filter, & adjust bands every 30 mi (48 km)

  Transmission, manual & transfer case, Pickup, Montero—Change lubricant every 30 mi (48 km)

W Spark plugs — Replace every 15 mi (24 km)

  Upper control arm bushings, Truck —
  Lubricate every 7.5 mi (12 km)

KEY TO LUBRICANTS
See other Mitsubishi charts

CRANKCASE
Gasoline engine:
  1985-86 . . . . **SE, SF**
  1987-89 . . . . **SF, SF/CC**
Diesel engine . . . . **CD**

CAPACITY, Refill:	Liters	Qt
2WD:		
1985-88 2.0L Pickup	3.5	3.7
1989 2.0L Pickup	3.8	4.0
1985-87 2.3L Diesel	5.1	5.3
1985-89 2.4L Van	3.5	3.7
1985-88 2.6L	3.8	4.0
1989 2.6L	4.0	4.2
4WD:		
1985-87 2.3L Diesel	5.5	5.7
1985-88 2.6L	5.3	5.6
1989 2.6L	4.5	4.8
V6 Montero	4.3	4.5

Capacity shown is without filter. When replacing filter, additional oil may be needed

Gasoline engine:
Above 32°F (0°C) 20W-20, 20W-40, 20W-50
Above –10°F (–23°C) . 10W-30, 10W-40, 10W-50
Below 60°F (16°C) 5W-20*, 5W-30, 5W-40
* Not recommended for sustained high-speed driving

Diesel engine:
32° to 104°F (0° to 40°C) 30
Above 14°F (–10°C) 20W-40
Above 5°F (–15°C) 15W-40
–4° to 104°F (–20° to 40°C) 10W-30
Below 50°F (10°C) 5W-30

TRANSMISSION, Automatic . . . . **AF, AP**
CAPACITY, Initial Refill*:	Liters	Qt
All models	4.7	5.0
* With the engine at operating temperature, shift transmission through all gears. Check fluid level in NEUTRAL and add fluid as needed

TRANSMISSION, Manual
1985-86 . . . . 80W, 75W-85W **GL-4**
1987-89: 2WD . . . . 75W-85W **GL-4†**
    4WD . . . . 80W, 75W-85W **GL-4†**
† 1989, add one bottle of friction modifier, Mitsubishi Part No. ME581050, to lubricant when servicing transmission

CAPACITY, Refill:	Liters	Pt
4-speed	2.1	4.4
5-speed: 2WD	2.3	4.8
4WD	2.2	4.6

TRANSFER CASE . . 80W, 75W-85W **GL-4**
CAPACITY, Refill:	Liters	Pt
All models	2.2	4.6

DIFFERENTIALS
Limited-Slip . . . . **GL-5★**
Standard: Pickup, Montero . . **GL-4, GL-5**
  Van **GL-5**
Above –10°F (–23°C), 90, 85W-90, 80W-90; –30° to –10°F (–34° to –23°C), 80W, 80W-90; below –30°F (–34°C), 75W

CAPACITY, Refill:	Liters	Pt
Front:	1.1	2.3
Pickup, Montero:		
Front	1.1	2.3
Rear, 4-cyl. Pickup . . .	1.5	3.2
Rear, 4-cyl. Montero . . .	1.8	3.8
Rear, V6	2.6	5.4
Van	1.5	3.2

SERVICE AT TIME OR MILEAGE—WHICHEVER OCCURS FIRST

MIIPM6   MIIPM6

W SERVICE TO MAINTAIN EMISSION WARRANTY

MI — MILES IN THOUSANDS
KM — KILOMETERS IN THOUSANDS

EVERY 12 MO/7.5 MI — 12 KM
Crankcase . . . . change oil

Oil filter . . . . replace
Every second oil change, but at least every 12 months

EVERY 12 MO/15 MI — 24 KM
Disc brake pads . . . . inspect
Also inspect brake hoses

Ball joints . . . . lubricate **LM**
With fittings only

Cooling system . . . . inspect
Service as required

Drive shaft boots . . . . inspect

Power steering fluid . . . . check **AF**

Transmission, automatic . . . . . check level

EVERY 15 MI — 24 KM
W Idle speed, 2.6L . . . . check/adjust

W Jet valve clearance
    2.6L . . . . inspect/adjust

EVERY 24 MO/30 MI — 48 KM
Ball joint, steering linkage seals &
    drive shaft boots . . . . inspect

Drum brakes . . . . inspect
Linings, wheel cylinders

Drive shaft joints . . . . lubricate **LM**

Exhaust system . . . . inspect

Front wheel bearings,
    1990 . . . . clean/repack **LM**
Inspect for leaks. Inspect & repack whenever rotors are removed

Coolant . . . . drain/flush/refill **EC**

EVERY 30 MI — 48 KM
Differential(s) . . . . check level

Limited-Slip differential . . change lubricant

Transmission, automatic &
    transfer case, 4WD . . . change lubricant

Transmission, manual &
    transfer case . . . . check level

W Air cleaner filter . . . . replace

W Choke & linkage 2.6L . . . . clean **PC**

Drive belts . . . . replace
Water pump & alternator only

W Fuel hoses . . . . check
1991-92 only

W Spark plugs . . . . replace

EVERY 60 MO/50 MI — 80 KM
W EGR valve, 4-cyl. . . . . replace
At mileage interval only 2.6L, also clean sub-EGR valve

W Fuel filter, 2.6L . . . . replace

W Fuel tank, lines,
    connections, cap . . . . inspect

W Fuel, & fuel
    vapor hoses . . . . check/replace
1990 only

EVERY 60 MO/60 MI—96 KM
W Crankcase ventilation, vacuum,
    water hoses . . . . replace
1990-91 only

W Distributor cap & rotor . . . . inspect

W Evaporative emissions
    control system . . . . inspect

W Ignition wires . . . . replace

W Intake air temperature
    control system, 1990 . . . . inspect

W Vacuum control system solenoid
    valve air filter, 2.6L . . . . replace

EVERY 60 MI — 96 KM
Timing belt . . . . replace

EVERY 80 MI—128 KM
W Crankcase emission
    control system . . . . check/clean **PC**

W Oxygen sensor . . . . replace

EVERY 100 MI — 160 KM
W Canister . . . . replace

SEVERE SERVICE
W Air cleaner filter, PCV system & brake
    system — Service more frequently

W Crankcase — Change oil every 3 mo/3 mi
    (4.8 km) & filter every second oil change

W Spark plugs — Replace every 15 mi (24 km)

Transmission, automatic — Change fluid, fil-
    ter, & adjust bands every 30 mi (48 km)

Transmission, manual & transfer case, Pick-
    up, Montero — Change lubricant every 30
    mi (48 km)

KEY TO LUBRICANTS

AF	DEXRON®-II Automatic Transmission Fluid
AP	Mitsubishi Plus ATF
CD	Motor Oil, API Service CD
EC	Ethylene Glycol Coolant Mix 50% to 70% with water
GL-4	Gear Oil, API Service GL-4
GL-5	Gear Oil, API Service GL-5
GL-5 ★	Special Lubricant for Limited-Slip Differentials Mitsubishi Part No. 8149630EX
LM	Lithium Grease, EP
PC	Carburetor Cleaner
SG	Motor Oil, API Service SG

CRANKCASE . . . . SG, SG/CD

CAPACITY, Refill:	Liters	Qt
2.4L	3.5	3.7
2.6L	4.5	4.8
3.0L	4.3	4.5

Capacity shown is without filter. When replacing filter, additional oil may be needed
Above 32°F (0°C) 20W-20, 20W-40, 20W-50
Above −10°F (−23°C) . 10W-30, 10W-40, 10W-50
Below 60°F (16°C) 5W-20*, 5W-30, 5W-40
* Not recommended for sustained high-speed driving

TRANSMISSION, Automatic . . . . AP

CAPACITY, Initial Refill*:	Liters	Qt
Pickup	1.9	2.0
Montero, Van	4.7	5.0

* With the engine at operating temperature, shift transmission through all gears. Check fluid level in NEUTRAL and add fluid as needed

TRANSMISSION, Manual
1990-91 . . . . 80W, 75W-85W **GL-4**†
1992 . . . . 75W-90, 75W-85W **GL-4**†
†Add one bottle of friction modifier, Mitsubishi Part No. ME581050, to lubricant when servicing transmission

CAPACITY, Refill:	Liters	Pt
4-cyl.	2.2	4.6
V6	2.5	5.2

TRANSFER CASE
1990-91 . . . . 80W, 75W-85W **GL-4**
1992 . . . . 75W-90, 75W-85W **GL-4**

CAPACITY, Refill:	Liters	Pt
All models	2.2	4.6

DIFFERENTIALS
Limited-Slip . . . . **GL-5 ★**
Standard **GL-5**
Above −10°F (−23°C), 90, 85W-90, 80W-90; −30° to −10°F (−34° to −23°C), 80W, 80W-90; below −30°F (−34°C), 75W

CAPACITY, Refill:	Liters	Pt
Front:		
Pickup	2.6	5.4
Montero	1.1	2.3
Rear:		
Pickup: 2WD	1.5	3.2
4WD	2.6	5.4
Montero: 4-cyl.	1.8	3.8
V6	2.6	5.4
Van	1.5	3.2

HOOD RELEASE: Inside

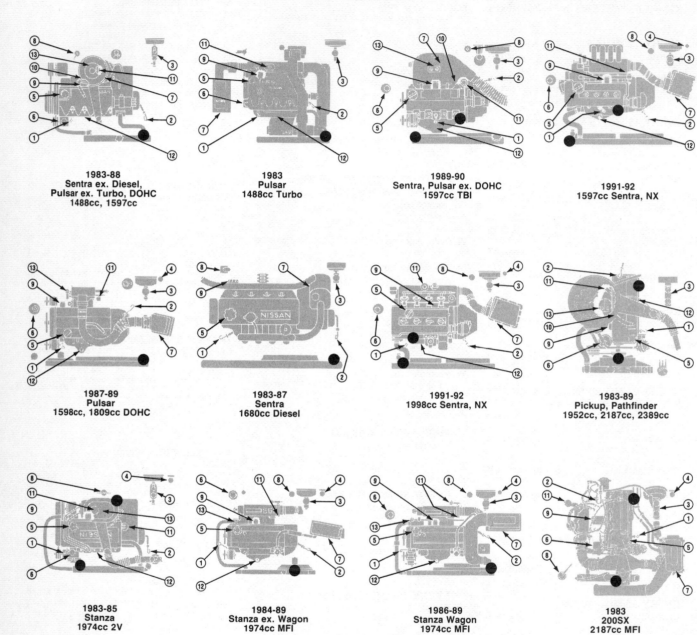

1983-88
Sentra ex. Diesel,
Pulsar ex. Turbo, DOHC
1488cc, 1597cc

1983
Pulsar
1488cc Turbo

1989-90
Sentra, Pulsar ex. DOHC
1597cc TBI

1991-92
1597cc Sentra, NX

1987-89
Pulsar
1598cc, 1809cc DOHC

1983-87
Sentra
1680cc Diesel

1991-92
1998cc Sentra, NX

1983-89
Pickup, Pathfinder
1952cc, 2187cc, 2389cc

1983-85
Stanza
1974cc 2V

1984-89
Stanza ex. Wagon
1974cc MFI

1986-89
Stanza Wagon
1974cc MFI

1983
200SX
2187cc MFI

① Crankcase dipstick
② Transmission dipstick
③ Brake fluid reservoir
④ Clutch fluid reservoir
⑤ Oil fill cap
⑥ Power steering reservoir
⑦ Air filter

⑧ Fuel filter
⑨ Oil filter
⑩ PCV filter
⑪ EGR valve
⑫ Oxygen sensor
⑬ PCV valve

● Cooling system drain   ○ Cooling system drain, some models

SERVICE LOCATIONS — ENGINE AND CHASSIS

HOOD RELEASE: Inside

1984-88
200SX
1809cc Turbo, 1974cc FI

1990-92
Axxess, Stanza
2389cc

1987-88
Van
2389cc

1990-91
Pickup, Pathfinder
2389cc

1989-90
240SX
2389cc

1991-92
240SX
2389cc DOHC

1983-84
280ZX, 810 Maxima
2393cc, 2753cc

1983-84
810 Maxima
Diesel
2793cc

1985-88
Maxima
2960cc

1989-91
Maxima
2960cc

1987-88
200SX V6,
1984-89
300ZX
2960cc

1990-92
300ZX
2960cc DOHC

1986-89
V6 Pickup, Pathfinder
2960cc TBI

1990-92
Pickup, Pathfinder
2960cc MFI

● Cooling system drain   ○ Cooling system drain, some models

SERVICE LOCATIONS — ENGINE AND CHASSIS

**0 FITTINGS
0 PLUGS**

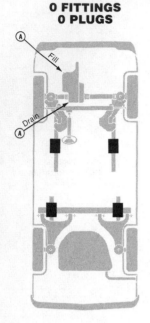

**1983-92
Sentra, Pulsar**

**0 FITTINGS
0 PLUGS**

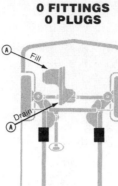

**1983-86
Stanza
(ex. Wagon)**

**0 FITTINGS
0 PLUGS**

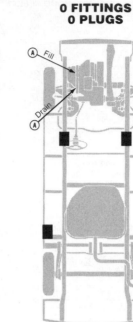

**1986-89
Stanza Wagon 2WD**

**0 FITTINGS
0 PLUGS**

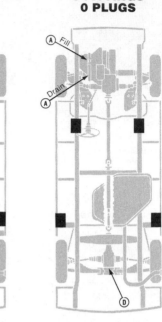

**1986-89
Stanza Wagon 4WD**

**0 FITTINGS
0 PLUGS**

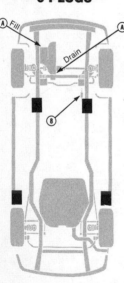

**1990
Axxess
2WD**

**0 FITTINGS
0 PLUGS**

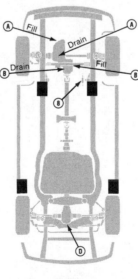

**1990
Axxess
4WD**

**0 FITTINGS
0 PLUGS**

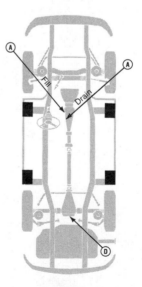

**1989-92
240SX**

**8-12
PLUGS**

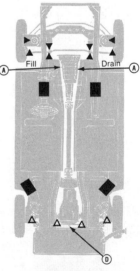

**1983 200SX,
1983-84 810, Maxima**

Ⓐ Manual transmission/transaxle, drain & fill

Ⓑ Transfer case, drain & fill

Ⓒ Automatic transaxle final drive, NOT USED

Ⓓ Differential, drain & fill

Ⓔ Fuel filter

CAUTION: On front wheel drive vehicles the center of gravity is further forward than on rear wheel drive vehicles. When removing major components from the rear of the vehicle while it is on a hoist, the vehicle must be supported in a manner to prevent it from tipping forward.

■ Lift adapter position　　▲ Plug　　△ Plug, some models

SERVICE LOCATIONS — ENGINE AND CHASSIS

DNIDP-4   DNIDP-4

**0 FITTINGS
0 PLUGS**

**0-2
PLUGS**

**4-8
PLUGS**

**0 FITTINGS
0 PLUGS**

**0 FITTINGS
0 PLUGS**

1984 200SX ex. Turbo

**1985-92
Maxima FWD,
1987-92 Stanza**

**1984 Turbo
1985-88 All**

**1983
280ZX**

**1990-92
300ZX**

**1984-89
300ZX**

**0 FITTINGS
0 PLUGS**

**11
PLUGS
0-4
FITTINGS**

**11
PLUGS**

**0 FITTINGS
4 PLUGS**

**1 FITTING
4 PLUGS**

**1987-88
Van**

**1983-86 early
4WD Pickup**

**1983-86 early
2WD Pickup**

**1986 late-92
2WD Pickup, Pathfinder**

**1986 late-92
4WD Pickup, Pathfinder**

CAUTION: On front wheel drive vehicles the center of gravity is further forward than on rear wheel drive vehicles. When removing major components from the rear of the vehicle while it is on a hoist, the vehicle must be supported in a manner to prevent it from tipping forward.

■ Lift adapter position   ▲ Plug   △ Plug, some models   • Fitting   ○ Fitting, some models

NISSAN
1983 All Models Except Pickup

DNIPM4   DNIPM4

MI—MILES IN THOUSANDS
KM—KILOMETERS IN THOUSANDS

1.5L & 2.8L TURBO,
EVERY 6 MO/3.75 MI—6 KM

Crankcase . . . . change oil
Change filter every other oil change

2.8L DIESEL,
EVERY 6 MO/5 MI—8 KM

Crankcase . . . . change oil

Oil filter . . . . replace
Change filter every other oil change

EVERY 6 MO/7.5 MI—12 KM

Crankcase . . . . change oil
Ex. 2.8L Diesel & Turbo

Oil filter ex. Diesel & Turbo . . . . . . replace

EVERY 12 MONTHS
Underbody . . . . flush/clean

EVERY 12 MO/15 MI—24 KM
Brake system . . . . change fluid
Inspect linings, drums & disc pads

Clutch, fuel & exhaust systems . . . inspect
Leaks, cracks, wear, free play

Differential . . . . check level

Front suspension & steering
linkage . . . . inspect

Tires . . . . rotate
Check balance & alignment

Transmission/Transaxle,
manual & automatic . . . . check level

Automatic temperature control air
cleaner 210 . . . . inspect

Brake & clutch master cylinders . . . . . . **HB**
Check systems

Choke 210 . . . . inspect

Cooling system hoses &
connections 210 . . . . inspect

Drive belts 210 . . . . inspect/adjust

Engine 210 . . . . major tune-up
Replace points, plugs. Check dwell, timing, distributor
cap (ex. Calif.), rotor & wires, choke, idle speed & mixture, valve clearance. Lubricate distributor cam & shaft

Fuel filter Diesel . . . . replace
49 states & Canada

Idle speed & mixture Canada . . . . . inspect

Idle speed Diesel . . . . inspect
49 states & Canada

Idle speed gasoline . . . . adjust

Ignition wires 210 . . . . inspect

Power steering reservoir . . check level **AF**
Inspect lines

Valves . . . . adjust

Body . . . . lubricate
Includes cables, linkages, locks, latches, hinges, seat
belts

EVERY 24 MO/30 MI—48 KM
Cooling system . . . . . . change coolant **EC**

Front wheel bearings . . . . inspect **LM**

Rear axle drive shaft joints . . . . . lubricate
280ZX

Air cleaner element . . . . replace

Air conditioning system . . . . inspect

Air induction valve filter . . . . . . replace
Engines with reed valve system only

Automatic temp. control
air cleaner ex. 210 . . . . inspect

Cable harness & connectors . . . inspect
280ZX, 810

Carbon canister filter 210 . . . . replace

Choke mechanism . . . . inspect
310, 510, Sentra, Pulsar U.S. models

Drive belts . . . . inspect

Engine ex. 210 . . . . major tune-up
Replace spark plugs. U.S., inspect distributor cap, rotor, wires & choke

Fuel filter, Calif. Diesel . . . . replace

Fuel lines . . . . inspect

Fuel vapor lines . . . . inspect

Idle speed Diesel, Calif. . . . . inspect

Injection nozzle tips . . . . inspect
Diesel, clean & service

Ignition system . . . . inspect
Check advance mechanism; inspect wires

Oxygen sensor . . . . inspect
280ZX, 810

PCV hoses . . . . inspect

Rubber hoses, 2.8L Diesel . . . . . . inspect

Timing FI Diesel . . . . inspect

EVERY 30 MI—48 KM
Idle speed 810 Diesel . . . . adjust

EVERY 60 MI—96 KM
Timing belts . . . . replace
2.8L Diesel engine

SERVICE AS REQUIRED
Fuel filter . . . . replace

SEVERE SERVICE
Crankcase—Gasoline, change oil every
3 mo/3 mi (5 km) ex. Turbo models. Diesel,
change filter every oil change

PCV filter 210, 310, 510, Sentra, Pulsar,
Pickup—In adverse weather conditions, inspect & replace if clogged

Transmission, manual & automatic;
differential—Change fluid or lubricant every
24 mo/30 mi (48 km)

KEY TO LUBRICANTS
See other Nissan charts

CRANKCASE

Gasoline engine		**SG**
Diesel engine	**SG/CD,**	**SG/CE**

CAPACITY, Refill:	Liters	Qt
Sentra, Pulsar: Gas	3.4	3.6
Diesel	3.6	3.8
Stanza	3.5	3.7
810 Maxima	4.5	4.8
Diesel	5.7	6.0
280ZX	4.0	4.2
Turbo	4.7	5.0
Stanza	3.5	3.7
200SX	3.8	4.0
A12A, A14, A15 eng. . . .	2.7	2.9

Capacity shown is without filter. When replacing filter, additional oil may be needed

Gasoline engines:
Above 50°F (10°C)	20W-40, 20W-50
Above 0°F (−18°C)	10W-30*, 10W-40
Below 60°F (15°C)	5W-30

Diesel engines:
Above 32°F (0°C)	30
Above 20°F (−7°C)	15W-40
Above 0°F (−18°C)	10W-30
Below 60°F (15°C)	5W-30

* Preferred

TRANSMISSION/TRANSAXLE,

Automatic		**AF**
CAPACITY†:	Liters	Qt
Front wheel drive	6.0	6.3
1983 Maxima	4.3	4.5
Others	5.5	5.9

†Total (dry) fill shown, use less fluid when refilling

TRANSMISSION/TRANSAXLE, Manual

280ZX Turbo	80W-90	**GL-4, AF**
Others		**GL-4**

GL-4: Above 50°F (10°C), 140; 30° to 100°F (−1°
to 38°C), 90; 10° to 85°F (−12° to 29°C), 85W;
below 100°F (38°C), 75W-90, 80W-90; below 85°F
(29°C), 80W; below 50°F (10°C), 75W

CAPACITY, Refill:	Liters	Pt
280ZX, 810 Maxima:		
4-speed	1.7	3.6
5-speed	2.0	4.2
200SX	2.0	4.2
510:		
4-speed	1.5	3.1
5-speed	1.7	3.6
310, Sentra, Pulsar:		
4-speed	2.3	4.9
5-speed	2.7	5.8
210:		
4-speed w/A12A eng...	1.2	2.5
4-speed others	1.3	2.8
5-speed	1.2	2.5
Stanza	2.7.	5.8

DIFFERENTIAL **GL-5**

Above 50°F (10°C), 140; 30° to 100°F (−1° to
38°C), 90; 10° to 85°F (−12° to 29°C), 85W; below
100°F (38°C), 75W-90, 80W-90; below 85°F
(29°C), 80W; below 50°F (10°C), 75W

CAPACITY, Refill:	Liters	Pt
280ZX, w/MT	1.3	2.8
210	0.9	1.9
280ZX w/AT, 810 Maxima	1.0	2.1
510, 200SX	1.1	2.3

SERVICE AT TIME OR MILEAGE—WHICHEVER OCCURS FIRST

DNIPM5   Perform the following maintenance services at the intervals indicated to keep the vehicle warranties in effect.   DNIPM5

W SERVICE TO MAINTAIN EMISSION WARRANTY

MI — MILES IN THOUSANDS
KM — KILOMETERS IN THOUSANDS

Rear wheel lug nuts . . . . torque
At first 100 miles (80 kilometers), then every 600 miles (960 kilometers)

ALL DIESEL AND TURBO ENGINES, EVERY 6 MO/5 MI — 8 KM
W Crankcase . . . . change oil

W Oil filter . . . . replace
At first oil change then every other

EVERY 6 MO/7.5 MI — 12 KM
W Crankcase . . . . change oil
Ex. Diesel & Turbo

W Oil filter ex. Diesel & Turbo . . . . . replace
Maxima, at every oil change. Others, at every other oil change

Tires 1987-88 . . . . rotate

EVERY 12 MONTHS
Underbody . . . . flush/clean

EVERY 12 MO/15 MI — 24 KM
Brake system . . . . inspect
Inspect linings, drums & disc pads

Clutch & exhaust systems . . . . inspect
Leaks, cracks, wear, free play

Differential . . . . check level

Front suspension & steering
linkage . . . . inspect

Tires 1984-86 . . . . rotate
Check balance & alignment

Transmission/Transaxle,
manual & automatic . . . . check level

W Automatic temp. control
air cleaner, Micra . . . . inspect

Brake & clutch master cylinders . . . . . . HB
Check systems

W Choke mechanism, Micra . . . . inspect

W Fuel filter Diesel . . . . replace

Idle speed & mixture Canada . . . . . inspect
Micra, adjust ignition timing

Idle speed Diesel . . . . inspect
49 states & Canada

Idle speed gasoline U.S. . . . . inspect

Power steering reservoir . . check level AF
Inspect lines & hoses

W Spark plugs Canada . . . . replace

W Valve clearance . . . . adjust
4-cyl. only

Body . . . . lubricate
Includes cables, linkages, locks, latches, hinges, seat belts

1987-88, EVERY 24 MONTHS
Ignition wires . . . . inspect

EVERY 24 MO/30 MI — 48 KM
Brake fluid . . . . replace HB
Replace every 12 mo/15 mi (24 km) if vehicle is operated in humid climates

W Cooling system . . . . . . change coolant EC

Front wheel bearings, RWD . . . inspect LM

W Air cleaner element . . . . replace

Air conditioning system . . . . inspect

W Air induction valve filter . . . . replace
2V engines with reed valve system only

W Automatic temp. control
air cleaner . . . . inspect
Ex. Micra, DOHC Pulsar

Choke mechanism . . . . inspect
Sentra, Pulsar U.S. models

W Drive belts . . . . inspect

W Fuel & fuel vapor lines . . . . inspect

Idle speed Diesel . . . . inspect
California

W Idle speed control actuator &
vacuum control modulator
valve filters . . . . replace
Sentra, Pulsar 2V ex. Calif., Canada

Ignition system 1984-86 . . . . inspect
Check advance mechanism; inspect wires

Injection nozzle tips
1.7L Diesel . . . . inspect

W Oxygen sensor . . . . inspect
1984-87, as equipped

W PCV hoses . . . . inspect

Rubber hoses, 1.7 Diesel . . . . inspect

W Spark plugs U.S. . . . . replace
Ex. platinum tipped

Timing FI Diesel . . . . inspect

EVERY 60 MI — 96 KM
W Spark plugs . . . . replace
Platinum tipped only

Timing belts . . . . replace
1.7 Diesel eng., 1987-88 Sentra, Pulsar, 1986-88 V6

SERVICE AS REQUIRED
W Fuel filter . . . . replace

SEVERE SERVICE
W Crankcase—Gasoline, change oil every 3 mo/3 mi (5 km) ex. Turbo models change 1.8L oil every 3 mo/2.5 mi (4 km). Diesel, change filter every oil change

W PCV filter Sentra, Pulsar, Micra — In adverse weather conditions, inspect & replace if clogged

Steering, suspension, locks, hinges, exhaust, brake system--Inspect every 6 mo/7.5 mi (12 km)

Transmission, manual & automatic; differential—Change fluid or lubricant every 24 mo/30 mi (48 km) when towing a trailer or driving on rough or muddy roads

KEY TO LUBRICANTS
See other Nissan charts

CRANKCASE

Gasoline engine		**SG**
Diesel engine	**SG/CD, SG/CE**	

CAPACITY, Refill:	Liters	Qt
Micra: 1984-85	2.2	2.4
1986-88	2.6	2.8
Sentra, Pulsar: Gasoline:		
1984	3.3	3.5
1985-88	2.8	3.0
DOHC	3.4	3.6
Diesel	3.6	3.8
Stanza, Multi: 1984	3.5	3.7
1985-88	3.1	3.3
Maxima: 1984	4.5	4.8
1985-88	3.9	4.1
300ZX	3.7	3.9
200SX: 4-cyl.: 1984	3.6	3.8
1985-88 . . .	3.2	3.4
V6	3.8	4.0

Capacity is without filter. When replacing filter, additional oil may be needed

Gasoline engines:
Above 50°F (10°C) 20W-40, 20W-50
Above 0°F (−18°C) 10W-30*, 10W-40
Below 60°F (16°C) 5W-30*

Diesel engines:
Above 32°F (0°C) . . . . : 30
Above 20°F (−7°C) 15W-40
Above 0°F (−18°C) 10W-30*
Below 60°F (16°C) 5W-30*
* Preferred

TRANSMISSION/TRANSAXLE, Automatic . . . . AF

CAPACITY†:	Liters	Qt
Front wheel drive	6.0	6.3
Maxima, 300ZX, 200SX .	7.0	7.3
Others	5.5	5.9

† Total (dry) fill shown

TRANSMISSION/TRANSAXLE, Manual

1984-86 300ZX Turbo . .	80W-90 **GL-4, AF**
Others	**GL-4**

GL-4, GL-5: Above 50°F (10°C), 140; 30° to 100°F (−1° to 38°C), 90; 10° to 85°F (−12° to 29°C), 85W; below 100°F (38°C), 75W-90, 80W-90; below 85°F (29°C), 80W; below 50°F (10°C), 75W

CAPACITY, Refill:	Liters	Pt
Maxima RWD	2.0	4.2
Maxima FWD	4.7	10.0
300ZX	1.9	4.0
200SX	2.0	4.2
Sentra, Pulsar: SOHC:		
4-speed	2.3	4.9
5-speed	2.7	5.8
DOHC	4.7	10.0
Stanza 2WD, Micra	2.7	5.8
Stanza, Multi 4WD	4.7	10.0

TRANSFER CASE GL-5
Viscosities, see Transmission/Transaxle, Manual

CAPACITY, Refill:	Liters	Pt
Sentra 4WD	1.1	2.3
Stanza, Multi 4WD	1.1	2.3

DIFFERENTIAL
Limited-Slip . . . . 80W-90 **GL-5★**
90 may be used above 0°F (−18°C)
Standard **GL-5**
Viscosities, see Transmission/Transaxle, Manual

CAPACITY, Refill:	Liters	Pt
Maxima	1.0	2.1
300ZX	1.3	2.8
200SX: Standard	1.0	2.1
IRS type	1.3	2.8
Sentra 4WD	1.0	2.1
Stanza, Multi 4WD	1.0	2.1

SERVICE AT TIME OR MILEAGE—WHICHEVER OCCURS FIRST

DNIPM9   DNIPM9

Perform the following maintenance services at the intervals indicated to keep the vehicle warranties in effect.

W SERVICE TO MAINTAIN EMISSION WARRANTY

MI — MILES IN THOUSANDS
KM — KILOMETERS IN THOUSANDS

TURBO ENGINE,
EVERY 6 MO/5 MI — 8 KM
W Crankcase .... change oil

W Oil filter .... replace
At first oil change then every other

EVERY 6 MO/7.5 MI — 12 KM
W Crankcase .... change oil
Ex. Turbo

W Oil filter ex. Turbo .... replace
Maxima, at every oil change. Others, at first oil change
then every other

Tires .... rotate

EVERY 12 MONTHS
Underbody .... flush/clean

EVERY 12 MO/15 MI — 24 KM
Brake system .... inspect
Inspect linings, drums, disc pads, lines & hoses

Differential .... check level

Drive shaft boots, FWD .... inspect

Exhaust systems .... inspect

Transfer case .... check level

Transmission/Transaxle,
   manual & automatic .... check level

Brake & clutch master cylinders ...... HB
Check systems

Power steering reservoir .. check level AF
Inspect lines & hoses

Body .... lubricate
Includes cables, linkages, locks, latches, hinges. Also
inspect seat belts

EVERY 24 MO/30 MI — 48 KM
Suspension & steering
   linkage .... inspect

Cooling system ...... change coolant EC
1991-92, initial service at 48 mo/60 mi (96 km)

W Air cleaner element .... replace
At mileage interval only

Air conditioning system .... inspect

Drive belts 1989-90 .... inspect
Inspect every 12 mo/15 mi (24 km) thereafter

Fuel & fuel vapor lines .... inspect

Idle speed .... inspect
1991-92 Sentra 1.6L

PCV hoses .... inspect

W Spark plugs .... replace
Ex. platinum tipped. At mileage interval only

Super HICAS linkage .... inspect
1990-92 240SX, 300ZX Turbo with active suspension

EVERY 36 MONTHS
Ignition wires 1989 .... inspect

EVERY 60 MI — 96 KM
Drive belts 1991-92 .... inspect
Inspect every 12 mo/15 mi (24 km) thereafter

Spark plugs .... replace
Platinum tipped only

W Timing belt .... replace
V6 only

AT 120 MONTHS
Air bag system .... inspect

SERVICE AS REQUIRED
W Fuel filter .... replace

W Valve clearance 1.6L .... adjust

SEVERE SERVICE
W Crankcase—Gasoline, change oil & filter
every: Turbo, 3 mo/3 mi (5 km); others, 3 mo/
3.75 mi (6 km)

Steering, suspension, locks, hinges, exhaust, brake system—Inspect every 6 mo/
7.5 mi (12 km)

Transmission, manual & automatic; differential, transfer case—Change fluid or lubricant every 24 mo/30 mi (48 km) when towing
a trailer or driving on rough or muddy roads

KEY TO LUBRICANTS
See other Nissan charts

CRANKCASE .... SG

CAPACITY, Refill:	Liters	Qt
Sentra, Pulsar, NX 1.6L .	2.8	3.0
1.8L DOHC	3.4	3.6
2.0L	3.2	3.4
Stanza, Axxess	3.1	3.3
Maxima: SOHC	3.5	3.7
DOHC	3.4	3.6
Micra	2.6	2.8
300ZX: 1989	3.6	3.8
1990	3.7	3.9
Turbo	4.1	4.3
1991-92	3.0	3.2
240SX: 1989-91	3.2	3.4
1992	3.5	3.7

Capacity is without filter. When replacing filter, additional
oil may be needed
Above 20°F (10°C) 20W-40, 20W-50
Above 0°F (–18°C) .... 10W-30†, 10W-40
1989 All; 1990 Axxess, Stanza;
1990-92 300ZX:
Below 60°F (16°C) 5W-30
1990-92 Others:
All temperatures 5W-30*
*Preferred
†Preferred for all 1989, 1990 Stanza & Axxess, 1990-92
300ZX

TRANSMISSION,
TRANSAXLE, Automatic .... AF

CAPACITY Refill†:	Liters	Qt
Sentra, Pulsar, NX	6.3	6.6
4-speed	7.0	7.3
Micra	6.0	6.3
Axxess, Stanza,		
Maxima SOHC	7.4	7.8
Maxima DOHC	9.4	10.0
240SX	8.3	8.7
300ZX: 1989	7.0	7.4
1990-92	7.7	8.1

† Total (dry) fill shown

TRANSMISSION,
TRANSAXLE, Manual GL-4
Above 50°F (10°C), 140; 30° to 100°F (–1° to
38°C), 90; 10° to 85°F (–12° to 29°C), 85W; below
100°F (38°C), 75W-90, 80W-90; below 85°F
(29°C), 80W; below 50°F (10°C), 75W

CAPACITY, Refill:	Liters	Pt
Sentra, Pulsar, NX:		
1989-90:		
SOHC: 4-speed	2.7	5.8
5-speed	2.8	6.0
DOHC	4.7	10.0
1991-92 4-speed	2.8	6.0
5-speed: 1.6L	2.9	6.2
2.0L	3.6	7.6
Micra: 1989	2.6	5.5
1990-91	2.9	6.2
Stanza, Axxess, Maxima .	4.7	10.0
240SX	2.4	5.1
300ZX: 1989	2.0	4.2
Turbo	2.4	5.1
1990-92	2.8	6.0

TRANSFER CASE GL-5
Viscosities, see Transmission/Transaxle, Manual

CAPACITY, Refill:	Liters	Pt
Sentra 4WD	1.1	2.3
Axxess 4WD	1.6	3.5

DIFFERENTIAL
Limited-Slip .... 80W-90 GL-5★
90 may be used above 0°F (–18°C)
Standard GL-5
Viscosities, see Transmission/Transaxle, Manual

CAPACITY, Refill:	Liters	Pt
300ZX: 1989	1.3	2.8
1990-92	1.5	3.1
Turbo	1.8	3.8
240SX: 1989-90	1.8	3.8
1991-92	1.3	2.5
w/Limited-Slip	1.5	3.1
Sentra 4WD	1.0	2.1
Axxess 4WD	1.0	2.1

NISSAN
1983 Pickup

DNIPM7

DNIPM7

MI—MILES IN THOUSANDS
KM—KILOMETERS IN THOUSANDS

2.2L DIESEL, EVERY 3.0 MI—5.0 KM
Crankcase .... change oil

Injection pump
 diaphragm .... 2-4 drops **CO**

Oil filter .... replace
Every other oil change

2.5L DIESEL,
EVERY 6 MO/5 MI—8 KM
Crankcase .... change oil

Oil filter .... replace

EVERY 6 MO/7.5 MI—12 KM
Crankcase .... change oil
Ex. 2.2L, 2.5L Diesel

Oil filter ex. Diesel .... replace

EVERY 12 MONTHS
Underbody .... flush/clean

EVERY 12 MO/15 MI—24 KM
Brake system .... change fluid
Inspect linings, drums & disc pads

Clutch, fuel & exhaust systems ... inspect
Leaks, cracks, wear, free play

Differential .... check level

Front suspension & steering
 linkage .... inspect

Front wheel bearings .... inspect **LM**
Pickup 4WD

Tires .... rotate
Check balance & alignment

Transmission,
 manual & automatic .... check level

Brake & clutch master cylinders ...... **HB**
Check systems

Drive belts,
 Diesel 4-cyl. .... inspect/adjust

Fuel filter Diesel .... replace
49 states & Canada

Idle speed & mixture Canada ..... inspect

Idle speed Diesel .... inspect
49 states & Canada

Idle speed gasoline .... adjust

Power steering reservoir .. check level **AF**
Inspect lines

Rubber hoses .... inspect
Calif. Diesel

Valves .... adjust

Body .... lubricate
Includes cables, linkages, locks, latches, hinges, seat belts

EVERY 24 MO/30 MI—48 KM
Cooling system ...... change coolant **EC**

Front wheel bearings .... repack **LM**

Air cleaner element .... replace

Air conditioning system .... inspect

Air induction valve filter .... replace
Engines with reed valve system only

Drive belts .... inspect

Engine .... major tune-up
Replace spark plugs. U.S., inspect distributor cap, rotor, wires & choke

Fuel filter, Calif. Diesel .... replace

Fuel lines .... inspect

Fuel vapor lines .... inspect

Idle speed Diesel, Calif. .... inspect

Injection nozzle tips .... inspect
Diesel, clean & service

Ignition system .... inspect
Check advance mechanism; inspect wires

PCV hoses .... inspect

Timing FI Diesel .... inspect

SERVICE AS REQUIRED
Fuel filter .... replace

SEVERE SERVICE
Crankcase—Gasoline, change oil every 3 mo/3 mi (5 km). Diesel, change filter every oil change

PCV filter—In adverse weather conditions, inspect & replace if clogged

Transmission, manual & automatic; differential—Change fluid or lubricant every 24 mo/30 mi (48 km)

KEY TO LUBRICANTS

AF	Dexron Automatic Transmission Fluid. Dexron available from dealer, do not use DEXRON®-II
CC	Motor Oil, API Service CC
CD	Motor Oil, API Service CD
CE	Motor Oil, API Service CE
CO	Cod Liver Oil
EC	Ethylene Glycol Coolant Mix with water to desired freeze protection
GL-4	Gear Oil, API Service GL-4
GL-5	Gear Oil, API Service GL-5
HB	Hydraulic Brake Fluid, DOT 3
LM	Lithium Grease, No. 2
SE	Motor Oil, API Service SE
SF	Motor Oil, API Service SF
SG	Motor Oil, API Service SG

CRANKCASE
Gasoline engine .... **SG**
Diesel engine .... **SG/CD, CD**

CAPACITY, Refill:	Liters	Qt
Datsun Pickup: 2WD	3.7	3.9
4WD	4.0	4.3
Diesel	5.0	5.3
Nissan Pickup: 2WD	3.6	3.8
4WD	3.8	4.0
Diesel	4.6	4.8

Capacity shown is without filter. When replacing filter, additional oil may be needed

Gasoline engines:
Above 50°F (10°C) 20W-40, 20W-50
Above 0°F (−18°C) 10W-30*, 10W-40
Below 60°F (15°C) 5W-30
Diesel engines:
Above 32°F (0°C) 30
Above 20°F (−7°C) 15W-40
Above 0°F (−18°C) 10W-30
Below 60°F (15°C) 5W-30
* Preferred

TRANSMISSION, Automatic .... **AF**

CAPACITY, Refill†:	Liters	Qt
All	5.5	5.9

†Total (dry) fill shown. Use less fluid when refilling

TRANSMISSION, Manual **GL-4**
Above 50°F (10°C), 140; 30° to 100°F (−1° to 38°C), 90; 10° to 85°F (−12° to 29°C), 85W; below 100°F (38°C), 75W-90, 80W-90; below 85°F (29°C), 80W; below 50°F (10°C), 75W

CAPACITY, Refill:	Liters	Pt
4-speed	1.7	3.6
5-speed	2.0	4.2

TRANSFER CASE **GL-4**

CAPACITY, Refill:	Liters	Qt
All	1.4	3.0

Above 50°F (10°C), 140; 30° to 100°F (−1° to 38°C), 90; 10° to 85°F (−12° to 29°C), 85W; below 100°F (38°C), 75W-90, 80W-90; below 85°F (29°C), 80W; below 50°F (10°C), 75W

DIFFERENTIAL **GL-5**
Above 50°F (10°C), 140; 30° to 100°F (−1° to 38°C), 90; 10° to 85°F (−12° to 29°C), 85W; below 100°F (38°C), 75W-90, 80W-90; below 85°F (29°C), 80W; below 50°F (10°C), 75W

CAPACITY, Refill:	Liters	Pt
Pickup rear	1.2	2.5
W/dual rear wheel, rear	1.3	2.8
Front (4WD)	1.0	2.1
Transfer case (4WD) ..	1.4	3.0

SERVICE AT TIME OR MILEAGE—WHICHEVER OCCURS FIRST

DNIPM8   DNIPM8

Perform the following maintenance services at the intervals indicated to keep the vehicle warranties in effect.

W   SERVICE TO MAINTAIN EMISSION WARRANTY

MI—MILES IN THOUSANDS
KM—KILOMETERS IN THOUSANDS

Rear wheel lug nuts, DRW . . . . torque
At first 100 miles (80 kilometers), then every 600 miles (960 kilometers)
Torque to 166-203 ft lb (226-275 Nm)

SERVICE PERIODICALLY
Brake & clutch master
   cylinders . . . . check level **HB**

Power steering reservoir . . check level **AF**

Transmission, automatic . . . . . check level

ALL DIESEL ENGINES
EVERY 6 MO/5 MI—8 KM
W Crankcase . . . . change oil
Replace Diesel injection pump diaphragm oil **CO**

W Oil filter . . . . replace
At first oil change then every other

EVERY 6 MO/7.5 MI—12 KM
Propeller shaft, 4WD . . . . inspect

W Crankcase . . . . change oil
Ex. Diesel

W Oil filter ex. Diesel . . . . replace

EVERY 12 MONTHS
Underbody . . . . flush/clean

EVERY 12 MO/15 MI—24 KM
Brake system . . . . inspect
Inspect lines & hoses, linings, drums & disc pads

W Differential, transfer case . . check level

Exhaust system . . . . inspect

Front suspension & steering
   linkage . . . . inspect

Front wheel bearings . . . . inspect **LM**
Pickup 4WD

Power steering lines & hoses . . . . . inspect

Tires . . . . rotate
Check balance & alignment

Transmission, manual . . . . . . check level

Drive belts Diesel . . . . inspect/adjust

Fuel filter Diesel . . . . replace

Idle speed Diesel . . . . inspect
49 states & Canada

Idle speed gasoline U.S. . . . . inspect

Injection nozzle tips Diesel . . . . inspect

Rubber hoses . . . . inspect
Calif. Diesel

W Valve clearance . . . . adjust

Body . . . . lubricate
Includes cables, linkages, locks, latches, hinges. Also inspect seat belts

EVERY 24 MO/30 MI—48 KM
W Cooling system . . . . change coolant **EC**

Front wheel bearings . . . . inspect **LM**
4WD, repack **LM**

W Air cleaner element . . . . replace

Automatic temp. control
   air cleaner . . . . inspect

W Drive belts . . . . inspect
Gasoline

Fuel & fuel vapor lines . . . . inspect

Idle speed Diesel . . . . inspect
California

W PCV filter . . . . replace

PCV hoses . . . . inspect

W Spark plugs . . . . replace

Timing, diesel injection pump . . . . inspect

EVERY 50 MI—80 KM
Oxygen sensor . . . . replace

EVERY 60 MI—96 KM
Drive belts . . . . replace

W Spark plugs . . . . replace
Platinum tipped only

W Timing belt, V6 . . . . replace

SERVICE AS REQUIRED
W Fuel filter . . . . replace

SEVERE SERVICE
W Crankcase—Gasoline, change oil every 3 mo/3 mi (5 km). Diesel, change filter every oil change

Limited-Slip differential—Change lubricant every 12 mo/15 mi (24 km) when towing a trailer or driving on muddy roads

Steering, suspension, locks, hinges, exhaust, brake system—Inspect every 6 mo/7.5 mi (12 km)

Transmission, manual & automatic; transfer case, differential—Change fluid or lubricant every 24 mo/30 mi (48 km) when towing a trailer or driving on rough or muddy roads

KEY TO LUBRICANTS

AF	Dexron Automatic Transmission Fluid. Dexron available from dealer, do not use DEXRON®-II
CD	Motor Oil, API Service CD
CO	Cod Liver Oil
EC	Ethylene Glycol Coolant Mix with water to desired freeze protection
GL-4	Gear Oil, API Service GL-4
GL-5	Gear Oil, API Service GL-5
GL-5★	Special Lubricant for Limited-Slip Differentials
HB	Hydraulic Brake Fluid, DOT 3
LM	Lithium Grease, No. 2
SF	Motor Oil, API Service SF
SG	Motor Oil, API Service SG

CRANKCASE
Gasoline engine . . . . **SG**
Diesel engine . . . . **SF/CD, CD**

CAPACITY, Refill:	Liters	Qt
1984-85 Pickup: 2WD	3.6	3.8
4WD	3.8	4.0
Diesel	4.8	5.1
1986		
2WD	3.2	3.4
4WD	3.5	3.7
Diesel	4.8	5.1

Capacity shown is without filter. When replacing filter, additional oil may be needed

Gasoline engines:
Above 50°F (10°C) 20W-40, 20W-50
Above 0°F (–18°C) 10W-30*, 10W-40
Below 60°F (16°C) 5W-30

Diesel engines:
Above 32°F (0°C) 30
Above 20°F (–7°C) 15W-40
Above 0°F (–18°C) 10W-30*
Below 60°F (16°C) 5W-30*
*Preferred

TRANSMISSION, Automatic . . . . **AF**

CAPACITY, Total Fill†:	Liters	Qt
All	5.5	5.9

†Total (dry) fill shown. Use less fluid when refilling

TRANSMISSION, Manual **GL-4**
Above 50°F (10°C), 140; 30° to 100°F (–1° to 38°C), 90; 10° to 85°F (–12° to 29°C), 85W; below 100°F (38°C), 75W-90, 80W-90; below 85°F (29°C), 80W; below 50°F (10°C), 75W

CAPACITY, Refill:	Liters	Pt
4-speed	1.7	3.6
5-speed	2.0	4.2

TRANSFER CASE **GL-4**
See Transmission, Manual for viscosity

CAPACITY, Refill:	Liters	Pt
All	1.4	3.0

DIFFERENTIAL
Limited-Slip . . . . 80W-90 **GL-5★**
Standard **GL-5**
See Transmission, Manual for viscosity

CAPACITY, Refill:	Liters	Pt
Front: 4-cyl.	1.3	2.8
V6	1.5	3.2
Rear: 4-cyl.: 2WD	1.5	3.2
4WD	1.3	2.8
V6	2.8	5.9

SERVICE AT TIME OR MILEAGE—WHICHEVER OCCURS FIRST

DNIPM10   Perform the following maintenance services at the intervals indicated to keep the vehicle warranties in effect.   DNIPM10

W   SERVICE TO MAINTAIN EMISSION WARRANTY

MI—MILES IN THOUSANDS
KM—KILOMETERS IN THOUSANDS

Rear wheel lug nuts, DRW . . . . . . torque
At first 100 miles (80 kilometers), then every 600 miles
(960 kilometers)
Torque to 166-203 ft lb (226-275 Nm)

SERVICE PERIODICALLY
Brake & clutch master
   cylinders . . . . check level **HB**

Power steering reservoir . . check level **AF**

Transmission, automatic . . . . . check level

ALL DIESEL ENGINES
EVERY 6 MO/5 MI—8 KM
W Crankcase . . . . change oil
Replace Diesel injection pump diaphragm oil **CO**

W Oil filter . . . . replace
At first oil change then every other

EVERY 6 MO/7.5 MI—12 KM
Propeller shaft, 4WD . . . . inspect

W Crankcase . . . . change oil
Ex. Diesel

W Oil filter ex. Diesel . . . . replace

Tires . . . . rotate

EVERY 12 MONTHS
Underbody . . . . flush/clean

EVERY 12 MO/15 MI—24 KM
Brake system . . . . inspect
Inspect lines & hoses, linings, drums & disc pads

Differential, transfer case . . . . . check level

Exhaust system 1986-89 . . . . inspect

Front suspension & steering
   linkage 1986-89 . . . . inspect

Front wheel bearings . . . . inspect **LM**
Pickup 4WD

Power steering lines
   & hoses 1987-88 . . . . inspect

Transmission, manual . . . . . . check level

Drive belts Diesel . . . . inspect/adjust

Fuel filter Diesel . . . . replace

Idle speed Diesel . . . . inspect
49 states & Canada

Idle speed gasoline U.S. . . . . inspect
1986-89

Injection nozzle tips Diesel . . . . inspect

Rubber hoses . . . . inspect
Calif. Diesel

W Valve clearance . . . . adjust
1986-89 4-cyl.

Body 1986-88 . . . . lubricate
Includes cables, linkages, locks, latches, hinges. Also
inspect seat belts

1986-89, EVERY 24 MONTHS
Ignition wires . . . . inspect

EVERY 24 MO/30 MI—48 KM
Cooling system . . . . . . change coolant **EC**
1991-92, initial service at 48 mo/60 mi (96 km)

Front suspension &
   steering linkage 1990-92 . . . . inspect

Front wheel bearings . . . . inspect **LM**
4WD, repack **LM**

Limited-Slip differential . . change lubricant

W Air cleaner element . . . . replace

W Drive belts . . . . inspect
Gasoline

Fuel & fuel vapor lines . . . . inspect

Idle speed Diesel . . . . inspect
California

W PCV filter . . . . replace
Ex. 1990-92 V6. At mileage interval only

PCV hoses . . . . inspect

W Spark plugs . . . . replace
At mileage interval only

Timing, diesel injection pump . . . . inspect

EVERY 60 MI—96 KM
Idle speed, Van . . . . adjust

Oxygen sensor . . . . replace

W Spark plugs . . . . replace
Platinum tipped only

W Timing belt, V6 . . . . replace

SERVICE AS REQUIRED
W Fuel filter . . . . replace

SEVERE SERVICE
Air induction valve filter, 1990-92 4-cyl.—
Replace every 30 mi (48 km)

W Crankcase—Change oil & filter every:
1986-89, 3 mo/3 mi (5 km); 1990-92, 3 mo/
3.75 mi (6 km)

Limited-Slip differential—Change lubricant
every 12 mo/15 mi (24 km) when towing a
trailer or driving on muddy roads

Steering, suspension, locks, hinges, exhaust,
brake system—Inspect every 6 mo/7.5 mi (12
km)

Transmission, manual & automatic; transfer
case, differential—Change fluid or lubricant
every 24 mo/30 mi (48 km) when towing a
trailer or driving on rough or muddy roads

KEY TO LUBRICANTS
AF   Dexron Automatic Transmission
     Fluid. Dexron available from dealer,
     do not use DEXRON®-II
CD   Motor Oil, API Service CD
CO   Cod Liver Oil
EC   Ethylene Glycol Coolant
     Mix with water to desired freeze protection
GL-4   Gear Oil, API Service GL-4
GL-5   Gear Oil, API Service GL-5
GL-5★   Special Lubricant for Limited-Slip
     Differentials
HB   Hydraulic Brake Fluid, DOT 3
LM   Lithium Grease, No. 2
SG   Motor Oil, API Service SG

CRANKCASE
Gasoline engine . . . . **SG**
Diesel engine . . . . **SG/CD**

CAPACITY, Refill:	Liters	Qt
Van	3.7	3.9
1986-89 Pickup, Pathfinder:		
4-cyl.: 2WD	3.3	3.5
4WD	3.8	4.0
V6: 2WD	3.6	3.8
4WD	3.0	3.2
Diesel	6.7	7.1
1990-92: 2WD	3.5	3.7
4WD	2.9	3.1

Capacity shown is without filter. When replacing filter, additional oil may be needed

Gasoline engines:
Above 50°F (10°C) 20W-40, 20W-50
Above 0°F (–18°C) 10W-30*, 10W-40
Below 60°F (16°C), 1986-89 . . . . 5W-30
All temperatures 5W-30*

Diesel engines:
Above 32°F (0°C) 30
Above 20°F (–7°C) 15W-40
Above 0°F (–18°C) 10W-30*
Below 60°F (16°C) 5W-30
*1986-89, 10W-30 preferred; 1990-92, 5W-30 preferred

TRANSMISSION, Automatic . . . . AF

CAPACITY, Total Fill†:	Liters	Qt
Van	7.0	7.3
Pickup, Pathfinder:		
1986-87	7.5	7.8
4-speed	7.0	7.4
1988-89 2WD	7.0	7.4
4WD	8.5	9.0
1990-92 2WD	7.9	8.3
4WD	8.5	9.0

†Total (dry) fill shown. Use less fluid when refilling

TRANSMISSION, Manual GL-4
Above 50°F (10°C), 140; 30° to 100°F (–1° to
38°C), 90; 10° to 85°F (–12° to 29°C), below
100°F (38°C), 75W-90, 80W-90; below 85°F
(29°C), 80W; below 50°F (10°C), 75W

CAPACITY, Refill:	Liters	Pt
Van	2.0	4.2
Pickup, Pathfinder:		
4-cyl.: 2WD	2.0	4.2
4WD	4.0	8.4
V6: 2WD	2.4	5.0
4WD	3.6	7.6

TRANSFER CASE
1986-89 . . . . **GL-4**
See Transmission, Manual for viscosity
1990-92 . . . . **AF**

CAPACITY, Refill:	Liters	Pt
Pickup, Pathfinder	2.2	4.8

DIFFERENTIAL
Limited-Slip . . . . 80W-90 **GL-5★**
90 may be used above 0°F (–18°C)
Standard **GL-5**
See Transmission, Manual for viscosity

CAPACITY, Refill:	Liters	Pt
Van	1.3	2.8
Pickup, Pathfinder:		
Front: 4-cyl.	1.3	2.8
V6	1.5	3.2
Rear: 4-cyl.: 2WD	1.5	3.2
4WD	1.3	2.8
V6	2.8	5.9

SERVICE LOCATIONS — ENGINE AND CHASSIS

HOOD RELEASE: Inside

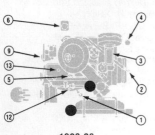

**1983-86
1.8L (112) 2V,
2.0L (122)
Code G, B, P**

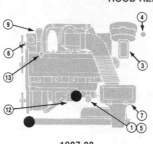

**1987-88
2.0L (122) Code 1**

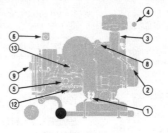

**1983-86
1.8L (112) FI Code 0,
1987-88
2.0L (122) OHC Code K**

1. Crankcase dipstick
2. Transmission dipstick
3. Brake fluid reservoir
4. Clutch fluid reservoir
5. Oil fill cap
6. Power steering reservoir
7. Air filter
8. Fuel filter
9. Oil filter
10. PCV filter
11. EGR valve
12. Oxygen sensor
13. PCV valve

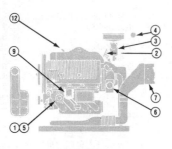

**1992
2.3L Code 3**

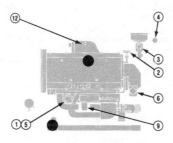

**1987-92 2.3L Code D
1989-92 2.3L Code A**

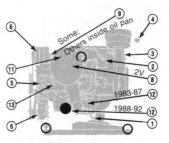

**1983-92
2.5L (151) Omega,
Ciera, Calais
Code R, U, 5
Air induction
system varies.**

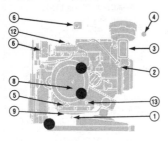

**1983-86
2.8L (173) 2V Code X, Z**

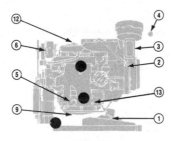

**1985-86
2.8L (173) FI
Code W**

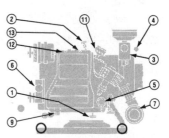

**2.8L Code W
1987 Ciera, Firenza
1988-89 Ciera, Cutlass Supreme
3.1L Code T
1989 Cutlass Supreme
1990-92 Ciera, Cutlass Supreme**

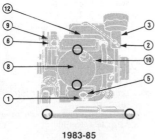

**1983-85
3.0L (181) 2V
Code E**

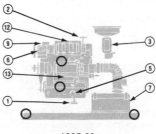

**1985-88
3.0L (181) FI
Code L**

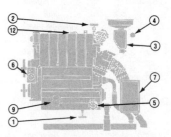

**1991-92 3.4L Code X
Cutlass Supreme**

● Cooling system drain   ○ Cooling system drain, some models

HOOD RELEASE: Inside

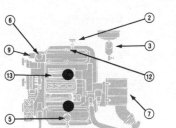

**1989-92
3.3L Code N
Achieva, Ciera, Calais**

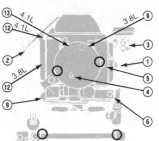

**1983-87
3.8L (231) 2V, 4.1L (252)
Code A, 4**

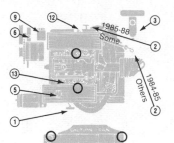

**1984-88
3.8L (231) FI Code 3
1986
3.8L FI Code B**

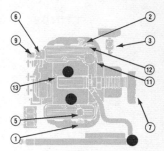

**1988-91 3.8L Code C
Ninety Eight, 88,
Toronado**

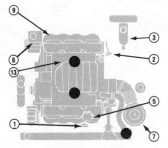

**1991-92 3.8L Code L
Ninety Eight, Toronado, Troféo**

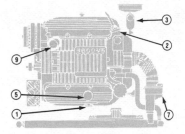

**1992
3.8L Code 1 Supercharged
Ninety-Eight**

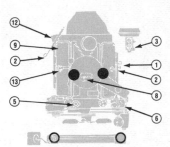

**4.3L (260), 5.0L (307)
ex. Toronado**

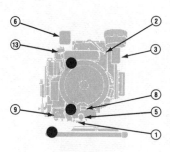

**1983-85
4.3L (262) V-6 Diesel
Code T**

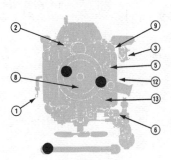

**1983-87
4.4L (267), 5.0L (305)**

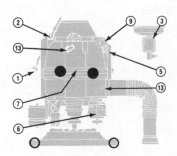

**1991-92 5.0L Code E
5.7L Code 7
Custom Cruiser**

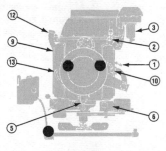

**1983-85
5.0L (307)**

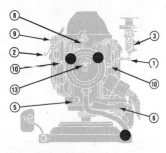

**1983-85
5.7L (350)
Diesel ex. Toronado
Code N**

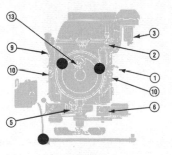

**1983-85
5.7L (350)
Toronado Diesel
Code N**

● Cooling system drain   ○ Cooling system drain, some models

OLDSMOBILE
1983-92 All Models Except Bravada, Silhouette

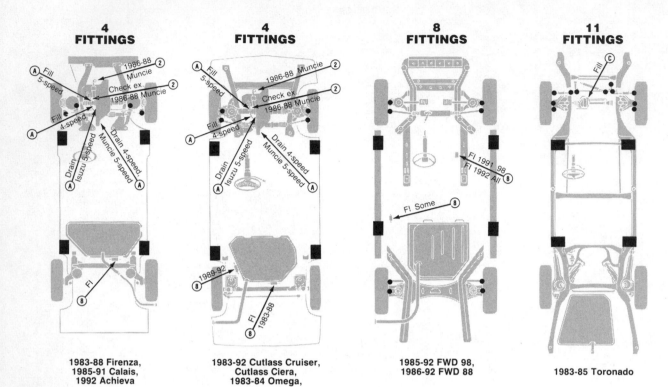

4 FITTINGS

1983-88 Firenza,
1985-91 Calais,
1992 Achieva

4 FITTINGS

1983-92 Cutlass Cruiser,
Cutlass Ciera,
1983-84 Omega,

8 FITTINGS

1985-92 FWD 98,
1986-92 FWD 88

11 FITTINGS

1983-85 Toronado

4 FITTINGS

1986-92 Toronado, Troféo

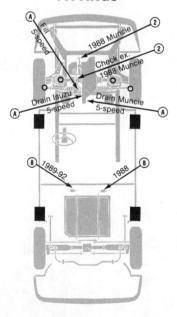

0-4 FITTINGS

1988-92 Cutlass Supreme

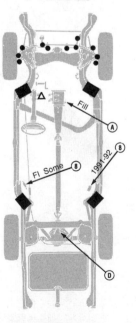

**11 FITTINGS
0-1 PLUGS**

1983-92 Custom Cruiser
1983-88 Cutlass RWD
1983-85 88
1983-84 98

Ⓐ Manual transmission/transaxle,
drain & fill
Ⓑ Transfer case, NOT USED
Ⓒ Automatic transaxle final drive,
drain & fill
Ⓓ Differential, drain & fill

② Transmission dipstick
⑧ Fuel filter

CAUTION: On front wheel drive vehicles the center of gravity is further forward than on rear wheel drive vehicles. When removing major components from the rear of the vehicle while it is on a hoist, the vehicle must be supported in a manner to prevent it from tipping forward.

▇ Lift adapter position   ▲ Plug   △ Plug, some models   • Fitting

OLDSMOBILE
1983 All Gasoline Models

SERVICE AT TIME OR MILEAGE—WHICHEVER OCCURS FIRST

OEPM8   OEPM8

MI—MILES IN THOUSANDS
KM—KILOMETERS IN THOUSANDS

EVERY 6 MONTHS
Brake master cylinder ..... check level **HB**

Clutch pedal free travel .... check/adjust
Front wheel drive models, every 5 mi (8 km)

Power steering reservoir ... check level **PS**

Transaxle or trans., auto. ..... check level

FIRST 7.5 MI—12 KM
Carburetor mounting bolts .... torque

Engine idle speed .... adjust
Without Idle Speed or Idle Air Control

Diff., Limited-Slip .... change lubricant
One time service only

Tires .... rotate
Radial tires, every 15 mi (24 km) after initial service.
Check brake pads. Lug nut torque, ft lb: Toronado, 140;
other front wheel drive 100; Delta 88 station wagon,
100; all others, 80 ex. 90 with aluminum wheels

FIRST 7.5 MI—12 KM;
THEN EVERY 24 MO/30 MI—48 KM
Choke & hoses .... check/clean

EVERY 12 MO/7.5 MI—12 KM
Crankcase .... change oil

Differential .... check level

Exhaust system .... inspect

Front suspension &
   steering linkage .... **4-11 fittings LB**

Oil filter .... replace
At first oil change, then at 12 mo/15 mi (24 km) intervals
only

Parking brake cables & guides .... coat **LB**
Check adjustment

Shift linkage .... coat **LB**
With floor shift, coat contact faces

Suspension & steering .... inspect
Also inspect front drive axle boots and seals

Transaxle or transmission ..... check level

Drive belts .... inspect/adjust

Throttle linkage .... inspect
Check for damage or binding

Body .... lubricate

EVERY 12 MONTHS
Cooling system .... inspect & tighten hoses
Wash radiator filler neck & cap; pressure test system.
Clean exterior of radiator core and air conditioning con-
denser

EVERY 24 MO/30 MI—48 KM
Cooling system .... change coolant **EC**
Flush system

EVERY 36 MO/30 MI—48 KM
Air cleaner element .... replace
Ex. 2.0L

EGR system .... clean/inspect

EVERY 30 MI—48 KM
Clutch cross shaft .... 1 plug **LB**

Front wheel bearings ex.
   front wheel drive ...... clean/repack **GC**
Service at mileage interval or at each brake reline,
whichever comes first. Tighten spindle nut to 12 ft lb
while turning wheel. Back off 1/2 turn & retighten finger
tight. End play, .001″-.005″

Fuel tank, cap & lines .... inspect

Ignition timing .... adjust
Inspect distributor cap, clean or replace

Ignition wires .... inspect/clean

PCV valve .... inspect
Blow out or replace hoses

Spark plugs .... replace

Vacuum advance system
   & hoses .... inspect
As equipped

EVERY 50 MI—80 KM
Air cleaner element, 2.0L .... replace

EVERY 100 MI—160 KM
Transaxle or trans., auto. .... change fluid
Clean sump screen or replace filter

SEVERE SERVICE
Crankcase—Change oil every 3 mo/3 mi
(4.8 km). Change filter at each oil change

Front wheel bearings—Repack every 15 mi
(24 km)

Transaxle or transmission, automatic—
Change fluid & filter or clean screen every
15 mi (24 km)

Differential—Change lubricant every 7.5 mi
(12 km) when towing a trailer

KEY TO LUBRICANTS

AF	DEXRON®-IIE Automatic Transmission Fluid
EC	Ethylene Glycol Coolant Mix with water to −34°F (−37°C) protection
GC	Wheel Bearing Grease, NLGI Category GC
GL-5	Gear Oil, API Service GL-5
GL-5★	Special Lubricant for Limited-Slip Differential
GLS	Gear Lubricant, Special GM Part No. 12345349
HB	Hydraulic Brake Fluid, DOT 3
LB	Chassis Grease, NLGI Category LB
PS	Power Steering Fluid
SG	Motor Oil, API Service SG Use Energy Conserving-II oils

CRANKCASE .... **SG**

CAPACITY, Refill:	Liters	Qt
4-cyl. 1.8L & 2.5L	2.8	3.0
Others	3.8	4.0

Capacity shown is without filter. When replacing filter, additional oil may be needed

Above 40°F (4°C)	30
Above 20°F (−7°C) 20W-20, 20W-40, 20W-50	
Above 10°F (−12°C)	15W-40
Above 0°F (−18°C)	10W-30*
Below 60°F (16°C)	5W-30△

△5W-30 may be used up to 100°F (38°C) in 4-cyl. & 2.8L
V-6 engines
*10W-30 preferred above 0°F (−18°C)

TRANSMISSION/TRANSAXLE,
   Automatic .... **AF**

CAPACITY, Initial Refill*:	Liters	Qt
Front wheel drive ex. Toronado	3.8	4.0
Toronado†	3.0	3.3
200 Transmission	3.3	3.5
250 Transmission	3.8	4.0
350 Transmission	3.0	3.3
700-R4 Transmission	4.7	5.0

*With the engine at operating temperature, shift transmission
through all gears. Let engine slow idle in PARK for 3 minutes
or more. Check fluid level and add fluid as needed
†Differential serviced separately

TRANSAXLE, Manual

4-speed	**AF**
5-speed	**GLS**

CAPACITY, Refill:	Liters	Pt
4-speed	2.8	6.0
5-speed	2.5	5.4

DIFFERENTIAL/FINAL DRIVE
Standard & Toronado . 80W, 80W-90* **GL-5**
Limited-Slip ..... 80W, 80W-90* **GL-5★**
*For vehicles normally operated in Canada, 80W only

CAPACITY, Refill:	Liters	Pt
Cutlass	1.7	3.5
Toronado	1.5	3.3
88, 98:		
7 1/2″ ring gear	1.7	3.5
8 1/2″, 8 3/4″ ring gear	2.0	4.3

LIMITED-SLIP IDENTIFICATION:
Tag under rear cover-attaching bolt

OLDSMOBILE
1983 All Diesel Models

MI—MILES IN THOUSANDS
KM—KILOMETERS IN THOUSANDS

EVERY 6 MONTHS
Brake master cylinder . . . . . check level **HB**

Power steering reservoir . . . check level **PS**

Transaxle or trans., auto. . . . . . check level

FIRST 5 MI—8 KM;
THEN EVERY 30 MI—48 KM
Engine idle speed . . . . adjust

FIRST 7.5 MI—12 KM
Diff., Limited-Slip . . . . change lubricant
One time service only

Tires . . . . rotate
Radial tires, every 15 mi (24 km) after initial service.
Check brake pads. Lug nut torque, ft lb: Toronado, 140;
other front wheel drive, 100; Delta 88 station wagon,
100; all others, 80 ex. 90 with aluminum wheels

EVERY 12 MO/5 MI—8 KM
Crankcase . . . . change oil

Differential . . . . check level

Exhaust pressure regulator valve &
   hoses, 6-cyl. . . . . inspect/test
After initial inspection, check again at 15 mi (24 km) &
every 15 mi (24 km) thereafter

Exhaust system . . . . inspect

Front suspension &
   steering linkage . . . . **4-11 fittings LB**

Oil filter . . . . replace

Parking brake cables & guides . . . . coat **LB**
Check adjustment

Suspension & steering . . . . inspect
Also inspect front drive axle boots and seals

Transaxle or transmission . . . . . check level

Drive belts . . . . inspect/adjust

Throttle linkage . . . . inspect
Check for damage or binding

Body . . . . lubricate

EVERY 12 MONTHS
Cooling system . . . . inspect & tighten hoses
Wash radiator filler neck & cap; pressure test system.
Clean exterior of radiator core and air conditioning con-
denser

EVERY 12 MO/15 MI—24 KM
Crankcase ventilation system . . . . . inspect
Clean filters in each valve cover, pipes & tubes

EVERY 24 MO/30 MI—48 KM
Cooling system . . . . change coolant **EC**
Flush system

EVERY 36 MO/30 MI—48 KM
EGR system . . . . clean/inspect

EVERY 30 MI—48 KM
Front wheel bearings ex.
   front wheel drive . . . . . clean/repack **GC**
Service at mileage interval or at each brake reline,
whichever comes first. Tighten spindle nut to 12 ft lb
while turning wheel. Back off 1/2 turn & retighten finger
tight. End play, .001″-.005″

Air cleaner element . . . . replace

Fuel filter . . . . replace

Injection pump timing . . . . adjust

EVERY 100 MI—160 KM
Transaxle or trans., auto. . . . . change fluid
Clean sump screen or replace filter

SEVERE SERVICE
Crankcase—Change oil every 3 mo/2.5 mi
(4 km). Change filter at each oil change

Front wheel bearings—Repack every 15 mi
(24 km)

Transaxle or transmission, automatic—
Change fluid & filter or clean screen every
15 mi (24 km)

Differential—Change lubricant every 7.5 mi
(12 km) when towing a trailer

KEY TO LUBRICANTS

AF	DEXRON®-IIE Automatic Transmission Fluid
CD	Motor Oil, API Service CD
EC	Ethylene Glycol Coolant Mix with water −34°F (−37°C) protection
GC	Wheel Bearing Grease, NLGI Category GC
GL-5	Gear Oil, API Service GL-5
GL-5 ★	Special Lubricant for Limited-Slip Differential
HB	Hydraulic Brake Fluid, DOT 3
LB	Chassis Grease, NLGI Category LB
PS	Power Steering Fluid
SG	Motor Oil, API Service SG Use Energy Conserving-II oils

CRANKCASE . . . . **SG/CD**

CAPACITY, Refill:	Liters	Qt
6-cyl.	5.6	6.0
8-cyl.	6.6	7.0

Includes filter

Above 32°F (0°C)	30♦
0° to 60°F (−18° to 16°C)	15W-40
Below 60°F (16°C)	10W-30

♦30 is preferred above 32°F (0°C), especially for continuous duty driving

TRANSMISSION/TRANSAXLE,
   Automatic . . . . **AF**

CAPACITY, Initial Refill*:	Liters	Qt
125 Transmission	3.8	4.0
325 Transmission†	3.0	3.3
350 Transmission	3.0	3.3

* With the engine at operating temperature, shift transmission
through all gears. Let engine slow idle in PARK for 3 minutes
or more. Check fluid level and add fluid as needed
†Differential serviced separately

DIFFERENTIAL/FINAL DRIVE

Standard & Toronado . 80W, 80W-90*	**GL-5**
Limited-Slip 80W, 80W-90*	**GL-5 ★**

* For vehicles normally operated in Canada, 80W only

CAPACITY, Refill:	Liters	Pt
Cutlass	1.7	3.5
Toronado	1.5	3.3
88, 98:		
7¹/₂″ ring gear	1.7	3.5
8¹/₂″, 8³/₄″ ring gear	2.0	4.3

LIMITED-SLIP IDENTIFICATION:
Tag under rear cover-attaching bolt

SERVICE AT TIME OR MILEAGE—WHICHEVER OCCURS FIRST

OEPM10   OEPM10

MI—MILES IN THOUSANDS
KM—KILOMETERS IN THOUSANDS

EVERY 6 MONTHS
Brake master cylinder .... check level **HB**

Clutch system .... check/adjust
Front wheel drive models, every 5 mi (8 km)

Power steering reservoir .. check level **PS**

FIRST 7.5 MI—12 KM
Carburetor or T.B.I. mounting
  bolts .... torque

Engine idle speed .... adjust
Without Idle Speed or Idle Air Control

Diff., Limited-Slip .... change lubricant
One time service only

Tires .... rotate
Radial tires, every 15 mi (24 km) after initial service.
Check brake linings. Lug nut torque, ft lb: 1985 FWD &
Custom Cruiser with 1/2″ studs, 100; all others, 80.
Toronado, 100; other front wheel drive, 100; Delta 88
station wagon, 100; all others, 80 ex. 90 with aluminum
wheels

FIRST 7.5 MI—12 KM;
THEN EVERY 24 MO/30 MI—50 KM
Choke & hoses .... check/clean

EVERY 12 MO/7.5 MI—12 KM
Brake system .... inspect
Check hydraulic system for leaks. Inspect brake linings

Crankcase .... change oil

Differential .... check level

Exhaust system .... inspect

Suspension &
  steering linkage ...... **4-11 fittings LB**

Oil filter .... replace

Parking brake cables & guides ... coat **LB**
Check adjustment

Shift linkage .... coat **LB**
With floor shift, coat contact faces

Suspension & steering .... inspect
Also inspect front drive axle boots and seals

Transaxle or transmission .... check level

Drive belts .... inspect/adjust

Throttle linkage .... inspect
Check for damage or binding

Body .... lubricate

EVERY 12 MONTHS
Cooling system ... inspect & tighten hoses
Wash radiator filler neck & cap; pressure test system.
Clean exterior of radiator core and air conditioning con-
denser. Inspect coolant, service as needed

EVERY 24 MO/30 MI—50 KM
Air pump belt .... inspect/adjust
Replace as needed

Cooling system ..... change coolant **EC**
Flush system

EVERY 36 MO/30 MI—50 KM
Air cleaner element .... replace
Ex. 2.0L

EGR system .... clean/inspect

EVERY 30 MI—50 KM
Clutch cross shaft .... **1 plug LB**

Front wheel bearings ex.
  front wheel drive ..... clean/repack **GC**
Service at mileage interval or at each brake reline,
whichever comes first. Tighten spindle nut to 12 ft lb
while turning wheel. Back off 1/2 turn & retighten finger
tight. End play, .001″-.005″

Fuel tank, cap & lines .... inspect

Distributor cap .... inspect

Ignition timing .... adjust
Inspect distributor cap, clean or replace

Ignition wires .... inspect/clean

PCV valve .... inspect
Blow out or replace hoses

Spark plugs .... replace

Thermostatic air cleaner .... inspect

Vacuum advance system
  & hoses .... inspect
As equipped

EVERY 50 MI—80 KM
Air cleaner element, 2.0L .... replace

EVERY 100 MI—160 KM
Transaxle or trans., auto. .... change fluid
Clean sump screen or replace filter

SEVERE SERVICE
Carburetor or T.B.I.—Torque mounting
bolts & adjust idle speed at 6 mi (10 km).
Inspect carburetor choke & hoses

Crankcase—Change oil every 3 mo/3 mi (5
km). Change filter at each oil change

Front suspension & steering linkage—
Lubricate every 6 mo/6 mi (10 km)

Front wheel bearings—Repack every 15 mi
(24 km) or every brake service, whichever
comes first

Transaxle or transmission, automatic—
Change fluid & filter or clean screen every
15 mi (24 km)

Differential—Change lubricant every 7.5 mi
(12 km) when towing a trailer

KEY TO LUBRICANTS

AF   DEXRON®-IIE Automatic Transmission
Fluid

EC   Ethylene Glycol Coolant
Mix with water −34°F (−37°C) protection

GC   Wheel Bearing Grease,
NLGI Category GC

GL-5   Gear Oil, API Service GL-5

GL-5★   Special Lubricant for Limited-Slip
Differential

GLS   Gear Lubricant, Special
4-speed, GM Part No. 1052931
5-speed, GM Part No. 12345349

HB   Hydraulic Brake Fluid, DOT 3

LB   Chassis Grease, NLGI Category LB

PS   Power Steering Fluid

SG   Motor Oil, API Service SG
Use Energy Conserving-II oils

CRANKCASE .... SG

CAPACITY, Refill♦:	Liters	Qt
4-cyl. 2.5L	2.8	3.0
Others	3.8	4.0

♦Capacity shown is without filter. When replacing filter,
additional oil may be needed

Above 40°F (4°C)	30
Above 20°F (−7°C)	20W-20
Above 10°F (−12°C)	15W-40
Above 0°F (−18°C)	10W-30
Below 60°F (16°C)	5W-30†

†5W-30 may be used up to 100°F (38°C) in 4-cyl. & 2.8L
V-6 engines

TRANSMISSION/TRANSAXLE,
Automatic .... AF

CAPACITY, Initial Refill*:	Liters	Qt
125 Transmission	3.8	4.0
200 Transmission	3.3	3.5
250 Transmission	3.8	4.0
325 Transmission†	3.0	3.3
440 Transmission	5.8	6.0

* With the engine at operating temperature, shift transmission
through all gears. Let engine slow idle in PARK for 3 minutes
or more. Check fluid level and add fluid as needed
†Differential serviced separately

TRANSAXLE, Manual .... GLS

CAPACITY, Refill:	Liters	Pt
4-speed	2.8	6.0
5-speed	2.5	5.4

DIFFERENTIAL/FINAL DRIVE
Standard &
  Toronado 80W, 80W-90* **GL-5**
Limited-Slip .... 80W, 80W-90* **GL-5★**
*For vehicles normally operated in Canada, 80W only

CAPACITY, Refill:	Liters	Pt
Toronado	1.5	3.3
Cutlass, 88, 98 RWD:		
7½″ ring gear	1.7	3.5
8½″, 8¾″ ring gear ...	2.0	4.3

LIMITED-SLIP IDENTIFICATION:
Tag under rear cover-attaching bolt

OLDSMOBILE
1984-85 All Diesel Models

OEPM11   OEPM11

MI—MILES IN THOUSANDS
KM—KILOMETERS IN THOUSANDS

EVERY 6 MONTHS
Brake master cylinder .... check level **HB**

Power steering reservoir .. check level **PS**

FIRST 5 MI—8 KM;
THEN EVERY 30 MI—50 KM
Engine idle speed .... adjust

FIRST 7.5 MI—12 KM
Diff., Limited-Slip .... change lubricant
One time service only

Tires .... rotate
Radial tires, every 15 mi (24 km) after initial service.
Check brake linings. Lug nut torque, ft lb: 1985 FWD &
Custom Cruiser with 1/2″ studs, 100; all others, 80.
Toronado, 100; Delta 88 station wagon, 100; all others,
80 ex. 90 with aluminum wheels

EVERY 12 MO/5 MI—8 KM
Brake system .... inspect
Check hydraulic system for leaks. Inspect brake shoes
or pads

Crankcase .... change oil

Differential .... check level

Exhaust pressure regulator valve &
   hoses .... inspect/test
After initial inspection, check again at 15 mi (24 km) &
every 15 mi (24 km) thereafter

Exhaust system .... inspect

Suspension &
   steering linkage ...... **4-11 fittings LB**

Oil filter .... replace

Parking brake cables & guides ... coat **LB**
Check adjustment

Suspension & steering .... inspect
Also inspect front drive axle boots and seals

Transaxle or transmission .... check level

Drive belts .... inspect/adjust

Throttle linkage .... inspect
Check for damage or binding

Water separator .... drain
As equipped

Body .... lubricate

EVERY 12 MONTHS
Cooling
   system .... inspect & tighten hoses
Wash radiator filler neck & cap; pressure test system.
Clean exterior of radiator core and air conditioning con-
denser

EVERY 12 MO/15 MI—24 KM
Crankcase ventilation system ..... inspect
Clean filters in each valve cover, pipes & tubes

EVERY 24 MO/30 MI—50 KM
Vacuum pump belt .... inspect/adjust
Replace as needed

Cooling system ...... change coolant **EC**
Flush system

EVERY 30 MI—50 KM
Front wheel bearings ex.
   front wheel drive ..... clean/repack **GC**
Service at mileage interval or at each brake reline,
whichever comes first. Tighten spindle nut to 12 ft lb
while turning wheel. Back off 1/2 turn & retighten finger
tight. End play, .001″-.005″

Air cleaner element .... replace

Fuel filter .... replace

Injection pump timing .... adjust

EVERY 100 MI—160 KM
Transaxle or trans., auto. .... change fluid
Clean sump screen or replace filter

SEVERE SERVICE
Crankcase — Change oil & filter every
3 mo/2.5 mi (4 km)

Front suspension & steering linkage—
Lubricate every 6 mo/5 mi (8 km)

RWD front wheel bearings—Repack every
15 mi (24 km) or at each brake service,
whichever comes first

Transaxle or transmission, automatic—
Change fluid & filter or clean screen every
15 mi (24 km)

Differential—Change lubricant every 7.5 mi
(12 km) when towing a trailer

KEY TO LUBRICANTS

AF	DEXRON®-IIE Automatic Transmission Fluid
CD	Motor Oil, API Service CD
EC	Ethylene Glycol Coolant Mix with water to –34°F (–37°C) protection
GC	Wheel Bearing Grease, NLGI Category GC
GL-5	Gear Oil, API Service GL-5
GL-5★	Special Lubricant for Limited-Slip Differential
HB	Hydraulic Brake Fluid, DOT 3
LB	Chassis Grease, NLGI Category LB
PS	Power Steering Fluid GM Part No. 1050017; Canada, 992646
SG	Motor Oil, API Service SG Use Energy Conserving-II oils

CRANKCASE .... **SG/CD**

CAPACITY, Refill:	Liters	Qt
Including filter		
6-cyl.	5.6	6.0
8-cyl.	6.6	7.0
Above 32°F (0°C)		30♦
0° to 60°F (–18° to 16°C)		15W-40
Below 60°F (–16°C)		10W-30

♦30 is preferred above 32°F (0°C), especially for continuous duty driving

TRANSMISSION/TRANSAXLE,
   Automatic .... **AF**

CAPACITY, Initial Refill*:	Liters	Qt
125 Transmission	3.8	4.0
325 Transmission†	3.0	3.3
350 Transmission	3.0	3.3
440 Transmission	5.8	6.0

* With the engine at operating temperature, shift transmission
   through all gears. Let engine slow idle in PARK for 3 minutes
   or more. Check fluid level and add fluid as needed
†Differential serviced separately

DIFFERENTIAL/FINAL DRIVE
Standard &
   Toronado 80W, 80W-90* **GL-5**
Limited-Slip ...... 80W, 80W-90* **GL-5★**

CAPACITY, Refill:	Liters	Pt
Cutlass	1.7	3.5
Toronado	1.5	3.3
88, 98 RWD		
7 1/2″ ring gear	1.7	3.5
8 1/2″, 8 3/4″ ring gear ...	2.0	4.3

* For vehicles normally operated in Canada, 80W only
LIMITED-SLIP IDENTIFICATION:
Tag under rear cover-attaching bolt

Copyright 1992 by H.M. Gousha, a division of Simon & Schuster

SERVICE AT TIME OR MILEAGE—WHICHEVER OCCURS FIRST

OEPM12   OEPM12

MI—MILES IN THOUSANDS
KM—KILOMETERS IN THOUSANDS

EVERY 6 MONTHS
Brake master cylinder .... check level **HB**

Clutch pedal
   free travel .... check/adjust
Front wheel drive models, every 5 mi (8 km)

Power steering reservoir .. check level **PS**

FIRST 7.5 MI—12 KM
Carburetor or T.B.I. mounting
   bolts .... torque

Engine idle speed .... adjust
Without Idle Speed or Idle Air Control

Diff., Limited-Slip .... change lubricant
One time service only

Tires .... rotate
Radial tires, every 15 mi (24 km) after initial service.
Check brake linings. Lug nut torque, ft lb: All FWD &
Custom Cruiser with 1/2″ studs, 100; all others, 80

FIRST 7.5 MI—12 KM;
THEN EVERY 24 MO/30 MI—50 KM
Choke & hoses .... check/clean

EVERY 12 MO/7.5 MI—12 KM
Brake system .... inspect
Check hydraulic system for leaks. Inspect brake linings

Crankcase .... change oil

Differential .... check level

Exhaust system .... inspect

Suspension &
   steering linkage ...... **4-11 fittings LB**

Oil filter .... replace

Parking brake cables & guides ... coat **LB**
Check adjustment

Shift linkage .... coat **LB**
With floor shift, coat contact faces

Suspension & steering .... inspect
Also inspect front drive axle boots and seals

Transaxle or transmission .... check level

Drive belts .... inspect/adjust

Throttle linkage .... inspect
Check for damage or binding

Body .... lubricate

EVERY 12 MONTHS
Cooling
   system........inspect & tighten hoses
Wash radiator filler neck & cap; pressure test system.
Clean exterior of radiator core and air conditioning con-
denser. Inspect coolant, service as needed

EVERY 24 MO/30 MI—50 KM
Air pump belt .... inspect/adjust
Replace as needed

Cooling system ..... change coolant **EC**
Flush system

EVERY 36 MO/30 MI—50 KM
Air cleaner element .... replace
Ex. 2.0L

EGR system .... clean/inspect

EVERY 30 MI—50 KM
Clutch cross shaft .... **1 plug LB**

Front wheel bearings ex.
   front wheel drive ..... clean/repack **GC**
Service at mileage interval or at each brake reline,
whichever comes first. Tighten spindle nut to 12 ft lb
while turning wheel. Back off 1/2 turn & retighten finger
tight. End play, .001″-.005″

Fuel tank, cap & lines .... inspect

Distributor cap .... inspect

Ignition timing .... adjust
Inspect distributor cap, clean or replace

Ignition wires .... inspect/clean

PCV valve .... inspect
Blow out or replace hoses

Spark plugs .... replace

Thermostatic air cleaner .... inspect

Vacuum advance system
   & hoses .... inspect
As equipped

EVERY 50 MI—80 KM
Air cleaner element, 2.0L .... replace

EVERY 100 MI—160 KM
Transaxle or trans., auto. ..... change fluid
Clean sump screen or replace filter

SEVERE SERVICE
Carburetor or T.B.I.—Torque mounting
bolts & adjust idle speed at 6 mi (10 km).
Inspect carburetor choke & hoses at 6 mi (10
km), then every 30 mi (50 km)

Crankcase—Change oil every 3 mo/3 mi (5
km). Change filter at each oil change

Front suspension & steering linkage—
Lubricate every 6 mo/6 mi (10 km)

Front wheel bearings RWD—Repack every
15 mi (24 km) or at every brake service,
whichever comes first

Transaxle or transmission, automatic—
Change fluid & filter or clean screen every
15 mi (24 km)

Differential—Change lubricant every 7.5 mi
(12 km) when towing a trailer

KEY TO LUBRICANTS

AF   DEXRON®-IIE Automatic Transmission
        Fluid

EC   Ethylene Glycol Coolant
        Mix with water to –34°F (–37°C) protection

GC   Wheel Bearing Grease,
        NLGI Category GC

GL-5   Gear Oil, API Service GL-5

GL-5★   Special Lubricant for Limited-Slip
            Differential

GLS   Gear Lubricant, Special
        4-speed, GM Part No. 1052931
        5-speed, GM Part No. 12345349

HB   Hydraulic Brake Fluid, DOT 3

LB   Chassis Grease, NLGI Cateogory LB

PS   Power Steering Fluid

SG   Motor Oil, API Service SG
        Use Energy Conserving-II oils

CRANKCASE .... **SG**

CAPACITY, Refill:	Liters	Qt
4-cyl. 2.5L	2.8	3.0
Others	3.8	4.0

Capacity shown is without filter. When replacing filter, additional oil may be needed

4-cyl., 2.8L V6 & 5.0L (305) V8:
Above 40°F (4°C) 30
Above 0°F (–18°C) 10W-30
All temperatures .... 5W-30†

All others:
Above 40°F (4°C) 30
Above 20°F (–7°C) 20W-20
Above 10°F (–12°C) 15W-40
Above 0°F (–18°C) .... 10W-30†
Below 60°F (–16°C) 5W-30
†Preferred

TRANSMISSION/TRANSAXLE,
   Automatic .... **AF**

CAPACITY, Initial Refill*:	Liters	Qt
125 Transmission	3.8	4.0
200 Transmission	3.3	3.5
440 Transmission	5.8	6.0

*With engine at operating temperature, shift transmission
through all gears. Let engine slow idle in PARK for 3 minutes
or more. Check fluid level and add fluid as needed

TRANSAXLE, Manual .... **GLS**

CAPACITY, Refill:	Liters	Pt
4-speed	2.8	6.0
5-speed:		
7-bolt alum. end cap	2.5	5.4
9-bolt steel end cap	1.9	4.0

DIFFERENTIAL
Standard 80W, 80W-90* **GL-5**
Limited-Slip ...... 80W, 80W-90* **GL-5★**
*For vehicles normally operated in Canada, 80W only

CAPACITY, Refill:	Liters	Pt
7½″ ring gear	1.7	3.5
8½″, 8¾″ ring gear	2.0	4.3

LIMITED-SLIP IDENTIFICATION:
Tag under rear cover-attaching bolt

SERVICE AT TIME OR MILEAGE—WHICHEVER OCCURS FIRST

OEPM13   OEPM13

Perform the following maintenance services at the intervals indicated to keep the vehicle warranties in effect.

W SERVICE TO MAINTAIN EMISSION WARRANTY

MI—MILES IN THOUSANDS
KM—KILOMETERS IN THOUSANDS

EVERY 6 MONTHS
Brake master cylinder . . . . check level **HB**

Clutch master cylinder . . . . check level **HB**

Power steering reservoir . . check level **PS**

FIRST 7.5 MI—12 KM
W Carburetor or T.B.I. mounting
   bolts, ex. 2.3L . . . . torque

W Engine idle speed, 1987-89 . . . . . adjust
   Without Idle Speed or Idle Air Control

   Diff., Limited-Slip . . . . change lubricant
   As equipped

   Tires . . . . rotate
   Initial service, then every 15 mi (24 km). Check brake linings

FIRST 7.5 MI—12 KM;
THEN EVERY 24 MO/30 MI—50 KM
W Choke & hoses . . . . check/clean
   As equipped

EVERY 12 MO/7.5 MI—12 KM
   Brake system . . . . inspect
   Check hydraulic system for leaks. Inspect brake linings

W Crankcase . . . . change oil

W Oil filter . . . . replace
   First oil change, then every other, but at least every 12 months

   Differential . . . . check level
   As equipped

W Exhaust system . . . . inspect

   Suspension &
      steering linkage . . . . . . **4-11 fittings LB**
   1991-92 every other oil change

   Parking brake cable guides . . . . . . coat **LB**
   Check adjustment

   Shift linkage . . . . coat **LB**
   With floor shift, coat contact faces

   Suspension & steering . . . . inspect
   Also inspect front drive axle boots and seals

   Transaxle or transmission . . . . check level

W Throttle linkage . . . . inspect
   Check for damage or binding

   Body . . . . lubricate

EVERY 12 MONTHS
W Cooling
      system . . . . . .inspect & tighten hoses
   Wash radiator filler neck & cap; pressure test system. Clean exterior of radiator core and air conditioning condenser. Inspect coolant, service as needed

EVERY 24 MO/30 MI—50 KM
   Drive belts . . . . inspect/adjust

W Cooling system . . . . change coolant **EC**
   Flush system

EVERY 36 MO/30 MI—50 KM
W Air cleaner element . . . . replace
   1987-90

   Crankcase inlet filter . . . . replace
   As equipped

W EGR system . . . . clean/inspect
   1987-90 engine codes H, K, R, U, Y, 1, 9

   Fuel tank, cap & lines . . . . inspect
   1987-90

EVERY 30 MI—50 KM
   Front wheel bearings ex.
      front wheel drive . . . . . clean/repack **GC**
   Service at mileage interval or at each brake reline, whichever comes first. Tighten spindle nut to 12 ft lb while turning wheel. Back off nut & retighten finger tight. Loosen nut just enough that hole in spindle lines up with slot in nut. (Not more than 1/2 flat). End play, .001″-.005″

W Air cleaner element . . . . replace
   1991-92

   EGR system . . . . clean/inspect
   1991-92 engine codes E, R, U, 7

W Distributor cap . . . . inspect
   Except distributorless ignition

   Fuel tank, cap & lines . . . . inspect
   1991-92

W Ignition timing . . . . adjust
   Except distributorless ignition

   Ignition wires . . . . inspect/clean
   As equipped

   PCV valve . . . . replace
   Some models blow out or replace hoses

W Spark plugs . . . . replace

W Thermostatic air cleaner . . . . . . inspect

W Vacuum advance system
      & hoses . . . . inspect
   1987 Canadian without Computer Command Control

FIRST 60 MI—100 KM;
THEN EVERY 15 MI—25 KM
   Camshaft timing belt . . . . inspect
   3.4L code X engine

EVERY 100 MI—160 KM
   Transaxle or trans., auto. . . . . change fluid
   Clean sump screen or replace filter

SEVERE SERVICE
W Carburetor or T.B.I., except 2.3L
   engine—Torque mounting bolts & adjust
   idle speed at 6 mi (10 km). Inspect carburetor choke & hoses at 6 mi (10 km), then
   every 30 mi (50 km)

W Crankcase—Change oil every 3 mo/3 mi
   (5 km). Change filter at each oil change

   Front suspension & steering linkage—
   Lubricate every oil change

   Front wheel bearings RWD—Repack every
   15 mi (24 km) or at every brake service,
   whichever comes first

   Tires, inspect/rotate at 6 mi (10 km), then
   every 15 mi (24 km)

   Transaxle or transmission, automatic—
   Change fluid & filter or clean screen every
   15 mi (24 km)

   Differential—Change lubricant every 7.5 mi
   (12 km) when towing a trailer

KEY TO LUBRICANTS
AF   DEXRON®-IIE Automatic Transmission
        Fluid

EC   Ethylene Glycol Coolant
        Mix with water to −34°F (−37°C) protection

GC   Wheel Bearing Grease,
        NLGI Category GC

GL-5 Gear Oil, API Service GL-5

GL-5★ Special Lubricant for Limited-Slip
          Differential

GLS Gear Lubricant, Special

HB   Hydraulic Brake Fluid, DOT 3

LB   Chassis Grease, NLGI Category LB

PS   Power Steering Fluid

SG   Motor Oil, API Service SG

CRANKCASE . . . . SG

CAPACITY, Refill:	Liters	Qt
1987 4-cyl. 2.5L Calais w/Auto. Trans., Ciera	**2.8**	**3.0**
3.4L V6	**4.7**	**5.0**
Others	**3.8**	**4.0**

Capacity shown is without filter. When replacing filter, additional oil may be needed

1987-88 3.0L V6, 3.8L V6; 1991-92 3.3L V6 3.8L V6:
Above 40°F (4°C) . . . . 30‡
Above 0°F (−18°C) . . . . 10W-30†
Below 60°F (16°C) 5W-30

1987-88 Others; 1989-90 All; 1991-92 Others
Above 40°F (4°C) . . . . 30‡
Above 0°F (−18°C) 10W-30
All temperatures . . . . 5W-30†

†Preferred
‡Use only if other specified grades are unavailable

TRANSMISSION/TRANSAXLE,
Automatic . . . . AF

CAPACITY, Initial Refill*:	Liters	Qt
125 (3T40)	**3.8**	**4.0**
200C	**3.3**	**3.5**
200-4R	**3.3**	**3.5**
440-T4 (4T60, 4T60E)	**5.8**	**6.0**
700-R4 (4L60)	**4.7**	**5.0**

*With engine at operating temperature, shift transmission through all gears. Let engine slow idle in PARK for 3 minutes or more. Check fluid level and add fluid as needed

TRANSAXLE, Manual . . . . GLS

CAPACITY, Refill:	Liters	Pt
Front wheel drive		
4-speed	**2.8**	**6.0**
5-speed:		
7-bolt alum. end cap . .	**2.6**	**5.4**
9-bolt steel end cap . .	**1.9**	**4.0**

DIFFERENTIAL
Standard 80W-90* **GL-5**
Limited-Slip . . . . 80W-90* **GL-5★**
*For vehicles normally operated in Canada, 80W only

CAPACITY, Refill:	Liters	Pt
7¹/₂″ ring gear	**1.7**	**3.5**
8¹/₂″, 8³/₄″ ring gear	**2.0**	**4.3**

LIMITED-SLIP IDENTIFICATION:
Tag under rear cover-attaching bolt

SERVICE LOCATIONS — ENGINE AND CHASSIS

HOOD RELEASE: Inside

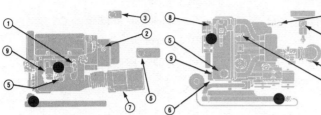
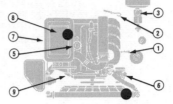
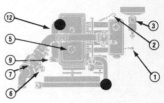

1989-91
4-cyl. 1905cc
DOHC version shown

1983-87
4-cyl. 1971cc FI

1985-91
4-cyl. 2155cc Turbo

1987-91
4-cyl. 2165cc FI

① Crankcase dipstick
② Transmission dipstick
③ Brake fluid reservoir
④ Clutch fluid reservoir
⑤ Oil fill cap
⑥ Power steering reservoir
⑦ Air filter
⑧ Fuel filter
⑨ Oil filter
⑩ PCV filter
⑪ EGR valve
⑫ Oxygen sensor
⑬ PCV valve

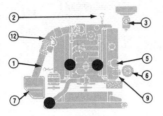
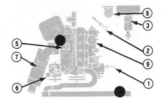
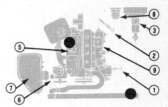

1987-89
V6 2849cc FI

1983
4-cyl. 2304cc Diesel

1983-85
4-cyl. 2304cc Turbo Diesel
1985-87
4-cyl. 2498cc Turbo Diesel

0 FITTINGS
0 PLUGS

1-3
FITTINGS

2-4
FITTINGS

1-5
FITTINGS

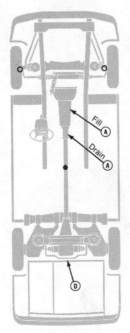

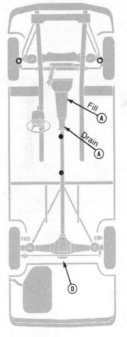
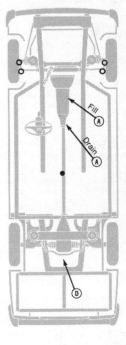

1989-91
405

1983-89
505 Sedan

1983-91
505 Wagon

1983-84
604

● Cooling system drain
• Fitting
○ Fitting, some models

Ⓐ Manual transmission/transaxle, drain & fill
Ⓑ Transfer case, NOT USED

Ⓒ Automatic transaxle final drive, NOT USED
Ⓓ Differential, drain & fill

PEUGEOT
1983-85 Diesel Engine Models

SERVICE AT TIME OR MILEAGE—WHICHEVER OCCURS FIRST

PTIPM1   PTIPM1

MI — MILES IN THOUSANDS
KM — KILOMETERS IN THOUSANDS

1983 NON-TURBO, EVERY 6 MO/5 MI — 8 KM
1983 TURBO, EVERY 3 MI — 5 KM
1984-85 EVERY 5 MI — 8 KM

Brake system .... inspect
Check lines & hoses for leaks & deterioration

Crankcase .... change oil

Chassis .... lubricate **LM**
Ball joints where applicable, driveshaft, torque tube

Differential .... check level

Oil filter .... replace

Transmission, manual .... check level

Battery .... check level

Brake/clutch reservoir .... check level **HB**

Cooling system .... inspect **EC**
Check level & concentration, clean radiator fins, pressure test at every other interval

Power steering .... check level
1983, **PS**; 1984-85 **AF**

Transmission, automatic ..... check level

Vacuum pump .... inspect
Check for leaks & cracks. 1983 check oil level **MO**

Windshield washers .... check level

Tires .... inspect/adjust
Check tread wear & inflation pressure

1983 TURBO, EVERY 15 MI — 24 KM

Chassis .... inspect
Check rubber boots on driveshaft, steering linkage, clutch slave cylinder

Air filter element .... replace
Non-Turbo only

Alternator mounting .... retorque

Rocker shaft retainer bolts ...... retorque

Vacuum pump bolts .... retorque

Valve clearance .... check/adjust

Brake system .... inspect
Check thickness of pads & shoes

Handbrake .... check/adjust

Steering column .... inspect
Check condition of flexible coupling

1983 TURBO, EVERY 15 MI — 24 KM
1983 NON-TURBO, EVERY 24 MO/20 MI — 32 KM
1984-85 TURBO, EVERY 20 MI — 32 KM

Differential .... change lubricant

Transmission, manual ... change lubricant

EVERY 24 MO/45 MI — 72 KM

Cooling system ...... change coolant **EC**

EVERY 30 MI — 48 KM

Brakes, rear .... clean/adjust
504 Wagon only

Air filter .... change oil **MO**
Oil bath type, change element as necessary

Air filter element .... replace
Dry element type

Brake/clutch fluid .... replace **HB**

Cooling fans .... inspect
Check operation of self-disengaging fan & AC fan

Drive belts .... check/adjust

Fuel filter .... replace

Idle speed .... check/adjust
1983-84 only

Kickdown cable .... check/adjust
Automatic transmission

Rocker shaft retainer bolts ...... retorque
1983 Non-Turbo only, 1984-85 all

Transmission, automatic .... change fluid

Valve clearance .... check/adjust
1983 Non-Turbo only, 1984-85 all

Vacuum pump .... change oil **MO**
1983 Turbo only

1983-85 EVERY 30 MI — 48 KM

Shock absorbers, struts .... inspect

Suspension .... inspect
Check condition & free play of bushings, hubs, ball joints, tie rod ends

1984-85 EVERY 60 MI — 100 KM

Air flow sensor plate .... clean
1984 Calif. only, 1985 all

SEVERE SERVICE

Crankcase oil — Change oil at half of recommended interval

Air filter — Clean or replace more frequently

Brake calipers — Lubricate every 6 mi (9.5 km) in areas subject to high salt usage or corrosive atmosphere

KEY TO LUBRICANTS

AF	DEXRON®-II, Automatic Transmission Fluid
CC	Motor Oil, API Service CC
CD	Motor Oil, API Service CD
EC	Engine Coolant Peugeot Part No. 9730.48 or 97.29
GL-5	Gear Oil, API Service GL-5
GL-5★	Special Lubricant for Limited-Slip Differential, API Service GL-5 with Limited-Slip additive Peugeot Part No. 97.37, or Mopar 405 7100
HB	Hydraulic Brake Fluid Heavy Duty, DOT 3 or DOT 4
LM	Lithium Multipurpose Grease
MO	Motor Oil, 10W-40 API Service CC, CD, SE/CC
PS	Power Steering Fluid GM 1050017 or equivalent
SE	Motor Oil, API Service SE

CRANKCASE .... **CD***
*CC may be used but requires reduced oil change interval, 3 mi (5 km)

CAPACITY, Refill*:

	Liters	Qt
All models	5.0	5.3

* Capacity shown includes filter

14° to 32°F (–10° to 0°C)	20
Below 14°F (–10°C)	10
All temperatures	10W-40
Above 14°F (–10°C)	15W-40
Below 14°F (–10°C)	10W-30

TRANSMISSION, Automatic .... **AF**
CAPACITY, Initial Refill†:

	Liters	Qt
All models	1.6	1.7

† Add specified quantity. With engine at operating temperature, shift transmission through all gears. Check fluid level in PARK and add fluid as needed

TRANSMISSION, Manual ... 10W-40 **CC**
CAPACITY, Refill:

	Liters	Pt
504	1.2	2.4
505, 604	1.6	3.4

DIFFERENTIAL .... 80W-90 **GL-5★**
CAPACITY, Refill:

	Liters	Pt
504	1.6	3.4
505, 604	1.6	3.3

SERVICE AT TIME OR MILEAGE—WHICHEVER OCCURS FIRST

PTIPM2   PTIPM2

Perform the following maintenance services at the intervals indicated to keep both the vehicle and emission warranties in effect.

MI — MILES IN THOUSANDS
KM — KILOMETERS IN THOUSANDS

1983-87 EVERY 6 MO/7.5 MI — 12 KM
1988 TURBO SEDAN,
EVERY 6 MO/5 MI — 8 KM
1988 2.2 FI, V6, TURBO WAGON,
EVERY 6 MO/7.5 MI — 12 KM
1989-91 EX. TURBO,
EVERY 7.5 MI — 12 KM
1989-91 TURBO,
EVERY 5 MI — 8 KM

Brake system .... inspect
Check lines & hoses for leaks & deterioration

Chassis .... lubricate **LM**
1983-86, ball joints where applicable, driveshaft bearing

Crankcase .... change oil

Oil filter .... replace
1989-91 2.2L Non-Turbo, every other oil change

Differential .... check level

Transmission, manual .... check level
505 models only

Battery .... check level
1983-85 only

Brake/clutch reservoir .... check level **HB**
1983-86 all models, 1988 Turbo Sedan only

Cooling system .... check level **EC**
1983-86 only, check concentration

Power steering .... check level
1983, **PS**; 1984-91 **AF**

Transmission, automatic ..... check level

Windshield washers .... check level

Tires .... inspect/adjust
Check tread wear & inflation pressure

Stereo .... clean/lubricate
Clean cassette head, lubricate antenna

EVERY 12 MO/15 MI — 24 KM
Differential .... change lubricant
1989-91, 505 Turbo only

Driveshaft .... lubricate **LM**
1987-91 505 only, wagon lube torque tube

Exhaust system .... inspect
1987-89 V6 only

Accelerator cable .... check/adjust
1987-91 505 Turbo only

Brake/clutch reservoir .... check level **HB**
1987-91 ex. 1988 Turbo Sedan

Cooling system .... inspect
Pressure test

Valve clearance .... check/adjust
1985-91 Turbo only

Brake pads .... inspect

Passive belt rails ...... clean/lubricate
405 models only

1983-91 EVERY 24 MO/22.5 MI — 36 KM
Differential .... change lubricant
505 ex. 1988-91 Turbo

Transmission, manual ... change lubricant
505 ex. 1988-91 Turbo

1983-88 EVERY 24 MO/45 MI — 72 KM
1989-91 EVERY 24 MO/30 MI — 48 KM
Cooling system ...... change coolant **EC**

EVERY 36 MO/30 MI — 48 KM
Differential .... change lubricant
1988-91 Turbo only

Transmission, automatic .... change fluid

Transmission, manual ... change lubricant
1988-91 Turbo only

Kickdown cable .... check/adjust

Air filter .... change oil **MO**
1983-86 oil bath type only

Air filter element .... replace
1985-91 dry element type only

Cooling fans .... check/adjust
Check self-disengaging fan & AC fan

Drive belts .... check/adjust

Oxygen sensor .... replace
1983-85 Non-Turbo only

Spark plugs .... replace

Valve clearance .... check/adjust
1983-91, 505 Non-Turbo only

1983-91 EVERY 36 MO/30 MI — 48 KM
Brake/clutch fluid .... replace **HB**

Shock absorbers/struts .... inspect

Suspension .... inspect
Check condition & free play of hubs, ball joints, tie rod ends

EVERY 98 MO/60 MI — 100 KM
Fuel filter .... replace

Oxygen sensor .... replace
1985 Turbo only

SEVERE SERVICE
Crankcase oil — Change oil at half of recommended interval

Automatic transmission, 405 — Change fluid every 15 mi (24 km)

Air filter — Clean or replace more frequently

Brake calipers — Lubricate every 6 mi (9.5 km) in areas subject to high salt usage or corrosive atmosphere

KEY TO LUBRICANTS

AF	DEXRON®-II, Automatic Transmission Fluid
CC	Motor Oil, API Service CC
CD	Motor Oil, API Service CD
EC	Engine Coolant Peugeot Part No. 9730.48 or 97.29
GL-5	Gear Oil, API Service GL-5
GL-5★	Special Lubricant for Limited-Slip Differential, API Service GL-5 with Limited-Slip additive Peugeot Part No. 97.37, or Mopar 405 7100
HB	Hydraulic Brake Fluid Extra Heavy Duty, DOT 3 or DOT 4
LM	Lithium Multipurpose Grease
MO	Motor Oil, 10W-40 API Service CC, CD, SE/CC
PS	Power Steering Fluid GM 1050017 or equivalent
SF	Motor Oil, API Service SF
SG	Motor Oil, API Service SG

CRANKCASE
1983-87 .... SF, SF/CC
1988 .... SF
1989-91 .... SF/CC, SF/CD, SG

CAPACITY, Refill*:	Liters	Qt
1983-87 1971cc	4.0	4.2
1985-91 2155cc Turbo ..	5.0	5.3
1987-89 2849cc	6.0	6.3
1987-91 2165cc	5.5	5.8
1989-91 1915cc SOHC ..	5.0	5.3
1989-91 1905cc DOHC ..	5.3	5.6

*Capacity shown includes filter
All temperatures 10W-40, 15W-40
Below 32°F (0°C) Turbo 10W-30

TRANSMISSION, Automatic ...... AF

CAPACITY, Initial Refill†:	Liters	Qt
1983-87 1971cc	1.6	1.7
1986-91 2155cc Turbo ..	2.6	2.8
1987-89 2849cc	2.6	2.8
1987-91 2165cc	2.6	2.8
1989-91 1905cc	2.4	2.5

† Add specified quantity. With engine at operating temperature, shift transmission through all gears. Check fluid level in PARK and add fluid as needed

TRANSMISSION, Manual
1983-84 .... 10W-40 **CC**
1985-87 .... 10W-40 **SF, SF/CC**
1988-91 505 models .... 10W-40 **SF**
1989-91 405 models 75W-80 **GL-5**

CAPACITY, Refill:	Liters	Pt
505 models	1.6	3.4
405 models	2.0	4.2

DIFFERENTIAL .... 80W-90 **GL-5★**

CAPACITY, Refill:	Liters	Pt
505 models	1.6	3.3

CHEK-CHART

HOOD RELEASE: Inside

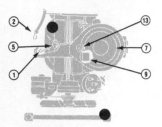

1983-87
1.6L (98) Code C

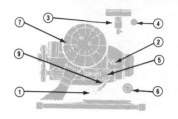

1988-92
1.6L Code 6
LeMans

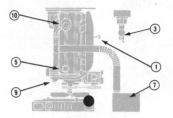

1983-86
1.8L (111) Diesel
Code D

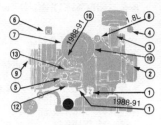

1983-86 1.8L (112) FI, OHC Code 0
1987-91 2.0L (122) OHC Code K

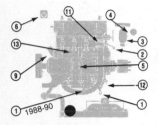

1983-86
1.8L (112) Turbo OHC Code J,
1987-90
2.0L (122) Turbo OHC Code M

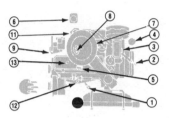

1983-86
1.8L (112) 2V,
2.0L (122)
Code G, P, B

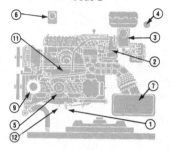

1992
2.0L Code H
LeMans, Sunbird

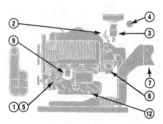

1992
2.3L Code 3
Grand Am

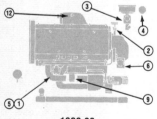

1988-92
2.3L Code A, D
Grand Am,
Grand Prix

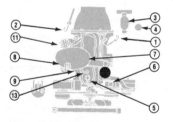

1983-86 2.5L (151)
Firebird

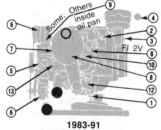

1983-91
2.5L Phoenix, 6000,
Fiero, Grand Am (2V shown)
Code R, U, 5
Air induction system varies

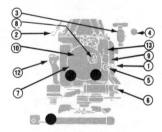

1983-84
2.8L 2V Code 1
Firebird

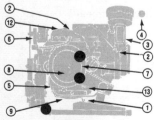

1983-86
2.8L 2V Code X, Z
Phoenix, 6000

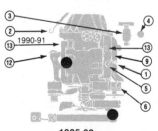

1985-92
2.8L FI Code S,
3.1L FI Code T
Firebird

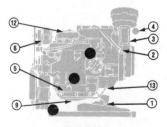

1985-86
2.8L FI Code W, 9
Fiero, 6000

1987-89 2.8L Code W, 9
6000, Grand Prix, Fiero
1988-92 3.1L (186) Code T

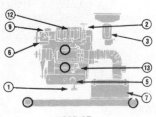

1985-87
3.0L FI Code L

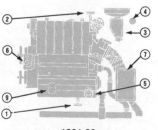

1991-92
3.4L Code X
Grand Prix

① Crankcase dipstick
② Transmission dipstick
③ Brake fluid reservoir
④ Clutch fluid reservoir
⑤ Oil fill cap
⑥ Power steering reservoir
⑦ Air filter
⑧ Fuel filter
⑨ Oil filter
⑩ PCV filter
⑪ EGR valve
⑫ Oxygen sensor
⑬ PCV valve

● Cooling system drain
○ Cooling system drain, some models

SERVICE LOCATIONS — ENGINE AND CHASSIS

PCDP-2 PCDP-2

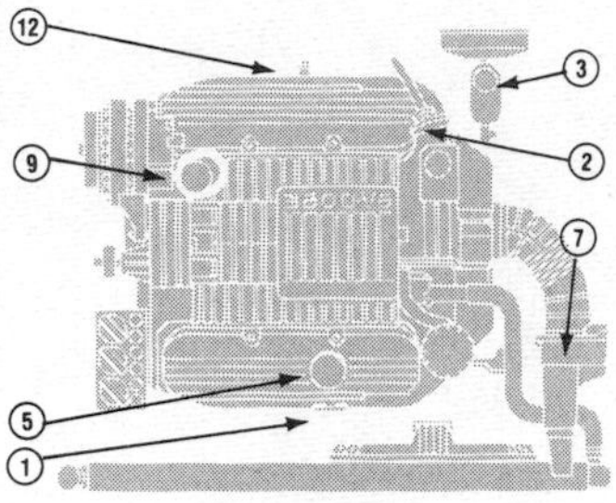

1992
3.8L FI Code 1
Bonneville

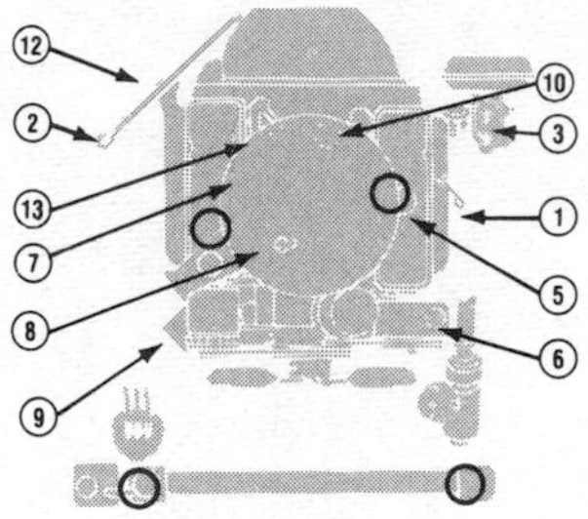

1983-87
3.8L 2V
Code A

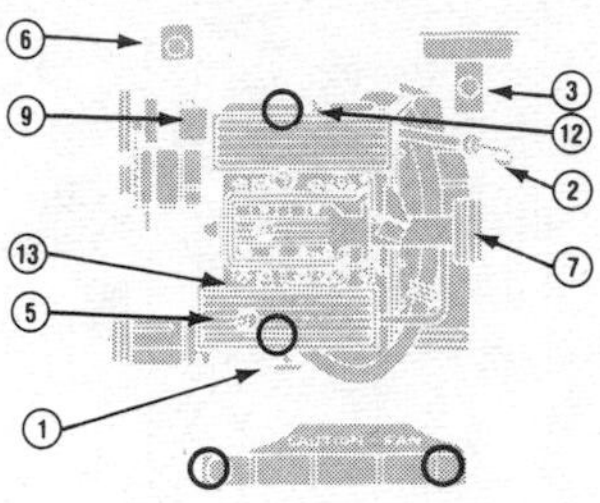

1987-88
3.8L FI
Code 3

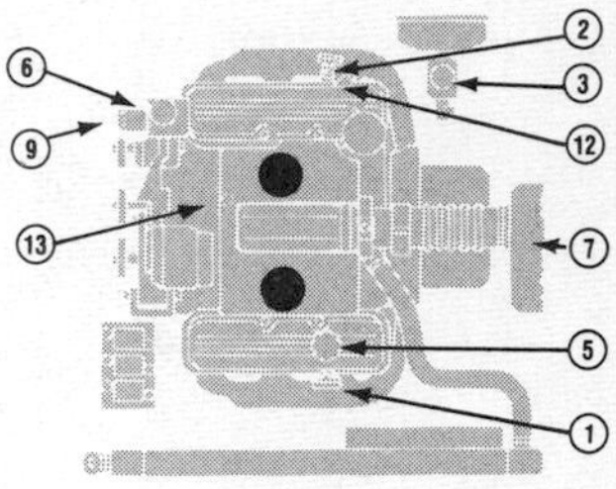

1988-90
3.8L Code C
Bonneville

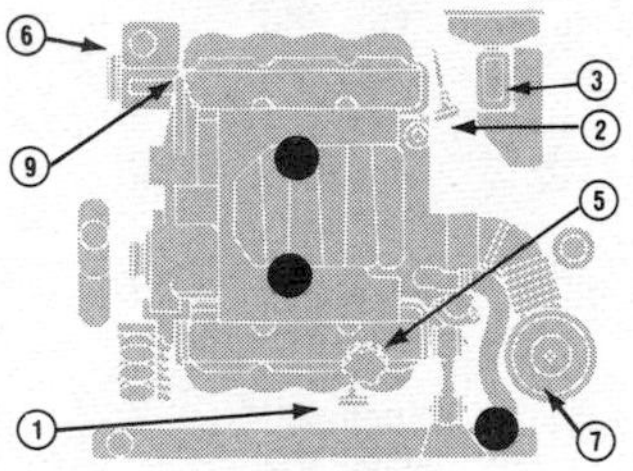

1991-92
3.8L Code L
Bonneville

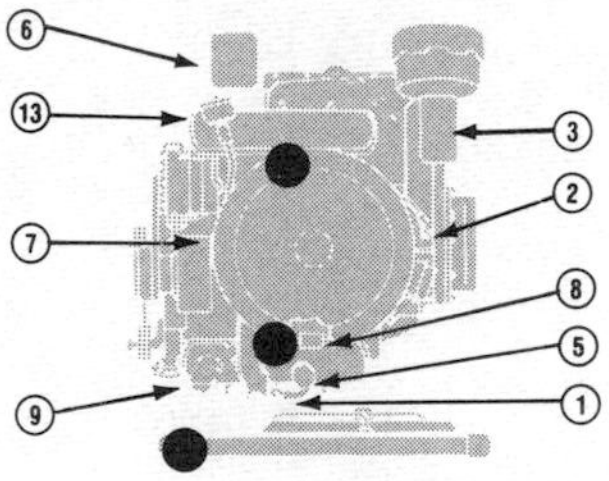

1983-85
4.3L (262) V-6 Diesel
Code T

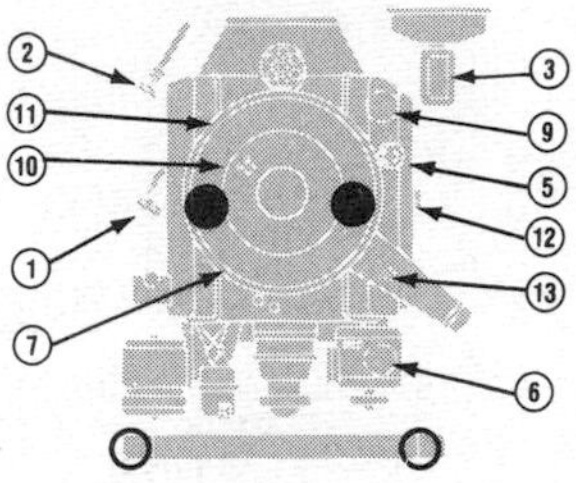

1988-92
5.0L (305) FI Code E
Firebird
Air induction
system varies

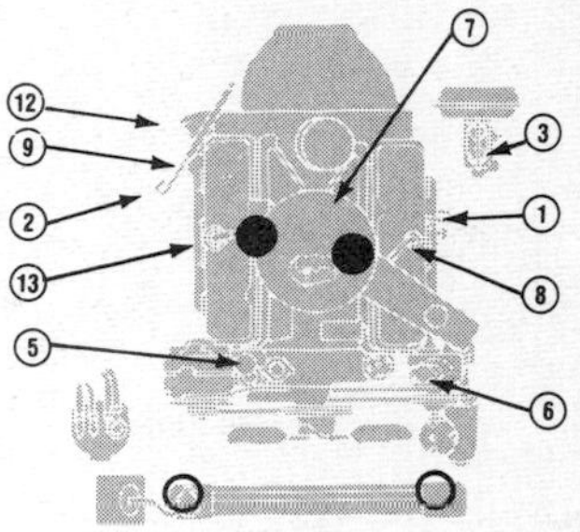

1986-89
5.0L (307) Code Y
Parisienne, Safari

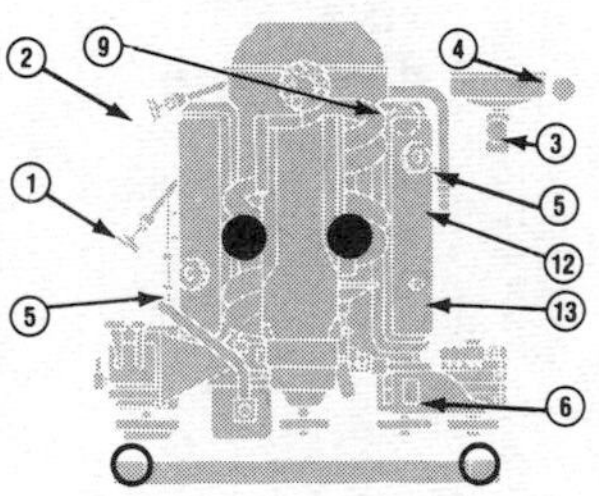

1985-92 5.0L (350) FI
Code F
1987-91 5.7L (350) FI
Code 8
Firebird

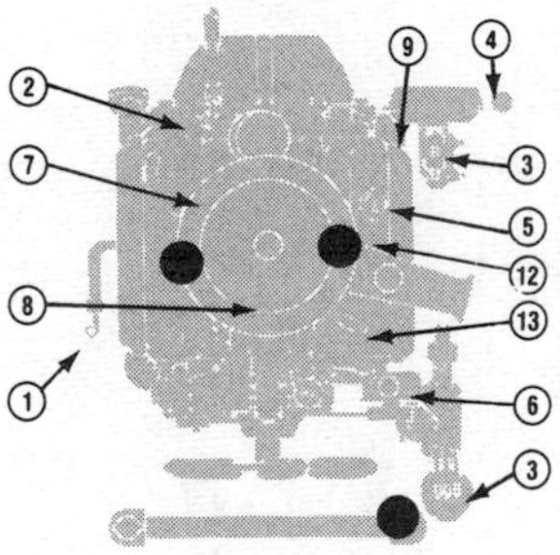

1983-87
5.0L (305) 4V,
5.7L (350) 4V

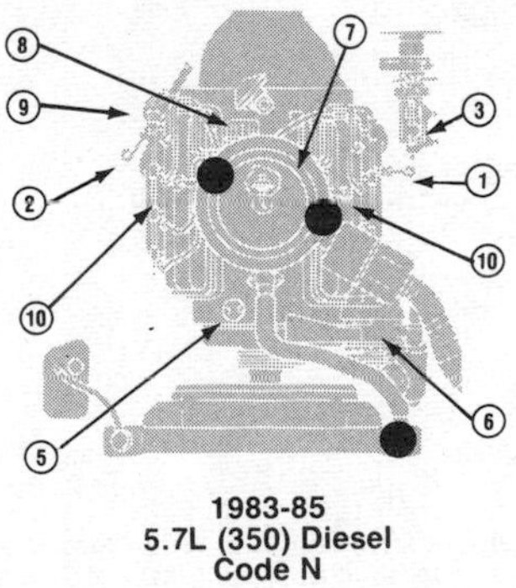

1983-85
5.7L (350) Diesel
Code N

6
FITTINGS

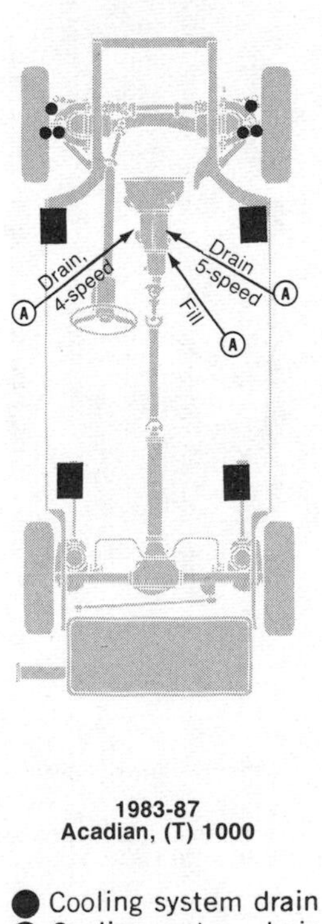

1983-87
Acadian, (T) 1000

0 FITTINGS
0 PLUGS

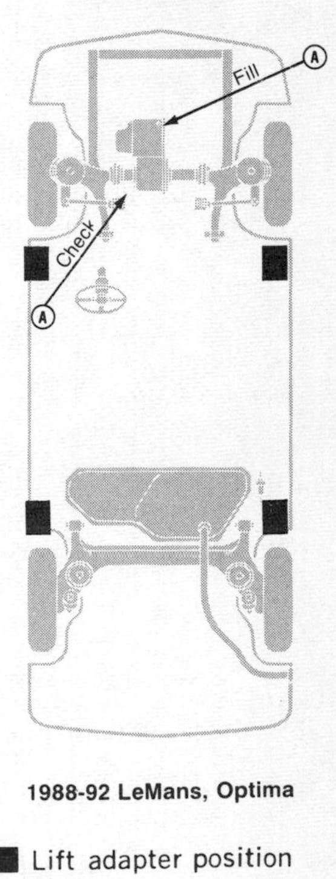

1988-92 LeMans, Optima

Ⓐ Manual transmission/transaxle, drain & fill
Ⓑ Transfer case, NOT USED
Ⓒ Automatic transaxle final drive, drain & fill
Ⓓ Differential, drain & fill

● Cooling system drain
○ Cooling system drain, some models

■ Lift adapter position
• Fitting

Copyright 1992 by H.M. Gousha, a division of Simon & Schuster

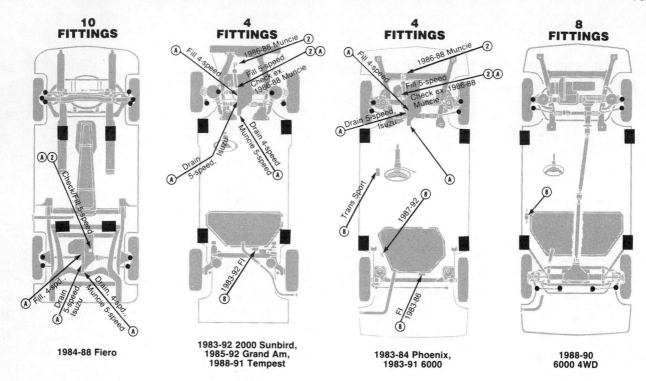

10 FITTINGS

1984-88 Fiero

4 FITTINGS

1983-92 2000 Sunbird,
1985-92 Grand Am,
1988-91 Tempest

4 FITTINGS

1983-84 Phoenix,
1983-91 6000

8 FITTINGS

1988-90
6000 4WD

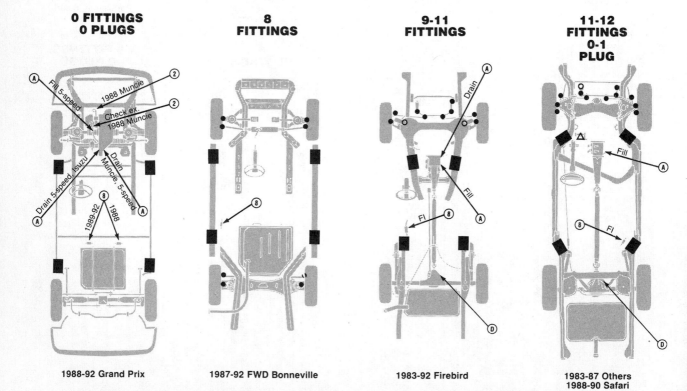

**0 FITTINGS
0 PLUGS**

1988-92 Grand Prix

8 FITTINGS

1987-92 FWD Bonneville

9-11 FITTINGS

1983-92 Firebird

**11-12 FITTINGS
0-1 PLUG**

1983-87 Others
1988-90 Safari

CAUTION: On front wheel drive vehicles the center of gravity is further forward than on rear wheel drive vehicles. When removing major components from the rear of the vehicle while it is on a hoist, the vehicle must be supported in a manner to prevent it from tipping forward.

Ⓐ Manual transmission/transaxle, drain & fill
Ⓑ Transfer case, drain & fill
Ⓒ Automatic transaxle final drive, drain & fill
Ⓓ Differential, drain & fill
② Transmission dipstick
⑧ Fuel filter

■ Lift adapter position   ▲ Plug   △ Plug, some models   • Fitting   ○ Fitting, some models

SERVICE AT TIME OR MILEAGE—WHICHEVER OCCURS FIRST

PCPM8   PCPM8

PCPM8

MI—MILES IN THOUSANDS
KM—KILOMETERS IN THOUSANDS

4-CYL. DIESEL,
EVERY 12 MO/3.75 MI—6 KM

Crankcase . . . . change oil

Oil filter . . . . replace
After initial service, replace every 12 mo or 7.5 mi (12 km)

Engine idle speed . . . . adjust
After initial service, adjust only every 30 mi (48 km)

EVERY 6 MONTHS

Brake master cylinder . . . . . check level **HB**

Clutch free pedal travel . . . . . check/adjust
Front wheel drive models, every 5 mi (8 km)

Power steering
reservoir . . . . check level **PS**

Transaxle or trans., auto . . . . . . check level

FIRST 7.5 MI—12 KM

Carburetor mounting bolts . . . . torque

Engine idle speed, gasoline . . . . adjust
Ex. engines with Idle Speed or Idle Air Control

Diff., Limited-Slip . . . . change lubricant

Tires . . . . rotate
Radial tires, every 15 mi (24 km) after initial service.
Check brake pads. Lug nut torque, ft lb: Acadian, 1000,
70; all front wheel drive, 100; all others, 80 ex. 90 with
aluminum wheels

Transmission, manual,
4-cyl. Diesel . . . . change lubricant
Service every 30 mi (48 km) thereafter

GASOLINE: FIRST 7.5 MI—12 KM;
THEN EVERY 24 MO/30 MI—48 KM
6-, 8-CYL. DIESEL: FIRST 5 MI—8 KM;
THEN EVERY 30 MI—48 KM

Choke & hoses, ex. Diesel . . . . .check/clean

Engine idle speed, Diesel . . . . adjust

GASOLINE,
EVERY 12 MO/7.5 MI—12 KM
DIESEL, EVERY 12 MO/5 MI—8 KM

Crankcase ex. 4-cyl. Diesel . . . . . change oil

Differential . . . . check level

Exhaust pressure regulator valve &
hoses, 6-cyl. Diesel . . . . inspect/test
After initial inspection, check again at 15 mi (24 km) &
every 15 mi (24 km) thereafter

Exhaust system . . . . inspect

Front suspension &
steering linkage . . . . **4-11 fittings LB**

Oil filter . . . . replace
6-, 8-cyl. Diesel, at every oil change; all others at first oil
change, then at 12 mo/15 mi (24 km) intervals only

Parking brake cables & guides . . . . coat **LB**
Check adjustment

Shift linkage . . . . coat **LB**
With floor shift, coat contact faces

Suspension & steering . . . . inspect
Also inspect drive axle boots and seals

Transaxle or transmission . . . . check level
Ex. 4-cyl. Diesel

Drive belts . . . . inspect/adjust

Throttle linkage . . . . inspect
Check for damage or binding

Body . . . . lubricate

EVERY 12 MONTHS

Cooling system . . . . inspect & tighten hoses
Wash radiator filler neck and cap; pressure test system. Clean exterior of radiator core and air conditioning
condenser

EVERY 12 MO/15 MI—24 KM

Crankcase ventilation system,
6-, 8-cyl. Diesel . . . . inspect
Clean filters in each valve cover, pipes, & tubes

EVERY 15 MI—24 KM

Valve clearance,
4-cyl. Diesel . . . . check/adjust

EVERY 24 MO/30 MI—48 KM

Cooling system . . . . change coolant **EC**
Flush system

EVERY 36 MO/30 MI—48 KM

Air cleaner element . . . . replace
Ex. Diesel, 1.6L & 2.0L

EGR system . . . . clean/inspect

EVERY 30 MI—48 KM

Clutch cross shaft . . . . **1 plug LB**

Front wheel bearings ex. front
wheel drive . . . . clean/repack **GC**
Service at mileage interval or at each brake reline,
whichever comes first. Tighten spindle nut to 12 ft lb
while turning wheel. Back off 1/2 turn & retighten finger
tight. End play, .001"-.005"

Fuel cap, tank & lines, ex. Diesel . . . inspect

Air cleaner element, Diesel . . . . replace

Fuel filter, Diesel. . . . . replace

Ignition timing . . . . adjust
Inspect distributor cap, clean or replace

Ignition wires. . . . . inspect/clean

Injection pump timing,
Diesel. . . . . check/adjust

PCV valve ex. Diesel. . . . . inspect
Blow out or replace hoses

Spark plugs . . . . replace

Vacuum advance system &
hoses. inspect
As equipped

EVERY 50 MI—80 KM

Air cleaner element, 1.6L, 2.0L . . . . .replace

EVERY 100 MI—160 KM

Transaxle or trans., auto . . . . . change fluid
Clean sump screen or replace filter

SEVERE SERVICE

Crankcase—Change oil: Gasoline, every 3
mo/3 mi (4.8 km); Diesel, every 3 mo/2.5 mi
(4 km). Change filter at each oil change

Front wheel bearings—Repack every 15 mi
(24 km)

Transaxle or transmission, automatic—
Change fluid & filter or clean screen every
15 mi (24 km)

Differential—Change lubricant every 7.5 mi
(12 km)

KEY TO LUBRICANTS
See inside front cover

CRANKCASE

Diesel engine . . . . SG/CD
Gasoline engine . . . . SG

CAPACITY, Refill△:	Liters	Qt
Diesel, including filter		
4-, 6-cyl.	5.8	6.0
8-cyl.	6.6	7.0
Gasoline		
4-cyl. 1.8L & 2.5L	2.8	3.0
Others.	3.8	4.0

△When replacing filter, up to 1.0L (1.0 qt) extra may be
needed

Diesel Engine:
4-cyl.
Above 32°F (0°C) . . . . 30♦
Above 15°F (–10°C) 15W-40
All temperatures 10W-30
6-, 8-cyl.
Above 32°F (0°C) . . . . 30♦
0° to 60°F (–18° to 16°C) 15W-40
Below 60°F (16°C) 10W-30
Gasoline Engine:
Above 40°F (4°C) 30
Above 20°F (–7°C) 20W-20, 20W-40, 20W-50
Above 10°F (–12°C) 15W-40
Above 0°F (–18°C) 10W-30*
Below 60°F (16°C) . . . . 5W-30†
† 5W-30 may be used up to 100°F (38°C) in 4-cyl. & 2.8L
V-6 engines
♦30 is preferred above 32°F (0°C), especially for continuous duty driving
* 10W-30 preferred above 0°F (–18°C)

TRANSMISSION/TRANSAXLE,
Automatic . . . . AF

CAPACITY, Initial Refill*:	Liters	Qt
Front wheel drive	3.8	4.0
180 Transmission	2.8	3.0
200 Transmission	3.3	3.5
250, 350 Transmission.	2.8	3.0
700-R4 Transmission.	4.7	5.0

* With the engine at operating temperature, shift transmission
through all gears. Let engine slow idle in PARK for 3 minutes
or more. Check fluid level and add fluid as needed
To drain, remove pan

TRANSMISSION/TRANSAXLE, Manual

FWD: 4-speed . . . . AF
5-speed . . . . GLS
RWD: 4-speed 80W, 80W-90* **GL-5**
5-speed 4-cyl. Diesel . . . . 5W-30 **SG**
5-speed others . . . . AF
* For vehicles normally operated in Canada, 80W only

CAPACITY, Refill:	Liters	Pt
FWD: 4-speed	2.8	6.0
5-speed	2.6	5.4
RWD: Acadian, 1000:		
4-speed	1.7	3.5
5-speed, Gasoline . . .	1.9	4.0
5-speed, Diesel	1.5	3.1
Firebird: 4-speed	1.7	3.5
5-speed	3.1	6.6

DIFFERENTIAL

Standard 80W, 80W-90* **GL-5**
Limited-Slip . . . . 80W, 80W-90* **GL-5★**
* For vehicles normally operated in Canada, 80W only

CAPACITY, Refill:	Liters	Pt
Acadian, 1000	0.8	1.7
Parisienne wagon or		
w/code L engine	1.9	4.0
Others	1.7	3.5

LIMITED-SLIP IDENTIFICATION:
Tag under rear cover-attaching bolt

SERVICE AT TIME OR MILEAGE—WHICHEVER OCCURS FIRST

PCPM9   PCPM9

MI—MILES IN THOUSANDS
KM—KILOMETERS IN THOUSANDS

1.8L TURBO,
EVERY 3 MO/3 MI—5 KM

Crankcase . . . . change oil

Oil filter . . . . replace
Initial service, then every other oil change

1.8L DIESEL,
EVERY 12 MO/3.75 MI—6 KM

Crankcase . . . . change oil

Engine idle speed . . . . adjust
After initial service, adjust every 30 mi (48 km)

Oil filter . . . . replace
After first two services, replace every other oil change

EVERY 6 MONTHS

Brake master cylinder . . . . . check level **HB**

Clutch free pedal travel . . . . check/adjust
Front wheel drive models, every 5 mi (8 km)

Power steering reservoir . . check level **PS**

FIRST 7.5 MI—12 KM

Carburetor or T.B.I. mounting
  bolts . . . . torque

Engine idle speed, gasoline . . . . . . adjust
Ex. engines with Idle Speed or Idle Air Control

Diff., Limited-Slip . . . . change lubricant

Tires . . . . rotate
Radial tires, every 15 mi (24 km) after initial service.
Check brake linings. Lug nut torque, ft lb: Acadian,
1000, 70; all front wheel drive, 100; all others, 80 ex. 90
with aluminum wheels

GASOLINE: FIRST 7.5 MI—12 KM;
THEN EVERY 24 MO/30 MI—50 KM

Choke & hoses . . . . check/clean

6- & 8-CYL. DIESEL: FIRST 5 MI—8 KM;
THEN EVERY 30 MI—48 KM

Engine idle speed . . . . adjust

GASOLINE,
EVERY 12 MO/7.5 MI—12 KM
4-CYL. DIESEL,
EVERY 12 MO/3.75 MI—6 KM
6-, & 8-CYL. DIESEL,
EVERY 12 MO/5 MI—8 KM

Brake system . . . . inspect
Check hydraulic system for leaks. Inspect brake linings

Crankcase ex. 1.8L Turbo
  & Diesel . . . . change oil

Differential . . . . check level

Exhaust pressure regulator valve &
  hoses, 6-cyl. Diesel . . . . inspect/test
After initial inspection, check again at 15 mi (24 km) &
every other oil change

Exhaust system . . . . inspect

Suspension &
  steering linkage . . . . . . **4-11 fittings LB**

Oil filter ex. 1.8L Turbo & Diesel . . replace
Diesel, at every oil change; all others at first oil change,
then at 15 mi (24 km) intervals only

Parking brake cables & guides . . . . coat **LB**
Check adjustment

Shift linkage . . . . coat **LB**
With floor shift, coat contact faces

Suspension & steering . . . . inspect
Also inspect drive axle boots and seals

Transaxle or transmission . . . . . check level

Drive belts . . . . inspect/adjust

Throttle linkage . . . . inspect
Check for damage or binding

Body . . . . lubricate

EVERY 12 MONTHS

Cooling system . . . . inspect & tighten hoses
Wash radiator filler neck & cap; pressure test system.
Clean exterior of radiator core & air conditioning con-
denser

EVERY 12 MO/15 MI—24 KM

Crankcase ventilation system,
  Diesel . . . . inspect
Clean filters in each valve cover, pipes & tubes

Valve clearance . . . . adjust
4-cyl. Diesel

EVERY 24 MO/30 MI—50 KM

Cooling system . . . . . . change coolant **EC**
Flush system

Vacuum/Air pump belts . . . . inspect/adjust
Replace as needed

EVERY 36 MO/30 MI—50 KM

Air cleaner element . . . . replace
Ex. Diesel, 1.6L & 2.0L

EGR system . . . . clean/inspect

EVERY 30 MI—50 KM

Clutch cross shaft . . . . **1 plug LB**

Front wheel bearings ex. front
  wheel drive . . . . clean/repack **GC**
Service at mileage interval or at each brake reline,
whichever comes first. Tighten spindle nut to 12 ft lb
while turning wheel. Back off 1/2 turn & retighten finger
tight. End play, .001″-.005″

Fuel cap, tank, & lines, ex. Diesel . . inspect

Air cleaner element, Diesel . . . . . . replace

Distributor cap . . . . inspect

Fuel filter, Diesel . . . . replace

Ignition timing . . . . adjust
Inspect distributor cap, clean or replace

Ignition wires . . . . inspect/clean

Injection pump timing,
  Diesel . . . . check/adjust

PCV valve ex. Diesel . . . . inspect
Blow out or replace hoses

Spark plugs . . . . replace

Thermostatic air cleaner . . . . inspect

Vacuum advance system &
  hoses . . . . inspect
As equipped

EVERY 50 MI—80 KM

Air cleaner element, 1.6L, 2.0L . . . . . replace

EVERY 100 MI—160 KM

Transaxle or trans., auto. . . . . change fluid
Clean sump screen or replace filter

SEVERE SERVICE

Carburetor or T.B.I.—Torque mounting
bolts & adjust idle speed at 6 mi (10 km),
also inspect carburetor choke & hoses

Crankcase—Change oil: Gasoline, every 3
mo/3 mi (5 km); Diesel: 4-cyl., every 3 mo/2
mi (3.2 km); 6- & 8-cyl., every 3 mo/2.5 mi (4
km). Change filter at each oil change

Front suspension & steering linkage—
Lubricate every: Gasoline, 6 mo/6 mi (10
km); Diesel, 6 mo/5 mi (8 km)

Front wheel bearings—Repack every 15 mi
(24 km) or at every brake service, whichever
comes first

Transaxle or transmission, automatic—
Change fluid & filter or clean screen every
15 mi (24 km)

Differential—Change lubricant every 7.5 mi
(12 km)

KEY TO LUBRICANTS
See inside front cover

CRANKCASE

Diesel engine . . . . SG/CD
Gasoline engine . . . . SG

CAPACITY, Refill:	Liters	Qt
Diesel, including filter:		
4- & 6-cyl.	5.8	6.0
8-cyl.	6.6	7.0
Gasoline:		
4-cyl. 2.5L	2.8	3.0
Others	3.8	4.0

Gasoline, capacity shown is without filter. When replacing
filter, additional oil may be needed

Diesel Engine:
4-cyl.
Above 32°F (0°C) . . . . 30♦
Above 15°F (−10°C) 15W-40
Below 100°F (38°C) 10W-30
6- & 8-cyl.
Above 32°F (0°C) . . . . 30♦
0° to 60°F (−18° to 16°C) 15W-40
Below 60°F (16°C) 10W-30
Gasoline Engine:
Above 40°F (4°C) 30
Above 20°F (−7°C) 20W-30
Above 10°F (−12°C) 15W-40
Above 0°F (−18°C) 10W-30
Below 60°F (16°C) . . . . 5W-30†
♦30 is preferred above 32°F (0°C), especially for continu-
  ous duty driving
†5W-30 may be used up to 100°F (38°C) in 4-cyl. & 2.8L
  6-cyl. engines

TRANSMISSION/TRANSAXLE,
  Automatic . . . . **AF**

CAPACITY, Initial Refill*:	Liters	Qt
125 Transmission	3.8	4.0
180 Transmission	2.8	3.0
200 Transmission	3.3	3.5
250 Transmission	3.8	4.0
350 Transmission	2.8	3.0
440 Transmission	6.0	6.3
700-R4 Transmission	4.7	5.0

* With the engine at operating temperature, shift transmission
through all gears. Let engine slow idle in PARK for 3 minutes
or more. Check fluid level and add fluid as needed

TRANSMISSION/TRANSAXLE, Manual
FWD . . . . **GLS**
RWD: Firebird 4-speed . . . . **AF**
  4-speed
    ex. Firebird 80W, 80W-90* **GL-5**
  5-speed 4-cyl.
    Diesel . . . . . 5W-30 **SF, SF/CC, SF/CD**
  5-speed others . . . . **AF**
* For vehicles normally operated in Canada, 80W only

CAPACITY, Refill:	Liters	Pt
FWD: 4-speed	2.8	6.0
5-speed	2.6	5.5
RWD: Acadian, 1000:		
4-speed	1.7	3.5
5-speed, Gasoline	1.9	4.0
5-speed, Diesel	1.5	3.1
Firebird: 4-speed	1.7	3.5
5-speed	3.1	6.6

DIFFERENTIAL
Standard 80W, 80W-90* **GL-5**
Limited-Slip . . . . . . 80W, 80W-90* **GL-5★**
* For vehicles normally operated in Canada, 80W only

CAPACITY, Refill:	Liters	Pt
Acadian, 1000	0.8	1.7
Parisienne:		
8¹/₂″ ring gear	1.9	4.2
8³/₄″ ring gear	2.4	5.4
Others	1.7	3.5

LIMITED-SLIP IDENTIFICATION:
Tag under rear cover-attaching bolt

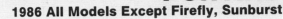

SERVICE AT TIME OR MILEAGE—WHICHEVER OCCURS FIRST

PCPM10   PCPM10

MI—MILES IN THOUSANDS
KM—KILOMETERS IN THOUSANDS

TURBOCHARGED ENGINES
EVERY 3 MO/3 MI—5 KM
Crankcase . . . . change oil

Oil filter . . . . replace
Initial service, then every other oil change

EVERY 6 MONTHS
Brake master cylinder . . . . check level **HB**

Clutch free pedal travel . . . . . check/adjust
Front wheel drive models, every 5 mi (8 km)

Power steering reservoir . . check level **PS**

FIRST 7.5 MI—12 KM
Carburetor or T.B.I. mounting
  bolts . . . . torque

Engine idle speed . . . . adjust
Ex. engines with Idle Speed or Idle Air Control

Diff., Limited Slip . . . . change lubricant
One time service only

Tires . . . . rotate
Radial tires, every 15 mi (24 km) after initial service.
Check brake linings. Lug nut torque, ft lb: Safari, Fiero,
all front wheel drive & Parisienne with 13/16″ lug nut,
100; all others, 80

EVERY 12 MO/7.5 MI—12 KM
Brake system . . . . inspect
Check hydraulic system for leaks. Inspect brake linings

Crankcase ex. 1.8L Turbo . . . . . change oil

Oil filter ex. 1.8L Turbo . . . . replace

Differential . . . . check level

Exhaust system . . . . inspect

Suspension &
  steering linkage . . . . . . **4-11 fittings LB**
Initial service at mileage interval

Parking brake cables & guides . . . coat **LB**
Check adjustment

Shift linkage . . . . coat **LB**
With floor shift, coat contact faces

Suspension & steering . . . . inspect
Also inspect drive axle boots and seals

Transaxle or transmission . . . . check level

Drive belts . . . . inspect/adjust

Throttle linkage . . . . inspect
Check for damage or binding

Body . . . . lubricate

EVERY 12 MONTHS
Cooling system . . . inspect & tighten hoses
Wash radiator filler neck and cap; pressure test system. Clean exterior of radiator core and air conditioning
condenser

EVERY 24 MO/30 MI—50 KM
Cooling system . . . . . change coolant **EC**
Flush system

Choke & hoses . . . . check/clean

Vacuum/Air pump belts . . . . inspect/adjust
Replace as needed

EVERY 36 MO/30 MI—50 KM
Air cleaner element . . . . replace
Ex. 1.6L & 2.0L

EGR system . . . . clean/inspect

EVERY 30 MI—50 KM
Clutch cross shaft . . . . **1 plug LB**

Front wheel bearings ex. front
  wheel drive . . . . clean/repack **GC**
Service at mileage interval or at each brake reline,
whichever comes first. Tighten spindle nut to 12 ft lb
while turning wheel. Back off 1/2 turn & retighten finger
tight. End play, .001″-.005″

Fuel cap, tank, and lines . . . . inspect

Distributor cap . . . . inspect

Ignition timing . . . . adjust
Inspect distributor cap, clean or replace

Ignition wires . . . . inspect/clean

PCV valve . . . . inspect
Blow out or replace hoses

Spark plugs . . . . replace

Thermostatic air cleaner . . . . inspect

Vacuum advance system &
  hoses . . . . inspect
As equipped

EVERY 50 MI—80 KM
Air cleaner element, 1.6L, 2.0L . . . .replace

EVERY 100 MI—160 KM
Transaxle or trans., auto. . . . . change fluid
Clean sump screen or replace filter

SEVERE SERVICE
Carburetor or T.B.I.—Torque mounting
bolts & adjust idle speed at 6 mi (10 km),
also inspect carburetor choke & hoses

Crankcase—Change oil & oil filter every 3
mo/3 mi (5 km)

Differential—Change lubricant every 7.5 mi
(12 km) when towing a trailer

Front suspension & steering linkage—
Lubricate every 6 mo/6 mi (10 km)

Front wheel bearings RWD—Repack every
15 mi (24 km) or at every brake service,
whichever comes first

Transaxle or transmission, automatic—
Change fluid & filter or clean screen every
15 mi (24 km)

KEY TO LUBRICANTS
See inside front cover

CRANKCASE		. . . . SG
CAPACITY, Refill:	**Liters**	**Qt**
4-cyl. 2.5L	2.8	3.0
Others	3.8	4.0

Capacity shown is without filter. When replacing filter, additional oil may be needed

4-cyl. 1.8L Turbo:
Above 40°F (4°C) 30
Below 40°F (4°C) . . . . 10W-30♦
V6 3.0L, 3.8L, V8 5.0L (307):
Above 40°F (4°C) 30
Above 20°F (−7°C) 20W-20
Above 10°F (−12°C) 15W-40
Above 0°F (−18°C) . . . . 10W-30♦
Below 60°F (16°C) 5W-30
All others:
Above 40°F (4°C) 30
Above 0°F (−18°C) 10W-30
All temperatures . . . . 5W-30♦
♦Preferred

TRANSMISSION,		
TRANSAXLE, Automatic		. . . . . . AF
CAPACITY, Initial Refill*:	**Liters**	**Qt**
125 Transmission	3.8	4.0
180 Transmission	2.8	3.0
200 Transmission	3.3	3.5
440 Transmission	5.8	6.0
700-R4 Transmission	4.7	5.0

*With the engine at operating temperature, shift transmission
through all gears. Let engine slow idle in PARK for 3 minutes
or more. Check fluid level and add fluid as needed

TRANSMISSION/TRANSAXLE, Manual		
FWD		GLS
RWD: 4-speed 80W, 80W-90*		GL-5
5-speed		AF

*For vehicles normally operated in Canada, 80W only

CAPACITY, Refill:	Liters	Pt
FWD: 4-speed	2.8	6.0
5-speed, Isuzu†	2.6	5.4
5-speed, Muncie‡:		
6000, Fiero	1.9	4.0
Others	2.1	4.4
RWD: Acadian, 1000	1.9	4.0
Firebird	3.1	6.6

† Has a 7-bolt aluminum end cap
‡ Has a 9-bolt steel end cap

DIFFERENTIAL		
Standard 80W, 80W-90*		GL-5
Limited-Slip 80W, 80W-90*		GL-5 ★

*For vehicles normally operated in Canada, 80W only

CAPACITY, Refill:	Liters	Pt
Acadian, 1000	0.8	1.7
Parisienne:		
8 1/2″ ring gear	1.9	4.0
8 3/4″ ring gear	2.4	5.4
Others	1.7	3.5

LIMITED-SLIP IDENTIFICATION:
Tag under rear cover-attaching bolt

CHEK-CHART

SERVICE AT TIME OR MILEAGE—WHICHEVER OCCURS FIRST

PCPM11   PCPM11

Perform the following maintenance services at the intervals indicated to keep the vehicle warranties in effect.

W   SERVICE TO MAINTAIN EMISSION WARRANTY

MI—MILES IN THOUSANDS
KM—KILOMETERS IN THOUSANDS

TURBOCHARGED ENGINES, EVERY 3 MO/3 MI—5 KM
W Crankcase . . . . change oil
W Oil filter . . . . replace

EVERY 6 MONTHS
Brake master cylinder . . . . check level **HB**
Clutch master cylinder . . . . check level **HB**
Power steering reservoir . . check level **PS**

FIRST 7.5 MI—12 KM
W Carburetor or T.B.I. mounting
bolts . . . . torque
W Choke & hoses . . . . check/clean
As equipped
W Engine idle speed . . . . adjust
Ex. engines with Idle Speed or Idle Air Control
Diff., Limited-Slip . . . . . . change lubricant
Tires . . . . inspect/rotate
Initial service then every 15 mi (24 km). Check brake linings

EVERY 12 MO/7.5 MI—12 KM
W Crankcase ex. Turbo . . . . . . change oil
W Oil filter ex. Turbo . . . . replace
First oil change, then every other, or 12 months
Brake system . . . . inspect
Check hydraulic system for leaks. Inspect brake linings
Differential . . . . check level
Exhaust system . . . . inspect
Suspension &
steering linkage . . . . . . **0-11 fittings LB**
Initial service at mileage interval
Parking brake cable guides . . . . . coat **LB**
Check adjustment
Shift linkage . . . . coat **LB**
With floor shift, coat contact faces
Suspension & steering . . . . inspect
Also inspect drive axle boots and seals
Transaxle or transmission . . . . check level
W Drive belts . . . . inspect/adjust
W Throttle linkage . . . . inspect
Check for damage or binding
Body . . . . lubricate

EVERY 12 MONTHS
W Cooling system   inspect & tighten hoses
Wash radiator filler neck and cap; pressure test system. Clean exterior of radiator core and air conditioning condenser

EVERY 24 MO/30 MI—50 KM
W Cooling system . . . . change coolant **EC**
Flush system

EVERY 36 MO/30 MI—50 KM
W Crankcase inlet air filter . . . . replace
As equipped
W EGR system . . . . clean/inspect
Engine VIN codes H, K, M, R, U, Y, 9
W Fuel cap, tank, and lines . . . . . . inspect

EVERY 30 MI—50 KM
Clutch cross shaft . . . . **1 plug LB**
Front wheel bearings ex. front
wheel drive . . . . clean/repack **GC**
Service at mileage interval or at each brake reline, whichever comes first. Tighten spindle nut to 12 ft lb while turning wheel. Back off & retighten finger tight. Loosen nut just enough that either hole in spindle lines up with slot in nut. (Not more than 1/2 flat).
W Air cleaner element . . . . replace
W Choke & hoses . . . . check/clean
As equipped
W Distributor cap . . . . inspect
Except distributorless ignition
W Ignition timing . . . . adjust
Except distributorless ignition
W Ignition wires . . . . inspect/clean
As equipped
W PCV valve . . . . replace
Blow out or replace hoses
W Spark plugs . . . . replace
W Thermostatic air cleaner . . . . . . inspect
W Vacuum advance system &
hoses . . . . inspect
As equipped

EVERY 50 MI—80 KM
W Air cleaner element . . . . replace
1.6L & 2.0L

EVERY 100 MI—160 KM
Transaxle or trans., auto. . . . . change fluid
Clean sump screen or replace filter

SEVERE SERVICE
W Carburetor or T.B.I.—Torque mounting bolts & adjust idle speed at 6 mi (10 km), also inspect carburetor choke & hoses
W Crankcase—Change oil & oil filter every 3 mo/3 mi (5 km)
Differential—Change lubricant every 7.5 mi (12 km) when towing a trailer
Suspension & steering linkage—Lubricate every other oil change
Front wheel bearings RWD—Repack every 15 mi (24 km) or at every brake service, whichever comes first
Tires—Rotate at 6 mi (10 km), then every 15 mi (24 km)
Transaxle or transmission, automatic—Change fluid & filter or clean screen every 15 mi (24 km)

KEY TO LUBRICANTS
AF   DEXRON®-IIE Automatic Transmission Fluid
EC   Ethylene Glycol Coolant
GC   Wheel Bearing Grease, NLGI Category GC
GLS   Gear Lubricant, Special
FWD, GM Part No. 12345349
Firebird, GM Part No. 1052931
GL-5   Gear Oil, API Service GL-5
GL-5★   Special Lubricant for Limited-Slip Differential
HB   Hydraulic Brake Fluid, DOT 3
LB   Chassis Grease, NLGI Category LB
PS   Power Steering Fluid
SG   Motor Oil, API Service SG

CRANKCASE . . . . SG

CAPACITY, Refill△:	Liters	Qt
2.5L 6000, Fiero, Grand Am w/AT	2.8	3.0
Others	3.8	4.0

Capacity shown is without filter. When replacing filter, additional oil may be needed
4-cyl. 2.0L Turbo:
Above 40°F (4°C) 30
All temperatures . . . . 10W-30♦
V6 3.0L, 3.8L
Above 40°F (4°C) 30
Above 0°F (−18°C) . . . . 10W-30♦
Below 60°F (16°C) 5W-30
Others:
Above 40°F (4°C) 30
Above 0°F (−18°C) 10W-30
All temperatures . . . . 5W-30♦
♦Preferred

TRANSMISSION/TRANSAXLE, Automatic . . . . AF

CAPACITY, Initial Refill*:	Liters	Qt
125 (3T40)	3.8	4.0
180 3L30	2.8	3.0
200C	3.3	3.5
440-T4 (4T60)	5.8	6.0
700-R4 (4L60)	4.7	5.0

* With the engine at operating temperature, shift transmission through all gears. Let engine slow idle in PARK for 3 minutes or more. Check fluid level and add fluid as needed

TRANSMISSION/TRANSAXLE, Manual
FWD . . . . **GLS**
RWD: 4-speed 80W, 80W-90* **GL-5**
5-speed:
Firebird . . . . **GLS**
Others . . . . **AF**
*For vehicles normally operated in Canada, 80W only

CAPACITY, Refill:	Liters	Pt
Acadian, 1000	1.9	4.0
Firebird	3.1	6.6
FWD: 4-speed	2.8	6.0
5-speed, Isuzu†	2.5	5.4
5-speed, Muncie‡:		
6000, Fiero	1.9	4.0
Others	2.1	4.4

† Has a 7-bolt aluminum end cap
‡ Has a 9-bolt steel end cap

DIFFERENTIAL
Standard 80W-90* **GL-5**
Limited-Slip . . . . 80W-90* **GL-5★**
*For vehicles normally operated in Canada, 80W only

CAPACITY, Refill:	Liters	Pt
Acadian, 1000	0.8	1.7
Safari:		
8½″ ring gear	1.9	4.0
8¾″ ring gear	2.4	5.4
Others	1.7	3.5

LIMITED-SLIP IDENTIFICATION:
Tag under rear cover-attaching bolt

SERVICE AT TIME OR MILEAGE—WHICHEVER OCCURS FIRST

PCPM12   PCPM12

Perform the following maintenance services at the intervals indicated to keep the vehicle warranties in effect.

W   SERVICE TO MAINTAIN EMISSION WARRANTY

MI—MILES IN THOUSANDS
KM—KILOMETERS IN THOUSANDS

TURBOCHARGED ENGINES, EVERY 3 MO/3 MI—5 KM
- W Crankcase . . . . change oil
- W Oil filter . . . . replace

EVERY 6 MONTHS
Brake master cylinder . . . . check level **HB**

Clutch master cylinder . . . . check level **HB**

Power steering reservoir . . check level **PS**

FIRST 7.5 MI—12 KM
- W Carburetor or T.B.I. mounting bolts . . . . torque
- W Choke & hoses . . . . check/clean
  As equipped
- W Engine idle speed . . . . adjust
  Ex. engines with Idle Speed or Idle Air Control

Diff., Limited-Slip . . . . change lubricant
One time service only

Tires . . . . inspect/rotate
Initial service then every 15 mi (24 km). Check brake linings

EVERY 12 MO/7.5 MI—12 KM
Brake system . . . . inspect
Check hydraulic system for leaks. Inspect brake linings LeMans, Optima, free reservoir cap breather hole from obstructions
- W Crankcase ex. Turbo . . . . change oil
- W Oil filter ex. Turbo . . . . replace
  First oil change, then every other, or 12 months

Differential . . . . check level
- W Exhaust system . . . . inspect

Suspension & steering linkage . . . . . . **4-11 fittings LB**
Initial service at mileage interval

Parking brake cable guides . . . . . . coat **LB**
Check adjustment

Shift linkage . . . . coat **LB**
With floor shift, coat contact faces

Suspension & steering . . . . inspect
Also inspect drive axle boots and seals

Transaxle or transmission . . . . check level
- W Drive belts . . . . inspect/adjust
  Except LeMans, Optima
- W Throttle linkage . . . . inspect
  Check for damage or binding

Body . . . . lubricate

EVERY 12 MONTHS
- W Cooling system   inspect & tighten hoses
  Wash radiator filler neck and cap; pressure test system. Clean exterior of radiator core and air conditioning condenser

EVERY 24 MO/30 MI—50 KM
- W Cooling system . . . . change coolant **EC**
  Flush system

Drive belts . . . . inspect/adjust
LeMans, Optima only
- W Drive belts . . . . inspect/adjust
  Replace as needed

EVERY 36 MO/30 MI—50 KM
- W Air cleaner element . . . . replace
- W Crankcase air filter . . . . replace
  As equipped
- W EGR system . . . . clean/inspect
  1988-90 engine VIN codes E, K, M, R, T (1988), U, Y, 7, 9

Fuel micro filter . . . . replace
LeMans, Optima only
- W Fuel cap, tank, and lines . . . . . inspect

EVERY 30 MI—50 KM
Clutch cross shaft . . . . **1 plug LB**

Front wheel bearings ex. front wheel drive . . . . clean/repack **GC**
Service at mileage interval or at each brake reline, whichever comes first. Tighten spindle nut to 12 ft lb while turning wheel. Back off & retighten finger tight. Loosen nut just enough that either hole in spindle lines up with slot in nut. (Not more than 1/2 flat).

EGR system . . . . clean/inspect
1991-92 engine VIN codes E, H, K, N, R, U, V, 1
- W Choke & hoses . . . . check/clean
  As equipped
- W Distributor cap . . . . inspect
  Except distributorless ignition
- W Ignition timing . . . . adjust
  Except distributorless ignition
- W Ignition wires . . . . inspect/clean
  As equipped
- W PCV valve . . . . replace
  Some models blow out or replace hoses
- W Spark plugs . . . . replace
- W Thermostatic air cleaner . . . . . inspect

FIRST 60 MI—100 KM; THEN EVERY 15 MI—25 KM
Camshaft timing belt . . . . inspect
3.4L Code X engine

EVERY 100 MI—160 KM
Transaxle or trans., auto. . . . . change fluid
Clean sump screen or replace filter

SEVERE SERVICE
- W Carburetor or T.B.I.—Torque mounting bolts & adjust idle speed at 6 mi (10 km), also inspect carburetor choke & hoses
- W Crankcase—Change oil & oil filter every 3 mo/3 mi (5 km)

Differential—Change lubricant every 7.5 mi (12 km) when towing a trailer

Suspension & steering linkage—Lubricate every other oil change

Front wheel bearings RWD—Repack every 15 mi (24 km) or at every brake service, whichever comes first

Tires—Rotate at 6 mi (10 km), then every 15 mi (24 km)

Transaxle or transmission, automatic—Change fluid & filter or clean screen every 15 mi (24 km)

KEY TO LUBRICANTS
AF	DEXRON®-IIE Automatic Transmission Fluid
EC	Ethylene Glycol Coolant
GC	Wheel Bearing Grease, NLGI Category GC
GLS	Gear Lubricant, Special GM Part No. 12345349
GL-5	Gear Oil, API Service GL-5
GL-5★	Special Lubricant for Limited-Slip Differential
HB	Hydraulic Brake Fluid, DOT 3
LB	Chassis Grease, NLGI Category LB
PS	Power Steering Fluid
SG	Motor Oil, API Service SG

CRANKCASE . . . . SG
CAPACITY, Refill:	Liters	Qt
3.4L DOHC	4.7	5.0
Others	3.8	4.0

Capacity shown is without filter. When replacing filter, additional oil may be needed

4-cyl. 2.0L Turbo:
Above 40°F (4°C) . . . . 30★
All temperatures . . . . 10W-30♦

1988 V6 3.0L, 3.8L
1990 Sunbird Turbo, Grand Prix Turbo
1991 3.1L V6 Turbo; V6 3.3L, 3.8L
Above 40°F (4°C) . . . . 30★
Above 0°F (−18°C) . . . . 10W-30♦
Below 60°F (16°C) 5W-30

Others:
Above 40°F (4°C) . . . . 30★
Above 0°F (−18°C) 10W-30
All temperatures . . . . 5W-30♦

♦Preferred
★Use only if other specified grades are unavailable

TRANSMISSION/TRANSAXLE, Automatic . . . . AF
CAPACITY, Initial Refill*:	Liters	Qt
125 (3T40)	3.8	4.0
200C	3.3	3.5
440-T4 (4T60, 4T60E)	5.8	6.0
700-R4 (4L60)	4.7	5.0
LeMans, Optima	3.8	4.0

*With the engine at operating temperature, shift transmission through all gears. Let engine slow idle in PARK for 3 minutes or more. Check fluid level and add fluid as needed

TRANSMISSION/TRANSAXLE, Manual
FWD . . . . GLS
RWD, 5-speed Firebird . . . . AF
CAPACITY, Refill:	Liters	Pt
FWD: 4-speed	2.8	6.0
5-speed, Isuzu†	2.5	5.4
5-speed, Muncie‡:		
6000, Fiero	1.9	4.0
Others	2.1	4.4
LeMans, Optima:		
4-speed	1.6	3.5
5-speed (1.6L engine) .	1.6	3.5
5-speed (2.0L engine) .	2.1	4.5
RWD, Firebird	2.8	6.0

† Has a 7-bolt aluminum end cap
‡ Has a 9-bolt steel end cap

DIFFERENTIAL
Standard 80W-90* GL-5
Limited-Slip . . . . 80W-90* GL-5★
*For vehicles normally operated in Canada, 80W only
CAPACITY, Refill:	Liters	Pt
Safari:		
8½″ ring gear	1.9	4.0
8¾″ ring gear	2.4	5.4
6000, 4WD rear	1.8	3.8
Others	1.7	3.5

LIMITED-SLIP IDENTIFICATION:
Tag under rear cover-attaching bolt

SERVICE LOCATIONS — ENGINE AND CHASSIS

HOOD RELEASE: Inside

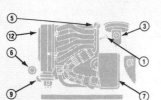

1983-88
4-cyl. 2479cc ex. Turbo & DOHC

1986-89
4-cyl. 2479cc Turbo

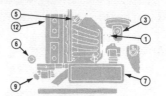

1987-88
4-cyl. 2479cc DOHC
1989
4-cyl. 2681cc DOHC
1989-92
4-cyl. 2990cc DOHC

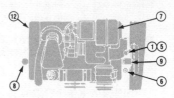

1983
6-cyl. 2994cc
1984-89
6-cyl. 3164cc
1990-92
6-cyl. 3600cc

① Crankcase dipstick
② Transmission dipstick
③ Brake fluid reservoir
④ Clutch fluid reservoir
⑤ Oil fill cap
⑥ Power steering reservoir
⑦ Air filter
⑧ Fuel filter
⑨ Oil filter
⑩ PCV filter
⑪ EGR valve
⑫ Oxygen sensor
⑬ PCV valve

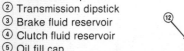

1983-89
6-cyl. 3299cc Turbo

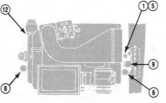

1983-84
V8 4664cc

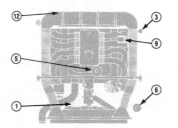

1985-92
V8 4957cc
(DOHC version shown)

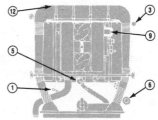

0 FITTINGS
0 PLUGS

0 FITTINGS
0 PLUGS

0 FITTINGS
0 PLUGS

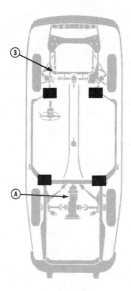

1983-89
911, 911 Turbo
1990-92
911 Carrera 2

1983-89
924S, 944, 944S, 944 Turbo
1990-91
944 S2
1992
968

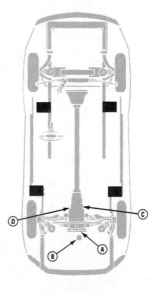

1983-92
928, 928S, 928S/4

Ⓐ Manual transmission/transaxle,
   drain & fill
Ⓑ Transfer case, NOT USED

Ⓒ Automatic transmission, check
Ⓓ Differential, drain & fill

■ Lift adapter position   ● Cooling system drain

SERVICE AT TIME OR MILEAGE—WHICHEVER OCCURS FIRST

PEIPM1   PEIPM1

Perform the following maintenance services at the intervals indicated to keep both the vehicle and emission warranties in effect

MI — MILES IN THOUSANDS
KM — KILOMETERS IN THOUSANDS

EVERY 7.5 MI — 12 KM

Crankcase . . . . change oil
1986-89 Turbo only

Oil filter . . . . replace
1986-89 Turbo only

EVERY 15 MI — 24 KM

Clutch pedal free play . . . . . . check/adjust

Clutch release lever . . . . lubricate
1986-88 only

Crankcase . . . . change oil
Inspect for leakage

Driveshaft boots . . . . inspect
1986-92 only

Oil filter . . . . replace

Exhaust system . . . . inspect
Turbo: check tightness of reactors, turbocharger, and wastegate

Front axle & steering . . . . inspect
Check tightness of components & condition of rubber boots & bushings

Front differential . . . . check level

Transaxle . . . . check level
Inspect for leakage

Accelerator linkage . . . . inspect
Check for smooth operation and full throttle opening, lubricate as necessary

Battery . . . . check level

Boost pressure safety switch . . . . . . check
Turbo only

Brake fluid reservoir . . . . . . check level **HB**
1986-92 only

Clutch hydraulic cylinders . . . . inspect

Crankcase ventilation system . . . . . inspect
Check hoses & connections, clean filter where applicable

Fuel lines & hoses . . . . inspect
1986-92 only

Fuel pump safety switch . . . . check
Turbo only

Ignition timing . . . . check/adjust
1986-87, Turbo only

Intake air hoses . . . . inspect
1986-92 only

On-board diagnostic
   system 1989-92 . . . . check/clear

Power steering 1989-92 . . . check level **AF**
Inspect steering pump drive belt

Valve clearance . . . . check/adjust

Windshield & headlight
   washers . . . . check level

Body . . . . check/lubricate
Check operation of all locks & hinges, lubricate door hinges & check rods

Brake system . . . . inspect
Check pad wear, condition of lines & hoses

Electrical equipment . . . . inspect
Check operation of lights, horns, buzzers, wipers, switches, instruments & power accessories

Handbrake . . . . check/adjust
1986-92 only

Headlights . . . . check/adjust

Seat belts 1990-92 . . . . inspect
Check condition and operation

Tires . . . . inspect/adjust
Check tread wear & inflation pressure

Weatherstrips . . . . clean/lubricate
Remove residue & coat with talcum powder, glycerine, or other suitable rubber lubricant

Wheel bearings, front . . . . . . check/adjust
1985-89 only

Wheel bearings, rear . . . . . . check/adjust
Turbo & Turbo look only

EVERY 24 MO

Brake fluid . . . . replace **HB**

EVERY 30 MI — 48 KM

Transaxle . . . . change lubricant
1983-85 only

Transmission, automatic . . . . change fluid

Air filter element . . . . replace
Replace air pump filter where applicable

Drive belts . . . . check/adjust

Ignition timing . . . . check/adjust
1988-89 Turbo only

Oxygen sensor . . . . replace
1983 only, reset mileage counter

Spark plugs . . . . replace

EVERY 48 MO

Air bag system . . . . inspect

EVERY 60 MI — 96 KM

Front differential . . . . change lubricant

Final drive, automatic
   transmission . . . . change lubricant

Transaxle . . . . change lubricant
1986-92 only

Fuel filter . . . . replace

Oxygen sensor . . . . replace
1986-89 only

SEVERE SERVICE

Crankcase — Change oil and filter more frequently

Air filter — Check/replace more frequently

Battery — Check level more frequently

Brakes — Inspect more frequently

Clutch — Check/adjust more frequently

Tires — Inspect more frequently

KEY TO LUBRICANTS

AF   DEXRON®-II Automatic Transmission Fluid

CD   Motor Oil, API Service CD

GL-5   Gear Oil, API Service GL-5

HB   Hydraulic Brake Fluid, Extra Heavy Duty, DOT 4

SF   Motor Oil, API Service SF

SG   Motor Oil, API Service SG

CRANKCASE . . . SF, SF/CD, SG, SG/CD

CAPACITY, Refill*:	Liters	Qt
2994cc, 3164cc, 3299cc .	10.0	10.6
3600cc	9.0	9.6

*Capacity shown includes filter. Add specified amount, run engine until oil is at operating temperature (above the white field at the bottom of the temperature gauge). Check dipstick with engine idling and add sufficient oil to bring level half way between the MIN & MAX marks. Allow engine to idle 30 seconds to stabilize level before rechecking. **DO NOT FILL TO MAX** unless the temperature gauge reading is higher than the first scale division.

2994cc, 3164cc, 3299cc:
Above 14°F (–10°C)	20W-50
Above 5°F (–15°C)	15W-40, 15W-50
–4° to 95°F (–20° to 35°C)	10W-40, 10W-50
–13° to 68°F (–25° to 20°C)	10W-30
–22° to 32°F (–30° to 0°C)	5W-30
Below 14°F (–10°C)	5W-20

3600cc:
Mineral base oils
Above 50°F (10°C)	15W-40, 20W-50, 40
Below 50°F (10°C) . . .	15W-40, 10W-40, 10W-30
Below 14°F (–10°C)	10W-30, 5W-30

Synthetic base oils
All temperatures	10W-40, 15W-40, 15W-50
Below 50°F (10°C)	10W-40, 10W-30, 5W-30

TRANSMISSION, Automatic . . . . **AF**

CAPACITY, Service Refill*:	Liters	Qt
1990-92 911 Carrera 2	3.0	3.2

*Add specified quantity. With engine at operating temperature, shift transmission through all gears. Check fluid level in PARK and add fluid as needed

TRANSAXLE, Manual

1983-86	90W	GL-5
1987-88 Turbo	90W	GL-5
1987-88 Non-Turbo	75W-90	GL-5
1989-92 All	75W-90	GL-5

CAPACITY, Refill:	Liters	Pt
1983-87 Non-Turbo	3.0	6.3
1988-89 2WD Non-Turbo . .	3.4	7.2
1983-89 Turbo	3.7	7.8
1989-92 4WD	3.8	4.0
1990-92 2WD	3.6	3.9

FINAL DRIVE, Automatic Transmission

1990-92	75W-90	GL-5

CAPACITY, Refill:	Liters	Pt
1990-92 911 Carrera 2 . .	0.9	2.0

FRONT DIFFERENTIAL . . . 75W-90 GL-5

CAPACITY, Refill:	Liters	Pt
1989-92 4WD	1.2	2.6

PORSCHE
1983-91 944 Series; 1986-88 924S Series
1992 968

CHEK-CHART

PEIPM2   PEIPM2

Perform the following maintenance services at the intervals indicated to keep both the vehicle and emission warranties in effect

MI — MILES IN THOUSANDS
KM — KILOMETERS IN THOUSANDS

1986-89 944 TURBO, EVERY 7.5 MI — 12 KM
Crankcase . . . . change oil
Check for leaks

Oil filter . . . . replace

EVERY 15 MI — 24 KM
Clutch disc wear . . . . check
1986 only

Crankcase . . . . change oil
Check for leaks

Driveshaft boots . . . . inspect
1986-92 only

Exhaust system . . . . inspect
1986-92 only

Final drive, automatic
    transmission . . . . check level
Check for leaks

Front axle & steering . . . . inspect
Check tightness of components & condition of rubber boots & bushings

Oil filter . . . . replace

Throttle linkage . . . . inspect
Check for smooth operation and full throttle opening; lubricate as neccessary

Transaxle, manual . . . . check level
Check for leaks

Transmission, automatic . . . . . check level
Check by viewing level in clear plastic reservoir mounted on the transmission case. Level must be between the MIN & MAX markings with engine idling at operating temperature. Check for leaks

Battery . . . . check level

Brake fluid reservoir . . . . check level
1986-92 only

Camshaft &
    balance shaft belts . . . . check/adjust

Cooling system . . . . inspect
Check tightness of hoses, clean radiator, check level EC

Crankcase ventilation
    system . . . . check/tighten
1986-91 only

Fuel lines & hoses . . . . inspect
1986-92 only

Headlight retractors . . . . lubricate

Intake air hoses . . . . inspect
1986-92 only

Power steering . . . . check level AF

Windshield & headlight
    washers . . . . check level/aim

Brake & clutch pedal
    free play . . . . check/adjust

Brake system . . . . inspect
Check pad wear, condition of lines & hoses

Body . . . . check/lubricate
Check operation and lubricate all locks, hinges & check rods

Diagnostic system . . . . check/clear

Electrical equipment . . . . inspect
Check operation of lights, horns, buzzers, wipers, switches, instruments & power accessories

Handbrake . . . . check/adjust
1986-92 only

Headlights . . . . check/adjust

Weatherstrips . . . . clean/lubricate
Remove residue & coat with talcum powder, glycerine, or other suitable rubber lubricant

Wheel bearings, front . . . . . . check/adjust
1985-92 only

Seat belts 1990-92 . . . . inspect
Check condition and operation

Tires . . . . inspect
Check tread wear & inflation pressure

EVERY 24 MO
Brake fluid . . . . replace HB

Engine coolant . . . . replace EC

EVERY 30 MI — 48 KM
Transaxle, manual . . . . . . change lubricant
1985 only

Transmission, automatic . . . . change fluid

Air filter element . . . . replace

Drive belts . . . . check/adjust

Spark plugs . . . . replace

EVERY 45 MI — 72 KM
Camshaft belt 1989-92 . . . . replace
Check & adjust tension after 2.5 mi (4 km)

EVERY 60 MI — 96 KM
Transaxle, manual . . . . . . change lubricant
1985-92 only

Final drive, automatic
    transmission . . . . change lubricant
1986-92 only

Fuel filter . . . . replace
1986-92 only

Oxygen sensor . . . . replace
1986-89 only

1987-89 FIRST 48 MO; THEN EVERY 24 MO
1990-92 EVERY 48 MO
Air bag system . . . . inspect

SEVERE SERVICE
Crankcase — Change oil and filter more frequently

Cooling system — Inspect more frequently

Air filter — Check/replace more frequently

Battery — Check level more frequently

Brakes — Inspect more frequently

Clutch — Check/adjust more frequently

Tires — Inspect more frequently

KEY TO LUBRICANTS

AF DEXRON®-II Automatic Transmission Fluid

CC Motor Oil, API Service CC

CD Motor Oil, API Service CD

EC Engine Coolant, Phosphate Free Ethylene Glycol
Mix with water to obtain proper protection level

GL-4 Gear Oil, API Service GL-4

GL-5 Gear Oil, API Service GL-5

HB Hydraulic Brake Fluid, Extra Heavy Duty, DOT 4

SF Motor Oil, API Service SF

CRANKCASE . . . . SF, SF/CC, SF/CD

CAPACITY, Refill*:	Liters	Qt
1983-85 944	5.5†	5.8†
1986 944 ex. Turbo	6.0†	6.3†
944 Turbo	6.5†	6.8†
1987-89:		
924S, 944 ex. Turbo . .	6.5†	6.8†
944 Turbo	7.0†	7.4†
1989-91 944S2:		
Aluminum sump	7.0	7.4
Plastic sump	8.0	8.4
1992 968	7.0	7.4

* Capacity shown includes filter
† When refilling, remove dipstick to provide adequate venting

Mineral base oils:
Above 60°F (16°C) 40
32° to 86°F (0° to 30°C) 30
14° to 50°F (–10° to 10°C) 20, 20W-20
Above 14°F (–10°C) 20W-40, 20W-50
Above 5°F (–15°C) 15W-40, 15W-50
32° to 100°F (0° to 38°C) 10W-40
–13° to 68°F (–25° to 20°C) 10W-30
–22° to 32°F (–30° to 0°C) 10W, 5W-30
Below 14°F (–10°C) 5W-20
Synthetic base oils:
32° to 105°F (0° to 42°C) 10W-30, 10W-40, 10W-50
All temperatures 5W-30, 5W-40, 5W-50

TRANSAXLE, Manual
1989 944, 944 Turbo 75W-90 **GL-5**
1992 968 . . . . 75W-90 **GL-5**
Others 80W, 80W-90 **GL-4**

CAPACITY, Refill:	Liters	Pt
1983-84 944	2.6	5.5
1985-89 944 ex. Turbo . .	2.0*	4.2*
1986-89 944 Turbo	2.2	4.6
1987-88 924S	2.0*	4.2*
1989-91 944S2	2.0	4.2
1992 968	2.8	5.8

* Proper level may be 1/4 in (6mm) below the fill plug, measure quantity and **do not overfill**

TRANSMISSION, Automatic . . . . . . AF
Final drive serviced separately

CAPACITY, Service Refill*:	Liters	Qt
1983-91	2.8	3.0

* Add specified quantity. With engine at operating temperature, shift transmission through all gears. Check fluid level in PARK and add fluid as needed

FINAL DRIVE, Automatic Transmission
1983-88, 1992 . . . . 90W **GL-5**
1989-91 . . . . 75W-90 **GL-5**

CAPACITY, Refill:	Liters	Pt
1983-91	1.0	2.1
1992	0.6	1.3

Copyright 1992 by H.M. Gousha, a division of Simon & Schuster

SERVICE AT TIME OR MILEAGE—WHICHEVER OCCURS FIRST

PEIPM3   PEIPM3

Perform the following maintenance services at the intervals indicated to keep both the vehicle and emission warranties in effect

MI — MILES IN THOUSANDS
KM — KILOMETERS IN THOUSANDS

EVERY 15 MI — 24 KM

Clutch . . . . inspect
Check disc for wear, check slave cylinder for leaks

Crankcase . . . . change oil
Check for leaks

Driveshaft boots . . . . inspect
1986-92 only

Exhaust system . . . . inspect
1986-92 only

Final drive, automatic
   transmission . . . . check level
Check for leaks

Front axle & steering . . . . inspect
Check tightness of components & condition of rubber boots & bushings

Oil filter . . . . replace

Transaxle, manual . . . . check level
Check for leaks

Transmission, automatic . . . . . check level
Check by viewing level in clear plastic reservoir mounted on the transmission case. Level must be between the MIN & MAX markings with engine idling at operating temperature. Check for leaks

Battery . . . . check/level

Brake fluid reservoir . . . . . . check level HB

Camshaft timing belt . . . . check/adjust

Cooling system . . . . inspect
Check tightness of hoses, clean radiator, check level EC

Crankcase ventilation system . . . . . inspect
1986-92 only

Fuel lines & hoses . . . . inspect
1986-92 only

Intake air hoses . . . . inspect
1986-92 only

Power steering . . . . check level AF
1990-92 check condition of drive belt

Throttle linkage . . . . inspect
Check for smooth operation and full throttle opening; lubricate as necessary

Windshield & headlight
   washers . . . . check level/aim

Brake & clutch pedal
   free play . . . . check/adjust

Brake system . . . . inspect
Check pad wear, condition of lines & hoses

Body . . . . check/lubricate
Check operation and lubricate all locks, hinges and check rods

Diagnosis system . . . . check/clear

Electrical equipment . . . . inspect
Check operation of lights, horns, buzzers, wipers, switches, instruments & power accessories

Handbrake . . . . check/adjust
1986-92 only

Headlights . . . . check/adjust

Limited-Slip differential
   regulator 1990-92 . . . . . . check level HB

Seat belts 1990-92 . . . . inspect
Check condition and operation

Tires . . . . inspect
Check tread wear & inflation pressure, 1990-92 check condition and operation of pressure warning system

Weatherstrips . . . . clean/lubricate
Remove residue & coat with talcum powder, glycerine, or other suitable rubber lubricant

Wheel bearings, front . . . . . . check/adjust
1985-92 only

EVERY 24 MO

Brake fluid . . . . replace HB

Engine coolant . . . . replace EC

Limited-Slip differential
   regulator fluid 1990-92 . . . . . replace HB

EVERY 30 MI — 48 KM

Final drive, automatic
   transmission . . . . change lubricant
1983-85 only

Transaxle, manual . . . . . change lubricant
1983-85 only

Transmission, automatic . . . . change fluid

Air filter element . . . . replace
Replace air pump filter where applicable

Drive belts . . . . check/adjust
Includes camshaft & balance shaft belts

Drive belt
   tensioner 1986-92 . . . . check/fill SF

Oxygen sensor . . . . replace
1983 only, reset mileage counter

Spark plugs . . . . replace

EVERY 48 MO

Air bag system . . . . inspect

EVERY 60 MI — 96 KM

Camshaft drive belt 1989-92 . . . . . replace
Check & adjust tension after 2.5 mi (4 km)

Final drive, automatic
   transmission . . . . change lubricant
1986-92 only

Transaxle, manual . . . . . . change lubricant
1986-92 only

Fuel filter . . . . replace

Oxygen sensor . . . . replace
1986-89 only

SEVERE SERVICE
Crankcase — Change oil and filter more frequently

Cooling system — Inspect more frequently

Air filter — Check/replace more frequently

Battery — Check level more frequently

Brakes — Inspect more frequently

Clutch — Check/adjust more frequently

Tires — Inspect more frequently

KEY TO LUBRICANTS

AF   DEXRON®-II Automatic Transmission Fluid

EC   Engine Coolant, Phosphate Free Ethylene Glycol
Mix with water to obtain proper protection level

GL-5   Gear Oil, API Service GL-5

HB   Hydraulic Brake Fluid, Extra Heavy Duty, DOT 4

SF   Motor Oil, API Service SF

CRANKCASE . . . . SF

CAPACITY, Refill:	Liters	Qt
All models	7.5	7.9

Capacity shown is without filter. When replacing filter, additional oil may be needed

Mineral base oils
Above 60°F (16°C)	40
32° to 86°F (0° to 30°C)	30
14° to 50°F (−10° to 10°C)	20, 20W-20
Above 14°F (−10°C)	20W-40, 20W-50
Above 5°F (−15°C)	15W-40, 15W-50
32° to 100°F (0° to 38°C)	10W-40
−13° to 68°F (−25° to 20°C)	10W-30
−22° to 32°F (−30° to 0°C)	10W, 5W-30
Below 14°F (−10°C)	5W-20

Synthetic base oils
32° to 105°F (0° to 42°C)	10W-30, 10W-40, 10W-50
All temperatures	5W-30, 5W-40, 5W-50

TRANSAXLE, Manual 75W-90 GL-5

CAPACITY, Refill:	Liters	Pt
1983-86 All models	3.8	8.0
1987-92 All models	4.5	9.6

TRANSMISSION, Automatic . . . . AF
Final drive serviced separately

CAPACITY, Service Refill*:	Liters	Qt
1983-86	5.5	5.8
1987-92	7.3	7.8

* Add specified quantity. With engine at operating temperature, shift transmission through all gears. Check fluid level in PARK and add fluid as needed

FINAL DRIVE, Automatic Transmission
1983-88	90W GL-5
1989-92	75W-90 GL-5

CAPACITY, Refill:	Liters	Pt
1983	2.0	4.3
1984-89	2.7	5.9
1990-92	3.0	6.3

HOOD RELEASE: Inside

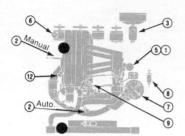

① Crankcase dipstick
② Transmission dipstick
③ Brake fluid reservoir
④ Clutch fluid reservoir
⑤ Oil fill cap
⑥ Power steering reservoir
⑦ Air filter
⑧ Fuel filter
⑨ Oil filter
⑩ PCV filter
⑪ EGR valve
⑫ Oxygen sensor
⑬ PCV valve

1983-88, 900
4-cyl. 1985cc 8-Valve
(Turbo version shown)

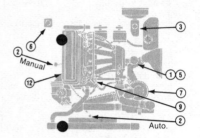

1985-92 900
4-cyl. 1985cc 16-Valve
(Turbo version shown)
1991-92 900
4-cyl. 2119cc

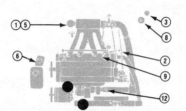

1986-90 9000
4-cyl. 1985cc 16-Valve
(Turbo version shown)

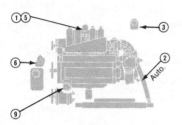

1990-92 9000
4-cyl. 2290cc
(Non-Turbo version shown)

0 FITTINGS
0 PLUGS

0 FITTINGS
0 PLUGS

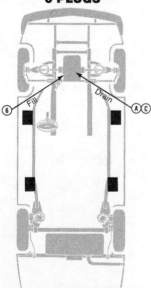

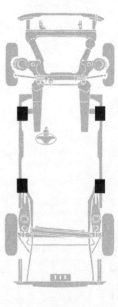

1983-92
900

1986-92
9000

■ Lift adapter position
● Cooling system drain

Ⓐ Manual transmission/transaxle, drain & fill
Ⓑ Transfer case, NOT USED

Ⓒ Automatic transaxle final drive, drain & fill
Ⓓ Differential, NOT USED

CHEK-CHART

SAAB
1983-84 All Models

SERVICE AT TIME OR MILEAGE—WHICHEVER OCCURS FIRST

SBIPM1

SBIPM1

MI — MILES IN THOUSANDS
KM — KILOMETERS IN THOUSANDS

NON-TURBO,
EVERY 6 MO/7.5 MI — 12.5 KM
TURBO, EVERY 6 MO/5 MI — 8 KM
Crankcase . . . . change oil

Oil filter . . . . replace

NON-TURBO,
EVERY 7.5 MI — 12.5 KM
TURBO, EVERY 6 MO/5 MI — 8 KM
Brake system . . . . inspect
Check thickness of brake pads, condition of lines & hoses, tightness of master cylinder & calipers

Chassis . . . . inspect
Check undercarriage for damage, drive shaft boots, ball joint & tie rod dust seals

Exhaust system . . . . inspect

Final drive . . . . check level
Automatic transmission only

Battery . . . . inspect
Check level, clean & tighten terminals, lubricate with petroleum jelly

Brake booster . . . . inspect
Check hoses & connections

Brake/clutch fluid . . . . check level **HB**

Cooling system . . . . inspect **EC**
Check condition & tightness of hoses, check level & concentration

Power steering . . . . check level **PS**

Transmission, automatic . . . . . check level

Transmission, manual . . . . check level

Electrical equipment . . . . inspect
Check function of all lights, buzzers, heater fan, horn, cooling fans & power accessories

Hand brake . . . . check

Tires . . . . inspect
Check treadwear & inflation pressure

Toe-in . . . . check/adjust

EVERY 12 MO/15 MI — 25 KM
Brake caliper slides . . . . lubricate **BL**

Front suspension . . . . inspect
Check ball joints & tie rod ends for wear

Fuel injection system . . . . inspect
Check hoses, wiring, components & connections for leakage, wear or damage

Headlights . . . . check/adjust

Shock absorbers . . . . check

Throttle linkage . . . . lubricate **MO**

Ventilation filter . . . . replace
W/o AC only

Wheel alignment . . . . check/adjust

EVERY 15 MI — 25 KM
Crankcase ventilation system . . . . . inspect

Drive belts . . . . check/adjust

Turbocharger . . . . inspect
Check operation of overpressure safety switch and charging pressure

Valve clearance . . . . check/adjust
Clean valve cover oil separator

FIRST 24 MO/30 MI — 50 KM;
THEN EVERY 12 MO
Drive belts . . . . check/adjust

Ignition wires . . . . inspect
Clean & check secondary leads for cuts, burns, or abrasions

FIRST 24 MO/30 MI — 50 KM;
THEN EVERY 12 MO/15 MI — 25 KM
Cooling system . . . . . . change coolant **EC**

EVERY 24 MO/30 MI — 50 KM
Brake fluid . . . . replace **HB**

EVERY 30 MI — 50 KM
Air filter element . . . . replace

Fuel filter . . . . replace

Oxygen sensor . . . . replace
Lubricate threads with anti-sieze compound, check operation of enrichment microswitch & reset service indicator lamp

Spark plugs . . . . replace

FIRST 48 MO/60 MI — 100 KM;
THEN EVERY 12 MO
Crankcase ventilation . . . . inspect

Evaporative emissions system . . . . inspect
Check canister, filler cap, lines, hoses & connections for leaks, damage & tightness

EVERY 60 MI — 100 KM
Charcoal canister . . . . replace

Distributor cap & rotor . . . . replace

Deceleration system . . . . check/adjust

Idle speed . . . . check/adjust

Ignition wires . . . . inspect
Check resistance of secondary wiring

Ignition timing . . . . check/adjust
Check advance mechanisms where applicable

SEVERE SERVICE
Crankcase — Change oil & filter: Non-Turbo every 4 mo/5 mi (8 km); Turbo every 4 mo/ 3.75 mi (6 km)

Air filter element — Replace

Fuel filter — Replace

Spark plugs — Replace

KEY TO LUBRICANTS

BL	Brake Lubricant	Saab Part No. 30 08 612
CC	Motor Oil, API Service CC	
CD	Motor Oil, API Service CD	
EC	Ethylene Glycol Coolant	Mix with water to desired freeze protection
FA	Automatic Transmission Fluid, Type F	
GL-4	Gear Oil, API Service GL-4	
GL-5	Gear Oil, API Service GL-5	
HB	Hydraulic Brake Fluid, DOT 4	
MO	Motor Oil	
PS	Power Steering Fluid	Saab Part No. 30 09 800 or GM 1050017
SF	Motor Oil, API Service SF	

CRANKCASE . . . . **SF/CC, SF/CD**

CAPACITY, Refill*:	Liters	Qt
Non-Turbo	3.8	4.0
Turbo	4.3	4.5

* Capacity shown includes filter
Above 0°F (−18°C) . . . . 10W-30†
Below 0°F (−18°C) 5W-30
† In extremely hot climates 15W-40 (only if API service classification is met)

TRANSMISSION, Automatic . . . . **FA**
Final drive serviced separately

CAPACITY, Total Fill†:	Liters	Qt
All	8.0	8.5

†Total capacity including torque converter is shown, when servicing, use less fluid than specified

TRANSAXLE, Manual . . . . . 10W-30 **SF♦**

CAPACITY, Refill:	Liters	Pt
All	2.5	5.3

♦Alternate, 75W **GL-4/GL-5**

FINAL DRIVE 80W **GL-4, GL-5**

CAPACITY, Refill:	Liters	Pt
All w/AT	1.3	2.6

SERVICE AT TIME OR MILEAGE—WHICHEVER OCCURS FIRST

W SERVICE TO MAINTAIN EMISSION WARRANTY

MI — MILES IN THOUSANDS
KM — KILOMETERS IN THOUSANDS

1985-87 NON-TURBO,
EVERY 12 MO/7.5 MI — 12.5 KM
1985-87 TURBO,
EVERY 6 MO/3.75 MI — 6 KM
1988-91, EVERY 12 MO/7.5 MI — 12.5 KM
1992, FIRST 5 MI — 8 KM;
THEN EVERY 12 MO/10 MI — 19 KM

W Crankcase . . . . change oil
W Oil filter . . . . replace

1985-91 EVERY 12 MO/7.5 MI — 12.5 KM
1992 FIRST 5 MI — 8 KM;
THEN EVERY 12 MO/10 MI — 19 KM

Brake system . . . . inspect
Check thickness of brake pads, condition of lines & hoses, tightness of master cylinder & calipers

Chassis . . . . inspect
Check undercarriage for damage, drive shaft boots, ball joint & tie rod dust seals, 1992 models; retighten suspension mounting points at first interval only

Exhaust system . . . . inspect
Final drive . . . . check level
900 w/automatic transmission only

Transmission, manual . . . . check level
Transmission, automatic . . . . check level
1992 9000, change lubricant at first interval only

Battery . . . . inspect
Check level, clean & tighten terminals, lubricate with petroleum jelly

Brake booster . . . . inspect
Check hoses & connections

Brake/clutch fluid . . . . check level **HB**

Cooling system . . . . inspect **EC**
Check condition & tightness of hoses, level & concentration

Drive belts 1992 . . . . inspect

Fuel injection system 1985-91 . . . . inspect
Check hoses, wiring, components & connections for leakage, wear or damage

Power steering . . . . check level **PS**

Body 1990 . . . . check/lubricate
Door stops, hinges, latches, locks, sunroof rails

Electrical equipment . . . . inspect
Check function of all lights, buzzers, heater fan, horn, cooling fans & power accessories

Hand brake . . . . check/adjust
1992 at first service, then every 30 mi (50 km)

Tires . . . . inspect
Check treadwear & inflation pressure, rotate 1989 only

Toe-in 1985-91 . . . . check/adjust

1985-87, 1991,
FIRST 24 MO/30 MI — 50 KM;
THEN EVERY 12 MO
1988-90, EVERY 30 MI — 50 KM

Drive belts . . . . check/adjust

Ignition wires 1985-89 . . . . inspect
Clean & check secondary leads for cuts, burns, or abrasions

1985-87, FIRST 24 MO/30 MI — 50 KM;
THEN EVERY 12 MO/15 MI — 25 KM
1988-91, EVERY 30 MI — 50 KM
1992, FIRST 36 MO/35 MI — 56 KM;
THEN EVERY 36 MO/30 MI — 50 KM

Cooling system . . . . . change coolant **EC**
If not using Saab approved coolant, reduce interval to 15 mi (25 km)

1985-87, 1991,
EVERY 24 MO/30 MI — 50 KM
1988-90, EVERY 30 MI — 50 KM
1992, FIRST 24 MO/35 MI — 56 KM;
THEN EVERY 24 MO/30 MI — 50 KM

Brake fluid . . . . replace **HB**

1985-91, EVERY 30 MI — 50 KM
1992, FIRST 35 MI — 56 KM;
THEN EVERY 30 MI — 50 KM

Brake caliper slides . . . . lubricate **BL**
1985-87, 900 only

Front suspension . . . . inspect
Check ball joints & tie rod ends for wear

W Air filter element . . . . replace
Fuel lines . . . . inspect
W Fuel filter 1985-91 . . . . replace

W Overpressure safety switch . . . . check
1985-91 turbocharged engines only. Not required for Calif. warranty

W Oxygen sensor . . . . replace
1985-87 8-valve engine only, lubricate threads with anti-sieze compound, check operation of enrichment microswitch & reset service indicator lamp

W Spark plugs . . . . replace
Throttle linkage 1985-89 . . . . lubricate **MO**
Transmission, automatic . . . . change fluid

W Valve clearance 1985-88 . . . . check/adjust
8-valve engine only

Body . . . . lubricate
Door stops, hinges, latches, locks, sunroof rails, convertible top mechanism

Headlights . . . . check/adjust
Shock absorbers . . . . check
Ventilation filter . . . . replace
9000 all, 900 w/o AC only

Wheel alignment . . . . check/adjust

1985-87, FIRST 48 MO/60 MI — 100 KM;
THEN EVERY 12 MO
1988-90, EVERY 60 MI — 100 KM
1991, FIRST 60 MO/60 MI — 100 KM;
THEN EVERY 12 MO
1992, FIRST 65 MI — 104 KM;
THEN EVERY 30 MI — 50 KM

W Crankcase ventilation . . . . inspect
Not required for Calif. warranty

W Evaporative emissions system . . . . inspect
Check canister, filler cap, lines, hoses & connections for leaks, damage & tightness
Not required for Calif. warranty

Ignition wires 1992 900 . . . . inspect

1985-91, EVERY 60 MI — 100 KM

W Charcoal canister . . . . replace
W Distributor cap & rotor . . . . replace
Not required for Calif. warranty

W Deceleration system 1985-88 check/adjust
W Idle speed 1985-88 . . . . check/adjust
W Ignition wires . . . . inspect
Check resistance of secondary wiring
Not required for Calif. warranty

Ignition timing . . . . check/adjust
1985-88 all, 1989 Turbo only, 1991 900 only

W Oxygen sensor . . . . replace
1988-89 all engines, 1985-87 16-valve engine only, lubricate threads with anti-sieze compound

1992, FIRST 65 MI — 104 KM

W Fuel filter . . . . replace
W Distributor cap & rotor 900 . . . . inspect
Drive belts . . . . replace

SEVERE SERVICE

Crankcase — Change oil & filter at half of specified interval

Spark plugs — Regap/replace every 15 mi (25 km)

Automatic transmission — Change fluid every 15 mi (25 km)

KEY TO LUBRICANTS

AF	DEXRON®-II Automatic Transmission Fluid
BL	Brake Lubricant Saab Part No. 30 08 612
CC	Motor Oil, API Service CC
CD	Motor Oil, API Service CD
EC	Ethylene Glycol Coolant Mix with water to desired freeze protection
FA	Automatic Transmission Fluid, Type F
GL-4	Gear Oil, API Service GL-4
GL-5	Gear Oil, API Service GL-5
HB	Hydraulic Brake Fluid, Extra Heavy Duty, DOT 4
MO	Motor Oil
PS	Power Steering Fluid Saab Part No. 30 09 800 or GM 1050017
SF	Motor Oil, API Service SF
SG	Motor Oil, API Service SG

CRANKCASE

1985-90 . . . . SF/CC, SF/CD*, SG*
1991-92 . . . . SF/CD, SG*
*Preferred

CAPACITY, Refill*:	Liters	Qt
2.0L SOHC	3.8	4.0
2.0L DOHC	4.0	4.2
Turbo◆	4.3	4.5
2.1L	4.0	4.2
2.3L	4.3	4.5

*Capacity shown includes filter
◆If oil cooler is drained add 0.5L (0.5 qt)
1985-91:
Above 0°F (–18°C) . . . . 10W-30†
Below 0°F (–18°C) 5W-30*
1992:
All temperatures 5W-30*,
5W-40*, 10W-30◆, 10W-40†

◆Preferred
†In extremely hot climates 10W-40, 15W-40, 15W-50 (only if API service classification **SF/CD**, **SG** is met)
*Must be fully or semisynthetic oil

TRANSMISSION, Automatic

900 3-speed . . . . **FA**
9000 4-speed . . . . **AF**
Does not include 3-speed final drive

CAPACITY, Total Fill†:	Liters	Qt
900 3-speed	8.0	8.5
9000 4-speed	8.2	8.6

†Total capacity including torque converter is shown, when servicing, use less fluid than specified

TRANSAXLE,

Manual . . . . 10W-30, 10W-40 SF, SG◆
CAPACITY, Refill:	Liters	Pt
All	2.5	5.3

◆Alternate 900 Series, 75W **GL-4/GL-5**

FINAL DRIVE, 900 Automatic

1985-91 . . . . 80W **GL-4**, **GL-5**
1992 . . 10W-30, 10W-40 **SF/CC**, **SF/CD**, **SG**
CAPACITY, Refill:	Liters	Pt
All	1.3	2.6

SERVICE AT TIME OR MILEAGE—WHICHEVER OCCURS FIRST

SNPM1   SNPM1

HOOD RELEASE: Inside

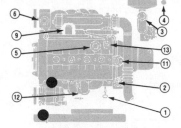

1991-92 1.9L SOHC
Code 9

1991-92 1.9L DOHC
Code 7

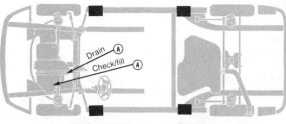

0 FITTINGS   0 PLUGS

● Cooling system drain   ■ Lift adapter position

KEY TO LUBRICANTS

AF   DEXRON®-IIE Automatic Transmission Fluid

EC   Saturn Part #21030365

HB   Hydraulic Brake Fluid DOT 3

LB   Chassis Grease, NLGI Category LB

MO   Motor Oil

PS   Power Steering Fluid
GM Part No. 9985010

SG   Motor Oil, API Service SG

① Crankcase dipstick
② Transmission dipstick
③ Brake fluid reservoir
④ Clutch fluid reservoir
⑤ Oil fill cap
⑥ Power steering reservoir
⑦ Air filter
⑧ Fuel filter
⑨ Oil filter
⑩ PCV filter
⑪ EGR valve
⑫ Oxygen sensor
⑬ PCV valve

Ⓐ Manual transmission/
  transaxle, drain & fill

CAUTION: On front wheel drive vehicles the center of gravity is further forward than on rear wheel drive vehicles. When removing major components from the rear of the vehicle while it is on a hoist, the vehicle must be supported in a manner to prevent it from tipping forward.

Perform the following scheduled maintenance service at the intervals indicated to keep the vehicle warranties in effect.

W   SERVICE TO MAINTAIN EMISSION WARRANTY

MI—MILES IN THOUSANDS
KM—KILOMETERS IN THOUSANDS

FIRST 6 MI—10 KM
Tires/wheels . . . . inspect/rotate
Then every 12 mi (20 km)

Transaxle,
  manual . . . . change filter & fluid

EVERY 6 MO/6 MI—10 KM
Axle boots . . . . inspect

Brake system . . . . inspect
Linings, hoses, lines, rotors, drums

W Crankcase . . . . change oil
Change filter every oil change

Exhaust system . . . . inspect

Parking brake . . . . inspect

Suspension . . . . Inspect
Bushings, ball joint seals

Brake master cylinder . . . . check level **HB**

Clutch master cylinder . . . . check level **HB**

Power steering . . . . check level

Shift linkage . . . . lubricate **LB**

Throttle cable linkage . . . . inspect

Transaxle . . . . check level

EVERY 12 MO
Chassis . . . . lubricate **MO**
Hood, door hinges, headlight doors, hood latch, rear folding seat, trunk lid hinge. Also, lubricate hood release pawl, door hold-open check link, sunroof track, and power passive restraint track with Lubriplate®70

EVERY 30 MI—50 KM
Transaxle, automatic . . . . change fluid

W Spark plugs . . . . replace

FIRST 30 MI—50 KM;
THEN EVERY 60 MI—100 KM
Automatic transaxle pressure
  filter . . . . replace

EVERY 24 MO/30 MI—50 KM
Cooling system hoses . . . . inspect

Drive belts . . . . inspect

EGR system . . . . inspect

Fuel system . . . . inspect
Tank, pipe/hose, cap

Vacuum lines & hoses . . . . inspect

EVERY 36 MO/30 MI—50 KM
W Air cleaner element . . . . replace

W Cooling system . . . . . . change coolant **EC**
Also replace radiator cap

EVERY 48 MO/60 MI—100 KM
Fuel filter . . . . replace

SEVERE SERVICE
W Crankcase—Change oil & oil filter every 3 mo/3 mi (5 km)

Tires—Inspect/rotate at 6 mi (10 km), then every 15 mi (25 km)

CRANKCASE . . . . **SG**
CAPACITY, Refill: Liters   Qt
All 3.8   4.0
Capacity shown is without filter. When replacing filter, additional oil may be needed
Above 40°F (4°C) 30*
Above 0°F (−18°C) 10W-30
All temperatures . . . . 5W-30* *
* Use only if other viscosities are not available
* * Preferred

TRANSAXLE, Automatic . . . . **AF**
CAPACITY, Initial Refill*:   Liters   Qt
All 3.6   3.8
* With the engine at operating temperature, shift transmission through all gears. Let engine slow idle in PARK for 3 minutes or more. Check fluid level and add fluid as needed

TRANSAXLE, Manual . . . . **AF**
CAPACITY, Refill: Liters   Pt
All 2.5   5.2

SUBARU
1983-92 All Models

HOOD RELEASE: Inside

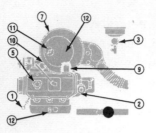

1987-92
3-cyl. 2V Justy

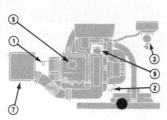

1990-92
3-cyl. FI Justy

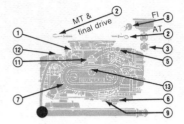

1983-87 4-cyl. OHV

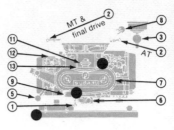

1985-88
4-cyl. 1.8L OHC 2V

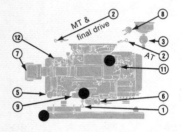

1985-92
4-cyl. 1.8L OHC FI

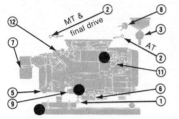

1984-90
4-cyl. 1.8L OHC Turbo

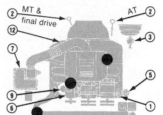

1990-92
4-cyl. 2.2L OHC
(Non-Turbo version shown)

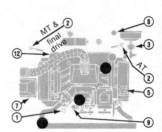

1988-89
6-cyl. 2.7L

0 FITTINGS
0 PLUGS

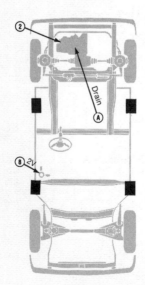

1987-92 Justy

0 FITTINGS
0 PLUGS

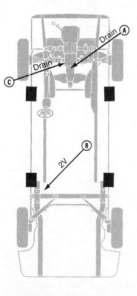

1983-92 2WD ex. Justy

0 FITTINGS
0 PLUGS

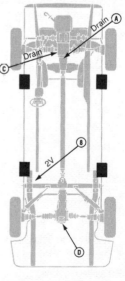

1983-92 4WD ex. Justy

① Crankcase dipstick
② Transmission dipstick
③ Brake fluid reservoir
④ Clutch fluid reservoir
⑤ Oil fill cap
⑥ Power steering reservoir
⑦ Air filter
⑧ Fuel filter
⑨ Oil filter
⑩ PCV filter
⑪ EGR valve
⑫ Oxygen sensor
⑬ PCV valve

Ⓐ Manual transmission/transaxle,
   drain & fill
Ⓑ Transfer case, NOT USED
Ⓒ Automatic transaxle final drive,
   drain & fill
Ⓓ Differential, drain & fill

CAUTION: On front wheel drive vehicles the center of gravity is further forward than on rear wheel drive vehicles. When removing major components from the rear of the vehicle while it is on a hoist, the vehicle must be supported in a manner to prevent it from tipping forward.

● Cooling system drain   ■ Lift adapter position

SERVICE AT TIME OR MILEAGE—WHICHEVER OCCURS FIRST

SUIPM2   SUIPM2

MI—MILES IN THOUSANDS
KM—KILOMETERS IN THOUSANDS

TURBO, EVERY 3 MO/3.75 MI—6 KM
Crankcase . . . . change oil
1984

Oil filter . . . . replace
1984 vehicles, initial service, then every other oil change

EVERY 7.5 MO/7.5 MI—12 KM
Crankcase . . . . change oil
Ex. 1984 Turbo

Oil filter . . . . replace
All ex. 1984 Turbo

Differential, front 1983 . . . . check level

Brake pads & discs . . . . inspect

Hill-holder system . . . . inspect/adjust
Ex. 1984

EVERY 15 MO/15 MI—24 KM
Brake system . . . . inspect
Check pads & discs, & operation of handbrake & servo system. Lubricate park brake lever of front disc caliper

Clutch & Hill-holder
   system 1984 . . . . inspect/adjust

Differential, front 1984 . . . . check level

Differential, rear . . . . check level

Suspension & steering . . . . inspect

Transaxle, manual . . . . check level

Cooling system . . . . inspect **EC**

Drive belts . . . . inspect/adjust
1983

Fuel filter . . . . replace
1983

Idle speed & mixture . . . . check/adjust
Speed only, 1983

Transmission, automatic . . . . . check level

Valve clearance . . . . inspect/adjust
Ex. 1983 AT equipped vehicles

Brake fluid . . . . replace **HB**
1983
Check system for leaks or damage

Wheel nuts . . . . torque
58-72 ft lb

Body . . . . lubricate **MO**
Hinges, door locks, hood & trunk lid, pedal assembly

EVERY 30 MO/30 MI—48 KM
Brake cylinder cups &
   dust seals . . . . replace

Brake drums & lining . . . . inspect

Brake fluid 1984 . . . . replace **HB**

Differential, front w/AT . . change lubricant

Differential, rear . . . . change lubricant

Transmission, automatic & transaxle,
   manual . . . . change lubricant

Wheel bearings
   front & rear . . . . inspect/repack **WB**
Ex. 1984

Wheel alignment . . . . check/adjust

Air & crankcase filter elements . . . replace
Air cleaner, PCV filter

Brake booster . . . . inspect
Vacuum hose & check valve

Choke mechanism . . . . lubricate

Cooling system . . . . . . change coolant **EC**

Drive belts 1984 . . . . inspect/replace

Evaporative fuel system
   hoses & connections . . . . inspect

Fuel filter 1984 . . . . replace

PCV valve . . . . replace

Spark plugs . . . . replace

Headlight aiming . . . . check/adjust

EVERY 60 MO/60 MI—96 KM
Wheel bearings 1984 . . . . repack **WB**

KEY TO LUBRICANTS

AF	DEXRON®-II Automatic Transmission Fluid
EC	Ethylene Glycol Coolant
GL-4	Gear Oil, API Service GL-4
GL-5	Gear Oil, API Service GL-5
GL-5★	Special Lubricant for Limited-Slip Differential
HB	Hydraulic Brake Fluid, DOT 3
MO	Motor Oil
PS	Power Steering Fluid Subaru Part No. K0209A0080
SF	Motor Oil, API Service SF
SG	Motor Oil, API Service SG
WB	Wheel Bearing Grease

CRANKCASE . . . . **SF**

CAPACITY, Refill:	Liters	Qt
1595cc	3.5	3.7
1781cc	4.0	4.2

Capacity shown is without filter. When replacing filter, additional oil may be needed
Above 90°F (32°C) 40
30° to 90°F (0° to 32°C) . . . 30, 20W-40, 20W-50
Below 90°F (32°C) . . . 10W-30, 10W-40, 10W-50
Below −10°F (−23°C) . . . . . . ex. Turbo 5W-30*
Below −13°F (−25°C) . . . . Turbo 5W-30*
*Not recommended for sustained high-speed driving

TRANSMISSION, Automatic . . . . **AF**
Front final drive serviced separately

CAPACITY, Initial Refill*:	Liters	Qt
All	2.5	2.6

*Add specified quantity. With engine at operating temperature, shift transmission through all gears. Check fluid level in PARK and add fluid as needed

TRANSAXLE, Manual **GL-5**
Above 30°F (0°C), 90; above −20°F (−30°C), 85W; below 90°F (32°C), 80W

CAPACITY, Refill:	Liters	Pt
1983 2WD	2.7	5.7
4WD	3.0	6.3
1984 2WD	2.5	5.2
4WD	2.8	6.0

FINAL DRIVE, Front **GL-5**
Above −10°F (−23°C), 90; −20° to 90°F (−30° to 32°C), 85W; below 60°F (16°C), 80W

CAPACITY, Refill:	Liters	Pt
All w/AT	1.2	2.5

DIFFERENTIAL, Rear (4WD) **GL-5**
Above 30°F (0°C), 90; above −20°F (−30°C), 85W; below 90°F (32°C), 80W

CAPACITY, Refill:	Liters	Pt
All models	0.8	1.7

SERVICE AT TIME OR MILEAGE—WHICHEVER OCCURS FIRST

SUIPM3   SUIPM3

Perform the following maintenance services at the intervals indicated to keep the vehicle warranties in effect.

W   SERVICE TO MAINTAIN EMISSION WARRANTY

MI—MILES IN THOUSANDS
KM—KILOMETERS IN THOUSANDS

EVERY 7.5 MO/7.5 MI—12 KM
W Crankcase . . . . change oil

W Oil filter 3-cyl. & Turbo . . . . replace
6-cyl. & 4-cyl. Non-Turbo, initial service, then every other oil change

Brake pads & discs . . . . inspect
Hatchback & Brat

Front & rear axle boots . . . . inspect
Hatchback & Brat

EVERY 15 MO/15 MI—24 KM
W Oil filter . . . . replace
4-cyl. Non-Turbo, 6-cyl.

Brake system . . . . inspect
Check pads & discs, & operation of handbrake & servo system. Lubricate park brake lever of front disc caliper

Clutch & Hill-holder
   system . . . . inspect/adjust

Suspension & steering . . . . inspect

W Cooling system . . . . inspect **EC**

Power steering . . . . check level
6-cyl. 2672cc **PS**, all others **AF**

W Valve clearance . . . . inspect/adjust
Justy & 1600cc engines only

Wheel nuts 1985-87 . . . . torque
58-72 ft lb

Body . . . . lubricate **MO**
Hinges, door locks, hood & trunk lid, pedal assembly

EVERY 30 MO/30 MI—48 KM
Brake drums & lining . . . . inspect

Brake fluid . . . . replace **HB**

Differential, front . . . . inspect

Differential, rear . . . . inspect

Transmission, automatic 2WD . . . . inspect

Transmission, automatic
   4WD . . . . change fluid

Wheel bearings front & rear
   1985-86 . . . . inspect/repack **WB**

W Air & crankcase filter elements . replace

Brake booster . . . . inspect
Vacuum hose & check valve

W Choke mechanism . . . . lubricate

W Cooling system . . . . change coolant **EC**

Drive belts . . . . inspect/replace

W Evaporative fuel system
      hoses & connections . . . . inspect

W Fuel filter . . . . replace

W Spark plugs . . . . replace

Headlight aiming . . . . check/adjust

EVERY 60 MO/60 MI—96 KM
W Canister . . . . replace
Federal 4WD ex. Turbo OHC

W Drive belts (inc. camshaft) . . . . . replace
OHC

W EGR . . . . inspect/clean
Federal 4WD ex. Turbo OHC

W Emissions hoses . . . . inspect
Federal 4WD ex. Turbo OHC

W Idle mixture . . . . inspect
Federal 4WD ex. Turbo OHC

W PCV valve . . . . replace
Federal 4WD ex. Turbo OHC

Wheel bearings front & rear
   1987-88 . . . . inspect/repack **WB**

SEVERE SERVICE
Crankcase—Change oil every 3 mo/3.75 mi (6 km), change filter at every other oil change

Brake fluid—Replace every 15 mo/15 mi (24 km)

Brake linings—Inspect every 7.5 mo/7.5 mi (12 km)

Front & rear axle boots—Inspect every 7.5 mo/7.5 mi (12 km)

Fuel filter—Replace as needed, inspect evaporative system hoses and connections

Steering & suspension—Inspect every 7.5 mo/7.5 mi (12 km)

Transmission, automatic—Change fluid every 15 mi (24 km)

Transmission, manual/Differentials, all—Change fluid every 30 mi (48 km)

KEY TO LUBRICANTS
See other Subaru chart

CRANKCASE . . . . SF, SG

CAPACITY, Refill*:	Liters	Qt
3-cyl. 1189cc	2.8	3.0
4-cyl. 1595cc	3.5	3.7
4-cyl. 1781cc	4.0	4.2
4-cyl. 2212cc	4.5	4.8
6-cyl. 2672cc	5.0	5.3
6-cyl. 3318cc	6.0	6.3

*Capacity shown is without filter. When replacing filter, additional oil may be needed

1985-87:
Above 90°F (32°C) 40
32° to 90°F (0° to 32°C) . . . 30, 20W-40, 20W-50
Below 90°F (32°C) . . . 10W-30, 10W-40, 10W-50
Below −10°F (−23°C) . . . . ex. Turbo 5W-30*
Below −13°F (−25°C) . . . . Turbo 5W-30*

1988-92:
Warm climate & H.D. applications 30, 40, 10W-50, 20W-40, 20W-50
−5° to 95°F (−21° to 35°C) 10W-30, 10W-40
Below 32°F (0°C) 5W-30*

*Not recommended for sustained high-speed driving

TRANSMISSION, Automatic . . . . AF
Does not include front differential

CAPACITY, Initial Refill*:	Liters	Qt
All ex. ECVT	2.5	2.6
ECVT 2WD	1.8	1.9
4WD	1.9	2.0

*Add specified quantity. With engine at operating temperature, shift transmission through all gears. Check fluid level in PARK and add fluid as needed

TRANSAXLE, Manual
Justy 75W-90 **GL4**
All others 75W-90 **GL-5**
Above 30°F (0°C), 90; above −20°F (−30°C), 85W; below 90°F (32°C), 80W

CAPACITY, Refill:	Liters	Pt
1985-89 Sedan & Wagon:		
2WD	2.6	5.4
4WD	3.3	7.0
Justy:		
1987-89 2WD	2.3	4.8
4WD	3.3	7.0
1990-92 2WD	2.1	4.4
4WD	2.8	6.0
XT Coupe:		
4-cyl. 2WD	2.6	5.4
4-cyl. 4WD	3.3	7.0
6-cyl. 4WD	3.5	7.4
Brat & Hatchback:		
2WD	2.5	5.2
4WD	2.8	6.0
Legacy:		
2WD	3.3	7.0
4WD	3.5	7.4
Loyale:		
2WD	2.6	5.4
4WD	3.3	7.0

DIFFERENTIAL, Front w/AT
1985-86 . . . . 75W-90 **GL-5**
1987-92 . . . . 80W-90 **GL-5**
Above 30°F (0°C), 90; above −20°F (−30°C), 85W; below 90°F (32°C), 80W

CAPACITY, Refill:	Liters	Pt
Ex. XT-Coupe	1.2	2.5
XT-Coupe	1.4	3.0

DIFFERENTIAL, Rear
Standard 75W-90 **GL-5**
Above 30°F (0°C), 90; above −20°F (−30°C), 85W; below 90°F (32°C), 80W

Limited-Slip . . . . 80W-90 **GL-5★**

CAPACITY, Refill:	Liters	Pt
All models	0.8	1.7

SERVICE LOCATIONS — ENGINE AND CHASSIS

TAIDP-1

TAIDP-1

HOOD RELEASE: Inside

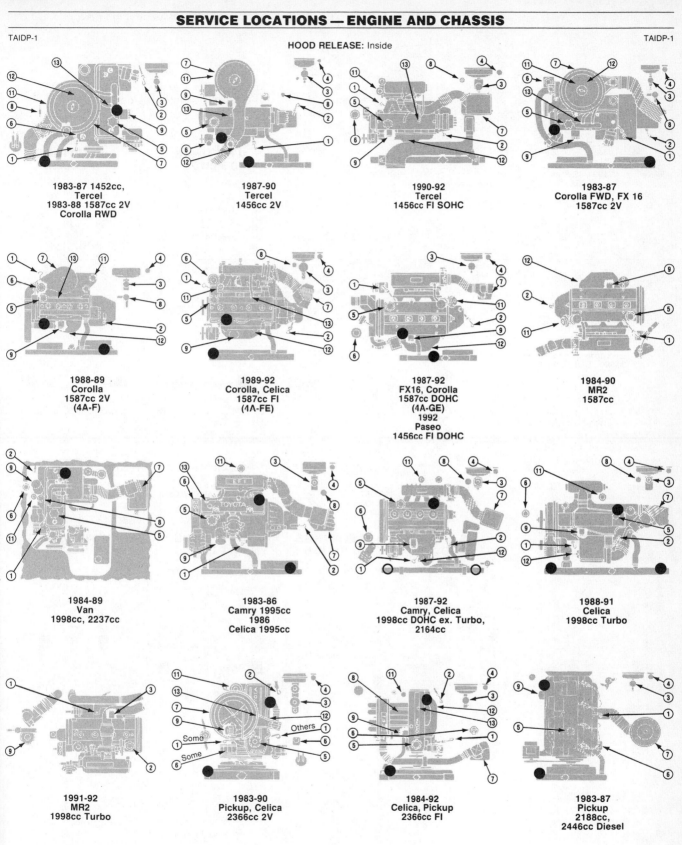

1983-87 1452cc,
Tercel
1983-88 1587cc 2V
Corolla RWD

1987-90
Tercel
1456cc 2V

1990-92
Tercel
1456cc FI SOHC

1983-87
Corolla FWD, FX 16
1587cc 2V

1988-89
Corolla
1587cc 2V
(4A-F)

1989-92
Corolla, Celica
1587cc FI
(4A-FE)

1987-92
FX16, Corolla
1587cc DOHC
(4A-GE)
1992
Paseo
1456cc FI DOHC

1984-90
MR2
1587cc

1984-89
Van
1998cc, 2237cc

1983-86
Camry 1995cc
1986
Celica 1995cc

1987-92
Camry, Celica
1998cc DOHC ex. Turbo,
2164cc

1988-91
Celica
1998cc Turbo

1991-92
MR2
1998cc Turbo

1983-90
Pickup, Celica
2366cc 2V

1984-92
Celica, Pickup
2366cc FI

1983-87
Pickup
2188cc,
2446cc Diesel

① Crankcase dipstick
② Transmission dipstick
③ Brake fluid reservoir
④ Clutch fluid reservoir
⑤ Oil fill cap

⑥ Power steering reservoir
⑦ Air filter
⑧ Fuel filter
⑨ Oil filter

⑩ PCV filter
⑪ EGR valve
⑫ Oxygen sensor
⑬ PCV valve

● Cooling system drain
○ Cooling system drain,
   some models

SERVICE LOCATIONS — ENGINE AND CHASSIS

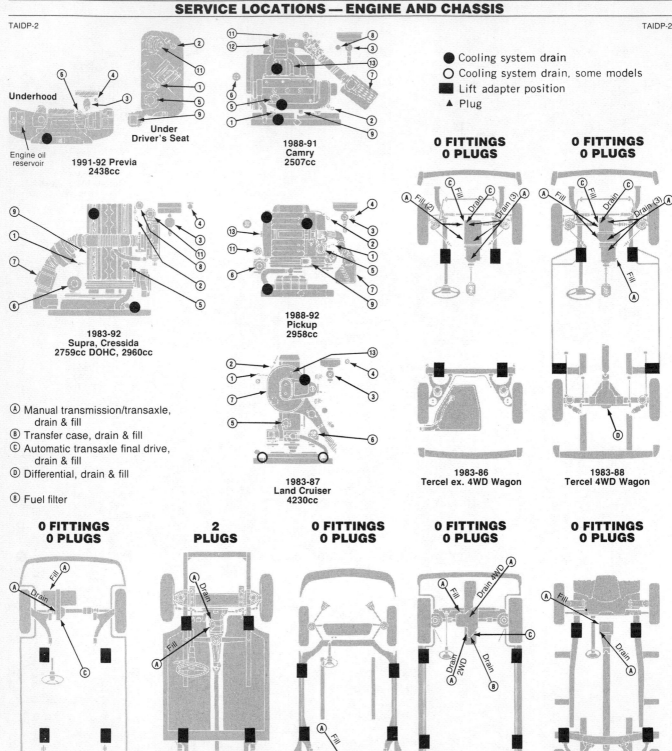

● Cooling system drain
○ Cooling system drain, some models
■ Lift adapter position
▲ Plug

Underhood

Engine oil reservoir

1991-92 Previa
2438cc

Under Driver's Seat

1988-91 Camry 2507cc

0 FITTINGS 0 PLUGS

0 FITTINGS 0 PLUGS

1983-92 Supra, Cressida 2759cc DOHC, 2960cc

1988-92 Pickup 2958cc

Ⓐ Manual transmission/transaxle, drain & fill
Ⓑ Transfer case, drain & fill
Ⓒ Automatic transaxle final drive, drain & fill
Ⓓ Differential, drain & fill

⑧ Fuel filter

1983-87 Land Cruiser 4230cc

1983-86 Tercel ex. 4WD Wagon

1983-88 Tercel 4WD Wagon

0 FITTINGS 0 PLUGS

2 PLUGS

0 FITTINGS 0 PLUGS

0 FITTINGS 0 PLUGS

0 FITTINGS 0 PLUGS

1987-92 Tercel ex. Wagon, Paseo

1983-87 Corolla RWD

1984-92 MR2

Camry, Corolla FWD, FX16 1987-92 Tercel ex. 4WD Wagon

1983-86 early Supra

CAUTION: On front wheel drive vehicles the center of gravity is further forward than on rear wheel drive vehicles. When removing major components from the rear of the vehicle while it is on a hoist, the vehicle must be supported in a manner to prevent it from tipping forward.

SERVICE LOCATIONS — ENGINE AND CHASSIS

TAIDP-3   TAIDP-3

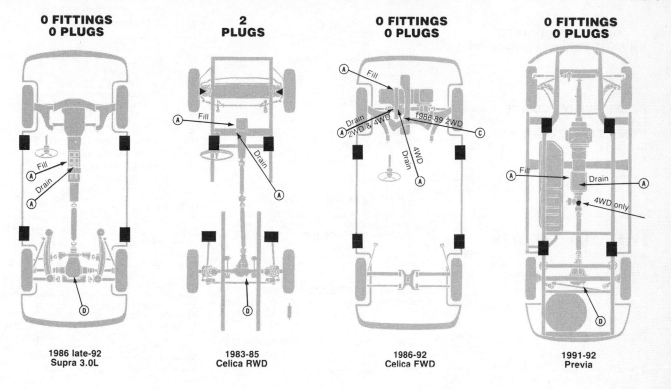

0 FITTINGS 0 PLUGS

1986 late-92
Supra 3.0L

2 PLUGS

1983-85
Celica RWD

0 FITTINGS 0 PLUGS

1986-92
Celica FWD

0 FITTINGS 0 PLUGS

1991-92
Previa

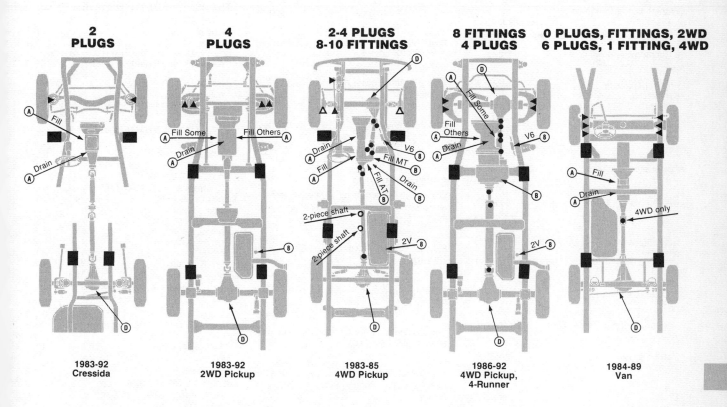

2 PLUGS

1983-92
Cressida

4 PLUGS

1983-92
2WD Pickup

2-4 PLUGS 8-10 FITTINGS

1983-85
4WD Pickup

8 FITTINGS 4 PLUGS

1986-92
4WD Pickup,
4-Runner

0 PLUGS, FITTINGS, 2WD 6 PLUGS, 1 FITTING, 4WD

1984-89
Van

CAUTION: On front wheel drive vehicles the center of gravity is further forward than on rear wheel drive vehicles. When removing major components from the rear of the vehicle while it is on a hoist, the vehicle must be supported in a manner to prevent it from tipping forward.

■ Lift adapter position   ▲ Plug   △ Plug, some models   ● Fitting   ○ Fitting, some models

TOYOTA
1983 All Models Except Land Cruiser, Pickup

MI—MILES IN THOUSANDS
KM—KILOMETERS IN THOUSANDS

DIESEL, EVERY 3 MO/3.75 MI—6 KM
GASOLINE,
EVERY 8 MO/10 MI—16 KM
Crankcase .... change oil

Oil filter .... replace

EVERY 12 MO/15 MI—24 KM
Brake system .... check
Fluid level **HB**, ex. Pickup, drums, linings, booster, parking brake, lines, pipes & hoses

Differential .... check level

Drive shaft boots FWD .... inspect

Transfer case .... check level

Transmission, transaxle,
   manual .... check level

Exhaust system .... inspect

Front suspension .... inspect
Ball joints, dust covers

Idle speeds .... check/adjust
One time service on vehicles with computer control

Power steering fluid ...... check level **AF**

Spark plugs .... replace
3A eng. only

Steering gear .... check level 90 **GL-4**
Check linkage & free play

Transmission, transaxle,
   automatic .... check level

Vacuum pump oil hose Diesel .... inspect

Valve clearance .... adjust
Except models with hydraulic lifters

Body .... inspect
Check nuts & bolts

EVERY 24 MO/30 MI—48 KM
Air cleaner element .... replace

Choke system .... inspect

Drive belts .... inspect
Ex. V-ribbed

Fuel lines & hoses .... inspect

Spark plugs .... replace
Ex. 3A eng. & platinum tipped

EVERY 36 MO/45 MI—72 KM
Front wheel bearings ... clean/repack **LM**
Torque to 19-23 ft lb. Back off & retighten finger tight. Service rear wheel bearings on cars with FWD

EVERY 48 MO/60 MI—96 KM
Charcoal canister .... inspect
Check fuel evaporative system, hoses & connections

Cooling system ...... change coolant **EC**

Drive belts, V-ribbed .... inspect

Fuel filter & cap gasket .... replace

Spark plugs .... replace
Platinum tipped only

Timing & compressor belts
   Diesel .... replace

Water sedimenter .... inspect

SEVERE SERVICE
Crankcase—Change oil & filter: Gasoline, every 3 mo/3.75 mi (6 km); Diesel, every 1.5 mo/1.875 mi (3 km)

Exhaust system—Inspect every 6 mo/7.5 mi (12 km)

Steering components—Inspect every 3 mo/3.75 mi (6 km)

Suspension & brake components—Inspect every 6 mo/7.5 mi (12 km)

Transmission, transaxle, transfer case & differential fluid—Change every 12 mo/15 mi (24 km)

Air cleaner element—Clean every 3 mo/3.75 mi (6 km)

Ignition wiring, distributor cap—Inspect every 12 mo/15 mi (24 km)

KEY TO LUBRICANTS
AF	DEXRON®-II Automatic Transmission Fluid
CC	Motor Oil, API Service CC
CD	Motor Oil, API Service CD
CE	Motor Oil, API Service CE
EC	Ethylene Glycol Coolant
	Maintain coolant protection to at least −34°F (−37°C)
FA	Automatic Transmission Fluid, Type F
GL-4	Gear Oil, API Service GL-4
GL-5	Gear Oil, API Service GL-5
HB	Hydraulic Brake Fluid, DOT 3
LM	Lithium Grease, with Moly
SE	Motor Oil, API Service SE
SF	Motor Oil, API Service SF
SG	Motor Oil, API Service SG

CRANKCASE
Gasoline engine .... **SG**
Diesel engine .... **SG/CD, SG/CE**

CAPACITY, Refill:	Liters	Qt
Camry	3.6	3.8
Corona, Celica	3.8	4.0
Cressida, Supra	4.7	4.9
Tercel, Corolla, Starlet ..	3.0	3.2

Capacity shown is without filter. When replacing filter, additional oil may be needed

Gasoline engines
Above 10°F (−12°C) 20W-40, 20W-50
Above −10°F (−23°C) . 10W-30, 10W-40, 10W-50
Below 50°F (10°C) 5W-30
Diesel engines
Above 50°F (10°C) 30
Below 85°F (30°C) 10W-30

TRANSMISSION/TRANSAXLE, Automatic
3-speed .... **AF**
4-speed .... **FA**
Differential is serviced separately in Camry and Tercel

CAPACITY, Initial Refill*:	Liters	Qt
Tercel	2.2	2.3
Others	2.4	2.5

*With the engine at operating temperature, shift transmission through all gears. Check fluid level in PARK and add fluid as needed

TRANSMISSION/TRANSAXLE, Manual
Camry .... **AF**
Tercel **GL-5**
Above 0°F (−18°C), 80W-90, 90; below 0°F (−18°C), 80, 80W-90
All others ... 75W-90, 80W-90 **GL-4, GL-5**

CAPACITY, Refill:	Liters	Pt
Celica, Supra	2.4	5.2
Corolla RWD	1.7	3.6
Corona, Camry	2.6	5.6
Cressida, Starlet	2.4	5.2
Tercel	3.3	7.0
4 × 4 wagon	3.9	8.2
Van	2.3	5.0

FINAL DRIVE, FWD w/AT
Camry .... **AF**
Tercel **GL-5**
Above 0°F (−18°C), 90; below 0°F (−18°C), 80W, 80W-90

CAPACITY, Refill:	Liters	Pt
Camry	2.0	4.2
Tercel	1.0	2.1

DIFFERENTIAL, Rear 90 **GL-5**
Below −10°F (−23°C), 80W, 80W-90

CAPACITY, Refill:	Liters	Pt
Cressida	1.2	2.6
Corona, Celica ex. Supra		
unitized type	1.2	2.6
Others	1.3	2.8
Supra	1.2	2.6
Corolla, Starlet	1.0	2.1
Tercel 4 × 4 wagon	1.0	2.1

SERVICE AT TIME OR MILEAGE—WHICHEVER OCCURS FIRST

TAIPM5 · TAIPM5

MI—MILES IN THOUSANDS
KM—KILOMETERS IN THOUSANDS

**1984 DIESEL ENGINES,
EVERY 4 MO/5 MI—8 KM
1985 DIESEL ENGINES,
EVERY 6 MO/5 MI—8 KM
GASOLINE,
EVERY 8 MO/10 MI—16 KM**

Crankcase . . . . change oil

Oil filter . . . . replace

**1984, EVERY 12 MO/15 MI—24 KM
1985, EVERY 18 MO/15 MI—24 KM**

Brake system . . . . check
Fluid level HB, drums, linings, booster, parking brake,
lines, pipes & hoses

Differential . . . . check level

Drive shaft boots FWD . . . . inspect

Transfer case . . . . check level

Transmission, transaxle,
manual . . . . check level

Front suspension . . . . inspect
Ball joints, dust covers

Idle speeds ex. EFI . . . . check/adjust
One time service on vehicles with 3A-C eng.

Power steering fluid . . . . . . check level AF

Spark plugs . . . . replace
3A eng. only

Steering gear . . . . check level 90 GL-4
Check linkage & free play

Transmission, transaxle,
automatic . . . . check level

Vacuum pump oil hose Diesel . . . . inspect

Valve clearance . . . . adjust
Except models with hydraulic lifters

**1984, EVERY 24 MO/30 MI—48 KM
1985, EVERY 36 MO/30 MI—48 KM**

Exhaust system . . . . inspect

Air cleaner element . . . . replace

Choke system . . . . inspect

Drive belts . . . . inspect
Except V-ribbed. Replace 1.8L diesel belts

Fuel lines & hoses . . . . inspect

Spark plugs . . . . replace
Except platinum tipped & 3A eng.

Body . . . . inspect
Check nuts & bolts

**1984, EVERY 36 MO/45 MI—72 KM
1985, EVERY 48 MO/40 MI—64 KM**

Front wheel bearings . . . clean/repack LM
Torque to 19-23 ft lb. Back off & retighten finger tight.
Service rear wheel bearings on cars with FWD.

Limited-Slip differential . . . . change oil

**1984, EVERY 48 MO/60 MI—96 KM
1985, EVERY 72 MO/60 MI—96 KM**

Charcoal canister . . . . inspect
Check fuel evaporative system, hoses & connections

Cooling system . . . . . . change coolant EC
Replace coolant every 24 mo/30 mi (48 km) thereafter

Drive belts, V-ribbed . . . . inspect

Fuel filter & cap gasket . . . . replace

Oxygen sensor . . . . replace
1985 FI Federal Pickup only

Spark plugs . . . . replace
Platinum tipped only

Timing & compressor belts
Diesel . . . . replace

Vacuum pump oil hose Diesel . . . . replace

Water sedimenter . . . . inspect

SEVERE SERVICE

Crankcase—Change oil & filter: Gasoline,
1984, every 3 mo/3.75 mi (6 km); 1985, every 6 mo/5 mi (8 km); Diesel, 1984, every 1.5 mo/1.875 mi (3 km); 1985, every 3 mo/2.5 mi (4 km)

Exhaust system—Inspect 1984, every 6 mo/7.5 mi (12 km); 1985, every 18 mo/15 mi (24 km)

Suspension steering & brake components—Inspect 1984, every 6 mo/7.5 mi (12 km); 1985, every 12 mo/10 mi (16 km)

Transmission, transaxle, transfer case & differential fluid—Change 1984, every 12 mo/15 mi (24 km); 1985 Tercel, Corolla, every 18 mo/15 mi (24 km); Others, every 24 mo/20 mi (32 km)

Air cleaner element—Clean 1984, every 3 mo/3.75 mi (6 km). 1985, inspect every 6 mo/5 mi (8 km)

Ignition wiring, distributor cap—Inspect 1984, every 12 mo/15 mi (24 km); 1985, every spring

KEY TO LUBRICANTS
See other Toyota charts

CRANKCASE
Gasoline engine . . . . SG
Diesel engine . . . . SG/CD, SG/CE

CAPACITY, Refill:	Liters	Qt
Supra	4.7	4.9
MR2	3.1	3.3
Camry:		
Gasoline	3.6	3.8
Turbo Diesel	3.8	4.0
Celica	3.8	4.0
Cressida	4.7	4.9
Starlet, Tercel	3.0	3.2
Corolla gasoline ex. FI . .	3.0	3.2
FI	3.4	3.6
Diesel	3.8	4.0

Capacity shown is without filter. When replacing filter, additional oil may be needed

Gasoline engines
Above 10°F (–12°C) 20W-40, 20W-50
Above –10°F (–23°C) 10W-30, 10W-40,
    10W-50
Below 50°F (10°C) 5W-30
Diesel engines
Above 50°F (10°C) 30
Above 10°F (–12°C) . . 15W-40, 20W-40, 20W-50
Above –10°F (–23°C) 10W-40, 10W-50
–10° to 85°F (–23° to 29°C) 10W-30
Below 32°F (0°C) 5W-30*
*Not recommended for continuous high speed driving

TRANSMISSION/TRANSAXLE,
   Automatic . . . . AF
Differential is served separately in Camry, Tercel, MR2,
and Corolla FWD

CAPACITY, Initial Refill*:	Liters	Qt
Tercel	2.2	2.3
4 × 4	4.2	4.4
Corolla FWD	3.1	3.3
Others	2.4	2.5

*With the engine at operating temperature, shift transmission through all gears. Check fluid level in PARK and add fluid as needed

TRANSMISSION/TRANSAXLE, Manual
Camry . . . . AF
Tercel GL-5
Above 0°F (–18°C), 90; below 0°F (–18°C), 80, 80W-90
All others . . . 75W-90, 80W-90 GL-4, GL-5

CAPACITY, Refill:	Liters	Pt
Celica, Supra	2.4	5.2
Corolla: RWD	1.7	3.6
FWD	2.6	5.6
Camry, MR2	2.6	5.6
Cressida, Starlet	2.4	5.2
Tercel	3.3	7.0
4 × 4 wagon	3.9	8.2

FINAL DRIVE, FWD w/AT
Camry, FWD Corolla, MR2 . . . . AF
Tercel GL-5
Above 0°F (–18°C), 90; below 0°F (–18°C), 80W, 80W-90

CAPACITY, Refill:	Liters	Pt
Camry	2.0	4.2
Corolla, MR2	1.4	3.0
Tercel	1.0	2.1

DIFFERENTIAL, Rear
Limited-Slip . . . . 90 GL-5 ★
Others 90 GL-5
Below –10°F (–23°C), 80W, 80W-90

CAPACITY, Refill:	Liters	Pt
Celica ex. Supra		
unitized type	1.2	2.6
Others	1.3	2.8
Supra, Cressida	1.2	2.6
Corolla RWD, Starlet . . .	1.0	2.1

SERVICE AT TIME OR MILEAGE—WHICHEVER OCCURS FIRST

TAIPM6

Perform the following maintenance services at the intervals indicated to keep the vehicle warranties in effect.

TAIPM6

W SERVICE TO MAINTAIN EMISSION WARRANTY

MI — MILES IN THOUSANDS
KM — KILOMETERS IN THOUSANDS

DIESEL & TURBO ENGINES,
EVERY 6 MO/5 MI — 8 KM
GASOLINE,
EVERY 12 MO/10 MI — 16 KM

W Crankcase . . . . change oil

W Oil filter . . . . replace
Supra Turbo, every other oil change

3A ENG.,
EVERY 18 MO/15 MI — 24 KM
ALL OTHERS,
EVERY 24 MO/20 MI — 32 KM

Brake system . . . . check
Fluid level **HB** disc pads & rotors, drums, linings, booster, parking brake, lines, pipes & hoses

Differential . . . . check level

Drive shaft boots FWD . . . . inspect

Transfer case . . . . check level

Transmission, transaxle,
    manual . . . . check level

Front suspension . . . . inspect
Ball joints, dust covers

Idle speed 3A eng. . . . . check/adjust
Adjust throttle positioner

Power steering fluid . . . . . . check level **AF**

W Spark plugs . . . . replace
3A eng. only

Steering gear . . . . check level 90 **GL-4**
Check linkage & free play

Transmission, transaxle,
    automatic . . . . check level

Vacuum pump oil hose Diesel . . . . inspect

W Valve clearance 3A eng. . . . . adjust

Body . . . . inspect
Torque nuts & bolts

EVERY 36 MO/30 MI — 48 KM

Exhaust system . . . . inspect

W Air cleaner element . . . . replace

Drive belts . . . . inspect
Ex. V-ribbed. Replace 1.8L Diesel belts

Fuel lines & hoses . . . . inspect

W Idle speeds ex. 3A eng. . . . . check/adjust
Adjust throttle positioner on carburetted engines

W Spark plugs . . . . replace
Ex. platinum tipped & 3A eng.

W Valve clearance . . . . adjust
Tercel, Corolla

ALL EX. 3A ENG.,
EVERY 48 MO/40 MI — 64 KM
3A ENG.,
EVERY 54 MO/45 MI — 72 KM

Front wheel bearings . . . clean/repack **LM**
Torque to 19-23 ft lb. Back off & retighten finger tight. Service rear wheel bearings on cars with FWD

Limited-Slip differential . . . . change oil

EVERY 72 MO/60 MI — 96 KM

Charcoal canister . . . . inspect
Check fuel evaporative system, hoses & connections

Cooling system . . . . . . change coolant **EC**
Replace coolant every 24 mo/30 mi (48 km) thereafter

Drive belts, V-ribbed . . . . inspect
Initial service, inspect every 12 mo/10 mi (16 km) thereafter

Fuel cap gasket . . . . replace

Oxygen sensor . . . . replace
All engines w/FI only

Spark plugs . . . . replace
Platinum tipped only

Timing & compressor belts
    Diesel . . . . replace

Vacuum pump oil hose Diesel . . . . replace

W Valve clearance . . . . adjust
MR2, Celica only
Except models with hydraulic lifters

Water sedimenter . . . . inspect

SEVERE SERVICE

W Crankcase — Change oil & filter: Gasoline, every 6 mo/5 mi (8 km); Diesel, every 3 mo/2.5 mi (4 km)

Exhaust system — Inspect every 18 mo/15 mi (24 km)

Suspension steering & brake components — Inspect every 12 mo/10 mi (16 km)

Transmission, transaxle, transfer case & differential fluid — Change every 24 mo/20 mi (32 km)

W Air cleaner element — Inspect every 6 mo/5 mi (8 km)

Timing belt — Replace every 60 mi (96 km)

KEY TO LUBRICANTS
See other Toyota charts

CRANKCASE

Gasoline engine . . . . **SG**
Diesel engine . . . . **SG/CD, SG/CE**

CAPACITY, Refill:	Liters	Qt
Supra, Cressida 2.8L	4.6	4.9
Cressida 3.0L	4.1	4.3
Supra 3.0L	3.7	3.9
Turbo	3.9	4.1
Camry: Gasoline	3.7	3.9
Turbo Diesel	3.8	4.0
Celica	3.7	3.9
4WD	3.3	3.6
Tercel, MR2	3.0	3.2
Corolla, FX: 2V	3.0	3.2
FI	3.4	3.6

Capacity shown is without filter. When replacing filter, additional oil may be needed

Gasoline engines
Above 10°F (−12°C) . . 15W-40, 20W-40, 20W-50
Above −10°F (−23°C) . 10W-30, 10W-40, 10W-50
Below 50°F (10°C) 5W-30

Diesel engines
Above 50°F (10°C) 30
Above 10°F (−12°C) . . 15W-40, 20W-40, 20W-50
−10° to 100°F (−23° to 38°C) 10W-30
Below 32°F (0°C) 5W-30

TRANSMISSION/TRANSAXLE, Automatic

Corolla 4WD . . . . **SLF***
*ATF Type T, Part No. 08886-00405
All others . . . . **AF**
Differential is serviced separately in 2WD Camry & Celica, FWD Corolla & FX 3-speed, and Tercel

CAPACITY, Initial Refill*:	Liters	Qt
Tercel	2.2	2.3
4WD	4.2	4.4
Corolla FWD, FX	2.3	2.4
w/OD	3.1	3.3
MR2	3.1	3.3
Supra 3.0L	1.6	1.7
1987-88 Cressida	1.6	1.7
Others	2.5	2.6

*With the engine at operating temperature, shift transmission through all gears. Check fluid level in PARK and add fluid as needed

TRANSMISSION/TRANSAXLE, Manual

Camry, Celica 2WD . . . . **AF**
Camry, Celica, Corolla
    4WD 75W-90, 80W-90 **GL-5**
May also use 90 above 0°F (−18°C); or 80W below 0°F (−18°C)
MR2 Supercharged,
    Supra Turbo 75W-90 **GL-5**
All others . . . 75W-90, 80W-90 **GL-4, GL-5**

CAPACITY, Refill:	Liters	Pt
Supra, Cressida	2.4	5.2
Turbo	3.0	6.4
MR2	2.6	5.6
Supercharged	4.2	8.8
Corolla: RWD	1.7	3.6
FWD	2.6	5.6
4WD	5.0	10.6
Camry, Celica	2.6	5.6
4WD	5.0	10.6
FX	2.6	5.6
Tercel	2.4	5.0
2WD wagon	3.4	7.2
4WD wagon	3.9	8.2

FWD, includes front differential and 4WD transfer case

TRANSFER CASE,
    4WD W/AT 75W-90, 80W-90 **GL-5**
May also use 90 above 0°F (−18°C); or 80W below 0°F (−18°C)

CAPACITY, Refill:	Liters	Pt
Corolla	0.8	1.6
Camry	0.7	1.4
Tercel 4WD wagon	1.0	2.1

FINAL DRIVE, FWD w/AT

Tercel 4WD wagon **GL-5**
Above 0°F (−18°C), 90; below 0°F (−18°C), 80W, 80W-90
Others . . . . **AF**
Corolla, FX w/3-speed; Camry & Celica 2WD w/AT, Tercel

CAPACITY, Refill:	Liters	Pt
Celica, Camry	1.6	3.4
Corolla, FX	1.4	3.0
Tercel ex. wagon	1.4	3.0

DIFFERENTIAL, Rear

Limited-Slip . . . . **GL-5★**
Standard **GL-5**
Above 0°F (−18°C), 90; below 0°F (−18°C), 80W, 80W-90

CAPACITY, Refill:	Liters	Pt
Celica, Camry 4WD rear . .	1.1	2.4
Supra, Cressida	1.2	2.6
Corolla RWD	1.0	2.1
w/Limited-Slip	1.3	2.8
Tercel wagon	1.0	2.1

SERVICE AT TIME OR MILEAGE—WHICHEVER OCCURS FIRST

TAIPM10   TAIPM10

Perform the following maintenance services at the intervals indicated to keep the vehicle warranties in effect.

W SERVICE TO MAINTAIN EMISSION WARRANTY

MI — MILES IN THOUSANDS
KM — KILOMETERS IN THOUSANDS

1989, AT FIRST 12 MO/10 MI — 16 KM
1990-92,
AT FIRST 12 MO/7.5 MI — 12 KM
Idle speed .... adjust
3E, 4A-F engines only

TURBO ENGINES,
EVERY 6 MO/5 MI — 8 KM
OTHERS,
1989, EVERY 12 MO/10 MI — 16 KM
1990-92,
EVERY 12 MO/7.5 MI — 12 KM
W Crankcase .... change oil
W Oil filter .... replace
Turbo, every other oil change

1989, EVERY 24 MO/20 MI — 32 KM
1990-92,
EVERY 24 MO/15 MI — 24 KM
Brake system .... check
Fluid level **HB**, disc pads & rotors, drums, linings, booster, parking brake, lines, pipes & hoses

Front suspension .... inspect
Ball joints, dust covers

Differential .... check level

Drive shaft boots FWD .... inspect

Transfer case .... check level

Transmission, transaxle, manual .... check level

Steering .... inspect
Check linkage & free play

Idle speed 1991-92 .... check/adjust

Power steering fluid:
1991-92 MR2 ...... check level **SLF***
All others .... check level **AF**
* Toyota Part No. 08886-01206

Transmission, transaxle, automatic .... check level

Body .... inspect
Torque nuts & bolts

EVERY 36 MO/30 MI — 48 KM
Differential, Limited-Slip . change lubricant

Exhaust system .... inspect

W Air cleaner element .... replace

Drive belts .... inspect
Except V-ribbed

Fuel lines & hoses .... inspect

Idle speed 1989 .... check/adjust
Adjust throttle positioner on carburetted engines

W Spark plugs .... replace
Except platinum tipped

Supercharger MR2 .... check level
Use Toyota Supercharger Oil, Part No. 08885-80108

W Valve clearance .... adjust
Tercel

1989, EVERY 48 MO/40 MI — 64 KM
1990-92,
EVERY 48 MO/30 MI — 48 KM
Wheel bearings .... clean/repack **LM**
Torque to 19-23 ft lb. Back off & retighten finger tight. Service rear wheel bearings on cars with FWD

Limited-Slip differential .... change oil

FIRST 36 MO/45 MI — 72 KM;
THEN EVERY 24 MO/30 MI — 48 KM
Cooling system,
1990-92 .... change coolant **EC**

EVERY 72 MO/60 MI — 96 KM
Charcoal canister .... inspect
Check fuel evaporative system, hoses & connections

Cooling system,
1989 .... change coolant **EC**
Replace coolant every 24 mo/30 mi (48 km) thereafter

Drive belts, V-ribbed .... inspect
Initial service, inspect every: 1989, 12 mo/10 mi (16 km); 1990-92, 12 mo/7.5 mi (12 km) thereafter

Fuel cap gasket .... replace

Spark plugs .... replace
Platinum tipped only

W Valve clearance .... adjust
All ex. Tercel
Except models with hydraulic lifters

EVERY 120 MO
Air bag system .... inspect
Initial service, then every 24 mo

SEVERE SERVICE
W Crankcase — Change oil & filter every: Turbo, 3 mo/2.5 mi (4 km); Others, 1989, 6 mo/5 mi (8 km); 1990-92, 6 mo/3.75 mi (6 km)

Exhaust system — Inspect every 18 mo/15 mi (24 km)

Suspension steering & brake components — Inspect every 12 mo/10 mi (16 km)

Transmission, transaxle, transfer case & differential — Change fluid or lubricant every: 1989, 24 mo/20 mi (32 km); 1990-92, 24 mo/15 mi (24 km)

W Air cleaner element — Inspect every: 1989, 6 mo/5 mi (8 km); 1991-92, 6 mo/3.75 mi (6 km)

Timing belt — Replace every 60 mi (96 km)

KEY TO LUBRICANTS
See other Toyota charts

CRANKCASE .... **SG**

CAPACITY, Refill:	Liters	Qt
Cressida, Supra	4.1	4.3
Turbo	4.3	4.5
Camry	3.7	3.9
3.0L	4.1	4.3
Celica: 1.6L	3.0	3.2
2.0L, 2.2L	3.7	3.9
Turbo: 1989	3.3	3.5
1990-92	3.6	3.8
Tercel	2.9	3.1
Corolla, 4AF, FE	3.0	3.2
4A-GE	3.4	3.6
MR2: 1989-90	3.0	3.2
1991-92 2.0L	3.6	3.8
2.2L	3.8	4.0

Capacity shown is without filter. When replacing filter, additional oil may be needed

1989-90:
Above 10°F (−12°C) .. 15W-40, 20W-40, 20W-50
Above −10°F (−23°C) . 10W-30, 10W-40, 10W-50
Below 50°F (10°C) 5W-30
1991-92:
Above 0°F (−18°C) 10W-30
Above 0°F (−18°C), 1991 ...... 10W-40
Below 50°F (10°C) 5W-30

TRANSMISSION/TRANSAXLE, Automatic
Corolla 4WD,
1990-91 Camry 4-cyl. 4WD ..... **SLF***
* ATF Type T, Part No. 08886-00405

All others .... **AF**
Differential is serviced separately in 2WD Camry & 1989 Celica, FWD Corolla 3-speed, and Tercel

CAPACITY, Initial Refill*:	Liters	Qt
Camry 1992 V6	2.9	3.1
Celica 1990-92, MR2	3.3	3.5
Corolla 2WD	2.3	2.4
w/OD or 4WD	3.1	3.3
Paseo	3.1	3.3
1990-91 Camry 4-cyl. 4WD	3.3	3.5
Supra, Cressida	1.6	1.7
Others	2.5	2.6

* With the engine at operating temperature, shift transmission through all gears. Check fluid level in PARK and add fluid as needed

TRANSMISSION/TRANSAXLE, Manual
FWD, includes front differential and 4WD transfer case
Tercel, Paseo 75W-90, 80W-90 **GL-4, GL-5**
Celica, Camry, Corolla 2WD:
1.6L 75W-90 **GL-4, GL-5**
2.0L ex. Turbo, 2.2L: 1989-90 ...... **AF**
1991-92 .... 75W-90 **GL-5**
V6 ...... 75W-90, 80W-90 **GL-4, GL-5**
Corolla, Celica, Camry
4WD 75W-90, 80W-90 **GL-4, GL-5**
May also use 90 above 0°F (−18°C), or 80W below 0°F (−18°C)
MR2 ex. Supercharged (1989-90),
Cressida, Supra ex.
Turbo . 75W-90, 80W-90 **GL-4, GL-5**
MR2 Supercharged & Turbo, Supra Turbo,
Celica 2WD Turbo 75W-90 **GL-5**

CAPACITY, Refill:	Liters	Pt
Supra, Cressida	2.4	5.2
Turbo	3.0	6.4
MR2 1989-90	2.6	5.6
Supercharged	4.2	8.8
Camry, Celica, Corolla:		
2WD 4-cyl.	2.6	5.6
2WD V6	4.2	8.8
4WD	5.0	10.6
Tercel, Paseo	2.4	5.0

TRANSFER CASE, 4WD w/AT
Camry, Corolla .. 75W-90, 80W-90 **GL-5**
May also use 90 above 0°F (−18°C); or 80W below 0°F (−18°C)

CAPACITY, Refill:	Liters	Pt
Camry, Corolla	0.7	1.4

FINAL DRIVE, FWD w/AT .... **AF**
Tercel, Corolla w/3-speed; Camry 1989 Celica 2WD, all V6

CAPACITY, Refill:	Liters	Pt
Camry, 1989 Celica		
2WD 4-cyl.	1.6	3.4
V6	1.0	2.2
Corolla, Tercel	1.4	3.0

DIFFERENTIAL, Rear
Limited-Slip .... **GL-5 ★**
Standard **GL-5**
Above 0°F (−18°C), 90; below 0°F (−18°C), 80W, 80W-90

CAPACITY, Refill:	Liters	Pt
Celica, Camry, Corolla:		
4WD rear	1.1	2.4
Supra, Cressida	1.2	2.6

SERVICE AT TIME OR MILEAGE—WHICHEVER OCCURS FIRST

TAIPM7   TAIPM7

MI—MILES IN THOUSANDS
KM—KILOMETERS IN THOUSANDS

DIESEL, EVERY 3 MO/3.75 MI—6 KM
Crankcase .... change oil

Oil filter .... replace

GASOLINE,
EVERY 8 MO/10 MI—16 KM
Crankcase .... change oil

Oil filter .... replace

EVERY 12 MO/15 MI—24 KM
Brake system .... check
Fluid level **HB**, drums, linings, booster, parking brake, lines, pipes & hoses

Transfer case .... check level

Exhaust system .... inspect

Front suspension .... inspect
Ball joints, dust covers, drive shaft boots

Steering gear .... check level 90 **GL-4**
Check linkage & free play

Vacuum pump oil hose
Diesel .... inspect

Valve clearance .... adjust

Body .... inspect
Check nuts & bolts

EVERY 24 MO/30 MI—48 KM
Cooling system ...... change coolant **EC**

Air cleaner element .... replace

Choke .... inspect

Drive belts .... inspect

Fuel lines & hoses .... inspect

Fuel supply system .... inspect

Spark plugs .... inspect

EVERY 48 MO/60 MI—96 KM
Cooling system .... inspect

Timing & compressor belts
Diesel .... replace
Canadian trucks every 100 mi (160 km)

Water sedimenter .... inspect

SEVERE SERVICE
Crankcase—Gasoline, change oil & filter every 3 mo/3.75 mi (6 km); Diesel, every 1.5 mo/1.875 mi (3 km)

Exhaust system—Inspect every 6 mo/7.5 mi (12 km)

Steering components—Inspect every 3 mo/3.75 mi (6 km)

Suspension & brake components—Inspect every 6 mo/7.5 mi (12 km)

Transmission/transaxle, manual & automatic, transfer case & differential fluid—Change every 12 mo/15 mi (24 km)

Air cleaner element—Clean every 3 mo/3.75 mi (6 km)

Ignition wiring, distributor cap—Inspect every 12 mo/15 mi (24 km)

KEY TO LUBRICANTS
AF	DEXRON®-II Automatic Transmission Fluid
CC	Motor Oil, API Service CC
CD	Motor Oil, API Service CD
CE	Motor Oil, API Service CE
EC	Ethylene Glycol Coolant Maintain coolant protection to at least –34°F (–37°C)
FA	Automatic Transmission Fluid, Type F
GL-4	Gear Oil, API Service GL-4
GL-5	Gear Oil, API Service GL-5
HB	Hydraulic Brake Fluid, DOT 3
LM	Lithium Grease, with Moly
SE	Motor Oil, API Service SE
SF	Motor Oil, API Service SF
SG	Motor Oil, API Service SG

CRANKCASE
Gasoline engine
All .... **SF**
Diesel engine
All .... **CC, SE/CC, SF/CC, SF/CD**

CAPACITY, Refill:	Liters	Qt
Pickup ex. Diesel	3.8	4.0
Diesel Pickup	4.8	5.1

Capacity shown is without filter. When replacing filter, additional oil may be needed

Gasoline engines
Above 40°F (4°C) 30
Above 10°F (–12°C) 20W-40, 20W-50
Above –10°F (–23°C) . 10W-30, 10W-40, 10W-50
Between 10° to 60°F (–12° to 16°C) 20
Below 50°F (10°C) 5W-30
Diesel engines
Above 50°F (10°C) 30
Below 85°F (30°C) 10W-30

TRANSMISSION, Automatic
3-speed .... **AF**
4-speed .... **FA**

CAPACITY, Initial Refill*:	Liters	Qt
All	2.4	2.5

* With the engine at operating temperature, shift transmission through all gears. Check fluid level in PARK and add fluid as needed

TRANSMISSION,
Manual 80W-90 **GL-4, GL-5**

CAPACITY, Refill:	Liters	Pt
2WD: 4-speed	2.7	5.8
5-speed, G series	2.2	4.6
W series	2.6	5.4
4WD: 4-speed	2.0	4.2
5-speed	1.8	3.8

TRANSFER
CASE 75W-90, 80W-90 **GL-4, GL-5**

CAPACITY, Refill:	Liters	Pt
All models	1.6	3.4

DIFFERENTIAL 90 **GL-5**
Below –10°F (–23°C), 80W, 80W-90

CAPACITY, Refill:	Liters	Pt
2WD: 7.5″ ring gear	1.7	3.6
8.0″ ring gear	1.8	3.8
4WD front & rear	2.2	4.6

SERVICE AT TIME OR MILEAGE—WHICHEVER OCCURS FIRST

TAIPM8   TAIPM8

MI—MILES IN THOUSANDS
KM—KILOMETERS IN THOUSANDS

1984 DIESEL ENGINES,
EVERY 4 MO/5 MI—8 KM
1985 DIESEL ENGINES,
EVERY 6 MO/5 MI—8 KM
GASOLINE,
EVERY 8 MO/10 MI—16 KM
Crankcase . . . . change oil

Oil filter . . . . replace

1984, EVERY 12 MO/15 MI—24 KM
1985, EVERY 18 MO/15 MI—24 KM
Brake system . . . . check
Fluid level **HB** drums, linings, booster, parking brake,
lines, pipes & hoses

Transfer case . . . . check level

Transmission, manual . . . . check level

Front suspension . . . . inspect
Ball joints, dust covers

Idle speeds ex. EFI . . . . check/adjust

Steering gear . . . . check level 90 **GL-4**
Check linkage & free play

Transmission, automatic . . . . . check level

Vacuum pump oil hose Diesel . . . . inspect

Valve clearance . . . . adjust
Except models with hydraulic lifters

1984, EVERY 24 MO/30 MI—48 KM
1985, EVERY 36 MO/30 MI—48 KM
Exhaust system . . . . inspect

Steering knuckle & propeller
   shafts 4 × 4 Pickup . . . . lubricate **LM**

Air cleaner element . . . . replace

Choke system . . . . inspect

Drive belts . . . . inspect
Ex. V-ribbed

Fuel lines & hoses . . . . inspect

Fuel supply system . . . . inspect

Spark plugs . . . . replace
Ex. platinum tipped

Body . . . . inspect
Check nuts & bolts

1984, EVERY 36 MO/45 MI—72 KM
1985, EVERY 48 MO/40 MI—64 KM
Front wheel bearings . . . clean/repack **LM**
Torque to 19-23 ft lb. Back off & retighten finger tight

1984, EVERY 48 MO/60 MI—96 KM
1985, EVERY 72 MO/60 MI—96 KM
Charcoal canister . . . . inspect
Check fuel evaporative system, hoses & connections

Cooling system . . . . . . change coolant **EC**
Replace coolant every 24 mo/30 mi (48 km) thereafter

Drive belts, V-ribbed . . . . inspect

Fuel filter & cap gasket . . . . replace

Oxygen sensor . . . . replace
1985 FI Federal Pickup only

Spark plugs . . . . replace
Platinum tipped only

Timing & compressor belts
   Diesel . . . . replace

Vacuum pump oil hose Diesel . . . . replace

Water sedimenter . . . . inspect

SEVERE SERVICE
Crankcase—Change oil & filter: Gasoline,
1984, every 3 mo/3.75 mi (6 km); 1985, every 6 mo/5 mi (8 km); Diesel, 1984, every 1.5
mo/1.875 mi (3 km); 1985, every 3 mo/2.5 mi
(4 km)

Exhaust system—Inspect 1984, every 6 mo/
7.5 mi (12 km); 1985, every 18 mo/15 mi (24
km)

Steering components—Inspect 1984, every
6 mo/7.5 mi (12 km)

Suspension & brake components—Inspect
1984, every 6 mo/7.5 mi (12 km); 1985, every 12 mo/10 mi (16 km)

Transmission, transfer case & differential
fluid—Change 1984, every 12 mo/15 mi (24
km); 1985, every 18 mo/15 mi (24 km)

Air cleaner element—Clean 1984, every 3
mo/3.75 mi (6 km). 1985, inspect every 6
mo/5 mi (8 km)

Ignition wiring, distributor cap—Inspect
1984, every 12 mo/15 mi (24 km); 1985, every spring

KEY TO LUBRICANTS
AF	DEXRON®-II Automatic Transmission Fluid
CC	Motor Oil, API Service CC
CD	Motor Oil, API Service CD
CE	Motor Oil, API Service CE
EC	Ethylene Glycol Coolant
	Maintain coolant protection to at least −34°F (−37°C)
GL-4	Gear Oil, API Service GL-4
GL-5	Gear Oil, API Service GL-5
HB	Hydraulic Brake Fluid, DOT 3
LM	Lithium Grease, with Moly
SF	Motor Oil, API Service SF
SG	Motor Oil, API Service SG

CRANKCASE
Gasoline engine . . . . **SG**
Diesel engine . . . . **SG/CD, SG/CE**

CAPACITY, Refill:	Liters	Qt
Pickup: Gasoline	3.8	4.0
Diesel	4.8	5.1
Van	3.0	3.2

Capacity shown is without filter. When replacing filter, additional oil may be needed

Gasoline engines
Above 10°F (−12°C) 20W-40, 20W-50
Above −10°F (−23°C) 10W-30, 10W-40,
                                                          10W-50
Below 50°F (10°C) 5W-30
Diesel engines
Above 50°F (10°C) . . . . 30†
Above 10°F (−12°C) . . 15W-40, 20W-40, 20W-50
Above −10°F (−23°C) 10W-40, 10W-50
−10° to 85°F (−23° to 29°C) 10W-30
Below 32°F (0°C) 5W-30*
* Not recommended for continuous high speed driving
† Not recommended for nonturbo pickup

TRANSMISSION, Automatic . . . . **AF**
CAPACITY, Initial Refill*:	Liters	Qt
All	2.4	2.5

*With the engine at operating temperature, shift transmis-
sion through all gears. Check fluid level in PARK and add
fluid as needed

TRANSMISSION, Manual
Truck 75W-90 **GL-4, GL-5**
Van 75W-90, 80W-90 **GL-4, GL-5**
CAPACITY, Refill:	Liters	Pt
Pickup:		
1984: 2WD: 4-speed	2.7	5.8
5-speed: G series . . .	2.2	4.6
W series	2.6	5.4
4WD	3.9	8.2
1985: Gas:		
2WD	2.4	5.0
4WD: W series	3.0	6.4
G series	3.9	8.2
Diesel:		
2WD: 4-speed	2.4	5.0
5-speed: G series .	2.2	4.6
W series	2.4	5.0
4WD	3.0	6.4
Van	2.3	5.0

TRANSFER
CASE 75W-90, 80W-90 **GL-4, GL-5**
CAPACITY, Refill:	Liters	Pt
All models	1.6	3.4

DIFFERENTIAL **GL-5**
Below −10°F (−23°C), 80W, 80W-90
CAPACITY, Refill:	Liters	Pt
Pickup:		
2WD: 7.5″ ring gear . .	1.7	3.6
8.0″ ring gear . .	1.8	3.8
4WD: Front	2.3	4.8
Rear	2.2	4.6
Van	1.5	3.1

SERVICE AT TIME OR MILEAGE—WHICHEVER OCCURS FIRST

TAIPM9   TAIPM9

Perform the following maintenance services at the intervals indicated to keep the vehicle warranties in effect.

W   SERVICE TO MAINTAIN EMISSION WARRANTY

MI—MILES IN THOUSANDS
KM—KILOMETERS IN THOUSANDS

FIRST 12 MO/7.5 MI—12 KM
Idle speed . . . . check/adjust

DIESEL & TURBO ENGINES,
EVERY 6 MO/5 MI—8 KM
GASOLINE:
EVERY 12 MO/10 MI—16 KM
W Crankcase . . . . change oil

W Oil filter . . . . replace

4WD, EVERY 18 MO/15 MI—24 KM
2WD, EVERY 24 MO/20 MI—32 KM
Brake system . . . . check
Fluid level **HB** disc pads & rotors, drums, linings, booster, parking brake, lines, pipes & hoses

Drive shaft boots 4WD . . . . inspect

Propeller shaft, 4WD Pickup,
   Van . . . . lubricate **LM**

Transfer case . . . . check level

Transmission, manual . . . . . . check level

Front suspension . . . . inspect
Ball joints, dust covers

Power steering fluid . . . . . . check level **AF**
Ex. Pickup

Steering gear . . . . check level 90 **GL-4**
Check linkage & free play

Transmission, automatic . . . . . check level

Vacuum pump oil hose Diesel . . . . inspect

Body . . . . inspect
Torque nuts & bolts

EVERY 36 MO/30 MI—48 KM
Exhaust system . . . . inspect

W Air cleaner element . . . . replace

Drive belts . . . . inspect
Ex. V-ribbed

Fuel lines & hoses . . . . inspect

W Idle speeds . . . . check/adjust
Adjust throttle positioner on carburetted engines

Spark plugs . . . . replace
Ex. platinum tipped

W Valve clearance . . . . adjust
4-cyl. ex. Van

Body . . . . inspect
Check nut & bolt torque

EVERY 48 MO/40 MI—64 KM
Front wheel bearings . . . clean/repack **LM**
Torque to 19-23 ft lb. Back off & retighten finger tight

EVERY 72 MO/60 MI—96 KM
Charcoal canister . . . . inspect
Check fuel evaporative system, hoses & connections

Cooling system . . . . . . change coolant **EC**
Replace coolant every 24 mo/30 mi (48 km) thereafter

Drive belts, V-ribbed . . . . inspect
Initial service, inspect every 12 mo/10 mi (16 km) thereafter

Fuel cap gasket . . . . replace

Oxygen sensor . . . . replace
1986-87 w/FI only

Spark plugs . . . . replace
Platinum tipped only

Timing & compressor belts
   Diesel . . . . replace

Vacuum pump oil hose Diesel . . . . replace

Valve clearance . . . . adjust
V6 engine

Water sedimenter . . . . inspect

EVERY 80 MI—126 KM
Oxygen sensor . . . . replace
1988-89

SEVERE SERVICE
W Crankcase—Change oil & filter: Gasoline, every: 6 mo/5 mi (8 km); Diesel, every 3 mo/2.5 mi (4 km)

Exhaust system—Inspect every 18 mo/15 mi (24 km)

Propeller shaft, 4WD — Lubricate every 12 mo/7.5 mi (12 km)

Suspension & brake components—Inspect every 12 mo/10 mi (16 km)

Transmission, transfer case & differential fluid or lubricant—Change every 24 mo/20 mi (32 km)

Wheel bearings — Repack every 36 mo/30 mi (48 km)

W Air cleaner element—Inspect every 6 mo/ 5 mi (8 km)

Timing belt — Replace every 60 mi (96 km)

KEY TO LUBRICANTS
See other Toyota charts

CRANKCASE
Gasoline engine . . . . **SG**
Diesel engine . . . . **SG/CD, SG/CE**

CAPACITY, Refill:	Liters	Qt
Pickup, 4-Runner		
4-cyl. Gasoline	3.8	4.0
Diesel	4.8	5.1
V6	4.0	4.2
Van	3.0	3.2

Capacity shown is without filter. When replacing filter, additional oil may be needed

Gasoline engines
Above 10°F (−12°C) . . 15W-40, 20W-40, 20W-50
Above −10°F (−23°C) . . 10W-30, 10W-40, 10W-50
Below 50°F (10°C) 5W-30

Diesel engines
Above 50°F (10°C) 30
Above 10°F (−12°C) . . 15W-40, 20W-40, 20W-50
−10° to 100°F (−23° to 38°C) 10W-30
Below 32°F (0°C) 5W-30

TRANSMISSION, Automatic . . . . **AF**

CAPACITY, Initial Refill*:	Liters	Qt
Pickup w/OD	4.5	4.8
Others	2.4	2.5

*With the engine at operating temperature, shift transmission through all gears. Check fluid level in PARK and add fluid as needed

TRANSMISSION, Manual
1986-88 . . . . 80W-90, 75W-90 **GL-4, GL-5**
1989: W series
   trans. . . 80W-90, 75W-90 **GL-4, GL-5**
Others 75W-90 **GL-4, GL-5**

CAPACITY, Refill:	Liters	Pt
4-Runner	3.0	6.4
Van	2.3	5.0
4WD	2.6	5.4
1986-88 Pickup, 2WD, 4-cyl.:		
R series	2.6	5.4
G series	2.2	4.6
W series	2.4	5.0
4WD R, W series	3.0	6.4
G series	3.9	8.2
V6, all	3.0	6.4
1989 Pickup, 2WD:		
G40, W46, W55	2.4	5.0
G57	2.2	4.6
R150	3.0	6.4
4WD: W56, R150	3.0	6.4
G58	3.9	8.2

TRANSFER CASE
Pickup, 4-Runner w/MT;
   Van 75W-90*, 80W-90 **GL-4, GL-5**
* 1989 V6 and Van; 75W-90 preferred
Pickup, 4-Runner w/AT . . . . **AF**

CAPACITY, Refill:	Liters	Pt
Pickup, 4-Runner		
1986-87	1.6	3.4
1988: 4-cyl. W56	1.6	3.4
A340H	0.8	1.6
V6	1.1	2.4
1989 MT: w/W56 trans. . . .	1.6	3.4
w/G56, R150 trans. . .	1.1	2.4
AT	0.8	1.6
Van	1.2	2.6

DIFFERENTIAL
4WD Pickup, 4-Runner w/Auto.
   Disc. Diff.† . . . . **GLS***
*Use Toyota Part No. 08885-80306
† Models with Automatic Disconnecting Differential do not have locking hubs
Others **GL-5**
Above 0°F (−18°C), 90; below 0°F (−18°C), 80W, 80W-90

CAPACITY, Refill:	Liters	Pt
Van	1.5	3.1
4WD front	1.3	2.4
4WD rear	1.9	3.7
Pickup, 4-Runner:		
2WD: 7.5″ ring gear . . .	1.4	2.8
8.0″ ring gear . . .	1.8	3.8
4WD: Front: 1986	2.3	4.8
1987-89	1.6	3.4
w/Auto. Disc. Diff. . .	1.9	4.0
Rear: Turbo, V6	2.4	5.0
Others	2.2	4.6

SERVICE AT TIME OR MILEAGE—WHICHEVER OCCURS FIRST

TAIPM11 · TAIPM11

Perform the following maintenance services at the intervals indicated to keep the vehicle warranties in effect.

W   SERVICE TO MAINTAIN EMISSION WARRANTY

MI—MILES IN THOUSANDS
KM—KILOMETERS IN THOUSANDS

FIRST 12 MO/7.5 MI — 12 KM
Idle speed . . . . check/adjust

EVERY 12 MO/7.5 MI—12 KM
W Crankcase . . . . change oil

W Oil filter . . . . replace

EVERY 24 MO/15 MI—24 KM
Brake system . . . . check
Fluid level **HB**, disc pads & rotors, drums, linings, booster, parking brake, lines, pipes & hoses

Differentials . . . . check level

Drive shaft boots 4WD . . . . inspect

Propeller shaft 4WD . . . . lubricate **LM**

Transfer case . . . . check level

Transmission, manual . . . . . . check level

Front suspension . . . . inspect
Ball joints, dust covers

Power steering fluid . . . . . . check level **AF**
Ex. Pickup

Steering gear . . . . check level
Check linkage & free play

Transmission, automatic . . . . . check level

Idle speed 1991 . . . . check/adjust

Body . . . . inspect
Torque nuts & bolts

EVERY 36 MO/30 MI—48 KM
Exhaust system . . . . inspect

W Air cleaner element . . . . replace

Drive belts . . . . inspect
Pickup, 4-Runner, initial service

Fuel lines & hoses . . . . inspect

Idle speeds 1990 . . . . check/adjust
Adjust throttle positioner on carburetted engines

Spark plugs . . . . replace
Ex. platinum tipped

W Valve clearance . . . . adjust
4-cyl. trucks

AT FIRST 36 MO/45 MI—72 KM
THEN, EVERY 24 MO/30 MI—48 KM
Cooling system . . . . . change coolant **EC**

PICKUP, 4-RUNNER:
2WD, EVERY 48 MO/30 MI—48 KM
4WD, EVERY 36 MO/30 MI—48 KM
Front wheel bearings . . . clean/repack **LM**
Torque to 19-23 ft lb. Back off & retighten finger tight

EVERY 72 MO/60 MI—96 KM
Charcoal canister . . . . inspect
Check fuel evaporative system, hoses & connections

Drive belts . . . . inspect
Inspect every 12 mo/7.5 mi (12 km) thereafter

Fuel cap gasket . . . . replace

W Spark plugs . . . . replace
Platinum tipped only

Valve clearance . . . . adjust
Previa & V6 engine

EVERY 80 MI—126 KM
Oxygen sensor . . . . replace

EVERY 120 MO
Air bag system . . . . inspect
Initial service, then every 24 mo

SEVERE SERVICE
W Crankcase—Change oil & filter every 6 mo/3.75 mi (6 km)

Exhaust system—Inspect every 24 mo/15 mi (24 km)

Propeller shaft, 4WD — Lubricate every 12 mo/7.5 mi (12 km)

Suspension & brake components—Inspect every 12 mo/7.5 mi (12 km)

Transmission, transfer case & differential fluid or lubricant—Change every 24 mo/15 mi (24 km)

Wheel bearings — Pickup, 4-Runner, re-pack every 36 mo/30 mi (48 km)

W Air cleaner element—Inspect every 6 mo/5 mi (8 km)

Timing belt, V6 — Replace every 60 mi (96 km)

KEY TO LUBRICANTS

AF	DEXRON®-II Automatic Transmission Fluid
EC	Ethylene Glycol Coolant Maintain coolant protection to at least –34°F (–37°C)
GL-4	Gear Oil, API Service GL-4
GL-5	Gear Oil, API Service GL-5
GLS	Gear Lubricant, Special Toyota Part No. 08885-80306
HB	Hydraulic Brake Fluid, DOT 3
LM	Lithium Grease, with Moly
SG	Motor Oil, API Service SG

CRANKCASE . . . . SG

CAPACITY, Refill:	Liters	Qt
Pickup, 4-Runner: 2WD . . .	4.0	4.2
4WD	4.2	4.4
Previa	5.5	5.8
Oil tank (underhood)	2.0	2.1

Capacity shown is without filter. When replacing filter, additional oil may be needed

1990:
Above 10°F (–12°C) . . 15W-40, 20W-40, 20W-50
Above –10°F (–23°C) . . 10W-30, 10W-40, 10W-50
Below 50°F (10°C) 5W-30
1991-92:
Above 0°F (–18°C) 10W-30
Above 0°F (–18°C), 1991 . . . . 10W-40
Below 50°F (10°C) 5W-30

TRANSMISSION, Automatic . . . . AF

CAPACITY, Initial Refill*:	Liters	Qt
Pickup, 4-Runner 2WD:		
4-cyl.	2.4	2.5
V6	1.6	1.7
4WD: 4-cyl.	1.6	1.7
V6	4.5	4.8
Previa	2.4	2.5

* With the engine at operating temperature, shift transmission through all gears. Check fluid level in PARK and add fluid as needed

TRANSMISSION, Manual
W series
trans. 80W-90, 75W-90 **GL-4, GL-5**
Others 75W-90, **GL-4, GL-5**

CAPACITY, Refill:	Liters	Pt
Pickup, 4-Runner 2WD: G40,		
W46, W55	2.4	5.0
G57	2.2	4.6
R150	3.0	6.4
4WD: W56, R150	3.0	6.4
G58	3.9	8.2
Previa: 2WD	2.2	4.6
4WD	2.6	5.4

TRANSFER CASE
Pickup, 4-Runner:
MT 75W-90 **GL-4, GL-5**
AT: 4-cyl. 75W-90 **GL-4, GL-5**
V6 . . . . **AF**
Previa 75W-90 **GL-4, GL-5**

CAPACITY, Refill:	Liters	Pt
Pickup, 4-Runner: MT:		
w/W56 trans.	1.6	3.4
w/G56, R150 trans. . . .	1.1	2.4
AT	0.8	1.6
Previa	1.3	2.8

DIFFERENTIAL
4WD Pickup, 4-Runner w/Auto.
Disc. Diff. . . . . **GLS***
Others **GL-5**
Above 0°F (–18°C), 90; below 0°F (–18°C), 80W, 80W-90
Models with Automatic Disconnecting Differential do not have locking hubs

CAPACITY, Refill:	Liters	Pt
Pickup, 4-Runner: 2WD:		
7.5″ RG	1.4	2.8
8.0″ RG	1.8	3.8
4WD: Front	1.6	3.4
w/Auto. Disc. Diff. . . .	1.9	4.0
Rear: 4-cyl.	2.2	4.6
V6	2.4	5.0
Previa: Front	1.1	2.2
Rear	1.5	3.2

VOLKSWAGEN
1983-92 All Models

SERVICE LOCATIONS — ENGINE AND CHASSIS

HOOD RELEASE: Vanagon, push button on rear lid; others, inside

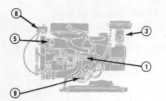

4-cyl. 1588cc Diesel
1983-84 Rabbit
1983-87, 1990-91 Jetta

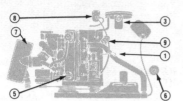

4-cyl. 1588cc
Turbo Diesel
1983-85 Quantum

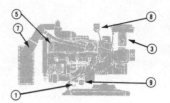

4-cyl. 1588cc Turbo Diesel
1983-84 Rabbit
1983-87 Jetta

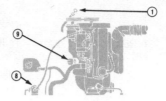

4-cyl. 1588cc Diesel
1983 Vanagon

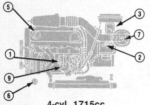

4-cyl. 1715cc
1983-84 Jetta,
Rabbit, Scirocco
4-cyl. 1780cc
1985-92 Jetta, Scirocco

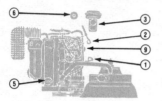

4-cyl. 1715cc
1983 Quantum
4-cyl. 1780cc
1984-86 Quantum

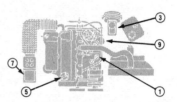

4-cyl. 1780cc
1987-92 Fox

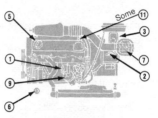

4-cyl. 1780cc
1985-92 Golf, GTI,
Jetta, Scirocco

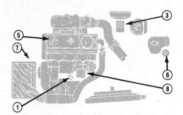

4-cyl. 1780 Supercharged
1989-92 Corrado

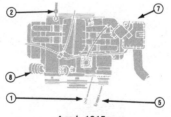

4-cyl. 1915cc
1984-85 Vanagon
4-cyl. 2109cc
1986-91 Vanagon

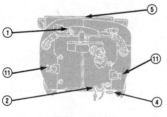

4-cyl. 1970cc
1983 Vanagon

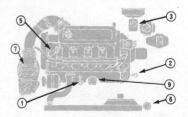

4-cyl. 1984cc
1990-92 Passat

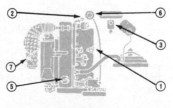

5-cyl. 2144cc
1983-84 Quantum
5-cyl. 2226cc
1985-88 Quantum

① Crankcase dipstick
② Transmission dipstick
③ Brake fluid reservoir
④ Clutch fluid reservoir
⑤ Oil fill cap
⑥ Power steering reservoir
⑦ Air filter
⑧ Fuel filter
⑨ Oil filter
⑩ PCV filter
⑪ EGR valve
⑫ Oxygen sensor
⑬ PCV valve

SERVICE LOCATIONS — ENGINE AND CHASSIS

0 FITTINGS
0 PLUGS

0 FITTINGS
0 PLUGS

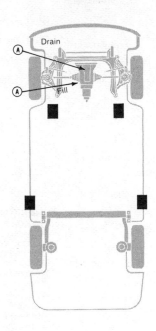

Fox

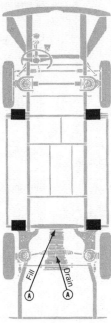

Vanagon

0 FITTINGS
0 PLUGS

0 FITTINGS
0 PLUGS

0 FITTINGS
0 PLUGS

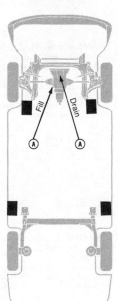

Quantum

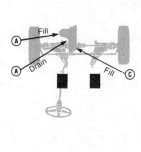

Rabbit, Scirocco,
Pickup, Jetta,
Golf

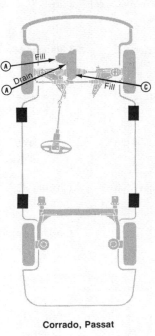

Corrado, Passat

CAUTION: On front wheel drive vehicles the center of gravity is further forward than on rear wheel drive vehicles. When removing major components from the rear of the vehicle while it is on a hoist, the vehicle must be supported in a manner to prevent it from tipping forward.

■ **Lift adapter position**

Ⓐ Manual transmission/transaxle, drain & fill
Ⓑ Transfer case, NOT USED

Ⓒ Automatic transaxle final drive, drain & fill
Ⓓ Differential, NOT USED

VOLKSWAGEN
1983 Air-Cooled Vanagon

VNIPM1   VNIPM1

MI—MILES IN THOUSANDS
KM—KILOMETERS IN THOUSANDS

EVERY 6 MO/7.5 MI—12 KM
Crankcase .... change oil

Oil filter .... replace
At first service interval only

Brake system ....inspect **HB**
Check fluid level, lining & pad thickness

EVERY 12 MO/15 MI—24 KM
Exhaust system .... check

Front axle & steering system ..... inspect
Check ball joints, dust seals, tie rods & ends

Front suspension .... 0-5 fittings **LM**

Oil filter .... replace

Transaxle or final drive ...... check level

Brake system .... inspect **HB**

Drive belts .... check/adjust

EGR system .... check
Ex. California. Reset mileage counter

Fuel filter ex. Calif. .... replace

Fuel supply system .... inspect

Idle speed .... check/adjust

Transmission, automatic ..... check level
Fluid warm, engine idling, in NEUTRAL. Maintain level between upper & lower marks on dipstick

Door & hood .... lubricate

PCV system .... inspect

Spark plugs .... replace
Ex. California

Steering .... check play

Steering & drive shafts ...... check boots

Tires & wheels .... inspect

Headlights .... check/adjust

EVERY 24 MONTHS
Brakes .... change fluid **HB**
Check operation of warning light switch on models so equipped

EVERY 24 MO/30 MI—48 KM
Oil strainer .... clean

Transmission, automatic .... change fluid
Remove & clean pan & strainer. Use new gasket

Air filter element .... replace

Compression .... check

Fuel filter .... replace

Oxygen sensor .... replace
California models only. Reset mileage counter

Spark plugs Calif. .... replace

Valve cover gaskets .... replace

SERVICE AS REQUIRED
Front suspension ball joints .. 4 plugs **LM**
If noise occurs, remove metal plugs, insert fittings & lubricate using low pressure. Reinstall plugs. Do not damage rubber seals

---

KEY TO LUBRICANTS

AF   DEXRON®-II Automatic Transmission Fluid

GL-4   Gear Oil, API Service GL-4

GL-5   Gear Oil, API Service GL-5

HB   Hydraulic Brake Fluid, DOT 4

LM   Lithium Grease

SF   Motor Oil, API Service SF

CRANKCASE .... SF

CAPACITY, Refill*:	Liters	Qt
All models	3.0	3.2

*Capacity shown is without filter. When replacing filter, additional oil may be needed

68° to 104°F (20° to 40°C)	40
32° to 86°F (0° to 30°C)	30
14° to 86°F (−10° to 30°C) 20W-40, 20W-50	
14° to 50°F (−10° to 10°C) 20W-20	
5° to 86°F (−15° to 30°C) 15W-40, 15W-50	
−4° to 50°F (−20° to 10°C) 10W-30, 10W-40	
−4° to 23°F (−20° to −5°C) 10W	
−22° to 14°F (−30° to −10°C) 5W-20	

TRANSMISSION, Automatic .... AF
Final drive serviced separately

CAPACITY, Initial Refill*:	Liters	Qt
All models	3.0	3.2

*Add specified quantity. With engine at operating temperature, shift transmission through all gears. Check level in NEUTRAL and add oil as needed
To drain, remove plugs

TRANSAXLE,
  Manual 80W, 80W-90 GL-4

CAPACITY, Refill:	Liters	Pt
All models	2.9	6.4

Drain thru one plug. Clean magnetic drain plugs. Fill slowly, allow 2 to 3 minutes for oil level to stabilize
Recheck level before replacing fill plug

FINAL DRIVE 90 GL-5

CAPACITY, Refill:	Liters	Pt
All models w/AT	1.2	2.6

Drain thru plug; clean magnetic drain plug

VOLKSWAGEN
1983-92 All Water-Cooled Gasoline Models

SERVICE AT TIME OR MILEAGE—WHICHEVER OCCURS FIRST

VNIPM2

W SERVICE TO MAINTAIN EMISSION WARRANTY

VNIPM2

MI—MILES IN THOUSANDS
KM—KILOMETERS IN THOUSANDS

EVERY 6 MO/7.5 MI—12 KM
Brake system . . . . inspect
Vanagon only. Check for damage or leaks. Check pad thickness

W Crankcase . . . . change oil

W Cooling system
1983-90 . . . . check level **EC**

W Oil filter . . . . replace
Initial service only

Clutch . . . . check/adjust
Ex. Vanagon, initial service only

EVERY 12 MO/15 MI—24 KM
Axle boots . . . . inspect

W Brake system . . . . inspect **HB**
Check fluid level, lining & pad thickness. Where applicable, check operation of pressure regulator

Clutch . . . . check/adjust
Ex. Quantum, Scirocco 16V, Vanagon

W Exhaust system . . . . inspect

W Fuel tank, lines, hoses
& connections 1983-88 . . . . . . inspect

Final drive, automatic . . . . check level

Front axle & steering system
boots & seals 1983-87 . . . . . . inspect

W Oil filter . . . . replace

Transaxle . . . . check level

W Air cleaner element 1983-88 . . . . . clean
Ex. Vanagon

Battery 1983-88 . . . . check level

W Compression 1983-88 . . . . check
Ex. Vanagon, 1983 carburetted & 1984 FI models

W Cooling system
1991-92 . . . . check level **EC**

Distributor cap & rotor
1983-85 Vanagon . . . . inspect
Ex. 1983 Calif. engines. Check ignition wires

Drive belts . . . . inspect/adjust
1983-85 Vanagon ex. Calif. 1984 carbureted engine

W EGR system 1983-88 . . . . check
Ex. Vanagon; reset EGR mileage counter where applicable. 1985-87 Canadian models only

Fuel filter 1983-84 . . . . replace
Ex. Calif. models & 1984 Quantum

Headlights 1983-88 . . . . adjust

W Idle speed & CO . . . . check/adjust
Not required for Calif. warranty. 1983-92 FI engines, check idle speed only

On-Board diagnosis
system . . . . check/clear

W PCV hoses 1983-88 . . . . inspect
1983-85 Vanagon & carburetted models only

Power steering . . . . . . check level **AF/PS**
All from 4-89 ex. Vanagon **PS**, others **AF**

W Spark plugs . . . . replace
1983 all ex. Calif. models, 1984-87 5-cyl. & 90 hp Canada only

Transmission, automatic . . . . . check level
Check final drive for leaks

W Valve clearance 1983-85 . . check/adjust
Ex. models w/hydraulic lifters, replace valve cover gasket

Door hinges & checks . . . . . . lubricate **MO**

Lights, accessories . . . . inspect

Sunroof rails . . . . clean/lubricate **SLS**

Supplemental restraint
system . . . . inspect

Tires & wheels . . . . inspect

EVERY 24 MONTHS
Brake fluid . . . . replace **HB**
Check operation of warning light switch; check brake pressure regulator where applicable

EVERY 24 MO/30 MI—48 KM
Front axle & steering system
boots & seals 1988-92 . . . . inspect

W Air cleaner element . . . . replace

W Fuel filter 1983-88 . . . . replace
Ex. 1984 Quantum & Scirocco. 1985-87 Cabriolet only

Transmission, automatic
1983-85 . . . . .change fluid
Clean pan, strainer; replace gasket

W Drive belts . . . . inspect/adjust

Oxygen sensor . . . . replace
1983-85 all, 1986-87 ex. Vanagon, Scirocco 16V
Reset mileage counter where applicable

W Spark plugs . . . . replace
Ex. 1992 Corrado

Valve cover gaskets . . . . replace
1983-88 Vanagon only

EVERY 60 MI—90 KM
Fuel filter . . . . replace
Scirocco & Quantum models

Oxygen sensor . . . . replace
1986-87 Vanagon & Scirocco 16V, 1988-91 all ex. Vanagon & Canada
Reset mileage counter where applicable

Spark plugs . . . . replace
1992 Corrado

EVERY 90 MI—144 KM
Oxygen sensor . . . . replace
1988-91 Vanagon ex. Canada

KEY TO LUBRICANTS

AF	DEXRON®-II Automatic Transmission Fluid
EC	Ethylene Glycol Coolant
GL-4	Gear Oil, API Service GL-4
GL-5	Gear Oil, API Service GL-5
HB	Hydraulic Brake Fluid, DOT 4
MO	Motor Oil
PS	Power Steering Fluid VW Part No. G002000, G002012
SF	Motor Oil, API Service SF
SG	Motor Oil, API Service SG
SLS	Silicone Spray

CRANKCASE . . . . SF, SG

CAPACITY, Refill:	Liters	Qt
4-cyl. engines:		
1983-86 Quantum	2.7	3.0
1983-91 Vanagon	3.8	4.2
1987-92 Fox	3.0	3.2
All others	3.5	3.7
5-cyl. engines:		
1983-86 Quantum	3.2	3.5
1987-88 Quantum	3.0	3.2
1993 EuroVan	4.0	4.2
V6 engines:		
1992 Passat	5.0	5.3

Capacity shown is without filter. When replacing filter, additional oil may be needed

1983-89:
68° to 104°F (20° to 40°C) 40
32° to 86°F (0° to 30°C) 30
14° to 50°F (−10° to 10°C) 20W-20
14° to 86°F (−10° to 30°C) . . . 20W-40, 20W-50
5° to 86°F (−15° to 30°C) . . . 15W-40, 15W-50
−4° to 50°F (−20° to 10°C) . . . 10W-30, 10W-40
−4° to 23°F (−20° to −5°C) 10W
−22° to 14°F (−30° to −10°C) 5W-20, 5W-30

1990-91:
Above 68° (20°C) 40
32° to 86°F (0° to 30°C) 30
Below 23°F (−5°C) 10W
14° to 50°F (−10° to 10°C) 20W-20
Above 14°F (−10°C) 20W-40, 20W-50
Above 5°F (−15°C) 15W-40, 15W-50
−4° to 60°F (−20° to 15°C) . . . 10W-30, 10W-40
Below 14°F (−10°C) 5W-20, 5W-30

1992:
Above 68° (20°C) 40
32° to 86°F (0° to 30°C) 30
Below 23°F (−5°C) 10W
14° to 50°F (−10° to 10°C) 20W-20
Above 14°F (−10°C) 20W-40, 20W-50
Above 5°F (−15°C) 15W-40, 15W-50
5° to 78°F (−15° to 25°C) . . . 10W-30, 10W-40
Below 78°F (25°C) 5W-30

TRANSMISSION, Automatic . . . . **AF**
Final drive serviced separately

CAPACITY, Initial Refill*:	Liters	Qt
All models	3.0	3.2

* Add specified quantity. With engine at operating temperature, shift transmission through all gears. Check level in PARK and add fluid as needed

TRANSAXLE, Manual
Vanagon 80W, 80W-90 **GL-4**
All others . . . . 75W-90 **GL-4†**
†Synthetic gear oil, VW Part No. G005000, if not available 80W **GL-4** may be used

CAPACITY, Refill:	Liters	Pt
Corrado, Passat	2.0	4.2
Fox	1.6	3.4
Quantum	1.9	4.2
Vanagon	2.5*	5.6*
Others: 4-speed	1.4	3.2
5-speed	1.9	4.2

* Correct oil level will be approximately 5/8 inch (15 mm) below the bottom of the fill plug opening

FINAL DRIVE
Corrado, Passat . . . . 75W-90 **GL-4†**
All others 90 **GL-5**
†Synthetic gear oil, VW Part No. G005000

CAPACITY, Refill:	Liters	Pt
All FWD w/AT	0.8	1.6
Vanagon	1.2	2.6

VOLKSWAGEN
1983-87, 1989-91 All Diesel Models

SERVICE AT TIME OR MILEAGE—WHICHEVER OCCURS FIRST

VNIPM3   **W** SERVICE TO MAINTAIN EMISSION WARRANTY   VNIPM3

MI—MILES IN THOUSANDS
KM—KILOMETERS IN THOUSANDS

TURBO DIESEL,
EVERY 6 MO/5 MI—8 KM
NON-TURBO DIESEL,
EVERY 6 MO/7.5 MI—12 KM
w Crankcase . . . . change oil

Clutch free play 1986-91 . . . . check/adjust
Initial service only

Fuel filter 1983-85 . . . . drain water

Oil filter 1983-85 . . . . replace
Initial service only. Models with raised bead on filter
sealing surface should have filter torqued to a minimum
of 24 Nm (18 ft lb) after 3-5 minutes of varied speed
engine operation

w Oil filter . . . . replace
1986-87 at each interval, 1990-91 at initial service only

EVERY 12 MO/15 MI—24 KM
Brake system . . . . inspect **HB**
Check fluid level, lining & pad thickness. Where appli-
cable, check operation of pressure regulator

Clutch pedal free play . . . . . . check/adjust

w Exhaust system . . . . inspect

Final drive, auto. trans. . . . . . . check level

Front axle, steering system,
& drive shaft boots & seals . . . . . inspect

Oil filter 1983-85, 1989-91 . . . . . . replace
Models with raised bead on filter sealing surface should
have filter torqued to a minimum of 24 Nm (18 ft lb) after
3-5 minutes of varied speed engine operation

Steering 1983-85 . . . . check play

Transaxle . . . . check level

w Cooling system . . . . . . check level **EC**

Fuel filter 1986-91 . . . . drain water

Headlights adjustment . . . . check

On-Board diagnosis
system . . . . check/clear

Power steering 1983-87 . . . check level **AF**

Power steering 1989-91 . . . check level **PS**

Transmission, automatic . . . . . check level

Door hinges & checks . . . . . . lubricate **MO**

Sunroof . . . . clean/lubricate **SLS**

Supplemental restraint
system . . . . inspect

Tires & wheels . . . . inspect

w PCV hoses . . . . inspect

Valve clearance 1983-85 . . . . check/adjust
Replace valve cover gasket

EVERY 24 MONTHS
Brake fluid . . . . replace **HB**
Check operation of warning light switch

EVERY 24 MO/30 MI—48 KM
Transmission,
automatic 1983-85 . . . . change fluid
Clean pan, strainer; replace gasket

w Air cleaner element . . . . replace

w Drive belts 1983 . . . . replace
1983, Jetta & Quantum only

Drive belts 1983-91 . . . . inspect/adjust
Ex. 1983 Jetta & Quantum

w Fuel filter . . . . replace

Idle speed . . . . check/adjust

w Timing belt, 1989-90 . . . . . check/adjust

SEVERE SERVICE
Crankcase—Change oil more frequently

KEY TO LUBRICANTS

AF	DEXRON®-II Automatic Transmission Fluid
CC	Motor Oil, API Service CC
CD	Motor Oil, API Service CD
EC	Ethylene Glycol Coolant
GL-4	Gear Oil, API Service GL-4
GL-5	Gear Oil, API Service GL-5
HB	Hydraulic Brake Fluid, DOT 4
MO	Motor Oil
PS	Power Steering Fluid VW Part No. G002000, G002012
SLS	Silicone Spray

CRANKCASE
Diesel engines . . . . CC, CD
Turbo Diesel engines . . . . CD

CAPACITY, Refill:	Liters	Qt
1983 Vanagon	3.5	3.7
1983-84 Jetta, Rabbit	3.5	3.7
1983-86 Quantum	2.7	3.0
1985-87 Golf	3.5	3.7
1985-91 Jetta	4.2	4.7

Capacity shown is without filter. When replacing filter, additional oil may be needed
1983-87:
68° to 104°F (20° to 40°C) 40
32° to 86°F (0° to 30°C) 30
14° to 86°F (−10° to 30°C) 20W-40, 20W-50
14° to 50°F (−10° to 10°C) 20W-20
5° to 86°F (−15° to 30°C) 15W-40, 15W-50
−4° to 50°F (−20° to 10°C) . . . 10W-30, 10W-40†
−20° to 23°F (−29° to −5°C) 10W
†10W-40 not recommended for 1986 models
1989-91:
Above 68°F (20°C) 40
32° to 86°F (0° to 30°C) 30
Below 23°F (−5°C) 10W
14° to 50°F (−10° to 10°C) 20W-20
Above 14°F (−10°C) 20W-40, 20W-50
Above 5°F (−15°C) 15W-40, 15W-50
Below 60°F (15°C) 10W-30, 10W-40

TRANSMISSION, Automatic . . . . **AF**
Final drive serviced separately

CAPACITY, Initial Refill*:	Liters	Qt
All models	3.0	3.2

*Add specified quantity. With engine at operating temper-
ature, shift transmission through all gears. Check fluid
level in PARK and add oil as needed

TRANSAXLE, Manual
Ex. Vanagon 80W **GL-4**
Vanagon 80W, 80W-90 **GL-4**

CAPACITY, Refill:	Liters	Pt
Golf, Jetta, Rabbit:		
4-speed	1.5	3.2
5-speed	2.0	4.2
Vanagon: 4-speed	2.5	5.6
5-speed	3.4	7.6
Quantum	1.6	3.4

*Correct oil level will be approximately 15 mm below bot-
tom of fill plug opening

FINAL DRIVE 90 **GL-5**

CAPACITY, Refill:	Liters	Pt
All FWD w/AT	0.8	1.6
Vanagon w/AT	1.2	2.6

SERVICE LOCATIONS — ENGINE AND CHASSIS

VOIDP-1   VOIDP-1

HOOD RELEASE: Inside

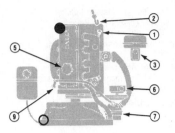

1983-84
2127cc 1V

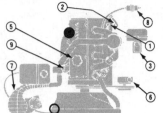

1983-85
2127cc Turbo

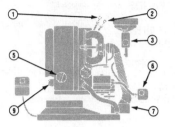

1983-92
2316cc Non-Turbo

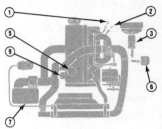

1985-92
2316cc Turbo

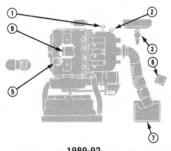

1989-92
2316cc DOHC

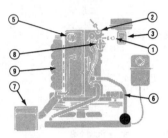

1983-84
2383cc
Diesel

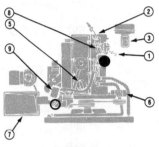

1984-86
2383cc
Turbo Diesel

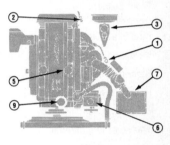

1992
2922cc DOHC

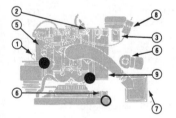

1983-86
2849cc

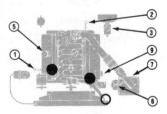

1987-90
2849cc

① Crankcase dipstick
② Transmission dipstick
③ Brake fluid reservoir
④ Clutch fluid reservoir
⑤ Oil fill cap
⑥ Power steering reservoir
⑦ Air filter
⑧ Fuel filter
⑨ Oil filter
⑩ PCV filter
⑪ EGR valve
⑫ Oxygen sensor
⑬ PCV valve

Ⓐ Manual transmission/transaxle, drain & fill
Ⓑ Transfer case, NOT USED
Ⓒ Automatic transaxle final drive, NOT USED
Ⓓ Differential, drain & fill

0 FITTINGS
0 PLUGS

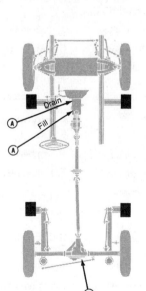

240 Series

0 FITTINGS
0 PLUGS

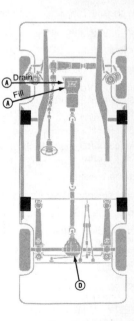

740, 760, 780, 900 Series

■ Lift adapter position   ● Cooling system drain   ○ Cooling system drain, some models

229

CHEK-CHART

SERVICE AT TIME OR MILEAGE—WHICHEVER OCCURS FIRST

VOIPM2   VOIPM2

MI—MILES IN THOUSANDS
KM—KILOMETERS IN THOUSANDS

1983-85, EVERY 6 MO/3.75 MI—6.25 KM
Crankcase GLT, Turbo . . . . change oil

Oil filter GLT, Turbo . . . . replace

EVERY 6 MO/7.5 MI—12.5 KM
Crankcase ex. GLT, Turbo . . . . change oil

Oil filter ex. Diesel, GLT, Turbo . . . replace

EVERY 7.5 MI—12.5 KM
Differential . . . . check level

Drive shaft, U-joints . . . . inspect

Exhaust pipe nuts GLT, Turbo . . . . . check

Front suspension
  & steering linkage . . . . inspect

Fuel filter, Diesel . . . . drain

Kickdown cable . . . . check/adjust

Steering gear . . . . inspect

Rear suspension . . . . check

Tires . . . . inspect

Transmission, manual . . . . . . check level

Wheel bearings . . . . check
1983: 10-slot wheel bearing nut, torque to 50 ft lb, then loosen 1/3 turn until slot aligns with cotter pin hole. 20-slot wheel bearing nut, torque to 42 ft lb, then loosen 1/2 turn; hand tighten until slot aligns with cotter pin hole

Battery . . . . check level

Brake system . . . . check level **HB**
Check operation, inspect hoses, check brake lights

Clamp screws GLT, Turbo . . . . check

Clutch fluid . . . . check level **HB**

Clutch pedal free play . . . . check

Coolant . . . . check level

Engine controls ex. Diesel . . . . inspect

Full load enrichment
  system GLT, Turbo . . . . check

Ignition timing . . . . check/adjust
Canada B21 only

Overload protection switch
  GLT, Turbo . . . . check

Parking brake . . . . check/adjust

Power steering pump . . . . . check level **FA**

Timing retard GLT, Turbo . . . . check

Transmission, automatic . . . . check level
Fluid warm, engine idling, in PARK. Level must not exceed upper mark on dipstick. Check gear selector

Turbo seal . . . . check

Body . . . . lubricate

EVERY 15 MI—25 KM
Brake pads & linings . . . . inspect

Brakes w/air dam . . . . . . change fluid **HB**
At least once a year

Exhaust system 1983 . . . . inspect

Carburetor damper . check level **AF** or **FA**
Canada B21 only

Choke & fast idle . . . . inspect
Canada B21 only

Distributor . . . . lubricate

Engine fuel filter, Diesel . . . . . drain water

Idle speed . . . . check/adjust
Canada B21 only

Oil filter, Diesel . . . . replace

PCV valve, Diesel . . . . clean/check

PCV system 1983-85
  Gasoline . . . . clean/check

Spark plugs . . . . replace
Canada only

Valve clearance, Diesel . . . . adjust

EVERY 22.5 MI—37.5 KM
Transmission, automatic . . . . change fluid

EVERY 30 MI—50 KM
Cooling system . . . . . . change coolant **EC**
NOTE: Diesel, pressure test system

Air cleaner element . . . . replace

Brake system 1984-85 . . . change fluid **HB**

Cooling system . . . . check
Check hoses & connections

Drive belts . . . . check/adjust

Engine controls, Diesel . . . . lubricate/set

Fuel filter, Diesel . . . . replace

Fuel lines, Diesel . . . . check

Idle speed, Diesel . . . . check/adjust

Injection pump controls
  1983-84 Diesel . . . . check

Oxygen sensor . . . . replace
Reset service indicator light

Spark plugs . . . . replace

Valve clearance, Gasoline . . . check/adjust

EVERY 45 MI—75 KM
Brake system 1983 . . . . . change fluid **HB**

Timing belt . . . . replace

Fuel filter 1983 . . . . replace

EVERY 60 MI—100 KM
Fuel filter (tank) . . . . replace

DIESEL, EVERY 75 MI—125 KM
Compression . . . . check

Injectors . . . . check

Timing gear belts,
  idler pulley . . . . replace

SEVERE SERVICE
Brake fluid—Change every 12 mo

Crankcase—Change oil and filter every 3 months

KEY TO LUBRICANTS
AF	DEXRON®-II Automatic Transmission Fluid
CC	Motor Oil, API Service CC
EC	Ethylene Glycol Coolant Mix 50/50 with water
FA	Automatic Transmission Fluid, Type F
GL-5	Gear Oil, API Service GL-5
GL-5★	Gear Oil For Limited-Slip Differential
HB	Hydraulic Brake Fluid, DOT 4
SF	Motor Oil, API Service SF

CRANKCASE . . . . SF/CC
CAPACITY, Refill:	Liters	Qt
4-cyl.	3.4	3.5
V6	6.0	6.3
6-cyl. Diesel	5.0	5.3

Capacity shown is without filter. When replacing filter, additional oil may be needed

Diesel Engines:
1983
Above 68°F (20°C) 40
Above 25°F (–4°C) 20W-50
Above 5°F (–15°C) 15W-50
32° to 86°F (0° to 30°C) 30
–13° to 68°F (–25° to 20°C) 10W-30
–13° to 86°F (–25° to 30°C) 10W-40
Below 68°F (20°C) 0W-30, 5W-30
1984-85
Above 5°F (–15°C) 15W-40
–13° to 68°F (–25° to 20°C) 10W-30
Below 60°F (16°C) 5W-30
Gasoline Engines:
1983
Above 50°F (10°C) 40
Above 25°F (–4°C) 20W-50
Above 5°F (–15°C) 15W-50
32° to 104°F (0° to 40°C) 30
–13° to 104°F (–25° to 40°C) . . 10W-30, 10W-40
Below 86°F (30°C) 0W-30, 5W-30
1984
Above 5°F (–15°C) 15W-40
Above –13°F (–25°C) 10W-40
–13° to 104°F (–25° to 40°C) 10W-30
Below 32°F (0°C) 5W-30
1985
Above 5°F (–15°C) 15W-40
–13° to 104°F (–25° to 40°C) 10W-30
Below 60°F (16°C) 5W-30

TRANSMISSION, Automatic
1983 All models . . . . **FA**
AW 70, 71 transmission (4-speed) may use **AF** if unit has been replaced or rebuilt

1984 AW, BW 55 . . . . **FA**
1984-85 All others . . . . **AF**
CAPACITY, Initial Refill*:	Liters	Qt
1983-84 AW 55, BW 55 . . .	3.5	3.7
1983-85 AW 70, AW 71 . . .	3.9	4.1

* Add specified quantity. With engine at operating temperatures, shift transmission through all gears. Check fluid level in PARK and add fluid as needed

TRANSMISSION, Manual . . . . **FA**
CAPACITY, Refill:	Liters	Pt
All models ex. w/OD	0.8	1.6
W/OD	2.3	4.8

DIFFERENTIAL
Standard 90 **GL-5**
Limited-Slip . . . . 90 **GL-5★**
GL-5 plus Volvo additive Part No. 1161129-0
Below 14°F (–10°C), 80W
CAPACITY, Refill:	Liters	Pt
Model 1030	1.3	2.8
Model 1031	1.6	3.4

SERVICE AT TIME OR MILEAGE—WHICHEVER OCCURS FIRST

VOIPM3

VOIPM3

MI—MILES IN THOUSANDS
KM—KILOMETERS IN THOUSANDS

EVERY 3.75 MI—6.25 KM
Crankcase, Turbo . . . . change oil

Oil filter, Turbo . . . . replace

EVERY 7.5 MI—12.5 KM
Clutch . . . . check free play
Proper play 1-3 mm (1/8-3/16")

Crankcase ex. Turbo . . . . change oil
At least every 6 mo

Differential . . . . check level

Oil filter, Gasoline ex. Turbo . . . . . replace
At least every 6 mo

Transmission, manual . . . . . . check level

Battery . . . . check level

Brake system . . . . check level HB
Check brakelight operation

Cooling system . . . . check level EC
Inspect hoses & connections

Fuel filter, Diesel . . . . drain water

Power steering . . . . . check level AF or FA

Throttle cable, Gasoline . . . . check/adjust
With accelerator pedal fully depressed, distance between cable housing and clip on cable should be 50.4-52.6 mm (1.98-2.07")

Transmission, automatic . . . . . check level

EVERY 15 MI—25 KM
Brake system . . . . inspect
Check calipers for leaks, discs for wear, & pad thickness, minimum 2 mm (5/64")

Oil filter, Diesel . . . . replace
At least every 6 mo

Shock absorbers . . . . inspect

Steering rack boots . . . . inspect

Suspension components . . . . retorque
One time service only. Control arm inner mount, 85 Nm (63 ft lb); control arm strut inner mount with 17 mm hex, 85 Nm (63 ft lb), with 19 mm hex, 140 Nm (103 ft lb); control arm strut outer mount, 95 Nm (70 ft lb); steering rack, 44 Nm, (32 ft lb); rear axle clamps, 45 Nm (33 ft lb)

Tires . . . . inspect
Check tread depth & wear pattern

Crankcase vent system, Diesel . . . inspect

Front suspension crossmember . . retorque
One time service only. Torque to 95 Nm (70 ft lb)

Valve clearance, Diesel . . . . adjust

Hood, trunk . . . . lubricate
Hinges, locks, safety catch

Parking brake . . . . check/adjust
Adjustment setting, 2-8 notches

EVERY 22.5 MI—37.5 KM
Transmission, automatic . . . . change fluid

EVERY 30 MI—50 KM
Brake hoses . . . . inspect

Front suspension . . . . inspect
Check steering wheel & rack freeplay, wheel bearing play, tie rod ends, ball joints, & control arm bushings

Fuel lines . . . . inspect

Rear suspension . . . . inspect
Check trailing arms, subframe, torque rods, Panhard rod, anti-roll bar, spring mountings & condition

Air filter . . . . replace

Brake system . . . . change fluid HB
1984-85 vehicles

Cold start device,
Diesel . . . . check operation

Cooling system . . . . . change coolant EC
At least every 2 years. Diesel, pressure test system

Drive belts . . . . check/adjust

Engine controls, Diesel . . . . check/adjust

Fuel filter . . . . replace

Idle speed, Diesel . . . . check/adjust

Injection pump timing . . . . . check/adjust

Kickdown cable, auto. trans. . . . . . adjust
Diesel models only. With accelerator pedal fully depressed, distance between cable housing & clip on cable should be 50.4-52.6 mm (1.98-2.07")

Oxygen sensor . . . . replace

Oxygen sensor indicator . . . . adjust
1984-85 vehicles

Spark plugs . . . . replace

Valves, Gasoline . . . . adjust

Doors . . . . lubricate
Hinges, doorsteps (paraffin wax), latches

EVERY 45 MI—75 KM
Brake system 1983 . . . . . change fluid HB
At least every 3 years. If equipped with air dam, at least every 12 mo

Timing belt, Turbo . . . . replace
1985 vehicles

EVERY 60 MI—100 KM
PCV system, Gasoline . . . . inspect
Clean calibrated nipple on start injector pipe

EVERY 75 MI—125 KM
Timing belt, injection pump belt &
pulley, Diesel . . . . replace

SEVERE SERVICE
Brake fluid—Change every 12 mo

Crankcase—Change oil every 3 mo/7.5 mi (12.5 km). Change filter: Gasoline, every oil change; Diesel, every other oil change

Air filter—Replace more often

KEY TO LUBRICANTS

AF	DEXRON®-II Automatic Transmission Fluid
CC	Motor Oil, API Service CC
CD	Motor Oil, API Service CD
EC	Ethylene Glycol Coolant Mix 50/50 with water
FA	Automatic Transmission Fluid, Type F
GL-5	Gear Oil, API Service GL-5
GL-5★	Gear Oil For Limited-Slip Differential
HB	Hydraulic Brake Fluid, DOT 4
SF	Motor Oil, API Service SF

CRANKCASE
Diesel engine . . . . CD, SF/CD
Gasoline engine . . . . . SF, SF/CC, SF/CD

CAPACITY, Refill:	Liters	Qt
4-cyl. 2.3L, Turbo	3.4	3.6
6-cyl. 2.4L Diesel	5.0	5.3
V6 2.8L	6.0	6.3

Capacity shown is without filter. When replacing filter, additional oil may be needed. Models with oil cooler, additional oil is required if cooler is drained

Diesel Engines:
Above 0°F (−18°C) 15W-40
−13° to 68°F (−25° to 20°C) 10W-30
Below 60°F (16°C) 5W-30

Gasoline Engines:
Above 0°F (−18°C) 15W-40
−13° to 104°F (−25° to 40°C) 10W-30
Below 60°F (16°C) 5W-30

TRANSMISSION, Automatic
1983 All . . . . FA
AW 70, 71 transmission (4-speed) may use AF if unit has been replaced or rebuilt
1984 AW, BW 55 . . . . FA
1984-85 All others . . . . AF

CAPACITY, Initial Refill*:	Liters	Qt
AW 70, AW 71	3.9	4.1
BW 55	3.5	3.7
ZF 4HP22	2.0	2.2

*Add specified quantity. With engine at operating temperature, shift transmission through all gears. Check fluid level in PARK and add fluid as needed

TRANSMISSION, Manual . . . . FA
CAPACITY, Refill:	Liters	Pt
4-speed	2.3	4.8
5-speed	1.3	2.8

DIFFERENTIAL
Standard GL-5
Limited-Slip . . . . GL-5★
GL-5 plus Volvo additive Part No. 1161129-0
Above 14°F (−10°C), 90; below 14°F (−10°C), 80W

CAPACITY, Refill:	Liters	Pt
Model 1030	1.3	2.8
Model 1031	1.6	3.4
Model 1035	1.4	3.0

VOLVO
1986-92 All Models

SERVICE AT TIME OR MILEAGE—WHICHEVER OCCURS FIRST

VOIPM4   VOIPM4

Perform the following maintenance services at the intervals indicated to keep the vehicle warranties in effect.

W SERVICE TO MAINTAIN EMISSION WARRANTY

MI—MILES IN THOUSANDS
KM—KILOMETERS IN THOUSANDS

1992 TURBO & 6-CYL. 2.9L, EVERY 5 MI—8 KM

W Crankcase . . . . change oil
6-cyl. at first service interval only

W Oil filter . . . . replace
6-cyl. at first service interval only

1986-91, EVERY 6 MO/5 MI—8 KM
1992, EVERY 12 MO/10 MI—16 KM

Brake master cylinder . . . . check level HB

Brake pads 1991 . . . . inspect

W Crankcase . . . . change oil
At least every 6 mo, reset service indicator

Differential 1986-90 . . . . check level
Ex. 1989 models w/Regina Bendix injection, 1990 700 Series

W Oil filter . . . . replace
At least every 6 mo

Tires . . . . inspect
Check pressure, tread depth & wear pattern

Transmission, manual . . . . . . check level
1986-90 Ex. 1989 models w/Regina Bendix injection, 1990 700 Series

Fuel filter, Diesel . . . . drain water

Power antenna . . . . lubricate

Power steering . . . . check level AF

Transmission, automatic . . . . . check level

Windshield washers . . . . check/fill

EVERY 12 MO/10 MI—16 KM

Brake system . . . . inspect/adjust
Check thickness of pads & linings, check condition of hoses & lines, check power booster, check parking brake cables & adjust

Clutch pedal free play . . . . check

Differential 1989-92 . . . . check level
1989 models w/Regina Bendix injection, 1990 700 Series only

Drive shaft, U-joints . . . . inspect

Exhaust system . . . . inspect

Front suspension & steering linkage
240 Series . . . . inspect

Rear suspension 240 Series . . . . . check

Shock absorbers 240 Series . . . . . inspect

Steering gear 240 Series . . . . inspect

Suspension components
700, 900 series . . . . retorque
One time service only. Control arm inner mount, 85 Nm (63 ft lb); control arm strut inner mount with 14 mm hex, 85 Nm (63 ft lb), with 19 mm hex, 140 Nm (103 ft lb); control arm strut outer mount, 95 Nm (70 ft lb); steering rack, 44 Nm, (32 ft lb); rear axle clamps, 45 Nm (33 ft lb)

Transmission, manual 1989-92 check level
1989 models w/Regina Bendix injection, 1990 700 Series only

Turbo to exhaust nuts . . . . retorque

Wheel bearings
240 Series . . . . inspect/adjust

Battery . . . . check level

Coolant . . . . check level

Cooling system . . . . pressure test

Fuel lines & hoses . . . . inspect

Kickdown cable . . . . check/adjust
Not required for 1992 960 models

Throttle cable,
1986-88 Gasoline . . . . check/adjust
With accelerator pedal fully depressed, distance between cable housing and clip on cable should be 50.4-52.6 mm (1.98-2.07")

Timing belt, 1992 4-cyl. . . . . check/adjust
At first service interval only

Body . . . . lubricate

Electrical equipment . . . . inspect

Service indicator . . . . reset

Windshield wipers . . . . inspect

EVERY 24 MO/20 MI—32 KM

Automatic transmission
1987-92 . . . . .replace fluid
Ex. models with AW30-40 transmission

Shock absorbers . . . . inspect
1992 700, 900 retorque at first service interval only

Steering gear . . . . inspect

PCV flame guard 1986-90 . . . . clean
4-cyl. non-turbo engine only

Body, 1992 . . . . inspect
Visually check for corrosion

1986, EVERY 25 MI—40 KM

Automatic transmission . . . . . change fluid

EVERY 36 MO/30 MI—48 KM

W Air filter element . . . . replace

Brake fluid . . . . replace HB
At least every 24 mo

W Cooling system . . . . change coolant EC
At least every 24 mo

W Drive belts, ex. 960 . . . . . . check/adjust

Drive shaft center support . . . . . . inspect

W Fuel filter, Diesel . . . . replace
Inspect fuel lines

Front suspension
& steering . . . . inspect
1991 740, 940 retorque

Oxygen sensor 1986 . . . . replace
Reset service indicator light

Rear suspension 700, 900 Series . inspect

W Spark plugs . . . . replace

Timing belt, 960 . . . . replace

W Valve clearance . . . . check/adjust

Wheel bearings . . . . inspect/adjust

EVERY 60 MO/50 MI—80 KM

Balance shaft belt DOHC . . . . replace

Timing belt, 4-cyl. . . . . replace
Readjust after 5 mi (8 km)

EVERY 72 MO/60 MI—96 KM

Drive belts, 960 . . . . replace

W Fuel filter . . . . replace

W EGR system 1991 . . . . inspect/clean

W PCV system . . . . inspect/clean

EVERY 80 MI—128 KM

Timing belt, Diesel . . . . replace

SEVERE SERVICE

Crankcase — Change oil & filter every 3 mo

Spark plugs — Replace: 240 every 10 mi (16 km), 740 every 15 mi (24 km)

Brake fluid — Replace every 15 mi (24 km)

KEY TO LUBRICANTS

AF	DEXRON®-II Automatic Transmission Fluid
CC	Motor Oil, API Service CC
CD	Motor Oil, API Service CD
EC	Ethylene Glycol Coolant Mix 50/50 with water
FA	Automatic Transmission Fluid, Type F
GL-5	Gear Oil, API Service GL-5
GL-5★	Gear Oil for Limited-Slip Differential
HB	Hydraulic Brake Fluid, DOT 4
SF	Motor Oil, API Service SF
SG	Motor Oil, API Service SG

CRANKCASE

1986 Diesel engine . . . . CD, SF/CD
1986-90 Gasoline engine . . . SF, SF/CC, SF/CD, SG
1991-92 . . . . SG, SG/CD

CAPACITY, Refill:	Liters	Qt
4-cyl. 2.3L, SOHC	3.4	3.6
4-cyl. 2.3L, DOHC	3.5	3.7
6-cyl. 2.4L Diesel	5.0	5.3
V6 2.8L	5.5	5.8
6-cyl. 2.9L	5.2	5.5

Capacity shown is without filter. When replacing filter, additional oil may be needed. On models with oil cooler, additional oil may be needed if cooler is drained

Diesel Engines:
Above 0°F (–18°C) 15W-40
–13° to 68°F (–25° to 20°C) 10W-30
Below 68°F (20°C) 5W-30

Gasoline Engines:
Above 0°F (–18°C) 15W-40
–4° to 104°F (–20° to 40°C) 10W-30
Below 68°F (20°C) 5W-30

TRANSMISSION, Automatic . . . . AF

CAPACITY, Initial Refill*:	Liters	Qt
1986-91 AW70, AW71, AW72	3.4	3.6
1986-92 ZF4HP22	2.0	2.2
1992 AW70, AW71	1.9	2.0
1992 AW30-34	3.0	3.3

*Add specified quantity. With engine at operating temperature, shift transmission through all gears. Check fluid level in PARK and add oil as needed

TRANSMISSION, Manual . . . . FA

CAPACITY, Refill*:	Liters	Pt
1986-90 M46 4-speed w/OD	2.3	4.8
1987-92 M47 5-speed	1.6	3.2
1991-92 M46 4-speed w/OD	2.6	5.6

DIFFERENTIAL

Standard GL-5
Eaton Automatic Lock GL-5
Dana Limited-Slip . . . . GL-5★
GL-5 plus Volvo additive Part No. 1161129-0
Above 14°F (–10°C), 90; below 14°F (–10°C) 80W

CAPACITY, Refill*:	Liters	Pt
Type 1030	1.3	2.8
Type 1031, 1041	1.6	3.4
Type 1035, 1045	1.4	3.0

KEY TO LUBRICANTS		
AF	DEXRON®-II Automatic Transmission Fluid Infiniti, use DEXRON® only. Do not use DEXRON®-II	
CC	Motor Oil, API Service CC	
CD	Motor Oil, API Service CD	
FA	Automatic Transmission Fluid, Type F	
GL-4	Gear Oil, API Service GL-4	
GL-5	Gear Oil, API Service GL-5	
GL-5★	Special Lubricant for Limited-Slip Differential	
SF	Motor Oil, API Service SF	
SG	Motor Oil, API Service SG	
SLF	Special Lubricant—Fluid Toyota ATF Type T or T-II	

MODEL — CAPACITY — LUBRICANT

ACURA—NSX

CRANKCASE .... SG

CAPACITY, Refill:	Liters	Qt
NSX (incl. filter)	5.0	5.3

TRANSAXLE, Automatic .... AF

CAPACITY, Initial Refill*:	Liters	Qt
NSX	2.9	3.1

*With engine at operating temperature, shift transmission through all gears. Turn engine off and check fluid level within one minute

TRANSAXLE, Manual .... SG
Above 15°F (−10°C), 30; above −5°F (−20°C), 20W-40; all temperatures, 10W-30, 10W-40

CAPACITY, Refill:	Liters	Pt
NSX	2.7	5.8

ALFA ROMEO

CRANKCASE
1992-91 .... 10W-40 SG
1990-83 .... 10W-50, 15W-50 SF

CAPACITY, Refill:	Liters	Qt
1992-83 All 4-cyl.	6.6	7.1
All V6	7.0	7.4

Capacity is without filter. When replacing filter, additional oil may be needed

TRANSMISSION, Automatic .... AF

CAPACITY, Initial Refill*:	Liters	Qt
1992-91 164	3.5	3.7
1989-87 Milano	1.7	1.8

*With the engine at operating temperature, shift transmission through all gears. Check fluid level in PARK and add fluid as needed

TRANSMISSION/TRANSAXLE, Manual 80W-90 GL-5

CAPACITY, Refill:	Liters	Pt
1992-91 164	1.8	3.8
1992-83 Spider	1.9	3.8
1989-87 Milano	2.4	4.8
1987-83 GTV6	2.9	6.0

DIFFERENTIAL 80W-90 GL-5

CAPACITY, Refill:	Liters	Pt
1992-83 All	1.4	3.0

DAIHATSU

CRANKCASE .... SF, SF/CC, SG

CAPACITY, Refill:	Liters	Qt
1991-89 1295cc, 1589cc	3.3	3.5
1991-88 993cc	2.7	2.9

Capacity is without filter. When replacing filter, additional oil may be needed
Above 10°F (−12°C), 15W-40, 20W-40, 20W-50
Above 0°F (−18°C), 10W-30, 10W-40, 10W-50
Below 50°F (10°C), 5W-30

TRANSMISSION/TRANSAXLE, Automatic .... AF

CAPACITY, Initial Refill*:	Liters	Qt
1991-89	1.5	1.6

*With the engine at operating temperature, shift transmission through all gears. Check fluid level in PARK and add fluid as needed

TRANSMISSION/TRANSAXLE, Manual GL-4
75W-85, 75W-90

CAPACITY, Refill:	Liters	Pt
1991-90 Rocky	1.7	3.8
1991-88 Charade	2.4	4.5

TRANSFER CASE 75W-85, 75W-90 GL-4

CAPACITY, Refill:	Liters	Pt
1991-90 Rocky: Part time	1.4	3.0
Full time	1.7	3.8

DIFFERENTIAL
Standard 80W-90, 90 GL-5
Limited-Slip .... 80W-90, 90 GL-5★

CAPACITY, Refill:	Liters	Pt
Rocky: Front	0.9	2.0
Rear	2.0	4.2

MODEL — CAPACITY — LUBRICANT

INFINITI

CRANKCASE .... SG
Above 50°F (10°C), 20W-40, 20W-50
Above 10°F (−18°C), 10W-30, 10W-40
Below 60°F (16°C), Q45, 5W-30
All temperatures, G20, M30, 5W-30*
*Preferred

CAPACITY, Refill:	Liters	Qt
G20	3.2	3.4
M30	4.0	4.2
Q45	5.6	5.9

Capacity is without filter. When replacing filter, additional oil may be needed

TRANSMISSION/TRANSAXLE, Automatic .... AF

CAPACITY, Total Fill:	Liters	Qt
G20	7.0	7.4
M30	8.3	8.7
Q45	10.2	10.7

TRANSAXLE, Manual GL-4
Above 50°F (10°C), 140; 32° to 104°F (0° to 40°C), 90; 14° to 86°F (−10° to 30°C), 85W; below 104°F (40°C), 75W-90, 80W-90; below 86°F (30°C), 80W; below 50°F (10°C), 75W

CAPACITY, Refill:	Liters	Pt
G20	3.6	7.7

DIFFERENTIAL GL-5
Viscosities — See Manual Transaxle.

CAPACITY, Refill:	Liters	Pt
M30	1.3	2.8
Q45	1.5	3.1

JAGUAR

CRANKCASE .... SG

CAPACITY, Refill:	Liters	Qt
1992-90 6-cyl. 4.0L	8.0	8.5
1992-83 V12 5.3L	10.0	10.5
1989-88 6-cyl. 3.6L	8.0	8.5
1987-84 6-cyl. 4.2L	7.5	7.8
1983 6-cyl. 4.2L	8.3	8.8

Includes filter
1992-90:
Above 14°F (−10°C), 15W-40, 15W-50, 20W-40, 20W-50
Above −4°F (−20°C), 10W-60
−4° to 105°F (−20° to 40°C), 10W-30, 10W-40, 10W-50
Below 14°F (−10°C), 5W-20, 5W-30, 5W-40
All temperatures, 5W-50
1989-83:
Above 14°F (−10°C), 10W-40, 10W-50, 15W-50, 20W-40, 20W-50
−4° to 50°F (−20° to 10°C), 10W-30, 10W-40, 10W-50
Below 14°F (−10°C), 5W-20, 5W-30

TRANSMISSION, Automatic
Borg Warner .... FA
Hydra-Matic, ZF .... AF

CAPACITY, Total Fill:	Liters	Qt
1992-90 Al 6-cyl. 4.0L	10.2	10.8
1990-83 XJS	9.1	9.5
1989-83 XJ6, Vanden Plas	8.0	8.4

DIFFERENTIAL 90 GL-5
Powr-Lok .... 90 GL-5★

CAPACITY, Refill:	Liters	Pt
1992-88 XJS	1.6	3.4
All 4-door models	2.1	4.4
1987-83 All models	1.5	3.3

LEXUS

CRANKCASE .... SG

CAPACITY, Refill:	Liters	Qt
ES250	3.7	3.9
ES300	4.1	4.3
LS400: 1992-91	5.0	5.3
1990	4.7	5.0
SC300, SC400	4.5	4.8

Capacity is without filter. When replacing filter, additional oil may be needed

MODEL — CAPACITY — LUBRICANT

MODEL — CAPACITY — LUBRICANT

LEXUS Continued
CRANKCASE Continued
ES250, 1990:
  Above 10°F (−12°C), 15W-40, 20W-40, 20W-50
  Above 0°F (−18°C), 10W-30, 10W-40, 10W-50
  Below 50°F (10°C), 5W-30
ES250, 1991; ES300:
  Above 0°F (−18°C), 10W-30
  Below 50°F (10°C), 5W-30
SC300, SC400, LS400:
  Above 0°F (−18°C), 10W-30
  Below 100°F (38°C), 5W-30*
*Preferred

TRANSMISSION/TRANSAXLE, Automatic
ES250, ES300, SC300 . . . . **AF**
LS400, SC400 . . . . **SLF**

CAPACITY, Initial Refill*:	Liters	Qt
ES250†	2.5	2.6
ES300	3.1	3.3
LS400	2.0	2.1
SC300	1.6	1.7
SC400	1.9	2.0

*With engine at operating temperature, shift transmission through all gears.
  Check fluid level with engine idling in PARK and add fluid as needed
†Final drive serviced separately

TRANSAXLE, Manual 75W-90, 80W-90 **GL-4, GL-5**

CAPACITY, Refill:	Liters	Pt
ES250, ES300	4.2	8.8

FINAL DRIVE, Front . . . . **AF**

CAPACITY, Refill:	Liters	Pt
ES250	1.0	2.2

DIFFERENTIAL, Rear **GL-5**
Above 0°F (−18°C), 90; below 0°F (−18°C), 80W, 80W-90

CAPACITY, Refill:	Liters	Pt
LS400, SC300, SC400	1.3	2.6

RANGE ROVER
CRANKCASE . . . . **SF, SF/CC**

CAPACITY, Refill:	Liters	Qt
1992-87	5.7	6.0

Includes filter
  Above 32°F (0°C), 20W-40, 20W-50
  Above 14°F (−10°C), 15W-40, 10W-50
  Below 14°F (−10°C), 5W-20, 5W-30, 5W-40
  Above −4°F (−20°C), 10W-40, 10W-50
  −4° to 50°F (−20° to 10°C), 10W-30

TRANSMISSION, Automatic . . . . **AF**

CAPACITY, Total Fill:	Liters	Qt
1992-87	9.1*	10.0*

*Dry or total fill shown, use less fluid when refilling

TRANSFER CASE
1992-89 . . . . **AF**
1988-87 . . . . **GL-4, GL-5**
  Above −4°F (−20°C), 90; below 50°F (10°C), 80W

CAPACITY, Refill:	Liters	Pt
1992-89	1.7	3.6
1988-87	2.5	5.3

DIFFERENTIAL 80W, 90 **GL-4, GL-5**

CAPACITY, Refill:	Liters	Pt
1992-87:		
Front	1.7	3.6
Rear	1.7	3.6

STERLING
CRANKCASE . . . . **SG**

CAPACITY, Refill:	Liters	Qt
All	4.5	4.8

Includes filter
1991-89:
  Above 20°F (−8°C) 10W-30
  All temperatures, 5W-30*
1988-87:
  Above 32°F (0°C), 15W-40, 15W-50, 20W-40, 20W-50
  Above −5°F (−20°C), 10W-40, 10W-50
  Below 15°F (−10°C), 5W-20, 5W-30, 5W-40
  −5° to 85°F (−20° to 30°C), 10W-30*
  All temperatures, 5W-50
*Preferred

STERLING Continued
TRANSAXLE, Automatic . . . . **AF**

CAPACITY, Initial Refill*:	Liters	Qt
All	3.2	3.4

*With engine at operating temperature shift transmission through all gears.
  Turn engine off and check fluid level within one minute

TRANSAXLE, Manual
1991-89 . . . . 5W-30 **SF, SF/CD**
1988-87 . . . . 10W-30 **SF, SF/CD**

CAPACITY, Refill:	Liters	Pt
All	2.2	4.6

SUZUKI
CRANKCASE . . . . **SG**

CAPACITY, Refill:		Liters	Qt
1992-86	Samurai	3.5	3.7
	Sidekick	4.0	4.2
	Swift	3.1	3.3
1988-85	Forsa	3.5	3.7
1985-83	LJ80, 81	3.0	3.2

Capacity is without filter. When replacing filter, additional oil may be needed
Swift:
  Above 0°F (−18°C), 10W-30
  All temperatures, 5W-30*
*Preferred, especially below 32°F (0°C)

Samurai, Sidekick:
  Above 14°F (−10°C), 20W-50
  Above 0°F (−18°C), 15W-40, 15W-50
  Above −4°F (−20°C), 10W-40, 10W-50
  −4° to 86°F (−20° to 30°C), 10W-30
  Below 86°F (30°C), 5W-30

Forsa:
  Above 40°F (4°C), 30
  Above 20°F (−7°C), 20W-20
  Above 10°F (−12°C), 15W-40
  Above 0°F (−18°C), 10W-30
  Below 100°F (38°C), 5W-30

LJ80, 81:
  Above 20°F (−7°C), 20W-40, 20W-50
  0° to 80°F (−18° to 27°C), 10W-30, 10W-40
  Below 20°F (−7°C), 5W-20, 5W-30

TRANSMISSION/TRANSAXLE, Automatic . . . . **AF**

CAPACITY, Initial Refill*:	Liters	Qt
Sidekick	2.8	3.0
Swift	0.8	0.8
Forsa	1.5	1.6

*With the engine at operating temperature, shift transmission through all
  gears. Check fluid level in PARK and add fluid as needed

TRANSMISSION/TRANSAXLE, Manual
Samurai, Sidekick, Swift 75W-80, 75W-90* **GL-4**
  Above 5°F (−15°C), 80W-90
Forsa 75W-85, 80W, 80W-90, 90 **GL-4**
LJ80, 81 . . . . 90 **GL-4**
*Preferred

CAPACITY, Refill:		Liters	Pt
1992-89	Sidekick: 2WD	1.9	4.0
	4WD	1.5	3.2
	Swift	2.4	4.9
1992-86	Samurai	1.3	2.7
1988-85	Forsa	2.3	4.8
1985-83	LJ80, 81	1.0	2.1

TRANSFER CASE
Samurai, Sidekick 75W-80, 75W-90* **GL-4**
  Above 5°F (−15°C), 80W-90
LJ80, 81 . . . . 90 **GL-4**
*Preferred

CAPACITY, Refill:		Liters	Pt
1992-89	Sidekick	1.7	3.6
1992-86	Samurai	0.8	1.7
1985-83	LJ80, 81	0.9	1.9

DIFFERENTIAL
Samurai, Sidekick 75W-80, 75W-90 **GL-5**
  Above 5°F (−15°C), 80W-90
LJ80, 81 . . . . 90 **GL-5**

CAPACITY, Refill:		Liters	Pt
1992-90	Samurai: Front	2.0	4.2
	Rear	1.5	3.2
1992-89	Sidekick: Front	1.0	2.1
	Rear	2.2	4.6
1989-86	Samurai: Front	1.7	3.6
	Rear	1.5	3.2
1985-83	LJ80, 81	1.3	2.8

THIS SECTION CONTAINS:

- **COOLING SYSTEM CAPACITIES**

- **FUEL TANK CAPACITIES**

- **AIR CONDITIONING SYSTEM REFRIGERANT CAPACITIES**

- **COOLING SYSTEM AIR BLEED CHART**

- **TIRE SIZES & PRESSURES WHEEL RIM SIZES**

- **WHEEL NUT TORQUE**

Column 1

MAKE, YEAR & MODEL	LITERS	QUARTS

PASSENGER CARS

ACURA

1992	Legend	8.5	9.0
	Vigor	7.5	8.0
1991	Integra: MT	6.0	6.5
	AT	6.5	7.0
	NSX: MT	16.0	17.0
	AT	16.5	17.5
1991-88	Legend: MT	9.0	9.5
	AT	8.5	9.0
1990	Integra: MT	5.0	5.5
	AT	5.5	6.0
1989-86	Integra	5.5	6.0
1987-86	Legend	8.5	9.0

AMERICAN MOTORS

1988-85	Eagle	13.0	14.0
1984	4-cyl.	8.5	9.0
	6-cyl.	13.0	14.0
1983	Eagle: 4-cyl.	6.0	6.5
	6-cyl.	13.0	14.0
	Spirit, Concord: 4-cyl.	6.0	6.5
	6-cyl.	10.5, 13.0*	11.0, 14.0*

AUDI

1992	V8 Quattro	8.5	9.0
	100	12.0	12.5
1991-90	Coupe Quattro	8.0	8.5
	V8 Quattro	10.5	11.0
1991-89	100, 200, Quattro	8.0	8.5
1991-88	80, 90, Quattro: 4-cyl.	7.0	7.5
	5-cyl.	8.0	8.5
1988-85	5000 Turbo Quattro	8.0	8.5
1988-84	5000S, 5000 Turbo	8.0	8.5
1987-86	4000S	6.5	7.0
	Coupe GT	7.0	7.5
1987-84	4000 Quattro	8.0	8.5
1985-84	Coupe GT	8.0	8.5
	4000S	7.0	7.5
1986-83	Quattro	9.5	10.0
1983	4000 4-cyl.	7.0	7.5
	4000 5-cyl., Coupe	8.0	8.5
	4000 Diesel	6.0	6.5
	5000 ex. Turbo	8.0	8.5
	5000 Turbo	9.5	10.0

BMW

1992-91	318i	6.5	7.0
	325 Series	10.5	11.0
	535i	12.0	12.5
	850i	13.0	13.5
	M3	9.5	10.0
	M5	13.5	14.0
1992-89	525i	10.5	11.0
1992-88	750iL	15.0	16.0
1990-85	325e, 535i, 635CSi, 735i, 735iL	12.0	13.0
1988-85	528e	11.0	11.5
1986-85	524td	12.0	13.0
1985-83	318i	7.0	7.5
1984-83	528e, 533i	12.0	13.0
	633CSi, 733i	12.0	13.0
1983	320i	7.0	7.5

BUICK CENTURY, REGAL

1992	Regal: 3.1L	12.0	12.5
	3.8L	10.5	11.0
	Century: 2.5L	9.5	10.0
	3.3L	12.0	13.0
1991-89	Century: 4-cyl.	9.0	9.5
	V6 3.3L	12.5	13.0
1989-88	Regal	12.0	12.5
1988-86	Century: 4-cyl.	9.0	9.5
	V6: 2.8L (173)	12.0	12.5
	3.8L (231)	11.5	12.0
1987-86	Regal: V6 ex. Turbo	12.5	13.0
	V6 Turbo	11.5	12.0
	V8 5.0L (307)	14.0, 15.0*	15.0, 16.0*
	V8 5.0L (305) Canada	14.5, 15.0	15.5, 16.0*
1985	Century V6: 3.0L (181)	12.0, 12.5*	12.5, 13.0*
	4.3L (262) Diesel	12.0	12.5
	Somerset Regal: 4-cyl.	6.0	7.0
	V6	9.5, 10.5*	10.0, 11.0*
1985-84	Century: 4-cyl.	9.0	9.5
	3.8L (231)	11.5, 12.0*	12.0, 12.5*
	Regal: V6 ex. Diesel & Turbo	12.5	13.0
	Diesel	14.0	15.0
	Turbo	12.5, 12.0*	13.5, 13.0*

Column 2

MAKE, YEAR & MODEL	LITERS	QUARTS

BUICK CENTURY, REGAL Continued

1984	V6: 3.0L (181)	13.5, 13.0*	14.5, 13.0*
	4.3L (262) Diesel	13.0, 12.5*	13.5, 13.0*
1983	Century: 4-cyl.	9.0, 9.5*	9.5, 10.0*
	V6: 3.0L (181)	13.5, 13.0*	14.5, 13.5*
	Diesel		13.5
	Regal: V6 ex. Diesel & Turbo	12.5	13.0
	Turbo	13.0	13.5
	Diesel	14.0	15.0
	Regal V8 Diesel	16.5	17.5

BUICK ELECTRA, LE SABRE, REATTA, RIVIERA, ROADMASTER, ESTATE WAGON

1992	Roadmaster	16.0	17.0
	w/HD radiator	16.5	17.5
1992-88	Reatta, Riviera	12.5	13.0
1992-87	LeSabre	12.5	13.0
	Electra, Park Avenue	12.5	13.0
1991	Roadmaster, Estate Wagon	16.0	17.0
1990-88	Estate Wagon	15.5	16.0
1987	Estate Wagon	15.0, 14.5*	16.0, 15.5*
	Riviera	11.5	12.0
1986	LeSabre, Estate Wagon	15.0, 14.5*	16.0, 15.5*
	Electra, Park Avenue, Riviera	11.5	12.0
1985	LeSabre, Estate Wagon: V6	12.5	13.0
	V8 ex. Diesel	15.0	16.0
	Diesel	17.5, 17.0*	18.5, 18.0*
	Electra, Park Avenue	12.5	13.5
	Riviera: Turbo	12.0	13.0
	V8 ex. Diesel	14.5	15.5
	V8 Diesel	17.0	18.0
1984	Turbo V6 (Riviera)	12.0	13.0
	H.D. Cooling	13.0	13.5
1984-83	V6 ex. Turbo	12.5	13.0
	V8: ex. Riviera	14.5, 15.5*	15.5, 16.0*
	Riviera	15.5	16.5
	Diesel	17.0	18.0
1983	Turbo V6 (Riviera)	13.0, 13.5*	13.5, 14.0*

BUICK SKYLARK, SOMERSET

1992	4-cyl.	10.0	10.5
	V6	12.5	13.0
1991-89	4-cyl.	10.0	10.5
	V6	12.0	12.5
1988-86	4-cyl.	7.5	8.0
	V6	9.5, 10.5*	10.0, 11.0*
1985	Somerset: 4-cyl.	7.5	8.0
	V6 3.0L (181)	9.5, 10.5*	10.0, 11.0*
1985-83	Skylark: 4-cyl.	9.0	9.5
	V6	11.0	11.5

BUICK SKYHAWK

1989-86	All	7.5	8.0
1985-83	4-cyl.: 1.8L (112)	7.5	8.0
	2.0L (121)	9.0	9.5

CADILLAC

1992	Allanté	10.0	11.0
	Eldorado, Seville	11.5	12.0
1992-91	Brougham	16.0	16.5
1992-90	DeVille, Fleetwood	11.5	12.0
1991	Allanté	10.5	11.5
	Eldorado, Seville	10.0	10.5
1990	Brougham, Eldorado:		
	V8 5.0L (307)	14.5	15.0
	V8 5.7L (350)	16.0	16.5
	Seville	11.5	12.0
1990-87	Allanté	11.5	12.0
1989	Seville, Eldorado	10.5	11.0
1989-87	Brougham	14.5	15.5
	DeVille, Fleetwood	12.5	13.5
1988	Cimarron	10.5	11.0
	Seville, Eldorado	12.5	13.5
1987-86	Seville, Eldorado	11.5	12.5
	Cimarron: 4-cyl.	9.0	9.5
	V6	10.5	11.0
1985	V6 Diesel	13.0	13.5
	V8 ex. Diesel:		
	Seville, Eldorado	11.0	12.0
	Fleetwood, DeVille	12.5	13.0
	Fleetwood Brougham	10.5	11.0
1985-83	V8 5.7L (350) Diesel:		
	Seville, Eldorado	17.5	18.5
	Others	22.5	23.5
1984-83	4-cyl. 2.0L (121) Cimarron:		
	MT	8.0	8.5
	AT	8.5	9.5
	V8 6.0L (368)	20.0	21.5
	V8 4.1L (250):		
	Seville, Eldorado	11.0	12.0
	Others	10.5	11.0

Column 3

MAKE, YEAR & MODEL	LITERS	QUARTS

CHEVROLET IMPALA, CAPRICE

1992	V8 5.0L	16.0	10.5
	W/H.D. radiator	16.5	17.5
	V8 5.7L	16.5	17.5
1991	V8	15.5	16.5
1990	V8: 5.0L (305): Sedan	15.5	16.5
	Wagon	15.0	16.0
	W/HD radiator	16.5	17.5
	5.7L (350)	14.0	15.0
1989-88	V6	11.5	12.0
1988-86	V8	16.0	17.0
1987-85	V6	11.5	12.5
1985	V8 ex. Diesel	16.0	16.5
	Diesel	17.5	18.0
1984	V8 5.0L (305)	14.5	15.5
1984-83	Diesel	17.0	18.0
	V6: 3.8L (229)	13.5	14.0
	3.8L (231)	11.0	11.5
1983	V8 5.0L (305)	14.0	15.0

CHEVROLET CAMARO

1992	V6 3.1L	14.0	15.0
	V8 5.7L	16.0	16.5
1992-91	V8 5.0L (305)(F)	17.0	18.0
1991-90	V6	13.5	14.5
	V8: 5.0L (305)(E)	16.5, 17.0*	17.5, 18.0*
	5.7L (350)	15.0, 15.5*	16.0, 16.5*
1990	V8: 5.0L (305)(F)	16.0, 16.5*	17.0, 17.5*
1989-86	V6	11.5	12.5
	V8: 5.0L (305)(H)	14.5	15.5
	5.0L (305)(F,G)	16.0	17.0
	5.7L (350)	16.0	17.0
1986	4-cyl.	9.5	10.0
1985	4-cyl.	12.0, 12.5*	12.5, 13.0*
	V6	12.0	12.5
	V8	16.5	17.0
1984	4-cyl.	8.5	9.0
	V6	12.0	12.5
	V8: 5.0L (305)	14.5, 15.0*	15.0, 15.5*
	5.0L (305) H.O.	15.0, 16.0*	16.0, 16.5*
1983	4-cyl.	12.0, 12.5*	12.5, 13.0*
	V6	12.0	12.5
	V8	14.0, 15.0*	15.0, 15.0*

CHEVROLET CELEBRITY

1990	4-cyl.	9.0, 9.5*	9.5, 10.0*
	V6	12.5	13.0
1989-85	4-cyl.	9.0	9.5
	V6 Gas	12.0	12.5
1985	V6 Diesel	12.5	13.0
1984-83	4-cyl.	8.5, 9.0*	9.0, 9.5*
	V6: Gas	11.5, 12.0*	12.0, 12.5*
	Diesel	12.0, 12.5*	12.5, 13.0*

CHEVROLET CAVALIER

1992	4-cyl.	13.5	14.0
1992-90	4-cyl.	11.0	11.5
1991	V6	12.5	13.0
1990	V6	10.5	11.0
1989-85	4-cyl.	9.0	9.5
	V6	10.5	11.0
1984	All	9.0	9.5
1983	All	9.0, 9.5*	9.5, 10.0*

CHEVROLET CHEVETTE

1987	All	8.5, 9.0*	9.0, 9.5*
1986-83	All	8.5	9.0

CHEVROLET CITATION

1985-83	4-cyl.	8.5	9.0
	V6	10.0, 11.5*	10.5, 11.0*

CHEVROLET CORSICA, BERETTA

1992	4-cyl.: 2.2L	9.0	9.5
	2.3L	10.0	10.5
	V6: MT	11.0	12.0
	AT	11.5	12.5
1991-90	4-cyl.	9.0	9.5
	V6: MT	11.0	12.0
	AT	11.5	12.5
1989-88	V6: MT	15.0	16.0
	AT	15.5	16.5
1989-87	4-cyl.	12.5, 13.5*	13.0, 14.0*
1987	V6: MT	15.0	16.0
	AT	16.0	17.0

CHEVROLET CORVETTE

1992-91	All ex. ZR-1	14.0	14.5
	ZR-1	17.0	18.0
1990	All	15.5	16.5
1989-85	All	13.5	14.0
1984	All	14.0	14.5

COOLING SYSTEM CAPACITIES

Capacities are rounded off to the nearest half unit

(Includes heater. *Indicates with air conditioning)

MAKE, YEAR & MODEL	LITERS	QUARTS	MAKE, YEAR & MODEL	LITERS	QUARTS	MAKE, YEAR & MODEL	LITERS	QUARTS
CHEVROLET LUMINA			**DODGE Continued**			**FORD MUSTANG Continued**		
1992 4-cyl.	9.0	9.5	1991 Monaco	9.0	9.5	1983 4-cyl.	8.0, 8.5*	8.5, 9.0*
V6: 3.1L	12.0	12.5	Dynasty: 2.5L, 3.0L	9.0	9.5	V6	10.0	10.5
3.4L: AT	12.0	12.5	3.3L	8.5	9.0	V8	12.5, 13.0*	13.0, 13.5*
MT	12.5	13.0	1991-89 Colt ex. wagon: 1.5L	5.0	5.5	**FORD PROBE**		
1991 4-cyl.	9.5	10.0	1.6L	6.0	6.5	1992-89 All	7.5	8.0
V6: Euro	12.0	12.5	Colt wagon	5.0	5.5	**FORD TAURUS**		
Z34: MT	12.5	13.0	1991-85 Colt Vista	7.0	7.5	1992-86 4-cyl.	8.0	8.5
AT	12.0	12.5	1990 Dynasty: 4-cyl.	9.0	9.5	V6 3.0L	10.5	11.0
APV	12.5	13.5	V6	8.5	9.0	SHO	11.0	11.5
W/rear AC	14.0	15.0	Monaco	8.0	8.5	V6 3.8L	12.0	12.5
1990 4-cyl.	9.0	9.5	1989-88 4-cyl. ex. Dynasty	8.5	9.0	**FORD TEMPO**		
V6	12.0	12.5	Dynasty	9.0	9.5	1992 All w/MT	7.5	8.0
CHEVROLET MALIBU,			1989-85 Diplomat	14.5, 15.5*	15.5, 16.5*	All w/AT	8.0	8.5
MONTE CARLO			1989-84 Conquest	9.0	9.5	1991 All	7.5	8.0
1988-87 V6	12.5	13.0	1988-85 Colt	5.0	5.5	1990-88 All w/MT	7.0	7.5
V8	15.5	16.5	1987-86 4-cyl. 2.2L (135),			All w/AT	7.5	8.0
1986-85 V6	12.0	12.5	2.5L (153)	8.5	9.0	1987-86 All w/MT	8.0, 7.0*	8.5, 7.5*
V8 ex. H.O.	15.5	16.0	1986-83 4-cyl. 1.6L (98)	6.5	7.0	All w/AT	8.0, 7.5*	8.5, 8.0*
H.O.	16.0	16.5	1985-83 4-cyl.: 1.7L (105)	5.5	6.0	1985 All ex. Diesel	7.0	7.5
1984 V6: 3.8L (229)	14.5	15.0	2.2L (135), 2.6L (156)	8.5	9.0	Diesel	7.5	8.0
3.8L (231)	11.0	11.5	1984 Colt Vista	6.5	7.0	1984 All ex. Diesel	7.5	8.0
V8: 5.0L (305)	15.5	16.5	1984-83 Diplomat	14.0, 14.5*	15.0, 15.5*	Diesel	8.5	9.0
5.0L (305) H.O.	16.0	16.5	Colt	4.5	5.0	**FORD THUNDERBIRD**		
1984-83 V8 Diesel	16.5	17.5	1983 6-cyl.	11.0, 12.0*	11.5, 12.5*	1992 V6 3.8L	12.0	12.5
1983 V6: 3.8L (229)	14.0	15.0	Challenger	9.0	9.5	1992-91 V8 5.0L	13.5	14.0
3.8L (231)	11.5	12.0	**EAGLE**			1991 V6 3.8L	11.5	12.0
V6 Diesel	14.0	15.0	1992 Summit wagon: 1.8L	6.0	6.5	1990-89 V6 3.8L (232): EFI	11.0	11.5
V8 5.0L (305)	15.5	16.5	2.4L	6.5	7.0	S/C	11.5	12.0
CHEVROLET NOVA			Talon	7.0	7.5	1988-87 V6 3.8L (232)	11.5	12.0
1988-85 All	6.0	6.5	Premier	8.0	8.5	1988-86 4-cyl. Turbo	9.5	10.0
CHEVROLET SPECTRUM			1992-91 Summit	5.0	5.5	1988-84 V8 5.0L (302)	13.5	14.0
1989-88 All ex. Turbo	6.5	7.0	1991 Premier	9.0	9.5	1986-84 V6 3.8L (232)	11.0	11.5
Turbo	7.0	7.5	Vista wagon	7.0	7.5	1985-84 4-cyl. Turbo	10.0	11.0
1987-85 All	6.5	7.0	Talon: 1.8L	6.0	6.5	1983 4-cyl. Turbo	8.5	9.0
CHEVROLET SPRINT			2.0L	7.0	7.5	V6 3.8L (232)	10.0, 10.5*	10.5, 11.0*
1991-85 All	4.0	4.5	1990 Talon	7.0	7.5	V8 5.0L (302)	12.5, 12.5*	13.0, 13.5*
CHRYSLER, IMPERIAL			1990-88 Premier	8.0	8.5	**GEO**		
1992 Imperial: 3.3L	9.0	9.5	Summit: 1.5L	5.0	5.5	1992 Storm: MT	7.0	7.0
3.8L	8.5	9.0	1.6L	6.0	6.5	AT	7.5	7.5
LeBaron: Coupe & conv.	8.5	9.0	1989-88 Medallion	6.5	7.0	1992-91 Prizm	5.5	6.0
Sedan: 2.5L	8.5	9.0	**FORD CROWN VICTORIA, LTD**			1992-89 Metro	4.0	4.5
3.0L	9.0	9.5	1992-88 All	13.5	14.0	1991-90 Storm: 4-cyl. SOHC	7.0	7.5
New Yorker	9.0	9.5	1987 V8: 5.0L (302)	13.5	14.0	4-cyl. DOHC: MT	7.0	7.5
Town & Country van	8.0	8.5	5.8L (351)	14.0	15.0	AT	7.5	8.0
1991 New Yorker, Imperial,			1986 LTD: 4-cyl. 2.3L (140)	9.0, 9.5*	9.5, 10.0*	1990-89 Prizm	6.0	6.5
Town & Country wagon	8.5	9.0	V6 3.8L (232)	11.0	11.5	1989 Spectrum	6.5	7.0
Lebaron, TC by Maserati	8.5	9.0	1985-84 LTD: 4-cyl. 2.3L (140)	8.5, 9.5*	9.0, 10.0*	**HONDA**		
1990 New Yorker, Imperial:			V6 3.8L (232)	11.0	11.5	1992 Prelude	7.5	8.0
V6 3.0L	9.0	9.5	V8	13.5	14.0	Civic	5.0	5.0
V6 3.3L	8.5	9.0	Crown Victoria:			1992-86 Accord: MT	6.5	7.0
Town & Country wagon:			5.0L (302) w/EFI	13.5	14.5	AT	7.0	7.5
V6 3.0L	9.5	10.0	Ex. EFI	15.0	16.0	1991 Civic Hatchback	5.0	5.5
V6 3.3L	8.0	8.5	5.8L (351)	15.5	16.5	Civic Sedan	5.5	6.0
1990-89 TC by Maserati	8.5	9.0	1983 LTD: 4-cyl. 2.3L (140)	8.0, 8.5*	8.5, 9.0*	CRX: Std., HF	5.0	5.5
1990-82 LeBaron	8.5	9.0	6-cyl. 3.3L (200)	8.0	8.5	Si	5.5	6.0
1989 New Yorker	9.0	9.5	V6 3.8L (232)	10.0	11.0	Prelude	6.5	7.0
Fifth Avenue: W/AC	15.5	16.5	Crown Victoria:			1991-90 Civic wagon: 2WD	5.5	6.0
W/o AC	14.5	15.5	5.0L (302)	12.5	13.0	4WD: MT	5.5	6.0
1989-87 Conquest	9.0	9.5	5.8L (351) Canada	13.0	14.0	AT	6.0	6.5
1988 New Yorker ex. Turbo	9.0	9.5	**FORD ESCORT, EXP**			1990-89 Civic	5.5	6.0
Turbo	8.5	9.0	1992-91 All w/MT	5.0	5.5	CRX: Std., Si	5.5	6.0
Fifth Avenue	15.5	16.5	All w/AT	6.0	6.5	HF	5.0	5.5
1987-85 New Yorker (FWD)	8.5		1990-87 All w/MT	8.0, 6.5*	8.5, 7.0*	Prelude ex. Fl: MT	7.0	7.5
Fifth Ave.	14.5, 15.5*	15.5, 16.5*	All w/AT	8.0, 7.0*	8.5, 7.5*	AT	7.5	8.0
1986-83 E Class, Laser	8.5	9.0	1986 All ex. Diesel: w/MT	7.5, 6.5*	8.0, 7.5*	Prelude w/Fl	8.0	8.5
1984 Fifth Avenue	14.0, 14.5*	15.0, 15.5*	w/AT	7.5, 7.0*	8.0, 7.5*	1988 Civic ex. wagon	4.5	5.0
1984-83 Cordoba, Fifth Ave.:			Diesel	7.5		Civic wagon	5.5	6.0
6-cyl.	11.0, 12.0*	11.5, 12.5*	1985 All ex. Diesel	6.5	7.0	CRX: Si	4.0	4.5
V8	14.0, 14.5*	15.0, 15.5*	Diesel	7.5	8.0	HF	4.5	5.0
Imperial	14.5	15.5	1984 All w/o EFI ex. Diesel	7.0	7.5	Prelude: S: MT	6.0	6.5
DAIHATSU			All w/EFI ex. Diesel	7.5	8.0	AT	7.0	7.5
1991-89 Charade: 3-cyl.	4.0	4.5	Diesel	8.5	9.0	Si	7.0	7.5
4-cyl.	5.5	6.0	1983 All	6.5, 7.5*	7.0, 8.0*	1987-86 Civic: 1300	4.5	5.0
DODGE			**FORD FAIRMONT**			1500	5.5	6.0
1992 Monaco	8.0	8.5	1983 4-cyl.	8.0, 8.5*	8.5, 9.0*	CRX: HF	4.5	5.0
Dynasty: 2.5L	8.5	9.0	6-cyl.	8.0	8.5	Others	5.5	6.0
3.0L, 3.3L	9.0	9.5	**FORD FESTIVA**			Prelude: MT	7.0	7.5
Colt Vista: 1.8L	6.0	6.5	1992-88 All	5.0	5.5	AT	6.5	7.0
2.4L	6.5	7.0	**FORD MUSTANG**			1985-84 Accord	7.0	7.5
Colt	5.0	5.5	1992-87 4-cyl.	9.5	10.0	1985-83 Prelude: MT	7.0	7.5
1992-91 Stealth	8.0	8.5	1992-84 V8 5.0L (302)	13.5	14.0	AT	7.5	8.0
1992-90 4-cyl. Daytona, Omni,			1986-84 4-cyl.: ex. Turbo	9.5	10.0	Civic: 1300, CRX HF	4.5	5.0
Shadow, Spirit	8.5	9.0	Turbo	10.5	11.0	1500	5.5	6.0
V6 3.0L ex. Monaco	9.0	9.5	V6 3.8L (232)	11.0	12.0	1983 Accord	5.5	6.0

COOLING SYSTEM CAPACITIES

(Includes heater. *Indicates with air conditioning)

Capacities are rounded off to the nearest half unit

HYUNDAI

MAKE, YEAR	MODEL	LITERS	QUARTS
1992	Elantra	6.0	6.5
	Scoupe	5.5	5.5
	Sonata: 2.0L	7.5	8.0
	3.0L	9.0	9.5
1992-86	Excel	5.0	5.5
1991	Scoupe	5.0	5.5
1991-89	Sonata: 4-cyl.	7.0	7.5
	V6	9.0	9.5
1987-85	Stellar	6.0	6.5
1987-84	Pony	6.0	6.5

INFINITI

MAKE, YEAR	MODEL	LITERS	QUARTS
1992	M30	9.0	9.5
1992-91	G20: MT	6.0	6.5
	AT	6.5	7.0
1992-90	Q45	10.5	11.0
1991-90	M30	8.5	9.0

ISUZU

MAKE, YEAR	MODEL	LITERS	QUARTS
1992-90	Stylus: MT	7.0	7.5
	AT	7.5	8.0
	Impulse: SOHC: MT	7.0	7.5
	AT	7.5	8.0
	DOHC	7.5	8.0
1989-88	I-Mark ex. Turbo	6.5	7.0
	I-Mark Turbo	7.0	7.5
1989-87	Impulse	9.0	9.5
1987-83	All: Gas	6.5	7.0
	Diesel	7.0	7.5
1986-84	Impulse	7.5	8.0

JAGUAR

MAKE, YEAR	MODEL	LITERS	QUARTS
1992	XJS: 4.0L	11.5	12.5
	5.3L	20.0	21.0
1992-91	XJ6	12.5	13.0
1990	XJ6	9.5	10.0

LEXUS

MAKE, YEAR	MODEL	LITERS	QUARTS
1992	ES 300, SC 300	8.5	9.0
	SC 400	11.0	11.5
1992-90	LS 400	10.5	11.0
1991-90	ES 250	9.5	10.0

LINCOLN

MAKE, YEAR	MODEL	LITERS	QUARTS
1992-88	Mark VII, Town Car	13.5	14.0
	Continental	11.5	12.0
1987-86	All	13.5	14.0
1985	6-cyl. 2.4L (146) Diesel	11.0	12.0
	V8: Town Car	13.5	14.5
	Trailer Tow	15.0	15.5
	Continental & Mark VII	13.5	14.0
1984	6-cyl. 2.4L (146) Diesel	11.5	12.5
	V8: Town Car	14.0	14.5
	Others ex. Diesel	13.5	14.0
	Diesel	11.0	12.0
1983	All	12.5	13.0

MAZDA

MAKE, YEAR	MODEL	LITERS	QUARTS
1992-91	Miata	4.5	5.0
	MX-3, Precidia: 4-cyl.	6.0	6.5
	V6	7.5	8.0
	929, Serenia	9.5	10.0
	RX-7 ex. Turbo	7.0	7.5
	RX-7 Turbo	8.5	9.0
1992-90	Protegé, 323: MT	5.0	5.5
	AT	6.0	6.5
	MX-6, 626	7.5	8.0
1990	MX-5 Miata	4.5	5.0
	929	9.5	10.0
1990-89	RX-7	8.5	9.0
1989	929: MT	9.0	9.5
	AT	9.5	10.0
1989-88	323 ex. Turbo: MT	5.0	5.5
	AT	6.0	6.5
	323 Turbo	6.0	6.5
	626	8.0	7.5
1988-87	RX-7 Turbo	8.5	9.0
1988-86	RX-7 ex. Turbo	7.5	8.0
1987-86	323: MT	5.0	5.5
	AT	5.5	6.0
1987-83	626 Gas	7.0	7.5
1985	626 Diesel	9.0	9.5
1985-83	GLC: MT	5.5	6.0
	AT	6.0	6.5
	RX-7	9.5	10.0

MERCEDES-BENZ

MAKE, YEAR	MODEL	LITERS	QUARTS
1992	300SE	14.5	15.5
	400SE, 500SEL	16.5	17.5
	600SEL	20.0	21.0

MERCEDES-BENZ Continued

MAKE, YEAR	MODEL	LITERS	QUARTS
1991	190E 2.3	9.5	10.0
	300CE, D, E, E 4MATIC, SE, SEL	9.5	10.0
	300SL	11.5	12.0
	350SD, SDL	10.0	10.5
	500SL	15.0	16.0
1991-89	420SEL, 560SEC, SEL	13.0	13.7
1990-89	190E	10.0	10.5
	300 Series	10.0	10.5
1988	190D 2.5	8.5	9.0
	190E 2.6	10.0	10.5
	260E, 300E, 300CE	10.0	10.5
	300SEL, 300TE	10.0	10.5
1988-87	190E 2.3L	8.5	9.0
	420SEL, 560SL, 560SEL, 560SEC	13.0	13.5
1987	190E 2.3-16	8.0	8.5
	190E 2.6L, 260E	9.0	9.5
1987-86	300D, 300TD, 300SDL	10.0	10.5
	300E	9.0	9.5
1986	190D, 190E	8.0	8.5
1985-83	300D, 300CD, 300SD	12.5	13.0
	380 Series	12.5	13.0
1983	240D	10.0	10.5

MERCURY CAPRI

MAKE, YEAR	MODEL	LITERS	QUARTS
1992-91	All ex. Turbo	5.0	5.5
	Turbo	6.0	6.5
1986-84	4-cyl. ex. Turbo	9.5	10.0
	4-cyl. Turbo	10.5	11.0
	V6 3.8L (232)	11.0	12.0
	V8 5.0L (302)	13.5	14.0
1983	4-cyl.	8.0, 8.5*	8.5, 9.0*
	Turbo	9.0	9.5
	6-cyl. 3.3L (200)	8.0	8.5
	V6	10.0	10.5
	V8	12.5, 13.0*	13.0, 13.5*

MERCURY COUGAR

MAKE, YEAR	MODEL	LITERS	QUARTS
1992-91	V6 3.8L EFI	11.5	12.5
	V8 5.0L	13.5	14.0
1990-89	V6 3.8L (232) EFI	11.0	11.5
	V6 3.8L (232) S/C	11.5	12.0
1988-86	V6 3.8L (232)	11.0	12.0
	V8 5.0L (302)	13.5	14.0
1985-84	4-cyl. Turbo	10.0	11.0
	V6 3.8L (232)	11.0	11.5
	V8 5.0L (302)	13.5	14.0
1983	4-cyl. Turbo	8.5	9.0
	V6 3.8L (232)	10.0, 10.5*	10.5, 11.0*
	V8 5.0L (302)	12.5, 12.5*	13.0, 13.5*

MERCURY LYNX, LN7

MAKE, YEAR	MODEL	LITERS	QUARTS
1987	All AT	8.0, 7.0*	8.5, 7.5*
	All MT	8.0, 6.5*	8.5, 7.0*
1986	All ex. Diesel: MT	7.5, 6.5*	8.0, 7.0*
	AT	7.5, 7.0*	8.0, 7.5*
	Diesel	7.0	7.5
1985	All ex. Diesel	6.5	7.0
	Diesel	7.5	8.0
1984	All ex. Diesel	7.0	7.5
	All w/EFI ex. Diesel	7.5	8.0
	Diesel	8.5	9.0
1983	All	6.5, 7.5*	7.0, 8.0*

MERCURY MARQUIS, GRAND MARQUIS

MAKE, YEAR	MODEL	LITERS	QUARTS
1992-88	All	13.5	14.0
1987-86	Grand Marquis V8:		
	5.0L (302)	13.5	14.5
	5.8L (351)	14.0	15.0
	w/Trailer Tow	15.0	16.0
1986	Marquis: 4-cyl.	9.0, 9.5*	9.5, 10.0*
	V6 3.8L (232)	11.0	11.5
1985-84	Marquis: 4-cyl.	8.5, 9.5*	9.0, 10.0*
	V6 3.8L (232)	11.0	11.5
	V8	13.5	14.0
	Grand Marquis:		
	5.0L (302) w/EFI	13.5	14.5
	Ex. EFI	15.0	16.0
	5.8L (351)	15.5	16.5
1983	Marquis: 4-cyl.	8.0, 8.5*	8.5, 9.0*
	6-cyl.	8.0	8.5
	V6	10.0	11.0
	Grand Marquis:		
	5.0L (302)	12.5	13.0
	5.8L (351) Canada	13.0	14.0

MERCURY SABLE

MAKE, YEAR	MODEL	LITERS	QUARTS
1992-86	3.0L (183)	10.5	11.0
	3.8L (232)	11.5	12.0
1987-86	4-cyl. 2.5L (153)	8.0	8.5

MERCURY TOPAZ

MAKE, YEAR	MODEL	LITERS	QUARTS
1992	All MT	7.5	8.0
	All AT	8.0	8.5
1991	All	7.5	8.0
1990-88	All MT	7.0	7.5
	All AT	7.5	8.0
1987-86	All ex. Diesel: MT	8.0, 7.0*	8.5, 7.5*
	AT	8.0, 7.5*	8.5, 8.0*
	Diesel	7.0	7.5
1985	All ex. Diesel	7.0	7.5
	Diesel	7.5	8.0
1984	All ex. Diesel	7.5	8.0
	Diesel	8.5	9.0

MERCURY TRACER

MAKE, YEAR	MODEL	LITERS	QUARTS
1992-88	MT	5.0	5.5
	AT	6.0	6.5

MERCURY ZEPHYR

MAKE, YEAR	MODEL	LITERS	QUARTS
1983	4-cyl.	8.0, 8.5*	8.5, 9.0*
	6-cyl.	8.0	8.5

MERKUR

MAKE, YEAR	MODEL	LITERS	QUARTS
1989	Scorpio	8.5	9.0
	XR4ti	10.5	11.0
1988	All	8.5	9.0
1987-85	XR4ti	10.0	10.5

MITSUBISHI

MAKE, YEAR	MODEL	LITERS	QUARTS
1992	Diamante	8.0	8.5
	Expo LRV	6.0	6.5
	Expo	6.5	7.0
1992-91	3000GT	8.0	8.5
	Eclipse: 1.8L	6.0	6.5
	2.0L	7.0	7.5
1992-90	Mirage	5.0	5.5
	Precis	5.5	6.0
1992-85	Galant	7.0	7.5
1989	Mirage: 1.5L	5.0	5.5
	1.6L	6.0	6.5
1989-88	Sigma	9.0	9.5
1989-83	Starion	9.0	9.5
1988	Cordia, Tredia	7.5	8.0
1988-85	Mirage	5.0	5.5
1987-83	Cordia, Tredia	7.0	7.5

NISSAN

MAKE, YEAR	MODEL	LITERS	QUARTS
1992-91	Maxima SOHC	9.0	9.5
	Maxima DOHC	11.5	12.0
	Sentra, NX Coupe:		
	1.6L	5.0	5.5
	2.0L	5.5	6.0
1992-90	240SX	6.5	7.0
	300ZX	9.0	9.5
1992-89	Stanza	7.5	8.0
1990	Axxess	7.5	8.0
	Maxima	8.5	9.0
	Pulsar NX: MT	5.5	6.0
	AT	6.0	6.5
1990-89	Sentra: 2WD	5.5	6.0
	4WD	6.0	6.5
1989	240 SX	6.0	6.5
	Pulsar NX: 1.6L	5.5	6.0
	1.8L	6.0	6.5
1989-88	300ZX ex. Turbo	10.5	11.0
1989-85	Maxima	9.0	9.5
1988	Stanza ex. wagon	7.5	8.0
	Stanza wagon	6.5	7.0
	W/o heater	5.5	6.0
	300ZX Turbo	11.0	11.5
1988-87	200SX V6	9.0	9.5
1988-84	200SX ex. V6	8.5	9.0
1988-83	Sentra, Pulsar ex. DOHC:		
	MT	4.5	5.0
	AT	5.0	5.5
	Pulsar DOHC	5.5	6.0
1987-84	Stanza:		
	MT, wagons	6.5	7.0
	AT	7.0	7.5
1987-83	Sentra Diesel	7.0	7.5
1986-84	300ZX ex. Turbo	10.5	11.0
	Turbo	11.0	11.5
	Micra	8.5	9.0
1984-83	Maxima: Gas	11.0	11.5
	Diesel	10.5	11.0
1983	280ZX	10.5	11.0
	Stanza	7.5	8.0
	200SX	9.5	10.0

Capacities are rounded off to the nearest half unit

(Includes heater. *Indicates with air conditioning)

MAKE, YEAR & MODEL	LITERS	QUARTS
OLDSMOBILE 88, NINETY-EIGHT, TORONADO TROFÉO		
1992-91 Eighty-Eight, Ninety-Eight ...12.0		13.0
Custom Cruiser............16.0		17.0
W/H.D. Cooling 16.5		17.5
1992-88 Toronado, Troféo 12.0		13.0
1990 Eighty-Eight 12.0		12.5
1990-87 Custom Cruiser......14.5, 15.5*		15.5, 16.5*
1990-86 Ninety Eight 12.0		12.5
1989-86 Delta 88 ....12.5		13.0
1987 Toronado 11.0		11.5
1986 Toronado 11.5		12.0
1985 Delta 88: V6 ....12.0		13.0
V8 ex. Diesel.....15.0, 14.5*		15.5, 15.0*
V8 Diesel.............17.0		18.0
Ninety-Eight: V6: 3.8L (231) .11.5,12.0*		12.0, 13.0*
3.0L (181) 12.0, 11.5*		12.0, 13.0*
Diesel 12.0		12.5
Toronado: V8 ex. Diesel 15.5		16.5
Diesel 17.0		18.0
1984 All ex. Toronado:		
V6 3.8L (231) 12.0		13.0
V8 ex. Diesel.........14.5		15.5
Toronado: V6 4.1L (252) 12.0		12.5
V8 ex. Diesel.........15.5		16.5
All Diesels 17.0		18.0
1983 V6 ....12.5		13.0
V8: 5.0L (307) ...14.5, 15.5*		15.5, 16.0*
Diesel 17.0		18.0
OLDSMOBILE CUTLASS, CUTLASS CIERA, VISTA-CRUISER		
1992 Cutlass Ciera, Cutlass Cruiser:		
4-cyl. 2.5L 7.5		8.0
V6 3.3L 9.0		9.5
1992-90 Cutlass Supreme 12.0		12.5
1991-90 Ciera, Cutlass Cruiser:		
4-cyl. 2.5L 7.5		8.0
V6 3.3L 9.5, 10.0*		10.0, 10.5*
1989 V6 3.3L 11.5, 12.0*		12.0, 13.0*
Cutlass Supreme 11.5, 12.0*		12.0, 12.5*
1989-88 Ciera, Cutlass Cruiser:		
4-cyl. 2.5L (151).........9.0		9.5
W/HD cooling 11.5		12.0
V6 2.8L (173) 11.5		12.0
W/HD cooling 12.0		12.5
1988 Ciera, Cutlass Cruiser:		
V6 3.8L (231) 11.5, 12.0*		12.0, 12.5*
Cutlass Supreme Classic 14.0, 15.0*		15.0, 15.5*
1987-86 Ciera, Cutlass Cruiser:		
4-cyl. 2.5L (151) ...9.0, 9.5*		9.5, 10.0*
V6: 2.8L (173) 11.5		12.0
3.8L (231) 11.5, 12.0*		12.0, 13.0*
Cutlass Supreme, 442:		
V6 3.8L (231) 12.0		13.0
V8 5.0L (307)(Y).....14.0, 14.5*		15.0, 15.5*
V8 5.0L (307) H.O. 14.5		15.5
V8 5.0L (305)(H) Canada ..14.5, 15.0*		15.5, 16.0*
1985 Ciera: 4-cyl. 9.0, 9.5*		9.5, 10.0*
V6: 2.8L (173) Canada ...11.5		12.0
3.0L (181) 12.5		13.0
3.8L (231) 11.5, 12.0*		12.0, 13.0*
Diesel 12.0, 12.5*		12.5, 13.0*
Cutlass Supreme:		
V6 3.8L (231) 12.0		13.0
V6 Diesel............14.0		15.0
V8 ex. Canada 15.0		15.5
V8 Canada 14.5		15.5
V8 Diesel...........16.5		17.5
1984 4-cyl..............9.0		9.5
V6: 3.0L (181) 12.0, 11.5*		12.5, 12.0*
3.8L (231)(3) 11.5, 12.0*		12.0, 12.5*
3.8L (231)(A) 12.0		13.0
4.3L (262) Diesel: Cutlass .14.0, 13.5*		14.5, 14.0*
Ciera 11.5, 12.0*		12.5, 13.0*
V8: 5.0L (307) 14.5		15.5
5.7L (350) Diesel 16.5		17.5
1983 4-cyl..........9.0, 9.5*		9.5, 10.0*
V6: 2.8L (173) 11.5, 12.0*		12.0, 12.5*
3.0L (181) 13.5, 12.5*		14.5, 13.5*
3.8L (231) 12.0		13.0
Diesel: Ciera 12.5, 13.0*		13.0, 14.0*
Supreme 14.0		15.0
V8: 5.0L (305) 14.5, 15.0*		15.5, 16.0*
5.0L (307) 14.0, 14.5*		15.0, 15.5*
Diesel 16.5		17.0

MAKE, YEAR & MODEL	LITERS	QUARTS
OLDSMOBILE FIRENZA		
1988-87 4-cyl.: 2.0L (121)(1)........11.0		12.0
2.0L (121)(K) 7.5		8.0
V6 2.8L (173) 11.5		12.0
1986-83 4-cyl. 1.8L (112) 7.5		8.0
4-cyl. 2.0L (121) 9.0, 9.5*		9.5, 10.0*
V6 2.8L (173) 10.0, 10.5*		10.5, 11.0*
OLDSMOBILE ACHIEVA, OMEGA, CALAIS		
1992-89 4-cyl. ex. H.O. 10.0		10.5
4-cyl. H.O. 10.5		11.0
V6.................10.5		11.0
1988-86 4-cyl.............7.5		8.0
V6.................9.5		10.0
1985 4-cyl..........9.0, 9.5*		9.5, 10.0*
V6 ....12.0, 11.5*		13.0, 12.0*
1984 4-cyl..........8.5, 9.0*		9.0, 9.5*
V6: 2.8L (173)(X):		
AT 9.5, 10.0*		10.0, 10.5*
MT 9.5, 11.5*		10.0, 12.0*
2.8L (173)(Z) 10.0		10.5
1983 4-cyl..........9.0, 9.5*		9.5, 10.0*
V6 ....11.0, 11.5*		11.5, 12.0*
PEUGEOT		
1992-90 405 8-valve eng. 6.5		7.0
405 16-valve eng. 7.0		7.5
1991-88 505: 4-cyl. 2.2L ex. Turbo ..7.5		8.0
V6 2.8L...........9.5		10.0
4-cyl. 2.2L Turbo 9.5		10.0
1989 405 4-cyl. 1.9L: 8-valve ...6.5		7.0
16-valve..........7.0		7.5
1987 505 V6 2.8L 9.5		10.0
4-cyl. 2.2L: Sedan 8.5		9.0
Wagon 9.5		10.0
1987-85 505 gas Turbo 9.5		10.0
1986 505 ex. Turbo 8.5		9.0
1985-84 505 Turbo Diesel 10.0		10.5
Gas engine MT 7.0		7.5
Gas engine AT 7.5		8.0
1984 604 Turbo Diesel 10.0		10.5
1983 505 gas engine..........7.0		7.5
All Diesel 10.0		10.5
604 ....10.5		11.0
PLYMOUTH		
1992 Acclaim 2.5L 8.5		9.0
3.0L..............9.0		9.5
Colt Vista: 1.8L 6.0		6.5
2.4L..............6.5		7.0
Colt 5.0		5.5
Laser 1.8L 5.0		5.5
2.0L..............7.0		7.5
1992-90 Sundance 8.5		9.0
1991-90 Acclaim.............8.5		9.0
Laser: 1.8L 5.0		6.5
2.0L.............7.0		7.5
1991-89 Colt ex. wagon: 1.5L 5.0		5.5
1.6L 6.0		6.5
Colt wagon..........7.0		7.5
1991-88 Horizon 4-cyl............8.5		9.0
1991-85 Colt Vista 7.0		7.5
1989-86 Caravelle, Reliant K, Sundance		
4-cyl. 2.2L (135),		
2.5L (153) 8.5		9.0
1989-85 Gran Fury, Caravelle Salon..14.5, 15.5*		15.5, 16.5*
1989-84 Conquest..............9.0		9.5
1988-85 Colt 5.0		5.5
1986-83 4-cyl. 1.6L (98) 6.5		7.0
1985-83 1.7L (107) 5.5		6.0
2.2L (135), 2.6L (156).....8.5		9.0
1984 Colt Vista 6.5		7.0
1984-83 V8 ....14.0, 14.5*		15.0, 15.5*
Colt ex. Vista, Conquest 4.5		5.0
1983 Sapporo............9.5		10.0
6-cyl.............10.5, 11.5*		11.5, 12.5*
PONTIAC CATALINA, BONNEVILLE, SAFARI, LAURENTIAN, PARISIENNE		
1992 Bonneville 12.0		13.0
1991-87 Bonneville 12.5		13.0
1989 Safari V8............16.0		17.0
1988-87 Safari V8...........14.5		15.0
1986-85 Parisienne:		
V6 4.3L (262) 11.5		12.0
V8 ex. Diesel.......14.5		15.0
1986-83 V6 ex. Parisienne 12.5		13.0
V8 5.0L (305) 14.5, 15.0*		15.5, 16.0*
1985 V8 5.7L (350) Diesel 17.0		18.0

MAKE, YEAR & MODEL	LITERS	QUARTS
PONTIAC CATALINA, BONNEVILLE, SAFARI, LAURENTIAN, PARISIENNE Continued		
1984-83 V6 Parisienne 13.5		14.0
V8 Diesel ex. Parisienne 16.5		17.0
Parisienne 17.0		18.0
PONTIAC FIERO		
1988-84 All.................13.0		14.0
PONTIAC FIREBIRD		
1992-91 V6 3.1L (191).............14.0		14.5
V8: 5.0L (305)(F) 17.0		18.0
5.7L (350) 15.5		16.5
1992-90 V8: 5.0L (305)(E)....16.5, 17.0*		17.5, 18.0*
1990 V6 3.1L (191) 13.5		14.5
5.0L (305)(F) ...16.0, 16.5*		17.0, 17.5*
5.7L(350) 15.0, 15.5*		16.0, 16.5*
1989-87 V6 2.8L (173) 11.5		12.5
V8: 5.0L (305)(E),(H) 14.5		15.5
5.0L (305)(F), 5.7L (350) ..16.0		17.0
1986-85 4-cyl..............12.0		13.0
V6................11.5		12.5
V8................16.0		17.0
1984-83 4-cyl. 2.5L (151) 12.0		13.0
V6................12.0		13.0
V8 5.0L (305).........16.5		17.0
PONTIAC FIREFLY		
1991-85 All..................4.0		4.5
PONTIAC GRAND PRIX		
1992-91 4-cyl. 2.3L (138) 9.0		9.5
V6: 3.1L (191) 12.0		12.5
3.4L (207): AT 12.0		12.5
MT 12.5		13.0
1990 4-cyl. 2.3L 8.5		9.0
V6: 3.1L ex. Turbo 12.0		12.5
3.1LTurbo 12.5		13.0
1989-88 V6 2.8L (173) 12.0		12.5
1987 83 V6 ....12.5		13.0
V8 5.0L (305) 14.5, 15.0*		15.5, 16.0*
1984-83 V8 Diesel 16.5		17.0
PONTIAC LE MANS, GRAND AM, 6000		
1992 Grand Am..............10.0		10.5
1992-88 LeMans...............7.5		8.0
1991 Grand AM:		
4-cyl. 2.3L ex. H.O., 2.5L .10.0		10.5
4-cyl. 2.3L H.O. 10.5		11.0
1991-90 6000: 4-cyl. 9.0, 12.5*		9.5, 13.0*
V6 ....11.5		12.5
1990 Grand AM:		
4-cyl. 2.3L ex. H.O. 7.0		7.5
4-cyl. 2.3L H.O., 2.5L 7.5		8.0
1989-87 6000: 4-cyl. 9.0		9.5
V6 ....11.5		12.5
1989-85 Grand AM 4-cyl. & V6 ......7.5		8.0
6000: 4-cyl. 9.0		9.5
V6 ex. MFI 11.0		11.5
V6 w/MFI & Diesel 12.0		12.5
1984 V6 2.8L (173)(Z) 11.5		12.0
1984-83 4-cyl. 2.5L (151) 9.0		9.5
V6 2.8L (173)		
ex. 1984 Code Z 10.5, 11.0*		11.0, 11.5*
V6 4.3L (262) Diesel 12.5, 13.0*		13.0, 14.0*
PONTIAC (T)1000		
1987 4-cyl. 1.6L (98) 8.5, 9.0*		9.0, 9.5*
1986-83 All 8.5		9.0
PONTIAC SUNBURST		
1987-85 All 6.5		7.0
PONTIAC VENTURA, PHOENIX, (J)2000, SUNBIRD (FWD)		
1992-91 Sunbird: 4-cyl. 11.0		11.5
V6................13.5		14.0
1990-83 (J)2000, Sunbird 7.5		8.0
1984-83 Phoenix 4-cyl. 9.0		9.5
V6................11.0		11.5
PONTIAC TRANS SPORT		
1992 3.1L: W/heater 11.5		12.5
W/AC.............12.0		13.0
W/rear AC 13.5		14.5
W/rear heater 13.0		14.0
3.8L: W/AC..........11.0		11.5
W/rear AC or rear heater ..12.5		13.5
1991-90 All 12.5		13.0
W/rear AC 14.0		14.5

COOLING SYSTEM CAPACITIES
(Includes heater. *Indicates with air conditioning)

Capacities are rounded off to the nearest half unit

MAKE, YEAR & MODEL	LITERS	QUARTS
PORSCHE		
1990 944S2	8.0	8.5
1990-82 928, 928S4	16.0	17.0
1989-84 944, 944S, 944 Turbo	8.5	9.0
1988-87 924S	8.5	9.0
1983 944	7.5	8.0
RENAULT		
1987 GTA	6.5	7.0
1987-85 Alliance/Encore	6.5	7.0
Fuego, Sportwagon	7.0	7.5
1984 Encore	4.0, 4.5*	4.5, 5.0*
1984-83 Alliance	4.0, 4.5*	4.5, 5.0*
Fuego, 18i	7.0	7.5
5, Le Car	6.0	6.5
SAAB		
1992-86 9000	9.0	9.5
1992-83 900	10.0	10.5
SATURN		
1992-91 All	6.5	7.0
SUBARU		
1992 SVX	7.0	7.5
1992-90 Justy: FWD, MT w/carb.	4.5	5.0
Others w/FI	5.0	5.5
Legacy: FWD	6.0	6.0
4WD	7.0	7.5
Loyale ex. Turbo	5.5	6.0
Turbo	6.0	6.5
1991-88 XT: 1800cc	5.5	6.0
2700cc	7.0	7.5
1989-87 Justy	4.5	5.0
1989-83 1600	5.5	6.0
1800 ex. Turbo	5.5	6.0
Turbo	6.0	6.5
SUZUKI		
1992 Swift: 1.3L	4.5	5.0
1.6L	5.0	5.0
Sidekick	5.5	5.5
1992-88 Samurai	5.0	5.5
1991-89 Sidekick	5.0	5.5
Swift	4.5	5.0
1988-85 Forsa	4.5	4.5
1985-81 LJ80, 81	4.0	4.0
TOYOTA		
1992 Camry: 2.2L	6.5	6.5
3.0L	8.5	9.0
Celica: 1.6L MT	5.0	5.5
AT	5.5	6.0
2.0L	6.5	7.0
2.2L MT	6.0	6.5
AT	6.5	7.0
Corolla: FWD	5.5	6.0
4WD	6.0	6.5
MR2: 2.0L	13.5	14.5
2.2L	13.0	13.5
Paseo	5.0	5.5
1992-90 Cressida	8.5	9.0
1992-89 Supra	8.0	8.5
1991-90 Celica: 1.6L	5.5	6.0
2.2L	6.0	6.5
2.0L Turbo	6.5	7.0
Corolla	6.0	6.5
1991-89 Camry, 4-cyl.	6.5	7.0
V6	9.5	10.0
Tercel	5.0	5.5
1989 Corolla: 2V	5.5	6.0
FI	6.0	6.5
MR2	13.0	13.5
1989-88 Celica	6.0	6.5
Turbo	6.5	7.0
1989-87 Cressida	8.0	8.5
1988-87 Tercel ex. wagon	4.5	5.0
Tercel wagon	5.0	5.5
1988-87 Camry	6.5	7.0
Supra	8.0	8.5
MR2: AT	11.5	12.0
MT	11.0	11.5
Corolla: Sedan, Liftback	6.0	6.5
Sport Coupe	5.5	6.0
1987 Celica: FE	6.5	7.0
GE	7.0	7.5
1986-83 Tercel	5.0	5.5
Camry Gas	7.0	7.5
Camry Diesel	8.5	9.0
Supra	8.0	8.5
1986 Celica	7.0	7.5

MAKE, YEAR & MODEL	LITERS	QUARTS
TOYOTA Continued		
1986-85 Cressida	8.5	9.0
MR2	13.0	13.5
1986-84 Corolla RWD	5.5	6.0
Corolla FWD Gas: MT	5.5	6.0
AT	6.0	6.5
Diesel	7.0	7.5
1985-83 Celica	8.5	9.0
1984-83 Starlet	5.0	5.5
Cressida	9.0	9.5
1983 Corolla	5.0	5.5
VOLKSWAGEN		
1992 Corrado	7.0	7.5
Cabriolet	5.0	5.0
1992-91 Passat	7.0	7.5
1992-88 Golf, GTI, Jetta	7.0	7.5
Fox: W/o AC	6.0	6.5
W/AC	6.5	7.0
1990 Corrado, Jetta	6.5	7.0
1990-88 Cabriolet, Scirocco	4.5	5.0
1988 Quantum	8.0	8.5
1987 Fox	6.5	7.0
1987-86 Golf, GTI, Cabriolet	7.0	7.5
Jetta Gas & Diesel	7.0	7.5
Quantum, Scirocco	7.0	7.5
1985 Quantum: 4-cyl. Gas	6.0	6.5
5-cyl. Gas	8.0	8.5
Diesel	7.0	7.5
1985-84 Golf, Rabbit ex. Conv.	6.5	7.0
1985-83 Jetta Diesel	6.5	7.0
Rabbit Conv., Scirocco, Jetta ex. Diesel	4.5	5.0
1984 Quantum: 4-cyl. Gas	6.0	6.5
5-cyl. Gas	5.5	6.0
Diesel	6.5	7.0
1983 Quantum: 4-cyl. Gas	5.0	5.5
5-cyl. Gas	4.5	5.0
Diesel	6.0	6.5
VOLVO		
1992 240, 960	10.0	10.5
1992-91 940	9.5	10.0
1992-85 740 Gasoline	9.5	10.0
1991-85 200 Series: MT	9.5	10.0
AT	9.0	9.5
1990 760, 780: 4-cyl. Turbo	10.0	10.5
V6	9.5	10.0
1989 760, 780: 4-cyl.	9.5	10.0
V6	10.0	10.5
1987-86 760 GLE	10.0	10.6
760 Turbo	9.5	10.0
1986 740 Diesel: MT	11.0	11.5
AT	10.0	10.5
1985-83 760: MT	11.0	11.5
AT	10.0	10.5
1984-83 240 Series	9.5	10.0

LIGHT TRUCKS, UTILITY VEHICLES, VANS

MAKE, YEAR & MODEL	LITERS	QUARTS
CHEVROLET/GMC TRUCKS		
Astro, Safari		
1992-85 4-cyl.	9.5	10.0
W/rear heater	12.0	13.0
V6	12.5	13.5
W/rear heater	15.5	16.5
Blazer, Jimmy		
1991 V8 5.7L	16.5, 17.5*	17.5, 18.5*
V8 6.2L Diesel	22.5, 23.5*	24.0, 25.0*
V8 7.4L	21.5, 22.5*	23.0, 24.0*
1990-88 6-cyl. 4.8L	14.5, 15.5*	15.5, 16.5*
V8 5.7L	16.5, 17.5*	17.5, 18.5*
V8 6.2L Diesel	23.5	25.0
1987-83 6-cyl. 4.1L	14.0	15.0
V6 4.3L	10.5	11.0
V8 5.0L, 5.7L	16.5, 17.5*	17.5, 18.5*
V8 6.2L Diesel	23.5	25.0
V8 7.4L	22.0, 23.0*	23.0, 24.5*
Chevrolet Lumina, GMC APV		
1992 3.1L	12.0	13.0
W/AC	12.0	13.0
W/rear AC	13.5	14.5
W/rear heater	13.0	14.0
3.8L	11.0	11.5
W/rear AC or heater	12.5	13.5
1991 All	12.5	13.5
W/rear AC	14.0	15.0
1990 All	12.5	13.5

MAKE, YEAR & MODEL	LITERS	QUARTS
CHEVROLET/GMC TRUCKS Continued		
C, K, R, V Series Pickups, Suburban		
1992-88 V6 4.3L	10.5	11.0
6-cyl. 4.8L	14.5, 15.5*	15.5, 16.5*
V8 5.0L, 5.7L	16.5, 17.0*	17.5, 18.0*
HD 3500, 1992	25.0, 25.5*	26.5, 27.0*
V8 6.2L Diesel	23.5	25.0
V8 6.5L Diesel	25.0	26.5
V8 7.4L	22.0, 23.5*	23.5, 25.0*
HD 3500, 1992	25.0, 27.0*	26.5, 28.5*
1987-85 V6 4.3L	10.5	11.0
6-cyl. 4.8L	14.5	15.5
V8 5.0L, 5.7L	16.5, 17.0*	17.5, 18.0*
V8 6.2L Diesel	23.5	25.0
V8 7.4L	22.0, 23.0*	23.0, 24.5*
1984-83 6-cyl. 4.1L	14.0, 14.5*	15.0, 15.5*
6-cyl. 4.8L	14.5, 15.0*	15.5, 16.0*
V8 5.0L, 5.7L	16.5, 17.0*	17.5, 18.0*
V8 6.2L Diesel	23.5*	25.0
V8 7.4L	21.5, 23.0*	23.0, 24.5*
G Series Vans		
1992-90 V6 4.3L	10.5	11.0
W/rear heater	13.0	14.0
V8 5.0L, 5.7L	16.0	17.0
W/rear heater	18.5	20.0
V8 6.2L (C) Diesel	22.5	24.0
W/rear heater	25.5	27.0
V8 6.2L (J) Diesel	24.0	25.5
W/rear heater	27.0	28.5
V8 7.4L	22.0	23.5
W/rear heater	24.5	26.0
1989-85 V6 4.3L	10.5	11.0
V8 5.0L, 5.7L	16.0	17.0
W/rear heater	18.5	20.0
V8 6.2L Diesel	22.5	24.0
V8 7.4L	22.0	23.5
1984-83 6-cyl. 4.1L	16.0	17.0
V8 5.0L, 5.7L	18.0, 19.0*	19.0, 20.0*
V8 6.2L Diesel	22.5	24.0
S Series Pickups, Sonoma, S Blazer & Jimmy, Syclone, Typhoon		
1992-87 4-cyl. 2.5L	11.0	11.5
V6 2.8L	10.0	10.5
V6 4.3L, 1992-90	11.5	12.0
V6 4.3L, 1989-88	13.0	13.5
1986-83 4-cyl. 1.9L	9.0	9.5
4-cyl. 2.2L Diesel	11.0, 11.5*	11.5, 12.0*
4-cyl. 2.5L	11.5	12.0
V6 2.8L	11.5	12.0
DODGE & PLYMOUTH TRUCKS		
FWD Caravan & Voyager		
1992 4-cyl. 2.5L	9.0	9.5
V6 3.0L, 3.3L	9.5	10.0
1991-84 4-cyl. 2.2L, 2.5L	8.0	8.5
4-cyl. 2.6L	9.0	9.5
V6 3.0L, 3.3L	9.5	10.0
B Series Vans		
1992 V6 3.9L	14.0	14.5
V8 5.2L	15.5	16.5
V8 5.9L	14.0	15.0
1991-88 V6 3.9L	13.5	14.5
V8 5.2L	15.5	16.5
V8 5.9L Gas	14.5	15.5
1987-83 6-cyl. 3.7L	12.5	13.5
V8 5.2L	15.5	16.5
V8 5.9L	14.0	15.0
Dakota		
1992-87 4-cyl. 2.5L	9.5	10.0
V6 3.9L	13.5	14.0
V8 5.2L	13.5	14.5
D, W Series Pickups; Ramcharger		
1992 V6 3.9L	14.0	15.0
6-cyl. 5.9L Diesel: MT	15.0	16.0
AT	16.0	17.0
V8 5.2L	16.0	17.0
V8 5.9L Gas	14.5	15.5
1991-88 V6 3.9L	14.0	15.0
6-cyl. 5.9L Diesel: MT	15.5	16.5
AT	16.5	17.5
V8 5.2L	16.0	17.0
V8 5.9L Gas	14.5	15.5
1987-83 6-cyl. 3.7L	11.5, 12.5*	12.0, 13.0*
V8 5.2L	15.0, 16.0*	16.0, 17.0*
V8 5.9L	13.5, 14.5*	14.5, 15.5*

Capacities are rounded off to the nearest half unit

(Includes heater. *Indicates with air conditioning)

DODGE & PLYMOUTH TRUCKS

MAKE, YEAR & MODEL	LITERS	QUARTS
Continued		
Ram 50, Raider		
1992-90 4-cyl. 2.4L	6.0	6.5
V6 3.0L	8.5	9.0
1989-87 Ram 50: 2.0L	7.0	7.5
2.6L	8.0	8.5
Raider: 4-cyl.	8.0	8.5
V6	9.0	9.5
1986-83 Ram 50: Gas	9.0	9.5
Diesel	8.0	8.5

FORD TRUCKS

MAKE, YEAR & MODEL	LITERS	QUARTS
Aerostar		
1992-88 V6 3.0L	11.0	11.5
V6 4.0L	12.0	12.5
1987-86 4-cyl. 2.3L: MT	6.5	7.0
AT	7.0	7.5
V6 2.8L	7.5	8.0
V6 3.0L	11.0	11.5
E Series Vans		
1992 6-cyl. 4.9L	15.0, 18.0*	16.0, 19.0*
V8 5.0L	17.5, 18.5*	18.5, 19.5*
V8 5.8L	20.0, 21.0*	21.0, 22.0*
V8 7.3L Diesel	29.0	31.0
V8 7.5L	27.0	29.0
1991-87 6-cyl. 4.9L	14.0, 17.0*	15.0, 18.0*
V8 5.0L	16.5, 17.5*	17.5, 18.5*
V8 5.8L	19.0, 20.0*	20.0, 21.0*
V8 6.9L, 7.3L Diesel	29.0	31.0
V8 7.5L	26.0	28.0
1986-83 6-cyl. 4.9L	14.0, 16.5*	15.0, 17.5*
V8 5.0L: MT	14.0, 16.5*	15.0, 17.5*
AT	16.5, 17.5*	17.5, 18.5*
W/XC	17.5	18.5
V8 5.8L: MT	14.0	15.0
AT	19.0, 20.0*	20.0, 21.0*
V8 6.9L Diesel	29.0	31.0
V8 7.5L	26.0	28.0
F Series Pickups, Bronco		
1992-88 6-cyl. 4.9L V8 5.0L: MT	12.0, 13.0*	13.0, 14.0*
AT	13.0, 14.0*	14.0, 15.0*
V8 5.8L: MT	14.0, 15.0*	15.0, 16.0*
AT	15.0, 16.0*	16.0, 17.0*
V8 6.9L, 7.3L Diesel	27.0	29.0
V8 7.5L	17.0	18.0
1987 6-cyl. 4.9L	12.0	13.0
W/XC	14.0	15.0
V8 5.0L: MT	12.0, 13.0*	13.0, 14.0*
AT	13.0	14.0
V8 5.8L: MT	14.0, 15.0*	15.0, 16.0*
AT	15.0	16.0
V8 6.9L Diesel	27.0	29.0
V8 7.5L	17.0	18.0
1986-83 V6 3.8L	9.5, 10.5*	10.0, 11.0*
6-cyl. 4.9L, V8 5.0L	12.0	13.0
W/XC	13.0	14.0
V8 5.8L	14.0	15.0
W/XC	15.0	16.0
V8 6.9L Diesel	29.0	31.0
V8 7.5L	17.0	18.0
Ranger, Explorer, Bronco II		
1992-90 4-cyl. 2.3L	6.0, 6.5*	6.5, 7.0*
V6 2.9L	6.5, 7.5*	7.0, 8.0*
V6 3.0L	9.0, 9.5*	9.5, 10.0*
V6 4.0L Explorer	7.0, 8.0*	7.5, 8.5*
V6 4.0L Ranger	7.5, 8.0*	8.0, 8.5*
1989-85 4-cyl. 2.0L	6.0	6.5
4-cyl. 2.3L Gas	6.0, 6.5*	6.5, 7.0*
4-cyl. 2.3L Diesel	11.5, 12.5*	12.0, 13.0*
V6 2.8L, 2.9L	7.0, 7.5*	7.5, 8.0*
1984-83 4-cyl. 2.0L	6.0	6.5
4-cyl. 2.2L Diesel	9.5, 10.0*	10.0, 10.5*
4-cyl. 2.3L	6.5	7.0

GEO

MAKE, YEAR & MODEL	LITERS	QUARTS
1992-90 Tracker	5.0	5.5
1989 Tracker	5.5	6.0

ISUZU TRUCKS

MAKE, YEAR & MODEL	LITERS	QUARTS
1992 Trooper: MT	9.0	9.5
AT	8.5	9.0
1992-91 Rodeo: 2.6L	9.0	9.5
3.1L	11.0	11.5
1992-89 Pickup, Amigo: 4-cyl.	9.0	9.5
V6	11.0	11.5
1991-90 Trooper, Trooper II: 4-cyl.	8.0	8.5
V6	10.0	10.5
1988 Trooper II	8.0	8.5
1987-83 Trooper II: Gas	8.0	8.5
Diesel	10.5	11.0
Pickup: Gas	8.0	8.5
Diesel: MT	9.0	9.5
AT	10.5	11.0

JEEP

MAKE, YEAR & MODEL	LITERS	QUARTS
1992-88 Cherokee, Wagoneer:		
4-cyl.	9.5	10.0
6-cyl.	11.5	12.0
Comanche: 4-cyl.	9.5	10.0
6-cyl.	11.5	12.0
1992-87 Wrangler: 4-cyl.	8.5	9.0
6-cyl.	10.0	10.5
1991-85 Grand Wagoneer, J10/20		
Truck: 6-cyl. 4.2L (258)	10.0	10.5
V8 5.9L (360)	13.0	14.0
1987-85 Comanche:		
4-cyl.: 2.5L (150)	9.5	10.0
2.1L (126) Turbo Diesel	8.5	9.0
6-cyl. 4.0L (242)	11.5	12.0
1987-85 Cherokee, Wagoneer:		
4-cyl. ex. Diesel	9.5	10.0
4-cyl. Turbo Diesel	8.5	9.0
V6 2.8L (173),		
6-cyl. 4.0L (242)	11.5	12.0
1986-85 CJ-7, Scrambler: 4-cyl.	8.5	9.0
6-cyl. 4.2L (258)	10.0	10.5
1984 4-cyl.	8.5	9.0
V6 2.8L (171)	11.5	12.0
1984-83 6-cyl. 4.2L (258)	10.0	10.5
V8: 5.0L (304)	12.5	13.0
5.9L (360)	13.0	14.0
1983 4-cyl. 2.5L (151)	7.5	8.0

MAZDA TRUCKS

MAKE, YEAR & MODEL	LITERS	QUARTS
1992-91 Navajo	8.0	8.5
1992-89 MPV: 4-cyl.	7.0	7.5
V6 w/MT	9.5	10.0
V6 w/AT	10.0	10.5
B2200, B2600 2WD	7.5	8.0
B2600 4WD	7.0	7.5
1988-87 B2200	7.5	8.0
B2600	9.0	9.5
1987-86 B2000	7.5	8.0
1984-83 B2000	7.0	7.5
B2200	10.5	11.0

MITSUBISHI TRUCKS

MAKE, YEAR & MODEL	LITERS	QUARTS
1992-90 Truck: 2.4L	6.0	6.5
3.0L	8.5	9.0
1991-89 Montero: 4-cyl.	9.0	9.5
V6	9.5	10.0
1991-88 Van	8.0	8.5
W/rear heater	8.5	9.0
1989-87 Pickup ex. 2.0L	8.0	8.5
Pickup w/2.0L	7.0	7.5
1988-87 Montero	8.0	8.5
1986-83 Pickup: Gas	9.0	9.5
Diesel	8.0	8.5

NISSAN/DATSUN TRUCKS

MAKE, YEAR & MODEL	LITERS	QUARTS
1992 Pickup, Pathfinder: 2WD	10.5	11.5
4WD	11.5	12.5
1991-90 Pickup, Pathfinder: 4-cyl.	7.0	7.5
V6	9.5	10.0
1990-88 Van: W/front heater	8.5	9.0
W/front & rear heater	9.0	9.5
W/o heater	7.0	7.5
1989-86 D21 Pickup, Pathfinder:		
4-cyl.: Gas	8.0	8.5
Diesel	12.0	13.0
V6	10.0	10.5
Van	9.0	9.5
1986-83 Nissan Pickup:		
MT	10.0	10.5
AT	9.5	10.0
Diesel	10.5	11.0
1983 Datsun Pickup	10.0	10.5

OLDSMOBILE TRUCKS

MAKE, YEAR & MODEL	LITERS	QUARTS
1992 Silhouette 3.1L:		
Copper-Brass	12.0	12.5
Aluminum	11.0	11.5
W/rear AC:		
Copper-Brass	13.5	14.5
Aluminum	12.5	13.5
Silhouette 3.8L	11.0	11.5
W/rear AC	12.5	13.5
1992-91 Bravada	11.5	12.0
1991 Silhouette	12.5	13.5
1990 Silhouette	10.0	12.0

PONTIAC TRUCKS

MAKE, YEAR & MODEL	LITERS	QUARTS
1992 Trans Sport: 3.1L:		
Copper-Brass	12.0	12.5
Aluminum	11.0	11.5
W/rear AC:		
Copper-Brass	13.5	14.5
Aluminum	12.5	13.5
3.8L	11.0	11.5
W/rear AC	12.5	13.5
1991 Trans Sport	13.0	13.5
W/rear AC	14.0	15.0
1990 Trans Sport	10.0	10.5

TOYOTA TRUCKS

MAKE, YEAR & MODEL	LITERS	QUARTS
1992 4-Runner: 2.4L: MT	8.5	9.0
AT: W/o rear heater	9.0	9.5
W/rear heater	9.5	10.0
3.0L	10.0	10.5
Pickup: 2.4L: MT	8.5	9.0
AT	9.0	9.5
3.0L	10.5	11.0
1992-91 Previa	11.5	12.0
W/towing opt.	12.5	13.0
Land Cruiser	18.5	19.5
1991-89 4-Runner & Pickup:		
4-cyl. w/MT	8.5	9.0
4-cyl. w/AT	9.0	9.5
V6	10.5	11.0
1990-89 Land Cruiser	19.5	20.5
1989-87 Van: 2WD	8.5	9.0
4WD	7.5	8.0
1988-85 Pickup, Gas	8.5	9.0
1986 Pickup, Diesel	10.5	11.0
Van	8.5	9.0
1985-84 Pickup: Gas	7.0	7.5
1984-83 Pickup: Gas	8.5	9.0
Diesel	10.0	10.5

VOLKSWAGEN TRUCKS

MAKE, YEAR & MODEL	LITERS	QUARTS
1992-88 Vanagon	16.0	17.0
1987-83 Vanagon, Gas	17.5	18.5
1985-83 Vanagon, Diesel	16.0	17.0
1983 Pickup	6.5	7.0

FUEL TANK CAPACITIES

Capacities are rounded off to the nearest half unit

BUICK

MAKE, YEAR & MODEL	Liters	Gal
Century		
1983-88 All ex. 4.3L Diesel	59	15.5
1983-85 4.3L Diesel	62	16.5
1989 All ex. 5.7L Diesel	51.5	13.5
5.7L Diesel	68	18
1990-92 All	59.5	15.5
Electra		
1983-84 5.7L Diesel	83	22
Ex. wagon	95	25
Wagon	83	22
1985-90 All	68	18
Estate Wagon		
1983-90 All	83	22
Le Sabre		
1983-85 5.7L Diesel	98	26
1983-84 Ex. wagon	95	25
Wagon	83	22
1985 Others	95	25
1986-88 All	83.5	22
1989-92 All	68	18
Park Avenue		
1991-92 All	68	18
Reatta		
1988-89 All	71	19
1990 All	68	18
1991 All	71	19
Regal		
1983-84 All	75	20
1985-87 All	68	18
1988 All ex. 2.8L	68	18
2.8L	62	16
1989-90 All	62	16
1991 All	64	16.5
1992 All	62	16
Riviera		
1983-85 All ex. 5.7L Diesel	79	21
5.7L Diesel	86	23
1986-88 All	68	18
1989 All	71	19
1990 All	68	18
1991 All	71	19
1992 All	68	18
Roadmaster		
1992 Sedan	87	23
1991-92 Wagon	83	22
Skyhawk		
1983-89 All	51	13.5
Skylark		
1983-85 2.5L	55	14.5
2.8L	57	15
1986-91 All	51.5	13.5
1992 All	57.5	15
Somerset		
1985-87 All	51.5	13.5

CADILLAC

MAKE, YEAR & MODEL	Liters	Gal
Allanté		
1987-92 All	83	22
Brougham		
1985 All ex. 5.7L Diesel	93	24.5
5.7L Diesel	98	26
1986-87 W/tt	94	25
W/o tt	78	20.5
1988-92 All	94.5	25
Cimarron		
1983-87 All	53	14
DeVille		
1983 All ex. 5.7L Diesel	95	25
5.7L Diesel	94.5	25
1984-85 All ex. Diesel	93	24.5
1984 5.7L Diesel	93	24.5
1985 4.3L Diesel	79.5	21
1986-91 All	68	18
Eldorado		
1983-85 All ex. 5.7L Diesel	77	20.5
1983-84 5.7L Diesel	86.5	23
1986-87 All	68	18
1988-89 All	71	19
1990 All	95	25
1991-92 All	71	19
Fleetwood		
1983 All ex. 5.7L Diesel	95	25
5.7L Diesel	102	27
1984-85 All ex. Diesel	93	24.5
1984 5.7L Diesel	98	26

CADILLAC Continued

MAKE, YEAR & MODEL	Liters	Gal
Fleetwood Continued		
1985 4.3L Diesel	98	26
1986-91 All	68	18
Fleetwood Brougham		
1983 All ex. 5.7L Diesel	95	25
5.7L Diesel	102	27
1984-85 All ex. Diesel	93	24.5
1984 5.7L Diesel	98	26
1986-88 All	68	18
1989-90 All	94	25
Limousine		
1983 All	94.5	25
1984 All	93	24.5
Seville		
1983-85 All ex. 5.7L Diesel	77	20.5
1983-84 5.7L Diesel	86.5	23
1986-87 All	68	18
1988-89 All	71	19
1990 All	68	18
1991-92 All	71	19

CHEVROLET

MAKE, YEAR & MODEL	Liters	Gal
Beretta		
1987-89 All	51.5	13.5
1990-92 All	59	15.5
Camaro		
1983-84 2.5L	58.5	15.5
Others	60	16
1985-86 5.0L	60	16
Others	58.5	15.5
1987-88 All	60	16
1991-92 All	58.5	15.5
Caprice		
1983-89 Sedan ex. Diesel	95	25
1983-85 Sedan Diesel	98	26
1990 Sedan	92	24.5
1991-92 Sedan	87.5	23
1983-89 Wagon	85	22
1990 Wagon	83.5	22
1991 Wagon	87.5	23
1992 Wagon	83.5	22
Cavalier		
1983-86 All	53	14
1987-91 All	51.5	13.5
1992 All	57.5	15
Celebrity		
1983-86 2.8L	62	16.5
1983-85 4.3L Diesel	63	16.5
1983-86 Others	59.5	15.5
1987-90 All	59.5	16
Chevette		
1983-86 All	47.5	12.5
1987 All	46	12
Citation		
1983-85 2.5L	55	14.5
2.8L	57	15
Corsica		
1987-89 All	51.5	13.5
1990-92 All	59	15.5
Corvette		
1984-92 All	75.5	20
El Camino		
1983-84 5.7L Diesel	83	22
Standard tank	66	17.5
Optional tank	83.5	22
1985-87 4.3L standard tank	67	17.5
Standard tank	68.5	18
Optional tank	83.5	22
Impala		
1983-85 Sedan ex. Diesel	95	25
Sedan Diesel	98	26
Wagon	85	22
Lumina		
1990-92 2.5L	65	17
3.1L	62	16.5
1991 Others	62	16.5
Lumina APV		
1990-92 All	76	20
Malibu		
1983 Sedan Diesel	75	20
Sedan, wagon	68.5	18
Monte Carlo		
1983-84 Diesel	75	20
1985-87 3.8L	66.5	17.5

CHEVROLET Continued

MAKE, YEAR & MODEL	Liters	Gal
Monte Carlo Continued		
1985-88 4.3L	66.5	17.5
1983-88 Others	68.5	18
Nova		
1985-88 All	50	13
Spectrum		
1985-88 All	42	11
Sprint		
1985-87 All	32	8.5
1988 All	31	8
All	33	8.5
1989-90 All	40	10

CHRYSLER

MAKE, YEAR & MODEL	Liters	Gal
Conquest		
1987-89 All	75	20
Cordoba		
1983 All	68	18
Daytona		
1984-91 All	53	14
E Class		
1983 All	49	13
1984 All	53	14
Executive Sedan		
1983 All	49	13
1984-85 All	53	14
Fifth Avenue		
1983-89 All	68	18
Imperial		
1983 All	68	18
1990-91 All	61	16
Laser		
1984-86 All	53	14
LeBaron		
1983 All	49	13
1984-88 All	53	14
1990-91 Coupe, convertible	53	14
1992 Coupe, convertible	61	16
1990 Sedan	61	14
1991 Sedan	61	16
1992 Sedan	53	14
New Yorker		
1983 All	68	18
1984-88 All	53	14
1989 All	60	16
1990-92 All	61	16
Newport		
1983-87 All	68	18
TC		
1991 All	53	14
Town & Country		
1990-92 All	76	20

DODGE

MAKE, YEAR & MODEL	Liters	Gal
400		
1983 All	49	13
600		
1983 All	49	13
1984-88 All	53	14
Aries		
1983 All	49	13
1984-89 All	53	14
Caravan		
1984 All	53	14
1985-86 All	57	15
1987 All	76	20
1988-90 Standard tank	57	15
Optional tank	76	20
Challenger		
1983 All	60	16
Charger		
1983-87 All	49	13
Colt		
1983-84 Standard tank	40	10.5
Optional tank	50	13
1985-88 All	45	12
1989-90 1.5L ex. wagon	50	13
1.5L wagon	47	12.5
1.6L	50	13
1.8L	47	12.5
1992 All	50	13
Conquest		
1984-86 All	75	20

DODGE Continued

MAKE, YEAR & MODEL	Liters	Gal
Daytona		
1984-92 All	53	14
Diplomat		
1983-89 All	68	19
Dynasty		
1988-92 All	61	16
Lancer		
1985-89 All	53	14
Mirada		
1983 All	68	19
Monaco		
1990-92 All	64.5	17
Omni		
1983-90 All	49	13
Rampage		
1983-84 All	49	13
Shadow		
1987-88 All	49	13
1991-92 All	53	14
Spirit		
1989-92 All	61	16
Stealth		
1991-92 All	75	20
Vista		
1984-85 All	50	13
1986-90 2WD	50	13
4WD	55	14.5
1992 1.8L	55	14.5
2.4L	60	16

DODGE IMPORT TRUCKS & UTILITY VEHICLES

MAKE, YEAR & MODEL	Liters	Gal
Raider		
1987-88 All	60	16
1989 2.6L	60	16
3.0L	75	20
Ram 50		
2WD		
1983-86 Standard	57	15
Optional	68	18
1987-88 Standard	52	14
Optional	69	18
1989 All	52	13.5
1990-92 Standard body	52	13.5
Long body	69	18
4WD		
1983-88 All	68.5	18
1989 All	59.5	15.5
1990-92 Standard body	60	16
Long body	75	20

EAGLE

MAKE, YEAR & MODEL	Liters	Gal
Eagle Wagon		
1988 All	83	22
Medallion		
1988-89 All	66	17.5
Premier		
1988-91 All	64.5	17
Summit		
1989-92 All ex. 1992 wagon	50	13
1992 Wagon ex. 2.4L	55	14.5
Wagon 2.4L	60	16
Talon		
1990-92 All	60	16

FORD

MAKE, YEAR & MODEL	Liters	Gal
Crown Victoria		
1983-85 Sedan	68	18
Wagon	70	18.5
Others	75.5	20
1986-88 All	68	18
All	75.5	20
1989-91 5.8L	75.5	20
1989 Others	68	18
1990-91 5.0L	68	18
1992 All	75.5	20
EXP		
1984-88 All	49	13
Escort		
1983-88 All	49	13
1989 All	49	11.5
1990 Standard tank	49	13
Wagon 5-speed AC	43.5	11.5
Others	43.5	11.5

MAKE, YEAR & MODEL	Liters	Gal
FORD Continued		
Escort Continued		
1991-92 1.8L	.50	13
1.9L	.45	12
Fairmont		
1983 All	.60	16
Festiva		
1988-92 All	.38	10
LTD		
1983-86 All	.60.5	16
Mustang		
1983-92 All	.58.5	15.5
Probe		
1989-92 All	.57	15
Taurus		
1989-92 3.0L SHO	.69.5	18.5
1986-92 Others	.60.5	16
1992 Optional tank	.69.5	18.5
Tempo		
1984-85 All	.57.5	15
1986-89 2WD	.58	15.5
1990-91 2WD	.60	16
1986 4WD	.49	13
1987-90 4WD	.53.5	14
1991 All	.54	14
1992 All	.60	16
Thunderbird		
1983-85 2.3L turbo	.68	18
Others	.78.5	20.5
1986 2.3L turbo	.72	19
Others	.85	22.5
1987-88 All	.83.5	22
1989-91 All	.72	19
1992 All	.68	18
GEO		
Metro		
1989-92 All	.40	10
Prizm		
1989-92 All	.50	13
Spectrum		
1989 All	.42	11
Storm		
1990-92 All	.47	12.5
Tracker		
1989-92 All	.42	11
HONDA		
Accord		
1983-90 All	.60	16
1991 Coupe	.60	16
1991-92 Others	.64.5	17
Civic		
1983 All	.42	11
1984-92 All	.45.5	12
CRX		
1984-86 HF	.38	10
1987-91 HF	.40	10.5
1984-86 ex. HF	.41	11
1987-91 ex. HF	.45	12
1985-89 FI	.45	12
Prelude		
1983-92 All	.60	16
LINCOLN		
Continental		
1983 All	.85.5	22.5
1984-85 All	.68	18
1986-87 All	.77	20.5
1988-92 All	.70	18.5
Mark VII		
1985 5.0L HO	.68	18
1984-85 Others	.84.5	22.5
1986-90 All	.83.5	22
1991-92 All	.79.5	21
Town Car		
1984-85 5.0L	.84.5	22.5
All	.68	18
1986-87 All	.68	18
1988 All	.83.5	22
1989-90 All	.68	18
1991-92 All	.75.5	20

MAKE, YEAR & MODEL	Liters	Gal
MAZDA		
323		
1986-87 All	.45	12
1988 All	.48	12.5
1989 2WD	.48	12.5
4WD	.50	13
1990 Hatchback	.50	13
Sedan	.55	14.5
1991 All	.50	13
626		
1983-88 All	.60	16
1989 2-wheel steering	.61	16
4-wheel steering	.57	15
1990-92 All	.60	16
929		
1988-92 All	.70	18.5
B2000 pickup		
1983-84 Short bed	.56	15
Long bed	.66	17.5
1986-87 Standard tank	.55	14.5
Optional tank	.60	16
B2200 pickup		
1983-84 Short bed	.56	15
Long bed	.66	17.5
1989-92 Short bed	.56	15
1987-92 Long bed	.66	17.5
B2600 pickup		
1989-92 Short bed	.56	15
1987-92 Long bed	.66	17.5
GLC		
1983-85 Ex. wagon	.42	11
Wagon	.45	12
MPV		
1989 All	.74	19.5
1990 All	.60	16
All	.74	19.5
1991 2WD	.60	16
2WD	.74	19.5
4WD	.75	20
MX-3		
1992 All	.50	13
MX-6		
1989 4-wheel steering	.57	15
1988-92 Others	.60	16
Miata		
1990-91 All	.45	12
Navajo		
1991 All	.73	19.5
Protegé		
1990 All	.55	14.5
1991 2WD	.55	14.5
4WD	.60	16
1992 All	.55	14.5
RX-7		
1983-87 All	.63	16.5
1988 All	.63	14
1989-91 All	.70	18.5
MERCURY		
Capri		
1983-86 All	.58.5	15.5
1991-92 All	.42	11
Cougar		
1984-85 2.3L turbo	.68	18
3.8L	.79.5	21
1983-85 Others	.78	20.5
1986 2.3L turbo	.72	19
Others	.85	22.5
1987-88 All	.83.5	22
1989-92 All	.72	19
Grand Marquis		
1983-85 Sedan	.68	18
Wagon	.70	18.5
Others	.75.5	20
1986-88 5.8L HO	.75.5	20
Others	.68	18
1989-90 5.8L	.75.5	20
1989 Others	.68	18
1990-91 5.0L	.68	18
1991 5.8L sedan	.75.5	20
1992 All	.75.5	20
LN7		
1983 All	.49.5	13

MAKE, YEAR & MODEL	Liters	Gal
MERCURY Continued		
Lynx		
1983-87 All	.49	13
1986 All	.38	10
Marquis		
1983-85 All	.60.5	16
Sable		
1990 3.8L	.70.5	18.5
1986-90 Others	.60.5	16
1991-92 Standard tank	.60.5	16
Optional tank	.69.5	18.5
Topaz		
1984-89 All	.58	15.5
1991 All Wheel Drive	.54	14
1990-92 Others	.60	16
Tracer		
1988-92 All	.45	12
Zephyr		
1983 All	.60	16
MERKUR		
Scorpio		
1988-89 All	.64	17
XR4ti		
1985-89 All	.57	15
MITSUBISHI		
3000GT		
1991-92 All	.75	20
Cordia		
1983-88 All	.49.5	13
Diamante		
1992 All	.72	19
Eclipse		
1990-92 All	.60	16
Expo		
1992 All	.60	16
Expo LRV		
1992 All	.55	15
Galant		
1985-89 All	.60	16
1990-92 2WD	.60	16
4WD	.62	16.5
Mirage		
1985-88 All	.45	12
1989-92 All	.50	13
Montero		
1983-88 All	.60	16
1989 2.6L	.60	16
1989-90 2-door	.75	20
4-door	.92	24.5
1992 All	.92	24.5
Pickup		
1983 2WD standard tank	.57	12.5
2WD optional tank	.68	15
4WD	.68	15
1984-85 Standard tank	.57	15
Optional tank	.68	18
1985-86 Others	.68	18
1987-88 2WD standard tank	.52	13.5
4WD standard tank	.59.5	15.5
1988 2WD optional tank	.69	18
4WD optional tank	.75	20
1989 Standard tank	.52	13.5
Optional tank	.69	18
1990 All	.52	14
1991 Ext. cab 3.0L	.75	20
Short bed 3.0L	.60	16
Long bed 3.0L	.75	20
1991-92 Long bed 2.4L	.69	18
Ext. cab 2.4L	.69	18
Short bed 2.4L	.52	13.5
1992 3.0L	.60	16
Precis		
1987-88 All	.40	10.5
1989-92 All	.45	12
Sigma		
1989-90 All	.60	16
Starion		
1983-89 All	.75	20
Tredia		
1983-88 All	.50	13
Van		
1987-90 All	.54	14

MAKE, YEAR & MODEL	Liters	Gal
NISSAN		
200SX		
1983 Ex. hatchback	.53	14
Hatchback	.60	16
1984-88 All	.53	14
240SX		
1989-92 All	.60	16
280ZX		
1983 All	.80	21
300ZX		
1984-92 All	.72	19
310		
1983 All	.50	13
810		
1983 Ex. wagon	.62	16.5
1983 Wagon	.60	15.5
Axxess		
1990 All	.65	17
Maxima		
1983-84 Ex. wagon	.62	16.5
Wagon	.60	15.5
1985-87 All	.60	16
1988 All	.65	17
1989-92 All	.70	18.5
Micra		
1984-85 All	.53	14
Multi		
1986-88 All	.60	16
NX		
1991 All	.50	13
1992 NX1600	.50	13
NX2000	.50	13
Pathfinder		
1987-92 Standard tank	.60	16
Optional tank	.80	21
Pickup		
1983-86 2WD short wheelbase	.50	13
2WD long wheelbase	.64	17
4WD short wheelbase	.60	16
4WD long wheelbase	.80	21
1987 All	.60	16
1988 All	.80	21
1989-92 Standard tank	.60	16
Optional tank	.80	21
Pulsar		
1983-90 All	.50	13
Sentra		
1983-86 All	.40	10.5
All	.50	13
1987-88 All	.53	14
1989-91 2WD	.50	13
1989-90 4WD	.47.5	12.5
1992 All	.50	13
Stanza		
1983-84 All	.54	14.5
1985-86 Ex. wagon	.54	14.5
Wagon	.60	16
1987-89 All	.60	16
1990-92 All	.62	16.5
Van		
1987-88 All	.65	17
OLDSMOBILE		
88		
1983-85 5.7L Diesel	.98	26
Others	.95	25
1986-92 All	.68	18
Achieva		
1992 All	.57.5	15
Bravada		
1991-92 All	.76	20
Calais		
1985-91 All	.51.5	13.5
Ciera		
1983 3.0L	.59	15.5
Others	.62	16.5
1984 3.0L	.62	16.5
1984-85 4.3L Diesel	.62.5	16.5
1984 Others	.59	15.5
1985 Ex. Diesel	.62	16
1986 2.8L	.62	16.5
1986-92 Others	.59.5	16

FUEL TANK CAPACITIES
Capacities are rounded off to the nearest half unit

MAKE, YEAR & MODEL		Liters	Gal
OLDSMOBILE Continued			
Custom Cruiser			
1983-92	All	.83	22
Cutlass			
1983	Wagon	.69	18
	Ex. wagon	.75	19.5
1984-85	All	.68.5	18
1985	Diesel	.75	20
1986-88	All	.68.5	18
1988	2.8L	.62	16
	5.0L	.68.5	18
1989-90	All	.62	16.5
1991-92	Wagon	.59.5	15.5
	Ex. wagon	.62	16.5
Firenza			
1983	All	.51.5	13.5
1984	All	.53	14
1986-88	All	.51.5	13.5
Ninety-Eight			
1983-84	5.7L Diesel	.98	26
	Others	.95	25
1985	4.3L Diesel	.98.5	26
	Others	.59.5	16
1986-92	All	.68	18
Omega			
1983-84	2.8L	.57	15
	Others	.55	14.5
Silhouette			
1990-92	All	.76	20
Toronado			
1983	Ex 5.7L Diesel	.79	21
1983-85	5.7L Diesel	.86	22.5
1984-85	Others	.80	21
1986-92	All	.68	18
Troféo			
1987-92	All	.68	18
PLYMOUTH			
Acclaim			
1989-92	All	.61	16
Caravelle			
1983-87	All	.68	18
1988	All	.53	14
1989	All	.63	18
Colt			
1983-84	Standard tank	.40	10.5
	Optional tank	.50	13
1985-88	All	.45	12
1989-90	1.5L wagon	.47	12.5
	1.5L ex. wagon	.50	13
	1.6L	.50	13
	1.8L	.47	12.5
1992	All	.50	13
Colt Vista — see Vista			
Conquest			
1984-86	All	.75	20
Gran Fury			
1983-88	All	.68	18
1989	All	.63	18
Horizon			
1983-90	All	.49	13
Laser			
1990-92	All	.60	16
Reliant			
1983	All	.49	13
1984-88	All	.53	14
Sapporo			
1983	All	.60	16
Scamp			
1983	All	.49	13
Sundance			
1987-92	All	.53	14
Turismo			
1983-87	All	.49	13

MAKE, YEAR & MODEL		Liters	Gal
PLYMOUTH Continued			
Vista			
1984-88	All	.50	13
1989-90	2WD	.50	13
	4WD	.55	14.5
1992	2.4L	.60	16
	Others	.55	14.5
Voyager			
1984-86	All	.57	15
1987	All	.76	20
1988-90	Standard tank	.57	15
	Optional tank	.76	20
1991	2WD	.76	20
	All Wheel Drive	.68	18
1992	Standard tank	.76	20
	Optional tank	.68	18
PONTIAC			
1000			
1983-87	All	.47.5	12.5
2000			
1983	All	.53	14
6000			
1983-85	4.3L Diesel	.63	16.5
1983-86	2.8L	.62	16.5
	Others	.59.5	15.5
1987-88	All	.59.5	16
1989	STE	.58.5	15.5
	Ex. STE	.59.5	15.5
1990	2WD	.59.5	15.5
	4WD	.54	14.5
1991	All	.59.5	15.5
Acadian			
1983-87	All	.47.5	12.5
Bonneville			
1983-84	5.7L Diesel	.75	20
	Sedan	.66	17.5
	Wagon	.69.5	18.5
1985-92	All	.68.5	18
Fiero			
1984-86	All	.38.5	10
1987-88	All	.45	12
Firebird			
1983-86	All	.60	16
1987-92	All	.58.5	15.5
Grand Am			
1985-91	All	.51.5	13.5
1992	All	.57.5	15
Grand LeMans			
1983	Sedan Diesel	.75	20
	Others	.69	18
Grand Prix			
1983-84	5.7L Diesel	.75	20
	Others	.66	17.5
1987	4.3L	.66	17.5
1985-88	Others	.68.5	18
1989-92	All	.62	16.5
LeMans			
1988-92	All	.50	13
Parisienne			
1983-85	5.7L Diesel	.102	27
1983-86	Sedan	.95	25
	Wagon	.83	22
Phoenix			
1983-84	2.5L	.55	14.5
	Others	.57	15
Safari			
1987-89	All	.84	22
Sunbird			
1984-91	All	.51.5	13.5
1992	All	.57.5	15
Sunburst			
1985-87	All	.42	11
Tempest			
1988-89	All	.51.5	13.5
1990	All	.59	15.5
Trans Sport			
1990-92	All	.76	20

MAKE, YEAR & MODEL		Liters	Gal
SUBARU			
3-Door			
1985-89	All	.60	16
4-Door			
1985-89	All	.60	16
Brat			
1983-84	All	.55	14.5
1985-87	All	.60	16
Hatchback			
1983-84	2WD	.50	13
	4WD	.45	12
1985-89	All	.60	16
Justy			
1987-88	All	.60	16
1989-92	All	.35	9
Legacy			
1990-92	All	.60	16
Loyale			
1990-92	All	.60	16
SVX			
1992	All	.70	18
Sedan			
1983-84	2WD	.60	16
	4WD	.55	14.5
1985-88	All	.60	16
Wagon			
1983-84	2WD	.60	16
	4WD	.55	14.5
1985-88	All	.60	16
XT			
1985-91	All	.60	16
TOYOTA			
4-Runner			
1988	2WD	.73	19.5
1985-91	Others	.65	17
1992	Standard	.65	17
	W/wide tires	.71	19
Camry			
1983-86	All	.55	14.5
1987-91	All	.60	16
1992	All	.70	18.5
Celica			
1983-91	All	.60	16
1992	2WD	.60	16
	4WD	.68	18
Corolla			
1983	Wagon	.62	16
	Ex. wagon	.50	13
1984-92	All	.50	13
Cressida			
1983-85	All	.65	17
1986	All	.70	18.5
1987	Sedan	.70	18.5
	Wagon	.69	18
1988-92	All	.70	18.5
Land Cruiser			
1983	Wagon	.90	24
	Ex. wagon	.85	22.5
1984-87	All	.90	24
1991-92	All	.95	25
MR2			
1985-89	All	.41	11
1991-92	All	.54	14.5
Paseo			
1992	All	.45	12
Pickup			
1983-86	Long bed	.61	16
1983-88	2WD short bed	.52	14
1987-90	4WD	.65	17
	Long bed	.65	17
1991-92	2WD short bed	.52	13.5
1989-92	2WD others	.65	17
	4WD short wheelbase	.65	17
1991-92	4WD others	.73	19.5

MAKE, YEAR & MODEL		Liters	Gal
TOYOTA Continued			
Previa Van			
1991-92	All	.75	20
Starlet			
1983-84	All	.40	10
Supra			
1983-86	All	.61	16
1987-92	All	.70	18.5
Tercel			
1983-85	2WD	.45	12
1984-86	4WD wagon	.50	13
1987-88	Ex. wagon	.45	12
1986-88	Wagon	.50	12
1989-92	All	.45	12
Van			
1984-89	All	.60	16
VOLKSWAGEN			
Cabriolet			
1985-92	All	.52	13.5
Corrado			
1990	All	.55	14.5
Fox			
1987-90	All	.47	12.5
GTI			
1985-90	All	.55	14.5
Golf			
1985-90	All	.55	14.5
Jetta			
1983-84	All	.40	10.5
1985-92	All	.55	14.5
Passat			
1990-92	All	.70	18.5
Pickup			
1983-85	All	.57	15
Quantum			
1983-85	All	.60	16
1986-88	2WD	.60	16
	4WD	.70	18.5
Rabbit			
1983-84	Convertible	.40	10.5
	Ex. convertible	.38	10
	Others	.42	11
Scirocco			
1983-85	All	.40	10.5
1986-89	All	.52	14
Vanagon			
1983-88	All	.60	16
1989-90	Syncro	.60	16
	Ex. Syncro	.70	18.5
VOLVO			
240 Series			
1983-85	Ex. Diesel	.60	16
1986-92	All	.60	16
740 Series			
1989-92	All	.60	16
760 Series			
1983-84	All	.82	21.5
1989-90	All	.80	21
1990	Wagon	.60	16
	Ex. wagon	.80	21
780			
1989-90	All	.80	21
940 SE			
1991	Sedan	.80	21
	Wagon	.60	16
1992	All	.60	16
960			
1992	Sedan	.80	21
	Wagon	.60	16
Diesel			
1983-85	All	.82	21.5

Column 1

MAKE, YEAR & MODEL	Kg.	Oz.
ACURA		
1992 Vigor	0.8	30
1991-86 All models	0.9	33
AUDI		
1992 100	1.1	39
1991-89 100, 200, V8 Quattro	1.1	38
1990-82 80, 90 4000, Coupe, Quattro	1.0	36
1988-84 5000	1.1	39
1983 5000	1.4	49
AMERICAN MOTORS		
1988-83 All models	0.9	34
AMC/RENAULT		
1989-83 Medallion, Alliance, Encore	0.8	28
1988 Eagle Wagon	0.9	34
BMW		
1992 325i	1.2	42
1992-85 5-Series, 7-Series, 850i:		
W/small condenser, 21.5" width	1.5	53
W/large condenser, 22.4" width	1.9	68
1991-87 M3	0.9	30
1991-83 3-Series ex. M3	1.0	34
1990-83 6-Series: w/o rear AC	1.1	38
W/rear AC	1.7	59
1984-83 5-Series	1.3	45
7-Series	1.2	42
BUICK		
1992 Century	1.2	44
Skylark	1.2	42
LeSabre, Park Ave.	1.1	46
1992-91 Roadmaster	1.4	50
1992-89 Reatta, Riviera	1.1	38
1992-88 Regal (FWD)	1.0	36
Electra	1.1	38
1991-89 Century	1.1	40
1991-86 LeSabre	1.1	38
Skyhawk: 1.8L	1.1	40
2.0L	1.0	36
Skylark, Somerset	1.0	36
1990-83 Estate Wagon, Regal (RWD)	1.6	54
1988-86 Century	1.1	40
Riviera	1.1	40
1987-85 Electra	1.3	44
1985-83 LeSabre, Riviera	1.6	54
Century, Skyhawk, Skylark	1.3	44
1984-83 Electra	1.6	54
CADILLAC		
1992 Fleetwood Brougham	1.4	49
1991-88 Eldorado, Seville	1.1	38
1991-87 Allanté	1.1	38
1991-85 Fleetwood Brougham	1.5	53
1990-89 DeVille, Fleetwood (FWD)	1.3	44
1988-85 Cimarron	1.0	36
1987-86 Eldorado, Seville	1.3	44
1984-83 Cimarron	1.3	44
DeVille, Eldorado, Fleetwood, Seville	1.6	56
CHEVROLET		
1992 Beretta, Corsica	1.2	42
1992-91 Caprice	1.4	50
1992-90 Lumina	1.0	36
1992-88 Camaro, Corvette	1.0	36
1992-86 Cavalier	1.0	36
1991-89 Beretta, Corsica	1.3	44
1990-86 Celebrity	1.1	40
1990-82 Caprice	1.6	54
1989-87 Spectrum	0.8	28
1988-87 Beretta, Corsica, Corvette	1.0	36
1988-85 Sprint	0.7	24
1988-83 Monte Carlo	1.6	54
1987-83 Camaro	1.4	48
Chevette	1.0	36
1986-85 Spectrum	0.7	24
1986-83 Impala, Malibu	1.6	54
1985-83 Cavalier, Celebrity, Corvette	1.3	44
Citation	1.3	44
CHEVROLET/GMC TRUCKS		
1992 G-Series: Front	1.5	42
Front & Rear	2.2	76
Safari: Front	1.0	36
Rear	1.7	60
Yukon, Suburban: Front	1.4	48
Front & Rear	1.9	68
Lumina APV: Front	1.4	50
Rear	1.8	65
1991-90 Lumina APV	1.4	48
Astro, Safari: Front	1.4	48
Rear	1.7	60

Column 2

MAKE, YEAR & MODEL	Kg.	Oz.
CHEVROLET/GMC TRUCKS Continued		
1991-88 C, K, S Series	1.1	37
W/roof-mounted unit:		
G Series ex. 7.4L engine	2.0	69
7.4L engine	1.9	64
R, V Series	2.4	92
Ex. roof-mounted unit:		
G Series ex. 7.4L engine	1.4	48
7.4L engine	1.1	40
R, V Series	1.4	50
1989 Astro, Safari: Front	1.0	36
Rear	1.7	60
1988-85 Astro, Safari: Front	0.9	32
Rear	1.4	48
1987 S Series	1.1	37
Others	1.6	56
1987-86 W/roof-mounted unit: G Series	2.0	72
Others	2.4	94
1985-83 W/roof-mounted unit: C, K Series	2.4	94
G Series	2.0	72
Ex. roof-mounted unit: S Series	1.1	37
Others	1.4	48
CHRYSLER/DODGE/PLYMOUTH		
1992 All FWD: W/o rear AC	0.9	32
W/rear AC	1.2	43
1992-90 Monaco	1.0	36
Laser	1.0	33
1991 Dynasty, New Yorker, Fifth Ave., Imperial	1.0	34
Others	0.9	32
1990-88 All other FWD models	1.1	38
1989-83 All RWD models	1.2	41
1987-83 Omni, Horizon, Charger, Turismo	1.0	34
All other FWD models	1.1	38
CHRYSLER/DODGE/PLYMOUTH IMPORT		
1992 Colt Vista	0.8	30
Colt	1.0	36
1992-91 Stealth	1.0	34
1992-83 Others	0.9	32
1991-90 Ram 50	0.9	30
DODGE/PLYMOUTH TRUCKS		
1992 Ram 50 pickup	0.8	30
Ramcharger	1.3	44
1992-91 Dakota	1.2	40
B-Series van	1.3	44
w/rear unit	1.8	62
1992-90 Caravan, Mini Ram, Voyager	0.9	32
w/rear unit	1.2	43
1992-88 D, W-Series pickup	1.3	44
1990-87 Dakota	1.3	44
1990-83 B-Series van	1.4	48
W/rear unit	1.8	62
1989-84 Caravan, Mini-Ram, Voyager	1.1	38
W/rear AC	1.3	44
1987-83 D, W-Series pickup	1.1	40
EAGLE		
1992 Summit	0.8	30
1992-90 Talon	0.9	32
1992-88 Premier	1.0	36
1991-84 Summit	1.0	36
FORD/MERCURY		
1992 Capri	0.7	25
Tracer, Escort	1.0	34
Mustang	1.4	42
Taurus, Sable	1.1	40
Crown Victoria, Marquis	1.1	41
1992-88 Festiva	0.7	25
Escort, Tempo, Topaz	1.1	36
Probe	1.1	40
Thunderbird, Cougar	1.1	40
1991 Capri	0.6	22
1991-88 Mustang	1.2	40
Sable, Taurus	1.3	44
3.8L engine	1.1	40
1991-88 Crown Victoria, Marquis	1.4	48
1989-87 Tracer	0.9	31
1987-84 Escort, EXP, Lynx, Tempo, Topaz, Taurus, Sable	1.1	40
1987-83 Crown Victoria, Grand Marquis	1.5	54
Capri, Cougar, LTD, Marquis, Mustang, Thunderbird	1.1	38
1983 Escort, EXP, Lynx, LN7	1.1	38
FORD TRUCKS		
1992 Bronco, F-Series pickup	1.3	44
1992-89 Aerostar	1.5	56
1992-83 Bronco II, Explorer, Ranger	0.9	32
E-Series van: Main unit	1.6	54
Auxiliary unit	2.0	70

Column 3

MAKE, YEAR & MODEL	Kg.	Oz.
FORD TRUCKS Continued		
1991-84 Bronco, F-Series pickup	1.4	48
1988-86 Aerostar	1.4	54
1983 Bronco, F-Series pickup	1.6	54
GEO		
1992-91 Storm, Tracker	0.6	21
1992-89 Prizm	0.8	27
Metro	0.5	18
1990-89 Tracker	0.7	25
HONDA		
1992 Civic	0.6	23
Accord	0.9	32
1991-88 Accord, Civic, CRX, Prelude	0.9	32
1987-84 Civic, CRX	0.8	28
1987-83 Prelude	0.8	28
Others	0.7	25
HYUNDAI		
1992 Elantra	0.9	32
1992-89 Sonata	0.9	32
1992-86 Excel, Scoupe	0.9	32
INFINITI		
1992-91 G20	0.8	28
1992-90 M30	0.9	32
Q45	1.2	41
ISUZU		
1992 Amigo, Pickup, Trooper	0.9	30
Impulse, Stylus	0.6	21
1992-91 Rodeo	1.0	35
1991-90 Impulse, Stylus	0.8	26
1991-84 Trooper	1.0	33
1990-88 Pickup	1.0	33
1989-85 I-Mark (FWD)	0.8	28
1989-83 Impulse	1.0	35
1987-83 Pickup, I-Mark (RWD)	0.9	30
JEEP		
1992-89 Grand Wagoneer, Wrangler, YJ	0.9	32
Comanche, Cherokee, Wagoneer	1.1	38
1988-84 Cherokee, Comanche, Wagoneer, Wrangler	0.9	32
Grand Wagoneer, J10, J20	1.0	36
1987-83 CJ5, CJ7	1.1	40
1983 Cherokee, Wagoneer, J10, J20	1.0	36
LEXUS		
1992 ES 300, SC 300, SC 400	1.0	35
1992-90 LS 400	1.0	36
1991-90 ES 250	0.7	27
LINCOLN		
1992 Mark VII	1.2	42
1992-88 Town Car	1.2	40
1992-88 Continental	1.1	40
1991-85 Mark VII	1.1	38
1990-83 Town Car	1.4	48
1987-83 Continental, Mark VI	1.1	38
MAZDA		
1992 Protegé, MX-3	0.8	27
1992-91 929	0.8	26
MX-6, 626	0.9	32
Pickup	0.7	26
1991 MPV: Single system	1.1	37
Twin system	1.5	51
1991-90 Miata	0.8	28
1991-88 323, Protegé	0.8	27
1990-89 MPV: Single system	1.2	42
Twin system	1.4	49
1990-88 626, MX-6	1.0	35
929	1.1	39
RX-7, Pickup	0.8	28
MERCEDES-BENZ		
1992 300SD, SE, 400SE, 500SEL, 600SEL	1.2	41
W/rear AC	1.4	48
1991-86 300E, CE	1.1	38
300SE, SEL, SDL; 420SEL; 560SEC, SEL	1.5	54
1989-87 260E	1.1	38
1989-86 190E 2.6L	1.1	38
560SL	1.0	36
1988-84 190D	1.1	38
1987-86 190E 16 valve	0.8	30
1987-84 190E 2.3L SOHC	1.1	38
1985-84 500SEC, SEL	1.5	54
1985-83 380SE, SEC, SEL	1.5	54
380SL, SLC	1.0	36
300D, CD, TD	1.1	40
300SD	1.5	54
1984-83 240D	1.1	40

AIR CONDITIONING SYSTEM REFRIGERANT CAPACITIES*
*Factory installed, or factory supplied systems only

MAKE, YEAR & MODEL		Kg.	Oz.
MITSUBISHI			
1992	Diamante	1.0	37
	Expo	0.8	30
	Precis	0.9	35
1992-91	3000GT	1.0	34
1992-90	Mirage	1.0	36
	Eclipse, Galant	0.9	33
	Pickup	0.8	30
	Sigma	0.9	32
1991-87	Precis	0.8	30
1990-87	Van/wagon: W/single unit	0.9	32
	W/dual units	1.5	51
1989-87	Mirage	0.9	32
1989-86	Cordia, Galant, Tredia, Sigma	0.9	32
1989-83	Starion Pickup, Montero	0.9	32
1987	Van/Wagon w/single unit	0.7	25
1986-85	Mirage	0.7	25
1985-83	Cordia, Tredia, Galant	0.7	25
NISSAN/DATSUN			
1992-91	Maxima	0.9	33
	Sentra, NX	0.7	25
	240SX	0.9	32
	Stanza	0.8	28
	300ZX	0.8	28
1992-83	Pickup, Pathfinder	0.9	32
1990	Axxess	0.9	32
	300ZX w/o Turbo	0.9	32
	300ZX Turbo	0.8	30
1990-89	240SX	1.0	36
1990-83	Sentra, Stanza	0.9	32
	Maxima	1.0	36
1989-84	300ZX	1.0	36
1989-83	Pulsar	0.9	32
1988-87	Van	1.5	53
1988-83	200SX	0.9	32
1983	280ZX, 510	1.0	36
OLDSMOBILE			
1992	Toronado, Troféo	1.1	38
	Achieva	1.2	42
	Cutlass Ciera, Cutlass Cruiser	1.2	44
	Eighty-Eight	1.3	46
	Ninety-Eight	1.3	46
1992-91	Custom Cruiser	1.4	50
1992-90	Silhouette	1.4	50
	W/rear AC	1.8	66
1992-88	Cutlass (FWD)	1.0	36
1991-88	Ninety-Eight	1.1	38
1991-86	Calais	1.0	36
	Ciera	1.1	40
	Delta 88	1.1	38

MAKE, YEAR & MODEL		Kg.	Oz.
OLDSMOBILE Continued			
1990-88	Custom Cruiser	1.6	54
1989-86	Toronado	1.1	40
1988-86	Firenza: 1.8L	1.1	40
	2.0L	1.0	36
1988-83	Cutlass (RWD)	1.6	54
1987-85	Ninety-Eight	1.3	44
1985-83	Ciera, Firenza	1.3	44
	Delta 88	1.6	54
	Omega	1.3	44
	Toronado	1.6	54
1984-83	Ninety-Eight	1.6	54
PEUGEOT			
1992-83	405, 505	1.0	35
PONTIAC			
1992	Bonneville	1.3	46
1992-90	Trans Sport	1.4	50
	W/rear AC	1.8	65
	Grand Am	1.2	42
1992-89	Firebird, LeMans	1.0	36
1992-88	Grand Prix	1.0	36
	Sunbird	1.0	36
1991-87	Bonneville	1.1	38
1991-86	6000	1.1	40
1990-88	Safari	1.6	54
1990-85	Grand Am	1.0	36
1989-88	Safari	1.6	54
1988	Fiero	1.1	38
	Firebird, LeMans	1.0	36
1988-84	Fiero	1.1	40
1987-83	Firebird	1.4	48
	Sunbird, (J)2000	1.2	44
	Parisienne, Safari	1.6	56
	Grand Prix	1.5	52
	(T)1000	1.0	36
1986-83	Bonneville, LeMans, Catalina	1.5	52
1985-83	6000, Phoenix	1.3	44
PORSCHE			
1990-89	911 Carrera 4	0.9	33
	944S2	0.9	33
1989	928S4 w/rear evaporator	1.1	40
1989-85	944 from 1-85	0.9	33
1989-84	911	1.3	47
1988-87	924S	0.9	33
1988-84	928 w/rear evaporator	1.2	42
1985-83	944 to 2-85	1.1	40
1984-83	928	1.0	37
1983	911	1.2	44

MAKE, YEAR & MODEL		Kg.	Oz.
SAAB			
1992	9000 w/rear AC	1.4	48
1992-91	9000 w/o rear AC	1.1	39
1992-83	900	1.0	36
1990-86	9000	1.1	38
SUBARU			
1992	SVX	0.6	22
1992-90	Legacy	0.9	32
	Loyale	0.8	30
1991-86	XT Coupe	0.7	27
1989-88	Sedan, Wagon: Hitachi	0.7	27
	Panasonic	0.8	29
1987-83	Sedan, Wagon	0.7	27
SUZUKI			
1992-90	Sidekick	0.6	21
	Swift	0.5	18
TOYOTA			
1992	Camry	1.0	35
	Land Cruiser	0.9	32
	Paseo	0.7	27
	Celica, Corolla, Supra, Tercel	0.7	25
	Pickup, 4-Runner	0.8	28
1992-91	Previa	1.0	34
	W/rear AC	1.2	42
1992-90	Cressida, MR2	0.8	30
1991-90	Camry, Celica, Corolla, Supra, Tercel	0.7	25
	Pickup, 4-Runner, Land Cruiser	0.8	28
1989-84	Van: W/dual AC	1.4	50
	W/single AC	0.7	25
1989-83	Others	0.7	25
VOLKSWAGEN			
1992-90	Corrado	1.1	38
1992-86	Vanagon	1.5	51
1992-85	Cabriolet, Scirocco	1.1	40
	Golf, GTI, Jetta	1.1	38
1988-87	Fox	1.2	42
1988-83	Quantum	1.0	34
1985-83	Jetta	1.2	43
1984-83	Jetta, Rabbit, Dasher	0.9	33
	Scirocco	1.0	34
VOLVO			
1992-88	760	1.1	38
1992-87	740, 780	1.2	40
1992-83	240 Series	1.1	38
1987-83	740, 760	1.2	40

COOLING SYSTEM AIR BLEED CHART

A number of models have cooling systems that cannot be completely filled with coolant through the radiator filler. The result can be air pockets that restrict coolant flow which may result in engine overheating and damage. The manufacturers provide air bleeds or procedures to purge the air from the system. When servicing a cooling system, refer to the following chart. If the model you are servicing is shown on the chart, bleed air from the system by loosing the air bleed and filling the system until coolant runs from the air bleed with no bubbles in it. Some systems require special procedures aside or in addition to this. These will be reflected in the chart along with the type of bleeder, it's location, coolant fill point and whether or not the engine needs to be running.

MAKE MODEL ENGINE	BLEEDER TYPE	LOCATION	FILL POINT	BLEED W/ ENGINE @ RPM	SPECIAL NOTICE
ACURA					
1986-91 All	screw	thermostat housing	radiator	off	—
AUDI					
4000 4-cyl.	thermo switch	engine outlet flange	reservoir	off	—
BMW					
All SOHC 6-cyl.	screw	thermostat housing	radiator	fast idle	—
CHRYSLER CORPORATION					
1985-86 4-cyl. 1.6L	vacuum valve	thermostat housing	radiator	off	Recheck cold
1992 1.8L Vista	bolt	thermostat housing	thermo housing & radiator	off	Fill through housing until full. Install bolt and top-off radiator. With engine warm rev 3 times and let cool, add coolant as needed

MAKE MODEL ENGINE	BLEEDER TYPE	LOCATION	FILL POINT	BLEED W/ ENGINE @ RPM	SPECIAL NOTICE
CHRYSLER CORPORATION Continued					
1985-92 4-cyl. 2.2L, 2.5L	vacuum valve or plug	thermostat housing	radiator	off	Recheck cold
1991-92 2.2L Turbo III	sending unit	thermostat housing	radiator	off	Recheck cold
1991-92 3.0L Stealth	—	—	radiator	—	With engine warm, race to 3000 rpm several times and recheck coolant level when cold
1990-92 V6 3.3L, 3.8L	sending unit	cylinder head	radiator	off	Recheck cold
EAGLE, DODGE					
1988-89 Medallion	screw	1. upper hose 2. heater hose 3. AT oil cooler	reservoir	off	—
1988-92 Premier, Monaco, V6	valve	thermostat housing	reservoir	off	Bleed twice, before & after running

MAKE MODEL ENGINE	BLEEDER TYPE	LOCATION	FILL POINT	BLEED W/ ENGINE @ RPM	SPECIAL NOTICE
FORD MOTOR COMPANY					
1986-91 Taurus, Sable, 4-cyl.	plug	thermostat housing	radiator	off	Reinstall plug after filling radiator before starting engine
1983-92 4-cyl. 2.3L OHC All passenger cars & Aerostar	heater hose	thermostat housing	radiator	—	Disconnect hose at water outlet connection and fill radiator until coolant is visible at the connection or reaches radiator cap filler neck
GENERAL MOTORS					
1983-92 All 4-cyl. 1.8L, 2.0L OHC; 2.5L w/thermostat twist cap	caps	radiator & thermostat housing	thermo	—	Fill through thermostat housing until coolant reaches top of radiator neck. Recheck cold
1984-85 Fiero	caps	radiator & thermostat housing	thermo	2000	Fill through thermostat housing until coolant reaches top of radiator, replace caps. Run engine for three minutes and then fast idle for 15-20 seconds. Top off through thermostat housing
1986-88 Fiero	caps	radiator & thermostat housing	radiator	off	Fill cooling system through radiator until full. Replace cap and run engine until warm. Add coolant through thermostat housing as needed
1987-89 V6 2.8L FWD ex. Century, Celebrity, Ciera, 6000	valve	thermostat housing	radiator	off	With high-mounted by-pass hose (above radiator), also remove hose from pipe
1986-87 V6 3.0L, 3.8L Electra, LeSabre, 88, 98, Bonneville	hose	heater outlet	radiator	3000	Rev to 3000 RPM & top off
1989-92 V6 3.1L ex. Century, Celebrity, Ciera, 6000	valves	1. thermostat housing 2. throttle body return pipe	radiator	off	Close valves when coolant flows from vent, continue filling, idle engine to operating temperature and top off
1991-92 V6 3.4L	valves	1. thermostat housing 2. heater inlet pipe	radiator	off	Fill radiator neck until full. Allow system to stabilize and add coolant as needed. Install radiator cap and close air bleeds. Fill coolant reservoir to proper level
1988-91 V6 3.8L Code C, 1989-90 V6 3.3L	—	—	radiator	—	With AC on, rev engine to 3000 RPM at least five times to purge trapped air
1991-92 3.8L Code L, 1	plug	thermostat housing	radiator	idle	Turn AC on, temp. on high. Rev engine to 3000 rpm five times and slowly open air bleed
1992 5.7L Code P Corvette	screw	1. thermostat housing 2. throttle body	radiator	off	—
Cadillac, all FWD V8	—	—	radiator	—	Run engine at 2000 rpm for 10 minutes with cap off
HONDA					
1983-91 All	screw	thermostat housing	radiator	off	—
MAZDA					
1986-88 RX-7	plug	radiator flange	radiator	idle	—

MAKE MODEL ENGINE	BLEEDER TYPE	LOCATION	FILL POINT	BLEED W/ ENGINE @ RPM	SPECIAL NOTICE
MITSUBISHI					
1992 1.8L Expo	bolt	thermostat housing	thermo housing & radiator	off	Fill through housing until full. Install bolt and top-off radiator. With engine warm rev 3 times and let cool, add coolant as needed
1991-92 3.0L 3000GT	—	—	radiator	—	With engine warm, race to 3000 rpm several times and recheck coolant level when cold
NISSAN					
1989-90 Sentra, Pulsar	plug	cylinder head	radiator	off	Recheck cold
1991-92 Sentra, NX: 1.6L	bolts(2)	1. cylinder head 2. heater hose outlet			1.6L & 2.0L: Fill until coolant flows from bleeders, then close. Jam open cap valve with a U-shaped wire. Run engine allowing remaining air to vent into coolant reservoir
2.0L	1. bolt 2. pipe cap	thermostat housing & heater hose	radiator	off	(See above)
1990-92 Axxess, Stanza	bolt	intake manifold plenum	radiator	off	Bolt located next to PCV valve. Recheck cold
1987-88 200SX V6	plug	right head	radiator	off	Plug is by PCV hose
1989-90 240SX	bolt	thermostat housing	radiator	off	Recheck cold
1990-91 300ZX	plug	radiator top tank	radiator	off	Recheck cold
1985-88 Maxima	bolt	heater pipe	radiator	off	Recheck cold
1989-92 Maxima	bolt	intake manifold plenum	radiator	off	Bolt located next to PCV valve. Recheck cold
1986-89 Pickup V6	plug	heater pipe	radiator	off	Plug is by battery
1990-92 Pickup: 4-cyl.	bolt	#1 intake manifold runner	radiator	off	Recheck cold
V6	bolt	intake manifold plenum	radiator	off	Bolt located next to PCV valve. Recheck cold
RENAULT					
1985-87 Alliance, Encore, GTA 1.7L, 2.0L	screw	radiator	tank	off	Recheck cold
SAAB					
900	screw	thermostat housing	tank	off	—
SUBARU					
1990-92 Legacy ex. Turbo	plug	radiator top tank	radiator	off	—
TOYOTA					
1984-89 MR2	valves	1. radiator 2. heater 3. water inlet	engine compartment filler cap	off	Fit hoses to bleeders to allow level to rise to height of filler cap
1989-91 Camry V6	valve	thermostat housing	radiator	off	—
VOLKSWAGEN					
1983-84 Jetta, Rabbit, Scirocco	hose	upper radiator	radiator	off	—
1984-91 Vanagon	valve	radiator	tank	fast idle	Raise front of vehicle 16" (40 cm). Open bleed connection in the engine compartment
1987-91 Fox	thermo switch	cylinder head	tank	off	—

TIRES
PASSENGER CAR

Tire sizes and tire pressures represent the car manufacturer's recommendations (for normal speeds).
†Sustained high speeds: **Numeric and Alphanumeric** sizes, add 4 psi (do not exceed 32 psi for load range ''B'', 36 psi for load range ''C'', 40 psi for load range ''D''); **P-Metric** sizes, add 3 psi (do not exceed 35 psi for Standard Load, 41 psi for Extra Load ''XL'' tire).
European metric sizes have maximum inflation pressure of either 32 or 36 psi, depending on construction. Refer to maximum inflation limit stamped on tire sidewall.
*For minimum load pressure, refer to tire decal. •Cars equipped with Trailer Tow Option, refer to tire decal.

MAKE	YEAR	MODEL	ORIGINAL EQUIPMENT SIZE Std.	Optional	PRESSURE†• Max. Load* F-R	RIM WIDTH
ACURA						
	1992	Legend	205/60VR15		32-30	6½-JJ
		Vigor	205/60R15		30-28	6-JJ
	1991	NSX: Front	205/50ZR15		35	6½-JJ
		Rear	225/50ZR16		35	8-JJ
	1991-90	Integra: RS, LS	195/60R14		32-32	5½-JJ
		GS	P195/60R14		35-35	5½-JJ
		Legend: Coupe	205/60VR15		32-30	5½-JJ
		Sedan	205/60R15		32-32	5½-JJ
	1989-86	Integra	195/60R14		32-32	5½-JJ
		Legend	205/60R15		32-32	5½-JJ
AMERICAN MOTORS						
	1988	Eagle 4WD wagon	P195/75R15		29-29	6-JJ
	1987-83	Eagle sedan, wagon . . .	P195/75R15	P215/65R15	29-29	6-JJ
	1984-83	Eagle Liftback: 4-cyl. . . .	P195/75R15	P215/65R15	26-30	6-JJ
		6-cyl.	P195/75R15	P215/65R15	29-29	6-JJ
	1983	Spirit, Concord	P195/75R15	P215/65R15	29-29	6-JJ
AUDI						
	1992	100	195/65HR15		—	5½-J
		100S, 100CS	195/65HR15		—	6-J
		V8 Quattro	215/60VR15		36-36	7½-J
	1991	Coupe Quattro	205/60VR15		32-32	7-J
		V8 Quattro	215/60HR15		36-36	7½-J
		80	175/70TR14		32-32	5½-J
		80 Quattro, 90	175/70TR14		34-34	6-J
		90 Quattro, 20V	205/50VR15		34-34	7-J
		100, 100 Quattro	195/65HR15		32-32	6-J
		200	205/60VR15		32-32	6-J
		200 Quattro	215/60VR15	215/60HR15	36-36	7½-J
	1990	Coupe Quattro	205/60VR15		30-30	7-J
		V8 Quattro	215/60ZR15		30-30	7-J
		100, 100 Quattro	205/60VR15		30-30	6-J
		200, 200 Quattro	205/60VR15		30-30	6-J
	1990-88	80	175/70R14		32-32	5½-J
		80 Quattro	195/60VR14		34-34	6-J
		90, 90 Quattro	195/60VR14		34-34	6-J
	1989	100E	185/70HR14		32-32	5½-J
		100, 200 & Quattro	P205/60VR15		30-30	6-J
	1988	5000S	185/70HR14		32-28	6-J
		5000S Quattro	205/60VR15		30-30	6-,7-J
		5000CS Turbo	205/60VR15		29-26	6-J
		5000CS Turbo Quattro . .	205/60VR15		30-30	6-J
	1987-86	4000 S	185/70SR14		26-26	6-J
		4000 CS Quattro	195/60HR14		28-28	6-J
		5000 S	185/70SR14		32-28	6-J
		5000 CS Turbo	205/65VR15		30-28	6-J
		5000 CS Turbo Quattro . .	205/60HR15		32-32	6-,7-J
		Coupe GT	185/60HR14		28-28	6-J
	1985	Quattro	215/50VR15		28-28	8-J
	1985-83	4000	175/70SR13		26-26	5-,5½-J
				185/60HR14	26-26	6-J
		Coupe	175/70SR13		26-26	5½-J
				185/60HR14	26-26	6-J
		5000 Turbo Gas	205/60HR15		26-26	6-J
	1984-83	5000 Turbo Diesel	185/70SR14		30-34	6-J
		5000 ex. Turbo	185/70SR14		28-28	5½-J
				185/70HR14	28-28	6-J
		Quattro	205/60HR15		26-25	6-,7-J
BMW						
	1992	325i	205/60R15		33-39	7-J
		318i, 325i conv.	195/65HR14			6-J
		525i	205/65R15	225/60HR15	33-41	6½-,7-J
				240/45ZR15	33-41	195 mm
		535i	225/60VR15		—	7-J
		M5	235/45ZR17		41-44	8-J
		735i, 735iL	225/60VR15		—	7-J
		750iL	225/60ZR15		—	7-J
		850i	235/50ZR16		—	7½-J
	1991	318i	195/65HR14		30-36	5½-J
				205/55R15	33-39	7-J
		318iS	195/65HR14		33-39	6½-J
				205/55R15	33-39	7-J
		525i	205/65R15		33-41	7-J
				225/60R15	33-41	7-J
				240/45ZR415	33-41	195 mm
		535i	225/60ZR15		35-44	7-J
				240/45ZR415	35-44	195 mm
				205/65R15	35-44	6½-J[1]

MAKE	YEAR	MODEL	ORIGINAL EQUIPMENT SIZE Std.	Optional	PRESSURE†• Max. Load* F-R	RIM WIDTH
BMW Continued						
	1991	M5	235/45ZR17		41-44	8-J
				225/50R16	36-44	7-J
		735i, 735iL, 750iL	225/60ZR15		35-44	7-J
		850i	235/50ZR16		30-36	7½-J
				225/55R16	30-36	7½-J
	1991-90	M3	205/55VR15		33-41	7-J
		325i, 325i conv.	195/65R14		33-39	6-J
				195/65R-14	33-39	6½-J
		325iS	195/65R14		32-41	6½-J
		325iX	205/55R15		32-41	7-J
	1990	525i	205/65VR15		33-41	7-J
		535i, 735i, 735iL, 750iL . .	225/60VR15		35-44	7-J
	1989	525i	205/65VR15	225/60VR15	33-41	6½-J[1]
				240/45VR415	33-41	195 mm
				220/55R390	36-44	165 mm
		535i	225/60VR15		35-44	6½-J[1]
				240/45VR415	35-44	195 mm
				220/55R390	35-44	165 mm
		735i, 735iL	205/65VR15	225/60R15	32-39	6½-J[1]
				240/45VR415	32-39	195 mm
				220/55R390	32-39	165 mm
		750iL	225/60ZR415		32-36	7-J
				240/45ZR415	32-36	195 mm
	1988	325iX, M3	205/55VR15		33-41	7-J
		L6, 635CSi	220/55VR390		33-36	165 mm
				195/70R14	33-36	6-,6½-J
				220/55VR390	33-36	165 mm
				200/60R390	33-36	165 mm
		M6	240/45VR415		36-41	195 mm
				220/55R390	36-41	165 mm
				220/55VR390	36-41	165 mm
		735i, 750iL	225/60VR15	205/65VR15	39-46	6½-,7-J
				240/45VR415	39-46	195 mm
				220/55R390	39-46	165 mm
	1988-87	325i, 325iS	195/65VR14	195/65R14	33-39	5½-,6-J
		M5	225/50VR16		37-41	7½-J
				220/55R390	37-44	165 mm
				220/55VR390	37-44	165 mm
	1988-85	325, 325e, 325es	195/65HR14		32-36	5½-,6-J
		528e	195/70R14	195/70HR14	29-32	6-,6½-J
				200/60HR390	29-32	165 mm
		535is	195/70VR14		36-36	6-,6½-J
				200/60HR390	36-36	165 mm
	1987-85	635CSi	205/70R14		33-36	6-,6½-J
	1986-85	524td	195/70HR14		29-32	6-,6½-J
				200/60HR390	29-32	165 mm
				200/60HR390	33-36	165 mm
				220/55VR390	33-36	165 mm
		735i, L7	205/70HR14		33-36	6½-J
				220/55VR390	33-36	165 mm
	1985	318i	175/70HR14		29-35	5½-J
				195/60HR14	29-35	5½-,6-J
	1984-83	318i	185/70SR13		27-27	5½-J
		320i, 528e	195/70HR14		29-29	6-,6½-J
				200/60HR390	29-29	165 mm
		533i	195/70VR14		33-33	6-,6½-J
				200/60VR15	33-33	165 mm
		633CSi	205/70VR14		32-32	6½-J
				220/55VR390	32-32	165 mm
		733i	205/70HR14		32-32	6½-J
				220/55VR390	32-32	165 mm

1 Alloy wheels, 7-J

BUICK ELECTRA, LE SABRE, RIVIERA, PARK AVENUE, ROADMASTER, ESTATE WAGON

MAKE	YEAR	MODEL	Std.	Optional	F-R	RIM WIDTH
	1992	LeSabre	P205/70R15		30-30	6-JJ
				P215/60R16	30-30	6½-JJ
		Park Avenue	P215/70R15		30-30	6-JJ
				P215/60R16	32-30	6½-JJ
		Regal	P205/70R14	P205/70R15	—	—
		GS, GT		P225/60R16	—	—
		Riviera	P215/65R15		28-26	6-JJ
		Roadmaster	P225/70R15		30-30	7-J
		Wagon	P225/70R15	P235/70R15	30-35	7-JJ
	1991	Roadmaster Estate Wagon	P225/75R15		30-35	7-J
		LeSabre	P205/75R14	P215/65R15	30-30	6-JJ
		Park Avenue	P205/70R15	P215/65R15	30-30	6-JJ
	1991-90	Riviera	P205/70R15	P215/65R15	28-26	6-JJ

14 Copyright 1992 by H.M. Gousha, a division of Simon & Schuster

Tire sizes and tire pressures represent the car manufacturer's recommendations (for normal speeds).
†Sustained high speeds: **Numeric and Alphanumeric** sizes, add 4 psi (do not exceed 32 psi for load range "B", 36 psi for load range "C", 40 psi for load range "D"); **P-Metric** sizes, add 3 psi (do not exceed 35 psi for Standard Load, 41 psi for Extra Load "XL" tire).
European metric sizes have maximum inflation pressure of either 32 or 36 psi, depending on construction. Refer to maximum inflation limit stamped on tire sidewall.
* For minimum load pressure, refer to tire decal. ●Cars equipped with Trailer Tow Option, refer to tire decal.

MAKE YEAR MODEL	ORIGINAL EQUIPMENT SIZE Std.	Optional	PRESSURE†● Max. Load* F-R	RIM WIDTH
BUICK ELECTRA, LE SABRE, RIVIERA, PARK AVENUE, ROADMASTER, ESTATE WAGON Continued				
1990 Electra ex. T Type, Ultra	P205/75R14	P215/65R15	30-30	6-JJ
Electra Ultra	P205/70R15		30-30	6-JJ
1990-89 LeSabre ex. T Type, wagon	P205/75R14		30-30	6-JJ
1990-86 T Type	P215/65R15		30-30	6-JJ
1990-85 Electra & LeSabre wagons	P225/75R15		30-35	7-JJ
1989 Electra ex. T Type, wagon	P205/75R14		30-30	6-JJ
Riviera	P205/70R15	P215/65R15	30-30	6-JJ
1988 All ex. wagon, Riviera, T Type	P205/75R14	P215/65R15	35-35	6-JJ
1988-86 Riviera	P205/75R14	P215/65R15	35-35	6-JJ
1987-86 All ex. T Type, wagon	P205/75R14	P205/70R15	35-35	6-JJ
		P215/65R15	35-35	6-JJ
1985 LeSabre ex. wagon	P205/75R15	P215/75R15	35-35	6-,7-JJ
Electra ex. wagon	P205/75R15	P215/65R15	30-30	6-JJ
1985-83 Riviera	P205/75R15	P225/70R15	30-30	6-JJ
1984 LeSabre	P205/75R15		35-35	6-JJ
		P215/75R15	35-35	7-JJ
Electra ex. wagon	P215/75R15		35-35	6-JJ
		P225/75R15	35-35	7-JJ
Electra wagon	P225/75R15		30-35	6-JJ
1983 LeSabre ex. wagon	P205/75R15	P215/75R15	35-35	6-JJ
Electra ex. wagon	P215/75R15	P225/75R15	35-35	6-JJ
LeSabre, Electra wagons	P225/75R15		30-35	7-JJ
BUICK CENTURY, REGAL				
1992 Century	P185/75R14		32-32	5½-JJ
1992-89 Regal ex. GT	P205/70R14		30-30	5½-JJ
		P205/70R15	30-30	6-JJ
Regal GT	P215/60R16		30-30	6½-JJ
1991-88 Century ex. GT	P185/75R14	P195/75R14	35-35	5½-JJ
1989-88 Century GT	P215/60R14		35-35	6½-JJ
1988 Regal ex. GT	P205/70R14		35-35	5½-JJ
Regal GT	P195/70R15		35-35	6-JJ
1987-86 Century T Type	P215/60R14		35-35	6½-JJ
1987-85 Century ex. T Type	P185/75R14	P195/75R14	35-35	5½-JJ
Regal ex. T Type, Turbo	P195/75R14	P205/70R14	35-35	6-,7-JJ
Regal T Type, Turbo	P215/65R15		35-35	7-JJ
1985 Century T Type	P195/70R14		35-35	5½-JJ
		P215/60R14	35-35	6½-JJ
1984 Century ex. T Type, Diesel	P185/75R14	P195/75R14	35-35	5½-JJ
Century T Type	P195/70R14	P215/60R14	35-35	6½-JJ
Century Diesel	P195/75R14		35-35	5½-JJ
Regal ex. T Type	P195/75R14	P205/70R14	35-35	6-JJ
Regal T Type	P215/65R15		35-35	6-JJ
Regal wagon	P195/75R14	P205/70R14	30-35	6-JJ
1983 Century ex. T Type, Diesel	P185/75R14	P195/75R14	35-35	5½-JJ
Century T Type, Diesel	P195/75R14		35-35	5½-JJ
Regal ex. wagon	P195/75R14	P185/75R14	35-35	6-JJ
		P205/70R14	35-35	6-JJ
Regal wagon	P195/75R14	P205/70R14	30-35	6-JJ
BUICK REATTA				
1991 All	P215/60R16		30-30	6-JJ
1990-88 All	P215/65R15		30-30	6-JJ
BUICK SKYHAWK				
1989 All ex. S/E	P185/80R13		35-35	5½-JB
S/E	P215/60R14		30-30	6-JJ
1988 All	P185/80R13	P205/70R13	35-35	5½-JB
		P215/60R14	35-35	6-JJ
1987 All	P175/80R13	P195/70R13	35-35	5½-JB
		P205/60R14	35-35	6-JJ
Turbo ex. wagon	P205/60R14		35-35	6-JJ
1986-85 All ex. T Type	P175/80R13	P195/70R13	35-35	5½-JB
T Type	P195/70R13		35-35	5½-JB
		P205/60R14	30-30	6-JJ
1984 T Type ex. Turbo	P195/70R13		35-35	5½-JB
Turbo	P205/60R14		30-30	6-JJ
1984-82 All ex. T Type	P175/80R13		35-35	5-JB
		P195/70R13	35-35	5½-JB
1983 T Type	P195/70R13		35-35	5½-JB

MAKE YEAR MODEL	ORIGINAL EQUIPMENT SIZE Std.	Optional	PRESSURE†● Max. Load* F-R	RIM WIDTH
BUICK SKYLARK, SOMERSET				
1992 Skylark	P185/75R14		35-35	6-JJ
1991 All ex. Gran Sport Coupe	P185/75R14		35-35	6-JJ
		P195/70R14	30-30	6-JJ
Gran Sport Coupe	P215/60R14		30-30	5½-JB
1990-89 All	P185/80R13		35-35	5½-JB
		P205/70R13	30-30	5½-JB
		P215/60R14	30-30	6-JJ
1988-86 All ex. T Type	P185/80R13	P205/70R13	35-35	5½-JB
T Type	P215/60R14		35-35	6-JJ
1985 All	P185/80R13	P205/70R13	35-35	5½-JB
1984-83 T Type	P215/60R14		35-35	6½-JJ
All ex. T Type	P185/80R13	P205/70R13	35-35	5½-JB
CADILLAC				
1992 Fleetwood, 60 Special	P205/70R15		30-30	6-JJ
DeVille: Coupe, Sedan	P205/70R15		30-30	6-JJ
Touring Sedan	P215/60R16		32-30	6½-JJ
Seville, Eldorado	P225/60R16		28-26	7-JJ
1992-91 Brougham	P225/75R15		30-30	7-JJ
1992-90 Allanté	P225/55VR16		28-24	7-JJ
1991 Eldorado	P205/70R15		28-26	6-JJ
		P215/65R15	28-26	7-JJ
		P215/60R16	28-26	7-JJ
DeVille, Fleetwood	P205/70R15		30-30	6-JJ
Seville	P205/70R15		28-26	6-JJ
		P215/60R16	28-26	7-JJ
		P215/65R15	28-26	7-JJ
1990 Eldorado	P225/75R15		32-32	6-JJ
DeVille, Fleetwood	P205/70R15	P215/75R15	30-30	5½-JJ
Seville	P205/70R15		28-26	5½-JJ
		P215/65R15	28-26	6-JJ
		P215/60R16	28-26	6-JJ
Brougham	P225/75R15		32-32	6-JJ
1989 Allanté	P225/55VR16		30-26	6-JJ
Eldorado, Seville	P205/75R14		35-35	5½-JJ
		215/65R15	35-35	6-JJ
DeVille, Fleetwood	P205/75R15		30-30	5½-JJ
1989-88 Brougham	P225/75R15		35-35	6-JJ
1988 Eldorado, Seville, DeVille, Fleetwood	P205/75R14		30-30	5½-JJ
		P215/65R15	32-32	6-JJ
		P215/60R14	35-35	6-JJ
Cimarron	P195/70R14		30-30	6-JJ
1988-87 Allanté	P225/60VR15		30-26	7-JJ
1987 Eldorado, Seville	P205/75R14		30-30	6-JJ
		P215/60VR16	32-30	6-JJ
Brougham	P215/75R15		32-32	6-JJ
		P225/75R15	35-35	6-JJ
1987-86 DeVille, Fleetwood	P205/75R14	P215/65R15	30-30	6-JJ
Cimarron	P195/70R13		35-35	5½-JB
		P205/60R14	35-35	6-JJ
1986 Eldorado, Seville	P205/75R14		32-26	5½-,6-JJ
		P215/60R15	32-30	6-JJ
1985 Eldorado, Seville Coupe, Sedan	P205/75R15		30-30	6-JJ
Biarritz Convertible	P205/70R15		28-24	6-JJ
DeVille, Fleetwood (FWD)	P205/75R15	P215/65R15	30-30	6-JJ
Fleetwood Brougham (RWD)	P215/75R15		32-32	6-JJ
1985-83 Cimarron	P195/70R13		35-35	5½-JB
1984 Eldorado, Seville: Coupe, Sedan	P205/75R15		28-32	6-JJ
Biarritz Convertible	P225/75R15		32-32	6-JJ
1984-83 DeVille, Brougham	P215/75R15		32-32	6-JJ
1983 Eldorado, Seville: W/o Tour. Susp. Pkg.	P205/75R15		28-32	6-JJ
W/Tour. Susp. Pkg.	P225/70R15		28-24	6-JJ
CHEVROLET IMPALA, CAPRICE				
1992 Caprice: Sedan	P215/75R15		30-30	7-JJ
Classic LTZ	P235/70VR15		30-30	7-JJ
Wagon	P225/75R15		30-35	7-JJ
1991 All ex. wagon	P205/75R15	P215/75R15	30-30	7-JJ
		P225/70R15	30-30	7-JJ
Wagon	P225/70R15		30-35	7-JJ
1990-83 All ex. wagon	P205/75R15		35-35	6-JJ
		P225/70R15	30-30	7-JJ
Wagon	P225/75R15		30-35	7-JJ

TIRES
PASSENGER CAR

Tire sizes and tire pressures represent the car manufacturer's recommendations (for normal speeds).
†Sustained high speeds: Numeric and Alphanumeric sizes, add 4 psi (do not exceed 32 psi for load range "B", 36 psi for load range "C", 40 psi for load range "D"); P-Metric sizes, add 3 psi (do not exceed 35 psi for Standard Load, 41 psi for Extra Load "XL" tire).
European metric sizes have maximum inflation pressure of either 32 or 36 psi, depending on construction. Refer to maximum inflation limit stamped on tire sidewall.
*For minimum load pressure, refer to tire decal. •Cars equipped with Trailer Tow Option, refer to tire decal.

CHEVROLET BERETTA, CORSICA

MAKE YEAR MODEL	ORIGINAL EQUIPMENT SIZE Std.	Optional	PRESSURE†• Max. Load* F-R	RIM WIDTH
1992 Beretta GT	P205/60R15		30-30	7-JJ
GTZ	P205/55VR16	P205/55R16	30-30	7-JJ
1992-91 Beretta ex. GT, GTZ	P185/75R14		30-30	6-JJ
		P195/70R14	30-30	6-JJ
Corsica LT	P185/75R14		30-30	6-JJ
		P205/60R15	30-30	6-JJ
1991-90 Beretta GTZ	P205/55VR16		30-30	7-JJ
1991-89 Beretta GT	P205/60R15		30-30	6-,7-JJ
1990 Beretta Convertible	P205/60R15		30-30	7-JJ
1990-89 Beretta ex. GT	P195/70R14		35-35	6-JJ
Corsica ex. LTZ	P185/75R14	P195/70R14	30-30	6-JJ
Corsica LTZ	P205/60R15		30-30	6-JJ
1988-87 Beretta	P195/70R14		35-35	6-JJ
		P205/60R15	30-30	6-,7-JJ
Corsica	P185/80R13		35-35	5½-JB
		P195/70R14	35-35	6-JJ
		P205/60R15	35-35	6-JJ

CHEVROLET CAMARO

MAKE YEAR MODEL	Std.	Optional	Pressure F-R	Rim Width
1992 Camaro RS	P215/65R15		30-30	7-JJ
		P235/55R16	30-30	8-JJ
1992-91 Z28 Coupe	P235/55R16		30-30	8-JJ
		P245/50ZR16	30-30	8-JJ
Z28 Convertible	P245/50ZR16		30-30	8-JJ
1991-90 RS Coupe	P215/65R15		30-30	7-JJ
1990 IROC-Z Coupe	P215/65R15		35-35	7-JJ
		P245/50ZR16	30-30	8-JJ
IROC-Z Convertible	P245/50ZR16		30-30	8-JJ
1989 RS Coupe, convertible	P215/65R15		30-30	7-JJ
IROC-Z	P215/65R15		35-35	7-JJ
		P245/50ZR16	30-30	8-JJ
1988 Sport Coupe	P215/65R15		30-30	7-JJ
IROC-Z	P215/65R15		35-35	7-JJ
		P245/50VR16	35-35	8-JJ
1987 Sport Coupe	P215/65R15		35-35	7-JJ
LT w/V6 2.8L	P205/70R14		30-30	7-JJ
LT w/V8 5.0L	P195/70R14		30-30	7-JJ
Z28 Sport Coupe	P215/65R15		35-35	7-JJ
Z28 w/IROC pkg.	P245/50VR16		30-30	8-JJ
1986 Sport Coupe	P215/65R15		35-35	7-JJ
Berlinetta	P205/70R14		35-35	7-JJ
1986-85 Z28	P215/65R15	P235/60VR15	35-35	7-JJ
W/IROC/FE2 susp.	P245/50VR16		30-30	8-JJ
1985-83 Sport Coupe	P195/75R14		35-35	6-JJ
		P205/70R14	35-35	7-JJ
1984-83 Sport Coupe w/Z28	P215/65R15		35-35	7-JJ
Berlinetta	P205/70R14		35-35	7-JJ

CHEVROLET CAVALIER, CITATION

MAKE YEAR MODEL	Std.	Optional	Pressure F-R	Rim Width
1992 Cavalier	P185/75R14		35-35	6-JJ
RS with Z51 Package	P195/70R14		30-30	6-JJ
1992-91 Z24 Coupe	P205/60R15		30-30	6-JJ
1991 All ex. Z24 Coupe	P185/75R14	P195/70R14	35-35	6-JJ
1990 All ex. Z24 Coupe	P185/80R13		35-35	5½-JB
Z24 Coupe	P215/60R14		35-35	6-JJ
1989 Coupe & Sedan ex. RS	P185/80R13		35-35	5½-JB
RS Coupe & Sedan	P195/70R14		30-30	6-JJ
Wagon ex. RS	P185/80R13		35-35	5½-JB
		P195/70R14	30-30	6-JJ
RS Wagon	P195/70R14		30-30	6-JJ
Z24	P215/60R14		30-30	6-JJ
1988 All ex. Z24	P185/80R13	P205/70R13	35-35	5½-JB
		P215/60R14	35-35	6-JJ
Z24	P215/60R14		30-30	6-JJ
1987-86 Cavalier ex. Z24	P175/80R13	P195/70R13	35-35	5½-JB
		P215/60R14	30-30	6-JJ
Cavalier Z24 Sport Coupe	P215/60R14		30-30	6-JJ
1985 Citation	P185/80R13		35-35	5½-JB
		P205/70R13	30-30	5½-JB
with X-11 Package	P215/60R14		35-35	6½-JJ
1985-83 Cavalier	P175/80R13		35-35	5-,5½-JB
		P195/70R13	35-35	5½-JB
1984-83 Citation	P185/80R13	P205/70R13	35-35	5½-JB
with X-11 Package	P215/60R14		35-35	6½-JJ

CHEVROLET CELEBRITY, MALIBU, MONTE CARLO, EL CAMINO

MAKE YEAR MODEL	Std.	Optional	Pressure F-R	Rim Width
1990 Celebrity ex. Eurosport	P185/75R14		35-35	5½-JJ
		P195/75R14	35-35	6½-JJ
Eurosport	P195/75R14		25-35	6½-JJ
		P195/70R14	30-30	6½-JJ
1989-85 Celebrity ex. Diesel & Eurosport	P185/75R14		35-35	5½-JJ
		P195/75R14	35-35	5½-,6½-JJ
Eurosport	P195/75R14	P195/70R14	30-30	5½-,6½-JJ
1988 Monte Carlo ex. SS	P195/75R14		35-35	6-JJ
		P205/70R14	35-35	6½-JJ
Monte Carlo SS	P215/65R15		32-32	7-JJ
1987-84 Monte Carlo ex. SS	P195/75R14		35-35	6-JJ
		P205/70R14	35-35	6-,6½-JJ
Monte Carlo SS	P215/75R14		32-32	7-JJ
1987-82 El Camino, Caballero	P205/75R14		35-35	6-JJ
1985 Diesel	P195/75R14		35-35	5½-,6½-JJ
1984 Celebrity ex. wagon	P185/80R13		35-35	5½-JB
		P195/75R14	35-35	5½-,6½-JJ
		P195/75R14	35-35	5½-JJ
Celebrity wagon	P185/75R14	P195/75R14	35-35	5½-JJ
1983 Celebrity	P185/80R13	P205/70R13	35-35	5½-JB
		P195/75R14	35-35	5½-JJ

CHEVROLET CHEVETTE

MAKE YEAR MODEL	Std.	Optional	Pressure F-R	Rim Width
1987-86 All ex. Diesel	P155/80R13		30-35	5-JB
1986 Diesel	P155/80R13		35-35	5-JB
1985-83 All	P155/80R13	P175/70R13	30-30	5-JB,5-JJ

CHEVROLET CORVETTE

MAKE YEAR MODEL	Std.	Optional	Pressure F-R	Rim Width
1992 Coupe, Conv.	P275/40ZR17		35-35[4]	9½-JJ
ZR-1 Coupe: Front	P275/40ZR17		35	9½-JJ
Rear	P315/35ZR17		35	11-JJ
1991-89 All	P275/40ZR17		35-35[4]	9½-JJ
Optional (rear ZR1)		P315/35ZR17	35	11-JJ
1988 All	P255/50ZR16		35-35	8½-JJ
		P275/40ZR17	35-35	9½-JJ
1987 Hatchback	P255/50VR16		35-35	8½-JJ[3]
Convertible	P255/50VR16		35-35	9½-JJ
1986 All	P255/50VR16		35-35	[2]
1985 All	P255/50VR16		32-32	[2]
1984 All	P255/50VR16		35-35	[2]
1983 All	P215/65R15		35-35	[1]
		P255/50R16	35-35	[2]

1 Front rim, 7-JJ; rear rim, 7½-JJ   2 Front rim, 8½-JJ; rear rim, 9½-JJ
3 With Handling Package, 9½-JJ   4 Convertible, 30-30

CHEVROLET LUMINA

MAKE YEAR MODEL	Std.	Optional	Pressure F-R	Rim Width
1992 Euro	P205/70R15		30-30	6-JJ
		P215/65R16	30-30	6½-JJ
1992-91 Z34	P225/60R16		30-30	6½-JJ
1992-90 All ex. Euro & Z34	P195/75R14		30-30	5½-JJ
1991 Euro	P205/70R15		30-30	6-JJ
		P225/60R16	30-30	6½-JJ
1990 Euro	P205/65R15		35-35	6-JJ
		P215/60R16	35-35	6-JJ

CHEVROLET NOVA

MAKE YEAR MODEL	Std.	Optional	Pressure F-R	Rim Width
1988 All	155/80R13		29-29	5-JB
		P175/70R13	26-26	5-JB
		P175/70HR13	32-32	5-JB
1987-85 All	P155/80R13		29-29	4½-JB
		P175/70R13	26-26	5-J

CHEVROLET SPECTRUM

MAKE YEAR MODEL	Std.	Optional	Pressure F-R	Rim Width
1988 All ex. Turbo	P155/80R13		35-35	4½-J
		P175/70R13	35-35	5-J
Turbo	P185/60R14		35-35	5½-JJ
1987-85 All	P155/80R13		30-30	4½-J

CHEVROLET SPRINT

MAKE YEAR MODEL	Std.	Optional	Pressure F-R	Rim Width
1988 All ex. Turbo	P145/80R12		32-32	4-B
Turbo	P165/70R12		26-26	4½-B
1987 ER Models	P145/80R12		35-35	4-B
1987-85 All ex. ER Models	P145/80R12		32-32	4-B

Tire sizes and tire pressures represent the car manufacturer's recommendations (for normal speeds).
†Sustained high speeds: **Numeric and Alphanumeric** sizes, add 4 psi (do not exceed 32 psi for load range "B", 36 psi for load range "C", 40 psi for load range "D"); **P-Metric** sizes, add 3 psi (do not exceed 35 psi for Standard Load, 41 psi for Extra Load "XL" tire).
European metric sizes have maximum inflation pressure of either 32 or 36 psi, depending on construction. Refer to maximum inflation limit stamped on tire sidewall.
*For minimum load pressure, refer to tire decal. •Cars equipped with Trailer Tow Option, refer to tire decal.

MAKE	YEAR	MODEL	ORIGINAL EQUIPMENT SIZE Std.	Optional	PRESSURE†• Max. Load* F-R	RIM WIDTH	MAKE	YEAR	MODEL	ORIGINAL EQUIPMENT SIZE Std.	Optional	PRESSURE†• Max. Load* F-R	RIM WIDTH
CHRYSLER							**DODGE**						
	1992	LeBaron coupe, conv.	P195/70R14		29-29	5½-JJ		1992	Colt, GL	P155/80R13	P175/70R13	29-29	4½-,5-J
				P205/60R15	29-29	6-JJ			Monaco LE	P195/70R14		30-30	5½-JJ
		LX		P205/60R15	29-29	6-JJ					P205/60R15	30-30	6-JJ
		LeBaron sedan	P195/70R14		32-32	5½-JJ			Monaco ES	P205/70R14		30-30	5½-JJ
				P205/60R15	32-32	6-JJ					P205/60R15	30-30	6-JJ
		LX	P205/60R15		32-32	6-JJ			Shadow: America	P185/70R14		32-32	5½,6-JJ
	1992-91	New Yorker	P195/75R14		32-32	5½-JJ			ES	P195/60R15		35-35	6-J
		Town & Country wagon	P205/70R15		35-35	6-JJ					P205/60R14	32-32	6-JJ
	1992-90	Imperial	P195/75R14		32-32	5½-JJ			Others	P185/70R14		32-32	5½-,6-JJ
	1991	LeBaron coupe & conv.:									P205/60R14	32-32	6-JJ
		Highline	P195/70R14		29-29	5½-JJ		1992-91	Daytona ex. IROC, ES	P185/70R14	P205/60R14	32-32	5½-JJ
		Premium LX	P205/60R15		29-29	6-JJ					P205/60R14	32-32	5-,6-JJ
		GTC	P205/60R15		29-29	6-JJ					P205/55VR16	32-32	6-JJ
	1991-89	TC	P205/60VR15		35-35	6-JJ			Daytona ES	P205/60R15		32-32	6-JJ
	1990	LeBaron coupe & conv.:							Daytona IROC	P205/55R16		32-32	6-JJ
		Highline	P195/70R14		29-29	5½-JJ			Stealth	P205/65R15		29-26	6½-JJ
		Premium, GT	P205/60R15		29-29	6-JJ			Stealth ES, R/T FWD	P225/55VR16		32-29	8-JJ
		GTC	P205/55R16		29-29	6-JJ			Stealth R/T Turbo 4WD	P245/45ZR17		32-29	8½-JJ
		New Yorker & 5th Ave.	P195/75R14		29-32	5½-JJ		1992-90	Spirit	P185/70R14		32-32	5½-JJ
		Town & Country wagon	P205/75R15	P195/75R15	35-35	6-JJ					P205/60R15	32-32	6-JJ
	1989	Le Baron coupe,							Spirit ES	P205/60R15		35-35	6-JJ
		conv. ex. GTC	P195/70R14		29-29	5½-JJ			Spirit LE	P195/70R14		32-32	5½-JJ
		GTC coupe, conv.	P205/55R16		29-29	6-J					P205/60R15	32-32	6-JJ
		LeBaron sedan ex. GTS	P195/70R14		29-29	5½-JJ			Spirit R/T	P205/60R15		32-32	6-JJ
		LeBaron GTS	P205/60R15		35-35	6-JJ		1992-89	Dynasty	P195/75R14		32-32	5½-JJ
		New Yorker	P195/75R14		29-29	5½-JJ		1991	Daytona Shelby	P205/55VR16		32-32	6-JJ
		Fifth Avenue	P205/75R15		35-35	7-JJ			Monaco LE	P195/70R14		32-32	5½-JJ
	1989-88	Conquest: Front	205/55VR16		27	7-JJ			Monaco ES	P205/70R14		32-32	5½-JJ
				225/50VR16	27	8-JJ			Shadow ex. ES	P185/70R14		32-32	5½-JJ
		Rear	225/50VR16		27	8-JJ			Shadow ES	P195/60HR15		35-35	6-JJ
				245/45VR16	27	9-JJ		1990	Shadow	P195/70R14		32-32	5½-JJ
	1988	LeBaron coupe, conv.	P195/70R14		29-29	5½-JJ					P195/60R15	35-35	6-JJ
				P205/60R15	29-29	6-JJ		1990-89	Colt ex. Turbo, wagon	P155/80R13		29-29	4½-,5-J
		New Yorker ex. Turbo	P195/75R14		29-29	5½-JJ					145SR13	32-32	4½-J
		New Yorker Turbo	P185/75R14		26-32	5½-JJ			Colt Turbo	195/60R14		29-29	5½-JJ
	1988-87	LeBaron ex. coupe, GTS	P185/70R14		26-29	5½-JJ			Colt wagon: FWD	P175/70R14		26-26	5-J
		LeBaron GTS	P185/70R14	P195/70R14	35-35	5½-JJ			4WD	P185/70R14		26-29	5-,5½-JJ
				P205/60R15	35-35	6-JJ			Colt Vista: FWD	P165/80R13	P185/70R13	29-29	5-J
	1988-85	Fifth Ave., Newport	P205/75R15		35-35	7-JJ			4WD	P185/70R14		29-35	5½-JJ
	1987	Conquest	P215/64R15		28-28	6½-JJ			Daytona	P185/70R14		32-32	5½-JJ
		W/Intercooler: Front	205/55VR16		28	7-J					P205/60R15	32-32	6-JJ
		Rear	225/50VR16		28	8-J					P225/50R15	32-32	6½-JJ
		LeBaron coupe	P185/75R14	P195/70R14	29-29	5½-JJ			Daytona ES	P205/60R15		32-32	6-JJ
				P205/60HR14	35-35	6-JJ			Daytona Shelby	P205/55R16		32-32	6-JJ
	1987-83	New Yorker	P185/75R14		26-32	5½-JJ		1989	Aries	175/80R13		35-35	5-JB
	1986-85	Laser	P185/70R14	P195/70R14	35-35	5½-JJ					P185/70R14	35-35	5½-JJ
		Laser XE	P205/60HR15	P225/50VR15	35-35	5-JJ			Lancer, Lancer ES	P195/70R14		29-29	5½-JJ
		LeBaron ex. Hatchback	P185/70R14		26-29	5½-JJ					P205/60R15	29-29	6-JJ
		LeBaron Hatchback	P185/70R14	P195/70R14	29-32	5½-JJ			Lancer Shelby	P205/60R15		29-29	6-JJ
				P205/60HR15	29-32	6-JJ			Omni	P165/80R13		35-35	5-JB
	1986-84	Executive Sedan	P185/75R14		29-32	5½-JJ			Shadow: H Series	P185/70R14		35-35	5½-JJ
	1984	Laser, Laser XE	P185/70R14		35-35	5½-JJ					P195/60R15	35-35	6-JJ
	1984-83	E Class	P185/70R14		26-32	5½-JJ			L Series	P175/80R13		35-35	5-JB
		LeBaron	P185/70R14		29-29	5½-JJ			Spirit, Spirit LE	P195/70R14		32-32	5½-JJ
		New Yorker 5th Ave.,							Spirit ES	P205/60R15		32-32	6-JJ
		Newport	P205/75R15		29-29	7-JJ		1989-85	Diplomat	P205/75R15		35-35	7-JJ
	1983	Cordoba	P195/75R15		29-29	5½-JJ		1988	Dynasty	P195/75R14		29-29	5½-JJ
				P205/75R15	29-29	7-JJ			Daytona	P185/70R14	P195/70R14	32-32	5½-JJ
				P215/70R15	29-29	7-JJ					P205/60HR14	32-32	6-JJ
		Imperial	P205/75R15		29-29	7-JJ			Daytona Pacifica	P205/60R15		32-32	6-JJ
									Daytona Shelby Z	P225/50VR15		32-32	6½-JJ
									Aries ex. wagon	P175/80R13		35-35	5-JB
											P185/70R14	35-35	5½-JJ
									Aries wagon	P185/70R14		35-35	5½-JJ
									Shelby CSX	P205/60VR15		35-35	6-JJ
DAIHATSU								1988-87	Shadow: H Series	P185/70R14		35-35	5½-JJ
	1991-90	Charade SE: Sedan	P155/80R13		29-26	4½-J					P205/50VR15	35-35	6-JJ
		Hatchback	P145/80R13		29-26	4½-J			L Series	P165/80R13		35-35	5-JB
		Charade SX: Sedan	P165/70R13		29-26	5-J			Omni, Charger ex. Shelby	P165/80R13		35-35	5-JB
		Hatchback	P155/80R13		29-26	4½-J		1988-85	Colt	P145/80R13		31-31	4½-J
				P165/70R13	29-26	5-J					P155/80R13	26-26	5-J
		Rocky 4×4	P205/75R15	P225/75R15	35-35	6-J					P175/70R13	26-26	5-J
	1989	Charade: CES	P145/80R13		29-26	4½-J					185/60R14	26-26	5½-J
		CLS, CLX	P155/80R13		29-26	4½-J			Lancer ex. ES	P185/70R14	P195/70R14	29-32	5½-JJ
		w/alum. engine	P165/80R13		29-26	5-J					P205/60R15	29-32	6-JJ
	1988	Charade: CLS, CLX	P145/80R13	P155/80R13	29-26	4½-J			Lancer ES	P195/70R14		29-32	5½-JJ
		CSX	P165/70R13		29-26	5-J					P205/60R15	29-32	6-JJ
				P145/80R13	29-26	4½-J		1988-84	Colt Vista: 2WD	P165/80R13	P185/70R13	26-26	5-J
									4WD	P185/70R14		26-26	5½-JJ

TIRES
PASSENGER CAR

Tire sizes and tire pressures represent the car manufacturer's recommendations (for normal speeds).
†Sustained high speeds: **Numeric and Alphanumeric** sizes, add 4 psi (do not exceed 32 psi for load range ''B'', 36 psi for load range ''C'', 40 psi for load range ''D''). **P-Metric** sizes, add 3 psi (do not exceed 35 psi for Standard Load, 41 psi for Extra Load ''XL'' tire).
European metric sizes have maximum inflation pressure of either 32 or 36 psi, depending on construction. Refer to maximum inflation limit stamped on tire sidewall.
*For minimum load pressure, refer to tire decal.   ●Cars equipped with Trailer Tow Option, refer to tire decal.

MAKE	YEAR	MODEL	ORIGINAL EQUIPMENT SIZE Std.	Optional	PRESSURE†● Max. Load* F-R	RIM WIDTH
DODGE Continued						
1988-83	600 ex. convertible		P185/70R14		26-32	5¹/₂-JJ
1987-85	Daytona ex. Turbo		P185/70R14	P195/70R14	35-35	5¹/₂-JJ
	Daytona Turbo		P205/60HR15		35-35	6-JJ
				P225/50VR15	35-35	6¹/₂-JJ
	Shelby Charger		P205/50VR15		35-35	6-JJ
1987-84	Aries		P175/80R13		35-35	5-JB
				P185/70R14	35-35	5¹/₂-JJ
1986	Conquest		P215/60R15		28-28	6¹/₂-JJ
	W/Intercooler: Front		205/55VR16		28	7-J
	Rear		225/50VR16		28	8-J
1986-85	Omni ex. GLH		P165/80R13	P175/75R13	35-35	5-JB
	Omni GLH		P195/50R15		35-35	6-JJ
	Charger ex. 2.2, Shelby		P165/80R13		35-35	5-JB
				P195/60R14	35-35	5¹/₂-JJ
	Charger 2.2		P195/60R14		35-35	5¹/₂-JJ
	600 Convertible		P195/60VR15		26-29	6-JJ
1985	Conquest		P195/70R14		28-28	6-J
				P215/60VR15	28-28	6¹/₂-JJ
1984	Conquest		P195/70R14		27-27	6-J
				P215/60R15	27-27	6¹/₂-JJ
	Daytona ex. Turbo		P185/70R14		35-35	5¹/₂-JJ
	Daytona Turbo		P195/60R15		35-35	6-JJ
	Omni		P165/80R13		35-35	5-JB
	Charger ex. Shelby		P195/60R14		35-35	5¹/₂-JJ
	Shelby Charger		P195/50R15		35-35	6-JJ
	Diplomat		P205/75R15		29-29	7-JJ
1984-83	Colt ex. Vista		155SR13		31-31	4-,4¹/₂-J
				P175/70R13	24-24	4¹/₂-J
1984-82	400		P185/70R14		29-29	5¹/₂-JJ
1983	Aries		P175/75R13	P195/70R13	35-35	5-JB
				P185/70R14	35-35	5¹/₂-JJ
	Challenger		195/70SR14		24-24	5¹/₂-JJ
	Diplomat		P195/75R15	P205/75R15	29-29	5¹/₂-,7-JJ
	Mirada		P195/75R15		29-29	5¹/₂-JJ,7-JJ
				P205/75R15	29-29	7-JJ
				P215/75R15	29-29	7-JJ
	Omni ex. Charger 2.2		P175/75R13		35-35	5-JB
				P195/60R14	35-35	5¹/₂-JJ
	Charger 2.2		P195/60R14		35-35	5¹/₂-JJ
EAGLE						
1992	Summit: 3-dr.		P155/80R13		29-29	4¹/₂-JB
	4-dr.		P155/80R13		29-29	5-JB
	Summit ES: 3-dr.		P175/70R13		29-29	4¹/₂-JB
	4-dr.		P175/70R13		29-29	5-JB
	Talon: FWD		P205/55R16		29-26	6-JJ
				P205/55VR16	29-26	6-JJ
	Turbo		P205/55VR16		29-26	6-JJ
	4WD		P205/55VR16		32-29	6-JJ
	Summit Wagon FWD: MT		P185/75R14		30-30	5¹/₂-JJ
	AT & 4WD		P205/70R14		30-30	5¹/₂-JJ
1992-90	Premier ES		P205/60R15		30-30	6-JJ
	Premier LX		P195/70R14		30-30	5¹/₂-JJ
				P205/60R15	30-30	6-JJ
1991	Summit		P155/80R13		30-30	5-JB
	Summit ES		P175/70R13		30-30	5-JB
	Talon ex. Turbo		P205/55R16		30-30	6-JJ
	Turbo		P205/55VR16		30-30	6-JJ
1990	Summit: DL		P155/80R13		30-30	5-JB
	LX		P175/70R13		29-29	5¹/₂-JB
	ES		P195/60R14		29-29	5¹/₂-JJ
1989	Premier		P195/70R14	P205/70R14	30-30	5¹/₂-,6-JJ
				P215/60R-15	30-30	6-JJ
	Summit: DL		P155/80R13		30-30	4¹/₂-,5-JB
	LX		P175/70R13		29-29	5-JB
				P195/60R14	29-29	5¹/₂-JJ
1989-88	Eagle 4WD wagon		P195/75R14		29-29	6-JJ
	Medallion		P185/65R14	P195/60R14	33-33	5¹/₂-JJ
1988	Premier ex. ES		P185/75R14	P195/70R14	30-30	5¹/₂-JJ
	Premier ES		P205/70HR14		30-30	6-JJ
FORD CROWN VICTORIA, LTD						
1992	Crown Victoria		P215/70R15	P225/70R15	31-35	6¹/₂-JJ
1991-88	Crown Victoria sedan		P215/70R15		31-35	6-JJ [2]
	Wagons		P215/70R15		27-35	6¹/₂-JJ
1987-86	Crown Victoria sedan		P205/75R15	P215/70R15	31-35	6-,6¹/₂-JJ
	Country Squire		P205/75R15	P215/70R15	27-35	6-,6¹/₂-JJ
1986-85	LTD ex. wagon		P195/75R14	P205/70R14	30-30	5-,5¹/₂-JJ
				P205/70HR14	30-30	5¹/₂-JJ

MAKE	YEAR	MODEL	ORIGINAL EQUIPMENT SIZE Std.	Optional	PRESSURE†● Max. Load* F-R	RIM WIDTH
FORD CROWN VICTORIA, LTD Continued						
1986-85	LTD wagon		P195/75R14	P205/70R14	28-35	5-,5¹/₂-JJ
1985	Crown Victoria		P215/75R14		31-35¹	6¹/₂-JJ
				P205/75R15	31-35	6-,6¹/₂-JJ
				P215/70R15	31-35	6-,6¹/₂-JJ
1984-83	LTD ex. Crown Victoria		P185/75R14	P195/75R14	30-30	5-,5¹/₂-JJ
				P205/70R14	35-35	5¹/₂-JJ
	Crown Victoria		P215/75R14	P225/75R14	31-35	6¹/₂-JJ
				P205/75R15	31-35	6-,6¹/₂-JJ
	Wagon ex. Country Squire		P185/75R14	P195/75R14	28-35	5-,5¹/₂-JJ
	Country Squire		P215/75R14	P225/75R14	27-35	6¹/₂-JJ
				P205/75R15	27-35	6-,6¹/₂-JJ

1 Wagon, 27-35   **2** Aluminum wheels, 6¹/₂-JJ

FORD ESCORT, EXP						
1992	LX sedan		P175/65R14		32-32	5-JJ
	LX-E		P185/60R14		32-32	5¹/₂-JJ
	GT		P185/60R15		32-32	5¹/₂-JJ
	All others		P175/70R13		32-32	5-JJ
1991	GT		P185/60HR15		32-32	6-JJ
1991-89	All ex. GT		P175/70R13		32-32	5-,5¹/₂-JJ
1990-89	GT		P195/60R15		30-30	6-JJ
1988	Escort ex. Pony, GT		P165/80R13		30-30	4¹/₂-,5-JB
	Pony		P175/80R13		35-35	4¹/₂-JJ
	EXP		P185/70R14		30-30	5¹/₂-JJ
1988-86	GT		P195/60HR15		30-30	6-JJ
1987	Escort ex. GT		P165/80R13		30-30	4¹/₂-,5-JB
				P175/80R13	35-35	5-JB
	EXP ex. GT		P185/70R14		30-30	5-JJ
1986	All ex. GT		P165/80R13		30-30	4¹/₂-,5-JB
				P175/80R13	35-35	5-JB
1985-84	All ex. EXP		P165/80R13	P175/80R13	35-35	4¹/₂-,5¹/₂-JB
				P165/80R13	30-30	5-,5¹/₂-JB
				165/70R365‡	30-30	135 mm
				185/65R365‡	28-28	135 mm
	EXP		P165/80R13		30-30	5-,5¹/₂-JB
				165/70R365‡	30-30	135 mm
				185/65R365‡	28-28	135 mm
1983	All ex. EXP		P165/80R13		35-35¹	4¹/₂-,5-JB
				165/70R365‡	30-30	135 mm
	EXP		P165/80R13		30-30	5-JB
				P175/80R13	30-30	5¹/₂-JB
				165/70R365‡	30-30	135 mm

1 Wagon, 30-30

FORD FAIRMONT						
1983	Fairmont ex. wagon		P175/75R14	P185/75R14	35-35	5-,5¹/₂-JJ
				190/65R390‡	28-28	150 mm
FORD FESTIVA						
1992	GL		165/70SR12		32-32	4¹/₂-J
1992-90	L		145/SR12		32-32	4-B
1991-90	L Plus, LX		165/70SR12		29-29	4¹/₂-B¹
1989-87	L		145/SR12		32-29	4-B
				165/70SR12	32-29	4¹/₂-J
	LX		165/70SR12		32-29	4¹/₂-J

1 Aluminum wheels, 4¹/₂-J

FORD MUSTANG						
1992-91	4-cyl.		P195/75R14		35-35	5¹/₂-JJ
				P205/65R15	35-35	7-JJ
	V8		P225/55ZR16		30-30	7-JJ
1990-88	4-cyl.		P195/75R14		35-35	5-JJ
				P195/75R14	35-35	5¹/₂-JJ
	V8		P225/60VR15		30-30	7-JJ
1987	All ex. GT		P195/75R14		35-35	5-JJ
	GT		P225/60VR15		30-30	7-JJ
1986-85	All ex. SVO		P195/75R14		30-30	5-JJ
				P205/70R14	30-30	5¹/₂-JJ
				P205/70VR14	35-35	5¹/₂-JJ
				P225/60VR15	30-30	7-JJ
1986-84	SVO		P225/50VR16		28-28	7-JJ
1984-83	All ex. SVO		P185/75R14	P195/75R14	35-35	5-,5¹/₂-JJ
				P205/70HR14	35-35	5¹/₂-JJ
				220/55R390‡	30-30	165 mm

Tire sizes and tire pressures represent the car manufacturer's recommendations (for normal speeds).
†Sustained high speeds: **Numeric and Alphanumeric** sizes, add 4 psi (do not exceed 32 psi for load range ''B'', 36 psi for load range ''C'', 40 psi for load range ''D''); **P-Metric** sizes, add 3 psi (do not exceed 35 psi for Standard Load, 41 psi for Extra Load ''XL'' tire).
European metric sizes have maximum inflation pressure of either 32 or 36 psi, depending on construction. Refer to maximum inflation limit stamped on tire sidewall.
*For minimum load pressure, refer to tire decal. ●Cars equipped with Trailer Tow Option, refer to tire decal.

MAKE	YEAR	MODEL	ORIGINAL EQUIPMENT SIZE Std.	Optional	PRESSURE†● Max. Load* F-R	RIM WIDTH
FORD PROBE						
	1992	GL	P195/70R14		32-26	6-JJ
	1992-91	GT	P205/60VR15		32-26	6-JJ
	1992-90	LX	P195/70R14		32-26	5¹/₂-JJ
				P205/60HR15	32-26	6-JJ
	1991-90	GL	P185/70R14		32-26	5¹/₂-JJ
				P195/70R14	32-26	6-JJ
	1990-89	GT	P195/60VR15		32-26	6-JJ
	1989	GL, LX	P185/70R14		32-26	5¹/₂-JJ
				P185/70HR14	32-26	6-JJ
FORD TAURUS						
	1992	L, GL	P195/70R14	P205/70R14	35-35	5¹/₂-JJ
		LX	P205/65R15		35-35	6-JJ
		SHO	P215/60R16		35-35	6-JJ
	1991	SHO	P215/60R16		35-35	7-JJ
	1991-89	All ex. SHO	P205/70R14		35-35	5¹/₂-JJ
				P205/65R15	35-35	5¹/₂-,6-JJ
	1990-89	SHO	P215/65VR15		35-35	6-JJ
	1988	All	P205/70R14		35-35	5¹/₂-JJ
				P205/65R15	35-35	6-JJ
	1987-86	All	P195/70R14	P205/70R14	35-35	5¹/₂-JJ
				P205/65R15	35-35	6-JJ
FORD TEMPO						
	1992	LX, GL	P185/70R14		30-30	5¹/₂-JJ
		GLS	P185/60R15		30-30	6-JJ
	1991-90	All	P185/70R14		30-30	5¹/₂-JJ
	1989-88	GL, LX & All Wheel Drive	P185/70R14		30-30	5¹/₂-JJ
		GLS	P185/70R14		30-30	6-JJ
	1987-86	All	P185/70R14		30-30	5¹/₂-JJ
	1985	All	P175/80R13		30-30	5-,5¹/₂-JB
				P185/70R14	30-30	6-JJ
	1984	All	P175/80R13		30-30	5-JB
				185/65R365‡	30-30	135 mm
	1983	All	P175/80R13		35-35	5-JB
FORD THUNDERBIRD						
	1992-91	Super Coupe	P225/60ZR16		30-30	7-JJ
	1992-89	All ex. Super Coupe	P205/70R15		30-30	6-JJ
				P215/70R15	30-30	6¹/₂-JJ
	1990-89	Super Coupe	P225/60VR16		30-30	7-JJ
	1988-87	Turbo Coupe	P225/60VR16		30-30	7-JJ
	1988-86	All ex. Turbo Coupe	P215/70R14		30-30	5¹/₂-JJ
	1986	Turbo Coupe	P225/60VR15		30-30	7-JJ
	1985	All ex. Turbo Coupe	P205/70R14	P215/70R14	30-30	5¹/₂-JJ
					30-30	5¹/₂-JJ
		Turbo Coupe	P225/60VR15		30-30	7-JJ
	1984-83	All	P195/75R14	P205/70R14	30-30	5¹/₂-JJ
				P205/70HR14	35-35	5¹/₂-JJ
				220/55R390‡	30-30	165 mm

‡ These metric diameter tires and rims are NOT interchangeable with any 13", 14" or 15" diameter tires or rims. Do NOT attempt to mount 365 mm tires (approx. 14³/₈" dia.) or 390 mm tires (approx. 15³/₈" dia.) on any 14" or 15" rims. Do NOT attempt to mount nominal 14" or 15" diameter tires on 365 mm or 390 mm diameter rims.

MAKE	YEAR	MODEL	ORIGINAL EQUIPMENT SIZE Std.	Optional	PRESSURE†● Max. Load* F-R	RIM WIDTH
GEO METRO						
	1992-91	Convertible	P165/65R13		30-30	4¹/₂-JB
	1992-89	All ex. convertible	P145/80R12		32-32	4-B
GEO PRIZM						
	1992	All ex. LSi, GSi	P155/80R13		35-35	5-J
		LSi	P175/70R13		29-25	5-JJ
	1992-91	GSi	P185/60R14		30-30	5-JJ
	1991	Notchback ex. GSi	P155/80R13		35-35	4¹/₂-JB
				P175/70R13	29-25	5-J
		Hatchback ex. GSi	P175/70R13		29-25	5-J
	1990	All ex. GSi	P175/70R13		29-25	5-J
		GSi	P185/60R14		30-30	5¹/₂-JJ
	1989	All	P175/70R13		29-29	5-J
GEO STORM, SPECTRUM						
	1992-91	GSi	P205/50VR15		35-35	6-JJ
	1992-90	All ex GSi	P185/60R14		30-30	5¹/₂-JJ
	1990	GSi	P185/60VR14		35-35	5¹/₂-JJ
	1989	All	P155/80R13		35-35	4¹/₂-JB

MAKE	YEAR	MODEL	ORIGINAL EQUIPMENT SIZE Std.	Optional	PRESSURE†● Max. Load* F-R	RIM WIDTH
HONDA						
	1992	Prelude S	185/70R14		30-30	5¹/₂-JJ
		Si, 4WS, SR	205/55R15		32-32	6¹/₂-JJ
		Civic: 3 dr.	P165/70SR13		35-32	4¹/₂-J
				P175/70SR13	32-32	5-J
				P185/60HR14	28-32	5-J
		4 dr.	P175/70SR13		32-32	5-J
				P175/70HR14	32-32	5-J
	1992-90	Accord: DX, LX	P185/70R14		32-32	5-J
		EX, SE	P195/60R15		26-26	5¹/₂-JJ
	1991	Prelude	195/60R14		28-26	5¹/₂-JJ
	1991-90	Civic EX sedan	175/65R14		32-32	5-J
	1991-89	Civic: Std. hatchback	P165/70R13		35-32	4¹/₂-J
		CX, DX sedan, hatchback	P175/70R13		32-32	5-J
		Si hatchback	185/60R14		28-26	5-J
		LX sedan	175/70R13		32-32	5-J
		Wagon, 2WD & wagovan	P175/70R13		32-32	5-J
		Wagon, 4WD	P175/70R14		32-32	5-J
	1991-88	CRX: HF	P165/70R13		35-32	4¹/₂-J
		DX, std. coupe 1.5	P175/70R13		28-28	5-J
		Si	185/60R14		24-24	5-J
	1990-88	Prelude S	185/70R13		28-26	4¹/₂-J
		Prelude Si	195/60R14		28-26	6-J
	1989-88	Accord ex. LXi	P185/70R13		26-26	4¹/₂-J
		Accord LXi	195/60R14		26-26	6-J
	1988-86	Civic: Hatchback	P165/70R13	P175/70R13	35-32	4¹/₂-J
					32-32	4¹/₂-J
		Sedan, wagon: 2WD	P175/70R13		32-32	4¹/₂-J
		4WD	165SR13		32-32	4¹/₂-J
	1987-86	CRX: HF	P165/70R13		35-32	4¹/₂-J
		W/FI	185/60R14		24-24	5-J
		Others	175/70R13		28-28	4¹/₂-J
	1987-84	Accord	P185/70R13		26-26	5-J
	1987-83	Prelude	185/70SR13		26-26	5-J
	1985-84	Civic, CRX: 1300, HF	165/70R13		24-24	4¹/₂-J
		1500 ex. S	P175/70R13		26-26	4¹/₂-J
		1500S	175/70SR13		26-26	4¹/₂-J
	1983	Civic: 1300, 4-speed	155SR12		24-24	4¹/₂-J
		1300, 5-speed	165/70R13		26-26	4¹/₂-J
		1500 ex. wagon	155SR13	165/70SR13	26-26	4¹/₂-J
		1500 wagon	155SR13		32-32	4¹/₂-J
		Accord	185/70SR13		26-26	4¹/₂-J
HYUNDAI						
	1992	Elantra	P175/65R14		32-32	5¹/₂-,6-J
				P185/60R14	32-32	5¹/₂-,6-J
		Scoupe ex. LS	P175/70R13		28-28	5-J
		Scoupe LS	P185/60R14		28-28	4¹/₂-J
	1992-91	Excel, GL	P155/80R13		28-28	4¹/₂-J
				P175/70R13	28-28	5-J
		Excel GS, GLS	P175/70R13		28-28	5-J
		Sonata	P195/70SR14		30-30	5-J
				P205/60HR15	30-30	6-JJ
	1991	Scoupe ex. LS	P175/70R13	P185/60RH14	25-25	5-J
		Scoupe LS	P185/60HR14		25-25	5-J
	1990-89	Excel	P155/80R13		30-30	4¹/₂-J
				P175/70R13	30-30	5-J
		Sonata	P185/70R13		30-30	5-J
				P195/70R14	30-30	5¹/₂-JJ
	1988	Stellar 2.0	P185/70R13		28-28	5-J
	1988-86	Excel	155/SR13		28-28	4¹/₂-J
				175/70SR13	28-28	5-J
	1986-85	Stellar	165/SR13		28-28	4¹/₂-J
	1986-84	Pony	P155/80R13		28-28	4¹/₂-J
INFINITI						
	1992-91	G20	195/60R14		35-35	6-JJ
	1991-90	M30	P215/60R15		35-35	6¹/₂-JJ
		Q45	P215/65R15		35-35	6¹/₂-JJ
ISUZU						
	1992-91	Impulse RS	205/50VR15		29-29	6-JJ
	1992-90	Stylus S	P175/70R13		30-30	5-J
		Stylus XS	P185/60R14		29-26	5-J
		Impulse XS	P185/60HR14		29-29	5¹/₂-JJ
	1989	I-Mark LS, RS	P185/60R14		29-26	5-J
		I-Mark XS	P175/70R13		30-30	5-J
		I-Mark S	P155/80R13		30-30	4¹/₂-J
		Impulse	205/60R14		29-29	6-JJ

TIRES
PASSENGER CAR

Tire sizes and tire pressures represent the car manufacturer's recommendations (for normal speeds).
†Sustained high speeds: **Numeric** and **Alphanumeric** sizes, add 4 psi (do not exceed 32 psi for load range ''B'', 36 psi for load range ''C'', 40 psi for load range ''D''). **P-Metric** sizes, add 3 psi (do not exceed 35 psi for Standard Load, 41 psi for Extra Load ''XL'' tire).
European metric sizes have maximum inflation pressure of either 32 or 36 psi, depending on construction. Refer to maximum inflation limit stamped on tire sidewall.
*For minimum load pressure, refer to tire decal. •Cars equipped with Trailer Tow Option, refer to tire decal.

MAKE YEAR MODEL	ORIGINAL EQUIPMENT SIZE Std.	Optional	PRESSURE†• Max. Load* F-R	RIM WIDTH
ISUZU Continued				
1988 I-Mark	P175/70R13		30-30	5-J
I-Mark S	P155/80R13		30-30	4½-J
I-Mark Turbo	P185/60R14		30-30	5-J
Impulse ex. Turbo	P195/86R14	205/60R14	29-29	6-JJ
Impulse Turbo	205/60R14		29-29	6-JJ
1987-85 I-Mark FWD	P155/80R13		30-30	4½-J
		P175/70R13	30-30	5-J
1985-83 I-Mark FWD	155SR13		24-24	5-J
		175/70SR13	24-24	5½-J
JAGUAR				
1992 XJS	235/60ZR15		28-28	6½-J
	235/60VR15		28-28	6½-J
		215/65R15	28-28	6½-J
		225/55ZR16	26-28	—
1992-91 XJ6	205/70VR15		27-30	7-J
		215/65	27-30	7-J
1990-88 XJ6, Vanden Plas	205/70VR15		27-30	6-JK
1989 XJS	235/60VR15		27-30	6½-JK
1987-85 XJ6	215/70VR15		27-26	6-JK
1987-83 XJS	215/70VR15		26-24	6-JK
1984 XJ6	215/70VR15		27-26	6-JK
1983 XJ6	205/70VR15		27-30	6-JK
LADA				
1987-83 Niva	175/SR16		29-27	5-J
1985-83 Signet, 1.3, 1.5 sedan	165/SR13		26-28	5-J
LEXUS				
1992 SC 300, SC 400	225/55VR16		32-32	7-JJ
ES 300	P205/65VR15		32-32	6-JJ
1992-90 LS 400	205/65VR15		30-30	6½-JJ
1991-90 ES 250	195/60VR15		32-29	5½-JJ
LINCOLN				
1992-91 Mark VII	P225/60R16		30-30	7-JJ
1992-90 Town Car	P215/70R15		30-34	6-6½-JJ
1992-88 Continental	P205/70R15		30-30	6½-JJ
1990-89 Mark VII ex. LSC	P215/70R15		30-30	6-JJ
1990-88 Mark VII LSC	P225/60R16		30-30	7-JJ
1989-85 Town Car	P215/70R15		30-34	6-6½-JJ
1988-85 Mark VII ex. LSC	P215/70R15		26-26	5½-,6-JJ
1987-85 Continental	P215/70R15		26-26	5½-,6-JJ
Mark VII LSC	P215/65R15		30-30	6-JJ
1984 Town Car	P215/70R15		30-34	6-6½-JJ
Mark VII, Continental	P215/70R15		26-26	5½-,6-JJ
		P215/65R15	30-30	5½-,6-JJ
1983 Lincoln, Mark VI	P205/75R15		30-34	6-6½-JJ
Continental	P205/75R15		26-26	5½-,6-JJ
MAZDA				
1992 929	P205/65R15		28-28	6-JJ
MX-6, 626: W/o Turbo	P185/70SR14		32-26	5½-J
	P195/60HR15		32-26	6-JJ
W/Turbo	P195/60VR15	P205/60VR15	32-36	6-JJ
Protegé: SOHC	P175/70SR13		32-32	5-J
DOHC	P185/60HR14		32-32	5½-JJ
MX-3	P185/65SR14		32-32	5½-JJ
MX-3 GS	P205/55VR15		28-28	6-JJ
323	155/80SR13		32-32	5-J
1992-90 MX-5 Miata	185/60R14		26-26	5½-J
MX-6: DX, LX	185/70R14		26-26	5½-JJ
GT	195/60R15		26-26	6-JJ
		P205/60R15	32-26	6-JJ
1991 RX-7 ex. Turbo, conv.	205/60VR15		32-32	6-JJ
RX-7 Turbo, convertible	205/55VR16		32-32	7-JJ
1991-90 323	P155/80R13		32-32	4½-J
323 SE	P175/70R13		32-32	5-J
Protegé: DX, SE	P175/70R13		32-32	5-J
LX	P185/60R14		32-32	5½-JJ
4WD	P185/65R14		32-32	5½-JJ
626: DX, LX	185/70SR14		32-26	5½-J
GT	195/60HR15		32-26	6-JJ
929	P195/65R15		30-30	6-JJ
929S	P205/60R15		32-32	6-JJ
1990-89 RX-7 ex. Turbo:				
GTU, GXL	205/60VR15		32-32	6-JJ
Convertible	205/60VR15		32-32	6½-JJ
RX-7 Turbo	205/55VR16		32-32	7-JJ

MAKE YEAR MODEL	ORIGINAL EQUIPMENT SIZE Std.	Optional	PRESSURE†• Max. Load* F-R	RIM WIDTH
MAZDA Continued				
1990-89 MPV: 2WD	P205/70R14		32-32	5½-JJ
		P215/65R15	30-30	6-JJ
4WD	P215/65R15		30-30	6-JJ
		P205/75R14	32-32	5½-JJ
1989 323 ex. Turbo	155SR13		29-26	4½-JJ
		175/70SR13	29-26	5-J
323 Turbo	185/60R14		29-26	5½-J
626 ex. Turbo	P185/70R14		32-26	5½-JJ
		P195/60R15	32-26	6-JJ
929	P195/65R15		30-30	6-JJ
1988 323: Base, SE	155SR13		29-26	4½-JJ
LX, wagon	175/70SR13		29-26	5-J
GT	185/60R14		29-26	5½-J
626, MX-6 ex. Turbo	185/70SR14		28-26	5½-JJ
Turbo	195/60HR15		28-26	6-JJ
929	P195/65R15		32-32	6-JJ
RX-7: SE	185/70HR14		32-32	5½-JJ
GTU, GXL, conv.	205/60VR15		32-32	6-J
Turbo	205/55VR16		32-32	7-JJ
1987-86 323	6.15-13		29-26	4½-J
		155SR13	29-26	4½-J
		175/70SR13	29-26	5-J
		185/60R14	29-26	5½-J
626	165SR14		28-26	5-J
		185/70SR14	28-26	5½-JJ
		185/70HR14	28-26	5½-JJ
		195/60R15	28-26	6-J
RX-7	205/60VR15		32-32	6-JJ
		185/70HR14	32-32	5½-JJ
		205/55VR16	32-32	7-JJ
1985-84 RX-7	165HR13		27-27	5-J
		185/70HR13	27-27	5½-JJ
		205/60VR14	28-28	5½-JJ
1985-83 626	185/70SR14		28-26	5-J
		165SR14	28-26	5½-JJ
GLC ex. Sports model	6.15-13, 155-13	155SR13	26-26	4½-J
1983 RX-7	165HR13		26-26	5-J
		185/70HR13	26-26	5½-JJ
GLC Sports model	175/70SR13		26-26	5-J
MERCEDES-BENZ				
1992 190E 2.3L	185/65R15		29-33	6-J
190E 2.6L	185/65R15	205/55R15	—	6-J
300D 2.5 Turbo	195/65HR15		—	6½-J
300E, 300CE	195/65R15		—	6½-J
		205/65R15	—	7-J
300SD, 300SE	225/60VR16		—	7½-J
300SL, 500SL	225/55ZR16		30-35	8-J
300TE, 400E	195/65VR15		—	6½-J
400SE, 500SEL, 600SEL	235/60ZR16		—	7½-J
500E	225/55ZR16		—	8-J
1992-87 190E 2.6L	185/65VR15		29-33	6-J
1992-86 300E	195/65VR15		29-35	6½-J
1991 190E 2.3L	185/65R15		29-33	6-J
350SD, SDL Turbo	205/65R15		30-35	6½-J
1991-90 300SL, 500SL	225/55ZR16		30-35	8-J
300SE, 300SEL	205/65R15		30-35	6½-JJ
1991-88 300CE, 300TE	195/65VR15		29-35	6½-J
1991-86 420SEL, 560SEL, 560SEC	205/65VR15		30-35	6½-J
1990-86 560SL	205/65VR15		29-35	7-J
1989-86 300SEL	205/65VR15		30-35	6½-J
1989-87 260E	195/65VR15		29-35	6½-J
1989-86 190D, 190E	185/65R15		28-32	6-J
1987 300SDL	205/65R15		30-35	7-J
1987-86 190E-16	205/55VR15		35-41	7-J
300D, 300TD	195/65R15		29-35	6½-J
1985 300SD	205/70HR14		28-30	6½-J
1985-84 190E, 190D	175/70R14		28-32	5-J
1985-83 380SE, 380SEL, 380SEC	205/70HR14		28-30	6½-J
380SL	205/70HR14		32-36	6½-J
300D, 300CD, 300TD	195/70SR14		28-32	6-J
1984-83 300SD	195/70SR14		28-30	6-J
1983 240D	175SR14		28-32	5½-J

Tire sizes and tire pressures represent the car manufacturer's recommendations (for normal speeds).
†Sustained high speeds: **Numeric and Alphanumeric** sizes, add 4 psi (do not exceed 32 psi for load range ''B'', 36 psi for load range ''C'', 40 psi for load range ''D''); **P-Metric** sizes, add 3 psi (do not exceed 35 psi for Standard Load, 41 psi for Extra Load ''XL'' tire).
European metric sizes have maximum inflation pressure of either 32 or 36 psi, depending on construction. Refer to maximum inflation limit stamped on tire sidewall.
*For minimum load pressure, refer to tire decal. •Cars equipped with Trailer Tow Option, refer to tire decal.

MAKE YEAR MODEL	O.E. Std.	Optional	PRESS Max Load F-R	RIM WIDTH
MERCURY MARQUIS, GRAND MARQUIS				
1992 Grand Marquis	P215/70R15	P225/70R15	31-35	6¹/₂-JJ
1991-88 Grand Marquis sedan	P215/70R15		31-35	6-JJ³
Wagon	P215/70R15		27-35	6¹/₂-JJ
1987-86 Grand Marquis sedan	P205/75R15	P215/70R15	31-35	6¹/₂-JJ
Wagon	P205/75R15	P215/70R15	27-35	6¹/₂-JJ
1986 Marquis	P195/75R14	P205/70R14	30-30¹	5-,5¹/₂-JJ
1985 Marquis	P195/75R14		30-30¹	5-,5¹/₂-JJ
		P205/70R14	30-30¹	5¹/₂-JJ
		220/55R390‡	30-30	150 mm
Grand Marquis	P215/75R14		31-35²	6-JJ
		P205/75R15	31-35²	6-,6¹/₂-JJ
		P215/70R15	31-35²	6-,6¹/₂-JJ
1984-83 All ex. wagon: Marquis	P185/75R14		30-35	5-,5¹/₂-JJ
		P195/75R14	30-30	5-,5¹/₂-JJ
		P205/70R14	35-35	5¹/₂-JJ
Grand Marquis	P215/75R14	P225/75R14	31-35	6¹/₂-JJ
		P205/75R15	31-35	6-,6¹/₂-JJ
Wagon ex. Colony Park	P185/75R14	P195/75R14	28-35	5-,5¹/₂-JJ
w/Trailer Tow		P205/75R14	28-35	6¹/₂-JJ
Colony Park Wagon	P215/75R14	P225/75R14	27-35	6¹/₂-JJ
		P205/75R15	27-35	6-,6¹/₂-JJ

1 Wagon, 28-35 **2** Wagon, 27-35 **3** Aluminum wheels, 6¹/₂-JJ

MAKE YEAR MODEL	O.E. Std.	Optional	PRESS F-R	RIM WIDTH
MERCURY CAPRI				
1992 All ex. XR2	P185/60R14		32-29	5¹/₂-JJ
XR2	P195/50R15		32-29	6-JJ
1991 All	P185/60R14		32-29	5¹/₂-JJ
1986 All ex. 5.0L	P195/75R14	P205/70R14	35-35	5¹/₂-JJ
5.0L	P225/60VR15		30-30	7-JJ
1985 All ex. RS	P195/75R14		30-30	5-JJ
		P205/70R14	30-30	5¹/₂-JJ
		P205/70VR14	35-35	5¹/₂-JJ
		220/55VR390‡	30-30	150 mm
RS 5.0L	P225/60VR15		30-30	7-JJ
		220/55VR390‡	30-30	150 mm
1984-83 All	P185/75R14		35-35	5-,5¹/₂-JJ
		P205/70HR14	35-35	5-,5¹/₂-JJ
		P195/75R14	30-30	5-,5¹/₂-JJ
		220/55R390‡	30-30	165 mm
MERCURY COUGAR, XR-7				
1992 XR7	P225/60ZR16		30-30	7-JJ
1992-89 All ex. XR-7	P205/70R15		30-30	6-JJ
		P215/70R15	30-30	6¹/₂-JJ
XR-7	P225/60VR16		30-30	7-JJ
1988-87 All ex. XR-7	P215/70R14	P215/70HR14	30-30	5¹/₂-JJ
1988-85 XR-7	P225/60VR15		30-30	7-JJ
1986 All ex. XR-7	P215/70R14	P215/70HR14	30-30	5¹/₂-JJ
		220/55R390‡	26-26	150 mm
1985 All ex. XR-7	P205/70R14	P215/70R14	30-30	5¹/₂-JJ
		P215/70HR14	30-30	5¹/₂-JJ
		220/55VR390‡	26-26	150 mm
1984-83 All	P195/75R14	P205/70R14	30-30	5¹/₂-JJ
		P205/70HR14	35-35	5¹/₂-JJ
		220/55R390‡	30-30	165 mm
MERCURY LYNX, LN7				
1987-86 All ex. XR3	P165/80R13		30-30	4¹/₂-,5-JB
		P175/80R13	35-35	4¹/₂-,5-JB
XR3	P195/60HR15		30-30	6-JJ
1985 All	P165/80R13		35-35	4¹/₂-5¹/₂-JB
		P175/80R13	35-35	4¹/₂-JB
		165/70R365‡	30-30	135 mm
1984 L, GS Series	P165/80R13		35-35	4¹/₂-,5-JB
		P175/80R13	35-35	5-JB
LTS, RS Series	165/70R365‡		30-30	135 mm
1983 All ex. wagon, LN7	P165/80R13		35-35	4¹/₂-,5-JB
		165/70R365‡	30-30	135 mm
Wagon	P165/80R13		30-30	4¹/₂-,5-JB
LN7	P165/80R13		30-30	5-,5¹/₂-JB
		165/70R365‡	30-30	135 mm
MERCURY, ZEPHYR				
1983 All	P175/75R14	P185/75R14	35-35	5-,5¹/₂-JJ
		190/65R390‡	28-28	150 mm
MERCURY SABLE				
1992 All	P205/65R15		35-35	6-JJ
1991-86 All	P205/70R14		35-35	5¹/₂-JJ
		P205/65R15	35-35	6-JJ

MAKE YEAR MODEL	O.E. Std.	Optional	PRESS F-R	RIM WIDTH
MERCURY TOPAZ				
1992 GS, LS	P185/70R14		30-30	5¹/₂-JJ
LTS, XR5	P185/60R15		30-30	6-JJ
1991-88 All	P185/70R14		30-30	5¹/₂-JJ
1987-86 All ex. GT, Sport GS	P185/70R14		30-30	5¹/₂-JJ
GT, Sport GS	185/65R365‡		30-30	135 mm
1985 All	P175/80R14		30-30	5-,5¹/₂-JB
		185/65R365‡	30-30	135 mm
1984 All	P175/80R13		30-30	5-JB
		185/65R365‡	30-30	135 mm
1983 All	P175/80R13		35-35	5-JB
MERCURY TRACER				
1992 Notchback	P175/70R13		32-32	5-JJ
LTS	P185/60R15		32-32	5¹/₂-JJ
1992-91 Wagon	P175/65R14		32-32	5-JJ
1991 All ex. LTS, wagon	P175/70R13		32-32	5-JJ
		P175/65R14	32-32	5-JJ
LTS	P185/60HR14		32-32	5-JJ
1990-88 All	P175/70R13		29-29	5-JJ
MERKUR				
1989-88 Scorpio	205/60HR15		32-32	6-J
1989-87 XR4Ti	195/60HR15		32-32	5¹/₂-J

‡ These metric diameter tires and rims are NOT interchangeable with any 13″, 14″ or 15″ diameter tires or rims. Do NOT attempt to mount 365 mm tires (approx. 14³/₈″ dia.) or 390 mm tires (approx. 15³/₈″ dia.) on any 14″ or 15″ rims. Do NOT attempt to mount nominal 14″ or 15″ diameter tires on 365 mm or 390 mm diameter rims.

MAKE YEAR MODEL	O.E. Std.	Optional	PRESS F-R	RIM WIDTH
MITSUBISHI				
1992 Diamante	205/65VR15		32-26	6-JJ
Expo	205/70R14		—	5¹/₂-JJ
Expo LRV: 2WD	185/75R14		—	5¹/₂-JJ
4WD	205/70R14		—	5¹/₂-JJ
1992-91 3000 GT ex. Turbo	225/55VR16		32-29	8-J
3000 GT Turbo	245/45ZR17		32-29	8¹/₂-J
Galant sedan	185/70SR14		29-26	5¹/₂-JJ
Galant Sport Sedan: GS	195/65R14		30-26	5¹/₂-JJ
GSR, GSX, VR-4	195/60R15		32-29	6-JJ
Mirage GS	195/60R14		29-29	5¹/₂-JJ
1992-90 Eclipse, Eclipse GS 1.3L	185/70R14		29-26	5¹/₂-JJ
Eclipse GS, GSX 2.0L 16V	205/55R16		32-29	6-JJ
Mirage ex. 1991 GS	P155/80R13	P175/70R13	29-29	4¹/₂-J, 5-J
1992-88 Precis	P155/80R13		28-28	4¹/₂-J
		175/70R13	32-32	5-J
1990-89 Galant	P185/70R14		32-32	5¹/₂-JJ
		P195/60R15	32-32	6-JJ
1989 Mirage	P155/80R13		32-32	5-J
		P195/60R14	32-32	5¹/₂-JJ
		P175/70R13	32-32	5-J
Sigma	195/60R15		32-32	6-JJ
1989-88 Starion: Front	205/55VR16		32	7-JJ
		225/50VR16	32	8-JJ
Rear	225/50VR16		32	8-JJ
		245/45VR16	32	9-JJ
1988 Cordia	195/60R14		32-32	5¹/₂-JJ
Galant	195/60R15		32-32	6-JJ
Mirage	P145/80R13		32-32	4¹/₂-J
		P155/80R13	32-32	5-J
		P175/70R13	32-32	5-J
		P185/60R14	32-32	5¹/₂-JJ
Tredia	P185/70R13		32-32	5-J
		195/60R14	32-32	5¹/₂-JJ
1987 Precis	P155/80R13		30-30	4¹/₂-J
		P175/70R13	30-30	5-J
Starion	215/60R15		32-32	6¹/₂-JJ
1987-86 Tredia	P165/80R13		32-32	4¹/₂-J
	P185/70R14		32-32	5-J
		195/60R14	32-32	5¹/₂-JJ
Cordia	P185/70R14		32-32	5-J
		195/60R14	32-32	5¹/₂-JJ
1987-85 Mirage	P145/80R13		32-32	4¹/₂-J
		P155/80R13	32-32	5-J
		185/60R14	32-32	5¹/₂-JJ
Galant	185/70HR14		32-32	5¹/₂-JJ
		195/60R15	32-32	6-JJ
1986 Starion	205/55VR16		32-32	7-JJ
		225/55VR16	32-32	8-JJ

Tire sizes and tire pressures represent the car manufacturer's recommendations (for normal speeds).
†Sustained high speeds: **Numeric and Alphanumeric** sizes, add 4 psi (do not exceed 32 psi for load range "B", 36 psi for load range "C", 40 psi for load range "D"); **P-Metric** sizes, add 3 psi (do not exceed 35 psi for Standard Load, 41 psi for Extra Load "XL" tire).
European metric sizes have maximum inflation pressure of either 32 or 36 psi, depending on construction. Refer to maximum inflation limit stamped on tire sidewall.
*For minimum load pressure, refer to tire decal. •Cars equipped with Trailer Tow Option, refer to tire decal.

MAKE YEAR	MODEL	ORIGINAL EQUIPMENT SIZE Std.	Optional	PRESSURE†• Max. Load* F-R	RIM WIDTH
MITSUBISHI Continued					
1985-83	Tredia, Cordia	P165/80R13		32-32	4½-J
			P185/70R13	32-32	5-J
			P185/70HR13	32-32	5-J
	Starion	P195/70R14		32-32	6-J
			P215/60VR15	32-32	6½-JJ
NISSAN					
1992	Maxima DOHC MT	P205/65VR15		—	6-,6½-JJ
	Stanza	P195/65HR14		—	5½-,6-JJ
1992-91	NX Coupe	P195/55R14		26-26	6-JJ
	Sentra E: Man. Trans.	P155/80R13	P175/70R13	26-26	5-J
	Auto. Trans.	P175/70R13		26-26	5-J
	Sentra XE, GXE, SET	P175/70R13		26-26	5-J
	Sentra SE-R	P185/60R14		26-26	5½-JJ
	Maxima	P205/65R15		26-26	6-,6½-JJ
1992-90	300ZX ex. Turbo	P225/50R16		26-26	7½-JJ
	Turbo: Front	P225/50ZR16		26	7½-JJ
	Rear	P245/45ZR16		26	8½-JJ
1992-89	240 SX	195/60R15	205/60R15	26-26	6-JJ
	Sentra: Std., E	P155SR13		26-26	5-J
	SE Coupe	185/60R14		26-26	5½-JJ
	Maxima SE	P205/65R15		26-26	6½-JJ
	Maxima GXE	P205/65R15		26-26	6-JJ
1991-90	Stanza	195/65R14		26-26	5½-JJ
	Pulsar NX	185/70R13		26-26	5-JJ
1990	Axxess	P195/70R14		26-26	5½-JJ
	Sentra XE	P155/80R13	P175/70R13	26-26	5-J
1989	Sentra XE	P175/70R13		26-26	5-JJ
1989-88	300 ZX ex. Turbo	P215/60R15		26-26	6½-JJ
	300 ZX Turbo	225/65VR16		26-26	7-JJ
	Pulsar ex. SE	185/70R13		26-26	5-J
	Pulsar SE	195/60R14		26-26	6-JJ
1989-86	Stanza sedan	P185/70R14		29-29	5-J, 5½-JJ
1988-87	Sentra: 2WD	P155/80R13		29-26	5-J
			P175/70R13	29-29	5-J
	Aluminum wheels	185/60R14		29-26	5½-J
			P175/70R13	29-29	5-J
	4WD	P175/70R13		26-26	5-J
1988-86	Stanza wagon	185/70SR14		29-29	5-J
	Aluminum wheels	185/70SR14		29-29	5½-JJ
1988-85	200 SX	185/70SR14		26-26	5-J
			195/60R15	28-28	6-JJ
			P195/60R15	26-26	6-JJ
			205/60R15	28-28	6-JJ
	Maxima	195/60R15		33-29	6-JJ
1986	Sentra	155SR13		26-26	4½-J
			175/70SR13	26-26	5-J
1986-84	300 ZX	P195/70R14		28-28	5½-JJ
			P215/60R15	28-28	6½-JJ
			225/50VR16	28-28	7-JJ
1986-83	Pulsar	175/70SR13		26-26	4½-J
1985-83	Sentra	155-13/ 6.15-13		24-24	4½-J
			155SR13	26-26	4½-J
			175/70SR13	26-26	5-J
	Stanza	165SR13		26-26	4½-J
			185/70SR13	26-26	5-J
1984	Micra	P155/80R12		32-32	4-,4½-J
	200SX	185/70SR14		26-26	5-J
	Turbo	195/60HR15		26-26	5½-JJ
1984-83	Maxima	185/70SR14		28-28	5-J
	280ZX ex. Turbo	195/70HR14		28-28	5½-,6-JJ
			P205/70R14	28-28	6-JJ
	280ZX Turbo	P205/60R15		28-28	6-JJ
1983	200SX	185/70SR14		26-26	5-,5½-J
	Maxima	185/70SR14		28-28	5-J
OLDSMOBILE 88, NINETY-EIGHT, TORONADO					
1992	Eighty-Eight Royale	P205/70R15		30-30	6-JJ
			P225/60R16	30-30	7-JJ
	Ninety-Eight:				
	Regency	P205/70R15		30-30	6-JJ
	Touring Sedan	P225/60R16		30-30	7-JJ
1992-91	Toronado ex. Troféo	P215/65R15		28-26	6-JJ
	Troféo	P215/60R16		28-26	7-JJ
1992-89	Custom Cruiser	P225/75R15		30-35	7-JJ

MAKE YEAR	MODEL	ORIGINAL EQUIPMENT SIZE Std.	Optional	PRESSURE†• Max. Load* F-R	RIM WIDTH
OLDSMOBILE 88, NINETY-EIGHT, TORONADO Continued					
1991	Eighty-Eight Royale	P205/75R14	P205/70R15	30-30	6-JJ
			P215/65R15	30-30	6-JJ
	Ninety-Eight:				
	Regency Elite	P205/70R15		30-30	6-JJ
	Touring Sedan	P215/65R16		30-30	7-JJ
1990	Toronado ex. Troféo	P205/70R15		28-26	6-JJ
			P205/75R15	30-30	6-JJ
			P215/65R15	30-30	6-JJ
	Troféo	P215/60R16		30-30	6-JJ
1990-89	Eighty-Eight Royale, Ninety-Eight	P205/75R14	P215/65R15	30-30	6-JJ
1989	Touring Sedan	P215/60R16		30-30	7-JJ
	Toronado ex. Troféo	P205/70R15		28-26	6-JJ
			P215/65R15	30-30	6-JJ
1989-88	Toronado Troféo	P215/65R15		30-30	6-JJ
1988	Touring Sedan	P215/65R15		30-30	6-JJ
1988-86	Delta 88, Ninety-Eight	P205/75R14		30-30	6-JJ
			P205/70R15	30-30	7-JJ
			P215/65R15	30-30	6-JJ
	Custom Cruiser	P225/75R15		30-35	7-JJ
	Toronado ex. Troféo	P205/70R14		30-30	5½-JJ
			P215/65R15	30-30	6-JJ
1985	Ninety-Eight	P205/75R14		30-30	6-JJ
1985-84	Delta 88 ex. wagon	P205/75R15	P215/75R15	35-35	7-JJ
	Delta 88 wagon	P225/75R15		35-35	7-JJ
1985-82	Toronado	P205/75R15		30-30	6-JJ
			P225/70R15	28-24	6-JJ
	Custom Cruiser	P225/75R15		30-35	6-JJ
1984	Ninety-Eight	P215/75R15	P225/75R15	35-35	6-JJ
1983	Delta 88	P205/75R15	P215/75R15	35-35	6-JJ
	Ninety-Eight	P215/75R15	P225/75R15	35-35	6-JJ
OLDSMOBILE CUTLASS, CIERA, CUTLASS CRUISER					
1992	Ciera	P185/75R14		32-32	5½-JJ
			P195/70R14	30-30	6-JJ
			P195/75R14	30-30	6-JJ
	Cutlass Cruiser	P185/75R14		30-35	5½-JJ
			P195/70R14	30-35	6-JJ
	Cutlass Supreme S	P205/70R15	P225/60R16	30-30	6-,6½-JJ
			P225/60R16	30-30	6½-JJ
	Cutlass Supreme SL	P215/60R16	P225/60R16	30-30	6½-JJ
	Cutlass Supreme International	P225/60R16		30-30	6½-JJ
1991	Cutlass Cruiser	P185/75R14		30-35	5½-JJ
			P195/70R14	30-35	6-JJ
			P195/75R14	30-35	6-JJ
1991-90	Cutlass Supreme	P195/75R14		30-30	5½-JJ
	Convertible	P215/65R15		30-30	6-JJ
	Cutlass Supreme SL	P205/70R15		35-35	6-JJ
1991-89	Cutlass Supreme International	P215/60R16		35-35	6½-JJ
1991-88	Ciera ex. International	P185/75R14	P195/70R14	35-35	5½-JJ
			P215/60R14	35-35	6-JJ
1990-88	Ciera International	P215/60R14		35-35	6-JJ
	Cutlass Cruiser	P185/75R14		35-35	5½-,6-JJ
1989	Cutlass Supreme	P195/75R14		30-30	5½-JJ
			P215/65R15	30-30	6-JJ
1988	Cutlass Supreme	P195/75R14	P205/75R14	35-35	6-JJ
			P215/65R15	35-35	6-JJ
1987-85	Cutlass ex. Ciera, 442	P195/75R14	P205/75R14	35-35	6-JJ
			P205/70R14	35-35	6-JJ
	Cutlass Ciera	P185/75R14	P195/75R14	35-35	5½-JJ
			P195/70R14	35-35	5½-JJ
			P215/60R14	30-30	6-JJ
	Cutlass 442	P215/65R15		30-30	7-JJ
1984	Cutlass Ciera	P185/75R14	P195/70R14	35-35	5½-JJ
	Optional ex. wagon		P195/75R14	35-35	5½-JJ
1984-83	Cutlass ex. Ciera, Cruiser	P195/75R14	P205/75R14	35-35	6-JJ
			P205/70R14	35-35	6-JJ
1983	Cutlass Ciera ex. Diesel	P185/80R13	P205/70R13	35-35	5½-JB
			P185/75R14	35-35	5½-JJ
			P195/70R14	35-35	5½-JJ
	Cutlass Ciera Diesel	P185/75R14	P195/70R14	35-35	5½-JJ
	Cutlass Cruiser ex. Diesel	P195/75R14	P205/75R14	30-35	6-JJ
			P205/70R14	30-35	6-JJ
	Cutlass Cruiser Diesel	P195/75R14	P205/75R14	32-35	6-JJ
			P205/70R14	32-35	6-JJ

Tire sizes and tire pressures represent the car manufacturer's recommendations (for normal speeds).
†Sustained high speeds: **Numeric and Alphanumeric** sizes, add 4 psi (do not exceed 32 psi for load range ''B'', 36 psi for load range ''C'',
40 psi for load range ''D''); **P-Metric** sizes, add 3 psi (do not exceed 35 psi for Standard Load, 41 psi for Extra Load ''XL'' tire).
European metric sizes have maximum inflation pressure of either 32 or 36 psi, depending on construction. Refer to maximum inflation limit stamped on tire sidewall.
*For minimum load pressure, refer to tire decal.   •Cars equipped with Trailer Tow Option, refer to tire decal.

MAKE	YEAR	MODEL	ORIGINAL EQUIPMENT SIZE Std.	Optional	PRES-SURE†• Max. Load* F-R	RIM WIDTH
OLDSMOBILE ACHIEVA, CALAIS						
	1992	Achieva	P185/70R14	P195/70R14	35-35	6-JJ
			P185/75R14	P195/70R14	35-35	6-JJ
				P205/55R16	35-35	6-JJ
	1991	Calais S	P185/75R14		35-35	6-JJ
				P215/60R14	30-30	6-JJ
				P205/60R15	35-35	6-JJ
	1991-90	Calais	P185/75R14		35-35	5¹/₂-JJ
		Calais SL	P195/70R14		35-35	6-JJ
				P215/60R14	30-30	6-JJ
	1991-89	Calais International	P205/55R16		35-35	6-JJ
	1990	Calais S	P185/75R14		35-35	5¹/₂-JJ
				P215/60R14	30-30	6-JJ
	1989	Calais, Calais S	P185/80R13		35-35	5¹/₂-JB
				P195/70R14	30-30	6-JJ
				P215/60R14	30-30	6-JJ
		Calais SL	P195/70R14	P215/70R14	30-30	6-JJ
	1988	All ex. International	P185/80R13	P205/70R13	35-35	5¹/₂-JB
				P195/70R14	35-35	6-JJ
				215/60R14	35-35	6-JJ
		International	P215/60R14		35-35	6-JJ
	1987-86	All	P185/80R13		35-35	5¹/₂-JB
				P205/70R13	30-30	5¹/₂-JB
				P195/70R14	30-30	6-JJ
				P215/60R14	30-30	6-JJ
	1985	All	P185/80R13	P205/70R13	35-35	5¹/₂-JB
OLDSMOBILE FIRENZA						
	1988	All	P185/80R13		35-35	5¹/₂-JB
				P195/70R14	35-35	6-JJ
				P215/60R14	35-35	6-JJ
	1987	All ex. GT	P175/80R13	P195/70R13	35-35	5¹/₂-JB
		GT	P205/60R14		30-30	6-JJ
	1986-85	All	P175/80R13	P195/70R13	35-35	5¹/₂-JB
				P205/60R14	30-30	6-JJ
	1984-83	All	P175/80R13		35-35	5-,5¹/₂-JB
				P195/70R13	35-35	5¹/₂-JB
OLDSMOBILE OMEGA						
	1984-83	All	P185/80R13	P205/70R13	35-35	5¹/₂-JB
PEUGEOT						
	1992-89	405 S, DL	185/65R15		30-32	5¹/₂-J
	1991	MI16	195/55VR15		33-33	6-J
	1991-89	505 sedan: S2.2i, S2.8i	185/65R15		29-32	6-J
		STX, Turbo	205/60R15		29-32	6-J
		505 wagon	195/65R15		28-32	6-J
	1990-89	405 MI16	195/60VR14		28-31	6-J
	1988	505: DL, GLS: Sedan	185/70R14		28-31	5¹/₂-J
		Wagon	195/70R14		26-36	6-J
		STI, GLX	185/65R15		29-32	6-J
		STX	205/60R15		29-32	6-J
		Turbo Sedan	205/60R15		29-31	6-J
		Turbo Wagon	205/60R15		29-34	6-J
	1987	505: GLS	185/65R15		29-32	6-J
		STI, STX	205/60R15		29-32	6-J
	1986	505: Sedan	185/70R14		31-34	5¹/₂-J,6-J[1]
				195/60R15	34-35	6-J
		Wagon	195/70R14		26-37	6-J
		Turbo Sedan	205/60R15		29-31	6-J
		Wagon	205/60R15		29-37	6-J
	1985	505 Gas: Sedan, GL	175SR14		27-32	5¹/₂-J
		S	175SR14		27-32	6-J
		STI	190/65HR390‡		25-30	150 mm
		Wagon	185/SR14		24-29	5¹/₂-J
		505 Turbo: Gas	195/60HR15		29-30	6-J
		Diesel GL	185/70R14		27-30	5¹/₂-J
		S	185/70R14		27-30	5¹/₂-J
		STI	190/65H15		29-30	6-J
	1984	505 Diesel	185SR14		25-29	5¹/₂-J
		505 Gas	175SR14		27-32	5¹/₂-J
				190/65HR390‡	25-30	150 mm
	1983	505	175SR14		28-32	5-J
				175HR14	28-32	5-J
				190/65HR390‡	25-30	150 mm
		604	195/65HR390‡		28-32	150 mm
		504 Diesel wagon	185SR14		24-40	5-J

MAKE	YEAR	MODEL	ORIGINAL EQUIPMENT SIZE Std.	Optional	PRES-SURE†• Max. Load* F-R	RIM WIDTH
PLYMOUTH						
	1992	Acclaim	P185/70R14		35-35	5¹/₂-JJ
				P195/70R14	32-32	5¹/₂-JJ
		Colt Vista wagon FWD: MT	P185/75R14		28-28	5¹/₂-JJ
		AT & 4WD	205/70R14		26-26	5¹/₂-JJ
	1992-91	Colt Hatchback ex. GL	P155/80R13		29-29	4¹/₂-JB
		GL	P175/70R13		29-29	5-JJ
	1992-90	Laser 1.8L	P185/70R14		29-26	5¹/₂-JJ
		Laser 2.0L ex. Turbo	P205/55R16	205/55VR16	29-26	6-JJ
		Laser Turbo	P205/55VR16		32-29	6-JJ
	1992-89	Sundance	P185/70R14		35-35	5¹/₂-JJ
		Sundance Duster	P195/60R15		35-35	6-JJ
	1991-89	Acclaim	P185/70R14		32-32	5¹/₂-JJ
				P195/70R14	29-32	6-JJ
		Acclaim LE	P195/70R14		29-32	5¹/₂-JJ
		Acclaim LX	P205/60R15		29-32	6-JJ
		Colt Vista Wagon: FWD	P165/80R13	P185/70R13	29-29	5-J
		4WD	P185/70R14		29-35	5¹/₂-JJ
	1990	Colt Hatchback ex. GT	P155/80R13		35-35	4¹/₂-JB
		GT	P175/70R14		35-35	5-J
				P195/60HR14	35-35	6¹/₂-JJ
	1990-89	Colt DL Wagon: FWD	P175/70R13		26-26	5-J
		4WD	P185/70R14		26-29	5-J
		Horizon America	P165/80R13		35-35	5-JB
	1989	Colt Hatchback: ex. E, GT	145/80R13		32-32	4¹/₂-JB
		E, GT	P155/80R13		29-29	5-JB
		GT Turbo	195/60R14		29-29	5¹/₂-JJ
		Reliant America	P175/80R13		35-35	5-JB
				P185/70R14	35-35	5¹/₂-JJ
	1989-84	Gran Fury	P205/75R15		35-35	7-JJ
	1988	Colt: E	P145/80R13		31-31	4¹/₂-J
				P155/80R13	31-31	5-J
		DL wagon	P175/70R13		26-26	5-J
		Premier	185/60R14		26-26	5¹/₂-JJ
		Reliant ex. wagon	P175/80R13		35-35	5-JB
				P185/70R14	35-35	5¹/₂-JJ
		Reliant wagon	P185/70R14		35-35	5¹/₂-JJ
	1988-87	Sundance: L series	P165/80R13		35-35	5-JB
		H series	P185/70R14		35-35	5¹/₂-JJ
				P205/50VR15	35-35	6-JJ
		Horizon, Turismo	P165/80R13		35-35	5-JB
	1988-85	Caravelle	P185/70R14		32-32	5¹/₂-JJ
	1988-84	Colt Vista: 2WD	P165/80R13		29-29	5-J
				P185/70R13	26-26	5-J
		4WD	P185/70R14		29-35	5¹/₂-JJ
	1987-85	Colt	P145/80R13		31-31	4¹/₂-J
				P155/80R13	26-26	5-J
				185/60HR14	26-26	5¹/₂-J
	1987-84	Reliant	P175/80R13		35-35	5-JB
				P185/70R14	26-35	5¹/₂-JJ
	1986	Conquest	P215/60R15		28-28	6¹/₂-JJ
		W/Intercooler:				
		Front		205/55VR16	28	7-J
		Rear		225/50VR16	28	8-J
	1986-85	Turismo ex. 2.2	P165/80R13		35-35	5-JB
				P195/60R14	35-35	5¹/₂-JJ
	1986-84	Horizon	P165/80R13	P175/75R13	35-35	5-JB
	1986-83	Turismo 2.2	P195/60R14		35-35	5¹/₂-JJ
	1985	Conquest	P195/70R14		28-28	6-J
				P215/60VR14	28-28	6¹/₂-JJ
	1984	Colt ex. Vista	155SR13		31-31	4-,4¹/₂-J
				P175/70R13	24-24	4¹/₂-J
				6.00-14/C	26-26	5-J
		Conquest		195/70R14	27-27	6-JJ
				P215/60R15	27-27	6¹/₂-JJ
		Turismo ex. 2.2	P165/80R13		35-35	5-JB
	1983	Gran Fury, Caravelle	P195/75R15		29-29	5¹/₂-JJ
				P205/75R15	29-29	7-JJ
		Horizon ex. Turismo 2.2	P175/75R13		35-35	5-JB
				P195/60R14	35-35	5¹/₂-JJ
		Reliant	P175/75R13	P185/70R13	35-35	5-JB
				P185/70R14	35-35	5¹/₂-JJ
		Sapporo		195/70SR14	24-24	5-,5¹/₂-JJ
PONTIAC BONNEVILLE, GRAND SAFARI, PARISIENNE						
	1992	Bonneville SE	P215/65R15		30-30	6-JJ
				P225/60R16	30-30	7-JJ
		Bonneville SSE	P225/60R16		30-30	7-JJ
		Bonneville SSEi	P225/60ZR16		30-30	7-JJ
	1991	Bonneville LE	P215/65R15		30-30	6-JJ
				P215/60R16	30-30	7-JJ

1 Alloy wheels, 4¹/₂-J

Tire sizes and tire pressures represent the car manufacturer's recommendations (for normal speeds).
†Sustained high speeds: **Numeric and Alphanumeric** sizes, add 4 psi (do not exceed 32 psi for load range "B", 36 psi for load range "C", 40 psi for load range "D"); **P-Metric** sizes, add 3 psi (do not exceed 35 psi for Standard Load, 41 psi for Extra Load "XL" tire).
European metric sizes have maximum inflation pressure of either 32 or 36 psi, depending on construction. Refer to maximum inflation limit stamped on tire sidewall.
*For minimum load pressure, refer to tire decal. ●Cars equipped with Trailer Tow Option, refer to tire decal.

MAKE YEAR MODEL	ORIGINAL EQUIPMENT SIZE Std.	Optional	PRESSURE†● Max. Load* F-R	RIM WIDTH
PONTIAC BONNEVILLE, GRAND SAFARI, PARISIENNE Continued				
1991-90 Bonneville SE, SSE	P215/60R16		30-30	7-JJ
1990 Bonneville LE	P205/75R14		35-35	6-JJ
1989-88 Bonneville LE	P205/75R14	P205/70R15	35-35	6-JJ
		P215/65R15	30-30	6-JJ
Bonneville SE	P215/65R15		30-30	6-JJ
Bonneville SSE	P215/60R16		30-30	7-JJ
1989-87 Safari wagon	P225/75R15		30-35	7-JJ
1987 Bonneville ex. LE, wagon	P205/75R14	P205/70R15	35-35	6-JJ
		P215/65R15	30-30	6-JJ
Bonneville LE	P215/65R15		30-30	6-JJ
1986-85 Parisienne ex. wagon	P205/75R15	P215/75R15	35-35	6-JJ
		P225/70R15	35-35	7-JJ
1986-84 Bonneville	P195/75R14	P205/75R14	35-35	6-JJ
Parisienne wagon	P225/75R15		24-32	7-JJ
1984 Bonneville w/Diesel	P205/75R14		35-35	6-JJ
Parisienne ex. wagon	P205/75R15		35-35	6-JJ
		P225/70R15	35-35	7-JJ
1983 Bonneville	P195/75R14	P205/75R14	35-35	6-JJ
Wagon	P195/75R14	P205/75R14	30-35	6-JJ
PONTIAC FIERO				
1988 Coupe	P185/75R14		35-35	6-JJ
		P195/70R14	30-30	6-JJ
Formula GT Coupe:				
Front	P205/60R15		30	7-JJ
Rear	P215/60R15		30	7-JJ
1987 Coupe	P185/75R14		35-35	6-JJ
Sport Coupe	P185/75R14		35-35	6-JJ
		P195/70R14	30-30	6-JJ
SE Coupe	P195/70R14		30-30	6-JJ
GT Coupe: Front	P205/60R15		30	7-JJ
Rear	P215/60R15		30	7-JJ
1986 Coupe	P185/75R14		35-35	6-JJ
SE Coupe	P195/70R14	P215/60R14	30-30	6-JJ
Sport Coupe	P185/75R14	P195/70R14	35-35	6-JJ
1985 All ex. GT, SE	P185/80R13		35-35	5½-JB
		P195/70R14	30-30	6-JJ
		P215/60R14	30-30	6-JJ
GT	P215/60R14		30-30	6-JJ
SE	P195/70R14		30-30	6-JJ
1984 Fiero Coupe, Spt. Coupe	P185/80R13		35-35	5½-JB
		P215/60R14	35-35	6-JJ
Fiero SE	P215/60R14		30-30	6-JJ
PONTIAC FIREBIRD, TRANS AM				
1992-91 Firebird Trans Am	P215/60R16	P245/50ZR16	30-30	8-JJ
1992-90 Firebird Formula, GTA	P245/50ZR16		30-30	8-JJ
1992-87 Firebird	P215/65R15		30-30	7-JJ
1990 Firebird Trans Am	P215/65R15		30-30	7-JJ
		P245/50ZR16	30-30	8-JJ
1989 Firebird Formula, Trans Am GTA	P245/50ZR16		30-30	8-JJ
Trans Am	P215/65R15		30-30	7-JJ
		P245/50ZR16	30-30	8-JJ
1988 Firebird Formula, Trans Am GTA	P245/50VR16		30-30	7-JJ
1988-87 Trans Am	P215/65R15	P245/50VR16	30-30	7-JJ
1986 All ex. Trans Am	P215/65R15	P235/65R15	30-30	7-JJ
Trans Am	P215/65R15	P235/60VR15	30-30	7-JJ
		P245/50VR16	30-30	8-JJ
1985 All ex. Trans Am	P195/75R14	P205/70R14	35-35	6-JJ
Trans Am	P215/65R15		35-35	7-JJ
		P235/60VR15	30-30	7-JJ
		P245/50VR16	30-30	8-JJ
1984 Firebird	P195/75R14		35-35	6-JJ
		P205/70R14	35-35	7-JJ
Trans Am, SE	P205/70R14	P215/65R15	35-35	7-JJ
W/16" wheels	P245/50R16		30-30	8-JJ
1983 Firebird	P195/75R14		35-35	6-JJ
Trans Am, SE	P205/70R14	P215/65R15	35-35	7-JJ
PONTIAC FIREFLY				
1988 All ex. Turbo	P145/80R12		35-35	4-B
Turbo	P165/70R12		26-26	4½-B
1987 ER Models	P145/80R12		35-35	4-B
1987-85 All ex. ER Models	P145/80R12		32-32	4-B

MAKE YEAR MODEL	ORIGINAL EQUIPMENT SIZE Std.	Optional	PRESSURE†● Max. Load* F-R	RIM WIDTH
PONTIAC GRAND PRIX				
1992 STE, GT	P225/60R16		30-30	8-JJ
GTP	P245/50ZR16		30-30	8-JJ
1992-91 LE, SE Sedan	P205/70R15		30-30	6-JJ
		P215/60R16	30-30	6½-JJ
SE Coupe	P205/70R15		30-30	6-JJ
		P215/60R16	30-30	6½-JJ
		P225/60R16	30-30	8-JJ
1991 STE, GT	P215/60R16		30-30	6½-JJ
		P225/60R16	30-30	8-JJ
GTP	P225/60R16		30-30	8-JJ
1990 LE Coupe	P205/65R15		30-30	6-JJ
LE Sedan	P195/75R14		30-30	5½-JJ
		P205/65R15	30-30	6-JJ
1990-89 SE, STE	P215/60R16		30-30	6½-JJ
Turbo	P245/50ZR16		30-30	8-JJ
1989 All ex. SE, STE, Turbo	P195/75R14	P195/70R15	30-30	6-JJ
		P215/60R16	30-30	7-JJ
1988 All ex. SE	P195/75R14	P195/70R15	35-35	6-JJ
		P215/65R15	30-30	7-JJ
SE	P215/65R15		30-30	7-JJ
1987-85 All ex. SJ	P195/75R14	P205/75R14	35-35	6-JJ
		P215/65R15	30-30	7-JJ
SJ	P195/75R14	P205/75R14	35-35	6-JJ
		P215/65R15	30-30	7-JJ
1984-83 All w/handling pkg. or Diesel	P205/75R14		35-35	6-JJ
All w/o handling pkg. or Diesel	P195/75R14	P205/75R14	35-35	6-JJ
		P205/70R14	35-35	6-JJ
PONTIAC 1000				
1987 1000	P155/80R13		30-35	5-JB,5-JJ
1986-85 1000	P155/80R13	P175/70R13	30-30	5-,5½-JB
1984-83 1000	P155/80R13	P175/70R13	30-30	5-JB,5-JJ
PONTIAC 6000, LE MANS, GRAND AM				
1992 Grand Am SE	P185/75R14		35-35	6-JJ
		P195/70R14	30-30	6-JJ
		P195/65R15	30-30	6-JJ
Grand Am GT	P205/55R16		35-35	6-JJ
Le Mans	P175/70R13		35-35	5-JB
1991-90 6000 LE	P185/75R14		35-35	5½-JJ
6000 SE	P195/70R15		30-30	6-JJ
Grand Am LE	P185/75R14		35-35	5½-JJ
		P195/70R14	30-30	6-JJ
Grand Am SE	P205/55R16		35-35	6-JJ
1991-89 LeMans ex. SE or GSE	P175/70R13		35-35	5-JB
1990-89 LeMans SE, GSE	P185/60R14		35-35	6-JJ
1989-88 6000 SE	P195/70R14		30-30	6-JJ
6000 STE	P195/70R15		35-35	6-JJ
1989-87 Grand Am ex. SE	P185/80R13		35-35	5½-JB
		P195/70R14	30-30	6-JJ
		P215/60R14	30-30	6-JJ
Grand Am SE	P215/60R14		30-30	6-JJ
6000 ex. SE, STE	P185/75R14		35-35	5½-,6-JJ
		P195/70R14	30-30	6-JJ
Wagon	P185/75R14		35-35	5½-,6-JJ
1988 LeMans	P175/70R13		35-35	5-JB
1987 6000 SE, STE	P195/70R14		30-30	6-JJ
1986 6000 SE, STE	P185/75R14	P195/70R14	35-35	5½-JJ
6000 STE	P195/70R14		30-30	6-JJ
1986-85 Grand Am	P185/80R13	P205/70R13	35-35	5½-JB
		P215/60R14	35-35	6-JJ
1985 6000 ex. STE	P185/75R14	P195/75R14	35-35	5½-,6-JJ
		P195/70R14	35-35	6-JJ
		P195/75R14	35-35	5½-,6-JJ
1985-83 6000 STE	P195/70R14		35-35	6-JJ
1984 6000 ex. STE	P185/75R14	P195/70R14	35-35	5½-JJ
		P195/75R14	35-35	6-JJ
1983 6000 ex. Diesel, STE	P185/80R13	P205/70R13	35-35	5½-JB
		P185/75R14	35-35	5½-JJ
		P195/70R14	35-35	5½-JJ
6000 Diesel	P195/75R14		35-35	5½-JJ
PONTIAC SUNBURST				
1987-85 All	P155/80R13		30-30	4½-J

Tire sizes and tire pressures represent the car manufacturer's recommendations (for normal speeds).
†Sustained high speeds: **Numeric and Alphanumeric** sizes, add 4 psi (do not exceed 32 psi for load range "B", 36 psi for load range "C", 40 psi for load range "D"); **P-Metric** sizes, add 3 psi (do not exceed 35 psi for Standard Load, 41 psi for Extra Load "XL" tire).
European metric sizes have maximum inflation pressure of either 32 or 36 psi, depending on construction. Refer to maximum inflation limit stamped on tire sidewall.
* For minimum load pressure, refer to tire decal.   ●Cars equipped with Trailer Tow Option, refer to tire decal.

MAKE	YEAR	MODEL	ORIGINAL EQUIPMENT SIZE Std.	Optional	PRESSURE†● Max. Load* F-R	RIM WIDTH
PONTIAC PHOENIX, 2000 SUNBIRD, SUNBIRD (FWD)						
	1992	Sunbird SE	P185/75R14		35-35	6-JJ
				P195/70R14	30-30	6-JJ
	1992-91	Sunbird, Sunbird LE	P185/75R14		35-35	6-JJ
				P195/70R14	30-30	6-JJ
	1991	Sunbird SE	P195/70R14		30-30	6-JJ
	1991-89	Sunbird GT, Turbo	P215/60R14		30-30	6-JJ
	1990	Sunbird LE, SE	P185/75R14		35-35	5½-JJ
				P195/70R14	30-30	6-JJ
	1989	Sunbird LE	P185/80R13		35-35	5½-JB
				P195/70R14	30-30	6-JJ
		Sunbird SE	P195/70R14	P215/60R14	30-30	6-JJ
	1988	Sunbird, SE ex. Turbo ..	P185/80R13		35-35	5-JB
				P195/70R14	35-35	5½-JJ
	1988-86	Sunbird SE Turbo, GT	P215/60R14		30-30	6-JJ
	1987-86	Sunbird, SE ex. Turbo ..	P175/80R13		35-35	5-JB
				P195/70R13	35-35	5½-JB
				P215/60R14	30-30	6-JJ
	1985	Sunbird ex. SE (Turbo) ..	P175/80R13	P195/70R13	35-35	5½-JB
				P205/60R14	30-30	6-JJ
		Sunbird SE (Turbo)	P205/60R14		30-30	6-JJ
	1984	2000 Sunbird, LE	P175/80R13	P195/70R13	35-35	5½-JB
				P205/60R14	35-35	6-JJ
		2000 Sunbird SE & Turbo	P205/60R14		35-35	6-JJ
	1984-83	Phoenix SJ, SE	P195/70R14		35-35	5½-JJ
		Phoenix ex. SJ, SE	P185/80R13	P205/70R13	35-35	5½-JB
	1983	2000	P175/80R13	P195/70R13	35-35	5½-JB
PORSCHE						
	1991	911 Turbo Coupe: Front	205/50ZR17		36	7-JJ
		Rear	P255/40ZR17		43	9-J
	1991-90	911 Carrera: Front	205/55ZR16		36	6-J
		Rear	225/50ZR16		43	8-J
		944S: Front	205/55ZR16		36	7-J
		Rear	225/50ZR16		36	8-J
		928: Front	225/50ZR16		29	7½-J
		Rear	245/45ZR16		43	9-J
	1989	911 Carrera: Front	205/55ZR16		29	6-J
		Rear	225/50ZR16		36	8-J
		911 Turbo: Front	205/55ZR16		29	7-J
		Rear	245/45ZR16		43	9-J
		928S4: Front	225/50ZR16		29	7-J
		Rear	245/45ZR16		43	8-J
		944	215/60ZR15		29-36	7-J
		944 Turbo: Front	225/50ZR16		36	7-J
		Rear	245/45ZR16		36	9-J
	1989-87	928S4: Front	225/50VR16		36	7-J
		Rear	245/45VR16		43	8-J
	1988	911 Carrera: Front	195/65VR15		29	7-J
		Rear	215/60VR15		36	8-J
	1988-87	924S	195/65VR15	205/55VR16	29-36	6-J
	1988-86	944	215/60VR15		29-36	7-J
		944 Turbo: Front	205/55VR16		36	7-J
		Rear	225/50VR16		36	8-J
		911 Turbo: Front	205/55VR16		29	7-J
		Rear	245/45VR16		43	9-J
	1987	911 Carrera: Front	185/70VR15	195/65VR15	29	6-J
		Rear	215/60VR15		36	7-J
	1986	928S	225/50VR16		36-44	7-J
	1986-83	911SC, Carrera: Front ...	185/70VR15		29	6-J
		Rear	215/60VR15		34	7-J
		Optional: Front	205/55VR16		29	6-J
		Rear	255/50VR16		34	7-J
	1985	944	185/70VR15		29-29	7-J
	1985-83	911 Turbo: Front	205/55VR16		29	7-J
		Rear	225/50VR16		43	8-J
		928	215/60VR15	225/50VR16	36-36	7-J
	1984-83	944	215/60VR15	205/55VR16	29-36	7-J
RENAULT						
	1987	Medallion: Sedan	P185/65R14	P195/60R14	33-33	5½-JJ
		Wagon	P185/65R14	P195/60R14	33-38	5½-JJ
		GTA sedan	195/50VR15		30-35	6-JJ
		GTA convertible	195/50VR15		30-30	6-JJ
	1987-85	Alliance ex. GTA, Encore	P155/80R13	P175/70R13	30-30	5-JB
				P185/60R14	28-28	5½-JJ
	1986-85	Sportwagon	P185/65R14		31-35	5½-JJ
	1985	Fuego	P185/65R14	P195/60R14	32-32	5½-JJ
RENAULT Continued						
	1984	Fuego	185/70R13		32-32	5½-JJ
				185/65R365‡	32-32	135 mm
		Sportwagon	175/70R13		32-35	5½-JJ
				185/65R365‡	32-35	135 mm
	1984-83	Alliance, Encore	P155/80R13	P175/70R13	30-30	5½-JB
		Fuego	185/70R13		28-32	5-JB
				165/70R365‡	28-32	135 mm
		Le Car	145SR13		32-32	4½-JB
SAAB						
	1992	900, 900S	185/65R15		36-36	5½-J
		900 Turbo	195/60R15		36-36	5½-J
		9000	195/65TR15		33-33	6-J
		9000 CD Turbo	195/65VR15		33-33	6-J
		9000 5-dr. Turbo	205/50ZR16		38-38	6½-J
	1991	900T Convertible	185/65R15		36-36	5½-J
		900 SPG Turbo	195/60VR15		38-39	5½-J
		9000 ex. Turbo	195/65R15		32-32	6-J
		9000 5-dr. Turbo	205/50ZR16		36-36	6½-J
		9000 CD Turbo	195/65R15		35-35	6-J
	1991-90	900 Series: 900, 900S	185/65R15		32-33	5½-J
		900 Turbo ex. SPG ...	185/65R15		35-36	5½-J
	1990	900 SPG	195/50ZR16		38-39	5½-J
		9000 Series: 9000S	195/65R15		38-38	6-J
		9000 Turbo	195/65VR15		32-32	6-J
		SPG	205/50ZR16		36-36	6-J
	1989-88	900 Series: All ex. Turbo	185/65R15		32-33	5½-J
		Turbo	185/65R15	195/60VR15	35-36	5½-J
		9000 Series: All ex. Turbo	185/65R15		32-33	6-J
		Turbo	205/55VR15	195/65VR15	36-36	6-J
	1987	900 Series:				
		W/8-valve engine.	185/65R15		32-33	5½-J
		W/16-valve engine:				
		All ex. SPG	195/60R15		35-36	5½-J
		SPG Turbo	195/60VR15		36-36	6-J
		9000 Series: All ex. Turbo	195/60R15		35-36	6-J
		Turbo	205/55VR15		36-36	6-J
	1986	900 Series:				
		W/8-valve engine	185/65R15		32-33	5½-J
		W/16-valve engine	195/60R15		35-36	5½-J
		W/Turbo	195/60R15		35-36	5½-J
		9000 Series:				
		Aluminum wheels	195/60VR15		38-38	6-J
		Steel wheels	185/65R15		38-38	5½-J
	1985	900, 900S	185/65R15		27-29	5½-J
		900 Turbo	195/60R15		27-29	5½-J
	1984-83	900 ex. Turbo 3-dr.	185/65SR15		27-29	5½-J
		900 Turbo 3-dr.	195/60HR15		27-29	5½-J
SATURN						
	1992-91	SL, SL1 Sedan	P175/70R14		30-28	5-JJ
		SL2 Sedan, SC Coupe ...	P195/60R15		30-28	6-JJ
STERLING						
	1988-87	825S-SL	195/65VR15		32-32	6-J
SUBARU						
	1992	Legacy: 4-dr.: FWD	P185/70HR14		30-29	5-,5½-JJ
		AWD	P185/70HR14		32-32	5-J,5½-JJ
		AWD Turbo	P195/60HR15		32-32	6-JJ
		Wagon: FWD	P185/70HR14		30-32	5-J,5½-JJ
		AWD	P185/70HR14		32-35	5-J,5½-JJ
		Loyale: 4-dr.	175/70SR13		28-28	5-J
		Wagon: FWD	175/70SR13		28-32	5-J
		4WD	165/SR13		28-32	5-J
		SVX	P225/50VR16		33-28	7½-JJ
	1992-91	Justy ex. GL	145/SR12		28-28	4-JB
		Justy GL	165/65SR13		28-28	5-J
	1991	Legacy: L	175/70R14		30-29	5-J
		LS, LSi	185/70R14		32-32	5½-J
		Loyale: FWD	175/70R13		28-28	5-J
		4WD	165/70R13		28-32	5-J
		XT GL	185/70R13		28-28	5-J
	1991-88	XT-6 FWD	195/60R14		33-28	5½-JJ
		XT-6 4WD	205/60R14		33-28	5½-JJ
	1990	Legacy: FWD	P175/70R14		30-29	5-J
		4WD	P185/70R14		32-32	5½-J
		Loyale ex. Turbo,				
		4WD wagon	175/70SR13		28-28	5-J
		4WD wagon	165/SR13		28-32	5-J

Tire sizes and tire pressures represent the car manufacturer's recommendations (for normal speeds).
†Sustained high speeds: **Numeric and Alphanumeric** sizes, add 4 psi (do not exceed 32 psi for load range "B", 36 psi for load range "C", 40 psi for load range "D"); **P-Metric** sizes, add 3 psi (do not exceed 35 psi for Standard Load, 41 psi for Extra Load "XL" tire).
European metric sizes have maximum inflation pressure of either 32 or 36 psi, depending on construction. Refer to maximum inflation limit stamped on tire sidewall.
*For minimum load pressure, refer to tire decal. •Cars equipped with Trailer Tow Option, refer to tire decal.

MAKE	YEAR	MODEL	ORIGINAL EQUIPMENT SIZE Std.	Optional	PRESSURE†• Max. Load* F-R	RIM WIDTH
SUBARU Continued						
	1990	Loyale Turbo:				
		FWD	175/70R13		28-28	5-J
		4WD	185/70HR13		28-28	5-J
		XT	185/70R13		28-28	5-J
	1990-89	Justy: DL FWD	145SR12		28-28	4-JB
		4WD	P165/65R13		28-28	5-JB
		GL	P165/65R13		28-28	5-JB
	1989-88	XT: DL	165SR13		28-28	5-J
		GL	185/70HR13		28-28	5-J
		Others ex. XT-6:				
		2WD: DL ex. wagon	155SR13		28-28	4½-J
		DL wagon	P155/80R13		28-32	5-J
		GL	175/70SR13		28-28	5-J
		GL-10, Turbo	175/70HR13		28-28	5-J
		4WD: DL ex. Hatchback	155SR13		28-28	5-J
		DL Hatchback	165SR13		28-28	4½-J
		GL ex. wagon	175/70SR13		28-28	5-J
		GL wagon	185/70SR13		28-32	5-J
		Turbo	185/70HR13		28-28	5-J
	1988-87	Justy	145SR12		28-28	4-JB
	1987-85	2WD: DL, Std. Model	155SR13		26-26[1]	4½
		GL, GL-10	175/70HR13		28-28[1]	5-J
		XT Coupe DL	165SR13		28-28	5-J
		GL, Turbo	185/70HR13		28-28	5-J
		4WD: DL, Std. Model	165SR13		28-28	4½-J
		GL, Turbo Brat	185/70HR13		28-28	5-J
		XT Turbo	185/70HR13		26-28	5-J
	1984-83	2WD: DL, Std. Model	155SR13		26-26[1]	4½
		GL	175/70SR13		26-26[1]	5-J
		4WD: DL, Std. Model	165SR13		26-26[1]	4½-J
		GL, Brat	185/70SR13		26-26[1]	5-J

1 Wagon and Brat with full load, 32

MAKE	YEAR	MODEL	ORIGINAL EQUIPMENT SIZE Std.	Optional	PRESSURE†• Max. Load* F-R	RIM WIDTH
SUZUKI						
	1992	Samurai: 2WD	P195/75R15		20-26	5½-J
		4WD	P205/70R15		20-26	5½-J
		Swift 4-dr. Canada 1.3L				
		ex. GT	P165/65R13		26-26	4½-J
		Swift: 1.6L	P165/65R14		28-28	—
		Ex. GT	P155/70R13		29-29	4½-J
		Sidekick: 2WD	P195/75R15		23-23	5½-JJ
		4WD	P205/75R15		23-23	5½-JJ
	1992-91	Swift GT	P175/60R14		26-26	5-J
	1991	Samurai	P195/75R15		20-26	5½-J
		Sidekick: 2WD	P195/75R15		26-26	5½-JJ
		4WD	P205/75R15		23-23	5½-JJ
		Swift ex. GT	P155/70R13		28-28	4½-J
	1990-89	Sidekick	205/75R15		23-23	6-JJ
		Swift: GLX	P155/70R13		28-28	5-J
		GTI	P175/60R14		26-26	5-J
	1990-86	Samurai	P205/70R15		20-26	5½-J
	1988-85	SA310	P145/80R12		31-31	4½-B
		W/Turbo	P165/70R12		26-26	4½-B
TOYOTA						
	1992	Camry: 2.2L	P195/70HR14		29-29	5½-JJ
		3.0L	P205/65HR15		32-32	6-JJ
		Celica: 1.6L	P185/65R14		29-28	6-JJ
		2.0L	215/50VR15		32-30	6½-JJ
		2.2L	205/60HR14		29-28	6-JJ
				205/55VR15	33-32	6-JJ
				215/50VR15	32-30	6½-JJ
		MR2: 2.0L Front	195/60VR14		29	6-JJ
		Rear		205/60VR14	33	7-JJ
		2.2L Front	195/60HR14		29	6-JJ
		Rear		205/60HR14	33	7-JJ
		Paseo	175/65HR14		26-26	5½-J
				185/60HR14	26-26	5½-J,JJ
		Tercel	P145/80R13		32-32	4½-J
				155/SR13	32-32	4½-J
		Canada	P155/80R13		32-32	4½-J
	1992-91	Supra	205/55R16	225/50ZR16	33-36	7-J
	1992-90	Corolla FWD	155SR13		28-28	5-J
				P155/80R13	29-29	5-J
				175/70SR13	28-28	5-J
				P175/70R13	29-29	5-J
				185/60R14	26-26	5½-JJ
		Corolla 4WD: Sedan	165SR13		32-32	5-J
		Wagon	165SR13		32-32	5-J

MAKE	YEAR	MODEL	ORIGINAL EQUIPMENT SIZE Std.	Optional	PRESSURE†• Max. Load* F-R	RIM WIDTH
TOYOTA Continued						
	1992-89	Cressida	195/65R15		32-32	6-JJ
	1991	Celica	165SR13		30-29	5-JJ
				185/70R13	28-26	5½-JJ
				185/65R13	32-29	5½-JJ
				215/50VR15	30-28	6½-JJ
		Celica GT-S	215/50VR15		32-30	6½-JJ
				185/70SR13	26-26	5-J
	1991-89	Tercel	P145/80R13		32-32	4½-J
				P155/80R13	28-28	5-J
				155/SR13	28-28	5-J
		Camry, 4-cyl.	185/70SR14	P185/70R14	30-30	5½-JJ
		V6	195/60R15		32-28	5½-JJ
	1990	Supra	205/55R16	225/50R16	36-32	7-JJ
		Celica: ST	165SR13		30-29	5-JJ
		GT	185/65R14		32-29	6-JJ
		GT-S	215/50VR15		32-30	6½-JJ
	1989	Supra	225/50VR16		32-32	7-JJ
		Corolla 4WD	165SR13		30-30	5-J
				185/70SR13	26-26	5-J
		MR2	185/60R14		30-30	5½-JJ
	1989-87	Corolla FWD	155/SR13		28-28	4½-J
				175/70SR13	26-26	5-J
				P155/80R13	28-28	4½-J
				P175/70HR13	32-32	5½-J
				P185/60HR14	32-32	5½-J
	1989-86	Celica	165SR13		30-26	5-J
				185/70SR13	28-26	5½-J
				205/60R14	26-26	6-JJ
				205/60VR14	30-30	6-JJ
	1988	Cressida	205/60R15		30-30	6-JJ
	1988-87	Tercel ex. wagon	145/80R13		32-32	4½-J
				155/SR13	28-28	4½-J
		Tercel Wagon	155/SR13		28-28	4½-J
				175/70SR13	26-26	5-J
		Camry	185/70SR14		30-30	5½-JJ
		Corolla FX16	P175/70HR13		28-28	5-J
				P185/60HR14	28-28	5½-J
		MR2	185/60R14		30-30	5-J
				185R14LT/D	26-65	5½-JJ
	1988-86	Supra 3.0L	225/50VR16		28-28	7-JJ
	1987-85	Corolla RWD	185/70SR13		28-28	5-J
		Corolla GTS	195//60R14		26-26	5½-J
		Cressida	195/70SR14		28-28	5½-J
				205/60R15	28-28	6-JJ
	1986	Camry	185/70SR13		30-30	5-J
		Tercel	145SR13		28-28	4½-J
				P195/75R14	35-35	4½-J
				175/70SR13	40-40	5½-JJ
		Corolla FWD	155R13	P155/80R13	28-28	4½-J
				175/70SR13	26-26	5-J
	1986-85	MR2	185/60R14		30-30	5-J
		Supra 2.8L	205/60R15		27-27	6-JJ
				225/60R14	27-27	7-JJ
	1985-84	Corolla: FWD Gas	155SR13		28-28	5-J
				175/70SR13	26-26	5-J
		Diesel	165SR13		28-28	5-J
		Celica	175SR14	185/70SR14	27-27	5½-J
				225/60HR14	27-27	7-JJ
	1985-83	Tercel ex. wagon	145SR13		32-32	4½-J
				155SR13	26-26	4½-J
				165/70SR13	28-28	5-J
		Tercel wagon	155SR13		28-28	4½-J
				175/70SR13	26-26	5-J
		Camry	165SR13		30-30	5-J
				185/70SR13	30-30	5½-J
	1984-83	Corolla RWD	165/SR13		26-26	4½-J
				185/70SR13	26-26	5-J
		Cressida	195/70SR14		27-27	5½-J
		Starlet	145SR13		28-28	4½-J
		Supra	195/70SR14		27-27	5½-J
				225/60HR14	27-27	7-JJ
	1983	Celica	185/70SR14		26-26	5½-J
			175SR14		26-26	5½-J
VOLKSWAGEN						
	1992	Golf GL	175/70R13		—	5½-J
	1992-91	Cabriolet	185/60R14		29-26	6-J
		Corrado	205/50VR15		33-29	6½-J
		Fox: 2-door	155/80SR13		24-26	5-J
		Sedan & Wagon	175/70SR13		24-28	5-J

Tire sizes and tire pressures represent the car manufacturer's recommendations (for normal speeds).
†Sustained high speeds: **Numeric and Alphanumeric** sizes, add 4 psi (do not exceed 32 psi for load range ''B'', 36 psi for load range ''C'', 40 psi for load range ''D''); **P-Metric** sizes, add 3 psi (do not exceed 35 psi for Standard Load, 41 psi for Extra Load ''XL'' tire). **European metric** sizes have maximum inflation pressure of either 32 or 36 psi, depending on construction. Refer to maximum inflation limit stamped on tire sidewall.
*For minimum load pressure, refer to tire decal.   •Cars equipped with Trailer Tow Option, refer to tire decal.

MAKE	YEAR	MODEL	ORIGINAL EQUIPMENT SIZE Std.	Optional	PRES-SURE†• Max. Load* F-R	RIM WIDTH	MAKE	YEAR	MODEL	ORIGINAL EQUIPMENT SIZE Std.	Optional	PRES-SURE†• Max. Load* F-R	RIM WIDTH
VOLKSWAGEN Continued							**VOLVO**						
	1992-91	Golf: GTI	185/60R14		29-25	6-J		1992	960	195/65R15		36-36	6-J
		GTI w/16V	195/50VR15		29-29	6½-J		1992-91	240: Sedan	185/70R14		36-36	5½-J
		Jetta: GL, Carat	185/60R14		32-32	6-J			Wagon	185R14		36-36	5½-J
		GLI 16V	185/55VR15		33-33	6-J			940 GLE	185/65R15		36-36	6-J
	1992-90	Passat CL, GL	195/60VR14		33-33	6-J			940 Turbo	205/55VR16		36-36	6½-J
	1991	Golf GL	175/70SR13		29-25	5½-J		1991	740 Turbo	195/60R15		36-36	6-J
	1991-90	Jetta Diesel	185/60R14		29-29	6-J			940 SE	195/65R15		36-36	6-J
	1990	Cabriolet	185/60R14		28-28	6-J		1991-90	740 ex. Turbo	185/65R15		36-36	6-J
		Corrado	195/50VR15		41-36	6-J		1990	740 Turbo	205/55VR16		36-36	6½-J
		Golf: GL	175/70R13		29-25	5½-J			780	195/65HR15		36-36	7-J
		GTI	185/60R14		29-25	6-J		1990-86	240 Sedan: (U.S.)	185/70R14		36-36	5½-J
		GTI w/16V	195/50VR15		29-25	6½-J			(Canada)	P185/75R14		35-35	5½-J
		Jetta: Carat, GL	185/60VR14		29-29	6-J			240 Wagon: (U.S.)	185/SR14		36-36	5½-J
		GLI w/16V	185/55VR15		29-29	6-J			(Canada)	P185/75R14		35-35	5½-J
	1990-88	Fox: 2-door	155/SR13		24-26	5-J			760 GLE	185/65R15		36-36	6-J
		4-door	175/70SR13		24-26	5½-J			760 Turbo	195/60R15		36-36	6-JJ
		Fox wagon	175/70SR13		24-28	5½-J		1989	780 ex. Turbo	205/60R15		36-36	6-JJ
	1989	Cabriolet	185/60HR15		28-28	6-J			780 Turbo	205/60R15		36-36	7-JJ
	1989-88	Jetta Carat, GLI w/16V	185/60HR14		29-29	6-J		1989-86	740 GL, GLE, Diesel	185/70R14		30-36	6-J
	1989-87	Golf GL, Jetta, Jetta GL	175/70SR13		29-25	5½-J			740 Turbo	195/60R15		36-36	6-J
		Golf GT, GTI, GLI	185/60HR14		29-26	6-J		1988-87	780	205/60R15		36-36	6-JJ
		W/16-valve eng.	205/55VR14		29-25	6-J		1985-83	All ex. 700 Series:				
	1988	Quantum GL	195/60HR14		30-30	6-J			Sedan: DL (U.S.)	175R-14		26-27	5½-J
		Syncro	195/60HR14		30-33	6-J			GL (U.S.)	185/70R14		26-27	5½-J
	1988-86	Cabriolet	175/70SR13	185/60HR14	28-28	5½-,6-J			DL, GL Canada)	P185/75R14		26-28	5½-J
	1987	Fox: 2-door	155/80SR13		24-26	5-J			Diesel	185/70R14		26-27	5½-J
		4-door, wagon	175/70SR13		24-28	5-J			GLT, Turbo	195/60R15		26-27	6-J
		Scirocco w/16 valve eng.	185/60HR14		29-26	6-J			Wagon: DL, GL (U.S.)	185R-14		27-30	5½-J
		Quantum	185/70SR13		30-30	5½-J			DL, GL (Canada)	P185/75R14		26-30	5½-J
		Syncro, optional	195/60HR14		30-33	6-J			Diesel	185R-14		26-30	5½-J
		Scirocco	175/70SR13		29-26	5½-J			GLT, Turbo	195/60R15		27-27	6-J
	1986	Scirocco	175/70HR13		27-27	5½-J			700 Series ex. Diesel	185/65R15		28-28	6-J
		Quantum	195/60HR14		28-28	6-J			700 Series Diesel	185/70R14		25-25	6-J
	1986-85	Golf, Jetta	155/80SR13		29-26	5-J							
				175/70SR13	29-26	5½-J							
		GTI, GLI	185/60HR14		29-26	6-J							
	1984	Jetta GLI	185/60HR14		27-31	6-J							
	1984-83	Rabbit: L, LS	155/80R13		27-31	5-J							
		LS Optional	175/70R13		27-31	5-J							
		GL	175/70R13		27-31	5-J	**YUGO**						
		GTI	185/60HR14		27-31	6-J		1990	All	155/70R13		24-27	5-K
		Convertible	175/70SR13		27-27	5-J		1989-86	All ex. GVX	145SR13		24-27	4½-J
		Jetta, Scirocco	175/70SR13		27-27	5½-J			GVX	155/70SR13		24-27	5-K
		Quantum	185/70SR13		28-28	5½							

Tire sizes and tire pressures represent the car manufacturer's recommendations (for normal speeds).
†Sustained high speeds: **Numeric and Alphanumeric** sizes, add 4 psi (do not exceed 32 psi for load range "B", 36 psi for load range "C", 40 psi for load range "D"). **P-Metric** sizes, add 3 psi (do not exceed 35 psi for Standard Load, 41 psi for Extra Load "XL" tire).
*For minimum load pressure, refer to tire decal.

MAKE	YEAR	MODEL	GVWR	ORIGINAL EQUIPMENT SIZE Std.	Optional	PRESSURE† Max. Load* F-R	RIM WIDTH

CHEVROLET, GMC TRUCKS (ex. Blazer, Jimmy)

MAKE	YEAR	MODEL	GVWR	Std.	Optional	Pressure F-R	RIM WIDTH
	1992	Lumina APV		P205/70R15		36-36	6-JJ
		C1500 Pickup		P225/75R15	P235/75R15	36-36	7-JJ
					P225/70R15	36-36	7-JJ
		C1500 Suburban		P235/75R15XL		35-35	7-JJ
		C2500 Pickup		LT225/75R16/C		36-36	6½-JJ
					LT225/75R16/D	36-36	6½-JJ
					LT245/75R16/E	36-36	6½-JJ
		C2500 Suburban		LT245/75R16E		36-36	6½-JJ
		K1500 Pickup		LT225/75R16/C		36-36	6½-JJ
		K2500 Pickup		LT225/75R16/C,D		36-36	6½-JJ
					LT245/75R16/C,E	36-36	6½-JJ
					LT265/75R16/C	36-36	6½-JJ
		K1500 Yukon		LT225/75R16/D		36-36	6½-JJ
		K2500 Yukon		LT245/75R16E		36-36	6½-JJ
		G10, -1500 Van		P205/75R15		35-35	6-JJ
		G20, -2500 Van		P225/75R15		35-35	6-JJ
		M10, -15 Astro, Safari:					
		Regular Van		P205/75R15		35-35	6-JJ
		2WD		P245/60R15		35-35	6½-JJ
		All others		P215/75R15		35-35	6-JJ
		S10, 15 Pickup:					
		2WD		P195/75R14	P215/65R15	36-36	6-JJ
		4WD		P205/75R15	P205/75R14	36-36	6-JJ
					P235/75R15	36-36	6-JJ
		S10, 15 Blazer		P205/75R15	P205/75R14	36-36	6-JJ
		4WD			P235/75R15	36-36	7-JJ
	1991-90	APV Cargo Van		P205/70R14		35-35	6-JJ
		Lumina APV		P205/70R14		35-35	6-JJ
					P195/70R15	35-35	6-JJ
	1991-89	C-1500 Pickup:					
		Regular Cab	5600-6100	P225/75R15		35-35	6-JJ
					P235/75R15	35-35	6-JJ
		Extended Cab	6200	P235/75R15		35-35	6-JJ
	1991-88	K-1500 Pickup:					
		Regular Cab	5600	LT225/75R16C		45-45	6.50,7.00
				LT265/75R16		35-35	7.00
		Extended Cab	6200	LT245/75R16/C		45-45	6.50
		C-2500 Pickup	7200	LT225/75R16/D		50-65	6.50
				LT245/75R16/C		40-55	6.50
				LT245/75R16/E		45-55	6.50
		K-2500 Pickup: Reg. Cab		LT225/75R16/D		55-65	6.50
				LT245/75R16/E		45-55	6.50
		Extended Cab		LT245/75R16/C		45-50	6.50
		G10, -1500 Van, Vandura	4900	P195/75R15	P205/75R15	35-35	6-,6½-JJ
					P215/75R15	35-35	6-,6½-JJ
		G20, -2500 Van, Vandura	6600	P225/75R15	P235/75R15	35-35	6-,6½-JJ
		G10, -1500 Sportvan	5600, 6000	P205/75R15	P215/75R15	35-35	6-,6½-JJ
		G20, -2500 Sportvan	6600, 6850	P225/75R15	P235/75R15	35-35	6-,6½-JJ
		Suburban: R, V10, -1500		P235/75R15		32-35	6,7,8-JJ
					P235/75R15XL	35-41	6,7,8-JJ
		R-, V20, -2500		LT235/85R16/E		45-55	6.50
	1990	M10, -15 Astro, Safari:					
		Regular Van		P205/75R15		35-35	6-JJ
					P215/75R15	35-35	6-JJ
					P245/60HR15	35-35	6½-JJ
		Extended Van		P215/75R15		35-35	6-JJ
					P245/60HR15	35-35	6½-JJ
		S10, -15 Pickup: 2WD		P195/75R14	P205/75R14	35-35	6-JJ
					P215/65R15	35-35	7-JJ
		4WD		P205/75R15	P205/75R15	35-35	6-JJ
					P235/75R15	35-35	7-JJ
		G10, -1500 Van, Vandura		P205/75R15	P215/75R15	35-35	6-JJ
	1989	M10, -15 Astro, Safari Van		P205/75R15		35-35	6-JJ
					P245/60HR15	35-35	6-JJ
		S10, -15 Pickup: 2WD		P195/75R14	P205/75R14	35-35	6-JJ
					P215/65R15	35-35	7-JJ
		4WD		P195/75R15	P205/75R15	35-35	6-JJ
					P235/75R15	35-35	7-JJ
	1988	M10/15 Astro, Safari Van		P195/75R15	P205/75R15	35-35	6-,6½-JJ
					P245/60R15	35-35	6½-JJ
		S10, -15 Pickup: 2WD		P195/75R14	P205/75R14	35-35	6-JJ
					P215/65R15	35-35	7-JJ
		4WD		P195/75R15		35-35	6-JJ
					P205/75R15	35-35	6-,7-JJ
					P235/75R15	35-35	7-JJ
		C-1500 Pickup: Regular Cab, Gas	5200, 5600	P205/75R15		35-35	6-JJ
					P225/75R15	32-35	6-,7-JJ
					P235/75R15	32-35	7-JJ
		Regular Cab, Diesel	5200, 5600	P235/75R15		35-35	6-JJ
		Extended Cab	6000	P235/75R15		35-35	7-JJ

CHEVROLET, GMC TRUCKS (ex. Blazer, Jimmy) Continued

MAKE	YEAR	MODEL	GVWR	Std.	Optional	Pressure F-R	RIM WIDTH
	1987-85	M10/15 Astro, Safari Van		P195/75R15	P205/75R15	35-35	6-JJ
		G10, -1500 Van, Vandura		P195/75R15	P205/75R15	35-35	6-JJ
					P215/75R15	35-35	6-JJ
					P225/75R15	35-35	6-JJ
					P235/75R15	35-35	6-JJ
	1987-83	S10, -15 Pickup: 2WD		P195/75R14	P205/75R14	35-35	6-JJ
					P215/65R15	35-35	7-JJ
					P225/75R15	35-35	6-JJ
					P235/75R15	35-35	6-JJ
		4WD		P195/75R15	P205/75R15	35-35	6-JJ
					P235/75R15	35-35	7-JJ
		R10, C10, -1500 Pickup		P195/75R15	P205/75R15	35-35	6-JJ
					P225/75R15	35-35	6-JJ
					P235/75R15	35-35	6-JJ
					LR60-15	32-32	7-JJ
						35-35	6-JJ
		V10, K10, -1500 Pickup		P235/75R15	LR60-15	32-32	7-JJ
					31×10.50R15LT	35-35	7-JJ
		G10, -1500 Sportvan, Rally		P205/75R15	P215/75R15	35-35	6-JJ
					P225/75R15	35-35	6-JJ
					P235/75R15	35-35	6-JJ
		Suburban: R10, C10, -1500		P235/75R15		35-35	6-JJ
					P235/75R15XL	41-41	6-JJ
		V10, K10, -1500		P215/75R15	P235/75R15	35-35	6-JJ
					P235/75R15XL	41-41	6-JJ
	1984-83	G10, -1500 Van, Vandura		FR78-15		32-32	6-JJ
					P205/75R15	35-35	6-JJ
					P215/75R15	35-35	6-JJ

CHEVROLET BLAZER, GMC JIMMY

MAKE	YEAR	MODEL	GVWR	Std.	Optional	Pressure F-R	RIM WIDTH
	1992	K1500 Blazer, Jimmy		LT225/75R16/C		35-35	7-JJ
	1991-90	S/T10, -15		P205/75R15		35-35	6-JJ[1]
					P235/75R15	35-35	7-JJ
		V10, -1500		P235/75R15		35-35	6-JJ
					31X10.5R15	35-35	7.00[2]
	1989-88	V10, -1500		P235/75R15		35-35	6-JJ
					P235/75R15XL	41-41	6-JJ
	1989-83	S10, -15		P195/75R15	P205/75R15	35-35	6-JJ
					P235/75R15	35-35	7-JJ
	1987	V10, -1500		P215/75R15		35-35	6-JJ
					P235/75R15	35-35	7-JJ
	1986-83	K10, -20; K1500-2500		P215/75R15	P235/75R15	35-35	6-JJ

1 Rally & aluminum wheels, 15″×7″ **2** Rally wheels, 15″×8″

DODGE-PLYMOUTH TRUCKS

MAKE	YEAR	MODEL	GVWR	Std.	Optional	Pressure F-R	RIM WIDTH
	1992	Caravan, CV, Voyager:					
		Short WB		P195/75R14		35-35	5½-JJ
					P205/70R14	35-35	5½,6-JJ
		Long WB & 4WD		P205/70R15		35-35	6-JJ
		Dakota		LT215/75R15D		35-40	6-JJ
				P185/75R14SL			6-JJ
				P205/75R15			6-JJ
	1992-91	B150	5300	P205/75R15	P225/75R15	35-35	6½-,7-JJ
					P235/75R15XL	35-41	6½-,7-JJ
		B250	6010	P225/75R15		35-35	6½-,7-JJ
					P235/75R15XL	35-41	6½-,7-JJ
		Ram 50: 2WD ex. LE		P195/75R14		35-35	6-JJ
					P205/75R14	35-35	6-JJ
		LE		P205/75R14		35-35	6-JJ
		PowerRam 50: 4WD		P225/75R15		35-35	6-JJ
	1992-90	Ram Pickup: D150S	5200	P205/75R15		35-35	6-,6½-,7-JJ
					P235/75R15XL	35-41	6-,6½-,7-JJ
		D150	5500	P215/75R15		35-35	6-,6½-,7-JJ
					P235/75R15XL	35-41	6-,6½-,7-JJ
		W150 W150S	6400	P235/75R15XL		35-41	6-,6½-,7-JJ
		D250, W250	7500	LT215/85R16/D		50-65	6.00
					LT235/85R16/E	45-80	6.00
		Ram Club Cab Pickup:					
		D150, W150	6200, 6400	P235/75R15XL		35-41	6-,6½-,7-JJ
		D250, W250	7400, 7500	LT215/85R16/D		50-65	6.00
			8510, 7500	LT235/85R16/E		45-80	6.00
	1992-86	AD150, AW150	5600	P235/75R15XL		35-41	6½-JJ[1]
			6000, 6400	P235/75R15XL		41-41	6½-JJ[1]
	1991	Dakota: 2WD ex. Sport Cab		P195/75R15	P205/75R15	30-35	6-JJ
					P215/75R15	30-35	6-JJ
		4WD ex. Sport Cab		P205/75R15	P215/75R15	35-35	6-JJ
					P235/75R15XL	35-35	6-JJ
		2WD Sport Cab		P215/75R15		35-35	6-JJ
		4WD Sport Cab		P235/75R15XL		35-41	6-JJ

Tire sizes and tire pressures represent the car manufacturer's recommendations (for normal speeds).
†Sustained high speeds: **Numeric and Alphanumeric** sizes, add 4 psi (do not exceed 32 psi for load range "B", 36 psi for load range "C", 40 psi for load range "D"); **P-Metric** sizes, add 3 psi (do not exceed 35 psi for Standard Load, 41 psi for Extra Load "XL" tire).
*For minimum load pressure, refer to tire decal.

DODGE-PLYMOUTH TRUCKS Continued

MAKE	YEAR	MODEL	GVWR	EQUIP. Std.	SIZE Optional	PRESSURE† Max. Load* F-R	RIM WIDTH
1991		Caravan, Voyager FWD:					
		Base, Std. LE		P195/75R14	P205/70R14	35-35	5 1/2-JJ
					P205/70R15	35-35	6 1/2-JJ
		Others		P205/70R15		35-35	6 1/2-JJ
		Caravan, Voyager 4WD		P205/70R15		35-35	6 1/2-JJ
		Caravan Cargo Van:					
		2WD	4220	195/75R14		35-35	5 1/2-JJ
			5060		LT195/75R15	36-36	6.00
		2WD	5290	LT195/75R15		36-36	6.00
		4WD	4220	P205/70R15		35-35	6-JJ
1991-89		Caravan, Voyager	4060-4910	P195/75R14	P205/70R14	35-35	5 1/2-JJ
					LT195/75R14	36-36	6.00
					P205/70R15	35-35	6 1/2-JJ
			5040-5090	LT195/75R15		36-36	6.00
1990-89		Dakota: 2WD	1250	P195/75R15	P205/75R15	30-35	6-JJ
					P215/75R15	30-35	6-JJ
		4WD		P195/75R15	P205/75R15	35-35	6-JJ
					P235/75R15XL	35-41	6-JJ
1990-83		B150, PB150					
		Van, wagon	4700, 5100	P195/75R15	P205/75R15	35-35	5 1/2-JJ
					P225/75R15	35-35	6 1/2-JJ,7-JJ
					P235/75R15XL	35-41	6 1/2-JJ,7-JJ
			5300, 5350, 5400, 6010	P205/75R15		35-35	5 1/2-JJ
					P235/75R15XL	35-41	6 1/2-JJ,7-JJ
		B250, PB250	6010, 6050, 6100	P225/75R15	P235/75R15	35-35	6 1/2-JJ,7-JJ
					P235/75R15XL	41-41	6 1/2-JJ HD
			6400	P235/75R15	P235/75R15XL	41-41	6 1/2-JJ HD
		Maxivan	6400	P235/75R15XL		41-41	6 1/2-JJ HD
1989		Raider: 2.6L (156)		P225/75R15		35-35	6-JJ
		3.L (181)		P235/75R15		35-35	6-JJ
					P235/75R15	35-35	6-JJ
		D100, D150	6300, 6400	P205/75R15		35-35	5 1/2-JJ
					P235/75R15XL	35-41	6 1/2-JJ
		W100, W150	6300, 6400	P235/75R15XL		35-41	6 1/2-JJ
		D250, W250	6600, 6900	LT215/85R16/C		45-50	6.00
				LT215/85R16/D		45-65	6.00
				LT235/85R16/E		45-80	6.00
				7.50-16LT/D		50-60	6.00
		D250	7500	LT235/85R16/E		45-80	6.00
				7.50-16LT/D		45-60	6.00
		W250	7500	LT215/85R16/D		55-65	6.00
				LT235/85R16/E		45-80	6.00
				7.50-16LT/D		45-60	6.00
		D250, W250	8510	LT235/85R16/E		45-80	6.00
1988-87		Raider		P225/75R15		26-35	6-JJ
		Ram 50 Pickup: 2WD		P195/75R14		26-35	6-JJ
					LT195/75R14	36-65	6.00
		4WD		P225/75R15		26-35	6-JJ
		Caravan, Voyager, Mini Ram	4040, 4510	P195/75R14	P205/70R14	35-35	5 1/2-JJ
		Mini Ram	4880	LT195/75R14		36-36	5.50
		Dakota: 2WD	1250	P195/75R14		35-35	6-JJ
					P205/75R15	35-35	6-JJ
					P215/75R15	35-35	6-JJ
					LT215/75R15	35-35	6.00 HD
			1800	P205/75R15	P215/75R15	35-35	6-JJ
		4WD	1450	P195/75R15	P205/75R15	35-35	6-JJ
					P235/75R15XL	35-41	6-JJ
			2000	P235/75R15XL		35-41	6-JJ
1988-86		D100, D150	4950	P195/75R15	P205/75R15	35-35	6 1/2-JJ
					P235/75R15XL	41-41	6 1/2-JJ
			5000	P205/75R15		35-35	6 1/2-JJ
					P235/75R15XL	41-41	6 1/2-JJ
			5900	P235/75R15XL		41-41	6 1/2-JJ
		W100, W150	6300, 6400	P235/75R15XL		41-41	6 1/2-JJ
1986-84		Caravan, Voyager, Mini Ram Van		P185/75R14	P195/75R14	35-35	5 1/2-JJ
					P205/70R14	35-35	5 1/2-JJ
1986 82		D150, W150	4800	P195/75R15	P205/75R15	35-35	5 1/2-JJ
					P235/75R15	35-35	6 1/2-JJ
					P255/70R15	35-35	6 1/2-JJ
			5850, 6050	P235/75R15	P255/70R15	35-35	6 1/2-JJ
					LR60-15	32-32	7-JJ
		W150	6010	P235/75R15		35-35	6 1/2-JJ
1985		AD150		P235/75R15		35-35	6 1/2-JJ
					P255/70R15	35-35	7-JJ
		AW150		P235/75R15XL		41-41	6 1/2-JJ
1984		AD150, AW150		P235/75R15	P255/70R15	35-35	6 1/2-JJ
1984-83		Rampage Scamp		P175/75R13		35-35	5-JB
					P195/60R14	35-35	5 1/2-JJ
		Rampage Sport, Scamp GT		P195/60R14		35-35	5 1/2-JJ
1983		AD150, PD100	5300	P235/75R15		35-35	6 1/2-JJ
					P255/70R15	35-35	7-JJ
		AW150, PW150	5850, 6010	P235/75R15		35-35	6 1/2-JJ
					P255/70R15	35-35	7-JJ

1 Aluminum or spoked wheels, 15"×7"

FORD TRUCKS (ex. Bronco, Explorer)

MAKE	YEAR	MODEL	GVWR	EQUIP. Std.	SIZE Optional	PRESSURE† Max. Load* F-R	RIM WIDTH
	1992	F-150 Pickup:					
		4×2	5250-5450	P215/75R15SL		35-35	6-J
			5250-6250	P235/75R15XL		35-41	6-,7 1/2-J
		4×4	6100-6250	P235/75R15XL		35-41	6-,7 1/2-J
					P265/75R15SC	30-30	7 1/2-J
		F-250 Pickup:					
		4×2	6600	LT215/85R16D		51-58	7-K
					LT235/85R16E	44-57	7-K
					7.50R16D	40-50	7-K
			8600	LT235/85R16E		44-80	7-,7 1/2-K
					LT235/85R16E	58-80	7-K
			8600-8800	LT235/85R16E		51-80	7-,7 1/2-K
		4×4	8800	LT235/85R16E		51-80	7-,7 1/2-K
		E-150 Van, Wagon	5500	P215/75R15SL		35-35	6-,7-J
					P225/75R15SL	35-35	6-J
					P235/75R15XL	41-41	6-J
			6500-6700	P235/75R15XL		41-41	6-,7-J
		E-250 Van, Wagon	7200	LT225/75R16D		50-55	7-K,7-J
					LT225/75R16E	50-55	7-K
			8450	LT225/75R16E		55-80	7-K,7-J
			8550	LT225/75R16E		55-80	7-K
			7300	LT215/85R16E		50-60	7-K,7-J
					LT225/75R16E	50-60	7-K
		Ranger: 4×2	4100-4440	P195/70R14SL		35-35	5 1/2,6-JJ
			4100-4700	P215/70R14SL		35-35	5 1/2,6-JJ
		4×4	4400-4980	P215/75R15SL		35-35	6-,7-JJ
			4640-4980	P235/75R15SL		30-35	7-JJ
	1992-88	Aerostar		P215/70R14		35-35	5 1/2,6-JJ
					P215/75R14	35-35	6-JJ
	1991-90	Ranger 4×2 Pickup		P195/70R14	P215/70R14	35-35	5 1/2-JJ
	1991-89	Ranger 4×4 Pickup		P215/75R15		35-35	6-JJ
					P235/75R14	35-35	6-JJ
		F-250	under 8500	LT215/85R16E		57-51	6.00
					LT235/85R16E	44-44	6.00
					7.50R-16LT/D	45-50	6.00
		E150 Regular Van		P215/75R15		35-35	6-JK
					P225/75R15	35-35	6-JK
					P235/75R15XL	41-41	6-JK
		E150 Super Van, Wagon		P235/75R15XL		41-41	6-JK
	1991-84	F-150 4×2 Regular Cab	5250, 6250	P215/75R15		35-35	5 1/2,6-JK
					P235/75R15XL	35-41	6-JK
		F-150 4×2 Supercab	6050-6250	P235/75R15XL		35-41	6-JK
		F-150 4×4	6100-6450	P235/75R15XL		35-41	6-JK
	1989	Ranger "S" Pickup		P195/70R14	P215/70R14	35-35	5 1/2-JJ
		Ranger 4×2 Pickup ex. "S"			P215/70R14	35-35	5 1/2-JJ
	1988	Ranger "S" Pickup		P195/70R14	P215/70R14	35-35	5 1/2-JJ
		Ranger 4×2 Pickup		P195/70R14	P215/70R14	35-35	5 1/2-JJ
		4×4 Pickup		P215/70R14		35-35	5 1/2-JJ
	1988-85	F-250 Regular Cab	6300-6600	LT215/85R16/C	LT215/85R16/D	51-51	6.00
					LT235/85R16/D,E	44-44	6.00
					7.50R16LT/D	45-50	6.00
	1988-84	F-150 Regular Cab	4700-4900	P195/75R15	P215/75R15	35-35	5 1/2,6-JK
					P235/75R15XL	35-41	6-JK
		E-150 Vans	5200-5300	P205/75R15		35-35	5 1/2,6-JK
					P225/75R15	35-35	6-JK
					P235/75R15XL	41-41	6-JK
		Club Wagon	6200-6600	P235/75R15XL		41-41	6-JK
	1987	Ranger "S" 4×2 Pickup		P185/75R14	P195/75R14	35-35	5-JJ
					P205/75R14	35-35	5 1/2-JJ
	1987-86	Aerostar	4020, 4120, 4400	P185/75R14	P195/75R14	35-35	5-,5 1/2-JJ
					P205/75R14	35-35	5 1/2-JJ
			4500	P195/75R14	P205/75R14	30-35	5 1/2-JJ
			4680-5040	P205/75R14		31-35	5 1/2-JJ
		Ranger Pickup		P195/75R14		35-35	5-JJ
					P205/75R14	35-35	5 1/2-JJ
					P215/75R14	35-35	5 1/2-JJ
	1985	Ranger 4×2 Pickup		P185/75R14	P195/75R14	35-35	5-,5 1/2-JJ
					P205/75R14	35-35	5 1/2-JJ
		Ranger 4×2 Chassis Cab		195/75R14	P205/75R14	35-35	5 1/2-JJ
					P215/75R14	35-35	6-JJ
		Ranger 4×4 Pickup		P195/75R15	P205/75R15	35-35	5-,5 1/2-JJ
					P215/75R15	35-35	5 1/2-JJ
	1984-83	Ranger 4×2 Pickup		P185/75R14	P195/75R14	35-35	5-JJ
					P205/75R14	35-35	5 1/2-JJ
					P205/75R14XL	41-41	5 1/2-JJ
		Ranger 4×2 Chassis Cab		P195/75R14	P205/75R14	35-35	5 1/2-JJ
					P205/75R14XL	41-41	5 1/2-JJ
		Ranger 4×4 Pickup		P195/75R15	P205/75R15	35-35	5 1/2-JJ
		E-150 Van, Wagon	5850-6200	P225/75R15		35-35	6-JK
					P235/75R15XL	35-41	6-JK
	1983	F-150 4×4	6450	P235/75R15XL		35-41	6-JK
					10-15LT/C	45-45	8.00
					10R-15LT/C	45-50	8.00

Tire sizes and tire pressures represent the car manufacturer's recommendations (for normal speeds).
†Sustained high speeds: **Numeric and Alphanumeric** sizes, add 4 psi (do not exceed 32 psi for load range "B", 36 psi for load range "C", 40 psi for load range "D"); **P-Metric** sizes, add 3 psi (do not exceed 35 psi for Standard Load, 41 psi for Extra Load "XL" tire).
*For minimum load pressure, refer to tire decal.

FORD BRONCO, BRONCO II, EXPLORER

MAKE YEAR MODEL GVWR	Std.	Optional	PRESSURE† Max. Load* F-R	RIM WIDTH
1992 Explorer	P225/70R15SL		30-35	6-,7-JJ
	P235/75R15SL		26-26	6-,7-JJ
Bronco	235/75R15XL		38-41	6-,7½-J
		31x10.5RX15C	35-40	7½-J
		P265/75R15SC	30-30	7½-J
1991 Explorer	P225/70R15	P235/75R15	35-35	6-JJ
1991-89 Bronco	P235/75R15XL		35-41	6-JK
		31x10.50R15/C	40-40	8-JJ
Bronco II	P205/75R15		35-35	6-JJ
1988 Bronco Cust., XLT	P235/75R15XL		35-41	6-JK
Eddie Bauer		P235/75R15XL	35-41	8-JK
Bronco II	P195/75R15			5½-,6-JJ
		P205/75R15	35-35	6-,7-JJ
1987-85 Bronco	P235/75R15XL		35-41	6-JK
		31×10.50R15/C	40-40	7-JJ
Bronco II	P195/75R15	P205/75R15	35-35	5½-,6-JJ
1984 Bronco II	P195/75R15		35-35	5½-K
		P205/75R15	35-35	5½-,6-JK
1984-83 Bronco	P215/75R15		35-35	5½-K
		P235/75R15XL	35-41	6-JK

GEO TRACKER

MAKE YEAR MODEL GVWR	Std.	Optional	PRESSURE† Max. Load* F-R	RIM WIDTH
1992-91 2WD	P195/75R15		23-23	5½-JJ
4WD	P205/75R15		23-23	5½-JJ
1990 All	P205/75R15		23-23	5½-JJ

ISUZU TRUCKS

MAKE YEAR MODEL GVWR	Std.	Optional	PRESSURE† Max. Load* F-R	RIM WIDTH
1992 Trooper	P245/70R16		30-35	7-JJ
1992-91 Rodeo ex. 4WD XS	P225/75R15		26-26	6-JJ
		31×10.5R15	29-29	7-JJ
4WD XS	31×10.5R15		29-29	7-JJ
1992-89 Amigo	P225/75R15		26-26	6-JJ
		31X10.5R15	29-29	7-JJ
1992-88 Pickup: ½ ton 2WD	P195/75R14		29-35	5-J
		P205/75R14	29-35	5½-JJ
½ ton 4WD	P225/75R15		26-26	6-JJ
		31×10.5R15	29-29	7-JJ
1991-88 Pickup 1 ton 2WD	185/R-14/8		26-65	5-J
Trooper, Trooper II	P235/75R15		35-35	6-JJ
		31×10.5R15	28-28	7-JJ
1987-86 Pickup	P195/75R14		35-35	5-J
		P215/75R14	35-35	5½-JJ
1987-84 Trooper	P225/75R15		28-35	6-JJ
1985-84 Pickup: 4×2	P195/75R14		28-35	5-J
4×4	F70-14		20-28	5½-JJ
1983 Pickup	F70-14		32-32	5½-JJ
		P195/75R14	35-35	5-J

JEEP

MAKE YEAR MODEL GVWR	Std.	Optional	PRESSURE† Max. Load* F-R	RIM WIDTH
1992 Cherokee	P195/75R15		—	6-,7-JJ[1]
		P215/75R15	—	7-JJ[1]
		P225/75R15	—	7-JJ
		P225/70R15	—	7-JJ
Comanche	P195/75R15		—	6-JJ
	P205/75R15		—	7-JJ
	P225/70R15		—	7-JJ
		P225/75R15	—	7-JJ
		P215/75R15	—	7-JJ
1992-90 Wrangler, YJ 4150	P215/75R15	P225/75R15	30-30	7-JJ
Maryland only	P205/75R15		30-30	6-JJ
1991-90 Cherokee, Comanche, Wagoneer 4640, 4850	P195/75R15		33-33	6-JJ[1]
		P205/75R15	30-30	6-,7-JJ[1]
		P215/75R15	30-30	7-JJ
		P225/70R15	30-35	7-JJ
		P225/75R15	30-30	7-JJ
1991-85 Grand Wagoneer	P235/75R15		35-35	6-,7-JJ
1989-88 Wrangler	P205/75R15	P215/75R15	30-30	7-JJ
		P225/75R15	30-30	7-JJ
1989-86 Comanche, Cherokee	P195/75R15		33-33	6-JJ
		P205/75R15	30-30	6-,7-JJ
		P215/75R15	30-30	6-,7-JJ
		P225/75R15	30-30	7-JJ
		P225/70R15	30-30	7-JJ
		P215/65R15	30-30	6-JJ
1989-84 Wagoneer	P205/75R15		30-30	6-,7-JJ
1988 Truck: J10(26)	P225/75R15		35-35	6-JJ
		P235/75R15	35-35	8-JJ
J20(27)	9.50×16.5LT/D		45-60	6.75
1987 J10 Truck 6025, 6200	P225/75R15	P235/75R15	35-35	6-JJ
J20 Truck 7600, 8400	9.50×16.5LT/D		45-60	6.75
Wrangler	P215/75R15	P225/75R15	35-35	6-JJ
1986 J10 Truck 5975	P225/75R15		35-35	6-JJ
6200	P235/75R15		35-35	6-JJ
1986-84 CJ-7, Scrambler	P205/75R15	P215/75R15	35-35[2]	5½-,7-JJ
		P235/75R15	35-35[2]	5½-,7-JJ
1985 J10 Truck	P225/75R15		35-35	6-,7-JJ
		P235/75R15	35-35	7-JJ
1985-84 Cherokee	P195/75R15	P205/75R15	30-30	6-JJ
		P215/75R15	30-30	7-JJ

JEEP Continued

MAKE YEAR MODEL GVWR	Std.	Optional	PRESSURE† Max. Load* F-R	RIM WIDTH
1984 J-10, Grand Wagoneer	P225/75R15		32-32	6-JJ[1]
		P235/75R15	32-32	6-JJ
		10R15LT	35-35	6-JJ
1983 CJ-5, CJ-7, Scrambler 3750, 4150	G78-15		24-24	6-L[1]
		P235/75R15	35-35	7-JJ
		H78-15, -15/D	28-28	6-L[1]
		L78-15	24-24	7-JJ
J-10 Truck 6200	P225/75R15		32-32	6-L[1]
		H78-15	32-32	6-L[1]
		10R15LT	35-35	8-JJ[1]
Cherokee, Wagoneer 6200	P225/75R15		35-35	6-L[1]
		P235/75R15	35-35	7-JJ
		L78-15, -15/C	28-28	8-JJ[1]
		10R15LT	35-35	8-JJ[1]

1 Aluminum wheel is 15×7.00
2 Scrambler, 30-35

MAZDA TRUCKS

MAKE YEAR MODEL GVWR	Std.	Optional	PRESSURE† Max. Load* F-R	RIM WIDTH
1992 MPV: 2WD	P205/70R14		35-35	5½-JJ
		P215/65R15	35-35	6-JJ
4WD	P215/65R15		35-35	6-JJ
1992-91 Navajo	P225/70R15		35-35	7-JJ
		P235/75R15	35-35	7-JJ
B2200, B2600i 2WD	P205/75R14		26-34	5½-JJ
B2600I 4WD	P215/75R15		28-31	6-JJ
		P235/75R15	28-31	6-JJ
1991 MPV: 2WD	P205/70R14		35-35	5½-JJ
		P215/65R15	32-32	6-JJ
4WD	P215/65R15		35-35	6-JJ
		P205/75R14	35-35	5½-JJ
1991-90 MPV: 2WD	P205/70R14		32-32	5½-JJ
		P215/65R15	32-32	6-JJ
4WD	P215/65R15		35-35	6-JJ
1989 MPV	P205/70R14		35-35	5½-JJ
		P215/65R15	32-32	6-JJ
1989-88 B2200: 2WD	P205/75R14		26-34	5½-JJ
		P225/70HR14	26-34	6-JJ
B2600 4WD	P215/75R15		26-34	6-JJ
		P235/75R15	26-34	6-JJ
1987-86 B2000	P205/75R14		26-34	5½-JJ
1984 B2000, B2200, B2400	6.00-14LT/C		26-45	4½-J
		P205/75R14	26-34	5½-JJ
1983 B2000, B2200	6.00-14LT/C		26-45	4½-JJ
		195SR14	26-32	5½-JJ
		ER70-14	26-32	5½-JJ
		P205/75R14	26-34	5½-JJ

MITSUBISHI TRUCKS

MAKE YEAR MODEL GVWR	Std.	Optional	PRESSURE† Max. Load* F-R	RIM WIDTH
1992-89 Pickup: 2WD	P195/75R14		26-35	6-JJ
		P205/75R14	26-35	6-JJ
4WD	P225/75R15		26-35	6-JJ
1991 Montero	P225/75R15		26-35	6-JJ
		LT195/75R14	36-36	6-JJ
1990-89 Montero 2-dr.: 2.6L engine	P225/75R15		26-35	6-JJ
3.0L engine	P235/75R15		26-35	6-JJ
Montero 4-dr.	P235/75R15		26-35	6-JJ
1990-87 Van, Wagon	P205/75R14		29-29	5½-JJ
1989-87 Pickup: 2WD	LT195/75R14/D		36-65	5-J
		P195/75R14	26-35	6-JJ
		P205/75R14	26-35	6-JJ
4WD	P225/75R15		26-35	6-JJ
1986-83 Pickup: 2WD	6.00-14LT/C		26-26	5-J
		185/SR14	22-22	6-J
4WD	GR78-15		22-22	6-JJ
Montero	215SR15		26-26	6-JJ

NISSAN/DATSUN TRUCKS

MAKE YEAR MODEL GVWR	Std.	Optional	PRESSURE† Max. Load* F-R	RIM WIDTH
1992 Pickup: 2WD E	P195/75R14		28-28	5-,6-JJ
		LT195/75R14	36-36	5-J
4WD: E	P215/75R15		28-28	5½-K,6-JJ
XE	P235/75R15		28-28	6-JJ
		P215/75R15	28-28	5½-K
SE	P235/75R15		28-28	6-JJ
		31x10.5R15LT	28-28	7-JJ
Pathfinder 4WD: E	P215/75R15		28-28	5½-K,6-JJ
XE	P215/75R15		28-28	6-JJ
SE	P235/75R15		28-28	5½-K
		P215/75R15	28-28	6-JJ
		31x10.5R15LT	28-28	7-JJ
1992-91 Pickup 2WD SE	P215/75R14		28-28	6-JJ
Pathfinder 2WD	P235/75R15		28-28	6-JJ
		P215/75R15	28-28	5½-K
Pickup 4WD	P215/75R15	P235/75R15	28-28	6-JJ
		31x10.5R15	28-28	7-JJ
1991 Pickup 2WD E	P195/75R14		28-28	5-J
		P215/75R14	28-28	6-JJ
		LT195/75R14	36-36	5-J

Tire sizes and tire pressures represent the car manufacturer's recommendations (for normal speeds).
†Sustained high speeds: **Numeric and Alphanumeric** sizes, add 4 psi (do not exceed 32 psi for load range "B", 36 psi for load range "C", 40 psi for load range "D"); **P-Metric** sizes, add 3 psi (do not exceed 35 psi for Standard Load, 41 psi for Extra Load "XL" tire).
*For minimum load pressure, refer to tire decal.

MAKE YEAR	MODEL GVWR	ORIGINAL EQUIPMENT SIZE Std.	Optional	PRESSURE† Max. Load* F-R	RIM WIDTH
NISSAN/DATSUN TRUCKS Continued					
1990	Pickup: 2WD	P195/75R14		28-28	5-J,6-JJ
			P215/75R14	28-28	6-JJ
			LT195/75R14	36-36	5-J
	4WD, Pathfinder	P215/75R15		28-28	5½-K
			P215/75R15	28-28	6-JJ
			P235/75R15	28-28	6-JJ[1]
			31X10.5R15	28-28	7-JJ
1990-87	Van	P195/75R14	P205/70R14	24-24	5½-JJ
1989-88	Pickup: 2WD	P185/75R14	P195/75R14	24-24	5-J
			P215/75R14	28-28	6-JJ
	4WD, Pathfinder	P215/75R15		28-28	5½-K
			P235/75R15	28-28	6-JJ
			31×10.5R15	28-28	7-JJ
1989-86½	Pickup HD, Cab & Chassis	LT195/75R14		36-36	5-J
1987-86½	Pickup 2WD	7.00-14		24-24	5-J
			P195/75R14	24-24	5-J
			P215/75R14	28-28	6-JJ
	Pickup 4WD	P215/75R15		28-28	5½-K
			P235/75R15	28-28	5½-K
	Aluminum Wheels	31×10.5R15LT		28-28	7-JJ
1986½-85	Pickup 2×4	P195/75R14		24-24	5-J
			P205/75R14	24-24	5½-J
	HD models	LT195/75R14		36-36	5-J
			P185/80R14	27-27	5-J
	Pickup 4×4	P215/75R15		28-28	5½-J
			P225/75R15	28-28	5½-J
1984	Pickup 2×4	185SR14		24-24	5-J
			195SR14	24-24	5-J
	HD models	E78-14		26-40	5-J
			P185/80R14	27-27	5-J
	Pickup 4×4	P215/75R15		28-28	5½-J
1983	Pickup 2×4:				
	Std. & longbed	7.00-14		22-22	5-J
	King Cab	185SR14		24-24	5-J
			195SR14	24-24	5-J
	HD models	E78-14LTD		26-40	5-J
	Pickup 4×4:				
	Std. & longbed	G78-15		28-28	5½-K
	King Cab	GR78-15		28-28	5½-K, 6-JJ

1 Aluminum wheels, 7-JJ

MAKE YEAR	MODEL GVWR	ORIGINAL EQUIPMENT SIZE Std.	Optional	PRESSURE† Max. Load* F-R	RIM WIDTH
OLDSMOBILE					
1992	Silhouette	P205/70R15		35-35	6-JJ
1991	Bravada	P235/75R15		35-35	7-JJ
	Silhouette	P205/70R14	P205/65R15	35-35	6-JJ
1990	Silhouette	P205/70R14	P195/70R15	35-35	6-JJ
PONTIAC TRANS SPORT					
1992	Trans Sport	P205/70R15		35-35	6-JJ
			P205/60R15	35-35	6-JJ
1991	Trans Sport	P205/70R14		30-30	5½-JJ
			P205/65R15	30-30	6-JJ
	Trans Sport SE	P205/65R15		30-30	6-JJ
1990	Trans Sport	P205/70R14		30-30	5½-JJ
	Trans Sport SE	P195/70R15		30-30	6-JJ
RANGE ROVER					
1989-87	All	205R16		28-38	7-JJ
TOYOTA TRUCKS					
1992	4-Runner: 2.4L	P225/75R15		26-29	7-JJ
	3.0L	31x10.5R15LT		26-29	7-JJ
	Pickup: 2WD: 2.4L	P195/75R14		29-35	5-J
			P205/75R14	29-35	6-JJ
	3.0L	185/R14-LT6PR		42-42	5-J
			185/R14-LT8PR	39-65	5½-J
			P215/65R15	29-35	6-JJ
	4WD: 2.4L	P225/75R15		26-29	6-,7-JJ
	3.0L	31x10.5R15LT		26-29	6-,7-JJ
1992-91	Previa	P205/75R14		35-35	6-JJ
			P215/65R15	35-35	6-JJ
	Land Cruiser	P235/75R15XL		29-35	6-JJ
			31×10.5R15LT	30-40	7-JJ

MAKE YEAR	MODEL GVWR	ORIGINAL EQUIPMENT SIZE Std.	Optional	PRESSURE† Max. Load* F-R	RIM WIDTH
TOYOTA TRUCKS Continued					
1991-90	Pickup, 2WD	P195/75R14		29-35	5-J
			P205/75R14	29-35	6-JJ
			P215/65R15	29-35	6-JJ
			185R14LT/C	32-32	5-J
			185R14LT/D	29-65	5½-J
	Pickup, 4WD &				
	4-Runner: 4-cyl.	P225/75R15		26-29	6-JJ
	V6	P225/75R15		26-29	6-JJ
			31X10.5R15LT	26-29	7-JJ
1990-88	Land Cruiser	P225/75R15XL		32-41	6-JJ
1989	Van: 2WD ex. Panel	P195/75R14		35-35	5½-JJ
	Panel	P175R14/6		40-40	5-J
	4WD	P205/75R14		35-35	5½-JJ
	4-Runner	P225/75R15		26-29	6-JJ[4]
	Pickup, 2WD: 4-cyl.: 2V	7.00-14LT/C		24-36	5-,5½-JJ
			P195/75R14	29-35	5-,5½-JJ
	FI	P195/75R14		29-35	5-,5½-JJ
			P205/75R14	29-35	6-JJ
	V6	P205/75R14		29-35	6-JJ
			185R14LT/C	32-32	5-,5½-JJ
			185R14LT/D	29-65	5½-JJ
			P215/65R15	29-35	6-JJ
	Pickup, 4WD	P225/75R15	10.5R15LT	26-29	6-JJ[4]
1988	Van: Deluxe pass.	175/R14LT		35-35	5½-J
	LE pass.	P195/75R14		35-35	5½-JJ
	Cargo	P195/75R14		35-35	5½-J
	4WD	P205/75R14		35-35	5½-JJ
	4-Runner ex. Turbo	P225/75R15		26-29	6-JJ
	4-Runner SR5 Turbo	P225/75R15		26-29	7-JJ
	Pickup: ½ Ton	7.00-14LT		24-36	5-J
			185/R14LT/C	29-29	5-J
			185/R14LT/D	26-65	5½-J
			P195/75R14	29-35	5-J
			205/70SR14	28-32	6-JJ
	1-Ton	185/R14LT/D		26-65	5½-J
	1-Ton Cab & Chassis	185/R14LT/C		29-29	5-J
1987	Van: 2WD	P195/75R14		35-35	5½-J
	Cargo	175/R14LT		41-41	5½-JJ
1987-85	Van, 4WD	P205/75R14		35-35	5½-J
	Pickup: ½ Ton	7.00-14LT		24-36	5-J
			P195/75R14	29-35	5-J[1,2]
			205/70SR14	28-32	6-JJ
	1 Ton, Cab & Chassis	185R14LT/C		29-29	5-J
			185R14LT/D	26-65	5½-J[3]
	4WD, 4-Runner	P225/75R15		26-29	6-JJ[4]
1987-84	Land Cruiser	HR78-15		26-32	6-JJ
1986	Van, 2WD	P185/75R14		35-35	5-J
			P195/75R14	35-35	5½-J
			175R14-6P	40-40	5½-JJ
1985-84	Van	P185/75R14		34-34	5½-J
1984-83	Pickup, 2WD: ½ Ton	7.00-14LT		24-36	5-J
			ER78-14	28-32	5-J
	¾ Ton, Cab & Chassis	7.50-14LT		24-36	5-J
	SR5	P195/75R14		29-35	5½-JJ[2]
			205/70SR14	28-32	6-JJ
			ER78-14	28-32	5½-JJ
	Pickup, 4WD	H78-15B	HR78-15B	24-28	6-JJ[3]
1983	Land Cruiser	H78-15B		26-30	6-JJ[3]

1 With FI, 5½-JJ 2 Aluminum wheels, 6-JJ 3 May use 5½-JJ
4 Aluminum wheels, 7-JJ

MAKE YEAR	MODEL GVWR	ORIGINAL EQUIPMENT SIZE Std.	Optional	PRESSURE† Max. Load* F-R	RIM WIDTH
VOLKSWAGEN TRUCKS					
1991	Vanagon ex. Syncro	185R14/C		36-40	5½-J
			205/70R14	36-40	6-JJ
	Vanagon Syncro	185R14/C		36-40	5½-J
			205/70R14/C	40-48	6-J
1990	Vanagon 7-seater				
	ex. GL	185/70R14/C		40-48	5½-J
	Vanagon GL Syncro	205/70R14		36-40	5½-J
1990-88	Vanagon & Camper GL	185/R14C		40-48	5½-J
			205/70R14	30-40	6-J
	Vanagon & Camper Syncro	205/70R14		36-40	6-J
1987	Vanagon	185R14LT/C		39-48	5½-J
	Syncro, optional	205/70R14		36-44	5½-,6-J
1986-85	Vanagon	185R-14C		38-44	5½-J
			205/70R14	27-31	5½-J
1984-83	Vanagon	185R-14C		38-44	5½-J
	Vanagon Camper	185R-14C		30-40	5½-J
1983	Pickup	165/70R13		29-29	5½-J
	Pickup Optional	175/70R14		29-29	5½-J

WHEEL NUT TORQUE

WHEEL NUT TIGHTENING SEQUENCE

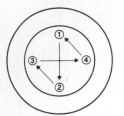

4-nut wheel

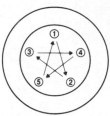

5-nut wheel

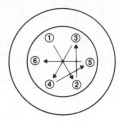

6-nut wheel

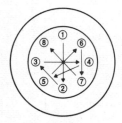

8-nut wheel

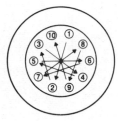

10-nut wheel

IMPORTANT:

Check all parts, including wheels, studs and mounting faces of hub and wheels, for dirt, rust or damage. Use a wire brush to remove dirt and rust, replace any damaged parts. Careless installation of wheels on a vehicle is a major cause of tire and wheel problems. Proper installation, including nut torque, is essential to safe, economical, trouble-free service. Use only the specified sizes and types of studs & nuts.

Tighten the nuts a quarter turn at a time following the criss-cross sequence shown at left. This is very important. Failure to tighten nuts in the criss-cross sequence will cause misalignment of wheel. Continue until all nuts are tightened to the torque specified in the table. Caution: improper torque can cause distortion, fatigue cracks or alignment problems. After running the vehicle for a short distance, check the nuts for tightness. Parts will usually seat naturally and torque on nuts will drop. Retighten all nuts to specified torque.

MAKE	YEAR	MODEL	TORQUE Ft/lbs
PASSENGER CARS			
ACURA			
	1992	Vigor	80
	1991-86	All	80
AMERICAN MOTORS			
	1988-83	All	75
AUDI			
	1992	100, V8 Quattro	80
	1991-88	All	80
	1987-83	4000, 5000, Quattro	80
BMW			
	1992-85	All	81
	1984-83	With wheel nuts	59-65
		With wheel bolts	65-80
BUICK			
	1992-89	All	100
	1988	All ex. Regal	100
		Regal	92
	1987	All	100
	1986	Regal	60-80
		Others	80-100
	1985	Somerset, Skyhawk, Skylark, Century, Electra, Park Ave., Riviera	100
		Others	80
	1984-83	Regal	80
		W/aluminum wheels	105

MAKE	YEAR	MODEL	TORQUE Ft/lbs
BUICK Continued			
	1984-83	LeSabre, Electra:	
		Standard: 7/16"-20	80
		1/2"-20	105
		Aluminum wheels: 7/16"-20	80
		1/2"-20	105
		Others	105
CADILLAC			
	1992-83	All	100
CHEVROLET			
	1992	All	100
	1992-91	Lumina	100
	1991-89	Camaro, Corvette	100
	1991-87	Corsica, Beretta	100
		Caprice ex. wagon: W/3/4" studs	80
		W/13/16" studs	100
		Caprice wagon	100
	1991-84	Cavalier, Citation, Celebrity	100
	1990	Lumina	92
	1988	Spectrum	65
		W/aluminum wheels	87
	1988-87	Nova	65-87
		Sprint	43
	1988-86	Camaro, Monte Carlo	80
	1988-84	Corvette	80
	1987-85	Chevette	80
		Spectrum	65
	1986	Caprice: W/1/2" studs	100
		W/7/16" studs	80
	1986-85	Nova	75
		Sprint	45
	1985-83	Camaro, Malibu, Monte Carlo	80
		W/aluminum wheels	90
		Caprice, Impala ex. wagon	80
		Wagon	100
		Citation, Cavalier, Celebrity	100
	1984-83	Chevette	70

MAKE	YEAR	MODEL	TORQUE Ft/lbs
CHEVROLET Continued			
	1983	Citation	100
		Chevrolet ex. wagon	80
		Chevrolet wagon	100
		Camaro, Chevelle, Corvette, Malibu, Monza, Nova, Vega	80
		With aluminum or gold style wheels	90
CHRYSLER, IMPERIAL			
	1992-90	All	95
	1989-87	Conquest	65-80
		All Other Rear-Wheel Drive models	90
	1989-84	All Front-Wheel Drive models	95
	1986-83	All Rear-Wheel Drive models	85
	1983	All Front-Wheel Drive models	80
DAIHATSU			
	1991	Charade, Rocky	65-87
	1990-89	All	63
DODGE			
	1992	Monaco	63
		Colt Vista	65-80
	1992-91	Stealth	87-101
		Colt ex. Vista	65-80
	1992-90	Monaco	63
	1992-84	FWD models ex. Colt, Vista	95
	1991	Monaco	90
		Colt Vista: Steel wheels	50-57
		Aluminum wheels	65-80
	1990-87	Colt, Vista	65-80
	1989-87	All RWD models	90
	1986-84	Colt, Vista, Conquest w/alum. wheels	65-80
	1986-83	All Other RWD models ex. Challenger	85
	1984-83	Colt, Vista, Conquest w/steel wheels	51-58
	1983	Colt, Challenger w/aluminum wheels	58-73
		Other FWD models	80

MAKE	YEAR	MODEL	TORQUE Ft/lbs
EAGLE			
	1992-90	Talon	85-100
	1992-89	Summit	65-80
	1991	Premier	90
	1990-89	Premier	63
FORD			
	1992-90	All ex. Escort, Festiva, Probe	85-105
		Escort	65-87
	1992-89	Probe	65-87
	1992-88	Festiva	65-87
	1989-83	All ex. Festiva, Probe	85-105
GEO			
	1992-90	Storm	87
	1992-89	Prizm	76
		Metro	45
	1989	Spectrum	65
		W/aluminum wheels	87
HONDA			
	1991-84	Civic, CRX, Accord, Prelude	80
	1983	Civic	50-65
		Prelude, Accord	72-88
HYUNDAI			
	1992-90	All	65-80
	1989-86	Steel wheels	50-57
		Aluminum wheels	65-72
INFINITI			
	1991-90	Q45	72-87
		M30	76-90
ISUZU			
	1992-90	Stylus	87
	1992-88	Impulse	87
	1989-88	I-Mark: W/steel wheels	65
		W/aluminum wheels	87
	1987-85	I-Mark FWD: W/steel wheels	60
		W/aluminum wheels	87
	1987-84	Impulse	80-94
	1985-83	I-Mark RWD: W/steel wheels	50
		W/aluminum wheels	90
JAGUAR			
	1992-89	All	65-75
	1988	XJ6 & Vanden Plas	75
	1987-83	All ex. alloy wheels	40-60
		With alloy wheels	50
LEXUS			
	1992-90	All	76
LINCOLN			
	1992-83	All	85-105
MAZDA			
	1992-83	All	65-87
MERCEDES-BENZ			
	1992	300SD, SE, 400SE, 500SEL, 600SEL	110
	1991-83	All	80

MAKE	YEAR	MODEL	TORQUE Ft/lbs
MERCURY			
	1992-91	All ex. Capri, Tracer	85-105
		Capri, Tracer	65-87
	1990	All	85-105
	1989-88	Tracer	65-87
	1989-83	All ex. Tracer	85-105
MERKUR			
	1989-88	Scorpio	52-73
	1989-85	XR4Ti	75-101
MITSUBISHI			
	1992-91	All ex. Eclipse, 3000GT	65-80
		Eclipse, 3000GT	87-101
	1990-87	All	65-80
	1986-84	All w/aluminum wheels	65-80
	1984-83	All w/steel wheels	51-58
	1983	All w/aluminum wheels	58-73
NISSAN			
	1992-90	All	72-87
	1989-86	All ex. 200SX	72-87
		200SX	87-108
	1985-83	All ex. 1986-83 pickup w/steel wheels	58-72
OLDSMOBILE			
	1992-90	All	100
	1989	All ex. Calais	100
		Calais	80
	1988-87	Ciera, Custom Cruiser, Firenza	100
		Calais, Cutlass, Delta 88, Ninety-Eight	80
	1986	Cutlass Supreme	80
		Custom Cruiser: W/1/2" studs	100
		W/7/16" studs	80
		Others, FWD	100
	1985	Cutlass Supreme, Delta 88, Calais	80
		Others	100
	1984	Cutlass ex. Ciera	80
	1984-83	Omega, Ciera, Firenza	100
		Custom Cruiser, Ninety-Eight	100
		88 ex. Custom Cruiser	80
		Toronado	100
	1983	Cutlass ex. Ciera	80
		With aluminum wheels	90
PEUGEOT			
	1992-89	405	55-66
	1991-89	505: Alloy wheels	59-66
		Steel wheels	41-48
	1988-87	Alloy wheels	50-58
		Steel wheels	39-47
	1986-83	Alloy wheels	51-62
		Steel wheels	44
PLYMOUTH			
	1992	Colt Vista	65-80
	1992-91	Acclaim, Sundance	95
	1992-90	Laser	85-100
	1991	Colt ex. Vista	65-80
		Colt Vista: Steel wheels	50-59
		Aluminum wheels	65-80
	1990	All ex. Laser	95
	1989-87	Colt, Vista	65-80
		Other FWD models	95
		All RWD models	90
	1986-84	FWD models ex. Colt, Vista	95
		Colt, Vista, Conquest w/alum. wheels	65-80
	1986-80	All Other RWD models ex. Sapporo	85
	1984-83	Colt, Vista, Conquest, Sapporo w/steel wheels	51-58
	1983	Colt, Sapporo w/alum. wheels	58-73

MAKE	YEAR	MODEL	TORQUE Ft/lbs
PONTIAC			
	1992-90	All ex. LeMans	100
		LeMans	65
	1989	Bonneville, Firebird, Safari	100
		Grand Am	100
		Grand Prix	103
	1989-88	LeMans	65
		Sunbird, 6000	100
	1988	Bonneville, Firebird	80
	1988-87	Firefly	43
		Grand Prix, Firebird	80
	1988-86	Fiero	100
		Sunburst	65
	1987	Bonneville, Grand Am, Safari	100
	1987-83	1000	80
		2000, 6000, Phoenix, Sunbird	100
	1986	Parisienne: W/1/2" studs	100
		W/7/16" studs	80
	1986-85	Firefly	45
	1986-84	Bonneville, Grand Prix, Firebird	80
	1985-84	Fiero	80
		Parisienne: W/3/4" nut	80
		W/13/16" nut	100
	1983	Bonneville, Grand Prix, Firebird	80
		W/aluminum wheels	100
PORSCHE			
	1990	911 Carrera 4	94
	1990-87	924S	96
	1988-83	944	96
		911, 928	96
	1983	924: Steel wheels	80
		Alloy wheels	96
RENAULT			
	1989-88	Medallion	63
	1987	GTA	65
	1987-85	Alliance, Encore	63
	1986-83	Fuego, 18i	60
	1984-83	Alliance, Encore	55
SAAB			
	1992-90	900, 9000	80-90
	1989-87	900	70-90
	1989-86	9000 w/aluminum wheels	75-90
	1986-83	99, 900	65-80
SATURN			
	1992-91	All	100
SUBARU			
	1992	SVX	72-87
		All others	58-72
	1991-83	All	58-72
SUZUKI			
	1992-91	Swift	36.5-50.5
		Sidekick, Samurai	58-79.5
	1990	All	36.5-50.5
	1988-85	Forsa	29-50
	1985-83	LJ80, 81	37-57
TOYOTA			
	1992-83	All	76
VOLKSWAGEN			
	1992-90	Cabriolet, Fox, Jetta	80
	1992-87	Fox, Golf, GTI	80
	1986-83	Dasher, Rabbit, Scirocco, Jetta, Quantum, Golf	80

WHEEL NUT TORQUE

MAKE	YEAR	MODEL	TORQUE Ft/lbs
VOLVO			
	1992	240	85
		740, 940, 960	63
	1991-86	All	63
	1985-83	All ex. 700 Series	72-100
		700 Series	63

LIGHT TRUCKS

CHEVROLET, GMC TRUCKS

MAKE	YEAR	MODEL	TORQUE Ft/lbs
	1992	S Series Pickups	95
		Safari, M Van	100
		S Series Jimmy, Sonoma	95
	1992-91	C-, K10-20	120
		C-, K30; R-, V30; SRW	120
		DRW w/8 lug nuts	140
		DRW w/10 lug nuts	175
	1992-90	Lumina APV	100
	1992-89	Van: G10, -15; G20, -25	100
		G30, -35 w/SRW	120
		G30, -35 w/DRW	140
	1991	R-, V10	100
		R-, V20	120
	1991-90	S Series: 2WD	80
		4WD	100
	1990	C-, K-Pickup, Sierra	105
		C-, K-35 w/DRW	125
		R-, V-Pickup: SRW	120
		DRW	140
	1989	Pickups, Sierra: SRW	120
		DRW	140
		Safari	102
	1989-88	S Series	73
		W/aluminum wheels	90
	1988	R-, V-Pickup: W/SRW	103
		W/DRW	140
		C-, K10, -15, Sierra: W/SRW	90
		W/DRW	125
		Astro, Safari	102
		Van: G10, -15; G20, -25	102
		G-30, -35: 5 bolts	117
		8 bolts	139
	1988-87	R-, V- Blazer, Jimmy, Suburban:	
		2WD	103
		4WD	88
		W/aluminum wheels, 6 lug nuts	103
	1987	R-, V- Pickup: 2WD	88
		4WD	80
		Van: G-10, -15; G20, -25	88
		G-30, -35	103
		W/8 lug nuts	125
	1987-86	S-10, -15	90
	1986-84	C-K Models, Blazer, Jimmy, Suburban:	
		W/5 lug nuts: 1/2"	100
		9/16"	120
		W/6 lug nuts	90
		W/8 lug nuts	140
		G10, -15; G20, -25	100
		G30, -35: W/5 lug nuts	120
		Dual wheels w/8 lug nuts	140
	1985-83	S10, -15	81
		W/optional wheels	100
	1983	C-K Models, Blazer, Jimmy, Suburban:	
		W/5 lug nuts	100
		W/6 lug nuts	90
		W/8 lug nuts	120
		G-10, -15; G20, -25	100
		G-30, -35	120
		W/dual wheels	140

DODGE, PLYMOUTH TRUCKS

MAKE	YEAR	MODEL	TORQUE Ft/lbs
	1992	Dakota	85-110
	1992-90	Ram 50 w/steel wheels	87-101
		Caravan, Voyager	95
	1992-86	Ram, Power Ram, Ramcharger,	
		Ram Van & Wagon:	
		Cone Type Nut 1/2-20	85-115
		Cone Type Nut 5/8-18	175-225
		Flanged Type Nut 5/8-18	300-350
	1991-90	Dakota	95
	1989-87	Dakota	85
		Ram 50	87-101
		Raider	72-87
	1988-86	Caravan, Voyager, Mini Ram Van,	
		Dakota	95
	1986-84	Ram 50 w/alum. wheels	65-80
	1985-83	150-350 ex. Van:	
		Cone Type Nut 1/2-20	85-115
		Cone Type Nut 5/8-18	175-225
		Flanged Type Nut 5/8-18	300-350
		B100-250 Vans:	
		W/Cone Type Nut 1/2-20	85-125
	1984-83	Ram 50 w/steel wheels	51-58
	1983	Ram 50 w/alum. wheels	58-73

FORD TRUCKS

MAKE	YEAR	MODEL	TORQUE Ft/lbs
	1992-91	Explorer	100
	1992-87	E-, F-150, Bronco, Bronco II,	
		Aerostar, Ranger	100
		E-, F-250, F-350	140
	1986-85	E-, F-150, -200, Bronco	85-115
		E-, F-250, -350 (Single Rear)	115-175
		E-, F-350 (Dual Rear)	125-155
	1986-83	Bronco, Bronco II, Ranger,	
		E-100-150-250, F-100-150-250	85-115
		E-350, F-350 (Single Rear)	115-175
	1984-83	E-350, F-350 (Dual Rear)	175-260

GEO TRACKER

MAKE	YEAR	MODEL	TORQUE Ft/lbs
	1992	All	60
	1991-89	All	37-58

ISUZU TRUCKS

MAKE	YEAR	MODEL	TORQUE Ft/lbs
	1992	Amigo: Steel wheels	66
		Pickup: Steel wheels	66
		Trooper	87
	1992-91	Rodeo: Steel wheels	66
		Aluminum wheels	87
	1992-90	Amigo: Aluminum wheels	86
	1992-89	Pickup: Aluminum wheels	87
	1991-90	Amigo: Steel wheels	72
		Trooper, Trooper II:	
		Steel wheels	58-87
		Aluminum wheels	80-94
	1991-89	Pickup: Steel wheels	72
	1988	Trooper: Steel wheels	65
		Aluminum wheels	87
	1987-83	Pickup, Trooper	58-87

JEEP

MAKE	YEAR	MODEL	TORQUE Ft/lbs
	1992	All	95-110
	1991-90	Wrangler, YJ	80
		Cherokee, Comanche,	
		Wagoneer, Grand	
		Wagoneer	75

JEEP Continued

MAKE	YEAR	MODEL	TORQUE Ft/lbs
	1989-84	Cherokee, Comanche,	
		Wagoneer, Wrangler	75
		Grand Wagoneer, Trucks	
		(under 8400 GVW)	75
		Trucks (over 8400 GVW)	130
	1986-84	CJ Series	80
	1983	CJ Series	65-80
		Cherokee, Wagoneer and	
		Trucks (under 8400 GVW)	65-90
		Trucks (over 8400 GVW)	110-150

MAZDA TRUCKS

MAKE	YEAR	MODEL	TORQUE Ft/lbs
	1992-88	Styled wheel	87-108
		Design wheel	65-87
	1987-86	B2000	87-108
	1984-83	Pickup	72-80
		W/aluminum wheels	87-94

MITSUBISHI TRUCKS

MAKE	YEAR	MODEL	TORQUE Ft/lbs
	1992	Truck	87-101
	1991-90	Truck, Van, Wagon	87-101
		Montero	72-87
	1989	Montero, Truck, Van, Wagon	87-101
	1988-87	Montero, Truck, Van, Wagon	72-87
	1986-84	All w/aluminum wheels	65-80
	1984-83	All w/steel wheels	51-58
	1983	All w/aluminum wheels	58-73

NISSAN/DATSUN TRUCKS

MAKE	YEAR	MODEL	TORQUE Ft/lbs
	1992-87	Pickup, Pathfinder	87-108
	1991-87	W/dual wheels	166-203
	1986-83	Pickup w/steel wheels	87-108

OLDSMOBILE TRUCKS

MAKE	YEAR	MODEL	TORQUE Ft/lbs
	1992-91	Bravada	100

PONTIAC TRUCKS

MAKE	YEAR	MODEL	TORQUE Ft/lbs
	1992-90	Trans Sport	100

TOYOTA TRUCKS

MAKE	YEAR	MODEL	TORQUE Ft/lbs
	1992	4 Runner	76
	1992-91	4WD Pickup, Previa	76
	1992-89	Pickup, 2WD: W/SRW	101
		W/DRW	170
	1992-88	Land Cruiser	116
	1991-88	4Runner, Van	76
	1990-89	4WD Pickup	101
	1988	Pickup: W/SRW	76
		W/DRW	141
	1987-83	Pickup w/dual wheels	126
		All others	65-86

VOLKSWAGEN TRUCKS

MAKE	YEAR	MODEL	TORQUE Ft/lbs
	1990	Vanagon	130
	1988-83	Vanagon	123
	1986-83	Pickup	80

Introduction

Good performance, maximum fuel economy, and reduced exhaust emissions are achieved by performing engine and other underhood vehicle maintenance according to the manufacturers' specifications. Recommended service intervals are listed on the service charts in the first half of this guide. Inspection and adjustment specifications for tune-ups are listed in the *Underhood Service Specifications*. Use the following "Underhood Service Instructions" to supplement the *Underhood Service Specifications*.

Contents

Vehicle Emission Control Information (VECI) Decals

Federal law requires that all late-model vehicles display an underhood VECI decal or label providing emission control information, including the types of emission control systems used, vacuum hose routings, spark plug type and gap, base ignition timing, and idle speed setting procedures, if applicable. Because manufacturers may change specifications during the model year, always follow the decal.

Engine Identification

Underhood service specifications may vary depending on the engine, transmission, and accessories fitted on the vehicle. To locate the correct specifications, identify the engine using the Vehicle Identification Number (VIN). Identifying the engine is explained in the *Engine Identification* table at the beginning of each manufacturer's *Underhood Service Specification* section.

Underhood Service Illustrations

Immediately following the *Engine Identification* information in each manufacturer's *Underhood Service Specifications* section are illustrations that show engine cylinder numbering sequence, firing order, distributor position, number-one tower on the distributor or coil pack, and direction of distributor rotation. Ignition timing marks are also shown as they would appear to you while you adjust the timing. Arrows indicate the direction of crankshaft rotation.

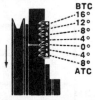

Engine diagrams contain service information.

ELECTRICAL AND IGNITION SYSTEMS

BATTERY

Battery service involves certain safety hazards because the battery contains an acidic electrolyte solution and produces explosive hydrogen gas during charging. When you service a battery, wear safety glasses to protect your eyes. Avoid wearing rings or a metal watch band, which can create accidental shorts. Work in a well-ventilated area, and keep sources of spark or open flame away from the battery to prevent explosions. When you remove or install battery cables, always disconnect the ground cable first and reconnect it last.

BATTERY GROUP NUMBERS AND CAPACITIES

The *Underhood Service Specifications* list batteries by their Battery Council International (BCI) group number and by their cold-cranking capacity (cranking performance). The BCI group number indicates battery size, shape, and terminal configuration. The cold-cranking capacity, which is determined by the manufacturer, is the amount of current flow the battery can deliver for 30 seconds at 0°F (–18°C) while maintaining at least 1.2 volts per cell, or a total of 7.2 volts for a 12-volt battery.

A replacement battery must have the specified BCI number. The new battery's cranking performance rating must be equal to or higher than that of the original battery.

BATTERY MAINTENANCE

There are three types of batteries in use today: conventional, low maintenance, and maintenance-free. Conventional and low-maintenance batteries have filler caps that allow you to add water to the cells. Check the water level periodically. Maintenance-free batteries have small gas vents, which prevent gas build-up in the case. You cannot add water to these batteries. Some manufacturers make recombinant, maintenance-free batteries that are completely sealed (no vents). You cannot add water to these batteries either.

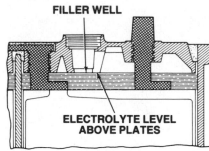

Electrolyte should completely cover the battery plates.

BATTERY INSPECTION

- Check the battery for cracks, loose terminals, damage, and dirt or grease.
- Check for corrosion around the terminals, holddown strap, and battery tray.
- If the battery has filler caps, check that the electrolyte level is above the plates and even with the bottom of the filler wells.
- Check for loose or corroded cable connections and worn insulation.
- Inspect the holddown and tray for looseness, damage, corrosion, and missing parts.
- If the battery has a heat shield, make sure it is in place.

BATTERY TESTING

Battery condition is determined by performing a state-of-charge test and capacity test. Three methods are used to determine a battery's state-of-charge: the specific gravity test, the state-of-charge indicator, and the open-circuit voltage test. The capacity test determines the battery's ability to provide cranking current while maintaining a specified voltage.

State-Of-Charge Tests

Specific gravity test

If a battery has removable cell caps, use the specific gravity test to determine the state-of-charge. Remove the cell caps, and insert a hydrometer into the first cell.

OPEN CIRCUIT VOLTAGE	BATTERY SPECIFIC GRAVITY*	STATE OF CHARGE	CHARGING TIME TO FULL CHARGE AT 80° F**					
			at 60 amps	at 50 amps	at 40 amps	at 30 amps	at 20 amps	at 10 amps
			FULL CHARGE					
12.6	1.265	100%						
12.4	1.225	75%	15 min.	20 min.	27 min.	35 min.	48 min.	90 min.
12.2	1.190	50%	35 min.	45 min.	55 min.	75 min.	95 min.	180 min.
12.0	1.155	25%	50 min.	65 min.	85 min.	115 min.	145 min.	280 min.
11.8	1.120	0%	65 min.	85 min.	110 min.	150 min.	195 min.	370 min.

*Correct for temperature.   **If colder, it'll take longer.

Battery charging times vary with state of charge, temperature, and charging rate.

Draw enough electrolyte into the hydrometer to float the indicator. Hold the hydrometer at eye level and take the temperature and specific gravity readings. Repeat this procedure for all remaining cells.

Using the specific gravity reading, determine the battery state-of-charge from the chart on this page. If the battery has a specific gravity reading of 1.225 (75-percent state-of-charge) or less, recharge it before performing the capacity test. If the specific gravity varies more than 50 points (0.050) between any two cells, replace the battery.

State-of-charge indicators

Some maintenance-free batteries have a built-in state-of-charge indicator. Depending upon the specific gravity of the electrolyte, the balls inside the indicator cage float or sink, changing the appearance of the indicator. The colored dot can be green, red, blue, or can have a red dot inside a larger blue dot. Interpret the state-of-charge indicator as described below:

- **Colored dot visible** — The battery is at or above a 65-percent state-of-charge and is ready for a capacity test.
- **Colored dot not visible (black dot), or red dot visible inside larger clear area** — The battery is below a 65-percent state-of-charge and must be charged before the capacity test.
- **Clear or light yellow** — The electrolyte level is too low for a state-of-charge reading. Do not recharge the battery. Replace it.

Open-circuit voltage test

To test the state-of-charge on a battery without cell caps, use the open-circuit voltage test. Battery temperature should be 60° to 100°F (16° to 38°C). Allow the battery voltage to stabilize for at least 10 minutes with no load applied. If the vehicle has high parasitic drains, disconnect the battery ground cable to remove load. If you have recently recharged the battery, apply a load for 15 seconds to remove surface charge. Then use a digital voltmeter (DVOM) to measure the open-circuit battery voltage to the nearest tenth of a volt. Use the chart to determine the state-of-charge. Remember that fully charged recombinant, maintenance-free batteries may develop an open-circuit voltage as high as 13.2 volts.

Battery Capacity Test

The capacity (load) test determines a battery's maximum deliverable cranking current by simulating a hard-start cranking condition. A Charging-Starting-Battery (CSB) tester is used to place resistance across a fully charged battery for a predetermined time. Then a voltage reading is taken. See the chart for minimum test

BATTERY TEMPERATURE °F (°C)	MINIMUM TEST VOLTAGE
70° (21°) or above	9.6 volts
60° (16°)	9.5 volts
50° (10°)	9.4 volts
40° (4°)	9.3 volts
30° (−1°)	9.1 volts
20° (−7°)	8.9 volts
10° (−12°)	8.7 volts
0° (−18°)	8.5 volts

Battery temperature affects minimum test voltage in the battery capacity test.

voltage. Test equipment for battery capacity testing varies in design. Consult the manufacturer's operating instructions for details. If the battery fails the capacity test, replace it.

BATTERY CHARGING

Whenever possible, use a slow battery charging rate (5 to 15 amperes) rather than a fast rate (50 to 60 amperes). Fast-charging may overheat the battery and cause damage, particularly on recombinant batteries or if the battery has a low state-of-charge. Never charge a frozen battery. Never use a fast charger as a booster to start an engine.

Wash dirt and corrosion from the battery, and make sure the electrolyte level is above the tops of the plates. Disconnect both battery cables before hooking up the charger to avoid damaging the car's electronic circuitry. Leave the battery cell caps in place, but be sure the gas vents are open. Charge the battery in a well-ventilated area away from sparks or open flames. Never disconnect the charger cables while the charger is operating.

The battery is fully charged when all cells are gassing and the specific gravity does not increase for three consecutive hours. Unless otherwise stated on the case, a fully charged battery should have a specific gravity reading of at least 1.265. Approximate charging times are shown on the accompanying chart.

CHARGING SYSTEM

Alternator current output, voltage regulator settings, and other charging system test data vary depending on vehicle de-

sign. Manufacturers' specifications for alternators and regulators are listed in the *Underhood Service Specifications* charts. If the system is undercharging, the alternator light on the dash will turn on and the battery will not be fully charged. If the system is overcharging, the battery will be overcharged. Perform the inspections and tests below. Check the results against manufacturers' specifications.

PRECAUTIONS

When testing the charging system, beware of moving parts and high electrical current that can injure you as well as damage electronic components in the vehicle. Remember these safety precautions when working with charging systems:

- Keep hands, hair, jewelry, and clothing away from moving parts. Remove all jewelry when servicing the battery or charging system.
- Keep the ignition switch OFF, except when specified to do otherwise during test procedures.
- Disconnect the battery ground (−) cable before removing leads from the alternator.
- Remember that the alternator output terminal has voltage present at all times when system connections are in place.
- Never operate an alternator without an external load connected.
- Keep the CSB analyzer carbon pile off (open) except when specified during actual procedures.

CHARGING SYSTEM INSPECTION

Many charging system problems are easily repaired. Before diagnosis:

- Check the battery electrolyte level, state-of-charge, and capacity as described earlier.
- Inspect the alternator drive belt for wear, damage, and correct tension. When adjusting the belt, never pry against the alternator's thin aluminum housing.
- Inspect system wiring and connections. Make sure that fusible links and fuses are intact.
- Check the alternator and regulator mountings for loose or missing bolts and screws.

CHARGING SYSTEM TESTS, GENERAL PROCEDURES

A Charging-Starting-Battery (CSB) analyzer or a carbon pile, voltmeter, and ammeter are needed for the following charging system tests. The wide variety of alternators and analyzers makes it impossible to give a single set of instructions that applies to every alternator. However, the following procedures are generally appropriate.

Connecting the Meters

Using the illustration as a guide, connect the test meters. Refer to the "Charging System Tests, Special Instructions" for variations on this setup:

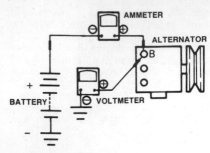

Use this illustration as a guide for charging system tests.

1. Disconnect the ground cable at the battery.
2. Disconnect the battery positive lead at the alternator terminal.
3. Connect the ammeter positive (+) lead to the alternator battery terminal, and connect the ammeter negative (–) lead to the alternator battery positive lead. This connects the ammeter in series with the battery and alternator.
4. Connect a voltmeter either:
   - At the battery positive terminal and ground
   - At the alternator battery terminal and ground, or
   - At the terminal connector (see special instructions) and ground.
5. Reconnect the battery ground cable.
6. Connect the carbon pile leads across the battery terminals to load the battery, or turn on vehicle electrical accessories to load the battery during the alternator output test.

Alternator Current Output Test

1. Start the engine and run it at the manufacturer's recommended rpm for the output test. Use the carbon pile or turn on the air conditioner, headlights, and other electrical accessories to load the charging system.
2. Compare the ammeter reading to the value in the *Underhood Service Specifications*.

Voltage Regulator Setting

1. Run the engine at the recommended test speed. After the alternator charges the battery, the ammeter reading should drop to about 5 amps.
2. Read the voltage and record the temperature. Compare with manufacturers' specifications for voltage setting.

CHARGING SYSTEM TESTS, SPECIAL INSTRUCTIONS

CHRYSLER and CHRYSLER IMPORTS Alternator Tests

Alternator with transistorized regulator:
1. Connect ammeter as described in the general procedures.
2. Connect the voltmeter positive (+) lead to the alternator battery lead,

and connect the voltmeter negative (–) lead to ground.
3. Disconnect the green field wire at the alternator.
4. Connect a jumper wire between ground and the field terminal on the alternator. *Do not ground the blue wire.*

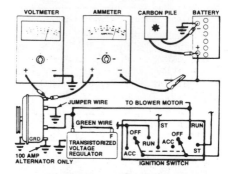

On a Chrysler alternator with a transistorized voltage regulator, connect the meters as shown for the current output test.

5. Reconnect the battery ground cable.
6. Connect a carbon pile across the battery terminals.
7. Adjust the engine speed and carbon pile according to the manufacturer's instructions.
8. Compare the ammeter reading to specifications for current output.
9. Connect the voltmeter positive (+) lead to the battery positive (+) terminal, and connect the voltmeter negative (–) lead to ground.
10. Run the engine at 1250 rpm with all accessories off.
11. Compare the voltmeter reading to specifications for regulator voltage setting.

Alternator with computerized regulator:

In most circumstances, use the computer diagnostics to check for faults in the charging system. It is possible to test the current output and voltage regulator setting according to the procedure above by replacing step 4 with the following step:

4. Connect a jumper wire between ground and at terminal R3 on the dash side of the 8-way black connector. *Do not ground the blue wire at terminal J2.*

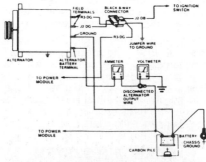

Do not ground the blue wire at terminal J2 when performing the current output test on a Chrysler alternator with a computerized regulator.

Mitsubishi alternator with internal IC regulator:

1. Connect ammeter as described in the general procedures.
2. Connect the voltmeter positive (+) lead to the alternator battery terminal, and connect the voltmeter negative (–) lead to ground.
3. Conduct the current output test with the engine at the manufacturer's recommended rpm. Adjust the carbon pile across the battery until the voltmeter reads 13.5 volts.
4. Compare the ammeter reading to specifications for current output.
5. Connect the voltmeter positive (+) lead to the L-terminal on the alternator, and connect the voltmeter negative lead to ground.

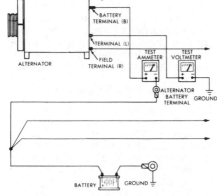

Use this illustration as a guide for testing the internal IC voltage regulator on a Mitsubishi alternator.

6. Turn the ignition switch to RUN, but do not start the engine. Short across the ammeter test leads with a jumper wire and start the engine.
7. Remove the jumper wire from the ammeter test leads and immediately increase engine speed to between 2,000 and 3,000 rpm.
8. Observe the voltmeter reading and compare with voltage regulator setting specification.

FORD Alternator Tests

Alternator with external or integral voltage regulator:
1. With the ignition switch OFF, connect the voltmeter positive (+) lead to the battery positive (+) terminal, and connect the voltmeter negative (–) lead to the battery negative (–) terminal.
2. Note the voltmeter reading (base battery voltage).
3. Run the engine at 1500 rpm with all electrical accessories OFF.
4. Note the voltmeter reading (no-load charging voltage).
5. Turn all electrical accessories on high.
6. Increase the engine speed to 2000 rpm.
7. Note the voltmeter reading (loaded charging voltage).
8. Compare the three voltmeter readings with voltage regulator setting specifications.

GM Alternator Tests

10-SI, 12-SI, 15-SI, and 27-SI alternators:

1. Connect ammeter as described in the general procedures.
2. Conduct the current output test with the engine at the manufacturer's recommended rpm. Adjust the carbon pile to obtain the maximum ammeter reading.

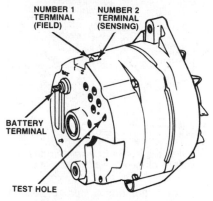

This illustration shows the terminals on GM 10-SI, 12-SI, 15-SI, and 27-SI alternators.

3. Compare the ammeter reading to specifications for current output.
4. Run the engine at moderate speed (approximately 2000 rpm) with all accessories off.
5. Measure voltage across the battery terminals, and compare with manufacturer's voltage regulator setting specifications.

CS series alternators:

1. Connect an ammeter and voltmeter as described in the general procedures.

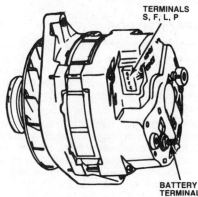

This illustration shows the terminals on GM CS series alternators.

2. Conduct the current output test with the engine at the manufacturer's recommended rpm. Adjust the carbon pile to obtain a voltmeter reading of 13 volts at maximum charging current.
3. Compare the ammeter reading to specifications for current output.
4. Run the engine at moderate speed (approximately 2000 rpm) with all accessories off.
5. Measure the voltage across the battery, and compare with manufacturer's voltage regulator setting specifications.

HONDA Alternator Tests

1983-1987 all models, except 1983-1987 Prelude: Conduct tests as described in the general procedures.

1983-1987 Prelude:

1. Hook up meters as described in the general procedures. Do not exceed 19 volts during testing.
2. For voltage regulator setting:
   - Fuel injected engines: Take voltage reading across the battery (no load).
   - Carburetted engines: Remove the regulator and condenser, but leave the 6-pin connector connected. Measure voltage between

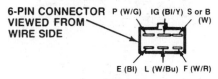

For some Honda carburetted engines you must test the voltage regulator at the connector.

E (ground) and F with engine idling. The voltage reading should meet voltage regulator setting specifications.

1988-1991 all models: The manufacturer recommends that you use the SUN VAT-40 tester or equivalent.

NISSAN Alternator Tests

1983-1991 all models:

1. Conduct current output test as described in the general procedure.
2. Conduct the voltage regulator test with the voltmeter connected at the alternator battery terminal and ground.

TOYOTA Alternator Tests

1983-1991 all models: Conduct tests as described in the general procedures.

VOLKSWAGEN Alternator Tests

1983-1991 all models:
The manufacturer recommends using the VAT-40 or equivalent for alternator tests. Use the illustration and instructions below as a guide:

1. Disconnect the battery ground and positive cables.
2. Connect the battery cutout switch to the battery positive pole.
3. Turn the battery cutout switch to ON. Connect the battery positive terminal to the battery cutout switch.
4. Connect the ammeter, voltmeter, and load resistance. Be sure that the load resistor is connected to the battery positive terminal.

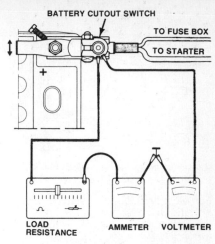

Use this illustration as a guide for testing Volkswagen charging systems.

5. Connect battery ground strap.
6. Run engine at recommended rpm and apply load to obtain maximum ammeter reading (about 20 amps).
7. Turn battery cutout switch to OFF.
8. Adjust load until ammeter reads about 60 percent of maximum rated output amperage.
9. Read the voltmeter for regulator voltage setting.

STARTING SYSTEM

The cranking voltage test and current draw test values for the starter motor are listed in the *Underhood Service Specifications*. Perform one or both of the starting system tests as recommended by the vehicle manufacturer.

TESTING PRECAUTIONS

Before testing the starting system, use the following list as a guide to ensure that you perform the tests safely:

- Make sure that the transmission is in PARK or NEUTRAL. Set the parking brake, and block the drive wheels.
- Always disconnect the battery ground cable before making or breaking connections at the starter motor, solenoid, or relay.
- Do not crank the starter motor for more than 15 seconds at a time. Allow two minutes between tests for the starter motor to cool.
- Disable the ignition system so the engine will not start.

DISABLING THE IGNITION SYSTEM

Starting system test readings are made while the starter motor is cranking. The engine must not start during these tests or the results will be inaccurate. To prevent the engine from starting, disable the ignition system by grounding the high tension lead between the coil and distributor, or by bypassing the ignition switch with a remote starter switch. For older GM vehicles, after installing the remote starter switch, turn the ignition key ON while performing the tests. Cranking with the key OFF can damage the ignition switch.

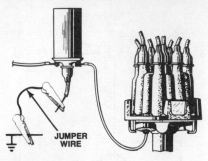

Grounding the coil wire disables some ignition systems.

For electronic ignition systems, disconnect the wiring harness connector(s) from the distributor or coil pack, or disconnect the wire from the negative (–) coil primary terminal. When disabling an electronic ignition, tape the wire ends so that the disconnected wires do not contact ground.

If the vehicle uses a starter relay, connect a remote starter switch according to the manufacturer's instructions. If the car uses a solenoid on the starter motor, connect the switch leads between the battery positive stud and the starting safety switch terminal on the starter solenoid.

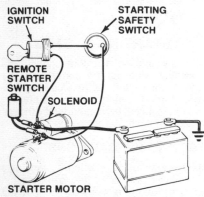

Use a remote starter switch when performing starting system tests.

CRANKING VOLTAGE TEST

The cranking voltage test measures the battery voltage available at the starter during cranking. To check the starter cranking voltage:

1. Bypass the ignition switch with a remote starter switch, or disable the ignition system to prevent the engine from starting.
2. Connect the voltmeter negative (–) lead to ground, and the voltmeter positive (+) lead to the battery positive (+) stud on the solenoid.
3. Crank the engine, and observe the voltmeter reading.
4. Compare the voltmeter reading to cranking voltage specifications.

If the reading is at or above specifications, but the engine still cranks poorly, there is likely a problem in the starter motor. If the reading is below specifications with a fully charged battery, perform a cranking current test. This test determines if the problem is due to high resistance in the starter circuit, or overloading of the starter caused by engine problems.

CRANKING CURRENT TEST

The cranking current test measures the amount of current needed by the starter circuit to crank the engine. The test procedure for performing the cranking current test varies depending on the type of test equipment you are using.

Cranking Current Test with a Series Ammeter or CSB Analyzer

1. Bypass the ignition switch with a remote starter switch, or disable the ignition.

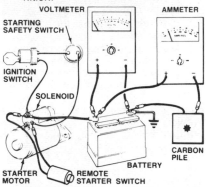

Connect test meters for a cranking current test using a series ammeter as shown.

2. If you are using a CSB analyzer, follow the manufacturer's instructions for hooking up the tester. Then continue to step 3. If you are using test meters and a carbon pile, connect the voltmeter and series ammeter as described below, using the illustration as a guide.
   a. Connect the voltmeter positive (+) lead to the battery positive (+) terminal. Connect the voltmeter negative (–) lead to the battery negative (–) terminal.
   b. Set the carbon pile to its maximum resistance (open).
   c. Connect the ammeter positive (+) lead to the battery positive (+) terminal. Connect the ammeter negative (–) lead to one lead of the carbon pile.
   d. Connect the other lead of the carbon pile to the battery negative (–) terminal.
3. While cranking the engine, watch and note the voltmeter reading.
4. With the starter motor off, adjust the carbon pile until the voltmeter reading matches the reading taken in step 3.
5. Note the ammeter reading. Then set the carbon pile back to the open position.
6. Compare the ammeter reading to the manufacturer's specifications. The table below summarizes the most probable causes of a current draw that is too low or too high.

PROBLEM	PROBABLE CAUSE
High current draw	Short in starter. Starter or engine binding.
Low current draw	High resistance in starting system. Battery is undercharged or defective.

Cranking Current Test with an Inductive Ammeter

1. Bypass the ignition switch with a remote starter switch, or disable the ignition system.
2. Connect the ammeter inductive pickup to the battery (+) cable. Be sure the arrow on the inductive pickup is pointing in the proper direction as specified on the ammeter.

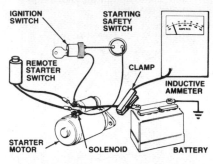

Connect test meters for a cranking current test using an inductive ammeter as shown.

3. Crank the engine for 15 seconds while watching the ammeter reading.
4. Compare the ammeter reading to specifications. The PROBLEM/PROBABLE CAUSE chart summarizes current draw problems.

IGNITION SYSTEM

The ignition system secondary circuit consists of the spark plugs, ignition cables, distributor cap and rotor (if equipped), and ignition coil or coil pack secondary windings. The primary circuit consists of the coil primary windings, ignition points or other switching device, resistor (not on all vehicles), ignition switch, and battery.

SPARK PLUGS

Inspect and replace spark plugs at the intervals listed on the service charts. When replacing the plugs, refer to the *Underhood Service Specifications* for the correct spark plug gap and installation torque.

Use a spark plug socket with a rubber insert when removing or installing plugs. Before removing spark plugs from an engine with aluminum cylinder heads, allow the engine to cool to prevent damaging the threads in the head.

Removing Spark Plugs

1. Disconnect the cables by pulling the spark plug boot and twisting gently. Do not pull the cable. On some vehicles, you must turn the spark plug boot at least one-half turn before removing the cable. Use insulated spark plug pliers when working near hot manifolds.
2. Loosen each plug one turn with a spark plug socket. Then blow away any dirt from around the plugs with compressed air. Do not allow debris to fall into the cylinder when you remove the plug.

3. Place the plugs in a tray or holder to keep them in order by cylinder number. You can determine engine condition and plug operating conditions by examining the deposits on the plugs.

4. If the plugs have gaskets, make sure that the old gasket comes out with the plug.

Gapping Spark Plugs

When installing new plugs, do not assume that they are correctly gapped. Always check them before installation. When adjusting the plug gap, do not bend the electrode by tapping it on the workbench, as this may damage the plug internally.

1. Use a round-wire feeler gauge to check the plug gap, not a flat "blade" feeler gauge.
2. If the gap does not meet the underhood service specifications, adjust it with a special bending tool that is usually provided with round-wire feeler gauges.
3. Check the gap and adjust as needed.

Installing Spark Plugs

If the plugs were difficult to remove, clean the cylinder head plug holes with a thread chaser before installing new plugs. If the vehicle you are working on has aluminum heads, use the thread chaser carefully, as it removes aluminum quickly and can damage the plug holes.

Be sure that the spark plug and cylinder head threads are clean and dry. Use anti-seize compound on the threads when installing plugs in aluminum cylinder heads.

1. Install the plugs by hand. Use a piece of rubber tubing on the plug insulator to turn plugs in hard-to-reach areas. If a plug does not turn easily, remove and reinstall it, as it may be cross threaded.
2. Tighten the plugs with a torque wrench. Torque values are listed in the *Underhood Service Specifications*.

IGNITION CABLES

Ignition cables used in late-model vehicles have carbon-impregnated fiber cores. These cores act as resistors to suppress radio frequency interference (RFI), which can disrupt electronic control system signals as well as radio reception. Never use metal-core ignition cables on late-model vehicles unless specified by the vehicle manufacturer.

Check the manufacturer's recommendations for ignition cable diameter. Some cables are 7 mm in diameter, but many electronic ignition systems require 8 mm cables. Never substitute 7 mm cables for 8 mm cables, as 8 mm cables are designed to withstand the extremely high voltages found in electronic ignition systems. Ignition systems on late-model cars can carry 40 kV (40,000 volts) or more.

Check ignition cable resistance with an ohmmeter. Most manufacturers recommend a maximum resistance of between 5000 to 12,000 ohms per foot. If any of the wires have high or infinite resistance, replace them.

DISTRIBUTOR CAP AND ROTOR

Some vehicles do not use a distributor in the ignition system secondary circuit. If the vehicle has a distributor, inspect the distributor cap and rotor for defects. If you find defects, replace both the cap and rotor as a set. Inspect a distributor cap for:

- Cracks
- Carbon tracks from arcing current
- A sticking or worn carbon button
- Burned or corroded terminals inside the cap
- Corrosion inside the ignition cable towers.

Inspect a distributor rotor for:

- A bent or broken contact strip
- Continuity
- A burned or eroded tip
- A cracked or broken positioning lug
- Carbon tracks or cracks on the body
- Insufficient tension on the spring at the top of the rotor.

Check the *Underhood Service Specifications* for the tests recommended by the vehicle manufacturer.

IGNITION COIL

Ignition coils come in many shapes and sizes, and can be located in a number of places in late-model cars. Before testing a coil, make these preliminary checks and replace any coil that is damaged:

- Make sure the coil is mounted securely and all connections are clean and tight.
- Check for a cracked or burned high voltage tower.
- Check for dents or cracks in the housing.
- Check for oil leakage if the coil is an oil-filled type.
- If the coil has a wiring harness connector, check the connector for damage, and be sure it is securely attached.

Ignition Coil Resistance

In most cases, to test an ignition coil, check the resistance of the primary and secondary windings with an ohmmeter. The resistance values and test temperatures specified by vehicle manufacturers are listed in the *Underhood Service Specifications*. Determine the type of coil you are working on, and use the appropriate procedure to test it.

Testing an oil-filled coil

The oil-filled coil was standard equipment on ignition systems of the past, and many vehicles still use them. Test the primary and secondary resistance of an oil-filled coil as follows:

1. With ignition OFF, disconnect all primary and secondary wiring from the coil. Set the ohmmeter on a low scale.

2. Measure the coil primary resistance between the positive (+) and negative (–) terminals.

3. Compare the reading to the manufacturer's specifications. If the reading is not within specifications, replace the coil.

4. Set the ohmmeter to a high scale.

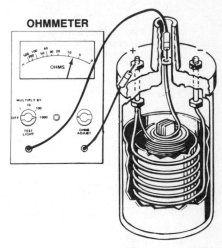

OHMMETER

Test the secondary winding of an oil-filled coil as illustrated.

5. Measure the coil secondary resistance between the center tower and both the positive (+) and negative (–) terminals.

6. Compare the lowest reading from step 5 to the manufacturer's specifications. If the reading is not within specifications, replace the coil.

Coil identification and testing

Use the illustrations to help identify the coil you are working on. Test coil resistance with an ohmmeter using the general instructions that follow, as well as any notes in the *Underhood Service Specifications*. Compare the results with specifications, and replace the coil or coils if defective. For the examples below, unless otherwise specified, check primary resistance between the positive and negative terminals. Check secondary resistance between the negative and high voltage terminals.

CHRYSLER, CHRYSLER IMPORTS and EAGLE Coil Testing

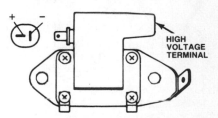

HIGH VOLTAGE TERMINAL

1987-91 1468cc, 1997cc Colt, Summit, Vista w/FI.

PRIMARY RESISTANCE

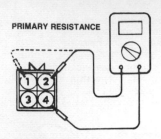

1989-90 1597cc Colt, Summit; 1990-91 1997cc Laser, Talon, coil primary resistance.

HIGH VOLTAGE TERMINAL

1988-89 Tracer, 1989-91 Probe Turbo, 1991 Capri

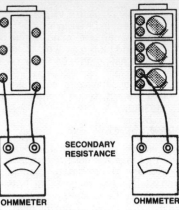

SECONDARY RESISTANCE

OHMMETER   OHMMETER

To check primary resistance on **Types I and II coils,** lift the coil cover, remove the wires from the primary terminals, and measure the resistance between the two terminals. Do the same for the remaining coils. Check secondary resistance as illustrated.

PRIMARY RESISTANCE

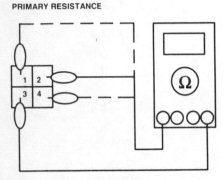

1991 2972cc DOHC Stealth, coil primary resistance.

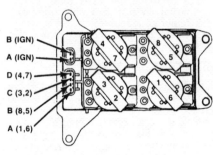

B (IGN)
A (IGN)
D (4,7)
C (3,2)
B (8,5)
A (1,6)

1990-91 5.7L DOHC, coil connectors.

GM Coil Testing

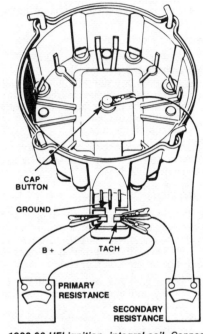

CAP BUTTON

GROUND

B +   TACH

PRIMARY RESISTANCE

SECONDARY RESISTANCE

1983-90 HEI ignition, integral coil. Connect the ohmmeter according to the illustration and measure primary and secondary resistance.

CYLINDERS 3 AND 6   B+

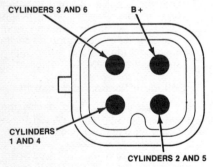

CYLINDERS 1 AND 4

CYLINDERS 2 AND 5

1990-91 2.2L Turbo, 3.3L, 3.8L DIS, coil.

FORD Coil Testing

HIGH VOLTAGE TERMINAL

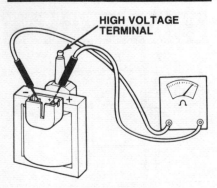

1983-88 TFI ignition.

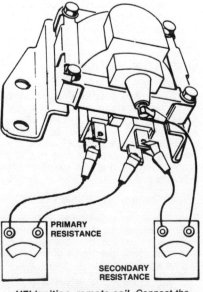

PRIMARY RESISTANCE

SECONDARY RESISTANCE

HEI ignition, remote coil. *Connect the ohmmeter according to the illustration and measure primary and secondary resistance.*

HONDA Coil Testing

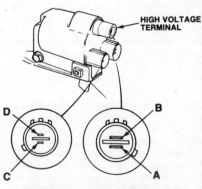

HIGH VOLTAGE TERMINAL

D   B

C   A

1986-87 Civic, CRX. 1986-89 Accord, Prelude w/FI. Measure primary resistance between terminals A and D. Measure secondary resistance between A and the high voltage terminal.

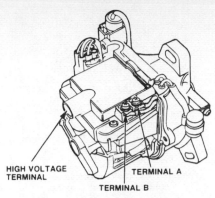

1988-91 Civic, CRX. Measure primary resistance between terminals A and B. Measure secondary resistance between A and the high voltage terminal.

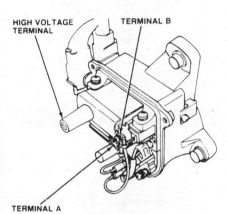

1990-91 Accord. Measure primary resistance between terminals A and B. Measure secondary resistance between A and the high voltage terminal.

NISSAN Coil Testing

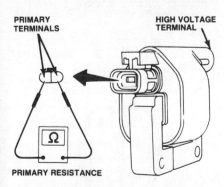

Most Nissan models. Check for more than one coil. Disconnect the coil power transistor(s). Measure primary resistance as illustrated. Measure secondary resistance between the high voltage terminal and each of the primary terminals. Compare the lowest reading with manufacturer's specifications for secondary resistance. Coil connectors may vary slightly between models.

TOYOTA Coil Testing

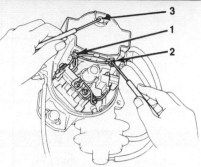

SECONDARY RESISTANCE

Most Toyota 4-cyl. models. Check primary resistance between points 1 and 2. Check secondary resistance between points 2 and 3.

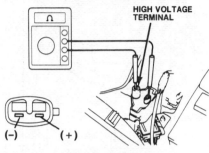

SECONDARY RESISTANCE

1989-91 Camry V6, 1991 Previa. Check primary resistance between positive (+) and negative (–) connector terminals. Check secondary resistance as shown.

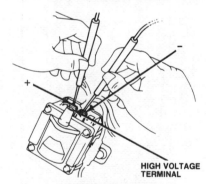

PRIMARY RESISTANCE

1983-86 Celica/Supra. Check primary resistance as shown. Check secondary resistance between the high voltage terminal and each primary terminal.

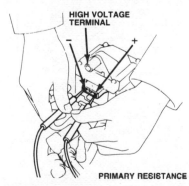

PRIMARY RESISTANCE

1987-91 Supra. Check primary resistance as shown. Check secondary resistance between the high voltage terminal and each primary terminal.

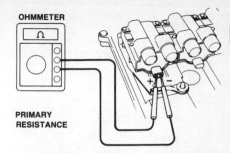

PRIMARY RESISTANCE

1987-91 Supra Turbo. With this coil, you cannot measure the secondary resistance.

VOLKSWAGEN Coil Testing

Use the test procedure for oil-filled coils.

DISTRIBUTOR PICKUP RESISTANCE AND AIR GAP

Mechanical breaker points have been replaced by electronic switching devices, such as optical sensors, magnetic-pulse generators, and Hall-effect switches. Check distributor or ignition pickup resistance and air gap in these systems, as indicated in the *Underhood Service Specifications.* Use the illustrations and instructions that follow as a guide.

CHRYSLER Pickup Coils

Check and adjust the pickup air gap as follows:
1. Align a tooth on the reluctor with the pickup coil.
2. Use non-magnetic feeler gauges to check the air gap.
3. To adjust the gap, align one reluctor blade with the pickup coil.
4. Loosen the pickup coil adjustment lock screw.
5. With a screwdriver blade inserted in the adjustment slot, shift the distributor plate so the correct size feeler gauge contacts the reluctor blade and the pickup coil.
6. Tighten the lock screw. No force should be required to remove the feeler gauge.
7. Apply vacuum to the distributor vacuum advance unit, and move the pickup plate through its range of travel. Watch the pickup coil to be sure it does not hit the reluctor. Recheck the air gap. If the pickup plate is loose, overhaul the distributor.

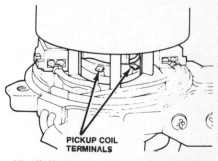

All w/2.6L engines. Measure the resistance between the pickup coil terminals by inserting the ohmmeter leads through the openings in the distributor.

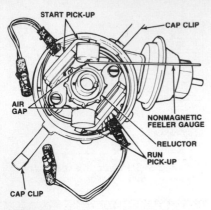

6-cyl. & V8, use a non-magnetic feeler gauge to check the pickup air gap. Measure pickup coil resistance at two-terminal connector(s).

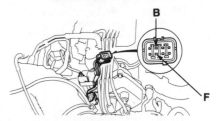

1989-91 Probe Turbo. At the distributor connector, measure the resistance between terminals A and B, C and D, and E and F.

GM Pickup Coils

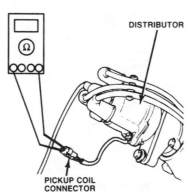

Connect the ohmmeter as shown in the illustration, and measure pickup coil resistance.

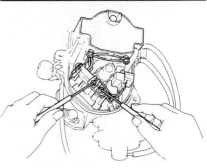

1988-91 CRX, Civic. Measure resistance between terminals D and E.

1990-91 Accord. Disconnect the TDC/CRANK/CYL 8-pin connector, and check resistance between terminals F and B.

FORD Pickup Coils

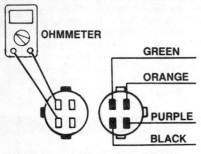

Dura-Spark ignition. Disconnect the distributor harness. Measure resistance between the orange and purple wire sockets at the connector.

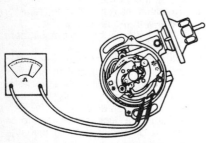

1983-88 TFI-I ignition. Disconnect the ignition module from the distributor. Measure the resistance between the points indicated.

1991 Geo Metro.

HONDA Pickup Coils

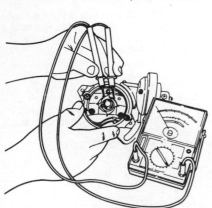

1989-91 Probe 4-cylinder. With the distributor cap and rotor removed, measure the resistance between the points indicated.

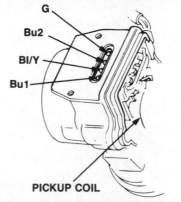

1986-89 w/FI Accord, Prelude. Remove igniter cover and pull igniter out. Check resistance between terminals G and Bu².

TOYOTA Pickup Coils

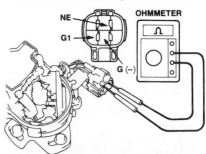

Most Toyota 4-cyl. models. Check resistance between the points indicated.

1989-91 Corolla. Disconnect the distributor connector and check the resistance between terminals G1 and G–, and Ne and G–.

1986-89 Celica, 3S-GE engine. Disconnect the connector and check the resistance between terminals G1 and G–, G2 and G–, and Ne and G–.

1987-89 Celica, 3S-FE engine. Disconnect the connector and check the resistance between terminals G and G–, and Ne and G–.

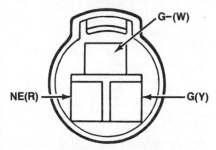

1983-86 Celica/Supra. Disconnect the connector and check the resistance between terminals G and G–, and Ne and G–.

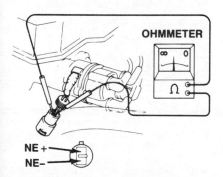

1983-91 Pickup 4-cyl. Check the resistance between the two terminals.

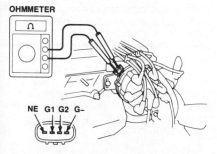

1986-91 Supra. Disconnect the connector, and check the resistance between terminals G1 and G–, G2 and G–, and Ne and G–.

IGNITION RESISTORS

AUXILIARY BALLAST RESISTOR

NORMAL BALLAST RESISTOR

Some manufacturers recommend checking the ignition resistor. Measure the resistance between the terminals.

FORD Ignition Resistors

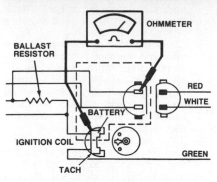

1983-90 Dura-Spark ignition. Place ohmmeter on the coil BATT terminal and the connector, as shown.

VOLKSWAGEN Ignition Resistors

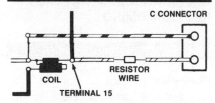

If the vehicle has an ignition resistor wire, remove connector C from the fuse relay panel, remove the resistor wire from coil terminal 15 — positive (+) terminal, and connect the ohmmeter at each end of the wire to measure the resistance.

IGNITION TIMING

Modern vehicles may have spark distribution systems with or without distributors. If the vehicle has a distributor, you can usually check and adjust the base timing. If the vehicle does not have a distributor, you must service it according to the manufacturer's instructions. For GM and Chrysler vehicles without distributors, you cannot check or adjust the base timing. On Ford vehicles, you can check the timing, but it is not adjustable.

The most common method for checking base timing is with a timing light. Always read the VECI decal for the most current timing procedures and specifications.

Use the illustrations and general instructions in this section as well as any notes listed with the *Underhood Service Specifications* for base timing.

CHECKING BASE IGNITION TIMING

Timing mark illustrations are located at the beginning of each *Underhood Service Specifications* section. Check and adjust base timing with the engine running at or near idle, unless otherwise specified.

Checking Base Timing

Using a timing light

1. Run the engine until it reaches normal operating temperature.
2. Connect a tachometer and timing light according to the equipment manufacturer's instructions. Attach the timing light pickup to the number 1 cylinder ignition cable or spark plug boot. Never puncture the ignition cable or spark plug boot to connect the timing light pickup.
3. Locate the timing marks. Wipe off any dirt, and use white chalk or paint on the marks to make them visible.
4. Disconnect hoses or electrical connectors, as specified on the VECI decal.
5. Set the parking brake, start the engine, and operate it at idle or the engine speed listed in the *Underhood Service Specifications*.
6. Aim the timing light, and observe the position of the marks. Compare the results with specifications, and adjust if needed.

Using a magnetic timing meter

In order to use a magnetic timing meter, the vehicle must have a receptacle designed for the probe:

1. Insert the magnetic timing meter probe into the receptacle on the engine, and attach any other meter connectors according to the manufacturer's instructions.

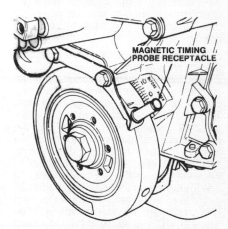

This is a typical magnetic timing probe receptacle.

2. Set the offset on the meter before checking the timing, or be sure to calculate the offset when reading the timing measurements.
3. Disconnect hoses or electrical connectors, as specified on the VECI decal.
4. Set the parking brake, start the engine, and operate it at idle or at the engine speed listed in the *Underhood Service Specifications*.
5. Read the timing value on the meter's digital display. Compare results with specifications, and adjust if needed.

SETTING THE BASE TIMING

Ignition System with a Distributor

1. Refer to the VECI decal for instructions on checking the base timing.
2. To adjust the base timing, loosen the distributor holddown bolt just enough so that you can turn the distributor.

3. To advance timing, rotate the distributor against rotor rotation. To retard timing, rotate the distributor in the direction of rotor rotation.
4. Tighten the hold-down bolt, and recheck the timing.

Ignition System without a Distributor

Distributorless ignition system timing is computer controlled. Information received from various engine sensors, such as camshaft or crankshaft position sensors, is processed by the engine computer. On domestic vehicles, timing is usually not adjustable. Instead, you must troubleshoot the system using the computer diagnostic routines and codes. Check the special instructions and the *Underhood Service Specifications* for more information on distributorless ignition systems.

CHECKING IGNITION TIMING ADVANCE

Check the timing advance after setting base timing. If the advance does not meet specifications, you will have to repair, replace, or adjust the mechanical advance mechanisms. In the case of computer controlled ignition systems, the computer may be faulty or may have to be reprogrammed.

In the *Underhood Service Specifications*, the advance ranges listed as "Total" under Distributor Timing Advance are the combined centrifugal and vacuum advances at a steady, no-load 2500 rpm. This "Total" *does not include* the initial advance (base timing). "Total" is the same figure you will get if you first set the base timing, and then use a dial-back-to-zero timing light, which is dialed back to the base timing setting. For example, if a distributor/vacuum advance unit adds 25 degrees of advance to the base timing at 2500 rpm, and the base timing is 5 degrees BTDC, you will read 25 degrees of spark advance when you dial the timing light back to 5 degrees BTDC. The specification you will find listed as "Total" under Distributor Timing Advance is 25 degrees.

When applicable, the *Underhood Service Specifications* are given for total advance and centrifugal advance. Subtracting the centrifugal advance from total advance gives the vacuum advance at 2500 rpm.

1. Connect a tachometer and timing light or meter as instructed in the base timing procedure. Be sure the base timing is correct before checking timing advance.
2. Disconnect and plug the vacuum lines at the distributor to disable the vacuum advance or advance/retard unit.
3. Set the engine idle speed to 2500 rpm.
4. Read the centrifugal advance timing. If you are using a timing meter, subtract the base timing from the new timing reading to obtain the centrifugal advance. If you are using a dial-back-to-zero timing light, dial the

light back to the base timing setting and read the degrees of centrifugal advance from the timing light. Check the centrifugal advance value against specifications.

5. Check the vacuum advance by connecting a vacuum pump to the advance diaphragm, and drawing about 15 to 20 in-Hg (380 to 510 mm-Hg). Engine speed should increase, and the timing should advance. Check against the "Total" advance specifications.
6. If the vehicle has a dual-diaphragm vacuum unit on the distributor, check the secondary retard or subadvance by connecting a vacuum pump to the diaphragm. Engine speed should decrease or increase respectively.

SPECIAL INSTRUCTIONS FOR CHECKING AND ADJUSTING IGNITION TIMING

CHRYSLER Ignition Timing

Domestics

Chrysler's DIS (distributorless ignition system) timing cannot be adjusted.

Electronic Ignition System (EIS), was used in vehicles through 1987. One variation has a magnetic pulse distributor with either one or two pickups, and was used on cars and trucks built in the early 1980s. This system was slowly phased out so that by 1987, it was used mainly on trucks. Another version of EIS was used with the Mitsubishi 2.6L engine in FWD vehicles from 1981 to 1987. This system uses a distributor with a built-in IC ignitor, and has centrifugal and vacuum advance. Both variations of the EIS system are used with carburetted engines.

- After warming the engine, quickly open the throttle to be sure it does not stick. The idle speed screw should be against its stop.
- Disconnect and plug the vacuum line at the distributor.
- If needed, adjust the rpm with the idle speed screw, and check timing.

Electronic spark control (ESC) and *electronic spark advance (ESA)* use magnetic pickup or Hall-effect distributors. These ignition systems are found on both car-

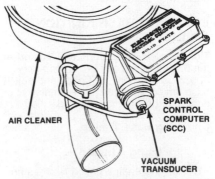

For some Chrysler carburetted engines with ESC or ESA, disconnect and plug the hose at the vacuum transducer on the SCC.

buretted and fuel injected engines. Computers used to control spark timing are either the spark control computer (SCC), single module engine controller (SMEC), or single board engine controller (SBEC).

- For carburetted engines, disconnect and plug the hose at the vacuum transducer as equipped on the SCC.
- If the vehicle has a carburetor switch, ground it. For fuel injected engines, disconnect the engine coolant sensor lead wire.

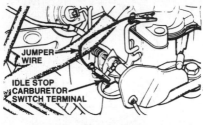

For other Chrysler carburetted engines with ESC or ESA, ground the carburetor switch.

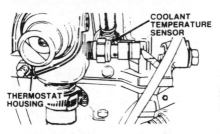

For Chrysler fuel injected engines with ESC or ESA, disconnect the engine coolant sensor lead wire connector.

- Erase fault codes from the computer after setting the timing.

Imports

Several ignition timing systems are used on Chrysler imports. One type has mechanical and vacuum advance, and is used on carburetted engines. Another uses mechanical and vacuum advance as well as rudimentary computer timing controls, and is used on 1984 to 1988 1.6L turbo engines and 1984 to 1989 2.6L turbo engines. Another system has full electronic spark timing (EST), and is used on fuel injected engines.

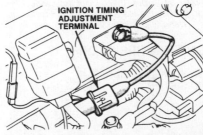

For Chrysler vehicles with EST and distributor, ground the ignition timing adjustment terminal.

- For engines with EST, connect a jumper wire to the ignition timing adjustment terminal, and ground it.
- For engines without EST, disconnect the white-striped vacuum hose from

the vacuum diaphragm at the distributor, and plug the hose end.
- On later models with mechanical and vacuum advance, as well as rudimentary computer timing controls, disconnect the high altitude pressure sensor and ground it.

For imports with distributorless ignition systems (DIS):

- Connect a jumper wire to the ignition timing adjustment terminal, and ground it.

For Chrysler imports with distributorless ignition systems, ground the ignition timing adjustment terminal.

- To adjust the timing, loosen the nut securing the crank angle sensor, and rotate it.

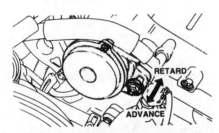

To adjust the timing on Chrysler imports with distributorless ignition systems, rotate the crank angle sensor.

FORD Ignition Timing

On Ford's DIS (distributorless ignition system) and EDIS (electronic distributorless ignition system), you can check, but you cannot adjust ignition timing. Timing cannot be checked or adjusted on EEC-III systems through 1984. On all other systems (TFI-I, TFI-IV, Dura-Spark-II, and EEC-IV with distributor), timing is adjustable.

- For non-EEC systems, remove the vacuum hoses from the distributor vacuum advance, and plug the hoses. If the car has a barometric

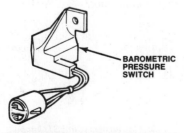

Ford non-EEC system with a barometric pressure switch.

pressure switch, disconnect the switch from the ignition module and jumper the connector pins (yellow and black wires).
- For some non-EEC systems (1983-1984), disconnect the wire from the MCU to the ignition module, and jumper pins at the ignition module.
- For EEC-IV systems (except DIS and EDIS), disconnect the single-wire inline spout connector near the distributor, or remove the shorting bar from the double-wire spout connector.

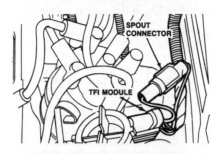

For Ford EEC-IV systems (except DIS and EDIS), disconnect the single wire inline spout connector near the distributor.

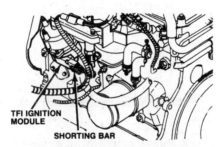

On some other EEC-IV systems (except DIS and EDIS), remove the shorting bar from the double wire spout connector.

- If the vehicle has a "positive buy" distributor (identified by the Torx head bolt), adjust the timing no more than six degrees.

GM Ignition Timing

On ignition systems with distributors, GM uses the HEI (High-Energy Ignition) system. There are many variations of the HEI ignition system, and therefore, many variations on procedures to check and adjust ignition timing.

Use the notes with the *Underhood Service Specifications* and the VECI decal, which is located on the radiator support or the hood, to check and adjust the ignition timing.

To check the base timing on most carburetted engines, you must disconnect the four-wire connector at the distributor, or ground the test terminal of the diagnostic connector. Note, however, that grounding the test terminal on some engines will put the system into a fixed timing setting that is *not* base timing.

On fuel injected engines, you cannot disconnect the four-wire distributor connector to check the base timing because the

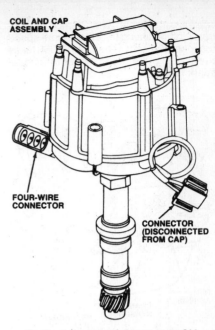

To check the base timing on most GM carburetted engines with HEI, disconnect the four-wire connector at the distributor.

computer needs a trigger signal to time the injector(s). On these engines, you must open a bypass connector in the distributor wiring harness, jumper across

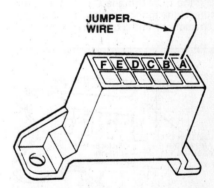

On some GM fuel-injected engines with HEI, jumper across two terminals of the diagnostic connector.

two terminals of the diagnostic connector, or ground a special connector in the engine compartment.

GM currently has three types of distributorless ignition systems:

The *C³I (Computer-Controlled Coil Ignition) system* uses coils, an ignition module, camshaft sensors (some) and

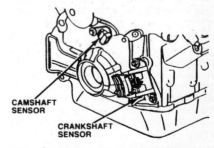

This C³I ignition system uses crankshaft and camshaft sensors, which send ignition timing data to the computer.

crankshaft sensors. The C³I module controls ignition timing until the engine speed reaches 400 rpm. Then the ECM takes over, using the EST mode to control spark timing.

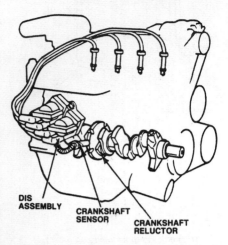

This illustration shows the major components of GM's DIS system.

The DIS (Direct Ignition System) uses a crankshaft sensor, coils, a DIS module, and the ECM (Engine Control Module) to control the ignition timing. The DIS module controls timing until the engine speed

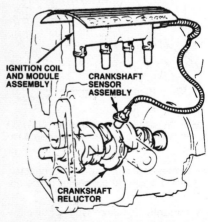

This illustration shows the major components of GM's IDI system.

reaches 400 rpm. Then the ECM takes over using the EST mode to control spark timing.

The IDI (Integrated Direct Ignition) system uses a crankshaft sensor, coils, an ignition module, a conductor housing, and the ECM (Engine Control Module) to control the ignition timing. The ignition module controls timing until the engine speed reaches 700 rpm. Then the ECM takes over using the EST mode to control spark timing.

Checking and adjusting these ignition systems by conventional methods is not possible.

HONDA Ignition Timing

- Remove the rubber cover from the inspection window to reveal the timing marks.

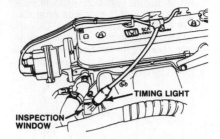

On Honda vehicles, you must remove the rubber cover from the inspection window to reveal the timing marks.

- On fuel injected vehicles, locate the service connector.
  — On 1990 and later vehicles, the connector is located in the far right corner under the dashboard. Remove the blue rubber cover, and jumper the terminals.

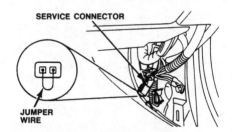

On 1990 and later Honda vehicles, the service connector is located in the far right corner under the dashboard. On earlier Honda vehicles, the connector is behind the coil.

  — On earlier fuel-injected vehicles, the connector is located behind the ignition coil. Remove the yellow rubber cover, and jumper the terminals.
- In most cases, for carburetted engines, do not remove the vacuum hoses. However, on some carburetted engines, you must remove the vacuum lines, plug them, and take a timing reading, which should be about 4° BTDC. These vehicles are indicated with an asterisk (*) in the Underhood Service Specifications.

NISSAN Ignition Timing

Use the notes on the Underhood Service Specifications page and the information below as a guide:

- For many Nissan vehicles manufactured in the early 1980s, disconnect and plug the distributor vacuum hoses before checking the timing.
- Check the timing with the vacuum sensor hose connected, but disconnect the sensor hose before adjusting the timing.

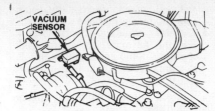

For some Nissans, disconnect the vacuum sensor hose before adjusting the timing.

- Connect the timing light inductive clamp to the high tension wire between the number 1 coil and spark plug.

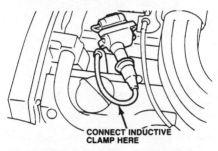

On this Nissan, connect the timing light inductive clamp to the high tension wire between the #1 coil and spark plug.

- Check the timing with the throttle sensor connected, but disconnect the throttle sensor before adjusting the timing.

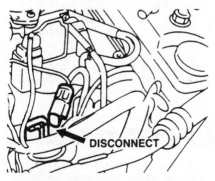

On this Nissan, disconnect the throttle sensor before adjusting the timing.

TOYOTA Ignition Timing

- Vehicles that do not have a vacuum advance diaphragm on the distributor have EST (electronic spark timing). Use a jumper wire to connect terminals TE1 and E1, or T and E1 (depending on the model), at the check connector.

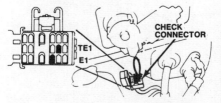

For Toyota vehicles with EST, jumper terminals TE1 and E1, or T and E1 (depending on the model), at the check connector.

- On some vehicles with vacuum advance, you must disconnect and plug the vacuum hose at the inner diaphragm, but leave other hoses connected, as mentioned in the notes on the *Underhood Service Specifications* page. Unless otherwise specified, for all other vehicles with vacuum advance, disconnect and plug the vacuum hoses at the distributor.

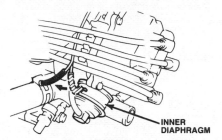

For some Toyota vehicles with vacuum advance, disconnect and plug the vacuum hose at the inner diaphragm, but leave other hoses connected.

VOLKSWAGEN Ignition Timing

Use the notes on the *Underhood Service Specifications* page and the information below as a guide:

- 1985-89 **Scirocco, Cabriolet**
  — CIS: Disconnect and plug vacuum hose.
  — CIS-E: Leave hoses connected.
- 1985-90 **Golf, Jetta, GTI**
  — CIS: Disconnect and plug vacuum hose.
  — CIS-E: Check the idle or throttle switch to be sure that it is closed.
  — Digifant II: Remove cap from CO tap tube and connect special tester.
- 1983-84 **Pickup, Jetta, Rabbit, Scirocco**
  — CIS with transistorized ignition: Disconnect plugs from idle stabilization unit, and connect them together.
  — Carburetted with transistorized ignition: Disconnect and plug vacuum retard hose.
  — CIS without transistorized ignition: Leave hoses connected.
  — 1983 **Rabbit, Jetta, Scirocco:** Disconnect plugs from idle stabilization unit and connect them together.
  — 1983 **Rabbit GTI:** Leave hoses connected.
- 1983-89 **Vanagon**
  — Air-cooled AFC, California: Disconnect plugs from idle stabilization unit and connect them together.
  — Air-cooled AFC, USA: Disconnect vacuum hose.
  — Water-cooled Digijet: Disconnect plugs from idle stabilization unit and connect them together.
  — Water-cooled Digifant: Disconnect temperature sensor II.

- 1983-88 **Quantum**
  — 4 CIS, 1983-84: Leave hoses connected.
  — 4 CIS-E: Disconnect vacuum hoses.
  — 5 CIS: Leave hoses connected.
  — 5 CIS-E: Disconnect vacuum hoses.
  — Synchro: Leave hoses connected.
- 1987-89 **Fox**
  — CIS/CIS-E: Disconnect vacuum hoses.
- 1990-91 **Passat:** Leave hoses connected.
- 1990-91 **Corrado:** Disconnect coolant temperature sensor.

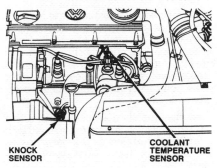

KNOCK SENSOR   COOLANT TEMPERATURE SENSOR

1990 Corrado. Disconnect the coolant temperature sensor.

FUEL SYSTEMS

The *Underhood Service Specifications* contain fuel system pressures and idle speed settings for vehicles with and without computer controls. Test procedures differ for carburetted, throttle-body injected, and multi-point injected engines.

FUEL PUMP PRESSURE

If you suspect that the fuel system is causing a driveability problem, check the fuel pump pressure to ensure that fuel delivery is adequate.

PRESSURE TEST FOR CARBURETTED FUEL SYSTEMS

Test fuel pump pressure with a pressure gauge attached to the fuel line at the carburetor inlet. Use a short connecting hose. If the fuel pump has a vapor return line, clamp the line during the test.

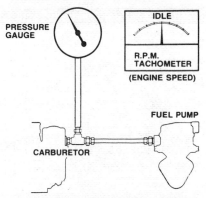

PRESSURE GAUGE   IDLE   R.P.M. TACHOMETER (ENGINE SPEED)   FUEL PUMP   CARBURETOR

Tee a pressure gauge into the fuel line to pressure test the fuel pump.

1. Run the engine for a few minutes. Then turn it off.
2. Disconnect the fuel line at the carburetor, and tee a pressure gauge into the fuel line.
3. Start the engine and run it at the specified engine speed. Note the pressure reading on the gauge, and compare it to the specification.
4. Stop the engine and watch the pressure gauge. If the fuel pump valves are sealing properly, the reading should remain constant for several minutes.

PRESSURE TEST FOR FUEL-INJECTED SYSTEMS

CAUTION: The electric fuel pumps used in fuel injected systems produce high fuel pressure at the injectors. Before teeing into the fuel lines of an injected system, relieve excess pressure in the lines. If you do not release system pressure, fuel will spray from the lines when you disconnect them.

Relieving Fuel Pressure

Most throttle-body injection systems operate at 10 to 20 psi or higher. Multi-point fuel injection systems operate at 30 psi or more. You must release system pressure by opening a special pressure release valve, by bleeding pressure from a vacuum operated pressure regulator, by disconnecting the electrical connector at the fuel pump, or by removing the fuel pump fuse.

If the system has a Schrader valve or test port, as do some Ford and GM injection systems, and you have a pressure gauge with a pressure release button, use the following procedure to release pressure:

1. Loosen the fuel tank cap to release any in-tank pressure.
2. Attach the pressure gauge to the Schrader valve on the throttle body or fuel rail.
3. Place the fuel drain tube in a suitable container and press the pressure release button.

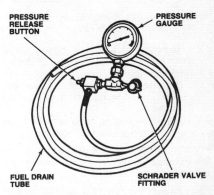

PRESSURE RELEASE BUTTON   PRESSURE GAUGE   FUEL DRAIN TUBE   SCHRADER VALVE FITTING

A gauge with a pressure release button can be used to release fuel system pressure.

If the system uses a fuel pressure regulator controlled by manifold vacuum, as do some Honda vehicles, release residual pressure as follows:

1. Loosen the fuel tank cap to release any in-tank pressure.

2. Remove the manifold vacuum hose from the regulator, and attach a hand-operated vacuum pump to the regulator.
3. Apply 25 in-Hg of vacuum to the regulator for 30 seconds. This bleeds any residual pressure back to the fuel tank through the return line.

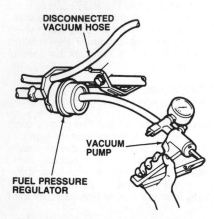

If the vehicle has a vacuum-controlled fuel pressure regulator, use a vacuum pump to release residual pressure.

4. Remove the hand vacuum pump, and reattach the manifold vacuum line.

On some Chrysler and GM vehicles, you must release pressure by disconnecting the electrical connector at the fuel pump, or for some Ford vehicles by disconnecting the inertia switch:

1. Start the engine.

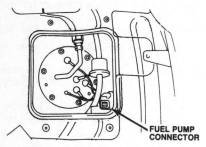

On some vehicles, disconnect the fuel pump electrical connector to release pressure.

2. Remove the electrical connector at the fuel pump, or disconnect the inertia switch.
3. The engine will stall after a few seconds, and fuel pressure will be released.
4. Crank the engine once or twice to be sure that pressure is released.

For some VW and GM vehicles, release the residual pressure by removing the fuse or fuel pump relay:

1. Loosen the fuel tank cap to release any in-tank pressure.
2. Remove the fuel pump fuse from the vehicle's fuse block, or disconnect the relay.
3. Start the engine, and let it run until it stalls.
4. Crank the engine once or twice to purge any remaining pressure from the system.

For some Chrysler vehicles, you must ground the injector terminal to release system pressure:

1. Loosen the fuel tank cap to release any in-tank pressure.
2. Disconnect the injector wiring harness, and use a jumper wire to ground terminal 1 on the connector.
3. Connect another jumper wire to terminal number 2, and touch the wire to the battery positive terminal for no more than 5 seconds. This releases system pressure.

Pressure Test Procedure

After relieving fuel system pressure, connect the pressure gauge in the fuel line. Some vehicles have a special test port where you can connect the gauge and test the fuel pressure. However, in some cases, you will have to use an adapter or a section of fuel line to connect the pressure gauge.

Use the procedure and illustrations that follow, as well as the notes included with the *Underhood Service Specifications* as a guide when testing fuel system pressure.

1. Relieve fuel system pressure, as explained earlier.
2. Connect the fuel pressure test gauge in the fuel line.
3. Start the engine, and run it at the correct engine speed.
4. Note the pressure reading on the gauge, and compare it to specifications. Throttle-body injection system pressure should remain relatively constant regardless of engine speed. Multi-point injection system pressure should vary with manifold vacuum.

Pressure Test Gauge Connections

Use the following illustrations to locate test ports in various fuel injected systems.

CHRYSLER Fuel Pressure Tests

Domestics

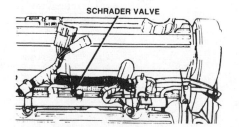

For Chrysler domestic engines with multi-point fuel injection, the Schrader valve is on the fuel rail.

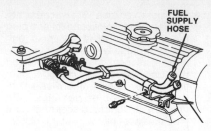

For engines with throttle-body injection, measure the pressure using a tee connector at the fuel supply hose.

Imports

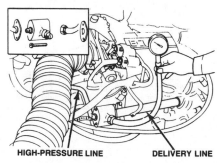

Connect the fuel pressure gauge between the fuel delivery line and the high pressure line. You will need an adapter to do this.

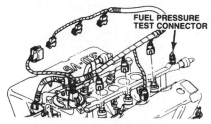

For models with multi-point injection, the test connector is on the fuel rail.

FORD Fuel Pressure Tests

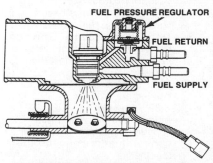

For Ford's throttle body injection system, measure the pressure at the fuel supply line with a tee connector and pressure gauge.

A few CFI systems have a test connector similar to the one used on multi-point injected systems.

GM Fuel Pressure Tests

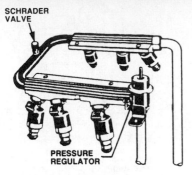

For GM vehicles with multi-point injection, use the Schrader valve connector on the fuel rail.

For GM vehicles with TBI, remove the section of hose between the fuel line and the throttle body, and connect the adapter and gauge.

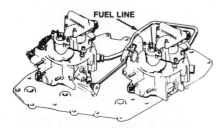

For GM cars with Crossfire TBI injection, connect the adapter and gauge at the fuel line between the throttle body assemblies.

HONDA Fuel Pressure Tests

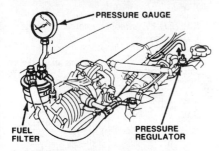

Remove the bolt from the outlet line on top of the fuel filter. Thread an adapter in its place, and connect the pressure gauge.

NISSAN Fuel Pressure Tests

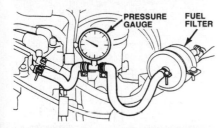

Remove the fuel outlet line at the fuel filter, and connect the gauge between the fuel filter outlet port and the fuel outlet line.

TOYOTA Fuel Pressure Tests

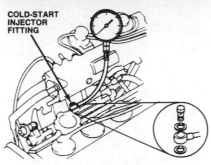

For Toyota engines, check the fuel pressure at the cold start injector. You will need a pressure gauge with a banjo fitting or an adapter.

VOLKSWAGEN Fuel Pressure Tests

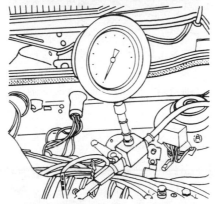

For the Bosch K-Jetronic or KE-Jetronic systems, you need a gauge with an adapter and an inline valve, so that you can shut off pressure when needed. Connect the adapter inline between the fuel distributor and the control pressure regulator.

IDLE SPEED CHECK AND ADJUSTMENT

During a tune-up, the idle speed usually is not adjusted on late-model cars. In fact, adjustment screws are often sealed at the factory. If the vehicle is not idling correctly, it is likely due to other factors, such as faulty sensors or vacuum leaks.

Vehicle manufacturers' instructions for idle speed check and adjustment vary. Read the VECI decal for specific information. However, observe these basic guidelines before setting the idle speed:

- Compression pressure must be within specifications.
- Mechanical valve lifters must be correctly adjusted.
- The ignition system must be in good operating condition.
- The manifold heat control valve must be working properly.
- Fuel pump pressure and volume must be within specifications.
- The engine must be at normal operating temperature.
- The vapor purge hose must be disconnected and plugged.
- The parking brake must be set and the drive wheels blocked.

- The PCV and EGR valves must be connected and functioning properly.

Idle speed may be manually adjusted or computer-controlled. The fuel systems may be carburetted or fuel injected. In manually adjustable systems, the idle speed is regulated by an adjusting screw that acts as a stop to open or close a throttle plate or air inlet at the intake manifold. You can find this adjustment on both carburetted and fuel injected engines.

In computer-controlled systems, the computer signals a stepper motor to open or close a throttle plate or valve, which opens or closes an air inlet. You will find computer-controlled idle speed on both carburetted and fuel injected engines.

IDLE SPEED CHECK AND ADJUSTMENT ON SYSTEMS WITHOUT COMPUTER CONTROLS

Always refer to the VECI decal before adjusting idle speed.

Carburetted Engines

Both slow (curb) and fast idle speeds are provided in the *Underhood Service Specifications*. Check the notes included with the specifications, and check the illustrations that follow.

1. Connect a tachometer.
2. Disconnect and plug any vacuum hoses, as needed.
3. Turn the idle speed adjusting screw on the throttle linkage clockwise to increase speed, or counterclockwise to decrease speed.

On carburetted engines, adjust the idle speed by turning the idle speed adjusting screw.

4. Adjust fast idle speed. Be sure the adjusting screw is on the step of the cam as specified in the *Underhood Service Specifications*.
5. Disconnect the tachometer.

Fuel Injected Engines

Although it is uncommon in late-model cars, some fuel injected vehicles have a manual idle speed adjustment, such as this Nissan.

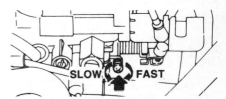

Like a carburetted system, some fuel injected systems have a manual idle speed adjustment.

1. Warm the engine to operating temperature, and connect the tachometer.
2. Run the engine at 2,000 rpm for 2 minutes.
3. Race the engine 2 or 3 times up to about 3,000 rpm. Then allow the vehicle to idle for 1 minute.
4. With the parking brake engaged, move the shifter into DRIVE, and check the idle speed.
5. Adjust the idle speed as needed by turning the idle adjusting screw.

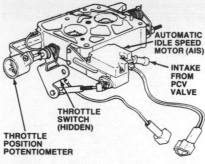

1983-84 4-cylinder, with computer control, with AIS (automatic idle speed) motor.

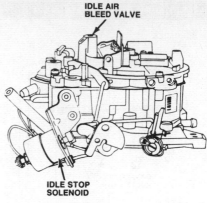

1983-87 6- and 8-cylinder, without computer controls.

IDLE SPEED CHECK AND ADJUSTMENT ON SYSTEMS WITH COMPUTER CONTROLS

Carburetted Engines

Computer-controlled carburetted engines usually have a manually adjustable idle speed stop screw and a solenoid or stepper motor to change the idle speed setting, as needed. Use the notes that are included with the *Underhood Service Specifications*, and the illustrations that follow to set the idle speed.

Fuel Injected Engines

Procedures for adjusting idle speed in fuel injected engines vary, depending on the type of system used. Some systems are completely computer controlled, and you cannot manually adjust the idle speed. For other systems, you must jumper the diagnostic connector or disengage a stepper motor or solenoid before manually adjusting the idle speed.

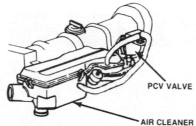

1986-90 4-cylinder, TBI, with computer controls.

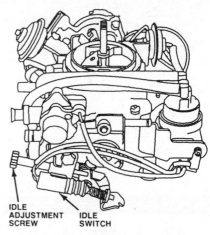

FORD Idle Speed Adjustment

1.3L (81) 2V, without computer controls.

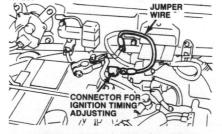

1986-90 4-cylinder except 1.8L, 2.0L, with computer control.

SPECIAL INSTRUCTIONS FOR CHECKING AND ADJUSTING THE IDLE SPEED

Use the notes with the *Underhood Service Specifications* and the illustrations that follow to adjust the idle speed.

CHRYSLER Idle Speed Adjustment

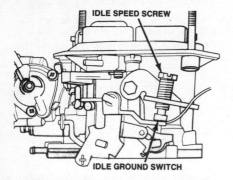

1984-87 4-cylinder 1.6L (97), 1.7L (105), 2.2L (135) 2V, without computer controls.

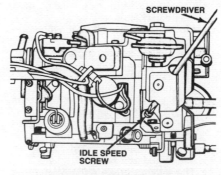

1985-87 4-cylinder 2.6L (156).

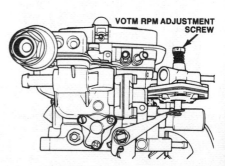

1986-90 2.0L, with computer control.

1.6L (98) 2V, without computer controls.

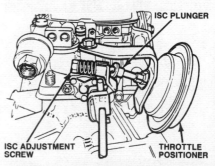

1.6L (98) 2V, 1.9L (113) 2V, with computer controls.

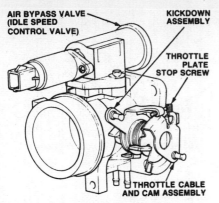

AIR BYPASS VALVE (IDLE SPEED CONTROL VALVE)

KICKDOWN ASSEMBLY

THROTTLE PLATE STOP SCREW

THROTTLE CABLE AND CAM ASSEMBLY

1.6L (98) MFI, 1.9L (113) MFI, with computer controls.

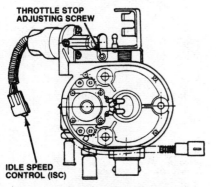

THROTTLE STOP ADJUSTING SCREW

IDLE SPEED CONTROL (ISC)

1.9L (113) TBI, 2.3L (140) HSC TBI, 2.5L (153), with computer controls.

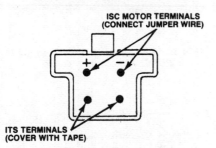

ISC MOTOR TERMINALS (CONNECT JUMPER WIRE)

ITS TERMINALS (COVER WITH TAPE)

2.0L (122), with computer controls.

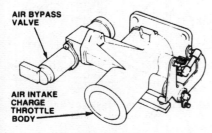

AIR BYPASS VALVE

AIR INTAKE CHARGE THROTTLE BODY

2.3L (140) OHC and Turbo, 2.9L, with computer controls.

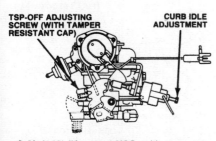

TSP-OFF ADJUSTING SCREW (WITH TAMPER RESISTANT CAP)

CURB IDLE ADJUSTMENT

2.3L (140) IV except HSC, with computer controls.

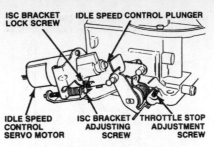

ISC BRACKET LOCK SCREW

IDLE SPEED CONTROL PLUNGER

IDLE SPEED CONTROL SERVO MOTOR

ISC BRACKET ADJUSTING SCREW

THROTTLE STOP ADJUSTMENT SCREW

2.8L (171), with computer controls.

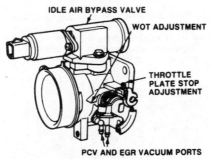

IDLE AIR BYPASS VALVE

WOT ADJUSTMENT

THROTTLE PLATE STOP ADJUSTMENT

PCV AND EGR VACUUM PORTS

3.0L (182) except SHO, 2.9L (179), 3.0L (182), 4.0L, 7.5L (460) FI, and 1989-90 4.9L, 5.0L, 5.8L, with computer controls.

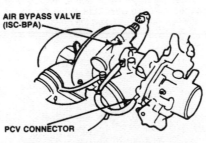

AIR BYPASS VALVE (ISC-BPA)

PCV CONNECTOR

3.0L (182) SHO, with computer controls.

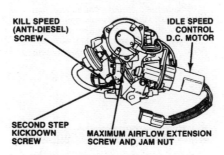

KILL SPEED (ANTI-DIESEL) SCREW

IDLE SPEED CONTROL D.C. MOTOR

SECOND STEP KICKDOWN SCREW

MAXIMUM AIRFLOW EXTENSION SCREW AND JAM NUT

4.9L (300) 1V, with computer controls.

IDLE AIR SET SCREW

1985-90 4.9L (300), 5.0L (302), 5.8L (351) FI, with computer controls.

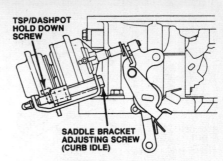

TSP/DASHPOT HOLD DOWN SCREW

SADDLE BRACKET ADJUSTING SCREW (CURB IDLE)

5.0L (302) CFI, and 5.0L 2V, without computer controls.

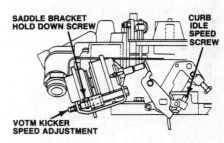

SADDLE BRACKET HOLD DOWN SCREW

CURB IDLE SPEED SCREW

VOTM KICKER SPEED ADJUSTMENT

5.8L (351), without computer controls.

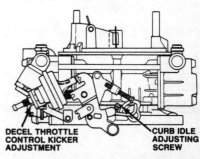

DECEL THROTTLE CONTROL KICKER ADJUSTMENT

CURB IDLE ADJUSTING SCREW

1983-87 7.5L, without computer controls.

GM Idle Speed Adjustment

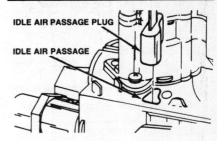

IDLE AIR PASSAGE PLUG

IDLE AIR PASSAGE

1983-86 with TBI, with computer controls.

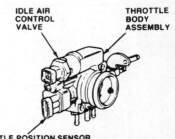

IDLE AIR CONTROL VALVE

THROTTLE BODY ASSEMBLY

THROTTLE POSITION SENSOR

1983-86 with MFI, 1987-89 with TBI or MFI.

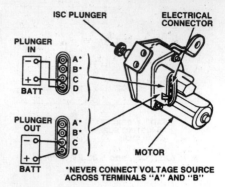

All carburetted engines with ISC, with computer controls.

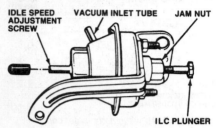

All carburetted engines with ILC, with computer controls.

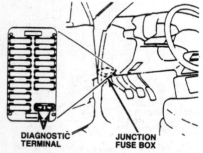

1989-91 1.0L TBI Geo, with computer control.

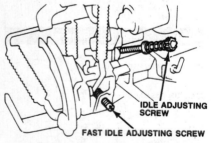

1.6L Nova 2V, without computer control.

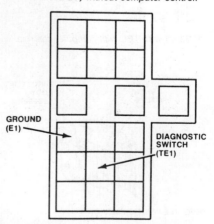

1.6L Geo Prizm, with computer control.

HONDA Idle Speed Adjustment

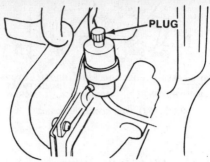

To check and adjust the idle speed in Honda models with automatic transmission built in the late 1980s, remove the air filter from the frequency solenoid valve, and plug the opening in the frequency solenoid valve.

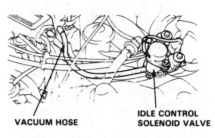

In late-model Hondas with fuel injection, remove the upper vacuum hose from the idle control solenoid valve, and clamp the end of the hose shut. Also plug the opening at the intake manifold.

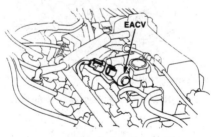

For other late-model Hondas with fuel injection, disconnect the 2-pin connector from the EACV before checking and adjusting the idle. After making adjustments, remove the backup fuse in the underhood relay box to reset the ECU.

NISSAN Idle Speed Adjustment

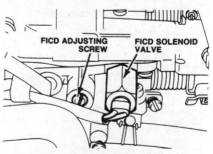

For fuel injected vehicles that do not use a computer-controlled idle speed system, set the fast idle using the FICD adjusting screw.

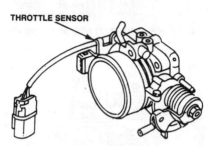

1984-87 E16, 2V, with computer control.

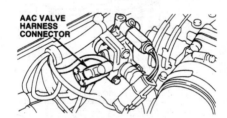

1987-90 E16 FI, 1989-91 KA24, with computer control.

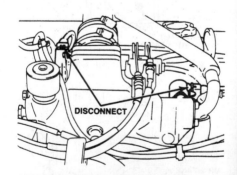

1984-89 VG30 Turbo, 1987-89 CA16, CA18 DOHC, with computer control.

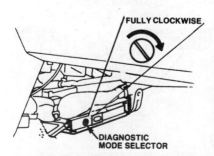

1987-88 CA18 Turbo, 1987-89 CA20 Stanza, with computer control.

1989-90 VG30 Maxima, with computer control.

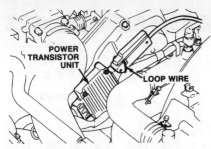

POWER TRANSISTOR UNIT — LOOP WIRE

1990 300ZX, with computer control.

TOYOTA Idle Speed Adjustment

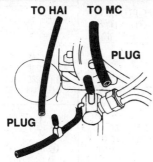

TO HAI — TO MC — PLUG — PLUG

1983-90 2366cc 2V, without computer controls.

IDLE SPEED ADJUSTING SCREW

1983-91 All FI, without computer controls.

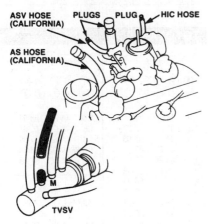

ASV HOSE (CALIFORNIA) — PLUGS — PLUG — HIC HOSE — AS HOSE (CALIFORNIA) — M — TVSV

1983-90 1452cc, 1587cc, 2V.

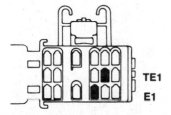

TE1 — E1

For vehicles with computer controls, jumper terminals T and E1 or TE1 and E1 before checking and adjusting the idle speed.

VOLKSWAGEN Idle Speed Adjustment

Before adjusting the idle speed on vehicles with ISS, disconnect the plugs on the idle stabilizer and connect them together. (See VOLKSWAGEN Ignition Timing section for illustration.)

ENGINE MECHANICAL

When working on the engine, refer to the manufacturer's service literature for the necessary specifications. The information in this section is limited to torque values for cylinder heads, intake and exhaust manifolds, crankshaft pulleys or dampers, and water pumps, valve clearance, compression pressure, and belt tension. Refer to the "Tightening Torques" table for more information.

CYLINDER HEAD BOLT TORQUE

The *Underhood Service Specifications* list recommended torque values for cylinder head bolts. The illustrations below show head bolt torque patterns that are recommended by the manufacturers. The engine size (in liters), the engine code (if available), and the engine year are listed under each head bolt tightening sequence. Ⓕ indicates the front of the engine, if the engine is used in longitudinal and transverse applications.

CHRYSLER (domestics & imports)

Sequence: Ⓕ ⑧⑥①③⑨ / ⑩④②⑤⑦

Liters	Code	Year
1.4	A	84
1.5	A	91
1.5	K	85-88
1.6	B	84
2.4	W	90-91

Sequence: ⑨⑤①④⑧ / ⑩⑥②③⑦

Liters	Code	Year
1.6	A	83-86

Sequence: ⑩④②⑥⑧ / ⑦⑤①③⑨

Liters	Code	Year
1.7	B	83

Sequence: ⑦⑤②④⑩ / ⑨③①⑥⑧

Liters	Code	Year
1.5	X	89-90
1.6 T	F	84-88
1.6	Y	89-90
1.6 T	Z	89
1.8	T	89-91
2.0	R	90-91
2.0 T	U	90-91

Sequence: ⑨③①⑥⑧ / ⑦⑤②④⑩

Liters	Code	Year
2.0	V	89-91

Sequence: ⑦⑥①③⑨ / ⑩④②⑤⑧

Liters	Code	Year
2.0	D	84-89

Sequence: Ⓕ ⑩⑥②③⑦ / ⑨⑤①④⑧

Liters	Code	Year
2.2 T	A	87-91
2.2 T	C	90
2.2	C	83-88
2.2	D	83-91
2.2 T	E	84-88
2.5 T	J	89-91
2.5	K	86-91
2.5	P	91

Sequence: ⑪⑧⑥①③⑨ / ⑪⑩④②⑤⑦

Liters	Code	Year
2.0	5	83
2.6	E	84-89
2.6	G	83-87
2.6 T	H	84-87
2.6 T	N	87-89
2.6	7	83

Sequence: ⑥②③⑦ / ⑤①④⑧   Ⓕ ⑨④①⑤ / ⑦③②⑥

Liters	Code	Year
3.0	B	91
3.0 T	C	91
3.0	S	89-91
3.0	3	87-91

Sequence: ⑦③②⑥ / ⑧④①⑤

Liters	Code	Year
3.0	U	90-91

Sequence: ⑦③①⑤ / ⑧④②⑥

Liters	Code	Year
3.3	R	90-91
3.9	M	87-88
3.9	X	88-91

Sequence: ⑬⑨⑤①③⑦⑪ / ⑭⑩⑥②④⑧⑫

Liters	Code	Year
3.7	H	83-87
3.7	J	83
3.7	K	83
3.7	L	83

Sequence: ⑨⑦③①⑤ / ⑧④②⑥

Liters	Code	Year
3.8	L	91

Sequence: ⑫⑧④①⑤⑨⑬ / ⑪⑦③②⑥⑩⑭

Liters	Code	Year
4.0	S	91

Sequence: ⑦③①⑤⑨ / ⑧④②⑥⑩

Liters	Code	Year
5.2	N	83
5.2	P	83-89
5.2	R	83-86
5.2	S	83-89
5.2	T	83-87
5.2	U	83
5.2	Y	88-91
5.9	I	83-88
5.9	V	83-85
5.9	W	83-85, 91
5.9	Z	90-91
5.9	5	89-91

Sequence: ⑩③④⑨ / ⑭⑧①⑤⑪ / ⑬⑦②⑥⑫

Liters	Code	Year
5.9	7	91

Sequence: ㉒⑭⑥③⑪⑲ / ㉖⑱⑩②⑦⑮㉓ / ㉕⑰⑨①⑧⑯㉔ / ㉑⑬⑤④⑫⑳

Liters	Code	Year
5.9 TD	8	89-91

FORD

Sequence: ⑨③①⑤⑦ / ⑧⑥②④⑩

Liters	Code	Year
1.6	2	83-85
1.6 HO	4	83-85
1.6	5	83-85, 88-89
1.6 T	8	84-85
1.9	J	86-91
1.9	9	85-90

Sequence: ⑧④①⑤⑨ / ⑦③②⑥⑩

Liters	Code	Year
1.3	H	89-91
1.3	K	88-89
1.6	2	91
1.6 T	6	91
1.8	8	91
2.0 D	H	84-87

Sequence: ⑩⑥②③⑦ / ⑨⑤①④⑧

Liters	Code	Year
2.2	C	89-91
2.2 T	L	89-91
2.3	R	84-87
2.3 HO	S	85,86, 88-90
2.3	X	85-90
2.5	D	86-90

Sequence: ⑥②③⑦ / ⑧④①⑤

Liters	Code	Year
2.3 HSO	S	91
2.3 HSC	X	91
2.5	N,D	91

Sequence: ⑨⑤①③⑦ / ⑧④②⑥⑩

Liters	Code	Year
2.3	A	84-91 OHC
2.3	A	83
2.3	M	91
2.3 T	T	84-88 OHC
2.3	TW	84-89 OHC
2.3	W	83
2.3 LP	6	83-84
4.6	W	91

Sequence: ⑧①④⑥ / ⑤③②⑦

Liters	Code	Year
2.9	V	88-89
2.9	T	91

Sequence: ⑥④②⑧ / ⑤①③⑦

Liters	Code	Year
3.0	U	86-91

Sequence: ⑤③①⑦ / ⑥②④⑧

Liters	Code	Year
3.0 HO	Y	89-91

Sequence: ⑦③①⑤ / ⑧④②⑥

Liters	Code	Year
3.8	C	89
3.8	R	88-91
3.8	4	88-91

Sequence: ⑤①③⑦ / ⑥②④⑧

Liters	Code	Year
3.8	3	83-87

⑤①③⑦
⑥④②⑧

| 4.0 | X | 91 |

⑪⑦③②⑥⑩⑭
⑬⑨⑤①④⑧⑫

| 4.9 | Y | 91 |

⑨⑤①③⑦
⑩⑥②④⑧

5.0 HO	E	87-91
5.0	F	83-91
5.0	M	84-87
5.0	N	91
5.0 HO	T	91
5.8	G	83-91
5.8	H	91
7.5	G	91

⑮⑪⑦③②⑥⑩⑭
⑯⑧①⑨⑰
⑫④⑤⑬

| 7.3 D | M | 88-91 |

⑬⑨⑤①④⑧⑫
⑭⑩⑥②③⑦⑪

| 4.1 | D | 83-85 |
| 4.8 | T | 83-89 |

⑬⑤⑫
⑦①⑨⑩
⑨④②⑧
⑪⑥⑭

| 4.3 D | T | 83-85 |
| 4.3 D | V | 83-84 |

Check for concealed pipe plugs.

⑬⑤②⑩
⑰⑨①⑥⑭
⑯⑫⑧④③⑦⑪⑮

5.0	E	88-91
5.0	F	83-91
5.0	G	84-88
5.0	H	83-87, 90-91
5.0	S	83-84
5.0	7	83
5.7	K	87-91
5.7	L	83-86
5.7	M	83-88, 91
5.7	7	91
5.7	8	83-91

⑨③①⑤⑦ LF
⑧⑥②④⑩
⑧⑥②④⑩ RT
⑨③①⑤⑦

⑦⑤①③⑨
⑧⑥②④⑩

5.0	Y	83-90
5.0	9	83-87
5.7 D	N	83-85

| 5.7 | J | 89-91 |

⑭⑩⑥②③⑦⑪⑮
⑰⑨①⑤⑧⑯
⑬⑤④⑫

| 6.2 D | C | 83-91 |
| 6.2 D | J | 83-91 |

⑫③
⑯⑨①⑤
⑮⑧②⑦⑭
⑪⑤④⑩

| 7.4 | N | 87-91 |
| 7.4 | W | 83-89, 91 |

GM

⑦③②⑥⑩
⑧④①⑤⑨

| 1.6 | C | 83-87 |
| 1.9 | A | 83-85 |

⑧⑥①③⑨
⑩④②⑤⑦

| 1.6 | 4 | 85-88 |

⑧④①⑤⑨
⑦③②⑥⑩

1.6	6	91
1.8 T	J	84-86
1.8	0	83-86
2.0	K	87-91
2.0 T	M	87-90
2.0	1	87-89
2.0	6	91
2.2	G	90-91

(F) ⑨⑤①③⑦
⑩⑥②④⑧

| 2.0 | B | 83-84 |
| 2.0 | P | 83-86 |

⑦③①⑥⑩
⑨⑤②④⑧

| 2.3 | A | 90-91 |
| 2.3 | D | 88-91 |

(F) ⑦④①⑤⑧
⑨③②⑥⑩

2.5	A	91
2.5	E	85-91
2.5	F, 2	83-86
2.5	R, 5	83-91
2.5	U	85-91

(F) ⑥②③⑦
⑤①④⑧

2.8	B	83-89
2.8	L	84
2.8	R	86-91
2.8	S	85-89
2.8	W	85-89
2.8	X	83-86
2.8	Z	83-84
2.8	1	83-84
2.8	9	85-88
3.1	D	90-91
3.1	T	89-91
3.4	X	91

⑥①③⑦
⑧④②⑤

3.0	E	83-85
3.0	L	85-88
3.3	N	89-91
3.8	A	83-87
3.8	B	86
3.8	C	88-91
3.8	L	91
3.8	3	84-88
3.8	7	86-87
3.8	9	84-85
4.1	4	83-84

⑧⑤⑨
⑫④①⑬
⑪⑦③②⑥⑩

4.3	B	90-91
4.3	N	85-86
4.3	Z	85-91

⑦⑥①⑤⑧
⑩③②④⑨

| 4.1 | 8 | 83-87 |

⑥③①④⑤
⑩⑦②⑧⑨

4.1	7	87-88
4.5	3	90
4.5	5	88-90
4.5	8	90-91
4.9	B	91

HONDA

⑦③②⑥⑩
⑧④①⑤⑨

1.3	D13A2	87
1.3	EV1	84-86
1.5	D15A2	87
1.5	D15A3	87
1.5	EW3	85-86
1.5	EW1	84-86

⑧⑥②④⑩
⑨③①⑤⑦

1.5	D15B1	88-89
1.5	D15B2	88-90
1.5	D15B6	89
1.6	D16A6	88-89
1.8	A18A1	87
1.8	ES1	83-84
1.8	ES2	85
1.8	ES3	85
1.8	ET2	85-86
2.0	A20A1	87-89
2.0	A20A3	87-89
2.0	BT	86
2.0	B20A3	88-89
2.0	B20A5	88-89
2.2	F22A1	90
2.2	F22A4	90

⑨③①⑤⑦
⑧⑥②④⑩

1.3	EJ1	83
1.5	EM1	83
1.8	EK1	83

NISSAN

⑨③①⑥⑧
⑦⑤②④⑩

1.5	E15	83
1.5	E15ET	83
1.6	E16	83
1.6	E16i	87-88
1.6	E16S	84-87
2.4	KA24E	89-91
2.4	KA24DE	91

⑪
⑬⑨③①⑥⑧
⑭⑦⑤②④⑩
⑫⑮

| 1.6 | GA16 | 89-91 |

⑨③①⑤⑦
⑧⑥②④⑩

1.6	CA16DE	87
1.7 D	CD17	83-87
1.8	CA18DE	88-89

⑦③①⑤⑨
⑧④②⑥⑩

1.8	CA18ET	86-88
2.0	CA20	83
2.0	CA20E	85-89
2.0	CA20S	84-85
2.0	Z20	83-86
2.2	Z22	83
2.2	Z22E	83
2.4	Z24	83-86
2.4	Z24i	86-89

⑦③①⑤⑨
⑧④②⑥⑩

| 2.0 | SR20DE | 91 |

⑰⑮⑬⑪⑫⑭⑯⑱
⑦⑤③①⑤⑨
⑩⑧⑥②④⑥

| 2.2 D | SD22 | 83 |
| 2.5 D | SD25 | 83-87 |

⑭⑩⑥②④⑧⑫
⑬⑨⑤①③⑦⑪

2.4	L24E	83-84
2.8	L28E	83
2.8 T	L28ET	83
2.8 D	LD28	83

⑥④②⑧ RT
⑦①③⑤

⑦①③⑤ LF
⑥④②⑧

| 3.0 | VG30DE | 90-91 |
| 3.0 | VG30DETT | 90-91 |

⑪⑦③①⑥⑩
⑬⑤④②⑫ RT
⑨③②⑧
⑧⑥②③⑬ LF
⑩⑥①③⑦⑪

3.0	VG30E	84-91
3.0	VG30ET	84-87
3.0	VG30i	87-89

TOYOTA

⑧⑥①③⑨
⑩④②⑤⑦

1.3	4KE	83-84
1.5	3A	83-87
1.5	3AC	83-88
1.6	4A-C	83-87
1.6	4A-FE	89-91
2.0	2S-E	83-86
2.0	3S-FE	87-91
2.0	3S-GE	86-89
2.0 T	3S-GTE	89-91
2.2	5S-FE	91
2.4	2TZ-FE	91

⑦③①⑥⑩
⑨⑤②④⑧

1.6	4A-GE	88-91
1.6	4A-GEC	85-87
1.6	4A-GELC	87-89
1.6 S	4A-GZE	88-89
1.6	4A-LC	87-88

⑨④②⑤⑨
⑩⑥①③⑦

| 1.6 | 4A-F | 88-89 |

⑨③①⑥⑧
⑦⑤②④⑩

| 1.5 | 3E | 87-90 |
| 1.5 | 3E-E | 90-91 |

⑰⑪⑨③①⑥⑧⑭⑯
⑮⑬⑦⑤②④⑩⑫⑱

1.8 D	1C	84-86
1.8 TD	1C-T	84-85
2.0 D	2CT	86

⑬ ⑫ ⑪
⑧ ⑥ ① ③ ⑨
⑩ ④ ② ⑤ ⑦

2.0   3YE-C   84-85
2.2   4Y-EC   86-89

⑱ ⑫ ⑩ ③ ① ⑤ ⑦ ⑬ ⑮
⑯ ⑭ ⑧ ⑥ ② ④ ⑨ ⑪ ⑰

2.2 D   L   83
2.4 D   2L   84-85
2.4 TD   2LT   85-86

⑩ ④ ② ⑤ ⑦
⑧ ⑥ ① ③ ⑨

2.4   22R   83-90
2.4   22R-E   83-91
2.4 T   22R-TE   86-88

⑬ ⑦ ③ ① ⑥ ⑩ ⑫
⑪ ⑨ ⑤ ② ④ ⑧ ⑭

2.8   5M-GE   83-88

⑦ ② ④ ⑥
(F) ⑤ ③ ① ⑧
⑧ ① ③ ⑤
⑥ ④ ② ⑦

2.5   2VZ-E   89
2.5   2VZ-FE   90-91

⑧ ② ④ ⑥
⑤ ③ ① ⑦

3.0   3VZ-E   89-91

⑫ ⑧ ④ ② ⑤ ⑨ ⑬
⑭ ⑩ ⑥ ① ③ ⑦ ⑪

3.0   7M-GE   86-91
3.0   7M-GET   87-91

⑮ ⑨ ⑤ ① ④ ⑧ ⑫
⑬ ⑪ ⑦ ③ ② ⑥ ⑩ ⑭

4.0   3F-E   88-91
4.4   2F   83-87

VOLKSWAGEN

⑩ ④ ① ⑥ ⑧   ⑧ ② ④ ⑥
⑦ ⑤ ② ③ ⑨   ⑤ ③ ① ⑦

All 4-cylinder engines, Vanagon diesels, and 5-cylinder Quantum.   Vanagon, air- and water-cooled, with engine out of car only.

VALVE CLEARANCE CHECK AND ADJUSTMENT

Manufacturers specify whether you must check the clearances with the engine hot or cold. "Hot" valve clearances are checked with the engine at operating temperature, and "cold" valve clearances are checked with the engine at ambient air temperature.

POSITIONING THE VALVES

Check clearances with a feeler gauge, and adjust the valves. There are two common methods for adjusting valves — with shims and with adjusting screws located on the rocker arms.

The "running mate" method of positioning the valves works for engines with an even number of cylinders.

1. Write down the engine firing order. Write the second half of the firing order below the first half. For example, if the firing order is 1 5 4 2 6 3 7 8, write: 1 5 4 2
         6 3 7 8.
The "running mates" are 1 and 6, 5 and 3, 4 and 7, and 2 and 8.
2. To position the valves for adjustment, rotate the engine in its normal direction until the exhaust valve for cylinder number six just closes. (The rocker arm for the exhaust valve for cylinder number six will feel slightly loose. If the vehicle does not have rocker arms, check for any clearance between the camshaft lobe and lifter with a feeler gauge. When there is clearance, the exhaust valve is closed). Then check and adjust the intake and exhaust valves of the running mate, cylinder number one, using the manufacturer's recommended adjustment method. Two methods are described in the following sections.
3. Rotate the engine in its normal direction until the exhaust valve for cylinder number five just closes. Check and adjust the valves of the running mate, cylinder number three.
4. Continue this method until all of the valves are checked and adjusted.

SHIM METHOD

Some engines have replaceable adjustment shims between the camshaft lobes and the valve lifters.

1. Check the valve clearances.
2. If the clearance must be adjusted, use a special tool to push the lifter down. Remove the adjusting shim with a screwdriver or magnet.

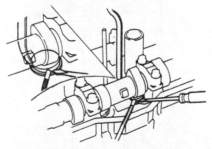

On this over-head cam engine, use shims to adjust the valve clearance.

3. Select the proper shim size to return the valve clearance to specifications, and install the shim.
4. Recheck the clearance.

ADJUSTING SCREW METHOD

On some engines, to adjust the valve clearance you must thread a screw on the rocker arm in or out to obtain the proper clearance. Most adjustment screws are secured with a locknut, but some are held in place with an interference fit in the rocker arm.

1. Check the valve clearances.
2. Use a box-end wrench and screwdriver to adjust the clearance.

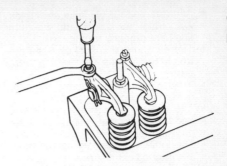

For some engines, adjust the valve clearance by turning the screw on the rocker arm and securing the locknut.

3. Check the clearance and tighten the locknut once the adjustment is correct.
4. Recheck the clearance.

COMPRESSION TEST

The minimum compression pressures and maximum variations allowed by vehicle manufacturers are listed in the *Underhood Service Specifications*. The maximum variation is the difference in compression between the highest and lowest cylinders. Some automakers give the allowable variation as a percentage.

BELT TENSION

As part of a tune-up, or after installing a new belt, check and adjust tension. There may be three belt tension specifications — one for used belts, one for new belts, and one for belts that use automatic tensioners. If the vehicle has a flat serpentine belt, use a tension gauge designed for that type of belt. Correct tensions are listed in the *Underhood Service Specifications*.

ENGINE COMPUTER SYSTEMS

Computerized engine control systems regulate spark timing, fuel delivery, engine idle speed, emission control devices, torque converter lockup, and many other systems and components. Electronic engine control systems vary from one model to another, but every system is made up of three distinct types of components: input sensors, a central computer, and output control devices.

On some systems, the central computer contains a replaceable computer chip called a Programmable Read Only Memory (PROM) or calibration module. This chip contains special instructions for particular driving conditions. Revised PROM's are sometimes issued by vehicle manufacturers to resolve driveability problems.

Before testing the computerized engine control system, be sure that:

- The battery is in good condition.
- The starting and charging systems are operating properly.

- All fuses and fusible links are intact.
- All wiring harnesses and vacuum lines are properly routed.
- The air and fuel supply systems are free of restrictions and working properly.
- Emission control systems are connected and operating properly.
- The coolant is at the proper level, and the thermostat is opening at the proper temperature.
- The ignition secondary components are in good condition.
- The base timing and idle speed are set to specification.
- The engine is in good mechanical condition.

Use the instructions in the *Underhood Service Specifications* and in the following section as a guide when reading trouble codes. Code definitions are listed in the *Underhood Service Specifications* for each manufacturer. Generally, problems indicated by trouble codes should be repaired beginning with the lower code numbers and working up from there.

Remember that trouble codes only indicate the circuit in which a problem is detected. They do not pinpoint individual components.

SPECIAL INSTRUCTIONS FOR ENGINE COMPUTER SELF-DIAGNOSTICS

CHRYSLER Engine Computers

DIAGNOSTIC TESTS:

For Chrysler domestics, you must use a special diagnostic tester or the CHECK ENGINE, POWER LOSS, or POWER LIMITED light on the dash board when retrieving trouble codes. To activate the diagnostics system, rapidly turn the ignition switch ON-OFF-ON-OFF-ON. Leave the ignition switch ON, and watch the warning lamp on the dash or the LED on the logic module. Either indicator will flash the 2-digit trouble codes. Code 55 signals the end of the test.

Chrysler domestics. If you use the Chrysler test meter attached to the diagnostic connector in the engine compartment, follow the manufacturer's instructions.

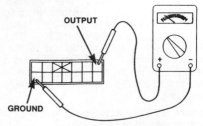

Chrysler imports and some Eagle models. *Connect a voltmeter to the diagnostic connector. Count the needle sweeps on the voltmeter to obtain trouble codes.*

SENSOR TESTS:

Chrysler domestics. Set the special diagnostics tester to the "Read Sensor Values" mode.

Chrysler imports and some Eagle models. You must use the ECI checker to test some sensors, such as the barometric pressure sensor and the motor position sensor. The ECI checker allows you to test the sensor without disconnecting it from the wiring harness. However, some sensors can be checked with a volt-ohmmeter.

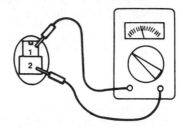

Coolant temperature sensor. *Measure the resistance between the two terminals.*

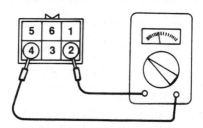

Intake air temperature sensor, 4-cylinder engines with FI. *Measure the resistance between terminals 2 and 4 of the connector.*

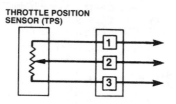

TPS voltage. *Measure between terminals 1 and 2. The third terminal is the 5 volt reference signal.*

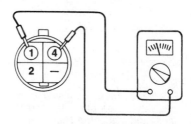

Motor position sensor. *Measure the resistance between terminals 1 and 4 of the ISC motor connector for motor position sensor resistance.*

FORD Engine Computers

DIAGNOSTIC TESTS:

For Ford vehicles covered in this guide, you will find three types of computerized engine control systems: MCU, EEC-III, and EEC-IV.

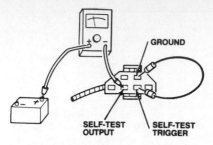

MCU engine control system. *Use an analog voltmeter and jumper wire to read trouble codes.*

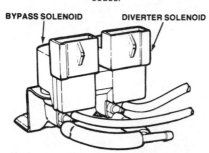

EEC-III system. *Display trouble codes using two vacuum gauges teed into the thermactor air control solenoid lines, or on self-powered test lamps connected to the solenoids.*

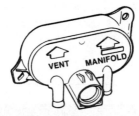

EEC-III self-test. *Connect a hand vacuum pump to the B/MAP sensor "Vent" port. Pump the vacuum down to 20 inches-Hg, and hold it for 8 seconds.*

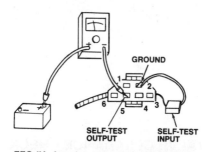

EEC-IV. *Attach a voltmeter to the self-test connector, and use a jumper wire to connect the self-test input lead to the number 2 slot of the connector.*

SENSOR TESTS:

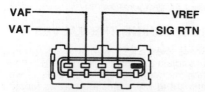

Vane air temperature sensor. *Measure the resistance between the VAT terminal and a good ground. Also, measure the voltage of the vane airflow sensor between terminal VAF and ground.*

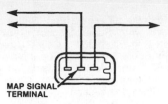

MAP sensor. Measure the voltage between the center terminal and ground.

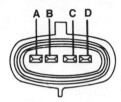

Mass airflow sensor. Measure the voltage between terminal D and ground.

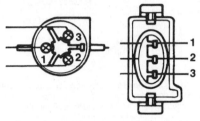

Throttle position sensor. Measure the voltage between terminal 2 and ground.

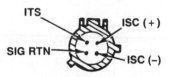

Idle speed control motor. Measure resistance between terminals ISC (+) and ISC (–).

GM Engine Computers

DIAGNOSTIC TESTS:

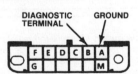

GM vehicles with computer controls, except vehicles with CRT diagnostic displays, early 1980s light-duty trucks, and most GM imports. Connect a jumper wire between the ground terminal (A) and the diagnostic terminal (B).

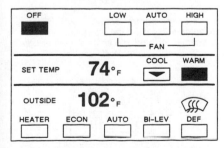

Vehicles with CRT diagnostic displays. To activate the self-diagnostic system, press the OFF and WARM buttons at the same time on the climate control system keypad.

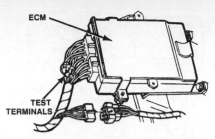

Light trucks manufactured in the early 1980s. Activate the CHECK ENGINE light by connecting the test terminals, which are taped on the harness near the ECM.

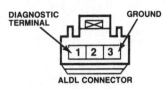

Some GM imports, such as Geo Storm. Connect a jumper wire between the diagnostic terminal (1) and ground (3).

SENSOR TESTS:

MAP sensor. Test at the three terminal connector. One terminal has reference voltage. Check voltage between terminals A and B.

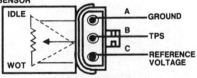

Throttle position sensor. Test the throttle position sensor voltage between terminals A and B.

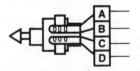

Idle speed controller. Test the resistance between terminals A and B, and between terminals C and D.

HONDA Engine Computers

DIAGNOSTIC TESTS:
Honda uses three methods to display trouble codes in late-model vehicles, as explained in the *Underhood Service Specifications*.

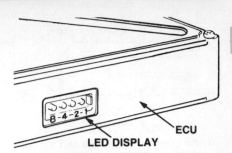

1985 Accord; 1985-87 Civic CRX, Hatchback, Sedan, Wagon with FI.

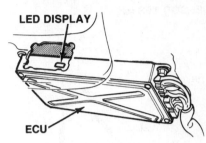

1986-87 Accord and Prelude with FI.

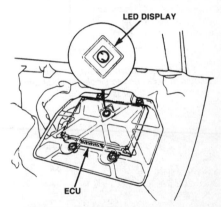

1988-90 Civic, CRX, Prelude, Accord.

SENSOR TESTS:

Crankshaft sensor. For 1985-87 1488cc w/FI engines, measure resistance between the blue and brown wire terminals.

NISSAN Engine Computers

Nissan uses two basic types of ECU.

DIAGNOSTIC TESTS:

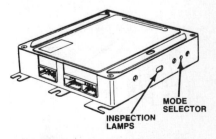

Select the troubleshooting mode using the screw on the side of the ECU.

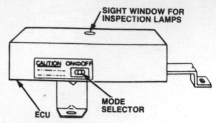

Use the toggle switch on the side of the ECU to activate the troubleshooting mode.

SENSOR TESTS:

Fuel temperature sensor. Measure resistance between the single terminal and a good ground.

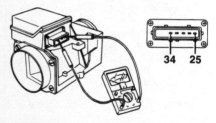

Manifold air temperature sensor. Measure the resistance between terminals 34 and 25 of the airflow meter.

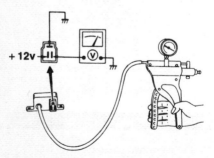

Vacuum sensor. Check voltage between the terminal illustrated and a good ground.

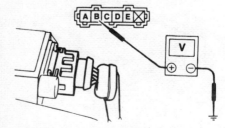

Airflow meter, 300 ZX. Measure the voltage between terminal B and a good ground.

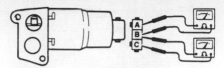

Idle speed control actuator, 1988 Sentra. Measure resistance between terminals A and B, and between terminals B and C.

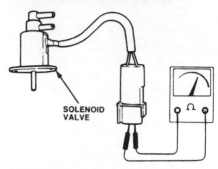

Idle speed control actuator, 1987 Maxima. Measure resistance at the two-terminal connector.

TOYOTA Engine Computers

DIAGNOSTIC TESTS:

Toyota uses four methods to display trouble codes in late-model vehicles, as explained in the *Underhood Service Specifications*.

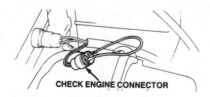

CHECK ENGINE CONNECTOR

1987-88 FX16; 1985-89 Van; 1985-86 Pickup with FI, Supra 2.8; 1985 Celica, Corolla GTS; 1983-84 Camry.

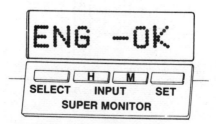

1985-90 Cressida, Supra with Super Monitor.

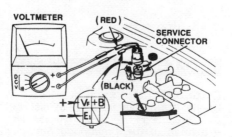

1983-84 Cressida, Supra.

For 1989-90, all except Van, Supra and Cressida with Super Monitor; 1987-88 Pickup with FI; 1986-88 Celica, Corolla with FI; Supra 3.0 without Super Monitor; 1985-87 Camry, MR2, Cressida without Super Monitor; see the connector in the "Fuel Systems" section.

SENSOR TESTS:

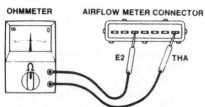

Manifold air temperature sensor. For all fuel injected engines, measure resistance between terminals E2 and THA of the airflow meter connector.

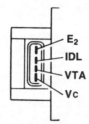

Throttle position sensor. Measure the resistance between terminals E2 and VTA.

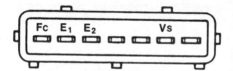

Air flow meter. Measure the resistance between terminals E2 and VS while moving the plate.

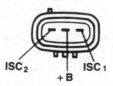

Idle speed control actuator, with three terminals. Measure the resistance between the center terminal and either the left or right terminal.

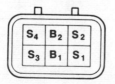

Idle speed control actuator, with six terminals. Measure the resistance between B1 and S1 or S3, and between B2 and S2 or S4.

VOLKSWAGEN Engine Computers

DIAGNOSTIC TESTS:

This is the rocker switch used to obtain codes in some VW vehicles.

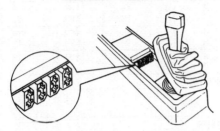

For some Volkswagens, use a diagnostic tester to obtain trouble codes. The tester hook-ups are located in a variety of places, depending on the model.

SENSOR TESTS:

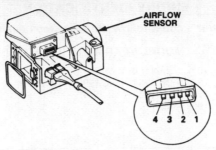

Intake air temperature sensor and airflow sensor. Measure the intake air temperature and flow sensor resistance at the same connector.

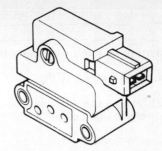

Differential pressure regulator. Check resistance at the two terminal connector.

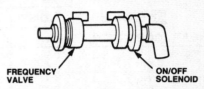

Frequency valve. Test resistance at the spade terminal on the frequency valve.

ACURA
1986-92 Integra, Legend, Vigor

ENGINE IDENTIFICATION

To identify an engine by the manufacturer's code, follow the four steps designated by the numbered blocks.

V.I.N. PLATE LOCATION:

Left side of hood support member. Also top left side of instrument panel.

1 MODEL YEAR IDENTIFICATION:

10th character of V.I.N.
1992 — N; 1991 — M; 1990 — L;
1989 — K; 1988 — J; 1987 — H;
1986 — G.

2 ENGINE CODE LOCATION:

Integra, first five characters of engine number, located on flange under the distributor.

Legend, first five characters of engine number, located on timing chain cover below engine oil fill cap.

4 ENGINE IDENTIFICATION

YEAR	3 ENGINE CODE	CYL.	DISPL. liters	cc	Fuel System	HP
1992	—	5	2.5	2451	MFI	176
	C32A1	6	3.2	3206	MFI	200
1991	B18A1	4	1.8	1834	MFI	130
	C32A1	6	3.2	3206	MFI	200
1990	B18A1	4	1.8	1834	MFI	130
	C27A1	6	2.7	2675	MFI	160
1989	D16A1	4	1.6	1590	MFI	118
	C27A1	6	2.7	2675	MFI	161

4 ENGINE IDENTIFICATION

YEAR	3 ENGINE CODE	CYL.	DISPL. liters	cc	Fuel System	HP
1988	D16A1	4	1.6	1590	MFI	118
	C27A1	6	2.7	2675	MFI	161
1987	D16A1	4	1.6	1590	MFI	118
	C25A1	6	2.5	2494	MFI	NA
1986	D16A1	4	1.6	1590	MFI	118
	C25A1	6	2.5	2494	MFI	NA

MFI — Multiport Fuel Injection.

UNDERHOOD SERVICE SPECIFICATIONS

AAITU1   AAITU1

CYLINDER NUMBERING SEQUENCE

4-CYL. FIRING ORDER: 1 3 4 2

V6 FIRING ORDER: 1 4 2 5 3 6

— Front of car —

| 1986-87 1590cc Integra | 1988-89 1590cc Integra | 1990-91 1834cc Integra | 1992 2451cc Vigor | 1986-90 2494cc, 2675cc Legend |

TIMING MARK

(Set timing on red mark)

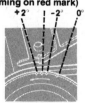 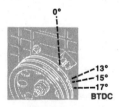

1986-91
1590cc,
1834cc Integra

1986-92
2494cc,
2675cc, 3206cc Legend

ELECTRICAL AND IGNITION SYSTEMS

BATTERY

BCI equivalent shown, size may vary from original equipment. Check clearance before replacing, holddown may need to be modified.

Engine	Year	STANDARD BCI Group No.	STANDARD Crank Perf.	OPTIONAL BCI Group No.	OPTIONAL Crank Perf.
Integra	1986-89	45*	410	--	—
Integra	1990-91	25	435	—	—
Legend	1986-89	24F	580	—	—
Legend	1990	24F	585	—	—
Legend	1991	24	585	—	—

* Best fit estimate, check polarity before connecting cables.

ALTERNATOR

Application	Year	Rated Output	Test Output (amps & eng. rpm)
1590cc	1986-87	55	58-68 @ 2000
		65	58-68 @ 2000
1590cc	1988-89	65	40-50 @ 2000
1834cc	1990-91	70	74-85 @ 2000
2494cc, 2675cc	1986-90	70	74-85 @ 2000
3206cc	1991-92	110	102 @ 2000

REGULATOR

Application	Year	Test Temp. (deg. F/C)	Voltage Setting
All	1986-87	—	13.9-15.1

UNDERHOOD SERVICE SPECIFICATIONS

AAITU2   AAITU2

STARTER

Engine	Year	Cranking Voltage (min. volts)	Max. Ampere Draw @ Cranking Speed
All	1986-90	8.0	350

SPARK PLUGS

Engine	Year	Gap (inches)	Gap (mm)	Torque (ft-lb)
1590cc, 1834cc	1986-91	.039-.043	1.0-1.1	13
2494cc	1986-87	.039-.043	1.0-1.1	13
2675cc	1988-90	.039-.043	1.0-1.1	16
2451cc	1992	.039-.043	1.0-1.1	13
3206cc	1991-92	.039-.043	1.0-1.1	13

IGNITION COIL
Resistance (ohms @ 70°F or 21°C)

Engine	Year	Windings	Resistance (ohms)
1590cc	1986-87	Primary	1.215-1.485
		Secondary	9040-13,560
1590cc	1988-89	Primary	.3-.5
		Secondary	9440-14,160
1834cc	1990-91	Primary	.6-.8
		Secondary	9760-14,640
2494cc, 2675cc	1986-89	Primary	.3-.4
		Secondary	9040-13,560†
2675cc	1990	Primary	.35-.42
		Secondary	16,000-24,000
3206cc	1991-92	Primary	0.9-1.1

† Measured between upper right side cavity terminal and secondary terminal.

BASE TIMING
At slow idle and Before Top Dead Center, unless otherwise specified.

1986-87 models, disconnect and plug distributor advance hoses.

1988-89 1590cc, remove the main fuse box cover and jumper terminals Br and Br/Bl.

1834cc, connect a jumper between the green and brown terminals of the light grey timing connector under dash.

2675cc, access the ignition timing adjuster in the control box by the brake master cylinder. Turn the screw on the unit to adjust timing. Rivets must be drilled from timing adjuster mounting to gain access to screw.

Engine/Model	Year	Man. Trans. (degrees)	Auto. Trans. (degrees)
1590cc	1986-87	0 ± 2	0 ± 2
1590cc	1988-89	12 ± 2	12 ± 2
1834cc	1990-91	16 ± 2	16 ± 2
2451cc	1992	15 ± 2	15 ± 2
2494cc	1986-87	3	3
w/vacuum hoses connected	1986-87	23 ± 2	18 ± 2
2675cc	1988-90	15 ± 2	15 ± 2
3206cc	1991-92	15 ± 2	15 ± 2

DISTRIBUTOR PICKUP

Engine	Year	Resistance (ohms)
1590cc: Pickup coil	1986-87	650-850
Crank angle sensor	1986-87	650-850
1590cc: Pickup coil	1988-89	350-550
Crank angle sensor	1988-89	700-1000
1834cc*: TDC sensor	1990-91	350-700
Cylinder sensor	1990-91	350-700
Crank angle sensor	1990-91	350-700
2494cc: Pickup coil	1986-87	650-850
Crank angle sensor	1986-87	500-1200
2675cc Cylinder sensor	1988-90	500-1000

* Measured between each of three pairs of terminals on distributor connector.

FUEL SYSTEM

FUEL SYSTEM PRESSURE

Engine	Year	Pressure PSI†	Pressure PSI■	Fuel Pump PSI
All	1986-90	36-41	35-37	64-85

† With vacuum hose to fuel pressure regulator disconnected.
■ With vacuum hose to fuel pressure regulator connected.

IDLE SPEED W/COMPUTER CONTROL
1590cc, 1834cc: With engine idling, disconnect the AIS connector. Adjust speed to specified setting value. Reconnect AIS and remove "Hazard" fuse at battery + post for 10 seconds minimum. Check that idle speed is at specified checking value. Fast idle is not adjustable. 1988, turn on headlights and rear window defroster. Verify that Electrical load speed-up is at specified value. Turn on AC, blower on high, verify that AC speed-up speed is at specified value.

2494cc, 2675cc: Check engine speed at idle against specified checking value. If yellow LED on ECU under passenger section is blinking, turn idle screw 1/4 turn clockwise. If yellow LED is on but not blinking, turn idle screw 1/4 turn counterclockwise. Check yellow LED again after 30 seconds and repeat procedure until it is off.

Engine	Year	Trans- mission	Checking Speed	Setting Speed	Fast Idle (Cold)
1590cc	1986-87	MT	500-600	750-850	1250-2250
1590cc	1986-87	AT	500-600 N	750-850 N	1250-2250 N
1590cc	1988	MT	650-750	500-600	1250-2250
1590cc	1989	MT	700-800	500-600	1250-2250
Elect. & AC Speed-up	1988-89	MT	700-800	—	—
1590cc	1988-89	AT	650-750 N	500-600 N	1250-2250 N
Elect. & AC Speed-up	1988	AT	700-800 N	—	—
1834cc	1990-91	MT	700-800	600-700	100-1800
Elect. & AC Speed-up	1990-91	MT	700-800	—	—
1834cc	1990-91	AT	700-800 N	600-700 N	1000-1800 N
Elect. & AC Speed-up	1990-91	AT	700-800 N	—	—
2451cc	1992	MT	650-750	—	—
2451cc	1992	AT	650-750 N	—	—
2494cc	1986-87	MT	670-770	—	1100-1900
2494cc	1986-87	AT	670-770 N	—	1100-1900 N
2675cc	1988-89	MT	630-730	—	1100-1900
2675cc	1988-90	AT	630-730 N	—	1100-1900 N
3206cc	1991-92	MT	600-700	—	1300-1700
3206cc	1991-92	AT	550-650 P	—	1300-1700 N

ENGINE MECHANICAL

TIGHTENING TORQUES
Some fasteners are tightened in more than one step.

		Torque Ft-lbs/Nm				
Engine	Year	Cylinder Head	Intake Manifold	Exhaust Manifold	Crankshaft Pulley	Water Pump
1590cc	1986-89	22/30, 48/66	16/22	23/32	83/115	9/12
1834cc	1990-91	22/30, 61/85	17/23	23/32	87/120	9/12
2494cc, 2675cc	1986-90	29/40, 56/78	16/22	25/34	123/170	9/12, small 16/22, large
3206cc	1991-92	29/40, 56/78	16/22	25/34	174/240	—

VALVE CLEARANCE
Engine cold.
Measured between camshaft and rocker arm.

Engine	Year	Intake (inches)	Intake (mm)	Exhaust (inches)	Exhaust (mm)
1590cc	1986-89	.005-.006	.13-.17	.006-.007	.15-.19
1834cc	1990-91	.006-.007	.15-.19	.007-.008	.17-.21
2451cc	1992	.010-.011	.24-.28	.011-.012	.28-.32

ACURA
1986-92 Integra, Legend, Vigor

COMPRESSION PRESSURE

Engine	Year	PSI	Maximum Variation PSI
1590cc	1986-89	134-192	28
1834cc	1990-91	135-185	28
2494cc	1986-87	135-178	28
2675cc	1988	134-171	28
2675cc	1989-90	142-171	28

BELT TENSION

Deflection method: Deflection midway between pulleys with an applied load of 22 pounds on longest belt segment.

Engine	Year	Alternator	Power Steering	Air Cond.
1590cc (inches)	1986-89	1/4-3/8	3/4-7/8	1/4-3/8
(mm)	1986-89	7-10	18-22	7-10
1834cc (inches)	1990-91	5/16-7/16	1/4-5/16	1/4-3/8
(mm)	1990-91	8.5-10.5	6-8	7-9
2494cc, 2675cc (inches)	1986-90	3/4-7/8	3/4-5/16	1/4-3/8
(mm)	1986-90	18-22	19-24	7-10

ENGINE COMPUTER SYSTEM

COMPUTER DIAGNOSTIC CODES

Turn ignition on and move passenger seat fully rearward to observe LED flashing light on the ECU (Integra, Legend Sedan) or pull down carpet on passenger side under dash (Legend Coupe). The codes will be displayed by the number of times the light flashes followed by a brief pause between cycles. Remove "Hazard" fuse at battery + terminal (4-cyl.) or "Alternator Sense" fuse in the underhood relay box (V6) for ten seconds minimum to erase codes.

LED on or off steadily, ECU
Code 1 Oxygen sensor or circuit (4-cyl.)
Code 1 Front oxygen sensor (V6)
Code 2 Rear oxygen sensor (V6)
Codes 3, 5 Manifold absolute pressure sensor or circuit
Code 4 Crank angle sensor
Code 6 Coolant temperature sensor or circuit
Code 7 Throttle angle sensor or circuit
Code 8 TDC sensor or circuit
Code 9 Crank angle sensor or circuit
Code 10 Intake air temperature sensor or circuit
Code 12 EGR control system
Code 13 Atmospheric pressure sensor or circuit
Code 14 Idle control system
Code 15 Ignition output signal
Code 16 Fuel injector (4-cyl.)
Code 17 Vehicle speed sensor or circuit (4-cyl.)
Code 18 Ignition timing adjustment (V6)
Code 19 Lock up control solenoid valve (4-cyl.)
Code 20 Electric load (4-cyl.)
Code 21 Front spool solenoid valve (3.0L)
Code 22 Front valve timing oil pressure switch (3.0L)

COMPUTER DIAGNOSTIC CODES Continued

Code 23 Front knock sensor (3.0L)
Code 30 AT FI signal A (3.0L)
Code 31 AT FI signal B (3.0L)
Code 35 TC standby signal (3.0L)
Code 36 TC FC signal (3.0L)
Code 41 Front oxygen sensor heater (3.0L)
Code 42 Rear oxygen sensor heater (3.0L)
Code 43 Fuel supply system (4-cyl.)
Code 43 Front fuel supply system (3.0L)
Code 44 Rear fuel supply system (3.0L)
Code 45 Front fuel metering (3.0L)
Code 46 Rear fuel metering (3.0L)
Code 47 Fuel pump (3.0L)
Code 51 Rear spool solenoid valve (3.0L)
Code 52 Rear valve timing oil pressure switch (3.0L)
Code 53 Rear knock sensor (3.0L)
Code 54 Crank angle B (3.0L)
Code 59 No. 1 cylinder position (3.0L)

SENSORS, INPUT

TEMPERATURE SENSORS

Engine	Year	Sensor	Resistance Ohms @ deg. F/C
All	1986-90	Coolant, Manifold Air	15,000-20,000 @ -4/-20
			5000-7000 @ 32/0
			2000-4000 @ 68/20
			900-1200 @ 104/40
			300-400 @ 176/80
			100-300 @ 248/120

MANIFOLD ABSOLUTE AND BAROMETRIC PRESSURE SENSORS
5 volts reference.

Engine	Year	Voltage @ in./mm Hg
All	1986-90	2.7-2.9 @ 0/0
		2.3-2.5 @ 5/125
		1.8-2.0 @ 10/250
		1.4-1.6 @ 15/375
		0.9-1.1 @ 20/500

THROTTLE POSITION SENSOR

Engine	Year	Voltage Idle	WOT
1590cc	1986-89	0.5	4.5
1834cc	1990-91	0.3	4.5
2494cc, 2675cc	1986-90	0.5	4.0

ACTUATORS, OUTPUT

IDLE SPEED CONTROL

Engine	Year	Resistance (ohms)
All	1986-87	6-20
All	1988-90	8-15

ENGINE IDENTIFICATION

To identify any engine by the manufacturer's code, follow the four steps designated by the numbered blocks.

1 **MODEL YEAR IDENTIFICATION:** Refer to illustration of Vehicle Identification Number (V.I.N.), the year is indicated by the last digit of the model year or as a code letter.

2 **ENGINE CODE LOCATION:** Refer to V.I.N. plate illustration. The engine code is indicated as a letter or number.

3 **ENGINE CODE:** In the vertical "CODE" column, find the engine code determined in Step 2.

4 **ENGINE IDENTIFICATION:** On the line where the engine code appears, read to the right to identify the engine.

V.I.N. PLATE LOCATION:

On top left side of instrument panel

Model year of vehicle:
1988 — Model year is J.
1987 — Model year is H.
1986 — Model year is G.
1985 — Model year is F.
1984 — Model year is E.
1983 — Model year is D.

MODEL YEAR AND ENGINE IDENTIFICATION:

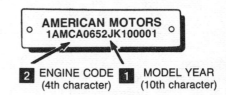

2 ENGINE CODE (4th character)   **1** MODEL YEAR (10th character)

4 ENGINE IDENTIFICATION

YEAR	**3** ENGINE CODE	CYL.	DISPL. liters	cu. in.	Fuel System	HP
1988	C	6	4.2	258	2V	112
1987	C	6	4.2	258	2V	112
1986	C	6	4.2	258	2V	112
1985	C	6	4.2	258	2V	112

4 ENGINE IDENTIFICATION

YEAR	**3** ENGINE CODE	CYL.	DISPL. liters	cu. in.	Fuel System	HP
1984	U	4	2.5	150	1V	105
	C	6	4.2	258	2V	112
1983	B	4	2.5	151	2V	80
	C	6	4.2	258	2V	108, 115†

1V — One Venturi Carburetor.   2V — Two Venturi Carburetor.
† Engine horsepower varies with model installation.

UNDERHOOD SERVICE SPECIFICATIONS

AMTU1   AMTU1

CYLINDER NUMBERING SEQUENCE

4-CYL. FIRING ORDER: 1 3 4 2

6-CYL. FIRING ORDER: 1 5 3 6 2 4

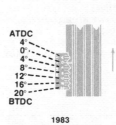

— Front of car —

1983-84 2.5L (150) AMC   1983 2.5L (151) GM   1983-88 4.2L (258)

TIMING MARK

BTDC 24° 20° 16° 12° -8° -4° 0° ATDC

ATDC 4° 0° 4° 8° 12° 16° 20° BTDC

1983-84 2.5L (150) AMC
1983-88 4.2L (258)

1983 2.5L (151) GM

ELECTRICAL AND IGNITION SYSTEMS

BATTERY

Engine	Year	STANDARD BCI Group No.	Crank. Perf.	OPTIONAL BCI Group No.	Crank. Perf.
4-cyl.	1983	55	380	56	450
	1984	55	370	—	—
6-cyl.					
Concord	1983	54	330	56	450
Eagle	1983-86	54	320	56	450
Eagle	1987-88	55	420	56	450

ALTERNATOR

Application (rated output)	Test Output (amps @ 2000 rpm)	Field Current Draw (amps @ volts)
1983 (42, 56, 66, 78 amps)	32, 46, 56, 68	4-5
1984-88 (56, 66, 68, 78)	46, 56, 58, 68	4-5

REGULATOR

Application	Test Temp. (deg. F/C)	Voltage Setting
1983-88 Delco	0-50/−18 to 10	14.3-15.3
	50-100/10-38	13.9-14.9
	100-150/38-66	13.4-14.4
	150-200/66-93	13.0-14.1

AMERICAN MOTORS
1983-88 Concord, Eagle, Spirit

UNDERHOOD SERVICE SPECIFICATIONS

AMTU2

STARTER

Engine	Year	Cranking Voltage (min. volts)	Ampere Draw @ Cranking Speed
4-cyl.	1983	9.6	—
4-cyl.	1984	9.6	150-180
6-cyl.	1983-88	9.6	150-180

SPARK PLUGS

Engine	Year	Gap (inches)	Gap (mm)	Torque (ft-lb)
2.5L (151)	1983	.060	1.52	10
2.5L (150)	1983-84	.033-.038	.84-.96	27
4.2L (258)	1983-88	.033-.038	.84-.96	7-15

IGNITION COIL

Resistance (ohms at 75°F or 24°C)

1983 4-cyl. GM eng.: Primary, 0-2; Secondary, 6000-30,000.

1983-84 4-cyl. AMC eng.: Primary, 1.13-1.23; Secondary, 7700-9300.

1983-88 6-, 8-cyl. eng.: Primary, 1.13-1.23; Secondary, 7700-9300.

DISTRIBUTOR PICKUP

Application	Resistance (ohms)	Air Gap (in./mm)
1983 2.5L (151)	500-1500	—
1983-88 2.5L (150), 4.2L (258)	400-800	.017 min.

IGNITION RESISTOR

Engine	Type	Resistance (ohms)	Temperature (deg. F/C)
4-cyl.			
1983-84	Wire	1.3-1.4	75/24
6-cyl.			
1983-88	Wire	1.3-1.4	75/24

BASE TIMING

Set timing at Before Top Dead Center and at slow idle, unless otherwise specified. Disconnect and plug distributor vacuum hose. 1983 6-cyl., disconnect yellow and blue wire connector at control module and place a jumper wire between the terminals on the module.

Timing MUST be set to specifications shown on emission label if different from setting listed.

Engine	Year	Man. Trans. (degrees) @ RPM	Auto. Trans. (degrees) @ RPM
2.5L (151)	1983	10 ±1	10 ±1
California	1983	12 ±1	12 ±1
2.5L (150)	1983-84	12 ±1	12 ±1
High Altitude	1983-84	19 ±1	19 ±1
4.2L (258)	1983	6 ±2 @ 1600	6 ±2 @ 1600
High Altitude	1983	13 ±2 @ 1600	13 ±2 @ 1600
4.2L (258)	1984-88	9 ±2 @ 1600	9 ±2 @ 1600
High Altitude	1984-88	16 ±2 @ 1600	16 ±2 @ 1600

DISTRIBUTOR TIMING ADVANCE

Engine degrees at engine rpm, no load, in addition to basic timing setting.

Engine	Transmission	Year	Distributor Number	Degrees @ 2500 RPM Total	Degrees @ 2500 RPM Centrifugal
2.5L (151)	MT & AT	1983	1110598	22.5-30.5	5-9
2.5L (151)	MT & AT	1983	1103527	24.4-32.4	6.9-10.9
2.5L (150)	MT & AT	1983-84	3242700	19.8-28.8	4.8-8.8
4.2L (258)	MT & AT	1983-84	3242409	30-40	10-14
4.2L (258)	MT & AT	1985-88	89933002353	29.0-38.5	7.5-12.0

FUEL SYSTEM

FUEL PUMP

Engine	Year	Pressure PSI	Pressure RPM	Volume Pints	Volume Sec.	Volume RPM
4-cyl. GM	1983	6.5-8.0	idle	1	30	idle
4-cyl. AMC	1983-84	4-5	idle	1	30	idle
6-cyl.	1983-88	4-5	idle	1	30	idle

IDLE SPEED W/O COMPUTER CONTROL

Preferred setting is the midpoint of range given.

Make all adjustments with engine at operating temperature.

Slow idle:

1983 2.5L (151) eng., disconnect and plug purge hose at canister and disconnect deceleration valve hose. With E2SE carb., insert dwell meter probes into sockets No. 6 (+) and No. 13 (–) of diagnostic connector. When dwell begins to vary at least 15° adjustments can be made. Remove air cleaner to adjust.

1983-88 6-cyl., disconnect solevac electrical and vacuum leads. Set idle speed to specification. Apply manifold vacuum to vacuum actuator and set actuator speed to specification. With AC, turn unit on, apply battery voltage to the solenoid electrical connector and adjust speed to specification.

All engines equipped with shutdown solenoids, electrically disconnect the solenoid and set shutdown speed to specification.

All engines with AC speedup solenoids (ex. 1983-84 6-cyl.), turn AC unit on and set speedup speed to specification with solenoid plunger fully extended.

Fast idle:

258 engs. set fast idle with TCS and EGR systems disabled.

151 eng. set fast idle to specification.

Engine	Year	SLOW Man. Trans.	SLOW Auto. Trans.	FAST Man. Trans.	FAST Auto. Trans.	Step of Cam
2.5L (151)	1983	800-1000	600-800 D	2400-2600	2600-2800 P	
base idle	1983	500	500 D			
AC speed-up	1983	1250	950 D			
2.5L (150)	1983-84	700-800	650-750 D	1900-2100	2200-2400 P	Second
base idle	1983-84	450-550	450-550 D			
AC speed-up	1983-84	900-1000	800-900 D			
4.2L (258) Eagle	1983	530-670†	530-670 D†	1600-1800	1750-1950 P	Second
High Altitude	1983	630-770†	580-720 D†	1600-1800	1750-1950 P	Second
California	1983	580-720†	480-620 D†	1600-1800	1750-1950 P	Second
Spirit, Concord	1983	580-720†	480-620 D†	1600-1800	1750-1950 P	Second
High Altitude	1983	630-770†	580-720 D†	1600-1800	1750-1950 P	Second
4.2L (258)	1984	550-650⊙	450-550 D⊙	1600-1800	1750-1950 P	Second
4.2L (258)	1985-88	630-730◆	550-650 D◆	1600-1800	1750-1950 P	Second
High Altitude	1985-88	650-750◆	550-650 D◆	1600-1800	1750-1850 P	Second

† Holding solenoid: MT 4-cyl. 600 ±50; AT 4-cyl. 500 ±50. MT 6-cyl. 750, vacuum actuator 900; AT 6-cyl. 650, vacuum actuator 800.

⊙ Holding solenoid: MT, 700-800; AT, 600-700 D. Vacuum actuator: MT, 900-1000; AT, 750-850 D.

◆ Holding solenoid: MT, 850-950; AT, 750-850 D. Vacuum actuator: MT, 1050-1150; AT, 850-950 D.

UNDERHOOD SERVICE SPECIFICATIONS

AMTU3   AMTU3

ENGINE MECHANICAL

TIGHTENING TORQUES

Engine	Year	Torque Ft-lbs/Nm				
		Cylinder Head	Intake Manifold	Exhaust Manifold	Crankshaft Pulley	Water Pump
2.5L (150)	1984	85/115	23/31	23/31	80/108	13/18
2.5L (151)	1983	92/125	37/50	35/47	160/220	17/23
4.2L (258)	1983-88	85/115	23/31	23/31	80/108	13/18

COMPRESSION PRESSURE

At cranking speed or specified rpm, engine temperature normalized, throttle open.

Engine	Year	PSI	Maximum Variation PSI
2.5L (151)	1983	140 @ 160 rpm	*
2.5L (150)	1984	155-185	30
All Others	1983-88	120-150	30

* Lowest cylinder pressure must be more than 70% of highest cylinder pressure.

BELT TENSION

A belt in operation 10 minutes is considered a used belt.
Use a strand tension gauge. Measurements are in pounds.

Engine	Year	Alternator	Power Steering	Air Cond.	Air Pump
USED BELTS					
4-cyl.	1983-84	90-115	90-115	90-115	40-60
6-cyl.	1983-87	90-115	90-115	90-115	90-115
w/power steering	1984-87	60-70	60-70	60-70	60-70
w/Serpentine belt	1983-87	140-160	140-160	140-160	140-160
NEW BELTS					
4-cyl.	1983-84	125-155	125-155	125-155	40-60
6-cyl.	1983-88	125-155	125-155 ★	125-155	125-155 ★
w/power steering	1984-88	65-75	65-75	65-75	65-75
w/Serpentine belt	1983-88	180-200	180-200	180-200	180-200

★ When power steering and air pump are on the same belt: Used, 60-70; New, 65-75.

ENGINE COMPUTER SYSTEM

COMPUTER DIAGNOSTIC CODES
4-CYL.

Code 12 No tach signal (diagnostic circuit OK)
Code 13 Oxygen sensor circuit
Code 14 Shorted coolant sensor circuit
Code 15 Open coolant sensor circuit

COMPUTER DIAGNOSTIC CODES Continued

Codes 21 & 22 Grounded wide open throttle (WOT) switch circuit
Code 22 Grounded adaptive vacuum or WOT switch circuit
Code 23 Open or grounded mixture control solenoid
Code 44 Lean oxygen sensor
Codes 44 & 45 Faulty oxygen sensor
Code 45 Rich oxygen sensor
Code 51 Faulty PROM or installation
Codes 52 & 53 Light on—Intermittent ECM problem
   Light off—Faulty ECM
Code 54 Faulty MC solenoid and/or ECM
Code 55 Faulty oxygen sensor or ECM
6-CYL.
Code 11 No tach signal
   Loss of full battery voltage or bad ground
   Shorted "check engine" display circuit
   Defective ECM
Code 12 Faulty coolant temperature switch
   Faulty thermal electric switch
   Defective ECM
Code 14 Faulty WOT or adaptive vacuum switch circuit
   Defective ECM
Code 21 Faulty OL3 vacuum switch or circuit
   Faulty adaptive vacuum switch or circuit
   Manifold or ported vacuum leak
   Defective ECM
Code 23 OL4 and adaptive vacuum switches defective
   WOT switch defective
   Manifold vacuum not present at vacuum switches
   Defective ECM
Code 24 Faulty coolant temperature switch for manifold heater
   OL1, 2 & 4 switches input wire open circuit

SENSORS, INPUT
TEMPERATURE SENSORS

Engine	Year	Sensor	Resistance Ohms @ deg. F/C
4- & 6-cyl.	1983-88	Coolant	continuity below 100/38 no continuity above 100/38

ACTUATORS, OUTPUT
MIXTURE SOLENOID

Engine	Year	Resistance (Ohms)
2.5L (151)	1983	20 min.
2.5L (150), 4.2L (258)	1983-88	50-95

ENGINE IDENTIFICATION

To identify an engine by the manufacturer's code, follow the four steps designated by the numbered blocks.

V.I.N.
PLATE LOCATION:

1987-83: Top left side of instrument panel, visible through windshield.

1 MODEL YEAR IDENTIFICATION:

1987-83 — 10th character of V.I.N.
1987 — H; 1986 — G; 1985 — F;
1984 — E; 1983 — D.

2 ENGINE CODE LOCATION:

1987-83 — 4th character of V.I.N.

4 ENGINE IDENTIFICATION

	3 ENGINE		DISPL.			
YEAR	CODE	CYL.	liters	cc	Fuel System	HP
1987	D	4	1.4	1397	TBI	56
	A	4	1.7	1721	TBI	78
	V	4	2.0	1965	TBI	95
1986	D	4	1.4	1397	TBI	56
	A	4	1.7	1721	TBI	78
1985	D	4	1.4	1397	TBI	56
	A	4	1.7	1721	TBI	78

4 ENGINE IDENTIFICATION

	3 ENGINE		DISPL.			
YEAR	CODE	CYL.	liters	cc	Fuel System	HP
1984	D	4	1.4	1397	TBI	60
	E	4	1.4	1397	MFI	60
1983	D	4	1.4	1397	TBI	60
	E	4	1.4	1397	MFI	60

T — Turbo. MFI — Multiport Fuel Injection.
TBI — Throttle Body Injection.

UNDERHOOD SERVICE SPECIFICATIONS

RTITU1

CYLINDER NUMBERING SEQUENCE

4-CYL. FIRING ORDER: 1 3 4 2

——— Front of car ———

1983-87 Alliance, Encore 1.4L	1985-87 Alliance, Encore 1.7L 1987 GTA 2.0L

RTITU1

TIMING MARK

0 8 BTDC

1983-87 Alliance, Encore, GTA

ELECTRICAL AND IGNITION SYSTEMS

BATTERY
BCI equivalent shown, size may vary from original equipment. Check clearance before replacing, holddown may need to be modified.

		STANDARD		OPTIONAL	
Engine/Model	Year	BCI Group No.	Crank. Perf.	BCI Group No.	Crank. Perf.
1.4L	1983-87	58	390	58	475
1.7L	1985-87	58	425	58	475
2.0L	1987	58	425	58	475

ALTERNATOR

Application	Rated Output (amps)	Test Output (amps)
1.4L	50, 70	43, 61 @ 1400
1.7L, 2.0L	60, 75	53, 61 @ 1400

REGULATOR

Application	Test Temp. (deg. F/C)	Voltage Setting
1983-87 All	68/20	12.5-15.0

STARTER

Engine	Year	Cranking Voltage (min. volts)	Ampere Draw @ Cranking Speed
1.4L	1985	9.0	150
1.4L	1986-87	9.6	120
1.7L	1985	9.0	200
1.7L, 2.0L	1986-87	9.6	120

SPARK PLUGS

Engine	Year	Gap (inches)	Gap (mm)	Torque (ft-lb)
1.4L	1983-87	.022-.026	.55-.65	18-22
1.7L	1985-87	.031	.80	21
2.0L	1987	.031	.80	21

IGNITION COIL
Resistance (ohms @ 70°F or 21°C)

Engine	Year	Windings	Resistance (ohms)
All	1983-87	Primary	0.4-0.8
		Secondary	2500-5500

BASE TIMING
Set timing at Before Top Dead Center at idle speed or less.

Engine	Year	Man. Trans. (degrees)	Auto. Trans. (degrees)
1.4L	1983-85	8 ±1*	8 ±1*
1.4L	1986-87	10 ±3*	10 ±3*
1.7L	1985-87	6 ±3*	6 ±3*
2.0L	1987	10 ±1*	10 ±1*

* Not adjustable.

UNDERHOOD SERVICE SPECIFICATIONS

RTITU2   RTITU2

FUEL SYSTEM

FUEL SYSTEM PRESSURE

CARBURETTED & TBI

Engine	Year	PSI	RPM
1.4L	1983-87	14.5	—
1.7L, 2.0L	1985-87	17.4	—

MFI

Engine	Year	Pressure Idle PSI*	Pressure Idle PSI**
1.4L Calif.	1983-84	—	33-39

* Pressure regulator vacuum disconnected.
**Pressure regulator vacuum connected.

IDLE SPEED W/O COMPUTER CONTROL

Engine	Year	SLOW Man. Trans.	SLOW Auto. Trans.	FAST Man. Trans.	FAST Auto. Trans.
1.4L Calif.	1983-84	600-700	600-700 D	—	—

IDLE SPEED W/COMPUTER CONTROL

1.4L, 1.7L: Run engine, then turn ignition off, ISC should fully extend. Disconnect the unit and adjust to setting speed. Turn engine off and reconnect unit. Start engine and verify checking speed is at specified value.

Engine	Year	Transmission	Setting Speed	Checking Speed	AC Speed-up
1.4L ex. Calif.	1983-84	MT	3300-3700	600-700	—
1.4L ex. Calif.	1983-84	AT	3300-3700 N	600-700 D	—
1.4L	1985-87	MT	3300-3700	700-800	—
Canada	1985-87	MT	3100-3500	400-800	—
1.7L	1985-87	MT	2900-3200	600	—
1.7L	1985-87	AT	2900-3200 N	900-950 D	—

ENGINE MECHANICAL

TIGHTENING TORQUES

Engine	Year	Torque Ft-lbs/Nm Cylinder Head	Intake Manifold	Exhaust Manifold	Crankshaft Pulley	Water Pump
1.4L	1983-87	42/57	12/17	12/17	81/110	—
1.7L, 2.0L	1985-87	†	16/22	16/22	7/95	—

† Tighten to 22/31, then 52/71. After three minutes, loosen and retorque to 15/20 and turn 123°.

VALVE CLEARANCE

Engine cold.

Engine	Year	Intake (inches)	Intake (mm)	Exhaust (inches)	Exhaust (mm)
1.4L	1983-87	.006	.15	.008	.20
1.7L, 2.0L	1985-87	.008	.20	.015	.40

BELT TENSION

Deflection method: Table lists deflection under moderate pressure applied midway between pulleys.

Strand Tension method: Use a strand tension gauge. Measurements are in pounds.

Engine	Year	Alternator	Power Steering	Air Cond.
Deflection method				
1.4L	1983-87	4.5	3.5-4.5	3.5-4.5
Strand Tension method				
1.4L	1983-87	80-95	90-115	90-115
1.7L, 2.0L w/Serpentine belt	1985-87	140-160	140-160	180-200

ENGINE COMPUTER SYSTEM

COMPUTER DIAGNOSTIC CODES

1983-85 All w/TBI
Install test bulb in sockets 2 & 4 of large test connector (1983-84) or between terminals J2-24 & J1-G at back of ECU harness connector (1985). Push WOT switch lever and with ISC plunger collapsed, have a helper turn ignition switch to ON position.

Code 1 Manifold air/fuel temperature sensor
Code 2 Coolant temperature sensor
Code 3 Wide open throttle & closed throttle switch
Code 4 Closed throttle switch & high air flow
Code 5 Wide open throttle & closed air flow
Code 6 Oxygen sensor

SENSORS, INPUT

TEMPERATURE SENSORS

Engine	Year	Sensor	Resistance Ohms @ deg. F/C
1.4L TBI	1983-84	Coolant, MAT	300-300,000 300-300,000
1.4L, 1.7L, 2.0L	1985-87	Coolant, MAT	13,500 @ 20/-7 7500 @ 40/4 3400 @ 70/20 1600 @ 100/38 450 @ 160/70 185 @ 212/100

MANIFOLD ABSOLUTE PRESSURE SENSOR

Engine	Year	Voltage
1.4L, 1.7L	1985-87	4-5, ign. on 1.5-2.1, idle

CRANKSHAFT SENSOR

Measured between brown and blue terminals of crank angle sensor.

Engine	Year	Resistance (ohms)
1.4L, 1.7L, 2.0L	1983-87	125-275

ACTUATORS, OUTPUT

COMPUTER TIMING ADVANCE

Alliance, Encore: To check advance schedule, disconnect and plug the vacuum hose at the control unit. Apply 10″ of vacuum to the unit and check against the specification listed at 1600 rpm.

The Advance Curve Characteristic Number is affixed to the ignition control module.

Engine	Transmission	Year	Adv. Curve Char. Number	Degrees
1.4L Alliance, Encore	MT & AT	1983-85	RE-028, 021B	17.5-21.0

AUDI
1983-92

ENGINE IDENTIFICATION

To identify an engine by the manufacturer's code, follow the four steps designated by the numbered blocks.

V.I.N. PLATE LOCATION:

Top of instrument panel or windshield pillar visible through windshield on driver's side.

1 MODEL YEAR IDENTIFICATION:

10th character of V.I.N.
1992 — N; 1991 — M; 1990 — L;
1989 — K; 1988 — J; 1987 — H;
1986 — G; 1985 — F; 1984 — E;
1983 — D.

2 ENGINE CODE LOCATION:

Prefix to engine number:

Code 3B engines — Stamped on side of engine block, passenger's side rear.

All other engines — Stamped on side of engine block below number 2 and 3 spark/glow plugs.

4 ENGINE IDENTIFICATION

YEAR	3 ENGINE CODE	CYL.	DISPL. liters	cc	Fuel System	HP
1992	NG	5	2.3	2309	CIS-E	130
	7A	5	2.3	2309	AFC	164
	AAH	6	2.8	2771	M	172
	PT	8	4.2	4172	M	276
1991	MC	5	2.2 T	2226 T	CIS	157
	3B	5	2.2 T	2226 T	M	217
	NF, NG	5	2.3	2309	CIS-E	130
	7A	5	2.3	2309	AFC	164
	PT	8	3.6	3562	M	240
1990	3A	4	2.0	1984	CIS-E	108
	MC	5	2.2 T	2226 T	CIS	157
	NF, NG	5	2.3	2309	CIS-E	130
	7A	5	2.3	2309	AFC	164
	PT	8	3.6	3562	M	240
1989	3A	4	2.0	1984	CIS-E	108
	MC	5	2.2 T	2226 T	CIS	157
	NF, NG	5	2.3	2309	CIS-E	130
1988	3A	4	2.0	1984	CIS-E	108
	MC	5	2.2 T	2226 T	CIS	157
	NF, NG	5	2.3	2309	CIS-E	130
1987	MG	4	1.8	1780	CIS-E	105
	MC	5	2.2 T	2226 T	CIS	157
	NF	5	2.3	2309	CIS-E	130
1986	MG	4	1.8	1780	CIS-E	105
	WE	5	2.1	2144	CIS	108
	KX	5	2.2	2226	CIS-E	110

4 ENGINE IDENTIFICATION

YEAR	3 ENGINE CODE	CYL.	DISPL. liters	cc	Fuel System	HP
1986 Cont'd.	KZ	5	2.2	2226	CIS-E	115
	MC	5	2.2 T	2226 T	CIS	157
1985	MG	4	1.8	1780	CIS-E	105
	DE	5	2.0 TD	1986 TD	VE	90
	WE	5	2.1	2144	CIS	108
	KH	5	2.1 T	2144 T	CIS	142
	WX	5	2.1 T	2144 T	CIS	160
	KX	5	2.2	2226	CIS-E	110
	KZ	5	2.2	2226	CIS-E	115
	MC	5	2.2 T	2226 T	CIS	157
1984	JN	4	1.8	1780	CIS-E	88
	DE	5	2.0 TD	1986 TD	VE	90
	WD, WE, WU	5	2.1	2144	CIS	108
	KH	5	2.1 T	2144 T	CIS	142
	WX	5	2.1 T	2144 T	CIS	160
	KX	5	2.2	2226	CIS-E	110
	JT	5	2.2	2226	CIS-E	115
1983	JK	4	1.6 D	1588 D	VE	54
	CY	4	1.6 TD	1588 TD	VE	70
	WT	4	1.7	1715	CIS	79
	DE	5	2.0 TD	1986 TD	VE	90
	WD, WE	5	2.1	2144	CIS	108
	WX	5	2.1 T	2144 T	CIS	160

AFC — Air Flow Control.   CIS — Continuous Injection System.
CIS-E — CIS Electronic.   D — Diesel.   M — Motronic.
T — Turbo.   TD — Turbo Diesel.   VE — Diesel Injection.

UNDERHOOD SERVICE SPECIFICATIONS

AIITU1   AIITU1

CYLINDER NUMBERING SEQUENCE

4-CYL. FIRING ORDER: 1 3 4 2

5-CYL. FIRING ORDER: 1 2 4 5 3

V6 FIRING ORDER: 1 4 3 6 2 5

V8 FIRING ORDER: 1 5 4 8 6 3 7 2

──── Front of car ────

All 4-cyl. Gasoline   All 5-cyl. Gasoline   V6 2.8 liter   V8 3.6, 4.2 liter

─── TIMING MARK ───

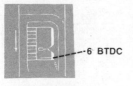
1.8, 2.0 liter w/MT

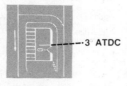
1.8, 2.0 liter w/AT

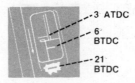
2.1, 2.2, 2.3 liter

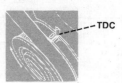
V8 3.6 liter

ELECTRICAL AND IGNITION SYSTEMS

BATTERY
BCI equivalent shown, size may vary from original equipment. Check clearance before replacing, holddown may need to be modified.

Engine	Year	STANDARD BCI Group No.	STANDARD Crank Perf.	OPTIONAL BCI Group No.	OPTIONAL Crank Perf.
1588cc Diesel	1983	49	650	—	—
1715cc	1983	42	435	—	—
Canada	1983	41	500	—	—
1780cc	1984-87	42	435	—	—
Canada	1984-87	41	500	—	—
1984cc	1988-90	41	500	—	—
1986cc Diesel	1983-84	49	650	—	—
2144cc	1983-85	41*	500	—	—
2226cc	1984-91	41*	500	—	—
2309cc: 80, 90	1988-91	41	500	—	—
100, 200	1989-91	41*	500	—	—
5000	1988	41*	500	—	—
Coupe Quattro	1990-91	41	650	—	—
3562cc V8 Quattro	1990	41*	650	—	—
3562cc	1991	49*	720	—	—

* Battery is vented to outside of vehicle.

ALTERNATOR

Engine	Year	Rated Output	Test Output (amps @ rpm)
1588cc Diesel	1983	45	—
w/AC	1983	65	44 @ 3000
1715cc	1983	55	35 @ 3000
w/AC	1983	65	44 @ 3000
1780cc	1984-87	65	44 @ 3000
1984cc	1988-89	90	74 @ 3000
1986cc Turbo Diesel	1983-84	90	60 @ 3000
2144cc ex. Turbo	1983-84	75	50 @ 3000
w/AC	1983-84	90	60 @ 3000
2144cc Turbo	1983-85	90	60 @ 3000
2226cc	1984-86	90	60 @ 3000
2226cc	1987-90	90	74 @ 3000
2226cc Turbo	1991	110	95 @ 3000
2309cc	1987-91	110	95 @ 3000

REGULATOR

Application	Year	Test Temp. (deg. F/C)	Voltage Setting
All	1983	Normal	12.5-14.5
All	1984-92	Normal	13.5-14.5

STARTER

Engine	Year	Cranking Voltage (min. volts)	Ampere Draw @ Cranking Speed
All	1983-92	8.0	—

SPARK PLUGS

Engine	Year	Gap (inches)	Gap (mm)	Torque (ft-lb)
1715cc	1983	.028-.031	.70-.80	14
1780cc	1984-85	.028-.031	.70-.80	14
1780cc	1986-87	.028-.035	.70-.90	14
1984cc	1988-89	.028-.035	.70-.90	14
2144cc 5000 ex. Turbo	1983-85	.028-.031	.70-.80	14
Turbo	1983-85	.024-.031	.60-.80	14
2144cc 4000, Coupe	1983-84	.032-.035	.80-.90	14
2226cc	1984-85	.028-.031	.70-.80	14
2226cc ex. Turbo	1986-87	.028-.035	.70-.90	14
Turbo, Code MC	1986-91	.024-.031	.60-.80	14
Turbo, Code WX	1986-88	.028-.035	.70-.90	14
DOHC Turbo, Code 3B	1991	.020-.028	.50-.70	22
2309cc	1987-91	.028-.035	.70-.90	14

SPARK PLUGS Continued

Engine	Year	Gap (inches)	Gap (mm)	Torque (ft-lb)
2771cc	1992	.028-.035	.70-.90	15
3562cc	1990	.028-.035	.70-.90	22
4172cc	1992	.028-.035	.70-.90	22

IGNITION COIL

Engine	Year	Windings	Resistance (ohms)
All ex. Turbo	1983-84	Primary	0.52-0.76
		Secondary	2400-3500
Turbo	1984-85	Primary	0.50-1.50
		Secondary	6500-8000
2.2L Code KZ	1985-86	Primary	0.5-1.5
		Secondary	5000-6000
Others ex. Turbo	1985-86	Primary	0.52-0.76
		Secondary	2400-3500
Turbo	1986-87	Primary	0.50-1.50
		Secondary	5000-9000
All ex. Code 7A	1988-91	Primary	0.50-1.50
		Secondary	5000-9000
Code 7A	1990-91	Primary	0.0-1.0
		Secondary	6500-8500
V6 2.8L	1992	Primary	0.5-1.2
		Secondary	9000-14,000

BASE TIMING
Set timing Before Top Dead Center, unless otherwise specified.

All Engines: Connect tachometer and timing light; check idle speed, observe timing mark.

Engines w/ISS (Integrated Idle Stabilizer): Disconnect plugs from stabilizer and connect them together.

Engine	Year	Man. Trans. (degrees) @ Idle	Auto. Trans. (degrees) @ Idle
1780cc	1984-87	6 ± 2	6 ± 2
1984cc	1988-89	6 ± 2	6 ± 2
2144cc Turbo	1983	—	21 @ 3000 rpm
2144cc U.S.	1983	6	3 ATDC
Canada	1983	3 ATDC	3 ATDC
2144cc: 4000, Coupe	1984	6 ± 2	3 ± 2
5000	1984	6 ± 2	6 ± 2
Canada	1984	3 ± 2 ATDC	3 ± 2 ATDC
2144cc Turbo	1984-86	6 ± 2*	6 ± 2*
Canada	1984-86	3 ± 1*	3 ± 1*
2226cc	1984-87	6 ± 2	6 ± 2
Canada	1986	6 ± 2	3 ± 2
2226cc SOHC Turbo	1986-91	0*	0*
2309cc SOHC	1987-91	15 ± 2	15 ± 2
2309cc DOHC	1990-91	0*	0*
3562cc	1990-91	—	0*

* Checking figure only, timing is non-adjustable.

DISTRIBUTOR TIMING ADVANCE
Engine degrees at engine rpm, no load, in addition to basic timing.

Engine	Trans-mission	Year	Distributor Number	Degrees @ 2500 RPM Total	Degrees @ 2500 RPM Centrifugal
1715cc	MT & AT	1983	049905205Q	26.2-33.0	16.2-21.0
Canada	MT & AT	1983	049905205R	21-30	17-22
Canada	MT	1983	035905206B	26.2-33.0	16.2-21.0
1780cc	MT & AT	1984	026905205L	24-32	14-19
2144cc Turbo U.S.	MT & AT	1983	035905205H	16-24	10-15
Canada	MT & AT	1983	035905206J	16-24	10-15
2144cc ex. Turbo U.S.	MT & AT	1983-84	035905205J	27-36	10-14
Canada	MT & AT	1983-86	035905205R	27-36	10-14
2226cc	MT & AT	1983-86	035905205AM	25.5-34.3	15.5-20.3

UNDERHOOD SERVICE SPECIFICATIONS

FUEL SYSTEM

FUEL PRESSURE PROCEDURE

AFC System:
1. Connect appropriate pressure gauge to test port of fuel rail and open gauge valve.
2. Bridge diagnostic connector A, terminal 1 negative (–) with diagnostic connector B, terminal 1. Energize fuel pump, listen for pump to run and remove jumper after a minimum of 4 seconds, read system pressure.

CIS Systems:
1. With engine at operating temperature, connect appropriate pressure gauge between fuel distributor and warm-up regulator.
2. Set gauge valve to open position, start engine and run at idle, allow pressure to stabilize, read control pressure.
3. Set gauge valve to closed position, allow pressure to stabilize, read system pressure.
4. Set gauge to open position, switch off ignition, after 10 minutes read residual pressure.

CIS-E Systems:
1. With engine at operating temperature, connect appropriate pressure gauge between cold start line and lower chamber test fittings of the fuel distributor.
2. Disconnect electrical connector from the differential pressure regulator.
3. Set gauge valve to open position, remove fuel pump relay and bridge terminals to energize pump, allow pressure to stabilize, read system pressure.
4. Set gauge valve to closed position, energize fuel pump, read differential pressure.
5. Set gauge valve to open position, energize fuel pump for 30 seconds, after 10 minutes read residual pressure.

Motronic Systems:
1. Connect appropriate pressure gauge to test port of fuel rail.
2. Disconnect vacuum hose from pressure regulator, start engine and run at idle, allow pressure to stabilize and take reading.
3. Reconnect vacuum to pressure regulator and check gauge reading.
4. Switch ignition off, after 10 minutes read residual pressure.

FUEL PRESSURE: AFC, MOTRONIC

Engine	Year	System Pressure		Residual Pressure PSI
		W/o vacuum PSI	W/vacuum PSI	
2226cc	1991	43-46	35-39	36-40
2309cc	1990-91	—	55-61	46
2771cc	1992	55-61	48-54	32-44
3562cc	1990-91	58-62	49-54	43-50
4172cc	1992	58-62	49-54	43-50

FUEL PRESSURE: CIS, CIS-E

Engine	System	Year	Pressure			
			System PSI	Control PSI	Differential PSI	Residual PSI
1715cc	CIS	1983-84	68-78	49-55	—	38
1780cc	CIS-E	1984-87	75-82	—	68-79	38
1984cc	CIS-E	1988-90	88-96	—	81-91	48
2144cc	CIS	1983-85	68-78	49-55	—	35-38
2226cc	CIS-E	1983-86	75-82	—	68-79	38
2309cc	CIS-E	1987-91	89-94	—	81-90	51

IDLE SPEED

All Engines: Must be at operating temperature, all electrical equipment switched off, cooling fan not running. If equipped with ISS (idle speed stabilizer), disconnect both electrical plugs and connect them together. If equipped with idle speed boost valve, pinch off hose to valve.

1984 2144cc Code WU: Disconnect multiplug from ignition coil, reinstall plug so that lead to idle stabilizer (green/white wire) is open. Disconnect and plug crankcase breather hoses, disconnect intake hose to canister.

1984-85 2144cc Turbo Code KH: Disconnect green wire from ignition coil terminal 1, disconnect and plug crankcase breather hoses at valve cover, remove plug from canister vent pipe at intake boot.

1985-91 2226cc Turbo Code MC: Disconnect crankcase breather hoses and plug outlets on valve cover, remove plug from canister vent pipe at intake boot.

All Other Engines: Disconnect crankcase breather hoses, remove plug from fitting of canister vent hose.

IDLE SPEED Continued

Engine	Year	Manual Transmission	Automatic Transmission
1588cc Diesel	1983	800-850	800-850 N
1588cc Turbo Diesel	1983	900-1000	900-1000 N
1715cc	1983	850-1000	850-1000 N
1780cc	1984	850-1000	850-1000 N
1780cc	1985-87	800-900	800-900 N
1984cc	1988-90	780-900	780-900 N
1986cc Diesel	1983-84	720-880	720-880 N
2144cc ex. California	1983	775-925	850-1000 N
California	1983	880-1000	880-1000 N
2144cc, all	1984-86	750-850	750-850 N
2226cc ex. Turbo	1984-86	750-850	750-850 N
2226cc Turbo before 2/86	1985-86	780-820	780-820 N
2226cc Turbo after 1/86	1986-89	750-850	670-770 D
2226cc SOHC Turbo	1990-91	700-740	700-740 N
2226cc DOHC Turbo	1991	770-830	—
2309cc Code NF	1987-91	670-770	670-770 N
2309cc Code NG	1988-91	720-860	720-860 N
2309cc DOHC	1990-91	750-850	750-850 N
2771cc	1992	700-800	700-800 N
3562cc	1990-91	—	660-720 N
4172cc	1992	—	660-720 N

IDLE MIXTURE

Engine	Year	Idle CO%
1715cc	1983	0.3-1.2*
Canada	1983	0.5-0.9
Canada w/MT	1983	1.0-1.5
1780cc	1984-87	0.3-1.2*
1984cc	1988-89	0.3-1.2
2144cc	1983	0.3-1.2*
Canada w/AT	1983	0.5-0.9
w/MT	1983	1.0-1.5
2144cc Turbo	1983	0.4-1.2*
2144cc	1984	0.6-1.0*
Canada	1984	0.3-0.7
2144cc Turbo	1984-85	0.8-1.2*
2226cc	1984-87	0.6-1.0*
2226cc Turbo	1986	0.8-1.2*
2226cc SOHC Turbo	1987-91	0.3-1.2
2226cc DOHC Turbo	1991	0.5-0.9
2309cc Code NF	1987-91	0.3-1.2
2309cc Code NG	1988-89	0.6-1.0
2309cc DOHC	1990-91	0.5-1.0
2771cc	1992	0.3-1.2
3562cc	1990-91	0.5-0.9
4172cc	1992	0.5-0.9

* Oxygen sensor disconnected.

ENGINE MECHANICAL

TIGHTENING TORQUES

Engine	Year	Torque Ft-lbs/Nm				
		Cylinder Head	Intake Manifold	Exhaust Manifold	Crankshaft Pulley	Water Pump
DIESEL ENGINES						
4-cyl. 1.6L:						
12-point bolt	1983-84	30/40	18/25	18/25	15/20	7/10
2nd stage		44/60				
Warm retorque†		+180°				
All	1985	30/40	18/25	18/25	15/20	7/10
2nd stage		44/60				
3rd stage		+180°				
Warm retorque†		+90°				
5-cyl. 2.0L	1983-85	44/60	18/25	18/25	258/350●	15/20
2nd stage ★		+180°				
Warm retorque		+90°				

UNDERHOOD SERVICE SPECIFICATIONS

AIITU4   AIITU4

TIGHTENING TORQUES Continued

		Torque Ft-lbs/Nm				
Engine	Year	Cylinder Head	Intake Manifold	Exhaust Manifold	Crankshaft Pulley	Water Pump
GASOLINE ENGINES						
4-cyl. 1.7L	1983	30/40	18/25	18/25	15/20	7/10
2nd stage		44/60				
3rd stage ★		+180°				
4-cyl. 1.8L	1984-87	44/60	—	—	15/20	7/10
2nd stage ★		+180°				
4-cyl. 2.0L	1988-89	44/60	6mm bolt 7/10	18/25	15/20	15/20
			8mm bolt 18/25			
2nd stage ★		+180°				
5-cyl. 2.1L:						
Ex. Turbo	1983-84	44/60	—	18/25	258/350•	15/20
2nd stage ★		+180°				
Turbo	1983-85	44/60	—	26/35	258/350•	15/20
2nd stage ★		+180°				
5-cyl. 2.2L:						
Ex. Turbo	1984-87	44/60	—	18/25	258/350•	15/20
2nd stage ★		+180°				
SOHC Turbo	1985-91	44/60	—	26/35	258/350•	15/20
2nd stage ★		+180°				
DOHC Turbo	1991	30/40	18/25	26/35	258/350•	16/22
2nd stage		44/60				
3rd stage ★		+180°				
5-cyl. 2.3L:						
SOHC	1987-91	44/60	15/20	18/25	258/350•	15/20
2nd stage ★		+180°				
DOHC	1990-91	29/40	15/20	18/25	15/20	15/20
2nd stage		44/60				
3rd stage ★		+180°				
V6 2.8L	1992	44/60	15/20	15/20	258/350•	7/10
2nd stage ★		+180°				
V8 3.6L	1990-91	30/40	11/15	18/25	258/350•	7/10
2nd stage		44/60				
3rd stage ★		+180°				

† With engine at operating temperature, repeat after 1000 miles of service.
★ Two at 90° is permissible, must be in one even motion.
• Valid only when using special extension, Audi Part No. 2079.

VALVE CLEARANCE

Engine at normal operating temperature.

Engine	Year	Intake (inches)	Intake (mm)	Exhaust (inches)	Exhaust (mm)
All w/o hydraulic	1983-86	.008-.012	.20-.30	.016-.020	.40-.50

COMPRESSION PRESSURE

At cranking speed, engine temperature normalized, throttle open.

Engine	Year	PSI @ RPM	Maximum Variation PSI
1588cc Diesel	1983	406-493	72
1715cc	1983	131-174	44
1780cc	1984-87	131-174	44
1984cc	1988-89	152-196	44
1986cc Diesel	1983-85	398-483	71
2144cc	1983-84	120-170	42
2144cc, 2226cc Turbo	1983-88	102-131	29
2226cc w/o Turbo	1985-87	120-174	44
2226cc SOHC Turbo	1989-91	123-144	44
2226cc DOHC Turbo	1991	131-189	44
2309cc	1987-88	145-203	44
2309cc SOHC	1989-91	160-172	44
2771cc	1992	160-232	44
3562cc	1990-91	145-190	44

BELT TENSION

Deflection method: Measured at midpoint of longest belt segment.

Engine	Year	Alternator	Power Steering	Air Cond.
All (inches)	1983-87	3/8-9/16	3/8-9/16	3/8-9/16
All (mm)	1983-87	10-15	10-15	10-15
All (inches)	1988-91	1/8-1/4	1/8-1/4	1/8-1/4
All (mm)	1988-91	2-5	2-5	2-5

ENGINE COMPUTER SYSTEM

COMPUTER DIAGNOSTIC CODES

All Models:
Drive car at least 5 minutes and leave running at idle, Turbo engines must exceed 3000 rpm and 17 psi of boost. For a no-start condition, crank engine over for a minimum of 6 seconds and leave ignition switched on.

1984cc 1988-90:
1. Connect tester, Audi Part No. US1115, between test lead (next to fuel distributor) and positive battery terminal, codes displayed by tester.
2. Install spare fuse in top of fuel pump relay for 4 seconds.
3. Repeat step 2 to access additional codes, leave fuse in place 10 seconds to erase memory.

Code	Application	Definition
1111	Control Unit	Defective unit or circuit
2113	Speed Sensor	No signal from hall sender
2121	Idle Switch	Defective switch or circuit
2123	Throttle Switch	Defective switch or circuit
2141	Knock Control	Excessive detonation signal
2142	Knock Control	No signal, defective sensor or circuit
2231	Idle Control	Idle speed outside control limits
2232	Air Flow Sensor	No signal, defective sensor or circuit
2312	Coolant Temperature	No signal, defective sensor or circuit
2341	Oxygen Sensor	System operating outside control limits
2342	Oxygen Sensor	No signal, defective sensor or circuit
2343	Fuel Mixture	System running too lean
2344	Fuel Mixture	System running too rich
4431	Idle Stabilizer	No signal, defective valve or circuit
4444	No Faults	Stored memory clear
0000	End Diagnosis	No additional stored codes

2144cc Turbo 1985, 2226cc Turbo 1985-88:
1. Codes will be displayed on instrument cluster warning lamps.
2. Bridge test contacts of the fuel pump relay for 4 seconds.
3. Repeat step 2 to access additional codes.

2226cc SOHC Turbo w/1 knock sensor 1989-91:
1. Connect tester, Audi Part No. US1115, between positive (+) cavity of diagnostic terminal A (light color) and cavity of terminal B (dark color). Codes displayed by tester, California models flash ENGINE light on dash.
2. Momentarily (4 seconds) connect jump wire between negative (−) cavity of diagnostic terminal A and terminal B.
3. Repeat step 3 for additional codes.

Code	Application	Definition
1111	Control Unit	Defective unit or circuit
2111	RPM Sensor	Defective sensor or circuit
2112	Timing Sensor	Defective sensor or circuit
2113	Hall Sender	Defective sender or circuit
2121	Idle Switch	Defective switch or circuit
2123	Throttle Switch	Defective switch or circuit
2141	Knock Control	Excessive detonation signal
2142	Knock Control	No signal, defective sensor or circuit
2221	Vacuum Control	No vacuum to control unit
2222	Pressure Sensor	Defective control unit pressure sensor
2312	Coolant Temperature	No signal, defective sensor or circuit
2322	Intake Air	No signal, defective sensor or circuit
2342	Oxygen Sensor	No signal, defective sensor or circuit
4444	No Faults	Stored memory clear
0000	End Diagnosis	No additional stored codes

2226cc SOHC Turbo w/2 knock sensors 1990-91:
1. Connect tester, Audi Part No. US1115, between positive diagnostic terminals 1 and 3, codes displayed by tester, California models flash ENGINE light on dash.
2. Momentarily (4 seconds) connect jump wire between diagnostic terminals 2 and 1.
3. Repeat step 3 for additional codes.

Code	Application	Definition
1111	Control Unit	Defective unit or circuit
2111	RPM Sensor	Defective sensor or circuit
2112	Timing Sensor	Defective sensor or circuit
2113	Hall Sender	Defective sender or circuit
2121	Idle Switch	Defective switch or circuit
2123	Throttle Switch	Defective switch or circuit
2141	Knock Control	Detonation from sensor No. 1
2142	Knock Control	Defective sensor No. 1 or circuit
2143	Knock Control	Detonation from sensor No. 2
2144	Knock Control	Defective sensor No. 2 or circuit
2214	RPM Signal	Idle speed too high
2221	Vacuum Control	No vacuum to control unit

UNDERHOOD SERVICE SPECIFICATIONS

AIITU5   AIITU5

COMPUTER DIAGNOSTIC CODES Continued

Code	Application	Definition
2222	Pressure Sensor	Defective control unit pressure sensor
2224	Manifold Pressure	Turbo control circuit
2312	Coolant Temperature	No signal, defective sensor or circuit
2322	Intake Air	No signal, defective sensor or circuit
2342	Oxygen Sensor	No signal, defective sensor or circuit
4444	No Faults	Stored memory clear
0000	End Diagnosis	No additional stored codes

2226cc DOHC Turbo 1991:
1. Special test equipment, Audi Part No. VAG1551, required.

Code	Application	Definition
1111	Control Unit	Defective unit or circuit
2111	RPM Sensor	Defective sensor or circuit
2112	Timing Sensor	Defective sensor or circuit
2113	Hall Sender	Defective sender or circuit
2121	Idle Switch	Defective switch or circuit
2123	Throttle Switch	Defective switch or circuit
2141	Knock Control	Detonation from sensor No. 1
2142	Knock Control	Defective sensor No. 1 or circuit
2143	Knock Control	Detonation from sensor No. 2
2144	Knock Control	Defective sensor No. 2 or circuit
2212	Throttle Valve	Potentiometer voltage out of range
2214	RPM Signal	Idle speed too high
2221	Vacuum Control	No vacuum to control unit
2222	Pressure Sensor	Defective control unit pressure sensor
2223	Altitude Sensor	Defective sensor or circuit
2224	Manifold Pressure	Turbo control circuit, overboost
2231	Idle Speed	Idle speed out of range
2234	System Voltage	System voltage out of range
2312	Coolant Temperature	No signal, defective sensor or circuit
2322	Intake Air	No signal, defective sensor or circuit
2324	Air Mass Sensor	Defective sensor or circuit
2341	Oxygen Sensor	System operating outside of limits
2342	Oxygen Sensor	No signal, defective sensor or circuit
2413	Mixture Control	System running too rich
3424	Fault Lamp	System not operating
4343	Canister Purge	Defective solenoid or circuit
4411	Fuel Injector #1	Defective injector or circuit
4412	Fuel Injector #2	Defective injector or circuit
4413	Fuel Injector #3	Defective injector or circuit
4414	Fuel Injector #4	Defective injector or circuit
4421	Fuel Injector #5	Defective injector or circuit
4431	Idle Stabilizer	Defective stabilizer or circuit
4442	Wastegate	Defective frequency valve or circuit
4444	No Faults	Stored memory clear
0000	End Diagnosis	No additional stored codes

2309cc 1987-88:
1. Codes will be displayed on instrument cluster warning lamps.
2. Install spare fuse in top of fuel pump relay for 4 seconds.
3. Repeat step 2 to access additional codes, leave fuse in place 10 seconds to erase memory.

2309cc SOHC 1989-91:
1. Connect tester, Audi Part No. US1115, between positive (+) cavity of diagnostic terminal A (light color) and cavity of terminal B (dark color). Codes displayed by tester, California models flash ENGINE light on dash.
2. Momentarily (4 seconds) connect jump wire between negative (−) cavity of diagnostic terminal A and terminal B.
3. Repeat step 3 for additional codes.

Code	Application	Definition
1111	Control Unit	Defective unit or circuit
1213	Speed Sensor	Transmission sensor or circuit
2121	Idle Switch	Defective switch or circuit
2122	Hall Sender	Defective sender or circuit
2123	Throttle Switch	Defective switch or circuit
2132	Control Unit	No signal from ignition to injection
2141	Knock Control	Excessive detonation signal
2142	Knock Control	No signal, defective sensor or circuit
2223	Altitude Sensor	No signal, defective sensor or circuit
2231	Idle Control	Idle speed too high
2232	Air Flow Sensor	No signal, defective sensor or circuit
2233	Reference Voltage	No reference signal to control units
2312	Coolant Temperature	No signal, defective sensor or circuit

COMPUTER DIAGNOSTIC CODES Continued

Code	Application	Definition
2341	Oxygen Sensor	System operating outside of limits
2342	Oxygen Sensor	No signal, defective sensor or circuit
2343	Fuel Mixture	System running too lean
2344	Fuel Mixture	System running too rich
2411	EGR System	System malfunction, California only
4431	Idle Stabilizer	No signal, defective valve or circuit
4444	No Faults	Stored memory clear
0000	End Diagnosis	No additional stored codes

2309cc DOHC 1990-91:
1. Connect tester, Audi Part No. US1115, between positive (+) cavity of diagnostic terminal A (light color) and cavity of terminal B (dark color). Codes displayed by tester, California models flash ENGINE light on dash.
2. Momentarily (4 seconds) connect jump wire between negative (−) cavity of diagnostic terminal A and terminal B.
3. Repeat step 3 for additional codes, or to erase memory after code 0000.

Code	Application	Definition
1111	Control Unit	Defective unit or circuit
1231	Speed Sensor	Transmission sensor or circuit
2111	Speed Sensor	Engine sensor or circuit
2112	Reference Sensor	Ignition sensor or circuit
2113	Hall Sender	Defective sender or circuit
2114	Distributor	Ignition out of adjustment
2121	Idle Switch	Defective switch or circuit
2141	Knock Control	Detonation from sensor No. 1
2142	Knock Control	Defective sensor No. 1 or circuit
2143	Knock Control	Detonation from sensor No. 2
2144	Knock Control	Defective sensor No. 2 or circuit
2212	Throttle Valve	Potentiometer voltage out of range
2232	Air Mass Sensor	Sensor voltage out of range
2233	Air Mass Sensor	Reference voltage high
2234	Control Unit	Supply voltage low
2242	CO Potentiometer	Potentiometer voltage low
2312	Coolant Temperature	Defective sensor or circuit
2342	Oxygen Sensor	Defective sensor or circuit
4431	Idle Stabilizer	Defective valve or circuit
4444	No Faults	Stored memory clear
0000	End Diagnosis	No additional stored codes

V8 3562cc 1990-91:
1. Bridge upper cavities of diagnostic terminals 1 & 4 with test light, Audi special tool No. US1115.
2. Crank engine for 5 seconds and leave the ignition switched on.
3. Momentarily (4 seconds) connect jump wire between the lower cavities of diagnostic terminals 1 & 2.
4. Test light flashes codes, California models flash ENGINE light on dash.
5. Repeat step 3 for additional codes, or to erase memory after code 0000.

Code	Application	Definition
1111	Control Unit	Defective unit or circuit
2111	Speed Sensor	Engine sensor or circuit
2112	Reference Sensor	Ignition sensor or circuit
2113	Hall Sender	Defective sender or circuit
2114	Hall Reference	Check, camshaft timing out of phase
2121	Idle Switch	Defective switch, adjustment, or circuit
2123	Full Throttle Switch	Defective switch, adjustment, or circuit
2141	Knock Regulation	Detonation, fuel quality or control unit
2142	Knock Sensor No. 1	Loose or defective sensor, circuit
2144	Knock Sensor No. 2	Loose or defective sensor, circuit
2231	Idle Stabilizer	Air leak, defective valve or circuit
2232	Airflow Meter	Defective sensor or circuit
2234	System Voltage	Check charging system, out of range
2312	Coolant Temperature	Defective sensor or circuit
2314	Transmission	Defective engine to transmission circuit
2322	Air Temperature	Defective sensor or circuit
2341	Oxygen Sensor	Defective sensor or circuit
2342	Oxygen Sensor	Defective sensor heating circuit
3424	Warning Lamp	Defective circuit, California only
4411	Fuel Injector	Check 1 & 5 injectors and circuit
4412	Fuel Injector	Check 2 & 7 injectors and circuit
4413	Fuel Injector	Check 3 & 6 injectors and circuit
4414	Fuel Injector	Check 4 & 8 injectors and circuit
4431	Idle Stabilizer	Defective valve, adjustment or circuit
4343	Canister Purge	Check solenoid and circuit
0000	End Diagnosis	No additional stored codes

UNDERHOOD SERVICE SPECIFICATIONS

SENSORS, INPUT
TEMPERATURE SENSORS

Engine	Year	Sensor	Resistance Ohms @ deg. F/C
1780cc	1984-86	Coolant	2500 @ 68/20
1984cc	1988-90	Coolant	5000-6500 @ 32/0
			1500-2000 @ 86/30
			500-650 @ 140/60
			200-300 @ 194/90
2226cc, all	1984-89	Coolant	6000 @ −4/−20
			1000 @ 68/20
			130 @ 176/80
2144cc w/o Turbo	1984-85	Coolant	2500 @ 68/20
2309cc, all	1987-91	Coolant	5000-6500 @ 32/0
			1500-2000 @ 86/30
			500-650 @ 140/60
			200-300 @ 194/90
2771cc	1992	Coolant	2500 @ 68/20
			330 @ 176/80
3562cc	1990-91	Coolant	11,000 @ −4/−20
			1250 @ 68/20
			600 @ 140/60
			200 @ 212/100
		Intake Air	420 @ −4/−20
			480 @ 68/20
			550 @ 140/60
			620 @ 212/100

AIRFLOW SENSOR

Engine	Year	Resistance Ohms @ Terminals	Voltage @ Terminals
4-cyl. 1.8L	1984-86	less than 1000† @ 2 & 3 more than 4000 @ 1 & 2	
4-cyl. 2.0L	1988-90	0-0.8 @ 3 & ground	4.35-5.35 @ 1 & 3 0-200 mV @ 2 & 3♦
5-cyl. 2.2L w/o Turbo	1984-86	less than 1000† @ 2 & 3 more than 4000 @ 1 & 2	
5-cyl. 2.3L	1987-91	0-0.8 @ 3 & ground	4.35-5.35 @ 1 & 3 0-200 mV @ 2 & 3♦
V8 3.6L	1990-91	— 3-5 @ 1 & 3●	2.5 @ 1 & 3★

† Resistance will gradually increase to 4000 ohms when sensor plate is lifted.
♦ With sensor plate in closed position.
★ Engine idling or ignition on, engine off.
● Engine at higher than idle rpm.

THROTTLE POTENTIOMETER

Engine	Year	Resistance Ohms @ Terminals	Throttle Position
5-cyl. DOHC Turbo	1991	1500-2600 @ 1 & 2	closed
		750-1300 @ 3 & 3	closed
		3600 max. @ 3 & 3	open
V6 2.8L	1992	1500-2600 @ 1 & 2	closed
		750-1300 @ 2 & 3	closed
		3600 max. @ 2 & 3	open

REFERENCE, SPEED AND TIMING SENSORS

Engine	Year	Resistance (ohms)
2226cc	1986-91	1000
2309cc DOHC	1990-91	1000
3562cc	1990-91	1000

ACTUATORS, OUTPUT
CONTROL PRESSURE REGULATOR

Engine	Year	Resistance (ohms)
1715cc	1983	16-22
2144cc, all	1983	16-22
2226cc Turbo	1986-89	14-22

DIFFERENTIAL PRESSURE REGULATOR

Engine	Year	Resistance (ohms)
1780cc	1984-86	17.5-21.5
1984cc	1988-90	15-25
2226cc	1984-86	17.5-21.5

IDLE STABILIZER

Engine	Year	Resistance (ohms)
2144cc, all	1983	24
2226cc ex. Turbo	1984-86	24-30
2226cc DOHC Turbo	1991	7.5-8.5
3562cc	1990-91	7.5-8.5

FREQUENCY VALVE

Engine	Year	Resistance (ohms)
2144cc, all	1983	2-3

COMPUTER TIMING ADVANCE

Engine	Year	Transmission	Distributor Number	Advance Degrees @ RPM
1780cc	1985-87	MT & AT	026905205S	22 ± 2 @ 3000*
2144cc Turbo	1983	MT & AT	035905206L	—
2144cc Turbo	1984	MT & AT	035905205AJ	—
2144cc Turbo	1985	MT & AT	035905206AF	—
2226cc Turbo	1986-91	MT & AT	035905206AF	—

* Vacuum hose(s) disconnected.

COMPONENT OUTPUT TEST

5-cyl. 2309cc DOHC, V8 3562cc 1990-91:
1. With test equipment connected to access diagnostic codes, switch ignition on without starting engine.
2. Momentarily connect jump wire (5-cyl., 4 seconds; V8, 10 seconds) to begin sequence.
3. Codes will be displayed on light and component activated.
4. Check for component function, then repeat step 2 to continue sequence.

Code	Application	Procedure
4433	Fuel Pump	Listen for pump to run (5-cyl. only)
4411	Injector No. 1	Wide open throttle and listen or feel for pulse
4412	Injector No. 2	Wide open throttle and listen or feel for pulse
4413	Injector No. 3	Wide open throttle and listen or feel for pulse
4414	Injector No. 4	Wide open throttle and listen or feel for pulse
4421	Injector No. 5	Wide open throttle and listen or feel for pulse
4422	Injector No. 6	Wide open throttle and listen or feel for pulse
4423	Injector No. 7	Wide open throttle and listen or feel for pulse
4424	Injector No. 8	Wide open throttle and listen or feel for pulse
4431	Idle Stabilizer	Listen for switch to cycle on and off
4443	Canister Purge	Listen for solenoid to cycle on and off
0000	End Sequence	Disconnect diagnostic equipment

ENGINE IDENTIFICATION

To identify an engine by the manufacturer's code, follow the four steps designated by the numbered blocks.

V.I.N. PLATE LOCATION:

All — Left side of instrument panel, visible through windshield.

1 MODEL YEAR IDENTIFICATION:

10th character of V.I.N.

1992 — N; 1991 — M; 1990 — L;
1989 — K; 1988 — J; 1987 — H;
1986 — G; 1985 — F; 1984 — E;
1983 — D.

2 ENGINE CODE LOCATION:

Prefix to engine number, stamped on engine block.

4 ENGINE IDENTIFICATION

YEAR	3 ENGINE CODE	CYL.	DISPL. liters	cc	Fuel System	HP
1992	M42	4	1.8	1796	FI	134
	M20	6	2.5	2494	FI	168
	M50	6	2.5	2494	FI	189
	M30	6	3.5	3428	FI	208
	M70	12	5.0	4988	FI	296
1991	M42	4	1.8	1796	FI	134
	S14	4	2.3	2302	FI	192
	M20	6	2.5	2494	FI	168
	M50	6	2.5	2494	FI	189
	M30	6	3.5	3428	FI	208
	B36	6	3.5	3535	FI	311
	M70	12	5.0	4988	FI	296
1990	S14	4	2.3	2302	FI	192
	M20E	6	2.5	2494	FI	168
	M30E	6	3.5	3428	FI	208
	S38	6	3.5	3453	FI	256
	M70	12	5.0	4988	FI	296
1989	S14	4	2.3	2302	FI	192
	M20E	6	2.5	2494	FI	168
	M30E	6	3.5	3428	FI	208
	S38	6	3.5	3453	FI	256
	M70	12	5.0	4988	FI	296
1988	S14	4	2.3	2302	FI	192
	M20E	6	2.5	2494	FI	167

4 ENGINE IDENTIFICATION

YEAR	3 ENGINE CODE	CYL.	DISPL. liters	cc	Fuel System	HP
1988 Cont'd.	M20E	6	2.7	2693	FI	121
	M30E	6	3.5	3428	FI	182, 208†
	S38	6	3.5	3453	FI	256
	M70	12	5.0	4988	FI	300
1987	M20E	6	2.7	2693	FI	121
	M30E	6	3.4	3428	FI	184
1986	M21D	6	2.4 TD	2443 TD	FI	114
	M20E	6	2.7	2693	FI	121
	M30E	6	3.5	3428	FI	184
1985	M10E	4	1.8	1766	FI	101
	M21D	6	2.4 TD	2443 TD	FI	114
	M20E	6	2.7	2693	FI	121
	M30E	6	3.5	3428	FI	184
1984	M10E	4	1.8	1766	FI	101
	M20E	6	2.7	2693	FI	121
	M30E	6	3.2	3210	FI	181
1983	M10E	4	1.8	1766	FI	101
	M20E	6	2.7	2693	FI	121
	M30E	6	3.2	3210	FI	181

† Engine horsepower varies with model installation.
TD — Turbo Diesel.   FI — Fuel Injection

UNDERHOOD SERVICE SPECIFICATIONS

BWITU1   BWITU1

CYLINDER NUMBERING SEQUENCE

4-CYL. FIRING ORDER
1 3 4 2

6-CYL. FIRING ORDER
1 5 3 6 2 4

12-CYL. FIRING ORDER
1 7 5 11 3 9 6 12 2 8 4 10

———— Front of car ————

| 1.8 liter 1983-85 | 6-cyl. Gasoline | V12 5.0 liter |

TIMING MARK

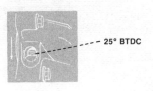

— 25° BTDC

1983-85
1.8 liter

- — 22° BTDC

1983-84
3.2 liter

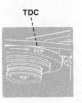

TDC

1983-92
2.7, 3.5 liter

ELECTRICAL AND IGNITION SYSTEMS

BATTERY

BCI equivalent shown, size may vary from original equipment. Check clearance and polarity before replacing, holddown may need to be modified.

Engine/Model	Year	STANDARD BCI Group No.	STANDARD Crank. Perf.	OPTIONAL BCI Group No.	OPTIONAL Crank. Perf.
All 4-cyl.	1983-85	42	495	—	—
All 6-cyl.	1983-85	47	370	—	—
2443cc Diesel	1985-86	49	740	—	—
All gasoline	1986	48	495	—	—
635CSi	1987	48	495	—	—
528e	1987-88	48	740	—	—
325e	1987-88	48	495	—	—
735i, 750iL	1987-92	†	690	—	—
325i	1987-92	†	495	—	—
535i	1987-92	†	740	—	—
635CSi, M6	1988-89	†	740	—	—
M5	1988-91	†	740	—	—
525i	1989-92	†	495	—	—
318i	1991-92	†	495	—	—

† Special low profile battery, no BCI equivalent.

ALTERNATOR

Application	Year	Rated Output	Test Output (amps @ eng. rpm)
1766cc	1983-85	65	65 @ 6000
1796cc	1991-92	80	—
2302cc	1988-91	90	—
2443cc Turbo Diesel	1985-86	80	—
2494cc SOHC	1988-92	80	—
2494cc DOHC w/MT	1991-92	90	—
2494cc DOHC w/AT	1991-92	105	—
2693cc	1983-88	80	—
2693cc	1987-88	90	—
3210cc	1983-84	80	—
3428cc	1985-87	80	—
3428cc ex. 735i	1988-90	90	—
3428cc 735i	1988-90	114	—
3428cc	1991-92	140	—
3453cc	1988-90	90	—
4988cc	1988-90	114	—
4988cc	1991-92	140	—

REGULATOR

At 1500 rpm, no load.

Application	Year	Test Temp. (deg. F/C)	Voltage Setting
All	1983-92	68/20	13.5-14.6

STARTER

Engine	Year	Cranking Voltage (min. volts)	Ampere Draw @ Cranking Speed
1766cc	1983	9.0	160
All 6-cyl.	1983-92	9.0	200

SPARK PLUGS

Engine/Model	Year	Gap (inches)	Gap (mm)	Torque (ft-lb)
1766cc 320i	1983	.024-.028	.60-.70	18-22
1766cc 318i	1983	.027-.031	.70-.80	18-22
1766cc 318i	1984-85	.024-.028	.60-.70	18-22
1796cc	1991-92	.024-.032	.60-.80	18-22
2302cc DOHC	1988-91	.024-.028	.60-.70	18-22
2494cc SOHC	1988-92	.028-.032	.70-.80	18-22
2693cc	1983-88	.028-.032	.70-.80	18-22
3210cc	1983-84	.028-.032	.70-.80	18-22
3428cc	1985-92	.028-.032	.70-.80	18-22
3453cc DOHC	1987-90	.024-.028	.60-.70	18-22
4988cc	1988-92	.028-.032	.70-.80	18-22

IGNITION COIL

Resistance (ohms at 68°F or 20°C)

Engine	Year	Windings	Resistance (ohms)
1766cc	1983-85	Primary	0.82
		Secondary	8250
1796cc	1991-92	Primary	0.40-0.80
		Secondary	—
2302cc	1988-91	Primary	0.37
		Secondary	9000
2494cc SOHC	1988-92	Primary	0.50-0.82
		Secondary	6000-8200
2693cc	1983-88	Primary	0.50
		Secondary	6000
3210cc	1983-84	Primary	0.50
		Secondary	6000
3428cc	1985-92	Primary	0.45-0.55
		Secondary	5400-6600
3453cc	1988-90	Primary	0.37
		Secondary	9000
4988cc	1988-92	Primary	0.45-0.55
		Secondary	5400-6600

IGNITION PICKUP

Application	Year	Resistance (ohms)	Air Gap (in./mm)
1766cc	1983-85	990-1210	.012-.028/.30-.70
2494cc	1988-92	1000-12000	.012-.028/.30-.70
3428cc	1985-92	1000-12000	.012-.028/.30-.70
4988cc	1988-92	1000-12000	.012-.028/.30-.70

BASE TIMING

Engine warm and distributor vacuum hose(s) disconnected and plugged.

1983-84 1766cc: Timing mark on flywheel is at 25° BTDC, a timing light with adjustable advance meter must be used.

Engine/Model	Year	Man. Trans. (degrees) @ RPM	Auto. Trans. (degrees) @ RPM
1766cc 320i	1983	25 ±1 @ 2200	25 ±1 @ 2200
1766cc 318i	1983-84	15 @ 2000	15 @ 2000
1766cc 318i	1985	25 @ 2200	25 @ 2200
1796cc	1991-92	11 ±3 @ 850*	11 ±3 @ 850*
2302cc DOHC	1988-91	0 ±3 @ 880*	
2494cc SOHC	1988-92	10 ±5 @ 760*	10 ±5 @ 760*
2693cc	1983-87	8 ±4 @ 700*	8 ±4 @ 700*
2693cc	1988	6 ±2 @ 700*	6 ±2 @ 700*
3210cc	1983-84	10 ±3 @ 700*	10 ±3 @ 700*
3428cc	1985-92	10 ±2 @ 800*	10 ±2 @ 800*
3453cc DOHC	1987-90	2 @ 840	—

* Checking figure only, timing is not adjustable.

DISTRIBUTOR TIMING ADVANCE

Engine degrees at engine rpm, no load, in addition to base timing setting.

Engine	Transmission	Year	Distributor Number	Degrees @ 2500 RPM Total	Degrees @ 2500 RPM Centrifugal
1766cc 320i	MT & AT	1983	0237002049	43-50	25-28
1766cc 318i	MT & AT	1983	0237002080	35-46	17-24

FUEL SYSTEM

FUEL PRESSURE

With engine at normal operating temperature and idling.

Engine	Year	Control Pressure PSI	System Pressure PSI
1766cc 320i	1983	54	68-75
1766cc 318i	1983-85	42-44	40-47

FUEL PRESSURE Continued

Engine	Year	Control Pressure PSI	System Pressure PSI
2302cc	1988-91	42-44	40-47
2494cc	1988-92	42-44	40-47
2693cc	1983-88	35-37	33-38
3210cc	1983-84	35-37	33-38
3428cc	1988-92	42-44	40-47
3453cc	1988-90	42-44	40-47
4988cc	1988-92	42-44	40-47

IDLE SPEED W/O COMPUTER CONTROL

Engine/Model	Year	Manual Transmission	Automatic Transmission
1766cc 320i	1983	800-900	900-1000 N
1766cc 318i	1983	650-750	650-750 N
AC speed-up	1983	800-900	800-900 N
1766cc	1984-85	800-900	800-900 N
AC speed-up	1984-85	800-900	800-900 N
2443cc Turbo Diesel	1985-86	700-800	700-800 N
AC speed-up	1985-86	950-1050	950-1050 N

IDLE SPEED W/COMPUTER CONTROL

Checking speed given, when adjusting, set to midpoint of range.

Engine	Year	Trans-mission	Slow Idle	Fast Idle	AC Speed-up
1766cc	1983-85	MT & AT	800-900	900-1000	800-900
1796cc	1991-92	MT & AT	810-890	870-960	—
2302cc	1988-91	MT	840-920	—	—
2494cc	1988-92	MT & AT	680-760	—	—
2693cc	1983-88	MT & AT	650-750	900-1000	800-900
3210cc	1983-84	MT & AT	650-750	900-1000	800-900
3428cc	1988-92	MT & AT	750-850	—	—
3453cc	1988-90	MT	750-850	—	—
3535cc	1991	MT	930-1010	—	—
4988cc	1988-92	AT	750-850	—	—

IDLE MIXTURE

1983-87: All vehicles with oxygen sensor, disconnect oxygen sensor and take sample from access port located upstream of the catalytic converter.

Engine	Year	Idle CO%
1766cc	1983-85	0.2-1.2
1796cc	1991-92	0.2-1.2
2302cc DOHC	1987-91	0.2-1.2
2494cc	1987-92	0.2-1.2
2693cc	1983-87	0.2-1.2
3210cc	1983-84	0.2-1.2
3428cc	1985-87	0.2-1.0
3428cc	1988-92	0.5-1.5
3453cc DOHC	1987-90	0.6-1.2
3535cc	1991	0.2-1.2
4988cc DOHC	1988-92	0.2-1.2

ENGINE MECHANICAL

TIGHTENING TORQUES

Engine	Year	Cylinder Head	Intake Manifold	Exhaust Manifold	Crankshaft Pulley	Water Pump
1766cc	1983-85	43/60	22-24/	16-18/	130-140/	6mm,
2nd stage†		+30-36°	30-33	22-25	180-200	6-7/
3rd stage♦		+20-30°				8-10;
						8mm,
						14-17/
						20-24

TIGHTENING TORQUES Continued

Engine	Year	Cylinder Head	Intake Manifold	Exhaust Manifold	Crankshaft Pulley	Water Pump
1796cc DOHC	1991-92	25/35	10-12/	16-18/	217-231/	6mm,
2nd stage		+90°	13-17	22-25	300-320	6-7/
3rd stage		+90°				8-10;
						8mm,
						15-17/
						20-24
2303cc DOHC	1988-91	36/50	6mm,	6mm●,	311-325/	6mm,
2nd stage		58-80	6.5-7.0/	6.5-7.0/	430-450	6-7/
3rd stage†		72/100	9-10;	9-10;		8-10;
			8mm,	8mm,		8mm,
			14-17/	16-18/		14-17/
			20-24	22-25		20-24
2443cc Diesel	1985-86	40/55	6mm●,	6mm●,	283-311/	6mm,
2nd stage†		+70-76°	6.5-7.0/	7-9/	390-430	6-7/
3rd stage♦		+85-95°	9-10;	10-12;		8-10;
			8mm,	8mm,		8mm,
			14-17/	14-17/		14-17/
			20-24	20-24		20-24
2494cc SOHC	1988-92	Hex,	22-24/	16-18/	283-311/	6mm,
2nd stage†		29/40	30-33	22-25	390-430	6-7/
3rd stage♦		43/60				8-10;
		+20-30°;				8mm,
		Torx,				14-17/
		22/30				20-24
2nd stage†		+90°				
3rd stage♦		+90°				
2693cc	1983-88	29/40	22-24/	16-18/	283-311/	6mm,
2nd stage†		43/60	30-33	22-25	390-430	6-7/
3rd stage♦		+20-30°				8-10;
						8mm,
						14-17/
						20-24
3210cc	1983-84	43/60	22-24/	16-18/	311-325/	6mm,
2nd stage†		+30-36°	30-33	22-25	430-450	6-7/
3rd stage♦		+30-40°				8-10;
						8mm,
						14-17/
						20-24
3428cc	1985-92	43/60	22-24/	16-18/	311-325/	6mm,
2nd stage†		+30-36°	30-33	22-25	430-450	6-7/
3rd stage♦		+30-40°				8-10;
						8mm,
						14-17/
						20-24
3453cc DOHC	1988-90	36/50	6mm,	6mm●,	311-325/	6mm,
2nd stage		58-80	6.5-7.0/	6.5-7.0/	430-450	6-7/
3rd stage†		72/100	9-10;	9-10;		8-10;
			8mm,	8mm,		8mm,
			14-17/	16-18/		14-17/
			20-24	22-25		20-24
4988cc	1988-92	22/30	14-17/	6mm●,	311-325/	6mm,
2nd stage†		+120°	20-24	6.5-7.0/	430-450	6-7/
				9-10;		8-10;
				8mm,		8mm,
				16-18/		14-17/
				22-25		20-24

† Allow cylinder head to settle for 15 minutes before bringing to torque.
♦ Run engine to operating temperature, about 25 minutes, before bringing to torque.
● Retorque after 1200 miles of service.

VALVE CLEARANCE

Engine cold, unless otherwise specified. Maximum coolant temperature; 95°F/ 35°C gasoline engines; 122°F/50°C Diesel engines.

Engine	Year	Intake (inches)	Intake (mm)	Exhaust (inches)	Exhaust (mm)
1766cc	1983	.006	.15	.006	.15
2302cc DOHC	1988-91	.010-.014	.26-.35	.010-.013	.26-.29
2443cc Turbo Diesel	1985-86	.012	.30	.012	.30
2494cc SOHC	1987-92	.010	.25	.010	.25
2693cc	1983-88	.010	.25	.010	.25
3210cc	1983-84	.012	.30	.012	.30
3428cc	1985-92	.012	.30	.012	.30
3453cc DOHC	1988-90	.012-.014	.30-.35	.012-.014	.30-.35

UNDERHOOD SERVICE SPECIFICATIONS

BWITU4   BWITU4

COMPRESSION PRESSURE

At cranking speed, engine temperature normalized, throttle open.

Engine	Year	PSI	Maximum Variation Percent*
All ex. Diesel	1983-92	142-156	60
Diesel	1985-86	284 min.	60

* Lowest cylinder pressure must be at least 60% of highest cylinder pressure.

ENGINE COMPUTER SYSTEM

COMPUTER DIAGNOSTIC CODES

1989-91 325i, 325iX: To activate, turn ignition switch to the ''ON'' position, codes will be displayed as flashes of the ''Check Engine'' light. Light will stay on continuously when all codes have been displayed. To clear memory, start engine 5 to 10 times.

Code	Indicated Fault
1	Air flow sensor
2	Oxygen sensor
3	Coolant temperature sensor
4	Idle speed controller

1989-92 All with Bosch Motronic systems M1.2, M1.3 or M1.7: To activate, turn ignition switch to the ''ON'' position and depress accelerator pedal 5 times to wide open throttle position. Codes will be displayed as flashes of the ''Check Engine'' light. To clear memory, use BMW tester or momentarily disconnect multi-pin connector from control unit. For 12 cylinder engines, codes beginning with 1 indicate a fault on the right (cylinders 1-6) bank, codes beginning with 2 indicate a fault on the left (cylinders 7-12) bank, to access codes for left bank, depress accelerator 6 times.

Code	Indicated Fault
1000, 2000	End of diagnosis
1211, 2211	Control unit
1215, 2215	Air flow sensor
1216, 2216	Throttle potentiometer
1221, 2221	Oxygen sensor
1222, 2222	Oxygen sensor regulation
1223, 2223	Coolant temperature sensor
1224, 2224	Air temperature sensor
1231, 2231	Battery voltage out of range
1232, 2232	Idle switch
1233, 2233	Full throttle switch
1251, 2251	Fuel injectors, final stage 1
1252, 2252	Fuel injectors, final stage 2
1261, 2261	Fuel pump relay
1262, —	Idle speed controller
1263, 2263	Canister purge valve
1264, 2264	Oxygen sensor heating relay
1444, 2444	No faults in memory

1991-92 All with Bosch Motronic system M3.1: To activate, depress accelerator pedal 5 times to wide open throttle position. Code will be displayed by flashes of the ''Check Engine'' light. To clear memory, use BMW Tester No. 2013, momentarily disconnect the vehicle battery, or control unit. Memory will automatically clear if vehicle is started 60 times with no repeat of failure.

Code	Indicated Fault
1211	Control unit
1215	Air mass/flow meter
1216	Throttle potentiometer
1221	Oxygen sensor circuit
1222	Oxygen sensor control out of range
1223	Coolant temperature circuit
1224	Intake air temperature circuit
1231	Battery voltage out of range
1251	Fuel injector, cylinder No. 1
1252	Fuel injector, cylinder No. 2
1253	Fuel injector, cylinder No. 3
1254	Fuel injector, cylinder No. 4
1255	Fuel injector, cylinder No. 5
1256	Fuel injector, cylinder No. 6
1261	Fuel pump relay
1262	Idle speed control valve
1263	Canister purge valve
1264	Oxygen sensor heating relay
1444	No faults in memory

SENSORS, INPUT

COOLANT TEMPERATURE SENSOR

Engine	Year	Resistance Ohms @ deg. F/C
All ex. Diesel:		
W/o DME	1983-85	7000-11,600 @ 14/–10
		2100-2900 @ 66-70/19-21
		270-400 @ 174-178/60-63
W/DME	1983-92	8200-10,500 @ 14/–10
		2200-2700 @ 66-70/19-21
		300-360 @ 174-178/60-63
2443cc Diesel	1985-86	1009-1259 @ 68/20
		638-770 @ 86/30
		245-299 @ 140/60
		103-125 @ 194/90

AIR TEMPERATURE SENSOR

Engine	Year	Resistance Ohms @ deg. F/C
All w/DME	1983-92	8200-10,500 @ 14/–10
		2200-2700 @ 66-70/19-21
		760-910 @ 120-124/49-52
		300-360 @ 174-178/60-63

CRANKSHAFT POSITION SENSOR

Engine	Year	Resistance Ohms
All w/DME	1983-92	70-90

DME PULSE SENDER

Engine	Year	Resistance Ohms
1796cc	1991-92	480-600
2302cc	1988-91	864-1056
2494cc	1988-92	494-546
2693cc	1983-88	486-594
3210cc	1983-84	486-594
3428cc	1985-92	486-594
3453cc	1988-90	864-1056
3535cc	1991	950-970
4988cc	1988-92	486-594

THROTTLE POTENTIOMETER

Engine	Year	Resistance Ohms	Throttle Position
1796cc	1991-92	3200-4800	closed
		800-1200	open

ACTUATORS, OUTPUT

IDLE SPEED CONTROLLER

Engine	Year	Resistance Ohms @ Terminals
1796cc	1991-92	6-10
All others w/DME	1983-92	40 @ 1 & 3
		20 @ 1 & 2, 2 & 3

ENGINE IDENTIFICATION

To identify any engine by the manufacturer's code, follow the four steps designated by the numbered blocks.

1 MODEL YEAR IDENTIFICATION: Refer to illustration of Vehicle Identification Number (V.I.N.). The year is indicated by a code letter.

2 ENGINE CODE LOCATION: Refer to V.I.N. plate illustration. The engine code is indicated as a letter or number.

3 ENGINE CODE: In the "CODE" column, find the engine code determined in Step 2.

4 ENGINE IDENTIFICATION: On the line where the engine code appears, read to the right to identify the engine.

V.I.N. PLATE LOCATION:

On top left side
of instrument panel

Model year of vehicle:
1992 — Model year is N.
1991 — Model year is M.
1990 — Model year is L.
1989 — Model year is K.
1988 — Model year is J.
1987 — Model year is H.
1986 — Model year is G.
1985 — Model year is F.
1984 — Model year is E.
1983 — Model year is D.

MODEL YEAR AND ENGINE IDENTIFICATION:

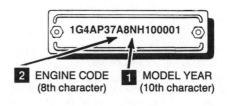

2 ENGINE CODE (8th character) **1 MODEL YEAR** (10th character)

YEAR	CODE	CYL.	liters	cu. in.	Fuel System	HP
1992	3	4	2.3	138	MFI	120
	R	4	2.5	151	TBI	110
	T	6	3.1	191	TBI	140
	N	6	3.3	204	MFI	160
	1	6	3.8	231	MFI	205
	L	6	3.8	231	MFI	170
	E	8	5.0	305	TBI	170
	7	8	5.7	350	TBI	180
1991	D	4	2.3	138	MFI	160
	R, U	4	2.5	151	TBI	110
	T	6	3.1	191	TBI	140
	N	6	3.3	204	MFI	160
	C	6	3.8	231	MFI	165
	L	6	3.8	231	MFI	170
	E	8	5.0	305	TBI	170
1990	D	4	2.3	138	MFI	160
	R, U	4	2.5	151	TBI	110
	T	6	3.1	191	MFI	135
	N	6	3.3	204	MFI	160
	C	6	3.8	231	MFI	165
	L	6	3.8	231	MFI	170
	Y	8	5.0	307	4V	140
1989	1	4	2.0	122	TBI	90
	D	4	2.3	138	MFI	150
	R	4	2.5	151	TBI	98
	U	4	2.5	151	TBI	110
	W	6	2.8	173	MFI	130
	T	6	3.1	191	MFI	140
	N	6	3.3	204	MFI	160
	C	6	3.8	231	MFI	165
	Y	8	5.0	307	4V	140
1988	K	4	2.0	122	TBI	96
	1	4	2.0	122	TBI	90
	D	4	2.3	140	MFI	150
	R, U	4	2.5	151	TBI	98
	W	6	2.8	173	MFI	125
	L	6	3.0	181	MFI	125
	3	6	3.8	231	MFI	150
	C	6	3.8 HO	231 HO	MFI	165
	Y	8	5.0	307	4V	140
1987	K	4	2.0	122	TBI	96
	M	4	2.0 T	122 T	MFI	165
	1	4	2.0	122	TBI	90
	R, U	4	2.5	151	TBI	98
	W	6	2.8	173	MFI	125
	L	6	3.0	181	MFI	125
	A	6	3.8	231	2V	110

YEAR	CODE	CYL.	liters	cu. in.	Fuel System	HP
1987 Cont'd.	3	6	3.8	231	MFI	150
	7	6	3.8 T	231 T	MFI	245
	H	8	5.0	305	4V	155
	Y	8	5.0	307	4V	140
1986	0	4	1.8	112	TBI	84
	J	4	1.8 T	112 T	MFI	150
	P	4	2.0	122	TBI	88
	R, U	4	2.5	151	TBI	92
	X	6	2.8	173	2V	112
	L	6	3.0	181	MFI	125
	A	6	3.8	231	2V	110
	B	6	3.8	231	MFI	140
	3	6	3.8 HO	231 HO	MFI	150
	7	6	3.8 T	231 T	MFI	235
	H	8	5.0	305	4V	155
	Y	8	5.0	307	4V	140
1985	0	4	1.8	112	TBI	85
	J	4	1.8 T	112 T	MFI	150
	P	4	2.0	122	TBI	88
	R, U	4	2.5	151	TBI	92
	X	6	2.8	173	2V	112
	W	6	2.8	173	MFI	130
	E	6	3.0	181	2V	110
	L	6	3.0	181	MFI	125
	A	6	3.8	231	2V	110
	3	6	3.8	231	MFI	125
	9	6	3.8 T	231 T	MFI	200
	T	6	4.3 D	262 D	MFI	85
	H	8	5.0	305	4V	155
	Y	8	5.0	307	4V	140
	N	8	5.7 D	350 D	MFI	105
1984	0	4	1.8	112	TBI	84
	J	4	1.8 T	112 T	TBI	150
	P	4	2.0	122	TBI	86
	B	4	2.0	122	2V	88
	R	4	2.5	151	TBI	92
	X	6	2.8	173	2V	112
	Z	6	2.8 HO	173 HO	2V	135
	E	6	3.0	181	2V	110
	A	6	3.8	231	2V	110
	3	6	3.8	231	MFI	125
	9	6	3.8 T	231 T	MFI	190, 200†
	4	6	4.1	252	4V	125
	T, V	6	4.3 D	262 D	MFI	85
	H	8	5.0	305	4V	145
	Y	8	5.0	307	4V	140
	N	8	5.7 D	350 D	MFI	105

ENGINE IDENTIFICATION Continued

4 ENGINE IDENTIFICATION

| 3 ENGINE | | | DISPL. | | Fuel | |
YEAR	CODE	CYL.	liters	cu. in.	System	HP
1983	0 4		1.8	112	TBI	84
	P 4		2.0	122	TBI	86
	B 4		2.0	122	2V	88
	R 4		2.5	151	TBI	92
	5 4		2.5	151	2V	92
	X 6		2.8	173	2V	112
	Z 6		2.8 HO	173 HO	2V	135
	E 6		3.0	181	2V	110
	A 6		3.8	231	2V	110
	3 6		3.8 T	231 T	4V	180

4 ENGINE IDENTIFICATION

| 3 ENGINE | | | DISPL. | | Fuel | |
YEAR	CODE	CYL.	liters	cu. in.	System	HP
1983	4 6		4.1	252	4V	125
Cont'd.	T, V 6		4.3 D	262 D	MFI	85
	H 8		5.0	305	4V	145
	Y 8		5.0	307	4V	140
	N 8		5.7 D	350 D	MFI	105

TBI — Throttle Body Injection. MFI — Multiport Fuel Injection.
2V — Two Venturi Carburetor. 4V — Four Venturi Carburetor.
HO — High Output. T — Turbocharged. D — Diesel.
† Engine horsepower varies with model installations.

UNDERHOOD SERVICE SPECIFICATIONS

BKTU1   BKTU1

CYLINDER NUMBERING SEQUENCE
4-CYL. FIRING ORDER: 1 3 4 2

— Front of car —

| 1983-86 1.8L (112) FI; 1987-88 2.0L (122) OHC | 1983-86 2.0L (122) | 1987-89 2.0L (122) ex. OHC | 1988-91 2.3L Code D, 1992 2.3L Code 3 | 1983-86 2.5L (151) | 1987-92 2.5L (151) |

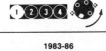

2.8L & 3.1L V6 FIRING ORDER 1 2 3 4 5 6

All Other V6 FIRING ORDER: 1 6 5 4 3 2

— Front of car —

| 1983-86 2.8L (173) | 1987-89 2.8L (173) Code W, 1989-92 3.1L Code T | 1983-85 3.0L (181) 2V Code E | 1989-92 3.3L Code N | 1985-88 3.0L (181) FI, 1986-88 3.8L (231) FI Code 3 Some | 1986-88 3.8L (231) FI Code 3 Some |

All Other V6 FIRING ORDER: 1 6 5 4 3 2

— Front of car —

| 1988-91 3.8L Code C, 1990-92 3.8L Code L Some | 1990-92 3.8L Code L Some, 1992 3.8L Code 1 | 1983-87 231 2V, 4.1L (252) | 1984-85 3.8L (231) Turbo | 1986-87 3.8L (231) Turbo | 1984-85 3.8L (231) FI |

8-CYL. FIRING ORDER: 1 8 4 3 6 5 7 2

— Front of car —

| 1983-90 5.0L (307) | 1991 5.0L Code E, 1992 5.7L Code 7 | 1983-87 5.0L (305) |

UNDERHOOD SERVICE SPECIFICATIONS

BKTU2   TIMING MARK   BKTU2

1983-86
1.8L (112) FI, OHC

1983-86
2.0L (122)

1987-88
2.0L (122) OHC

1983-86
2.5L (151)

1983-86
2.8L (173)

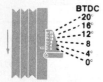

1983-85
3.0L (181) 2V,
1984-85
3.8L (231) FI

4.1L (252);
1983-87
3.8L (231) 2V

1991
5.0L Code E,
1992
5.7L Code 7

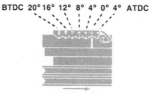

1983-86
5.0L (305)

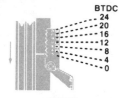

1983-90
5.0L (307)

ELECTRICAL AND IGNITION SYSTEMS

BATTERY

Engine	Year	STANDARD BCI Group No.	STANDARD Crank. Perf.	OPTIONAL BCI Group No.	OPTIONAL Crank. Perf.
1.8L (112)	1983	70	405	75	500
1.8L (112)	1984	74	500	75	465
1.8L (112)	1985	75	630	—	—
2.0L (122) U.S.	1983	70	405	75	500
2.0L (122) Canada	1983	75	500		
2.0L (122)	1984	71	390	75	500
2.0L (122)	1985-86	75	500	75	570
2.0L (122) MT	1987-89	75	525	75	630
AT	1987-89	75	630	—	—
2.0L (122) OHC	1987-88	75	630	—	—
2.3L	1988-92	75	630	—	—
2.5L (151)	1983	70	405	75	500
2.5L (151)	1984	71	390	75	500
2.5L (151)	1985-92	75	630	—	—
2.8L (173)	1983	70	315	75	500
2.8L (173)	1984-85	71	390	75	500
2.8L (173)	1986	75	430	75	500
2.8L (173)	1987-88	75	525	75	570
Canada	1988	75	570		
3.0L (181)	1983	70	315	75	500
3.0L (181)	1984	70	390	75	500
3.0L (181)	1985-88	75	630	—	—
3.1L	1989-92	75	525	—	—
3.3L	1989-92	75	630	—	—
3.8L (231) Regal	1983	70	315	78	550
LeSabre & Turbo	1983	71	390	78	550
3.8L (231)	1984	71	390	75	500
MFI	1984	75	625	75	500
SFI Turbo	1984	75	500	75	630
3.8L (231) Regal	1985-86	75	500	75	630
3.8L (231) All Others	1986	78	630	78	730
3.8L (231) Regal RWD	1987-88	75	525	75	630
3.8L (231) Century, Electra, LeSabre, Park Ave.	1987-91	75	630	78	730
Riviera	1987	75	630	75	730
Riviera	1988	78	630	—	—
Riviera	1989	75	730	—	—
Reatta	1988-89	78	770	—	—
Riviera, Reatta	1990-91	78	770	—	—
Regal	1990-91	75	630	—	—
4.1L (252) Regal	1983-84	70	315	74	550
4.1L (252) Others	1983-84	71	390	78	550
4.3L (262)†					
Regal	1983-85	78	550	78	550
Century	1983	76	750	75	500
Century	1984-85	76	770	76	1075

BATTERY Continued

Engine	Year	STANDARD BCI Group No.	STANDARD Crank. Perf.	OPTIONAL BCI Group No.	OPTIONAL Crank. Perf.
5.0L (305) Canada	1983-85	71	390	78	550
5.0L (305) Canada	1986-87	70	525	75	570
5.0L (307)	1983-84	71	390	78	550
5.0L (307) Estate Wagon	1986	75	500	78	515
5.0L (307) Regal	1986-88	75	430	75	525
5.0L (307) Estate Wagon	1987-89	70	525	75	570
5.0L	1990-91	75	525	—	—
5.7L (350)† Diesel	1983	78	550	78	550
5.7L (350)† Diesel	1984	78	450	78	550

† Diesel engines use two batteries.

ALTERNATOR

See UNDERHOOD SERVICE INSTRUCTIONS at the beginning of this section for test/adjustment diagrams.

Year	Rated Output (amps)	Test Output (amps)	Field Current Draw (max. amps)
1983-85	42, 56, 66, 70, 78, 80, 85, 94, 97, 108	†	4-5
1986	56, 66, 70, 78, 85, 94	†	
1986	100, 108, 120	△	
1987-88	78, 94	†	—
1987-92	74, 85, 100, 105, 108, 120, 124	△	—

† Increase engine speed until maximum alternator output is obtained (approximately 2000 rpm); output must be within 10 amps of rated output.
△ At moderate engine speed, output must be within 15 amps of rated output.

REGULATOR

Application	Test Temp. (deg. F/C)	Voltage Setting	Field Relay Closing Volts
1983-85	Warm	12.5-15.4	—
1986-92	Warm	13.5-16.0	—

STARTER

Engine	Year	Cranking Voltage (min. volts)*	Ampere Draw @ Cranking Speed
All	1983-92	9.0	—

* At 75°F (23°C) or higher.

UNDERHOOD SERVICE SPECIFICATIONS

SPARK PLUGS

Engine	Year	Gap (inches)	Gap (mm)	Torque △ (ft-lb)
1.8L (112), 2.0L (122)	1983-89	.035	.89	7-15
2.3L	1988-92	.035	.89	20
2.5L (151)	1983-92	.060	1.52	15
2.8L (173)	1983-89	.045	1.14	7-15
3.0L (181)	1983-84	.080	2.03	7-15
3.0L (181) 2V	1985	.060	1.52	15
3.0L (181) FI	1985	.040	1.02	20
3.0L (181) FI	1986-88	.045	1.14	7-15
3.1L	1989-92	.045	1.14	11
3.3L	1989-91	.060	1.52	20
3.3L	1992	.060	1.52	11
3.8L (231) 2V	1983	.080	2.03	7-15
3.8L (231) 2V	1984-87	.060	1.52	7-15
3.8L (231) FI	1984-85	.080	2.03	15
3.8L (231) FI Code 3	1986-87	.045	1.14	7-15
3.8L Code C, L	1988-92	.060	1.52	11
3.8L (231) Turbo	1983	.060	1.52	7-15
3.8L (231) Turbo	1984-85	.045	1.14	7-15
3.8L (231) Turbo	1986-87	.035	.89	7-15
4.1L (252)	1983-84	.080	2.03	7-15
5.0L (305)	1983-85	.045	1.14	15
5.0L (305), 5.7L	1986-92	.035	.89	11
5.0L (307)	1983-84	.080	2.03	25
5.0L (307) Canada	1984	.060	1.52	25
5.0L (307)	1985-90	.060	1.52	25

△ New plugs.

IGNITION COIL

See UNDERHOOD SERVICE INSTRUCTIONS at the beginning of this section for test/adjustment diagrams.

Application	Year	Resistance (ohms) Primary●	Secondary■
All w/distributor	1983-92	0-2	6,000-30,000
3.0L, 3.8L: Type I coils*	1984-92	.5-.9	10,000-13,000
Type II coils*	1986-88	—	5,000-10,000
Type II coils*	1990-92	.3-.5	5,000-7,000
3.3L	1989-92	.5-.9	5,000-8,000
2.0L, 2.5L, 2.8L	1987-90	—	5,000-10,000
2.3L	1988-92	—	20,000 max.

* Type I coils, 3 coil towers on each side of coil pack.
  Type II coils, 6 coil towers on one side of coil pack.
● Without distributor, measured between the two coil primary power wires on each coil.
■ Without distributor, measured across each coils two towers with spark plug wires removed.

DISTRIBUTOR PICKUP

See UNDERHOOD SERVICE INSTRUCTIONS at the beginning of this section for test/adjustment diagrams.

Engine	Year	Resistance (ohms)	Air Gap (in./mm)
All	1983-92	500-1500	—

BASE TIMING

See UNDERHOOD SERVICE INSTRUCTIONS at the beginning of this section for test/adjustment diagrams.

Set timing at slow idle and Before Top Dead Center, unless otherwise specified. Disconnect and plug distributor vacuum hose at distributor.

1983-90 all carburetted with C-3 System, disconnect 4-wire connector at distributor. Timing MUST be set to specifications shown on emission label if different from setting listed. If "Check Engine" light comes on during procedure, remove ECM fuse to clear.

1983-86 1.8L (112) FI, 2.5L (151) engines, ground diagnostic connector.

1983-86 2.0L (122) FI, 2.8L (173) FI, 1991-92 5.0L, 5.7L, disconnect EST bypass connector (tan/black wire).

All w/o distributor not adjustable.

BASE TIMING Continued

Engine	Year	Man. Trans. (degrees) @ RPM	Auto. Trans. (degrees) @ RPM
1.8L (112) FI	1983-86	8	8 D
2.0L (122)	1983	0	0
Canada	1983	0 @ 850	0 @ 850 N
w/decal DDB	1983	—	2 @ 850 N
2.0L (122)	1984-86	6	6 D
Canada	1984	4 @ 850	0 @ 850 D
2.0L (122) OHC	1987	8	8 D
2.5L (151)	1983-86	8	8
Canada	1983	10	8 @ 750 N
2.8L (173)	1983-84	10	10
High output	1983-84	10	10
Canada	1983-84	6 @ 650	10 @ 750 N
Wagons	1984	—	6 @ 750 N
2.8L (173) 2V & FI	1985-86	10	10
Canada 2V	1985-86	6 @ 650	6 @ 750 N
4-speed AT	1985-86	—	10 @ 750 N
3.0L (181) 2V	1983-84	—	15 P
3.8L (231) 2V	1983-87	—	15 D
3.8L (231) FI	1984-85	—	15
4.1L (252)	1983-84	—	15 P
4.3L (262) Diesel Regal	1984-85	—	5 @ 1300 P◆
4.3L (262) Diesel Century, Electra	1984-85	—	6 @ 1300 P◆
5.0L (305)	1983-87	—	4
5.0L, 5.7L	1991-92	—	0 @ 500 D
5.0L (307)	1983-90	—	20 @ 1100 P
Canada	1983-84	—	12 @ 1100 P
Canada	1985	—	8 @ 1100 P
Canada	1987	—	8 @ 1500 P

DISTRIBUTOR TIMING ADVANCE

Engine degrees at engine rpm, no load, in addition to basic timing setting.
Mechanical advance distributors only.

Engine	Transmission	Year	Distributor Number	Degrees @ 2500 RPM Total	Centrifugal
2.0L (122)	MT & AT	1983-84	1103548, 92	32.9-40.9	10.9-14.9
2.5L (151)	MT	1983	1103471	30.5-40.5	8.5-14.5
2.5L (151)	AT	1983	1103528	27.8-35.8	9.8-13.8
2.8L (173)	MT	1983-84	1103525	35-43	17-21
2.8L (173)	AT	1983-84	1103523	34.9-42.9	12.9-16.9
2.8L (173)	AT	1984	1103586	35-43	17-21
2.8L (173)	MT	1985	1103617	45-53	17-21
2.8L (173)	AT	1985	1103618	41.9-49.9	12.9-16.9
2.8L (173)	AT	1985-86	1103619	35-43	17-21
3.8L (231)	AT	1983-84	1110766	31.0-37.8	9.0-11.8
3.8L (231)	AT	1985-87	1103612	20.3-28.3	2.3-6.3
5.0L (305)	AT	1983-84	1103282	29.8-37.8	11.8-15.8
5.0L (307)	AT	1983-84	1103490	43.5-51.5	15.5-19.5
5.0L (307)	AT	1985-86	1103607	23-27	9-11
5.0L (307)	AT	1987	1103718	41.2-49.2	19.2-23.2

FUEL SYSTEM

FUEL SYSTEM PRESSURE

See UNDERHOOD SERVICE INSTRUCTIONS at the beginning of this section for test/adjustment diagrams.

All carburetted models, test pump with gauge at carburetor height. On cars equipped with vapor return system, squeeze off return hose to obtain accurate reading.

All models with TBI, pressure measured at fuel inlet of TBI unit.

All models with MFI, pressure measured at fuel rail.

CARBURETTED, TBI

Engine	Year	PSI	RPM
1.8L (112) FI	1983-86	9.0-13.0	ign. on
1.8L (112) 2V, 2.0L (122) 2V	1983-84	4.5	idle
2.0L (122) FI	1983-89	9.0-13.0	Idle
	1987-89	13 min.†	idle
2.5L (151) 2V	1983	6.5-8.0	idle

UNDERHOOD SERVICE SPECIFICATIONS

FUEL SYSTEM PRESSURE Continued
CARBURETTED, TBI Continued

Engine	Year	PSI	RPM
2.5L (151) FI	1983-92	9.0-13.0	idle
	1987-92	13 min.†	idle
2.8L (173)	1983	6.0-7.5	idle
2.8L (173) 2V	1984-86	5.5-6.5	idle
3.0L (181) 2V	1983-85	5.5-6.5	idle
3.8L (231) 2V	1983-87	5.5-6.5	idle
4.1L (252)	1983-84	5.5-6.5	idle
4.3L (262) Diesel	1983-85	5.8-8.7	ign. on
5.0L (305)	1983-87	5.5-6.5	idle
5.0L, 5.7L	1991-92	9.0-13.0	idle
		13 min.†	idle
5.0L (307)	1983-90	5.5-6.5	idle
5.7L (350) Diesel	1983-85	5.5-6.5	idle

FUEL INJECTED (MFI)

Engine	Year	Pressure (PSI) Ign. on	Idle	Fuel Pump†
1.8L (112) Turbo	1984-86	30-40	24-37	60 min.
2.0L (122) Turbo	1987	35-38	25-30	65 min.
2.3L (138)	1988-92	40.5-47	30.5-44	47 min.
2.8L (173)	1985-87	40.5-47	30.5-44	60 min.
3.0L (181)	1985-86	37-43	31-40	75 min.
3.0L (181)	1987	34-43	29-34	75 min.
3.0L (181)	1988	40-47	31-42	75 min.
3.1L	1989-92	40.5-47	30.5-44	47 min.
3.3L (181)	1989	40-44	32-46	50 min.
3.3L	1990-92	40-47	31-44	47 min.
3.8L (231)	1984-86	34-43	24-37	75 min.
3.8L (231)	1987	34-43	29-34	75 min.
3.8L (231) Code 3	1988	34-40	25-35	75 min.
3.8L (231) Code C	1988-90	40-47	37-43	75 min.
3.8L Code L	1990-92	40-47	31-42	47 min.

† With fuel return line briefly restricted.

IDLE SPEED W/O COMPUTER CONTROL

1983-85 Diesel Engines: Start engine and allow it to warm up to operating temperature. Connect tachometer following manufacturer's instructions. Adjust screw on injection pump to obtain specified slow idle.

Turn ignition off and then attach jumper wire across fast idle switch connector terminals. Turn ignition on and adjust idle solenoid (energized) to obtain specified fast idle.

1983-87 Gasoline Engines: Make all adjustments with engine at operating temperature, choke fully open, and electric cooling fan off (if equipped). Engines with idle speed control, idle adjustments are not recommended during tune-up.

Engines with C-4 system, connect dwell meter to carburetor fuel valve lead and ground. Set meter to 6-cylinder scale. When needle begins to vary engine is in closed loop mode and is ready to adjust. Disconnect and plug canister purge vacuum hose.

Adjust idle solenoid screw, plunger fully extended, or carburetor idle speed screw to specification. If equipped with idle stop solenoid, disconnect the electrical or vacuum lead and adjust carburetor body screw to specification.

Engines equipped with speed-up solenoid, turn A/C on and disconnect compressor clutch wire or apply vacuum or battery voltage to solenoid. Adjust solenoid to specification with plunger fully extended.

To set fast idle, disconnect and plug EGR and distributor vacuum hose (as equipped). Set choke cam on specified step and adjust engine speed to specification.

Engine	Year	SLOW Man. Trans.	SLOW Auto. Trans.	FAST Man. Trans.	FAST Auto. Trans.	Step of Cam
2.0L (122) Canada	1983	900	900 D	2400	2600 P▲	High
base idle	1983	850	850 N			
speed-up	1983	1150	1250 D			
w/decal DXD	1983	—	900 D	—	3000 P	High
shutdown idle	1983	—	850 N			
speed-up	1983	—	1250 D			
2.0L (122) Canada	1984	900	800 D	3000	3000 P	High
base idle	1984	850	750 N			
speed-up	1984	1150	1250 D			
w/AC	1984	—	900 D	—	3000 P	High
base idle	1984	—	850 N			
speed-up	1984	—	1250 D			

IDLE SPEED W/O COMPUTER CONTROL Continued

Engine	Year	SLOW Man. Trans.	SLOW Auto. Trans.	FAST Man. Trans.	FAST Auto. Trans.	Step of Cam
2.5L (151) Canada	1983	750	750 D	2600	2600 P	High
base idle	1983	700	700 D			
speed-up	1983	1000	900 D			
w/AC	1983	—	800 D	—	2600 P	High
base idle	1983	—	750 D			
speed-up	1983	—	900 D			
2.8L (173)	1983	775	600 D	2500	2500 P	High
solenoid	1983	1100	750 D			
5-speed	1983	800	—	2600	—	High
solenoid	1983	1000	—			
Canada	1983	700	700 D	2000	2000 P	High
solenoid	1983	1050	900 D			
2.8L (173) HO	1983-84	800	725 D	2600	2700 P	High
solenoid	1983-84	1100	850 D			
2.8L (173) 2V	1984-86	800	600 D	2500	2500 P	High
solenoid	1984-86	1100	750 D			
Canada	1984	700	700 D	2000	2000	High
solenoid	1984	1050	900 D			
Canada	1985-86	700	700 D	2600	2700	High
solenoid	1985-86	1050	900 D			
3.8L (231) 2V Canada	1983-86	—	550 D	—	2000 P	High
solenoid	1983-85	—	670 D			
solenoid	1986	—	750 D			
3.8L (231) 2V Canada	1987	—	550 D	—	2200 P	High
solenoid	1987	—	750 D			
3.8L (231) Turbo	1983	—	650 D	—	2500 P	High
solenoid	1983	—	750 D			
w/decal BUD	1983	—	600 D	—	2600 P	High
solenoid	1983	—	700 D			
4.3L (262) Diesel						
Century, Electra	1983-85	—	675 D		775 D	—
Regal	1983-84	—	660 D	—	775 D	—
5.0L (305)	1983-86	—	500 D	—	1850 P	High
solenoid	1983-84	—	600 D			
solenoid	1985-87	—	650 D			
5.0L (307) Canada	1983-85	—	550 D		750 D	Low
solenoid, All	1983-85	—	700 D			
5.0L (307) Canada	1987	—	500 D		725 D	Low
AC speed-up	1987	—	650 D			
5.7L (350) Diesel	1983-85	—	600 D		750 D	

▲ With decal DXD, 3000 P.

IDLE SPEED W/COMPUTER CONTROL

See UNDERHOOD SERVICE INSTRUCTIONS at the beginning of this section for test/adjustment diagrams.

Midpoint of range given is the preferred setting speed.

Idle speed is adjustable only if a specification is given under "Minimum Speed".

All 1983-86 w/TBI: Gain access to throttle stop screw. With engine at operating temperature, disconnect idle air controller and install special tool to seal idle air passage of throttle body. Turn throttle stop screw to specified mimimum speed value.

All 1983-86 w/MFI; All 1987-92 w/TBI or MFI: When specifications appear in Minimum Speed column, disconnect PCV valve hose and allow engine to draw air for two minutes. Disconnect IAC electrical lead and adjust setting speed to specified value. Others, ground diagnostic lead and turn ignition on for 30 seconds. Remove IAC electrical lead and remove ground from diagnostic connector. Start engine and adjust setting speed to specified value.

All carburetted w/ISC: With engine at operating temperature, turn ignition off and disconnect harness from ISC. Apply 12 volts (+) to third terminal from top of ISC (C), and ground the fourth terminal from top (D) only long enough to retract ISC plunger. With engine running, set minimum idle to specified value by adjusting carb base screw. Apply 12 volts (+) to fourth terminal from top of ISC (D) and ground the third terminal from top (C) only long enough to fully extend ISC plunger. Set maximum speed to specified value by turning ISC plunger head.

Never apply voltage to first two upper terminals (A & B) or damage to the unit will result.

All carburetted w/ILC: Disconnect and plug vacuum hoses at EGR and canister purge valves. With engine at operating temperature, remove vacuum hose from ILC and plug. Set maximum speed to specified value by holding hex nut and turning plunger shaft. Reconnect ILC vacuum hose and check that minimum speed is at specified value. To adjust, remove rubber and metal plugs from rear center outlet tube, insert a 3/32″ allen wrench. Remove ILC hose and plug. Connect a remote vacuum source and apply vacuum to the unit. Adjust carb base screw to obtain specified shutdown value.

IDLE SPEED W/COMPUTER CONTROL Continued

ALL FUEL INJECTED

Engine	Year	Minimum Speed Man. Trans.	Minimum Speed Auto. Trans.	Checking Speed Man. Trans.	Checking Speed Auto. Trans.
1.8L (112) incl. Turbo	1983-84	775-825	675-725 N	—	—
1.8L (112) incl. Turbo	1985	775-825	675-725 N	900-1000	675-775 D
1.8L (112) incl. Turbo	1986	775-825	675-725 N	900-1000	775-875 D
2.0L (122)	1983-86	625-675	625-675 D	—	—
2.0L (122)	1988-89	450-650	450-650 N	—	—
2.0L (122) OHC	1987-88	450-600	450-600 N	800	800 N
Turbo	1987	550-650	550-650 N	—	—
2.3L	1990-92	—	—	—	800 N max.
2.5L (151)	1983-84	750-800	475-525 N	—	—
2.5L (151)	1985	750-800	475-525 N	900-1000	675-775 D
2.5L (151)	1986	750-800	475-525 N	850-950	750-850 D
2.5L (151)	1987	550-650	550-650 N	750-850	750-850 D
2.5L (151)	1988-92	550-650	550-650 N	800	800 N max.
2.8L (173)	1985-86	600-700	500-600 D	—	—
2.8L (173)†	1987	625-725	500-600 D	—	—
2.8L††	1987-89	—	—	—	650-750 D
3.0L (181)	1985-88	—	450-550 D	—	—
3.1L	1989-90	—	—	750-950	650-750 D
3.1L	1991-92	—	—	—	700-800 N
3.3L	1989	—	—	—	650-750 N
3.3L Century	1990	—	—	—	650-750 N
3.3L Skylark	1990	—	—	—	675-750 D
3.3L	1991-92	—	—	—	650-750 N
3.8L (231) FI Code B, 3 & Turbo	1984-88	—	450-550 D	—	—
3.8L	1988-89	—	—	—	650-750 N
3.8L Code C	1990-91	—	—	—	650-850 N
3.8L Code L	1990-92	—	—	—	650-750 N
5.0L	1991	—	—	—	500-600 D

† With mass airflow sensor.
†† Speed density system.

ALL CARBURETTED

Engine	Year	Trans.	Min. Speed	Max. Speed	Fast	Step of Cam
3.0L (181)	1983	AT	500 D	1300 P	2400 P	High
3.0L (181)	1984-85	AT	500 D	1350 P	2400 P	High
3.8L (231)	1983	AT	450 D	900 D	2200 P	High
3.8L (231)	1984-85	AT	450 D	1000 D	2200 P	High
3.8L (231)	1986-87	AT	450 D	900 D	2200 P	High
4.1L (252)	1983-84	AT	470 D	900 D	2200 P	High
w/decal BGC, BGD	1983	AT	470 D	900 D	2100 P	High
5.0L (307)	1983-84	AT	500 D	725 D	700 D	Low
Base idle	1983-84	AT	500 D	—		
5.0L (307)	1985-90	AT	450 D	700 D	550 D	Low
Base idle	1985-90	AT	450 D	—		

ENGINE MECHANICAL

TIGHTENING TORQUES

See UNDERHOOD SERVICE INSTRUCTIONS at the beginning of this section for test/adjustment diagrams.
Some fasteners are tightened in more than one step.
Some values are specified in inches.

Engine	Year	Torque Ft-lbs/Nm Cylinder Head	Intake Manifold	Exhaust Manifold	Crankshaft Pulley	Water Pump
1.8L (112) OHC	1983-86	18/25, +60°, +60°, +60°, plus 30°-50° eng. warm	25/34	16/22	20/27	19/25
1.8L (112 2V, 2.0L (122)	1983-84	65-75/88-107	20-25/27-34	22-28/30-38	66-85/90-115	12-21/16-28
2.0L (122)	1985-86	65-75/81-102	18-25/24-34	34-44/46-60	66-89/90-120	12-21/16-28

TIGHTENING TORQUES Continued

Engine	Year	Torque Ft-lbs/Nm Cylinder Head	Intake Manifold	Exhaust Manifold	Crankshaft Pulley	Water Pump
2.0L (122) ex. OHC	1987-89	73-83/99-113◉, 62-70/85-95†	15-22/20-30	6-13/8-18	66-89/90-120	15-22/20-30
2.0L (122) OHC	1987-88	18/25, +60°, +60°, +60°, plus 30°-50° eng. warm	16/22	16/22	20/27	18/25
2.3L	1987-89	26/35, +90°	18/25	27/37	74/100, +90°	10/12, cover 19/26, others
2.3L	1990-91	26/35, +110°◆	18/25	31/42, nuts 106"/12, studs	74/100, +90°	106"/12, cover 19/26, others
2.3L	1992	□	18/25	31/42, nuts 106"/12, studs	79/100, +90°	106"/12, cover 19/26, others
2.5L (151)	1983	85/115	29/40	44/60	200/260	25/34
2.5L (151)	1984	92/125	29/40	44/60	200/260	25/34
2.5L (151)	1985-86	18/25, 22/30‡	25/34	25/43* 37-50**	162/220	25/34
2.5L	1987-92	18/25, 26/35●, +90°	25/34	25/43* 37/50**	162/220	25/34
2.8L (173) Century, Skylark	1983-86	70/95	20-25/27-34	22-28/30-38	66-84/90-115	8/10, M6 15/22, M8 25/34, M10
2.8L, 3.1L Regal	1987-92	33/45, +90°	16/22, 23/32	19/25	77/105	7/10
3.0L (181) 2V	1983-84	80/108, after 15 minutes, 80/108	45/61	25/34	225/306	7/10
3.0L (181) FI	1985-88	25/34, +90°, +90°†	32/44	37/50	200/270	8/11
3.3L	1989-90	35/47, +130°■	88"/10	30/41	219/297	8/10
3.3L	1991-92	35/47, +130°■	88"/10	38/52	111/150, +76°	29/39
3.8L (231) 2V & 4V Turbo, 4.1L (252)	1983-84	80/108, after 15 minutes, 80/108	45/61	25/34	225/306	7/10
3.8L (231) 2V	1985	72/98	35/47	20/27	200/270	7/10
3.8L (231) 2V	1986	25/34, +90°, +90°†	45/66	20/27	200/270	19/26
3.8L (231) 2V	1987	25/34, +90°, +90°†	32/44	37/50	219/297	10/13
3.8L (231) FI	1984	80/108, after 15 minutes, 80/108	13/18	25/34	225/306	7/10
3.8L (231) Code B, 3	1985-88	25/34, +90°, +90°†	32/44	37/50	200/270	8/11
3.8L Code C	1988	25/34, +90°, +90°†	8/10	41/55	219/297	8/10
3.8L	1989-90	35/47, +130°■	8/10	41/55	219/297	8/10
3.8L	1991-92	35/47, +130°■	88"/10	41/55	76/105, +76°	84"/10, short 29/38, long
4.3L (262) Diesel	1983-85	142/193★	41/55	28/39	200-350/275-475	13/18, short 21/28, long
4.4L (267), 5.0L (305)	1983-84	65/88	30/40	20/27	60/81	30/40
5.0L (305)	1985-87	60-75/81-102	25-45/34-61	20-32/27-43* 14-26/19-35**	65-75/87-102	25-35/34-47

TIGHTENING TORQUES Continued

Engine	Year	Torque Ft-lbs/Nm				
		Cylinder Head	Intake Manifold	Exhaust Manifold	Crankshaft Pulley	Water Pump
5.0L, 5.7L	1991-92	68/92	35/47	20/27, studs 36/45, bolts	70/95	30/41
5.0L (307)	1983-86	60/81, 125/169	40/54	25/34	200-310/ 270-400	13/18
5.0L (307)	1987-88	90/122, 130/176	40/54	25/34	200-310/ 270-400	7/10
5.0L (307)	1989-90	40/54, +95°, first and last bolts on exhaust manifold side +120°, all others	40/54	25/34	200-310/ 270-400	11/14
5.7L (350) Diesel	1983-85	100/136, 130/176	40/54	25/34	200-310/ 270-400	13/18

† To 60/81 maximum.
* Four outer bolts.
** Three inner bolts.
‡ Turn last bolt on left (number nine) to 29/40. Then turn all except number nine 120° turn number nine 90°.
□ Tighten six center bolts to 26/35. Tighten two bolts at front of head to 15/20. Tighten two bolts at rear of head to 22/30. Turn all bolts 90°. Back off all bolts one turn and repeat procedure.
★ Eight central bolts, three upper and lower, 59/80.
⊙ Long bolts.
♦ Turn two bolts at front of engine (outside of valve cover) 100°.
● Turn last bolt on left (number nine) to 18/25.
■ Tighten four inner bolts an additonal 30°.

COMPRESSION PRESSURE

At cranking speed or specified rpm, engine temperature normalized, throttle open.

Engine	Year	PSI	Maximum Variation PSI
All gasoline	1983-92	100 min.	†
All diesel	1983	275 min.	†
All diesel	1984-85	300 min.	★

† Lowest cylinder pressure must be more than 70% of highest cylinder pressure.
★ Lowest cylinder pressure must be more than 80% of highest cylinder pressure at 200 rpm minimum.

BELT TENSION

All Except With Automatic Tensioner

1986-91: A belt in operation for 1 minute is considered a used belt.

1984-85: A belt in operation for 3 minutes is considered a used belt.

Use a strand tension gauge. Measurements are in pounds.

Engine	Year	Alternator	Power Steering	Air Cond.	Air Pump
Used Belts					
1.8L	1983-86	75	100	75	—
2.0L	1983-86	75	70	100	—
2.0L OHC	1987	75	100	75	—
2.0L OHC	1988	—	—	80	—
2.3L	1987-91	—	110	—	—
2.5L Code R	1983-86	75	70	75	—
2.5L Code U	1985-87	90	110	90	—
2.5L Code U	1988-91	90	90	90	—
2.8L 2V	1983-86	70	70	70	45
2.8L FI	1985-86	150	150	100	—
3.0L, 3.8L FI	1983-85	70	90	90	45
3.8L 2V, 4.1L	1983-87	70	80	80	45
4.3L Diesel	1983-85	—	—	—	75
5.0L (307), 5.7L Diesel	1983-84	80	90	90	45
Cogged or 3/8" belt	1983-84	55	—	—	70
5.0L (307), 5.7L Diesel	1985-90	110	110	110	55
Cogged or 3/8" belt	1985-90	90	—	—	90
New Belts					
1.8L	1983-86	145	165	155	—
2.0L	1983-86	145	165	165	—
2.0L OHC	1987	145	165	155	—
2.0L OHC	1988	—	—	155	—
2.3L	1987-91	—	110	—	—
2.5L Code R	1983-86	145	145	165	—
2.5L Code U	1985-91	165	180	165	—

BELT TENSION Continued

Engine	Year	Alternator	Power Steering	Air Cond.	Air Pump
2.8L 2V	1983-86	145	135	145	100
2.8L FI	1983-86	210	205	165	—
3.0L, 3.8L FI	1983-85	145	165	165	75
3.8L 2V, 4.1L	1983-87	125	135	135	80
4.3L Diesel	1983-85	—	—	—	45
5.0L (307), 5.7L Diesel	1983-88	160	170	170	80
Cogged or 3/8" belt	1983-88	145	—	—	145
5.0L (307)	1989-90	150	165	165	135
Cogged	1989-90	135	—	—	—

All With Automatic Tensioner

If index marks on tensioner are outside the range, replace the belt. If marks are within range and belt tension is below specified value, replace tensioner.

Engine	Year	Tension
2.3L	1987-92	50 min.
2.5L Ciera	1987-88	40 min.
2.5L Ciera	1989-91	50-70
2.8L	1987	70 min.
2.8L	1988-89	50-70
3.0L	1985-86	67 min.
3.0L	1987-88	79 min.
3.1L	1989-92	50-70
3.3L	1989-92	67 min.
3.8L Code C, B, 3	1986-91	67 min.
4.3L Diesel	1983-85	100-140
5.0L, 5.7L	1991-92	105-125

ENGINE COMPUTER SYSTEM

COMPUTER DIAGNOSTIC CODES

See UNDERHOOD SERVICE INSTRUCTIONS at the beginning of this section for test/ adjustment diagrams.

All ex. 1986-92 Riviera, Reatta w/CRT
Connect a jumper between A and B terminals on under dash connector (identified by a slot between the terminals on single-row connectors, or two upper right hand cavities on two-row connectors). Turn ignition switch on. Code 12 will flash three times, then codes in memory will be displayed. Do not run engine with jumper connected.

Remove ECM fuse for a minimum of ten seconds to clear memory.

1986-89 Riviera, Reatta w/CRT
To enter diagnostic modes, turn ignition switch on and push "off" and "warm" buttons simultaneously for three seconds and release. Any stored codes will be displayed.

To clear ECM codes, press the "HI" switch after the ECM message is displayed. After accessing the ECM system, continually press the "LO" switch after each message until "CLEAR CODES" is displayed, then press "HI" button. Press the "BI LEVEL" button to exit diagnostics.

The computer system monitors other systems and functions besides ECM trouble codes. See Service Manual for details.

1990 Riviera, Reatta
Ground terminal D of diagnostic connector.

All ex. 1986-89 Riviera, Reatta
Code 12 No tach reference to ECM
Code 13 Oxygen sensor circuit
Code 14 Coolant sensor circuit (high temperature indicated)
Code 15 Coolant sensor circuit (low temperature indicated)
Code 16 System voltage (high or low)
Code 17 Spark interface circuit
Code 21 Throttle position sensor circuit (1983)
Code 21 Throttle position sensor (voltage high) (1984-90)
Code 22 Throttle position sensor (voltage low) (1984-90)
Code 23 Open or ground MC solenoid (carburetted)
Code 23 Manifold air temperature, (low temperature indicated) (FI)
Code 24 Vehicle speed sensor
Code 25 Manifold air temperature, (high temperature indicated)
Code 26 Quad driver circuit
Code 27 Second gear switch circuit
Code 28 Third gear switch circuit

COMPUTER DIAGNOSTIC CODES Continued

Code 29 Fourth gear circuit open
Code 31 Wastegate overboost (1984-87 Turbo)
Code 31 Canister purge solenoid (carburetted)
Code 31 Park/neutral switch circuit (1988-91 FI)
Code 31 EGR circuit (1988-90 TBI)
Code 32 Barometric or altitude sensor (carburetted)
Code 32 EGR system failure (FI)
Code 33 MAP, voltage high (FI) or MAF, (high air flow indicated, 3.3L, 3.8L)
Code 34 MAP sensor voltage low (FI) or MAF, (low air flow indicated, 3.3L, 3.8L)
Code 34 MAP sensor voltage high or low (FI)
Code 35 Idle speed or idle air control circuit
Code 36 Transaxle shift control (1991)
Code 36 Mass air flow burn off circuit (1987-90)
Code 36 Closed throttle air flow (1984-86)
Code 37 MAT sensor temperature too high (1984-86)
Code 38 MAT sensor temperature too low (1984-86)
Code 38 Brake switch circuit (1988-90)
Code 40 Power steering pressure switch open (1984-87)
Code 41 No distributor reference pulses to ECM (carburetted)
Code 41 CAM sensor circuit (3.3L, 3.8L Code 3, C)
Code 41 Cylinder select error (Others, FI)
Code 42 EST or EST bypass circuit grounded or open
Code 43 ESC retard signal
Code 44 Air/fuel mixture lean
Codes 44 & 45 Faulty O_2 sensor
Code 45 Air/fuel mixture rich
Code 46 Power steering pressure switch circuit (1988-90)
Code 47 AC clutch and cruise circuit
Code 48 Misfire
Code 51 Faulty PROM or installation
Code 52 CALPAK error
Code 53 Alternator voltage out of range (MFI)
Code 53 EGR vacuum sensor vacuum incorrect (carburetted)
Code 54 Fuel pump circuit, low voltage (FI)
Code 54 Shorted MC solenoid or faulty ECM (carburetted)
Code 55 Grounded V-REF, faulty O_2 sensor or ECM
Code 58 PASS key fail enable circuit
Code 61 Degraded oxygen sensor (ex. 3.8L Code L)
Code 61 Cruise vent solenoid (3.8L Code L)
Code 62 Transmission gear switch (ex. 3.8L Code L)
Code 62 Cruise vac solenoid (3.8L Code L)
Code 63 EGR flow problem - small
Code 64 EGR flow problem - medium
Code 65 EGR flow problem - large (w/CRT only)
Code 65 Fuel injector circuit (ex. CRT & 3.8L Code L)
Code 65 Cruise servo position (3.8L Code L)
Code 66 A/C pressure switch
Code 67 Cruise switches circuit
Code 68 Cruise system problem
Code 69 AC head pressure switch

1987-89 Reatta, 1986-89 Riviera
Code E013 Open oxygen sensor circuit
Code E014 Coolant sensor circuit, high temperature
Code E015 Coolant sensor circuit, low temperature
Code E016 System voltage out of range
Code E021 TPS, voltage high
Code E022 TPS, voltage low
Code E023 MAT, low temperature
Code E024 Vehicle speed sensor
Code E025 MAT, high temperature
Code E026 Quad driver error
Code E027 Second gear switch circuit
Code E028 Third gear switch circuit
Code E029 Fourth gear switch circuit
Code E031 Park/Neutral switch
Code E034 MAF sensor frequency low
Code E038 Brake switch circuit
Code E039 Torque converter clutch circuit
Code E041 Cam sensor circuit
Code Code E042 EST or bypass circuit
Code E043 ESC system
Code E044 Lean exhaust
Code E045 Rich exhaust
Code E046 Power steering, switch circuit
Code E047 ECM-BCM Data
Code E048 Misfire
Code E063 EGR flow problem, small
Code E064 EGR flow problem, medium
Code E065 EGR flow problem, large

SENSORS, INPUT
TEMPERATURE SENSORS

Engine	Year	Sensor	Resistance Ohms @ deg. F/C
All	1983-90	Coolant,	13,500 @ 20/-7
	1983-92	Manifold Air*	7500 @ 40/4
			3400 @ 70/20
			1800 @ 100/38
			450 @ 160/70
			185 @ 210/100
All	1991-92	Coolant	28,700 @ -4/-20
			12,300 @ 23/-5
			7200 @ 41/5
			3500 @ 68/20
			1460 @ 104/40
			470 @ 158/70
			180 @ 210/100

* As equipped, not used on all engines.

MANIFOLD ABSOLUTE, VACUUM, AND BAROMETRIC PRESSURE SENSORS
See UNDERHOOD SERVICE INSTRUCTIONS at the beginning of this section for test/adjustment diagrams.

Engines may use one, or a combination of these sensors. All sensors appear the same. Manifold Absolute Pressure sensors have a vacuum line connected between the unit and manifold vacuum. On Barometric Pressure sensors, the line is not used and the connector is either open or has a filter installed over it. Pressure sensors also have a vacuum line between the sensor and intake manifold and only appear on carburetted models.

Barometric Pressure Sensors: Measure voltage with ignition on and engine off.

Manifold Absolute Pressure Sensors: Measure voltage with ignition on and engine off. Start engine and apply 10 in./250 mm Hg to unit, voltage should be: 3.8L Turbo 4V, 0.9-1.7 volts less; others, 1.5 volts minimum less.

Pressure Sensors: Measure voltage as indicated.

5 volts reference.

Engine	Year	Sensor	Voltage @ Altitude/Condition
All, as equipped	1983-90	Barometric	3.8-5.5 @ 0-1000
			3.6-5.3 @ 1000-2000
			3.5-5.1 @ 2000-3000
			3.3-5.0 @ 3000-4000
			3.2-4.8 @ 4000-5000
			3.0-4.6 @ 5000-6000
			2.9-4.5 @ 6000-7000
			2.5-4.3 @ 7000-
3.8L 4V Turbo	1983	Manifold Absolute	1.7-3.2 @ 0-1000
			1.6-3.0 @ 1000-2000
			1.5-2.8 @ 2000-3000
			1.4-2.7 @ 3000-4000
			1.3-2.6 @ 4000-5000
			1.2-2.5 @ 5000-6000
			1.1-2.4 @ 6000-7000
			0.5-2.3 @ 7000-

Engine	Year	Sensor	Voltage @ Vacuum In Hg/kPa
Others	1983-91	Manifold Absolute	1.0-1.5 @ idle / 4.5-4.8 @ WOT
All	1992	Manifold Absolute	4.9 @ 0/0
			3.8 @ 6/20
			2.7 @ 12/40
			1.7 @ 18/60
			0.6 @ 24/80
			0.3 @ 30/100

Engine	Year	Sensor	Voltage @ Condition
2.5L 2V, 2.8L 2V, 5.0L	1983-90	Vacuum	.50-.64 @ ign. on / 1.7 3.0*

* 10 in./250 mm applied to unit.

BUICK
1983-92

UNDERHOOD SERVICE SPECIFICATIONS

SENSORS, INPUT Continued

CRANKSHAFT SENSORS
Air gap is measured between crankshaft sensor and interrupter rings.

Resistance is measured at room temperature.

Engine	Year	Resistance (ohms)	Air Gap (in./mm)
2.0L ex. OHC, 2.8L, 3.1L	1987-92	900-1200	—
2.3L	1988-90	900-1200	—
2.3L	1991-92	500-900	—
2.5L	1987-92	800-900	—
3.0L, 3.3L, 3.8L w/C³I	1984-92	—	.025/.65

THROTTLE POSITION SENSOR (TPS)
See UNDERHOOD SERVICE INSTRUCTIONS at the beginning of this section for test/ adjustment diagrams.

Verify that minimum idle is at specified value.

Make all checks/adjustments with engine at operating temperature.

Carburetted Models: Remove aluminum plug covering the adjustment screw. Remove the screw and connect a digital voltmeter to the TPS black wire (–) and either of the two other colored wires (+). If voltage is approximately 5 volts, this is the reference voltage source. Connect DVOM to the other wire in this case. Apply thread locking compound to the screw and with ignition on and engine not running (as applies), quickly adjust screw to obtain specified voltage at indicated condition.

Fuel Injected Models: Disconnect harness connector from TPS. Using three six-inch jumper wires, reconnect harness to TPS. With ignition on and engine not running (as applies), connect a digital voltmeter to black wire (–) and either of the two other colored wires (+). If voltage is approximately 5 volts, this is the reference voltage source. Connect DVOM to the other wire in this case. Check reading against specified value. If TPS is adjustable, loosen the unit retaining screws and rotate the unit to reach specified value.

Engine	Year	TPS Voltage Idle	WOT (approx.)
1.8L (112)	1983-86	.20-1.250*	5.0
2.0L (122) FI	1983-84	.525	—
2.0L (122)	1985-86	.20-1.250*	5.0
2.0L	1987-89	.33-1.33*	5.0
2.0L OHC	1987-89	.20-1.250*	5.0
2.3L	1988-89	.51	—
2.3L	1990-91	.40-.90*	4.7 min.
2.5L (151)	1983-89	.20-1.250*	5.0
2.5L	1991-92	.35-1.33	5.0
2.8L (173)	1983	.26△	—
2.8L (173)	1984	.30△	—
2.8L (173) 2V	1985	.27	—
2.8L (173) 2V	1986	.30	—
2.8L (173) FI	1985-89	.55	—
3.0L (181)	1983	.51◆	—
3.0L (181)	1984	.65🔳◆	—
3.0L (181) 2V	1985	.60🔳◆	—

SENSORS, INPUT Continued

THROTTLE POSITION SENSOR (TPS) Continued

Engine	Year	TPS Voltage Idle	WOT
3.0L (181) FI	1985	.50	—
3.0L (181) FI	1986-88	.55	—
3.1L	1989-92	.29-.98*	4.8 min.
3.3L	1989-92	.40	4.5 min.
3.8L (231) 2V	1983	.86●	—
3.8L (231) 2V	1984-87	.46◆	—
3.8L (231) Turbo	1983	.36◆	—
3.8L (231) FI & Turbo	1984-92	.40	5.1
4.1L (252)	1983	.97●	—
4.1L (252)	1984	.57◆	—
5.0L (307)	1983	.46◆	—
5.0L (307)	1984-90	.41◆	5.0 approx.
5.0L, 5.7L	1991-92	.20-.95	5.0 approx.

- ● High step of fast idle cam.
- ◆ Idle speed or Load compensator (ISC, ILC) retracted.
- * Not adjustable.
- △ With anti-diesel solenoid disconnected.
- 🔳 With 3-speed, .57.

ACTUATORS, OUTPUT

IDLE SPEED CONTROL
See UNDERHOOD SERVICE INSTRUCTIONS at the beginning of this section for test/ adjustment diagrams.

All engines with ISC.

Measured between terminals A & B and C & D.

Engine	Year	Resistance (ohms)
All carburetted	1983-90	10 min.
2.8L, 3.1L Century, Regal	1988-89	.48-.58
3.8L Code C	1988-89	.48-.58
All others, TBI & MFI	1983-89	20 min.
2.3L, 2.5L, 3.1L, 3.8L Electra, LeSabre	1990	.40-.80
3.8L Reatta, Rivera	1990	.48-.56
All	1991-92	.40-.80

MIXTURE CONTROL SOLENOID-CARBURETTED ENGINES
On some engines, the ECM will be damaged if the resistance of the mixture control solenoid is less than specified.

Engine	Year	Resistance (ohms)
All	1983-90	10 min.

ENGINE IDENTIFICATION

To identify any engine by the manufacturer's code, follow the four steps designated by the numbered blocks.

1 **MODEL YEAR IDENTIFICATION:** Refer to illustration of the Vehicle Identification Number (V.I.N.), the year is indicated by a code letter which is the 10th character of the V.I.N.

2 **ENGINE CODE LOCATION:** Refer to illustration of V.I.N. plate for location and designation of engine code.

3 **ENGINE CODE:** In the vertical "CODE" column, find the engine code determined in Step 2.

4 **ENGINE IDENTIFICATION:** On the line where the engine code appears, read to the right to identify the engine.

V.I.N. PLATE LOCATION:

On top left side of instrument panel.

Model year of vehicle:
1992 — Model year is N.
1991 — Model year is M.
1990 — Model year is L.
1989 — Model year is K.
1988 — Model year is J.
1987 — Model year is H.
1986 — Model year is G.
1985 — Model year is F.
1984 — Model year is E.
1983 — Model year is D.

MODEL YEAR AND ENGINE IDENTIFICATION:

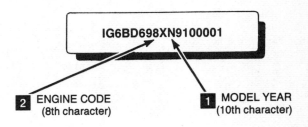

IG6BD698XN9100001

2 ENGINE CODE (8th character)

1 MODEL YEAR (10th character)

YEAR	**3** ENGINE CODE	CYL.	**4** ENGINE IDENTIFICATION DISPL. liters	cu. in.	Fuel System	HP
1992	8	8	4.5	273	MFI	200
	B	8	4.9	300	MFI	200
	E	8	5.0	305	TBI	170
	7	8	5.7	350	TBI	185
1991	8	8	4.5	273	MFI	200
	B	8	4.9	300	MFI	200
	E	8	5.0	305	TBI	170
	7	8	5.7	350	TBI	180
1990	8	8	4.5	273	MFI	200
	5	8	4.5	273	MFI	180
	Y	8	5.0	307	4V	140
	7	8	5.7	350	TBI	180
1989	5	8	4.5	273	TBI	155
	5	8	4.5	273	MFI	200
	Y	8	5.0	307	4V	140
1988	W	6	2.8	173	MFI	125
	7	8	4.1	250	MFI	170
	5	8	4.5	273	TBI	155
	Y	8	5.0	307	4V	140
1987	1	4	2.0	122	TBI	90
	W	6	2.8	173	MFI	135
	8	8	4.1	250	TBI	130
	7	8	4.1	250	MFI	170
	Y	8	5.0	307	4V	140

YEAR	**3** ENGINE CODE	CYL.	**4** ENGINE IDENTIFICATION DISPL. liters	cu. in.	Fuel System	HP
1986	P	4	2.0	122	TBI	85
	W	6	2.8	173	MFI	120
	8	8	4.1	250	TBI	130, 135†
	Y	8	5.0	307	4V	140
1985	P	4	2.0	122	TBI	88
	W	6	2.8	173	MFI	125
	8	8	4.1	250	TBI	125, 135†
	T	6	4.3 D	262 D	MFI	85
	N	8	5.7 D	350 D	MFI	105
1984	P	4	2.0	122	TBI	88
	B	4	2.0	122	2V	88
	8	8	4.1	250	TBI	135
	N	8	5.7 D	350 D	MFI	105
	9	8	6.0	368	MFI	140
1983	P	4	2.0	122	TBI	86
	B	4	2.0	122	2V	88
	8	8	4.1	250	TBI	135
	N	8	5.7 D	350 D	MFI	105
	9	8	6.0	368	MFI	140

D — Diesel.   TBI — Throttle Body Injection.
MFI — Multiport Fuel Injection.   2V — Two Venturi Carburetor.
4V — Four Venturi Carburetor.
† Horsepower varies with model installation.

UNDERHOOD SERVICE SPECIFICATIONS

CCTU1   CCTU1

CYLINDER NUMBERING SEQUENCE

4-CYL. FIRING ORDER: 1 3 4 2

6-CYL. FIRING ORDER: 1 6 5 4 3 2

1 4 6 3 2 5

——— Front of car ———

| 1983-86 2.0L (122) | 1987 2.0L (122) | 1985-86 2.8L (173) | 1987-88 2.8L (173) |

UNDERHOOD SERVICE SPECIFICATIONS

CCTU2   CCTU2

CYLINDER NUMBERING SEQUENCE

8-CYL. FIRING ORDER:
6.0L (368)
1 5 6 3 4 2 7 8
All Others
1 8 4 3 6 5 7 2

Front of car

| 4.1L (250), 4.5L (273),
4.9L (300)
FWD | 1983-85
4.1L (250)
RWD | 1986-90
5.0L (307) | 1990-92
5.7L (350),
1991-92
5.0L (305) | 1983-84
6.0L (368)
Gasoline |

TIMING MARK

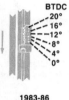

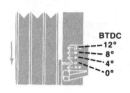

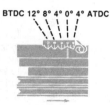

| 1983-86
2.0L (122) | 1985-86
2.8L (173) | 1983-88
4.1L (250),
1988-92
4.5L (273),
1991-92
4.9L (300) | 1990-92
5.7L (350),
1991-92
5.0L (305) | All Other
8-cyl. |

ELECTRICAL AND IGNITION SYSTEMS

BATTERY

Engine	Year	STANDARD BCI Group No.	STANDARD Crank. Perf.	OPTIONAL BCI Group No.	OPTIONAL Crank. Perf.
2.0L (122)	1983	70	405	75	500
Canada	1983	78	550	—	—
Other Gasoline	1983	78	515	—	—
2.0L (122)	1984	70	405	75	500
Late models	1984-86	75	500	75	630
Other Gasoline	1984-85	78	515	78	770
4.3L (262) Diesel	1985	76	1075	—	—
5.7L (350) Diesel	1983-85	78	550*	—	—
4.1L (250) DeVille	1986	78	515	78	730
4.1L (250) Eldorado	1986	78	515	78	630
4.1L (250) Fleetwood	1986	78	515	78	770
Canada	1986	78	550	78	770
5.0L (307) Fleetwood Brougham	1986	78	515	78	730
2.0L (122), 2.8L (173)	1987	75	525	75	630
Canada	1987	75	630	—	—
4.1L (250) Allanté	1987	78	770	—	—
Eldorado, Seville	1987	78	540	78	730
Fleetwood, DeVille	1987	78	540	78	730
Canada	1987	78	540	78	770
5.0L (307)	1987	78	540	78	730
Canada	1987	78	540	78	770
2.8L (173)	1988	78	770	—	—
4.1L (250) Allanté	1988	78	770	—	—
4.5L (279) Fleetwood, DeVille	1988	78	770	—	—
Eldorado, Seville	1988	78	730	—	—
4.5L, 4.9L Allanté	1989-92	78	770	—	—
Eldorado, Seville	1989-92	78	770	—	—
DeVille, Fleetwood	1989-92	78	540	78	770
5.0L, 5.7L	1988-92	78	730	—	—

* Requires two batteries.

ALTERNATOR

See UNDERHOOD SERVICE INSTRUCTIONS at the beginning of this section for test/adjustment diagrams.

Application	Rated Output (amps)	Test Output (amps)
1983-85	78, 80, 100	†
1986-87	78, 97	†
1986-87	100, 108, 120	△
1988-90	78, 100, 120	△
1991 Allanté	120	90 @ 1500
Brougham: 5.0L	100	△
5.7L	120	△
All others	140	*

† Increase engine speed until maximum alternator output is obtained (approx. 2000 rpm); output must be within 10 amps of rated output.
△ Run engine at moderate speed, output must be within 15 amps of rated output.
* Output at 2000 rpm must be 90% of rated output.

REGULATOR

Application	Test Temp. (deg. F/C)	Voltage Setting
1983-85	Warm	12.5-15.5
1986-92	Warm	13.5-16.0

STARTER

Engine	Year	Cranking Voltage (min. volts)	Ampere Draw @ Cranking Speed
All	1983-92	9.6	—

SPARK PLUGS

Engine	Year	Gap (inches)	Gap (mm)	Torque (ft-lb)
4-cyl.	1983-86	.035	.89	15
V6 2.8L (173)	1985-87	.045	1.14	15
V8	1983-89	.060	1.52	15

SPARK PLUGS Continued

Engine	Year	Gap (inches)	Gap (mm)	Torque △ (ft-lb)
V8: 4.5L	1990-92	.060	1.52	11
4.9L	1991-92	.060	1.52	23
5.0L	1990	.060	1.52	25
5.0L	1991-92	.035	.89	22
5.7L	1990-92	.035	.89	22

IGNITION COIL
Winding resistance (ohms at 80°F or 27°C)
See UNDERHOOD SERVICE INSTRUCTIONS at the beginning of this section for test/adjustment diagrams.

1983-84 8-cyl. eng. ex. 4.1L (250): Primary, 0.4-0.5; Secondary, 8000-9500.
1983-92 All others w/distributor: Primary, 0-2; Secondary, 6000-30,000.
1987-88 2.8L: Primary, NA; Secondary, 5000-10,000.

DISTRIBUTOR PICKUP
See UNDERHOOD SERVICE INSTRUCTIONS at the beginning of this section for test/adjustment diagrams.

Engine	Year	Resistance (ohms)	Air Gap (in./mm)
All w/distributor	1983-92	500-1500	—
2.8L (173)	1987-88	900-1200*	—

* Crankshaft sensor.

BASE TIMING
See UNDERHOOD SERVICE INSTRUCTIONS at the beginning of this section for test/adjustment diagrams.

All except computer controlled eng., disconnect and plug distributor vacuum hose.

1983-84: 6.0L (368) FI eng., disconnect pink/black wire with connector from tan/black wire by distributor.
1983-86: 1.8L (112) 2V, 2.0L (122) 2V, 4.1L (252), disconnect 4-wire connector at distributor.
1983-84: 4.1L (250), disconnect green reference signal connector.
1983-86: 2.0L (122) FI, 2.8L (173) FI; **1990-92:** 5.0L (305), 5.7L (350), disconnect EST bypass connector (single connector tan/black wire).
1985-92: 4.1L (250), 4.5L (279), 4.9L, 5.0L (307), connect a jumper between terminals A & B of the diagnostic connector.

If "Check Engine" light comes on during this procedure, remove ECM fuse to clear.

Engine	Year	Man. Trans. (degrees) @ RPM	Auto. Trans. (degrees) @ RPM
2.0L (122)	1983	0	0
Canada	1983	0 @ 850	0 @ 850 P
w/decal DBB	1983	—	2 @ 850 P
2.0L (122)	1984-86	6	6 D
Canada	1984	4 @ 850	0 @ 850 P
2.8L (173)	1985-86	10	10 D
4.1L (250)	1983-88	—	10 @ 900 P max.
4.5L (279)	1988-89	—	10 @ 900 P max.
4.5L, 4.9L	1990-92	—	10● @ 800 P max.
5.0L (305)	1991	—	0 @ 500 D
5.0L (307)	1986-90	—	20 @ 1100 P
5.7L (350)	1990-91	—	0 @ 500 D
6.0L (368) FI	1983-84	—	10

● 4.9L using regular fuel, 6°.

DISTRIBUTOR TIMING ADVANCE
Engine degrees at engine rpm, no load, in addition to basic timing setting.
Mechanical advance distributors only.

Engine	Transmission	Year	Distributor Number	Degrees @ 2500 RPM Total	Degrees @ 2500 RPM Centrifugal
2.0L (122)	MT & AT	1983	1103535	32.9-40.9	10.9-14.9
2.0L (122)	MT & AT	1983-84	1103548, 92	32.9-40.9	10.9-14.9

FUEL SYSTEM

FUEL SYSTEM PRESSURE
See UNDERHOOD SERVICE INSTRUCTIONS at the beginning of this section for test/adjustment diagrams.
Carburetted models, pinch off fuel return line.
All models with TBI, pressure measured at fuel inlet of TBI unit.
All models with MFI, pressure measured at fuel rail.

Engine	Year	Pressure PSI	Pressure RPM
2.0L (122)	1983-86	9-13	ign. on
Canada	1983-84	5.5-7.0	idle
2.8L (173)	1985-88	40.5-47.0	ign. on
	1985-88	30.5-44.0	idle
	1985-88	60 min.	■
4.1L (250), 4.5L (279) TBI	1983-89	9-12	—
4.5L, 4.9L	1990-92	40-50	ign. on
		32-38	idle
5.0L	1991-92	9-13	idle
		13 min.■	idle
5.0L (307)	1986-90	5.5-6.5	idle
350 (R), 6.0L (368), 425 FI	1983-84	37-42†	idle
	1983-84	27-32●	idle
5.7L (350) Diesel	1983-85	5.8-8.7	—
5.7L Gas	1990-92	9-13	idle
		13 min.■	idle

† With no vacuum at pressure regulator.
● With 20 in. Hg applied to the pressure briefly.
■ Fuel pump pressure with fuel return line briefly restricted.

IDLE SPEED W/O COMPUTER CONTROL
Disconnect and plug parking brake vacuum hose at vacuum release cylinder.

Engines Without Fuel Injection:
Check idle and if not at specified slow idle rpm, adjust idle speed screw or solenoid adjustment nut to obtain specified rpm.

Air-conditioned models equipped with idle speed-up solenoid, turn AC on, disconnect compressor clutch wire and with solenoid fully extended, adjust solenoid to obtain specified rpm. Turn air conditioner off and reconnect compressor lead.

Set fast idle to specified rpm.

Engines With Fuel Injection:
Adjust idle bypass screw to specified slow idle.

1983-85 Diesel eng.:
Adjust screw on injection pump to set idle speed. To set fast idle, install a jumper wire between the terminals of the cold advance switch. Disconnect EGR and adjust fast idle solenoid to specification.

Engine	Year	SLOW Man. Trans.	SLOW Auto. Trans.	FAST Man. Trans.	FAST Auto. Trans.	Step of Cam
2.0L (122) Canada	1983	900	900 D	2400	2600 P	High
base idle	1983	850	850 N			
speed-up	1983	1150	1250 D			
w/decal DXD	1983	—	900 D	—	3000 P	High
base idle	1983	—	800 N			
speed-up	1983	—	1250 D			
2.0L (122) Canada	1984	900	800 D	3000	3000 P	High
base idle	1984	850	750 N			
speed-up	1984	1150	1250 D			
w/AC	1984	—	900 D	—	3000 P	High
base idle	1984	—	850 N			
speed-up	1984	—	1250 D			
4.3L (262) Diesel	1985	—	675 D	—	775 D	—
5.7L (350) Diesel	1983-85	—	600 D	—	750 D	—

IDLE SPEED W/COMPUTER CONTROL
See UNDERHOOD SERVICE INSTRUCTIONS at the beginning of this section for test/adjustment diagrams.

Carburetted
1986-90 5.0L (307): Disconnect and plug vacuum hoses at EGR and canister purge valves. With engine at operating temperature, remove vacuum hose from ILC and plug. Set maximum speed to specified value by holding hex nut and turning plunger shaft. Reconnect ILC vacuum hose and check that minimum speed is at specified value. To adjust, remove rubber and metal plugs from rear center outlet tube, insert a 3/32" Allen wrench. Remove ILC hose and plug. Connect a remote vacuum source and apply vacuum to the unit. Adjust carb base screw to obtain specified base value.

UNDERHOOD SERVICE SPECIFICATIONS

IDLE SPEED W/COMPUTER CONTROL Continued

Fuel injected

1983-86 2.0L (122): Gain access to throttle stop screw. With engine at operating temperature, disconnect idle air controller and install special tool to seal idle air passage of throttle body. Turn throttle stop screw to specified minimum speed value.

1985-87 2.8L (173) FI, 1987 2.0L (122): Ground diagnostic lead and turn ignition on for 30 seconds. Remove IAC electrical lead and remove ground from diagnostic connector. Start engine and set minimum speed to specified value.

1983-85 4.1L (250) and 6.0L (368): Retract ISC plunger by hand and disconnect ISC connector. Set minimum speed to specified value. Check TPS voltage for recommended setting. 6.0L (368) only: disconnect TPS connector and open throttle by hand to approximately 1500 rpm. Close throttle and turn ignition off. ISC plunger should extend fully. Disconnect ISC and start engine. Set maximum speed to specified value.

1986-89 4.1L (250), 4.5L (279) TBI: With engine at operating temperature, turn engine off and disconnect harness from ISC. Apply 12 volts (+) to third from top of ISC (C), and ground the fourth terminal from top (D) only long enough to retract ISC plunger. Start engine and check minimum speed against specified checking value. If not, set minimum idle to specified value by adjusting base screw.

1987-92 4.1L, 4.5L MFI, 4.9L, 5.7L: With ISC fully retracted, idle should be at specified checking value.

ALL CARBURETTED

Engine	Year	Trans.	Min. Speed	Max. Speed	Fast	Step of Cam
5.0L (307)	1986-90	AT	450 D	700 D	550 D	Low
base idle	1986-90	AT	450 D			

ALL FUEL INJECTED

Engine	Year	Transmission	Minimum Speed	Checking Speed
2.0L (122)	1983-86	MT	625-675	—
2.0L (122)	1983-86	AT	625-675 D	—
2.0L (122)	1987	MT	575-625	—
2.0L (122)	1987	AT	575-625 N	—
2.8L (173)	1985-86	MT	600-700	—
2.8L (173)	1985-86	AT	500-600 D	—
2.8L (173)	1987	MT	625-725	—
2.8L (173)	1987	AT	500-600 D	—
2.8L (173)	1988	MT	—	750-950
2.8L (173)	1988	AT	—	650-750 D
4.1L (250)	1983-85	AT	450 N	—
4.1L (250) TBI	1986-87	AT	525 N	475-550 N
4.1L (250) MFI	1987-88	AT	500 N	450-550 N
4.5L (279) TBI	1988-89	AT	525 N	475-550 N
4.5L	1989	AT	500 N	500-600 N
4.5L, 4.9L: Allanté	1990-92	AT	550 N	500-600 N
Others	1990-92	AT	525 N	500-550 N
5.0L	1991-92	AT	—	500-600 D
5.7L	1990-92	AT	—	500-600 D
6.0L (368)	1983-85	AT	350-400 N	1400-1600 N

ENGINE MECHANICAL

TIGHTENING TORQUES

See UNDERHOOD SERVICE INSTRUCTIONS at the beginning of this section for test/adjustment diagrams.

Some fasteners are tightened in more than one step.

Engine	Year	Torque Ft-lbs/Nm				
		Cylinder Head	Intake Manifold	Exhaust Manifold	Crankshaft Pulley	Water Pump
1.8L (112) 2V, 2.0L (122)	1983-84	65-75/ 88-107	20-25/ 27-34	22-28/ 30-38	66-85/ 90-115	12-21/16-28
2.0L (122)	1985-86	65-75/ 88-107	18-25/ 24-34	34-44/ 46-60	66-89/ 90-120	12-21/16-28
2.8L (173)	1985-86	77/105	13-25/ 18-34	19-31/ 25-42	67-85/ 90-115	6-9/8-12
2.8L (173)	1987-88	33/45, +90°	15/20, 24/33	20-30/ 15-22	76/103	7/10, short 18/24, long
4.1L (250)	1983-85	38/50, 74/100†	**	18/25	—	7/10, short 30/40, long
4.1L (250)	1986-88	38/50, 68/90†	**	18/25	—	7/10, short 30/40, long

TIGHTENING TORQUES Continued

Engine	Year	Torque Ft-lbs/Nm				
		Cylinder Head	Intake Manifold	Exhaust Manifold	Crankshaft Pulley	Water Pump
4.3L (262) Diesel	1985	142/193‡	41/55	28/39	200-350/ 275/475	13/18, short 21/28, long
4.5L, 4.9L	1989-92	38/50, 68/90†	♦	18/25	70/95	5/7, short 30/40, long
5.0L (305), 5.7L Gas	1990-91	70/95*	35/45	26/35	70/95	10/14, short 22/30, long
5.0L (307)	1986	60/81, 125/169	40/54	25/34	200-310/ 270-400	13/18
5.0L (307)	1987-88	90/122, 130/176	40/54	25/34	200-310/ 270-400	7/10
5.0L (307)	1989-90	40/54, +95°, first and last bolts on exhaust manifold side +120°, all others	40/54	25/34	200-310/ 270-400	11/14
5.7L (350) Diesel	1983-85	100/136, 130/176	40/54	25/34	200-310/ 270-400	13/18

† After tightening all bolts to this specification, tighten numbers 1, 3, & 4 (upper row, center three bolts on each head) to 90/120.

‡ Eight central bolts, three upper and lower, 59/80.

** Tighten four center bolts to 15/20. Tighten eight outer bolts to 22/30. Then tighten all bolts to 22/30.

♦ Tighten four center bolts to 8/12. Tighten eight outer bolts to 12/16. Then tighten all bolts to 12/16.

* Over three phases.

COMPRESSION PRESSURE

At cranking speed, engine temperature normalized, throttle open.

Engine	Year	PSI	Maximum Variation PSI
4.1L (250), 4.5L (279), 4.5L, 6.0L (368), 425	1983-92	140-165	*
All others, gasoline	1983-92	100 min.	*
Diesel	1983	275 min.	*
Diesel	1984-85	300 min.	†

* Lowest cylinder pressure must be more than 70% of highest reading cylinder pressure.

† Lowest cylinder pressure must be more than 80% of highest cylinder pressure at 300 rpm minimum.

BELT TENSION

A belt that has been pretensioned is considered a used belt.

Use a strand tension gauge. Measurements are in pounds.

Engine	Year	Alternator	Power Steering	Air Cond.	Air Pump
USED BELTS					
All	1983-86	67	67	90	67
All w/serpentine	1985-91	70-120*	70-120*	70-120*	—
4.5L, 4.9L	1992	110*	110*	110*	—
NEW BELTS					
All	1983-86	168	168	146	168
All w/serpentine	1985-91	70-120*	70-120*	70-120*	—
4.5L, 4.9L	1992	110*	110*	110*	—

* Automatic tensioner operating range.

ENGINE COMPUTER SYSTEM

COMPUTER DIAGNOSTIC CODES

See UNDERHOOD SERVICE INSTRUCTIONS at the beginning of this section for test/adjustment diagrams.

4-cyl., 5.0L, 5.7L

Connect a jumper between A and B terminals on under dash connector (identified by a slot between the terminals or is two upper right hand cavities on a two row connector). Turn ignition on. Code 12 will flash three times, then the codes in memory will be displayed.

Remove ECM fuse for a minimum of ten seconds to clear memory.

UNDERHOOD SERVICE SPECIFICATIONS

COMPUTER DIAGNOSTIC CODES Continued

4.1L, 4.5L, 4.9L, 6.0L
Turn ignition on. Press ''OFF'' and ''WARMER'' buttons on Climate Control at the same time. Codes will be displayed on Climate Control indicator. Press ''Reset'' and ''Recall'' buttons (1983-86) or ''Auto'' (1987-88) to exit diagnostic mode. Clear codes by pressing ''OFF'' and ''HI'' buttons at same time.
Codes will be displayed with either an ''E'' or ''EO'' preceeding them.
1989-91, complicated procedure required to display BCM codes and ''snapshot'' parameters. See manufacturers service data.

1983-92 4-cyl., 5.0L, 5.7L
Code 12 No tach reference to ECM
Code 13 Oxygen sensor circuit
Code 14 Shorted coolant sensor circuit
Code 15 Open coolant sensor circuit
Code 21 Throttle position sensor voltage high
Code 22 Throttle position sensor voltage low
Code 23 Open or ground MC solenoid (carburetted)
Code 23 MAT sensor voltage high (FI)
Code 24 Vehicle speed sensor circuit
Code 25 MAT sensor voltage low (FI)
Code 31 Canister purge solenoid
Code 32 Barometric or altitude sensor (4-cyl.)
Code 32 EGR vacuum control (V6 2.8L MFI)
Code 33 MAP sensor voltage high (4-cyl. 2.0L)
Code 33 Mass airflow sensor frequency high (V6 2.8L MFI)
Code 34 MAP sensor voltage low (4-cyl. 2.0L)
Code 34 Mass airflow sensor frequency low (V6 2.8L MFI)
Code 34 MAP or vacuum sensor circuit (carburetted)
Code 35 Idle speed control switch circuit shorted
Code 41 No distributor reference pulses to ECM 1983-86
Code 41 Cylinder select error (1988)
Code 42 EST or EST bypass circuit grounded or open
Code 43 ESC retard signal too long
Code 44 Air/fuel mixture lean
Codes 44 & 45 Faulty oxygen sensor
Code 45 Air/fuel mixture rich
Codes 51 & 52 Faulty PROM or installation
Code 53 Alternator voltage high (FI)
Code 53 EGR vacuum valve sensor (carburetted)
Code 54 Shorted MC solenoid or faulty ECM (carburetted)
Code 54 Fuel pump circuit voltage low (FI)
Code 55 Grounded V-REF, faulty oxygen sensor or ECM
Code 61 Degraded oxygen sensor

4.1L, 4.5L, 4.9L, 6.0L
Code 12 No tach signal
Code 13 Oxygen sensor not ready (left sensor Allanté)
Code 14 Shorted coolant sensor circuit
Code 15 Open coolant sensor circuit
Code 16 Alternator voltage out of range
Code 17 Shorted crank signal circuit (TBI)
Code 17 Right oxygen sensor not ready (Allanté)
Code 18 Open crank signal circuit
Code 19 Shorted fuel pump circuit
Code 20 Open fuel pump circuit
Code 21 Shorted throttle position sensor circuit
Code 22 Open throttle position sensor circuit
Code 23 EST/bypass circuit shorted or open
Code 24 Speed sensor circuit problem
Code 25 Modulated displacement failure
Code 26 Shorted throttle switch circuit
Code 27 Open throttle switch circuit
Code 28 Shorted third or fourth gear circuit (TBI)
Code 30 ISC circuit problem (TBI)
Code 30 RPM error (MFI)
Code 31 Shorted MAP sensor circuit
Code 32 Open MAP sensor circuit
Code 33 MAP/Barometric sensor correlation
Code 34 MAP signal out of range
Code 35 Shorted Barometric sensor circuit
Code 36 Open Barometric sensor circuit
Code 37 Shorted MAT sensor circuit
Code 38 Open MAT sensor circuit
Code 39 VCC engagement problem
Code 40 Power steering pressure switch circuit
Code 41 Cam sensor circuit
Code 42 Left oxygen sensor lean (MFI)
Code 43 Left oxygen sensor rich (MFI)
Code 44 Lean exhaust signal (right sensor with MFI)
Code 45 Rich exhaust signal (right sensor with MFI)

COMPUTER DIAGNOSTIC CODES Continued

Code 46 Right to left bank fueling imbalance
Code 47 ECM/BCM data problem
Code 48 EGR system fault
Code 50 Second gear pressure switch
Code 51 PROM error indicator
Code 52 ECM memory reset indicator
Code 53 Distributor signal interrupt
Code 55 TPS misadjusted
Code 58 Anti-theft system
Code 59 VCC temperature sensor circuit
Code 60 Transmission not in drive
Code 61 Cruise control circuit; Allanté, vent solenoid, others, set & resume engaged simultaneously
Code 62 Cruise control circuit; Allanté, vacuum solenoid circuit, others, vehicle speed exceeds maximum limit
Code 63 Cruise control circuit; Vehicle speed & set speed tolerance exceeded
Code 64 Cruise control circuit; Vehicle acceleration exceeds maximum limit
Code 65 Cruise control circuit; Allanté, servo position sensor, others coolant temperature exceeds maximum limit
Code 66 Cruise control circuit; Engine RPM exceeds maximum limit
Code 67 Cruise control circuit; Switch circuit shorted
Code 68 Cruise control circuit; Switch circuit shorted
Code 70 Intermittent TPS
Code 71 Intermittent MAP
Code 73 Intermittent coolant sensor
Code 74 Intermittent MAT
Code 75 Intermittent speed sensor
Code 80 Fuel system rich
Code 85 Throttle body service required
Code 96 Torque converter overstress
Code 97 P/N D/R engagement problem
Code 98 P/N D/R engaged problem

SENSORS, INPUT

TEMPERATURE SENSORS

Engine	Year	Sensor	Resistance Ohms @ deg. F/C
All	1983-90	Coolant, Manifold Air*	13,500 @ 20/−7
			7500 @ 40/4
			3400 @ 70/20
			1800 @ 100/38
			450 @ 160/70
			185 @ 210/100
5.0L, 5.7L	1991-92		12,300 @ 23/−5
			7280 @ 41/5
			3520 @ 68/20
			1459 @ 104/40
			467 @ 160/70
			177 @ 210/100

* As equipped, not used on all engines.

MANIFOLD ABSOLUTE, VACUUM, AND BAROMETRIC PRESSURE SENSORS
See UNDERHOOD SERVICE INSTRUCTIONS at the beginning of this section for test/adjustment diagrams.

Engines may use one, or a combination of these sensors. All sensors appear the same. Manifold Absolute Pressure sensors have a vacuum line connected between the unit and manifold vacuum. On Barometric Pressure sensors, the line is not used and the connector is either open or has a filter installed over it. Pressure sensors also have a vacuum line between the sensor and intake manifold and only appear on carburetted models.

Barometric Pressure Sensors: Measure voltage with ignition on and engine off.

Manifold Absolute Pressure Sensors: Measure voltage with ignition on and engine off. Start engine and apply 10 in./250 mm Hg to unit, voltage should be 1.2-2.3 volts less (except 5.0L, 5.7L) or 1.5 volts minimum less (5.0L, 5.7L).

Pressure Sensors: Measure voltage as indicated.
5 volts reference.

Engine	Year	Sensor	Voltage @ in./mm Hg
4.1L (250), 4.5L, 4.9L	1983-92	Manifold Absolute	0.5-0.9 @ 11-15/275-375
			4.5-5.0 @ 28-31/700-775
5.0L, 5.7L	1990-92	Manifold Absolute	1-2 @ idle
			4.0-4.8 @ WOT

UNDERHOOD SERVICE SPECIFICATIONS

CCTU6   CCTU6

SENSORS, INPUT Continued

MANIFOLD ABSOLUTE, VACUUM, AND BAROMETRIC PRESSURE SENSORS Continued

Engine	Year	Sensor	Voltage @ Altitude
All others, as equipped	1983-90	Barometric, Manifold Absolute	3.8-5.5 @ 0-1000
			3.6-5.3 @ 1000-2000
			3.5-5.1 @ 2000-3000
			3.3-5.0 @ 3000-4000
			3.2-4.8 @ 4000-5000
			3.0-4.6 @ 5000-6000
			2.9-4.5 @ 6000-7000
			2.5-4.3 @ 7000-

Engine	Year	Sensor	Voltage @ Altitude
1.8L 2V, 5.0L 4V	1983-90	Vacuum	.50-.64 @ ign. on 1.7-3.0*

* 10 in./250 mm applied to unit.

CRANKSHAFT SENSORS
Resistance is measured at room temperature.

Engine	Year	Resistance (ohms)
2.8L	1987-88	900-1200

THROTTLE POSITION SENSOR (TPS)
See UNDERHOOD SERVICE INSTRUCTIONS at the beginning of this section for test/adjustment diagrams.

Verify that minimum idle is at specified value.

Make all checks/adjustments with engine at operating temperature.

Carburetted Models: Remove aluminum plug covering the adjustment screw. Remove the screw and connect a digital voltmeter to black wire (−) and either of the two other colored wires (+). If voltage is approximately 5 volts, this is the reference voltage lead. Connect DVOM to other wire in this case. Apply thread locking compound to the screw and with ignition on and engine not running (as applies), quickly adjust screw to obtain specified voltage at indicated condition.

1983-89 All V8 Engines w/FI: With ignition on and engine not running, connect digital voltmeter positive lead to pin A (blue-dark wire) and connect negative lead to pin B (black wire). Check reading against specified value and rotate sensor to adjust.

1983-88 All 4-cyl. & V6 Engines w/FI: Disconnect harness connector from TPS. Using three six-inch jumper wires, reconnect harness to TPS. With ignition on and engine not running (as applies), connect a digital voltmeter to black wire (−) and either of the two other colored wires (+). If voltage is approximately 5 volts, this is the reference voltage lead. Connect DVOM to other wire in this case. Check reading against specified value. If TPS is adjustable, loosen the unit retaining screws and rotate the unit to reach specified value.

SENSORS, INPUT Continued

THROTTLE POSITION SENSOR (TPS) Continued

Engine	Year	TPS Voltage†	Condition
2.0L (122) FI	1983-84	.525	●
2.0L (122)	1985-87	.20-1.25*	—
2.8L (173)	1985-88	.55	—
4.1L (250), 4.5L (279), 4.9L	1983-90	.50	—
5.0L	1991-92	.30-1.0*	—
5.0L (307)	1986-90	.41	◆
5.7L	1990	.20-1.25*	—
5.7L	1991-92	.30-1.0*	—
6.0L (368) FI	1983-84	.50	—

● At slow idle with speed motor (ISC) fully retracted.
† ±.10 carburetted engines, ±.05 fuel injected engines.
* Not adjustable.
◆ Idle load compensator retracted.

ACTUATORS, OUTPUT

IDLE SPEED CONTROL
See UNDERHOOD SERVICE INSTRUCTIONS at the beginning of this section for test/adjustment diagrams.

All engines with ISC.

Measured between terminals A & B and C & D.

Engine	Year	Resistance (ohms)
4.1L (250), 4.5L, 4.9L	1983-92	4-100
5.0L, 5.7L	1990-92	40-80
All others, TBI & MFI	1983-89	20 min.
All carburetted	1983-90	10 min.

MIXTURE CONTROL SOLENOID-CARBURETTED ENGINES
On some engines, the ECM will be damaged if the resistance of the mixture control solenoid is less than specified.

Engine	Year	Resistance (ohms)
5.0L	1986-89	10 min.
5.0L	1990	20-26

ENGINE IDENTIFICATION

To identify any engine by the manufacturer's code, follow the four steps designated by the numbered blocks.

1 MODEL YEAR IDENTIFICATION: Refer to illustration of Vehicle Identification Number (V.I.N.). The year is indicated by a code letter.

2 ENGINE CODE LOCATION: Refer to V.I.N. plate illustration. The engine code is indicated as a letter or number.

3 ENGINE CODE: In the "CODE" column, find the engine code determined in Step 2.

4 ENGINE IDENTIFICATION: On the line where the engine code appears, read to the right to identify the engine.

V.I.N. PLATE LOCATION:

On top left side of instrument panel.

Model year of vehicle:
1992 — Model year is N.
1991 — Model year is M.
1990 — Model year is L.
1989 — Model year is K.
1988 — Model year is J.
1987 — Model year is H.
1986 — Model year is G.
1985 — Model year is F.
1984 — Model year is E.
1983 — Model year is D.

MODEL YEAR AND ENGINE IDENTIFICATION:

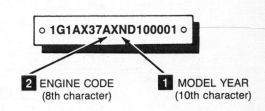

2 ENGINE CODE (8th character) **1 MODEL YEAR** (10th character)

YEAR	3 ENGINE CODE	CYL.	DISPL. liters	DISPL. cu. in.	Fuel System	HP
1992	4	4	2.2	133	MFI	110
	A	4	2.3	138	MFI	180
	R	4	2.5	151	TBI	105
	T	6	3.1	191	MFI	140
	X	6	3.4	204	MFI	210
	E	8	5.0	305	MFI	170
	F	8	5.0	305	TBI	130
	7	8	5.7	350	TBI	180
	8	8	5.7	350	MFI	245
	P	8	5.7	350	MFI	300
	J	8	5.7	350	MFI	375
1991	G	4	2.2	133	TBI	95
	A	4	2.3	138	MFI	140
	R	4	2.5	151	TBI	110
	T	6	3.1	191	MFI	140
	X	6	3.4	207	MFI	200, 210†
	E	8	5.0	305	MFI	170
	F	8	5.0	305	TBI	205, 230†
	J	8	5.7	350	MFI	375
	7	8	5.7	350	TBI	195
	8	8	5.7	350	MFI	245
1990	G	4	2.2	133	TBI	95
	A	4	2.3	138	MFI	180
	R	4	2.5	151	TBI	110
	T	6	3.1	191	MFI	135, 140
	Z	6	4.3	262	TBI	140
	E	8	5.0	305	TBI	170
	F	8	5.0	305	MFI	195, 230†
	Y	8	5.0	307	4V	140
	7	8	5.7	350	TBI	190
	8	8	5.7	350	MFI	240, 245†
	J	8	5.7	350	MFI	380
1989	1	4	2.0	122	TBI	90
	R	4	2.5	151	TBI	110
	W	6	2.8	173	MFI	125-130†
	S	6	2.8	173	MFI	135
	Z	6	4.3	262	TBI	140
	E	8	5.0	305	TBI	170
	F	8	5.0	305	MFI	195-230†
	Y	8	5.0	307	4V	140
	7	8	5.7	350	TBI	190
	8	8	5.7	350	MFI	230-245†
	J	8	5.7	350	MFI	385
1988	1	4	2.0	122	TBI	90
	R	4	2.5	151	TBI	98
	W	6	2.8	173	MFI	125-130†
	S	6	2.8	173	MFI	135
	Z	6	4.3	262	TBI	140-145†
	H	8	5.0	305	4V	150, 170†
	G	8	5.0 HO	305 HO	4V	180
	E	8	5.0	305	TBI	170

YEAR	3 ENGINE CODE	CYL.	DISPL. liters	DISPL. cu. in.	Fuel System	HP
1988 Cont'd.	F	8	5.0	305	MFI	190-215†
	Y	8	5.0	307	4V	140
	8	8	5.7	350	MFI	225-240†
1987	C	4	1.6	98	2V	65
	1	4	2.0	122	TBI	90
	R	4	2.5	151	TBI	98
	W	6	2.8	173	MFI	125, 130†
	S	6	2.8	173	MFI	135
	A	6	3.8	231	2V	110
	Z	6	4.3	262	TBI	140, 145†
	H	8	5.0	305	4V	150-170†
	G	8	5.0 HO	305 HO	4V	180
	F	8	5.0	305	MFI	190, 215†
	Y	8	5.0	307	4V	140
	6	8	5.7	350	4V	180
	8	8	5.7	350	MFI	225, 240†
1986	C	4	1.6	98	2V	65
	D	4	1.8 D	111 D	MFI	51
	P	4	2.0	122	TBI	88
	R	4	2.5	151	TBI	92
	2	4	2.5	151	TBI	88
	X	6	2.8	173	2V	112
	W	6	2.8	173	MFI	120, 125†
	S	6	2.8	173	MFI	135
	A	6	3.8	231	2V	110
	Z	6	4.3	262	TBI	140
	H	8	5.0	305	4V	150-165†
	G	8	5.0 HO	305 HO	4V	180, 190†
	F	8	5.0	305	MFI	210
	Y	8	5.0	307	4V	140
	6	8	5.7	350	4V	165
	8	8	5.7	350	MFI	230
1985	C	4	1.6	98	2V	65
	D	4	1.8 D	111 D	TBI	51
	P	4	2.0	122	TBI	88
	R, 2	4	2.5	151	TBI	92
	X	6	2.8	173	2V	112
	W	6	2.8	173	MFI	125, 135†
	S	6	2.8	173	MFI	135
	A	6	3.8	231	2V	110
	Z	6	4.3	262	TBI	130
	T	6	4.3 D	262 D	MFI	85
	H	8	5.0	305	4V	150-165†
	G	8	5.0 HO	305 HO	4V	180, 190†
	F	8	5.0	305	MFI	215
	6	8	5.7	350	4V	165
	8	8	5.7	350	MFI	230
	N	8	5.7 D	350 D	MFI	105
1984	C	4	1.6	98	2V	65
	D	4	1.8 D	111 D	TBI	51
	P	4	2.0	122	TBI	86

ENGINE IDENTIFICATION Continued

4 ENGINE IDENTIFICATION

YEAR	3 ENGINE CODE	CYL.	DISPL. liters	cu. in.	Fuel System	HP
1984 Cont'd.	B	4	2.0	122	2V	88
	R, 2	4	2.5	151	TBI	92
	1	6	2.8	173	2V	107
	X	6	2.8	173	2V	112
	Z	6	2.8 HO	173 HO	2V	135
	9	6	3.8	229	2V	110
	A	6	3.8	231	2V	110
	T	6	4.3 D	262 D	MFI	85
	H	8	5.0	305	4V	145
	G	8	5.0 HO	305 HO	4V	190
	S	8	5.0	305	TBI	165
	N	8	5.7 D	350 D	MFI	105
	6	8	5.7	350	4V	N/A
	8	8	5.7	350	TBI	205
1983	C	4	1.6	98	2V	65
	D	4	1.8 D	111 D	MFI	51
	P	4	2.0	122	TBI	86
	B	4	2.0	122	2V	88

4 ENGINE IDENTIFICATION

YEAR	3 ENGINE CODE	CYL.	DISPL. liters	cu. in.	Fuel System	HP
1983 Cont'd.	R, 2	4	2.5	151	TBI	92
	5, F	4	2.5	151	2V	92, 94†
	X	6	2.8	173	2V	112
	1	6	2.8	173	2V	107
	Z	6	2.8 HO	173 HO	2V	135
	9	6	3.8	229	2V	110
	A	6	3.8	231	2V	110
	T, V	6	4.3 D	262 D	MFI	85
	H	8	5.0	305	4V	145
	7	8	5.0 HO	305 HO	4V	190
	S	8	5.0	305	TBI	165
	N	8	5.7 D	350 D	MFI	105
	6	8	5.7	350	4V	N/A

TBI — Throttle Body Injection.
2V — Two Venturi Carburetor.
D — Diesel.
MFI — Multiport Fuel Injection.
4V — Four Venturi Carburetor.
HO — High Output.
† Engine horsepower varies with model installation.

UNDERHOOD SERVICE SPECIFICATIONS

CTTU1   **CYLINDER NUMBERING SEQUENCE**   CTTU1

4-CYL. FIRING ORDER:
1 3 4 2

— Front of car —

| 1983-87 1.6L (98) | 1983-86 2.0L (122) | 1987-89 2.0L (122) Code 1, 1990-91 2.2L Code G, 1992 2.2L Code 4 | 1990-92 2.3L Code A | 1983-86 Camaro 2.5L (151) | 1983-86 2.5L (151) FWD | 1987-92 2.5L (151) |

2.8L (173) FIRING ORDER: 1 2 3 4 5 6

All Other V6 FIRING ORDER: 1 6 5 4 3 2

— Front of car —

1 4 6 3 2 5

| 1983-86 2.8L (173) ex. Camaro | 1987-89 2.8L (173) ex. Camaro, 1990-92, 3.1L Code T (FWD), 1991-92 3.4L Code X | 1983-89 2.8L (173) Camaro, 1990-92 3.1L Code T (RWD) | 1983-84 3.8L (229) | 1983-87 3.8L (231) | 1985-87 4.3L (262) | 1988-90 4.3L (262) |

8-CYL. FIRING ORDER:
1 8 4 3 6 5 7 2

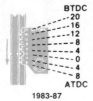
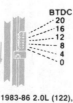
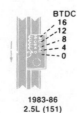

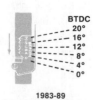

— Front of car —

| 1986-90 5.0L (307) | 1983-86 8-cyl., 1987-91 5.7L (350) Code 8 | 1987-92 8-cyl. ex.: 5.0L (307), 5.7L (350) Corvette Code 8, J | 1989-92 Corvette 5.7L (350) Code J |

TIMING MARK

| 1983-87 1.6L (98) | 1983-86 2.0L (122), 1987-89 4.3L (262) | 1983-86 2.5L (151) | 1983-86 2.8L (173) ex. Camaro | 1983-89 2.8L (173) Camaro | 1990-92 3.1L FI Code T RWD Camaro |

CHEK-CHART

CHEVROLET
1983-88 All Models Except Nova, Spectrum, Sprint
1989-92 All Models Except Geo, Sprint, Lumina APV

UNDERHOOD SERVICE SPECIFICATIONS

CTTU2   CTTU2

TIMING MARK

1983-87
3.8L (231)

1985-86, 90 4.3L (262),
1985-90 5.0L (305),
1991-92 5.0L Code E, F

1983-84
3.8L (229), 4.4L (267),
5.0L (305)

1986-90
5.0L (307)

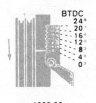

1983-92
5.7L (350) FI
Camaro & Corvette ex. Code J,
1989-92
5.7L FI Code 7 (Police)

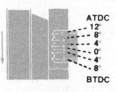

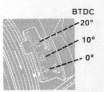

1990-92
5.7L DOHC Code J
Corvette

ELECTRICAL AND IGNITION SYSTEMS

BATTERY

Engine	Year	STANDARD BCI Group No.	STANDARD Crank. Perf.	OPTIONAL BCI Group No.	OPTIONAL Crank. Perf.
1.6L (98) MT	1983-85	70	310	71	390
1.6L (98) AT	1983-85	70	355	71	390
1.6L (98) MT	1986	70	310	70	405
1.6L (98) AT	1986	70	355	70	405
1.6L (98) Canada	1986	70	405	—	—
1.6L (98) MT	1987	70	330	70	425
1.6L (98) AT	1987	70	385	70	425
1.8L (111) Diesel	1983-85	74	550	—	—
1.8L (111) Diesel	1986	78	515	—	—
2.0L (122)	1983-84	70	405	75	500
2.0L (122) Canada	1983-84	75	500	75	630
2.0L (122)	1986	75	500	75	630
2.0L (122) MT	1987	70	525	75	630
2.0L (122) AT	1987	75	570	75	630
2.0L (122) MT	1988-89	75	525	75	630
2.0L (122) AT	1988-89	75	630	—	—
2.2L Cavalier	1990-91	75	630	—	—
2.2L Corsica, Beretta:					
MT	1990-91	75	525	75	630
AT	1990-91	75	630	—	—
2.2L	1992	75	525	75	630
2.3L	1990-92	75	630	—	—
2.5L (151)	1983-85	70	405	75	500
Can. Camaro	1983-84	75	500	—	—
2.5L (151)	1986-92	75	630	—	—
2.8L (173)	1983-84	70	405	75	500
2.8L (173) Camaro	1986	70	525	75	570
2.8L (173) 2V					
ex. Canada	1986	70	405	78	730
Canada	1986	75	630	78	730
2.8L (173) FI	1986	75	500	75	630
2.8L (173): Cavalier	1987-88	75	525	75	630
Celebrity	1987	75	525	75	570
Celebrity	1988	75	525	75	630
Camaro	1987-88	75	525	75	570
Corsica, Beretta	1987-88	70	525	75	630
2.8L: Cavalier	1989	75	630	—	—
Celebrity, Camaro	1989	75	525	75	570
Corsica, Beretta	1989	70	525	75	630
3.1L MFI Cavalier	1990-91	75	630	—	—
Others	1990-91	75	525	75	630
3.1L	1992	75	525	—	—
3.4L DOHC	1991	75	630	—	—
3.4L DOHC	1992	75	690	—	—
3.8L (229)	1983	70	355	75	500
3.8L (229)	1984	70	405	75	500
3.8L (231)					
Impala, Caprice	1983	71	390	78	550
3.8L (231)					
Impala, Caprice	1984	70	355	75	500
3.8L (231) All Others	1983-84	70	315	78	550
3.8L (231)	1985	75	500	78	550
3.8L (231)	1986	75	500	75	630
3.8L (231)	1987	75	525	75	630

BATTERY Continued

Engine	Year	STANDARD BCI Group No.	STANDARD Crank. Perf.	OPTIONAL BCI Group No.	OPTIONAL Crank. Perf.
4.3L (262) Diesel					
Celebrity	1983	76	750	75	500
4.3L (262) Diesel					
Malibu, Monte Carlo	1983	75	500	78	550
4.3L (262) Diesel	1984-85	78	770	76	1075
4.3L (262)	1986	75	630	75	570
4.3L (262): Monte Carlo	1987	75	525	75	630
Caprice	1987	75	630	—	—
4.3L (262)	1988-90	75	630	—	—
4.3L	1992	75	525	—	—
5.0L (305) Caprice	1983	70	355	75	500
5.0L (305) All Others	1983-84	70	405	75	500
5.0L (305) HO	1984	75	500	—	—
5.0L (305) 4V, TBI	1986-90	70	525	75	570
5.0L	1991-92	75	525	—	—
5.0L (305) FI	1987	75	500	—	—
5.0L (305) MFI	1988-92	75	525	75	570
5.7L (350) Diesel	1983	75	500	78	550
5.7L (350) Diesel	1984-85	70	405	78	550
5.7L (350) Camaro	1987-91	75	630	—	—
5.7L (350) Corvette	1984-85	75	500	—	—
5.7L (350) Corvette	1986-87	75	630	—	—
5.7L (350) Corvette	1988-89	75	525	—	—
DOHC	1989	75	630	—	—
5.7L Corvette	1990-92	75	525	—	—
DOHC	1990-92	75	690	—	—
5.7L (350) Caprice	1986-92	78	730	—	—
5.7L (350) All Others	1983	71	350	73	465

ALTERNATOR
See UNDERHOOD SERVICE INSTRUCTIONS at the beginning of this section for test/adjustment diagrams.

Year	Rated Output (amps)	Test Output (amps)	Field Current Draw (amps)
1983	42, 55, 56, 63, 78, 85	†	4-5
1984	37, 42, 50, 56, 66, 78, 94, 97	†	4-5
1985	42, 56, 66, 78, 94, 97, 108, 120	†	4-5
1986	42, 56, 66, 70, 78, 94, 97	†	4-5
1986	85, 105	△	5.5-7.0
1987-88	78, 94	†	4-5
1987-89	85, 100, 105, 108, 120	△	—
1990-92	74, 80, 85, 100, 105, 120, 124	△	—

† Increase engine speed until maximum output is obtained (approximately 2000 rpm); output must be within 10 amps of rated output.
△ Output at 2000 rpm must be within 15 amps of rated output.

Copyright 1992 by H.M. Gousha, a division of Simon & Schuster

63

UNDERHOOD SERVICE SPECIFICATIONS

CTTU3   CTTU3

REGULATOR

Application	Test Temp. (deg. F/C)	Voltage Setting
1983-84	Warm	12.5-15.4
1986-92	Warm	13.5-16.0

STARTER

Engine	Year	Cranking Voltage (min. volts)	Ampere Draw @ Cranking Speed
All	1983-92	9.0*	—

* At 70°F (21°C) or higher.

SPARK PLUGS

Engine	Year	Gap (inches)	Gap (mm)	Torque (ft-lb)
4-cyl.				
2.2L	1992	.045	1.14	11
2.3L	1990-92	.035	.89	20
2.5L (151)	1983-91	.060	1.52	11
All Others	1983-91	.035	.89	11
6-cyl.				
2.8L (173)	1983-89	.045	1.14	7-15
3.1L	1990-92	.045	1.14	11
3.4L	1991-92	.045	1.14	11
3.8L (229)	1983-84	.045	1.14	7-15
3.8L (231) 2V	1983	.080	2.03	7-15
3.8L (231) 2V	1984-87	.060	1.52	7-15
4.3L (262)	1985-92	.035	.89	11
8-cyl.				
	1983-85	.045	1.14	7-15
HO or FI	1984-85	.035	.89	7-15
Canada, all	1983-85	.045	1.14	7-15
8-cyl. ex. 5.0L (307)	1986-91	.035	.89	22
5.0L (307)	1986-90	.060	1.52	20
8-cyl.: 5.7L Code P	1992	.050	1.26	11
All Others	1992	.035	.89	11

IGNITION COIL

See UNDERHOOD SERVICE INSTRUCTIONS at the beginning of this section for test/adjustment diagrams.

Winding Resistance (ohms at 75°F or 24°C)

Engine	Year	Windings	Resistance (ohms)
All w/distributor	1983-92	Primary	0-2
		Secondary	6000-30,000
2.0L, 2.5L, 2.8L			
DIS coils	1987-90	Secondary	5000-10,000*
2.3L	1990-92	Secondary	20,000 max.*
5.7L DOHC	1990	Primary	.35-1.45†
		Secondary	5000-6500*

* Measured across each coils towers with spark plug wires removed.
† Measured between A terminal of 2-pin connector and each terminal on 4-pin connector.

DISTRIBUTOR PICKUP

See UNDERHOOD SERVICE INSTRUCTIONS at the beginning of this section for test/adjustment diagrams.

Application	Year	Resistance (ohms)	Air Gap (in./mm)
All	1983-92	500-1500	—

BASE TIMING

See UNDERHOOD SERVICE INSTRUCTIONS at the beginning of this section for test/adjustment diagrams.

Set timing at slow idle and Before Top Dead Center, unless otherwise specified. Disconnect and plug distributor vacuum hose at distributor on vehicles without computer control.

1983-86 2.5L (151) & 3.8L (229) engines, ground diagnostic connector.

1983-86 2.0L (122) FI, 2.8L (173) FI, 5.7L (350) FI, 5.0L (305) CFI engines, disconnect bypass connector (tan/black wire).

1987-92 all models w/distributor & FI, disconnect timing connector, single wire connector in engine harness between distributor and ECM.

1983-90 all others w/carburetor, disconnect 4-wire connector at distributor.

Timing MUST be set to specifications on emission label, if different from setting listed. If "Check Engine" light comes on during procedure, remove ECM fuse to clear.

BASE TIMING Continued

Engine	Year	Man. Trans. (degrees) @ RPM	Auto. Trans. (degrees) @ RPM
1.6L (98)	1983	6	6
w/5-speed	1983	8	—
Canada	1983	6	10
1.6L (98)	1984-87	8	8
Canada	1984-87	8	12
w/leaded fuel	1984-86	4	—
2.0L (122)	1983	0	0
Canada	1983	0 @ 850	0 @ 850 N
w/decal DBB	1983	—	2 @ 850 N
2.0L (122)	1984-86	6	6 D
Canada	1984	4 @ 850	0 @ 850 N
2.5L (151)	1983-86	8	8 D
Canada	1983	10	8 @ 750 N
2.8L (173)	1983-86	10	10
Canada Camaro	1983	10	16
Canada Others	1983-86	6 @ 650	10 @ 750 N
Wagons	1984	—	6 @ 750 N
2.8L (173) Camaro	1987-89	10	10 D
3.1L Camaro	1990-92	10	10 D
3.8L (229)	1983-84	—	0 @ 1200 P
3.8L (231)	1983-87	—	15 D
4.3L (262) Gasoline	1985-92	—	0 D
5.0L (305)	1983-84	6	6
Canada	1983-84	4 @ 500	4 @ 500
5.0L (305) 4V	1985-87	0	0
Canada	1985-87	4 @ 500	4 @ 500 D
HO & FI	1985-87	6	6 D
5.0L (305) 4V	1988	—	6 @ 600 D
5.0L (305) TBI	1988-92	0	0 D
5.0L (305) MFI	1989-92	6	6 D
5.0L (307)	1986-90	—	20 @ 1100 P
Canada	1986-87	—	8 @ 1500 P
5.7L (350) Police	1983-88	6	6
Canada	1983-87	—	2
5.7L (350) MFI	1984-92	6	6 D
5.7L TBI	1989-92	—	0 D

DISTRIBUTOR TIMING ADVANCE

Engine degrees at engine rpm, no load, in addition to basic timing setting. Mechanical advance distributors only.

Engine	Transmission	Year	Distributor Number	Degrees @ 2500 RPM Total	Degrees @ 2500 RPM Centrifugal
1.6L (98)	MT & AT	1983-84	1113504	24.3-32.3	6.3-10.3
1.6L (98)	MT	1984	1113511	28.3-36.3	6.3-10.3
1.6L (98)	MT & AT	1984	1113565, 66	26.2-34.2	4.2-8.2
1.6L (98)	MT	1985-87	1113613	24.2-32.2	6.2-10.2
1.6L (98)	MT	1985-87	1113615	28.3-36.3	6.3-10.3
1.6L (98)	AT	1985-87	1113614	25.3-33.3	2.3-6.3
1.6L (98)	MT & AT	1985-87	1113616	24.3-32.3	6.3-10.3
2.0L (122)	MT & AT	1983-84	1113535, 48, 92	32.9-40.9	10.9-14.9
2.5L (151)	MT	1983	1113471	30.5-40.5	8.5-14.5
2.5L (151)	AT	1983	1103528	27.8-35.8	9.8-13.8
2.5L (151)	AT	1983	1103545	22.8-30.8	4.8-8.8
2.8L (173)	MT & AT	1983-84	1103523	34.9-42.9	12.9-16.9
2.8L (173)	MT	1983-84	1103525	35-43	17-21
2.8L (173)	AT	1983	1103522	27.2-35.2	5.2-9.2
2.8L (173)	AT	1984	1103586	25-33	17-21
2.8L (173)	MT	1985	1103617	45-53	17-21
2.8L (173)	AT	1985-86	1103618	41.9-49.9	12.9-16.9
2.8L (173)	AT	1985	1103619	35-43	17-21
3.8L (231)	AT	1983-84	1110766	31.0-37.8	9.0-11.8
3.8L (231)	AT	1985-87	1103612	20.3-28.3	2.3-6.3
5.0L (305)	MT & AT	1983-87	1103282	29.8-37.8	11.8-15.8
5.0L (307)	AT	1986	1103607	23-27	9-11
5.0L (307)	AT	1987	1103718	30-38	12-16
5.7L (350)	AT	1983-87	1103282	29.8-37.8	11.8-15.8
5.7L (350)	AT	1983-87	1103339	22.3-30.3	14.3-18.3

CHEK-CHART

CHEVROLET
1983-88 All Models Except Nova, Spectrum, Sprint
1989-92 All Models Except Geo, Sprint, Lumina APV

UNDERHOOD SERVICE SPECIFICATIONS

CTTU4   CTTU4

FUEL SYSTEM

FUEL SYSTEM PRESSURE
See UNDERHOOD SERVICE INSTRUCTIONS at the beginning of this section for test/adjustment diagrams.

Carburetted models, pinch off fuel return line.

All models with TBI, pressure measured at fuel inlet of TBI unit.

All models with MFI, pressure measured at fuel rail.

CARBURETTED & TBI, DIESEL

Engine	Year	PSI	RPM
4-cyl.			
1.6L (98)	1983	2.5-6.5	idle
1.6L (98)	1984-87	5.5-6.5	idle
1.8L (111) Diesel	1983-85	5.8-8.7	idle
2.0L (122) 2.2L	1983-91	9.0-13.0	ign. on
		13 min.	idle
2.5L (151) 2V	1983	6.5-8.0	idle
2.5L (151) ex. Lumina	1983-90	9.0-13.0	ign. on
	1987-90	13 min.†	idle
2.5L Lumina	1990-92	26-32	idle
6-cyl.			
2.8L (173)	1983	6.0-7.5	idle
2.8L (173) 2V	1984-86	5.5-6.5	idle
3.8L (229)	1983-84	5.5-6.5	idle
3.8L (231)	1983-86	5.5-6.5	idle
4.3L (262) Diesel	1983-85	5.8-8.7	ign. on
4.3L (262) Gas	1985-92	9-13	idle
		13 min.†	idle
8-cyl.			
4.4L (267), 5.0L (305) 4V, 5.0L (307), 5.7L (350) 4V	1983-88	5.5-6.5	idle
5.0L (305) FI	1983-84	9-13	ign. on
5.0L (305), 5.7L TBI	1988-90	9-13	ign. on
		13 min.†	idle
5.7L (350) Diesel	1983-85	5.5-6.5	idle

† With fuel return line briefly restricted.

GASOLINE MFI

Engine	Year	Ign. On	Pressure (PSI) Idle	Fuel Pump†
2.3L	1990-92	40.5-47	30.5-44	60 min.
2.8L (173), 3.1L	1985-92	40.5-47	30.5-44	47 min.
5.0L (305)	1985-92	40.5-47	30.5-44	60 min.
5.7L (350) Corvette	1985	34-39	24-36	60 min.
5.7L (350) ex. DOHC	1986-92	40.5-47	30.5-44	47 min.
5.7L DOHC	1990-92	48-55	38-52	55 min.

† With fuel return line briefly restricted.

IDLE SPEED W/O COMPUTER CONTROL
Set idle with Air-Conditioning unit turned OFF (unless otherwise specified on engine label).

1983-85 Diesel Engines: Start engine and allow it to warm up to operating temperature. Connect tachometer following manufacturer's instructions. Adjust screw on injection pump to obtain specified slow idle.

1.8L (111) eng.: Apply vacuum to fast idle actuator. Loosen locknut and adjust knurled nut to specification.

5.7L (350) eng.: Turn ignition off and then attach jumper wire across fast idle switch connector terminals. Turn ignition on and adjust idle solenoid (energized) to obtain specified fast idle.

1983-88 Others: Make all adjustments with engine at operating temperature, choke fully open, and electric cooling fan off (if equipped). Engines with idle speed control, idle adjustments not recommended during tune-up.

Engines with C-4 system, connect dwell meter to carburetor fuel valve lead and ground. Set meter to 6-cylinder scale. When needle begins to vary engine is closed loop mode and is ready to adjust.

All other engines, disconnect and plug vacuum hoses indicated on emissions label.

Adjust idle solenoid screw, plunger fully extended, or carburetor idle speed screw to specification. If equipped with idle stop solenoid, disconnect the electrical lead and adjust carburetor body screw to specification.

Engines equipped with air conditioning speed-up solenoid, turn A/C on and disconnect compressor clutch wire. Adjust solenoid to specification with plunger fully extended.

To set fast idle, set choke cam on specified step and adjust engine speed to specification.

IDLE SPEED W/O COMPUTER CONTROL Continued

Engine	Year	SLOW Man. Trans.	SLOW Auto. Trans.	FAST Man. Trans.	FAST Auto. Trans.	Step of Cam
1.6L (98)	1983	800	700 D	2500	2500 P	High
solenoid	1983	1150	875 D			
w/5-speed	1983	950	—	2500	—	High
solenoid	1983	1150	—			
Canada	1983	700	700 D	2500	2500 P	High
1.6L (98) 4-speed	1984-87	800	700 D	2500	2500 P	High
solenoid	1984-87	1250	875 D			
Canada	1984-87	700	700 D	2700	2800 P	High
w/leaded fuel	1984-86	850		2300	—	High
1.6L (98) 5-speed	1984-85	1000	—	2500	—	High
solenoid	1984-85	1250				
Canada	1984-85	1000	—	2700	—	High
solenoid	1984-85	1000				
1.6L (98) 5-speed	1986-87	900	—	2500	—	High
solenoid	1986-87	1250	—			
Canada	1986-87	900	—	2700	—	High
solenoid	1986-87	1000				
1.8L (111) Diesel	1983-86	625	725 N	950	950 P	—
2.0L (122) Canada	1983	900	900 D	2400	2600 D	High
base idle	1983	850	850 N			
speed-up	1983	1150	1250 D			
w/decal DXD	1983	—	900 D	—	3000 P	High
base idle	1983	—	800 N			
speed-up	1983	—	1250 D			
2.0L (122) Canada	1984	900	800 D	3000	3000 P	High
base idle	1984	850	750 N			
speed-up	1984	1150	1250 D			
w/AC	1984	—	900 D	—	3000 P	High
base idle	1984	—	850 N			
speed-up	1984	—	1250 D			
2.5L (151) Canada	1983	750	750 D	2600	2600 P	High
base idle	1983	700	700 D			
speed-up	1983	1000	900 D			
w/AC	1983	—	800 D	2600 P	High	
base idle	1983	—	750 D			
speed-up	1983	—	900 D			
2.8L (173) ex. HO						
Camaro	1983	800	600 D	2600	2600 P	High
solenoid	1983	1000	750 D			
Canada	1983	700	700 D	2000	2000 N	High
solenoid	1983	1200	950 D			
Citation, Celebrity	1983	775	600 D	2500	2500 P	High
solenoid	1983	1100	750 D			
5-speed	1983	800	—	2600	—	High
solenoid	1983	1000	—			
Canada	1983	700	700 D	2000	2000 P	High
solenoid	1983	1050	900 D			
Canada Camaro	1983	700	700 D	2000	2000 N	High
solenoid	1983	1200	950 D			
2.8L (173) HO	1983-84	800	725 D	2600	2700 P	High
solenoid	1983-84	1100	850 D			
2.8L (173) ex. HO						
Camaro	1984	800	600 D	2600	2500 P	High
solenoid	1984	1100	750 D			
Canada	1984	700	700 D	2000	2000 N	High
solenoid	1984	1200	920 D			
Citation, Celebrity	1984	800	600 D	2500	2500 P	High
solenoid	1984	1100	750 D			
Canada	1984	700	700 D	2000	2000 P	High
solenoid	1984	1200	900 D			
2.8L (173) 2V	1985-86	—	600 D	—	2500 P	High
solenoid	1985-86	—	750 D			
Canada	1985-86	—	700 D	—	2700 P	High
solenoid	1985-86	—	900 D			
3.8L (231) Canada	1983-86	—	550 D	—	2000 P	High
AC speed-up	1983-85	—	670 D			
AC speed-up	1986	—	750 D			
3.8L (231) Canada	1987	—	550 D	—	2200 P	High
solenoid	1987	—	750 D			
4.3L (262) Diesel	1983-85	—	675 D	—	775 D	—
5.0L (305) 4V ex. HO	1983-88	700	500 D	1800	2200 P	High
solenoid	1983-88	800	650 D			
Canada ex. Camaro	1983-87	—	500 D	—	1850 P	High
solenoid	1983-84	—	600 D			
solenoid	1985-87	—	650 D			

UNDERHOOD SERVICE SPECIFICATIONS

CTTU5   CTTU5

IDLE SPEED W/O COMPUTER CONTROL Continued

Engine	Year	SLOW Man. Trans.	SLOW Auto. Trans.	FAST Man. Trans.	FAST Auto. Trans.	Step of Cam
5.0L (305) 4V ex. HO						
Canada Camaro	1983-87	650	550 D	1500	1850 P	High
solenoid	1983-87	750	650 D			
5.0L (305) HO	1983-88	700	600 D	1800	2200 P	High
AC speed-up	1983-88	800	650 D			
5.0L (307) Canada	1987	—	500 D	—	725 D	Low
solenoid	1987	—	650 D			
5.7L (350) Diesel	1983-85	—	600 D		750 D	—
5.7L (350) Police	1983-87	—	500 D	—	2200 P	High
solenoid	1983-87	—	650 D			
Canada	1983-87	—	600 D	—	1850 P	High
solenoid	1983-87	—	650 D			

IDLE SPEED W/COMPUTER CONTROL

See UNDERHOOD SERVICE INSTRUCTIONS at the beginning of this section for test/adjustment diagrams.

Midpoint of range given is the preferred setting speed.

1983-86 All w/single TBI: Gain access to throttle stop screw. With engine at operating temperature, disconnect idle air controller and install special tool to seal idle air passage of throttle body. Turn throttle stop screw to specified minimum speed value.

1983-84 All w/dual TBI: Disconnect IAC electrical lead. Start engine and let idle stabilize. Remove cap on rear TBI unit and connect a water manometer. Adjust minimum speed to achieve 6" H_2O on scale in drive. Reinstall cap on rear unit and remove cap on front TBI unit. If reading is not 6" H_2O, adjust balance screw on linkage. Disconnect manometer and set minimum speed on rear TBI unit to specified value.

1983-86 All w/FI except TBI; 1987-90 All w/FI & TBI when specifications appear in Minimum Speed column: Ground diagnostic lead and turn ignition on for 30 seconds. Remove IAC electrical lead and remove ground from diagnostic connector. Start engine and set minimum speed to specified value.

All carburetted w/ISC: With engine at operating temperature, turn ignition off and disconnect harness from ISC. Apply 12 volts (+) to third terminal from top of ISC (C), and ground the fourth terminal from top (D) only long enough to retract ISC plunger. With engine running, set minimum idle to specified value by adjusting carb base screw. Apply 12 volts (+) to fourth terminal from top of ISC (D) and ground the third terminal from top (C) only long enough to fully extend ISC plunger. Set maximum speed to specified value by turning ISC plunger head.

Never apply voltage to first two upper terminals (A & B) or damage to the unit will result.

All carburetted w/ILC: Disconnect and plug vacuum hoses at EGR and canister purge valves. With engine at operating temperature, remove vacuum hose from ILC and plug. Set maximum speed to specified value by holding hex nut and turning plunger shaft. Reconnect ILC vacuum hose and check to see that minimum speed is at specified value. To adjust, remove rubber and metal plugs from rear center outlet tube, insert a 3/32" allen wrench. Remove ILC hose and plug. Connect a remote vacuum source and apply vacuum to the unit. Adjust carb base screw to obtain specified shutdown value.

ALL FUEL INJECTED

Engine	Year	Minimum Speed Man. Trans.	Minimum Speed Auto. Trans.	Checking Speed Man. Trans.	Checking Speed Auto. Trans.
2.0L (122)	1983-86	625-675	625-675 D	—	—
2.0L (122)	1987-89	450-650	450-650 N	—	—
2.2L	1990-91	450-650	450-650 N	—	—
2.2L	1992	—	—	525-675	525-675 N
2.5L (151)	1983-84	750-800	475-525 N	—	—
2.5L (151)	1985	750-800	475-525 N	900-1000	675-775 D
2.5L (151)	1986	750-800	475-525 N	850-950	750-850 D
2.5L (151)	1987	550-650	550-650 N	750-850	750-850 D
2.5L (151)	1988-92	550-650	550-650 N	800 max.	800 N max.
2.8L (173)	1985-86	600-700	500-600 D	—	—
2.8L (173)†	1987	625-725	500-600 D	—	—
Camaro	1987	600-700	500-600 D	—	—
2.8L ex. Camaro††	1987-89	—	—	750-950	650-750 D
Camaro	1988-89	600-700	500-600 D	—	—
3.1L	1990	—	—	750-950	650-750 D
Camaro	1990	—	—	800 max.	800 N max.
3.1L, 3.4L	1991-92	—	—	800-900	700-800 D
3.4L	1991	—	—	600-700	600-700 D
4.3L (262)	1985-86	—	500-600 D	—	—
4.3L (262)	1987-89	—	400-450 N	—	—
4.3L	1990-92	—	—	—	500-600 D
5.0L (305)	1983-84	—	475 D	—	—
5.0L (305)	1985	—	450-550 D	—	—

IDLE SPEED W/COMPUTER CONTROL Continued

ALL FUEL INJECTED

Engine	Year	Minimum Speed Man. Trans.	Minimum Speed Auto. Trans.	Checking Speed Man. Trans.	Checking Speed Auto. Trans.
5.0L (305)	1986	—	400 D	—	—
5.0L (305) MFI	1987-88	400	400 N	—	—
5.0L MFI	1989	400-450	400-450 N	—	—
5.0L MFI	1990-91	—	—	600-800	600-800 N
5.0L (305) TBI	1988-89	400-450	400-450 N	—	—
5.0L TBI	1990-92	—	—	550-750	500-600 N
5.7L (350)	1983-84	—	475 D	—	—
5.7L (350)	1985-86	450	400 D	—	—
5.7L (350)	1987-88	450	450 N	—	—
5.7L MFI	1989	—	400-450 N	—	—
5.7L MFI ex. DOHC	1990-92	—	—	600-800	600-800 N
5.7L TBI	1989	—	450-500 D	—	—
5.7L TBI	1990-92	—	—	—	500-600 D

† Mass airflow system.
†† Speed density system.

ALL CARBURETTED

Engine	Year	Trans.	Min. Speed	Max. Speed	Fast	Step of Cam
3.8L (229)	1983-84	AT	475 D	750 D	2200 P	High
w/AC	1983-84	AT	475 D	800 D	2200 P	High
3.8L (231)	1983	AT	450 D	900 D	2200 P	High
3.8L (231)	1984-86	AT	450 D	1000 D	2200 P	High
5.0L (307)	1986-90	AT	450 D	700 D	550 D	Low
base idle	1986-90	AT	450 D	—	—	—

ENGINE MECHANICAL

TIGHTENING TORQUES

See UNDERHOOD SERVICE INSTRUCTIONS at the beginning of this section for test/adjustment diagrams.

Some fasteners are tightened in more than one step.

Engine	Year	Torque Ft-lbs/Nm Cylinder Head	Intake Manifold	Exhaust Manifold	Crankshaft Pulley	Water Pump
1.6L (98)	1983-87	75/100	18/24	18/24	100/135	15/20
1.8L (111)						
Diesel	1983-86	21-36/ 28-48, 90-105/ 122-142	30/40	—	—	15/20
1.8L (112) 2V, 2.0L (122)	1983-84	65-75/ 88-107	20-25/ 27-34	22-28/ 30-38	66-85/ 90-115	12-21/ 16-28
2.0L (122)	1985-86	65-75/ 88-107	18-25/ 24-34	34-44/ 46-60	66-89/ 90-120	12-21/ 16-28
2.0L (122)	1987-89	73-83/ 99-113⊙ 62-70/ 85-95◆	15-22/ 20-30	6-13/ 8-18	66-89/ 90-120	15-22/ 20-30
2.2L	1990	41/55, +45°, +45°, +20°⊙, +10°◆	18/25	10/13	85/115	18/25
2.2L	1991	43/58◆, 46/63⊙, +90°	18/25	10/13	77/105	22/30
2.2L	1992	43/58◆, 46/63⊙, +90°	22/30	10/13	37/50	22/30◆ 18/25⊙
2.3L	1990-91	26/35, +110°◆◆	18/25	27/37 △ 10/13 ▲	74/100	10/12, cover 19/26, others
2.3L	1992	□	18/25	31/42, nuts 106"/12, studs	74/100, +90°	10/12, cover 19/26, others

CHEK-CHART

CHEVROLET
1983-88 All Models Except Nova, Spectrum, Sprint
1989-92 All Models Except Geo, Sprint, Lumina APV

UNDERHOOD SERVICE SPECIFICATIONS

CTTU6   CTTU6

TIGHTENING TORQUES Continued

Engine	Year	Cylinder Head	Intake Manifold	Exhaust Manifold	Crankshaft Pulley	Water Pump
			Torque Ft-lbs/Nm			
2.5L (151)	1983	85/115	29/40	44/60	200/260	25/34
2.5L (151)	1984	92/125	29/40	44/60	200/260	25/34
2.5L (151)	1985-86	18/25, 22/30‡	25/34	25/43*, 37-50**	162/220	25/34
2.5L	1987-92	18/25, 26/35●, +90°	25/34	25/43*, 37-50**	162/220	25/34
2.8L (173) Celebrity, Citation, Camaro	1983-86	70/95	20-25/27-34	22-28/30-38	66-84/90-115	8/10, M6 15/22, M8 25/34, M10
2.8L (173) Cavalier	1985-86	77/105	13-25/18-34	9-31/25-42	67-85/90-115	6-9/8-12
2.8L	1987-89	33/45, +90°	15/20, 24/33	20-30/15-22	76/103	7/10, short 18/24, long
3.1L MFI ex. Camaro	1990-92	33/45, +90°	15/20, 24/33	18/25	75/102	88″/10
3.1L Camaro	1990-92	40/55, +90°	15/21●●, 19/26■	25/34	70/95	88″/10◆ 25/34⊙
3.4 DOHC	1991-92	37/50, +90°	18/25	116″/13	37/50	89″/10
3.8L (231)	1983-84	80/108, after 15 minutes, 80/108	45/61	25/34	225/306	88″/10
3.8L (231) 2V	1985	72/98	35/47	20/27	200/270	88″/10
3.8L (231) 2V	1986	25/34, +90°, +90°‡	45/66	20/27	200/270	19/26
3.8L (231) 2V	1987	25/34, +90°, +90°‡	32/44	37/50	219/297	10/13
4.3L (262), 5.0L (305), 5.7L (350) ex. Corvette	1985-88	60-75/81-102	25-45/34-61	20-32/27-43* 14-26/19-35**	65-75/87-102	25-35/34-47
4.3L, 5.0L, 5.7L ex. Corvette	1989-92	68/93	35/47	20/27* 26/35**	70/95	30/40
4.3L (262) Diesel	1983-85	142/193★	41/55	28/39	200-350/275-475	13/18, short 21/28, long
4.4L (267), 5.0L (305), 5.7L (350)	1983-84	65/88	30/40	20/27	60/81	30/40
5.0L (307)	1986	60/81, 125/169	40/54	25/34	200-310/270-400	13/18
5.0L (307)	1987-88	90/122, 130/176	40/54	25/34	200-310/270-400	88″/10
5.0L (307)	1989-90	40/54, +95°, first and last bolts on exhaust manifold side +120°, all others	40/54	25/34	200-310/270-400	11/14◆ 22/30⊙
5.7L (350) Corvette	1984-88	60-75/81-101	35/47	20/27	60/81	30/40
5.7L Corvette SOHC	1989-91	68/93	35/47	20/27* 26/35**	70/95	30/40
5.7L Corvette SOHC	1992	65/88	71″/8, 35/48	20/35	70/95	88″/10◆ 35/47⊙
5.7L DOHC	1990-92	45/60, 74/100, 118/160	20/26	11/15	148/200	20/26
5.7L (350) Diesel	1983-85	100/136, 130/176	40/54	25/34	200-310/270-400	13/18

TIGHTENING TORQUES Continued

* Four outer bolts.
** Three inner bolts.
‡ Turn last bolt on left (number nine) to 29/40. Then turn all except number nine 120°, turn number nine 90°.
□ Tighten six center bolts to 26/35. Tighten two at front of head to 15/20. Tighten two at rear of head to 22/30. Then turn all bolts 90°. Loosen all bolts one turn and repeat procedure.
★ Eight central bolts, three upper and lower, 59/80.
⊙ Long bolts.
◆ Short bolts.
◆◆ Turn first two bolts on front of engine (#7 & #9) 100°.
● Turn last bolt on left (number nine) to 18/25.
△ Nuts.
▲ Studs.
●● Center two.
■ Others.

VALVE CLEARANCE
Engine cold unless otherwise specified.

Engine	Year	Intake (inches)	Intake (mm)	Exhaust (inches)	Exhaust (mm)
1.8L (111) Diesel	1983-86	.010	.25	.014	.35

COMPRESSION PRESSURE
At cranking speed or specified rpm, engine temperature normalized, throttle open.

Engine	Year	PSI	Maximum Variation PSI
4-cyl.			
1.8L (111) Diesel	1983-86	370-441 @ 200 min.	—
All Others	1983-91	100 min.	*
6-cyl.			
4.3L (262) Diesel	1983	275 min.	*
4.3L (262) Diesel	1984-85	300 min.	†
All Others	1983-91	100 min.	*
8-cyl.			
5.7L (350) Diesel	1983	275 min.	*
5.7L (350) Diesel	1984-85	300 min.	†
All Others	1983-91	100 min.	*

* Lowest cylinder pressure must be more than 70% of highest cylinder pressure.
† Lowest cylinder pressure must be more than 80% of highest cylinder pressure at 200 rpm min.
● Lowest cylinder pressure must be more than 6.5% of highest cylinder pressure.

BELT TENSION
All Except With Automatic Tensioner

1983: A belt in operation 15 minutes is considered used.
1984-87: A belt in operation 3 minutes is considered used.
Use a strand tension gauge. Measurements are in pounds.

Engine	Year	Alternator	Power Steering	Air Cond.	Air Pump
Used Belts					
1.6L	1983-87	70	70	90	—
2.0L	1983-86	75	70	100	—
2.3L	1990-91	—	110	—	—
2.5L	1983-86	75	70	75	—
2.8L 2V	1983-86	70	70	70	45
2.8L FI	1985-86	210	205	165	—
3.8L 2V	1983-87	70	80	80	45
4.3L Diesel	1983-85	—	—	—	45
4.3L Gas	1985-87	70	70	70	90
5.0L (305) 4V	1983-87	70	70	90	70
5.0L (305) FI	1985-87	90	70	90	70
5.0L (307), 5.7L Diesel	1985-88	80	90	90	45
Cogged or ³/₈″ belt	1985-88	55	—	—	70
5.7L Diesel	1983-84	80	90	90	45
Cogged belt	1983-81	55	—	—	—
New Belts					
1.6L	1983-87	145	145	165	—
2.0L	1983-86	145	145	165	—
2.3L	1990-91	—	110	—	—
2.5L	1983-86	145	145	165	—
2.8L 2V	1983-86	145	135	145	100

UNDERHOOD SERVICE SPECIFICATIONS

BELT TENSION Continued

Engine	Year	Alternator	Power Steering	Air Cond.	Air Pump
2.8L FI	1985-86	150	150	110	—
3.8L 2V	1983-87	125	135	135	80
4.3L Diesel	1983-85	—	—	—	75
4.3L Gas	1985-87	145	145	165	145
5.0L (305) 4V	1983-87	145	145	165	145
5.0L (305) FI	1985-87	135	145	165	145
5.0L (307), 5.7L Diesel	1985-88	160	170	170	80
Cogged or 3/8" belt	1985-88	145	—	—	145
5.7L Diesel	1983-84	160	170	170	80
Cogged belt	1983-84	145	—	—	—

All With Automatic Tensioner

If index marks on tensioner are outside the range, replace the belt. If marks are within range, and belt tension is below specified value, replace tensioner.

Engine	Year	Tension
2.0L, 2.2L	1989-92	67-77
2.3L	1990-92	50 min.
2.5L Celebrity	1987-88	40 min.
2.5L	1989-92	50-70
2.8L	1987	70 min.
2.8L FWD	1988-89	50-70
2.8L Camaro	1989	116-142
W/AC	1989	103/127
3.1L FWD	1989-92	50-70
3.1L Camaro	1990	116-142
W/AC	1990	103-127
3.1L Camaro	1991-92	95-140
W/AC	1991-92	85-110
5.0L, 5.7L	1988-92	99-121
5.7L Corvette	1991	60-90
5.7L Corvette	1989-90	120-140

ENGINE COMPUTER SYSTEM

COMPUTER DIAGNOSTIC CODES

See UNDERHOOD SERVICE INSTRUCTIONS at the beginning of this section for test/adjustment diagrams.

Connect a jumper between A and B terminals on under dash connector (identified by a slot between the terminals or is two upper right hand cavities of the two row connector). Turn ignition switch on. Code 12 will flash three times, then codes in memory will be displayed. Do not run engine with jumper connected.

Remove the ECM fuse for a minimum of ten seconds to clear memory.

Code 12 No tach signal to ECM
Code 13 Oxygen sensor circuit
Code 14 Coolant sensor circuit (high temperature indicated)
Code 15 Coolant sensor circuit (low temperature indicated)
Code 16 DIS or Opti-Spark ignition circuit
Code 21 Throttle position sensor circuit (1983)
Code 21 Throttle position sensor voltage high (1984-86)
Code 22 Throttle position sensor voltage low
Code 23 Open or grounded MC solenoid (carburetted)
Code 23 Manifold air temperature circuit (low temperature indicated)
Code 24 Vehicle speed sensor circuit
Code 25 Manifold air temperature, high temperature indicated
Codes 26, 27, 28 Quad driver circuit
Code 31 Camshaft sensor (FI)
Code 31 Canister purge solenoid (carburetted)
Code 32 Barometric or altitude sensor (carburetted)
Code 32 EGR failure (FI)
Code 32 EGR vacuum control (MFI)
Code 33 MAP, MAF sensor circuit voltage (high) (FI)
Code 34 MAP, MAF sensor circuit voltage (low) (FI)
Code 34 Vacuum sensor circuit (carburetted)
Code 35 Idle speed or idle air control circuit
Code 36 MAF burn off circuit (ex. Corvette)
Code 36 DIS or Opti-Spark ignition circuit (Corvette)
Code 39 Transaxle clutch switch circuit
Code 41 No distributor reference pulses to ECM (1985-89 carburetted)
Code 41 Cylinder select error (1987-88 FI)
Code 42 EST or EST bypass circuit grounded or open

COMPUTER DIAGNOSTIC CODES Continued

Code 43 ESC signal
Code 44 Air/fuel mixture lean (left on Corvette V8)
Codes 44 & 45 Faulty oxygen sensor
Code 45 Air/fuel mixture rich (left on V8 DOHC)
Code 46 No vehicle anti-theft signal
Code 51 Faulty PROM, MEM-CAL, ECM or installation
Code 52 Fuel CALPAK (ex. Corvette)
Code 52 Oil temperature sensor (Corvette)
Code 53 EGR vacuum sensor vacuum incorrect (carburetted)
Code 53 Alternator voltage out of range (FI ex. 5.0L TBI)
Code 53 Vehicle anti-theft circuit (5.0L TBI)
Code 54 Fuel pump circuit (FI)
Code 54 Faulty MC solenoid or faulty ECM (carburetted)
Code 55 Grounded V-REF, faulty oxygen sensor, ECM (ex. V8 DOHC)
Code 55 Fuel lean monitor (Corvette)
Code 56 Vacuum sensor circuit
Code 61 Degraded oxygen sensor (ex. Corvette)
Code 61 Secondary part throttle valve system (Corvette)
Code 62 Transaxle switch circuit (ex. Corvette)
Code 62 Engine oil temperature sensor (Corvette)
Code 63 MAP sensor voltage high (ex. Corvette)
Code 63 Right side oxygen sensor, circuit open (Corvette)
Code 64 MAP sensor voltage low (ex. DOHC)
Code 64 Right side oxygen sensor, lean (Corvette)
Code 65 Right side oxygen sensor, rich (Corvette)
Code 66 AC pressure sensor
Code 67 AC pressure sensor or clutch circuit
Code 68 AC relay circuit
Code 69 AC clutch circuit
Code 72 Gear selector switch

SENSORS, INPUT

TEMPERATURE SENSORS

Engine	Year	Sensor	Resistance Ohms @ deg. F/C
All	1983-90	Coolant	13,500 @ 20/–7
	1983-92	Manifold Air*	7500 @ 40/4
			3400 @ 70/20
			1800 @ 100/38
			450 @ 160/70
			185 @ 210/100
All	1991-92	Coolant	28,700 @ –4/–20
			12,300 @ 23/–5
			7280 @ 41/5
			3500 @ 68/20
			1460 @ 104/40
			467 @ 158/70
			177 @ 212/100

* As equipped, not used on all engines. Specifications also apply to V8 DOHC oil temperature sensor.

MANIFOLD ABSOLUTE, VACUUM, AND BAROMETRIC PRESSURE SENSORS
See UNDERHOOD SERVICE INSTRUCTIONS at the beginning of this section for test/adjustment diagrams.

Engines may use one, or a combination of these sensors. All sensors appear the same. Manifold Absolute Pressure sensors have a vacuum line connected between the unit and manifold vacuum. On Barometric Pressure sensors, the line is not used and the connector is either open or has a filter installed over it. Pressure sensors also have a vacuum line between the sensor and intake manifold and only appear on carburetted models.

Barometric Pressure Sensors: Measure voltage with ignition on and engine off.

Manifold Absolute Pressure Sensors: Measure voltage with ignition on and engine off. Start engine and apply 10 in./250 mm Hg to unit, voltage should be: 1.5 volts minimum less.

Pressure Sensors: Measure voltage as indicated.

5 volts reference.

Engine	Year	Sensor	Voltage @ Altitude/Condition
All, as equipped	1983-90	Barometric	3.8-5.5 @ 0-1000
			3.6-5.3 @ 1000-2000
			3.5-5.1 @ 2000-3000
			3.3-5.0 @ 3000-4000
			3.2-4.8 @ 4000-5000
			3.0-4.6 @ 5000-6000
			2.9-4.5 @ 6000-7000
			2.5-4.3 @ 7000-

SENSORS, INPUT Continued

MANIFOLD ABSOLUTE, VACUUM, AND BAROMETRIC PRESSURE SENSORS Continued

Engine	Year	Sensor	Voltage @ Vacuum In Hg/kPa
All, as equipped	1983-91	Manifold Absolute	1.0-2.0 @ idle 4.0-4.8 @ WOT
All, as equipped	1992	Manifold Absolute	4.9 @ 0/0 3.8 @ 6/20 2.7 @ 12/40 1.7 @ 18/60 0.6 @ 24/80 0.3 @ 30/100

Engine	Year	Sensor	Voltage @ Altitude
2.5L 2V, 2.8L 2V, 5.0L 4V, 5.7L 4V	1983-90	Vacuum	.50-.64 @ ign. on 1.7-3.0*

* 10 in./250 mm applied to unit.

CRANKSHAFT SENSORS
Resistance is measured at room temperature.

Engine	Year	Resistance (ohms)
2.0L, 2.8L, 3.1L	1987-92	900-1200
2.2L	1991-92	800-1200
2.3L	1990	900-1200
2.3L	1991-92	500-900
2.5L	1987-92	800-900

THROTTLE POSITION SENSOR (TPS)
See UNDERHOOD SERVICE INSTRUCTIONS at the beginning of this section for test/adjustment diagrams.

Verify that minimum idle is at specified value.

Make all checks/adjustments with engine at operating temperature.

Carburetted Models: Remove aluminum plug covering the adjustment screw. Remove the screw and connect a digital voltmeter to black wire (–) and either of the other two colored wires (+). If voltage is approximately 5 volts, this is the reference voltage lead. Connect DVOM to other wire in this case. Apply thread locking compound to the screw and with ignition on and engine not running (as applies), quickly adjust screw to obtain specified voltage at indicated condition.

Fuel Injected Models: Disconnect harness connector from TPS. Using three six-inch jumper wires reconnect harness to TPS. With ignition on and engine not running (as applies), connect a digital voltmeter to black wire (–) and either of the other two colored wires (+). If voltage is approximately 5 volts, this is the reference voltage lead. Connect DVOM to other wire in this case. Check reading against specified value. If TPS is adjustable, loosen the unit retaining screws and rotate the unit to reach specified value.

Engine	Year	TPS Voltage† Idle	WOT
1.6L (98)	1983-87	.92●	—
2.0L (122) FI	1983-84	.525	—
2.0L (122)	1985-86	.20-1.25*	—
2.0L, 2.2L	1987-92	.33-1.33*	5.0
2.3L	1990-92	.40-.90	4.9
2.5L (151)	1983-91	.20-1.25*	4.5
2.8L (173)	1983	.26▲	—
2.8L (173)	1984	.30	—
2.8L (173) 2V	1985-86	.27	—
2.8L (173) FI	1985-88	.55	—
2.8L, 3.1L	1989	.29-.98*	4.8
Camaro	1989	.55	—

SENSORS, INPUT Continued

THROTTLE POSITION SENSOR (TPS) Continued

Engine	Year	TPS Voltage† Idle	WOT (approx.)
3.1L	1990-92	.29-.98*	4.8
3.4L DOHC	1991-92	.29-.98	4.8
3.8L (229)	1983-84	.36♦	—
3.8L (231) 2V	1983	.86●	—
3.8L (231) 2V	1984	.46♦	—
4.3L (262)	1985-86	.525	—
4.3L (262)	1987-90	.20-1.25*	5.0
4.3L	1992	.20-.95*	5.0
5.0L (305) 4V	1983	.51	—
5.0L (305) 4V	1984-87	.48	—
5.0L (305) 4V	1988	.50	★
5.0L (305) MFI	1985-89	.54	—
5.0L MFI	1990-91	.20-.96*	5.0
5.0L MFI	1992	.36-.62*	5.0
5.0L TBI	1988-89	.20-1.25*	5.0
5.0L TBI	1990-91	.45-1.25	5.0
5.0L TBI	1992	.20-.95*	5.0
5.0L MFI	1990-91	.36-.96*	4.6
5.0L (307)	1986-90	.41	—
5.7L (350) Corvette	1983-84	.525	—
5.7L (350) Corvette, Camaro	1985-89	.54	—
5.7L MFI	1990	.20-.96	4.6
5.7L MFI	1991	.36-.96*	5.0
5.7L Camaro	1992	.36-.62*	5.0
Corvette	1992	.30-.90*	5.0
5.7L DOHC	1990	.54	5.0
5.7L DOHC	1991-92	.23-59*	5.0
5.7L (350) Police	1983	.51	—
5.7L (350) Police	1984-88	.48	—
5.7L Police	1989	.20-1.25*	5.0
5.7L Police	1990-91	.45-1.25*	5.0
5.7L Police	1992	.20-.95*	5.0

● High step of fast idle cam.
♦ Idle speed or Load Compensator (ISC or ILC) retracted.
† ±.10 carburetted, ±.05 fuel injected engines.
* Not adjustable.
▲ With idle solenoid disconnected.

ACTUATORS, OUTPUT

IDLE SPEED CONTROL
See UNDERHOOD SERVICE INSTRUCTIONS at the beginning of this section for test/adjustment diagrams.

All engines with ISC.

Measured between terminals A & B and C & D.

Engine	Year	Resistance (ohms)
2.8L Celebrity	1988-89	48-58
All Other TBI & MFI	1983-89	20 min.
All TBI & MFI	1990-92	40-80
DOHC V8	1990	20 min.
All carburetted	1983-89	10 min.

MIXTURE CONTROL SOLENOID-CARBURETTED ENGINES
On some engines, the ECM will be damaged if the resistance of the mixture control solenoid is less than specified.

Engine	Year	Resistance (ohms)
All	1983-90	10 min.

ENGINE IDENTIFICATION

To identify an engine by the manufacturer's code, follow the four steps designated by the numbered blocks.

1 MODEL YEAR IDENTIFICATION: Refer to illustration of Vehicle Identification Number (V.I.N.). The year is indicated by a code letter.

2 ENGINE CODE LOCATION: Refer to illustration of V.I.N. plate for location and designation of engine code.

3 ENGINE CODE: In the "CODE" column, find the engine code determined in Step 2.

4 ENGINE IDENTIFICATION: On the line where the engine code appears, read to the right to identify the engine.

V.I.N. PLATE LOCATIONS:

All except Forward Control (P) Models — V.I.N plate is attached to top left of instrument panel and viewed from outside through windshield.

Forward Control (P) Models — V.I.N plate is attached to front of dash and toe panel.

Model year of vehicle:
1992 — Model year is N.
1991 — Model year is M.
1990 — Model year is L.
1989 — Model year is K.
1988 — Model year is J.
1987 — Model year is H.
1986 — Model year is G.
1985 — Model year is F.
1984 — Model year is E.
1983 — Model year is D.

MODEL YEAR AND ENGINE IDENTIFICATION:

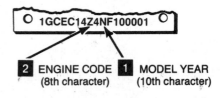

2 ENGINE CODE (8th character) **1 MODEL YEAR** (10th character)

4 ENGINE IDENTIFICATION

YEAR	3 ENGINE CODE	CYL.	DISPL. liters	DISPL. cu. in.	Fuel System	HP
1992	A	4	2.5	151	TBI	105
	R	6	2.8	173	TBI	125
	D	6	3.1	191	TBI	120
	L	6	3.8	231	MFI	165
	W	6	4.3	262	CPI	195, 200
	Z	6	4.3	262	TBI	150, 155, 160†
	H	8	5.0	305	TBI	170, 175†
	K	8	5.7	350	TBI	190, 195, 210†
	C	8	6.2 D	379 D	MFI	140, 145
	J	8	6.2 D	379 D	MFI	150, 155
	F	8	6.5 D	379 D	MFI	190
	N	8	7.4	454	TBI	230, 255†
1991	A	4	2.5	151	TBI	105
	R	6	2.8	173	TBI	125
	D	6	3.1	191	TBI	120
	Z	6	4.3	262	TBI	150, 155, 160†
	B	6	4.3 HO	262 HO	TBI	170
	H	8	5.0	305	TBI	170, 175†
	K	8	5.7	350	TBI	190, 195, 210†
	J	8	6.2 D	379 D	MFI	150, 155
	C	8	6.2 D	379 D	MFI	140, 145
	N	8	7.4	454	TBI	230, 255
1990	E	4	2.5	151	TBI	94, 96†
	R	6	2.8	173	TBI	125
	D	6	3.1	191	TBI	120
	Z	6	4.3	262	TBI	150, 155, 160†
	B	6	4.3 HO	262 HO	TBI	175
	H	8	5.0	305	TBI	170, 175†
	K	8	5.7	350	TBI	190, 195, 210†
	J	8	6.2 D	379 D	MFI	150, 155†
	C	8	6.2 D	379 D	MFI	135, 140, 145†
	N	8	7.4	454	TBI	230
1989	E	4	2.5	151	TBI	92
	R	6	2.8	173	TBI	125
	Z	6	4.3	262	TBI	150, 160†
	T	6	4.8	292	1V	115
	H	8	5.0	305	TBI	170, 175†
	K	8	5.7	350	TBI	190, 195, 210†
	C	8	6.2 D	379 D	MFI	126, 130†
	J	8	6.2 D	379 D	MFI	143, 148†
	N	8	7.4	454	TBI	230
	W	8	7.4	454	4V	230
1988	E	4	2.5	151	TBI	92, 96†
	R	6	2.8	173	TBI	125
	Z	6	4.3	262	TBI	150, 160
	T	6	4.8	292	1V	115

YEAR	3 ENGINE CODE	CYL.	DISPL. liters	DISPL. cu. in.	Fuel System	HP
1988 Cont'd.	H	8	5.0	305	TBI	170, 175†
	K	8	5.7	350	TBI	185-210†
	M	8	5.7	350	4V	185
	C	8	6.2 D	379 D	MFI	126, 130†
	J	8	6.2 D	379 D	MFI	143, 148†
	N	8	7.4	454	TBI	230
	W	8	7.4	454	4V	230
1987	E	4	2.5	151	TBI	92, 96†
	R	6	2.8	173	TBI	125
	T	6	4.8	292	1V	115
	Z	6	4.3	262	TBI	150, 160†
	H	8	5.0	305	TBI	160, 185†
	M	8	5.7	350	4V	185
	K	8	5.7	350	TBI	185-210†
	C	8	6.2 D	379 D	MFI	130
	J	8	6.2 D	379 D	MFI	145, 148†
	W	8	7.4	454	4V	230
	N	8	7.4	454	TBI	230
1986	E	4	2.5	151	TBI	92
	R	6	2.8	173	TBI	125
	N	6	4.3	262	4V	155
	Z	6	4.3	262	TBI	145
	T	6	4.8	292	1V	115
	F	8	5.0	305	4V	155
	H	8	5.0	305	4V	160
	L	8	5.7	350	4V	165
	M	8	5.7	350	4V	185
	K	8	5.7 LP	350 LP	4V	185
	C	8	6.2 D	379 D	MFI	130
	J	8	6.2 D	379 D	MFI	145, 148†
	W	8	7.4	454	4V	240
1985	A	4	1.9	119	2V	82
	Y	4	2.0	122	2V	N/A
	S	4	2.2 D	133 D	MFI	62
	E	4	2.5	151	TBI	92
	B	6	2.8	173	2V	110
	D	6	4.1	250	2V	N/A
	N	6	4.3	262	4V	150
	T	6	4.8	292	1V	115
	F	8	5.0	305	4V	155
	H	8	5.0	305	4V	160
	K	8	5.7 LP	350 LP	4V	N/A
	L	8	5.7	350	4V	165
	M	8	5.7	350	4V	165
	C	8	6.2 D	379 D	MFI	130
	J	8	6.2 D	379 D	MFI	135
	W	8	7.4	454	4V	230
1984	A	4	1.9	119	2V	82
	Y	4	2.0	122	2V	83
	S	4	2.2 D	133 D	MFI	62
	B	6	2.8	173	2V	112
	D	6	4.1	250	2V	110
	T	6	4.8	292	1V	120
	F, H	8	5.0	305	4V	155, 160†

CHEVROLET/GMC TRUCKS
1983-92 All Models
Includes Oldsmobile Bravada and Silhouette, Pontiac Trans Sport

ENGINE IDENTIFICATION Continued

4 ENGINE IDENTIFICATION

3 ENGINE			DISPL.		Fuel System	HP
YEAR	CODE	CYL.	liters	cu. in.		
1984 Cont'd.	K	8	5.7 LP	350 LP	4V	N/A
	L, M	8	5.7	350	4V	165
	C	8	6.2 D	379 D	MFI	130
	J	8	6.2 D	379 D	MFI	135
	W	8	7.4	454	4V	230
1983	A	4	1.9	119	2V	80
	Y	4	2.0	122	2V	83
	B	6	2.8	173	2V	112
	D	6	4.1	250	2V	110
	T	6	4.8	292	1V	120

4 ENGINE IDENTIFICATION

3 ENGINE			DISPL.		Fuel System	HP
YEAR	CODE	CYL.	liters	cu. in.		
1983 Cont'd.	F, H	8	5.0	305	4V	140
	L, M	8	5.7	350	4V	165
	C	8	6.2 D	379 D	MFI	130
	J	8	6.2 D	379 D	MFI	135
	W	8	7.4	454	4V	240

D — Diesel.   FI — Fuel Injection.   LP — LPG powered conversion.
CPI — Central Port Injection.   MFI — Multiport Fuel Injection.
TBI — Throttle Body Injection.   1V — One Venturi Carburetor.
2V — Two Venturi Carburetor.   4V — Four Venturi Carburetor.
† Engine horsepower varies with model installation.

UNDERHOOD SERVICE SPECIFICATIONS

GMTTU1   GMTTU1

CYLINDER NUMBERING SEQUENCE

L-4-CYL. FIRING ORDER:
1 3 4 2

2.8L, 3.1L V6 FIRING ORDER:
1 2 3 4 5 6

4.3L (262) V6 FIRING ORDER:
1 6 5 4 3 2

L-6 FIRING ORDER:
1 5 3 6 2 4

V8 FIRING ORDER:
1 8 4 3 6 5 7 2

1983-85 1.9L (119)

1983-84 2.0L (122)

1985-92 2.5L (151)

Front of car

2.8L (173)

1990-92 3.1L Lumina APV, Silhouette, Trans Sport

1992 3.8L Code L Lumina APV, Silhouette, Trans Sport

1985-86 4.3L (262) 4V Code N

1986-92 4.3L (262) FI Code W, Z

Front of car
4.1L (250), 4.8L (292)

1983-86 Gasoline

1987-92 Gasoline

TIMING MARK

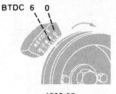

BTDC 6 0

1983-85 1.9L (119)

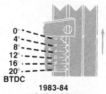

0° 4° 8° 12° 16° 20° BTDC

1983-84 2.0L (122)

BTDC 12° 8° 4° 0°

1985-86 2.5L (151), 1986-92 4.3L (262) FI ex. G Van, 1987-92 5.0L (305), 5.7L (350)

BTDC 12 8 4 0

1987-88 2.5L (151)

12° 8° 4° 0° 4°

1989-92 2.5L Code A, E

BTDC 20° 16° 12° 8° 4° 0°

2.8L (173)

BTDC 16 12 8 4 0

1990-92 3.1L Lumina APV, Silhouette, Trans Sport

ATDC 8° 4° 0° 4° 8° 12° BTDC

1988-92 4.3L G Van

0° 4° 8° ATDC

1983-85 4.1L (250), 1983-90 4.8L (292)

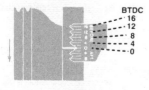

BTDC 16 12 8 4 0

1985-86 4.3L (262) 4V

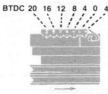

BTDC 20 16 12 8 4 0 4 ATDC

1983-86 5.0L (305), 5.7L (350)

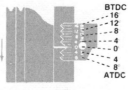

BTDC 16 12 8 4 0 4 ATDC

1983-89 7.4L (454)

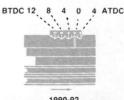

BTDC 12 8 4 0 4 ATDC

1990-92 7.4L FI Code N

CHEVROLET/GMC TRUCKS
1983-92 All Models
Includes Chevrolet Lumina APV, Oldsmobile Bravada & Silhouette; Pontiac Trans Sport

UNDERHOOD SERVICE SPECIFICATIONS

GMTTU2 GMTTU2

ELECTRICAL AND IGNITION SYSTEMS

BATTERY

Engine	Year	STANDARD BCI Group No.	STANDARD Crank Perf.	OPTIONAL BCI Group No.	OPTIONAL Crank Perf.
4-cyl.					
1.9L (112)	1983-85	70	315	78	515
2.0L (122)	1983-84	70	405	78	515
2.5L (151)	1985-86	70	405	—	—
2.5L (151)	1987-92	75	525	78	630
6-cyl.					
2.8L (173)	1983	70	315	74	465
2.8L (173)	1984-85	70	405	78	515
2.8L (173) Canada	1984-85	75	500	78	515
2.8L (173)	1986	70	525	78	515
2.8L (173)	1987	75	430	75	525
2.8L (173)	1988-92	75	525	78	630
3.1L FWD Vans	1990-92	75	525	—	—
3.8L FWD Vans	1992	70	630	—	—
4.1L (250)					
2WD Pickup	1983-84	70	405	31	625
4WD Pickup	1983-84	70	405	78	515
4.1L (250) Vans	1983-84	70	405	78	515
4.3L (262)	1985-86	75	500	78	515
4.3L (262)	1987-90	75	525	78	630
4.3L S Series	1991-92	75	525	78	630
Others	1991-92	78	630	—	—
4.8L (292)					
Vans & 4WD	1983-86	70	405	78	515
All Others	1983-84	71	390	31	625
8-cyl.					
5.0L (305)					
Calif. Vans	1983-86	71	390	78	515
5.0L (305) All Others	1983-86	70	405	78	515
5.0L (305): MT	1987-89	75	430	78	630
AT	1987-89	75	525	78	630
5.0L	1990	75	525	78	630
5.0L	1991-92	78	630	—	—
5.7L (350) Vans	1983-85	71	390	31	625
5.7L (350) Step Vans	1983-86	71	390	78	515
5.7L (350) Pickups	1983-86	70	405	78	515
5.7L (350)	1987-90	75	525	78	630
5.7L	1991-92	78	630	—	—
6.2L (379) Diesel	1983-85	78	550†	—	—
6.2L (379) Diesel	1986	78	515†	—	—
6.2L (379) Diesel					
Pickups	1987-92	75	570†	—	—
Vans	1987-92	78	540†	—	—
6.5L Diesel	1992	75	570†	—	—
7.4L (454) Pickups	1983-85	70	405	78	515
7.4L (454) All Others	1983-85	71	390	78	515
7.4L (454) All	1986	78	515	—	—
7.4L (454) All	1987-92	78	630	—	—

† Two batteries required.

ALTERNATOR

See UNDERHOOD SERVICE INSTRUCTIONS at the beginning of this section for test/adjustment diagrams.
Some models, rated output can be verified by stamping on end frame.

Application	Rated Output (amps)	Test Output (amps)
1983-84	37, 42, 63, 78	*
1985	37, 42, 56, 66, 78, 80, 85	*
1986 S Series, Astro, Safari	85, 100	*
1986 All Others	66, 78, 85, 94, 100	*
1987-92	66, 70, 81, 94	*
	85, 100, 105	†
	120, 124	†

* Output at 2000 rpm must be within 10 amps of rated output.
† Output at 2000 rpm must be within 15 amps of rated output.

REGULATOR

Application	Test Temp. (deg. F/C)	Voltage Setting
1983-86	—	12.5-15.4
1987-92	—	13.5-16.0

STARTER

Engine	Year	Cranking Voltage (min. volts)	Ampere Draw @ Cranking Speed
All	1983-92	9.0	—

SPARK PLUGS

Engine	Year	Gap (inches)	Gap (mm)	Torque (ft-lb)
4-cyl. 1.9L (119)	1983-85	.044	1.1	—
4-cyl. 2.0L (122)	1983-84	.035	.89	7-15
4-cyl. 2.5L (151)	1985-86	.060	1.52	7-15
V6 2.8L, 3.1L	1983-92	.045	1.14	7-15
V6 3.8L	1992	.060	1.52	.20
V6 4.3L	1985-92	.035	.89	7-15
6-cyl.	1983-89	.035	.89	17-27
8-cyl.	1983-86	.045	1.14	17-27
8-cyl.: Light-Duty	1987-88	.035	.89	22
Heavy-Duty	1987-88	.045	1.14	22
8-cyl.	1989-92	.035	.89	22

IGNITION COIL

See UNDERHOOD SERVICE INSTRUCTIONS at the beginning of this section for test/adjustment diagrams.
Winding Resistance (ohms at 75°F or 24°C)

3.8L: Primary resistance measured across each coil's two primary power wires. Secondary resistance measured across companion coil towers with spark plug wires removed.

Engine	Year	Windings	Resistance (ohms)
1.9L (119)	1983	Primary	.90-1.40
		Secondary	7300-11,100
1.9L (119)	1984-85	Primary	1.13-1.53
		Secondary	10,200-13,800
3.8L Type I*	1992	Primary	.50-1.0
		Secondary	10,000-13,000
Type II	1992	Primary	.30-.50
		Secondary	5000-7000
All Others	1983-92	Primary	0-2
		Secondary	6000-30,000

* Type I coils have three coil towers on each side.
  Type II coils have six coil towers on each side.

DISTRIBUTOR PICKUP

See UNDERHOOD SERVICE INSTRUCTIONS at the beginning of this section for test/adjustment diagrams.

Engine	Year	Resistance (ohms)	Air Gap (in./mm)
1.9L (119)	1983-85	—	.008-.016/ .2-.4
3.8L	1992	—	.025/.65
All Others	1983-92	500-1500	—

BASE TIMING

See UNDERHOOD SERVICE INSTRUCTIONS at the beginning of this section for test/adjustment diagrams.
Set timing at slow idle and Before Top Dead Center, unless otherwise specified.
2.5L (151), ground diagnostic connector under dash. Average pulses of cylinders 1 & 4.
2.8L (173), 3.1L TBI, place system in bypass mode, disconnect tan/black wire by ECM in passenger compartment.
2.8L (173) 2V EST, disconnect 4-wire connector at distributor.
4.3L (262) FI, place system in bypass mode, disconnect tan/black wire at distributor.
All V8 w/FI, place system in bypass mode, disconnect tan/black wire inboard of bulkhead.
All others, disconnect & plug distributor vacuum hose(s).

CHEVROLET/GMC TRUCKS
1983-92 All Models
Includes Chevrolet Lumina APV, Oldsmobile Bravada & Silhouette; Pontiac Trans Sport

UNDERHOOD SERVICE SPECIFICATIONS

BASE TIMING Continued

Engine	Year	Man. Trans. (degrees)	Auto. Trans. (degrees)
1.9L (119)	1983-85	6	6
2.0L (122)	1983-84	2	2
2.5L (151)	1985-90	8	8 D
2.8L (173)	1983-85	8	12
High Altitude	1983	12	12
California	1983-85	10	10
High Altitude	1984	10	14
High Altitude	1985	10	12
2.8L (173)	1986-91	10	10 P
3.1L FWD Vans	1990-92	—	10 D
4.1L (250)	1983-84	10	10
4.1L (250) California	1983-84	6	6
4.3L (262)	1985	0	0
Calif., High Altitude	1985	4	4
4.3L (262) Astro, Safari	1986	0	0 P
4.3L (262) Others	1986	0	0
Calif., High Altitude	1986	4	4
4.3L (262)	1987-91	0	0 P
4.8L (292)	1983-89	8	8
5.0L (305)	1983	4	4
w/label DCK	1983	2	—
w/dist. 1103436	1983	8	8
California	1983	—	8
5.0L (305) w/dist. 1103460	1984-86	—	6
w/dist. 1103465	1984-86	4	4
5.0L (305) TBI	1987-91	0	0 P
5.7L (350) Light-duty●	1983-84	4	4
w/label CFA, DDW	1983	6	6
California	1983-84	6	6
5.7L (350) Heavy-duty●	1983-85	8	8
California	1984	8	6
5.7L (350) Light-duty●	1985	8	8
High Altitude	1985	10	10
California	1985	6	6
Canada	1985	10	10
5.7L (350) Light-duty●	1986	4	8
California	1986	6	6
High Altitude	1986	10	10
5.7L (350) Heavy-duty	1986	4	4
California	1986	—	6
5.7L (350) TBI	1987-91	0	0 P
5.7L (350) 4V	1987-89	4	4
7.4L (454) Heavy-duty●	1983-90	4	4

● **Light-duty emission models:** 1983-86, GVW of 8500 lb or less. **Heavy-duty emission models:** 1983-86, GVW of 8501 lb or over.

DISTRIBUTOR TIMING ADVANCE

Degrees advance at engine rpm, no load, in addition to basic timing.

Mechanical advance distributors only.

Engine	Trans-mission	Year	Distributor Number	Degrees @ 2500 RPM Total	Degrees @ 2500 RPM Centrifugal
1.9L (119)	AT	1983-84	94230979	27-35	8-12
1.9L (119)	MT	1983-84	94240905	27-35	8-12
1.9L (119) Calif.	MT & AT	1983-84	94230990	22-30	8-12
2.0L (122)	MT	1983	1103536	32.2-40.2	10.2-16.2
2.0L (122)	AT	1983	1103441	35.6-43.6	13.6-17.6
2.0L (122)	MT	1984	1103547	33.5-41.5	11.5-15.5
2.0L (122)	AT	1984	1103546	33.6-41.6	11.6-15.6
2.8L (173)	MT	1983-84	1103520	30.9-38.9	12.9-16.9
2.8L (173)	AT	1983-84	1103521	26.9-34.9	8.9-12.9
2.8L (173)	MT	1985	1103620, 35	31.2-39.2	13.2-17.2
2.8L (173)	AT	1985	1103621	29-37	11-15
4.1L (250)	MT & AT	1983-84	1111388	30.6-38.6	12.6-16.6
4.1L (250)	MT & AT	1983-84	1103481	22-31	8-13
4.1L (250)	MT	1983-84	1103482	30-39	8-13
4.1L (250)	MT & AT	1983-84	1103483	26-35	8-13
4.1L (250)	MT & AT	1983	1103488	16-25	8-13
4.3L (262)	MT & AT	1985-86	1103572	16.2-24.2	8.2-12.2
4.3L (262)	MT & AT	1985-86	1103631	22.3-30.3	8.3-12.3
4.8L (292)	MT & AT	1983-85	1110753	20.6-28.6	12.6-16.6
4.8L (292)	MT & AT	1985-87	1103636	20.8-28.8	9.8-13.8
5.0L (305)	MT & AT	1983-86	1103465	26.7-34.7	8.7-12.7
5.0L (305)	MT & AT	1983-84	1103436	32.5-40.5	14.5-18.5
5.0L (305)	MT & AT	1985	1103604	29.3-37.3	11.3-15.3

DISTRIBUTOR TIMING ADVANCE Continued

Engine	Trans-mission	Year	Distributor Number	Degrees @ 2500 RPM Total	Degrees @ 2500 RPM Centrifugal
5.0L (305)	MT	1985-86	1103641	26.9-34.9	8.9-12.9
5.7L (350)	MT & AT	1983	1103353	32.3-40.3	6-10
5.7L (350)	MT & AT	1983-84	1103375	19.0-27.4	11.0-15.4
5.7L (350)	MT & AT	1983-87	1103420	13.5-23.0	5.5-11.0
5.7L (350)	MT & AT	1985	1103384	28-36	15-19
5.7L (350)	MT & AT	1983-86	1103436	32.3-40.3	14.3-18.3
5.7L (350)	MT & AT	1983	1103378	11.8-15.8	11.8-15.8
5.7L (350)	MT & AT	1985-89	1103606	23.2-31.2	15.2-19.2
7.4L (454) 4V	MT & AT	1983-89	1103376	17.4-25.9	9.4-13.9

FUEL SYSTEM

FUEL SYSTEM PRESSURE
See UNDERHOOD SERVICE INSTRUCTIONS at the beginning of this section for test/adjustment diagrams.

Engine	Year	PSI
All carburetted & TBI:		
4-cyl. 1.9L (119)	1983-85	4.0-6.5
4-cyl. 2.0L (122)	1983-84	5.5-6.5
4-cyl. 2.5L (151)	1985-92	9-13
		13 min.●
V6 2.8L (173)	1983-85	6-7.5
V6 2.8L (173), 3.1L	1985-92	9-13
		13 min.●
V6 4.3L (262) 4V	1985-86	4.0-6.5
V6 4.3L (262) FI	1985-92	9-13
		13 min.●
6-cyl.	1983-86	4.5-6.0
8-cyl.	1983-85	7.5-9.0*
8-cyl. 4V	1986-87	4-6.5
8-cyl. TBI	1987-92	9-13
		13 min.●
8-cyl. Diesel	1983-92	5.5-6.5

* With vapor return line, 5.5-7.0.
● With fuel return line briefly restricted.

		Pressure		
Engine	Year	Ign. On	Idle	Fuel Pump†
All MFI:				
3.8L	1992	40-47	30-44	47 min.

† With fuel return line briefly restricted.

IDLE SPEED W/O COMPUTER CONTROL
Disconnect and plug hoses as indicated on emission label.

Adjust idle to specified rpm by adjusting idle solenoid screw (plunger fully extended) or throttle stop screw.

Air-conditioned models equipped with idle speed-up solenoid, turn AC on, disconnect compressor clutch wire with solenoid fully extended, adjust solenoid to obtain specified rpm. Turn air conditioner off and reconnect compressor wire.

Electrically disconnect idle shutdown solenoid, if so equipped, and adjust idle speed screw or solenoid hex-head screw to obtain SHUTDOWN IDLE SPEED of 450 rpm, unless specified otherwise. Reconnect solenoid lead.

Reconnect hoses, unless specified otherwise on label or footnoted below. On models equipped with CEC solenoid, disconnect electrical lead.

Set fast idle to specified rpm with transmission in NEUTRAL or PARK, unless otherwise specified.

Engine	Year	SLOW Man. Trans.	SLOW Auto. Trans.	FAST Man. Trans.	FAST Auto. Trans.	Step of Cam
1.9L (119)	1983	800	900 P	3200	3200 P, N	First
	1984-85	900	900 P	—	—	—
AC speed-up	1983-85	900	900 P			
California	1983-85	900	900 P	3200	3200 P, N	First
AC speed-up	1983-85	900	900 P			
2.0L (122)	1983	800	800 D	2600	2600 P, N	High
AC speed-up	1983	1075	—			
2.0L (122)	1984	800	800 D	3000	2600 P, N	High
AC speed-up	1984	1075	925 D			

CHEVROLET/GMC TRUCKS
1983-92 All Models
Includes Chevrolet Lumina APV, Oldsmobile Bravada & Silhouette; Pontiac Trans Sport

UNDERHOOD SERVICE SPECIFICATIONS

GMTTU4   GMTTU4

IDLE SPEED W/O COMPUTER CONTROL Continued

Engine	Year	SLOW Man. Trans.	SLOW Auto. Trans.	FAST Man. Trans.	FAST Auto. Trans.	Step of Cam
2.2L (133) Diesel	1984	800	—	925	—	
2.8L (173)	1983	650	650 D	1800	2100 P, N	High
Solenoid	1983	850	850 D			
High Altitude	1983	700	700 D	1800	2100 P, N	High
Solenoid	1983	850	850 D			
California	1983-85	750	650 D	2100	2100 P, N	High
Solenoid	1983-85	950	850 D			
2.8L (173)	1984	700	600 D	2100	2100 P, N	High
Solenoid	1984	850	850 D			
High Altitude	1984	700	700 D	2100	2100 P, N	High
Solenoid	1984	850	850 D			
2.8L (173)	1985	700	700 D	2300	2100 P, N	High
Solenoid	1985	1100	850 D			
4.1L (250)	1983	550	525 D △	2000	2200 P, N	High
AC speed-up	1983	750 ■	650 D			
High Altitude	1983	600	550 D	2000	2200 P, N	High
AC speed-up	1983	750	650 D			
California	1983	750	650 D	2100	2100 P, N	High
AC speed-up	1983	850	750 D			
shutdown idle	1983	—	500 D			
4.1L (250)	1984	550	525 D	2000	2200 P, N	High
AC speed-up	1984	700	650 D			
High Altitude	1984	600	600 D	2000	2200 P, N	High
AC speed-up	1984	700	650 D			
California	1984	700	650 D	2000	2200 P, N	High
AC speed-up	1984	850	700 D			
shutdown idle	1984	—	500 D			
4.3L (262) 4V	1985-86	600	500	1800	2200 P, N	High
AC speed-up	1985-86	800	700 D			
High Altitude	1985-86	600	500	1800	1800 P, N	High
AC speed-up	1985-86	850	750 D			
California	1985-86	600	500	1800	1800 P, N	High
AC speed-up	1985-86	800	700 D			
4.8L (292)	1983-89	700	700 N	2400	2400 P, N	High
shutdown idle	1983-89	450	450 N			
5.0L (305)	1983	600	500 D	1300	1600 P, N	High
AC speed-up	1983	700	600 D			
California	1983	—	550 D	—	1800 P, N	High
AC speed-up	1983	—	600 D			
5.0L (305)						
Fed., Canada	1984-85	700	500 D	1500	1600 P, N	High
AC speed-up	1984-85	800	650 D			
w/labels						
XDW, XDX	1984	700	—	1600	—	High
AC speed-up	1984	800	—			
5.0L (305) Calif.	1984-86	—	550 D	—	1800 P, N	High
AC speed-up	1984-86	—	650 D			
5.0L (305)						
Fed., Canada	1986	700	550 D	1700	1800 P, N	High
AC speed-up	1986	800	650 D			
High Altitude	1986	700	600 D	1500	1500 P, N	High
5.7L (350)						
Light-duty	1983	600	500 D	1300	1600 P, N	High
AC speed-up	1983	750	600 D			
High Altitude	1983	700	600 D	1600	1600 P, N	High
California	1983	—	550 D	—	1800 P, N	High
AC speed-up	1983	—	650 D			
Canada	1983	700	500 D	1600	1600 P, N	High
AC speed-up	1983	—	600 D			
5.7L (350) Light-duty	1984-85	700	550 D	1300	1600 P, N	High
AC speed-up	1984-85	800	650 D			
High Altitude	1984-85	700	600 D	1400	1400 P, N	High
California	1984-85	—	550 D	—	1800 P, N	High
AC speed-up	1984-85	—	650 D			
5.7L (350) Heavy-duty●	1983-85	700	700 N	1900	1900 P, N	High
5.7L (350) Light-duty●	1986	700	550 D	1500	1600 P, N	High
AC speed-up	1986	800	650 D			
High Altitude	1986	700	600 D	1400	1400 P, N	High
5.7L (350) Heavy-duty●	1986-89	600	700 N	1900	1900 P, N	High
AC speed-up	1986-89	800				
Calif. P Series	1986	—	700 N	—	1900 P, N	High
Calif. Others	1986	—	550 D	—	1800 P, N	High
AC speed-up	1986	—	650 D			
Canada	1987	700	700 N	1900	1900 N	High
6.2L (379)	1983-89	650	650 D	800	800 P, N	—

IDLE SPEED W/O COMPUTER CONTROL Continued

Engine	Year	SLOW Man. Trans.	SLOW Auto. Trans.	FAST Man. Trans.	FAST Auto. Trans.	Step of Cam
7.4L (454) Heavy-duty●	1983-86	700	700 N	1900	1900 P, N	High
7.4L	1987-89	600	700 N	1900	1900 N	High

● **Light-duty emission models:** 1983-86, GVW of 8500 lb or less. **Heavy-duty emission models:** 1983-86, GVW of 1801 lb or over.

△ With labels DKD, DKF, DWS, DWT, 475 D.

■ Pickups and Vans with pulse air, 700.

IDLE SPEED W/COMPUTER CONTROL

See UNDERHOOD SERVICE INSTRUCTIONS at the beginning of this section for test/adjustment diagrams.

1985-86 2.5L (151) FI: Remove air cleaner assembly and disconnect Idle Air Control (IAC) multi-plug. Start engine and allow idle to stabilize. Install special tool in the idle air passage of the throttle body and turn throttle stop screw to obtain the specified setting speed.

1987-90 All; 1991-92 S Series & 7.4L: Ground diagnostic terminal (see COMPUTER DIAGNOSTIC CODES), turn ignition on but do not start engine. Wait 30 seconds then disconnect the IAC connector. Remove ground from the diagnostic terminal, start engine and turn throttle stop screw to obtain the specified setting speed.

Engine	Year	Transmission	Setting Speed	Checking Speed
2.5L (151) FI	1985-86	MT	750-800	900-1000
2.5L (151) FI	1985-86	AT	475-525 N	675-775 D
2.5L (151)	1987-89	MT	550-650	900
2.5L (151): 2WD	1987-89	AT	450-550 N	800 D
4WD	1987-89	AT	450-550 N	650 D
2.5L (151) Vans	1987-90	MT	550-650	800
2.5L (151) Vans	1987-90	AT	450-550 N	750 D
2.5L S Series	1990	MT	550-650	950
2.5L S Series	1990	AT	450-550 N	800 D
2.5L	1991-92	MT	550-650	900
2.5L	1991-92	AT	450-550 N	800 D
2.8L (173) FI	1985-86	MT & AT	700 N	—
2.8L (173)	1987-92	MT	650-750	800
2.8L (173)	1987-89	AT	650-750 N	800 D
3.1L FWD Vans	1990-92	AT	650-750 N	600-700 D
3.8L	1992	AT	—	650-750 N
4.3L (262) FI	1986	AT	400-500 D	—
4.3L (262)	1987-89	MT	400-500	500-550
4.3L (262)	1987-89	AT	350-550 D	500-550 D
S Series	1988-89	AT	425-525 N	500-550 D
4.3L LD	1990	MT	400-525	550
S Series	1990	MT	400-525	600
4.3L LD	1990	AT	350-450 D	540 D
S Series	1990	AT	425-525 N	500 D
HO Vans	1990	AT	425-525 D	590 D
4.3L LD	1991-92	MT	—	550
S Series	1991-92	MT	400-525	600
4.3L LD	1991-92	AT	—	540 D
	1992	AT	—	525 D
S Series	1991-92	AT	350-450 D	525 D
HO Van	1991-92	AT	—	590 D
4.3L HD	1990	MT	400-525	650
4.3L HD	1990	AT	350-450 N	650 D
4.3L HD	1991	MT	—	650
4.3L HD	1991	AT	—	500 D
	1992	AT	—	550 D
5.0L (305)	1987-90	MT	475-525	600●
5.0L (305)	1987-90	AT	400-450 D	500 D
5.0L	1991-92	MT	—	600
5.0L	1991-92	AT	—	500 D
5.7L (350) LD	1987-89	MT	475-525	600
5.7L (350) LD	1987-89	AT	400-450 D	500 D
5.7L LD	1990	MT	475-525	650
5.7L LD	1990	AT	400-450 D	525 D
5.7L LD	1991-92	MT	—	600
5.7L LD	1991-92	AT	—	525 D
5.7L (350) HD	1987-90	MT	525-575	650†
5.7L (350) HD	1987-90	AT	425-475 D	550 D
5.7L HD	1991-92	MT	—	600
5.7L HD	1991-92	AT	—	550 D
7.4L (454)	1987-92	MT	675-725	800
7.4L (454)	1987-89	AT	675-725 D	750 D
7.4L	1990-92	AT	600-650 D	750 D

● 1987-89 C10 Fed. 3-speed AT w/o AIR: 425-475 setting; 550 D checking.

† G Van or Suburban w/single catalytic converter, 600.

CHEK-CHART

CHEVROLET/GMC TRUCKS
1983-92 All Models
Includes Chevrolet Lumina APV, Oldsmobile Bravada & Silhouette; Pontiac Trans Sport
UNDERHOOD SERVICE SPECIFICATIONS

GMTTU5　　　　　　　　　　　　　　　　　　　　　　　　　　　GMTTU5

ENGINE MECHANICAL

TIGHTENING TORQUES
See UNDERHOOD SERVICE INSTRUCTIONS at the beginning of this section for test/adjustment diagrams.

Some fasteners are tightened in more than one step.

Engine	Year	Cylinder Head	Intake Manifold	Exhaust Manifold	Crankshaft Pulley	Water Pump
		Torque Ft-lbs/Nm				
1.9L (119)	1983-85	61/83, 72/98	16/22	16/22	87/118	—
2.0L (122)	1983-84	65-75/ 88-107	22-29/ 30-40	19-29/ 26-40	66-89/ 90-120	14-22/ 20-30
2.2L (134) Diesel	1983-85	40-47/ 54-64, 61-69/ 83-93	10-17/ 14-23	10-17/ 14-23	124-151/ 168-205	24-38/ 33-52
2.5L (151)	1985-87	18/25, 22/30‡	25/34	32/43* 36/50**	162/220	25/34
2.5L	1988-92	18/25, 26/35●, +90°	25/34	32/43* 26/35**	162/220	17/23
2.8L (173)	1983-85	70/95	13-15/ 18-34	20-30/ 27-41	48-55/ 65-75	8/10, short 15/20, long
2.8L (173)	1986-87	70/95	23/31	25/34	70/95	8/10, short 18/24, long
2.8L	1988-92	40/55, +90°	15/21	25/34	70/95	7/10, short 18/24, long
3.1L	1990-92	41/55, +90°	13/18, 19/26	24/33	70/95	89"/10
3.8L	1992	35/47 +130°⊙	88"/10, lower 22/30, upper	38/52	110/150, +76°	84"/10, short 29/39, long
4.1L (250), 4.8L (292)	1983-85	95/130■	38/52	38/52	50/70	15/20
4.1L (250), 4.8L (292)	1986-89	95/130■	38/52	38/52	50/70	15/20
4.3L (262)	1985	65/90	30/41	20/28	60/86	30/40
4.3L (262), 5.0L (305), 5.7L (350)	1986-92	65/90	35/48	26/36, center two 20/28, others	70/95	30/40
5.0L (305), 5.7L (350)	1983-85	65/90	30/40	20/28	60/81	30/40
6.2L (379) Diesel	1984-85	20/25, 50/65, +90°♦	25-37/ 34-50	18-33/ 25-45	140-162/ 190-220	25-37/ 34-50
6.2L (379) Diesel	1986-90	20/25, 50/65, +90°	31/42	26/35	85/115	30/40
7.4L (454)	1983-91	80/110	30/40	40/50, steel 18/24, iron	85/115	30/40

* Four outer bolts.
** Three inner bolts.
‡ Turn last bolt on left (number nine) to 29/40. Then turn all except number nine 120°, turn number nine 90°.
● Turn last bolt on left (number nine) to 18/25.
⊙ Turn four center bolts an additional 30°.
■ Left side, front bolt is tightened to 85/115.
♦ To 105/135 minimum.

VALVE CLEARANCE
Engine cold.

Engine	Year	Intake (inches)	Intake (mm)	Exhaust (inches)	Exhaust (mm)
1.9L (119)	1983-85	.006	.15	.010	.25
2.2L (133) Diesel	1984-85	.016	.40	.016	.40

COMPRESSION PRESSURE
At cranking speed, engine temperature normalized, throttle open.

Engine	Year	PSI	Maximum Variation PSI
4-cyl.:			
1.9L (119)	1983-85	119-170	8.5
2.2L (134) Diesel	1984-85	441	—
Others	1983-91	100 min.	*
6-cyl., V6, V8: Gasoline	1983-91	100 min.	*
Diesel	1983	275 min.	*
	1984-88	300 min.	†
	1989-92	380 min.	†

* Lowest cylinder pressure must be more than 70% of highest cylinder pressure.
† Lowest cylinder pressure must be more than 80% of highest cylinder pressure at 200 rpm minimum.

BELT TENSION
A belt operated one engine revolution is considered a used belt.

Engine	Year	Alternator	Power Steering	Air Cond.	Air Pump
Strand Tension					
USED BELTS					
2.8L (173)	1983-86	65-80	65-80	65-80	45
6.2L (379)	1983-86	70-80	70-80	90-100	—
All Others	1983-86	70-80	70-80	90-100	70-80
4.8L (292)	1987-89	90	90	90	90
V6, V8 Gasoline	1987-91	90	67	90	67
V8 Diesel	1987-91	67	67	90	—
All Serpentine	1985-91	*	*	*	—
NEW BELTS					
All	1983-86	120-130	120-130	135-145	120-130
4.8L (292)	1987-89	169	169	169	169
V6, V8 Gasoline	1987-91	135	146	169	146
V8 Diesel	1987-91	146	146	169	—
All Serpentine	1985-91	*	*	*	—

* Serpentine, automatic tensioner.

ENGINE COMPUTER SYSTEM

COMPUTER DIAGNOSTIC CODES
See UNDERHOOD SERVICE INSTRUCTIONS at the beginning of this section for test/adjustment diagrams.

Connect a jumper between A and B terminals on under dash connector (identified by a slot between the terminals, or is two upper right hand cavities on 2-row connector). Turn ignition switch on. Code 12 will flash three times, then codes in memory will be displayed. Do not run engine with jumper connected.

Remove ECM fuse for a minimum of 10 seconds to clear memory.

Code 12 No tach reference to ECM
Code 13 Oxygen sensor circuit
Code 14 Shorted coolant sensor circuit
Code 15 Open coolant sensor circuit
Code 21 Throttle position sensor circuit
Code 23 Open or ground MC solenoid (carburetted)
Code 23 MAT sensor temperature low (FI, gasoline)
Code 23 TPS not calibrated (Diesel)
Code 24 Vehicle speed sensor circuit
Code 25 MAT sensor temperature high (FI)
Code 31 MAP sensor too low (Diesel)
Code 32 Barometric or altitude sensor (carburetted)
Code 32 EGR vacuum switch circuit (FI)
Code 33 MAP sensor voltage high
Code 34 MAP or vacuum sensor circuit (carburetted)
Code 34 MAP sensor voltage low (FI)
Code 35 Idle speed control switch circuit shorted
Code 41 No distributor reference pulses to ECM
Code 42 EST or EST bypass circuit grounded or open
Code 43 ESC retard signal too long
Code 44 Air/fuel mixture lean
Codes 44 & 45 Faulty oxygen sensor
Code 45 Air/fuel mixture rich
Code 51 Faulty PROM or installation
Code 53 EGR vacuum sensor vacuum incorrect (1982-88)
Code 53 System over voltage (4-cyl.)
Code 53 Faulty PROM (V6, V8 gas)
Code 53 5 volt V-REF overload (V8 Diesel)
Code 54 Shorted MC solenoid or faulty ECM
Code 55 Grounded V-REF, faulty oxygen sensor or ECM

CHEVROLET/GMC TRUCKS
1983-92 All Models
Includes Chevrolet Lumina APV, Oldsmobile Bravada & Silhouette; Pontiac Trans Sport

UNDERHOOD SERVICE SPECIFICATIONS

GMTTU6   GMTTU6

SENSORS, INPUT

TEMPERATURE SENSORS

Engine	Year	Sensor	Resistance Ohms @ deg. F/C
All	1983-90	Coolant, Manifold Air*	13,500 @ 20/−7
			7500 @ 40/4
			3400 @ 70/20
			1800 @ 100/38
			450 @ 160/70
			185 @ 210/100
All	1991-92	Coolant, Manifold Air*	28,700 @ −4/−20
			12,300 @ 23/−5
			7200 @ 41/5
			3500 @ 68/20
			1460 @ 104/40
			470 @ 158/70
			180 @ 210/100

  * As equipped, not used on all engines.

MANIFOLD ABSOLUTE, VACUUM, AND BAROMETRIC PRESSURE SENSORS
See UNDERHOOD SERVICE INSTRUCTIONS at the beginning of this section for test/adjustment diagrams.

Engines may use one, or a combination of these sensors. All sensors appear the same. Manifold Absolute Pressure sensors have a vacuum line connected between the unit and manifold vacuum. On Barometric Pressure sensors, the line is not used and the connector is either open or has a filter installed over it. Pressure sensors also have a vacuum line between the sensor and intake manifold and only appear on carburetted models.

Barometric Pressure Sensors: Measure voltage with ignition on and engine off.

Manifold Absolute Pressure Sensors: Measure voltage with ignition on and engine off. Start engine and apply 10 in./250 mm Hg to unit, voltage should be 1.5 volts minimum less.

Pressure Sensors: Measure voltage as indicated.

5 volts reference.

Engine	Year	Sensor	Voltage @ Altitude or Condition
All, as equipped	1983-90	Barometric	3.8-5.5 @ 0-1000
			3.6-5.3 @ 1000-2000
			3.5-5.1 @ 2000-3000
			3.3-5.0 @ 3000-4000
			3.2-4.8 @ 4000-5000
			3.0-4.6 @ 5000-6000
			2.9-4.5 @ 6000-7000
			2.5-4.3 @ 7000-
All	1983-92	Manifold Abolute	1.0-1.5 idle
			4-4.8 WOT

Engine	Year	Sensor	Voltage @ Altitude
All, as equipped	1983-88	Vacuum	.50-.64 @ ign. on
			1.7-3.0*

  * 10 in./250 mm applied to unit.

SENSORS, INPUT Continued

THROTTLE POSITION SENSOR (TPS)
See UNDERHOOD SERVICE INSTRUCTIONS at the beginning of this section for test/adjustment diagrams.

Verify that idle is at specified value.

Make all checks/adjustments with engine at operating temperature.

Carburetted Models: Remove aluminum plug covering the adjustment screw. Remove the screw and connect a digital voltmeter from the TPS center terminal to the bottom terminal. Apply thread locking compound to the screw and with ignition on and engine not running (as applies), quickly adjust screw to obtain specified voltage at indicated condition.

Fuel Injected Models: Disconnect harness multi-plug from TPS. Using three six-inch jumper wires, reconnect harness to TPS. With ignition on and engine not running, connect a digital voltmeter to terminals A and B of TPS harness. If TPS is adjustable, loosen the unit retaining screws and rotate the unit to obtain the specified value.

Engine	Year	TPS Voltage† Idle	WOT
2.5L (151)	1985-91	.20-1.25*	—
2.5L	1992	.60-1.25	4.5 min.
2.8L (173)	1983-86	.26	—
2.8L (173)	1987-92	.48	—
3.1L FWD Vans	1990-92	.20-1.25	—
3.8L	1992	.40	5.1
4.3L (262) 4V	1985-86	.25	—
4.3L (262) TBI	1986-91	.20-1.25*	—
5.0L (305)	1983	.51	—
California	1983	.40	—
5.0L (305)	1984-87	.48	—
California	1984-87	.41	—
5.7L (350)	1983	.40	—
5.7L (350)	1984-87	.41	—
8-cyl. w/TBI	1988-91	.20-1.25†	4.5 min.

  † ±.10.
  * Not adjustable.

ACTUATORS, OUTPUT

IDLE SPEED CONTROL
See UNDERHOOD SERVICE INSTRUCTIONS at the beginning of this section for test/adjustment diagrams.

All engines with ISC.

Measured between terminals A & B and C & D.

Engine	Year	Resistance (ohms)
All TBI	1983-89	20 min.
All	1990-92	40-80

MIXTURE CONTROL SOLENOID-CARBURETTED ENGINES
On some engines, the ECM will be damaged if the resistance of the mixture control solenoid is less than specified.

Engine	Year	Resistance (ohms)
1.9L	1983-85	20 min.
All others	1983-89	10 min.

ENGINE IDENTIFICATION

To identify any engine by the manufacturer's code, follow the four steps designated by the numbered blocks.

1 MODEL YEAR IDENTIFICATION: Refer to illustration of Vehicle Identification Number (V.I.N.), the year is indicated by a code letter which is the 10th character of the V.I.N.

2 ENGINE CODE LOCATION: Refer to illustration of V.I.N. plate for location and designation of engine code.

3 ENGINE CODE: In the vertical "CODE" column, find the engine code determined in Step 2.

4 ENGINE IDENTIFICATION: On the line where the engine code appears, read to the right to identify the engine.

V.I.N. PLATE LOCATION:

On top left side
of instrument panel

Model year of vehicle:
1992 — Model year is N.
1991 — Model year is M.
1990 — Model year is L.
1989 — Model year is K.
1988 — Model year is J.
1987 — Model year is H.
1986 — Model year is G.
1985 — Model year is F.
1984 — Model year is E.
1983 — Model year is D.

MODEL YEAR AND ENGINE IDENTIFICATION:

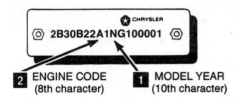

2 ENGINE CODE (8th character) **1 MODEL YEAR** (10th character)

4 ENGINE IDENTIFICATION

YEAR	3 ENGINE CODE	CYL.	DISPL. liters	DISPL. cu. in.	Fuel System	HP
1992	D	4	2.2	135	TBI	93
	A	4	2.2 T	135 T	MFI	224
	B	4	2.5	152	TBI	100
	W	4	2.5	152	TBI	100
	K	4	2.5	152	TBI	100
	J	4	2.5 T	152 T	MFI	152
	P	4	2.5 T	152 T	MFI	152
	3	6	3.0	182	MFI	141, 142†
	V	6	3.0	182	MFI	141, 142†
	U	6	3.0	182	MFI	150
	R	6	3.3	201	MFI	147, 150†
	L	6	3.8	230	MFI	150
1991	D	4	2.2	135	TBI	122
	A	4	2.2 T	135 T	MFI	224
	K	4	2.5	152	TBI	100
	J	4	2.5 T	152 T	MFI	152
	3	6	3.0	182	MFI	141
	R	6	3.3	201	MFI	147, 150†
	L	6	3.8	230	MFI	150
1990	D	4	2.2	135	TBI	93
	C	4	2.2 T	135 T	MFI	174
	K	4	2.5	152	TBI	100
	J	4	2.5 T	152 T	MFI	150
	3	6	3.0	182	MFI	141, 142†
	R	6	3.3	201	MFI	147, 150†
1989	D	4	2.2	135	TBI	93
	A	4	2.2 T	135 T	MFI	174
	K	4	2.5	152	TBI	100
	J	4	2.5 T	152 T	MFI	150
	3	6	3.0	182	MFI	141
	P, 4	8	5.2	318	2V	140
	S	8	5.2	318	4V	175
1988	D	4	2.2	135	TBI	93
	E	4	2.2 T	135 T	MFI	149
	A	4	2.2 T	135 T	MFI	174
	K	4	2.5	152	TBI	96
	3	6	3.0	182	MFI	136
	P, 4	8	5.2	318	2V	147
	S, 8	8	5.2	318	4V	175
1987	C	4	2.2	135	2V	96
	D	4	2.2	135	TBI	97
	E	4	2.2 T	135 T	MFI	146
	A	4	2.2 T	135 T	MFI	174

4 ENGINE IDENTIFICATION

YEAR	3 ENGINE CODE	CYL.	DISPL. liters	DISPL. cu. in.	Fuel System	HP
1987 Cont'd.	K	4	2.5	152	TBI	100
	G	4	2.6	156	2V	104
	3	6	3.0	182	MFI	140
	P, 4	8	5.2	318	2V	140
	S, 8	8	5.2	318	4V	175
1986	A	4	1.6	97	2V	64
	C	4	2.2	135	2V	96, 110†
	D	4	2.2	135	TBI	97
	E	4	2.2 T	135 T	MFI	145
	K	4	2.5	152	TBI	100
	G	4	2.6	156	2V	104
	P	8	5.2	318	2V	140
	R, S	8	5.2	318	4V	175
1985	A	4	1.6	97	2V	64
	C	4	2.2	135	2V	96, 110†
	D	4	2.2	135	TBI	99
	E	4	2.2 T	135 T	MFI	145
	G	4	2.6	156	2V	99, 101†
	P	8	5.2	318	2V	140
	R, S	8	5.2	318	4V	175
1984	A	4	1.6	97	2V	64
	C	4	2.2	135	2V	96, 110†
	D	4	2.2	135	TBI	99
	E	4	2.2 T	135 T	MFI	142
	G	4	2.6	156	2V	101
	P	8	5.2	318	2V	130
	R, S	8	5.2	318	4V	165
1983	A	4	1.6	97	2V	62
	B	4	1.7	105	2V	63
	C	4	2.2	135	2V	94
	D	4	2.2	135	TBI	97
	G	4	2.6	156	2V	93
	H, J	6	3.7	225	1V	90
	K, L	6	3.7	225	2V	N/A
	P	8	5.2	318	2V	130
	N	8	5.2	318	TBI	140
	R, S	8	5.2	318	4V	165

T — Turbocharged.   TBI — Throttle Body Injection.
MFI — Multiport Fuel Injection.   1V — One Venturi Carburetor.
2V — Two Venturi Carburetor.   4V — Four Venturi Carburetor.
† Engine horsepower varies with model installation.

UNDERHOOD SERVICE SPECIFICATIONS

CRTU1

CYLINDER NUMBER SEQUENCE

CRTU1

4-CYL. FIRING ORDER:
1 3 4 2

V6 FIRING ORDER:
1 2 3 4 5 6

6-CYL. FIRING ORDER:
1 5 3 6 2 4

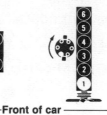

8-CYL. FIRING ORDER:
1 8 4 3 6 5 7 2

— Front of car —

1983-86 1.6L (97)	1983 1.7L (105)	1989-92 2.2L 16V DOHC Turbo

— Front of car —

2.2L (135) ex. 16V DOHC, 2.5L (153)	1983-87 2.6L (156)

— Front of car —

1987-92 3.0L (183)	3.3L, 3.8L	1983 3.7L (225)	1983-89 5.2L (318)

— TIMING MARK —

1983-86 1.6L (97) when viewed at drive belt end of engine

1989-92 2.2L, 2.5L w/AT, 2.2L DOHC Turbo w/MT

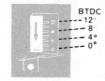

1983 1.7L (105) w/MT, 1983-89 2.2L (135), 2.5L (153) w/MT ex. 2.2L DOHC Turbo

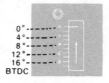

1983 1.6L (97) when viewed at bellhousing, 1983-88 2.2L (135) w/AT

2.6L (156)

3.0L (183)

No Timing Marks on Engine

3.3L, 3.8L

1983 3.7L (225)

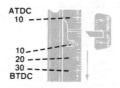

1983-85 5.2L (318), 5.9L 360

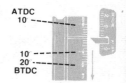

1986-89 5.2L (318)

ELECTRICAL AND IGNITION SYSTEMS

BATTERY

Engine	Year	STANDARD BCI Group No.	STANDARD Crank. Perf.	OPTIONAL BCI Group No.	OPTIONAL Crank. Perf.
1.6L (97)	1983-86	26	335	25	430
Canada	1985-86	25	430	—	500
1.7L (105)	1983	26	335	25*	430
2.2L (135) Aries, Reliant	1983-85	26	335	24*	500
2.2L (135) Aries, Reliant	1986	26	335	34	400
2.2L (135) Lancer, LeBaron, GTS, 400, Caravelle	1983-85	26	335	24	500
w/RWD	1983-84	25	430	24	500
w/RWD & Canada	1985-86	34	400	34	500
2.2L (135) E-Class, 600	1983-85	25	370	24	500
2.2L (135) Aries, Reliant	1986	34	400	34	500
2.2L (135) FI, TBI	1983-85	24	500	—	—
2.2L (135) Omni, Horizon	1983-85	26	335	25*	430
2.2L (135) Mini-Vans	1986	26	335	34	400
Canada	1986	34	400	—	—
2.2L (135) Aries, Reliant	1987	26	335	34	400
Turbo models	1987	34	400	34	500
All Others	1987	26	335	25	370

BATTERY Continued

Engine	Year	STANDARD BCI Group No.	STANDARD Crank. Perf.	OPTIONAL BCI Group No.	OPTIONAL Crank. Perf.
2.2L (135) TBI	1988-90	34	400	—	—
2.2L TBI	1991	34	500	—	—
2.2L (135) Turbo	1988-91	34	500	—	—
2.5L (153) All Models	1986-87	34	400	34	500
2.5L (153) All Models	1988-90	34	500	—	—
2.5L	1991	34	625	—	—
2.6L (156)	1983	25	370	24*	500
2.6L (156)	1984-85	26	335	25	430
w/RWD	1984-85	25	430	24	500
2.6L (156) Mini-Vans	1986	26	335	34	500
Canada	1986	34	400	34	500
3.0L (183)	1987	34	400	—	—
3.0L (183)	1988-90	34	500	—	—
3.0L	1991	34	500	—	—
Chrysler Models	1991	34	625	—	—
Monaco	1991	34	625	—	—
Stealth SOHC	1991	25	420	24	585
DOHC	1991	24	490	24	585
3.3L	1990-91	34	500	—	—
Chrysler Models	1991	34	625	—	—
3.7L (225)	1983	25	430	24	500
3.8L	1991	34	625	—	—
5.2L (318)	1983-85	25	430	24	500
Imperial	1983	24	500	—	—
5.2L (318)	1985-87	34	400	34	500
5.2L (318)	1988-89	34	500	34	625

* Check hood clearance.

UNDERHOOD SERVICE SPECIFICATIONS

CRTU2   CRTU2

ALTERNATOR

See UNDERHOOD SERVICE INSTRUCTIONS at the beginning of this section for test/adjustment diagrams.

With 15 volts at alternator and at 1250 rpm unless otherwise specified.

Application	Year	Rated Output (amps)	Test Output (amps @ rpm)
Bosch alt.	1984-86	65	50
	1989-91	75	68
	1984-86	90	78-85 @ 1000
	1989-92	90	84-88
	1988	35/75	30
	1984-86	40/90	87
	1987-88	40/90	40
	1984-86	40/100	87
Chrysler alt.			
Yellow tag	1983-87	60	45
Brown tag	1983-87	78	56
Yellow tag	1983-87	114	97
	1984-88	40/90	87
	1984-88	50/120	98
Delco alt. (Monaco)	1990-91	85	70 @ 2000
	1990-91	96	78 @ 2000
	1990-91	105	84 @ 2000
Mitsubishi alt.	1990	65	46 @ 2500
	1983-87	75	63-70 @ 1000
	1990	75	53 @ 2500
	1986-87	90	80-91 @ 1000
Nippondenso alt.	1989-92	75	68
4-cyl.	1989-92	90	87
V6	1989-92	90	90
	1989-92	120	98
	1987-88	40/90	87

REGULATOR

Application	Test Temp. (deg. F/C)	Voltage Setting
1983-87 Chrysler, not computer regulated	−20/−29	14.9-15.9
	80/27	13.9-14.6
	140/60	13.3-13.9
	Above 140/60	Less than 13.9
1983-87 Mitsubishi	68/20	14.1-14.7
1984-85 Bosch	77/25	13.8-14.2
1990-91 Monaco	—	13.5-16.0
1985-89 Computer regulated	—	14.5-15.0
1990-92 Computer regulated	0-50/−18 to 10	14.5-15.0
	50-100/10-38	13.9-14.5
	100-150/38-66	13.8-14
	150-200/66-93	13.8 max.

STARTER

Engine at operating temperature.

Engine	Year	Cranking Voltage (min. volts)	Ampere Draw @ Cranking Speed
4-cyl.:			
1.6L (97), 1.7L (105)	1983-85	7.5	120-160
2.2L (135)	1983-86	7.5	120-160
2.6L (156)	1983-84	—	150-210
2.6L (156)	1985-86	7.5	120-160
4-cyl., V6	1987	7.5	150-220
All Others	1983-87	9.5	180-200
All ex. Monaco	1988-92	7.5	150-220
Monaco	1990-91	9.6	250 max.

SPARK PLUGS

Engine	Year	Gap (inches)	Gap (mm)	Torque (ft-lb)
2.2L (135), 2.5L (153)	1983-89	.035	.89	20
2.2L, 2.5L	1990-92	.033-.038	.8-.9	20
2.6L (156)	1983	.041	1.04	20
2.6L (156)	1984-87	.035-.040	.89-1.02	20
3.0L (183)	1987-92	.039-.043	1.0-1.1	20
3.3L, 3.8L	1990-92	.048-.053	1.2-1.3	20
3.7L (225)	1983	.035	.89	10
5.2L (318) Others	1983-89	.035	.89	30

IGNITION COIL

See UNDERHOOD SERVICE INSTRUCTIONS at the beginning of this section for test/adjustment diagrams.

Application	Year	Windings	Resistance (ohms)
Prestolite	1983-84	Primary	1.60-1.79
		Secondary	9400-11,700
	1985-91	Primary	1.34-1.55
		Secondary	9400-11,700
Essex, Echlin	1983-91	Primary	1.34-1.62
		Secondary	9000-12,200
Mitsubishi 2.6L	1983-87	Primary	.70-.85
		Secondary	9000-11,000
Diamond: Oil filled	1988-91	Primary	1.34-1.55
		Secondary	15,000-19,000
Epoxy	1990-92	Primary	.97-1.18
		Secondary	11,000-15,300
Diamond: 2.2L Turbo, 3.3L, 3.8L DIS	1990-92	Primary	.52-.63†
		Secondary	11,600-15,800††
Marshal 3.3L DIS	1990	Primary	.53-.65†
		Secondary	7000-9000††
Toyodenso 4-cyl.	1991-92	Primary	.95-1.20
		Secondary	11,300-13,300
V6	1990-92	Primary	.51-.61
		Secondary	11,500-13,500

† Measured between B+ (upper right) and each of the other three terminals on four wire coil connector.

†† Measured between high voltage terminals of each bank of coils with spark plug wires removed.

DISTRIBUTOR PICKUP

See UNDERHOOD SERVICE INSTRUCTIONS at the beginning of this section for test/adjustment diagrams.

Application	Resistance (ohms)	Air Gap (in./mm)
Distributor without Hall Effect		
1983-89 6- & 8-cyl. single pickup	150-900	.006/.15
1983-89 6- & 8-cyl. dual pickups:		
Start	150-900	.006/.15
Run	150-900	.012/.30
1983-86 2.6L (156)	920-1120	—

IGNITION RESISTOR

See UNDERHOOD SERVICE INSTRUCTIONS at the beginning of this section for test/adjustment diagrams.

Engine	Type	Resistance (ohms)	Temperature (deg. F/C)
All w/EI	1983	1.12-1.38	70-80/ 21-27
5.2L (318) FI	1983	1.12-1.38 Coil side	70-80/ 21-27

BASE TIMING

See UNDERHOOD SERVICE INSTRUCTIONS at the beginning of this section for test/adjustment diagrams.

Set timing at Before Top Dead Center and at slow idle unless otherwise specified.

1990-92 1.8L, 2.0L: Ground ignition timing connector and adjust timing. Remove ground and verify that timing is at ''Check'' specification.

All others: Disconnect and plug vacuum hoses at distributor or ESC (Electronic Spark Control) unit, as equipped. W/FI, disconnect coolant temperature sensor.

Engine	Year	Man. Trans. (degrees)	Auto. Trans. (degrees)
1.6L (97)	1983-86	12 ±2	12 ±2
1.7L (105)	1983	20♦ ±2	12 ±2
2.2L (135) 2V	1983-87	10 ±2	10 ±2
Canada w/decal 154	1983	12 ±2	12 ±2
High Altitude	1983	6 ±2	6 ±2
Vans	1986-87	6 ±2	6 ±2
2.2L (135) HO	1983-86	15 ±2	—
2.2L (135) TBI	1983-84	6 ±2	6 ±2
2.2L (135) TBI	1985-92	12 ±2	12 ±2
2.2L (135) Turbo	1984-90	12 ±2	12 ±2
2.5L (153)	1986-92	12 ±2	12 ±2

BASE TIMING Continued

Engine	Year	Man. Trans. (degrees)	Auto. Trans. (degrees)
2.6L (156)	1983-87	—	7 ±2
High Altitude	1986-87	—	12 ±2
3.0L (183) ex. Monaco	1987-92	12 ±2	12 ±2
3.7L (225)	1983	16 ±2	16 ±2
Canada	1983	—	12 ±2
5.2L (318) 2V	1983-84	—	16† ±2
5.2L (318) 2V	1985-89	—	7 ±2
Canada	1985-87	—	12 ±2
5.2L (318) 4V	1983-89	—	16 ±2
5.2L (318) FI	1983	—	12 ±2

† If equipped with 3-port vacuum switch on driver's side front of intake manifold, set to 12°.

♦ With module 4318113, set to 12°.

DISTRIBUTOR TIMING ADVANCE

Engine degrees at engine rpm, no load, in addition to basic timing setting.

Engine	Trans-mission	Year	Distributor Number	Degrees @ 2500 RPM Total	Degrees @ 2500 RPM Centrifugal
2.6L (156)	AT	1983	4243694, 707	28.2-36.2	10.2-14.2
2.6L (156)	AT	1983	4243708	23.2-31.2	10.2-14.2
2.6L (156)	AT	1984-87	4243251	20.5-28.5	7.5-11.5
2.6L (156)	AT	1984-87	4243134, 792	25.5-33.5	7.5-11.5
3.7L (225)	AT	1983	4145612, 717	24.4-32.4	4.4-8.4

FUEL SYSTEM

FUEL SYSTEM PRESSURE

See UNDERHOOD SERVICE INSTRUCTIONS at the beginning of this section for test/adjustment diagrams.

FI, with vacuum hose connected to fuel pressure regulator.

Engine	Year	Pressure PSI	Pressure RPM
4-cyl.			
All carburetted	1983-87	4.5-6.0	idle
TBI	1983-84	34-38	idle
TBI	1985-91 (early)	13.5-15.5	idle
TBI	1991-92 (late)	38-40	idle
EFI Turbo	1984-86	51-55	idle
EFI Turbo	1987-92	53-57	idle
6-cyl.			
All	1983	4.0-5.5	idle
All	1987-92	46-50	idle
8-cyl.			
5.2L (318), 5.9L (360)	1983-89	5.8-7.3	idle
FI	1983	7.5-11.5	—

IDLE SPEED W/O COMPUTER CONTROL

Label Number: Refers to last two large digits of part number on the left side of label.

Specifications on emissions label must be used if different from those given.

1983-86 If idle speed changes after switches and vacuum hoses are reconnected do not readjust.

4-cyl. 1.6L (97), 1.7L (105), 2.2L (135) 2V: 1983-86 Remove PCV valve from grommet.

1984-87 Disconnect oxygen system test connector located on left fender shield on feedback equipped carbs.

Disconnect and plug EGR and distributor or Spark Control Computer (SCC) vacuum hoses.

Disconnect radiator fan switch and install a jumper between the female terminals.

Ground the carb idle stop switch.

1983 with AC: Remove adjusting screw and spring on top of solenoid. Switch AC unit on and set blower to low. When compressor clutch is cycling, adjust idle speedup speed to specification. Turn AC unit off and replace adjusting screw and spring with engine not running. De-energize radiator fan and start engine, adjust idle speed to specification.

IDLE SPEED W/O COMPUTER CONTROL Continued

1983 without AC: Set idle speed to specification. Electrically disconnect solenoid and set shutdown speed to specification.

1984-87 Set idle speed to specification, remove red wire from 6-way connector on carb side and set shutdown idle speed to specification.

To set fast idle, place fast idle cam on specified step and adjust fast idle speed to specification.

4-cyl. 2.6L (156):

1984 With feedback control, start engine and disconnect oxygen sensor.

1985-87 With feedback control, remove idle switch electrical connector.

All models, set idle speed to specification.

With AC, turn unit on and set speedup speed to spec. with compressor cycling.

6- & 8-cyl.:

1983-87 Disconnect and plug canister control hose and disconnect oxygen sensor electrical lead.

Disconnect and plug EGR, distributor of SCC vacuum hoses. Air cleaner may be removed but plug the air cleaner vacuum hose and leave the SCC electrical leads connected. Ground carb idle stop switch.

With AC, turn unit on and disconnect the compressor clutch electrical lead. Set speedup speed to specification. Turn AC unit off and set idle speed to specification. 1985-86 Remove adjusting screw and spring on solenoid, insert an allen wrench to adjust.

Without AC, set idle speed to specification.

Engine	Year	SLOW Man. Trans.	SLOW Auto. Trans.	FAST Man. Trans.	FAST Auto. Trans.	Step of Cam
1.6L (97)	1983	800	1000 N	1400	1600 N	Low
shutdown idle	1983	700	700 N			
1.6L (97)	1984-86	850	1000 N	1400	1600 N	Low
shutdown idle	1984-86	700	700 N			
Canada	1986	850	—	1200	—	Low
shutdown idle	1986	700	—			
1.7L (105)	1983	850	900 N	1400	1400 N	Low
shutdown idle	1983	700	700 N			
speed-up	1983	850	900 N			
2.2L (135) 2V ex. HO	1983	775	900 N	1400	1500 N	Low
w/decal 171	1983	—	900 N	—	1600 N	Low
High Altitude	1983	900	850 N	1350	1375 N	Low
w/decal 170, 264	1983	—	850 N	—	1275 N	Low
shutdown idle	1983	—	700 N			
Canada	1983	900	900 N	1400	1400 N	Low
w/decal 154	1983	950	—	1400	—	Low
shutdown idle	1983	700	700 N			
2.2L (135) 2V ex. HO	1984	800	900 N	1700	1850 N	Low
High Altitude	1984	800	900 N	1500	1600 N	Low
Rampage, Vans	1984	850	1000 N	1500	1700 N	Low
Omni, Horizon	1984	800	900 N	1500	1600 N	Low
High Altitude	1984	800	900 N	1700	1850 N	Low
California	1984	800	900 N	1500	1600 N	Low
w/VOS	1984	800	900 N	1700	1850 N	Low
Rampage	1984	800	900 N	1700	1850 N	Low
shutdown idle, all	1984	600	600 N			
Canada	1984	900	900 N	1700	1850 N	Low
Leaded fuel	1984	800	900 N	1500	1700 N	Low
shutdown idle	1984	700	700 N			
2.2L (135) 2V ex. HO	1985	800	900 N	1700	1850 N	Low
shutdown idle	1985	700	700 N			
Canada	1985	900	900 N	1700	1850 N	Low
shutdown idle	1985	700	700 N			
2.2L (135) 2V ex. HO	1986	800	900 N	1700	1850 N	Low
w/decal 941	1986	900	—			
Vans	1986	850	900 N	1700	1850 N	Low
shutdown idle, all	1986	700	700 N			
w/decal 939, 940	1986	800	—	1800	—	Low
shutdown idle	1986	700	—			
Canada	1986	900	900 N	1700	1850 N	Low
Vans	1986	850	900 N	1700	1850 N	Low
shutdown idle, all	1986	700	700 N			
2.2L (135) 2V	1987	800	900 N	1800	1950 N	Low
shutdown idle	1987	700	700 N			
w/decal 593	1987	900	900 N	1700	1850 N	Low
shutdown idle	1987	700	700 N			
Vans	1987	800	900 N	1700	1850 N	Low
shutdown idle	1987	700	700 N			

IDLE SPEED W/O COMPUTER CONTROL Continued

Engine	Year	SLOW Man. Trans.	SLOW Auto. Trans.	FAST Man. Trans.	FAST Auto. Trans.	Step of Cam
2.2L (135) 2V HO	1983	900	—	1400	—	Low
2.2L (135) 2V HO	1984	850	—	1700	—	Low
California	1984	850	—	1600	—	Low
shutdown idle, all	1984	600	—			
2.2L (135) 2V HO	1985	900	—	1700	—	Low
shutdown idle	1985	700	—			
2.2L (135) 2V HO	1986	850	—	1700	—	Low
shutdown idle	1986	700	—			
2.6L (156)	1983	—	800 N	—	—	—
speed-up	1983	—	900 N	—	—	—
2.6L (156)	1984-85	—	800 N	—	950 N	—
w/decal 842, 843, 875, 885	1984-85	—	800 N	—	950 N	—
speed-up	1984-85	—	900 N			
Canada	1984-85	—	800 N	—	1300 N	—
speed-up	1984-85	—	900 N			
2.6L (156)	1986	—	800 N	—	1300 N	—
speed-up	1986	—	900 N			
High Altitude	1986	—	850 N	—	950 N	—
speed-up	1986	—	900 N			
Canada	1986	—	600 N	—	950 N	—
speed-up	1986	—	900 N			
2.6L (153)	1987	—	850 N	—	950 N	—
w/decal 506	1987	—	800 N	—	1300 N	—
w/decal 942	1987	—	850 N	—	1300 N	—
AC speed-up	1987	—	900 N			
California	1987	—	800 N	—	950 N	—
AC speed-up	1987	—	900 N			
Canada	1987	—	800 N	—	1300 N	—
AC speed-up	1987	—	900 N			
3.7L (225) 1V	1983	—	725 N	—	2000 N	2nd high
solenoid	1983	—	900 N			
3.7L (225) 2V Canada	1983	—	750 N	—	1600 N	Second
w/decal 163	1983	—	700 N	—	1600 N	Second
solenoid	1983	—	900 N			
5.2L (318) 2V	1983	—	650 N	—	1400 N	Second
solenoid	1983	—	900 N			
California	1983	—	600 N	—	1400 N	Second
solenoid	1983	—	900 N			
Canada	1983	—	730 N	—	1500 N	Second
5.2L (318) 2V	1984	—	675 N	—	1400 N	Second
solenoid	1984	—	850 N			
Canada	1984	—	730 N	—	1500 N	Second
5.2L (318) 2V	1985	—	680 N	—	1700 N	Low
solenoid	1985	—	850 N			
Canada	1985	—	730 N	—	1600 N	Low
5.2L (318) 2V	1986-89	—	630 N	—	1700 N	Second
solenoid	1986-89	—	775 N			
Canada	1986-87	—	730 N	—	1600 N	Second
Solenoid	1986-87	—	850 N			
5.2L (318) 4V	1983-84	—	650 N	—	1400 N	Second
solenoid	1983-84	—	850 N			
5.2L (318) 4V	1985-86	—	750 N	—	1450 N	Second
solenoid	1985-86	—	800 N			
5.2L (318) 4V	1987	—	650 N	—	1450 N	Second
w/decal 549, 946	1987	—	750 N	—	1450 N	Second
solenoid	1987	—	900 N			
5.2L (318) 4V	1988-89	—	750 N	—	1450 N	Second
solenoid	1988-89	—	900 N			

VOS Vacuum Operated Secondary.

IDLE SPEED W/COMPUTER CONTROL

See UNDERHOOD SERVICE INSTRUCTIONS at the beginning of this section for test/adjustment diagrams.

Idle speed must be within 100 rpm of specification listed.

1983-84 4-cyl., with engine at operating temperature and not running, install a jumper wire to make fan run continuously. Remove brown wire with white tracer from throttle body 6-way connector. Start engine and apply battery voltage for 5 seconds to wire to fully close AIS. Place transmission in drive and adjust idle stop on throttle body to specification. Reconnect the AIS wire and verify checking speed is at specified value.

IDLE SPEED W/COMPUTER CONTROL Continued

1986-92 4-cyl.; V6: With TBI, remove PCV valve and install special tool C-5004 (0.125" orifice) into hose. With MFI, disconnect idle purge line from throttle body. Start engine and using Diagnostic Readout Box, access "Minimum Airflow Idle Speed." If checking speed is not within specification range, replace the throttle body.

1983 V8: With engine at operating temperature, turn ignition on and start engine. Throttle arm of AIS motor should rotate so that it is pointing towards the front of the engine. Adjust screw on end of AIS motor linkage to specification.

Engine	Year	Transmission	Setting Speed	Checking Speed	Idle Speed
2.2L (135) TBI	1983	AT	650-675 N	—	—
2.2L (135) TBI	1984	MT	790-810	—	850
2.2L (135) TBI	1984	AT	715-735 N	—	700 N
2.2L (135) TBI	1985	MT	—	—	850
2.2L (135) TBI	1985	AT	—	—	750 N
2.2L (135) TBI	1986	MT	—	1100-1300	900
2.2L (135) TBI	1986	AT	—	1100-1300 N	700 N
W/decal 974, 995, 998	1986	AT	—	1100-1300 N	725 D
2.2L (135) TBI	1987	MT	—	1100-1300	900
2.2L (135) TBI	1987	AT	—	1100-1300 N	900 N
California w/decal 143, 144, 145, 146, 147, 537	1987	AT	—	1100-1300 N	900 N
w/decal 897, 997	1987	AT	—	1100-1300 N	725 D
Canada	1987	AT	—	1100-1300 N	700 N
w/decal 945, 98	1987	AT	—	1100-1300 N	725 D
2.2L (135) TBI	1988-90	MT	—	1100-1300	850
2.2L (135) TBI	1988-90	AT	—	1100-1300 N	850 N
2.2L TBI	1991-92	MT	—	1100-1300	—
2.2L TBI	1991-92	AT	—	1100-1300 N	—
2.2L (135) Turbo	1984	MT	750-800	—	950
2.2L (135) Turbo	1984	AT	750-800 N	—	800 N
2.2L (135) Turbo	1985	MT	900-950	—	900
2.2L (135) Turbo	1985	AT	900-950 N	—	800 N
2.2L (135) Turbo	1986-87	MT	—	650-900	900
2.2L (135) Turbo	1986-87	AT	—	650-900 N	800 N
w/decal 594, 595	1987	AT	—	650-900 N	900 N
2.2L (135) Turbo†	1987	MT	—	650-900	900
2.2L (135) Turbo†	1987	AT	—	650-900 N	900 N
2.2L (135) Turbo	1988-89	MT	—	650-900	900
2.2L (135) Turbo	1988-89	AT	—	650-900 N	900 N
2.2L Turbo	1990	MT	—	650-1050	950
2.2L Turbo	1990	AT	—	650-1050 N	900 N
2.2L Turbo	1991	MT	—	550-900	—
2.2L Turbo	1992	MT	—	650-1150	—
2.5L (153) TBI	1986	MT	—	1050-1250	900
2.5L (153) TBI	1986	AT	—	1050-1250 N	700 D
w/decal 975, 996, 999	1986	AT	—	1050-1250 N	725 D
2.5L (153) TBI	1987	MT	—	1050-1250	900
2.5L (153) TBI	1987	AT	—	1050-1250 N	900 N
w/decal 999	1987	AT	—	1050-1250 N	725 D
2.5L (153) TBI	1988-91	MT	—	1050-1250	850
2.5L (153) TBI	1988-91	AT	—	1050-1250 N	850 N
2.5L Turbo	1989	MT	—	650-900	900
2.5L Turbo	1989	AT	—	650-900 N	900 N
2.5L Turbo	1990-91	MT	—	650-1200	—
2.5L Turbo	1990-91	AT	—	650-1200 N	—
2.5L Turbo	1992	MT	—	700-1400	—
2.5L Turbo	1992	AT	—	700-1400 N	—
3.0L (183)	1987	AT	—	850-1050 N	700 N
California	1987	AT	—	850-1050 N	750 N
Canada	1987	AT	—	850-1050 N	800 N
3.0L (183)	1988	AT	—	850-1050 N	800 N
3.0L	1989	AT	—	850-1050 N	700 N
Vans	1989	AT	—	850-1050 N	800 N
3.0L	1989-90	MT	—	750-950	800
3.0L	1989-90	AT	—	750-950 N	700 N
3.0L ex. Monaco	1991-92	MT	—	750-950	—
	1991-92	AT	—	750-950 N	—
3.3L, 3.8L	1990	AT	—	700-950 N	750 N
3.3L, 3.8L	1991-92	AT	—	700-950 N	—
5.2L (318) FI	1983	AT	530-630 D	—	—

† With intercooler.

ENGINE MECHANICAL

TIGHTENING TORQUES
See UNDERHOOD SERVICE INSTRUCTIONS at the beginning of this section for test/adjustment diagrams.

Some torque values are specified in inches.

Engine	Year	Cylinder Head	Intake Manifold	Exhaust Manifold	Crankshaft Pulley	Water Pump
				Torque Ft-lbs/Nm		
1.6L (97)	1983-86	52/70	45/61	45/61	100-136	30/41
1.7L (105)	1983	60/82, +90°	200″/23	200″/23	20/25	250″/28
2.2L (135), 2.5L (153)	1983-92	45/61, 65/89, 65/89, +90°†	200″/23	200″/23	20/25	250″/28-upper 3 40/54-lower 1
2.6L (156)	1983-87	69/94*, 76/103**	150″/17	150″/17	87/118	204″/23
3.0L (183) ex. Monaco	1987-90	70/95*	174″/20	191″/22	110/150	240″/27
3.0L ex. Monaco	1991-92	80/108*	174″/20	200″/22	110/150	23/27
3.0L Monaco	1990-91	●	11/15	13/18	133/180	20/27
3.3L, 3.8L	1990-92	45/61, 65/89, 65/89, +90°	200″/23	200″/23	40/54	105″/12
3.7L (225)	1983	70/95	200″/23-bolts 240″/27-nuts		—	30/41
5.2L (318)	1983-84	95/130	45/61	20/27-bolts 15/20-nuts	100/136	30/41
5.2L (318)	1985-86	105/143	45/61	20/27-bolts 15/20-nuts	100/136	30/41
5.2L (318)	1987-88	105/143	35/47	20/27-bolts 15/20-nuts	100/136	30/41
5.2L (318)	1989	105/143	40/54	20/27-bolts 15/20-nuts	100/136	30/41

* Cold.
** Hot.
† Torque should be above 90/122 after this step or replace bolt.
● Tighten to 44/60, loosen each bolt individually and retorque to 30/40. Turn an additional 160-200°.

VALVE CLEARANCE
Engine hot.

Engine	Year	Intake (inches)	Intake (mm)	Exhaust (inches)	Exhaust (mm)
1.6L (97)	1983-86	.012	.30	.014	.35
1.7L (105)	1983	.008-.012	.20-.30	.016-.020	.41-.51
2.6L (156)	1983-84	.006†	.15	.010	.25
2.6L (156)	1985-87	.006	.15	.010†	.25†

† Includes jet valve.

COMPRESSION PRESSURE
At cranking speed, engine temperature normalized, throttle open.

Engine	Year	PSI	Maximum Variation PSI
4-cyl.	1983-84	100 min.	25
2.2L (135)	1983-84	130-150	20
2.6L (156)	1983-84	149	15
4-cyl.	1985-91	100 min.	*
2.6L (156)	1985-87	149	15
V6: 3.0L ex. Monaco	1987-91	178	14
3.0L Monaco, 3.3L, 3.8L	1990-91	100 min.	*
6-cyl.	1983	100 min.	25
8-cyl.	1983-84	100 min.	40
8-cyl.	1985-89	100 min.	25

* Lowest cylinder must be 75% of highest.

BELT TENSION
A belt in operation 15 minutes is considered a used belt.

Engine	Year	Alternator	Power Steering or Idler	Air Cond.	Air Pump
Strand Tension					
1.6L (97) new	1983-85	115	95	95	95
1.6L (97) used	1983-85	80	70	70	70
1.6L (97) new	1986	95	105	—	105
1.6L (97) used	1986	60	70	—	70
1.7L (105) new	1983	65	80	90	70
1.7L (105) used	1983	40	50	45	40
2.2L (135) new	1983	110	75	40	45
2.2L (135) used	1983	80	55	30	35
2.2L (135) new	1984-92	105	95	95	—
2.2L (135) used	1984-92	80	80	80	—
2.5L (153) new	1986-92	115	105	105	—
2.5L (153) used	1986-92	80	80	80	—
2.6L (156) new	1983	—	110	—	—
2.6L (156) used	1983	—	75	—	—
2.6L (156) new	1984-85	115	95	115	—
2.6L (156) used	1984-85	80	80	80	—
V6 3.0L ex. Monaco new	1987-92	*	*	125	—
V6 3.0L ex. Monaco used	1987-92	*	*	80	—
V6 3.0L Monaco new	1990-91	180-200	180-200	180-200	—
V6 3.0L Monaco used	1990-91	140-160	140-160	140-160	—
V6 3.3L, 3.8L	1990-92	*	*	*	—
6- & 8-cyl. new	1983-88	120	120	120	120
6- & 8-cyl. used	1983-88	70	70	70	70
Deflection†					
1.6L (97) new	1983-86	1/4″	1/4″	1/4″	1/4″
1.6L (97) used	1983-86	5/16″	5/16″	5/16″	5/16″
1.7L (105) new	1983	1/8″	1/4″	—	3/16″
1.7L (105) used	1983	1/4″	5/16″	—	7/32″
2.2L (135) new	1983	1/8″	1/4″	5/16″	7/32″
2.2L (135) used	1983	1/4″	7/16″	3/8″	1/4″
2.2L (135) new	1984-90	1/8″	5/16″	5/16″	3/16″
2.2L (135) used	1984-90	1/4″	7/16″	7/16″	1/4″
2.5L (153) new	1986-90	1/8″	1/4″	5/16″	1/4″
2.5L (153) used	1986-90	1/4″	7/16″	7/16″	3/16″
2.6L (156) new	1983	3/16″	1/4″	1/4″	5/16″
2.6L (156) used	1983	1/4″	3/8″	5/16″	3/8″
2.6L (156) new	1984-87	3/16″	1/4″	1/4″	—
2.6L (156) used	1984-87	1/4″	3/8″	5/16″	—
3.0L (183) ex. Monaco	1987-91	*	*	1/4″-5/16″	—
3.3L, 3.8L	1990-91	*	*	*	—
6- & 8-cyl. all	1983-89	—	—	—	—

† At 10 lb of force on midpoint of belt.
* Serpentine belt with automatic tensioner.

ENGINE COMPUTER SYSTEM

COMPUTER DIAGNOSTIC CODES
See UNDERHOOD SERVICE INSTRUCTIONS at the beginning of this section for test/adjustment diagrams.

1983-92 FI: Turn ignition switch on-off-on-off-on and observe POWER LOSS or CHECK ENGINE light on instrument panel.

1985-87 1.6L 2V, 2.2L 2V: Connect Digital Readout Box (DRB) to diagnostic connector. Place idle speed screw on high step of cam and turn ignition to ''Run'' position with engine off.

1985-87 1.6L 2V, 2.2L 2V:
Code 11 Mixture control solenoid
Code 13 Canister purge solenoid
Code 14 Power to computer memory
Code 17 Throttle control solenoid
Code 18 Vacuum operated secondary control solenoid
Code 21 Distributor pickup
Code 22 Oxygen sensor
Code 24 Computer vacuum transducer
Code 25 Radiator fan temp. sensor
Code 26 Coolant temp. sensor
Code 28 Speed sensor
Code 31 Power to computer interrupted
Codes 32, 33 Computer failure
Code 55 End of message
Code 88 Start of message

UNDERHOOD SERVICE SPECIFICATIONS

CRTU6   CRTU6

COMPUTER DIAGNOSTIC CODES Continued

2.2L (135), 2.5L (153) TBI & Turbo
Code 11 Ignition reference circuit
Code 12 Standby memory (1983-90)
Code 13 MAP sensor vacuum circuit
Code 14 MAP sensor electrical circuit
Code 15 Speed/distance sensor
Code 16 Battery voltage loss (1984-89)
Code 17 Engine running too cool
Code 21 Oxygen sensor
Code 22 Coolant temperature sensor
Code 23 Throttle body temperature sensor (1983-90 TBI)
Code 23 Charge temperature circuit MFI, 1991 TBI
Code 24 Throttle position sensor
Code 25 Automatic idle speed control circuit
Code 26 Peak injector current not reached (1984-87 TBI, 1988-90)
Code 26 Number one injector circuit MFI
Code 27 Fuel injector circuit control
Code 27 Number two injector circuit (1984-87 MFI)

Code 31 Canister purge solenoid
Code 32 Power loss lamp
Code 33 Air conditioner WOT relay (1983-88)
Code 33 Air conditioner clutch relay (1989-91)
Code 34 EGR solenoid circuit (1983-87)
Code 34 Speed control solenoid driver circuit (1988-91)
Codes 34 & 36 Spare driver circuit
Code 35 Fan control relay circuit
Code 36 Wastegate solenoid circuit
Code 37 Shift indicator lamp ex. MFI (1983-88)
Code 37 Barometric read solenoid circuit MFI (1983-88)
Code 37 Torque converter part throttle unlock solenoid circuit (1989-91)
Code 41 Charging system over voltage (1984-91)
Code 41 Alternator field circuit (1990-91)
Code 42 Automatic shutdown relay circuit
Code 43 Interface circuit between Logic and Power modules (1983-87)
Code 43 Spark interface circuit (1988-89)
Code 43 Ignition coil circuit (1990-91 3.3L)
Code 44 Logic module (1983-84)
Code 44 Battery temperature out of range (1985-87)
Code 44 Loss of voltage to logic board (1988-89)
Code 45 Boost limit exceeded
Code 46 Battery voltage too high
Code 47 Battery voltage too low
Code 51 Closed loop fail system circuit (1983-84)
Code 51 Oxygen sensor lean (1985-87)
Code 52 Logic module (1983-84)
Code 52 Oxygen sensor rich (1985-87)
Code 53 Logic module (1983-88)
Code 53 Internal engine controller fault (1989)
Code 54 Distributor sync pick-up circuit
Code 55 End of message
Code 61 Baro read solenoid
Code 62 EMR mileage accumulator circuit
Code 63 Fault code error (1983-90)
Code 63 Controller failure, EEPROM write denied (1991)
Code 64 Variable nozzle turbo solenoid
Code 77 Speed control power relay
Code 88 Start of message

SENSORS, INPUT

TEMPERATURE SENSORS

Engine	Year	Sensor	Resistance Ohms @ deg. F/C
1.6L (97)	1983-86	Coolant*	22,000-382,000 @ −40-20/−40 to −7
			3300-36,000 @ 50-100/10-38
			140-3900 @ 140-245/60-110
2.2L (135) 2V	1985-87	Coolant†	20-200 @ 150/66 max.
			100-1500 @ 150-200/66-93
			400-6000 @ 200/93 min.
		Coolant††	22,000-382,000 @ 200/93 min.
			3300-36,000 @ 50-100/10-38
			176-3900 @ 140-245/60-110
	1983-84	Coolant	9000-11,000 @ −4-20/−20 to −7
			3000-8000 @ room temp.
			800-1000 @ operating temp.

SENSORS, INPUT Continued

TEMPERATURE SENSORS Continued

Engine	Year	Sensor	Resistance Ohms @ deg. F/C
2.2L (135) TBI & Turbo, 2.5L (153), 3.3L, 3.8L	1985-92	Coolant, Charge	7000-13,000 @ 70/21
			700-1000 @ 200/93
	1985-91	Throttle body■	5600-14,600 @ 70/21
			400-1500 @ 200/93
	1983-84	Coolant	9000-11,000 @ −4-20/−20 to −7
			3000-8000 @ room temp.
			800-1000 @ operating temp.
3.0L (183)	1988-92	Coolant	7000-13,000 @ 70/21
			700-1000 @ 200/93
3.7L (225)	1983	Coolant	500-1100 @ 90/32 max.
			1300 min. @ operating temp.
		Charge	100 max. @ 60/16
			no continuity @ operating temp.
5.2L (318)	1988-89	Charge	6000 min. @ 70/21
			2500 max. @ 200/93
	1983-87	Coolant	500-1100 @ 90/32 max.
			1300 min. @ operating temp.
		Charge	100 max. @ 60/16
			no continuity @ operating temp.

* Measured between single upper and lower right terminal.
† Measured between single upper and lower left terminal of 3-terminal connector. Some specifications apply to two terminal connectors.
†† Measured between single upper and lower right terminal of three terminal connector.
■ 1985-91 early TBI only.

MANIFOLD ABSOLUTE PRESSURE SENSORS

Apply 5″ (125mm) of vacuum to sensor and measure voltage. Apply 20″ (500mm) of vacuum to unit. Change in voltage should be within range listed below.

Engine	Year	Voltage Change
2.2L (135) Turbo	1986-88	1.1-1.4
2.2L (135), 2.5L (153) TBI	1986-88	2.3-2.9
2.5L (153), 3.0L (183) Vans	1987-88	2.3-2.9

THROTTLE POSITION TRANSDUCER (TPT)

1983 5.2L (318) FI: Special EFI tester required.

1983-85 2.2L (135) FI & Turbo: Connect voltmeter (+) to orange wire with blue tracer of the throttle body connector. Connect voltmeter (−) to ground. Turn ignition switch to run position. Check voltage against specification with engine not running.

Engine	Year	TPS (voltage)† Idle	WOT
2.2L (135) FI, 2.5L (153)	1983-89	0.5-1.5	3.5
5.2L (318) FI	1983	4.5	—

† ±.05.

ACTUATORS, OUTPUT

IDLE SPEED SOLENOID

Engine	Year	Resistance (ohms)
1.6L (97), 1.7L (105), 2.2L (135) 2V	1983-87	20-100
3.7L (225), 5.2L (318)	1983-89	15-35

COMPUTER TIMING ADVANCE

Specifications are in addition to basic timing.
Perform all tests with engine at operating temperature.

1983-87: Carburetted, disconnect and plug vacuum hose at computer. Apply 16″ of vacuum to the transducer and increase engine speed to 2000 RPM. Verify that idle speed screw is not contacting the carb ground switch and check advance against specification after time indicated has elapsed.

1983-90: With FI, increase engine speed to 2000 RPM and check advance.

UNDERHOOD SERVICE SPECIFICATIONS

ACTUATORS, OUTPUT Continued
COMPUTER TIMING ADVANCE Continued

Engine	Year	Trans-mission	Computer Number	Time (minutes)	Advance
1.6L (97)	1984-86	MT & AT	All	0	29-37
1.7L (105)	1983	MT	All	0	26-34
2.2L (135) 2V	1983	MT & AT	All	0	24-34
California	1983	MT	All	0	24-32
California	1983	AT	All	0	30-38
High Altitude	1983	MT & AT	All	0	30-38
2.2L (135) 2V	1984	MT & AT	All	0	36-46
2.2L (135) 2V ex. Vans	1985-86	MT & AT	All	0	36-44
California	1985-86	MT	All	0	36-44
California	1985-86	AT	All	0	32-40
2.2L (135) Vans	1985	MT & AT	All	0	34-42
California High Alt.	1985	MT & AT	All	0	37-45
2.2L (135) Vans	1986	MT & AT	All	0	19-27
California High Alt.	1986	MT	All	0	23-31
California High Alt.	1986	AT	All	0	18-26
2.2L (135) HO	1985-86	MT	5226449	0	34-42
	1985-86	MT	5227079	0	39-47
California	1985-86	MT	All	0	32-40
2.2L (135) 2V	1987	MT	All	0	37-45
California	1987	AT	All	0	32-40
Others	1987	AT	All	0	36-44
2.2L (135) TBI	1983-84	MT & AT	All	0	36-44
2.2L (135) TBI	1985	MT	All	0	30-38
2.2L (135) TBI	1985	AT	All	0	36-44
2.2L (135) TBI	1986-87	MT	All	0	23-31
2.2L (135) TBI	1986-87	AT	All	0	33-41
2.2L (135) TBI	1988-89	MT	All	0	22-30
2.2L (135) TBI	1988-89	AT	All	0	29-37
2.2L TBI	1990-92	MT	All	0	17-25
2.2L TBI	1990-92	AT	All	0	12-20
2.2L (135) Turbo	1984-87	MT & AT	All	0	33-41
2.2L (135) Turbo I	1988	MT	All	0	29-35
2.2L (135) Turbo I	1988	AT	All	0	21-29

ACTUATORS, OUTPUT Continued
COMPUTER TIMING ADVANCE Continued

Engine	Year	Trans-mission	Computer Number	Time (minutes)	Advance
2.2L (135) Turbo II	1988-89	MT & AT	All	0	36-44
2.2L Turbo	1990	MT & AT	All	0	29-37
2.5L (153)	1986-87	MT	All	0	15-23
2.5L (153)	1986-87	AT	All	0	23-31
2.5L (153) Vans	1986-87	MT & AT	All	0	33-41
2.5L (153) Vans	1988-89	MT	All	0	24-32
2.5L (153) Vans	1988-89	AT	All	0	29-37
2.5L (153) Others	1988-89	MT	All	0	24-32
2.5L (153) Others	1988-89	AT	All	0	26-34
2.5L	1990-92	MT & AT	All	0	17-25
2.5L Turbo	1990-92	MT	All	0	21-29
2.5L Turbo	1990-92	AT	All	0	26-34
3.0L (183)	1987	AT	All	0	26-34
3.0L (183)	1988	AT	All	0	34-42
3.0L	1990-92	MT	All	0	30-38
3.0L	1990-92	AT	All	0	34-42
3.3L	1990-91	AT	All	0	24-32
California	1990-91	AT	All	0	33-41
3.7L (225)	1983	AT	All	1	10-18
California	1983	AT	All	1	4-12
5.2L (318) 2V	1983	AT	All	0	26-34
Canada	1983	AT	All	0	21-29
5.2L (318) 2V	1984	AT	All	0	47-55
Canada	1984	AT	All	0	35-43
5.2L (318) 2V	1985-89	AT	All	0	42-50
Canada	1986-88	AT	All	0	38-46
5.2L (318) 4V	1983	AT	All	0	16-24
Canada	1983	AT	All	0	21-29
5.2L (318) 4V	1984	AT	All	0	37-45
5.2L (318) 4V	1985-87	AT	All	0	34-42
5.2L (318) 4V	1988	AT	All	0	42-50
5.2L (318) 4V	1989	AT	All	0	34-42
5.2L (318) FI	1983	AT	All	0	19-27

CHRYSLER, DODGE, PLYMOUTH
1983-92 Challenger, Champ, Colt, Conquest, Laser (1990-92), Ram 50, Raider, Sapporo, Stealth, Vista

ENGINE IDENTIFICATION

To identify an engine by the manufacturer's code, follow the two steps designated by the numbered blocks.

V.I.N. PLATE LOCATION:
Left side of instrument panel visible through windshield.

1 MODEL YEAR IDENTIFICATION:
10th character of V.I.N.
1992 — N; 1991 — M; 1990 — L;
1989 — K; 1988 — J; 1987 — H;
1986 — G; 1985 — F; 1984 — E;
1983 — D.

2 ENGINE CODE LOCATION:
8th character of V.I.N.

4 ENGINE IDENTIFICATION

YEAR	CODE	CYL.	liters	cc	Fuel System	HP
1992	A	4	1.5	1468	MFI	92
	D	4	1.8	1834	MFI	113
	T	4	1.8	1755	MFI	92
	R	4	2.0	1997	MFI	135
	U	4	2.0 T	1997 T	MFI	195
	W	4	2.4	2350	MFI	116
	S	6	3.0	2972	MFI	164
	B	6	3.0	2972	MFI	222
	C	6	3.0 T	2972 T	MFI	300
1991	A	4	1.5	1468	MFI	92
	T	4	1.8	1755	MFI	92
	V	4	2.0	1997	MFI	96
	R	4	2.0	1997	MFI	135
	U	4	2.0 T	1997 T	MFI	190, 195†
	W	4	2.4	2350	MFI	107
	S	6	3.0	2972	MFI	164
	B	6	3.0	2972	MFI	222
	C	6	3.0 T	2972 T	MFI	300
1990	X	4	1.5	1468	MFI	75, 81†
	Y	4	1.6	1597	MFI	123
	T	4	1.8	1755	MFI	87, 92†
	V	4	2.0	1997	MFI	96
	R	4	2.0	1997	MFI	135
	U	4	2.0 T	1997 T	MFI	190, 195†
	V	4	2.0	1997	MFI	96
	W	4	2.4	2350	MFI	107
	S	6	3.0	2972	MFI	143
1989	X	4	1.5	1468	MFI	75, 81†
	Y	4	1.6	1597	MFI	113
	Z	4	1.6 T	1597 T	MFI	135
	T	4	1.8	1755	MFI	87
	V	4	2.0	1997	MFI	99
	D	4	2.0	1997	2V	90
	E	4	2.6	2555	2V	109
	N	4	2.6 T	2555 T	TBI	188
	S	6	3.0	2972	MFI	143
1988	K	4	1.5	1468	2V	68
	K	4	1.5	1468	MFI	N/A
	F	4	1.6 T	1597 T	TBI	105

4 ENGINE IDENTIFICATION

YEAR	CODE	CYL.	liters	cc	Fuel System	HP
1988 Cont'd.	D	4	2.0	1997	2V	90
	D	4	2.0	1997	MFI	96
	E	4	2.6	2555	2V	109
	N	4	2.6 T	2555 T	TBI	176
1987	K	4	1.5	1468	2V	68
	F	4	1.6 T	1597 T	TBI	105
	D	4	2.0	1997	2V	90
	E	4	2.6	2555	2V	109
	H	4	2.6 T	2555 T	TBI	145
	N	4	2.6 T	2555 T	TBI	176
1986	K	4	1.5	1468	2V	68
	F	4	1.6 T	1597 T	TBI	102
	D	4	2.0	1997	2V	88, 90†
	E	4	2.6	2555	2V	106, 108†
	H	4	2.6 T	2555 T	TBI	145
1985	K	4	1.5	1468	2V	68
	F	4	1.6 T	1597 T	TBI	102
	D	4	2.0	1997	2V	88, 90†
	J	4	2.3 TD	2346 TD	MFI	63
	E	4	2.6	2555	2V	106, 108†
	H	4	2.6 T	2555 T	TBI	145
1984	A	4	1.4	1410	2V	64
	B	4	1.6	1597	2V	72
	F	4	1.6 T	1597 T	TBI	102
	D	4	2.0	1997	2V	88, 90†
	J	4	2.3 TD	2346 TD	MFI	63
	E	4	2.6	2555	2V	106, 108†
	H	4	2.6 T	2555 T	TBI	145
1983	2	4	1.4	1410	2V	64
	3	4	1.6	1597	2V	72
	5	4	2.0	1997	2V	88, 90†
	9	4	2.3 TD	2346 TD	MFI	80
	7	4	2.6	2555	2V	100, 105†

† Engine horsepower varies with model installation.
T — Turbo.   TD — Turbo Diesel.   2V — Two Venturi Carburetor.
TBI — Throttle Body Injection.   MFI — Multiport Fuel Injection.

UNDERHOOD SERVICE SPECIFICATIONS

CRITU1   CRITU1

CYLINDER NUMBERING SEQUENCE

FIRING ORDER: 4-cyl. 1 3 4 2

— Front of car —

1983-90 1.4L, 1.5L; 1983-84 1.6L; 1984-88 1.6L Turbo	1991-92 1.5L	1989-90 1.6L Turbo, 1990-92 2.0L DOHC	1992 1.8L Vista	2.0L-2V FWD	1.8L Laser, 2.0L FI ex. DOHC & RWD	2.0L RWD, 2.6L	1992 2.4L Vista	2.4L Ram 50

6-cyl. 1 2 3 4 5 6

— Front of car —

3.0L ex. Stealth	1991-92 Stealth 3.0L SOHC	1991-92 Stealth 3.0L DOHC

CHRYSLER, DODGE, PLYMOUTH
1983-92 Challenger, Champ, Colt, Conquest, Laser (1990-92), Ram 50, Raider, Sapporo, Stealth, Vista

UNDERHOOD SERVICE SPECIFICATIONS

CRITU2   CRITU2

TIMING MARK

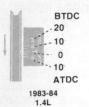

1983-84
1.4L

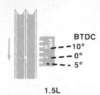

1.5L

1.6L FWD Turbo,
2.0L Vista,
1.8L, 2.0L DOHC, 2.4L

1.6L RWD,
2.0L ex. DOHC Vista,
2.6L

3.0L ex.
Stealth

1991-92 Stealth
3.0L

ELECTRICAL AND IGNITION SYSTEMS

BATTERY

BCI equivalent shown, size may vary from original equipment. Check clearance before replacing, holddown may need to be modified.

Engine	Year	STANDARD BCI Group No.	STANDARD Crank. Perf.	OPTIONAL BCI Group No.	OPTIONAL Crank. Perf.
1410cc, 1468cc, 1597cc	1983-86	25	500	—	—
Canada	1983-86	24	500	—	—
1468cc, 1597cc	1987-89	25	375	25	420
1468cc, 1597cc ex. Turbo	1990	25	355	—	—
1468cc	1991-92	25	350	25	430
Canada	1991-92	25	430	—	—
1597cc Turbo	1990	45	435	—	—
1755cc Colt Wagon	1989-90	45	435	—	—
1755cc Laser	1990-92	86	430	—	—
1997cc Pickup	1983-85	25	430	—	—
Canada	1983-85	24	500	—	—
1997cc Pickup	1986-87	25	430	25	500
1997cc Pickup	1988	25	430	—	—
1997cc Vista	1984-88	25	420	—	—
1997cc Vista	1989	45	435	25	420
Canada	1989	25	420	—	—
1997cc Laser	1990-91	86	430	—	—
1997cc Laser	1992	86	525	—	—
2346cc Diesel	1983-85	27	800	—	—
2350cc Pickup	1990-92	51	430	24	585
Canada	1990-92	24	490	24	585
2555cc Pickup	1983-85	25	430	—	—
Canada	1983-85	24	500	—	—
2555cc Pickup	1986-87	25	430	25	500
2555cc Pickup	1988	25	430	—	—
2555cc Pickup, Raider	1989	45	435	24	585
2555cc Conquest	1984-89	25	420	—	—
2972cc Raider	1989	24	490	—	—
2972cc Pickup	1990-91	24	490	24	585
2972cc Stealth	1991-92	24	490	—	—

ALTERNATOR

Engine	Year	Rated Output (amps)	Test Output (amps @ eng. rpm)
1410cc, 1597cc	1983	45	37-42 @ 1500
1410cc, 1597cc	1984	45	32 @ 1150
Turbo	1984	50	35 @ 1150
1468cc MT	1985-86	50	35 @ 1150
AT	1985-86	55	39 @ 1150
1468cc 2V MT	1987-89	60	42 @ 2500
AT	1987-89	65	45 @ 2500
1468cc FI	1988-89	75	52 @ 2500
1468cc	1990-92	65	46 @ 2500
		75	53 @ 2500
1597cc Turbo	1985-86	65	46 @ 1150
1597cc U.S.	1987-90	75	52 @ 2500
Canada	1987-90	65	45 @ 2500
1755cc Colt wagon	1989-90	75	52 @ 2500
1755cc, 1997cc Laser	1990-92	65	46 @ 2500
		75	53 @ 2500
		90	63 @ 2500
1834cc, 2350cc Vista, Colt	1992	60	42 @ 2500
		65	46 @ 2500
		75	53 @ 2500

ALTERNATOR Continued

Engine	Year	Rated Output (amps)	Test Output (amps @ eng. rpm)
1997cc, 2555cc Pickup	1983-86	45	41 @ 3000
1997cc, 2555cc Pickup	1987-89	45	31 @ 2500
		60	42 @ 2500
1997cc Vista	1984-91	65	45 @ 2500
Canada	1990-91	75	52 @ 2500
2346cc Diesel	1984-86	50	45 @ 3000
2350cc Pickup	1990-92	40	28 @ 2500
		45	31 @ 2500
		60	42 @ 2500
2555cc Challenger, Sapporo	1983	50	41-50 @ 2500
Canada	1983	55	42-50 @ 2500
2555cc Conquest	1984-86	65	59 @ 3000
2555cc Conquest	1987-89	65	45 @ 2500
2555cc Raider	1987-89	50	35 @ 2500
2972cc Raider	1989	75	52 @ 2500
2997cc Pickup	1990-91	65	45 @ 2500
2997cc Stealth	1991-92	90	63 @ 2500
		110	77 @ 2500

REGULATOR

Application	Test Temp. (deg. F/C)	Voltage Setting
1983 ex. truck	68/20	14.1-14.7
Truck	68/20	13.9-14.9
1984 all ex. Vista, Conquest	68/20	14.1-14.7
Vista, Conquest	68/20	13.9-14.9
1985-86 Colt, Vista	68/20	14.4-15.0
Conquest, Pickup	68/20	14.1-14.7
1987-88 Colt 2V, Turbo	−4/−20	14.4-15.6
	68/20	14.2-15.2
	140/60	13.8-15.1
	175/80	13.6-15.0
1987-92 Others	−4/−20	14.2-15.4
	68/20	13.9-15.9
	140/60	13.4-14.6
	175/80	13.1-14.5

STARTER

Engine	Year	Cranking Voltage (min. volts)	Ampere Draw @ Cranking Speed
All	1983-92	8.0	—

SPARK PLUGS

Engine	Year	Gap (inches)	Gap (mm)	Torque (ft-lb)
All ex. 1597cc Turbo	1983-85	.039-.043	1.0-1.1	18-21
Canada	1983-85	.028-.031	.70-.80	18-21
All ex. Turbo	1986-90	.039-.043	1.0-1.1	15-21
Turbo	1989-90	.028-.031	.70-.80	15-21

CHRYSLER, DODGE, PLYMOUTH
1983-92 Challenger, Champ, Colt, Conquest, Laser (1990-92), Ram 50, Raider, Sapporo, Stealth, Vista

UNDERHOOD SERVICE SPECIFICATIONS

CRITU3   CRITU3

IGNITION COIL

Engine	Year	Windings	Resistance (ohms)
1410cc, 1597cc			
Canada	1983	Primary	1.26-1.54
		Secondary	9000-11,000
1410cc, 1597cc AT	1984	Primary	1.10-1.30
		Secondary	11,600-15,800
Others	1983-84	Primary	1.04-1.27
		Secondary	7100-9600
1468cc 2V	1985-88	Primary	1.1-1.3
		Secondary	11,600-15,800
1468cc FI, 1755cc	1988-90	Primary	.72-.88
		Secondary	10,300-13,900
1468cc	1991-92	Primary	0.9-1.2
		Secondary	20,000-29,000
1597cc Turbo	1984-86	Primary	1.00-1.30
		Secondary	7100-9600
1597cc Turbo	1987-88	Primary	1.1-1.3
		Secondary	9400-12,600
1597cc, 1755cc	1989-90	Primary	.77-.95
		Secondary	10,300-13,900
1755cc Laser	1990-92	Primary	0.9-1.2
		Secondary	19,000-27,000
1834cc	1992	Primary	0.9-1.2
		Secondary	20,000-29,000
1997cc Vista	1985-86	Primary	1.20
		Secondary	13,500
1997cc Vista	1987-91	Primary	.72-.88
		Secondary	10,900-13,300
1997cc, 2555cc			
Pickup	1985	Primary	1.04-1.27
		Secondary	7100-9600
1997cc, 2555cc Pickup			
Coil No. E-064	1986	Primary	1.20
		Secondary	13,700
Coil No. E-089	1986	Primary	1.20
		Secondary	17,000
1997cc, 2555cc Pickup	1987-89	Primary	1.1-1.3
		Secondary	22,100-29,900
1997cc Laser	1990-91	Primary*	.77-.95
		Secondary*	10,300-13,900
1997cc Laser	1992	Primary	.70-.86
		Secondary	11,300-15,300
2350cc	1990-92	Primary	.72-.88
		Secondary	10,300-13,900
2555cc Raider	1987-89	Primary	1.1-1.3
		Secondary	14,500-19,500
2555cc Conquest	1984-86	Primary	1.04-1.27
		Secondary	7100-9600
2555cc Conquest	1987-89	Primary	1.12-1.38
		Secondary	9400-12,700
2972cc SOHC	1989-92	Primary	.72-.88
		Secondary	10,300-13,900
2972cc DOHC	1991-92	Primary	.67-.81**
		Secondary	11,300-15,300**

* Primary windings measured between terminals 2 & 1 and 2 & 4 of 4-terminal connector. Secondary windings measured between high voltage terminals of coil towers 1 & 4 and 2 & 3.

** Primary windings measured between terminals 1 & 3, 2 & 3, and 4 & 3 of 4-terminal connector. Secondary winds measured between each pair of coil high tension terminals with spark plug wires removed.

DISTRIBUTOR PICKUP

Application	Year	Resistance (ohms)	Air Gap (in./mm)
All	1983-84	920-1120	.008 min./.20
Pickup			
w/Mitsubishi distr.	1985-89	—	.031/.80
w/Nippon-Denso distr.;			
Vista	1985-89	130-190	.008-.015/.2-.4
Colt 2V	1985-88	—	.008/.20
Turbo	1985-88	920-1120	—
Conquest	1986-89	920-1120	—
All others ex. Vista	1985-88	920-1120	.008 min./.20

IGNITION POINTS

Engine	Year	Gap (inches)	Gap (mm)	Dwell (degrees)	Spring Tension (ounces)
1410cc Canada	1983	.018-.021	.45-.55	49-55	18-23

IGNITION RESISTOR

Engine	Year	Type	Resistance (ohms)	Temperature (deg. F/C)
All 2V as equipped	1983-89	Unit	1.20-1.50	68/20

BASE TIMING

Set timing at slow idle and Before Top Dead Center, unless otherwise specified.

1983-88 Models w/o EST: Disconnect and plug distributor vacuum hoses on models with dual diaphragm. 1987-88 high altitude models, ground ignition timing connector also. Models with dual diaphragm, timing will increase 5° over base specification when vacuum hoses are connected.

1987-92 Models w/EST: Remove cap from timing adjustment connector (twin lead harness, mounted on fender skirt) and ground left terminal under plastic lock. When reconnected, timing should be at "check" specification.

Engine	Year	Man. Trans. (degrees) @ RPM	Auto. Trans. (degrees) @ RPM
1410cc	1983	5 ±2	5 ±2
High Altitude	1983	10 ±2	10 ±2
1410cc ex. 4-speed	1984	5 ±2	—
4-speed	1984	10 ±2	—
1468cc	1985	3 ±2	3 ±2
1468cc 2V	1986-88	5 ±2	5 ±2
1468cc FI: Set	1989-92	5 ±2	5 ±2
Check	1989-92	10 ±2	10 ±2
High Altitude	1989-91	15 ±2	15 ±2
1597cc ex. Turbo	1983-84	5 ±2	5 ±2
High Altitude	1983	10 ±2	10 ±2
1597cc Turbo	1984-85	8 ±2	8 ±2
1597cc Turbo	1986-88	10 ±2	10 ±2
Canada	1986-88	8 ±2	8 ±2
1597cc: Set	1989-90	5 ±2	5 ±2
Check, ex. Wagon	1989-90	8 ±2*	8 ±2*
Check, Wagon	1989	15 ±2*	15 ±2*
1755cc Colt Wagon: Set	1989-90	5 ±2	5 ±2
Check	1989-90	15 ±2*	15 ±2*
1755cc Laser: Set	1990-92	5 ±2	5 ±2
Check	1990-92	10 ±2	10 ±2
1834cc: Set	1992	5 ±2	5 ±2
Check	1992	5 ±2	5 ±2
1995cc, 1997cc	1983-84	5 ±1	5 ±1
High Altitude	1983	10 ±1	10 ±1
Canada	1983	13 ±2	13 ±2
Canada	1984	5 ±2	5 ±2
1997cc	1985	5 ±2	5 ±2
1997cc Vista	1986-88	8 ±2	8 ±2
4WD	1986-88	5 ±2	5 ±2
1997cc Vista. Set	1989-91	5 ±2	5 ±2
Check	1989-91	10 ±2	10 ±2
High Altitude	1989-91	15 ±2	15 ±2
1997cc Pickup	1986	5 ±2	5 ±2
1997cc Pickup	1987-89	8 ±2	8 ±2
1997cc Laser: Set	1990-92	5 ±2	5 ±2
Check	1990-92	8 ±2	8 ±2
2350cc: Set	1990-92	5 ±2	5 ±2
Check	1990-92	8 ±2*	8 ±2*
2555cc 2V	1983-89	7 ±2	7 ±2
High Altitude	1983	12 ±2	12 ±2
2555cc FI	1984-89	10 ±2	10 ±2
2972cc: Set	1989-92	5 ±2	5 ±2
Check	1989	10 ±2	10 ±2
Check	1990-92	15 ±2	15 ±2

* At high altitudes, timing will be advanced further.

CHRYSLER, DODGE, PLYMOUTH
1983-92 Challenger, Champ, Colt, Conquest, Laser (1990-92), Ram 50, Raider, Sapporo, Stealth, Vista

UNDERHOOD SERVICE SPECIFICATIONS

CRITU4   CRITU4

DISTRIBUTOR TIMING ADVANCE

Engine degrees at engine rpm, no load, in addition to basic timing setting.

Mechanical advance distributors only.

Engine	Transmission	Year	Distributor Number	Degrees @ 2500 RPM Total	Centrifugal
1410cc	MT	1983	T3T05783	27.8-35.8	6.8-10.8
1410cc	MT	1983	T4T62176	24.8-32.8	6.8-10.8
1410cc	MT	1983	T4T63472	27.8-35.8	6.8-10.8
1410cc	MT	1984	T3T61872	25.9-31.7	7.9-9.7
1410cc	MT	1984	T3T62172	28.9-34.7	7.9-9.7
1468cc	MT & AT	1985	T3T62672, 73	22-30	1-5
1468cc	AT	1985	T3T62671	24-32	1-5
1468cc Canada	MT & AT	1985	T3T62180	28-36	2-6
1468cc	MT & AT	1986	T3T62678	28-36	7-11
1468cc	MT & AT	1986	T3T62677	25-33	7-11
1468cc 2V	MT	1987-88	T3T62688	21.9-29.9	0.9-4.9
1468cc 2V	MT	1987-88	T3T62681	18.9-26.9	0.9-4.9
1597cc	MT & AT	1983	T3T05778, 79	30.2-38.2	12.2-16.2
1597cc	MT & AT	1984	T3T61872	25.9-31.7	7.9-9.7
1597cc	MT & AT	1983	T4T62176	24.8-32.8	6.8-10.8
1597cc Turbo	MT & AT	1984-88	T3T63175	21.4-26.8*	8.4-9.8
1997cc	AT	1984	T4T62181	33.0-40.3	10.0-13.3
1997cc	MT	1984	T4T62182	31.0-38.3	10.0-13.3
1997cc	MT	1983-84	T4T62186	37.7-45.7	7.7-11.7
1997cc	MT	1983-84	T4T63474	37.7-45.7	7.7-11.7
1997cc	AT	1983-84	T4T62180	28.7-36.7	7.7-11.7
1997cc	MT & AT	1983-84	T4T62185	20.7-28.7	7.7-11.7
1997cc	MT & AT	1983-84	T4T62172	20-28	7-11
1997cc	MT	1984	T4T63473	40.0-47.3	10.0-13.3
1997cc Vista	MT	1984	T4T63473	26.5-34.5	8.5-12.5
1997cc Vista	MT	1984	T4T62172	26.5-34.5	8.5-12.5
1997cc Vista 2WD	AT	1984-85	T4T62181	33.0-40.3	10.0-13.3
1997cc Vista 2WD	MT	1985	MD084036	26.5-34.5	8.5-12.5
1997cc Vista 2WD	MT & AT	1985-86	100291-061	26.5-34.5	8.5-12.5
1997cc Vista 4WD	MT	1985-86	100291-116	33.8-41.8	7.8-11.8
1997cc Truck	MT & AT	1984-86	100291-057	35.5-43.5	7.5-11.5
1997cc Truck	MT	1984-86	110291-062	28.5-33.5	7.5-11.5
1997cc Truck	AT	1985-86	100291-064	25.8-33.8	7.8-11.8
1997cc Pickup	MT & AT	1987-89	MD110418	25.8-33.8	7.8-11.8
1997cc Pickup	MT & AT	1987-89	MD110419, 40	28.8-36.8	7.8-11.8
1997cc Pickup	MT & AT	1987	MD112111	33.8-41.8	7.8-11.8
1997cc Pickup	MT & AT	1988-89	MD125103	25.8-33.8	7.8-11.8
2555cc	MT & AT	1983	T4T60171	20.8-28.8	7.8-11.8
2555cc	MT & AT	1983-84	T4T62074	28.8-36.8	7.8-11.8
2555cc	MT & AT	1983-84	T4T62075, 78	25.8-33.8	7.8-11.8
2555cc	MT & AT	1983-84	T4T62076, 77	20.8-28.8	7.8-11.8
2555cc Turbo	MT & AT	1984-87	T4T63371	32.8-40.8	11.8-15.8
2555cc Turbo	MT & AT	1985-87	T4T63372	31.6-39.6	10.6-14.6
2555cc Turbo	MT & AT	1988-89	T4T63373	31.7-39.7	10.7-14.7
2555cc Truck	MT & AT	1984-86	T3T61971	33-41	5-9
2555cc Truck	MT & AT	1984-86	T3T61972	26-34	5-9
2555cc Truck	MT & AT	1985-86	T3T61973	26.4-34.4	8.4-12.4
2555cc Pickup	MT & AT	1987	T3T65472	25.8-33.8	4.8-8.8
2555cc Pickup	MT & AT	1987	T3T65473	30.8-33.8	4.8-8.8
2555cc Pickup	MT & AT	1987-89	T3T65572	22.8-30.8	4.8-8.8
2555cc Pickup	MT & AT	1988-89	T3T65476	22.8-30.8	4.8-8.8
2555cc Raider	MT & AT	1987	T3T61980	22.8-30.8	4.8-8.8
2555cc Raider	MT & AT	1987-89	T3T65571	25.8-33.8	4.8-8.8
2555cc Raider	MT & AT	1988-89	T3T65474	22.8-30.8	4.8-8.8

* Retard, 16-20 degrees @ 17.5 inches hg.

FUEL SYSTEM

FUEL SYSTEM PRESSURE

Engine	Year	Pressure PSI	RPM
Carburetted & TBI:			
1410cc, 1597cc	1983-84	3.7-5.1	idle
Others, 2V	1983-86	4.6-6.0	idle
1597cc, 2555cc TBI	1984-89	35-38	idle

FUEL SYSTEM PRESSURE Continued

Engine	Year	Pressure @ Idle PSI*	PSI**
Fuel Injected (MFI)			
1468cc FI	1988-92	47-50	38
1597cc	1989-90	47-50	38
1755cc, 1834cc	1989-92	47-50	38
1997cc	1987-92	47-50	38
Turbo	1990-91	36-38	27
Turbo MT	1992	36-38	27
Turbo AT	1992	41-46	33
2350cc	1990-92	47-50	38
2972cc	1989-92	47-50	38
Turbo	1991-92	43-45	34

  * Pressure regulator vacuum hose disconnected.

 ** Pressure regulator vacuum hose connected.

IDLE SPEED W/O COMPUTER CONTROL

Midpoint of range given is the preferred setting.

All 2V: Adjust throttle stop screw or idle speed screw to obtain specified idle rpm. With choke fully closed, adjust fast idle to specified rpm by adjusting fast idle screw under throttle lever (1987). Models with A/C (1983-86), turn A/C on and adjust idle up diaphragm to specification.

Midpoint of range given is the preferred setting.

Engine	Year	SLOW Man. Trans.	Auto. Trans.	FAST Man. Trans.	Auto. Trans.	Step of Cam
1410cc	1983	550-750*	—	—	—	—
Canada	1983	600-800	—			
AC speed-up	1983	850-950				
AC speed-up, Canada	1983	1050-1150	—			
1410cc w/o AC	1984	600-800	—	—	—	—
w/AC	1984	650-850	—			
Canada	1984	800-900	800-900 N			
1468cc	1985-86	600-800	650-850 N	—	—	—
PS, Elect. speed-up	1986	800-900	800-900 N			
AC speed-up	1985-86	800-900	800-900 N			
Canada	1985-86	800-900	800-900 N			
speed-up	1985-86	800-900	800-900 N			
1468cc	1987-88	600-800	650-850 N	2800	2700 N	2nd High
PS, Elect. speed-up	1987-88	750-950	750-950 N			
AC speed-up	1987-88	800-900	800-900 N			
1597cc	1983	550-750	650-850 N	—	—	—
AC speed-up	1983	850-950	900-1000 N			
Canada	1983	800-900	800-900 N			
AC speed-up	1983	1050-1150	1100-1200 N			
1597cc w/o AC	1984	—	650-850 N	—	—	—
w/AC	1984	—	750-950 N			
Canada	1984	800-900	800-900 N			
1997cc	1983	650-850	650-850 N	—	—	—
5-speed	1983	600-800	—			
California	1983	650-850	650-850 N			

CHRYSLER, DODGE, PLYMOUTH
1983-92 Challenger, Champ, Colt, Conquest, Laser (1990-92), Ram 50, Raider, Sapporo, Stealth, Vista

UNDERHOOD SERVICE SPECIFICATIONS

CRITU5   CRITU5

IDLE SPEED W/O COMPUTER CONTROL Continued

		SLOW		FAST		
Engine	Year	Man. Trans.	Auto. Trans.	Man. Trans.	Auto. Trans.	Step of Cam
1997cc						
Canada	1983	800-900	800-900 N			
AC speed-up	1983	850-900	850-900 N			
1997cc Pickup	1984	650-850	750-950 N	—	—	—
AC speed-up	1984	850-900	850-900 N			
w/5-speed	1984	800-900	—			
Canada	1984	800-900	800-900 N			
AC speed-up	1984	850-900	850-900 N			
1997cc Vista	1984	600-800	650-850 N	—	—	—
Speed-up	1984	600-800	650-850 N			
w/AC	1984	650-850	750-950 N			
Speed-up	1984	800-900	800-900 N			
1997cc Pickup	1985-86	650-850	650-850 N	—	—	—
AC speed-up	1985-86	850-900	850-900 N			
1997cc Pickup	1987-89	650-850	650-850 N	2500	2450 N	2nd High
AC speed-up	1987-89	850-950	850-950 N			
1997cc Vista 2WD	1985-86	600-800	—	—	—	—
Speed-up	1985-86	750	—			
AC speed-up	1985-86	800-900	—			
1997cc Vista 4WD	1985	700-800	—			
AC speed-up	1985	800-900	—			
2346cc Diesel	1983	700-850	—	—	—	—
2346cc Diesel	1984-85	700-800	—	—	—	—
2555cc truck	1983	650-850	700-900 N	—	—	—
Canada	1983	800-900	800-900 N			
AC speed-up	1983	850-900	850-900 N			
2555cc car	1983	650-850	700-900 N			
Canada	1983	800-900	800-900 N			
AC speed-up	1983	1000-1100	1000-1100 N			
2555cc truck	1984-86	650-850	700-900 N	—	—	—
AC speed-up	1984-86	850-900	850-900 N			
Canada	1984	800-900	800-900 N			
AC speed-up	1984	850-900	850-900 N			
2555cc Truck	1987-89	700-900	700-900 N	2350	2300 N	2nd High
AC speed-up	1987-89	850-950	850-950 N			
2555cc Raider	1987-89	700-900	700-900 N	2350	2300 N	2nd High
AC speed-up	1987-89	900-950	900-950 N			

* 600-800 w/4×2 Man. Trans., code 4, 5 or 6 of 12th VIN character.

IDLE SPEED W/COMPUTER CONTROL

Midpoint of range given is the preferred setting speed.

1989-92 1597cc 1997cc, 2972cc: Ground ignition timing connector and terminal 10 of self diagnostic connector.

1989-92 Others; 1988-86 All: Turn ignition to ON position for more than 15 seconds. Turn switch off and disconnect ISC servo harness connector. Ground red wire on computer side of ISC connector (1987-88 1597cc Turbo and 1987-89 2555cc Turbo only). Start engine and adjust speed to specified value.

Turn AC on and verify that speed-up speed is at specified value.

Engine	Year	Trans-mission	Setting Speed	Checking Speed	AC Speed-up
1468cc ex. Wagon	1989-91	MT	700-800	650-850	850
	1989-91	AT	700-800 N	650-850 N	700 D
1468cc, 1755cc Wagon	1988-90	MT	700	600-800	850
	1988-90	AT	700 N	600-800 N	650 D
1597cc Turbo	1986	AT	600 N	600-800 N	800-900 N
1597cc Turbo	1987-88	MT	700	600-800	850
	1987-88	AT	700 N	600-800 N	650 D
1597cc	1989-90	MT	750	650-850	850
	1989-90	AT	750 N	650-850 N	700 D
1755cc Laser	1990-92	MT	600-800	650-750	850
1755cc Laser	1990-92	AT	600-500 N	650-750 N	650 D
1834cc Vista, Colt	1992	MT	700-800	650-850	850
1834cc Vista, Colt	1992	AT	700-800 N	650-850 N	850 N
1997cc Vista	1985-86	AT	700 N	600-800 N	800-900 N
1997cc Vista	1987-88	MT & AT	700 N	600-800 N	850 N
1997cc Vista	1989-90	MT & AT	700 N	600-800 N	900 N
1997cc Vista	1991	MT	650-750	600-800	900
1997cc Vista	1991	AT	650-750 N	600-800 N	600 D
1997cc Laser	1990-92	MT	700-800	650-850	850
1997cc Laser	1990-92	AT	700-800 N	650-850 N	650 D
2350cc Pickup	1990-92	MT	700-800	650 850	900
2350cc Pickup	1990-92	AT	700-800 N	650-850 N	700 D
2350cc Vista, Colt	1992	MT	700-800	650-850	850
2350cc Vista, Colt	1992	AT	700-800 N	650-850 N	850 N
2555cc Turbo	1984-86	MT & AT	750 N	750-950 N	—
2555cc Turbo	1987-89	MT	850	750-950	1000
	1987-89	AT	850 N	750-950 N	750 D
2972cc	1989-92	MT	650-750	600-800	900
2972cc	1989-92	AT	650-750 N	600-800 N	650 D

ENGINE MECHANICAL

TIGHTENING TORQUES
See UNDERHOOD SERVICE INSTRUCTIONS at the beginning of this section for test/adjustment diagrams.

		Torque Ft-lbs/Nm				
Engine	Year	Cylinder Head	Intake Manifold	Exhaust Manifold	Crankshaft Pulley	Water Pump
1468cc	1985-92	51-54/ 69-74	12-14/ 16-19	12-14/ 16-19	9-11/ 12-15	9-11/ 12-15⊙
1597cc	1985-88	51-54/ 69-74	11-14/ 20-25	18-21/ 25-30	14-22/ 20-30	9-11/ 12-15⊙
1597cc	1989-90	65-72/ 90-100	11-14/ 15-19*	18-22/ 25-30	14-22/ 20-30	9-11/ 12-15⊙
1755cc Colt Wagon	1989-90	51-54/ 70-75	15-22/ 21-31	18-22/ 25-30	11-13/ 15-16	9-11/ 12-15⊙
1755cc Laser	1990-92	51-54/ 70-75	11-14/ 15-20	11-14/ 15-20	11-13/ 15-18	9-11/ 12-15
1834cc	1992	54/75□, 14/20, +90°, +90°	13/18	22/30	134/185	18/24
1997cc	1989-90	65-72/ 90-100	11-14/ 15-19	11-14/ 15-19	15-21/ 20-30	9-11/ 12-15⊙
1997cc Laser	1990-92	65-72/ 100-110	11-14/ 15-20•	11-14/ 15-20	14-22/ 20-30	9-11/ 12-15⊙
2350cc Pickup	1990-92	65-72/ 90-100	11-14/ 15-20	11-14/ 15-20	15-21/ 20-30	9-11/ 12-15⊙

CHRYSLER, DODGE, PLYMOUTH
1983-92 Challenger, Champ, Colt, Conquest, Laser (1990-92), Ram 50, Raider, Sapporo, Stealth, Vista

TIGHTENING TORQUES Continued

Engine	Year	Cylinder Head	Intake Manifold	Exhaust Manifold	Crankshaft Pulley	Water Pump
2350cc Vista, Colt	1992	76-83/ 105-115	13/18	13/18	18/25	10/14
2346cc Diesel	1983-86	76-83/ 103-112	11-14/ 15-19	11-14/ 15-19	123-137/ 167-186	—
2555cc	1983-89	65-72/ 90-100†	11-14/ 15-19	11-14/ 15-19	80-95/ 110-130	9-11/ 12-15
2972cc Pickup, Raider	1989-91	65-72/ 90-100	11-14/ 15-19	11-15/ 15-21	109-115/ 150-160	14-19/ 20-27
2972cc Stealth SOHC	1991-92	80/110	13/18	13/18	108-116/ 150-160	17/24
DOHC	1991-92	90/125	13/18	33/45††	130-137/ 180-190	17/24

* Short bolts.
● Long bolts, 22-30/30-42.
⊙ Short bolts, long bolts, 14-20/20-27.
† Small bolts forward of cam gear, 11-15/15-22.
†† Turbo, 13/18.
□ Then loosen all bolts.

VALVE CLEARANCE
Engine hot.

Engine	Year	Intake (inches)	Intake (mm)	Exhaust (inches)	Exhaust (mm)
All ex. Diesel†	1983-88	.006	.15	.010	.25
Jet valve	1983-84	.006	.15	—	—
Jet valve	1985-88	.010	.25	—	—
Diesel	1983-85	.010	.25	.010	.25
1468cc, 1755cc	1989-90	.006	.15	.010	.25
1468cc	1991-92	.006	.15	.010	.25

† 1985-89 2.0L & 2.6L except jet valve have hydraulic lifters.

COMPRESSION PRESSURE
At cranking speed (250-400 rpm), engine temperature normalized, throttle open.

Engine	Year	PSI	Maximum Variation PSI
Diesel	1983-85	384	—
All ex. Diesel & 2555cc Turbo	1984	170	—
1468cc	1985-88	171-192	14
1468cc	1989-92	137 min.	14
1597cc	1985-86	128-149	14
1597cc	1987-88	119-149	14
1755cc	1989-90	137 min.	14
1834cc	1992	142 min.	14
1997cc Vista	1985-88	149-171	14
1997cc Truck	1985-88	149-171	14
1997cc, 2350cc	1989-92	119 min.	14
2555cc Conquest	1984-88	113-142	14
2555cc Conquest	1989	97 min.	14
2555cc Truck	1985-87	156-171	14
2555cc Raider	1987	136-170	14
2555cc Truck, Raider	1988	149-170	14
2555cc Truck, Raider	1989	119 min.	14
2972cc Pickup, Raider	1989-91	119 min.	14
2972cc Stealth SOHC	1991-92	127 min.	14
DOHC	1991-92	139 min.	14
Turbo	1991-92	115 min.	14

BELT TENSION
1983-84 ex. Diesel: 1/4-3/8 inch or 6-10 millimeter deflection at midpoint of belt between water pump & alternator, under a 22-pound load.
1983-85 Diesel: 3/8-1/2 inch or 10-13 millimeter deflection at midpoint of belt under a 22-pound load.
1985-88 ex. Diesel: 1.5L, 7/32-9/32 inch or 5.5-7 0 millimeter deflection; 1.6L 1/4-5/16 inch or 6.5-8.0 millimeter deflection; others, 1/4-3/8 inch or 7-10 millimeter deflection.

ENGINE COMPUTER SYSTEM

COMPUTER DIAGNOSTIC CODES
See UNDERHOOD SERVICE INSTRUCTIONS at the beginning of this section for test/ adjustment diagrams.
1984-88 Colt Turbo
1984-86 Conquest
With ignition off, connect a voltmeter to the diagnostic connector located under battery (1.6L), or on right hand cowl by ECI computer (2.6L). Turn ignition on, codes will be displayed as sweeps of voltmeter needle.
1987-88 Vista, Conquest
1988 Colt w/FI
1989-92 All w/FI
Access connector in glove box or under dash on passenger side (early models) or by driver side kick panel by fuse block (late models). Connect an analog voltmeter to upper right cavity (+) and lower left (–). Turn ignition switch on. Codes will be displayed as pulses of voltmeter needle. Disconnect battery negative cable to erase codes.
1987-88 Vista, Colt:
Codes occur as fast (0) or slow (1) pulses over a ten second period. The following deciphers each code:

Colt			Vista		
Long pulse	=	1	00000	=	0
10	=	2	10000	=	1
100	=	3	01000	=	2
1000	=	4	11000	=	3
10000	=	5	00100	=	4
100000	=	6	01011	=	5
110	=	7	01100	=	6
1100	=	8	00011	=	7
11000	=	9	11101	=	8
110000	=	10			
1100000	=	11			
11110	=	12			
111100	=	13			
1111000	=	14			
000000000	=	15			

1988-89 1597cc Turbo;
1984-89 2555cc Turbo:
Code 1 Oxygen sensor and/or computer
Code 2 Ignition signal
Code 3 Airflow sensor
Code 4 Pressure sensor
Code 5 Throttle position sensor
Code 6 ISC motor position sensor
Code 7 Coolant temperature sensor
Code 8 Car speed signal
Vista:
Code 1 Oxygen sensor
Code 2 Crank angle sensor
Code 3 Airflow sensor
Code 4 Barometric pressure sensor
Code 5 Throttle position sensor
Code 6 ISC motor position sensor
Code 7 Engine temperature sensor
Code 8 TDC sensor
1989-91 All w/FI;
1988 Colt w/FI:
Continuous Flashing System normal
Code 11 Oxygen sensor (front on V6 Turbo)
Code 12 Airflow sensor
Code 13 Intake air temperature sensor
Code 14 TPS
Code 15 ISC motor position sensor
Code 21 Coolant temperature sensor
Code 22 Crank angle sensor
Code 23 TDC sensor
Code 24 Vehicle speed sensor
Code 25 Barometric pressure sensor
Code 31 Detonation sensor
Code 36 Ignition timing adjustment
Code 39 Oxygen sensor (rear on V6 Turbo)
Code 41 Injector
Code 42 Fuel pump
Code 43 EGR
Code 44 Ignition coil power transistor, cyl. 1 & 4 (V6)
Code 52 Ignition coil power transistor, cyl. 2 & 5 (V6)
Code 53 Ignition coil power transistor, cyl. 3 & 6 (V6)
Code 61 Transaxle and ECM interlink
Code 62 Warm-up valve position sensor
One Long Sweep, ECU

CHEK-CHART

CHRYSLER, DODGE, PLYMOUTH
1983-92 Challenger, Champ, Colt, Conquest, Laser (1990-92),
Ram 50, Raider, Sapporo, Stealth, Vista

UNDERHOOD SERVICE SPECIFICATIONS

CRITU7   CRITU7

SENSORS, INPUT

TEMPERATURE SENSORS
See UNDERHOOD SERVICE INSTRUCTIONS at the beginning of this section for test/adjustment diagrams.

Engine	Year	Sensor	Resistance Ohms @ deg. F/C
All	1983-92	Coolant	5900 @ 32/0
			2500 @ 68/20
			1100 @ 104/40
			300 @ 176/80
1468cc 2V, 1997cc 2V, 2555cc 2V	1985-86	Intake Air	2450 @ 68/20
1468cc FI, 1597cc DOHC, 1755cc, 1997cc FI, 2350cc, 2555cc Turbo, 2972cc	1987-92	Intake Air†	6000 @ 32/0
			2700 @ 68/20
			400 @ 176/80
1597cc Turbo	1985-88	Intake Air	2450 @ 68/20
2555cc Turbo	1984-86	Intake Air*	2450 @ 68/20
		Intake Air**	2500 @ 68/20

* Sensor on air intake pipe.
** Sensor on air cleaner housing.
† Measured between terminals 4 & 6 or 6 & 8 (bottom left and right) of airflow sensor.

PRESSURE SENSORS

Engine	Year	Sensor	Voltage @ in./mm Hg
1597cc Turbo	1987-88	Barometric	.79 @ 2.8/70
			1.84 @ 7/175
			4.00 @ 14.2/330
1997cc FI, 2555cc Turbo	1987-89	Barometric	.79 @ 2.8/70
			1.84 @ 7/175
			4.00 @ 14.2/330

THROTTLE POSITION SENSOR (TPS)
See UNDERHOOD SERVICE INSTRUCTIONS at the beginning of this section for test/adjustment diagrams.

All FI: Insert digital voltmeter probes along GW lead (+) and B lead (−) or GB lead (−) on TPS connector. With ignition switch on and engine not running, check reading against specification. Rotate unit to adjust.

All 2V: Connect digital voltmeter probes between two adjacent TPS bottom terminals. With ignition on and engine not running, check reading against specifications. Turn TPS linkage screw to adjust.

SENSORS, INPUT Continued

THROTTLE POSITION SENSOR (TPS) Continued

Model	Year	TPS Voltage
Colt 2V	1984-88	.25
Colt Turbo, Conquest	1984-86	.45-.51
Colt FI, Conquest	1987-92	.48-.52
Vista: w/MT	1984-86	.25
w/AT	1984-86	.445
Vista, Laser	1987-92	.48-.52
Pickup, Raider 4-cyl.	1985-89	.25
Pickup 4-cyl.	1990-92	.48-.52
Raider, Pickup, Stealth V6	1989-92	.4-1.0

MOTOR POSITION SENSOR
See UNDERHOOD SERVICE INSTRUCTIONS at the beginning of this section for test/adjustment diagrams.

Engine	Year	Resistance (ohms)
1468cc FI, 1755cc	1988-92	4000-6000
1997cc FI, 2350cc, 2555cc Turbo	1987-91	4000-6000

AIRFLOW SENSOR
Measured between red and black wire leads at idle.

Engine	Year	Volts
1597cc Turbo	1987-88	2.2-3.2

ACTUATORS, OUTPUT

IDLE SPEED CONTROL SOLENOID
At 68°F (20°C).

1987-88 1597cc, 1997cc FI, 1987-89 2555cc Turbo, 2972cc: Measured between two upper terminals.

Engine	Year	Resistance (ohms)
1468cc FI, 1755cc	1989-92	5-35
1597cc Turbo	1987-88	5-35
	1985-86	7-10
1997cc 2V AT	1985-86	7-10
1997cc FI, 2350cc	1987-92	5-35
2555cc Turbo	1987-89	5-35
	1983-86	7-10
1997cc DOHC, 2972cc	1988-92	28-33†

† Measured between middle and either left or right cavities in both rows of 6-terminal ISC connector.

MIXTURE CONTROL SOLENOID
Carburetted engines.

Engine	Year	Resistance (ohms)
1468cc, 1997cc, 2555cc	1987-89	54-66

CHEK-CHART

ENGINE IDENTIFICATION

To identify any engine by the manufacturer's code, follow the four steps designated by the numbered blocks.

1 **MODEL YEAR IDENTIFICATION:** Refer to illustration of Vehicle Identification Number (V.I.N.), the year is indicated by a code letter which is the 10th character of the V.I.N.

2 **ENGINE CODE LOCATION:** Refer to illustration of V.I.N. plate for location and designation of engine code.

3 **ENGINE CODE:** In the vertical "CODE" column, find the engine code determined in Step 2.

4 **ENGINE IDENTIFICATION:** On the line where the engine code appears, read to the right to identify the engine.

V.I.N. PLATE LOCATIONS:

Models 100-450
Left front door lock face or pillar.

V.I.N. also on top left side of instrument panel.

Model year of vehicle:
1992 — N; 1991 — M; 1990 — L;
1989 — K; 1988 — J; 1987 — H;
1986 — G; 1985 — F; 1984 — E;
1983 — D.

MODEL YEAR AND ENGINE IDENTIFICATION:

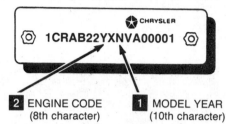

2 ENGINE CODE (8th character) **1** MODEL YEAR (10th character)

---

	3 ENGINE		**4** ENGINE IDENTIFICATION			
			DISPL.		Fuel	
YEAR	CODE	CYL.	liters	cu. in.	System	HP
1992	K	4	2.5	152	TBI	117
	X	6	3.9	238	MFI	180
	Y	8	5.2	318	MFI	230
	Z	8	5.9	360	TBI	190
	5	8	5.9	360	TBI	205
	8	6	5.9 TD	359 TD	MFI	160
1991	K	4	2.5	152	TBI	117
	X	6	3.9	238	TBI	125
	Y	8	5.2	318	TBI	165, 170†
	Z	8	5.9	360	TBI	190
	5	8	5.9	360	TBI	205
	8	6	5.9 TD	359 TD	MFI	160
1990	K	4	2.5	152	TBI	100
	X	6	3.9	238	TBI	125
	Y	8	5.2	318	TBI	170
	Z	8	5.9	360	TBI	190
	5	8	5.9	360	TBI	205
	8	6	5.9 TD	359 TD	MFI	160
1989	K	4	2.5	152	TBI	100
	X	6	3.9	238	TBI	125
	Y	8	5.2	318	TBI	170
	5, W	8	5.9	360	TBI	180-193†
	8	6	5.9 TD	359 TD	MFI	160
1988	C	4	2.2	135	2V	91
	M, X	6	3.9	238	TBI	125
	Y	8	5.2	318	TBI	170
	W	8	5.9	360	4V	185
	I	8	5.9	360	4V	185
1987	C	4	2.2	135	2V	96
	M	6	3.9	238	2V	125

	3 ENGINE		**4** ENGINE IDENTIFICATION			
			DISPL.		Fuel	
YEAR	CODE	CYL.	liters	cu. in.	System	HP
1987 Cont'd.	H	6	3.7	225	1V	90
	T	8	5.2	318	2V	145
	W	8	5.9	360	4V	180
	I	8	5.9	360	4V	175
1986	H	6	3.7	225	1V	90
	T	8	5.2	318	2V	145
	W	8	5.9	360	4V	180
	I	8	5.9	360	4V	175
1985	H	6	3.7	225	1V	90
	T	8	5.2	318	2V	145
	V	8	5.9	360	2V	170
	W	8	5.9	360	4V	180
	I	8	5.9	360	4V	175
1984	H	6	3.7	225	1V	85, 95†
	T	8	5.2	318	2V	135, 150†
	V	8	5.9	360	2V	170
	W	8	5.9	360	4V	175, 180†
	I	8	5.9	360	4V	175
1983	J	6	3.7	225	1V	90-100†
	M, L	6	3.7	225	2V	100, 105†
	T	8	5.2	318	2V	145, 150†
	U	8	5.2	318	4V	160-170†
	V	8	5.9	360	2V	170
	I	8	5.9	360	4V	170
	W	8	5.9	360	4V	180

TD — Turbo Diesel.   TBI — Throttle Body Injection.
MFI — Multiport Fuel Injection.   1V — One Venturi Carburetor.
2V — Two Venturi Carburetor.   4V — Four Venturi Carburetor.
† Engine horsepower varies with model installation.

UNDERHOOD SERVICE SPECIFICATIONS

CRTTU1   CRTTU1

CYLINDER NUMBERING SEQUENCE

FIRING ORDER:

4-CYL.
1 3 4 2

V6-CYL.
1 6 5 4 3 2

6-CYL.
1 5 3 6 2 4

8-CYL.
1 8 4 3 6 5 7 2

2.2L (135),
2.5L (153)

3.7L (225)

3.9L (239)

5.2L (318),
5.9L (360)

—— Front of car ——

UNDERHOOD SERVICE SPECIFICATIONS

CRTTU2 CRTTU2

TIMING MARK

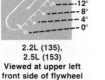

2.2L (135),
2.5L (153)
Viewed at upper left
front side of flywheel
housing

1983-87
3.7L (225)

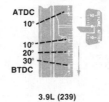

3.9L (239)

1983-85
5.2L (318), 5.9L (360)
(When viewed
from under hood)

1986-92
5.2L (318), 5.9L (360)
(When viewed
from under hood)

1983-92
5.2L (318),
5.9L (360) Some
(When viewed
from under vehicle)

ELECTRICAL AND IGNITION SYSTEMS

BATTERY

		STANDARD		OPTIONAL	
Engine	Year	BCI Group No.	Crank. Perf.	BCI Group No.	Crank. Perf.
All	1983-84	25	370	24	500
All	1985-86	34	400	34	500
All ex. Dakota	1987-91	34	500	34	625
Diesel	1989-91	31	1025	—	—
Dakota 4-cyl.	1987-88	26	335	34	400
Dakota 4-cyl.	1989-91	34	500	—	—
Dakota V6	1987-88	34	400	—	—
Dakota V6	1989-91	34	500	34	625

ALTERNATOR

See UNDERHOOD SERVICE INSTRUCTIONS at the beginning of this section for test/adjustment diagrams.

Test output minimum amps is measured at 15.0 volts, except 78, 114, or 117 ampere alternator which is 13.0 volts.

Application	Year	Rated Output	Test Output (amps @ 1250 rpm)
Tag Color (1983-87 models):			
Violet	1983-85	41	40
Yellow	1983-87	60	57
Yellow	1983-85	117	72
Yellow	1986	114	92
Brown	1985-87	78	57
50/120 alt.	1987	120	98
All Models (1988-92)			
Bosch: 75HS	1988-90	75	30
90HS	1988-89	90	75
Nippondenso: 75HS	1988-90	75	68
90HS	1988-90	90	87
120HS	1989-90	120	98
Nippondenso: 75HS	1991-92	75	75
90HS	1991-92	90	90
120HS	1991-92	120	120
Chrysler: 90RS	1988-89	90	87
120RS	1988-89	120	98

REGULATOR

1983-87, all ex. 1987 50/120 amp alternator.

Year	Test Temp. (deg. F/C)	Voltage Setting
1983-87	−20/−29	14.9-15.9
	80/27	13.9-14.6
	140/60	13.3-13.9
	Above 140/60	Less than 13.9
1988-89	—	*
1990-92	—	12.9-15.0*

* Regulated by computer.

STARTER

Engine at operating temperature.

Engine	Year	Cranking Voltage (min. volts)	Ampere Draw @ Cranking Speed
3.7L (225), 5.2L (318)	1983-86	·9.5	165-180
All Others	1983-86	9.5	180-200
2.2L (135)	1987	7.5	120-160
All Others	1987	9.5	180-200
All: Gasoline	1988-92	7.5	150-220
Diesel		8.0	450-550

SPARK PLUGS

Engine	Year	Gap (inches)	Gap (mm)	Torque (ft-lb)
4-cyl.	1987-92	.035	.89	20
3.7L (225)	1983-86	.035	.89	10
All Others	1983-92	.035	.89	30

IGNITION COIL

See UNDERHOOD SERVICE INSTRUCTIONS at the beginning of this section for test/adjustment diagrams.
Resistance (ohms at 70° to 80°F or 21° to 27°C)

Engine	Year	Windings	Resistance (ohms)
All w/Prestolite	1983-84	Primary	1.60-1.79
		Secondary	9400-11,700
All oil filled coils:			
Essex, UTC	1983-92	Primary	1.34-1.55
		Secondary	9000-12,200
Prestolite	1985-92	Primary	1.34-1.55
		Secondary	9400-11,700
Diamond	1988-92	Primary	1.34-1.55
		Secondary	15,000-19,000
All epoxy type:			
Diamond	1991-92	Primary	.96-1.18
		Secondary	11,300-15,300
Toyodenso	1991-92	Primary	.95-1.20
		Secondary	4300-13,300

DISTRIBUTOR PICKUP

See UNDERHOOD SERVICE INSTRUCTIONS at the beginning of this section for test/adjustment diagrams.

Engine	Year	Resistance (ohms)	Air Gap (in./mm)
3.7L (225), All V8 ex. EST.			
Single pickup	1983-87	150-900	.006/.15
Dual pickups:			
start	1983-86	150-900	.006/.15
run	1983-86	150-900	.012/.30
run 6-cyl.	1987-88	150-900	.012/.30
run 8-cyl.	1987-88	150-900	.008/.20

IGNITION RESISTOR

See UNDERHOOD SERVICE INSTRUCTIONS at the beginning of this section for test/adjustment diagrams.

Year	Resistance (ohms)	Temperature (deg. F/C)
1983-88 ex. ESC	1.12-1.38	70-80/ 21-27

DODGE/PLYMOUTH TRUCKS
1983-92 All Rear Wheel & 4-Wheel Drive Models

CHEK-CHART

UNDERHOOD SERVICE SPECIFICATIONS

BASE TIMING
See UNDERHOOD SERVICE INSTRUCTIONS at the beginning of this section for test/adjustment diagrams.

All carburetted. Set timing at slow idle and Before Top Dead Center, unless otherwise specified.

Distributor or Spark Control Computer vacuum hose disconnected and plugged.

Ground carb switch on models 1983-87 with computer.

1988-91 All, 1992 2.5L, 5.9L: Disconnect coolant temperature sensor.

1992 3.9L, 5.2L. Timing is not adjustable. Set timing marks to TDC and verify that rotor blade is aligned with notch on switch plate.

Engine	Year	Man. Trans. (degrees)	Auto. Trans. (degrees)
2.2L (135)	1987-88	6 ±2	6 ±2
w/decal 901, 02, 03, 04	1987-88	3 ±2	3 ±2
2.5L	1989-92	12 ±2	—
3.7L (225)	1983-87	12• ±2	16• ±2
3.9L (238)	1987	7 ±2†	7 ±2†
3.9L	1988-91	10 ±2	10 ±2
3.9L	1992	TDC*	TDC*
5.2L (318) 2V	1983-87	12 ±2	12 ±2
w/decal 950, 951	1987	8 ±2	8 ±2
Calif., High Altitude	1983-84	16 ±2	16 ±2
Calif., High Altitude	1985-86	8 ±2	8 ±2
5.2L (318) 2V HD♦	1983	2 ATDC ±2	2 ATDC ±2
5.2L (318) 2V HD♦	1984-86	8 ±2	8 ±2
5.2L (318) 2V HD♦	1987	—	10 ±2
5.2L (318) 4V LD♦	1983	12 ±2	16 ±2
5.2L (318) 4V HD♦	1983	8 ±2	8 ±2
5.2L (318) FI	1988-91	10 ±2	10 ±2
5.2L	1992	TDC*	TDC*
5.9L (360) 2V	1983	4 ±2	4 ±2
5.9L (360) 4V	1983	4 ±2	4 ±2
California	1983	10 ±2	10 ±2
5.9L (360)	1984	—	14 ±2
Heavy-duty♦	1984	—	4 ±2
5.9L (360)	1985-86	12 ±2	16 ±2
Heavy-duty♦	1985-86	10 ±2	10 ±2
w/decal SWG	1986	13 ±2	13 ±2
5.9L (360)	1987-88	12 ±2	12 ±2
California	1987	16 ±2	16 ±2
w/decal 564	1987	12 ±2	12 ±2
High Altitude	1988	13 ±2	13 ±2
Heavy-duty♦	1987-88	10 ±2	10 ±2
w/distr. 4145397	1987-88	13 ±2	13 ±2
5.9L FI	1989-92	10 ±2	10 ±2

♦ **Light-duty cycle:** GVW of 8500 or less; **Heavy-duty cycle:** GVW of 8501 lb or over.
• Timing may be readjusted to 8° MT, 12° AT if detonation is occurring.
† Timing may be readjusted to 3° if detonation is occurring.
* Not adjustable.

DISTRIBUTOR TIMING ADVANCE
Engine degrees at engine rpm, no load, in addition to basic timing setting.

Engine	Trans-mission	Year	Distributor Number	Degrees @ 2500 RPM Total	Centrifugal
5.2L (318)	MT & AT	1983-87	4111501	26.2-34.5	6.2-10.5
5.2L (318)	MT & AT	1983-84	4111783	27.4-35.4	12.4-16.4
5.2L (318)	MT & AT	1983-84	4111950, 5	28-35	8-11
5.2L (318)	MT & AT	1983-86	4145606	25.3-31.4	5.3-7.4
5.9L (360)	MT & AT	1983	4091661	26.8-34.8	14.8-18.8
5.9L (360)	MT & AT	1983-87	4111950, 5	28-35	8-11
5.9L (360)	MT & AT	1987	4145399	28-36	4-8
5.9L (360)	MT & AT	1987	4379070	22.6-30.6	7.6-11.6

FUEL SYSTEM

FUEL SYSTEM PRESSURE
See UNDERHOOD SERVICE INSTRUCTIONS at the beginning of this section for test/adjustment diagrams.

Engine	Year	Pressure PSI	RPM
2.2L (135)	1987-88	4.5-6.0	idle
2.5L (135)	1989-92	13.5-15.5	idle
3.7L (225)	1983-87	4.0-5.5	idle

FUEL SYSTEM PRESSURE Continued

Engine	Year	Pressure PSI	RPM
3.9L (238), 5.2L (318), 5.9L (360) ex. TBI	1983-87	5.75-7.25	idle
3.9L, 5.2L, 5.9L	1987-91	13.5-15.5	idle
3.9L, 5.2L	1992	37-41	idle
Diesel	1989-92	3.5	idle

IDLE SPEED W/O COMPUTER CONTROL
See UNDERHOOD SERVICE INSTRUCTIONS at the beginning of this section for test/adjustment diagrams.

1983-86, disconnect and plug canister control and EGR vacuum hoses. Remove PCV valve from grommet and allow it to draw underhood air. With ESC, ground carb switch and disconnect O₂ sensor.

1983-88, 6- & 8-cyl. models with solenoids. Turn A/C on, set blower to low, disconnect compressor clutch wire. Without A/C, apply battery voltage to solenoid. Adjust speed-up solenoid by removing adjusting screw and spring and inserting a 1/8" Allen wrench into socket and turning. Set idle speed by adjusting screw on carb body.

1987-88 4-cyl., energize radiator fan with a jumper wire. Remove PCV valve from grommet and disconnect vacuum kicker solenoid electrical lead. Disconnect oxygen sensor test connector on left fender shield. Adjust idle speed screw on top of solenoid to specified idle speed. Place fast idle cam on specified step and adjust to specified value. Disconnect idle solenoid electrical lead and set base idle to specified value.

Other models, set idle speed by turn screw on carb body. Set cam to specified step and adjust fast idle to specification.

Engine	Year	SLOW Man. Trans.	SLOW Auto. Trans.	FAST Man. Trans.	FAST Auto. Trans.	Step of Cam
2.2L (135)	1987-88	850	900 N	1750	1950	Low
base idle	1987-88	700	700 N			
3.7L (225) 2V	1983	700	—	1600	—	2nd High
3.7L (225) 1V	1983	600	650 N	1600	1600 P, N	2nd High
Solenoid	1983	800	800 N			
California	1983	750	750 N	1600	1600 P, N	2nd High
Solenoid	1983	850	850 N			
Canada	1983	725	750 N	1800	1600 P, N	2nd High
3.7L (225)	1984	700	725 N	1600	1600 P, N	2nd High
Solenoid	1984	800	800 N			
California	1984	700	725 N	1600	1600 P, N	2nd High
Solenoid	1984	850	850 N			
Canada	1984	725	750 N	1800	1600 P, N	2nd High
Heavy Duty♦	1984	700	—	1700	—	2nd High
3.7L (225)	1985-87	725	750 N	1600	1600 P, N	2nd High
Solenoid	1985-87	825	850 N			
Canada	1985-87	725	750 N	1800	1600 P, N	2nd High
Solenoid	1985-87	825	850 N			
California	1985-87	775	775 N	1600	1600 P, N	2nd High
Solenoid	1985-87	850	850 N			
3.9L (238) 4V	1987	700	700 N	1700	1800 N	2nd High
w/decal 575, 77, 78	1987	720	700 N	1800	1900 N	2nd High
5.2L (318) 2V	1983-84	750	750 N	1500	1500 P, N	2nd High
High Altitude	1983-84	800	800 N	1400	1400 P, N	2nd High
Solenoid	1983-84	850	850 N			
California	1983-84	740	700 N		1400 P, N	2nd High
Solenoid	1983-84	850	850 N			
Canada	1983-84	750	750 N	1500	1500 P, N	2nd High
Heavy Duty♦	1984	750	—	1500	—	2nd High
5.2L (318) 2V LD	1985	700	700 N	1600	1600 P, N	2nd High
Solenoid	1985	850	850 N			
High Altitude	1985	650	650 N	1400	1400 P, N	2nd High
Solenoid	1985	780	780 N			
California	1985	725	650 N	1625	1450 P, N	2nd High
Solenoid	1985	850	800 N			
5.2L (318) 2V HD	1985	750	750 N	1600	1450 P, N	2nd High
5.2L (318) LD	1986	700	700 N	1550	1550 P, N	2nd High
Solenoid	1986	875	875 N			
High Altitude	1986	650	650 N	1400	1400 P, N	2nd High
Solenoid	1986	780	780 N			
California	1986	650	650 N	1450	1450 P, N	2nd High
Solenoid	1986	850	800 N			
5.2L (318) HD	1986	—	700 N	—	1450 P, N	2nd High
w/decal 936, 937, 938	1986	—	650 N	—	1450 P, N	2nd High

UNDERHOOD SERVICE SPECIFICATIONS

CRTTU4   CRTTU4

IDLE SPEED W/O COMPUTER CONTROL Continued

Engine	Year	SLOW Man. Trans.	SLOW Auto. Trans.	FAST Man. Trans.	FAST Auto. Trans.	Step of Cam
5.2L (318) LD	1987	700	700 N	1550	1550 N	2nd High
Solenoid	1987	825	825 N			
w/decal 950, 51	1987	650	650 N	1450	1450 N	2nd High
Solenoid	1987	825	825 N			
w/decal 960	1987	—	650 N	—	1600 N	2nd High
Solenoid	1987	—	825 N			
High Altitude	1987	650	650 N	1400	1400 N	2nd High
Solenoid	1987	780	780 N			
California	1987	650	650 N	1450	1450 N	2nd High
Solenoid	1987	780	780 N			
5.2L (318) 4V	1983	750	750 N	1600	1600 P, N	2nd High
California	1983	750	750 N	1800	1800 P, N	2nd High
5.9L (360) 2V	1983	—	750 N	—	1600 P, V	2nd High
5.9L (360) LD♦	1984	—	760 N	—	1500 P, N	2nd High
High Altitude	1984	—	725 N	—	1600 P, N	2nd High
5.9L (360) 4V HD♦	1983-84	700	700 N	1500	1500 P, N	2nd High
California	1983-84	750	750 N	1700	1700 P, N	2nd High
5.9L (360) LD♦	1985-86	800	800 N	1350	1350 P, N	2nd High
Solenoid	1985-86	—	900 N			
High Altitude	1985	780	750 N	1600	1600 P, N	2nd High
High Altitude	1986	750	710 N	1600	1600 P, N	2nd High
5.9L (360) HD♦	1985-86	750	750 N	1350	1350 P, N	2nd High
Calif., Canada	1985-86	800	800 N	1350	1350 P, N	2nd High
5.9L (360) LD♦	1987	800	800 N	1400	1400 N	2nd High
Solenoid	1987	—	950 N			
California	1987	700	700 N	1350	1300 N	2nd High
Solenoid	1987	—	950 N			
w/decal 564	1987	800	800 N	1400	1400 N	2nd High
Solenoid	1987	—	950 N			
5.9L (360) HD♦	1987	800	800 N	1350	1350 N	2nd High
Solenoid	1987	800	850 N			
w/decal 472, 473	1987	—	900 N	—	1350 N	2nd High
California	1987	800	800 N	1350	1350 N	2nd High
5.9L (360) LD♦	1988	800	800 N	1400	1400 N	2nd High
w/decal 628, 630, 725, 727, 729	1988	750	750 N	1400	1400 N	2nd High
Solenoid	1988	800	850 N			
Canada	1988	800	800 N	1400	1400 N	2nd High
5.9L (360) HD	1988	800	800 N	—	—	—
Solenoid	1988	950	950 N			
California	1988	800	800 N	—	—	—

♦ **Light-duty cycle:** 1983 models, GVW of 8500 lb or less. **Medium-duty cycle:** GVW of 6001 to 8500 lb. **Heavy-duty cycle:** 1983-87 models with a GVW of 8501 lb or over.
* With carb. R9425A, R9426A, R9428A, and R9429A or with authorized electric choke control switch: Slow, 650; shutdown, 800.

IDLE SPEED W/COMPUTER CONTROL
See **UNDERHOOD SERVICE INSTRUCTIONS** at the beginning of this section for test/adjustment diagrams.

1988-91 V6, V8, 1992 5.9L: Run engine for two minutes and shut off. After 60 seconds, disconnect ISC and Coolant temp. sensor connectors. Adjust extension screw on ISC to adjust.

1989-92 4-cyl.: Connect DRB-II to ''check engine'' connector. Disconnect PCV valve and install special tool C-5004 (0.125" orifice) to PCV hose. Start engine and switch DRB to ''Min. Airflow Idle Spd.'' If minimum throttle body airflow is not correct, throttle body must be replaced.

Engine	Year	Setting Speed	Idle Speed	Checking Speed
2.5L	1989-90	—	850	1050-1250
2.5L	1991-92	—	—	1050-1250
3.9L Dakota	1988-89	2500-2600 (N)	750 (N)	—
3.9L Others: MT	1988	2500-2600 (N)	600	—
AT	1988	2500-2600 (N)	850 (N)	—
With decal 033, 034, 601, 603, 791	1988	2500-2600 (N)	750 (N)	—
3.9L	1989	2500-2600 (N)	750 (N)	—
3.9L	1990-91	2500-2600 (N)	—	—
5.2L	1988-89	2750-2850 (N)	700 (N)	—
5.2L	1990-91	2750-2850 (N)	—	—
5.9L LD	1989	2750-2850 (N)	800 (N)	—
High Altitude	1989	2750-2850 (N)	750 (N)	—
HD	1989	2750-2850 (N)	800 (N)	—
5.9L	1990-92	2750-2850 (N)	—	—

ENGINE MECHANICAL

TIGHTENING TORQUES
See **UNDERHOOD SERVICE INSTRUCTIONS** at the beginning of this section for test/adjustment diagrams.

Some fasteners are tightened in more than one step.
Some torques are specified in inches.

Engine	Year	Cylinder Head	Intake Manifold	Exhaust Manifold	Crankshaft Pulley	Water Pump
2.2L (135), 2.5L (153)	1987-92	45/61, 65/89, 65/89, +90°†	200"/23	200"/23	50/68	21/28-upper 40/54-lower
3.7L (225)	1983-85	35/47, 70/95	120"/14-nuts 240"/27-bolts 260"/23-studs		—	30/41
3.7L (225)	1986-87	35/47, 70/95	120"/14-nuts 260"/29-bolts 300"/34-studs		—	30/41
3.9L (238)	1987-91	50/68, 105/43	45/61	20/27-bolts 15/20-nuts	135/181	30/41
3.9L	1992	50/68, 105/143	72"/8, 12/16	25/36	135/181	30/40
5.2L (318), 5.9L (360)	1983-87	50/68, 105/43	45/61	20/27-bolts 15/20-nuts	100/136	30/41
5.2L, 5.9L	1988-91	50/68, 105/43	40/54	20/27-bolts 15/20-nuts	100/136	30/41
5.2L	1992	50/68, 105/143	72"/8 12/16	25/34	135/181	30/40
5.9L	1992	50/68, 105/143	25/34, 40/54	15/20-nuts 20/27-bolts	135/183	30/40
5.9L Diesel	1989	29/40, 62/85, 93/126	18/24	32/43	92/125	18/24

†Torque should be above 90/122 after this step or replace bolt.

COMPRESSION PRESSURE
At cranking speed, engine temperature normalized, throttle open.

Engine	Year	PSI	Maximum Variation PSI
6-cyl.	1983-86	100 min.	25
8-cyl.	1983-84	100 min.	40
All Gasoline	1985-92	100 min.	25

BELT TENSION
A belt in operation for 15 minutes is considered a used belt.

Strand Tension method: Use gauge. Measurements are in pounds. Used belts, 60-90; New belts, 100-140. 1990-91 Dakota V8, 1992 3.9L, 5.2L use automatic tensioner.

ENGINE COMPUTER SYSTEM

COMPUTER DIAGNOSTIC CODES
See **UNDERHOOD SERVICE INSTRUCTIONS** at the beginning of this section for test/adjustment diagrams.

All w/FI: Turn ignition switch on-off-on-off-on and observe. Check Engine light.
Code 11 Engine not cranked since battery disconnected
Code 12 Standby memory circuit
Code 13 MAP sensor vacuum circuit
Code 14 MAP sensor electrical circuit
Code 15 Speed/distance sensor circuit
Code 16 Battery voltage sense loss
Code 17 Engine running too cool
Code 21 Oxygen sensor circuit
Code 22 Coolant temperature sensor circuit
Code 23 Throttle body temperature circuit
Code 24 Throttle position sensor circuit
Code 25 Automatic idle speed control circuit
Code 26 Peak injector current not reached
Code 27 Fuel injector control problem
Code 31 Canister purge solenoid circuit

UNDERHOOD SERVICE SPECIFICATIONS

CRTTU5   CRTTU5

COMPUTER DIAGNOSTIC CODES Continued

Code 32 EGR diagnostics
Code 33 Air conditioner WOT relay circuit
Code 34 Speed control solenoid driver circuit
Code 35 Radiator for relay (4-cyl.)
Code 35 Idle switch (V6, V8)
Code 36 Air switching solenoid
Code 37 Torque converter lock-up solenoid
Code 41 Charging system over voltage
Code 42 Automatic shutdown relay circuit
Code 43 Ignition coil control
Code 44 Loss of F2 to logic board
Code 45 Automatic transmission overdrive circuit
Code 46 Battery over voltage
Code 47 Battery under voltage
Code 51 Oxygen sensor lean
Code 52 Oxygen sensor rich
Code 53 Logic module (1988)
Code 53 Engine controller fault
Code 55 End of message
Code 62 EMR mileage accumulator
Code 63 EEPROM write denied or fault code error
Code 88 Start of message

SENSORS, INPUT

TEMPERATURE SENSORS

Engine	Year	Sensor	Resistance Ohms @ deg. F/C
2.2L (135), 3.9L (238) 4V	1987-88	Coolant, Charge	5000-6000 @ 70/21 700-800 @ 200/93
2.5L (153), 3.9L (238), 5.2L (318), 5.9L (360)	1988-91	Coolant	7000-13,000 @ 70/21 700-1000 @ 200/93
		Throttle body (ex. V6)	5600-14,600 @ 70/21 400-1500 @ 200/93
2.5L, 5.9L	1992	Coolant	7000-13,000 @ 70/21 700-1000 @ 200/93
		Throttle body	5600-14,600 @ 70/21 400-1500 @ 200/93
3.7L (225), 5.2L (318), 5.9L (360)	1983-87	Coolant	22,000-382,000 @ −40° to 20°F 3300-36,000 @ 50 to 100°F 176-3900 @ 140 to 245°F
		Charge	100 max. @ 60/16 no continuity @ operating temp.
3.9L, 5.9L	1992	Coolant, Charge	29,330-35,990 @ @ 32/0 11,370-13,610 @ 68/20 4900-5750 @ 104/40 2310-2670 @ 176/80 640-720 @ 212/100 370-410 @ 248/210

MANIFOLD ABSOLUTE PRESSURE SENSOR
All Models with TBI.

1988-91 Apply 5″ (125mm) Hg to unit and record output voltage. Apply 20″ (500mm) Hg to unit, the difference in voltage should be 2.3-2.9.

Engine	Year	Voltage Idle	Voltage Ign. On
3.9L, 5.2L	1992	1.5-2.1	4.0-5.0

THROTTLE POSITION SENSOR
All with TBI.

Engine	Year	Voltage Idle	Voltage WOT
All	1987-91	0.5-1.5	4.0
3.9L, 5.2L	1992	0.2 min	4.8 max
5.9L	1992	0.5-1.5	4.0

ACTUATORS, OUTPUT

IDLE SPEED SOLENOID

Engine	Year	Resistance (ohms)
2.2L (135), 3.9L (238)	1987-88	20-100
3.7L (225), 5.2L (318) 4V	1983-87	15-35

COMPUTER TIMING ADVANCE

All specifications are in addition to basic timing.

Perform tests with engine at operating temperature.

Disconnect and plug vacuum hose at computer. Apply 16″ of vacuum to the transducer and increase engine speed to 2000 RPM. Verify that idle speed screw is not contacting the carb ground switch and check advance against specification after one minute, or time indicated has elapsed.

Engine	Year	Transmission	Computer Number	Advance
2.2L (135)	1987-88	MT & AT	All	17.5-25.5
2.5L	1989-90	MT & AT	All	24-32
6-cyl. 1V	1983	MT	All	21-29
6-cyl. 1V	1983	AT	All	18-26
California	1983	MT	All	12-20
California	1983	AT	All	0-8
6-cyl. 2V	1983	MT	All	24-32
5.2L (318) 2V	1983	MT	All	9-17
5.2L (318) 2V	1983	AT	All	4-12
6-cyl.	1984	MT	All	35-43
6-cyl.	1984	AT	All	39-47
California	1984	MT	All	33-41
California	1984	AT	All	17-25
Canada	1984	MT	All	33-41
Canada	1984	AT	All	37-45
3.9L (238) Fed., Canada	1987	MT	All	32-40
California	1987	MT	4379196	26-34
w/3.50 axle	1987	MT	4379198	22-30
All	1987	AT	All	34-42
3.9L (238) Dakota				
Fed., Canada	1987	MT	All	34-42
Fed., Canada	1987	AT	All	32-40
California	1987	MT	All	34-42
California	1987	AT	4379196	26-34
California	1987	AT	4379198	22-30
3.9L (238) Dakota	1989-90	MT & AT	All	31-39
5.2L (318) 2V	1984	MT & AT	All	38-48
6-cyl.	1985	MT	All	29-37
6-cyl.	1985	AT	All	34-42
California	1985	MT	4289637	30-38
California	1985	MT & AT	All Others	26-34
Canada	1985	MT & AT	All	37-45
5.2L (318) 2V	1985	MT & AT	All	30-38
California	1985	MT	4289617	26-34
California	1985	MT & AT	All Others	30-38
6-cyl.	1986-87	MT	All	29-37
California	1986-87	MT	All	26-34
6-cyl.	1986-87	AT	All	34-42
California	1986-87	AT	All	26-34
5.2L (318)	1986	MT & AT	All	41-49
High Alt.	1986	MT & AT	All	30-38
California	1986	MT	All	30-38
California	1986	AT	All	41-49
Ramcharger	1986	AT	All	38-46
5.2L (318)	1987	MT & AT	All	28-36
High Alt.	1987	MT	All	30-38
High Alt.	1987	AT	All	38-46
California	1987	MT	All	15-23
California	1987	AT	All	26-34
Ramcharger	1987	AT	All	22-30
3.9L, 5.2L	1988	MT & AT	All	20-35

ENGINE IDENTIFICATION

To identify an engine by the manufacturer's code, follow the four steps designated by the numbered blocks.

V.I.N.
PLATE LOCATION:
1992-88: Top left side of instrument panel, visible through windshield.

1 MODEL YEAR IDENTIFICATION:
1992-88 — 10th character of V.I.N.
1992 — N; 1991 — M; 1990 — L;
1989 — K; 1988 — J.

2 ENGINE CODE LOCATION:
1992-89 — 8th character of V.I.N.
1988 — 4th character of V.I.N.

4 ENGINE IDENTIFICATION

YEAR	3 ENGINE CODE	CYL.	DISPL. liters	cc	Fuel System	HP
1992	A	4	1.5	1468	MFI	92
	D	4	1.8	1797	MFI	113
	R	4	2.0	1997	MFI	135
	U	4	2.0 T	1997	MFI	195
	W	4	2.4	2396	MFI	116
	U	6	3.0	2970	MFI	150
1991	A	4	1.5	1468	MFI	92
	R	4	2.0	1997	MFI	135
	U	4	2.0 T	1997	MFI	190, 195
	U	6	3.0	2970	MFI	150
1990	X	4	1.5	1468	MFI	81
	Y	4	1.6	1597	MFI	113
	R	4	2.0	1997	MFI	135

4 ENGINE IDENTIFICATION

YEAR	3 ENGINE CODE	CYL.	DISPL. liters	cc	Fuel System	HP
1990 Cont'd.	U	4	2.0 T	1997	MFI	190
	U	6	3.0	2970	MFI	150
1989	X	4	1.5	1468	MFI	81
	Y	4	1.6	1597	MFI	113
	F	4	2.2	2165	MFI	103
	Z	4	2.5	2460	TBI	111
	U	6	3.0	2970	MFI	150
1988	F	4	2.2	2165	MFI	103
	Z	4	2.5	2460	TBI	111
	U	6	3.0	2970	MFI	150

T — Turbo.   MFI — Multiport Fuel Injection.
TBI — Throttle Body Injection.

UNDERHOOD SERVICE SPECIFICATIONS

EETU1   EETU1

CYLINDER NUMBERING SEQUENCE

4-CYL. FIRNG ORDER: 1 3 4 2

— Front of car —

| 1989-90 Summit 1.5L Code X | 1991-92 Summit 1.5L Code A | 1989-90 Summit 1.6L, 1990-92 Talon 2.0L | 1992 1.8L Code D Summit Wagon | 1988-90 Premier 2.5L | 1988-89 Medallion 2.2L | 1992 2.4L Code W Summit Wagon |

— TIMING MARK —

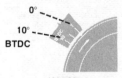

0°
10°
BTDC

1991-92
Summit Codes A, W

BTDC
— 10°
— 0°

1989-90
Summit Codes D, X

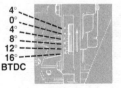

4°
0°
4°
8°
12°
16°
BTDC

2.2L

V6 FIRING ORDER:
1 6 3 5 2 4

Direct ignition
Distributor ignition

Front of car
1988-92 Premier 3.0L

ELECTRICAL AND IGNITION SYSTEMS

BATTERY
BCI equivalent shown, size may vary from original equipment. Check clearance before replacing, holddown may need to be modified.

Engine/Model	Year	STANDARD BCI Group No.	STANDARD Crank. Perf.	OPTIONAL BCI Group No.	OPTIONAL Crank. Perf.
1.5L, 1.6L Summit	1989-90	45	435	—	—
1.5L, 1.6L Summit	1991-92	25	35	25	430
1.8L Talon	1990-92	86	430	—	—
2.0L Talon	1990-92	86	525	—	—
2.0L Vista	1989-91	25	420	—	—
2.2L Medallion	1988-89	34	375	58	400
2.5L, 3.0L Premier	1988	58	390	34	525
2.5L, 3.0L Premier	1989-92	34	500	—	—

ALTERNATOR

Application	Year	Rated Output (amps)	Test Output (amps)
Medallion	1988-89	75	61 @ 1200
		90	76 @ 1200
Premier	1988-90	85, 96, 100, 105	*
Premier	1991-92	96	78 @ 2000

ALTERNATOR Continued

Application	Year	Rated Output (amps)	Test Output (amps)
Summit, Talon	1989-92	65	46 @ 2500
		75	53 @ 2500
		90	63 @ 2500
Vista	1989-91	65	46 @ 2500
		75	53 @ 2500

* Output at 2000 rpm must be within 15 amps of rated output.

REGULATOR

Application	Test Temp. (deg. F/C)	Voltage Setting
1988-89 Medallion	175/80	13.0-14.1
1988-91 Premier	—	13.5-16.0
1989-92 Summit, Talon, Vista	-4/-20	14.2-15.4
	68/20	13.9-14.9
	140/60	13.4-14.6
	175/80	13.1-14.5

STARTER

Engine	Year	Cranking Voltage (min. volts)	Ampere Draw @ Cranking Speed
1.5L, 1.6L, 1.8L, 2.0L, 2.4L	1989-92	8.0	—
2.2L	1988-89	9.6	160
2.5L, 3.0L	1988-92	9.6	130

EAGLE/RENAULT
1988-92 Medallion, Premier, Summit, Talon, Vista

SPARK PLUGS

Engine	Year	Gap (inches)	Gap (mm)	Torque (ft-lb)
1.5L, 1.6L	1989-92	.039-.043	1.0-1.1	15-21
1.8L, 2.0L ex. Turbo, 2.4L	1990-92	.039-.043	1.0-1.1	15-21
2.0L Turbo	1990-92	.028-.031	0.7-0.8	15-21
2.2L	1988-89	.036	.90	11
2.5L	1988-89	.036	.90	28
3.0L	1988-92	.035	.90	11

IGNITION COIL
Resistance (ohms @ 70°F or 21°C)

2.0L, 1991 3.0L (late): Primary windings measured between B+ terminal (upper right on connector) and each of the other three terminals. Secondary resistance measured at each coils high voltage terminals with spark plug wires removed.

Engine	Year	Windings	Resistance (ohms)
1.5L	1989-90	Primary	.72-.86
		Secondary	10,300-13,900
1.5L, 1.8L Wagon	1991-92	Primary	0.9-1.2
		Secondary	20,000-29,000
1.6L	1989-90	Primary	.77-.95
		Secondary	10,300-13,900
1.8L Talon	1990-92	Primary	0.9-1.2
		Secondary	19,000-27,000
2.0L Talon	1990-91	Primary	.72-.95
		Secondary	10,300-13,900
2.0L Vista	1989-91	Primary	.72-.88
		Secondary	10,900-13,300
2.0L	1992	Primary	.70-.86
		Secondary	11,300-15,300
2.2L, 2.5L, 3.0L (early)	1988-90	Primary	0.5-1.0
		Secondary	4500-5000
2.4L	1991	Primary	.72-.88
		Secondary	10,300-13,900

BASE TIMING
Set timing at Before Top Dead Center at idle speed or less.

1.5L, 1.6L, 1.8L, 2.0L, 2.4L: Ground ignition timing connector (on fender skirt or firewall). When disconnected, timing should be at "Check" value.

Engine	Year	Man. Trans. (degrees)	Auto. Trans. (degrees)
1.5L: Set	1989-92	5 ±2	5 ±2
Check	1989-92	10 ±2	10 ±2
1.6L: Set	1989-90	5 ±2	5 ±2
Check	1989-90	8 ±2	8 ±2
1.8L Talon: Set	1990-92	5 ±2	5 ±2
Check	1990-92	10 ±2	10 ±2
1.8L Wagon: Set	1992	5 ±2	5 ±2
Check	1992	5 ±2	5 ±2
2.0L ex. Vista, 2.4L: Set	1990-92	5 ±2	5 ±2
Check	1990-92	8 ±2	8 ±2
2.0L Vista: Set	1989-91	5 ±2	5 ±2
Check	1989-91	10 ±2	10 ±2

FUEL SYSTEM

FUEL SYSTEM PRESSURE

CARBURETTED & TBI

Engine	Year	PSI	RPM
2.5L	1988-89	14-15	idle

MFI

Engine	Year	Pressure @ idle PSI*	PSI**
1.5L, 1.6L, 1.8L, 2.0L ex. Turbo, 2.4L	1989-91	47-53	38
2.0L Turbo MT	1990-92	36-38	27
2.0L Turbo AT	1992	41-46	33
2.2L	1988-89	—	33-39

FUEL SYSTEM PRESSURE Continued
MFI Continued

Engine	Year	Pressure @ idle PSI*	PSI**
3.0L (early)	1988-91	—	28-30
3.0L (late)	1991-92	—	43

* Pressure regulator vacuum disconnected.
** Pressure regulator vacuum connected.

IDLE SPEED W/COMPUTER CONTROL
1.5L, 1.8L Talon: Turn ignition on for more than 15 seconds and turn off. Disconnect ISC and start engine. Set to specified value. Reconnect ISC and turn AC on, verify that speed increases to specified value.

2.0L: Ground ignition timing connector and terminal 10 of the self-diagnostic connector. Set speed to specified value. Reinstate connections and verify the speed increases to specified value with AC on.

2.5L: Fully extend ISC with tool #7086 and adjust to specified value.

1991-92 3.0L (late): Connect DRB-II and select base idle mode. Verify that idle is at specified checking speed. Replace throttle body if outside range.

Engine	Year	Transmission	Setting Speed	Checking Speed	AC Speed-up
1.5L, 1.6L	1989-92	MT	700-800	650-850	850
	1989-92	AT	700-800 N	650-850 N	850 N
1.8L Talon	1990-92	MT	650-750	600-800	850
	1990-92	AT	650-750 N	600-800 N	650 D
1.8L Wagon, 2.0L ex. Vista, 2.4L	1990-92	MT	700-800	650-850	850
	1990-92	AT	700-800 N	650-850 N	700 D
2.0L Vista	1989-91	MT	650-750	600-800	900
	1989-91	AT	650-750 N	600-800 N	600 D
3.0L (late)	1991-92	AT	—	565-665 D	—
2.5L	1988-89	MT	3500	750-800	—
	1988-89	AT	3500 N	750-800 N	—

ENGINE MECHANICAL

TIGHTENING TORQUES
1.5L, 1.6L, 1.8L, 2.0L, 2.4L cylinder head bolts are tightened with engine cold.

Engine	Year	Cylinder Head	Intake Manifold	Exhaust Manifold	Crankshaft Pulley	Water Pump
1.5L, 1.8L Talon	1989-92	51-54/ 69-74	12-14/ 16-19	12-14/ 16-19	9-11/ 12-15	9-11/ 12-15■ 14-20/ 20-27□
1.6L, 2.0L	1989-92	65-72/ 90-100	11-14/ 15-19■ 22-30/ 30-42□	18-22/ 25-30	14-22/ 22-30	9-11/ 12-15■ 14-20/ 20-27□
1.8L Wagon	1992	54/75† 14/20, +90°, +90°	13-18	22/30	134/185	18/24
2.2L	1985-89	69/93	—	—	96/130	—
2.4L Wagon	1992	76-83/ 105-115	13/18	13/18	18/25	10/14
2.5L	1988-89	110/149*	23/31	23/31	80/108	13/18
3.0L	1988-91	●	11/15	13/18	125/170	20/27

* Tighten bolt number eight (first bolt, right front side) to 100/136.
● Engines built before code 89616 (1988-90), tighten to 45/61. Back off and retighten to 15/19 and then turn 105°. Run engine for 15 minutes, let cool for six hours and tighten an additional 45°. Engines built from code 89616 (1990-91), tighten to 45/61. Back off and retighten to 30/40 then turn 160-200°.
■ Short bolts.
□ Long bolts.
† Then back off completely.

VALVE CLEARANCE
Engine cold.

Engine	Year	Intake (inches)	Intake (mm)	Exhaust (inches)	Exhaust (mm)
1.5L	1989-92	.003	.07	.007	.17

UNDERHOOD SERVICE SPECIFICATIONS

EETU3

EETU3

COMPRESSION PRESSURE
At cranking speed, engine warm, throttle open.

Engine	Year	PSI	Maximum Variation PSI
1.5L	1989-92	137 min.	14
1.6L	1989-90	171 min.	14
1.8L Talon	1990-92	131 min.	14
1.8L Wagon	1992	142 min.	14
2.0L Vista	1989-91	119 min.	14
2.0L ex. Vista	1990-91	137 min.	14
2.0L ex. Vista	1992	145 min.	14
2.0L Turbo	1990-91	114 min.	14
2.0L Turbo	1992	121 min.	14
2.4L	1992	119 min.	14
2.5L	1988-89	155-185	30
3.0L	1990-92	*	—

* Lowest cylinder pressure must be 75% of highest.

BELT TENSION
Use a strand tension gauge. Measurements are in pounds.

Engine	Year	Alternator	Power Steering	Air Cond.
Strand Tension method				
NEW BELTS:				
1.5L, 1.8L	1989-92	110-155	110-155	105-125
1.6L, 2.0L	1989-92	110-155	110-155	80-95
2.2L	1988-89	65-85	65-85	65-85
Serpentine	1988-89	140-160	140-160	140-160
2.5L, 3.0L	1988-92	180-200	180-200	180-200
USED BELTS:				
1.5L, 1.8L	1989-92	90	90	70-90
1.6L, 2.0L	1989-92	55-110	55-110	55-70
2.2L	1988-89	65-85	65-85	65-85
Serpentine	1988-89	140-160	140-160	140-160
2.5L, 3.0L	1988-92	140-160	140-160	140-160

ENGINE COMPUTER SYSTEM

COMPUTER DIAGNOSTIC CODES
1989-92 Summit, Talon, Vista
Access connector in or under glove box or by fuse block. Connect an analog voltmeter to upper right (+) and lower left (−) cavity. Turn ignition on, codes will be displayed as sweeps of voltmeter needle. Disconnect battery to erase codes.

1991-92 Premier (late)
Turn ignition switch on-off-on-off-on. Codes will be displayed on Check Engine light.

1989-92 Summit, Talon, Vista
Code 11 Oxygen sensor
Code 12 Airflow sensor
Code 13 Intake air temperature sensor
Code 14 Throttle position sensor
Code 15 Motor position sensor
Code 21 Coolant temperature sensor
Code 22 Crank angle sensor
Code 23 Top dead center sensor
Code 24 Vehicle speed sensor
Code 25 Barometric pressure sensor
Code 31 Detonation sensor
Code 36 Ignition timing adjustment
Code 41 Injector
Code 42 Fuel pump
Code 43 EGR
One long pulse ECM
Continuous pulsing System normal
1991-92 Premier (late)
Code 11 Ignition reference circuit
Code 13 MAP sensor vacuum circuit
Code 14 MAP sensor electrical circuit
Code 15 Speed/distance sensor circuit
Code 17 Engine running too cool
Code 21 Oxygen sensor circuit
Code 22 Coolant temperature sensor circuit
Code 23 Charge temperature circuit
Code 24 Throttle position sensor circuit
Code 25 Automatic idle speed control circuit
Code 26 Peak injector current not reached
Code 26 Injector circuit
Code 27 Fuel injection circuit control
Code 32 EGR system

COMPUTER DIAGNOSTIC CODES Continued
Code 33 Air conditioner clutch relay
Code 34 Speed control solenoid driver circuit
Code 35 Fan control relay circuit
Code 42 Automatic shutdown relay circuit
Code 43 Ignition coil circuit
Code 51 Oxygen sensor lean
Code 52 Oxygen sensor rich
Code 53 Internal engine controller fault
Code 54 Fuel sync pick-up circuit
Code 55 End of message
Code 63 EEPROM write denied
Code 77 Speed control power relay

SENSORS, INPUT
TEMPERATURE SENSORS

Engine	Year	Sensor	Resistance Ohms @ deg. F/C
1.5L, 1.6L, 1.8L, 2.0L, 2.4L	1989-92	Coolant	5900 @ 32/0 2500 @ 68/20 1100 @ 104/40 300 @ 176/80
		Intake Air*	6000 @ 32/0 2700 @ 68/20 400 @ 176/80
2.5L, 3.0L	1988-91 (early)	Coolant, MAT	13,500 @ 20/−7 7500 @ 40/4 3400 @ 70/20 1600 @ 100/38 450 @ 160/70 185 @ 212/100
3.0L	1991 (late)-92	Coolant, MAT	7000-13,000 @ 70/21 700-10,000 @ 200/93

* Measured between terminals 4 & 6 or 6 & 8 (bottom left and right) of airflow sensor connector.

MANIFOLD ABSOLUTE PRESSURE SENSOR

Engine	Year	Voltage
2.2L, 2.5L, 3.0L	1988-91 (early)	4-5, ign. on 1.5-2.1, idle

THROTTLE POSITION SENSOR

Engine	Year	Voltage Idle	WOT
1.5L, 1.6L, 1.8L Talon, 2.0L	1989-91	.48-.52	—
1.8L, 2.4L Wagon	1992	0.4-1.0*	—
2.5L	1988-89	—	4.6-4.7
3.0L	1988-91 (early)	0.5-1.0	—

* Not adjustable.

MOTOR POSITION SENSOR

Engine	Year	Resistance (ohms)
1.5L, 1.8L, 2.4L	1989-92	4,000-6,000

CRANKSHAFT SENSOR
Measured between brown and blue terminals of crank angle sensor.

Engine	Year	Resistance (ohms)
2.2L, 2.5L, 3.0L	1988-91 (early)	125-275

ACTUATORS, OUTPUT
IDLE SPEED CONTROL SOLENOID
At 68°F (20°C)
1.6L: Measured between middle and either left or right cavities in both rows of 6-terminal ISC connector.

Engine	Year	Resistance (ohms)
1.5L, 1.8L, 2.0L Vista	1989-92	5-35
1.6L, 2.0L Talon	1989-92	28-33*

* Measured between all three pairs of terminals on six-row connector.

FORD MOTOR COMPANY
1983-92 Ford, Lincoln, Mercury, Merkur

ENGINE IDENTIFICATION

To identify any engine by the manufacturer's code, follow the four steps designated by the numbered blocks.

1 MODEL YEAR IDENTIFICATION: Refer to illustrations of Vehicle Identification Number (V.I.N.).

2 ENGINE CODE LOCATION: Refer to illustration of V.I.N. plate for location and designation of engine code.

3 ENGINE CODE: In the vertical "CODE" column, find the engine code determined in Step 2.

4 ENGINE IDENTIFICATION: On the line where the engine code appears, read to the right to identify the engine.

V.I.N. PLATE LOCATION:

On top left side of instrument panel.

Model year of vehicle:
1992 — Model year is N.
1991 — Model year is M.
1990 — Model year is L.
1989 — Model year is K.
1988 — Model year is J.
1987 — Model year is H.
1986 — Model year is G.
1985 — Model year is F.
1984 — Model year is E.
1983 — Model year is D.

MODEL YEAR AND ENGINE IDENTIFICATION:

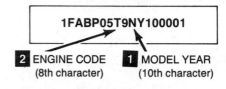

2 ENGINE CODE (8th character) **1 MODEL YEAR** (10th character)

4 ENGINE IDENTIFICATION

YEAR	3 ENGINE CODE	CYL.	DISPL. liters	DISPL. cu. in.	Fuel System	HP
1992	H	4	1.3	79	MFI	63
	Z	4	1.6	98	MFI	100
	6	4	1.6 T	98 T	MFI	132
	8	4	1.8	110	MFI	127
	J	4	1.9	113	TBI	88
	C	4	2.2	133	MFI	110
	L	4	2.2 T	133 T	MFI	145
	M*	4	2.3	140	MFI	105
	X	4	2.3	140	MFI	96
	U	6	3.0	182	MFI	135, 145†
	Y	6	3.0 SHO	182 SHO	MFI	220
	4	6	3.8	232	MFI	140, 160†
	R	6	3.8 S	232 S	MFI	210
	W	8	4.6	281	MFI	190-210
	E	8	5.0 HO	302 HO	MFI	225
	T	8	5.0 HO	302 HO	MFI	200
1991	H	4	1.3	79	MFI	63
	Z	4	1.6	98	MFI	100
	6	4	1.6 T	98 T	MFI	132
	8	4	1.8	110	MFI	127
	J	4	1.9	113	TBI	88
	C	4	2.2	133	MFI	110
	L	4	2.2 T	133 T	MFI	145
	M*	4	2.3	140	MFI	105
	X	4	2.3	140	MFI	98
	S	4	2.3	140	MFI	100
	N	4	2.5	153	MFI	90
	U	6	3.0	182	MFI	145
	Y	6	3.0 SHO	182 SHO	MFI	200
	4	6	3.8	232	MFI	140, 155†
	R	6	3.8 S	232 S	MFI	210
	W	8	4.6	281	MFI	185-200†
	E	8	5.0 HO	302 HO	MFI	225
	F	8	5.0	302	MFI	150-160†
	T	8	5.0 HO	302 HO	MFI	200
	G	8	5.8	351	2V	180
1990	H	4	1.3	79	MFI	63
	9	4	1.9	113	TBI	90
	J	4	1.9	113	MFI	110
	C	4	2.2	133	MFI	110
	L	4	2.2 T	133 T	MFI	145
	A*	4	2.3	140	MFI	88
	X	4	2.3	140	MFI	98
	S	4	2.3 HO	140 HO	MFI	100
	D	4	2.5	153	TBI	90
	U	6	3.0	182	MFI	140
	Y	6	3.0 SHO	182 SHO	MFI	220
	4	6	3.8	232	MFI	140
	R	6	3.8 S	232 S	MFI	210
	E	8	5.0 HO	302 HO	MFI	225
	F	8	5.0	302	MFI	150-160†
	G	8	5.8	351	2V	180
1989	K	4	1.3	79	2V	58
	H	4	1.3	79	MFI	63
	5	4	1.6	98	MFI	82

4 ENGINE IDENTIFICATION

YEAR	3 ENGINE CODE	CYL.	DISPL. liters	DISPL. cu. in.	Fuel System	HP
1989 Cont'd.	9	4	1.9	113	TBI	90
	J	4	1.9	113	MFI	110
	C	4	2.2	133	MFI	110
	L	4	2.2 T	133 T	MFI	145
	A*	4	2.3	140	MFI	88
	W*	4	2.3 T	140 T	MFI	145, 175†
	X	4	2.3	140	MFI	98
	S	4	2.3 HO	140 HO	MFI	100
	D	4	2.5	153	TBI	90
	V	6	2.9	179	MFI	144
	U	6	3.0	182	MFI	140
	Y	6	3.0 SHO	182 SHO	MFI	220
	4	6	3.8	232	MFI	140
	C‡, R	6	3.8 S	232 S	MFI	210
	F	8	5.0	302	MFI	150
	E	8	5.0 HO	302 HO	MFI	225
	G	8	5.8	351	2V	180
1988	K	4	1.3	79	2V	58
	5	4	1.6	98	MFI	82
	9	4	1.9	113	TBI	90
	J	4	1.9	113	MFI	110
	A*	4	2.3	140	MFI	90
	T*	4	2.3 T	140 T	MFI	150-190†
	W*	4	2.3 T	140 T	MFI	145, 175†
	X	4	2.3	140	MFI	98
	S	4	2.3 HO	140 HO	MFI	100
	D	4	2.5	153	TBI	90
	V	6	2.9	179	MFI	144
	U	6	3.0	182	MFI	140
	4	6	3.8	232	MFI	140
	F	8	5.0	302	MFI	150-160†
	E	8	5.0 HO	302 HO	MFI	225
	G	8	5.8 HO	351 HO	2V	180
1987	9	4	1.9	113	TBI	90
	J	4	1.9	113	MFI	115
	H	4	2.0 D	122 D	MFI	58
	R	4	2.3	140	1V	N/A
	X	4	2.3	140	TBI	86
	S	4	2.3	140	TBI	100
	A*	4	2.3	140	MFI	90
	W*	4	2.3 T	140 T	MFI	145, 175†
	T*	4	2.3 T	140 T	MFI	150, 190†
	D	4	2.5	153	TBI	90
	U	6	3.0	182	MFI	140
	3	6	3.8	232	TBI	120
	F	8	5.0	302	MFI	150, 160†
	M	8	5.0 HO	302 HO	MFI	200
	E	8	5.0 HO	302 HO	MFI	225
	G	8	5.8 HO	351 HO	2V	180
1986	9	4	1.9	113	2V	86
	J	4	1.9	113	MFI	108
	H	4	2.0 D	122 D	MFI	52
	R	4	2.3	140	1V	N/A
	X	4	2.3	140	TBI	86
	S	4	2.3 HO	140 HO	TBI	100

ENGINE IDENTIFICATION Continued

4 ENGINE IDENTIFICATION

YEAR	CODE	CYL.	liters	cu. in.	Fuel System	HP
1986 Cont'd.	A*	4	2.3	140	1V	88
	W*	4	2.3 T	140 T	MFI	145-175†
	T*	4	2.3 T	140 T	MFI	200
	D	4	2.5	153	TBI	92
	U	6	3.0	182	MFI	140
	3	6	3.8	232	2V	N/A
	3	6	3.8	232	TBI	120
	F	8	5.0	302	MFI	150, 160†
	M	8	5.0 HO	302 HO	MFI	200
	G	8	5.8 HO	351 HO	2V	180
1985	2	4	1.6	98	2V	70
	4	4	1.6 HO	98 HO	2V	78, 80†
	5	4	1.6	98	MFI	84
	8	4	1.6 T	98 T	MFI	120
	9	4	1.9	113	2V	86
	H	4	2.0 D	122 D	MFI	52
	R	4	2.3	140	1V	N/A
	X	4	2.3	140	TBI	86
	S	4	2.3 HO	140 HO	TBI	100
	A*	4	2.3	140	1V	88
	W*	4	2.3 T	140 T	MFI	145-155†
	T*	4	2.3 T	140 T	MFI	175
	L	6	2.4 TD	146 TD	MFI	115
	3	6	3.8	232	2V	N/A
	3	6	3.8	232	TBI	120
	F	8	5.0	302	MFI	140, 155†
	F	8	5.0	302	2V	140
	M	8	5.0 HO	302 HO	MFI	165, 180†
	M	8	5.0 HO	302 HO	4V	210
	G	8	5.8 HO	351 HO	2V	180
1984	2	4	1.6	98	2V	70
	4	4	1.6 HO	98 HO	2V	78, 80†
	5	4	1.6	98	MFI	84

4 ENGINE IDENTIFICATION

YEAR	CODE	CYL.	liters	cu. in.	Fuel System	HP
1984 Cont'd.	8	4	1.6 T	98 T	MFI	120
	H	4	2.0 D	122 D	MFI	52
	R	4	2.3	140	1V	84
	A*	4	2.3	140	1V	88
	6	4	2.3 LP	140 LP	1V	N/A
	W*	4	2.3 T	140 T	MFI	145
	T*	4	2.3 T	140 T	MFI	175
	L	6	2.4 TD	146 TD	MFI	115
	3	6	3.8	232	2V	N/A
	3	6	3.8	232	TBI	120
	F	8	5.0	302	MFI	140, 155†
	M	8	5.0 HO	302 HO	MFI	165
	M	8	5.0 HO	302 HO	4V	175, 205†
	G	8	5.8 HO	351 HO	2V	180
1983	2	4	1.6	98	2V	70
	4	4	1.6 HO	98 HO	2V	80
	5	4	1.6	98	MFI	82
	A	4	2.3	140	1V	90
	W	4	2.3 T	140 T	MFI	145
	6	4	2.3 LP	140 LP	1V	N/A
	X	6	3.3	200	1V	92
	3	6	3.8	232	2V	110
	F	8	5.0 HO	302 HO	TBI	130, 145†
	F	8	5.0 HO	302 HO	4V	175
	G	8	5.8	351	2V	165

† Varies with model installation.   * Overhead cam 2.3L only.
‡ Early production only.
D — Diesel.   HO — High Output.
LP — LPG powered conversion.
S — Supercharged.   SHO — Super High Output.
T — Turbo.   TD — Turbo Diesel.
TBI — Throttle Body Injection.   MFI — Multiport Fuel Injection.
1V — One Venturi Carburetor.   2V — Two Venturi Carburetor.
4V — Four Venturi Carburetor.

UNDERHOOD SERVICE SPECIFICATIONS

FDTU1   **CYLINDER NUMBERING SEQUENCE**   FDTU1

4-CYL. FIRING ORDER: 1 3 4 2

| 1987-92 1.3L Festiva, 1.6L Tracer | 1991-92 1.6L Capri | 1991-92 1.9L | 1989-92 2.2L ex. Turbo |

— Front of car —

| 1983-85 1.6L (98) | 1991-92 1.8L | 1985-90 1.9L (113) | 1989-92 2.2L Turbo |

4-CYL. FIRING ORDER: 1 3 4 2

— Front of car —

| 1983 2.3L (140) ex. Turbo | 1983-89 2.3L (140) Turbo | 1984-90 2.3L (140) ex. Tempo/Topaz & Turbo | 1991-92 2.3L Mustang | 2.3L (140) Tempo/Topaz, 2.5L (153) |

V6-CYL. FIRING ORDER: 1 4 2 5 3 6

— Front of car —

| 1988-90 2.9L (177) | 3.0L (183) ex. 1989-92 DOHC-SHO | 1989-92 3.0L DOHC-SHO | 1988-92 3.8L (232) | 1983 3.8L (232) | 1984-92 3.8L (232) ex. Supercharged | 1989-92 3.8L Supercharged |

FORD MOTOR COMPANY
1983-92 Ford, Lincoln, Mercury, Merkur

UNDERHOOD SERVICE SPECIFICATIONS

CYLINDER NUMBERING SEQUENCE

6-CYL. FIRING ORDER:
1 5 3 6 2 4

8-CYL. FIRING ORDER:
1983-92 4.6L, 5.0L (302) HO;
5.8L (351)
1 3 7 2 6 5 4 8

All Other 8-cyl.
1 5 4 2 6 3 7 8

Front of car

1983 3.3L (200)	1991-92 4.6L 8-cyl.	All 8-cyl. ex. 1991-92 4.6L

TIMING MARK

BTDC
16°
10°
6°
0°

1988-92 1.3L (81);
1988-89 1.6L (98);
1991-92 1.6L (98);
1991-92 1.8L (110)

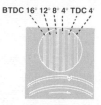

BTDC 16° 12° 8° 4° TDC 4°

1983-85 1.6L (98);
1985-92 1.9L (113)

ATDC
2°
0°
2°
6°
10°
12°
16°
BTDC

1989-92 2.2L

BTDC
30
20
10
0
10
ATDC

2.3L (140)
ex. Tempo/Topaz

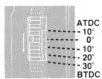

ATDC
10°
0°
10°
20°
30°
BTDC

1984
2.3L (140) Tempo/Topaz
w/MT

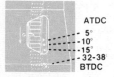

ATDC
5°
10°
15°
32-38
BTDC

1984
2.3L (140) Tempo/Topaz
w/AT (when initial
timing is 15°)

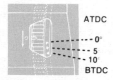

ATDC
0°
5
10
BTDC

1984
2.3L (140) Tempo/Topaz
w/AT (when initial
timing is 10°)

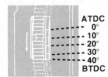

ATDC
0°
10°
20°
30°
40°
BTDC

1985-92
2.3L (140) Tempo/Topaz
w/MT

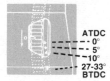

ATDC
0°
5°
10°
27-33°
BTDC

1985-92
2.3L (140)
Tempo/Topaz w/AT

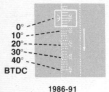

0°
10°
20°
30°
40°
BTDC

1986-91
2.5L (153)
w/MT

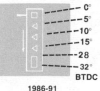

0°
5°
10°
15°
28
32°
BTDC

1986-91
2.5L (153)
w/AT

BTDC
33°
27°
20°
12°
0°

1988-90
2.9L (177)

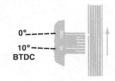

0°
10°
BTDC

1990-92 3.0L
Probe

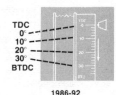

TDC
0°
10°
20°
30°
BTDC

1986-92
3.0L (182)
ex. 1989-92
DOHC-SHO
& 1990-92 3.0L Probe

0°
5°
10°
15°
BTDC

1989-92 3.0L
DOHC-SHO

BTDC
30°
20°
10°
0°
10°
20°
30°
ATDC

1989-92 3.8L
Supercharged

BTDC
14
10
6
2
0
2
ATDC

1983
3.3L (200)

0°
4°
8°
12°
BTDC

1983
3.8L (232)

BTDC
30°
20°
10°
0°
10°
ATDC

1984-92
3.8L (232);
ex. 1989-92
Supercharged;
All 8-cyl. ex. 1991-92 4.6L
(4.6L does not have timing marks)

ELECTRICAL AND IGNITION SYSTEMS

BATTERY

Engine	Year	STANDARD		OPTIONAL	
		BCI Group No.	Crank. Perf.	BCI Group No.	Crank. Perf.
1.3L (81)	1988	35	305	—	—
1.3L	1989-92	35	390	—	—
1.6L (98)	1988-89	35	390	—	—
1.6L (98) MT	1983	58	310	58	380
Power steering	1983	58	380	—	—
1.6L (98) AT	1983	58	410	—	—
1.6L (98) EFI	1983	58	410	—	—

BATTERY Continued

Engine	Year	STANDARD		OPTIONAL	
		BCI Group No.	Crank. Perf.	BCI Group No.	Crank. Perf.
1.6L (98) MT	1984-85	57	310	58	450
Power steering	1984-85	58	380	58	450
1.6L (98) Others	1984-85	58	410	58	450
1.6L	1987-89	35	390	—	—
1.6L	1991-92	35	460	—	—
1.8L	1991-92	35	460		
1.9L (113) 2V MT	1985-86	57	310	58	410
Power steering	1985-86	58	380	58	410
1.9L (113) 2V AT	1985-86	58	410	—	—
1.9L (113) EFI	1985-86	58	410	58	450

BATTERY Continued

Engine	Year	STANDARD BCI Group No.	STANDARD Crank. Perf.	OPTIONAL BCI Group No.	OPTIONAL Crank. Perf.
1.9L (113) TBI	1987-90	58	460	58	540
1.9L (113) FI	1987-90	58	540	—	—
1.9L	1991-92	35	460	—	—
2.0L (121) Diesel	1984-87	33	1050	—	—
2.2L	1989-92	56	505	—	—
2.3L (140) ex. Mustang, Capri:					
Manual ex. Canada	1983	61	310	62	380
Manual Canada	1983	62	380	63	450
Automatic	1983	62	380	63	450
2.3L (140) Mustang, Capri:					
Manual ex. Canada	1983	61	310	63	450
Manual Canada	1983	62	380	63	450
Automatic	1983	62	380	63	450
2.3L (140) OHC Mustang MT ex. High Alt., Canada	1984-86	61	310	63	380
2.3L (140) LPG	1984	63	450	—	—
2.3L (140) Police & Taxi	1984	24F	455	—	—
2.3L (140) All Others	1984-86	62	380	63	450
2.3L (140) Turbo	1985	63	450	64	535
T-Bird, Cougar	1985	64	535	—	—
2.3L (140) OHC ex. Turbo	1987-92	58	460	58	540
2.3L (140) HSC	1984-86	58	380	58	450
2.3L (140) HSC w/MT	1987-92	58	460	58	540
2.3L (140) HSC w/AT	1987-92	58	540	—	—
2.3L (140) Turbo	1987-88	58	540	—	—
2.4L (146) Diesel	1984	65	850	—	—
2.5L (153)	1986	58	380	58	540
2.5L (153) w/AC	1986	58	540	—	—
2.5L (153) w/MT	1987-89	58	540	65	850
2.5L (153) w/AT	1987-91	65	650	65	850
2.9L	1988-89	47	590	—	—
3.0L (182)	1986	58	380	58	540
3.0L (182) ex. SHO, Probe	1987-92	58	540	65	850
W/heated windshield	1986-92	65	850	—	—
3.0L Probe	1991-92	58R	540	—	—
3.0L SHO	1989-91	34	650	—	—
3.3L (200)	1983	61	310	62, 63	380, 450
3.8L (232) Mustang, Capri	1983	61	310	63	450
3.8L (232) All Others	1983	61	310	62	380
3.8L (232)	1984-87	62	380	63	450
3.8L (232) Police & Taxi	1984-85	24F	455	—	—
3.8L (232) RWD	1988-90	58	460	58	540
3.8L (232) FWD	1988-90	65	850	—	—
3.8L FWD	1991-92	65	650	—	—
3.8L RWD ex. Supercharged	1991	58	460	58	540
3.8L Supercharged: MT	1991-92	58	540	65	650
AT	1991-92	65	650	—	—
Cold climate	1991-92	65	650	—	—
4.6L	1991	65	650	65	850
4.6L	1992	58	540	65	650
w/heated windshield	1992	65	850	—	—
Town Car	1992	65	650	—	—
5.0L (302) Mustang, Capri	1983	61	310	63	450
5.0L (302) All Others	1983	63	450	—	—
5.0L (302)	1984-85	63	450	64	475
5.0L (302) Lincoln	1984-85	64	475	—	—
5.0L (302) Police	1984-85	24F	455	—	—
5.0L (302) Cougar, T-Bird	1986	63	450	65	850
5.0L (302) Lincoln, Grand Marquis	1986	64	535	—	—
5.0L (302) Canada & Police	1986	64	535	—	—
5.0L (302) All Others	1986	63	450	64	535

BATTERY Continued

Engine	Year	STANDARD BCI Group No.	STANDARD Crank. Perf.	OPTIONAL BCI Group No.	OPTIONAL Crank. Perf.
5.0L (302): Mustang Crown Victoria,	1987-88	58	540	—	—
Grand Marquis	1987	63	450	64	535
Town Car, Continental	1987	64	535	—	—
Thunderbird, Cougar	1987-88	58	540	—	850
Mark VII	1987-88	65	850	—	—
5.0L (302): Mustang Crown Victoria,	1989-92	58	540	—	—
Grand Marquis	1988-91	58	540	65	650
Thunderbird	1991-92	65	650	—	—
Town Car	1988-90	65	650	65	850
All w/heated windshield	1988-90	65	850	—	—
5.8L (351)	1983-86	64	475	—	—
5.8L (351)	1987-90	58	540	65	650

ALTERNATOR

See UNDERHOOD SERVICE INSTRUCTIONS at the beginning of this section for test/adjustment diagrams.

Ampere rating stamped on housing.

Application	Year	Rated Output	Test Output
All ex. Merkur	1983-89	40, 50, 60, 65, 70, 100	•
Merkur	1985-89	90	80-90 @ 2000
Festiva	1990-92	50	35 @ 3000
Capri	1991-92	85	70 @ 3000
Probe	1990-92	70, 80, 90	†
Escort, Tempo, Topaz	1990-92	60, 65, 75, 90	■
Taurus, Sable	1990-92	90, 100, 130	■
Thunderbird, Cougar	1990-92	65, 75, 95, 110	■
Mustang	1990-92	65, 75	■
Others	1990-92	65, 75, 85, 100	■

• 1983-89, if rated output cannot be obtained at 2000 rpm, eng. rpm may be increased to 2900 max. rpm.

† Output at 3000 rpm must be within 10% of rated output.

■ Output at 2000 rpm must be near rated output or higher.

REGULATOR

Model	Year	Test Temp. (deg. F/C)	Voltage Setting
Festiva, Tracer, Probe	1988-90	68/20	14.4-15.0
Festiva, Capri, Probe 4-cyl.; Escort, Tracer w/1.8L		68/20	14.1-14.7

All others: Measure battery voltage and record figure. With engine operating off idle and all secondary electrical systems turned off, regulated voltage should be no greater than 3.0 volts above recorded figure. Turn on headlights and set heater blower to high. Regulated voltage off idle should be no less than 0.5 volts above recorded figure.

STARTER

Application	Year	Cranking Voltage (min. volts)	Ampere Draw @ Cranking Speed
Gasoline Engines			
4 in. or 101 mm dia.	1983-86	9.6	150-250
4½ in. or 114 mm dia.	1983-86	9.6	150-210
Festiva	1988-92	8.0	150-250
Capri	1991-92	8.0	—
Tracer	1987-89	8.0	—
Scorpio	1988-89	10.5	200-300
All Others	1987-91	9.6	150-250
All Others	1992	9.6	130-220
Diesel engines All	1984-87	—	375 max.

FORD MOTOR COMPANY
1983-92 Ford, Lincoln, Mercury, Merkur

SPARK PLUGS

Engine	Year	Gap (inches)	Gap (mm)	Torque (ft-lb)
1.3L (81)	1988-92	.039-.043	1.0-1.1	11-17
1.6L (98)	1983-85	.042-.046	1.07-1.17	10-15
1.6L (98)	1988-92	.039-.043	1.0-1.1	11-17
1.8L	1991-92	.039-.043	1.0-1.1	11-17
1.9L (113)	1985-90	.042-.046	1.07-1.17	10-15
1.9L	1991	.052-.056	1.32-1.42	—
2.2L	1989-92	.039-.043	1.0-1.1	11-17
2.3L (140)	1983-86	.042-.046	1.07-1.17	10-15
Turbo & Propane	1983-86	.032-.036	.81-.91	10-15
2.3L (140)	1987-89	.042-.046	1.07-1.17	10-15
2.3L HSC	1990-91	.052-.056	1.32-1.42	7-15
2.3L OHC	1990-91	.042-.046	1.07-1.17	5-11
2.5L	1986-90	.042-.046	1.07-1.17	5-11
2.9L	1988-89	.042-.046	1.07-1.17	18-28
3.0L (182)	1986-91	.042-.046	1.07-1.17	10-15
3.3L (200)	1983	.048-.052	1.22-1.32	15-20
3.8L (232)	1983-85 early	.042-.046	1.07-1.17	5-11
3.8L (232)	1985 late-91	.052-.056	1.32-1.42	5-11
4.6L	1991	.052-.056	1.32-1.42	10-15
5.0L (302) ex. HO	1983-85	.048-.052	1.22-1.32	10-15
5.0L (302) HO	1983-85	.042-.046	1.07-1.17	10-15
5.0L (302)	1986	.048-.052	1.22-1.32	10-15
5.0L (302) HO	1987-91	.052-.056	1.32-1.42	10-15
Others	1987-91	.042-.046	1.07-1.17	10-15
5.8L (351)	1983-91	.042-.046	1.07-1.17	10-15

IGNITION COIL
See UNDERHOOD SERVICE INSTRUCTIONS at the beginning of this section for test/adjustment diagrams.

Application	Windings	Resistance (ohms)
1983-90 Dura-Spark ign.	Primary	0.8-1.6
	Secondary	7700-10,500
1983-88 TFI ign.†	Primary	0.3-1.0
	Secondary	8000-11,500
1988-89 1.3L, 1.6L	Primary	0.8-1.6
	Secondary	6000-30,000
1988-89 2.9L	Primary	0.3-1.0
	Secondary	8000-11,000
1989-90 2.2L	Primary	1.04-1.27
	Secondary	7100-9700
Turbo	Primary	.72-.88
	Secondary	10,300-13,900

† Identified by module mounted to distributor.

DISTRIBUTOR PICKUP
See UNDERHOOD SERVICE INSTRUCTIONS at the beginning of this section for test/adjustment diagrams.

Application	Resistance (ohms)	Air Gap (in./mm)
1983-90 1.6L, 1.9L w/TFI-1 ign.	650-1300	.017 min./ .43 min.
1983-92 All Others w/Dura-Spark ign.	400-1000*	.017 min./ .43 min.
All w/EEC IV	—	—
1989-92 2.2L	900-1200	—
Turbo	210-260	—

* With 250 watt heat lamp held 1 to 2 inches from coil for 5 to 10 minutes.

IGNITION RESISTOR
See UNDERHOOD SERVICE INSTRUCTIONS at the beginning of this section for test/adjustment diagrams.

Engine	Year	Type	Resistance (ohms)	Temperature (deg. F/C)
All w/Dura-Spark II, III	1983-92	Wire	0.8-1.6	—

BASE TIMING
See UNDERHOOD SERVICE INSTRUCTIONS at the beginning of this section for test/adjustment diagrams.

Set timing at Before Top Dead Center and at slow idle unless otherwise specified.

Disconnect and plug distributor vacuum hose.

On engines equipped with dual-mode ignition timing, disconnect the third three-pin connector from sensor.

Engines with ignition module basic part No. 12A244, disconnect the two-wire connector (yellow and black wires) and jump the module connector pins.

1983 1.6L w/EFI: Disconnect single white wire connector at distributor.

1984-92 with EEC IV: Disconnect single wire connector at distributor or remove shorting bar from double wire spout connector.

1988-89 1.3L 2V: Disconnect & plug distributor vacuum hose. At high altitude, disconnect barometric pressure sensor.

1989-92 1.3L FI: Ground one-pin self-test connector by master cylinder.

1987-89 1.6L: Disconnect distributor vacuum hose and black connector by distributor.

1989-92 1.6L, 2.2L ex. Turbo; disconnect and plug distributor vacuum hoses.

1989-92 1.8L, 2.2L Turbo, ground test connector.

1991-92 1.9L, 2.3L, 4.6L, install EDIS checker and press SAW button. Timing should be at Set Value. When button is released, timing should advance to Check Value.

Reset timing only if more than ±2 degrees from specification listed.

With ''Positive Buy'' (identified with a Torx-head distributor holddown bolt) ±4 degrees.

Timing must be set to specifications shown on emission decal if different from setting listed.

Engine	Year	Man. Trans. (degrees) @ RPM	Auto. Trans. (degrees) @ RPM
1.3L (81) 2V	1988-89	0 ±1	2 ±1
1.3L FI	1989-92	10 ±1	10 ±1
1.6L (98)	1983	8 @ 800	14 @ 800 N
w/decal DFR, DFS, DJV	1983	10 @ 800	10 @ 800 N
w/decal DPA	1983	12 @ 800	—
High Altitude	1983	12 @ 800	16 @ 800 N
California	1983	10 @ 800	10 @ 800 N
w/decal DGS	1983	8 @ 800	—
w/decal DPR	1983	12 @ 800	—
w/decal DJR, DJS	1983	—	14 @ 800 N
Canada	1983	12 @ 800	14 @ 800 N
w/decal DGK	1983	8 @ 800	—
w/decal DNU	1983	14 @ 800	—
w/decal DFU, DPS	1983	10 @ 800	10 @ 800 N
1.6L (98) FI	1983	10 @ 800	—
1.6L (98)	1984-85	8 @ 800	—
High Output	1984-85	12 @ 800	14 @ 800 N
FI & Turbo	1984-85	10	10
Canada	1984	14 @ 800	—
1.6L (98)	1987-89	2 ±2	2 ±2
1.6L	1991-92	2 ±1	2 ±
Turbo	1991-92	12 ±1	12 ±1
1.8L	1991-92	10 ±1	10 ±1
1.9L (113) 2V	1985-86	10 @ 750	10 @ 750 N
w/decal APJ	1986	8 @ 750	—
1.9L (113) TBI & FI	1986-92	10	10
1.9L	1991-92	10 ±2*	10 ±2*
Check	1991-92	15 min.	15 min.
2.2L	1989-90	6 ±1	6 ±1
Turbo	1989-90	9 ±1	
2.3L (140)	1983	9 @ 700	9 @ 700 N
2.3L (140) 1V ex. HSC	1984-85	10	10
Canada	1984	12 @ 700	12 @ 700 N
Canada	1985	10	10 @ 700 N
2.3L (140) 1V ex. HSC	1986	10	10
w/decal ALR	1986	8	8
2.3L (140) OHC FI	1987-90	10	10
2.3L OHC	1991-92	10*	10*
Check	1991-92	16 min.	16 min.
2.3L (140) Turbo ex. 1985 Merkur	1984-88	10	10
2.3L (140) Merkur	1985	13	10
2.3L (140) Propane	1984	—	12 @ 600 N
2.3L (140) HSC	1984	15	10
w/decal ACB, ANC	1984	15 @ 800	—
California	1984	15 @ 800	10
w/decal ANE	1984	—	15
Canada	1984	10 @ 800	10 @ 800 N
w/decal AVC, AVF	1984	15	15
2.3L (140) HSC 1V	1985-86	10 @ 800	10 @ 800 N

BASE TIMING Continued

Engine	Year	Man. Trans. (degrees) @ RPM	Auto. Trans. (degrees) @ RPM
2.3L (140) HSC 1V	1987	8 @ 800 N	8 @ 800 N
2.3L (140) HSC FI	1985-87	10	10
2.3L (140) HSC	1988	15	15
2.3L HSC	1989	10	10
2.3L HSC	1990-91	15	15
2.5L (153)	1986-91	10	10
2.9L	1988-89	10	10
3.0L (182)	1986-92	—	10
3.0L SHO	1989-92	10*	—
3.3L (200)	1983	—	10 @ 900 N
w/decal DGZ, DMP	1983	—	8 @ 900 N
High Altitude	1983	—	12 @ 900 N
3.8L (232)	1983	—	12 @ 800 N
w/decal BJT, BJU	1983	—	4 @ 800 N
w/decal DHU, DJD, DLY	1983	—	10 @ 800 N
High Altitude	1983	—	18 @ 800 N
California	1983	—	10 @ 800 N
w/decal DDM	1983	—	12 @ 800 N
w/decal DLE	1983	—	8 @ 800 N
3.8L (232) FI	1984-92	—	10
w/decal AJE	1984	—	6 @ 800
Supercharged	1989-92	10*	10*
3.8L (232) 2V	1984	—	12 @ 800 N
3.8L (232) 2V	1985-86	—	6 @ 800 N
4.6L	1991-92	—	10*
5.0L (302)	1983	10 @ 800	*
Canada	1983	10 @ 800	6 @ 800
5.0L (302)	1984	—	10
High Output	1984	10 @ 800	—
5.0L (302)	1985	—	10
w/decal CAZ, CBF, CHN, CHP	1985	—	8
5.0L (302) High Output	1985	12 @ 800	—
California	1985	10 @ 800	—
5.0L (302)	1986-92	10	10
5.8L (351)	1983	—	12 @ 600
5.8L (351)	1984-91	—	14 @ 600 N
Canada trailer tow	1984-87	—	12 @ 600 N

* Timing not adjustable.

DISTRIBUTOR TIMING ADVANCE

Engine degrees at engine rpm, no load, in addition to basic timing setting.

Mechanical advance distributors only.

Engine	Transmission	Year	Distributor Number	Degrees @ 2500 RPM Total	Degrees @ 2500 RPM Centrifugal
1.3L (81) 2V	MT	1988-89	—	30.9-39.9*	6.9-10.9
1.3L TBI	AT	1989	—	24-32*	6-10
1.6L (98)	MT	1983	E3EE-DA	24.9-34.3	7.4-11.8
1.6L (98)	MT	1983	E3EE-NA	35.0-44.5	5.5-10.0
1.6L (98)	MT	1983-85	E3EE-KA	26.8-36.9	5.3-10.4
1.6L (98)	AT	1983	E3EE-HA	33.5-43.2	4.0-8.7
1.6L (98)	AT	1983	E3EE-RA	26.6-35.8	5.1-9.3
1.6L (98)	MT	1983-85	E3EE-PA	23.5-33.1	6.0-10.6
1.6L (98)	MT	1983-85	E3EE-TA	26.7-37.0	5.2-10.5
1.6L (98)	AT	1984-85	E3EE-VA	22.0-31.3	4.5-8.8
1.6L (98)	AT	1984-85	E3EE YA	26.0-35.1	4.5-8.6
1.6L (98)	MT	1984-85	E4EE-FA	28.0-38.5	7.5-12.0
1.6L (98)	MT	1984-85	E4EE-GA	29.8-39.1	4.3-8.6
1.6L (98)	AT	1985	E5EE-BA	29.9-39.1	4.4-8.6
1.6L (98)	MT & AT	1988	E8GY-A	43.3-53.3*	12.3-16.3
1.9L (113)	MT	1985-86	E5EE-DB	30.3-39.5	4.8-9.0
1.9L (113)	MT	1985-86	E5EE-CB	24.9-35.5	4.4-9.0
2.2L ex. Turbo	MT & AT	1989-90	—	28.4-36.4†	10.4-14.4
2.3L (140)	MT & AT	1983	E3ZE-DA	23.5-33.0	6.5-10.5
2.3L (140)	AT	1983	E3ZE-EA	25.0-34.7	7.5-12.2
2.3L (140)	MT	1984	E4ZE-BA	14.2-21.8	0.7-5.3
2.3L (140)	AT	1984-85	E4ZE-CA	18.5-25.8	0-4.3
2.3L (140)	MT	1985	E43E-GA	17.3-26.9	3.8-8.2
2.3L (140)	MT & AT	1985-86	E43E-DA	17.5-26.6	4.0-8.1
2.3L (140) Propane	AT	1983	E3DX-AA	18.6-28.6	9.1-14.1
2.3L (140) HSC	MT	1984-87	E43E-DA	17.5-26.6	4.0-8.1
2.3L (140) HSC	AT	1984-86	E43E-GA	17.3-26.9	3.8-8.2

DISTRIBUTOR TIMING ADVANCE Continued

Engine	Transmission	Year	Distributor Number	Degrees @ 2500 RPM Total	Degrees @ 2500 RPM Centrifugal
3.3L (200)	AT	1983	E1BE-EA	24.5-33.5	7-11
3.3L (200)	AT	1983	E2BE-CA	23.0-32.6	5.5-10.1
3.8L (232)	AT	1983	E2SE-DA	26.2-35.6	4.7-9.1
3.8L (232)	AT	1984-86	E4AE-AA	31.0-40.4	5.5-9.9
5.0L (302)	AT	1983-85	E2VE-BA	23.1-32.7	5.6-10.2
5.0L (302)	MT	1983	E3ZE-HA	34.1-43.5	8.6-13.0
5.0L (302)	MT	1983	E3ZE-JA	25.6-35.4	8.1-12.9
5.0L (302)	MT	1984	E4ZE-DA	27.3-36.5	9.8-14.0
5.0L (302)	MT	1985	E5ZE-BA	27.5-36.8	10.0-14.3
5.8L (351) 2V W	AT	1983-87	E2AE-EA	27.9-38.0	6.4-11.5

* Both vacuum chambers activated.

† Vacuum retard, 4-8.

FUEL SYSTEM

FUEL SYSTEM PRESSURE

See UNDERHOOD SERVICE INSTRUCTIONS at the beginning of this section for test/adjustment diagrams.

Carburetted, pinch off fuel return line, if equipped.

All w/TBI, fuel pressure measured at inlet fitting on unit.

All w/FI, fuel pressure measured at fitting on fuel rail.

Engine	Year	Pressure PSI	Pressure RPM
Carburetted:			
1.3L (81)	1988-89	3-6	idle
1.6L (98) 2V, 1.9L (113) 2V	1983-86	4.5-6.5	idle
2.3L (140) 1V	1983-87	5-7	idle
3.3L (200), 250	1983	5-7	idle
3.8L (232) 2V	1983-86	6-8	idle
5.0L (302) ex. FI	1983-85	6-8	idle
351, 400	1983-88	6-8	idle
Fuel Injected: TBI			
1.9L (113)	1987-90	13-17	idle
2.3L (140) HSC	1985-87	13-16	idle
2.5L (153)	1986-90	13-17	idle
3.8L (232)	1984-87	25-45	idle
5.0L (302)	1983-84	39	idle
MFI			
1.3L	1989-92	35-40 / 25-31 / 69-85●	ign. on / idle / —
1.6L (98) FI & Turbo	1983-85	35-45 / 30-45	ign. on / idle
1.6L	1987-89	28-32* / 36-42†	idle
1.6L	1991-92	37-42 / 37-41 / 64-85●	ign. on / idle / —
1.8L	1991-92	38-46 / 30-37 / 64-85	ign. on / idle / —
1.9L, 2.3L OHC, 2.9L	1987-92	35-45 / 30-45	ign. on / idle
2.2L	1989-92	34-40 / 37-33 / 64-85●	ign. on / idle / —
2.3L HSC, 2.5L	1988-92	50-60 / 45-60	ign. on / idle
3.0L ex. SHO, 3.8L ex. Supercharged, 5.0L	1985-92	35-45 / 30-45	ign. on / idle
3.0L SHO	1989-92	30-45 / 28-33	ign. on / idle
3.8L Supercharged	1989-92	35-45 / 30-40	ign. on / idle

● Fuel pump pressure.

* Vacuum hose connected to fuel pressure regulator.

† Vacuum hose disconnected from fuel pressure regulator.

CHEK-CHART

UNDERHOOD SERVICE SPECIFICATIONS

FDTU6   FDTU6

IDLE SPEED W/O COMPUTER CONTROL

See UNDERHOOD SERVICE INSTRUCTIONS at the beginning of this section for test/adjustment diagrams.

1983:

Disconnect and plug parking brake release if so equipped. Make all adjustments with air cleaner and cooling fan off and engine at operating temperature.

Follow engine emission decal if procedure differs. With EEC, run engine for 5 minutes and then fast idle for 20 seconds.

Adjust solenoid throttle body or throttle plate adjusting screw to obtain curb idle. If more than 50 rpm from specification, automatic transmission linkage must be adjusted.

To obtain fast idle, disconnect and plug EGR and canister purge valve. Set to specified step of cam.

A/C speed-up, adjust with A/C and blower on maximum, with compressor clutch wire disconnected.

With VOTM, adjust with manifold vacuum applied to valve.

1984-87:

Make all adjustments with engine warm. If adjustment is more than 50 rpm, adjust transmission linkage (AT only).

1.6L (98) 2V, disconnect VOTM vacuum hose (AC only) and set idle speed to spec. With AC, reinstate VOTM vacuum hose and turn heater on, set temperature to cool and turn blower on high; when radiator fan comes on, set speed-up speed to spec. To set fast idle, disconnect and plug EGR vacuum hose.

2.3L (140) Canada, disconnect and plug VOTM (AC only) and place a jumper between the fan control and ground. Set idle speed to spec. To set fast idle, disconnect and plug the EGR vacuum hoses.

3.8L (232) 2V, set idle speed to spec. With AC, turn unit on MAX and disconnect the compressor clutch wire and set AC speed-up speed to spec. To set fast idle, disconnect and plug the EGR vacuum hose and electrically disconnect the canister purge solenoid.

5.0L (302) 2V & 4V, set idle speed to spec. To set fast idle, disconnect and plug the EGR vacuum hose.

5.0L (302) CFI, check engine rpm against spec. If reading is high, turn VOTM bracket adjusting screw counterclockwise 1 turn at a time until proper specification is met. If reading is too low, turn off engine and turn the bracket screw 1 turn clockwise, set against specification and repeat until proper specification is met. To set fast idle, disconnect and plug the EGR and CM vacuum hoses, disconnect the canister purge solenoid valve.

1984-90:

5.8L (351) engine, disconnect the VOTM vacuum hose (AC only). Set idle speed to spec. Apply manifold vacuum to the VOTM and set speed-up speed to spec. To set fast idle, disconnect and plug the EGR vacuum hose.

1988-89:

1.3L (81) 2V, set idle to specified value with cooling fan off. To set fast idle, disconnect fast idle pull-off solenoid vacuum hose and plug. Set fast idle cam on specified step and adjust to specified value. Electrically disconnect electric load vacuum solenoid and race engine momentarily. Set electric load speed-up to specified value. Electrically disconnect AC speed-up solenoid, race engine momentarily, and set AC speed-up to specified value.

1.6L (98), set idle to specified value with cooling fan off.

Engine	Year	SLOW Man. Trans.	SLOW Auto. Trans.	FAST Man. Trans.	FAST Auto. Trans.	Step of Cam
1.3L (81) 2V	1988-89	700-750	—	1650-2150	—	Second
Elect. speed-up	1988	750-850	—			
AC speed-up	1988	1200-1300	—			
1.6L (98)	1983	800	750 D	2400	2400 P	Kickdown
AC speed-up	1983	1200	—			
w/decal DFL	1983	650	—	2100	—	Kickdown
DGH, DGJ	1983	800	—	2200	—	Kickdown
AC speed-up	1983	1200	—			
High Altitude	1983	900	850 D	2400	2400 P	Kickdown
AC speed-up	1983	1500	—			
w/decal DPD	1983	900	—	2400	—	Kickdown
AC speed-up	1983	1200	—			
Canada	1983	800	750 D	2400	2400 P	Kickdown
AC speed-up	1983	1200	—			
1.6L (98)						
w/decal DGK	1983	800	—	2200	—	Kickdown
AC speed-up	1983	1200	—			
DNU	1983	750	—	2200	—	Kickdown
AC speed-up	1983	1200	—			

IDLE SPEED W/O COMPUTER CONTROL Continued

Engine	Year	SLOW Man. Trans.	SLOW Auto. Trans.	FAST Man. Trans.	FAST Auto. Trans.	Step of Cam
1.6L (98) w/decal AJK, CEC, CFN	1984-85	700	—	2200	—	Second
	1984-85	720	—	2200	—	Second
AC speed-up	1984-85	1200	—			
High Output	1984-85	800	—	2200	—	Second
1.6L (98)	1988	800-900	950-1050 N	—	—	
1.6L	1989	800-900	800-900 N	—	—	
2.0L (122) Diesel	1984-87	725-775	—	1450-1550		
AC speed-up	1984-87	725-775	—			
2.3L (140) Propane	1983-84	—	750 D	—	1000 P	Kickdown
2.3L (140)	1983	850	800 D	1800	2600 P	Kickdown
shutdown idle	1983	600	600 N			
California	1983	850	800 D	1800	2000 P	Kickdown
shutdown idle	1983	600	600 N			
2.3L (140) ex. HSC Canada	1984	850	800 D	2000	2200 P	Kickdown
shutdown idle	1984	700	700 N			
2.3L (140) ex. HSC Canada	1985	—	800 D	—	2200 P	Kickdown
shutdown idle	1985	—	700 N			
2.3L (140) HSC	1984	800	700 D	1900	2600 P	Kickdown
shutdown idle	1984	600	600 N			
w/decal AME, AMF, AUT, AUV, AZR, AZS, BAJ, BAK	1984	—	600 D	—	2600 P	Kickdown
shutdown idle	1984	600	600 N			
Canada	1984	800	700 D	2200	2600 P	Kickdown
shutdown idle	1984	600	600 N			
2.3L (140) HSC 1V	1985-87	800	730 D	2200	2200 P	Kickdown
shutdown idle	1985-87	600	600 N			
2.4L (146) Diesel	1984	—	700-800 N	—	900-1050 P	
2.4L (146) Diesel	1985	—	750-800 N	—	900-1050 P	
w/decal CNG, CNH, CNJ	1985	—	840 N	—	—	
3.3L (200)	1983	—	600 D	—	2000 P	Kickdown
shutdown idle	1983	—	450 N			
w/decal DGB, DGC	1983	—	550 D	—	2200 P	Kickdown
DMY	1983	—	550 D	—	2000 P	Kickdown
3.8L (232)	1983	—	550 D	—	2200 P	High
AC speed-up	1983	—	650 D			
shutdown idle	1983	—	450 D			
w/decal DEN, DHU, DJD	1983	—	550 D	—	2200 P	High
AC speed-up	1983	—	700 D			
shutdown idle	1983	—	450 D			
High Altitude	1983	—	550 D	—	2100 P	High
AC speed-up	1983	—	700 D			
shutdown idle	1983	—	450 D			
California	1983	—	550 D	—	2200 P	High
AC speed-up	1983	—	700 D			
shutdown idle	1983	—	450 D			
3.8L (232) 2V U.S.	1984	—	550 D	—	2200 P	High
AC speed-up	1984	—	650 D			
Canada	1984	—	600 D	—	2200 P	High
AC speed-up	1984	—	700 D			
3.8L (232) 2V	1985-86	—	650 D	—	2200 P	High
shutdown idle	1985-86	—	550 D			
w/AC	1985	—	600 D	—	2200 P	High
AC speed-up	1985	—	700 D			
5.0L (302) 2V	1983-85	700	550 D	2400	1500 P	High
5.0L (302) 4V	1983-85	700	—	2400	—	High
5.0L (302) FI	1983-84	—	550 D	—	2200 P	High
w/decal AEB, AKD, ADV, AFP, AKE	1984	—	550 D	—	2300 P	Kickdown
5.0L (302) FI:						
LTD, Marquis	1985	—	550 D	—	2500 P	High
T-Bird, Cougar	1985	—	550 D	—	2400 P	High
w/decal CAN, CHC	1985	—	550 D	—	2200 P	High

IDLE SPEED W/O COMPUTER CONTROL Continued

Engine	Year	SLOW Man. Trans.	SLOW Auto. Trans.	FAST Man. Trans.	FAST Auto. Trans.	Step of Cam
5.0L (302) FI:						
Crown Victoria, Grand Marquis, Town Car w/decal	1985	—	550 D	—	2300 P	High
BBE, CBB, CBC Continental	1985	—	550 D	—	2100 P	High
Mark VII w/decal CML, CRT, CNL, CRS	1985	—	550 D	—	2300 P	High
	1985	—	550 D	—	2400 P	High
5.8L (351)	1983	—	600 D	—	1500 P	Kickdown
AC speed-up	1983	—	700 D			
5.8L (351) Police	1984-91	—	600 D	—	1650 P	Kickdown
AC speed-up	1984-91	—	700 D			
5.8L (351) Can. trailer tow	1987	—	600 D	—	1550 P	Kickdown
AC speed-up	1987	—	700 D			

IDLE SPEED W/COMPUTER CONTROL

See UNDERHOOD SERVICE INSTRUCTIONS at the beginning of this section for test/adjustment diagrams.

Note: WIFI, if idle speed is higher than the specified checking speed, perform a system check before attempting to adjust the idle speed.

1.3L: Jumper test connector (black, 1-pin) to ground.

1.6L (98) 2V, 1.9L (113) 2V: With engine at operating temperature, disconnect and plug vacuum hose at thermactor air control valve bypass section. Disconnect and plug ISC vacuum hose and connect a vacuum pump to the unit. 1.9L, adjust maximum speed by turning full stroke adjustment screw on throttle lever. Apply enough vacuum to retract the unit. Set idle speed to specified minimum speed with cooling fan running by adjusting the throttle stop screw. Reconnect vacuum hose to ISC unit with transmission in Park. Place transmission in Drive and compare idle speed with specified checking speed. Adjust ISC screw to obtain specified value.

1983-90 1.6L (98) MFI ex. Tracer, 1.9L (113) MFI: With engine at operating temperature, disconnect and plug both EGR solenoid vacuum lines. Disconnect ISC electrical lead. Run engine at 2000 rpm for 60 seconds and return to idle. Adjust speed to specified setting speed within two minutes with engine cooling fan on. Repeat if two minutes is exceeded.

1991-92 1.6L Capri: Ground the self test connector (white, 1-pin).

1991-92 1.8L: Jumper terminal 10 of diagnostic connector to ground. Canada models, apply parking brake to turn off headlights.

1983-90 1.9L (113) TBI, 2.3L (140) HSC TBI, 2.5L (153): Idle engine for two minutes (AT in drive) and check idle speed. To adjust, set system in self test mode (see Computer Diagnostic Codes), turn key to run position. When ISC plunger fully retracts, turn key off and disconnect diagnostic mode. Electrically disconnect ISC and gain access to throttle stop screw. Start engine and set to specified setting speed.

1991-92 1.9L: Disconnect ISC air bypass solenoid. Run engine at 2000 rpm for one minute and check/set idle to specified value.

1989-92 2.2L: Ground STI (black, 1-pin) and set idle to specified setting speed.

1991 2.3L HSC: Disconnect SPOUT connector. Remove PCV valve and install special tool with .020 orifice. Disconnect ISC and run engine at 2500 rpm for 30 seconds. Set idle to specified setting speed.

2.3L (140) OHC & Turbo, 2.9L: With engine at operating temperature, disconnect ISC air bypass valve electrical connector. Disconnect cooling fan electrical connector. Run engine at 2000 rpm for two minutes (1983-90) or 1500 rpm for 30 seconds (1991). Return to idle and adjust speed to specified setting speed. Reconnect leads and verify that checking speed is at specified value.

2.3L (140) 1V ex. HSC: Hold open throttle to maintain 1000 rpm, and press on ISC motor shaft to retract it. Release throttle and quickly unplug ISC motor connector. Disconnect cooling for electrical lead. Run engine at 2000 rpm for one minute and return to idle. Check speed against specified minimum value. Remove cap to adjust throttle stop screw. Reconnect all leads and verify that idle speed is at specified checking value. To set maximum speed disconnect EGR vacuum and purge solenoid electrical leads. Run engine at 2200 rpm and verify that ISC motor has fully extended. Disconnect ISC motor and set maximum speed to specified value using an Allen wrench.

1986-90 3.0L (182) ex. SHO: Disconnect timing SPOUT and air bypass valve connectors. Remove PCV valve and install PCV tool (.20" orifice). Set idle to specified setting value. Reconnect connectors and verify checking value is correct.

3.0L SHO: Disconnect PCV and canister purge hoses from throttle body and connect PCV hose to canister purge nipple. Disconnect ISC electrical connector. Adjust idle to specified setting speed.

1984-87 3.8L (232) FI: Idle engine in Drive (w/AT) for one minute and compare speed with specified checking value.

IDLE SPEED W/COMPUTER CONTROL Continued

1988-90 3.8L (232): Set idle to specified setting speed after running engine at 2500 rpm for 30 seconds.

1985-88 5.0L (302) FI: Run engine at 1800 rpm for 30 seconds and allow to return to idle. Check idle against specified checking value. Turn throttle plate stop screw to obtain specified setting speed.

1989-92 5.0L Mustang, Mark VII: Insert a .025 feeler gauge between step screw and throttle level. Set idle to specified value and remove feeler.

ALL CARBURETTED
Checking Speed is the computer controlled idle speed value.

Engine	Year	Minimum Speed	Maximum Speed	Checking Speed	Fast	Step of Cam
1.6L (98)						
AT	1983	720 D	—	750 D	2400 N	Second
AT	1984	720 D	—	750 D	2600 N	Second
AT	1985	720 D	—	750 D	2400 N	Second
1.9L (113)						
MT	1985-86	720	1050	750	2200	Second
w/PS or AC	1985-86	720	1350	750	2200	Second
AT	1985-86	720 D	1800	750 D	2400 N	Second
2.3L (140) ex. HSC						
MT	1984	675-725	1400-2000	775-925	2000	Kickdown
AT	1984	675-725 N	1400-2200 N	675-825 D	2200 N	Kickdown
MT	1985-86	675-725	1800-2200	750-850	2000†	Kickdown
AT	1985-86	675-725 N	2000-2400 N	710-790 D	2200† N	Kickdown

† W/decal ALR, 1800 N.

ALL FUEL INJECTED
Checking speed is the computer controlled idle speed value.

Engine	Year	Transmission	Setting Speed	Checking Speed
1.3L	1989	AT	800-900 N	—
1.3L	1990-92	MT	680-720	800-900
		AT	830-870 N	800-900 N
1.6L (98)	1983-85	MT	800	—
		AT	750 D	—
1.6L (98) Turbo	1984-85	MT	800	—
1.6L	1991-92	MT	800-900	—
		AT	800-900 N	—
1.8L	1991-92	MT	700-800	—
		AT	700-800 N	—
1.9L (113) TBI	1987-90	MT	550-650	760-840
		AT	550-650 N	760-840 D
1.9L (113) MFI	1986-87	MT	925-1075	900
		AT	925-1075 N	800 D
1.9L (113) MFI	1988-90	MT	900-1000	900-1100
1.9L	1991-92	MT	650	730-930
		AT	650 N	730-930 N
2.2L	1989-92	MT	750	725-775
		AT	750 N	725-775 N
2.3L (140) HSC	1985	MT	725-775	725-775
		AT	570-630 D	570-630 D
w/decal CDL	1985	AT	770-830 D	770-830 D
2.3L (140) HSC HO	1985	MT	775-825	775-825
		AT	570-630 D	570-630 D
2.3L (140) HSC & HO	1986	MT	775-825	775-825
		AT	625-675 D	625-675 D
w/decal AHU, AHV	1986	AT	570-630 D	570-630 D
2.3L (140) HSC	1987	MT	735-785	835-885
	1987	AT	615-665 D	665-715 D
2.3L (140) HSC	1988-90	MT	1500-1600	810-890
		AT	975-1075 D	690-750 D
2.3L HSC	1991	MT	1525-1575	810-890
		AT	925-975 D	680-760 D
2.3L (140) OHC FI	1987-88	MT	500-550	690-750
		AT	500-550 N	690-750 D
w/Calibr. 8-06A-R10	1988	MT & AT	625-675 N	690-750 N
w/Calibr. 8-05A-R10	1988	MT & AT	575-625 N	690-750 N
2.3L OHC	1989-90	MT	575-625	770-830
	1989-90	AT	625-675 N	770-830 D
2.3L OHC	1991	MT	575-625	780
	1991	AT	625-675 N	720 D

IDLE SPEED W/COMPUTER CONTROL Continued

ALL FUEL INJECTED Continued

Engine	Year	Transmission	Setting Speed	Checking Speed
2.3L (140) Turbo	1983-88	MT	700-800	825-975
w/decal CDV, CDZ	1987	MT	725-775	825-975
2.3L (140) Turbo	1984-87	AT	700-800 N	925-1075 N
2.3L (140) Turbo	1988-89	AT	700-800 N	825-975 N
2.5L (153)	1986	MT	750-850	750-850
	1986	AT	650-750 D	650-750 D
2.5L (153)	1987-89	MT	675-725	775-825
		AT	625-675 D	675-725 D
2.5L	1991	AT	■	750 D
2.9L	1988-89	AT	675-725 N	800-900 N
3.0L (182)	1986	AT	595-655† D	625† D
3.0L	1987-90	AT	740-780 D	—
SHO	1989-90	MT	770-830	—
3.0L	1991	MT	■	800
3.0L SHO	1991-92	MT	770-850	—
3.8L (232)	1984-85	AT	—	500-600 D
Mustang, Capri	1984-85	AT	—	475-575 D
3.8L (232)	1986-87	AT	—	500-600 D
w/decal AAZ, ABA, ABJ, ABK, ABL	1986	AT	—	475-575 D
3.8L (232) RWD	1988	AT	530-570 D	500-600 D
3.8L (232) FWD	1988	AT	680-720 D	590-690 D
Calibration 8-16D, R	1988	AT	620-660 D	590-690 D
3.8L RWD	1989-90	AT	*	550-650 D
Supercharged	1989-90	MT	*	700-800
	1989-90	AT	*	550-650 D
3.8L FWD	1989-90	AT	*	650-750 D
Continental	1989-90	AT	*	620-720 D
3.8L Continental	1991	AT	■	625 D
Taurus, Sable	1991	AT	■	640 D
Police	1991	AT	■	700 D
Thunderbird, Cougar	1991	AT	■	600 D
4.6L	1991	AT	■	560 D
5.0L (302)	1986	AT	555-595 D	490-615 D
Mustang, Capri	1986	AT	555-595 D	550-700 D
5.0L (302) HO	1986	MT	680-720	625-775
		AT	605-645 D	550-700 D
5.0L (302): Mustang	1987-88	MT	680-720	625-775
	1987-88	AT	605-645 D	550-700 D
Mark VII HO	1987-88	AT	605-645 D	550-700 D
Crown Victoria, Grand Marquis, Town Car, Thunderbird, Cougar, Continental, Mark VII	1987-88	AT	555-595 D	525-650 D
5.0L: Mustang	1989-90	MT	*	625-775
	1989-90	AT	*	575-725 D
Mark VII	1989-90	AT	*	550-675 D
All others	1989-90	AT	*	525-650 D
5.0L: Mustang	1991-92	MT	625-725	
		AT	625-725 N	
Mark VII	1991-92	AT	625-725 N	
T-Bird, Cougar	1991-92	AT	■	610 D
Others	1991	AT	■	525-650 D

† If modification decal is present by emissions decal and indicates processor change, setting speed is 710 D; checking speed is 700 N & D.

* With engine off, back out throttle plate stop screw enough to clear throttle lever pad. Insert a .010″ feeler gauge between screw and pad. Turn screw in until contact is made, then turn in an addiitonal: 5.0L ex. HO, 1⅞ turns; all others, 1½ turns.

■ Idle speed is only adjustable with special tester.

ENGINE MECHANICAL

TIGHTENING TORQUES

See UNDERHOOD SERVICE INSTRUCTIONS at the beginning of this section for test/ adjustment diagrams.

Some fasteners are tightened in more than one step.

Some values are specified in inches.

TIGHTENING TORQUES Continued

Engine	Year	Cylinder Head	Intake Manifold	Exhaust Manifold	Crankshaft Pulley	Water Pump
1.3L (81) Festiva, 1.6L (98) Tracer	1988-92	35-40/ 50-60, 56-60/ 75/81	14-20/ 19-26	12-17/ 16-23	109-152″/ 12-17	14-19/ 19-26
1.6L Capri	1991-92	14-25/ 20-34, 56-60/ 75/81	14-19/ 19-25	28-34/ 38-46	109-152″/ 12-17	14-19/ 19-25
1.6L (98), 1.9L (113)	1983-89	44/60**, +90°, +90°	12-15/ 16-20	15-20/ 21-27	74-90/ 100-121	5-8/ 7-10
1.8L	1991-92	56-60/ 76-81	14-19/ 19-25	28-34/ 38-46	69-152″/ 12-17	14-19/ 19-25
1.9L	1990-92	44/60**, +90°, +90°	12-15/ 16-20	15-20/ 21-27	81-96/ 110-130	5-8/ 7-10
2.0L (121) Diesel	1984-87	22/30, +90°, +90°	11-17/ 16-23	16-20/ 22-27	116-123/ 160-170	23-34/ 32-47
2.2L	1989-92	57-64/ 80-86	14-22/ 19-30	16-21/ 22-28	9-13/ 12-17	14-19/ 19-25
2.3L (140) OHC: Ex. Turbo	1987-92	50-60/ 68-81, 80-90/ 108-122	20-29/ 26-38	15-17/ 20-23, 20-30/ 27-41	103-133/ 140-180	14-21/ 19-28
Ex. Turbo	1983-86	50-60/ 68-81, 80-90/ 108-122	14-21/ 19-28	5-7/ 7-9, 16-23/ 22-31	100-120/ 136-167	14-21/ 19-28
Turbo	1985-89	50-60/ 68-81, 80-90/ 108-122	14-21/ 19-28	16-23/ 22-31	100-120/ 136-162	14-21/ 19-28
Turbo	1983-84	50-60/ 68-81, 80-90/ 108-122	14-21/ 19-28	16-23/ 22-31	80-103/ 111-139	14-21/ 19-28
2.3L (140) HSC, 2.5L (153)	1984-92	51-59/ 70-80, 70-76/ 95-103	15-23/ 20-30	5-7/7-10, 20-30/ 27-41	111-139/ 140-170	15-23/ 20-30
2.9L Scorpio	1988-89	22/30, 51-55/ 70-75, +90°	3-6/4-8, 6-11/8-15 11-15/ 15-21, 15-18/ 21-25†	20-30/ 27-41	85-96/ 115-130	7-9/ 9-12
3.0L (182)	1986-92	37/50, 68/92	11/15, 18/25, 24/33	19/25	107/145	6-8/ 8-12
3.0L SHO	1989-92	37-50/ 49-69, 62-68/ 83-93	11-17/ 15-23	26-38/ 35-52	113-126/ 152-172	5-16 6-9
3.3L (200)	1983	50-55/ 68-75, 60-65/ 81-88, 70-75/ 95-102	18-24/ 23-33	18-24/ 24-33	85-100/ 115-136	12-18/ 16-24
3.8L (232)	1983	47/65, 55/75, 63/85, 74/101*	5/7, 10/14, 18/25	15-22/ 20-30	93-121/ 125-165	15-22/ 20-30
3.8L (232)	1984-92	37/50, 45/60, 51/70, 59/80*	7.5/10, 15/20, 24/32	15-22/ 20-30	93-121/ 125-165	15-22/ 20-30
4.6L	1991-92	15-22/ 20-30, +85-95°, +85-95°	15-22/ 20-30	15-22/ 20-30	114-121/ 155-165	15-22/ 20-30

TIGHTENING TORQUES Continued

Engine	Year	Torque Ft-lbs/Nm Cylinder Head	Intake Manifold	Exhaust Manifold	Crankshaft Pulley	Water Pump
5.0L (302)	1983-92	55-65/ 76-88, 65-72/ 88-98	23-25/ 31-34‡	18-24/ 24-32	70-90/ 95-122	12-18/ 16-24
5.8L (351)	1983-92	85/115, 95/129, 105-112/ 142-151	23-25/ 31-34‡	18-24/ 24-32	70-90/ 95-122	12-18/ 16-24

* Back off bolts 2-3 turns and repeat tightening procedures.
† Warm up engine and retorque to final specification.
**Back off bolts and retorque to 44/60.
‡ Retorque hot.

VALVE CLEARANCE
Engine cold except as noted.

Engine	Year	Intake (inches)	Intake (mm)	Exhaust (inches)	Exhaust (mm)
2.0L (121) Diesel	1984-87	.008-.011	.20-.30	.011-.015	.30-.40
2.4L (146) Diesel	1984-85	.012	.30	.012	.30

COMPRESSION PRESSURE
At cranking speed, engine temperature normalized, throttle open.

Engine	Year	PSI	Maximum Variation PSI
2.0L (121) Diesel	1984-87	384-427	—
2.4L (146) Diesel	1984-85	348	—
All Gasoline	1983-92	Lowest cylinder pressure must be more than 75% of highest cylinder pressure.	

BELT TENSION
A belt in operation 10 minutes is considered a used belt.

Deflection method: Table lists deflection at midpoint of belt segment.
Strand Tension method: Use a strand tension gauge. Measurements are in pounds.
With automatic tensioner: Inspect indicator marks and replace belt if index mark is not between reference marks.

Application	Year	Alternator	Power Steering	Air Cond.	Thermactor
Deflection method					
All* (inches)	1983-85	1/8-1/4	1/8-1/4	1/8-1/4	1/8-1/4
All* (mm)	1983-85	3-6	3-6	3-6	3-6
All◆ (inches)	1983-85	1/8-1/2	1/8-1/2	1/8-1/2	1/8-1/2
All◆ (mm)	1983-85	3-13	3-13	3-13	3-13
2.2L (inches)	1989-92	1/4-5/16	1/4-5/16	1/4-5/16	—
2.2L (mm)	1989-92	6-12	6-12	6-12	—
USED BELTS					
Strand Tension method					
V-ribbed V-6					
4 rib ex. AP	1983	100-130	100-130	100-130	—
4 rib AP	1983	—	—	—	90-120
5 rib	1983	120-150	120-150	120-150	120-150
6 rib	1983	130-160	130-160	130-160	130-160
w/tensioner	1983	80-140	80-140	80-140	80-140
V	1983	90-120	90-120	90-120	90-120
1/4″	1982-83	—	—	—	40-60
V-belts ex. AP	1984-90	80-100	80-100	80-100	—
V-belts AP	1984-90	—	—	—	40-60
Cogged	1984-90	110-130	110-130	110-130	110-130
V-ribbed (5 ribs)	1986-90	110-130	110-130	110-130	110-130
V-ribbed (6 ribs)	1984-90	140-160	140-160	140-160	140-160
Serpentine w/tensioner⊙	1984-85	80-140	—	—	—
Serpentine w/tensioner⊙	1986-90	100-180	—	—	—
1.3L	1991-92	95-110	90-110	90-110	—
1.6L	1991-92	110-132	110-132	110-132	—
1.8L	1991-92	68-85	95-110	95-110	—
3.0L					
w/o tensioner	1991-92	110-130	110-130	110-130	—
3.0L SHO	1991-92	148-192	112-157	112-157	—
5.0L Mustang	1991-92	100-150⊙	—	—	—

BELT TENSION Continued

Application	Year	Alternator	Power Steering	Air Cond.	Thermactor
NEW BELTS					
Strand Tension method					
V-ribbed					
4 rib ex. AP	1983	110-150	110-150	110-150	—
4 rib AP	1983	—	—	—	90-130
5 rib	1983	130-170	130-170	130-170	130-170
6 rib	1983	140-180	140-180	140-180	140-180
w/tensioner	1983	85-140	85-140	85-140	85-140
V	1983	120-160	120-160	120-160	120-160
1/4″	1983	—	—	—	50-80
V-belts ex. AP	1984-90	90-130	90-130	90-130	—
V-belts AP	1984-90	—	—	—	50-90
Cogged	1984-90	120-160	120-160	120-160	120-160
V-ribbed (6 ribs)	1984-90	150-190	150-190	150-190	150-190
Serpentine w/tensioner⊙	1984-85	80-140	—	—	—
Serpentine w/tensioner⊙	1986-90	100-130	—	—	—
1.3L	1991-92	110-130	110-125	110-125	—
1.6L	1991-92	110-132	110-132	110-132	—
1.8L	1991-92	86-103	110-132	110-132	—
3.0L					
w/o tensioner	1991-92	140-160	140-160	140-160	—
3.0L SHO	1991-92	220-265	148-192	148-192	—
5.0L Mustang	1991-92	100-150⊙	—	—	—

* Midpoint of free span less than 12 inches (305 millimeters).
◆ Midpoint of free span 12 inches (305 millimeters) or more.
⊙ Checking figure, not adjustable.

ENGINE COMPUTER SYSTEM

COMPUTER DIAGNOSTIC CODES
See UNDERHOOD SERVICE INSTRUCTIONS at the beginning of this section for test/ adjustment diagrams.

EEC III:
Run engine at 1800 rpm for one or two minutes until radiator hose pressurizes.
Tie two vacuum gauges into both smaller vacuum hoses at Thermactor Air Diverter and Air Bypass solenoids. Apply 20″ of vacuum to vent port of B/MAP sensor and hold for at least eight seconds. Throttle kicker will extend and hold for 90 seconds. When it retracts, service codes will be displayed. A five-second pause occurs between codes.

MCU:
Complicated procedure required to obtain valid codes. See shop manual.
With key off, locate self-test connector. Connect a jumper wire from the upper right cavity to the second lower cavity from left. Connect an analog VOM from battery (+) to lower second from right cavity (–). Disconnect PCV valve vacuum line of canister control valve (4- & 6-cyl.). Remove PCV valve from valve cover and uncap restrictor in thermactor vacuum control line (8-cyl. as equipped).

1983-90 EEC IV:
Complicated procedure required to obtain valid codes. See shop manual.
Continental w/message center: Hold "Select" "Check Out" and "Reset" down. Turn ignition switch on.
All others: With engine at operating temperature and ignition off, locate SELF-TEST connector under hood. Connect a jumper wire between input connector (single terminal) and upper right cavity on connector. Connect an analog VOM to battery (+) and second bottom right cavity on connector. On some models, the "CHECK ENGINE" light will flash codes. A four second delay separates individual codes. On Continental with message center, hold "SELECT," "CHECK OUT," and "RESET" buttons down to activate test. SELF-TEST codes are revealed in a series of three separate test procedures (key on engine off, engine running, and continuous) and must be accessed in order.

Key on engine off: Place transmission in park or neutral, set parking brake, turn off all electrical equipment, place octane switch (2.3L SVO Turbo) in premium position. Activate SELF-TEST and place ignition key in run position, do not depress throttle. Observe and record service codes.

Engine running: Deactivate SELF-TEST. Start engine and run at greater than 2000 rpm for 2 minutes. Turn engine off, wait ten seconds & reactivate SELF-TEST. Start engine without depressing throttle. An engine ID code will be displayed (**Code 2**—4-cyl., **Code 3**—6-cyl., **Code 4**—8-cyl.), depress and release brake pedal once. Observe and record service codes.

Continuous: Allow engine to run at idle after all codes have been displayed. After approximately 2 minutes, continuous codes will be displayed. System will remain in continuous mode until ignition is switched off or SELF-TEST is deactivated.

1983 All w/EEC III
Code 11 System OK
Code 12 RPM out of spec.
Code 15 Calibration assembly (memory)

COMPUTER DIAGNOSTIC CODES Continued

Code 21 Faulty engine coolant temperature wiring
Code 22 Barometric/MAP
Code 23 Throttle position sensor circuit
Code 24 Air charge temperature circuit faulty
Code 31 EGR sensor not moving open
Code 32 EGR sensor not closing
Code 41 Fuel mixture lean
Code 42 Fuel mixture rich
Code 43 Coolant temperature under 120°F
Code 44 Thermactor system

1983 4- & 6-cyl. w/MCU
Code 11 System OK
Code 33 Running test not initiated
Code 41 Fuel mixture lean
Code 42 Fuel mixture rich
Code 44 Thermactor
Code 45 Thermactor air diverter valve
Code 46 Thermactor air bypass valve
Codes 51 or 61 Low temperature vacuum switch
Codes 52 or 62 Idle tracking or wide open throttle switch
Codes 53 or 63 Closed switches
Codes 56 or 66 Closed throttle switch

1983-89 V8 w/MCU
Code 11 System OK
Code 12 RPM out of spec.
Code 25 Knock sensor
Code 41 Fuel mixture lean
Code 42 Fuel mixture rich
Code 44 Thermactor
Code 45 Thermactor always upstream
Code 46 Thermactor not bypassing
Code 51 Hi-low vacuum switch
Code 53 Dual temperature switch
Code 54 Mid-temperature switch
Code 55 Mid-vacuum switch
Codes 61 & 65 Mid-vacuum switch closed
Code 62 Barometric switch

1983-90 ALL W/EEC IV
Test condition: I—ignition on/engine off, R—engine running, C—continuous

Code Displayed	Test Condition	Results
11	I, R, C	System OK, test sequence complete
12	R	Idle speed control out of range
13	I, R, C	Normal idle out of range
14	I, C	Ignition profile pickup erratic
15	I	ROM test failure
15	C	Power interrupt to keep alive memory
16	R	Erratic idle, oxygen sensor out of range throttle not closing
17	R	Curb idle out of range
18	C	No ignition signal to ECM
18	R	SPOUT circuit open
19	I	No power to processor
19	R	Erratic idle speed or signal
19	C	CID sensor failure
21	I, R	Coolant temperature out of range
21	I, R, C	Coolant temperature sensor out of range
22	I, R, C	MAP, BARO out of range
23	I, R, C	Throttle position signal out of range
24	I, R	Air charge temperature low, improper sensor installation
25	R	Knock not sensed in test
26	I, R	Vane, Mass air flow sensor contamination or circuit
27	C	Vehicle speed sensor or circuit
28	I, R	Vane air temperature sensor adjustment or circuit
29	C	No continuity in vehicle speed sensor circuit
31	I, R, C	Canister or EGR valve control system
32	I, R, C	Canister or EGR valve control system
33	R, C	Canister or EGR valve not operating properly
34	I, R, C	Canister or EGR control circuit
35	I, R, C	EGR pressure feedback, regulator circuit
38	C	Idle control circuit
39	C	Automatic overdrive circuit
41	C	Oxygen sensor signal ex. 5.0L SEFI; 5.0L SEFI, fuel pressure out of range
41	R	Lean fuel mixture ex. 5.0L SEFI; 5.0L SEFI, injectors out of balance

COMPUTER DIAGNOSTIC CODES Continued

Code Displayed	Test Condition	Results
42	R	Fuel pressure out of range 5.0L SEFI only
42	R, C	Fuel mixture rich ex. 5.0L SEFI
43	C	Lean fuel mixture at wide open throttle
43	R	Engine too warm for test
44	R	Air management system inoperative
45	R	Thermactor air diverter circuit
45	C	DIS coil pack, 1 circuit failure
46	R	Thermactor air bypass circuit
46	C	DIS coil pack, 2 circuit failure
47	R	Low flow of unmetered air at idle
48	R	High flow of unmetered air at idle
48	C	DIS coil pack, 3 circuit failure
49	C	SPOUT signal defaulted to 10 degrees
51	I, C	Coolant temperature sensor out of range
52	I, R	Power steering pressure switch out of range
53	I, C	Throttle sensor input out of range
54	I, C	Vane air flow sensor, air charge temperature sensor
55	R	Charging system under voltage 1983-88 ex. 3.8L TBI
55	R	Open ignition key power circuit 1983-88 3.8L TBI only, 1989-90 All
56	I, R, C	Vane, Mass airflow sensor or circuit
57	C	Transmission neutral pressure switch circuit
58	I	CFI; idle control circuit, EFI; vane air flow circuit
58	R	Idle control/motor or circuit
58	C	Vane air temperature sensor or circuit
59	I, C	Transmission throttle pressure switch circuit ex. 3.0L SHO
59	I, C	Low speed fuel pump circuit 3.0L SHO, 3.8L Supercharge
61	I, C	Coolant temperature switch out of range
62	I	Transmission circuit fault
63	I, C	Throttle position sensor circuit
64	I, C	Vane air temperature, air charge temperature sensor
65	C	Fuel control system not switching to closed loop
66	I, C	No vane, mass airflow sensor signal
67	I, R, C	Neutral drive switch or circuit
67	C	AC clutch switch circuit
68	I, R, C	TBI; Idle tracking switch, EFI; Vane air temperature circuit
69	I, C	Vehicle speed sensor circuit
71	C	TBI; Idle tracking switch, EFI; Electrical interference
72	C	System power circuit, electrical interference
72	R	No MAP or mass airflow sensor change
73	I, R	Throttle position sensor or circuit
74	R	Brake on/off ground circuit fault
75	R	Brake on/off power circuit fault
76	R	No vane airflow change
77	R	Throttle "goose" test not performed
78	C	Power circuit
79	I	A/C clutch circuit
81	I	Thermactor air circuit, turbo boost circuit
82	I	Thermactor air circuit, integrated controller circuit
82	I	Supercharger bypass circuit
83	I	EGR control circuit 3.8L CFI, 2.3L EFI ex. turbo only
83	I	Cooling fan circuit 2.3L Turbo, 2.5L, 3.0L, 3.8L EFI only
83	I, C	Low speed fuel pump relay 1983-88, 1989-90 SHO
83	I, C	EGR solenoid circuit, 1989-90 ex. SHO
84	I, R	EGR control circuit
85	I, R	Canister purge circuit ex. 2.3L Turbo; 2.3L Turbo transmission shift control circuit
85	C	Excessive fuel pressure or flow
85	I	Canister purge circuit
86	C	Low fuel pressure or flow
87	I, R, C	Fuel pump circuit
88	I	2.3L Turbo; clutch converter circuit, others; integrated controller
89	I	Lock-up solenoid
91	R, C	Oxygen sensor, fuel pressure, injector balance
92	R	Fuel mixture rich, fuel pressure high
93	I	Throttle plate position or TPS sensor
94	R	Secondary air inoperative
95	I, C	Fuel pump circuit
95	R	Thermactor air diverter circuit
96	I, C	Fuel pump circuit
96	R	Thermactor air bypass circuit
98	R	Repeat test sequence 1983-88
99	R	Repeat test sequence 1983-88
99	R	System has not learned to control idle

UNDERHOOD SERVICE SPECIFICATIONS

SENSORS, INPUT

TEMPERATURE SENSORS
See UNDERHOOD SERVICE INSTRUCTIONS at the beginning of this section for test/adjustment diagrams.

1.3L VAT: Measured between upper terminal (GN/BK wire) of airflow sensor and ground.

1.6L VAT: Measured between terminal 25 (upper terminal on airflow connector) and ground.

2.2L VAT: Measured between first (R wire) and fifth (LG/W wire) of airflow sensor.

All others with EEC IV VAT: Measured between upper terminal (LG/P wire) of airflow sensor and ground.

Engine	Year	Sensor	Resistance Ohms @ deg. F/C
1.3L (81), 1.6L Capri, Tracer; 1.8L, 2.2L	1988-92	Coolant	14,600-17,800 @ -4/-20 2200-2700 @ 68/16 1000-1300 @ 104/40 500-640 @ 140/60 290-355 @ 176/80
1.6L (98), 1.9 (113), 2.3L (140), 2.5L (153), 2.9L (179), 3.0L (182), 3.8L (231), 5.0L (302)	1983-92*	Coolant, Air Charge	31,700-42,900 @ 68/20 13,650-18,650 @ 104/40 6500-8900 @ 140/60 3240-4440 @ 176/80 1770-2370 @ 212/100 980-1380 @ 248/115
All w/EEC III	1983	Coolant, Air Charge	1100-8000 1700-60,000
1.3L	1989	Vane Air	3000-6000 @ 40/4 2000-3000 @ 68/20 500-2000 @ 90/32
1.6L (98)	1987-89	Vane Air	5800 @ 32/0 2700 @ 65/18 300 @ 185/85 180 @ 220/105
1.3L, 1.6L, 1.8L, 2.2L	1989-92	Vane Air	13,000-17,000 @ -4/-20 4700-5700 @ 32/0 2100-2900 @ 68/20 950-1250 @ 104/40 500-700 @ 140/60 250-350 @ 176/80
1.6L (98) FI, 1.9L (119) MFI, 2.3L (140) Turbo	1983-90	Vane Air	2100-2900 @ 68/20 1100-1350 @ 104/40 500-700 @ 140/60 280-380 @ 176/80 120-160 @ 212/100 110-120 @ 248/115

* With EEC IV only.

MANIFOLD ABSOLUTE AND BAROMETRIC PRESSURE SENSORS
See UNDERHOOD SERVICE INSTRUCTIONS at the beginning of this section for test/adjustment diagrams.

1.3L: Measured between lower right terminal (BR/BK wire) and ground.

1.6L: Measured between terminals 45 and 46 (lower right and upper left).

2.2L: Measured between upper right (LG/Y wire) and lower left (Y wire).

All others with EEC IV: Measured between BK/W wire and ground.

Engine	Year	Voltage @ in./mm Hg
1.3L FI	1989	3.5-4.5 @ 0/0 2.5-3.5 @ 5/125 2.5 max. @ 30/750
1.6L, 2.2L	1987-89	0 @ 0/0 3.5-4.5 @ 30/750

Engine	Year	Sensor	Voltage @ Altitude
All ex. 1.3L, 1.6L, 1.8L, 2.2L	1983-90* 1991-92	MAP, BARO BARO	1.55-1.63 @ 0 1.52-1.60 @ 1000 1.49-1.56 @ 2000 1.46-1.54 @ 3000 1.43-1.51 @ 4000 1.39-1.48 @ 5000 1.36-1.45 @ 6000 1.34-1.43 @ 7000

SENSORS, INPUT Continued

MANIFOLD ABSOLUTE AND BAROMETRIC PRESSURE SENSORS Continued

Engine	Year	Sensor	Frequency HZ @ in./KPA
All ex. 1.3L, 1.6L, 1.8L, 2.2L	1991-92	MAP	159 @ 0/0 141 @ 6/20 125 @ 12/41 109 @ 18/61 95 @ 24/81 80 @ 30/102

Engine	Year	Sensor	Voltage @ in./mm Hg
1.6L	1991-92	MAP	3.26-4.42 @ 0/0 2.86-3.86 @ 15/17 2.26-3.06 @ 10/34 1.64-2.22 @ 15/51 1.07-1.45 @ 20/68 .49-.67 @ 25/85

Engine	Year	Resistance (ohms) @ Altitude
All w/EEC III	1983	7.6-8.4 @ 0-1500 7.2-8.1 @ 1500-2500 6.9-7.8 @ 2500-3500 6.7-7.3 @ 3500-4500 6.6-7.2 @ 4500-5500 6.3-7.0 @ 5500-6500 6.1-6.7 @ 6500-7500 5.4-6.7 @ 7500 and up

* With EEC IV only. Measured with ignition on and engine off.

MASS OR VANE AIRFLOW SENSOR
See UNDERHOOD SERVICE INSTRUCTIONS at the beginning of this section for test/adjustment diagrams.

Engines with multi-port injection.

1.6L MFI, 1.9L MFI, 2.3L MFI: Vane Airflow Sensors, measured between second upper terminal (W/BK wire) and ground.

3.0L SHO, 3.8L Supercharged, 5.0L MFI HO: Mass Airflow Sensors, measured between terminal D (upper most) and ground.

Engine	Year	Voltage Ign. On	Idle
1.6L, 1.9L, 2.3L	1983-88	.15-.50	1.50-2.70
1.9L, 2.3L	1989-91	.17-.50	1.10-1.70
3.0L SHO, 3.8L Supercharged, 5.0L HO	1986-91	.70 max.	.20-1.50

Engine	Year	Vane Position Closed	Open
1.3L	1989-91	.34-.46	3.6-4.4
1.3L	1992	4.5-5.0	0.5-1.5
1.6L	1991	1.9-2.1	7.8-8.0
1.6L	1992	3.0-3.3	7.0-8.0
1.8L	1991	3.6-4.4	0.4-1.1
1.8L	1992	4.5-5.0	0.5-1.5
2.2L	1989-91	3.0-3.3	5.0-7.0
2.2L	1992	3.0-3.3	7.0-8.0

Engine	Year	Voltage @ MPH/KPH
All ex. 1.3L, 1.6L, 1.8L, 2.2L	1992	0.8 @ idle 1.0 @ 20/32 1.7 @ 40/64 2.1 @ 60/96

THROTTLE POSITION SENSOR (TPS)
See UNDERHOOD SERVICE INSTRUCTIONS at the beginning of this section for test/adjustment diagrams.

Engines with EEC III: Turn ignition to RUN position and remove vacuum hose from throttle kicker as equipped. With engine not running, compare voltage reading against specifications and adjust as needed.

Engines with EEC IV: Connect positive (+) probe of DVOM along terminal "A" (upper) of TPS. Connect negative (-) probe along terminal "B" (middle, LG/DG wire) and turn ignition on but do not start engine. Adjust TPS to specified value.

UNDERHOOD SERVICE SPECIFICATIONS

SENSORS, INPUT Continued

THROTTLE POSITION SENSOR (TPS) Continued

Engine	Year	TPS Voltage Idle	WOT
All w/EEC III	1983	1.60-2.40	6.0 min.
1.6L (98) FI	1983-84	0.50-1.30*	—
1.9L TBI	1989-90	.39	4.84
1.9L MFI	1989-90	.24	4.84
1.9L	1991	.34	4.84
2.2L	1989-90	.36-.66	4.30
2.3L (140) Turbo	1983-84	0.25-1.40*	—
2.3L	1989-90	.20	4.84
2.3L OHC	1991	.34	4.84
2.3L HSC	1991	.20	9.84
2.5L	1989-91	.39	4.84
2.9L	1988-89	1.0 max.*	3.8-4.2
3.0L ex. SHO	1989-91	.34	4.84
3.0L SHO	1989-91	.23	4.89
3.8L, 4.6L, 5.0L	1989-91	.39	4.84
All others w/EEC IV	1984-88	0.9-1.1†	—

* Not adjustable.
† Adjustable units only.

CRANKSHAFT SENSOR

Engine	Year	Resistance (ohms)
All w/EEC III	1983	100-640
1.9L	1991-92	2300-2500
2.3L	1990-91	300-750
3.0L SHO	1989-91	300-750
3.8L Supercharged	1989-91	300-750
4.6L	1991	300-750
4.6L	1992	2300-2500

VEHICLE SPEED SENSOR

Engine	Year	Resistance (ohms)
All w/EEC IV	1983-92	190-250

ACTUATORS, OUTPUT

IDLE SPEED CONTROL
See UNDERHOOD SERVICE INSTRUCTIONS at the beginning of this section for test/adjustment diagrams.

All FI engines with ISC.

Engine	Year	Resistance (ohms)
All	1983-92	6-13

MIXTURE CONTROL SOLENOID-CARBURETTED ENGINES

Engine	Year	Resistance (ohms)
2.3L (140) 1V YFA	1983-86	30-60
3.8L (232), 5.0L (302) 2V 2150	1983-86	15-30

COMPUTER TIMING ADVANCE

1983-91 specifications are in addition to base timing.

Activate system test procedure. See ''COMPUTER DIAGNOSTIC CODES'' section. Check advance against specifications.

1992 degrees of advance are measured at indicated vehicle speed.

Test with engine at operating temperature.

Year	Engine	Advance
1983	All w/EEC III	27-33
1983-91	All w/EEC IV	17-23

Engine	Year	Degrees of Advance Idle	30 MDH/50 KPH	55 MPH/90 KPH
2.3L HSC	1992	15-20	35-39	41-45
2.3L Mustang MT	1992	18-20	22-28	22-32
AT	1992	12-18	22-28	28-31
3.0L ex. SHO MT	1992	22-26	38-42	42-46
AT	1992	22-26	44-48	47-51
3.0L SHO	1992	10-15	26-34	33-38
3.8L FWD	1992	25-30	34-38	40-45
Police	1992	21-25	36-40	38-42
RWD	1992	16-21	32-36	30-36
Supercharged MT	1992	18-22	32-34	31-35
AT	1992	18-23	28-33	28-33
5.0L Mustang	1992	16-20	32-36	36-42
T-Bird, Cougar	1992	19-23	33-37	40-44
Mark VII	1992	22-26	32-36	34-38

ENGINE IDENTIFICATION

To identify any engine by the manufacturer's code, follow the four steps designated by the numbered blocks.

1 **MODEL YEAR IDENTIFICATION:** Month and year of manufacture stamped on Vehicle Certification (V.C.) label.

2 **ENGINE CODE LOCATION:** Refer to illustrations of certification label.

3 **ENGINE CODE:** In the vertical "CODE" column, find the engine code determined in Step 2.

4 **ENGINE IDENTIFICATION:** On the line where the engine code appears, read to the right to identify the engine.

MODEL YEAR AND ENGINE IDENTIFICATION:

1 DATE OF MANUFACTURE

MODEL YEAR DESIGNATION:

Stated on Emission Control Information label in the engine compartment. Also indicated from 10th character of V.I.N.
1992 — N, 1991 — M, 1990 — L,
1989 — K, 1988 — J, 1987 — H,
1986 — G, 1985 — F, 1984 — E,
1983 — D.

VEHICLE CERTIFICATION LABEL — Attached to rear face of left door or pillar.

Vehicle Identification Number (V.I.N.) Also located on top left side of instrument panel

2 ENGINE CODE (8th character)

4 ENGINE IDENTIFICATION

YEAR	**3** ENGINE CODE	CYL.	DISPL. liters	cu. in.	Fuel System	HP
1992	A	4	2.3	140	MFI	100
	T	6	2.9	179	MFI	140
	U	6	3.0	182	MFI	145
	X	6	4.0	241	MFI	145, 160†
	Y	6	4.9	300	MFI	145, 160†
	N	8	5.0	302	MFI	185
	H	8	5.8	351	MFI	200
	M	8	7.3 D	445 D	MFI	160, 180†
	G	8	7.5	460	MFI	230
1991	A	4	2.3	140	MFI	100
	T	6	2.9	179	MFI	140
	U	6	3.0	182	MFI	145
	X	6	4.0	241	MFI	155, 160†
	Y	6	4.9	300	MFI	145, 150†
	N	8	5.0	302	MFI	185
	H	8	5.8	351	MFI	200
	M	8	7.3 D	445 D	MFI	160, 180†
	G	8	7.5	460	MFI	230
1990	A	4	2.3	140	MFI	100
	T	6	2.9	179	MFI	140
	U	6	3.0	182	MFI	145
	X	6	4.0	244	MFI	155, 160†
	Y	6	4.9	300	MFI	145, 150†
	N	8	5.0	302	MFI	185
	H	8	5.8	351	MFI	210
	M	8	7.3 D	445 D	MFI	160, 180†
	G	8	7.5	460	MFI	230
1989	A	4	2.3	140	MFI	100
	T	6	2.9	179	MFI	140
	U	6	3.0	182	MFI	145
	Y	6	4.9	300	MFI	145, 150†
	N	8	5.0	302	MFI	185
	H	8	5.8	351	MFI	210
	M	8	7.3 D	445 D	MFI	160, 180†
	G	8	7.5	460	MFI	230
1988	C	4	2.0	122	2V	80
	A	4	2.3	140	MFI	90
	T	6	2.9	179	MFI	140
	U	6	3.0	182	MFI	145
	Y	6	4.9	300	MFI	145, 150†
	N	8	5.0	302	MFI	185
	H	8	5.8	351	MFI	210
	M	8	7.3 D	445 D	MFI	160, 180†
	G	8	7.5	460	MFI	215, 235†
1987	C	4	2.0	122	2V	80
	A	4	2.3	140	MFI	88, 90†
	E	4	2.3 TD	143 TD	MFI	86
	T	6	2.9	179	MFI	140
	U	6	3.0	182	MFI	145
	Y	6	4.9	300	MFI	145, 150†
	N	8	5.0	302	MFI	185

4 ENGINE IDENTIFICATION

YEAR	**3** ENGINE CODE	CYL.	DISPL. liters	cu. in.	Fuel System	HP
1987 Cont'd.	H	8	5.8	351	4V	180, 190†
	1	8	6.9 D	421 D	MFI	150, 170†
	L	8	7.5	460	4V	240, 245†
	G	8	7.5	460	MFI	215, 235†
1986	C	4	2.0	122	1V	80
	A	4	2.3	140	MFI	88, 90†
	E	4	2.3 TD	143 TD	MFI	86
	S	6	2.8	171	2V	115
	T	6	2.9	179	MFI	140
	U	6	3.0	182	MFI	145
	Y	6	4.9	300	1V	116-125†
	N	8	5.0	302	MFI	185
	H	8	5.8	351	4V	210
	1	8	6.9 D	421 D	MFI	150, 170†
	L	8	7.5	460	4V	240, 245†
1985	C	4	2.0	122	1V	74
	A	4	2.3	140	MFI	88, 90
	E	4	2.3 TD	143 TD	MFI	86
	S	6	2.8	171	2V	115
	Y	6	4.9	300	1V	116-125†
	F	8	5.0	302	2V	145-150†
	N	8	5.0	302	MFI	190
	G	8	5.8	351	2V	150-165†
	H	8	5.8	351	4V	210
	1	8	6.9 D	421 D	MFI	150-170†
	L	8	7.5	460	4V	220-225†
1984	C	4	2.0	122	1V	73
	P	4	2.2 D	134 D	MFI	59
	A	4	2.3	140	1V	79, 82†
	S	6	2.8	171	2V	115
	Y	6	4.9	300	1V	116-125†
	F	8	5.0	302	2V	143-150†
	G	8	5.8	351	2V	149-165†
	G	8	5.8	351	4V	210
	1	8	6.9 D	421 D	MFI	150, 170†
	L	8	7.5	460	4V	220, 225†
1983	C	4	2.0	122	1V	73
	P	4	2.2 D	134 D	MFI	59
	A	4	2.3	140	1V	79, 82†
	S	6	2.8	173	2V	115
	3	6	3.8	232	2V	109
	Y	6	4.9	300	1V	116-121†
	F	8	5.0	302	2V	139-143†
	G	8	5.8	351	2V	139-152†
	1	8	6.9 D	421 D	MFI	146-161†
	L	8	7.5	460	4V	193, 202†

† Engine horsepower varies with model installation.
D — Diesel.   MFI — Multiport Fuel Injection.   TD — Turbo Diesel.
1V — One Venturi Carburetor.   2V — Two Venturi Carburetor.
4V — Four Venturi Carburetor.

UNDERHOOD SERVICE SPECIFICATIONS

CYLINDER NUMBERING SEQUENCE

4-CYL. FIRING ORDER:
1 3 4 2

— Front of car —

Aerostar
2.3L (140)

1983-88
Ranger/Bronco II
2.0L (122),
2.3L (140)

1989-92 2.3L

V6-CYL. FIRING ORDER:
1 4 2 5 3 6

6-CYL. FIRING ORDER:
1 5 3 6 2 4

8-CYL. FIRING ORDER:
351, 400
1 3 7 2 6 5 4 8

All Other 8-cyl.
1 5 4 2 6 3 7 8

— Front of car —

| 2.8L (171) | 2.9L (177) | 3.0L (183) | 3.8L (232) | 4.0L (245) | 1983-86 4.9L (300) | 1987-92 4.9L (300) | 8-cyl. |

TIMING MARK

Ranger/Bronco II
2.0L (122),
2.3L (140)

BTDC
30°
20°
10°
0°
10°
ATDC

2.8L (171),
2.9L (177)

BTDC
33°
27°
20°
12°
0°

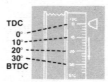

3.0L (183)

TDC
0°
10°
20°
30°
BTDC

4.0L (245)

0°
10°
BTDC

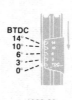

1983-86
4.9L (300)

BTDC
14°
10°
6°
3°
0°

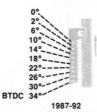

1987-92
4.9L (300)

0°
2°
6°
10°
14°
18°
22°
26°
30°
BTDC 34°

3.8L (232)

0°
4°
8°
12°
BTDC

8-cyl.

BTDC
30°
20°
10°
0°
10°
ATDC

ELECTRICAL AND IGNITION SYSTEMS

BATTERY

Engine	Year	STANDARD BCI Group No.	STANDARD Crank. Perf.	OPTIONAL BCI Group No.	OPTIONAL Crank. Perf.
Ranger, Bronco II, Explorer					
4-cyl.					
2.0L (122), 2.3L (140), 2.8L (171)	1983-86	63	380	64	535
Canada	1983-86	63	450	64	535
2.3L (140) Diesel	1985-87	63	450*	—	—
2.0L, 2.3L: MT	1987	62	380	63, 64	450, 535
AT	1987	63	450	64	535
2.0L, 2.3L: MT	1988	62, 63	380, 450	64	535
AT	1988	63	450	64	535
2.3L	1989-92	58	540	65	650
V-6					
2.8L (171)	1985	62	380	64	535
Canada	1985	63	450	64	535
2.9L (177)	1986-87	63	450	64	535
2.9L (177) Ranger	1988-92	58	540	65	650
Bronco II	1988-90	65	650	—	—
2.9L Explorer	1991-92	65	650	65	850
3.0L	1991-92	58	540	65	650
4.0L	1991-92	65	650	65	850

BATTERY Continued

Engine	Year	STANDARD BCI Group No.	STANDARD Crank. Perf.	OPTIONAL BCI Group No.	OPTIONAL Crank. Perf.
F-Series					
6-cyl., V-6					
All	1983	63	450	64	535
All	1984-85	62	380	24F	475
All	1986	62	380	64	535
All MT	1987	65	650	65	850
All AT	1987	65	850	—	—
All	1988-92	65	650	65	850
8-cyl.					
6.9L (421) Diesel	1983-86	27*	700	—	—
7.5L (460) MT	1983-85	62	380	64	535
7.5L (460) AT	1983-85	64	535	24F	350
7.5L (460)	1986	64	535	—	—
All Others 2V, MT	1983-85	61	310	62	380
All Others 2V, AT	1983-85	62	380	64	535
5.0L (302) FI, 5.8L (351)	1985-86	63	450	64	535
All gas	1987-92	65	650	65	850
All Diesel	1987-92	65	850	—	—
Aerostar					
2.3L (140), 2.8L (171) MT	1986-87	62	380	64	535
2.3L (140), 2.8L (171) AT	1986-87	63	450	64	535

UNDERHOOD SERVICE SPECIFICATIONS

FDTTU2   FDTTU2

BATTERY Continued

		STANDARD		OPTIONAL	
Engine	Year	BCI Group No.	Crank. Perf.	BCI Group No.	Crank. Perf.
3.0L (182)	1986-87	63	450	64	535
3.0L (182)	1988	64	535	—	—
3.0L	1989-92	65	650	—	—
Econoline					
All MT	1983	62	380	24F	500
All AT	1983	64	535	—	—
All	1984-85	24F	475	—	—
6-cyl. cargo vans	1986	62	380	64	535
5.0L (302), 5.8L (351) cargo vans	1986	63	450	64	535
7.5L (460), all passenger vans	1986-89	64	535	—	—
6 cyl., V8	1987-91	64	535	—	—
6 cyl., V8	1992	65	650	65	850
6.9L (421), 7.3L Diesel	1986-91	27*	700	—	—
7.3L Diesel: Left	1992	65	850	—	—
Right	1992	50	600	—	—
Auxiliary	1986-91	24F	350	—	—
Auxiliary	1992	50	400	—	—
Bronco					
All	1984-85	63	450	64	535
All 6-cyl.	1986	62	380	64	535
All 8-cyl.	1986	63	450	64	535
All	1987-91	65	650	65	850

* Requires two batteries.

ALTERNATOR
See UNDERHOOD SERVICE INSTRUCTIONS at the beginning of this section for test/adjustment diagrams.

Ampere rated output is stamped on housing.

Application	Rated Output	Test Output
1983	40, 60, 65, 75, 90	♦
1984-89 Rear term.	40, 60	♦
Side term.	70, 100	♦
Int. regl.	40, 60, 65	♦
1990-91 Ranger, Aerostar	75, 80	†
Bronco II	80	†
E-series	70, 100	†
F-series	60, 70, 75	†
Bronco	70, 75	†
1992 All	40, 60, 65, 75, 100, 130	†

♦ If rated output cannot be obtained at 2000 rpm, engine speed may be increased to a maximum of 2900 rpm.

† Output at 2000 rpm should be near or over the rated output.

REGULATOR
Measure battery voltage and record figure. With engine operating off idle and all secondary electrical systems turned off, regulated voltage should be no greater than 2.5 volts above recorded figure. Turn on headlights and set heater blower to high. Regulated voltage off idle should be no less than 0.5 volts above recorded figure.

STARTER

Application	Year	Cranking Voltage (min. volts)	Ampere Draw @ Cranking Speed	Engine RPM
4-cyl., V6	1983-90	9.6	150-200	180-250
4.0L	1990	9.6	140-200	170-220
4-cyl., V6	1991-92	9.6	140-200	170-250
6-cyl., V8: 4" or 101.60 mm dia.	1983-91	9.6	150-200	180-250
4½" or 114.3 mm dia.	1983-91	9.6	150-180	150-290
6-cyl. V8	1992	9.6	140-200	200-250
4-cyl. Diesel	1983-87	—	500 max.	150-220
8-cyl. Diesel	1983-91	—	430-530	170-230

SPARK PLUGS

Engine	Year	Gap (inches)	Gap (mm)	Torque (ft-lb)
2.0L (122)	1983-84	.032-.036	.81-.91	7-12
2.0L (122)	1985-88	.042-.046	1.07-1.17	5-10
2.3L (140)	1983-84	.032-.036	.81-.91	7-12
2.3L (140)	1985-88	.042-.046	1.07-1.17	5-10
3.8L (232)	1983	.042-.046	1.07-1.17	15-22
4.0L	1990-91	.052-.056	1.22-1.32	18-28
4.9L (300)	1983-87	.042-.046	1.07-1.17	15-20
All Others	1983-91	.042-.046	1.07-1.17	10-15

IGNITION COIL
See UNDERHOOD SERVICE INSTRUCTIONS at the beginning of this section for test/adjustment diagrams.

Winding Resistance (ohms at 75°F or 24°C)
1983-88 w/Dura-Spark: Primary, 0.8-1.6; Secondary, 7700-10,500.
1984-88 w/TFI (EEC IV): Primary, 0.3-1.0; Secondary, 8000-11,500.

DISTRIBUTOR PICKUP
See UNDERHOOD SERVICE INSTRUCTIONS at the beginning of this section for test/adjustment diagrams.

Engine	Year	Resistance (ohms)	Air Gap (in./mm)
Ex. EEC	1983-88	400-1000*	.017 min./.43 min.

* With 250 watt heat lamp held 1½ inches from coil for 5 minutes.

IGNITION RESISTOR
See UNDERHOOD SERVICE INSTRUCTIONS at the beginning of this section for test/adjustment diagrams.

Engine	Year	Type	Resistance (ohms)	Temperature (deg. F/C)
All w/Dura-Spark II	1983-88	Wire	0.8-1.6	—

BASE TIMING
See UNDERHOOD SERVICE INSTRUCTIONS at the beginning of this section for test/adjustment diagrams.

Set timing at Before Top Dead Center unless otherwise specified. Set timing below rpm setting listed or at idle if not specified.

Only reset timing if more than ±2 degrees from specifications listed.

With ''Positive Buy'' ignition, (identified by a Torx-head distributor holddown bolt) ±4 degrees.

Disconnect and plug distributor vacuum hose as equipped.

On engines equipped with dual-mode ignition timing disconnect third three-pin connector from sensor.

Engines with EEC III, system not adjustable.

Engines with ignition module part number 12A244, disconnect the two-wire connector (yellow & black wires) and jump the module connector pins.

Engines with EEC IV, disconnect single wire, connector or shorting bar from two-wire connector at distributor.

Engine	Year	Man. Trans. (degrees) @ RPM	Auto. Trans. (degrees) @ RPM
2.0L (122)	1983	6 @ 800	—
w/decal DMD, DME	1983	9 @ 800	—
2.0L (122)	1984	8 @ 800	—
w/decal ADL, ADK	1984	9 @ 800	—
2.0L (122)	1985-88	6 @ 800	—
2.2L Diesel	1983-84	2 ATDC	—
2.3L (140)	1983	6 @ 800	8 @ 800 N
High Altitude	1983	10 @ 800	10 @ 800 N
2.3L (140)	1984	6 @ 800	6 @ 800 N
High Altitude	1984	10 @ 800	10 @ 800 N
2.3L (140) FI	1985-89	10	10
2.3L	1989-92	10*	10*
2.8L (171)	1983-86	10	10
2.9L (177)	1986-92	10	10
3.0L (182)	1986-92	10	10
3.8L (232)	1983	2 @ 800	10 @ 800 N
4.0L	1990-92	10*	10*

Copyright 1992 by H.M. Gousha, a division of Simon & Schuster

UNDERHOOD SERVICE SPECIFICATIONS

FDTTU3   FDTTU3

BASE TIMING Continued

Engine	Year	Man. Trans. (degrees) @ RPM	Auto. Trans. (degrees) @ RPM
4.9L (300)	1983	6 @ 800	10 @ 800 N
w/decal DES	1983	10 @ 800	—
w/decal DHP	1983	8 @ 800	—
High Altitude	1983	10 @ 800	14 @ 800 N
4.9L (300)	1984	10	10
Heavy Duty	1984	12 @ 800	12 @ 800 N
High Altitude	1984	14	14
4.9L (300)	1985-92	10	10
w/decal CJU	1985	—	12
w/decal CJZ	1985	—	14
Heavy Duty	1985-86	6 @ 800	6 @ 800 N
5.0L (302)	1983-84	8 @ 800	8 @ 800 N
w/decal DHV	1983	—	*
High Altitude	1983-84	12 @ 800	12 @ 800 N
California	1983	—	*
California	1984	8 @ 800	10
Canada Heavy Duty	1984	6 @ 800	6 @ 800 N
5.0L (302)	1985-92	10	10
w/decal CKR, CLC	1985	8 @ 850	—
5.8L (351)	1983	*	10 @ 600 N
High Altitude	1983	*	14 @ 600 N
California	1983	—	*
5.8L (351) 2V: w/EEC III	1984-85	*	—
w/EEC IV	1984-85	10	10
Heavy Duty	1984-85	8 @ 700	8 @ 800 N
5.8L (351) 4V	1984-87	10 @ 800	10 @ 800 N
High Altitude	1984-87	14 @ 800	14 @ 800 N
Heavy Duty	1986	10† @ 900	10 @ 900 N
Heavy Duty	1987	—	8 @ 900 N
w/decal ANE, ANF, ANG, ANH, ANJ, APR, APO	1986	8† @ 900	8 @ 700 N
5.8L (351)	1988-92	10	10
7.5L (460) 4V	1983-87	8 @ 800	8 @ 800 N
High Altitude	1984-85	10 @ 800	10 @ 800 N
7.5L (460) FI	1987-92	10	10

* Timing not adjustable.

† When operated at high altitude, reset timing to 14°.

DISTRIBUTOR TIMING ADVANCE

Engine degrees at engine rpm, no load, in addition to basic timing setting.

Mechanical advance distributors only.

Engine	Trans-mission	Year	Distributor Number	Degrees @ 2500 RPM Total	Degrees @ 2500 RPM Centrifugal
2.0L (122)	MT	1983-84	E27E-BA	31.8-40.4	10.3-14.9
2.0L (122)	MT	1983-86	E37E-FA, GA	32.0-41.1	10.5-14.6
2.3L (140)	MT & AT	1983-84	E27E-AA	28.2-37.2	25.9-34.9
2.3L (140)	MT	1983-84	E27E-BA	31.8-40.4	10.3-14.9
2.3L (140)	MT & AT	1983-84	E37E-FA	32.0-41.1	10.5-14.6
3.8L (232)	MT	1983	E3TE-PA	40.7-50.5	11.2-16.0
3.8L (232)	AT	1983	E3TE-YA	25-35	3.5-8.5
4.9L (300)	MT & AT	1983-85	D5TE-FA	19.6-29.0	6.0-10.5
4.9L (300)	AT	1983-85	D9TE-ADA	12.2-21.2	6.7-10.7
4.9L (300)	MT	1983-85	D9TE-AEA	12-21	6.5-10.5
4.9L (300)	MT	1983	E2TE-RA	32.8-42.5	7.3-12.0
4.9L (300)	MT & AT	1983	E2TE-FA	37.0-46.6	7.5-12.1
4.9L (300)	MT	1983	E1TE-HA	33.0-42.7	7.5-12.2
4.9L (300)	AT	1983	E1TE-GA	28.2-38.1	6.7-11.6
4.9L (300) Propane	MT & AT	1983	E2TE-ABA	29.5-38.8	12.0-16.3
4.9L (300)	MT & AT	1983	E3UE-HA	37.4-46.6	7.6-12.1
4.9L (300)	AT	1983	E3TE-RA	33.9-43.2	4.4-8.7
4.9L (300)	AT	1983	E3TE-UA	34.7-44.2	5.2-9.6
4.9L (300)	AT	1983	E3TE-KA	34.0-43.3	4.5-8.8
4.9L (300) HD	MT & AT	1985-86	E4TE-EA	27.8-37.0	10.3-14.5
4.9L (300) HD	MT	1985-86	E5TE-MA	20.7-30.5	3.2-8.0
4.9L (300) HD	AT	1985-86	E5TE-NA	22.1-31.9	4.6-9.4
302	MT & AT	1983	D7TE-ADA	13.9-24.1	4.4-9.5
5.0L (302)	MT	1983	E3TE-UA	34.7-44.2	5.2-9.6
5.0L (302)	MT & AT	1983	E3TE-SA	30.5-39.8	5.0-9.3
5.0L (302)	AT	1983	E3TE-JA	25.7-35.4	8.2-12.9
5.0L (302)	AT	1983	E2TE-MA	20.1-30.0	6.6-11.5
5.0L (302)	AT	1983	E3TE-HA	30.2-40.0	4.7-9.5
5.0L (302)	AT	1983	E2TE-TA	38.6-48.4	9.1-13.9
5.0L (302)	AT	1983	E3UE-EA	22.1-31.8	4.6-9.3

DISTRIBUTOR TIMING ADVANCE Continued

Engine	Trans-mission	Year	Distributor Number	Degrees @ 2500 RPM Total	Degrees @ 2500 RPM Centrifugal
5.0L (302)	MT & AT	1983-84	D7TE-ADA	13.9-24.1	4.5-9.5
5.0L (302)	MT	1983-84	E3TE-ZA	24.8-34.0	7.3-11.5
5.0L (302)	AT	1983-84	E3TE-AAA	25.1-34.8	7.6-12.3
5.0L (302)	AT	1984	E43E-HA	28.7-37.7	7.2-11.2
351 Windsor	MT	1983	D7UE-LA	14.5-23.7	5.0-9.2
5.8L (351)W	MT	1983	E2TE-KA	12.7-22.1	7.2-11.6
5.8L (351)W	MT	1983	E2TE-SA	8.7-18.0	3.2-7.5
5.8L (351) 2V	MT & AT	1983-84	D7UE-LA	14.5-23.7	5.0-9.2
5.8L (351) 2V	MT & AT	1983-86	E2TE-UA	9.9-21.0	4.4-9.5
5.8L (351) 4V	AT	1984-86	E4TE-EA	27.8-37.0	10.3-14.5
5.8L (351) 4V	MT	1985-86	E5TE-NA	22.1-31.9	4.6-9.4
5.8L (351) 4V	AT	1985-86	E5TE-MA	20.7-30.5	3.2-8.0
5.8L (351) 4V	MT & AT	1985-87	E5TE-RA	23.0-32.5	9.5-14.0
460	AT	1983	D7TE-APA	28-38	10.6-15.5
7.5L (460)	MT & AT	1984-87	E3HE-BA	32.0-41.3	14.5-18.8
7.5L (460)	MT & AT	1984-87	E4HE-AA	34.0-43.3	10.5-14.8

FUEL SYSTEM

FUEL SYSTEM PRESSURE

See UNDERHOOD SERVICE INSTRUCTIONS at the beginning of this section for test/adjustment diagrams.

Engine	Year	Pressure PSI	Pressure RPM
Carburetted:			
4-cyl.	1983-88	5-7	idle
6-cyl.:	1983-86	5-7	idle
2.8L (171)	1983-86	4-6	idle
3.8L (232)	1983	6-8	idle
8-cyl.:			
2V & 4V Mech.	1983-87	6-8	idle
Elect.	1983-87	4-5	idle
Fuel Injected:			
2.3L (140)	1985-87	35-45	ign. on
		25-35	idle
2.3L (140)	1988-92	35-45	ign. on
		30-45	idle
2.9L (179), 3.0L (182)	1986-87	35-45	ign. on
		28-38	idle
2.9L (179), 3.0L (182), 4.0L	1988-92	35-45	ign. on
		30-45	idle
4.9L (300)	1987-92	50-60	ign. on
		45-60	idle
V8	1984-87	35-45	ign. on
		28-38	idle
V8	1988-92	35-45	ign. on
		30-45	idle

IDLE SPEED W/O COMPUTER CONTROL

See UNDERHOOD SERVICE INSTRUCTIONS at the beginning of this section for test/adjustment diagrams.

1983: Disconnect and plug vacuum brake release cylinder, if so equipped. If equipped with AUTOMATIC TRANSMISSION, linkage to carb must be adjusted if idle more than 50 rpm from spec. Follow emission decal if different.

Curb idle: Disconnect and plug air bypass valve vacuum hose. With EEC, run engine at idle for 5 minutes and fast idle for 20 seconds before adjusting idle. Adjust throttle stop screw or solenoid to spec.

Fast idle: Disconnect and plug EGR and canister purge vacuum hoses.

3.8 and 5.0 engine: Disconnect and plug thermactor air bypass valve.

AC: Set AC and blower on maximum. Disconnect compressor clutch wire.

VOTM: Apply manifold vacuum to valve and adjust.

1984-86: 2.0L, 2.3L, adjust hex rod at end of TSP with all vacuum hoses connected. To set fast idle, disconnect and plug the EGR vacuum hose.

2.2L diesel, turn the 10-mm bolt on the injection pump to set curb idle. To set fast idle, pull out choke fully and adjust the screw on the fast idle linkage.

1984-87: 5.0L 2V, adjust by turning the solenoid bracket screw. With AC, turn unit on to MAX, set blower on high and disconnect the compressor clutch wire. Set speed-up speed to spec. To set fast idle, disconnect and plug the EGR vacuum hose, disconnect the canister purge solenoid.

UNDERHOOD SERVICE SPECIFICATIONS

FDTTU4   FDTTU4

IDLE SPEED W/O COMPUTER CONTROL Continued

5.8L, disconnect and plug the VOTM. Run engine at 2000 rpm for several seconds and adjust idle speed to spec. To set fast idle, disconnect and plug the EGR vacuum hose and disconnect the canister purge solenoid.

7.5L, disconnect the canister purge vacuum hose. Set idle speed to spec. To set fast idle, disconnect and plug the EGR and distributor vacuum hoses. Apply manifold vacuum to distributor.

		SLOW		FAST		
Engine	Year	Man. Trans.	Auto. Trans.	Man. Trans.	Auto. Trans.	Step of Cam
2.0L (122)	1983-84	800	—	2000	—	Kickdown
shutdown idle	1983-84	600	—			
2.2L (134) Diesel	1983-84	780-830	—	1150-1250	—	—
2.3L (140)	1983-84	800	800 D	2000	2000 P	Kickdown
W/pwr. strg.	1983-84	850				
shutdown idle	1984	600	600 N			
w/decal DAB, DAR,						
DAS, DAT	1984	850	750 D	2000	2000 P	Kickdown
shutdown idle	1984	600	600 N			
2.3L (143) Diesel	1985-87	700-800	—	—	—	—
3.8L (232)	1983	700	600 D	2100	2200 P	High
shutdown idle	1983	550	550 N			
AC speed-up	1983	850	750 D			
4.9L (300)	1983	600	550 D	1600	1600 P	Kickdown
shutdown idle	1983	500	500 N			
AC speed-up	1983	—	600 D			
w/decal						
DES, DET	1983	500	—	1600	—	Kickdown
shutdown idle	1983	475	—			
DCA	1983	600	—	1600	—	Kickdown
shutdown idle	1983	500	—			
4.9L (300)						
Canada HD	1984-85	700	550 D	1600	1600 P	Kickdown
shutdown idle	1984-85	500	500 N			
4.9L (300) HD	1985-86	750	650 D	1450	1450 N	Kickdown
AC speed-up	1985-86	800	650 D			
shutdown idle	1985-86	500	500 N			
5.0L (302)	1983	700	600 D	2100	2250 P	High
AC speed-up	1983	800	675 D			
w/decal						
DHV	1983	—	650 D	—	2000 P	High
shutdown idle	1983	—	575 D			
California	1983	—	575 D	—	2000 P	High
5.0L (302)	1984	800	600 D	2100	2100 P	High
shutdown idle	1984	700	—			
w/AC	1984	700	—	2100	—	High
AC speed-up	1984	800	675 D			
California	1984	800	575 D	2100	2000 P	High
shutdown idle	1984	700	—			
w/AC	1984	700	—	2100	—	High
AC speed-up	1984	—	800			
Canada	1984	750	650 D	1250	1500 P	Kickdown
shutdown idle	1984	—	575 N			
5.8L (351)	1983	750	625 D	1700	2000 P	High
AC speed-up	1983	850	—			
shutdown idle	1983	—	575 D			
w/decal						
DEY, DFR	1983	600	—	1650	—	2nd High
California	1983	—	600 D	—	1650 P	2nd High
5.8L (351) 2V						
w/EEC III	1984	900	—	2000	—	High
shutdown idle	1984	600	—			
AC speed-up	1984	1400	—			
w/EEC IV	1984	750	600 D	2000	2000 P	High
Canada	1984	700	650 D	1500	1500 P	Kickdown
shutdown idle	1984	—	525 N			
5.8L (351) 4V	1984-85	—	650 D	—	1900 P	High
AC speed-up	1984	—	750 D			
AC speed-up	1985	—	700 D			
5.8L (351) LD	1986-87	—	650 D	—	2200 P	High
AC speed-up	1986-87	—	800 D			
Heavy Duty	1986	800	650 D	2200	2200 P	High
w/decal ANE, ANF,						
ANG, ANH, APR, APU	1986	—	700 D	—	2200 P	High
Heavy Duty	1987	—	700 D	—	2200 P	High
6.9L (421) Diesel	1983-85	600-700	600-700 N	850-900	850-900 N	—

IDLE SPEED W/O COMPUTER CONTROL Continued

		SLOW		FAST		
Engine	Year	Man. Trans.	Auto. Trans.	Man. Trans.	Auto. Trans.	Step of Cam
7.5L (460)	1983	—	650 D	—	1600 P	High
7.5L (460)	1984	—	600 D	—	1600 P	Kickdown
7.5L (460)	1985-87	800	650 D	2200	1600 P	Kickdown

IDLE SPEED W/COMPUTER CONTROL

See UNDERHOOD SERVICE INSTRUCTIONS at the beginning of this section for test/ adjustment diagrams.

Note: W/FI, if idle speed is higher than the specified checking speed, perform a system check before attempting to adjust the idle speed.

Midpoint of range given is the preferred setting speed.

2.0L (122): With engine at operating temperature and not running, disconnect the ISC electrical connector. Use jumper wires to connect one of the upper terminals (directly beneath plastic lock) to battery voltage (+), and the other terminal to ground (−).

Note: If voltage is applied to the lower terminals, damage to ISC will result. If the ISC extends, reverse the jumper wire connections. Start engine and verify that minimum speed is as specified. Fully extend the ISC with engine not running, and set maximum speed to specifications.

2.3L (140), 2.9L (179), 3.0L (182), 4.0L, 7.5L (460) FI: With engine at operating temperature and not running, disconnect air bypass valve electrical lead. Start engine, run at 2500 rpm for 30 seconds and check setting speed against specifications.

2.8L (171): Run engine at operating temperature, remove air cleaner, but leave air temperature sensor connected. Turn engine off, verify that ISC extends and disconnect the unit. Disconnect and plug EGR vacuum hose. Start engine and adjust ISC bracket to obtain maximum speed. Reconnect ISC and verify that checking speed is as specified. Hold throttle open slightly, push on ISC plunger to fully retract it, and disconnect the unit. Set minimum speed. Remove PCV valve and install PCV special tool (.20 orifice). Disconnect distributor timing connector and ISC. Start engine and set idle to specified setting value.

4.9L (300) 1V: To set minimum speed, jumper self test connector (see Computer Diagnostic Codes) and turn ignition switch to run position with engine off. After ISC retracts, turn ignition off and disconnect ISC. Start engine and set minimum speed to specified value. To set maximum speed, with engine at operating temperature and not running, remove air cleaner and disconnect coolant temperature sensor. Start engine and adjust maximum speed by turning ISC adjusting screw.

1985-88 4.9L (300) FI, 5.0L (302) FI, 5.8L (351) FI: With engine at operating temperature, run at 1800 rpm for 30 seconds and return to idle. Check that speed is at checking value. If speed is too high, disconnect battery positive (+) lead and reconnect. Repeat above procedure. If speed is still too high, check for trouble codes. If none are stored, back out idle air set screw and adjust to setting value. Adjustment must be made within 40 seconds or repeat previous procedure. 1988, after obtaining specified setting speed, back screw out an additional 1/2 turn.

1989-90 4.9L, 5.0L, 5.8L

1991 5.0L, 5.8L HD, 1992 5.0L: Install a .050 (4.9L, 5.0L w/AT) or .030 (5.0L w/MT, 5.8L) feeler gauge between throttle plate stop screw and throttle lever. Disconnect ISC electrical lead and start engine. Adjust idle to specified setting value.

ALL CARBURETTED

Checking Speed is the computer controlled idle speed value.

Engine	Year	Min. Speed	Checking Speed	Fast	Step of Cam	Max. Speed
2.0L (122)	1985-86	700 max.	775-875	1700	Kickdown	1800-2200
2.0L (122)	1987-88	700 max.	775-875	3200	High	1800-2200
2.8L (171) AT	1983-84	650 D	700-800 D	3000 P	High	2000 N
2.8L (171) MT	1983-86	750	800-900	3000	High	2000
2.8L (171) AT	1985-86	750 N	700-800 D	3000 P	High	2000 N

Engine	Year	Trans.	Minimum Speed	Maximum Speed	Checking Speed	Fast	Step of Cam
4.9L (300)	1984-85	MT	450-550	1500-1600	600-700*	1600	Kickdown
4.9L (300)	1984-85	AT	450-550 N	1500-1600 N	500-650 D*	1600	Kickdown
4.9L (300)	1986	MT	450-550	1500-1600	550-650	1600	Kickdown
California	1986	MT	450-550	1500-1600	600-700	1600	Kickdown

FORD TRUCKS
1983-92

IDLE SPEED W/COMPUTER CONTROL Continued

ALL CARBURETTED Continued

Engine	Year	Trans.	Minimum Speed	Maximum Speed	Checking Speed	Fast	Step of Cam
4.9L (300)	1986	AT	450-550 N	1500-1600 N	500-600 D	1600 P	Kickdown
California	1986	AT	450-550 N	1500-1600 N	500-650 D	1600 P	Kickdown

* With decal CCU, CCV, CDR, CDS, CLH, CLJ, CLK, CLR: MT, 550-650; AT, 500-600 D.

ALL FUEL INJECTED

1991-92 4.9L, 5.0L w/4-speed AT, 5.8L LD; 1992 4.0L, 5.8L: Idle speed is adjustable only when using special tester.

Engine	Year	Transmission	Setting Speed	Checking Speed
2.3L (140)	1985	MT	550-600†	575-725
		AT	550-600 N†	625-775 N
2.3L (140)	1986-88	MT	550-600†	645-795
2.3L (140) w/decal ABT, ABU, CBY, CBU, CBZ	1986-88	AT	550-600 N†	645-795 D
	1987-88	MT	550-600	725-875
	1987-88	AT	550-600 N	725-875 D
2.3L	1989-90	MT	550-600	645-795
		AT	550-600 N	575-725 D
2.3L	1991	MT	475-575	645-795
		AT	475-575 N	575-725 D
2.3L	1992	MT	450-750	—
		AT	500-800 N	—
2.9L (177)	1986-87	MT	700-800	850
California	1986-87	MT	700-800	900
	1986-87	AT	675-725 N	800 N
2.9L (177)	1987-88	MT	600-700	850
		AT	675-725 N	800 N
2.9L	1989-90	MT	700-750	650
	1989-90	AT	700-750 N	800 N
Calif.	1990	AT	700-750 N	650
2.9L	1991	MT	700-750	850
		AT	700-750 N	800 D
2.9L	1992	MT	450-750	—
3.0L (182)	1987-88	MT	700-750	750-850
		AT	600-650 D	650-750 D
3.0L	1989-90	MT	700-750	760-830
		AT	600-650 D	620-720 D
3.0L	1991-92	MT	550-650	—
		AT	550-650 N	—
4.0L	1990	MT	675	—
		AT	675 N	—
4.0L	1991	MT	625-775	—
		AT	525-775 N	—
4.9L (300) w/decal CEG, CEH, CEK, CEL, CEM, CEN, CEP	1987	MT	680-720	590-690
	1987	MT	680-720	650-750
w/decal CER, CES, CET, CEU, CFA	1987	MT	680-720	625-675
4.9L (300) w/decal CEG, CEH, CEK, CEL, CEM, CEN, CEP	1987	AT	580-620 D	525-625 D
	1987	AT	580-620 D	590-690 D
w/decal CER, CES, CET, CEU, CFA	1987	AT	580-620 D	625-675 D
4.9L (300)	1988	MT	625-675	625-725
w/4WD	1988	MT	570-750	650-750
4.9L (300)	1988	AT	625-725 N	525-625 D
4.9L (300) w/decal AEA, AEB, AEC, AED, AEE, AFC, AFG, AFT	1988	AT	725-775 N	590-690 D
4.9L w/calibr. 7-52ER, JR, KR, MR, QR, RR, ZR; 9-72JR	1989	MT	725-775	—
	1989	MT	625-675	—
4.9L w/calibr. 7-52ER, JR, KR, MR, QR, RR, ZR; 9-72JR	1989	AT	725-775 N	—
	1989	AT	625-675 N	—

IDLE SPEED W/COMPUTER CONTROL Continued

ALL FUEL INJECTED Continued

Engine	Year	Transmission	Setting Speed	Checking Speed
4.9L	1990	MT	675-725	650-750
w/decal DEN	1990	MT	675-725	625-725
w/decal DES, DEY, DEZ	1990	MT	675-725	590-690
4.9L	1990	AT	650-700 N	550-650 D
w/E40D trans.	1990	AT	650-700 N	525-625 D
4.9L	1991	MT	—	700
		AT	—	600 D
w/decal G5A, G5D, G5H, G5L		AT	—	575 D
w/decal GHZ, GFJ, G5J		AT	—	640 D
5.0L (302)	1985-87	MT	680-720	775
		AT	580-620 D	675 D
5.0L (302)	1988-90	MT	650-750	—
		AT	625-725 N	—
5.0L	1991-92	MT	550-850	—
3-speed	1991-92	AT	525-825 N	—
5.8L (351)	1988-90	MT	680-780	—
5.8L LD	1991	MT	630-930	—
		AT	680-980 N	—
5.8L (351)	1988-90	AT	730-830 N	—
w/4-speed AT	1989-90	AT	680-780 D	—
7.5L (460)	1987	MT	630-670	750
		AT	630-670 D	700 D
7.5L (460)	1988-90	MT	625-675	—
		AT	600-700 N	—
7.5L	1991-92	MT	500-800	—
		AT	500-800 N	—

† Reset to 600-650 (N) if carbon buildup problems in engine are incurred.

ENGINE MECHANICAL

TIGHTENING TORQUES
See UNDERHOOD SERVICE INSTRUCTIONS at the beginning of this section for test/adjustment diagrams.

Some fasteners are tightened in more than one step.

Some values are specified in inches.

Engine	Year	Torque Ft-lbs/Nm				
		Cylinder Head	Intake Manifold	Exhaust Manifold	Crankshaft Pulley	Water Pump
2.0L (122), 2.3L (140)	1983-92	50-60/ 68-81/ 80-90/ 108-122	5-7/ 7-9, 14-21/ 19-28	178-204"/ 20-23 20-30/ 27-41	103-133/ 140-180	15-22/ 19-29
2.2L (134) Diesel	1983-84	80-85/ 109-115	12-17/ 16-24	17-20/ 23-26	253-289/ 234-312	12-17/ 16-24
2.3L (140) Diesel	1985-87	76-83/ 103-112	11-14/ 15-19	11-14/ 15-19	123-137/ 167-186	—
2.8L (171)	1983-86	29-40/ 39-54, 40-51/ 54-69, 70-85/ 95-115	3-6/ 4-8, 6-11/ 8-15, 15-18/ 21-25	20-30/ 27-40	85-96/ 115-130	7-9/ 9-12
2.9L (179)	1986-92	22/30/ 51-55/ 70-75/ +90°	6-11/ 8-15, 15-18/ 21-25	20-30/ 27-40	85-96/ 115-130	7-9/ 9-12
3.0L (182)	1986-92	37/50, 68/92	11/15, 18/24	19/25	107-145	7/10
3.8L (232)	1983	47/65, 55/75, 63/85, 74/101	5/7, 10/14, 18/25	15-22/ 20-30	93-121/ 125-165	15-22/ 20-30
4.0L	1990-92	44/60, 59/80, +80-85°	6-11/ 8-15, 15-18/ 21-25	19/25	30-37/ 40-50, +80-90°	6-9/ 9-12

UNDERHOOD SERVICE SPECIFICATIONS

FDTTU6   FDTTU6

TIGHTENING TORQUES Continued

Engine	Year	Cylinder Head	Intake Manifold	Exhaust Manifold	Crankshaft Pulley	Water Pump
		Torque Ft-lbs/Nm				
4.2L (255), 5.0L (302)	1983-92	55-65/ 75-88, 65-72/ 88-97	23-25/ 32-33●	18-24/ 25-32	70-90/ 95-122	12-18/ 17-24
4.9L (300)	1983-92	50-55/ 67-75, 60-65/ 82-88, 70-85/ 94-115	22-32/ 30-43	22-32/ 30-43	130-150/ 177-203	12-18/ 17-24
5.8L (351)W	1983-92	85/115, 95/129, 105-112/ 143-151	23-25/ 32-33●	18-24/ 25-32	70-90/ 95-122	12-18/ 17-24
6.9L (421) Diesel	1985-87	40/54, 70/95, 80/108, 80/108	24/33	35/47	90/122	14/19
6.9L (421) Diesel	1983-84	40/54, 60/81, 75/102, 75/102	24/33	30/41	90/122	14/19
7.3L (445) Diesel	1988-92	65/88, 90/122, 100/135	24/33	35/47*	90/122	14/19
7.5L (460)	1983-92	70-80/ 95-108, 100-110/ 136-149, 130-140/ 177-189	8-12/ 11-16, 12-22/ 16-30, 22-35/ 30-47	22-30/ 30-48	70-90/ 95-122	12-18/ 16-24

* Retorque, again, to same specification.
● With FI, upper to lower manifold, 12-18/17.24.

VALVE CLEARANCE
Engine warm.

Engine	Year	Intake (inches)	Intake (mm)	Exhaust (inches)	Exhaust (mm)
2.2L (121) Diesel	1983-84	.012	.30	.012	.30
2.3L (143) Diesel	1985-87	.010	.25	.010	.25
2.8L (171)	1983-85	.014	.35	.016	.40

COMPRESSION PRESSURE
At cranking speed, engine temperature normalized, throttle open.

Engine	Year	PSI	Maximum Variation PSI
All ex. 4-cyl. Diesel	1983-92	Lowest reading cylinder must be more than 75% of the highest cylinder pressure.	
2.2L (134) Diesel	1983-84	384-427	43
2.3L (143) Diesel	1985-87	341-384	43

BELT TENSION
A belt in operation 10 minutes is considered a used belt.
1988-92 Automatic tensioner used.
Deflection method: Table lists deflection at midpoint of belt segment.
Strand Tension method: Use a strand tension gauge. Measurements are in pounds.

Application	Year	Alternator	Power Steering	Air Cond.	Therm-actor
USED BELTS					
Strand Tension method					
All 1/4"/6.35 mm	1983	—	—	—	40-60
All Others	1983	75-120	75-120	75-120	75-120
V-belts, ex. AP	1984-87	80-100	80-100	80-100	—
V-belts, AP	1984-87	—	—	—	40-60
Cogged	1984-87	110-130	110-130	110-130	110-130
V-ribbed	1984-87	140-160	140-160	140-160	140-160

BELT TENSION Continued

Application	Year	Alternator	Power Steering	Air Cond.	Therm-actor
Ranger, Bronco II: 4-cyl.	1988-92	140-160	—	—	—
V6	1988-92	110-130	—	—	—
Aerostar	1988-92	†	—	—	—
Others: 4.9L F-series	1988-92	90 min.†	—	—	—
Vans	1988-92	117 min.†	—	—	—
5.0L, 5.8L F-series	1988-92	75 min.†	—	—	—
Vans	1988-92	111 min.†	—	—	—
7.3L	1988-92	104 min.†	—	—	—
Vac. pump	1988-92	72 min.†	—	—	—
7.5L	1988-92	117 min.†	—	—	—
PS & AC	1988-92	94 min.†	—	—	—
NEW BELTS					
Strand Tension method					
All 1/4"/6.35 mm	1983	—	—	—	50-80
All Others	1983	120-160	120-160	120-160	120-160
V-belts, ex. AP	1984-87	90-130	90-130	90-130	—
V-belts, AP	1984-87	—	—	—	50-90
Cogged	1984-87	120-160	120-160	120-160	120-160
V-belts	1984-87	150-190	150-190	150-190	150-190
Ranger, Bronco II: 4-cyl.	1988-92	150-190	—	—	—
V6	1988-92	120-160	—	—	—
Aerostar	1988-92	†	—	—	—
Others: 4.9L F-series	1988-92	90 min.†	—	—	—
Vans	1988-92	117 min.†	—	—	—
5.0L, 5.8L F-series	1988-92	75 min.†	—	—	—
Vans	1988-92	111 min.†	—	—	—
7.3L	1988-92	140-180	—	—	—
Vac. pump	1988-92	90-130	—	—	—
7.5L	1988-92	160-200	—	—	—
PS & AC	1988-92	94 min.†	—	—	—

† Tension is correct if index mark on pulley is within range marks on tensioner.

ENGINE COMPUTER SYSTEM

COMPUTER DIAGNOSTIC CODES
See UNDERHOOD SERVICE INSTRUCTIONS at the beginning of this section for test/ adjustment diagrams.

EEC III: Run engine at 1800 rpm for one or two minutes until radiator hose pressurizes. Tie two vacuum gauges into both smaller vacuum hoses at Thermactor Air Diverter and Air Bypass solenoids. Apply 20" of vacuum to vent port of B/MAP sensor and hold for at least eight seconds. Throttle kicker will extend and hold for 90 seconds. When it retracts, diagnostic codes will be displayed. A five-second pause occurs between codes.

MCU: Complicated procedure required to achieve valid codes. See shop manual.
4-cyl. with EGR vacuum load control: tape control valve vent holes.
With key off, locate self-test connector. Connect a jumper wire from the upper right cavity to the second lower cavity from left. Connect an analog VOM from battery positive (+) terminal to lower second from right cavity (–). Disconnect PCV valve vacuum line of canister control valve (4- & 6-cyl.). Remove PCV valve from valve cover and uncap restrictor in Thermactor vacuum control line (8-cyl. as equipped).

1984-90 EEC IV:
Complicated procedure required to obtain valid codes. See shop manual. With engine at operating temperature and ignition off, locate SELF-TEST connector under hood. Connect a jumper wire between input connector (single terminal) and upper right cavity on connector. Connect an analog VOM to battery (+) and second bottom right cavity on connector. A four second delay separates individual codes. SELF-TEST codes are revealed in a series of three separate test procedures (key on engine off, engine running, and continuous) and must be accessed in order.

Key on engine off: Place transmission in park or neutral, set parking brake, turn off all electrical equipment, place octane switch (2.3L SVO Turbo) in premium position. Activate SELF-TEST and place ignition key in run position, do not depress throttle. Observe and record service codes.

Engine running: Deactivate SELF-TEST. Start engine and run at greater than 2000 rpm for 2 minutes. Turn engine off, wait ten seconds & reactivate SELF-TEST. Start engine without depressing throttle. An engine ID code will be displayed (**Code 2**—4-cyl., **Code 3**—6-cyl., **Code 4**—8-cyl.), depress and release brake pedal once. Observe and record service codes.

Continuous: Allow engine to run at idle after all codes have been displayed. After approximately 2 minutes, continuous codes will be displayed. System will remain in continuous mode until ignition is switched off or SELF-TEST is deactivated.

UNDERHOOD SERVICE SPECIFICATIONS

FDTTU7

COMPUTER DIAGNOSTIC CODES Continued

EEC III:
Code 11 System OK
Code 12 RPM out of specification
Code 15 Calibration assembly (memory)
Code 21 Faulty engine coolant temperature wiring
Code 22 Barometric/MAP
Code 23 Throttle position sensor circuit
Code 24 Air charge temperature circuit faulty
Code 31 EGR sensor not moving open
Code 32 EGR sensor not closing
Code 41 Fuel mixture lean
Code 42 Fuel mixture rich
Code 43 Coolant temperature under 120°F
Code 44 Thermactor system

MCU:
Code 11 System OK
Code 33 Running test not initiated
Code 41 Fuel mixture lean
Code 42 Fuel mixture rich
Code 44 Thermactor
Code 45 Thermactor air diverter valve
Code 46 Thermactor air bypass valve
Code 51 or 61 Low temperature vacuum switch
Code 52 or 62 Idle tracking or wide open throttle switch
Code 53 or 63 Closed switches
Code 56 or 66 Closed throttle switch

1983-86 ALL W/EEC IV
Test condition: I—ignition on/engine off, R—engine running, C—continuous

Code Displayed	Test Condition	Results
11	I, R, C	System OK, test sequence complete
12	R	Idle speed control out of range, off idle
13	R, C	Controlled idle out of range
14	C	Ignition profile pickup erratic
15	I	ROM test failure
15	C	Power interrupt to keep alive memory
16	R	Erratic idle, oxygen sensor out of range
18	C	No tach signal to ECM
18	R	Spout circuit open, ex. 4.0L
18	R	SAW circuit, 4.0L
18	C	Erratic IDM, input to ECM or spout circuit open
19	I	No power to processor
21	I, R	Coolant temperature out of range
21	C	Coolant temperature sensor out of range
22	I, R, C	MAP, BARO out of range
23	I, R	Throttle position sensor out of range
24	I, R	Air temperature low, improper sensor installation
25	R	Knock not sensed in test
26	I, R	MAF sensor circuit, 4.0L
26	I, R	Transmission oil temperature sensor, ex. 4.0L
28	C	Loss of primary tach—right side
29	C	Vehicle speed sensor circuit
31	I, R, C	EGR valve control, feedback sensor out of range, ex. V8
31	I, R	EVAP control system, V8
32	R, C	EGR, pressure feedback not controlling, 1985-89
33	R, C	EGR valve not closing
34	I, R, C	EGR control circuit, ex. V8
34	I, R, C	EVAP control system, V8
35	I, R, C	No EGR position signal, RPM too low, ex. V8
35	I, R, C	EVAP control system, V8
41	R	Fuel mixture lean
41	C	Oxygen sensor signal
42	R, C	Fuel mixture rich
43	R	Oxygen sensor cooled
44	R	Air management system inoperative
45	R	Thermactor air diverter circuit
45	C	Coil 1, 2, or 3 failure
46	R	Thermactor air bypass circuit
47	I	4WD switch closed
51	I, C	Coolant temperature sensor out of range
52	I, R	Power steering pressure switch out of range
53	I, C	Throttle sensor input out of range
54	I, C	Vane air flow sensor, air charge temperature sensor
55	R	Charging system under voltage
56	C	MAF sensor above voltage, 4.0L
56	I, C	Transmission oil temperature sensor, ex. 4.0L
58	R	Idle tracking switch circuit

COMPUTER DIAGNOSTIC CODES Continued

Code Displayed	Test Condition	Results
59	C	Transmission throttle pressure switch circuit (1985-88)
59	C	2-3 shift error (1989)
61	I, C	Coolant temperature switch out of range
62	I, R	Transmission 4/3 circuit fault
63	I, C	Throttle position sensor circuit
64	I, C	Vane air temperature, air charge temperature sensor
65	R	Charging system over voltage (1985-88)
65	R	Overdrive cancel switch not changing
66	C	MAF circuit below voltage, 4.0L
66	I, C	Transmission oil temperature sensor grounded, ex. 4.0L
67	I	Neutral drive switch
67	C	AC clutch switch circuit
68	I	Idle tracking switch (1985-88)
69	C	Vehicle speed sensor circuit
69	I	3-4 shift error
72	R	No MAP or MAF signal change
73	I, R	No throttle sensor change
74	R	Brake on/off ground circuit fault
75	R	Brake on/off power circuit fault
77	R	Throttle "goose" test not performed
78	C	Time delay relay or circuit
79	—	AC on during test
81	I	Thermactor air bypass circuit
82	I	Thermactor air system circuit
83	I	EGR control circuit
84	I	EGR vent circuit
85	I	Canister purge circuit
86	I	Shift solenoid circuit
87	I	Fuel pump circuit
88	I	Choke relay out of range
88	C	Loss of dual plug input control
89	I	Clutch converter overide circuit
91, 92	I	Shift solenoid circuit
93	I	Coast clutch solenoid
94	I	Converter clutch solenoid
95	I, C	Fuel pump circuit
96	I, C	Fuel pump circuit
97	I	Overdrive cancel indicator light circuit
98	R	Test failure, repeat sequence (1985-88)
98	I	Electronic pressure control driver
99	I, C	Electronic pressure control circuit

SENSORS, INPUT

TEMPERATURE SENSORS

Engine	Year	Sensor	Resistance Ohms @ deg. F/C
All w/EEC IV	1983-92	Coolant, Air Charge	31,700-42,900 @ 68/20
			13,650-18,650 @ 104/40
			6500-8900 @ 140/60
			3240-4440 @ 176/80
			1770-2370 @ 212/100
			980-1380 @ 248/115
All w/EEC III	1983	Coolant, Air Charge	1100-8000
			1700-60,000

MANIFOLD ABSOLUTE AND BAROMETRIC PRESSURE SENSORS
See UNDERHOOD SERVICE INSTRUCTIONS at the beginning of this section for test/adjustment diagrams.
With EEC IV, measured between BK/W wire and ground with ignition on and engine off.

Engine	Year	Sensor	Voltage @ Altitude
All w/EEC IV	1983-90	MAP, BARO	1.55-1.63 @ 0
	1991-92	BARO	1.52-1.60 @ 1000
			1.49-1.56 @ 2000
			1.46-1.54 @ 3000
			1.43-1.51 @ 4000
			1.39-1.48 @ 5000
			1.36-1.45 @ 6000
			1.34-1.43 @ 7000

UNDERHOOD SERVICE SPECIFICATIONS

FDTTU8   FDTTU8

SENSORS, INPUT Continued
MANIFOLD ABSOLUTE AND BAROMETRIC PRESSURE SENSORS Continued

Engine	Year	Sensor	Frequency Hz @	Vacuum In Hg/kPa
All	1991-92	MAP	159	0/0
			141	6/20
			125	12/40
			109	18/60
			95	24/80
			80	30/100

Engine	Year	Resistance (ohms) @ Altitude
All w/EEC III	1983	7.6-8.4 @ 0-1500
		7.2-8.1 @ 1500-2500
		6.9-7.8 @ 2500-3500
		6.7-7.3 @ 3500-4500
		6.6-7.2 @ 4500-5500
		6.3-7.0 @ 5500-6500
		6.1-6.7 @ 6500-7500
		5.4-6.7 @ 7500 and up

MASS AIRFLOW SENSOR
Voltage is measured at indicated vehicle speed.

Engine	Year	Voltage @	Speed MPH/KPH
All	1991-92	.80 @	0/0
		1.00 @	20/32
		1.70 @	40/64
		2.10 @	60/96

CRANKSHAFT SENSOR

Engine	Year	Resistance (ohms)
All w/EEC III	1983	100-640
4.0L	1990-92	2300-2500

VEHICLE SPEED SENSOR

Engine	Year	Resistance (ohms)
All w/EEC IV	1983-92	190-250

THROTTLE POSITION SENSOR (TPS)
See UNDERHOOD SERVICE INSTRUCTIONS at the beginning of this section for test/ adjustment diagrams.

Engines with EEC III: Turn ignition to RUN position and remove vacuum hose from throttle kicker, as equipped. With engine not running, compare voltage reading against specifications and adjust as needed.

Engines with EEC IV: Connect positive probe of DVOM along terminal A (upper) of TPS and connect negative probe along terminal B (middle). Turn ignition on but do not start vehicle. Adjust TPS to specified value.

Engine	Year	TPS Voltage Minimum	TPS Voltage Maximum
All w/EEC III	1983	1.60-2.40	6.0 min.
All w/EEC IV	1984-88	0.90-1.00†	—
2.3L	1989-90	.34	4.84
2.3L	1991	.20	4.84
2.3L	1992	.43-.57	3.6-4.8
2.9L	1989-91	.34	4.84
2.9L	1992	.43-.57	3.6-4.8
3.0L	1989-90	.34	4.84
3.0L	1991	.20	4.84
3.0L	1992	.43-.57	3.6-4.8

SENSORS, INPUT Continued
THROTTLE POSITION SENSOR (TPS) Continued

Engine	Year	TPS Voltage Minimum	TPS Voltage Maximum
4.0L	1990	.34	4.84
4.0L	1991	.20	4.84
4.0L	1992	.43-.57	3.6-4.8
4.9L	1989-90	.20	4.84
4.9L	1991	.34	4.84
4.9L	1992	.43-.57	3.6-4.8
5.0L	1989-90	.20	4.84
5.0L	1991	.34	4.84
5.0L	1992	.43-.57	3.6-4.8
5.8L, 7.5L	1989-90	.20	4.84
w/4-speed AT	1989-90	.34	4.84
5.8L, 7.5L	1991	.34	4.84
5.8L, 7.5L	1992	.43-.57	3.6-4.8

† Adjustable units only.

ACTUATORS, OUTPUT

IDLE SPEED CONTROL
See UNDERHOOD SERVICE INSTRUCTIONS at the beginning of this section for test/ adjustment diagrams.

All FI engines with ISC.

Engine	Year	Resistance (ohms)
All w/EEC IV	1983-92	6-13

MIXTURE CONTROL SOLENOID-CARBURETTED ENGINES

Engine	Year	Resistance (ohms)
4.9L 1V YFA	1983-86	30-60
5.0L, 5.8L 2V 2150	1983-86	15-30

COMPUTER TIMING ADVANCE
1983, 1992, specifications include initial timing.

1984-91, specifications are in addition to basic timing.

Test with engine at operating temperature.

1983-91, activate system test procedure. See ''Computer Diagnostic Codes'' section. Check advance against specifications.

1992, degrees of advance are measured at indicated vehicle speed.

Year	Engine	Advance
1983	All w/EEC III	27-33
1983-91	All w/EEC IV	17-23

Engine	Year	Degrees of Advance Idle	30 MPH/50 KPH	55 MPH/90 KPH
2.3L	1992	18-22	28-32	30-34
2.9L MT	1992	24-28	28-34	30-36
AT	1992	24-28	30-36	32-36
3.0L MT	1992	24-28	33-37	34-38
AT	1992	24-28	28-35	28-34
4.9L	1992	17-20	24-28	24-30
w/4-speed AT	1992	20-24	28-32	24-30
5.0L MT	1992	12-14	26-30	38-42
3-speed AT	1992	14-20	28-36	30-40
4-speed AT	1992	18-22	36-40	36-42
5.8L	1992	16-20	32-36	36-42
7.5L	1992	20-24	38-42	42-48
w/4-speed AT	1992	22-28	36-40	36-40

ENGINE IDENTIFICATION

To identify any engine by the manufacturer's code, follow the four steps designated by the numbered blocks.

1 MODEL YEAR IDENTIFICATION: Refer to illustration of Vehicle Identification Number (V.I.N.). The year is indicated by a code letter.

2 ENGINE CODE LOCATION: Refer to V.I.N. plate illustration. The engine code is indicated as a letter or number.

3 ENGINE CODE: In the "CODE" column, find the engine code determined in Step 2.

4 ENGINE IDENTIFICATION: On the line where the engine code appears, read to the right to identify the engine.

V.I.N. PLATE LOCATION:

On top left side
of instrument panel

Model year of vehicle:
1992 — Model year is N.
1991 — Model year is M.
1990 — Model year is L.
1989 — Model year is K.
1988 — Model year is J.
1987 — Model year is H.
1986 — Model year is G.
1985 — Model year is F.

MODEL YEAR AND ENGINE IDENTIFICATION:

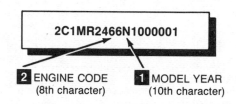

2C1MR2466N1000001

2 ENGINE CODE (8th character)   **1** MODEL YEAR (10th character)

4 ENGINE IDENTIFICATION

YEAR	3 ENGINE CODE	CYL.	DISPL. liters	cc	Fuel System	HP
1992	6 (Metro)	3	1.0	993	TBI	52
	5 (Prizm)	4	1.6	1588	MFI	130
	6 (Prizm)	4	1.6	1588	MFI	102
	6 (Storm)	4	1.6	1588	MFI	95
	8 (Storm)	4	1.8	1787	MFI	140
	U (Tracker)	4	1.6	1588	TBI	80
1991	6 (Metro)	3	1.0	993	TBI	55
	2	3	1.0 T	993 T	MFI	70
	5 (Prizm)	4	1.6	1588	MFI	130
	6 (Prizm)	4	1.6	1588	MFI	102
	5 (Storm)	4	1.6	1588	MFI	130
	6 (Storm)	4	1.6	1588	MFI	95
	U (Tracker)	4	1.6	1588	TBI	80
1990	6 (Metro)	3	1.0	993	TBI	49
	2	3	1.0 T	993 T	MFI	N/A
	5 (Prizm)	4	1.6	1588	MFI	130
	6 (Prizm)	4	1.6	1588	MFI	102
	6 (Storm)	4	1.6	1588	MFI	95
	5 (Storm)	4	1.6	1588	MFI	125
	U	4	1.6	1590	TBI	80
1989	6 (Metro)	3	1.0	993	TBI	49
	2	3	1.0 T	993 T	MFI	70
	7	4	1.5	1471	2V	70

4 ENGINE IDENTIFICATION

YEAR	3 ENGINE CODE	CYL.	DISPL. liters	cc	Fuel System	HP
1989 Cont'd.	6 (Prizm)	4	1.6	1588	MFI	102
	U	4	1.6	1590	TBI	80
1988	5	3	1.0	993	2V	46, 48
	2	3	1.0 T	993 T	MFI	70
	7	4	1.5	1471	2V	70
	9	4	1.5 T	1471 T	MFI	105
	4	4	1.6	1587	2V	74
	5	4	1.6	1587	MFI	110
1987	5	3	1.0	993	2V	48
	2	3	1.0 T	993 T	MFI	70
	7	4	1.5	1471	2V	70
	9	4	1.5 T	1471 T	MFI	105
	4	4	1.6	1587	2V	74
1986	5	3	1.0	993	2V	48
	7	4	1.5	1451	2V	70
	4	4	1.6	1587	2V	74
1985	M	3	1.0	993	2V	48
	K	4	1.5	1471	2V	70
	4	4	1.6	1587	2V	74

TBI — Throttle Body Injection.   MFI — Multiport Fuel Injection.
T — Turbo.   2V — Two Venturi Carburetor.

UNDERHOOD SERVICE SPECIFICATIONS

GOITU1   GOITU1

CYLINDER NUMBERING SEQUENCE
3-CYL. FIRING ORDER: 1 3 2
4-CYL. FIRING ORDER: 1 3 4 2

1985-88 Sprint, Firefly 1.0L

1989-91 Metro, Sprint, Firefly, 1992 Metro

1985 Spectrum, Sunburst 1.5L

1986-89 Spectrum, Sunburst 1.5L ex. Turbo

1985-88 Nova 1.6L 2V

1988 Nova 1.6L DOHC, 1989-92 Prizm 1.6L Code 5

1990-92 Storm 1.6L Code 5, 6; 1.8L Code 8

1989-92 Prizm 1.6L Code 6

1989-92 Tracker

── Front of car ──

CHEK-CHART

GEO/CHEVROLET - PONTIAC
1989-92 Metro, Prizm, Spectrum, Storm, Tracker, Sprint, Firefly
CHEVROLET - PONTIAC
1985-88 Sprint, Spectrum, Nova; Firefly, Sunburst

UNDERHOOD SERVICE SPECIFICATIONS

GOITU2   **TIMING MARK**   GOITU2

1985-91
Firefly, Sprint 1.0L,
1989-92
Metro

1985-88
Spectrum 1.5L

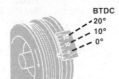

1985-88
Nova 1.6L 2V,
1989-92
Prizm Code 6,
1990-92 Storm Codes 5, 6, 8

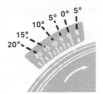

1988
Nova 1.6L DOHC
1990-92
Prizm Code 5

1989-92
Tracker 1.6L

ELECTRICAL AND IGNITION SYSTEMS

BATTERY

Engine	Year	STANDARD BCI Group No.	STANDARD Crank. Perf.	OPTIONAL BCI Group No.	OPTIONAL Crank. Perf.
1.0L	1985-89	45	410	—	—
1.0L	1990	26	440	—	—
1.0L	1991-92	26	390	—	—
1.5L	1985-89	21R	410	—	—
1.6L Nova	1985-88	35	310	—	—
1.6L Prizm	1989-92	35	370	—	—
1.6L, 1.8L Storm	1990-92	35	370	—	—
1.6L Tracker	1989	45	470	—	—
1.6L Tracker	1990-92	26	500	—	—

ALTERNATOR

Application	Year	Rated Output (amps)	Test Output (amps)
1.0L	1985-88	35	20 @ 2000
1.0L	1989-92	50	40 @ 2000
1.0L	1992	55	—
1.5L	1985-89	45, 60	30 @ 2000
1.6L Nova	1985-88	60	30 @ 2000
1.6L Prizm	1989-92	60	*
1.6L Storm	1990	61	30 @ 2000
1.6L Storm	1990	85	30 @ 2000
1.6L, 1.8L Storm:			
1.6L	1991-92	75	†
1.8L	1992	85	†
1.6L Tracker	1989-92	55	*

* Output at 2000 rpm must be within 10 amps of rated output.
† Output at 2000 rpm must be within 15 amps of rated output.

REGULATOR

Engine	Year	Test Temp. (def. F/C)	Voltage Setting
1.0L, 1.5L	1985-92	Cold	14.2-14.8
1.0L w/55A alt.	1992	—	14.7-15.0
1.6L Nova	1985-88	77/25	13.5-15.1
1.6L Prizm	1989-92	77/25	14.2-14.8
1.6L, 1.8L Storm	1990-92	—	13.5-16.0
1.6L Tracker	1989-92	68/20	14.4-15.0

STARTER

Engine	Year	Cranking Voltage (min. volts)	Ampere Draw @ Cranking Speed
1.0L MT	1985-88	9.5	270 max.
AT	1985-88	8.0	230 max.
1.0L	1992	9.0	150 max.
1.5L MT	1985-88	9.5	260 max.
AT, Turbo	1985-88	9.5	270 max.
1.6L, 1.8L Storm:			
MT, 1.6L	1990-92	8.7	230 max.
MT, 1.8L	1992	8.0	230 max.
AT, SOHC	1990-92	8.0	280 max.
AT, DOHC	1990-92	8.5	300 max.
1.6L Tracker	1989-92	7.7	300 max.

SPARK PLUGS

Engine	Year	Gap (inches)	Gap (mm)	Torque (ft-lb)
1.0L	1985-92	.039-.043	1.0-1.1	21
1.5L	1985-89	.039-.043	1.0-1.1	14
1.6L Nova	1985-88	.039-.043	1.0-1.1	11-15
1.6L Prizm	1989-92	.031	0.8	21
1.6L, 1.8L Storm	1990-92	.041	1.05	21
1.6L Tracker	1989-92	.028-.031	0.7-0.8	21

IGNITION COIL
Winding Resistance (ohms at 75°F or 24°C)

Engine	Year	Windings	Resistance (ohms)
1.0L 2V	1985-88	Primary	1.06-1.43
		Secondary	10,800-16,200
Turbo	1987-88	Primary	1.08-1.32
		Secondary	11,600-15,800
1.0L	1989-92	Primary	1.33-1.55
		Secondary	10,700-14,500
1.5L	1985	Primary	1.10-1.40
		Secondary	12,100-14,900
1.5L 2V	1986-87	Primary	1.2-1.5
		Secondary	10,200-13,800
1.5L 2V	1988-89	Primary	1.1-1.8
		Secondary	11,200-20,500
1.5L Turbo	1987-88	Primary	0-2
		Secondary	6,000-30,000
1.6L 2V	1985-88	Primary	0.3-0.5
		Secondary	7,500-10,500
1.6L FI	1988	Primary	0.5-0.7
		Secondary	11,000-16,000
1.6L Prizm Code 6	1989-91	Primary	1.3-1.6
		Secondary	10,400-14,000
1.6L Prizm Code 5	1990-91	Primary	0.4-0.5
		Secondary	10,200-13,800
1.6L Storm	1990	Primary	0-2
		Secondary	6,000-30,000
1.6L, 1.8L Storm	1991-92	Primary	1.2-1.5
		Secondary	10,200-13,800
1.6L Tracker	1989-90	Primary	1.35-1.65
		Secondary	11,000-14,500
1.6L Tracker	1991-92	Primary	0.7-1.2
		Secondary	10,200-14,000

DISTRIBUTOR PICKUP

Engine	Year	Resistance (ohms)	Air Gap (in./mm)
1.0L	1985-92	130-190	.008-.016/.2-.4
1.5L 2V	1985-89	140-180	.008-.016/.2-.4
1.5L Turbo	1987-88	500-1500	—
1.6L Nova, Prizm	1985-92	140-180	.008-.016/.2-.4
1.6L, 1.8L Storm	1990-92	500-1500	—
1.6L Tracker	1989-92	—	.008-.016/.2-.4

UNDERHOOD SERVICE SPECIFICATIONS

BASE TIMING

Set timing at slow idle and Before Top Dead Center, unless otherwise specified. 1.0L 2V, 1.5L leave all distributor hoses connected.

1989-92, 1.0L TBI ex. 1989-91 LSI, 1991-92 Tracker: Jumper terminals C and D of diagnostic connector by ignition coil (Metro) or battery (Tracker).

1.6L Nova, Prizm FI: Jumper terminals T and E1 (1985-88) or TE1 and E1 (1989-92) of diagnostic connector under hood.

1.6L Storm: Jumper far left and far right terminals of ALDL connector under dash.

1989-91, all others: Disconnect and plug distributor vacuum hoses. 1.0L LSI, when vacuum hose is connected, timing will increase to Check specification.

Engine	Year	Man. Trans. (degrees) @ RPM	Auto. Trans. (degrees) @ RPM
1.0L	1985-88	10 ±1	6 ±1
Canada	1985-86	10 ±1	4 ±1
Canada	1987-88	8 ±1	6 ±1
1.0L: Set	1989-92	6	6
Check, LSI	1989-91	12 ±1	12 ±1
1.5L	1985	5	10
1.5L 2V	1986-89	15	10
1.5L Turbo	1987-88	15	—
1.6L 2V Nova	1985-88	5	5
1.6L FI Nova, Prizm	1988-92	10	10
1.6L, 1.8L Storm	1990-92	10	10
1.6L Tracker	1989-92	8 ±1	8 ±1

DISTRIBUTOR TIMING ADVANCE

Engine degrees at engine rpm, no load, in addition to basic timing setting.

Mechanical advance distributors only.

Engine	Transmission	Year	Distributor Number	Degrees @ 2500 RPM Total	Degrees @ 2500 RPM Centrifugal
1.0L 2V	MT	1985-88	96052001	24-32	5-9
1.0L 2V leaded fuel	MT	1985-86	96053177	4.8-12.8	0.8-4.8
1.0L 2V leaded fuel	MT	1987-88	96055619	13.2-21.2	7.2-11.2
1.0L 2V ER	MT	1987-88	96056787	17-25	8-12
1.0L 2V	AT	1986-88	96054065	28.5-36.5	6.5-10.5
1.0L Turbo	MT	1987-88	96055620	20-28	6-10
1.5L 2V	MT	1985	94109580	31.1-38.1	5.1-8.1
1.5L 2V	MT	1986-89	94419559	30.5-38.5	4.5-8.5
1.5L 2V	AT	1985	94157468	29.1-36.1	5.1-8.1
1.5L 2V	AT	1986-89	94178219	28.5-36.5	4.5-8.5
1.6L Nova	MT & AT	1985	16050	34.5-42.5	8.5-12.5
1.6L	MT & AT	1986	16081	33.9-41.9	7.9-11.9
1.6L	MT & AT	1986-88	16082	14.8-22.8	2.8-6.8
1.6L Tracker	MT & AT	1989	96058488	19.8-27.8	7.3-11.3

FUEL SYSTEM

FUEL SYSTEM PRESSURE

At idle unless otherwise indicated.

Engine	Year	PSI	RPM
Carburetted & TBI:			
1.0L	1989-92	23.2-30.5	ign. on
		13-20	idle
1.6L Nova	1985-88	3.5	idle
1.6L Tracker	1989-92	34-40	idle
		57 min.†	—

Engine	Year	Pressure PSI*	Pressure PSI**	Fuel Pump†
MFI:				
1.0L Turbo	1987-91	25-33	35-43	—
1.5L Turbo	1987-88	28.4	35.6	—
1.6L Nova, Prizm	1988-92	30-33	38-44	57 min.
1.6L, 1.8L Storm	1990-92	35-42	25-30	65 min.

* Vacuum hose connected to fuel pressure regulator.
** Vacuum hose disconnected frzom fuel pressure regulator.
† Fuel pump pressure with return line restricted.

IDLE SPEED W/O COMPUTER CONTROL

See UNDERHOOD SERVICE INSTRUCTIONS at the beginning of this section for test/adjustment diagrams.

1.0L: Set idle speed with all accessories and cooling fan off. Set idle up with lights and heater on. To set fast idle, disconnect and plug coolant hoses at carburetor thermo element and set fast idle cam on index mark. Set fast idle with engine at operating temperature.

1.0L, 1.5L Turbo: Set idle to specified speed. To set electrical speed-up (1.0L), turn headlights on and adjust screw on solenoid. To set AC speed-up (1.0L), turn AC on and adjust screw on solenoid.

1.5L 2V: Disconnect and plug distributor vacuum, canister purge, EGR, ITC, vacuum hoses.

Air-conditioned models equipped with idle speed-up solenoid, turn AC on and with solenoid fully extended, adjust solenoid to obtain specified rpm.

1.6L Nova 2V: Set idle speed to specified value. To set fast idle, disconnect hose from M port of thermo vacuum switching valve. To set speed-up speed (first step), disconnect vacuum hose from rear of vacuum solenoid. Check speed-up speed against specified value. Reconnect hose and disconnect first hose by linkage to check second step speed-up speed.

1.6L Nova, Prizm FI: Set idle to specified value.

Engine	Year	SLOW Man. Trans.	SLOW Auto. Trans.	FAST Man. Trans.	FAST Auto. Trans.	Step of Cam
1.0L 2V	1985-88	700-800	800-900 N	2100-2700	2100-2700 N	High
Canada	1985-88	700-800	800-900 N	1500-2500	1500-2500 N	High
idle-up	1985-88	750-850	750-850 N			
1.0L ER	1986-88	650-750	—	2100-2700	—	High
idle-up	1986-88	750-850				
1.0L Turbo	1987-89	700-800				
Elect. speed-up	1987-89	750-850				
AC speed-up	1987-89	950-1050	—			
1.5L 2V	1985-89	750	1000 N			
AC speed-up	1985-89	850	980 N			
1.5L Turbo	1987-88	900-1000				
1.6L Nova	1985	650	800 N	3000	3000 N	High
Speed-up (1st step)	1985	800	900 N			
Speed-up (2nd step)	1985	1100-1500	1200-1600 N			
1.6L 2V Nova	1986-88	650	750 N	3000	3000 N	High
Speed-up (1st step)	1986-88	800	900 N			
Speed-up (2nd step)	1986-88	1200-1600	1300-1700 N			
1.6L FI Nova	1988	800	800 N	—	—	—

IDLE SPEED W/COMPUTER CONTROL

See UNDERHOOD SERVICE INSTRUCTIONS at the beginning of this section for test/adjustment diagrams.

1.0L TBI: Install a fuse into diagnostic connector in fuse block. Set idle to specified value. Turn AC on and adjust speed-up to specified value.

1.6L Prizm: Jumper terminals TE1 and E1 of diagnostic connector. Set idle to specified value. Turn AC on and verify that speed increases to speed-up speed.

1.6L Tracker: Set idle to specified value.

Engine	Year	Transmission	Checking Speed	Setting Speed	AC Speed-up
1.0L	1989-90	MT	—	700-800	850-950
1.0L	1989	AT	—	650-750 N	800-900 N
1.0L LSI	1990	AT	—	650-750 N	850-950
Others	1990	AT	—	800-900 N	800-900 N
1.0L XFI	1991-92	MT	—	650-750	850-950
Convertible	1991-92	MT	—	800-900	850-950
	1991-92	AT	—	800-900 N	800-900 N
Others	1991-92	MT	—	750-850	850-950
	1991-92	AT	—	800-900	800-900 N

CHEK-CHART

GEO/CHEVROLET - PONTIAC
1989-92 Metro, Prizm, Spectrum, Storm, Tracker, Sprint, Firefly
CHEVROLET - PONTIAC
1985-88 Sprint, Spectrum, Nova; Firefly, Sunburst

UNDERHOOD SERVICE SPECIFICATIONS

GOITU4   GOITU4

IDLE SPEED W/COMPUTER CONTROL Continued

Engine	Year	Transmission	Checking Speed	Setting Speed	AC Speed-up
1.6L Prizm code 6	1989-92	MT	—	800	900-1000
	1989-92	AT	—	800 D	900-1000 N
1.6L Prizm code 5	1990-92	MT	—	700	900-1000
	1990-92	AT	—	700 D	900-1000 N
1.6L, 1.8L Storm	1990-92	MT	800 max.	—	—
	1990-92	AT	800 N max.	—	—
1.6L Tracker	1989-92	MT	750-850	800	950-1050
	1989-92	AT	750-850 N	800 N	950-1050 N

BELT TENSION

Engine	Year	Alternator	Power Steering	Air Conditioning
Deflection method				
1.0L (inches)	1985-88	1/4-11/32	—	5/16-7/16
(mm)	1985-88	6-9	—	8-12
1.0L (inches)	1989-92	3/16-1/4	3/16-1/4	3/16-1/4
(mm)	1989-92	5-7	5-7	5-7
1.6L Tracker (inches)	1989-92	3/16-5/16	3/16-5/16	5/16-1/2
(mm)	1989-92	5-8	5-8	8-12
Strand Tension method				
1.5L	1985-89	70-110	70-110	70-110
1.6L Nova, Prizm	1985-92	110-150	60-100	60-100
1.6L, 1.8L Storm	1990-92	70-110	70-110	130-160

ENGINE MECHANICAL

TIGHTENING TORQUES
Some fasteners are tightened in more than one step.

Engine	Year	Torque Ft-lbs/Nm				
		Cylinder Head	Intake Manifold	Exhaust Manifold	Crankshaft Pulley	Water Pump
1.0L	1985-88	46-50/63-70	14-20/18-28	14-20/18-28	7-9/10-13	7-9/10-13
1.0L	1989-92	54/73	17/23	17/23	8/11	8/11
1.5L	1985-89	29/40, 58-79	17/23	17/23	108/147	17/23
1.6L 2V	1985-88	43/59	18/25	18/25	87/118	11/15
1.6L DOHC	1987-88	22/29, +90°, +90°	20/27	18/25	101/137	11/15
1.6L Prizm	1989-92	44/60	14/19•	18/25	87/118	11/15
1.6L, 1.8L Storm	1990-92	29/40, 58/79	17/23	30/39	87/118	17/23
1.6L Tracker	1989-92	54/73	17/23	17/23	8/11	8/11

• Code 6 engine, 20/27.

VALVE CLEARANCE
Engine cold, unless otherwise specified.

Engine	Year	Intake (inches)	Intake (mm)	Exhaust (inches)	Exhaust (mm)
1.0L: Hot	1985-88	.010	.25	.012	.30
Cold	1985-88	.006	.15	.008	.20
1.5L 2V Hot	1985-89	.006	.15	.010	.25
1.6L 2V Hot	1985-88	.008	.20	.012	.30
1.6L FI Nova, Prizm	1988-92	.006-.010	.15-.25	.008-.012	.20-.30
1.6L, 1.8L Storm:					
SOHC	1990-92	.004-.008	.10-.20	.008-.012	.20-.30
DOHC	1990-92	.006	.15	.010	.25
1.6L Tracker	1989-92	.005-.007	.13-.17	.006-.008	.15-.19

COMPRESSION PRESSURE
At cranking speed or specified rpm, engine temperature normalized, throttle open.

Engine	Year	PSI @ RPM	Maximum Variation PSI
1.0L	1985-92	156-199	14
1.5L	1985-89	128-179	•
1.6L Nova	1985-88	128-178	14
1.6L Prizm	1989-92	142-191	14
1.6L, 1.8L Storm	1990-92	142-191	14
1.6L Tracker	1989-92	170-199	14

• Lowest cylinder must be 65% of highest.

ENGINE COMPUTER SYSTEM

COMPUTER DIAGNOSTIC CODES
See UNDERHOOD SERVICE INSTRUCTIONS at the beginning of this section for test/adjustment diagrams.

1985-89 Spectrum, 1990-92 Storm
To activate diagnostic check, connect a jumper wire from terminals A & C of the ALDL connector (the two outer cavities of the three-terminal connector) located under the dash near the ECM. To clear memory, remove the ECM fuse for a minimum of ten seconds.

1985-86 Sprint
Place cancel switch located by the fuse box into the ''on'' position. ''SENSOR'' lamp on instrument cluster should light without flashing when ignition is switched on. Start engine and bring up to normal operating temperature, increase engine speed to 1500 to 2000 rpm. ''SENSOR'' lamp should flash, if not, check the following:
Oxygen sensor
Mixture control solenoid
Idle mixture and carburetor
Thermal switch
Wire connections for the emission control systems
ECM
Idle & WOT micro-switches
After diagnosis is complete, turn cancel switch off with engine running.

1987-88 Sprint
Reach under dash, under steering wheel and turn diagnostic switch on. Codes will be displayed on ''CHECK ENGINE'' light. Remove battery positive (+) terminal to clear codes.

1988 Nova FI
Turn ignition switch on and jumper both terminals of check engine connector by wiper motor. ''CHECK ENGINE'' light will flash codes. Remove ECM fuse for 10 seconds minimum to cancel codes.

1989-92 Prizm
Jumper terminals TE1 and E1 of diagnostic connector in engine compartment.

1989-92 Tracker
Turn ignition on and jumper both terminals of the underhood check engine connector (blue/yellow and black wires).

1989-92 Metro
Install a fuse in diagnostic cavity of fuse block. Codes will be displayed on ''CHECK ENGINE''.

1985-89 Spectrum 2V
Code 12 No tach signal to ECM
Code 13 Oxygen sensor circuit
Code 14 Shorted coolant sensor circuit
Codes 15 & 16 Open coolant sensor circuit
Code 21 Idle switch out of adjustment, or circuit open
Code 22 Fuel cut off relay, or open circuit
Code 23 Open or grounded M/C solenoid circuit
Code 25 Open or grounded vacuum switching valve
Code 42 Fuel cut off relay, or circuit grounded
Code 44 Lean oxygen sensor
Code 45 Rich system
Code 51 Faulty PROM, or improper installation
Code 53 Shorted switching unit, or faulty ECM
Code 54 Shorted M/C solenoid, or faulty ECM
Code 55 Faulty ECM

1987-88 Spectrum Turbo
Code 12 No distribution reference to ECM
Code 13 O_2 sensor circuit
Code 14 Shorted coolant sensor circuit
Codes 15 & 16 Open coolant sensor circuit

GEO/CHEVROLET - PONTIAC
1989-92 Metro, Prizm, Spectrum, Storm, Tracker, Sprint, Firefly
CHEVROLET - PONTIAC
1985-88 Sprint, Spectrum, Nova; Firefly, Sunburst

UNDERHOOD SERVICE SPECIFICATIONS

GOITU5   GOITU5

COMPUTER DIAGNOSTIC CODES Continued

Code 21 TPS voltage high
Code 22 TPS voltage low
Code 23 Manifold air temperature sensor
Code 24 Vehicle speed sensor
Code 25 Air or switching valve or circuit
Code 31 Wastegate control
Code 33 MAP sensor voltage high
Code 34 MAP sensor voltage low
Code 42 EST circuit
Code 43 Detonation sensor
Code 45 Rich O_2 sensor
Code 51 Faulty PROM or ECM

1987-88 Sprint 2V
Code 12 Diagnostic function working
Code 13 Oxygen sensor
Code 14 Coolant temperature sensor
Code 21 Throttle position switches
Code 23 Intake air temperature sensor
Code 32 Barometric pressure sensor
Code 51 ECM
Code 52 Fuel cut solenoid
Code 53 Secondary air sensor
Code 54 Mixture control solenoid
Code 55 Bowl vent solenoid

1987-88 Sprint Turbo
1989-92 Metro, Tracker, Storm
Code 12 Diagnostic function working
Code 13 Oxygen sensor
Code 14 Open coolant temperature sensor circuit
Code 15 Shorted coolant temperature sensor circuit
Code 21 Throttle position sensor circuit open
Code 22 Shorted throttle position sensor circuit
Code 23 Intake air temperature sensor circuit open
Code 24 Vehicle speed sensor
Code 25 Shorted intake air temperature circuit
Code 31 High turbo charger pressure (1987-88)
Codes 31 & 32 MAP or baromeutic pressure sensor (1989-92)
Code 33 Air flow meter (Turbo)
Code 33 MAP sensor (1990-92)
Code 41 Ignition signal
Code 42 Crank angle sensor (ex. Storm)
Code 42 EST (Storm)
Code 44 ECM idle switch circuit (1987-89)
Codes 44 & 45 Idle switch circuit (1992 Tracker)
Codes 44 & 45 Oxygen sensor (others)
Code 51 EGR system (ex. Storm)
Code 51 ECM (Storm)
Code 53 ECM ground circuit
On Steady ECM

1989-92 Prizm
1988 Nova FI
Continuous Flashing System normal
Codes 12 & 13 RPM signal
Code 14 Ignition signal
Code 21 Oxygen sensor
Code 22 Coolant temperature sensor
Code 24 Manifold air temperature sensor
Code 25 Air/fuel ratio lean
Code 26 Air/fuel ratio rich
Code 27 Sub oxygen sensor
Code 31 Mass air flow sensor
Code 41 Throttle position sensor
Code 42 Vehicle speed sensor
Code 43 Starter signal
Code 51 AC Switch signal
Code 71 EGR system

SENSORS, INPUT

TEMPERATURE SENSORS
1.0L Turbo: Manifold air temperature sensor measured between terminals 1 & 5 (first and last) of airflow meter.

1.6L Prizm DOHC: Manifold air temperature sensor measured between terminals E2 & THA (first and last) of airflow meter.

SENSORS, INPUT Continued

TEMPERATURE SENSORS Continued

Engine	Year	Sensor	Resistance Ohms @ deg. F/C
1.0L 2V	1987-88	Coolant, Manifold Air	6000 @ 32/0
			2000 @ 80/27
			1000 @ 120/49
			800 @ 140/60
			600 @ 165/74
			200 @ 212/100
1.0L Turbo	1987-91	Coolant	5600 @ 32/0
			2500 @ 68/20
			1200 @ 104/40
			600 @ 140/60
			320 @ 176/80
			180 @ 212/100
		Manifold Air	4000-7000 @ 32/0
			2000-3000 @ 68/20
			900-1300 @ 104/40
1.0L TBI, 1.6L Tracker, 1.6L Storm	1989-90	Coolant, Manifold Air	13,500 @ 20/−7
			7500 @ 40/4
			1800 @ 100/38
			450 @ 160/71
			185 @ 210/100
1.6L, 1.8L Storm	1991-92	Coolant, Manifold Air	13,500 @ 20/−7
			7500 @ 40/4
			1800 @ 100/38
			450 @ 160/71
			185 @ 210/100
1.0L TBI, 1.6L Tracker	1991-92	Coolant, Manifold Air	14,650 @ 0/−18
			8100 @ 20/−7
			4800 @ 40/4
			2500 @ 70/21
			1250 @ 100//38
			400 @ 160//71
			190 @ 210//99
1.5L 2V	1985-89	Coolant	2100-2900 @ 68/20
			1000 max. @ operating temp.
1.5L Turbo	1987-88	Coolant	5600 @ 32/0
			2500 @ 68/20
			1200 @ 104/40
			600 @ 140/60
			320 @ 176/80
			180 @ 212/100
		Manifold Air	9423 @ 32/0
			3515 @ 68/20
			1459 @ 104/40
			667 @ 140/60
			332 @ 176/80
			177 @ 212/100
1.6L FI Nova, Prizm	1987-92	Coolant	6000 @ 32/0
			2000 @ 80/27
			1000 @ 120/49
			800 @ 140/60
			600 @ 165/74
			200 @ 212/100
		Manifold Air	10,000-20,000 @ −4/−20
			4000-7000 @ 32/0
			2000-3000 @ 68/20
			900-1300 @ 104/40
			400-700 @ 212/100

MANIFOLD ABSOLUTE AND BAROMETRIC PRESSURE SENSORS
See UNDERHOOD SERVICE INSTRUCTIONS at the beginning of this section for test/adjustment diagrams.

Measure voltage with ignition on and engine off. With 10″ (250mm) Hg applied to unit, voltage will be 1.2-2.3 less.

		Voltage	
Engine	Year	Idle	WOT
1.5L Turbo	1987-88	1.0-1.5	4.0-4.5
1.0L	1991-92	1.0-1.5	3.0-4.0
1.6L Prizm, Tracker	1991-92	1.0-1.5	4.0-4.5

GEO/CHEVROLET - PONTIAC
1989-92 Metro, Prizm, Spectrum, Storm, Tracker, Sprint, Firefly
CHEVROLET - PONTIAC
1985-88 Sprint, Spectrum, Nova; Firefly, Sunburst

UNDERHOOD SERVICE SPECIFICATIONS

GOITU6   GOITU6

SENSORS, INPUT Continued

MANIFOLD ABSOLUTE AND BAROMETRIC PRESSURE SENSORS Continued

Engine	Year	Voltage @ Altitude (feet)
1.0L, 1.6L Storm	1989-90	3.6-4.4 @ 0
1.6L Tracker	1989-91	3.5-4.2 @ 1000
		3.4-4.1 @ 2000
		3.2-4.0 @ 3000
		3.1-3.8 @ 4000
		3.0-3.7 @ 5000
		2.9-3.6 @ 6000
		2.5-3.4 @ 7000-

THROTTLE POSITION SENSOR
See UNDERHOOD SERVICE INSTRUCTIONS at the beginning of this section for test/adjustment diagrams.

1.6L DOHC: Resistance measured between terminals E2 & VTA (first and third) of TPS.

Engine	Year	Voltage	
		Idle	WOT
1.0L TBI AT	1989-91	.54	4.9
1.0L TBI	1992	0.4-0.6	—
1.5L 2V	1985-89	0.8 max.	4.5
1.5L Turbo	1987-88	.45 max.	4.0
1.6L Prizm code 5	1990-92	0.6 max.	4.5
1.6L Storm	1990-92	.20-1.25	4.0 min.
1.6L Tracker	1989-90	.54	4.9
1.6L Tracker	1991	.70 max.	4.9 min.
1.6L Tracker	1992	0.4-0.6	4.9 min.

SENSORS, INPUT Continued

THROTTLE POSITION SENSOR Continued

Engine	Year	Resistance (ohms)	
		Idle	WOT
1.6L DOHC	1987-88	200-800	3300-10,000

ACTUATORS, OUTPUT

IDLE SPEED CONTROL
See UNDERHOOD SERVICE INSTRUCTIONS at the beginning of this section for test/adjustment diagrams.

1.5L Turbo, 1.6L Storm: Measured between terminals A & B and C & D of ISC.

Engine	Year	Resistance (ohms)
1.5L Turbo	1987-88	20 min.
1.6L Tracker	1989-90	5-10
1.6L Tracker	1991-92	10-16
1.6L Storm	1990-92	40-80

MIXTURE CONTROL SOLENOID

Engine	Year	Resistance (ohms)
1.5L 2V	1985-89	10 min.

HONDA
1983-92

ENGINE IDENTIFICATION

To identify an engine by the manufacturer's code, follow the four steps designated by the numbered blocks.

V.I.N. PLATE LOCATION:

Left side of hood support member.
Also top left side of instrument panel.

1 MODEL YEAR IDENTIFICATION:

10th character of V.I.N.
1992 — N; 1991 — M; 1990 — L;
1989 — K; 1988 — J; 1987 — H;
1986 — G; 1985 — F; 1984 — E;
1983 — D.

2 ENGINE CODE LOCATION:

First 3 characters (1983-86) or 5 characters of engine number stamped on right top side of engine block or (1987-92) on decal by left hood hinge.

4 ENGINE IDENTIFICATION

YEAR	3 ENGINE CODE	CYL.	DISPL. liters	cc	Fuel System	HP
1992	D15B8	4	1.5	1493	MFI	70
	D15Z1	4	1.5	1493	MFI	92
	D15B7	4	1.5	1493	MFI	102
	D16Z6	4	1.6	1590	MFI	125
	F22A1	4	2.2	2156	MFI	125
	F22A6	4	2.2	2156	MFI	135, 140†
	—	4	2.3	2259	MFI	160
1991	D15B6	4	1.5	1493	MFI	62
	D15B1	4	1.5	1493	TBI	70
	D15B2	4	1.5	1493	TBI	93
	D16A6	4	1.6	1590	MFI	105
	B20A5	4	2.0	1958	MFI	135
	B21A1	4	2.1	2056	MFI	140
	F22A1	4	2.2	2156	MFI	125
	F22A4	4	2.2	2156	MFI	130
	F22A6	4	2.2	2156	MFI	140
1990	D15B6	4	1.5	1493	MFI	62
	D15B1	4	1.5	1493	TBI	70
	D15B2	4	1.5	1493	TBI	93
	D16A6	4	1.6	1590	MFI	105
	B20A3	4	2.0	1958	2-1V	104
	B20A5	4	2.0	1958	MFI	135
	B21A1	4	2.1	2056	MFI	140
	F22A1	4	2.2	2156	MFI	125
	F22A4	4	2.2	2156	MFI	130
1989	D15B6	4	1.5	1493	MFI	62
	D15B1	4	1.5	1493	TBI	70
	D15B2	4	1.5	1493	TBI	92
	D16A6	4	1.5	1590	MFI	105
	A20A1	4	2.0	1955	2V	98
	A20A3	4	2.0	1955	MFI	120
	B20A3	4	2.0	1958	2-1V	104
	B20A5	4	2.0	1958	MFI	135
1988	D15B6	4	1.5	1493	MFI	62
	D15B1	4	1.5	1493	TBI	70
	D15B2	4	1.5	1493	TBI	92
	D16A6	4	1.6	1590	MFI	105
	A20A1	4	2.0	1955	2V	98
	A20A3	4	2.0	1955	MFI	120
	B20A3	4	2.0	1958	2-1V	104
	B20A5	4	2.0	1958	MFI	135

4 ENGINE IDENTIFICATION

YEAR	3 ENGINE CODE	CYL.	DISPL. liters	cc	Fuel System	HP
1987	D13A2	4	1.3	1342	3V	60
	D15A2	4	1.5	1488	3V	58-76†
	D15A3	4	1.5	1488	MFI	91
	A1B5	4	1.8	1830	2-1V	100
	A20A1	4	2.0	1955	2V	98
	A20A3	4	2.0	1955	MFI	110
1986	EV1	4	1.3	1342	3V	60
	EW1	4	1.5	1488	3V	65, 76
	EW3	4	1.5	1488	MFI	91
	ET2	4	1.8	1830	2-1V	100
	BS	4	2.0	1955	2V	98
	BT	4	2.0	1955	MFI	110
1985	EV1	4	1.3	1342	3V	60
	EV2•	4	1.3	1342	2V	N/A
	EW1	4	1.5	1488	3V	65, 76†
	EW2•	4	1.5	1488	2V	N/A
	EW3	4	1.5	1488	MFI	91
	EZ1•	4	1.6	1598	2V	N/A
	ES2	4	1.8	1830	2V	86
	ES3	4	1.8	1830	MFI	101
	ET2	4	1.8	1830	2-1V	100
	ET1•	4	1.8	1830	2-1V	N/A
1984	EV1	4	1.3	1342	3V	60
	EV2•	4	1.3	1342	2V	N/A
	EW1	4	1.5	1488	3V	76
	EW2•	4	1.5	1488	2V	N/A
	EZ1•	4	1.6	1598	2V	N/A
	ES1	4	1.8	1830	2V	86
	ES1	4	1.8	1830	2-1V	100
	ET1•	4	1.8	1830	2-1V	N/A
1983	EN1•	4	1.3	1335	2V	61
	EJ1	4	1.3	1335	3V	60
	EM1	4	1.5	1488	3V	67
	EL1•	4	1.6	1602	2V	N/A
	EK1	4	1.8	1751	3V	75
	ES1	4	1.8	1830	2-1V	100
	ET1•	4	1.8	1830	2-1V	N/A

† Engine horsepower varies with model installation.
• Canada only.   TBI — Throttle Body Injection.
MFI — Multiport Fuel Injection.   1V — One Venturi Carburetor.
2V — Two Venturi Carburetor.   3V — Three Venturi Carburetor.

UNDERHOOD SERVICE SPECIFICATIONS

HAITU1   HAITU1

CYLINDER NUMBERING SEQUENCE

4-CYL. FIRING ORDER: 1 3 4 2

1983 Civic
1335cc, 1488cc;
Accord, Prelude
1751cc

1984-87
Civic, CRX
1342cc,
1488cc 3V

1985-87 Civic, CRX
1488cc FI

1988-92 Civic,
CRX, 1493cc, 1590cc

1984-85 Accord
1830 2V

1984-85 Accord
1830cc FI

1983-90
Prelude
1830cc, 1958cc 2 × 1V;
1986-89 Prelude, Accord
1955cc

1988-91 Prelude
1998cc FI,
2056cc FI

1990-92 Accord, Prelude
2156cc

Front of car

UNDERHOOD SERVICE SPECIFICATIONS

HAITU2   HAITU2

TIMING MARK

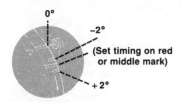

1983 Civic
w/MT;
1983-92 Accord,
Prelude w/MT

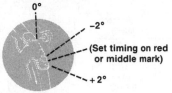

1983 Civic
w/AT;
1983-92 Accord,
Prelude w/AT

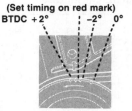

1984-92
Civic, CRX

ELECTRICAL AND IGNITION SYSTEMS

BATTERY

BCI equivalent shown, size may vary from original equipment.
Check clearance before replacing, holddown may need to be modified.

Engine	Year	STANDARD BCI Group No.	STANDARD Crank. Perf.	OPTIONAL BCI Group No.	OPTIONAL Crank. Perf.
Accord: Early	1983	45	410	—	—
Late	1983	26	405	—	—
Accord	1984-89	26	405	—	—
Accord	1990-92	24	550	—	—
Civic, CRX	1983-85	51	410	—	—
Civic: U.S. prod.	1986-89	52	405	—	—
Japan prod.	1986-89	51	410	—	—
Civic	1990-91	51	405	—	—
CRX	1986-91	51	410	—	—
Prelude	1983-89	26	405	—	—
Prelude	1990-91	24	585	—	—

ALTERNATOR

See UNDERHOOD SERVICE INSTRUCTIONS at the beginning of this section for test/adjustment diagrams.

Application	Year	Rated Output	Test Output (amps @ eng. rpm)
Civic	1983	45	45 @ 4500
Accord, Prelude	1983	60	60 @ 3500
Accord, Prelude	1984	70	61-68 @ 5000
Civic, CRX ex. HF	1984-87	55	50 @ 5000
CRX HF	1985-87	60	57-62 @ 1500
Prelude	1985-87	60	54-60 @ 1500
Accord	1985-87	65	58-64 @ 1500
Civic, CRX	1988-89	60	38-48 @ 2000
Prelude	1988-89	65	63-68 @ 2000
Accord	1988-89	70	75-86 @ 2000
Civic, CRX	1990-91	60	38-48 @ 2000
Accord	1990-91	80	78-95 @ 2000
Prelude	1990-91	70	70-80 @ 2000
Accord	1992	70	40 min. @ 2000
Civic	1992	80	30 min. @ 2000

REGULATOR

Application	Year	Test Temp. (deg. F/C)	Voltage Setting
All	1983-84	68/20	13.5-14.5
Accord, Civic	1985	140/60	13.9-15.1
Prelude	1985	68/20	14.5-15.1
All	1986-87	140/60	13.9-15.0
All	1988-91	—	12.5-14.5
All	1992	—	13.9-15.1

STARTER

Engine	Year	Cranking Voltage (min. volts)	Max. Ampere Draw @ Cranking Speed
1335cc	1983	8.0	230
1342cc	1984	8.0	350
1342cc MT	1985-87	8.5	230
California	1986	8.0	200

STARTER Continued

Engine	Year	Cranking Voltage (min. volts)	Max. Ampere Draw @ Cranking Speed
1488cc	1983	8.0	230
California	1983	8.0	200
1488cc	1984	8.0	350
1488cc MT	1985-87	8.5	230
AT	1985-87	8.0	350
California	1986-87	8.0	200
1493cc, 1590cc:			
0.8 kw	1988-91	8.0	200
1.0 kw	1988-91	8.5	230
1.2 kw	1988-91	8.0	280
1.4 kw	1988-91	8.0	350
1751cc	1983	8.0	230
1830cc, 1955cc	1983-87	8.0	350
1955cc, 1958cc, 2056cc, 2156cc	1988-91	8.5	350
All	1992	8.0	400

SPARK PLUGS

Engine	Year	Gap (inches)	Gap (mm)	Torque (ft-lb)
1335cc, 1488cc				
Canada	1983	.028-.031	.70-.80	13
1602cc	1983	.031-.035	.80-.90	11-18
All Others	1983-92	.039-.043	1.0-1.1	13

IGNITION COIL

See UNDERHOOD SERVICE INSTRUCTIONS at the beginning of this section for test/adjustment diagrams.

Resistance (ohms @ 70°F or 21°C)

1990 1958cc, 2056cc: Primary windings measured between terminals A & D of coil connector. Secondary windings measured between terminal A of coil connector and high voltage terminal.

Engine	Year	Windings	Resistance (ohms)
1335cc, 1488cc, 1602cc, 1830cc	1983	Primary	1.0-1.3
		Secondary	7400-11,000
1751cc	1983	Primary	1.06-1.24
		Secondary	7400-11,000
1342cc, 1488cc	1984	Primary	1.24-1.46
		Secondary	8000-12,000
1830cc	1984	Primary	1.06-1.24
		Secondary	7400-11,000
All	1985	Primary	1.06-1.24
		Secondary	7400-11,000
All w/carb	1986	Primary	1.06-1.24
		Secondary	7400-11,000
All w/FI	1986	Primary	1.215-1.485
		Secondary	11,074-11,526
All	1987	Primary	1.2-1.5
		Secondary	11,074-11,526
1493cc, 1590cc	1988-89	Primary	0.3-0.5
		Secondary	9440-14,160
1955cc	1988-89	Primary	1.2-1.5
		Secondary	11,074-11,526
1958cc	1988-89	Primary	1.2-1.5
		Secondary	9040-13,560

HONDA
1983-92

IGNITION COIL Continued

Engine	Year	Windings	Resistance (ohms)
1493cc, 1590cc	1990-91	Primary	0.6-0.8
		Secondary	9760-14,640
1958cc, 2056cc	1990-91	Primary	0.3-0.4
		Secondary	9040-13,560
2156cc	1990-91	Primary	0.6-0.8
		Secondary	12,880-19,320
1493cc, 1590cc	1992	Primary	0.6-0.8
		Secondary	13,200-19,800
2156cc	1992	Primary	0.6-0.8
		Secondary	14,400-21,600

DISTRIBUTOR PICKUP
See UNDERHOOD SERVICE INSTRUCTIONS at the beginning of this section for test/ adjustment diagrams.

Includes TDC, cylinder and crankshaft position sensors mounted in distributor.

Application	Resistance (ohms)	Air Gap (in./mm)
1983-85 All w/carb	—	†
1986-87 FI distributor pickup	650-850	†
1988-91 1493cc, 1590cc	350-550*	—
1992 1493cc, 1590cc	350-700	—
1988-90 1955cc FI, 1958cc 2×1V	650-850	†
1990-91 1958cc FI, 2056cc	700-1100	—
1990-91 2156cc	350-700*	—
1992 2156cc	260-500	—

† Equal space between pickup and reluctor on each side.
* On 5 terminal connectors, measured between two low, or two center terminals. On 7 terminal connectors, measured between each of three adjacent pairs of terminals.

BASE TIMING
See UNDERHOOD SERVICE INSTRUCTIONS at the beginning of this section for test/ adjustment diagrams.

At slow idle and Before Top Dead Center, unless otherwise specified.

1983-89: Leave distributor vacuum hoses, as equipped, connected.

1988-89: On models w/o vacuum advance (EST), remove yellow cap from timing connector (located in left rear engine compartment or by coil) and jumper the two terminals.

1990-92: Jumper terminals of 2-pin timing connector located on right side under dash.

Engine	Year	Man. Trans. (degrees)	Auto. Trans. (degrees)
1335cc Canada 2V	1983	2 ±2	8 ±2 D
1335cc CVCC	1983	20	—
w/5-speed	1983	18	—
1342cc	1984-87	21 ±2	—
California	1984-87	16 ±2	—
Canada	1984-87	12 ±2	12 ±2
1342cc	1987	14 ±2	—
1488cc Canada	1983	13 ±2	2 ATDC ±2
1488cc	1984-85	20 ±2	15 ±2
w/PS	1984-85	—	17 ±2
Canada 2V	1984-85	10 ±2	14 ±2
1488cc 3V ex. HF	1986-87	20 ±2*	15 ±2*
w/PS	1986-87	—	17 ±2*
Canada 2V	1986-87	10 ±2	14 ±2
1488cc 3V HF Federal	1986	21 ±2*	—
Federal	1987	26 ±2*	—
California	1986-87	16 ±2*	—
1488cc FI	1985-87	16 ±2*	—
California	1985-87	12 ±2*	—
1493cc	1988-91	18 ±2	18 ±2
1493cc HF	1988-91	14 ±2	14 ±2
1493cc: D15B8	1992	12 ±2	12 ±2
Others	1992	16 ±2	16 ±2
1590cc	1988-91	18 ±2	18 ±2
1590cc	1992	16 ±2	16 ±2
1598cc	1984-85	2 ±2	2 ±2 D
1602cc Canada	1983	5 ±2	5 ±2 D
1751cc	1983	16	16
California	1983	12	16
1830cc 2×1V	1983	10	12
California	1983	12	12
1830cc Canada	1983-85	22 ±2	12 ±2

BASE TIMING Continued

Engine	Year	Man. Trans. (degrees)	Auto. Trans. (degrees)
1830cc 2V	1984-85	22 ±2	18 ±2
California	1984-85	18 ±2	18 ±2
1830cc 2×1V	1984-87	20 ±2	12 ±2
1830cc FI	1985	18 ±2	18 ±2
1955cc 2V	1986-89	24 ±2*	15 ±2 D*
California	1986-89	20 ±2*	15 ±2 D*
1955cc FI	1986-88	15 ±2*	15 ±2*
1958cc 2×1V	1988-89	20 ±2*	15 ±2*
California	1988-89	15 ±2*	10 ±2*
1958cc FI, 2056cc, 2156cc	1988-92	15 ±2	15 ±2

* With vacuum hoses disconnected and plugged, 4° BTDC.

DISTRIBUTOR TIMING ADVANCE
Engine degrees at engine rpm, no load, in addition to base timing setting.

Mechanical advance distributors only.

Engine	Transmission	Year	Distributor Number	Degrees @ 2500 RPM Total	Degrees @ 2500 RPM Centrifugal
1335cc	MT	1983	D4R80-24, 26	26.3-32.5	7.3-11.5
Canada	MT & AT	1983		29-37	16-20
1342cc	MT	1984-85	D4R82-28	19.2-23.2	5.2-7.2
California	MT	1984-85	D4R82-27	23.7-27.7	5.2-7.2
1342cc Canada	MT & AT	1984-85		21-29	18-22
1342cc	MT	1986-87	D4R85-34	46.5-54.5	11-15
1488cc	MT & AT	1983	D4R80-27, 29, 30	26.5-33.0	7.5-12.0
Canada	MT	1983		29-37	16-20
Canada	AT	1983		34-42	16-20
1488cc 3V	MT	1984-85	D4R82-31	16.1-20.1	5.6-7.6
1488cc 3V	AT	1984-85	D4R82-30	21.1-25.1	6.6-8.6
Canada	MT & AT	1984	—	20-28	18-22
1488cc 3V ex. HF	MT	1985	D4R84-33	45.9-53.1	14.9-18.1
1488cc 3V ex. HF	AT	1985	D4R84-14	39.9-47.1	8.9-12.1
Canada	MT & AT	1985		19.5-27.5	18-22
1488cc 4WD Wagon	MT	1985	D4R84-40	—	—
1488cc HF	MT	1985	D4R84-44	44.4-51.6	11.4-14.6
1488cc HF	MT	1985	D4R84-43	39.4-44.6	11.4-14.6
1488cc FI	MT	1985-87	TD-05J	20-32	10-14
1488cc FI	MT	1985-87	TD-06J	18-28	10-14
1488cc ex. HF & 4WD	MT	1986-87	D4R85-18	48-56	10-14
1488cc ex. HF & 4WD	AT	1986-87	D4R85-17	31-39	6-10
1488cc HF	MT	1986-87	D4R85-10	—	—
1488cc HF	MT	1986-87	D4R85-23	33-41	6.5-10.5
1598cc Canada	MT & AT	1984	—	24-34	17-23
1598cc Canada	MT & AT	1985	—	25-33	18-22
1602cc Canada	MT	1983	—	28-36	20-24
1602cc Canada	AT	1983	—	24-32	20-24
1602cc Canada	MT	1984	—	24-32	16-20
1602cc Canada	AT	1984	—	22-30	19-23
1602cc Canada Accord	MT	1985	—	24-32	16-20
1602cc Canada	AT	1985	—	18.5-26.5	15.5-19.5
1751cc	MT	1983	D4R80-20	17.5-23.5	8.5-12.5
1751cc	MT	1983	D4R80-23	21.5-27.5	8.5-12.5
1751cc	AT	1983	D4R80-21, 22	20.0-25.5	7.0-10.5
1830cc	MT & AT	1983	All	14-20	5-9
1830cc Canada	MT	1983	—	43-51	24-28
1830cc Canada	AT	1983	—	33-41	24-28
1830cc 2V	MT	1984	D4R82-32/TD-01K	33.4-41.4	11.4-15.4
1830cc 2V	MT	1984	D4R83-03/TD-09K	20.9-29.9	11.4-15.4
1830cc 2V	AT	1984	D4R82-02/TD-08K	29.4-37.4	11.4-15.4
1830cc 2×1	MT	1984-87	D4R83-14/TD-13K	25.3-31.3	13.3-17.3
1830cc 2×1	AT	1984-87	D4R83-15/TD-14K	22.8-28.8	13.3-17.3
1830cc 3V	MT	1985	D4R84-22/TD-16K	27.4-38.6	8.4-11.6
1830cc 3V	MT	1985	D4R84-24/TD-18K	27.4-34.6	8.4-11.6
1830cc 3V	AT	1985	D4R84-23/TD-17K	27.4-34.6	8.4-11.6
1830cc FI	MT & AT	1985	TD-01L	27.4-35.4	9.4-13.4
1955cc 2V	MT	1986-89	D4R85-55/TD-41K		
1955cc 2V	MT	1986-89	D4R84-57/TD-43K	34.8-42.8	12.8-16.8
1955cc 2V	AT	1986-89	D4R84-58/TD-42K	29.5-37.5	11.5-15.5
1955cc FI	MT & AT	1986-87	TD-01N	14.6-22.6	6.6-10.6
1955cc FI	MT	1988-89	TD-06N/9N	19.5-23.5†	12-16
1958cc FI	AT	1988-89	TD-07N/10N	17.5-21.5†	10-14

† Subadvance, 11-15 @ 12".

FUEL SYSTEM

FUEL PUMP

See UNDERHOOD SERVICE INSTRUCTIONS at the beginning of this section for test/adjustment diagrams.

With fuel injection; pressure measured at fitting on fuel filter.

Engine	Year	Pressure	
		PSI	RPM
Carburetted:			
1335cc Canada	1983	2.1-2.8	idle
1342cc, 1488cc	1984	2.7-3.8	idle
1342cc, 1488cc 3V	1985-86	2.4-3.3	idle
1598cc	1984-85	2.4-3.1	—
1830cc 2V	1984-85	2.4-3.1	ign. on
1830cc 2×1	1984-86	2.1-2.8	ign. on
1955cc 2V	1986-87	2.6-3.3	idle
1958cc 2×1	1988-90	2.6-3.3	ign. on
All	1983	2.1-2.8	ign. on

Engine	Year	Pressure (PSI)	
		Idle*	Idle†
Fuel Injected:			
1488cc	1985-86	33-39	—
1488cc	1987	36-41	—
1493cc, 1590cc	1988-91	35-41	35-37
1493cc, 1590cc	1992	40-47	30-38
1830cc, 1955cc	1985-86	33-39	—
1955cc, 1958cc, 2056cc, 2156cc	1987-90	35-41	35-37
2156cc	1991-92	40-47	30-38

* With pressure regulator vacuum hose disconnected.

† With pressure regulator vaccum hose connected.

IDLE SPEED W/O COMPUTER CONTROL

See UNDERHOOD SERVICE INSTRUCTIONS at the beginning of this section for test/adjustment diagrams.

Preferred setting is the midpoint of range given.

1983-87:

1335cc, 1342cc, 1488cc:

Disconnect and plug air intake control vacuum hose.

Set idle speed by adjusting throttle stop screw.

Vehicles with manual transmission or 1984-87 automatic transmission with PS & AC have an idle control system.

Manual transmission, turn on headlights and set heater blower on high.

Adjust idle control screw on diaphragm linkage to idle speed.

Automatic transmission with PS & AC, turn wheels to full lock and adjust idle control screw on boost diaphragm linkage.

Turn on AC and adjust screw on boost diaphragm to specified speed-up speed.

To set fast idle, set cam on specified step and adjust to specification.

1751cc:

Disconnect and plug intake air control vacuum hose. With engine warm and electric cooling fan on, adjust idle to specification.

With AC, turn on and adjust screw on idle boost diaphragm to specification.

1984-89:

1830cc, 1955cc MT:

Disconnect and plug intake air control vacuum hose, with engine warm, set idle speed to specification.

Turn AC on and adjust speed-up speed to specified value.

1955cc AT:

Disconnect and plug intake air control vacuum hose. Remove filter from frequency solenoid valve and plug opening in valve. Lower idle speed as much as possible by adjusting throttle stop screw. Set base idle speed to specified value by adjusting screw on throttle cable linkage. Readjust throttle stop screw to idle speed specification. Place transmission in gear and adjust screw on boost diaphragm linkage to idle speed A. Place transmission in neutral and turn AC on. Set speed-up speed to specified value by adjusting screw on boost diaphragm.

IDLE SPEED W/O COMPUTER CONTROL Continued

Engine	Year	SLOW		FAST		Step of Cam
		Man. Trans.	Auto. Trans.	Man. Trans.	Auto. Trans.	
1335cc	1983	650-750	650-750 D	3000	3000 N	High
idle controller	1983	600-700	—			
speed-up	1983	650-750	650-750 D			
w/5-speed	1983	600-700	—	3000		High
idle controller	1983	600-700	—			
speed-up	1983	600-700	—			
Canada	1983	700-800	700-800 D	2100-3100	2100-3100	—
1342cc	1984-87	600-700	650-700 D	2500-3500	—	High
5-speed	1984	550-650	—	2500-3500	—	High
idle controller	1984-87	600-700	—			
speed-up	1984-87	700-800	—			
1342cc High Altitude	1984-87	750-850	—	2500-3500	—	High
idle controller	1984-87	750-850*	—			
speed-up	1984-87	750-850*	—			
1488cc	1983	650-750	650-750 D	2500-3500	2500-3500 N	High
idle controller	1983	600-700	—			
speed-up	1983	650-750	650-750 D			
1488cc	1984	650-750	600-700 D	2500-3500	2500-3500 N	High
idle controller	1984	650-750	—			
speed-up	1984	700-800	700-800 D			
California	1984	650-750	650-750 D	2500-3500	2500-3500 N	High
idle controller	1984	650-750	—			
speed-up	1984	700-800	700-800 D			
High Altitude	1984	700-800	650-750 D	2500-3500	2500-3500 N	High
idle controller	1984	700-800	—			
speed-up	1984	700-800	700-800 D			
1488cc HF	1985-87	530-630	—	2500-3500		High
idle controller	1985-87	600-700	—			
speed-up	1985-87	650-750	—			
California	1985-87	550-650	—	2500-3500	—	High
idle controller	1985-87	600-700	—			
speed-up	1985-87	650-750	—			
High Altitude	1985-87	700-800†	—	2500-3500		High
idle controller	1985-87	700-800†	—			
speed-up	1985-87	700-800†	—			

HONDA
1983-92

UNDERHOOD SERVICE SPECIFICATIONS

IDLE SPEED W/O COMPUTER CONTROL Continued

Engine	Year	SLOW Man. Trans.	SLOW Auto. Trans.	FAST Man. Trans.	FAST Auto. Trans.	Step of Cam
1488cc ex. HF	1984-87	650-750	600-700 D	2500-3500	2500-3500 N	High
idle controller	1984	650-750	—			
idle controller	1985-87	650-750	600-700 D			
speed-up	1984-87	700-800	700-800 D			
California	1984-87	650-750‡	650-750 D	2500-3500	2500-3500 N	High
idle controller	1984	650-750	—			
idle controller	1985	650-750	700-800 D			
idle controller	1986-87	650-750‡	650-750 D			
speed-up	1984-87	700-800	700-800 D			
High Altitude	1984-87	700-800	650-750 D	2500-3500	2500-3500 N	High
idle controller	1984	700-800	—			
idle controller	1985-87	700-800	650-750 D			
speed-up	1984-87	700-800	700-800 D			
1488cc Canada	1984-87	700-800	650-750 D	1500-2500	1500-2500 N	—
1598cc Canada	1984-85	700-800	650-750 D	1800	1800	—
1602cc Canada	1983	700-800	650-750 D	1500-2500	1500-2500	—
1751cc	1983	700-800	650-750	2000-3000	2000-3000 N	High
speed-up	1983	700-800	650-750 D			
1830cc 2×1	1983	750-850	700-800 D	2000-3000	2000-3000 N	High
speed-up	1983	700-800	650-750 D			
1830cc 2×1	1984-85	750-850	750-850 D	1400-2000	1500-2100 N	Third
speed-up	1984-85	750-850	750-850 D			
High Altitude	1984-85	700-800	700-800 D	1400-2000	1500-2100 N	Third
speed-up	1984-85	700-800	700-800 D			
Canada	1984-85	700-800	650-750 D	—	—	—
1830cc 2×1	1986-87	750-850	750-850 D	1250-2250	1200-2200 N	Third
speed-up	1986-87	750-850	750-850 D			
High Altitude	1986-87	700-800	700-800 D	1250-2250	1200-2200 N	Third
speed-up	1986-87	700-800	700-800 D			
1830cc 2V	1984-85	700-800	650-750 D	2000-3000	2000-3000 N	High
speed-up	1984-85	700-800	650-750 D			
High Altitude	1985	650-750*	650-750 D●	2000-3000	2000-3000 N	High
speed-up	1985	650-750	650-750 D			
1955cc 2V	1986	700-800	650-750 N†	2000-3000	2000-3000 N	High
idle control A	1986	—	550-650 D			
speed-up	1986-87	700-800	650-750 N			
base idle	1986-87	—	550-650 N			

IDLE SPEED W/O COMPUTER CONTROL Continued

Engine	Year	SLOW Man. Trans.	SLOW Auto. Trans.	FAST Man. Trans.	FAST Auto. Trans.	Step of Cam
1955cc 2V	1987-89	750-850	650-750 N	2000-3000	2000-300 N	High
idle control A	1987-89	—	650-750 D			
speed-up	1987-89	750-850	650-750 N			
base idle	1987-89	—	580-680 N			
1958cc 2×1	1988-90	750-850	700-800 D	1600-2000	1600-2000 N	Third
speed-up	1988-90	750-850	700-800 D			

* If adjusted at low altitude, 700-800.
● If adjusted at low altitude, 650-750.
† High altitude 600-700 N.
‡ 4WD Wagon, 700-800.

IDLE SPEED W/COMPUTER CONTROL

See UNDERHOOD SERVICE INSTRUCTIONS at the beginning of this section for test/ adjustment diagrams.

1985-87: Disconnect and plug vacuum hose at idle controller. Set speed to specified value. Turn AC on and verify that the speed-up speed is at specification. Check fast idle with engine cold.

1988-92: Electrically disconnect electronic air control valve (EACV). Set idle to set speed. Remove HAZARD fuse for 10 seconds to reset ECU. Verify that idle is at checking speed. Turn headlights and AC on to check speed-up.

Engine	Year	Transmission	Set Speed	Checking Speed	Speed-up Speed	Fast Idle (Cold)
1488cc FI	1985-87	MT	700-800	—	700-800	1250-2250
1493cc	1988	MT	575-675	675-775	730-830	1000-1800
1493cc	1988	AT	575-675 N	675-775 N	730-830 N	1000-1800 N
1493cc	1989-90	MT	575-675	700-800	750-850	1000-2000
1493cc	1989-91	AT	575-675 N	700-800 N	750-850 N	1000-2000 N
Canada	1990-91	MT	575-675	750-850	750-850	1000-2000
	1990-91	AT	575-675 N	750-850 N	750-850 N	1000-2000 N
1493cc HF	1988-89	MT	450-550	550-650	700-800	1000-1800 N
Calif., High Alt.	1988-89	MT	450-550	600-700	700-800	1000-1800
1493cc D15B8	1992	MT	370-470	620-720	700-800*	—
Canada	1992	MT	370-470	700-800	700-800*	—
1493cc D15Z1	1992	MT	370-470	550-650	650-750*	—
Canada	1992	MT	370-470	650-750	650-750*	—
1493cc D15B7	1992	MT	370-470	620-720	700-800*	—
	1992	AT	370-470 N	650-750 N	700-800 N*	—
Canada	1992	MT	370-470	700-800	700-800*	—
	1992	AT	370-470 N	700-800 N	700-800 N*	—
1590cc	1988-89	MT	500-600	700-800	730-830 N	1000-1800 N
1590cc	1989	AT	500-600 N	700-800 N	770-870 N	1000-2000 N
1590cc	1990-91	MT	500-600	700-800	730-830†	1000-2000
		AT	500-600 N	700-800 N	730-830 N†	1000-2000 N
1590cc	1992	MT	370-470	620-720	700-800*	—
	1992	AT	370-470	650-750 N	700-800*	—
Canada	1992	MT	370-470	700-800	700-800*	—
	1992	AT	370-470	700-800 N	700-800 N*	—
1830cc FI	1985	MT	700-800	—	750-850	1000-1800
1830cc FI	1985	AT	700-800 N	—	750-850 N	1000-1800 N
1955cc FI	1986-87	MT	700-800	—	700-800	1000-1800
1955cc FI	1986-87	AT	700-800 N	—	700-800 N	1000-1800 N
1955cc, 1958cc FI	1988-89	MT	600-800	700-800	700-800	1100-1900
1955cc, 1958cc FI	1988-89	AT	600-700 N	700-800 N	700-800 N	1100-1900 N
1958cc, 2056cc	1990	MT	600-700	720-820	720-820	1100-1900
1958cc, 2056cc	1990	AT	600-700 N	720-820 N	720-820 N	1100-1900 N
2156cc	1990-92	MT	500-600	650-750	720-820	1400
2156cc	1990-92	AT	500-600 N	650-750 N	720-820 N	1400 N

† AC speed-up, 760-860 (N). Wagon, 760-860 (N).
* Electrical speed-up listed; AC speed-up, 760-860.

UNDERHOOD SERVICE SPECIFICATIONS

ENGINE MECHANICAL

TIGHTENING TORQUES

See UNDERHOOD SERVICE INSTRUCTIONS at the beginning of this section for test/adjustment diagrams.

Some fasteners are tightened in more than one stage.

| | | Torque Ft-lbs/Nm | | | | |
Engine	Year	Cylinder Head	Intake Manifold	Exhaust Manifold	Crankshaft Pulley	Water Pump
1335cc, 1488cc	1983	22/32, 43/60	7/10, 16/22	7/10, 16/22	80/110	9/12
1342cc, 1488cc	1984-85	22/32, 43/60	16/22	18/22	83/115	9/12
1342cc, 1488cc	1986-87	22/32, 43/60	16/22	23/32	83/115	9/12
1493cc, 1590cc	1988-91	22/30, 47/65	16/22	23/32	119/165	9/12-short 33/45-long
1493cc D15B7, B8	1992	22/30, 47/65	17/23	23/32	134/185	9/12
1493cc D15Z1, 1590cc	1992	22/30, 53/73	17/23	23/32	134/185	9/12
1751cc	1983	22/32, 43/60	7/10, 16/22	7/10, 16/22	83/115	9/12
1830cc, 1955cc	1983-88	22/32, 49/68	16/22	23/32	83/115	9/12
1955cc	1989	22/32, 49/68	16/22	23/32	108/150	9/12
1958cc, 2056cc	1988-91	22/32, 49/68	16/22	23/32	108/150	9/12
2156cc	1990-92	29/40, 51/70, 78/108	16/22	23/32	159/220	9/12

VALVE CLEARANCE

Engine cold.

Engine	Year	Intake♦ (inches)	Intake♦ (mm)	Exhaust (inches)	Exhaust (mm)
1335cc, 1488cc	1983	.005-.007	.13-.17	.007-.009	.17-.23
1598cc, 1602cc Canada	1983	.005-.007	.13-.17	.010-.012	.25-.30
1342cc, 1488cc, 1493cc ex. HF	1984-92	.007-.009	.17-.22	.009-.011	.22-.27
1493cc HF	1988-90	.005-.007	.12-.17	.007-.009	.17-.22
1598cc Canada	1983	.005-.007	.13-.17	.010-.012	.25-.30
1751cc, 1830cc, 1955cc, 1958cc ex. FI	1988	.005-.007	.13-.17	.010-.012	.25-.30
1958cc FI, 2056cc	1988-90	.003-.005	.08-.12	.006-.008	.16-.20
2156cc	1990-92	.009-.011	.24-.28	.011-.013	.28-.32

♦ Includes auxiliary air valve where applicable.

COMPRESSION PRESSURE

At 400 rpm, unless otherwise specified, engine temperature normalized, throttle open.

Engine	Year	PSI	Maximum Variation PSI
1335cc	1983	164-192	28
Canada	1983	142-171	28
1342cc	1984-85	142-171	28
1342cc	1986-87	135-164	28
1488cc	1983	192	28
1488cc 3V	1984-86	135-164	28
1488cc HF	1985	142-171	28
1488cc FI	1986-87	156-185	28
1493cc	1988-92	135-185	28

COMPRESSION PRESSURE Continued

Engine	Year	PSI	Maximum Variation PSI
1590cc	1988-92	135-185	28
1602cc Canada	1983	142-171	28
1751cc	1983	185	28
1830cc	1984-85	156-184	28
1830cc	1986-87	125-156	28
1955cc 2V	1986-89	135-171	28
1955cc FI, 1958cc, 2056cc, 2156cc	1986-92	135-178	28

BELT TENSION

Deflection method: Deflection midway between pulleys with an applied load of 22 pounds on longest belt segment.

Engine	Year	Alternator	Power Steering	Air Cond.	Air Pump
Civic (inches)	1983	1/2-11/16	—	5/16-3/8	1/2-11/16
(mm)	1983	12-17	—	8-10	12-17
Civic (inches)	1984-85	9/32-3/8	3/4-7/8	9/32-11/32	—
(mm)	1984-85	7-10	18-22	7-9	—
Civic (inches)	1986-87	9/32-3/8	3/4-7/8	5/16-3/8	—
(mm)	1986-87	7-10	18-22	8-10	—
Civic, CRX (inches)	1988-92	3/8-7/16	3/8-1/2	3/8-7/16	—
(mm)	1988-92	9-11	9-12	9-11	—
Accord, Prelude (inches)	1983	9/16-11/16	—	1/2-5/8	9/16-11/16
(mm)	1983	14-17	—	12-16	14-17
Accord, Prelude (inches)	1984	1/4-11/32	3/4-7/8	3/8-1/2	—
(mm)	1984	6-9	18-22	10-12	—
Accord ex. FI, Prelude (inches)	1985	9/32-3/8	3/4-7/8	3/8-1/2	—
(mm)	1985	7-10	18-22	10-12	—
Accord FI (inches)	1985	1/8-1/4	3/4-7/8	3/8-1/2	—
(mm)	1985	3-6	18-22	10-12	—
Prelude ex. FI (inches)	1986-89	9/32-3/8	3/4-7/8	3/8-1/2	—
(mm)	1986-89	7-10	18-22	10-12	—
Accord, Prelude FI (inches)	1986-89	1/4-3/8	3/4-7/8	3/8-1/2	—
(mm)	1986-89	6-10	18-22	10-12	—
Accord, Prelude (inches)	1990-92	3/8-7/16	1/2-5/8	3/8-7/16	—
(mm)	1990-92	10-12	12.5-16	10-12	—

ENGINE COMPUTER SYSTEM

COMPUTER DIAGNOSTIC CODES

See UNDERHOOD SERVICE INSTRUCTIONS at the beginning of this section for test/adjustment diagrams.

1985 Accord, 1985-87 Civic CRX, Hatchback, Sedan, Wagon w/FI

When PGM-FI dash light is on consistently, access ECU under passenger's seat with ignition switch on. Four LED's numbered 8421 will display codes. After making repairs, disconnect the battery negative terminal for at least 10 seconds to reset the ECU memory.

Code 0 Dash warning light off: ECU power source.
ECU ground.
Faulty ECU.
Dash warning light on: ECU ground.
Faulty ECU.
Combination meter.
Warning light wire shorted.

Code 1 Oxygen sensor or circuit.
Misfiring spark plug.

Codes 2, 4, 84, 842, 8421 ECU faulty.

Code 21 MAP sensor or circuit.

Code 41 MAP sensor piping disconnected.

Code 42 Coolant temperature sensor or circuit.

Code 421 Throttle angle sensor or circuit.

COMPUTER DIAGNOSTIC CODES Continued

Codes 8, 81 Crank angle sensor or circuit.
Code 82 Intake air temperature sensor or circuit.
Code 821 Idle mixture adjuster sensor or circuit.
Code 841 Atmospheric pressure sensor or circuit.

1986-87 Accord, Prelude w/FI

When PGM-FI dash light is on consistently, access ECU under driver's seat with ignition switch on. Red LED will flash the number of times corresponding to each code with two second intervals between codes. After making repairs, disconnect #11 fuse for 10 seconds to reset memory.

Code 0 With dash warning light off: Faulty ECU.
         ECU ground.
         With dash warning light on: ECU power source.
         ECU ground.
         Combination meter.
         Warning light wire shorted.
         Faulty ECU.
Code 1 Oxygen sensor or circuit.
         Misfiring spark plug.
         Fuel system faulty.
Codes 2, 4, 11, 14 or higher ECU faulty.
Code 3 MAP sensor or circuit.
Code 5 MAP sensor piping disconnected.
Code 6 Coolant temperature sensor or circuit.
Code 7 Throttle angle sensor or circuit.
Codes 8, 9 Crank angle sensor or circuit.
Code 10 Intake air temperature sensor or circuit.
Code 12 EGR control system.
Code 13 Atmospheric pressure sensor or circuit.

1988-90 Civic, CRX, Prelude, Accord

When PGM-FI dash light is on consistently, access ECU under passenger side carpet under dash or kick panel and turn ignition on. LED will flash in short (ones) or long (tens) durations corresponding to each code with two second intervals between separate codes. After making repairs, remove battery negative cable for 10 seconds to reset ECU.

1992

Locate 2- and 3-pin connectors by passenger side kick panel. Jumper the terminals of the 2-pin connector only. Codes will be displayed on "Check" engine light. Remove "Back Up" fuse in fuse block to erase codes.

Civic, CRX, Accord, Prelude w/FI

Code 0 ECU.
Codes 1, 2 Oxygen content.
Codes 3, 5 Manifold absolute pressure.
Code 4 Crank angle.
Code 6 Coolant temperature.
Code 7 Throttle angle.
Code 8 TDC position.
Code 9 Cylinder position sensor.
Code 10 Intake air temperature.
Code 13 MAP sensor.
Code 14 Electronic air control.
Code 15 Ignition output signal.
Code 16 Fuel Injector.
Code 19 Lock-up control solenoid valve.
Code 20 Electric load.
Code 21 Spool solenoid valve.
Code 22 Valve timing oil pressure switch.
Codes 30, 31 AT-FI signal.
Code 41 Oxygen sensor heater.
Code 43 Fuel supply system.
Code 48 LAF sensor.

COMPUTER DIAGNOSTIC CODES Continued

Prelude 2 × 1V

Code 1 Oxygen content.
Code 2 Vehicle speed sensor.
Codes 3, 5 Manifold absolute pressure.
Code 4 Vaccum switch signal.
Code 6 Coolant temperature sensor.
Code 8 Ignition coil signal.
Code 10 Intake air temperature.
Code 14 Electronic air control.

SENSORS, INPUT

TEMPERATURE SENSORS

Engine	Year	Sensor	Resistance Ohms @ deg. F/C
All FI	1985-92	Coolant, Intake Air	15,000-20,000 @ −4/−20 5000-7000 @ 32/0 2000-4000 @ 68/20 900-1200 @ 104/40 300-400 @ 176/80 100-300 @ 248/115

MANIFOLD ABSOLUTE AND BAROMETRIC PRESSURE SENSORS

Engine	Year	Sensor	Voltage @ in./mm Hg
All FI	1985-92	MAP, Barometric	2.7-2.9 @ 0/0 2.3-2.5 @ 5/127 1.8-2.0 @ 10/255 1.4-1.6 @ 15/380 0.9-1.1 @ 20/510
1958cc 2×1V	1988-90	MAP	2.7-2.9 @ 0/0 2.3-2.5 @ 5/127 1.8-2.0 @ 10/255 1.4-1.6 @ 15/380 0.9-1.1 @ 20/510

THROTTLE POSITION SENSOR

Engine	Year	Resistance (ohms)	Voltage Idle	Voltage WOT
1488cc FI, 1955cc FI	1985-87	3200-7200†	.48-.52†	4.0†
All FI	1988-92	—	0.5*	4.5*

† Measured between yellow and green wires of TPS.
* Measured between left and right terminals of TPS connector.

CRANKSHAFT SENSOR

See UNDERHOOD SERVICE INSTRUCTIONS at the beginning of this section for test/adjustment diagrams.

Other ignition sensors, see Distributor Pickup.

Measured between brown and blue terminals of crank angle sensor.

Engine	Year	Resistance (ohms)
1488cc FI	1985-87	6500-8500

ACTUATORS, OUTPUT

IDLE SPEED CONTROL SOLENOID

Engine	Year	Resistance (ohms)
All FI	1987-90	8-15

ENGINE IDENTIFICATION

To identify an engine by the manufacturer's code, follow the steps designated by the numbered blocks.

V.I.N. PLATE LOCATION:
Top of instrument panel visible through windshield.

1 MODEL YEAR IDENTIFICATION:

Excel, Sonata — 10th character of V.I.N.
All others — Check emissions certification decal or 10th character of V.I.N.

1992 — N; 1991 — M; 1990 — L;
1989 — K; 1988 — J; 1987 — H;
1986 — G; 1985 — F; 1984 — E.

2 ENGINE CODE LOCATIONS:

Pony, uses 1.4L & 1.6L eng.
Stellar, 1985-86, uses 1.6L eng.; 1987-88, 8th character of V.I.N.
Others — 8th character of V.I.N.

4 ENGINE IDENTIFICATION

YEAR	3 ENGINE CODE	CYL.	DISPL. liters	cc	Fuel System	HP
1992	J	4	1.5	1468	MFI	81
	R	4	1.6	1597	MFI	105, 113
	F	4	2.0	1997	MFI	128
	T	6	3.0	2972	MFI	142
1991	J	4	1.5	1468	MFI	81
	S	4	2.4	2351	MFI	116
	T	6	3.0	2972	MFI	142
1990	J	4	1.5	1468	MFI	81
	S	4	2.4	2351	MFI	116
	T	6	3.0	2972	MFI	142
1989	J	4	1.5	1468	2V	68
	S	4	2.4	2351	MFI	116
	T	6	3.0	2972	MFI	142

4 ENGINE IDENTIFICATION

YEAR	3 ENGINE CODE	CYL.	DISPL. liters	cc	Fuel System	HP
1988	J	4	1.5	1468	2V	68
	F	4	2.0	1997	MFI	100
1987	—	4	1.4	1439	2V	70
	J	4	1.5	1468	2V	68
	—	4	1.6	1597	2V	74
	F	4	2.0	1997	2V	NA
1986	—	4	1.4	1439	2V	70
	J	4	1.5	1468	2V	68
	—	4	1.6	1597	2V	74
1985	—	4	1.4	1439	2V	70
	—	4	1.6	1597	2V	74
1984	—	4	1.4	1439	2V	70

MFI — Multiport Fuel Injection. **2V — Two Venturi Carburetor.**

UNDERHOOD SERVICE SPECIFICATIONS

HIITU1   HIITU1

CYLINDER NUMBERING SEQUENCE

4-CYL. FIRING ORDER: 1 3 4 2

V6 FIRING ORDER:
1 2 3 4 5 6

— Front of car —

| 1986-92 Excel, Scoupe 1468cc | 1984-87 Pony 1439cc; Pony, Stellar 1597cc | 1992 1597cc Elantra, 1997cc Sonata | 1989-91 Sonata 2351cc | 1989-92 Sonata 2972cc |

— TIMING MARK —

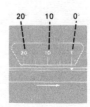

| 1986-92 Excel, Scoupe 1468cc, Elantra 1597cc, 1989-92 Sonata 1997cc, 2351cc | 1984-87 Pony 1439cc; Pony, Stellar 1597cc | 1989-92 Sonata 2972cc |

UNDERHOOD SERVICE SPECIFICATIONS

ELECTRICAL AND IGNITION SYSTEMS

BATTERY

Negative ground. BCI equivalent shown, size may vary from original equipment. Holddown and tray are designed to accept a Group 24 replacement battery.

Check clearance before replacing, holddown may need to be modified.

Engine	Year	STANDARD BCI Group No.	STANDARD Crank. Perf.	OPTIONAL BCI Group No.	OPTIONAL Crank. Perf.
1439cc	1984-87	45	420	—	—
1468cc	1986-91	25*	420*	—	—
Canada	1986-88	45	420	—	—
Canada	1989-91	24	580	—	—
1597cc Pony	1984-87	45	420	—	—
Stellar	1985-86	22NF	420	—	—
1997cc Stellar	1987	45	420	—	—
2350cc	1989-91	25	420	—	—
Canada	1989-91	24	580	—	—
2972cc	1990-91	24	540	—	—
Canada	1990-91	24	580	—	—

* Some models use a Group 35.

ALTERNATOR

Engine	Year	Rated Output (amps)	Test Output (amps)
1439cc	1984-87	70	—
1468cc	1986-88	55	—
1468cc	1986-88	60	—
1468cc	1989	60	42 @ 2500
1468cc	1990-92	75	53 @ 2500
1597cc	1985-87	50	—
1597cc	1985-87	60	—
1597cc	1986-87	70	—
1597cc	1986-87	55	—
1597cc	1992	75	53 @ 2500
1997cc	1987-88	70	—
1997cc	1992	75, 90	53 @ 2500
2350cc	1989-91	75	53 @ 2500
2972cc	1990-92	90	53 @ 2500

REGULATOR

Engine	Year	Voltage Setting	Test Temp. (deg. F/C)
1439cc	1984-87	14.4-14.6	86/30
1468cc	1986-88	14.4-14.6	86/30
1468cc	1989	14.4-15.6	−4/−20
		14.2-15.2	68/20
		13.8-15.1	140/60
		13.6-15.0	176/80
1597cc w/50 amp. alt.	1985-86	14.4-14.7	86/30
1597cc w/60 amp. alt.	1985-86	14.4-14.6	86/30
1997cc	1987-88	14.4-14.6	86/30
All others	1989-92	14.2-15.4	−4/−20
		13.9-14.9	68/20
		13.4-14.6	140/60
		13.1-14.5	176/80

STARTER

Engine	Year	Cranking Voltage (min. volts)	Ampere Draw @ Cranking Speed
1439cc, 1597cc	1984-87	9.0	150

SPARK PLUGS

Engine	Year	Gap (inches)	Gap (mm)	Torque (ft-lb)
1439cc	1984-87	.028-.031	.70-.80	18
1468cc ex. Canada	1986-87	.039-.043	1.0-1.1	15-21
1468cc Canada	1986-87	.028-.031	.70-.80	15-21
1468cc	1988-92	.039-.043	1.0-1.1	15-21
1597cc	1985-87	.028-.031	.70-.80	18
1597cc	1992	.039-.043	1.0-1.1	15-21

SPARK PLUGS Continued

Engine	Year	Gap (inches)	Gap (mm)	Torque (ft-lb)
1997cc	1987	.028-.031	.70-.80	18
1997cc	1992	.039-.043	1.0-1.1	15-21
2350cc	1989-91	.039-.043	1.0-1.1	15-21
2972cc	1990-92	.039-.043	1.0-1.1	15-21

IGNITION COIL

Winding resistance (ohms @ 68°F or 20°C)

1992 1597cc, 1997cc: Primary windings are measured between terminals 1 & 3 and 2 & 3 (diagonally) of 4-terminal coil connector. Secondary windings are measured between adjoining coil high tension towers.

Engine	Year	Windings	Resistance (ohms)
1439cc, 1597cc	1984-87	Primary	1.26-1.54
		Secondary	8,700-11,700
1468cc	1986-89	Primary	1.1-1.3
		Secondary	11,600-15,800
1468cc	1990-92	Primary	.72-.88
		Secondary	10,300-13,900
1597cc	1992	Primary	.77-.95
		Secondary	10,300-13,900
1997cc	1987	Primary	1.3-1.8
		Secondary	11,650-15,760
1997cc	1992	Primary	.77-.95
		Secondary	10,300-13,900
2350cc	1989-91	Primary	.72-.88
		Secondary	10,890-13,310
2972cc	1990-92	Primary	.72-.88
		Secondary	10,300-13,900

DISTRIBUTOR PICKUP

Engine	Year	Resistance (ohms)	Air Gap (in./mm)
1468cc	1986-89	—	.030/.80
1997cc	1987-88	—	.030/.80

IGNITION POINTS

Engine	Year	Gap (inches)	Gap (mm)	Dwell (degrees)	Spring Tension (ounces)
1439cc	1984-87	.018-.022	.45-.55	49-55	—
1597cc	1985-87	.018-.022	.45-.55	49-55	—

IGNITION RESISTOR

Engine	Year	Type	Resistance (ohms)	Temperature (deg. F/C)
1439cc, 1597cc	1984-87	Unit	1.2-1.5	68/20
1468cc	1986-89	Unit	1.2-1.6	68/20
1997cc	1987	Unit	1.15-1.55	68/20

BASE TIMING

Set timing at slow idle and Before Top Dead Center, unless otherwise specified.

Carburetted:
U.S. models except high altitude, leave vacuum hoses connected.
High altitude and Canadian models, disconnect and plug distributor vacuum hose.

Fuel Injected:
1468cc, 2350cc, ground ignition timing connector.
1597cc, 1997cc, 2972cc, jumper terminals of ignition timing connector.
All models, when ignition timing connector is ungrounded or not jumpered, timing should be at Check value.

Engine	Year	Man. Trans. (degrees)	Auto. Trans. (degrees)
1439cc	1984-87	5 ±1	5 ±1
1468cc	1986-87	5 ±2	5 ±2
California	1986-87	3 ±2	3 ±2
High Altitude	1986-87	8 ±2	8 ±2
Canada	1986-87	4 ±2	4 ±2
1468cc: Set	1988-89	5 ±2	5 ±2
1468cc: Set	1990-92	5 ±2	5 ±2
Check	1990-92	10 ±2	10 ±2

UNDERHOOD SERVICE SPECIFICATIONS

BASE TIMING Continued

Engine	Year	Man. Trans. (degrees)	Auto. Trans. (degrees)
1597cc	1985-87	5 ±2	5 ±2
1597cc: Set	1992	5 ±2	5 ±2
Check	1992	8 ±2	8 ±2
1997cc	1987-88	5 ±1	5 ±1
1997cc: Set	1992	5 ±2	5 ±2
Check	1992	8 ±2	8 ±2
2350cc: Set	1989-91	5 ±2	5 ±2
Check	1989-91	10 ±2	10 ±2
2972cc: Set	1990-92	5 ±2	5 ±2
Check	1990-92	—	15 ±2

DISTRIBUTOR TIMING ADVANCE
Engine degrees at engine rpm, no load, in addition to base timing setting.

Engine	Trans-mission	Year	Distributor Number	Degrees @ 2500 RPM Total	Degrees @ 2500 RPM Centrifugal
1439cc	MT & AT	1984-87	—	23.4-33.4	6.4-10.4
1468cc Fed.	MT	1986-87	21370	27-35	4-8
1468cc Fed.	AT	1986-87	21380	25-33	4-8
1468cc Calif.	MT & AT	1986-87	21350, 60	25-33	4-8
1468cc Canada	MT & AT	1986-87	—	29.9-37.9	3.9-7.9
1468cc Fed.	MT	1987-89	21430	24-32	3-7
1468cc Fed.	AT	1987-89	21440	21-29	3-7
1468cc Calif.	MT & AT	1987-89	21410, 20	21-29	3-7
1468cc Canada	MT	1987-88	—	21-25	0
1468cc Canada	AT	1987-88	—	18-22	0
1597cc	MT & AT	1985-87	—	23.4-33.4	6.4-10.4
1997cc	MT & AT	1987	—	21.4-29.4	1.4-5.4

FUEL SYSTEM

FUEL SYSTEM PRESSURE

Engine	Year	Pressure PSI	Pressure RPM
Carburetted:			
1439cc	1984-88	2.7-3.7	idle
1468cc	1986-89	2.8-3.6 ■	idle
1597cc	1985-87	3.7-5.1	idle
1997cc	1987	2.7-3.7	idle
Fuel Injected:			
1997cc	1988	35.6-38.4*	idle
		28.4†	idle
All	1989-92	46-49*	idle
		39 approx.†	idle

* Vacuum hose disconnected from fuel pressure regulator.
† Vacuum hose connected to fuel pressure regulator.
■ Fuel return line pinched off.

IDLE SPEED W/O COMPUTER CONTROL
To set idle speed, turn idle speed screw to obtain specified value. Adjust solenoids, as equipped, to obtain specified speed-up speed.

Midpoint of range given is the preferred setting speed.

Engine	Year	SLOW Man. Trans.	SLOW Auto. Trans.	FAST Man. Trans.	FAST Auto. Trans.	Step of Cam
1439cc	1984-87	800-850	800-850 N	—	—	—
1468cc U.S.	1986-87	600-800	650-850 N	—	—	—
Speed-up	1986-87	850	850 N			
1468cc Canada	1986-87	820-880	820-880 N	—	—	—
Speed-up	1986-87	890-910	940-960 N			
1468cc	1988	650-850	650-850 N	2800	2700 N	Second
	1989	700-900	700-900 N	2800	2700 N	Second
PS, Elec. speed-up	1988-89	750-950	750-950 N			
AC speed-up	1988-89	850-900	850-900 N			

IDLE SPEED W/O COMPUTER CONTROL Continued

Engine	Year	SLOW Man. Trans.	SLOW Auto. Trans.	FAST Man. Trans.	FAST Auto. Trans.	Step of Cam
1597cc	1985-87	800-850	800-850 N	—	—	—
1997cc	1987	725-775	725-775 N	—	—	—

IDLE SPEED W/COMPUTER CONTROL
1468cc, 2350cc: Turn ignition on for 20 seconds. Disconnect ISC and start engine. Adjust to specified setting speed.

1597cc, 1997cc, 2972cc: Jumper ignition timing connector terminals, and Self Diagnostic check terminal (10 and ground of ALDL).

Engine	Year	Setting Speed	Checking Speed
1468cc MT	1990-92	600-800	600-800
AT	1990-92	600-800 N	600-800 N
1597cc MT	1992	700-800	650-850
AT	1992	700-800 N	650-850 N
1997cc MT	1988	700	700-800
AT	1988	700 N	700-800 N
1997cc MT	1992	700-800	650-850
AT	1992	700-800 N	650-850 N
2350cc MT	1989-91	650-850	650-850
AT	1989-91	650-850 N	650-850 N
2972cc AT	1990-92	650-750 N	600-800 N

ENGINE MECHANICAL

TIGHTENING TORQUES

Engine	Year	Torque Ft-lbs/Nm Cylinder Head*	Intake Manifold	Exhaust Manifold	Crankshaft Pulley	Water Pump
1439cc, 1597cc	1984-87	52/71	13/17	13/17	47/64	22/29
1468cc	1986-91	51-54/ 69-74	12-14/ 16-19	12-14/ 16-20	9-11/ 12-15, small 51-72/ 70-100, large	9-11/ 12-15, short 14-20/ 20-27, long
1597cc	1992	65-72/ 88-98	11-14/ 15-20	18-22/ 25-30	14-22/ 20-29, small 80-94/ 110-130, large	9-11/ 12-15, short 14-20/ 20-26, long
1997cc	1987-88	69/93	13/18	13/18	18/25	—
1997cc	1992	76-83/ 105-115	11-14/ 15-20	11-14/ 15-20	14-22/ 20-29, small 80-94/ 110-130, large	9-11/ 12-15, small 14-20/ 20-29, long
2350cc	1989-91	65-72/ 90-100	11-14/ 15-19	11-14/ 15-19	14-22/ 20-30	9-11/ 12-15, short 14-20/ 20-27, long
2972cc	1990-91	65-72/ 88-98	11-14/ 15-20	11-14/ 15-20	108-116/ 147-157	14-20/ 20-26
2972cc	1992	76-83/ 105-115	11-14/ 15-20	11-16/ 15-22	108-116/ 147-157	14-20/ 20-26

* Engine cold.

VALVE CLEARANCE
Engine hot, measured at valve stem.

Engine	Year	Intake (inches)	Intake (mm)	Exhaust (inches)	Exhaust (mm)
1437cc, 1468cc, 1597cc, 1997cc SOHC	1984-92	.006	.15	.010†	.25†
2350cc	1989-91	—*	—*	—	—

† 2V engines, includes jet valve.
* Jet valve, .010 in./.25 mm.

COMPRESSION PRESSURE

At cranking speed, engine warm, throttle open.

Engine	Year	PSI	Maximum Variation PSI
1468cc	1986-89	164 @ 250	—
1468cc	1990-92	171-192	14
1597cc	1985-87	156	—
1597cc	1992	171-192	14
1997cc	1987-88	171 @ 250	—
1997cc	1992	171-192	14
2972cc	1990-91	149-170	14

BELT TENSION

Deflection method: With 22 pounds of pressure applied midway between pulleys on longest belt segment.

Engine	Year	Alternator	Power Steering	Air Cond.	Air Pump
All (mm)	1984-85	9	9	9	9
All (inches)	1984-85	3/8	3/8	3/8	3/8
All (mm)	1986-92	7-9	7-9	7-9	7-9
All (inches)	1986-92	1/4-3/8	1/4-3/8	1/4-3/8	1/4-3/8

ENGINE COMPUTER SYSTEM

COMPUTER DIAGNOSTIC CODES

1988 Stellar

With ignition off, connect an analog voltmeter to the diagnostic connector located behind right side strut tower. Turn ignition on. Codes will be displayed as sweeps of voltmeter needle.

The voltmeter will sweep in long (+) or short (–) pulses over a ten-second period. Each period is separated by six-second intervals. The following deciphers each code:

10000 = 1	**Code 1** Oxygen sensor
01000 = 2	**Code 2** Ignition signal
11000 = 3	**Code 3** Airflow sensor
00100 = 4	**Code 4** Atmospheric pressure sensor
10100 = 5	**Code 5** Throttle position sensor
01100 = 6	**Code 6** ISC motor position sensor
11100 = 7	**Code 7** Coolant temperature sensor
00010 = 8	**Code 8** TDC sensor
00000 = 9	**Code 9** Normal

1989 Sonata, 1990-92 All

Access diagnostic connector in glove box or driver's side kick panel and connect on analog voltmeter to the upper right (+) and lower left (–) cavities. Turn ignition on. Voltmeter will sweep in long pulses, indicating tenths; and short pulses, indicating ones.

Code 11 Oxygen sensor	**Code 24** Vehicle speed sensor
Code 12 Airflow sensor	**Code 25** Barometric pressure sensor
Code 13 Intake air temperature sensor	**Code 41** Injector
Code 14 Throttle position sensor	**Code 42** Fuel pump
Code 15 Motor position sensor	**Code 43** EGR
Code 21 Coolant temperature sensor	**Code 44** Ignition coil
Code 22 Crank angle sensor	**One long sweep**—ECU
Code 23 TDC sensor	**Continuous pulsing**—System normal

SENSORS, INPUT

TEMPERATURE SENSORS

Engine	Year	Sensor	Resistance Ohms @ deg. F/C
All	1986-92	Coolant	5900 @ 32/0
			2500 @ 68/20
			1100 @ 104/40
			300 @ 176/80
1468cc	1986-89	Intake Air	2450 @ 68/20
2350cc	1989	Intake Air†	5900 @ 32/0
			2500 @ 68/20
			1100 @ 104/40
			300 @ 176/80
All	1990-92	Intake Air*	5400-6600 @ 32/0
			2300-3000 @ 68/20
			310-430 @ 176/80

† Measured between terminals 2 & 4 of airflow sensor.
* Measured between terminals 4 & 6 (lower right & left) at airflow sensor.

SENSORS, INPUT Continued

PRESSURE SENSORS

Engine	Year	Sensor	Voltage @ in./mm Hg
All FI	1989-91	Barometric*	.79 @ 2.8/70
			1.84 @ 7/175
			4.00 @ 14.2/330

* Measured between terminals 5 & 6 (lower middle & lower left) of airflow sensor.

THROTTLE POSITION SENSOR

1986-89 1468cc: Back out speed screws enough to close throttle valve. Connect DVOM between two lower horizontal blades of TPS. Adjust screw on linkage to specified voltage.

1989-91 early 1468cc, 2350cc: Measure voltage along single upper (–) and lower left (+) terminals of TPS.

1991 late-92 1468cc, 1597cc, 1997cc: Measure voltage between first and third terminals of TPS connector.

2972cc: Measured between upper and lower right terminals of TPS connector.

Model	Year	TPS Voltage	
		Idle	WOT
1468cc	1986-89	.25	—
1468cc	1990-91	.48-.52	4.5-5.5
1597cc	1992	.48-.52	4.5-5.5
1997cc	1988	.50	—
1997cc	1992	.48-.52	4.5-5.5
2350cc	1989-91	.48-.52	—
2972cc	1989-92	.48-.52	4.5-5.5

AIRFLOW SENSOR

Measured between terminals 3 & 6 (upper and lower left) of airflow sensor.

Engine	Year	Volts
2350cc	1989	2.2-3.2
All	1990-91	2.7-3.2

Engine	Year	Frequency Hz @ RPM
1468cc, 1597cc	1992	27-33 @ idle
		60-80 @ 2000
1997cc	1992	25-50 @ idle
		70-90 @ 2000
2972cc	1992	30-45 @ idle
		85-105 @ 2000

ACTUATORS, OUTPUT

IDLE SPEED CONTROL SOLENOID

1468cc, 2350cc: Measured between two upper terminals of ISC connector.

1597cc, 1997cc, 2972cc: Measured between center and either left or right terminals on both rows of 6-terminal ISC connector.

Engine	Year	Resistance @ 68°F (20°C) (ohms)
1468cc, 2350cc	1989-92	5-35
1597cc, 1997cc, 2972cc	1990-92	28-33

MIXTURE CONTROL SOLENOID

Engine	Year	Resistance (ohms)
1468cc	1986-89	54-66

COMPUTER TIMING ADVANCE

With engine at operating temperature, check advance at idle and 2000 rpm. Specifications include initial timing. At high altitudes, add 5°.

Engine	Year	Degrees	
		Idle	2000
1468cc	1990-92	8-12	26-34
1597cc	1992	5-15	32-40
1997cc	1992	5-15	33-41
2350cc	1989-91	5-15	30-40
2972cc	1990-92	5-15	30-40

ENGINE IDENTIFICATION

To identify an engine by the manufacturer's code, follow the four steps designated by the numbered blocks.

V.I.N. PLATE LOCATION:

Top of instrument panel visible through windshield.

1 MODEL YEAR IDENTIFICATION:

10th character of V.I.N.

1992 — N; 1991 — M; 1990 — L;
1989 — K; 1988 — J; 1987 — H;
1986 — G; 1985 — F; 1984 — E;
1983 — D.

2 ENGINE CODE LOCATION:

8th character of V.I.N.

4 ENGINE / ENGINE IDENTIFICATION

YEAR	CODE	CYL.	DISPL. liters	cc	Fuel System	HP
1992	6	4	1.6	1588	MFI	95
	4	4	1.6 T	1588 T	MFI	160
	8	4	1.8	—	MFI	140
	L	4	2.3	2254	2V	96
	E	4	2.6	2559	MFI	120
	Z	6	3.1	3137	TBI	120
	—	6	3.2	—	MFI	—
1991	6	4	1.6	1588	MFI	95
	5	4	1.6	1588	MFI	130
	4	4	1.6 T	1588T	MFI	160
	L	4	2.3	2254	2V	96
	E	4	2.6	2559	MFI	120
	Z	6	3.1	3137	TBI	120
1990	6	4	1.6	1588	MFI	95
	5	4	1.6	1588	MFI	125
	L	4	2.3	2254	2V	96
	E	4	2.6	2559	MFI	120
	R	6	2.8	2827	TBI	120
1989	7	4	1.5	1471	2V	70
	9	4	1.5 T	1471 T	MFI	110
	5	4	1.6	1588	MFI	125
	F	4	2.0 T	1994 T	MFI	140
	L	4	2.3	2254	2V	96
	L	4	2.3	2254	MFI	110
	E	4	2.6	2559	MFI	120
	R	6	2.8	2827	TBI	120
1988	7	4	1.5	1471	2V	70
	9	4	1.5 T	1471 T	MFI	110
	F	4	2.0 T	1994 T	MFI	140
	L	4	2.3	2254	2V	96
	L	4	2.3	2254	MFI	110
	E	4	2.6	2559	MFI	120
1987	7	4	1.5	1471	2V	70
	9	4	1.5 T	1471 T	MFI	110

YEAR	CODE	CYL.	DISPL. liters	cc	Fuel System	HP
1987 Cont'd.	A	4	1.9	1949	2V	82
	A	4	1.9	1949	MFI	90
	F	4	2.0 T	1994 T	MFI	140
	S	4	2.2 D	2238 D	MFI	62
	U	4	2.2 TD	2238 TD	MFI	80
	L	4	2.3	2254	2V	96
1986	7	4	1.5	1471	2V	70
	A	4	1.9	1949	2V	82
	A	4	1.9	1949	MFI	90
	F	4	2.0 T	1994 T	MFI	140
	S	4	2.2 D	2238 D	MFI	62
	U	4	2.2 D	2238 D	MFI	80
	L	4	2.3	2254	2V	96
1985	K	4	1.5	1471	2V	70
	B	4	1.8	1817	2V	78
	A	4	1.9	1949	2V	82
	A	4	1.9	1949	MFI	90
	F	4	2.0 T	1994 T	MFI	140
	S	4	2.2 D	2238 D	MFI	62
1984	B	4	1.8	1817	2V	78
	P	4	1.8 D	1817 D	MFI	51
	A	4	1.9	1949	2V	82
	A	4	1.9	1949	MFI	90
	S	4	2.2 D	2238 D	MFI	62
1983	B	4	1.8	1817	2V	78
	P	4	1.8 D	1817 D	MFI	51
	A	4	1.9	1949	2V	82
	A	4	1.9	1949	MFI	90
	S	4	2.2 D	2238 D	MFI	62

TBI — Throttle Body Injection.
2V — Two Venturi Carburetor.
TD — Turbo Diesel.
MFI — Multiport Fuel Injection.
D — Diesel.   T — Turbo

UNDERHOOD SERVICE SPECIFICATIONS

IUITU1

CYLINDER NUMBERING SEQUENCE

4-CYL. FIRING ORDER: 1 3 4 2

6-CYL. FIRING ORDER: 1 2 3 4 5 6

— Front of car —

1983-85
I-Mark 1817cc Gasoline,
1983-87
Pickup 1817cc, 1949cc,
1983-87
Impulse 1949cc FI

1985
I-Mark 1471cc

1986-92
I-Mark, Impulse,
Stylus 1471cc,
1588cc DOHC

1990-92
Stylus
1588cc SOHC

1985-89
Impulse 1994cc Turbo,
1986-92
Amigo, Pickup,
Trooper, Rodeo
2254cc, 2559cc

Front of car

1989-92
Pickup, Trooper, Rodeo
2.8L, 3.1L

TIMING MARK

BTDC 20° 10° 0°

1985-89 I-Mark 1471cc,
1985-89 Impulse 1994cc Turbo,
1989-92
I-Mark, Impulse, Stylus 1588cc

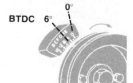

BTDC 6°   0°

1983-87
1817cc, 1949cc

BTDC 12 8 4 0

1986-92
Impulse, Trooper, Pickup
2254cc, 2559cc

BTDC
16°
12°
8°
4°
0°

1989-92
Pickup, Trooper, Rodeo
2.8L, 3.1L

ELECTRICAL AND IGNITION SYSTEMS

BATTERY

BCI equivalent shown, size may vary from original equipment. Check clearance before replacing, holddown may need to be modified.

	STANDARD		OPTIONAL	
Engine	BCI Group No.	Crank. Perf.	BCI Group No.	Crank. Perf.
1983-89 I-Mark: Gas	21R	320	—	—
Diesel	24	500	—	—
1983-85 Pickup, Trooper: Gas	21	320	—	—
Diesel	27	465	—	—
1986-88 Pickup, Trooper: Gas	21	320	25	380
Diesel	27	655	—	—
1989-92 Pickup, Trooper: MT	25	360	—	—
AT	24	585	—	—
Amigo	25	360	—	—
1983-87 Impulse	24	370	—	—
1988-89 Impulse: w/MT	25	360	—	—
w/AT	24	490	—	—
1990-92 Stylus, Impulse	35	350	—	—

ALTERNATOR

Application	Rated Output (amps @ eng. rpm)	Test Output (amps @ eng. rpm)
1983-89 Impulse	60	30 @ 2000
Turbo	75	30 @ 2000
I-Mark FWD	45,60	30 @ 2000
1990-92 Stylus, Impulse	75	*
1983-87 Pickup, Trooper 4-cyl.	40,50	30 @ 2000
1988-92 Amigo, Pickup, Trooper,		
Rodeo: 4-cyl.	50,60	30 @ 2000
V6	85	*

* Output at 2000 rpm must be within 15 amps of rated output.

REGULATOR

Application	Test Temp. (deg. F/C)	Voltage Setting
1983-84	70/21	13.8-14.8
1985-87 I-Mark FWD	—	14.2-14.8
Impulse	—	13.8-14.4
Turbo	—	14.05-15.03
I-Mark RWD, Pickup Gas	70/21	13.8-14.8
Pickup Diesel	—	14.0-14.6
1988-89 Impulse	—	14.05-15.03
Trooper V6	—	13.0-16.0
Others	—	14.2-14.8
1990-92 Amigo, Pickup	—	13.0-15.5
Rodeo, 4-cyl.	—	13.0-15.0
V6	—	13.0-16.0
Trooper, 4-cyl.	—	14.2-14.8
V6	—	13.0-16.0
Stylus, Impulse	—	13.0-16.0

STARTER

Model	Cranking Voltage (min. volts)	Maximum Ampere Draw
1983 I-Mark, Pickup Gas	7.4	200
I-Mark Diesel	7.5	300
Pickup Diesel	8.8	300
1983-87 Impulse	9.15	200
Turbo	8.0	230
1984-85 I-Mark RWD Gas	7.4	200
Diesel	7.5	300
1984-88 Pickup, Trooper Gas:		
1.9L	9.15	200
2.3L	8.0	230
Diesel	7.5	500
1985-89 I-Mark: MT	9.5	150
AT, Turbo	9.5	270
DOHC	8.0	280
1988-89 Impulse, Trooper 4-cyl.	8.0	230
Trooper V6	9.0	—

STARTER Continued

Model	Cranking Voltage (min. volts)	Maximum Ampere Draw
1990-92 Amigo, Pickup, Trooper:		
4-cyl.	8.0	230
V6	9.0	—
Rodeo, 4-cyl.	8.0	280
V6	9.0	—
Stylus, MT	8.7	230
AT	8.0	280
Impulse, MT	8.7	230
AT	8.5	330
Turbo	8.0	280

SPARK PLUGS

Engine	Gap (inches)	Gap (mm)	Torque (ft-lb)
1983-88 All	.039-.043	1.0-1.1	—
1989-90 2.8L	.045	1.14	—
Others	.039-.043	1.0-1.1	—
1991-92 1.6L, 1.8L	.040	1.05	14
Turbo	.030	.75	14
2.3L, 2.6L	.040	1.05	14
2.8L, 3.1L	.045	1.14	14
3.2L	.040	1.05	14

IGNITION COIL

Engine	Year	Windings	Resistance (ohms)
1471cc	1985	Primary	1.10-1.40
		Secondary	12,100-14,900
1471cc 2V	1986-89	Primary	1.2-1.5
		Secondary	10,200-13,500
1471cc Turbo, 1588cc	1987-89	Primary	0-2
		Secondary	6000-30,000
1588cc ex. Turbo, 1.8L	1990-92	Primary	1.2-1.5
		Secondary	10,200-13,800
1817cc, 1949cc, 1994cc, 2254cc FI	1983-89	Primary	1.13-1.53
		Secondary	10,200-13,800
2254cc 2V	1986-92	Primary	1.1-1.4
		Secondary	8600-13,000
2559cc	1988-92	Primary	.81-.99
		Secondary	7500-11,300
V6 2.8L, 3.1L	1989-92	Primary	0.6-1.0
		Secondary	6500-10,200

DISTRIBUTOR PICKUP

Model	Resistance (ohms)	Air Gap (in./mm)
1471cc 2V, 1817cc, 1949cc 2V	140-180	.008-.016/.2-.4
1471cc Turbo, 1588cc, 2.8L, 3.1L	500-1500	
2254cc 2V	—	.012-.020/.3-.5

BASE TIMING

1471cc 2V, 1817cc 2V, 1949cc 2V, 2254cc 2V: Disconnect and plug distributor vacuum hose.

1588cc, 1.8L: Jumper first and third terminals of ALDL connector by passenger side kick panel

Others: Set timing to specified value.

2.8L, 3.1L: Disconnect set timing connector by distributor.

Engine	Year	Man. Trans. (degrees)	Auto. Trans. (degrees)
1471cc: Set	1985-89	3 @ 600-700	3 @ 850-950 N
Check*	1985-89	15 @ 750	10 @ 1000
1588cc, 1.8L	1990-92	10 ± 1	10 ± 1
1817cc, 1949cc 2V	1983-87	6	6
High alt.	1983-87	10	10
1949cc FI, 1994cc, 2254cc FI	1983-89	12	12
2254cc 2V	1986-87	12	12
2254cc 2V	1988-92	6	6
2559cc	1988-92	12	12
2.8L, 3.1L	1989-92	10	10

* With vacuum hose connected.

UNDERHOOD SERVICE SPECIFICATIONS

IUITU3   IUITU3

DISTRIBUTOR TIMING ADVANCE

Engine degrees at engine rpm, no load, in addition to basic timing setting.
Mechanical advance distributors only.

Engine	Trans-mission	Year	Distributor Number	Degrees @ 2500 RPM Total	Centrifugal
1471cc	MT	1985	0311	31.1-38.1	5.1-8.1
1471cc	AT	1985	—	29.1-36.1	5.1-8.1
1471cc 2V	MT	1986-89	0401	30.5-38.5	4.5-8.5
1471cc 2V	AT	1986-89	0410	28.5-36.5	4.5-8.5
1817cc	MT & AT	1983-85	5930	26.5-34.5	7.5-11.5
1949cc 2V	MT	1983-87	0140	21.5-29.5	6.5-10.5
1949cc 2V	MT & AT	1983-86	0160	—	—
2254cc	MT	1986-87	8941672490	—	—
2254cc	MT	1986-87	8941367650	17.5-25.5	6-10
2254cc	MT & AT	1986-87	8941619730	24-32	7.5-11.5

FUEL SYSTEM

FUEL SYSTEM PRESSURE

Engine	Year	Pressure PSI	RPM
Carburetted & TBI:			
1471cc 2V	1985-89	3.8-4.7	idle
1817cc, 1949cc 2V	1983-87	3.6	idle
2.8L, 3.1L	1989-92	9-13	idle
		13-18 ★	idle

★ With fuel return hose briefly restricted.

Engine	Year	Pressure PSI*	Pressure PSI†	Fuel Pump PSI
1471cc Turbo	1987-89	35.6	28.4	—
1588cc ex. Turbo	1989-92	35-38	25-30	—
1588cc Turbo	1991-92	—	40-47	65
2559cc	1988-92	42	35	43

* Pressure regulator vacuum hose disconnected.
† Pressure regulator vacuum hose connected.

IDLE SPEED W/O COMPUTER CONTROL

1471cc 2V, 1817cc 2V, 1949cc 2V, 2254cc 2V: Disconnect and plug distributor, canister purge, and EGR vacuum hoses. Set idle to specified value. With AC, turn AC to maximum and adjust speed-up speed to specified value with solenoid fully extended.

1471cc Turbo, 1949cc FI, 1994cc, 2254cc FI: Disconnect wiring connector of vacuum solenoid valve and adjust idle speed by turning screw on throttle body.

2559cc: Disconnect and plug canister purge and EGR vacuum hoses. Disconnect pressure regulator vacuum solenoid valve electrical connector.

All Diesel: Set idle to specified value. To adjust fast idle, disconnect vacuum hoses from vacuum switch valve and connect together. Adjust speed by turning nut on vacuum switch. Midpoint of range given is the preferred setting.

Engine	Year	SLOW Man. Trans.	SLOW Auto. Trans.	FAST Man. Trans.	FAST Auto. Trans.	Step of Cam
1471cc 2V	1985-88	750	1000 N	—	—	—
speed-up	1985-88	850	980 N			
1471cc 2V	1989	750	1000 N	3700	4100	High
speed-up	1989	850	980 N			
1817cc I-Mark	1983-85	850-950	850-950 N	3200	3200 N	High
speed-up	1983-85	850-950	850-950 N			
1817cc Diesel	1983-84	575-675	675-775 N	900-950	900-950 N	—
1949cc Pickup	1983-87	750-850	850-950 N	3200	3200 N	High
Calif.	1983-87	850-950	850-950 N	3200	3200	High
speed-up, all	1983-87	850-950	850-950 N			
1949cc, 1994cc Impulse	1983-87	850-950	850-950			
2238cc Diesel	1983	700-800	700-800 N	900-950	900-950 N	

IDLE SPEED W/O COMPUTER CONTROL Continued

Engine	Year	SLOW Man. Trans.	SLOW Auto. Trans.	FAST Man. Trans.	FAST Auto. Trans.	Step of Cam
2254cc 2V	1986-87	750-850	850-950 N	—	—	
Calif.	1986-87	850-950	850-950 N	—	—	
speed-up, all	1986-87	850-950	850-950 N			
2254cc 2V	1988-92	850-950	850-950 N	2700-3000	2700-3000 N	High
2254cc FI	1988-89	850-950	850-950 N			
2559cc	1988-91	850-950	850-950 N	—	—	

IDLE SPEED W/COMPUTER CONTROL

1987-90 1471cc, 1588cc: ground test terminal on ALDL connector. Race engine over 2000 rpm and set idle to specified value.

1989-91 2.8L: Connect SCAN tool to ALDL. Select "Field Service" mode. After 45 seconds, disconnect IAC and exit mode. Disconnect distributor set timing connector and adjust idle speed.

Engine	Year	Setting Speed MT	Setting Speed AT	Checking Speed MT	Checking Speed AT
1471cc Turbo	1987-89	950	—	900-1000	—
1588cc	1989	900	—	—	—
1588cc	1990	950	950 N	—	—
1588cc	1991-92	—	—	800-900	890-990 N
Turbo	1991-92	—	—	850-950	
2.8L, 3.1L	1989-92	—	—	550-750	550-750 N
3.2L	1992	—	—	750	750 N

ENGINE MECHANICAL

TIGHTENING TORQUES

Some fasteners are tightened in more than one step.

Engine	Year	Torque Ft-lbs/Nm Cylinder Head	Intake Manifold	Exhaust Manifold	Crankshaft Pulley	Water Pump
1471cc	1985-89	29/39, 58/79	17/22	—	108/147	17/23
1588cc	1989-92	29/39, 58/79	17/22	30/39*	108/147	17/23
1817cc, 1949cc 2V	1983-87	44/60, 72/98	18/25	18/25	98/133	19/26
1817cc Diesel	1983-84	97/132	15/21	15/21	108/147	15/21
1949cc FI	1983-87	62/84, 72/98	18/25	18/25	98/133	19/26
1994cc	1985-89	58/79, 72/98	16/21	16/21	86/117	14/19
2238cc ex. Turbo	1983-87	45/61, 65/88	15/21	15/21	140/190	30/41
2238cc Turbo	1985-87	38/52, +120-150°	15/21	15/21	140/190	30/41
2254cc	1986-92	58/79, 72/98	16/21-nut 14/19-bolt	16/21	86/117	14/19
2559cc	1987-92	58/79, 72/98	16/21	33/44	86/117	14/19
2.8L, 3.1L	1989-91	40/55, +90°	19/26	25/34	70/95	7/10† 18/25††

* Turbo, 43/59.
† Small bolts.
†† Large bolts.

ISUZU
1983-92 All Models

VALVE CLEARANCE
Engine cold.

Model	Intake (inches)	Intake (mm)	Exhaust (inches)	Exhaust (mm)
1983-92 4-cyl. Gas: Ex. 2559cc	.006	.15	.010	.25
2559cc	.008	.20	.008	.20
1983-86 Diesel: 1817cc	.010	.25	.014	.35
2238cc	.016	.40	.016	.40

COMPRESSION PRESSURE
At cranking speed, engine warm, throttle open.

Engine	Year	PSI	Maximum Variation PSI
1471cc	1985-89	128-179	*
1588cc	1989-92	128 min.	*
1817cc 2V, 1949cc 2V	1983-87	119-171	8.5
1817cc Diesel	1983-84	370-441	—
1949cc FI, 1994cc	1983-89	125-178	*
2238cc Diesel	1983-87	398-441	—
2254cc 2V, 2559cc	1986-90	119-171	8.5
2254cc, 2559cc	1991-92	142-170●	—
2254cc FI	1988-89	125-178	14
2.8L, 3.1L	1989-92	100 min.	†

* Lowest cylinder pressure must be within 6.5% of average cylinder pressure.
† Lowest cylinder pressure must be within 75% of highest.
● 114 PSI minimum.

BELT TENSION

Model	Year	Alternator	Power Steering	Air Cond.	Air Pump
Tension method					
I-Mark	1985-89	70-110	70-110	70-110	70-110
Stylus, Impulse	1990-91	70-110	120-150	120-150	—
Deflection method					
All others (in.)	1983-92	3/8	3/8	3/8	3/8
(mm)	1983-92	10	10	10	10

ENGINE COMPUTER SYSTEM

COMPUTER DIAGNOSTIC CODES
1983-85 I-Mark
1983-87 Calif. Pickup
1984-91 Trooper, 1988-92 Amigo, Pickup, Rodeo 4-cyl.
1983-89 Impulse ex. 1985-89 Turbo: To activate, ground diagnostic connector under dash or, when equipped with two leads, connect them together. To erase codes, remove ECM fuse for 10 seconds minimum.

1985-89 Impulse Turbo: Access ECM, turn ignition on and observe that codes 2 & 6 are displayed on LED on ECM body. Depress accelerator pedal and see that code 6 is erased. Start engine and observe that code 2 is erased. If LED continues to flash, there is a failure in the system.
To decode LED pulses, pulse cycle is 11 seconds long; LED will flash 7 times, once each second with a four second delay between cycles. During any of the seven flashes, if the LED flashes 4 times quickly within a second a failure is indicated. Decode problem in following chart.

1985-89 I-Mark FWD:
To activate diagnostic check, connect a jumper wire from terminals ''A'' & ''C'' of the ALDL connector (the two outer cavities of the three terminal connector) located under the dash near the ECM. Code 12 will flash, indicating that the system has been activated, remove jumper wire before starting engine. To clear memory, remove the ECM fuse for a minimum of ten seconds.

1989-91 Trooper, 1991-92 Rodeo V6:
Jumper terminals ''A'' and ''B'' of ALDL connector under dash. Codes will be displayed on Check Engine light. Remove ELM fuse for 10 seconds to clear codes.

I-Mark 2V, 1983-92 Amigo, Pickup 2V, 1984-87 Trooper 2V, 1989-92 Trooper, Rodeo, Pickup V6
Code 12 No tach signal to ECM.
Code 13 Oxygen sensor circuit.
Code 14 Shorted coolant sensor circuit.
Codes 15, 16 Open coolant sensor circuit.

COMPUTER DIAGNOSTIC CODES Continued
Code 21 Idle switch out of adjustment, or circuit open.
Code 22 Fuel cut off relay, or open circuit.
Code 23 Open or grounded M/C solenoid circuit.
Code 24 Vehicle speed sensor.
Code 25 Open or grounded vacuum switching valve.
Code 33 MAP sensor, signal voltage high.
Code 34 MAP sensor, signal voltage low.
Code 42 Fuel cut-off relay, or circuit grounded (2V).
Code 42 EST circuit (FI).
Code 43 ESC circuit.
Code 44 Lean oxygen sensor.
Code 45 Rich system.
Code 51 Shorted fuel cut solenoid (4-cyl.).
Code 51 Faulty PROM, or improper installation.
Code 52 Faulty ECM or ROM (4-cyl.).
Code 52 CALPAK error (V6)
Code 53 Shorted switching solenoid.
Code 54 Shorted M/C solenoid (4-cyl.).
Code 54 Fuel pump circuit.
Code 55 Faulty ECM or oxygen sensor.

Impulse ex. 1985-89 Turbo, 1988-92 Amigo, Pickup, Trooper, Rodeo 2.6L
Code 12 No tach signal to ECM.
Code 13 Oxygen sensor circuit.
Code 14 Shorted coolant sensor circuit.
Code 15 Coolant sensor signal low.
Code 16 Open coolant sensor circuit.
Code 21 Idle and full-throttle switch activated.
Code 22 Starter signal.
Code 23 Power transistor circuit.
Code 24 Pressure regulator vacuum switching valve.
Code 26 Canister purge vacuum switching valve.
Code 26 Canister purge VSV driver transistor.
Code 32, 34 EGR temperature sensor.
Code 33 FI output terminal shorted or open.
Code 35 Power transistor circuit open.
Code 41 Crank angle sensor signal erratic.
Code 43 Idle contact switch always closed.
Code 44 Lean oxygen sensor.
Code 45 Rich system.
Codes 51, 52, 55 Faulty ECM.
Code 53 Pressure regulator VSV driver transistor.
Code 54 Power transistor or ground.
Code 61 Air flow sensor hot wire broken or harness open.
Code 62 Air flow sensor cold wire broken.
Code 63 Speed sensor signal not received.
Code 64 FI driver transistor or ground.
Code 65 Full throttle switch always activated.
Code 66 Knock sensor.
Code 71 TPS signal abnormal.
Code 72 EGR vacuum switching valve output terminal shorted or harness open.
Code 73 EGR vacuum switching valve transistor or ground.

Impulse 1985-88 Turbo
Code 1 Knock sensor circuit.
Code 2 Ignition signal circuit.
Code 3 Coolant temperature sensor circuit.
Code 4 Stepper motor circuit.
Code 5 TPS circuit.
Code 6 TPS signal erratic.
Code 7 Power supply voltage.

1987-89 1471cc Turbo
1989-92 1588cc
Code 12 No tach signal to ECM.
Code 13 Oxygen sensor circuit.
Code 14 Coolant sensor circuit (high temperature indicated).
Codes 15, 16 Open coolant sensor circuit (low temperature indicated).
Code 21 TPS voltage high.
Code 22 TPS voltage low.
Code 23 Manifold air temperature sensor (signal voltage high).
Code 24 Vehicle speed sensor.
Code 25 Manifold air temperature sensor (signal voltage high).
Code 31 Wastegate control.
Code 32 EGR failure.
Code 33 MAP sensor voltage high.
Code 34 MAP sensor voltage low.
Code 42 EST circuit.
Code 43 Detonation sensor.
Code 44 Lean oxygen sensor.
Code 45 Rich oxygen system.
Code 51 Faulty PROM, or installation. Faulty MEMCAL.

UNDERHOOD SERVICE SPECIFICATIONS

SENSORS, INPUT

TEMPERATURE SENSORS

Engine	Year	Sensor	Resistance Ohms @ deg. F/C
1471cc, 2254cc 2V	1985-89	Coolant	5600 @ 32/0
			2500 @ 68/20
			1200 @ 104/40
			600 @ 140/60
			320 @ 176/80
			180 @ 212/100
1588cc, 2.8L, 3.1L	1989-92	Coolant	13,500 @ 320/−7
		Manifold Air	7500 @ 40/4
			3400 @ 70/21
			1800 @ 100/38
			450 @ 160/71
			1850 @ 210/100
1994cc, 2254cc FI, 2559cc	1985-92	Coolant	7000-12,000 @ 14/−10
			3000-5000 @ 50/10
			2000-3000 @ 68/20
			700-1000 @ 122/50
			200-400 @ 176/80
2254cc 2V	1990-92	Coolant	4100-4750 @ 59/15
			78-84 @ 265/128
1471cc Turbo	1987-89	Manifold Air	9423 @ 32/0
			3515 @ 68/20
			1459 @ 104/40
			667 @ 140/60
			332 @ 176/80
			177 @ 212/100
1588cc, 2254cc, 2559cc	1989-92	EGR	200,000 @ −40/−40
			28,000 @ 32/0
			5800 @ 104/40
			1000 @ 212/100
			135 @ 392/200

MANIFOLD ABSOLUTE PRESSURE SENSOR

With engine running and 10 inches/250mm Hg applied to unit, 1.5-2.3 volts less.

Engine	Year	Volts @ Altitude
1588cc	1989-92	3.8-5.5 @ 1000 max.
		3.6-5.3 @ 1000-2000
		3.5-5.1 @ 2000-3000
		3.3-5.0 @ 3000-4000
		3.2-4.8 @ 4000-5000
		3.0-4.6 @ 5000-6000
		2.9-4.5 @ 6000-7000
		2.5-4.3 @ 7000 or over
2.8L, 3.1L	1989-92	1-2 @ idle
		4.0-4.8 @ WOT

SENSORS, INPUT Continued

MANIFOLD ABSOLUTE PRESSURE SENSOR Continued

Engine	Year	Volts @ in./mm Hg
2254cc 2V	1989-92	.12-.38 @ 5/125
		1.5-1.7 @ 12/300
		4.4-4.6 @ 28/700

THROTTLE POSITION SENSOR

1471cc Turbo, measured between red wire in TPS and ground.

Model	Year	TPS Idle	Voltage WOT
1471cc 2V	1985-89	†	—
1471cc Turbo	1987-89	0.35 ±0.04	4.0
1588cc	1989-92	1.25 max	4.0 min.
1994cc, 2254cc FI, 2559cc	1985-92	*	—
2.8L, 3.1L	1989-92	.48	—

* 2.6-4.6 volts difference between idle and WOT.
† 3000-6000 ohms at idle decreasing as throttle is opened. Measured between terminals 4 and 12 of carburetor connector.

ACTUATORS, OUTPUT

IDLE SPEED CONTROL SOLENOID

Engine	Year	Resistance (ohms)
1471cc Turbo, 2.8L, 3.1L	1987-92	20 min.‡
1588cc	1989-92	40-80

‡ Measured between terminals 1 & 2 and 3 & 4 of ISC.

AIR REGULATOR

Controls fast idle.

Engine	Year	Resistance (ohms)
2559cc	1988-92	45-50

MIXTURE CONTROL SOLENOID

Engine	Year	Resistance (ohms)
1471cc 2V	1987-89	10 min.
2254cc 2V	1986-92	20 min.

ENGINE IDENTIFICATION

To identify any engine by the manufacturer's code, follow the four steps designated by the numbered blocks.

1 MODEL YEAR IDENTIFICATION: Refer to V.I.N. plate. The year is indicated as a code letter.

2 ENGINE CODE LOCATION: Refer to V.I.N. plate. The engine code is indicated as a letter or number.

3 ENGINE CODE: In the vertical "CODE" column, find the engine code determined in Step 2.

4 ENGINE IDENTIFICATION: On the line where the engine code appears, read to the right to identify the engine.

V.I.N. PLATE LOCATIONS:
Under hood or top left side of instrument panel

Model year of vehicle:
1992 — Model year is N.   1987 — Model year is H.
1991 — Model year is M.   1986 — Model year is G.
1990 — Model year is L.   1985 — Model year is F.
1989 — Model year is K.   1984 — Model year is E.
1988 — Model year is J.   1983 — Model year is D.

1 MODEL YEAR IDENTIFICATION:
10th character of V.I.N.

2 ENGINE CODE LOCATION:
1992-89 — 8th character of V.I.N.
1988-83 — 4th character of V.I.N.

4 ENGINE IDENTIFICATION

YEAR	3 ENGINE CODE	CYL.	DISPL. liters	DISPL. cu. in.	Fuel System	HP
1992	P	4	2.5	150	MFI	123, 130†
	S	6	4.0	242	MFI	180, 190†
1991	P	4	2.5	150	MFI	126, 128†
	S	6	4.0	242	MFI	180, 190†
	7	8	5.9	360	2V	144
1990	E	4	2.5	150	TBI	117, 121†
	L	6	4.0	242	MFI	177
	T	6	4.2	258	2V	112
	7	8	5.9	360	2V	144
1989	E	4	2.5	150	TBI	117, 121†
	L	6	4.0	242	MFI	177
	M	6	4.2	258	2V	112
	7	8	5.9	360	2V	144
1988	H	4	2.5	150	TBI	117
	M	6	4.0	242	MFI	177
	C	6	4.2	258	2V	112
	N	8	5.9	360	2V	144
1987	B	4	2.1 D	126 D	MFI	85
	H	4	2.5	150	TBI	117
	M	6	4.0	242	MFI	173
	C	6	4.2	258	2V	112
	N	8	5.9	360	2V	144

4 ENGINE IDENTIFICATION

YEAR	3 ENGINE CODE	CYL.	DISPL. liters	DISPL. cu. in.	Fuel System	HP
1986	B	4	2.1 D	126 D	MFI	85
	U	4	2.5	150	1V	105
	H	4	2.5	150	TBI	97, 117†
	W	6	2.8	173	2V	110
	C	6	4.2	258	2V	112
	N	8	5.9	360	2V	144
1985	B	4	2.1 D	126 D	MFI	87
	U	4	2.5	150	1V	105
	W	6	2.8	173	2V	110
	C	6	4.2	258	2V	112
	N	8	5.9	360	2V	144
1984	U	4	2.5	150	1V	105
	W	6	2.8	173	2V	110
	C	6	4.2	258	2V	115
	N	8	5.9	360	2V	144
1983	B	4	2.5	151	2V	80
	C	6	4.2	258	2V	115
	N	8	5.9	360	2V	144

TBI — Throttle Body Injection.   **MFI** — Multiport Fuel Injection.
1V — One Venturi Carburetor.   **2V** — Two Venturi Carburetor.
† Engine horsepower varies with model installation.   **D** — Diesel.

UNDERHOOD SERVICE SPECIFICATIONS

JPTU1   **CYLINDER NUMBERING SEQUENCE**   JPTU1

4-CYL. FIRING ORDER:
1 3 4 2

2.8L (173) FIRING ORDER:
1 2 3 4 5 6

L-6 FIRING ORDER: 1 5 3 6 2 4

8-CYL. FIRING ORDER:
1 8 4 3 6 5 7 2

— Front of car —

| 1983-90 2.5L (150) AMC/Jeep | 1991-92 2.5L | 1983 2.5L (151) GM | 1984-86 2.8L (173) | 1987-92 4.0L (242) | 1983-90 4.2L (258) | 5.9L (360) |

TIMING MARK

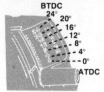

1983-92
2.5L (150) AMC/Jeep,
1987-92
4.0L (242),
1983-90
4.2L (258)

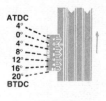

1983
2.5L (151) GM

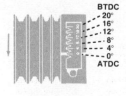

1984-86
2.8L (173)

5.9L (360)

UNDERHOOD SERVICE SPECIFICATIONS

ELECTRICAL AND IGNITION SYSTEMS

BATTERY

		STANDARD		OPTIONAL	
Engine	Year	BCI Group No.	Crank. Perf.	BCI Group No.	Crank. Perf.
Cherokee, Wagoneer	1984-87	58	425	—	—
Diesel	1985-87	24	815	—	—
CJ7, Scrambler	1984-87	55	420	54	450
Grand Wagoneer, Truck	1985-87	55	420	54	450
Cherokee, Wagoneer, Comanche	1988-91	58	390	58	475
	1992	58	430	58	500
Wrangler, YJ	1988-90	55	420	56	450
	1991	58	390	58	475
	1992	58	430	58	500
Grand Wagoneer	1988	56	450	—	—
Grand Wagoneer	1989-91	58	475	—	—

ALTERNATOR

Application	Rated Output (amps)	Test Output (amps @ 2000 rpm)
1983-85	42, 78	*
Optional	56, 85	*
1986-88 Gasoline	56, 66, 78	*
1986-87 Diesel	60, 70	*
1988-90		
4.2L, 5.9L	56, 66, 78, 94	*
2.5L, 4.0L	61, 74, 85, 100	*
1991-92 Grand Wagoneer	78	*
Others	75, 90	**

* Output at 2000 rpm must be within 10 amps of rated output.
** Output at 2000 rpm must be at rated output.

REGULATOR

Application	Test Temp. (deg. F/C)	Voltage Setting
1983-88 All gasoline, 1989-91 4.2L, 5.9L	0-50/ −18 to 10	14.3-15.3
	50-100/ 10-38	13.9-14.9
	100-150/ 50-66	13.4-14.4
	150-200/ 66-93	13.0-14.1
1985-87 Diesel	—	14.5-15.5
1989-90 2.5L, 4.0L	—	13.5-16.0
1991-92 2.5L, 4.0L	−40 to 20/ −40 to -7	14.5-15.0
	20-80/ −7 to 27	13.9-15.0
	80-140/ 27-60	13.2-14.4
	140-160/ 60-71	13.2-13.8

STARTER

Engine	Year	Cranking Voltage (min. volts)	Ampere Draw @ Cranking Speed
4-cyl., V-6 cyl.	1983-88	9.6	—
6-cyl.	1983-88	9.6	150-180
8-cyl.	1983-88	9.6	160-210
All	1989-92	9.6	160

SPARK PLUGS

Engine	Year	Gap (inches)	Gap (mm)	Torque (ft-lb)
2.5L (150)	1984-86	.035	.89	27
2.5L (151)	1983	.060	1.52	10
2.8L (173)	1984-86	.041	1.04	—
4.2L (258)	1983-86	.033-.038	.84-.97	11
8-cyl.	1983-86	.033-.038	.84-.97	28
All	1987-92	.035	.89	27

IGNITION COIL
Resistance (ohms at 75°F or 24°C)

Engine	Year	Windings	Resistance (ohms)
2.5L (151)	1983	Primary	0-2
		Secondary	6000-30,000
2.5L FI	1986-89	Primary	0.4-0.8
		Secondary	2500-5500
2.5L, 4.0L: Diamond	1991	Primary	.97-1.18
		Secondary	11,300-15,300
Toyodenso	1991	Primary	.95-1.20
		Secondary	11,300-13,300
2.8L (173)	1984-86	Primary	.90-1.40
		Secondary	7300-11,100
4.0L (242)	1987-90	Primary	0.4-0.8
		Secondary	2500-5500
All Others	1983-91	Primary	1.11-1.25
		Secondary	7700-9300

DISTRIBUTOR PICKUP

Application	Resistance (ohms)	Air Gap (in./mm)
1983 2.5L (151)	500-1500	—
1984-86 2.8L (173)	500-1500	—
1983-91 4.2L (258), 5.9L (300)	400-800	0.17/.28 min

IGNITION RESISTOR

Engine	Year	Type	Resistance (ohms)	Temperature (deg. F/C)
4.2L, 5.9L	1983-91	Wire	1.3-1.4	—

BASE TIMING
Carburetted models only.

Set timing at slow idle and Before Top Dead Center, unless otherwise specified. Disconnect and plug distributor vacuum line.

Timing MUST be set to specifications shown on emission label if different from setting listed.

Engine	Year	Man. Trans. (degrees)	Auto. Trans. (degrees)
2.5L (150) 1V	1984-86	12 ±2●	12 ±2●
High Altitude	1984-86	19 ±2●	19 ±2●
2.5L (151)	1983	12 ±2	—
2.8L (173)	1984-86	8 ±2	12 ±2
High Altitude	1984-86	17 ±2	19 ±2
California	1984-86	10 ±2	12 ±2
4.2L (258)	1983	6 ±2●	6 ±2●
High Altitude	1983	13 ±2●	13 ±2●
4.2L (258)	1984-91	9 ±2●	9 ±2●
High Altitude	1984-91	16 ±2●	16 ±2●
5.9L (360)	1983-84	10 ±1	10 ±1
High Altitude	1983-84	16 ±1	16 ±1
5.9L (360)	1985-89	12 ±2	12 ±2
High Altitude	1985-89	19 ±2	19 ±2
5.9L (360)	1990	—	10 ±2
High Altitude	1990	—	17 ±2

● At 1600 rpm.

DISTRIBUTOR TIMING ADVANCE

Engine degrees at engine rpm, no load, in addition to basic timing setting.

Mechanical advance distributors only.

Engine	Trans- mission	Year	Distributor Number	Degrees @ 2500 RPM Total	Degrees @ 2500 RPM Centrifugal
2.5L (150) 1V	MT & AT	1983-86	3242700	19.8-28.8	4.8-8.8
2.5L (151)	MT	1983	1110598	22.5-30.5	5-9
2.5L (151)	MT	1983	1103527	24.4-32.4	6.9-10.9
2.8L (173)	MT	1984	1103520	33-41	13-17
2.8L (173)	AT	1984	1103521	23-33	9-13
2.8L (173)	MT	1985-86	1103620	28.2-34.2	10.2-14.2
2.8L (173)	AT	1985-86	1103621	24-32	6-10
4.2L (258)	MT & AT	1983	3241333	29.3-40.3	9.3-14.3
4.2L (258)	MT & AT	1983	3241334	27.5-38.5	7.5-12.5
4.2L (258)	MT & AT	1983-84	3242409	30-40	10-14
4.2L (258)	MT & AT	1985-90	8933002353	23.5-31.5	6.5-10.5
5.9L (360)	MT & AT	1983-90	3233174	29.5-38.5	8-12
5.9L	AT	1990	53006450	27.5-37.5	7-12

FUEL SYSTEM

FUEL SYSTEM PRESSURE

Engine	Year	Pressure PSI	Pressure RPM	Volume Pints	Volume Sec.	Volume RPM
Carburetted & TBI						
4-cyl.	1983	6.5-8.0				
4-cyl. ex. FI	1984-86	4.0-5.0	idle	1	30	idle
4-cyl. w/FI	1986-90	14-15	—	—	—	—
6-cyl. 2V	1983-89	4-5	idle	1	30	idle
V-6 cyl.	1984-86	6.0-7.5	idle	—	—	—
8-cyl.	1983-91	5.0-6.5	idle	1	30	idle

Engine	Year	Pressure*	Pressure†
MFI			
2.5L, 4.0L	1987-92	39-41	31

* With pressure regulator vacuum hose connected.
† With pressure regulator vacuum hose disconnected.

IDLE SPEED W/O COMPUTER CONTROL

The midpoint of the ranges given is the preferred setting.

On all models disconnect decel valve and canister purge hoses. Do not allow vehicle to idle for more than three minutes.

4-cyl. 2V eng.: With A/C, adjust idle speed to specification, turn A/C on and adjust idle speed-up to specification. Without A/C, adjust idle speed to specification, disconnect solenoid electrical lead and set idle shutdown speed.

6-cyl. eng.: Disconnect and plug solenoid vacuum line. Disconnect solenoid electrical lead. Adjust idle speed. Apply vacuum to solenoid and set speed to specification. Apply battery voltage to solenoid and turn A/C on. Set speed-up to specification.

8-cyl. eng.: Adjust idle speed with solenoid fully extended. Electrically disconnect the solenoid and set shutdown speed to specification.

To set fast idle, disconnect and plug EGR vacuum hose.

Preferred setting is the midpoint of range given.

Engine	Year	SLOW Man. Trans.	SLOW Auto. Trans.	FAST Man. Trans.	FAST Auto. Trans.	Step of Cam
2.1L (124) Diesel	1985-87	750-850	750-850 D	—	—	—
speed-up	1985-87	1000-1200	1000-1200 N			
maximum speed	1985-87	4700-4800	4700-4800 P			
2.5L (150) 1V	1983-86	700-800	650-750 D	1900-2100	2200-2400 P	Second
shutdown idle	1983-86	450-550	450-550 N			
speed-up idle	1983-86	900-1000	800-900 D			
2.5L (151)	1983	800-1000	600-800 D	2300-2500	2500-2700 P	High

IDLE SPEED W/O COMPUTER CONTROL Continued

Engine	Year	SLOW Man. Trans.	SLOW Auto. Trans.	FAST Man. Trans.	FAST Auto. Trans.	Step of Cam
2.8L (173)	1984-86	650-750	650-750 D	2000-2200	2200-2400 P	High
solenoid	1984-86	1150-1250	1150-1250 N			
4.2L (258)	1983	530-670♦	430-570 D△	1600-1800	1750-1950 P	—
California	1983	580-720♦	480-620 D△	1600-1800	1750-1950 P	—
High Altitude	1983	630-770♦	580-720 D△	1600-1800	1750-1950 P	—
4.2L (258)	1984-90	630-730♦	550-650 D△	1600-1800	1750-1950 P	Second
High Altitude	1984-89	650-750♦	600-700 D△	1600-1800	1750-1950 P	Second
5.9L (360)	1983-91	550-650	550-650 D	1400-1600	1500-1700 P	Second
shutdown idle	1983-91	450-500	450-500 N			

♦ With Sole-Vac Vacuum actuator energized, 900 ±50.
Holding solenoid, 1100 ±50.
△ With Sole-Vac Vacuum actuator energized, 900 D ±50.
Holding solenoid, 800 D ±50.

IDLE SPEED W/COMPUTER CONTROL

2.5L: Disconnect ISC and fully extend plunger with special tool. Adjust plunger head screw to specified value.

4.0L: Set idle to specified value by adjusting stop screw.

Engine	Year	Checking Speed Man. Trans.	Checking Speed Auto. Trans.	Setting Speed Man. Trans.	Setting Speed Auto. Trans.
2.5L (150) FI	1986-90	750 min.	750 N min.	3500	3500 N
2.5L	1991	800	800 N	—	—
4.0L (242)	1987-89	700	700 N	700	700 N
4.0L	1990-91	550-650	550-650 N		

ENGINE MECHANICAL

TIGHTENING TORQUES

Engine	Year	Torque Ft-lbs/Nm Cylinder Head	Intake Manifold	Exhaust Manifold	Crankshaft Pulley	Water Pump
2.5L (150)	1984-87	85/115‡	23/31	23/31	80/108	13/18
2.5L (150)	1988-91	110/149**	23/31	23/31	80/108	22/30
2.5L (151)	1983	92/125	37/50	35/47	160/220	17/23
4.0L (242)	1987-92	100/149*	23/31	30/41, outer 23/31, center	80/108	22/30
4.2L (258)	1983-90	85/115	23/31	23/31	80/108	13/18
5.9L (360)	1983-91	110/149	43/58	15/20, outer 25/34, center	90/122	4/5

‡ Bolt number 8 (first bolt on left front), 75/102.
* Bolt number 11 (first bolt on right front), 100/136.
** Bolt number 8 (first bolt on left front, 100/136.

VALVE CLEARANCE

Engine cold.

Engine	Year	Intake (inches)	Intake (mm)	Exhaust (inches)	Exhaust (mm)
2.1L Diesel	1985-87	.008	.20	.010	.25

UNDERHOOD SERVICE SPECIFICATIONS

JPTU4

COMPRESSION PRESSURE

At cranking speed or specified rpm, engine temperature normalized, throttle open.

Engine	Year	PSI	Maximum Variation PSI
2.5L (150)	1984-89	155-185	30
2.5L	1990-92	120-150	30
2.5L (151)	1983	140 @ 160 rpm	†
4.0L (258)	1991-92	120-150	30
4.2L (258)	1983-90	120-150	30
5.9L (360)	1983-91	120-140	30
All Others	1985-86	—	†

† Lowest cylinder pressure must be more than 70% of highest cylinder pressure.

BELT TENSION

A belt is considered used once it has been pretensioned and run. Use a strand tension gauge. Measurements are in pounds.

Engine	Year	Alternator	Power Steering or Idler	Air Cond.	Air Pump
USED BELTS					
4-cyl. Gas	1983-89	90-115	90-115	90-115	90-115
6-cyl.	1983	90-115	90-115△	90-115	90-115△
Serpentine	1983	140-160			
All Others	1983-92	90-115	90-115	90-115	90-115
Serpentine	1985-91	140-160	—	—	—
NEW BELTS					
4-cyl.	1983-84	125-155	125-155	125-155	125-155
4-cyl. Gas	1985-87	120-160	120-140	120-160	—
6-cyl.	1983	125-155	125-155	125-155	140-160
Serpentine	1983	180-200	—	—	—
All Others	1983-92	125-155	125-155	125-155	125-155
Serpentine	1985-92	180-200	—	—	—

△ When air pump and power steering are on the same belt: Used, 60-70; New, 65-75.

ENGINE COMPUTER SYSTEM

COMPUTER DIAGNOSTIC CODES

1984-86 2.8L (173) Calif.: Connect a jumper between terminals 6 & 7 of the 15 terminal diagnostic connector.

"CHECK ENGINE" light will flash codes. Code 12 will flash three times, then other codes will be displayed.

Disconnect ECM fuse for 10 seconds to clear memory.

1991-92 2.5L, 4.0L: Connect Diagnostic Readout Box (DRB-II) to diagnostic connector. Turn ignition on and access "Read Fault Code Data".

1984-86 2.8L:
Code 12 No tach signal to ECM
Code 13 Oxygen sensor
Code 14 Shorted coolant temperature sensor
Code 15 Open coolant temperature sensor
Code 21 Throttle position sensor
Code 23 Open or grounded MC solenoid
Code 34 Vacuum sensor
Code 41 No distributor reference pulses to ECM
Code 42 EST or EST bypass circuit open or grounded
Code 44 Air/fuel mixture lean
Codes 44 & 45 Faulty oxygen sensor
Code 45 Air/fuel mixture rich
Code 51 Faulty PROM or installation
Code 54 Shorted MC solenoid or faulty ECM
Code 55 Grounded V-REF, faulty oxygen sensor or ECM

1991-92 2.5L, 4.0L:
Code 11 Ignition
Code 13 MAP sensor vacuum
Code 14 MAP sensor electrical
Code 15 Speed sensor
Code 17 Engine running too cool
Code 21 Oxygen sensor
Code 22 Coolant temperature sensor
Code 23 Charge temperature
Code 24 Throttle position sensor
Code 25 AIS control
Code 27 Fuel injector control
Code 33 Air conditioning clutch relay
Code 34 Speed control solenoid driver

JPTU4

COMPUTER DIAGNOSTIC CODES Continued

Code 35 Fan control relay
Code 41 Alternator field
Code 42 Automatic shutdown relay
Code 44 Battery temperature sensor
Code 46 Battery over voltage
Code 47 Battery under voltage
Code 51 Oxygen sensor lean
Code 52 Oxygen sensor rich
Code 53 Internal engine controller fault
Code 54 Distributor sync pickup
Code 62 EMR mileage accumulator
Code 63 Controller failure EEPROM write denied
Code 76 Fuel pump resistor bypass relay

SENSORS, INPUT

TEMPERATURE SENSORS

Engine	Year	Sensor	Resistance Ohms @ deg. F/C
2.5L 1V, 4.2L	1983-90	Coolant	continuity @ 100/38 max. no continuity above 100/38
2.5L FI, 4.0L	1986-90	Coolant, Manifold Air	13,500 @ 20/−7 7500 @ 40/4 3400 @ 70/20 1600 @ 100/38 450 @ 160/70 185 @ 212/100
2.5L, 4.0L	1991-92	Coolant, Manifold Air	85,850-108,390 @ −4/−20 49,250-61,430 @ 14/−10 17,990-21,810 @ 50/10 4900-5750 @ 104/40 1630-1870 @ 160/70 640-720 @ 212/100

PRESSURE SENSORS

Engine	Year	Sensor	Voltage
2.5L	1986-92	Barometric	4.0-5.0, ign. on 1.5-2.1, idle
4.0L	1987-88	Barometric	4.0-5.0, ign. on 0.5-1.5, idle
4.0L	1986-92	Barometric	4.0-5.0, ign. on 1.5-2.1, idle

CRANK ANGLE SENSOR

Engine	Year	Resistance (ohms)
2.5L FI, 4.0L	1986-91	125-275

THROTTLE POSITION SENSOR

2.5L: Connect DVOM across terminals A (+) and B (–) of TPS connector. Turn ignition on and fully open throttle plate. Check voltage against specified value.

4.0L: Connect DVOM between terminals C (+) and B (–). Measure voltage with throttle closed.

Engine	Year	Voltage Idle	Voltage WOT
2.5L (150) FI	1986-89	—	4.6-4.7
2.5L	1991-92	.20 min.	4.8 max.
4.0L	1987-89	0.8	—
4.0L MT	1990	0.85	—
AT	1990	4.15	—
4.0L	1991-92	.20 min.	4.8 max.

ACTUATORS, OUTPUT

MIXTURE CONTROL SOLENOID

Engine	Year	Resistance (ohms)
Carburetted:		
2.5L (151)	1983	20 min.
2.5L (150), 4.2L (258), 5.9L (360)	1983-91	50-95

ENGINE IDENTIFICATION

To identify an engine by the manufacturer's code, follow the four steps designated by the numbered blocks.

V.I.N. PLATE LOCATION:

On engine bulkhead or on top left side of instrument panel visible thru windshield.

1 MODEL YEAR IDENTIFICATION:

1992-83 — 10th character of V.I.N.
1992 — N; 1991 — M; 1990 — L;
1989 — K; 1988 — J; 1987 — H;
1986 — G; 1985 — F; 1984 — E;
1983 — D.

2 ENGINE CODE LOCATION:

1992-86 — 8th character of V.I.N.
1985-82 — 5th character of V.I.N.

4 ENGINE IDENTIFICATION

3 ENGINE	ROTORS	DISPL.		Fuel	
YEAR	CODE or CYL.	liters	cc	System	HP
1992	— 4	1.6	1597	MFI	82, 88
	— DOHC 4	1.6	1597	MFI	105, 116†
	— 4	1.8	1839	MFI	103
	— DOHC 4	1.8	1839	MFI	125
	— 6	1.8	1844	MFI	130
	— 4	2.2	2187	2V	85
	— 4	2.2	2187	MFI	91
	— 4	2.2	2187	MFI	110
	— 4	2.2 T	2187 T	MFI	145
	— 6	2.6	2606	MFI	121
	— 6	3.0	2954	MFI	155
	— DOHC 6	3.0	2954	MFI	195
	— 6	4.0	4016	MFI	155
1991	— 2	1.3	1308	MFI	160
	— 2	1.3 T	1308 T	MFI	200
	2 4	1.6	1597	MFI	82
	1, 2 4	1.6	1597	MFI	105, 116†
	4, 8 4	1.8	1839	MFI	103
	6 4	1.8	1839	MFI	125
	1, 2, A, B ... 4	2.2	2187	MFI	110
	3, 4, C, D ... 4	2.2 T	2187 T	MFI	145
	3 4	2.2	2187	2V	85
	3 4	2.2	2187	MFI	91
	4 4	2.6	2606	MFI	121
	— 6	3.0	2954	MFI	150, 158†
	— DOHC 6	3.0	2954	MFI	190
	— 6	4.0	4016	MFI	155
1990	1, 3 2	1.3	1308	MFI	160
	2, 4 2	1.3 T	1308 T	MFI	200
	2 4	1.6	1597	MFI	82
	1, 2 4	1.6	1597	MFI	116
	4, 8 4	1.8	1839	MFI	103
	6 4	1.8	1839	MFI	125
	3 4	2.2	2187	2V	85
	3 4	2.2	2187	MFI	91
	1, 2, A, B ... 4	2.2	2187	MFI	110
	3, 4, C, D ... 4	2.2 T	2187 T	MFI	145
	1, 4 4	2.6	2606	MFI	121
	2, 3 6	3.0	2954	MFI	150
	1 6	3.0	2954	MFI	158
	2 6	3.0	2954	MFI	190
1989	1, 3 2	1.3	1308	MFI	160
	2, 4 2	1.3 T	1308 T	MFI	200
	2 4	1.6	1597	MFI	82
	3 (2WD) 4	1.6 T	1597 T	MFI	132
	4 (2WD) 4	1.6 T	1597 T	MFI	132
	3 4	2.2	2187	2V	85
	1, 2, A, B ... 4	2.2	2187	MFI	110
	3, 4, C, D ... 4	2.2 T	2187 T	MFI	145
	1 4	2.6	2606	MFI	121

4 ENGINE IDENTIFICATION

3 ENGINE	ROTORS	DISPL.		Fuel	
YEAR	CODE or CYL.	liters	cc	System	HP
1989 Cont'd.	2 4	2.6	2606	MFI	121
	1 6	3.0	2954	MFI	158
	2 (2WD) 6	3.0	2954	MFI	150
	3 (4WD) 6	3.0	2954	MFI	150
1988	1 2	1.3	1308	MFI	146
	2 2	1.3 T	1308 T	MFI	182
	1 4	1.6	1597	MFI	82
	2 (2WD) 4	1.6 T	1597 T	MFI	132
	3 (4WD) 4	1.6 T	1597 T	MFI	132
	3 4	2.2	2184	2V	85
	A, B 4	2.2	2184	MFI	110
	C, D 4	2.2 T	2184 T	MFI	145
	2 4	2.6	2555	2V	102
	1 .... V6	3.0	2954	MFI	158
1987	1 2	1.3	1308	MFI	146
	2 2	1.3 T	1308 T	MFI	182
	1 4	1.6	1597	2V	N/A
	2 4	1.6	1597	MFI	82
	1 4	2.0	1998	2V	80
	1 4	2.0	1998	MFI	93
	3 4	2.0 T	1998 T	MFI	120
	F2 4	2.2	2184	2V	N/A
	G54B 4	2.6	2555	2V	N/A
1986	1 2	1.3	1308	MFI	146
	1 4	1.6	1597	2V	N/A
	2 4	1.6	1597	MFI	82
	1 4	2.0	1998	2V	80
	1 4	2.0	1998	MFI	93
	3 4	2.0 T	1998 T	MFI	120
1985	B 2	1.1	1146	4V	101
	B 2	1.3	1308	MFI	135
	D 4	1.5	1490	2V	68
	B 4	2.0 D	1998 D	MFI	N/A
	B 4	2.0	1998	2V	84
1984	B 2	1.1	1146	4V	101
	B 2	1.3	1308	MFI	135
	D 4	1.5	1490	2V	68
	C 4	2.0	1970	2V	73, 78†
	B 4	2.0	1998	2V	84
	D 4	2.2 D	2209 D	MFI	59
1983	B 2	1.1	1146	4V	100
	D 4	1.5	1490	2V	63, 68†
	C 4	2.0	1970	2V	74, 77†
	B 4	2.0	1998	2V	84
	D 4	2.2 D	2209 D	MFI	58

D — Diesel.   T — Turbo.   MFI — Multiport Fuel Injection.
2V — Two Venturi Carburetor.   4V — Four Venturi Carburetor.
† Engine horsepower varies with model installation.

UNDERHOOD SERVICE SPECIFICATIONS

MAITU1

Rotary engine
FIRING ORDER
1 2

CYLINDER NUMBERING SEQUENCE

Piston engine
4-CYL. FIRING ORDER: 1 3 4 2

MAITU1

1983-85
RX-7 1146cc, 1308cc
ex. w/coil ign.

1983
GLC RWD
1415cc, 1490cc

1983-85
GLC FWD 1490cc

1986-92
323 1597cc ex. Turbo,
1990-92 Protegé
1839cc SOHC

1988-89
323 1597cc Turbo

1990-92 Protegé
1834cc DOHC

1990-92
Miata 1597cc

1983-84
B2000, 626
1970cc

Front of car

UNDERHOOD SERVICE SPECIFICATIONS

MAITU2   MAITU2

CYLINDER NUMBERING SEQUENCE

Piston engine
4-CYL. FIRING ORDER: 1 3 4 2

V6 FIRING ORDER:
1 2 3 4 5 6

| 1983-85 626 1998cc 2V | 1986-87 626 1998cc FI Gasoline | 1986-87 1998cc Pickup, 1987-88 B2200, B2600 2184cc, 2555cc, 1989-92 B2200 2184cc | 1988-92 626, MX-6 2184cc ex. Turbo | 1988-92 626, MX-6 2184cc Turbo | 1988-92 MPV, 929 2954cc SOHC | 1990-92 929 2954cc DOHC |

— **Front of car** —

TIMING MARK

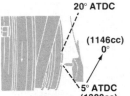

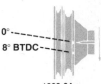

20° ATDC

(1146cc) 0°

5° ATDC (1308cc)

1983-85 RX-7 1146cc, 1984-90 1308cc

10° BTDC   0°

1983-85 GLC 1490cc, 1984-92 626, MX-6 1998cc, 2184cc, 1987-92 B2200 2184cc

10° BTDC   0°

1986-92 323, Miata 1597cc, 1990-92 Protegé 1834cc

0°

8° BTDC

1983-84 B2000 1970cc

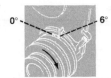

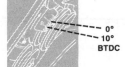

0°   6°

1983 626 1998cc, 1986-87 B2000 1998cc

BTDC
10°
0°
10°
ATDC

1987-88 B2600 2555cc

0°
10°
BTDC

1988-92 MPV, B2600, 929 2606cc, 2954cc, 1992 MX-3 1884cc

ELECTRICAL AND IGNITION SYSTEMS

BATTERY

BCI equivalent shown, size may vary from original equipment. Check clearance before replacing, holddown may need to be modified.

Model	Year	STANDARD BCI Group No.	STANDARD Crank Perf.	OPTIONAL BCI Group No.	OPTIONAL Crank Perf.
RX-7	1983-90	21R	320	35	405
Canada	1986-90	35	405	—	—
RX-7	1991	35	350	35	420
Canada	1991	35	420	—	—
GLC FWD	1983-85	21R	320	35	380
323, Protegé	1986-90	21R	320	35	380
323, Protegé	1991-92	35	350	—	—
Calif.	1991-92	21R	310	—	—
626	1983-84	21R	320	35	405
626, MX-6	1985-92	21R	320	35	360
Diesel	1985	27F	655	—	—
929	1988-91	21R	320	24F	585
Pickup Diesel	1983-84	27	600	—	—
Pickup	1983-85	27	370	—	—
Pickup: B2200	1986-88	21	320	24	515
B2600	1987-88	21R	320	24F	515
Pickup: B2200	1989-92	21	310	24	490
B2600	1989-92	21	310	24	585
MPV	1989-92	21R	310	24F	585
Navajo	1991-92	65	650	—	—

ALTERNATOR

Engine	Year	Rated Output (amps)	Test Output (amps @ rpm)
1146cc	1983	50	36 @ 2500
1146cc	1984-85	55	51 @ 2500
1308cc	1984-85	60	53 @ 2500
1308cc	1986-88	70	55 @ 2500
1308cc	1989-90	80	60 @ 2500
1490cc	1983-85	50	30 @ 2500
1597cc 2V	1986-87	55	42 @ 2500
1597cc FI	1986-87	60	45 @ 2500
1597cc FI	1988-89	60	60 @ 3000
1597cc Miata: MT	1990-92	60	60 @ 3000
AT	1990-92	65	65 @ 2500
1597cc MX-3	1992	70	70 @ 3000
1597cc Others	1990-92	65	65 @ 2500
1839cc	1990-91	65	65 @ 2500
1844cc	1992	90	90 @ 3000
1970cc Pickup	1983-84	35	30 @ 2500
1998cc 626	1983-87	65	51 @ 2500
1998cc Pickup	1986-87	55	50 @ 2500
2184cc FI	1988-89	70	65 @ 3000
2184cc 626, MX-6	1990-92	70	65 @ 3000
Turbo w/MT	1990-92	70	65 @ 3000
Turbo w/AT	1990-92	80	60 @ 2500
2184cc 2V, 2555cc	1987-92	55	50 @ 2500
2606cc: Pickup	1989-92	60	55 @ 3000
MPV	1989-92	70	70 @ 3000
2954cc	1988	65	60 @ 3000
2954cc	1989-91	70	60 @ 3000
2954cc 929	1992	90	90 @ 3000
4016cc	1991-92	95	—

UNDERHOOD SERVICE SPECIFICATIONS

MAITU3   MAITU3

REGULATOR

Application	Year	Voltage Setting	Test Temp. (deg. F/C)
Navajo	1991-92	•	—
All ex. Navajo	1990-92	14.1-14.7	68/20
323, 626, RX-7, MPV, Miata	1988-89	14.1-14.7	68/20
Pickup	1987-89	14.2-15.2	68/20
All Others	1986-89	14.4-15.0	68/20
RX-7	1984-85	14.2-15.2	68/20
GLC, 626	1984-85	14.4-15.0	68/20
Pickup	1984-85	14.1-14.7	68/20
All ex. 626	1983	14.1-14.7	68/20
626	1983	14.4-15.0	68/20

• Measure battery voltage and record figure. With engine operating off-idle and all secondary electrical systems turned off, regulated voltage should be no greater than 3.0 volts above recorded figure. Turn headlights on and set heater blower to high. Regulated voltage off idle should be no less than 0.5 volts above recorded figure.

STARTER

Engine	Year	Cranking Voltage (min. volts)	Ampere Draw @ Cranking Speed
All	1983-92	8.0	—

SPARK PLUGS

Engine/Model	Year	Gap (inches)	Gap (mm)	Torque (ft-lb)
Rotary Engines:				
All	1983-85	.053-.057	1.35-1.45	9-13
All	1986-88	.080	2.0	9-13
All	1989-90	.043-.067	1.1-1.7	9-13
Piston Engines:				
All	1983-85	.029-.033	.75-.85	11-17
1998cc 2V, 2184cc 2V	1986-92	.030-.033	.75-.85	11-17
All Others	1986-92	.039-.043	1.0-1.1	11-17

IGNITION COIL

Winding resistance (ohms @ 68°F or 20°C)

1597cc Miata: Primary resistance measured between terminals 1 & 2 and 1 & 3 of coil connector. Secondary resistance measured between two left or two right side high tension terminals of coils with spark plug wires removed.

1844cc: Primary resistance measured between first and third terminals of 3-terminal coil connector. Secondary resistance measured between terminal C (closest to coil tower) of 3-terminal coil connector and high tension terminal of coil with spark plug wire removed.

2954cc DOHC: Primary resistance measured between both pairs of terminals on coil.

Engine/Model	Year	Windings	Resistance (ohms)
1146cc	1983	Primary	.81-.99
		Secondary	7000
1146cc, 1308cc	1984-85	Primary	1.21-1.49
1308cc	1986-90	Primary	0.2-1.0
1490cc	1983-85	Primary	1.03-1.27
		Secondary	10,000-30,000
1597cc	1986-89	Primary	†
		Secondary	6000-30,000
1597cc Miata	1990-92	Primary	.78-.94
		Secondary	11,200-15,200
1597cc Others, 1839cc	1990-92	Primary	.81-.99
		Secondary	10,000-16,000
1844cc	1992	Primary	.58-.86
		Secondary	11,500-18,500
1998cc	1983-85	Primary	1.03-1.27
		Secondary	10,000-30,000
1998cc	1986-88		
Passenger Car		Primary	1.03-1.27
		Secondary	10,000-30,000
Pickup Truck		Secondary	8350-10,200
2184cc FI	1988-90	Primary	1.04-1.27
		Secondary	7100-9700
2184cc	1991-92	Primary	.77-.95
		Secondary	10,300-13,900
2184cc Turbo	1988-92	Primary	.72-.88
		Secondary	10,300-13,900
2184cc 2V	1987-92	Primary	1.0-1.3
		Secondary	6000-30,000

IGNITION COIL Continued

Engine/Model	Year	Windings	Resistance (ohms)
2555cc	1987-88	Primary	1.0-1.3
		Secondary	10,000-20,000
2606cc	1989-90	Primary	.77-.95 *
		Secondary	6000-30,000
2606cc	1991-92	Primary	.81-.99 *
		Secondary	6000-30,000
2954cc 929	1988-91	Primary	.72-.88
		Secondary	10,000-30,000
2954cc	1992	Primary	.70-1.1
		Secondary	9000-17,000
2954cc MPV	1989-90	Primary	.81-.99
		Secondary	6000-30,000

† Coil is defective if there is no continuity.

* Measured between two terminals on right side of high tension tower. When measured on left side, 0.9-1.1.

DISTRIBUTOR PICKUP

Application	Year	Resistance (ohms)	Air Gap (in./mm)
1146cc, 1308cc	1983-85	600-700	.020-.035/.50-.90
1970cc B2000	1983-84	945-1155	.008-.024/.20-.60
2184cc FI	1990-92	900-1200	—
2555cc B2600	1987-88	—	.031/.08
2606cc, mech. distr.	1989-90	900-1200	—
2954cc 929	1988-91	140-180*	—
2954cc MPV	1989-90	900-1200	—

* Measured between all three left and right terminals individually.

IGNITION RESISTOR

Application	Year	Type	Resistance (ohms)	Temperature (deg. F/C)
2555cc	1987-88	Unit	1.0-1.5	—

TIMING PROCEDURE

Both leading and trailing ignition systems must be timed on rotary engines.

Rotary engine leading ignition:
Disconnect and plug distributor vacuum hose(s). Loosen distributor lock nut and rotate to obtain specified timing.

Rotary engine trailing ignition:
1983-85, loosen vacuum unit attaching screws and move unit to obtain specified timing. Tighten screws and recheck timing.

1986-90, rotate crankshaft sensor to adjust.

Piston engines:
1988-91 626 Turbo, 929, MPV 6-cyl.: Ground test connector (green connector, 1 wire).

1990-92 323, Protegé, Miata

1992 MX-3 929: Ground diagnostic test terminal #10.

1992 4016cc: Connect EDIS checker and press SAW key. Timing should be at Set value. With button relaxed, timing should be at Check value.

All w/mechanical advance distributor: Disconnect and plug distributor vacuum hose(s). Loosen distributor lock nut and rotate to obtain specified timing.

Some models w/EST: When test terminal is ungrounded, verify that timing is at Check value.

BASE TIMING

Set timing at slow idle and Before Top Dead Center, unless otherwise specified.

Engine/Model	Year	Man. Trans. (degrees)	Auto. Trans. (degrees)
Rotary Engines:			
1146cc:			
Leading	1983-85	0 ±1	0 ±1
Trailing	1983-85	20 ATDC ±2	20 ATDC ±2
1308cc:			
Leading	1984-90	5 ATDC ±1	5 ATDC ±1
Trailing	1984-90	20 ATDC ±2	20 ATDC ±2
Piston Engines:			
1490cc ex. Wagon	1983-85	6 ±1	6 ±1
Wagon	1983	8 ±1	8 ±1
1597cc	1986-89	2 ±1	2 ±1
Turbo	1988-89	12 ±1	12 ±1

UNDERHOOD SERVICE SPECIFICATIONS

MAITU4   MAITU4

BASE TIMING Continued

Engine/Model	Year	Man. Trans. (degrees)	Auto. Trans. (degrees)
1597cc, 323	1990-92	7 ±1	7 ±1
1597cc Miata	1990	8 ±1	8 ±1
1597cc Miata	1991-92	10 ±1	8 ±1
1597cc MX-3	1992	10 ±1	10 ±1
1839cc	1990-92	5 ±1	5 ±1
DOHC	1990-92	10 ±1	10 ±1
1844cc	1992	10 ±1	10 ±1
Check	1992	6-18	6-18
1970cc Pickup	1983-84	8 ±1	8 ±1
1998cc	1983-87	6 ±1	6 ±1
2184cc FI	1988-92	6 ±1	6 ±1
Turbo	1988-92	9 ±1	9 ±1
2184cc 2V	1987-92	6 ±1	6 ±1
2555cc	1987-88	7 ±1	7 ±1
2606cc	1989-92	5 ±1	5 ±1
2954cc 929	1988-91	15 ±1	15 ±1
DOHC	1990	—	8 ±1
2954cc	1992	—	10 ±1
Check	1992	—	7-20
2954cc MPV	1989-91	11 ±1	11 ±1
4016cc	1991-92	10*	10*
Check	1991-92	15 min.	15 min.

* Not adjustable.

DISTRIBUTOR TIMING ADVANCE

Engine degrees at engine rpm, no load, in addition to base timing setting.

Mechanical advance distributors only.

Engine	Trans-mission	Year	Distributor Number	Degrees @ 2500 RPM Total	Degrees @ 2500 RPM Centrifugal
Rotary Engines:					
1146cc Leading	MT & AT	1983-85	—	19.8-26.0	10.8-13.0
Trailing	MT & AT	1983-85	—	37.0-47.4	9-15
1308cc Leading	MT	1984-85	—	21-29	13-17
Trailing	MT	1984-85	—	36-44	13-17
Piston Engines:					
1490cc	MT & AT	1983	D4R80-06	16-24	4-8
1490cc	MT & AT	1983-85	—	12.1-20.1	4.1-8.1
1597cc 2V	MT & AT	1986-87	—	34-42	18-22
1597cc FI	MT & AT	1986-87	—	45-53	19-23
1597cc FI	MT & AT	1988-89	—	34-42	8-12
1597cc Turbo	MT & AT	1988-89	—	17.8-25.8	4.8-8.8
1970cc	MT & AT	1983-84	T4T62571, 72	24-32	8-12
1998cc Federal	MT	1983-85	—	31.4-41.4	9.4-13.4
1998cc Federal	AT	1983-85	—	27.4-37.4	9.4-13.4
1998cc California	MT	1983-85	—	29.4-37.4	9.4-13.4
1998cc California	AT	1983-85	—	25.4-33.4	9.4-13.4
1998cc Pickup	MT	1986-87	—	30-38	10-14
1998cc 626	MT & AT	1986-87	—	27.2-35.2	9.2-13.2
1998cc Turbo	MT	1986-87	—	29-39	16-20
2184cc FI	MT & AT	1988-90	—	30.2-38.2	12.2-16.2
2184cc 2V	MT & AT	1987-90	—	25-33	9-13
2555cc	MT & AT	1987-88	—	25-33	4-8
2606cc†	MT & AT	1989-90	—	38-46*	24-28
2954cc MPV	MT & AT	1989-91	—	31-38	38-46

* Vacuum retard, 4-8.

† Late 1990 MPV has EST.

FUEL SYSTEM

FUEL PUMP

Engine	Year	Pressure (PSI) Fuel Pump	Pressure (PSI) Fuel Line†	Pressure (PSI) Fuel Line•
1146cc	1983-85	2.8-3.6	—	—
1308cc FI	1984-85	50-71	28.4	37
1308cc FI	1986-87	64-85.3	28.4	35.6-37
1308cc FI	1988	64-85.3	28.4	34.1-39.8
1308cc	1989-91	71-92	27-33	—
Turbo	1989-91	71-92	28.4	34-40
1490cc	1983	2.8-3.6	—	—
1490cc	1984-85	4.3-6.0	—	—

FUEL PUMP Continued

Engine	Year	Pressure (PSI) Fuel Pump	Pressure (PSI) Fuel Line†	Pressure (PSI) Fuel Line•
1597cc 2V	1986-87	4-5	—	—
1597cc FI	1986-89	64-85	24.6-31.3	34-41
1597cc, 1839cc, 1844cc	1990-92	64-85	30-38	38-46
1970cc	1983-84	2.8-3.6	—	—
1998cc	1983-84	2.8-4.3	—	—
1998cc 2V Pickup	1986-87	3.9-4.4	—	—
1998cc FI 626	1986-87	64-85	27-33	35-41
2184cc 2V Mech.	1987-92	3.7-4.7	—	—
Elect.	1987-92	2.8-3.6	—	—
2184cc FI	1988-92	64-85	27-33	34-40
2555cc	1987-88	2.8-3.6	—	—
2606cc, 2954cc	1988-91	64-85	28-38	38-46
2954cc 929	1992	64-92	30-38	38-46
4016cc	1991-92	—	30-45	35-45

† Vacuum hose connected to pressure regulator.

• Vacuum hose disconnected from pressure regulator.

IDLE SPEED W/O COMPUTER CONTROL

Midpoint of range given is the preferred setting.

1983-85 Rotary engine: To set curb idle, disconnect and plug idle compensator valve at air cleaner, adjust to specification. To set fast idle, disconnect choke diaphragm vacuum hose, apply vacuum to unit and measure clearance between choke valve and throttle bore. To set AC speed-up, disconnect AC relay electrical leads and apply battery voltage. Set speed-up to specification.

1986-88 Rotary engine: Bridge terminals of the initial set coupler, located by washer fluid bottle, and set idle speed to specification.

1989-90 Rotary engine: Ground test connector (single wire, green connector) by battery.

1983-92 Gasoline piston engines: To set idle speed, turn idle speed screw to obtain specified idle. To set fast idle, set cam on specified step and adjust to specified value. To set speed-up speed, activate vacuum ports on vacuum solenoid that correspond to each speed-up system. Adjust vacuum ports on solenoid to specified value.

1983-85 Diesel engine: With sufficient throttle cable length, turn screw on injection pump to obtain specified idle.

Engine	Year	SLOW Man. Trans.	SLOW Auto. Trans.	FAST Man. Trans.	FAST Auto. Trans.	Step of Cam
Rotary Engines:						
1146cc	1983-85	750	750 D	—	—	—
AC speed-up	1983-85	1200	1200 N	—	—	—
1308cc FI	1984-85	800	—	—	—	—
1308cc FI	1986-90	725-775	725-775 N	—	—	—
Speed-up	1986-90	800	750 D	—	—	—
Piston Engines:						
1490cc ex. Wagon	1983-85	850	750 D	—	—	Second
AC speed-up	1983-85	1200	1200 N	—	—	
1490cc Wagon	1983	800	750 D	—	—	Second
1597cc 2V	1986-87	800-900	950-1050 N	2000-2350	2200-2500 N	Third
Speed-up: AC	1986-87	1300-1400	1400-1500 N			
Elect. load	1986-87	950-1050	1100-1200			
PS	1986-87	1100-1300	1100-1300 N			
1597cc FI	1986-87	800-900	950-1050 N	—	—	
Speed-up: AC	1986-87	1250-1350	1450-1550 N			
Elect. load	1986-87	900-950	1050-1100 N			
PS	1986-87	1000-1100	1150-1250 N			
1970cc Pickup	1983-84	650	650 D	—	—	First
1998cc gasoline	1983-85	750	700 D	—	—	Second
1998cc Diesel	1985	800-850	—	1350-1650	—	—
AC speed-up	1985	900-950	—			
1998cc Pickup	1986-87	800-850	—	—	—	
Speed-up	1986-87	1300-1500	—			

IDLE SPEED W/O COMPUTER CONTROL Continued

Engine	Year	SLOW Man. Trans.	SLOW Auto. Trans.	FAST Man. Trans.	FAST Auto. Trans.	Step of Cam
1998cc 626	1986	750-800	900-950 N	—	—	—
1998cc 626	1987	800-850	900-950 N	—	—	—
Speed-up: AC	1986-87	1250-1350	1250-1350 N			
Elect. load, PS	1986-87	850-950	1000-1100 N			
2184cc 2V	1987-92	800-850	800-850 N	3000-4000	3000-4000 N	High
Speed-up: AC	1987-92	1300-1500	1300-1500 N			
Elect. load, PS	1987-92	—	920-970 N			
2555cc	1987-88	800-850	800-850 N	—	—	—
Speed-up	1987-88	1200-1400	1200-1400 N			

IDLE SPEED W/COMPUTER CONTROL

Midpoint of range given is the preferred setting speed.

Ground test connector (see Computer Diagnostic Codes) and set idle to specified value.

Engine	Year	Transmission	Setting Speed	Checking Speed	AC Speed-up
1597cc FI	1988-89	MT	800-900	—	—
		AT	800-900 N	—	—
1597cc Miata	1990-92	MT	850	800-900	—
		AT	850 N	800-900 N	—
1597cc 323	1990-92	MT	750	700-800	—
		AT	750 N	700-800 N	—
1597cc MX-3	1992	MT	700-800	700-800	800-900
		AT	700-800 N	700-800 N	750-850 N
1839cc	1990-92	MT	750	700-800	—
		AT	750 N	700-800 N	—
1844cc	1992	MT	640-700	640-700	720-780
		AT	640-700 N	640-700 N	720-760 N
2184cc FI	1988-89	MT	750	725-775	800
		AT	750 N	725-775 N	800 N
2184cc FI	1990-92	MT	750	725-775	800
		AT	750 N	725-775 N	850 N
2606cc	1989-92	MT	730-770	—	—
		AT	750-790 N	—	—
2954cc	1988-91	MT	630-670	—	—
		AT	630-670 N	—	—
DOHC	1990-91	AT	680-720 N	—	900 N
2954cc 929	1992	AT	680-720 N	—	—
2954cc MPV	1989-92	MT	780-820	—	—
		AT	780-820 N	—	—
4016cc	1991	MT	—	675	—
		AT	—	675 N	—

ENGINE MECHANICAL

TIGHTENING TORQUES

Some fasteners are tightened in more than one step.

Some values are specified in inches.

Engine	Year	Cylinder Head	Intake Manifold	Exhaust Manifold	Crankshaft Pulley	Water Pump
1308cc	1984-90	—	14-19/ 19-25	23-34/ 31-46	69-95″/ 7-11	13-20/ 18-26
1490cc	1983-85	56-59/ 78-82	14-19/ 19-26	14-17/ 19-23	80-87/ 110-120	14-22/ 19-31
1597cc, 1839cc, ex. DOHC	1986-92	56-60/ 76-81	14-19/ 19-25	12-17/ 16-23	109-152″/ 12-17	14-19/ 19-25

TIGHTENING TORQUES Continued

Engine	Year	Cylinder Head	Intake Manifold	Exhaust Manifold	Crankshaft Pulley	Water Pump
1597cc, 1839cc DOHC	1986-92	56-60/ 76-81	14-19/ 19-25	29-42/ 39-57	109-152″/ 12-17	14-19/ 19-25
1844cc	1992	17-19/ 23-26, +90°, +90°	14-19/ 19-25	14-19/ 19-25	116-123/ 157-167	14-19/ 19-25
1970cc Pickup	1983-85	65-69/ 90-95	14-19/ 19-25	16-21/ 22-28	116-123/ 157-167	14-19/ 19-25
1998cc	1983-87	59-64/ 80-86	14-19/ 19-25	16-21/ 22-28	9-13/ 12-17	14-19/ 19-25
1998cc Diesel	1985	22/30 +90°, +90°	14-19/ 19-25	16-21/ 22-28	17-23/ 23-33	28-38/ 38-53
2184cc FI	1988-92	59-64/ 80-86	14-22/ 19-30	25-36/ 34-49	109-152″/ 12-17	14-19/ 19-25
2184cc 2V	1987-92	59-64/ 80-86	14-22/ 19-30	16-21/ 22-28	9-13/ 12-17	9-13/ 12-17
2209cc Diesel	1983-84	80-85/ 110-120	12-17/ 16-24	12-17/ 16-24	145-181/ 200-250	12-17/ 16-24
2555cc	1987-88	65-72/ 88-98	11-14/ 15-19	11-14/ 15-19	90-94/ 108-128	104-122″/ 12-14
2606cc	1989-92	59-64/ 80-86	14-22/ 19-30	16-21/ 22-28	130-145/ 173-196	14-19/ 19-25
2954cc	1988-92	14/20 +90°, +90°	14-19/ 19-25	16-21/ 22-28	116-123/ 157-167	14-19/ 19-25

VALVE CLEARANCE

Engine hot.

Engine	Year	Intake (inches)	Intake (mm)	Exhaust (inches)	Exhaust (mm)
1272cc, 1415cc, 1490cc	1983-85	.010	.25	.012	.30
1796cc, 1970cc	1983-85	.012	.30	.012	.30
1597cc	1986-87	.012	.30	.012	.30
1998cc gasoline	1983-87	.012	.30	.012	.30
1998cc Diesel	1985	.008-.012	.20-.30	.012-.016	.30-.40
2209cc Diesel	1983-84	.012	.30	.012	.30
2555cc	1987-88	Hydraulic Lifters			
Jet Valve	1987-88	.010	.25	—	—

COMPRESSION PRESSURE

At cranking speed, engine warm, throttle open.

Engine/Model	Year	PSI	Maximum Variation PSI
Rotary Engines:			
All	1983-91	85 min.	21
Piston Engines:			
1490cc	1983-85	128-170	28
1597cc ex. MX-3	1986-92	135-192	28
MX-3	1992	142-186	28
1839cc	1990-91	128-182	28
1844cc	1992	142-193	28
1970cc	1983-84	128-171	28
1998cc gasoline	1983-87	115-164	28
Turbo	1986-87	110-156	28
1998cc, 2209cc Diesel	1983-85	384-427	—
2184cc FI	1988-92	114-162	28
Turbo	1988-92	98-139	28
2184cc 2V	1987-92	121-173	28
2555cc	1987-88	119-171	—
2606cc	1989-92	142-182	28
2954cc	1988-92	114-164	28
4016cc	1991-92	*	

* Lowest cylinder pressure should be within 75% of highest.

UNDERHOOD SERVICE SPECIFICATIONS

MAITU6   MAITU6

BELT TENSION

With 22 pounds of pressure applied midway between pulleys on longest belt segment.

Engine	Year	Alternator	Power Steering	Air Cond.	Air Pump
Deflection Method:					
USED BELTS					
1146cc (inches)	1983-85	1/2-11/16	—	3/8-9/16	7/16-1/2
(mm)	1983-85	13-17	—	10-14	11-13
1308cc (inches)	1983-85	1/2-11/16	—	3/8-9/16	7/16-1/2
(mm)	1983-85	13-17	—	10-14	11-13
1308cc (inches)	1986-88	9/16-11/16	9/16-11/16	9/16-11/16	9/16-11/16
(mm)	1986-88	14-17	14-17	14-17	14-17
1308cc (inches)	1989-90	1/2-5/8	7/16-1/2	1/4-5/16	3/8-7/16
(mm)	1989-90	12-15	11-13	6-8	9-11
1490cc (inches)	1983	7/16-1/2	—	3/8-9/16	5/16-3/8
(mm)	1983	11-13	—	10-14	8-10
1970cc (inches)	1983-84	1/2-9/16	—	—	1/2-9/16
(mm)	1983-84	12-14	—	—	12-14
1998cc (inches)	1983-85	5/16-3/8	3/8-7/16	—	3/8-7/16
(mm)	1983-85	6-7	10-12	—	10-12
1998cc (inches)	1986-87	5/16-7/16	5/16-7/16	5/16-7/16	5/16-7/16
(mm)	1986-87	8-10	8-10	8-10	8-10
2184cc FI (inches)	1988-92	5/16-3/8	5/16-3/8	5/16-3/8	—
(mm)	1988-92	7-9	7-9	7-9	—
2184cc 2V (inches)	1987-92	7/16-3/8	7/16-3/8	5/8-9/16	7/16-3/8
(mm)	1987-92	8-9	8-9	12-14	8-9
2555cc (inches)	1987-88	1/4-7/16	7/16-1/2	9/16-5/8	1/4-7/16
(mm)	1987-88	7-10	10-11	14-16	7-10
2954cc 929 (inches)	1988-90	3/8-7/16	3/8-7/16	3/8-7/16	—
(mm)	1988-90	10-12	9-11	9-11	—
Strand Tension Method:					
USED BELTS					
1597cc, 1839cc ex. Miata	1986-92	68-85	95-110	95-110	—
1597cc Miata	1990-92	95-110	95-110	95-110	—
1844cc	1992	50-70	40-55	50-70	—
2606cc	1989-92	103-123	93-106	126-143	—
2954cc 929	1991-92	92-110	92-110	92-110	—
2972cc MPV	1989-92	103-123	106-123	79-90	—
NEW BELTS					
1597cc, 1839cc ex. Miata	1986-92	85-103	110-132	110-132	—
1597cc Miata	1990-92	110-132	110-132	110-132	—
1844cc	1992	70-90	55-70	70-90	—
2606cc	1989-92	123-143	92-105	99-121	—
2954cc 929	1991-92	110-125	110-125	110-125	—
2972cc MPV	1989-92	123-143	125-143	92-106	—

ENGINE COMPUTER SYSTEM

COMPUTER DIAGNOSTIC CODES

1984-91 RX-7 FI,

1985-87 626 Connect digital code checker (tool #49 G018 9A0) to check connector located by battery (RX-7), or control unit (626).

1986-87 323, B2000 Connect system checker (tool #49 G030 920) to check connector located by control unit.

1987-92 B2200 Connect system checker (Tool #49 H018 9A1) to connector above right side wheel housing. Ground check connector (yellow/black) and turn ignition on.

1989-92 B2600,

1988-92 323, 626, 929, MPV Connect system checker (Tool #49 H018 9A1) to check connector loaded by battery and ground green single wire connector if equipped.

1984-88 RX-7 FI
Code 1 Crank angle sensor
Code 2 Air flow meter
Code 3 Coolant temperature sensor
Code 4 Intake air temperature sensor (air flow meter)
Code 5 Oxygen sensor
Code 6 Throttle sensor
Code 7 Boost pressure sensor
Code 9 Atmospheric pressure sensor
Code 12 Trailing side coil w/ignitor
Code 15 Intake air temperature (dynamic chamber, intake air pipe)

1989-91 RX-7
Code 1 Ignition coil, trailing side
Codes 2, 3 Crank angle sensor
Code 8 Airflow meter
Code 9 Coolant temperature sensor
Code 10 Intake air temperature sensor, airflow meter
Code 11 Intake air temperature sensor, engine

COMPUTER DIAGNOSTIC CODES Continued
Codes 12, 18 Throttle sensor
Code 13 MAP sensor
Code 14 Barometric sensor
Code 15 Oxygen sensor
Code 17 Feedback system
Codes 20, 27, 37 Metering oil pump
Code 25 Pressure regulator solenoid
Code 26 Step motor, metering oil pump
Code 30 Split air solenoid valve
Code 31 Relief solenoid
Code 32 Switch solenoid
Code 33 Port air solenoid
Code 34 Air bypass valve solenoid
Code 38 Warm-up solenoid
Code 40 Auxiliary port valve
Code 41 Intake control solenoid
Code 51 Fuel pump resistor
Code 71 Injector, front
Code 73 Injector, rear

1988-92 323, 626, 929, MPV, Miata, MX-3
Code 1 Ignition pulse
Codes 2, 3, 4 Distributor pickups or crankshaft sensor
Code 5 Knock sensor
Code 6 Speed sensor
Code 7 Knock sensor (right side, 929 DOHC)
Code 8 Air flow meter
Code 9 Coolant temperature sensor
Code 10 Intake air sensor in airflow meter
Code 11 Intake air sensor in intake manifold
Code 12 Throttle sensor
Code 14 Atmospheric pressure sensor
Code 15 Oxygen sensor (left side, DOHC 929)
Code 16 EGR position sensor
Code 17 Feedback system (left side, DOHC 929)
Code 23 Oxygen sensor (right side, DOHC 929)
Code 24 Feedback system (right side, DOHC 929)
Code 25 Pressure regulator solenoid
Codes 26, 27 Purge central solenoids
Code 28 EGR vacuum solenoid
Code 29 EGR vent solenoid
Code 34 ISC valve
Code 36 Oxygen sensor heater, right side
Code 37 Oxygen sensor heater, left side
Codes 40, 41 Induction control solenoid valves
Code 46 VRIS solenoid (V6)
Code 55 Pulse generator
Code 60 AT solenoid, 1-2 shift
Code 61 AT solenoid, 2-3 shift
Code 62 AT solenoid, 3-4 shift
Code 63 AT solenoid, lock-up
Code 65 AC signal
Code 67 Fan relay
Code 69 Fan coolant temperature sensor

1985-87 323, 626
Code 1 Ignition pulse
Code 2 Air flow meter
Code 3 Coolant temperature sensor
Code 4 Engine temperature sensor, 323
Code 4 Intake air temperature sensor, 626
Code 5 Feedback system
Code 6 Atmospheric pressure sensor, 323
Code 6 Throttle sensor, 626
Code 8 EGR sensor
Code 9 Atmospheric pressure sensor
Code 22 No. 1 cylinder sensor

1987-92 B2200 2V
Code 1 Ignition pulse, 1987-92
Code 1 Engine speed sensor, 1986-87
Code 2 Coolant temperature sensor
Code 3 Feedback system
Code 4 Vacuum sensor
Code 5 EGR position sensor
Code 9 Coolant temperature sensor or circuit
Code 13 Vacuum sensor or circuit
Code 14 Barometric pressure sensor or circuit
Code 15 O_2 sensor or circuit
Code 16 EGR control system
Code 17 Mixture control system
Code 18 Air/fuel solenoid or circuit

MAZDA
1983-92

COMPUTER DIAGNOSTIC CODES Continued

Code 22 Fuel out solenoid or circuit
Code 23 Coasting richer, solenoid or circuit
Code 26 Purge solenoid or circuit
Code 28 Duty solenoid valve or circuit
Code 29 Duty solenoid vent valve or circuit
Code 30 ACV solenoid valve or circuit
Code 35 Idle up solenoid or circuit
Code 45 Vacuum solenoid valve or circuit

SENSORS, INPUT

TEMPERATURE SENSORS

Intake air temperature sensor, measured between terminals E2 and THA of airflow sensor.

Engine	Year	Sensor	Resistance Ohms @ deg. F/C
1308cc, 1597cc, 1998cc, 2184cc, 2606cc, 2954cc	1984-92	Coolant	14,500-17,800 @ −4/−20
			2200-2700 @ 68/20
			1000-1300 @ 104/40
			500-640 @ 140/60
			280-350 @ 176/80
		Intake Air*	10,000-20,000 @ −4/−20
			4000-7000 @ 32/0
			2000-3000 @ 68/20
			900-1300 @ 104/40
			400-700 @ 140/60
1308cc, 2606cc MPV, 2954cc	1989-92	Intake Air†	29,000-37,000 @ 77/25
			3100-3900 @ 185/85
4016cc	1991-92	Coolant, Manifold Air	31,700-42,900 @ 68/20
			13,650-18,650 @ 104/40
			6500-8900 @ 140/60
			3240-4440 @ 176/80
			1770-23,700 @ 212/100
			980-13,800 @ 248/120

* Sensor contained in airflow meter.
† Sensor located on intake manifold.

PRESSURE SENSORS

1308cc: Measured between terminal D of pressure sensor and ground.

1597cc FI, 2184cc FI, 2606cc, 2954cc: Measured between L/O wire of sensor and ground with 4.5-5.5 volts reference.

Engine	Year	Sensor	Voltage @ Elevation
1597cc FI, 2184cc FI, 2606cc, 2954cc	1985-90	Barometric	3.5-4.5 @ 0 ft
			2.5-3.5 @ 6500 ft

Engine	Year	Sensor	Voltage @ in./mm Hg
1308cc	1989-90	Pressure	2.8-3.2 @ 3.9/100
Turbo	1989-90	Pressure	1.9-2.1 @ 3.9/100
1998cc, 2184cc 2V	1986-92	Pressure	1.4 min. @ 0/0
			4.9 max. @ 30/750

Engine	Year	Frequency Hz @	Vacuum In Hg/kPa
4016cc	1991-92	125-189	0/0
		120-162	6/20
		107-143	12/40
		94-124	18/60
		80-110	24/81
		68-92	30/102

SENSORS, INPUT Continued

THROTTLE POSITION SENSOR

Engine	Year	Voltage	
		Idle	WOT
1308cc	1990-91	.25-1.25	4.1-4.4
1597cc, 1839cc w/AT	1991-92	0.5	4.0
2184cc FI 626, MX-6	1990-92	.37-.66	3.58-5.17
2184cc FI Pickup	1990-92	.37-.66	4.5-5.5
2606cc MPV	1989-92	0.5	4.3
2606cc Pickup	1990-92	.37-.66	4.5-5.5
2954cc MPV	1989-92	0.3	4.0

CRANKSHAFT SENSOR

1308cc, measured between both right or both left cavities on unit.

Engine	Year	Resistance (ohms)
1308cc	1986-91	110-210
1844cc	1992	950-1250

AIRFLOW METER

Engine	Year	Resistance @ Ohms	Throttle Position
1308cc	1990-91	20-800	idle
		200-1000	WOT
1597cc, 1839cc, 2184cc FI, 2954cc	1990-92	20-600	idle
		20-1200	WOT

Engine	Year	Voltage @ MPH/KPH
4016cc	1991-92	.60 @ 0/0
		1.10 @ 20/32
		1.70 @ 40/64
		2.10 @ 60/96

VEHICLE SPEED SENSOR

Engine	Year	Resistance (ohms)
4016cc	1991-92	190-250

ACTUATORS, OUTPUT

IDLE SPEED CONTROL

At 68°F (20°C).

Engine	Year	Resistance (ohms)
1308cc	1990-91	10-13
1597cc	1986-89	5-20
1597cc, 1839cc	1990-92	10-13
2184cc FI	1988-92	6.3-9.9
2606cc	1989-92	7.7-9.3
2954cc	1988-92	10-13
4016cc	1991-92	7-13

CHEK-CHART

ENGINE IDENTIFICATION

To identify an engine by the manufacturer's code, follow the four steps designated by the numbered blocks.

V.I.N. PLATE LOCATION:
On left front pillar post visible through windshield.

1 MODEL YEAR IDENTIFICATION:
Seventh character of V.I.N., first character of emissions control label.
1992 — N; 1991 — M; 1990 — L;
1989 — K; 1988 — J; 1987 — H;
1986 — G; 1985 — F; 1984 — E;
1983 — D.

2 ENGINE CODE LOCATION:
Prefix to engine number, stamped on block.

4 ENGINE IDENTIFICATION

YEAR	3 ENGINE CODE	CYL.	DISPL. liters	cc	Fuel System	HP
1992	102.985	4	2.3	2299	FI	130
	602.962	5	2.5 TD	2497 TD	FI	121
	103.942, 103.940	6	2.6	2599	FI	158
	103.983, 103.985	6	3.0	2960	FI	177
	104.980, 104.981	6	3.0	2960	FI	217, 228†
	104.990	6	3.2	3199	FI	228
	603.971	6	3.5 TD	3449 TD	FI	148
	119.975, 119.971	8	4.2	4196	FI	268, 282†
	119.960	8	5.0	4973	FI	322
	119.970, 119.974	8	5.0	4973	FI	322
	120.980	12	6.0	5991	FI	402
1991	102.985	4	2.3	2299	FI	130
	602.962	5	2.5 TD	2497 TD	FI	121
	103.940, 103.942	6	2.6	2599	FI	158
	103.983	6	3.0	2962	FI	177
	104.980, 104.981	6	3.0	2962	FI	217, 228†
	603.970	6	3.5 TD	3449 TD	FI	134
	116.965	8	4.2	4196	FI	201
	119.960	8	5.0	4973	FI	322
	117.968	8	5.6	5547	FI	238
1990	103.940, 103.942	6	2.6	2599	FI	158
	103.983	6	3.0	2962	FI	177
	124.050	6	3.0	2962	FI	217
	104.981	6	3.0	2962	FI	228
	117.965	8	4.2	4196	FI	201
	119.960	8	5.0	4973	FI	322
	117.968	8	5.6	5547	FI	238
1989	602.911	5	2.5 D	2497 D	FI	90
	103.940, 103.942	6	2.6	2599	FI	158
	103.983	6	3.0	2962	FI	177
	117.965	8	4.2	4196	FI	201
	117.967	8	5.6	5547	FI	227
	117.968	8	5.6	5547	FI	238
1988	102.985	4	2.3	2299	FI	130
	602.911	5	2.5 D	2497 D	FI	93
	103.940, 103.942	6	2.6	2599	FI	158
	103.983	6	3.0	2962	FI	177
	117.965	8	4.2	4196	FI	201

4 ENGINE IDENTIFICATION

YEAR	3 ENGINE CODE	CYL.	DISPL. liters	cc	Fuel System	HP
1988 Cont'd.	117.967	8	5.6	5547	FI	227
	117.968	8	5.6	5547	FI	238
1987	102.985	4	2.3	2299	FI	130
	102.983	4	2.3	2299	FI	167
	602.911	5	2.5 D	2497 D	FI	93
	602.961	5	2.5 TD	2497 TD	FI	123
	103.940, 103.942	6	2.6	2599	FI	158
	103.983	6	3.0	2962	FI	177
	603.960, 603.963	6	3.0 TD	2996 TD	FI	143
	117.965	8	4.2	4196	FI	201
	117.967	8	5.6	5547	FI	227
	117.968	8	5.6	5547	FI	238
1986	102.985	4	2.3	2299	FI	120
	102.983	4	2.3	2299	FI	167
	602.911	5	2.5	2497 D	FI	93
	103.983	6	3.0	2962	FI	177
	603.961	6	3.0	2996 TD	FI	143
	603.962	6	3.0	2996 TD	FI	148
	116.965	8	4.2	4196	FI	201
	117.967	8	5.6	5547	FI	227
	117.968	8	5.6	5547	FI	238
1985	601.921	4	2.2	2197 D	FI	72
	102.961	4	2.3	2299	FI	120
	617.951, 617.952	5	3.0	2998 TD	FI	118, 123†
	116.962, 116.963	8	3.8	3839	FI	155
	117.963	8	5.0	4973	FI	184
1984	601.921	4	2.2	2197 D	FI	72
	102.961	4	2.3	2299	FI	113
	616.912	4	2.4	2399 D	FI	67
	617.951, 617.952	5	3.0	2998 TD	FI	120
	116.962, 116.963	8	3.8	3839	FI	155
	117.963	8	5.0	4973	FI	184
1983	616.912	4	2.4	2399 D	FI	67
	617.951, 617.952	5	3.0	2998 TD	FI	120
	116.962, 116.963	8	3.8	3839	FI	155

D — Diesel.   TD — Turbo Diesel.   FI — Fuel Injection.
† Engine horsepower varies with emission equipment package.

UNDERHOOD SERVICE SPECIFICATIONS

MZITU1 MZITU1

CYLINDER NUMBERING SEQUENCE

4-CYL. FIRING ORDER:
1 3 4 2

6-CYL. FIRING ORDER:
1 5 3 6 2 4

8-CYL. FIRING ORDER:
1 5 4 8 6 3 7 2

12-CYL. FIRING ORDER:
1 12 5 8 3 10 6 7 2 11 4 9

— Front of car —

| 2.3 liter | 2.8 liter | 2.6, 3.0 liter | 3.8, 4.2, 5.6 liter | 6.0 liter |

TIMING MARK

0°
5° BTDC
10° BTDC

2.3 liter

TDC
7°
11°

2.6, 3.0 liter

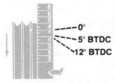

0°
5° BTDC
12° BTDC

3.8, 4.2, 5.6 liter

MERCEDES-BENZ
1983-92

ELECTRICAL AND IGNITION SYSTEMS

BATTERY

BCI equivalent shown, size may vary from original equipment.
Check clearance before replacing, holddown may need to be modified.

Engine/Model	Year	STANDARD BCI Group No.	STANDARD Crank. Perf.	OPTIONAL BCI Group No.	OPTIONAL Crank. Perf.
4-cyl.					
2.2L Diesel	1984-85	*	690	—	—
2.3L Gasoline	1984-87	47	460	—	—
2.3L Gasoline	1988-89	48	495	—	—
2.4L Diesel	1983	49	650	—	—
5-cyl.					
2.5L Diesel	1986-89	49	740	—	—
3.0L Turbo Diesel	1983-85	49	740	—	—
6-cyl.					
2.6L Gasoline	1987-91	48	495		
3.0L Gasoline	1986-89	48	495	—	—
3.0L Sedan, Coupe	1990-91	48	495	—	—
Roadster	1990-91	49	740	—	—
3.0L Diesel, Turbo Diesel	1986-87	49	740	—	—
8-cyl.					
3.8L Sedan, Coupe	1983-85	48	495	—	—
Roadster	1983-85	49	650	—	—
4.2L Sedan	1986-87	48	520	—	—
4.2L Sedan	1988-91	49	740	—	—
5.0L Sedan, Coupe	1984-85	48	495	—	—
5.0L Roadster	1990-91	49	740	—	—
5.6L Coupe, Roadster	1986-87	49	740	—	—
5.6L Sedan	1986-87	48	495	—	—
5.6L, all models	1988-91	49	740	—	—

* Special size (11.75″ × 7.0″ × 7.25″), no BCI equivalent.

ALTERNATOR

Application	Year	Rated Output (amps)	Test Output (amps @ rpm)
380 Series	1983	70	—
300D, SD	1983-85	55	55 @ 3100
380SE, SEL, SEC	1983-85	80	—
380SL	1983-85	70	—
500SEC, SEL	1984-85	80	—
190E	1984-85	65	—
190D	1984-85	55	55 @ 3100
190E, D, E-Sport	1986-90	70	70 @ 2480
260E, 300D, E, SDL, 560SL	1986-89	70	70 @ 2230
420SEL	1986-91	80	80 @ 2160
560SEC, SEL	1986-91	80	80 @ 2160
300SL, 500SL	1990-92	100	
300SE, SEL	1991	80	80 @ 2160
350SD, SDL	1991	80	80 @ 2160
190E 2.3, 300D	1991-92	70	70 @ 2230
300E, TE, 4MATIC	1991-92	80	80 @ 2160
400E, 500E	1992	110	—
300SE, 400SE, 500SEL, 600SEL	1992	120	120 @ 1970

REGULATOR

Application	Test Temp. (deg. F/C)	Voltage Setting
All models	Normal	13.0-14.5

STARTER

Engine	Year	Cranking Voltage (min. volts)	Ampere Draw @ Cranking Speed
4-cyl. gas	1984-88	8.0	—
6-cyl.	1986-89	8.0	—
V8	1983-89	7.5	—
Diesel engines	1983-87	7.8	—

SPARK PLUGS

Engine	Year	Gap (inches)	Gap (mm)	Torque (ft-lb)
All	1983	.032	.80	18-22
2299cc	1984-89	.032	.80	8-14
2299cc	1991-92	.032	.80	8-14
2599cc	1987-92	.032	.80	8-14
2962cc	1986-92	.032	.80	18-22
3839cc	1984-85	.039	.90	18-22
4196cc, 5547cc	1986-92	.032	.80	19-24
4973cc	1984-85	.032	.80	18-22
4973cc	1990-92	.032	.80	18-22

IGNITION COIL
Winding Resistance (ohms at 68°F or 20°C)

Engine	Year	Windings	Resistance (ohms)
4-cyl.	1984-85	Primary	.50-.90
		Secondary	6000-16,000
4-cyl.	1986-88	Primary	.30-.60
		Secondary	7000-13,000
6-cyl.	1986-89	Primary	.30-.60
		Secondary	7000-13,000
8-cyl.	1983-85	Primary	.30-.60
		Secondary	6000-15,000
8-cyl.	1986-87	Primary	.22-.27
		Secondary	8100-9900
8-cyl.	1988-89	Primary	.20-.40
		Secondary	7000-13,000

IGNITION PICKUP

Engine	Year	Resistance (ohms)	Air Gap (in./mm)
Gasoline	1983	500-700	.024/0.6

IGNITION RESISTOR

Year	Type	Resistance (ohms)	Temperature (deg. F/C)
1983-85	Wire	.4 & .6	68/20

TIMING PROCEDURE

1. Connect timing light to No. 1 spark plug wire.
2. Idle engine at normal operating temperature with vacuum hose(s) connected.
3. Adjust timing by turning distributor housing.

BASE TIMING

Set at Before Top Dead Center with engine idling, unless otherwise specified.

Engine	Year	Man. Trans. (degrees)	Auto. Trans. (degrees)
2.3L	1984-86	5 ±1	5 ±1
2.3L	1987-88	0 ±2†	0 ±2†
2.3L-16	1986-87	20†	20†
2.6L	1987	9 ±2†	9 ±2†
2.6L	1988-92	0 ±2♦	0 ±2♦
3.0L	1986-87	9 ±2†	9 ±2†
3.0L	1988-92	0 ±2♦	0 ±2♦
3.8L	1983-85	—	TDC*
4.2L	1986-87	—	12 ±2†
4.2L	1988-92	—	5 ±2♦
5.0L	1984-85	—	TDC†
5.6L	1986-87	—	12 ±2†
5.6L	1988-91	—	5 ±2♦

* With vacuum disconnected.
† For reference only, timing not adjustable.
♦ Reference figure at cranking speed, not adjustable.

DISTRIBUTOR TIMING ADVANCE

Engine degrees at engine rpm, no load, in addition to base timing setting.

Engine	Trans-mission	Year	Distributor Number	Degrees @ 2500 RPM Total	Degrees @ 2500 RPM Centrifugal
2.3L	MT & AT	1984-85	0237002094	30-38	16-20
2.3L	MT & AT	1984-85	0237002084	36-46	12-18
3.8L	AT	1983-85	0237401010	31.5-37.5	16.5-20.5

FUEL SYSTEM

FUEL PRESSURE

With engine at operating temperature, and idling.

Engine	Year	Control PSI	System PSI
4-cyl.			
2.3L	1984-85	—	77-80
2.3L	1986	—	83-96
2.3L	1987-88	—	77-80
6-cyl.			
2.6L	1987-89	—	77-80
3.0L	1986-89	—	77-80
8-cyl.			
3.8L, 5.0L	1983-85	49-55	73-80
4.2L, 5.6L	1986-89	—	90-92

IDLE SPEED W/O COMPUTER CONTROL

Engine	Year	Man. Trans.	Auto. Trans.
2.2L Diesel	1984-85	700-800	700-800 N
2.3L	1984-85	670-770	570-670 D
AC speed-up	1984-85	670-770	670-770 N
2.4L Diesel	1983	700-800	700-800 N
3.0L Diesel	1983	—	650-850 N
3.0L Turbo Diesel	1984-85	—	700-800 N
3.8L	1983-85	—	600-700 N
5.0L	1984-85	—	500-600 N

IDLE SPEED W/COMPUTER CONTROL

Engine	Year	Man. Trans.	Auto. Trans.
2.3L	1986	840-940	620-720 D
2.3L	1987-88	700-800	600-800 D
2.5L Diesel	1986-88	660-700	660-700 N
2.5L Turbo Diesel	1991-92	—	660-700 N
2.6L	1987-92	650-750	550-650 D
3.0L Gasoline	1986-92	600-700	500-600 D
3.0L Diesel	1986-87	610-650	610-650 N
3.5L Turbo Diesel	1991-92	—	610-650 N
4.2L	1986-92	—	450-550 D
5.0L	1990-92	—	450-550 D
5.6L	1986-91	—	500-600 D
6.0L	1992	—	500-650 D

IDLE MIXTURE

Engine	Year	A/F Ratio	Idle CO%
2.3L	1984-85	—	0.5-1.5
3.8L, 5.0L	1983-85	—	0.5-1.5

ENGINE MECHANICAL

TIGHTENING TORQUES

Engine	Year	Cylinder Head	Intake Manifold	Exhaust Manifold	Crankshaft Pulley	Water Pump
DIESEL ENGINES						
4-cyl. 2.2L	1984-85	18/25	—	—	236/320	7/10
2nd stage		30/40				
3rd stage†		90°, +90°				
4-cyl. 2.4L:						
16-point bolt	1983-84	30/40	—	—	199-243/	7/9
2nd stage		52/70			270-330	
3rd stage†		90°, +90°				
5-cyl. 2.5L	1986-89	18/25	—	—	236/320	7/10
2nd stage		30/40				
3rd stage†		90°, +90°				
5-cyl. 3.0L:						
16-point bolt	1983-85	30/40	—	—	199-243/	7/9
2nd stage		52/70			270-330	
3rd stage†		90°, +90°				
6-cyl. 3.0L	1986-87	18/25	—	—	236/320	7/10
2nd stage		30/40				
3rd stage†		90°, +90°				
GASOLINE ENGINES						
4-cyl. 2.3L	1984-88	52/70	—	—	148/200	7/10
2nd stage		90°, +90°			90°, +90°	
6-cyl. 2.6L,						
3.0L	1986-92	52/70	—	—	221/300	17/23
2nd stage		90°, +90°				
V8 3.8L	1983-85	22/30	—	—	199-243/	18/25
2nd stage♦		44/60			270-330	
V8 4.2L, 5.6L	1986-91	22/30	—	—	221/300	18/25
2nd stage♦		44/60				
V8 5.0L	1984-85	22/30	—	—	221/300	18/25
2nd stage♦		44/60				

† Allow cylinder head to settle 10 minutes before final torque.
♦ Tighten head to specification, allow to settle 10 minutes and retorque.

VALVE CLEARANCE

Engine cold.

Engine	Year	Intake (inches)	Intake (mm)	Exhaust (inches)	Exhaust (mm)
2.3L-16 valve	1986-87	.006	.15	.012	.30
2.4L Diesel	1983	.004	.10	.012	.30
3.0L All	1983-85	.004	.10	.014	.36

COMPRESSION PRESSURE

At cranking speed, engine temperature normalized, throttle open.

Engine	Year	PSI @ RPM	Max. variation PSI	Min. allowable PSI
Diesel	1983-88	320-350	43	218
	1989	319-435	—	260
Gasoline	1983-87	130-145	23	108
	1988-89	145-174	—	123

BELT TENSION

A belt in operation immediately after running is considered a used belt.
Strand Tension method: Measured in pounds with a strand gauge.

Engine	Year	New	Used
All V8:			
9.5mm belts	1988-89	66	44-45
12.5mm belts	1988-89	110	88-99

Deflection method: Table lists deflection at midpoint of longest belt segment under a 13 pound load.

Automatic tensioner assemblies are fitted to some late model vehicles.

MZITU4 MZITU4

BELT TENSION Continued

USED BELTS

Engine	Year	Alternator	Power Steering	Air Cond.	Air Pump
All 4-, 5-, & 6-cyl.:					
(inches)	1983-89	3/8*	3/16	3/8*	3/8*
(mm)	1983-89	10*	5	10*	10*
All V8:					
(inches)	1983-89	3/8	3/8	3/16	3/8
(mm)	1983-89	10	10	5	10

* Special tensioning tool required.

ENGINE COMPUTER SYSTEM

COMPUTER DIAGNOSTIC CODES

Start engine and run until oil temperature reaches operating range, 140°-168°F (60°-80°C). Connect an ''on-off ratio tester'' (Bosch model KDJE-P600) to the diagnostic socket in the engine compartment. Allow engine to run at idle, failure codes will be displayed as a percentage on the meter.

1986-87 2.3L ex. 16 valve, 1987 2.6L:

0%	No voltage to control unit or defective unit.
10%	Air flow sensor position indicator defective or polarity reversed.
20%	Full load contact polarity reversed or defective.
30%	Coolant temperature sensor circuit open or shorted or sensor defective.
40%	Air flow sensor circuit open or shorted or sensor defective.
50%	Oxygen sensor not at operating temperature, open circuit, sensor defective.
60%	Not used.
70%	No TD signal to control unit.

COMPUTER DIAGNOSTIC CODES Continued

80%	Altitude correction capsule circuit open or shorted or capsule defective.
90%	Not used.
100%	Lean fuel mixture, oxygen sensor circuit grounded, defective oxygen sensor, defective control unit or on-off ratio tester.
Oscillates	No malfunction of monitored signals.

SENSORS, INPUT

CRANKSHAFT SENSORS

Engine	Year	Position Sensor Resistance (ohms)	Reference Sensor Resistance (ohms)
4-cyl. 2.3L DOHC	1986-87	730-910	750
4-cyl. 2.3L SOHC	1986-88	680-1200	750
6-cyl. 2.6L	1987-89	680-1200	750
6-cyl. 3.0L	1986-89	730-910	750
V8 4.2L, 5.6L	1986-89	730-910	750

COMPUTER TIMING ADVANCE

Specifications include base timing.

Perform with engine at normal operating temperature.

Engine	Year	Degrees @ RPM Without Vacuum	Degrees @ RPM With Vacuum
2.3L-16 valve	1986-87	20 ±2 @ 4000	31 ±2 @ 4000
2.3L ex. 16 valve	1986-88	24 ±2 @ 3500	38 ±2 @ 3500
2.6L	1987-89	27 ±2 @ 3200	42 ±2 @ 3200
3.0L	1986-89	29 ±2 @ 3200	42 ±2 @ 3200
4.2L	1986-89	30 ±2 @ 3500	43 ±2 @ 3500
5.6L	1986-89	26 ±2 @ 3500	42 ±2 @ 3500

ENGINE IDENTIFICATION

To identify an engine by the manufacturer's code, follow the four steps designated by the numbered blocks.

V.I.N. PLATE LOCATION:

Left side of instrument panel visible through windshield.

1 MODEL YEAR IDENTIFICATION:

10th character of V.I.N.

1992 — N; 1991 — M; 1990 — L;
1989 — K; 1988 — J; 1987 — H;
1986 — G; 1985 — F; 1984 — E;
1983 — D.

2 ENGINE CODE LOCATION:

8th character of V.I.N.

4 ENGINE IDENTIFICATION

YEAR	3 ENGINE CODE	CYL.	DISPL. liters	cc	Fuel System	HP
1992	J	4	1.5	1468	MFI	81
	A	4	1.5	1468	MFI	92
	Y	4	1.6	1597	MFI	123
	T	4	1.8	1755	MFI	92
	D	4	1.8	1834	MFI	113
	V	4	2.0	1997	MFI	102
	R	4	2.0	1997	MFI	135
	U	4	2.0 T	1997 T	MFI	190
	W	4	2.4	2350	MFI	116
	S	6	3.0	2972	MFI	143, 151†
	B	6	3.0	2972	MFI	222
	C	6	3.0 T	2972 T	MFI	300
1991	J	4	1.5	1468	MFI	81
	A	4	1.5	1468	MFI	92
	Y	4	1.6	1597	MFI	123
	T	4	1.8	1755	MFI	92
	V	4	2.0	1997	MFI	102, 105†
	R	4	2.0	1997	MFI	135
	U	4	2.0 T	1997 T	MFI	190
	W	4	2.4	2350	MFI	116
	S	6	3.0	2972	MFI	143, 151†
	B	6	3.0	2972	MFI	222
	C	6	3.0 T	2972 T	MFI	300
1990	J	4	1.5	1468	MFI	81
	X	4	1.5	1468	MFI	81
	Y	4	1.6	1597	MFI	113
	T	4	1.8	1755	MFI	92
	V	4	2.0	1997	MFI	102
	R	4	2.0	1997	MFI	135
	U	4	2.0 T	1997 T	MFI	190
	W	4	2.4	2350	MFI	107, 116†
	S	6	3.0	2972	MFI	142, 143†
1989	J	4	1.5	1468	2V	70
	X	4	1.5	1468	MFI	81
	Z	4	1.6 T	1597 T	MFI	135
	D	4	2.0	1997	2V	88, 90
	V	4	2.0	1997	MFI	102
	R	4	2.0	1997	MFI	135
	L	4	2.4	2350	MFI	107
	E	4	2.6	2555	2V	109
	N	4	2.6 T	2555 T	TBI	188
	S	6	3.0	2972	MFI	NA
1988	K	4	1.5	1468	2V	68
	F	4	1.6 T	1597 T	MFI	105
	G	4	1.8 T	1795 T	TBI	116

4 ENGINE IDENTIFICATION

YEAR	3 ENGINE CODE	CYL.	DISPL. liters	cc	Fuel System	HP
1988 Cont'd.	D	4	2.0	1997	2V	88, 90†
	L	4	2.4	2350	MFI	110
	E	4	2.6	2555	2V	109
	N	4	2.6 T	2555 T	TBI	188
	S	6	3.0	2972	MFI	142
1987	K	4	1.5	1468	2V	68
	F	4	1.6 T	1597 T	TBI	102
	G	4	1.8 T	1795 T	TBI	116
	D	4	2.0	1997	2V	88, 90†
	L	4	2.4	2350	MFI	110
	E	4	2.6	2555	2V	106, 108†
	H	4	2.6 T	2555 T	TBI	145
	N	4	2.6 T	2555 T	TBI	176
1986	K	4	1.5	1468	2V	68
	F	4	1.6 T	1597 T	TBI	102
	G	4	1.8 T	1795 T	TBI	116
	D	4	2.0	1997	2V	88, 90†
	L	4	2.4	2350	MFI	110
	E	4	2.6	2555	2V	106, 108†
	H	4	2.6 T	2555 T	TBI	145
	N	4	2.6 T	2555 T	TBI	170
1985	K	4	1.5	1468	2V	68
	F	4	1.6 T	1597 T	TBI	102
	G	4	1.8 T	1795 T	TBI	116
	D	4	2.0	1997	2V	88, 90†
	J	4	2.3 TD	2346 TD	MFI	63
	L	4	2.4	2350	MFI	110
	E	4	2.6	2555	2V	106, 108†
	H	4	2.6 T	2555 T	TBI	145
1984	G	4	1.8 T	1795 T	TBI	116
	D	4	2.0	1997	2V	88, 90†
	J	4	2.3 TD	2346 TD	MFI	63
	E	4	2.6	2555	2V	106, 108†
	H	4	2.6 T	2555 T	TBI	145
1983	4	4	1.8	1795	2V	84
	5	4	2.0	1997	2V	88, 90†
	9	4	2.3 TD	2346 TD	MFI	80
	7	4	2.6	2555	2	100, 105†
	H	4	2.6 T	2555 T	TBI	145

TBI — Throttle Body Injection.   MFI — Multiport Fuel Injection.
2V — Two Venturi Carburetor.   T — Turbo.
TD — Turbo Diesel.   FI — Fuel Injection.
† Engine horsepower varies with model installation.

UNDERHOOD SERVICE SPECIFICATIONS

MIITU1

CYLINDER NUMBERING SEQUENCE
4-CYL. FIRING ORDER: 1 3 4 2

MIITU1

1991-92
Precis 1468cc,
1985-90
Mirage, Precis 1468cc,
1985-88
1597cc Turbo,
1983-88
Tredia, Cordia
1795cc Turbo,
1988-92
Galant, Eclipse
1997cc SOHC

1991-92
Mirage 1468cc

1989-92
Mirage 1597cc,
1989-92
Galant, Eclipse
1997cc DOHC

1992
Expo LRV 1834cc

1983-88
Tredia, Cordia 1997cc,
1984-87
Galant 2350cc

1987-90
Van 2351cc,
1983-89
Pickup 1997cc,
1990-92
Pickup 2351cc

1992
Expo 2350cc

1983-90
Pickup, Montero,
Starion 2555cc

—— Front of car ——

MITSUBISHI
1983-92

UNDERHOOD SERVICE SPECIFICATIONS

CYLINDER NUMBERING SEQUENCE

V6 FIRING ORDER: 1 2 3 4 5 6

1988-92
V6, Galant, Sigma,
Diamante SOHC

1989-92
Montero, Pickup V6

1991-92
3000GT,
Diamante DOHC

TIMING MARK

BTDC
10°

0°

1985-92
Mirage, Precis,
1983-88
Tredia, Cordia,
1984-90
Galant, Van,
1988-92
Galant, Eclipse,
1990-92 Pickup 4-cyl.,
1992 Expo

BTDC
10°
0°
10°
ATDC

1983-89 Pickup, Montero,
Starion 1997cc, 2555cc

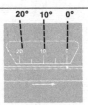

20° 10° 0°

1988-92
V6 Galant, Sigma,
Montero, Pickup,
Diamante, 3000GT

ELECTRICAL AND IGNITION SYSTEMS

BATTERY

BCI equivalent shown, size may vary from original equipment. Check clearance before replacing, holddown may need to be modified.

Application	Year	STANDARD BCI Group No.	STANDARD Crank. Perf.	OPTIONAL BCI Group No.	OPTIONAL Crank. Perf.
Cordia, Tredia:					
MT	1983	51	405	—	—
AT	1983	45	455	—	—
Turbo MT	1984	51	405	—	—
Others	1984	45	455	—	—
Others	1985-88	45	455	—	—
Diamante	1992	24	490	—	—
Eclipse	1990-92	86	430	—	—
Expo	1992	24	490	—	—
Expo LRV	1992	25	430	—	—
Galant	1985-92	51	405	—	—
Galant Sigma	1988-90	24	490	—	—
Mirage	1985-89	51	405	—	—
Turbo	1985-89	45	455	—	—
Turbo	1990	24	350	—	—
Turbo	1991-92	25	430	—	—
Precis	1987-90	21	400	—	—
Starion	1983-89	45	455	—	—
3000GT	1991-92	24	490	—	—
Pickup Gas	1983-85	51	405	27	585
Diesel	1983	27	585	—	—
Diesel	1984-85	29H	840	—	—
2.0L	1986-87	51	405	—	—
2.6L	1986-87	27	585	—	—
2.6L	1988-89	51	405	—	—
2WD	1990-92	51	405	—	—
4WD	1990-92	24	490	—	—
Montero	1983-91	51	405	—	—
Van	1987-90	51	405	—	—

ALTERNATOR

Engine	Year	Rated Output	Min. Test Output (amps. @ eng. rpm)
1468cc Precis	1987-89	55	55 @ 3000
	1987-89	60	60 @ 3000
1468cc Precis	1990-91	75	52 @ 2500
1468cc Mirage: MT	1985-86	50	35 @ 1150
AT	1985-86	55	39 @ 1150

ALTERNATOR Continued

Model	Year	Rated Output	Test Output (amps. @ eng. rpm)
1468cc Mirage: MT	1987-88	60	42 @ 2500
AT	1987-88	65	45 @ 2500
1468cc Mirage	1989-92	75	52 @ 2500
1597cc Turbo	1985-86	65	46 @ 1150
1597cc	1987-89	75	52 @ 2500
1597cc: MT	1990-92	65	46 @ 2500
AT	1990-92	75	52 @ 2500
1755cc, 1997cc Eclipse	1990-92	65	45 @ 2500
	1990-92	75	52 @ 2500
	1992	90	63 @ 2500
1795cc, 1997cc Tredia, Cordia	1983-88	65	45 @ 2500
1834cc, 2350cc Expo	1992	60	42 @ 2500
	1992	65	46 @ 2500
	1992	75	53 @ 2500
1997cc Galant	1989-92	75	53 @ 2500
1997cc, 2555cc Pickup	1983-92	45	31 @ 2500
2346cc Diesel	1983-85	50	45 @ 3000
2350cc Galant	1985-87	65	46 @ 2500
2350cc Van	1987-90	75	52 @ 2500
2350cc Pickup	1990-92	40	28 @ 2500
	1990-92	45	31 @ 2500
	1990-92	60	42 @ 2500
2555cc Starion	1983-86	65	59 @ 3000
2555cc Starion	1987-89	65	45 @ 2500
2555cc Starion	1987-89	75	52 @ 2500
2555cc Montero	1983-84	50	45 @ 3000
	1983-84	55	49 @ 3000
2555cc Montero	1985-91	50	31 @ 2500
	1985-91	55	38 @ 3000
2972cc Pickup	1990-92	65	46 @ 2500
2972cc Montero	1989-91	75	52 @ 2500
2972cc Sigma	1988-91	75	52 @ 2500
2972cc 3000GT	1991-92	90	63 @ 2500
	1991-92	100	77 @ 2500
2972cc Diamante	1992	90	63 @ 2500

REGULATOR

Application	Year	Test Temp. (deg. F/C)	Voltage Setting
Tredia, Cordia, Starion	1983	68/20	14.1-14.7
Pickup, Montero	1983	68/20	13.9-14.9
Starion	1984	68/20	14.1-14.7
All others	1984	68/20	13.9-14.9

UNDERHOOD SERVICE SPECIFICATIONS

MIITU3   MIITU3

REGULATOR Continued

Application	Year	Test Temp. (deg. F/C)	Voltage Setting
Starion, Pickup	1985	68/20	14.1-14.7
Mirage, Galant	1985-86	68/20	14.4-15.0
Tredia, Cordia, Montero	1985-86	68/20	13.9-14.9
Starion	1986	68/20	14.4-15.0
Pickup	1986	68/20	14.1-14.7
Mirage, Tredia, Cordia	1987-88	−4/−20	14.4-15.6
		68/20	14.2-15.2
		140/60	13.8-15.1
		175/80	13.6-15.0
Precis	1987-89	—	14.4-15.0
All others	1987-92	−4/−20	14.2-15.4
		68/20	13.9-15.9
		140/60	13.4-14.6
		175/80	13.1-14.5

STARTER

Engine	Year	Cranking Voltage (min. volts)	Ampere Draw @ Cranking Speed
All	1983-92	8.0	—

SPARK PLUGS

Engine	Year	Gap (inches)	Gap (mm)	Torque (ft-lb)
1597cc	1989	.028-.032	.7-.8	15-21
1997cc DOHC Turbo	1990-91	.028-.032	.7-.8	15-21
All others	1983-92	.039-.043*	1.0-1.1*	15-21

* With Nippondenso plugs, .035-.039 in. (0.9-1.0 mm).

IGNITION COIL

Ignition system without distributor, primary windings are measured between terminals 1 & 4 and 2 & 3 (diagonally) of 4-terminal coil connector. Secondary windings are measured between adjoining coil high tension towers.

Engine	Year	Windings	Resistance (ohms)
All	1983	Primary	1.04-1.27
		Secondary	7100-9600
1468cc 2V	1985-88	Primary	1.1-1.3
		Secondary	11,600-15,800
1468cc FI	1989-90	Primary	.72-.88
		Secondary	10,300-13,900
1468cc Precis	1991-92	Primary	.72-.88
		Secondary	10,300-13,900
1468cc Mirage	1991-92	Primary	0.9-1.2
		Secondary	20,000-29,000
1597cc Turbo	1985-86	Primary	1-1.3
		Secondary	7100-9600
1597cc Turbo	1987-88	Primary	1.1-1.3
		Secondary	9400-12,600
1597cc DOHC	1989-92	Primary	.77-.95
		Secondary	10,300-13,900
1755cc	1990-92	Primary	0.9-1.2
		Secondary	19,000-27,000
1795cc	1984-86	Primary	1.15
		Secondary	8350
1795cc Turbo	1987-88	Primary	1.13-1.37
		Secondary	9400-12,600
1834cc	1992	Primary	0.9-1.2
		Secondary	20,000-29,000
1997cc Tredia, Cordia; 2555cc Montero	1984-86	Primary	1.20
		Secondary	13,700
1997cc, 2555cc Pickup, 2555cc Starion	1984-85	Primary	1.04-1.27
		Secondary	7100-9600
1997cc Pickup, 2555cc Pickup, 2555cc Montero	1986	Primary	1.2
		Secondary	13,700
1997cc Tredia, Cordia	1987-88	Primary	1.08-1.32
		Secondary	11,700-15,700
1997cc, 2555cc Pickup	1987-89	Primary	1.1-1.3
		Secondary	22,100-29,900
1997cc SOHC	1989-92	Primary	.72-.88
		Secondary	10,900-13,300

IGNITION COIL Continued

Engine	Year	Windings	Resistance (ohms)
1997cc DOHC Eclipse	1992	Primary	.70-.86
		Secondary	11,300-15,300
1997cc DOHC Others	1989-92	Primary	.77-.95
		Secondary	10,300-13,900
2350cc	1985	Primary	1.20
		Secondary	13,700
2350cc	1986	Primary	1.20
		Secondary	26,000
2350cc	1987-92	Primary	.72-.88
		Secondary	10,300-13,900
2555cc Starion	1986	Primary	1.04-1.27
		Secondary	7100-9600
2555cc Montero	1987-89	Primary	1.1-1.3
		Secondary	14,500-19,500
2555cc Starion	1987-89	Primary	1.12-1.38
		Secondary	9400-12,700
2972cc ex. 3000GT	1988-92	Primary	.72-.88
		Secondary	10,300-13,900
2972cc 3000GT	1991-92	Primary	.67-.81
		Secondary	11,300-15,300

DISTRIBUTOR PICKUP

Engine	Year	Resistance (ohms)	Air Gap (in./mm)
All ex. Hall Effect:			
All	1983	920-1120	.030/.80
1997cc	1984	—	.030/.80
All others	1984	920-1120	.030/.80
1597cc, 1795cc, 2555cc Turbo	1985	920-1120	.030/.80
All others	1985	—	.030/.80
1468cc, 2350cc, 2555cc 2V	1986	—	.030/.80
1597cc, 2555cc, Turbo	1986	920-1120	—
1795cc	1986	920-1120	.030/.80
1997cc Tredia, Cordia	1986	130-190	.030/.80
1997cc Pickup	1986	—	.008-.015/.2-.4
1468cc, 2555cc 2V	1987-90	—	.030/.80
1595cc, 1795cc, 2555cc Turbo	1987-89	920-1120	—
1997cc Pickup, Tredia, Cordia	1987-89	130-190	.008/.015/.2-.4

IGNITION RESISTOR

Engine	Year	Type	Resistance (ohms)	Temperature (deg. F/C)
All, as equipped	1983-89	Unit	1.20-1.50	68/20

BASE TIMING

1986 1597cc high altitude, disconnect pressure sensor.

1987 88 1597cc high altitude, 2350cc high altitude, 2555cc high altitude, 2972cc: Disconnect ignition timing connector and jumper female terminal to ground.

1989-92 All w/FI: Ground ignition timing connector.

When disconnected, timing should advance to "Check" Specification.

All others, disconnect and plug distributor vacuum hoses.

Engine	Year	Man. Trans. (degrees) @ RPM	Auto. Trans. (degrees) @ RPM
1468cc: To 4/85	1985	3 ±2	3 ±2
From 4/85	1985	5 ±2	5 ±2
1468cc Mirage	1986-87	5* ±2	5* ±2
1468cc Precis	1987-89	5● ±2	5 ±2
California	1987	3 ±2	3 ±2
1468cc Precis	1988-89	5 ±2	5 ±2
1468cc 2V Mirage	1988-89	5* ±2	5* ±2
1468cc FI	1989-92	5 ±2	5 ±2
Check	1989-92	10 ±2	10 ±2
High Alt.	1989-92	15 ±2	15 ±2
1597cc	1985	8 ±2	8 ±2
1597cc	1986-88	10† ±2	10† ±2

UNDERHOOD SERVICE SPECIFICATIONS

BASE TIMING Continued

Engine	Year	Man. Trans. (degrees) @ RPM	Auto. Trans. (degrees) @ RPM
1597cc	1989-92	5 ±2	5 ±2
Check	1989-92	8 ±2	8 ±2
High Alt.	1989-92	13 ±2	13 ±2
1755cc	1990-92	5 ±2	5 ±2
Check	1990-92	10 ±2	10 ±2
1795cc	1983	5 ±2	5 ±2
California	1983	8 ±2	8 ±2
1795cc	1984-86	7 ±2	7 ±2
1795cc	1987-88	10 ±2	10 ±2
1834cc	1992	5 ±2	5 ±2
Check	1992	5 ±2	5 ±2
1997cc	1983-86	5 ±2	5 ±2
California	1985-86	8 ±2	8 ±2
1997cc 2V	1987-89	8 ±2	8 ±2
1997cc FI: SOHC	1989-92	5 ±2	5 ±2
Check	1989-92	10 ±2	10 ±2
High Alt.	1989-92	15 ±2	15 ±2
DOHC	1989-92	5 ±2	5 ±2
Check	1989	12 ±2	—
High Alt.	1989	17 ±2	—
Check	1990-92	8 ±2	8 ±2
Turbo	1990-91	5 ±2	5 ±2
Check Eclipse	1990-92	8 ±2	8 ±2
Check Galant	1990-92	12 ±2	12 ±2
2350cc	1985	5 ±2	5 ±2
2350cc	1986	8 ±2	8 ±2
2350cc	1987-92	5 ±2	5 ±2
Check	1989-92	8 ±2	8 ±2
High Alt.	1989-92	13 ±2	13 ±2
2555cc 2V	1983-90	7 ±2	7 ±2
2555cc Turbo	1983-89	10 ±2	10 ±2
2972cc	1988-92	5 ±2	5 ±2
Check	1988-92	15 ±2	15 ±2
High Alt.	1988-92	—	20 ±2

* With vacuum hose connected, high altitude, 10°.
† With pressure sensor connected, high altitude, 15°.
● Models without vacuum regulator valve, 7.

DISTRIBUTOR TIMING ADVANCE

Engine degrees at engine rpm, no load, in addition to basic timing setting.

Mechanical advance distributors only.

1983 1795cc, Idle advance, 10° @ 11.8″ Hg.

1984-88 1597cc, Vacuum retard, 16-20° @ 17.5″ Hg.

1984-88 1795cc, Vacuum retard, 6° @ 6″ Hg.

1983-89 2555cc Turbo, Vacuum retard, 7° @ 9″ Hg.

Engine	Trans- mission	Year	Distributor Number	Degrees @ 2500 RPM Total	Degrees @ 2500 RPM Centrifugal
1468cc	MT	1985	T3T62672, 73	24-32	1-5
1468cc	AT	1985	T3T62671	22-30	1-5
1468cc	MT & AT	1986	T3T62678	28-36	7-11
1468cc	MT & AT	1986	T3T62677	25-33	7-11
1468cc	MT & AT	1987-88	T3T62681	18.9-26.9	0.9-4.9
1468cc	MT	1987-88	T3T62680	21.9-4.9	0.9-4.9
1597cc Turbo	MT & AT	1984-88	T3T63175	31-39	10-14
1795cc 5-spd. Fed.	MT	1983	MD060266	35.7-43.7	9.7-13.7
1795cc 5-spd. Calif.	MT	1983	MD061223	30.7-38.7	9.7-13.7
1795cc 4×2 spd.:					
Fed.	MT	1983	MD013880	32.7-40.7	9.7-13.7
Calif.	MT	1983	MD062608	27.7-35.7	9.7-13.7
1795cc	AT	1983	MD062608	27.7-35.7*	9.7-13.7
1795cc	MT & AT	1984-88	T3T63171, 72	33-41*	10-14
1997cc FWD	MT & AT	1984	T3T61877	27.9-35.9	7.9-11.9
1997cc FWD	MT & AT	1984	T4T61876	25.9-33.9	7.9-11.9
1997cc FWD	MT & AT	1985-88	100291-057	35.5-43.5	7.5-11.5
1997cc FWD	MT & AT	1985-86	100291-060	25.9-33.9	7.9-11.9
1997cc Pickup	MT	1983-84	T4T62186	37.7-45.7	7.7-11.7
1997cc Pickup	MT	1983-84	T4T63474	37.7-45.7	7.7-11.7
1997cc Pickup	AT	1983-84	T4T62180	28.7-36.7	7.7-11.7
1997cc Pickup	MT & AT	1983-84	T4T62185	20.7-28.7	7.7-11.7
1997cc Pickup	MT & AT	1984-86	100291-062	37.5-45.5	7.5-11.5
1997cc Pickup	MT	1984-86	100291-063	28.5-33.5	7.5-11.5

DISTRIBUTOR TIMING ADVANCE Continued

Engine	Trans- mission	Year	Distributor Number	Degrees @ 2500 RPM Total	Degrees @ 2500 RPM Centrifugal
1997cc Pickup	AT	1986	100291-064	25.8-33.8	7.8-11.8
1997cc Pickup	MT & AT	1986	100291-057	35.5-43.5	7.5-11.5
1997cc Pickup	MT & AT	1987-89	MD110418	25.8-33.8	7.8-11.8
1997cc Pickup	MT & AT	1987-89	MD110419, 40	28.8-36.8	7.8-11.8
1997cc Pickup	MT & AT	1987	MD112111	33.8-41.8	7.8-11.8
1997cc Pickup	MT & AT	1988-89	MD125103	25.8-33.8	7.8-11.8
2350cc	AT	1985	MD084893	30.6-38.6	9.6-13.6
2350cc	MT & AT	1986	T4T63371	32.8-40.8	11.8-15.8
2555cc 2V	MT & AT	1983	T4T62074	28.8-36.8	7.8-11.8
2555cc 2V	MT & AT	1983-84	T4T62075, 78	25.8-33.8	7.8-11.8
2555cc 2V	MT & AT	1983-84	T4T62076, 77	20.8-28.8	7.8-11.8
2555cc 2V	MT	1983	T4T62186	37.8-45.8	7.8-11.8
2555cc 2V	MT & AT	1984-86	T3T61971, 72	33-41	5-9
2555cc 2V	MT & AT	1985-86	T3T61973	23-31	5-9
2555cc 2V	MT & AT	1987	T3T65472	25.8-33.8	4.8-8.8
2555cc 2V	MT & AT	1987	T3T65473	30.8-33.8	4.8-8.8
2555cc 2V	MT & AT	1987-89	T3T65572	22.8-30.8	4.8-8.8
2555cc 2V	MT & AT	1987	T3T61980	22.8-30.8	4.8-8.8
2555cc 2V	MT & AT	1987-90	T3T65571	25.8-33.8	4.8-8.8
2555cc 2V	MT & AT	1988-89	T3T65474, 76	22.8-30.8	4.8-8.8
2555cc Turbo	MT & AT	1984-87	T4T63371	32.8-40.8	11.8-15.8
2555cc Turbo	MT & AT	1985-89	T4T63372, 73	31.6-39.6	10.6-14.6

* Pressure retard 6° @ 6 PSI.

FUEL SYSTEM

FUEL SYSTEM PRESSURE

Engine	Year	Pressure PSI	Pressure RPM
1597cc Turbo, ex. DOHC 2555cc Turbo	1983-89	35-38♦	idle
2350cc	1985-88	35.5-38.5*	idle
		28.5†	idle
All others w/FI ex. Turbo	1988-92	47-50*	idle
		38†	idle
4-cyl. Turbo MT	1989-91	36-38*	idle
		27†	idle
4-cyl. Turbo AT	1992	41-46*	idle
		33†	idle
V6 Turbo	1992	43-45*	idle
		34†	idle

♦ Measured at TBI unit.
* Vacuum disconnected from fuel pressure regulator.
† Vacuum connected to fuel pressure regulator.

IDLE SPEED W/O COMPUTER CONTROL

Midpoint of range given is the preferred setting.

1468cc, 1986-88 1997cc Tredia, Cordia w/MT: Set idle speed to specified value. 1986-88, to set PS/Elect. speed-up, apply 12 volts to throttle opener solenoid and adjust to specified value. To set AC speed-up, turn AC on and adjust vacuum actuator to specified value.

All others: Set idle speed to specified value. Turn AC on and adjust speed-up speed as needed.

Engine	Year	SLOW Man. Trans.	SLOW Auto. Trans.	FAST Man. Trans.	FAST Auto. Trans.	Step of Cam
1468cc	1985-86	600-800	650-850 N	—	—	—
PS, Elect. speed-up	1986	800-900	800-900 N			
AC speed-up	1985-86	800-900	800-900 N	—	—	—
1468cc Mirage	1987-88	600-800	650-850	2800	2700 N	2nd High
PS, Elect. speed-up	1987-88	750-950	750-950 N			
AC speed-up	1987-88	800-900	800-900			

UNDERHOOD SERVICE SPECIFICATIONS

MIITU5   MIITU5

IDLE SPEED W/O COMPUTER CONTROL Continued

Engine	Year	SLOW Man. Trans.	SLOW Auto. Trans.	FAST Man. Trans.	FAST Auto. Trans.	Step of Cam
1468cc Precis	1987	700-900	650-850 N	2800	2700 N	2nd High
	1988-89	700-900	700-900 N	2800	2700 N	2nd High
PS, Elect. speed-up	1987-89	750-950	750-950 N			
AC speed-up	1987-89	850-900	850-900			
1795cc: Federal	1983	550-750	650-850 N	—	—	—
California	1983	600-800	600-800 N	—	—	—
All w/4×2 speed	1983	600-800	—	—	—	—
AC speed-up, all	1983	900-1000	800-900 N			
1997cc Pickup	1983-84	650-850	650-850 N	—	—	—
5-speed	1983-84	600-800	—	—	—	—
California	1983-84	650-850	650-850 N	—	—	—
AC speed-up	1983-84	850-900	850-900 N			
1997cc Tredia, Cordia	1984	650-850	750-950 N	—	—	—
AC speed-up	1984	800-900	630-650 D			
1997cc Pickup	1985-86	650-850	650-850 N	—	—	—
AC speed-up	1985-86	850-900	850-900 N			
1997cc Tredia, Cordia	1985-86	600-800	—	—	—	—
PS, Elect. speed-up	1985-86	750	—			
AC speed-up	1985-86	700-800	—			
1997cc Pickup	1987-89	650-850	650-850 N	2500	2450 N	2nd High
AC speed-up	1987-89	850-900	850-900 N			
1997cc Tredia, Cordia	1987-88	600-800	—	—	—	—
AC speed-up	1987-88	800-900	—			
2346cc Diesel	1983	700-850	—	—	—	—
2346cc Diesel	1984-85	700-800	—	—	—	—
AC speed-up	1984-85	850-900	—			
2555cc 2V	1983	650-850	700-900 N	—	—	—
AC speed-up	1983	850-950	850-950 N	—	—	—
2555cc Turbo	1983	750-850	—	—	—	—
2555cc 2V Pickup	1984	650-850	700-900 N	—	—	—
AC speed-up	1984	850-900	850-900 N	—	—	—
2555cc 2V Montero	1984	650-850	700-900 N	—	—	—
AC speed-up	1984	900-950	900-950 N	—	—	—
2555cc 2V	1985-86	650-850	700-900 N	—	—	—
AC speed-up	1985-86	850-900●	900 N●	—	—	—
2555cc 2V	1987-89	700-900	700-900 N	2350	2300 N	2nd High
AC speed-up, Pickup	1987-89	850-900	850-900 N			
AC speed-up, Montero	1987-89	900-950	900-950 N			

● Montero, 900-950 (N).

IDLE SPEED W/COMPUTER CONTROL

1989-92 All DOHC FI: Disconnect and ground female end of ignition timing connector. Ground terminal 10 of self-diagnostic connector (under dash). Set idle speed. Reinstate system, turn AC on and verify the speed-up is at specified value.

1989-92 All SOHC FI; 1984-88 1597cc, 1795cc Turbo, 2350cc, 2555cc Turbo: Verify that TPS voltage is at proper value. Turn ignition on for 20 seconds and turn off. Disconnect ISC servo. Ground red wire in connector (computer side of harness)(1987-88 1.6L Turbo, 1987-89 2.6L Turbo) and start engine. Set idle speed to specified value. Turn AC on and verify that AC speed-up speed is at specified value. This is not adjustable.

1985-86 Tredia, Cordia w/AT: Turn ignition on for 18 seconds and turn off. Disconnect ISC actuator and oxygen sensor, start engine. Set idle to specified value. Verify that base idle screw is 2/3 of a turn away from the setting speed. Turn AC on and verify that speed-up speed is at specified value.

Midpoint of range given is the preferred setting speed.

Engine	Year	Transmission	Setting Speed	Checking Speed	AC Speed-up
1468cc FI	1989-92	MT	700-800	650-850	850
	1989-92	AT	700-800 N	650-800 N	750 D
1597cc Turbo	1985-86	MT & AT	600 (N)	600-800 (N)	850 (N)
1597cc Turbo	1987	MT & AT	700 (N)	600-800 (N)	800-900 (N)
1597cc	1988	MT	700	600-800	800
	1988	AT	700 N	600-800 N	650 D
1597cc	1989-92	MT	700-800	650-850	850
	1989-92	AT	700-800 N	650-850 N	700 D
1755cc	1990-92	MT	650-750	600-800	850
	1990-92	AT	650-750 N	600-800 N	650 D
1795cc	1984-88	MT & AT	600 (N)	600-800 (N)	
1834cc	1992	MT	700-800	650-850	850
	1992	AT	700-800 N	650-850 N	850 N
1997cc Tredia, Cordia	1985-88	AT	700	600-800 (N)	800-900 (N)
1997cc SOHC	1989-92	MT	700-800	650-850	900
	1989-92	AT	700-800 N	650 850 N	700 D
1997cc DOHC	1990-92	MT	700-800	650-850	850
	1990-92	AT	700-800 N	650-850 N	700 D
Turbo, Galant	1990-92	MT	750-850	700-900	850
2350cc	1984-87	MT	650	650-850	—
2350cc	1984-87	AT	650 N	650-850 N	—
2350cc	1989-91	MT	700-800	650-850	900
	1992	MT	700-800	650-850	1000*
	1989-92	AT	700-800 N	650-850 N	700 D
2555cc Turbo	1984-86	MT & AT	750 (N)	750-950 (N)	
2555cc Turbo	1987-89	MT	850	750-950	1000
	1987-88	AT	850 N	750-950 N	750 D
2555cc Turbo	1989	MT	850	750-950	900
	1989	AT	850 N	750-950 N	650 D
2972cc	1988	MT & AT	650-750 (N)	600-800 (N)	900 (N)
2972cc SOHC	1989-92	MT	650-750	600-800	900
		AT	650-750 N	600-800 N	650 D

* Expo, 850.

ENGINE MECHANICAL

TIGHTENING TORQUES
Specifications for cylinder head bolts are for cold engine.

Engine	Year	Torque Ft-lbs/Nm Cylinder Head	Intake Manifold	Exhaust Manifold	Crankshaft Pulley	Water Pump
1468cc	1985-92	51-54/ 69-74	12-14/ 16-19	12-14/ 16-19	9-11/ 12-15	9-11/ 12-15, ⊙
1597cc	1985-88	51-54/ 69-74	11-14/ 20-25	18-21/ 25-30	14-22/ 20-30	9-11/ 12-15, ⊙
1597cc	1989-92	65-72/ 90-100	11-14/ 15-19* 22-30/ 30-42●	18-22/ 25-30	14-22/ 20-30	9-11/ 12-15, short 14-20/ 20-27, long
1795cc 2V, 1997cc Tredia, Cordia	1983-88	65-72/ 90-100	11-14/ 15-19	11-14/ 15-19	15-21/ 20-30	8-9/ 10-12, ⊙
1755cc	1990-92	51-54/ 69-74	12-14/ 16-19	12-14/ 16-19	9-11/ 12-15	9-11/ 12-15, ⊙
1795cc Turbo	1984-88	65-72/ 90-100	11-14/ 15-19	11-14/ 15-19	15-21/ 20-30	9-11/ 12-15, ⊙

UNDERHOOD SERVICE SPECIFICATIONS

MIITU6   MIITU6

TIGHTENING TORQUES Continued

Engine	Year	Cylinder Head	Intake Manifold	Exhaust Manifold	Crankshaft Pulley	Water Pump
			Torque Ft-lbs/Nm			
1834cc	1992	54/75■, 14/20, +90°, +90°	13/18	22/30	134/185	18/24
1997cc Pickup	1983-89	65-72/ 90-100	11-14/ 15-19	11-14/ 15-19	15-21/ 20-30	9-11/ 12-15
1997cc SOHC ex. Pickup	1989-92	65-72/ 90-100	11-14/ 15-19	11-14/ 15-19	15-21/ 20-30	9-11/ 12-15, ⊙
1997cc DOHC	1989-92	65-72/ 90-100	11-14/ 15-19* 22-30/ 30-42●	18-22/ 25-30	14-22/ 20-30	9-11/ 12-15, ⊙
2346cc Diesel	1983-85	76-83/ 103-112	11-14/ 15-19	11-14/ 15-19	123-137/ 167-186	—
2350cc ex. Expo	1985-92	65-72/ 90-100	11-14/ 15-20	11-14/ 15-20	15-21/ 20-30	9-11/ 12-15, ⊙
2350cc Expo	1992	76-83/ 105-115	13/18	13/18	18/25	10/14
2555cc	1983-90	65-72/ 90-100†	11-14/ 15-19	11-14/ 15-19	80-95/ 110-130	9-11/ 12-15
2972cc SOHC ex. Diamante	1989-91	65-72/ 90-100	11-14/ 15-19	11-15/ 15-21	109-115/ 150-160	14-19/ 20-27
2972cc SOHC Diamante	1992	76-83/ 105-115	—	14/19	108-116/ 150-160	17/24
2972cc DOHC Diamante	1992	76-83/ 105-115	—	21/30	130-137/ 180-190	17/24
2972cc DOHC 3000GT	1991-92	90-125	13/18	22/30	130-137/ 180-190	17/24

* Short bolts.
● Long bolts.
† Small bolts forward of cam gear, 11-15/15-22.
⊙ Short bolts. Long bolts, 14-20/20-27.
■ Then fully loosen.

VALVE CLEARANCE
Engine hot.

Application	Year	Intake (inches)	Intake (mm)	Exhaust (inches)	Exhaust (mm)
Tredia, Cordia	1983-84	.006	.15	.010	.25
Jet valve	1983-84	.010	.25	—	—
Pickup, Gas	1983-84	.006	.15	.010	.25
Jet valve	1983-84	.010	.25	—	—
Pickup, Diesel	1983-85	.010	.25	.010	.25
Starion	1983-85	.006	.15	.010	.25
Jet valve	1983-85	.010	.25	—	—
Tredia, Cordia, 1.8L	1985-86	.006	.15	.010	.25
2.0L	1985-86	*	*	*	*
Jet valve, all	1985-86	.010	.25	—	—
Galant	1985-87	*	*	*	*
Jet valve	1985-87	.010	.25	—	—
Pickup, Gas	1985-89	*	*	*	*
Jet valve	1985-89	.010	.25	—	—
Mirage, Precis	1985-92	.006	.15	.010	.25
Jet valve, 2V	1985-92	.010	.25	—	—
Starion	1986-89	*	*	*	*
Jet valve	1986-89	.010	.25	—	—
Tredia, Cordia, Van	1987-88	*	*	*	*
Jet valve	1987-88	.010	.25	—	—

* Hydraulic lifters except Jet valve.

COMPRESSION PRESSURE
At cranking speed, engine temperature normalized, throttle open.

Engine	Year	PSI @ 250 RPM	Maximum Variation PSI
1468cc	1985	164	—
1468cc Mirage	1986-88	171-192	14
1468cc Precis	1987-89	164	—
1468cc Precis	1990-92	171-192	14
1468cc Mirage	1989-92	137 min.	14
1597cc	1985	128	—
1597cc	1986-88	119-149	14
1597cc	1989	149 min.	14
1597cc	1990-91	171 min.	14
1597cc	1992	145 min.	14
1755cc	1990-92	131 min.	14
1795cc	1986-88	128-149	14
1834cc	1992	142 min.	14
1997cc	1986-88	149-171	14
1997cc	1989-92	125 min.	14
DOHC, Eclipse	1989-91	137 min.	14
DOHC, Galant	1990-92	159 min.	14
Turbo	1990-92	114 min.	14
2346cc Diesel	1983-85	384	—
2350cc	1985-88	149-171 min.	14
2350cc	1989-92	119 min.	14
2555cc	1983-87	140	—
2555cc 2V	1986-88	149-171	14
2555cc Turbo	1986-88	113-142	14
2555cc 2V	1989	119 min.	14
2555cc Turbo	1989	97 min.	14
2972cc	1988	149-170	14
2972cc SOHC Pickup, Montero	1989-91	119 min.	14
2972cc SOHC Diamante	1992	149 min.	14
2972cc DOHC	1991-92	139 min.	14
Turbo	1991-92	115 min.	14

BELT TENSION
With 22 lbs. of force applied at midpoint of belt.

Engine	Year	Alternator	Power Steering	Air Cond.	Air Pump
Deflection method:					
All Gas (inches)	1983-84	1/4-3/8	1/4-3/8	1/4-3/8	1/4-3/8
(mm)	1983-84	6-10	6-10	6-10	6-10
All Diesel (inches)	1983-85	3/8-1/2	3/8-1/2	3/8-1/2	3/8-1/2
(mm)	1983-85	10-13	10-13	10-13	10-13
1468cc (inches)	1985	7/32-9/32	7/32-9/32	7/32-9/32	7/32-9/32
(mm)	1985	5.5-7	5.5-7	5.5-7	5.5-7
1597cc (inches)	1985	1/4-5/16	1/4-5/16	1/4-5/16	—
(mm)	1985	6.5-8	6.5-8	6.5-8	—
All other gas (inches)	1985	1/4-3/8	1/4-3/8	1/4-3/8	1/4-3/8
(mm)	1985	7-10	7-10	7-10	7-10
1468cc (inches)	1986	7/32-9/32	7/32-9/32	1/8-5/32	7/32-9/32
(mm)	1986	5.5-7	5.5-7	2.5-4	5.5-7
1597cc (inches)	1986	1/4-5/16	1/4-5/16	1/8-5/32	—
(mm)	1986	6.5-8	6.5-8	2.5-4	—
1795cc, 1997cc Tredia, Cordia, 2350cc, 2555cc Starion (inches)	1986	1/4-3/8	1/4-3/8	3/8-7/16	1/4-3/8
(mm)	1986	7-10	7-10	9-11	7-10
1997cc Pickup (inches)	1986	1/4-3/8	7/32-11/32	1/4-3/8	1/4-3/8
(mm)	1986	7-10	6-9	7-10	7-10
2555cc Pickup (inches)	1986	1/4-3/8	3/8-7/16	5/16-3/8	1/4-3/8
(mm)	1986	7-10	9-12	8-10	7-10
2555cc Montero (inches)	1986	1/4-3/8	11/32-1/2	11/16-13/16	1/4-3/8
(mm)	1986	7-10	9-12	17-20	7-10
1468cc (inches)	1987	1/4-3/8	1/4-3/8	5/32-7/32	1/4-3/8
(mm)	1987	7-9	7-9	4-6	7-9
1597cc (inches)	1987	5/16-7/16	5/16-7/16	3/8-7/16	—
(mm)	1987	8-11	8-11	9-11	—
1997cc Tredia, Cordia (inches)	1987-88	9/32-11/32	9/32-11/32	11/32-1/2	9/32-11/32
(mm)	1987-88	7.5-9	7.5-9	9-11	7.5-9
1997cc Pickup (inches)	1987-89	1/4-3/8	7/32-3/8	1/4-11/32	1/4-3/8
(mm)	1987-89	7-10	7-10	6-9	7-10

MITSUBISHI
1983-92

UNDERHOOD SERVICE SPECIFICATIONS

BELT TENSION Continued

Engine	Year	Alternator	Power Steering	Air Cond.	Air Pump
2350cc (inches)	1987	5/16-7/16	5/16-7/16	3/8-7/16	—
(mm)	1987	8-11	8-11	9-11	—
2555cc Pickup					
(inches)	1987-89	1/4-3/8	3/8-7/16	11/16-13/16	1/4-3/8
(mm)	1987-89	7-10	9-12	17-20	7-20
2555cc Montero					
(inches)	1987-89	11/32-3/8	11/32-3/8	11/16-1/2	11/32-3/8
(mm)	1987-89	9-12	9-12	17-20	9-12
2555cc Starion					
(inches)	1987-89	1/4-3/8	11/32-1/2	1/4-3/8	—
(mm)	1987-89	7-10	9-12	7-10	—
1468cc Mirage					
(inches)	1988	7/32-9/32	7/32-9/32	5/32-7/32	7/32-9/32
(mm)	1988	5.5-7	5.5-7	4-6	5.5-7
1468cc Precis					
(inches)	1988-90	1/4-3/8	1/4-3/8	5/16-3/8	1/4-3/8
(mm)	1988-90	7-9	7-9	8-10	7-9
1597cc (inches)	1988	1/4-5/16	1/4-5/16	11/32-5/16	—
(mm)	1988	6.5-8	6.5-8	9-11	—
2350cc (inches)	1988-89	1/4-3/8	1/4-3/8	1/4-3/8	—
(mm)	1988-89	7-10	7-10	7-10	—
2972cc Sigma (inches)	1988-89	1/4-3/8	1/4-3/8	5/32-3/16	—
(mm)	1988-89	7-10	7-10	4-5	—
Strand Tension method:					
NEW					
1468cc FI	1989-92	110-155	110-155	104-126	—
1597cc	1989-92	110-155	110-155	82-96	—
1755cc, 1997cc	1989-92	110-155	110-155	104-126	—
1834cc: PS w/o AC	1992	145-190	145-190	—	—
PS w/AC	1992	165-175	165-175	165-175	—
2972cc Sigma	1989-92	155-200	155-200	155-200	—
2972cc Others	1989-92	110-155	110-155	104-126	—
USED					
1468cc FI	1989-92	90	90	71-88	—
1597cc	1989-92	90	90	55-68	—
1755cc, 1997cc	1989-92	55-110	55-110	71-88	—
1834cc: PS w/o AC	1992	90-130	90-130	—	—
PS w/AC	1992	110-140	110-140	110-140	—
2972cc Sigma	1989-92	110	110	110	—
2972cc Others	1989-92	55-110	55-110	71-86	—

ENGINE COMPUTER SYSTEM

COMPUTER DIAGNOSTIC CODES

1989-92 All; 1987-88 Galant, Starion, Van, Montero V6: Access diagnostic connector in or under glove box or by fuse block. Connect an analog voltmeter to upper right (+) and lower left (−) cavities. Turn ignition on with engine off.

1983-86 All with FI: With ignition off, connect a voltmeter to the diagnostic connector located under battery (1.6L), or on right hand cowl by ECI computer (1.8, 2.6L). Turn ignition on, codes will be displayed as sweeps of voltmeter needle.

1987-88 Mirage Turbo: Connect an analog voltmeter to ground (−) and single wire connector (+) on engine bulkhead by set timing connector. Turn ignition on but do not start engine.

1987-88 Tredia, Cordia: Connect an analog voltmeter to lower right (−) and upper (+) cavities of diagnostic connector. Turn ignition switch on but do not start engine.

All models, remove ECM fuse for 15 seconds minimum to clear codes.

All ex. 1987-88 Galant, Van, codes will be displayed as sweeps of the voltmeter needle. Needle will sweep only if a problem in the system has been detected by the ECM.

1989 Starion, 1987 Galant, 1987-88 Van, voltmeter needle will sweep and indicate short or long durations every 2 seconds for a 10 second cycle. If the needle does not sweep, the ECM has not detected a failure in the system.
The following deciphers each code:

0 = short sweep, 1 = long sweep

```
00000 = 0
10000 = 1
01000 = 2
11000 = 3
00100 = 4
10100 = 5
01100 = 6
11100 = 7
00010 = 8
```

COMPUTER DIAGNOSTIC CODES Continued

1989 All, 1988 Galant, voltmeter needle will sweep in long durations indicating the number of tens, or short durations, indicating the number of ones.

1989 Starion; 1983-88 All ex. 1988 Galant:
Code 1 Oxygen sensor and/or computer
Code 2 Ignition signal or crank angle sensor
Code 3 Airflow sensor
Code 4 Pressure sensor
Code 5 Throttle position sensor
Code 6 ISC motor position sensor
Code 7 Coolant temperature sensor
Code 8 Car speed signal or TDC sensor
1989-92 All others; 1988 Galant:
Code 9 No failure
Code 11 Oxygen sensor
Code 12 Air flow sensor
Code 13 Intake air temperature sensor
Code 14 TPS
Code 15 Motor position sensor
Code 21 Coolant temperature sensor
Code 22 Crank angle sensor
Code 23 TDC sensor
Code 24 Vehicle speed sensor
Code 25 Barometric pressure sensor
Code 31 Detonation sensor
Code 36 Ignition timing adjustment
Code 39 Oxygen sensor (front on Turbo)
Code 41 Injector
Code 42 Fuel pump
Code 43 EGR
Code 44 Ignition coil (ex. V6 DOHC)
Code 44 1-4 coil power transistor (V6 DOHC)
Code 52 2-5 coil power transistor (V6 DOHC)
Code 53 3-6 coil power transistor (V6 DOHC)
Code 61 Transmission & ECM Interlink
Code 62 Induction control valve position sensor
Code 71 Traction control vacuum solenoid valve
Code 72 Traction control vent solenoid valve

1 long sweep ECU
Rapid pulsing Normal state

SENSORS, INPUT

TEMPERATURE SENSORS

Engine	Year	Sensor	Resistance Ohms @ deg. F/C
All	1983-92	Coolant	5900 @ 32/0
			2500 @ 68/20
			1100 @ 104/40
			300 @ 176/80
1468cc, 1597cc Turbo, 1795cc Turbo	1984-86	Intake Air	2450 @ 68/20
1468cc FI, 1597cc, 2350cc, 2555cc Turbo, 2972cc	1987-92	Intake Air†	6000 @ 32/0
			2700 @ 68/20
			400 @ 176/80
1997cc, 2555cc	1983-86	Intake Air	2450 @ 68/20

† Measured between terminals 2 & 4 of airflow sensor.

PRESSURE SENSORS
Precis, measured between terminals 5 & 6 (lower middle and lower left) of airflow connector.

Engine	Year	Sensor	Voltage @ in./mm Hg
1597cc	1987-88	Barometric	.79 @ 2.8/70
			1.84 @ 7/175
			4.00 @ 14.2/330
1795cc Turbo	1984-88	Pressure	1.5-2.6, ign. on
			0.2-1.2 @ idle
2555cc Turbo	1987-89	Barometric	.79 @ 2.8/70
			1.84 @ 7/175
			4.00 @ 14.2/330
1468cc Precis	1990-92	Barometric	0.79 @ 3/150
			1.84 @ 7/350
			4.00 @ 15/760

UNDERHOOD SERVICE SPECIFICATIONS

SENSORS, INPUT Continued

AIRFLOW SENSOR
Except Precis, measured between red and black wire leads at idle.

Engine	Year	Volts
1597cc Turbo, 2350cc	1987-88	2.2-3.2
1795cc Turbo	1984-88	2.2-3.3
1468cc Precis	1990-91	2.7-3.2

Measured between terminals 3 & 6 (upper and lower left) of airflow sensor connector.

Engine	Year	Frequency (HZ) Idle	Frequency (HZ) @ 2000 RPM
1468cc Mirage	1990	24-40	63-83
1468cc Mirage	1991-92	30-45	80-110
1597cc Mirage	1990-92	27-33	60-80
1755cc	1990-92	25-40	67-88
1834cc	1992	23-49	51-91
1997cc SOHC	1990-92	25-50	70-130
1997cc DOHC	1990-92	25-50	70-90
1997cc Turbo	1990-92	25-50	50-85
2350cc Van	1990	40-60	120-140
2350cc Pickup	1990-91	45-65	100-130
2350cc Pickup	1992	40-60	85-105
2350cc Expo	1992	34-60	70-110
2972cc Pickup, Montero	1990	24-45	80-105
2972cc Pickup, Montero	1991-92	40-60	85-105
2972cc Sigma	1990	30-45	85-105
2972cc 3000GT, Diamante	1991-92	25-50	70-100

THROTTLE POSITION SENSOR (TPS)

All FI: Insert digital voltmeter probes along GW or blue lead (+) and B lead (−) (4-cyl.) on TPS connector. With ignition switch on and engine not running, check reading against specification at speed indicated. Rotate unit to adjust.

All 2V: Back off speed adjusting screw enough to fully close throttle valve. Connect digital voltmeter probes between two bottom terminals of TPS. With ignition on and engine not running, check reading against specifications at speed indicated. Rotate unit or turn TPS linkage screw to adjust.

Engine	Year	TPS Voltage	Setting Speed
1468cc 2V	1985-89	.25	—
1468cc FI	1989-92	.48-.52	—
1597cc	1985-86	.45-.49	600
1597cc	1987-92	.48-.52	700
1755cc	1984-88	.45-.49	600
1834cc, 2350cc Expo	1992	.40-.10*	—
1795cc	1990-91	.48-.52	700
1997cc Tredia, Cordia: w/MT	1984-88	.25	—
w/AT	1984-86	.445	700
w/AT	1987-88	.485	700
1997cc FI	1989-92	.48-.52	—
1997cc Pickup, 2555cc 2V	1985-89	.25	—
2350cc Galant	1985	.45-.49	650
2350cc Galant, Van, Pickup	1986-92	.48-.52	750
2555cc Turbo	1983-86	.45-.49	750
2555cc Turbo	1987-89	.48-.52	750
2972cc Sigma	1988-90	.48-.52	—
2972cc 3000GT, Montero	1989-92	.40-1.0*	—

* Not adjustable

SENSORS, INPUT Continued

MOTOR POSITION SENSOR

Engine	Year	Resistance (ohms)
All 4-cyl. SOHC ex. Turbo	1989-91	4000-6000

ACTUATORS, OUTPUT

IDLE SPEED CONTROL SOLENOID

Engine	Year	Resistance (ohms)
1468cc FI	1989-92	5-35
1597cc Turbo	1987-88	5-35
	1985-86	7-10
1597cc DOHC	1989-92	28-33†
1795cc Turbo	1984-88	5-35
1834cc, 1997cc SOHC	1990-92	5-35
1997cc, DOHC	1990-92	28-33†
2350cc	1985-92	5-35
2555cc Turbo	1987-89	5-35■
	1983-86	7-10
2972cc	1988-92	28-33†

† Measured between middle and either left or right cavities in both rows of ISC.
■ Measured between terminals 1 & 4 of ISC.

MIXTURE CONTROL SOLENOID

Engine	Year	Resistance (ohms)
1468cc 2V	1987-89	54-66
1795cc 2V, 1997cc	1983-89	54-66
2555cc 2V	1983-90	54-66

COMPUTER TIMING ADVANCE
With engine at operating temperature, check advance at idle and 2000 rpm. Specifications include initial timing. At high altitudes, add 5°.

Engine	Year	Degrees Idle	Degrees 2000 RPM
1468cc FI	1989-90	8-12	26-34
1468cc FI	1991-92	7-13	13-38
1597cc	1989	5-15	30-38
1597cc	1990-92	5-15	32-40
1755cc	1990-92	8-12	26-34
1834cc	1992	0-13	10-30
1997cc	1989-92	5-15	30-40
DOHC	1989-92	5-15	33-41
Turbo	1990-92	5-15	30-40
2350cc Van	1989	5-15	35-43
2350cc Pickup	1990-92	6-12	36-42
2350cc Expo	1992	0-16	33-53
2972cc Sigma	1989-90	13-20	27-31
Montero	1989	13-20	38-42
Montero, Pickup	1990-92	13-20	25-31
2972cc Diamante	1992	7-23	20-40
DOHC	1992	7-23	25-45
2972cc DOHC 3000GT	1991-92	7-23	30-40
Turbo	1991-92	7-23	28-35

ENGINE IDENTIFICATION

To identify an engine by the manufacturer's code, follow the four steps designated by the numbered blocks.

V.I.N.
PLATE LOCATION:

Cars — Chassis number appears on plate attached to instrument panel visible through windshield.

Trucks — Chassis number stamped on right or left hand frame side member and on plate in engine compartment of late models.

1 MODEL YEAR IDENTIFICATION:

1986-92 — 10th character of V.I.N.
1992 — N; 1991 — M; 1990 — L;
1989 — K; 1988 — J; 1987 — H;
1986 — G.

1985-83 — Cannot be determined from vehicle markings, except on emission label.

2 ENGINE CODE LOCATIONS:

1992-86 — 4th character of V.I.N.

1985-83 Pickup — Left side of engine block.

310 — Upper front of engine block.

1985-83 All Other Models — Upper right side of engine block. May also appear on plate attached to left side of engine bulkhead or left front wheelhouse visible when hood is raised.

4 ENGINE IDENTIFICATION

YEAR	3 ENGINE CODE	CYL.	DISPL. liters	cc	Fuel System	HP
1992	E (GA16)	4	1.6	1597	MFI	110
	G (SR20)	4	2.0	1998	MFI	140
	F (KA24)	4	2.4	2389	MFI	138, 140†
	S (KA24)	4	2.4	2389	MFI	134
	H (KA24)	4	2.4	2389	MFI	155
	H (VG30)	6	3.0	2960	MFI	153, 160
	E (VG30)	6	3.0	2960	MFI	190
	R (VG30)	6	3.0	2960	MFI	222
	C (VG30ET)	6	3.0 T	2960 T	MFI	300
1991	E (GA16)	4	1.6	1597	MFI	110
	G (SR20)	4	2.0	1998	MFI	140
	F (KA24)	4	2.4	2389	MFI	138
	H (KA24)	4	2.4	2389	MFI	155
	S (KA24)	4	2.4	2389	MFI	134
	H (VG30)	6	3.0	2960	MFI	153
	R (VG30)	6	3.0	2960	MFI	222
	C (VG30)	6	3.0 T	2960 T	MFI	300
1990	G (GA16)	4	1.6	1597	TBI	90
	F (KA24)	4	2.4	2389	MFI	138
	H (KA24)	4	2.4	2389	MFI	140
	S (KA24)	4	2.4	2389	MFI	134
	H (VG30)	6	3.0	2960	MFI	153
	H (VG30)	6	3.0	2960	MFI	165
	R (VG30)	6	3.0	2960	MFI	222
	C (VG30ET)	6	3.0 T	2960 T	MFI	300
1989	G (GA16)	4	1.6	1577	TBI	90
	C (CA18)	4	1.8	1809	MFI	125
	H (CA20)	4	2.0	1974	MFI	94
	N (Z24)	4	2.4	2389	TBI	106
	H (KA24)	4	2.4	2389	MFI	140
	H (VG30)	6	3.0	2960	TBI or MFI	145-160†
	C (VG30ET)	6	3.0 T	2960 T	MFI	205
1988	P (E16)	4	1.6	1597	TBI	69
	E (CA18)	4	1.8	1809	MFI	125
	C (CA18)	4	1.8 T	1809 T	MFI	125
	P (CA20)	4	2.0	1974	MFI	99
	H (CA20)	4	2.0	1974	MFI	94, 97†
	S, N (Z24)	4	2.4	2389	TBI	106
	H (VG30)	6	3.0	2960	TBI or MFI	145-165
	V (VG30)	6	3.0	2960	MFI	165
	C (VG30ET)	6	3.0 T	2960 T	MFI	205
1987	P (E16)	4	1.6	1597	2V	70
	P (E16)	4	1.6	1597	TBI	70
	E (CA16)	4	1.6	1598	MFI	N/A
	S (CD17)	4	1.7 D	1680 D	MFI	55
	C (CA18)	4	1.8 T	1809 T	MFI	120
	P, H (CA20)	4	2.0	1974	MFI	97, 102†
	N, S (Z24)	4	2.4	2389	TBI	106
	J (SD25)	4	2.5 D	2488 D	MFI	70
	H (VG30)	6	3.0	2960	TBI or MFI	140, 152†

4 ENGINE IDENTIFICATION

YEAR	3 ENGINE CODE	CYL.	DISPL. liters	cc	Fuel System	HP
1987 Cont'd.	V, H (VG30)	6	3.0	2960	MFI	140-160†
	C (VG30ET)	6	3.0 T	2960 T	MFI	205
1986	P (E16)	4	1.6	1597	2V	69
	S (CD17)	4	1.7 D	1680 D	MFI	55
	C (CA18)	4	1.8 T	1809 T	MFI	120
	F (Z20)	4	2.0	1952	2V	N/A
	P, H (CA20)	4	2.0	1974	MFI	97, 102†
	N (Z24)	4	2.4	2389	2V	103
	N (Z24)	4	2.4	2389	TBI	106
	J (SD25)	4	2.5 D	2488 D	MFI	70
	H (VG30E)	6	3.0	2960	TBI or MFI	152, 160†
	C (VG30ET)	6	3.0 T	2960 T	MFI	200
1985	E16	4	1.6	1597	2V	69
	CD17	4	1.7 D	1680 D	MFI	55
	CA18ET	4	1.8 T	1809 T	MFI	120
	Z20	4	2.0	1952	2V	N/A
	CA20	4	2.0	1974	2V	88
	CA20E	4	2.0	1974	MFI	97, 102†
	Z24	4	2.4	2389	2V	103
	SD25	4	2.5 D	2488 D	MFI	70
	VG30E	6	3.0	2960	MFI	152, 160†
	VG30ET	6	3.0 T	2960 T	MFI	200
1984	E16	4	1.6	1597	2V	69
	CD17	4	1.7 D	1680 D	MFI	55
	CA18ET	4	1.8 T	1809 T	MFI	N/A
	CA20	4	2.0	1974	2V	88
	CA20E	4	2.0	1974	MFI	97
	Z20	4	2.0	1952	2V	N/A
	Z24	4	2.4	2389	2V	103
	L24E	6	2.4	2393	MFI	120
	SD25	4	2.5 D	2488 D	MFI	70
	VG30E	6	3.0	2960	MFI	160
	VG30ET	6	3.0 T	2960 T	MFI	200
1983	E15	4	1.5	1488	2V	65
	E15ET	4	1.5 T	1488 T	2V	N/A
	E16	4	1.6	1597	2V	69
	CD17	4	1.7 D	1680 D	MFI	55
	Z20	4	2.0	1952	2V	N/A
	CA20	4	2.0	1974	2V	88
	Z22E	4	2.2	2187	MFI	102
	Z22	4	2.2	2187	2V	98
	SD22	4	2.2	2164	MFI	55
	Z24	4	2.4	2389	2V	103
	L24E	6	2.4	2393	MFI	120
	SD25	4	2.5 D	2488 D	MFI	70
	L28E	6	2.8	2753	MFI	145
	L28ET	6	2.8 T	2753 T	MFI	180
	LD28	6	2.8 D	2793 D	MFI	80

D — Diesel. T — Turbo. TBI — Throttle Body Injection.
MFI — Multiport Fuel Injection. 2V — Two Venturi Carburetor.
† Engine horsepower varies with model installation.

UNDERHOOD SERVICE SPECIFICATIONS

DNITU1   CYLINDER NUMBERING SEQUENCE   DNITU1

4-CYL. FIRING ORDER:
    1 3 4 2

Front of car

1983-90
310, Sentra, Pulsar
1488cc, 1597cc

1991-92
1597cc Sentra, NX

1991-92
1998cc Sentra, NX

1983-89
8-plug 200SX, 510, Pickup,
Pathfinder, Van 1809cc, 1952cc,
1974cc, 2187cc, 2389cc

1983-89
Stanza, Multi 1974cc

UNDERHOOD SERVICE SPECIFICATIONS

DNITU2

CYLINDER NUMBERING SEQUENCE

DNITU2

4-CYL. FIRING ORDER: 1 3 4 2

6 CYL. FIRING ORDER: 1 5 3 6 2 4

**1990-92
Pickup
2389cc**

**1989-92
240SX
2389cc**

**1990-92
Axxess, Stanza
2389cc**

**1983-84
810, Maxima, 280ZX
2393cc, 2753cc**

V6 FIRING ORDER: 1 2 3 4 5 6

**1984-89
300ZX, Pickup,
Pathfinder
2960cc**

**1990-92
Pickup, Pathfinder
2960cc**

**1985-88
Maxima 2960cc**

**1989-91
Maxima 2960cc SOHC**

— Front of car —

TIMING MARK

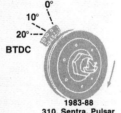

**1983-88
310, Sentra, Pulsar
1488cc, 1597cc**

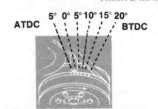

**1987-89 Pulsar 1598cc, 1809cc DOHC;
1984-88 200SX; 1983-89 Stanza 1809cc, 1974cc;
1989-92 Sentra, Pulsar 1597cc, 1998cc;
1989-92 240SX 2389cc;
1990-92 Stanza, Axxess 2389cc**

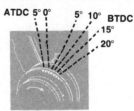

**1984-92
All 2960cc**

**1983-89 Pickup, Pathfinder
1952cc, 2187cc, 2389cc;
1983 200SX 2187cc;
1983-84 200ZX, 810 Maxima
2393cc, 2753cc**

ELECTRICAL AND IGNITION SYSTEMS

BATTERY

Specifications given are for the manufacturer's recommended replacement and may vary from the battery supplied as original equipment.

Model	Year	STANDARD BCI Group No.	STANDARD Crank. Perf.	OPTIONAL BCI Group No.	OPTIONAL Crank. Perf.
Sentra Gasoline	1983-88	35	380	—	—
Canada	1983-88	24F	435	—	—
Sentra Diesel	1983-87	27F	470	27F	655
Canada	1983-87	27F	655	—	—
Sentra	1989-90	35	350	24F	415
Canada	1989-90	24F	415	—	—
Sentra, NX	1991-92	35	490	—	—
Pulsar	1983-90	35	380	—	—
Canada	1983-90	24F	435	—	—
Micra	1983-86	22NF	340	—	—
Axxess	1990	35	350	—	—
Axxess					
Canada	1990-92	24F	415	—	—
Stanza	1983-86	25	380	—	—
Canada	1983-86	24	435	—	—
Stanza	1987-88	35	380	24F	435
Canada	1987-88	24F	435	—	—
Stanza wagon, Multi	1986-88	24F	435	—	—
Stanza	1989-92	35	350	24F	415
Canada	1989-92	24F	415	—	—
Maxima	1983-85	25	380	—	—
Canada	1983-85	27	470	—	—

BATTERY Continued

Model	Year	STANDARD BCI Group No.	STANDARD Crank. Perf.	OPTIONAL BCI Group No.	OPTIONAL Crank. Perf.
Maxima	1986-88	35	380	—	—
Canada	1986-88	27F	410	—	—
Maxima	1989-92	35	350	24F	585
Canada	1989-92	24F	585	27F	625
200SX	1983	25	350	—	—
Canada	1983	27	470	—	—
200SX	1984-88	25	350	—	—
Canada	1984-85	27	470	—	—
Canada	1986-88	24	415	—	—
240SX	1989-92	25	350	24	415
Canada	1989-92	24	415	—	—
280ZX	1983	25	350	—	—
Canada	1983	27	470	—	—
300ZX	1984-89	25	380	—	—
Canada	1984-89	27	470	—	—
300ZX: MT	1990-92	24F	415	—	—
AT	1990-92	24F	585	—	—
Pickup	1983-85	25	380	24	435
Diesel	1983-85	27	655	—	—
Canada	1983-85	24	435	—	—
Pickup, Pathfinder:					
4-cyl.	1986-92	25	380	25	435
V6	1986-92	25	380	27	470
Canada: 4-cyl.	1986-92	25	435	—	—
V6	1986-92	27	470	—	—
Pickup, Diesel	1986-87	24	610	—	—

UNDERHOOD SERVICE SPECIFICATIONS

DNITU3   DNITU3

ALTERNATOR
See UNDERHOOD SERVICE INSTRUCTIONS at the beginning of this section for test/adjustment diagrams.

Engine/Model	Year	Rated Output (amps)	Test Output (amps @ eng. rpm)
Axxess	1990-92	70	50 @ 2500
Maxima	1983-84	60	50 @ 2500
Maxima	1985-92	90	63 @ 2500
DOHC	1992	95	80 @ 2500
Micra	1984-91	50	42 @ 2500
NX: 1.6L	1991-92	70	50 @ 2500
2.0L	1991-92	80	63 @ 2500
Pickup	1983-86	50	40 @ 2500
		60	50 @ 2500
Pickup, Pathfinder	1986-89	60	50 @ 2500
Pickup, Pathfinder	1990-92	60	48 @ 2500
V6		70	50 @ 2500
Sentra, Pulsar	1983-86	50	42 @ 2500
		60	50 @ 2500
Sentra, Pulsar	1987-89	60	50 @ 2500
		70	50 @ 2500
Sentra, Pulsar	1990	65	50 @ 2500
Canada	1990	70	50 @ 2500
Sentra: 1.6L	1991-92	70	50 @ 2500
2.0L	1991-92	80	63 @ 2500
Stanza	1983-86	60	50 @ 2500
Stanza, Multi	1987-89	70	50 @ 2500
Stanza	1990-92	70	50 @ 2500
		80	60 @ 2500
200SX	1983-86	60	50 @ 2500
200SX	1987-89	70	50 @ 2500
240SX	1990-92	80	60 @ 2500
280ZX	1983	60	50 @ 2500
Turbo	1983	70	50 @ 2500
300ZX	1984-89	70	50 @ 2500
300ZX	1990-92	80	65 @ 2500
Turbo	1990-92	90	65 @ 2500

REGULATOR

Application	Year	Test Temp. (deg. F/C)	Voltage Setting
All	1983	68/20	14.4-15.0
Micra, 300ZX Turbo	1984-85	68/20	14.1-14.7
All Others	1984-85	68/20	14.4-15.0
Micra, 200SX, Stanza, Pickup 4-cyl.	1986	68/20	14.1-14.7
All Others	1986	68/20	14.4-15.0
4-cyl. Pickup	1987	68/20	14.4-15.0
All Others	1987	68/20	14.1-14.7
1974cc 200SX, Pickup	1988-89	68/20	14.4-15.0
All Others	1988-92	68/20	14.1-14.7

SPARK PLUGS

Engine/Model	Year	Gap (inches)	Gap (mm)	Torque (ft-lb)
Sentra, Pulsar, 310 Canada	1983-86	.031-.035	.80-.90	14-22
Pickup	1983-89	.031-.035	.80-.90	14-22
Pulsar DOHC	1987-89	.043†	1.1†	14-22
Pickup V6	1990-92	.031-.035	.80-.90	14-22
NX 1998cc w/o platinum spark plugs	1991-92	.031-.035	.80-.90	14-22
All Others	1983-92	.039-.043	1.0-1.1	14-22

† Do not adjust.

IGNITION COIL
See UNDERHOOD SERVICE INSTRUCTIONS at the beginning of this section for test/adjustment diagrams.

Resistance (ohms @ 68°F or 20°C).

Engine	Year	Windings	Resistance (ohms)
1237cc	1984-85	Primary	1.00-1.30
		Secondary	7300-11,000
1488cc, 1597cc	1983-86	Primary	1.04-1.27
		Secondary	7300-11,000

IGNITION COIL Continued

Engine	Year	Windings	Resistance (ohms)
1597cc	1987-90	Primary	0.84-1.02
		Secondary	8200-12,400
1597cc	1991-92	Primary	0.9 approx.
		Secondary	13,000 approx.
1952cc	1983-86	Primary	0.84-1.02
		Secondary	8300-12,600
1998cc	1991-92	Primary	1.0 approx.
		Secondary	10,000 approx.
2389cc 2V	1984-86	Primary	1.05-1.27
		Secondary	8400-12,600
2389cc FI	1986	Primary	0.8-1.0
		Secondary	7600-11,400
2389cc 240SX	1990-92	Primary	1.0 approx.
		Secondary	10,000 approx.
2389cc Axxess, Pickup, Stanza	1990-92	Primary	0.7 approx.
		Secondary	8000 approx.
2753cc Turbo	1983	Primary	0.63-0.77
		Secondary	7000-8600
2960cc	1984-86	Primary	0.8-1.0
		Secondary	7600-11,400
2960cc Maxima SOHC	1990-92	Primary	1.0 approx.
		Secondary	8200-12,400
2960cc Maxima DOHC	1992	Primary	0.8 approx.
2960cc Pickup, Pathfinder	1990-92	Primary	1.0 approx.
		Secondary	10,000 approx.
2960cc 300ZX	1990-92	Primary	0.7 approx.
		Secondary	8000 approx.
All Others	1983-86	Primary	0.84-1.02
		Secondary	8200-12,400
All Others	1987-89	Primary	0.8-1.0
		Secondary	7600-11,400

DISTRIBUTOR PICKUP

Engine	Year	Resistance (ohms)	Air Gap (in./mm)
All w/EI ex. Hall Effect	1983-86	—	.012-.020/.30-.50
1237cc	1984-91	970-1170	—

TIMING PROCEDURE
See UNDERHOOD SERVICE INSTRUCTIONS at the beginning of this section for test/adjustment diagrams.

1987 1597cc 2V: Check timing against specified value. Disconnect and plug vacuum sensor hose before adjusting.

1987-92 1597cc FI: Check timing against specified value. Disconnect throttle sensor harness before adjusting.

1987-89 1598cc, 1809cc DOHC: Remove spark plug/coil cover. Connect inductive clamp to wire between #1 coil and spark plug. Rotate crank angle sensor to adjust.

1990-92 1998cc, 2389cc: Disconnect throttle sensor harness before adjusting.

1992 Maxima DOHC: Disconnect throttle sensor harness before adjusting.

1990-92 2960cc 300ZX: Remove #1 coil from mount and install a longer high tension wire. Connect inductive clamp to high tension wire. Rotate crank angle sensor to adjust.

1983-86 All Others: Disconnect and plug distributor vacuum hose, as equipped.

1987-92 All Others: Set timing to specified value.

BASE TIMING
Set timing at slow idle and Before Top Dead Center, unless otherwise specified.

Engine/Model	Year	Man. Trans. (degrees) @ RPM	Auto. Trans. (degrees) @ RPM
1237cc	1984-85	2 ATDC ±2	2 ±2
1488cc	1983	2 ATDC ±2	2 ATDC ±2
Turbo	1983	—	15 ±2
1597cc	1983	5 ATDC ±2	5 ATDC ±2
1597cc	1984-85	15 ±2	8 ±2
California, Canada	1984-85	5 ATDC ±2	5 ATDC ±2
1597cc	1986	10 ±2	10 ±2
California, Canada	1986	5 ATDC ±2	5 ATDC ±2
1597cc 2V: Checking	1987	7 ±2	7 ±2
Adjusting	1987	2 ATDC	2 ATDC

UNDERHOOD SERVICE SPECIFICATIONS

DNITU4   DNITU4

BASE TIMING Continued

Engine/Model	Year	Man. Trans. (degrees) @ RPM	Auto. Trans. (degrees) @ RPM
1597cc FI: Checking	1987-90	7 ±5	7 ±5
Adjusting	1987-90	7	7
1597cc	1991-92	10 ±2	10 ±2
1598cc, 1809cc DOHC	1987-88	15 ±2	15 ±2
1809cc Turbo	1984-88	15 ±2	15 ±2
1974cc	1983-84	0 ±2	0 ±2
200SX from 6-84	1984	4 ±2	0 ±2
1974cc Stanza ex. Wagon	1985-86	4 ±2	0 ±2
Canada	1985-86	0 ±2	0 ±2
1974cc Stanza Wagon	1986	4 ±2	4 ±2
To improve driveability	1986	6 ±2	6 ±2
1974cc 200SX	1985-86	4 ±2	4 ±2
w/distr. 18F12	1986	15 ±2	15 ±2
1974cc	1987-89	15 ±2	15 ±2
1974cc Pickup	1983-86	5 ±2	—
1998cc	1991-92	15 ±2	15 ±2
2187cc, 2389cc 2V	1983-86	3 ±2	3 ±2
2187cc FI	1983	8 ±2	8 ±2
2389cc FI Pickup, Pathfinder	1986	5 ±2	5 ±2
2389cc Pickup	1987-92	10 ±2	10 ±2
2389cc Others	1989-90	15 ±2	15 ±2
2389cc 240SX	1991-92	20 ±2	20 ±2
2389cc Stanza	1991-92	15 ±2	15 ±2
2393cc	1983-84	8 ±2	8 ±2
2753cc	1983	8 ±2	8 ±2
2753cc Turbo	1983	20 ±3	20 ±3
2960cc ex. Pickup	1984-87	20 ±2	20 ±2
Turbo	1987	15 ±2	15 ±2
2960cc Pickup	1986-89	12 ±2	12 ±2
2960cc 200SX	1988	20 ±2	20 ±2
2960cc Maxima	1988-89	15 ±2	20 ±2
2960cc 300ZX	1988-89	15 ±2	20 ±2
Turbo	1988-89	10 ±2	15 ±2
2960cc Maxima, Pickup	1990-92	15 ±2	15 ±2
2960cc 300ZX	1990-92	15 ±2	15 ±2

DISTRIBUTOR TIMING ADVANCE

Engine degrees at engine rpm, no load, in addition to base timing setting.

Mechanical advance distributors only.

Engine	Transmission	Year	Distributor Number	Degrees @ 2500 RPM Total	Degrees @ 2500 RPM Centrifugal
1237cc	MT	1984-85	T4T83581	20-28	9-13
1237cc	AT	1984-85	T4T83582	10.2-18.2	5.2-9.2
1488cc	MT & AT	1983	D4R81-08	17.5-25.5	6.5-10.5
1488cc	MT	1983	D4R81-13	22.5-30.5	6.5-10.5
1488cc	MT	1983	D4R82-25	24.8-32.8	8.8-12.8
1597cc California	MT	1983-86	D4R82-12	25.2-33.2	7.2-11.2
1597cc	AT	1983	D4R82-13	18.2-26.2	7.2-11.2
1597cc	AT	1983	D4R82-14	20.2-28.2	7.2-11.2
1597cc Canada	MT	1983-86	D4R82-21	16.3-24.3	5.3-9.3
1597cc Canada	AT	1983-86	D4R82-22	10.3-18.3	5.3-9.3
1597cc California	AT	1984-86	D4R82-24	16.2-24.2	7.2-11.2
1974cc 200SX, Stanza	MT & AT	1983-84	D4N82-01, 02	38.5-46.5	5.5-9.5
1974cc 200SX, Stanza	AT	1983	D4N81-07	26.5-34.5	5.5-9.5
1974cc 200SX, Stanza	MT & AT	1984-86	D4N83-16	32.5-40.5	9.5-13.5
1974cc 200SX, Stanza	MT & AT	1984-85	D4N83-15	33-41	10-14
1974cc 200SX, Stanza	MT	1985-86	T0T80273	22.7-30.7	9.5-13.5
1974cc 200SX, Stanza	MT & AT	1986	D4N84-17,18,19	17-25	9.5-13.5
1974cc Pickup	MT	1983-84	D4N82-14	24-32	1-5
1974cc Pickup	MT	1985	D4N84-04	24.2-32.2	6.2-10.2
2187cc 2V	MT & AT	1983	D4N80-36	35.6-43.6	2.6-6.6
2187cc 2V	MT & AT	1983	D4N80-37	31.6-39.6	2.6-6.6
2187cc 2V	MT & AT	1983	D4N80-38	15.6-23.6	2.6-6.6
2187cc 2V	MT & AT	1983	D4N80-39	20.6-28.6	2.6-6.6
2187cc 2V	MT & AT	1983	D4N80-43	13.6-21.6	5.6-9.6
2187cc FI	MT & AT	1983	D4N81-01	23.6-31.6	5.6-9.6
2187cc FI	MT	1983	D4N81-01	23.6-31.6	5.6-9.6
2187cc FI	AT	1983	D4N81-02	18.6-26.6	5.6-9.6

DISTRIBUTOR TIMING ADVANCE Continued

Engine	Transmission	Year	Distributor Number	Degrees @ 2500 RPM Total	Degrees @ 2500 RPM Centrifugal
2389cc	MT & AT	1983	D4N82-08	27.9-35.9	9.3-11.3
2389cc	MT & AT	1983	D4N82-09	30.3-38.3	9.3-11.3
2389cc	MT & AT	1983-84	D4N82-10	17.3-25.3	9.3-11.3
2389cc	MT & AT	1983	D4N82-11	22.9-30.9	9.3-11.3
2389cc	MT & AT	1984	D4N83-11	33-41	10-14
2389cc	MT & AT	1984	D4N83-13	23-31	10-14
2389cc	MT & AT	1984	D4N83-14	28-36	10-14
2389cc	MT & AT	1985	D4N84-02	19.6-27.6	6.6-10.6
2389cc	MT & AT	1985-86	D4N84-01	24.6-32.6	6.6-10.6
2389cc	MT & AT	1985-86	D4N84-03	14.6-22.6	6.6-10.6
2389cc	MT & AT	1985-86	D4N84-05	29.6-37.6	6.6-10.6
2389cc	MT & AT	1985-86	D4N84-06	16.5-24.5	8.5-12.5
2389cc	MT	1986	D4N85-01	14.6-22.6	6.6-10.6
2389cc	MT & AT	1986	D4N85-02	12.1-21.1	6.6-10.6
2393cc	MT & AT	1983-84	D6K81-02	41.4-49.4	13.4-17.4
2753cc	MT & AT	1983	D6K82-01	40.9-48.9	12.9-16.9

FUEL SYSTEM

FUEL SYSTEM PRESSURE

See UNDERHOOD SERVICE INSTRUCTIONS at the beginning of this section for test/adjustment diagrams.

All carburetted & TBI, measured at fuel inlet fitting on unit.

All MFI, measured between fuel filter and metal pipe. Values are approximate pressure.

Engine	Year	Pressure PSI	Pressure RPM
Carburetted & TBI:			
All 2V	1983-87	2.8-3.8	idle
1597cc TBI	1987-88	14	idle
1597cc	1989-90	43†	idle
		34‡	idle
2389cc (early)	1986	14	idle
(late)	1986-89	36	idle
2960cc TBI	1986-89	36	idle

Engine	Year	Pressure†	Pressure‡	RPM
Fuel Injected (MFI):				
All	1983-85	37	30	idle
1597cc, 1998cc	1991-92	43	36	idle
1598cc	1987	36	28	idle
1809cc Turbo	1986-88	37	30	idle
1809cc DOHC	1988-89	43	36	idle
1974cc	1986-87	37	30	idle
1974cc	1986-89	43	37	idle
2389cc	1989-92	43	33	idle
2960cc	1986-88	37	30	idle
Turbo	1986-88	44	30	idle
2960cc Maxima	1989-92	43	36	idle
300ZX	1989	37	30	idle
Turbo	1989	44	30	idle
2960cc 300ZX	1990-92	43	36	idle
2960cc Pickup	1990-92	43	34	idle

† Without vacuum to fuel pressure regulator.
‡ With vacuum applied to fuel pressure regulator.

IDLE SPEED W/O COMPUTER CONTROL

See UNDERHOOD SERVICE INSTRUCTIONS at the beginning of this section for test/adjustment diagrams.

Preferred setting is the midpoint of ranges given.

With engine warm, turn idle speed adjusting screws to obtain specified rpm.

Allow engine to warm up, race engine several times. With FI, disconnect fast idle control device (FICD). Adjust throttle screw to obtain specified rpm.

Carburetted:

To set fast idle, open throttle valve and set to specified step of cam. Adjust fast idle screw to specification.

To set AC speed-up, turn AC on and set blower to high. Adjust speed-up device adjusting screw to specification.

UNDERHOOD SERVICE SPECIFICATIONS

DNITU5   DNITU5

IDLE SPEED W/O COMPUTER CONTROL Continued

Engine/Model	Year	SLOW Man. Trans.	SLOW Auto. Trans.	FAST Man. Trans.	FAST Auto. Trans.	Step of Cam
1237cc	1984-85	650-750	600-700 D	1800-2600	1900-2700 N	Second
1488cc ex. Turbo	1983	700-800	—	2400-3200	—	Second
AC speed-up	1983	750-850				
1597cc	1983	700-800	600-700 D	2300-3200	2300-3200 N	Second
AC speed-up	1983	750-850	580-660 D			
1597cc California	1984-85	700-800	600-700 D	2600-3400	2900-3700 N	Second
Canada	1984-85	700-800	600-700 D	1900-2700	2400-3200 N	Second
AC speed-up, all	1984-85	750-850	580-660 D			
1597cc Calif., Canada	1986	750-850	600-700 D	1800-2600	2300-3100 N	Second
AC speed-up	1986	750-850	600-700 D			
1597cc Calif., Canada	1987	700-900	600-800 D	1800-2600	2100-2900 N	High
AC speed-up	1987	700-900	600-800 D			
1680cc Diesel	1983-86	700-850	700-850 D	—	—	—
AC speed-up	1983-84	850-950	850-950 N			
AC speed-up	1985-86	800-850	900-950 N			
1680cc Diesel	1987	650-750	—	—	—	—
AC speed-up	1987	750-850				
1809cc Turbo	1984-86	700-800	650-750 D	—	—	—
AC speed-up†	1984-86	1000-1050	1050-1100 N			
High Altitude	1984-86	630-730	580-680 D			
1974cc 2V 200SX, Stanza	1983-84	550-750	550-750 D	—	—	—
AC speed-up	1983-84	800-900	800-900 D			
1974cc FI	1984-85	650-850	600-800 D	—	—	—
AC speed-up†	1984-85	800-900	600-800 D			
1974cc 200SX, Stanza	1986	650-850	600-800 D	—	—	—
w/distr. 18F12	1986	650-750	550-650 D			
AC speed-up, 200SX	1986	1000-1050	1050-1100 N			
AC speed-up, Stanza	1986	800-900	600-800 D			
1974cc 200SX	1987-88	700-800	700-800 D	—	—	—
AC speed-up	1987-88	1000-1050	750-850 D			
From VIN 18479, 18528	1987	—	700-800 D			
1974cc Pickup	1983	500-700	—	—	—	—
AC speed-up	1983	900	—			
1974cc Pickup	1984-86	600-800	—	—	—	—
AC speed-up	1984-86	800-900	—			
2164cc Diesel	1983	650-800	—	—	—	—
AC speed-up	1983	900	—			

IDLE SPEED W/O COMPUTER CONTROL Continued

Engine/Model	Year	SLOW Man. Trans.	SLOW Auto. Trans.	FAST Man. Trans.	FAST Auto. Trans.	Step of Cam
2187cc 2V 2WD	1983	750-850	550-750 D	—	—	—
AC speed-up	1983	800	800 N			
2187cc 2V 4WD	1983	700-900	550-750 D	—	—	—
AC speed-up	1983	950	950 N			
2187cc FI	1983	650-850	600-800 D	—	—	—
AC speed-up†	1983	900	1000 N			
2389cc 2WD	1983	700-900	550-750 D	—	—	—
California	1983	800-1000	550-750 D			
AC speed-up, all	1983	900	1000 N			
2389cc 2V 4WD	1983-86	700-900	550-750 D	—	—	—
AC speed-up	1983	900	1000 N			
AC speed-up	1984-86	800-900	800-900 N			
2389cc 2V 2WD	1984	550-750	550-750 D	—	—	—
California	1984	600-800	550-750 D			
AC speed-up, all	1984	800-900	800-900 N			
2389cc 2V 2WD	1985	600-800	550-750 D	—	—	—
Canada	1985	550-750	550-750 D			
AC speed-up, all	1985	900-1000	1000 N			
2389cc 2WD: U.S.	1986	700-900	550-750 D	2200-2600	2600-3000 N	Second
Cab & Chassis	1986	600-800	—	2200-2600	—	Second
Canada	1986	550-750	550-750 D	2200-2600	2200-2600 N	Second
AC speed-up, all	1986	800-900	800-900 N			
2389cc FI	1986	850-950	850-950 N	—	—	—
AC speed-up, early	1986	950-1050	950-1050 N			
AC speed-up, late	1986	850-950	850-950 N			
2389cc Van	1987-88	750-850	650-750 D	—	—	—
AC speed-up	1987-88	900-1000	900-1000 N			
2389cc Pickup 2WD	1987	750-850	600-700 D	—	—	—
AC speed-up	1987	850-950	850-950 N			
2389cc Pickup, Pathfinder 4WD	1987	750-850	600-700 D	—	—	—
AC speed-up	1987	850-950	850-950 N			
2389cc Pickup, Pathfinder	1988-89	750-850	600-700 D	—	—	—
AC speed-up	1988-89	850-950	850-950 N			
2393cc	1983	600-800	550-750 D	—	—	—
AC speed-up†	1983	800	750 N			
2393cc	1984	650-750	600-700 D	—	—	—
AC speed-up	1984	800	750 N			
2488cc Diesel	1983-86	650-800	—	—	—	—
AC speed-up	1986	800-900				
2753cc ex. Turbo	1983	600-800	600-800 D	—	—	—
AC speed-up†	1983	820	750 N			

UNDERHOOD SERVICE SPECIFICATIONS

DNITU6   DNITU6

IDLE SPEED W/O COMPUTER CONTROL Continued

Engine/Model	Year	SLOW Man. Trans.	SLOW Auto. Trans.	FAST Man. Trans.	FAST Auto. Trans.	Step of Cam
2793cc Diesel	1983	600-750	600-750 D	—	—	—
AC speed-up	1983	850-950	850-950 N			
2960cc ex. Pickup	1984-86	650-750	650-750 D	—	—	—
High Altitude	1984-86	600-700	600-700 D	—	—	—
AC speed-up, all	1984-85	750-850	750-850 D			
2960cc Pickup	1986-89	750-850	650-750 D	—	—	—
AC speed-up	1986-89	850-950	850-950 D			
2960cc 200SX	1987-88	650-750	650-750 D	—	—	—
High Alt.	1988	600-700	600-700 D	—	—	—
AC speed-up	1987-88	750-850	750-850 D			
2960cc Maxima	1987-88	700-800	650-750 D	—	—	—
High Alt.	1987-88	650-750	600-700 D	—	—	—
AC speed-up	1987-88	750-850	750-850 D			
2960cc 300ZX	1987-89	650-750	650-750 D	—	—	—
High Alt.	1987-89	600-700	600-700 D	—	—	—
AC speed-up, all	1987-89	750-850	750-850 D			

† Checking figure, cannot be adjusted.

IDLE SPEED W/COMPUTER CONTROL

See UNDERHOOD SERVICE INSTRUCTIONS at the beginning of this section for test/adjustment diagrams.

Midpoint of range given is the preferred setting speed.

1983 1488cc Turbo, 2753cc Turbo:
With engine at operating temperature, race several times and return to idle. Disconnect idle control valve and check speed against specified value.

1984-87 1597cc 2V Federal:
With engine at operating temperature, disconnect vacuum control modulator harness. Race engine several times and set idle speed to specified value. Switch engine off and reconnect vacuum control modulator harness. Restart engine, race several times, and check idle speed against specified value.

1987-92 1597cc FI, 1989-92 2389cc Stanza, 240SX, Axxess:
With engine at operating temperature disconnect throttle sensor harness connector. Start engine and set idle to specified setting speed. Turn engine off, reconnect harness and restart engine. Verify that idle speed is within checking speed. Turn on AC and verify that idle increases to specified value.

1984-89 2960cc Turbo, 1987-89 1598cc, 1809cc DOHC:
With engine at operating temperature, turn ignition off and disconnect automatic air control (AAC) valve harness. Start engine and set idle speed to specified value. Switch engine off and reconnect harness. Restart engine and check idle speed against specified value. Turn AC on and verify that speed-up is at specified value.

All engines, turn AC on and verify that speed-up speed is at specified value.

1987-88 1809cc Turbo, 1987-89 1974cc Stanza:
Disconnect throttle valve and automatic air control valve harness. Start engine and adjust idle to specified setting speed. Turn engine off, reconnect harness and restart engine. Verify that idle is at specified checking speed.

1989-90 2960cc Maxima:
Turn diagnostic selector on ECU fully clockwise and adjust idle to specified value. Turn AC on and verify that idle increases to specified value.

1991-92 2960cc Maxima:
Disconnect ISC and set idle to specified value.

1990-92 2960cc 300ZX:
Attach inductive clamp to loop wire on power transistor behind upper radiator hose. Set idle to specified value.

All models: After checking/adjusting idle speed, reinstate connections and turn AC on. Verify that speed increases to specified value.

IDLE SPEED W/COMPUTER CONTROL Continued

Engine	Year	Transmission	Setting Speed	Checking Speed	Speed-up Speed
1488cc Turbo	1983	AT	600-700 D	—	—
1597cc Federal	1984-86	MT	650-750	700-900	—
		AT	500-600 D	750-850 D	—
1597cc 2V Federal	1987	MT	700-750	700-900	900-1100
		AT	600-650 D	600-800 D	600-800 D
1597cc FI	1988	MT	750	700-900	900-1100
		AT	670 D	600-800 D	650-850 D
1597cc 2WD	1989-90	MT	675-775	700-900	950-1150
Sentra	1989	AT	575-675 D	600-800 D	950-1150 N
Sentra	1990	AT	750-850 N	800-1000 N	950-1150 N
Pulsar	1989-90	AT	575-675 D	650-850 D	900-1100 N
1597cc 4WD	1989-90	MT	675-775	700-900	900-1100
	1989	AT	575-675 D	600-800 D	900-1100 N
	1990	AT	750-850 N	800-1000 N	900-1000 N
1597cc U.S.	1991-92	MT	550-650	600-700	600-700
Canada	1991-92	MT	550-650	700-800	700-800
	1991-92	AT	675-775 N	750-850 N	750-850 N
1598cc DOHC	1987	MT	700-800	750-850	750-850
1809cc DOHC	1988-89	MT	700-800	750-850	950-1050
		AT	600-700	650-750 D	950-1050 N
1809cc Turbo	1987-89	MT	700	700-800	1000-1050
1974cc Stanza	1987-89	MT	650-750	700-800	950-1050
		AT	550-650 D	650-750 D	950-1050 N
1974cc Stanza Wagon	1987-88	MT	650-750	700-800	800-900
		AT	550-650 D	650-750 D	650-750 D
1998cc	1991-92	MT	700-800	750-850	800-900
		AT	700-800 N	750-850 N	800-900 N
2389cc 240SX From eng. KA24-012039	1989	MT	650-750	700-800	950-1050
	1989-90	MT	600-700	650-750	950-1050
	1989-90	AT	650-750 N	700-800 N	950-1050 N
2389cc Axxess, Stanza: U.S.	1990-92	MT	600-700	650-750	—
		AT	600-700 N	650-750 N	—
Canada	1990-92	MT	600-700	700-800	—
		AT	600-700 N	700-800 N	—
2389cc Pickup, Pathfinder	1990-91	MT	700-800	750-850	800-900
		AT	700-800 N	750-850 N	800-900 N
2389cc 240SX	1991-92	MT	600-700	650-750	950-1050
		AT	600-700 N	650-750 N	950-1050 N
2753cc Turbo	1983	MT	650-750	—	—
			600-700 D	—	—
2960cc Maxima SOHC	1989-91	MT	700	700-800	750-850
	1989-92	AT	700 N	700-800 N	750-850 N
2960cc Maxima DOHC	1992	MT	650-750	700-800	750-850
		AT	650-750 N	700-800 N	750-850 N
2960cc Trucks	1990-92	MT	700	700-800	750-850
		AT	700 N	700-800 N	750-850 N
2960cc 300ZX	1990-92	MT	650	650-750	750-850
		AT	720 N	720-820 N	750-850 N
Turbo	1984-89	MT	650	650-750	750-850
		AT	600 D	600-700 D	750-850 D
Turbo	1990-92	MT	650	650-750	800-900
		AT	700 N	700-800 N	800-900 N

ENGINE MECHANICAL

TIGHTENING TORQUES
See UNDERHOOD SERVICE INSTRUCTIONS at the beginning of this section for test/adjustment diagrams.

Some fasteners are tightened in more than one step.

Engine	Year	Torque Ft-lbs/Nm Cylinder Head	Intake Manifold	Exhaust Manifold	Crankshaft Pulley	Water Pump
1488cc, 1597cc Sentra, Pulsar, 310	1983-88	22/29, 51-54/ 69-74◆	12-15/ 16-21	12-15/ 16-21	80-94/ 108-127	6-10/9-14

UNDERHOOD SERVICE SPECIFICATIONS

DNITU7   DNITU7

TIGHTENING TORQUES Continued

		Torque Ft-lbs/Nm				
Engine	Year	Cylinder Head	Intake Manifold	Exhaust Manifold	Crankshaft Pulley	Water Pump
1597cc	1989-90	22/29, 47/64♦	12-15/ 16-21	12-15/ 16-21	98-112/ 132-155	4-6/6-8
1597cc	1991-92	22/29, 43/59⊙	12-15/ 16-21	12-15/ 16-21	98-112/ 132-152	5-6/6-8
1598cc, 1809cc DOHC	1987-89	22/29 76/103‡	14-19/ 20-25	27-35/ 37-48	105-112/ 142-152	12-14/16-20
1680cc Diesel	1983-86	43-51/ 59-69, 72-80/ 98-108	13-16/ 18-22	13-16/ 18-22	90-98/ 123-132	12-14/16-20
1809cc Turbo, 1974cc 200SX, Stanza	1984-89	22/29, 58/78●	14-19/ 19-25	14-22/ 20-29	90-98/ 123-132	12-14/16-20
	1983	51-58/ 69-79	13-16/ 18-22	13-17/ 18-24	87-101/ 118-137	9-12/12-16
1974cc, 2389cc Pickup	1983-88	22/29, 58/78*	12-14/ 16-20	13-16/ 18-22	90-98/ 123-132	12-15/16-20
1998cc	1991-92	29/39, 58/78△	13-15/ 15-21	27-35/ 37-48	105-112/ 142-152	12-15/ 16-21
2164cc Diesel	1983	22-29/ 29-39, 36-47/ 49-64 short; 43-58/ 59-78, 87-108/ 118-147 long	11-13/ 15-18	11-13/ 15-18	217-239/ 294-324	7-9/10-13 short; 14-18/20-25 long
2187cc 200SX	1983	51-58/ 69-79	12-15/ 16-22	12-15/ 16-22	87-116/ 118-158	5-6/6-8 short; 12-15/16-22 long
2187cc Pickup	1983	58/79	12-14/ 16-20	12-14/ 16-20	87-116/ 118-158	3-7/7-12 short; 7-12/12-16 long
2393cc	1983	58-65/ 78-88	—	—	101-116/ 137-157	5-6/6-8 short; 12-15/16-21 long
8mm nut		9-12/ 12-16	9-12/ 12-16			
8mm bolt		11-18/ 15-25	11-18/ 15-25			
10mm bolt		25-33/ 34-44	25-33/ 34-44			
2393cc	1984	22/29, 58/78	—	—	101-116/ 137-157	5-6/6-8 short; 12-15/16-21 long
8mm nut		9-12/ 12-16	9-12/ 12-16			
8mm bolt		11-18/ 15-25	11-18/ 15-25			
10mm bolt		25-33/ 34-44	25-33/ 34-44			
2389cc	1989-90	22/29, 58/78★	12-14/ 16-20, 17-20/ 24-27	12-14/ 16-20	105-112/ 142-152	12-15/16-21
2389cc Axxess, Stanza, Pickup	1991-92	22/29, 58/78‡	12-15/ 16-21	12-15/ 16-21	87-116/ 118-157	12-14/ 16-19
2389cc 240SX	1991-92	22/29, 58/78‡	—	27-35/ 37-48	105-112/ 142-152	12-14/ 16-19
2488cc Diesel	1985-87	22/29, 36/49 short; 43/59, 94-127 long	11-13/ 15-18	11-13/ 15-18	217-239/ 294-324	7-9/10-13 short; 14-18/20-25 long

TIGHTENING TORQUES Continued

		Torque Ft-lbs/Nm				
Engine	Year	Cylinder Head	Intake Manifold	Exhaust Manifold	Crankshaft Pulley	Water Pump
2753cc	1983	58-65/ 78-88	—	—	101-116/ 137-157	5-6/6-8 short; 12-15/16-21 long
8mm nut		9-12/ 12-16	9-12/ 12-16	—		
8mm bolt		11-18/ 15-25	11-18/ 15-25			
10mm bolt		25-33/ 34-44	25-33/ 34-44			
2793cc Diesel	1983	87-94/ 118-127	12-15/ 17-21 short; 25-33/ 34-44 long	12-15/ 17-21 short; 25-33/ 34-44 long	16-20/ 22-27	3-4/4-5 short; 6-9/9-12 long
2960cc Maxima SOHC, 300ZX, 200SX	1984-92	22/29, 43/59†	13-16/ 18-22	13-16/ 18-22	90-98/ 123-132	12-15/16-21
2960cc 300ZX DOHC	1990-92	29/39, 90/123■	12-14/ 16-20	17-20/ 24-27	159-174/ 216-235	12-14/ 16-19
2960cc Maxima DOHC	1992	29/39, +70° ▲	17-20/ 24-27	—	123-130/ 167-177	12-15/ 16-21
2960cc Pickup, Pathfinder	1986-92	22/29, 43/59†	12-14/ 16-20 17-20/ 24-27	13-16/ 18-22 17-20/ 24-27	90-98/ 123-132	12-15/16-21

† Loosen fasteners, retorque to 22/29, then turn an additional 60-65°.
* Loosen fasteners, retorque to 22/29, then turn an additional 90-95°.
★ Loosen fasteners, retorque to 22/29, then turn an additional 80-85° (or 54-61/74-83).
■ Loosen fasteners, retorque to 25-33/34-44, then turn bolts an additional 70° (or 90/123).
♦ Loosen fasteners, retorque to 22/29, then 51-54/69-74.
‡ Loosen fasteners, retorque to 22/29, then turn an additional 85-90°.
● Loosen fasteners, retorque to 22/29, then 54-61/74-83.
⊙ Loosen fasteners, retorque to 22/29, then turn an additional 50°. Small bolts outside of valve cover torque to 4-6/6-8.
△ Loosen fasteners, retorque to 29/39, then turn an additional 90°, and again turn 90°.
▲ Loosen fasteners, retorque to 29/39, then turn an additional 70°.

VALVE CLEARANCE
Set with engine hot.

Engine	Year	Intake (inches)	Intake (mm)	Exhaust (inches)	Exhaust (mm)
1237cc	1984-86	.010	.25	.012	.30
1488cc, 1597cc, Sentra, Pulsar, 310	1983-88	.011	.28	.011	.28
1597cc	1991-92	.015	.37	.016	.40
1680cc Diesel	1983-86	.010	.25	.018	.45
1809cc Turbo, 1974cc†, 2187cc, 2389cc	1983-89	.012	.30	.012	.30
2389cc 240SX	1991-92	.012-.015	.31-.39	.013-.016	.33-.41
2393cc, 2753cc, 2793cc	1983	.010	.25	.012	.30
2164cc, 2388cc Diesel	1983-86	.014	.35	.014	.35

† 1987-89 1974cc, hydraulic lifters.

COMPRESSION PRESSURE
At cranking speed, engine warm, throttle open.

Engine	Year	PSI	Maximum Variation PSI
1237cc Micra, 1488cc, 1597cc Sentra, Pulsar, 310	1983-90	142-181	14
1488cc Turbo	1983	158	*
1597cc	1991-92	164-192	14
1598cc, 1809cc DOHC	1987-89	156-185	14
1680cc Diesel	1984-87	427-469	†

UNDERHOOD SERVICE SPECIFICATIONS

DNITU8

DNITU8

COMPRESSION PRESSURE Continued

Engine	Year	PSI @ 250 RPM	Maximum Variation PSI
1809cc Turbo, 1974cc ex. Pickup	1983-89	128-171	14
1974cc, 2187cc, 2389cc Pickup	1983-89	128-171	*
1998cc	1991-92	149-178	14
2388cc Diesel	1983-87	356-427	*
2389cc 240SX	1989-90	142-192	14
2389cc 240SX	1991-92	151-179	14
2389cc Pickup	1990-92	142-192	14
2389cc Axxess, Stanza	1989-92	146-175	14
2393cc, 2753cc	1983-84	128-171	*
2393cc Diesel	1983	356-455	*
2960cc ex. Turbo	1984-89	128-179	14
Turbo	1984-89	121-169	14
2960cc 300ZX ex. Turbo	1990-92	142-186	14
2960cc Maxima DOHC	1992	142-183	14
2960cc Others	1990-92	128-173	14

* Lowest cylinder pressure must be more than 80% of highest cylinder pressure.
† Minimum pressure, 284 psi.

BELT TENSION

A belt in operation 20 minutes is considered a used belt.
Deflection midway between pulleys with an applied load of 22 lb.

Engine	Year	Alternator	Power Steering	Air Cond.	Air Pump
1488cc, 1597cc Sentra, Pulsar, 310 (inches)	1983-86	1/2-11/16	5/16-3/8	3/8-7/16	—
(mm)	1983-86	13-17	7-9	9-11	—
1597cc Sentra (inches)	1987-89	11/32-3/8	9/32-11/32	11/32-3/8	—
(mm)	1987-89	8.5-9.5	7-9	9-10	—
1597cc Pulsar (inches)	1987-89	11/32-3/8	13/32	1/2	—
(mm)	1987-89	8.5-9.5	10.5	12.5	—
1597cc Pulsar (inches)	1988-89	11/32-3/8	9/32-11/32	11/32-3/8	—
(mm)	1988-89	8.5-9.5	7-9	9-10	—
1597cc (inches)	1990-92	9/32-5/16	5/32-1/4	5/32-1/4	—
(mm)	1990-92	7-9	4-6	4-6	—
1598cc, 1809cc DOHC (inches)	1987-88	1/4-5/16	9/32-11/32	1/8-5/32	—
(mm)	1987-88	6-8	7-9	3-4	—
1680cc Diesel (inches)	1983-87	3/8-7/16	3/8-7/16	7/16-1/2	—
(mm)	1983-87	9-11	9-11	11-13	—
1974cc ex. Pickup 2V (inches)	1983-85	7/16-9/16	7/32-3/8	1/8-7/32	—
(mm)	1983-85	11-14	6-10	4-6	—
1809cc Turbo, 1974cc FI (inches)	1986	5/16-7/16	7/32-3/8	1/16-7/32	—
(mm)	1986	7-10	6-10	3-6	—
1974cc Stanza (inches)	1987-89	7/32-9/32	9/32-11/32	1/8-5/32	—
(mm)	1987-89	5-7	7-9	3-4	—
1809cc Turbo, 1974cc 200SX (inches)	1987-88	9/32-5/16	13/32-15/32	5/32-7/32	—
(mm)	1987-88	7-8	10-12	4-5	—
1974cc, 2389cc Pickup (inches)	1983-85	15/32-19/32	—	5/16-7/16	19/32-11/16
(mm)	1983-85	12-15	—	7-10	15-18
1974cc, 2389cc Pickup (inches)	1986	3/8-1/2	7/16-15/32	3/16-7/16	—
(mm)	1986	9-13	10-12	8-10	—
1998cc (inches)	1991-92	9/32-5/16	9/32-5/16	5/32-7/32	—
(mm)		7-8	7-8	4-5	—

BELT TENSION Continued

Engine	Year	Alternator	Power Steering	Air Cond.	Air Pump
2389cc Van (inches)	1987-88	5/16-3/8	11/32-13/32	7/16-1/2	—
(mm)	1987-88	8-10	9-10	11-13	—
2389cc Pickup (inches)	1987-92	7/32-9/32	3/8-7/16	9/32-3/8	—
(mm)	1987-92	5-7	9-11	7-9	—
2389cc Pickup (inches)	1983-86	5/16-9/16	—	5/16-9/16	5/16-9/16
(mm)	1983-86	8-12	—	8-12	8-12
2187cc 200SX (inches)	1983	15/32-19/32	19/32-11/16	7/16-1/2	—
(mm)	1983	12-15	15-18	10-13	—
2389cc 240SX (inches)	1989-92	9/32-5/16	5/16-3/8	9/32-5/16	—
(mm)	1989-92	7-8	8-9	7-8	—
2389cc Axxess (inches)	1990-92	7/32-5/16	7/32-5/16	5/32-7/32	—
(mm)	1990-92	5-6	5-6	4-5	—
2389cc Stanza (inches)	1990-92	1/4-9/32	1/4-9/32	3/16-1/4	—
(mm)	1990-92	6-7	6-7	5-6	—
2393cc, 2753cc (inches)	1983	5/16-7/16	7/16-9/16	7/32-5/16	—
(mm)	1983	7-10	10-14	5-7	—
2793cc Diesel (inches)	1983	7/16-1/2	5/16-3/8	15/32-1/2	—
(mm)	1983	11-13	8-9	12-13	—
2960cc (inches)	1984-85	7/32-3/8	7/32-7/16	7/16-1/2	—
(mm)	1984-85	6-9	5-10	10-12	—
2960cc, 300ZX (inches)	1986-92	5/16-3/8	1/2-5/8	3/8-7/16	—
(mm)	1986-92	7-9	13-16	9-11	—
2960cc, Maxima (inches)	1986-92	5/16-3/8	7/16-5/32	7/32-5/16	—
(mm)	1986-92	7-9	10-12	5-7	—
2960cc Pickup (inches)	1986-92	7/32-9/32	3/8-7/16	9/32-3/8	—
(mm)	1986-92	5-7	9-11	7-9	—
2960cc 200SX (inches)	1987-88	9/32-5/16	3/8-15/32	11/32-13/32	—
(mm)	1987-88	7-8	10-12	9-10	—

ENGINE COMPUTER SYSTEM

COMPUTER DIAGNOSTIC CODES
See UNDERHOOD SERVICE INSTRUCTIONS at the beginning of this section for test/adjustment diagrams.

1983-87 1488cc ex. Turbo, 1597cc 2V:
With ignition switch off, locate control unit and position it so the red and green LED lights can be seen. Turn switch on control unit on and switch on ignition. Check LED lights for interval.

1983-86 1488cc Turbo, 1974cc FI, 2960cc
1984-87 1809cc Turbo
1986 2389cc FI:
Turn ignition on and access ECU. Verify that LEDs stay on. Turn mode switch screw fully clockwise or, if equipped, turn mode switch on. LEDs will flash codes. Depress accelerator and release, shift transmission through all gears. Start engine, drive vehicle (E15 Turbo only), and turn AC, heater blower, light switches on and off. Codes displayed at this point (ex. 44) indicate system failures. Disconnect battery negative terminal to erase codes.

1987-89 All ex. 1987 1809cc Turbo & 1597cc 2V; 1989 Maxima:
1987-89 Pickup, Pathfinder, Van: With engine running, access ECU and turn diagnostic mode switch on. After LEDs flash three times turn switch off. After obtaining codes, turn mode switch on. After LEDs flash four times, turn mode switch and ignition switch off.

1990 300ZX, Stanza: With ignition on, access ECU under dash. Turn mode selector clockwise, after two seconds turn counterclockwise. Repeat procedure. Codes will be displayed on LEDs similar to other models.

1990 Others, 1991-92 Trucks & Maxima SOHC: With engine running access ECU and turn mode switch screw fully clockwise. After LEDs flash three times, turn switch fully counterclockwise.

All models: Codes will be displayed on LED and/or "Check" engine light, if equipped. Red LED flashes tens, green LED flashes ones.

UNDERHOOD SERVICE SPECIFICATIONS

COMPUTER DIAGNOSTIC CODES Continued

1990 300ZX, Stanza; 1991-92 All ex. Trucks & Maxima SOHC: After obtaining codes, turn mode switch clockwise after two seconds, counterclockwise.

1990 Others, 1991-92 Trucks & Maxima SOHC: After obtaining codes, turn mode switch fully clockwise. After LEDs flash four times, turn mode switch counterclockwise and turn ignition switch off.

1597cc ex. Turbo, 1983 1597cc all, 1984-86 1597cc California:
LED off: No problem in system.
LED on:
  Flashes slowly:
    Fuel mixture solenoid
    Vacuum switching solenoids (1.5L)
    Anti-diesel solenoid
  Flashes quickly:
    Oxygen sensor
    Engine temperature sensor

1983-86 1488cc Turbo, 1974cc FI, 2960cc
1984-87 1809cc Turbo
1986 2389cc FI:
Code 11 Crank angle sensor
Code 12 Airflow meter
Code 13 Engine temperature sensor
Code 14 Vehicle speed sensor
Code 21 Ignition signal
Code 22 Fuel pump circuit
Code 23 Throttle valve or idle switch
Code 24 Neutral/Park switch
Code 31 AC speed-up valve (with AC)
Code 31 System OK (without AC)
Code 32 Starter signal
Code 33 Oxygen sensor
Code 34 Detonation sensor
Code 41 Fuel temperature sensor
Code 42 Altitude sensor
Code 42 Throttle sensor (1986 Pickup)
Code 43 Battery voltage high/low
Code 43 Injector (1986 Pickup)
Code 44 System OK

1597cc Federal & 1987 1597cc Calif.:
Red LED off, Green LED on: No problem in system.
Red LED on, Green LED flashing quickly:
  Vacuum sensor
  Altitude sensor
  Engine temperature sensor
  Air temperature sensor
Red LED on, Green LED flashing slowly:
  Mixture heater relay
  Fuel mixture solenoid
  Coasting richer solenoid
  Anti-diesel solenoid
  Air injection control valve
  Idle speed control valve

1987-92 ex. 1987 1809cc Turbo:
Code 11 Crank angle sensor
Code 12 Air flow meter
Code 13 Water temperature sensor
Code 14 Vehicle speed sensor
Code 15 Mixture ratio control
Code 21 Ignition signal
Code 22 Fuel pump circuit
Code 23 Idle switch
Code 24 Neutral/clutch switch
Code 25 Idle speed control
Code 31 ECU
Code 32 EGR
Code 33 O₂ sensor 1987-89 (1987-91 300ZX left side)
Code 33 EGR sensor, 1990-91 others
Code 34 Detonation sensor
Code 35 Exhaust temperature sensor
Code 41 Air temperature sensor
Code 42 TPS (4-cyl.) or fuel temperature sensor (V6)
Code 43 Throttle sensor
Code 44, 55 System OK
Code 45 Injector leak
Code 51 Injector circuit
Code 53 O₂ sensor (300ZX right side)
Code 54 AT control unit to ECU problem
Code 55 No malfunction

SENSORS, INPUT

TEMPERATURE SENSORS
See **UNDERHOOD SERVICE INSTRUCTIONS** at the beginning of this section for test/adjustment diagrams.

Air temperature sensor, all models with FI, measured between first and last terminal of airflow meter.

Fuel temperature sensors are attached to the fuel pressure regulator.

Engine	Year	Sensor	Resistance Ohms @ deg. F/C
All	1984-92	Coolant	8000-10,000 @ 14/−10
			2100-2900 @ 68/20
			680-1000 @ 122/50
			300-330 @ 176/80
			140-150 @ 230/110
2389 FI, 2960cc	1984-89	Cylinder Head	8000-10,000 @ 14/−10
			2300-2700 @ 68/20
			700-900 @ 122/50
			300-330 @ 176/80
2187cc FI, 2753cc	1983-87	Cylinder Head	7000-11,400 @ 14/−10
			2100-2900 @ 68/20
			680-1000 @ 122/50
			250-400 @ 176/80
2960cc 300ZX	1984-92	Fuel	8000-10,000 @ 14/−10
2960cc Maxima	1985-88		2300-2700 @ 68/20
			700-900 @ 122/50
			300-330 @ 176/80
1809cc Turbo, 1974cc ex. Pickup	1984-89	Manifold Air	8000-10,000 @ 14/−10
			2300-2700 @ 68/20
			700-900 @ 122/50
			300-330 @ 176/80
1488cc Turbo, 1597cc 2V Fed., 1974cc Pickup, 2389cc SOHC	1983-92	Manifold Air	7000-11,400 @ 14/−10
			2100-2900 @ 68/20
			680-1000 @ 122/50
			250-400 @ 176/80
All, as equipped	1987-92	Exhaust Gas	77,000-94,000 @ 212/100

VACUUM SENSOR
See **UNDERHOOD SERVICE INSTRUCTIONS** at the beginning of this section for test/adjustment diagrams.

Engine	Year	Voltage @ in./mm Hg
1597cc 2V Fed.	1984-87	4 @ 0/0
		0.5 @ 26/650

THROTTLE POSITION SENSOR
5 volts reference.

1989-90 1597cc: 2WD measured between red wire and ground; 4WD, measured between white wire and ground.

1597cc TBI: Measured between white wire and ground.

1598cc, 1809cc DOHC: Measured between L/W wire and ground.

		Voltage	
Engine	Year	Idle	WOT
1597cc	1987-88	0.5	5.0
1597cc, 1998cc	1989-92	.45-.55	4.0
1578cc, 1809cc DOHC	1987-89	0.5	4.0
2389cc 240SX	1989-90	0.5	4.0
2389cc 240SX	1991-92	0.4-0.5	4.0
2389cc Stanza, Axxess	1990-92	0.4-0.5	5.0
2389cc, 2960cc Pickup	1986-92	0.5	4.0
2960cc 300ZX	1984-89	0.4	4.0
2960cc 300ZX	1990-92	0.4-0.5	4.0
2960cc Maxima	1989-92	0.5	4.2
2960cc 300ZX	1990	0.4-0.5	5.0

AIRFLOW METER
See **UNDERHOOD SERVICE INSTRUCTIONS** at the beginning of this section for test/adjustment diagrams.

Voltage between idle and WOT should increase evenly.

On three or four terminals, measured between terminal A (first) and ground. V6 w/five terminals, measured between B (second) and ground.

UNDERHOOD SERVICE SPECIFICATIONS

SENSORS, INPUT Continued

AIRFLOW METER Continued

Engine	Year	Voltage @ Idle	Voltage @ 2000 rpm
1597cc	1989-90	1.0 approx.	—
1597cc	1991-92	0.7-1.1	1.1-1.5
1598cc, 1809cc DOHC	1987-89	1.5 approx.	—
1998cc	1991-92	1.3-1.7	1.7-2.1
2389cc 240SX, Axxess	1989-90	1.0 approx.	—
2389cc Stanza	1990	0.8-1.5	—
2389cc Stanza	1991-92	1.3-1.8	1.8-2.2
2389cc 240SX	1991-92	1.0-1.5	1.4-1.9
2389cc Trucks	1991-92	1.0-3.0	—
2960cc	1987-88	2.0 approx.	—
2960cc Maxima SOHC	1989-92	1.0-1.3	1.8-2.0
DOHC	1992	0.8-1.5	1.4-1.8
2960cc 300ZX	1989	2.0 approx.	—
2960cc Pickup, Pathfinder	1990-92	1.5-2.0	
2960cc 300ZX	1990-92	0.8-1.5	1.4-1.8
Turbo	1990-92	0.9-1.4	1.4-1.8

ACTUATORS, OUTPUT

IDLE SPEED CONTROL
All FI engines with ISC.

Engine	Year	Resistance (ohms)
1597cc; 1598cc, 1809cc DOHC, 1998cc	1987-92	10 approx.
1597cc TBI	1987-88	9.5-10.5* 8.5-9.5†
1974cc	1985-89	30-40●
2389cc Pickup	1986-89	30-40
2389cc ex. Pickup	1989-92	10 approx.
2960cc Maxima	1985-88	40
2960cc Maxima SOHC	1989-92	27-40
2960cc 300ZX	1984-89	40

ACTUATORS, OUTPUT Continued

IDLE SPEED CONTROL Continued

Engine	Year	Resistance (ohms)
2960cc Pickup, Pathfinder	1986-89	30-40
2960cc All ex. Maxima SOHC	1990-92	10 approx.

* Measured between terminals A & B.
† Measured between terminals C & D.
● Measured between terminals A & B and B & C.

MIXTURE CONTROL SOLENOID-CARBURETTED ENGINES

Engine	Year	Resistance (ohms)
1597cc 2V Fed.	1984-87	30-50

AIR REGLATOR CONTROL VALVE
Controls fast idle on FI engines.

Engine	Year	Resistance (ohms)
1597cc	1991-92	70-80
1809cc Turbo, 1974cc, 2960cc	1984-89	30-50
2389cc 240SX	1989-92	70-80
2187cc, 2393cc, 2753cc	1983-84	25-90
2960cc Pickup, 300ZX	1990-92	70-80

COMPUTER TIMING ADVANCE
Include initial timing.

Engine	Year	Advance @	
		Idle	2000 rpm
1597cc	1991-92	10	20 min.
1998cc	1991-92	15	25 min.
2389cc Stanza	1991-92	15	25 min.
240SX	1991-92	20	25 min.
2960cc 300ZX	1990-92	15	25 min.
2960cc Maxima DOHC	1992	15	25 min.

CHEK-CHART ✓

ENGINE IDENTIFICATION

To identify any engine by the manufacturer's code, follow the four steps designated by the numbered blocks.

1 **MODEL YEAR IDENTIFICATION:** Refer to illustrations of Vehicle Identification Number (V.I.N.). The year is indicated by a code letter.

2 **ENGINE CODE LOCATION:** Refer to V.I.N. plate illustration. The engine code is indicated as a letter or number.

3 **ENGINE CODE:** In the "CODE" column, find the engine code determined in Step 2.

4 **ENGINE IDENTIFICATION:** On the line where the engine code appears, read to the right to identify the engine.

V.I.N. PLATE LOCATION:

On top left side of instrument panel.

Model year of vehicle:
1992 — Model year is N.
1991 — Model year is M.
1990 — Model year is L.
1989 — Model year is K.
1988 — Model year is J.
1987 — Model year is H.
1986 — Model year is G.
1985 — Model year is F.
1984 — Model year is E.
1983 — Model year is D.

MODEL YEAR AND ENGINE IDENTIFICATION:

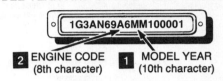

1G3AN69A6MM100001

2 ENGINE CODE (8th character) **1** MODEL YEAR (10th character)

4 ENGINE IDENTIFICATION

YEAR	3 ENGINE CODE	CYL.	DISPL. liters	cu. in.	Fuel System	HP
1992	3	4	2.3	138	MFI	120
	D	4	2.3	138	MFI	160
	A	4	2.3	138	MFI	180
	R	4	2.5	151	TBI	110
	T	6	3.1	191	MFI	140
	N	6	3.3	204	MFI	160
	X	6	3.4	207	MFI	200, 210
	1	6	3.8	231	MFI	205
	L	6	3.8	231	MFI	170
	E	8	5.0	305	TBI	170
	7	8	5.7	350	TBI	180
1991	D	4	2.3	138	MFI	160
	A	4	2.3	138	MFI	180
	R, U	4	2.5	151	TBI	110
	T	6	3.1	191	MFI	140
	N	6	3.3	204	MFI	160
	X	6	3.4	207	MFI	200, 210†
	C	6	3.8	231	MFI	165
	L	6	3.8	231	MFI	160
	E	8	5.0	305	TBI	170
1990	D	4	2.3	138	MFI	160
	A	4	2.3 HO	138 HO	MFI	180
	R, U	4	2.5	151	TBI	110
	T	6	3.1	191	MFI	135
	D	6	3.1	191	TBI	120
	N	6	3.3	204	MFI	160
	C	6	3.8	231	MFI	165
	Y	8	5.0	307	4V	140
1989	D	4	2.3	138	MFI	150
	A	4	2.3 HO	138 HO	MFI	180
	R	4	2.5	151	TBI	98
	U	4	2.5	151	TBI	110
	W	6	2.8	173	MFI	130
	T	6	3.1	191	MFI	140
	N	6	3.3	204	MFI	160
	C	6	3.8	231	MFI	165
	Y	8	5.0	307	4V	140
1988	K	4	2.0	122	TBI	96
	1	4	2.0	122	TBI	90
	D	4	2.3	140	MFI	150
	R, U	4	2.5	151	TBI	98
	W	6	2.8	173	MFI	130
	L	6	3.0	181	MFI	125
	3	6	3.8	231	MFI	150
	C	6	3.8 HO	231 HO	MFI	165
	Y	8	5.0	307	4V	140
1987	K	4	2.0	122	TBI	96
	1	4	2.0	122	TBI	90
	R, U	4	2.5	151	TBI	98
	W	6	2.8	173	MFI	125
	L	6	3.0	181	MFI	125
	A	6	3.8	231	2V	110
	3	6	3.8	231	MFI	150
	H	8	5.0	305	4V	155
	Y	8	5.0	307	4V	140
	9	8	5.0 HO	307 HO	4V	170

4 ENGINE IDENTIFICATION

YEAR	3 ENGINE CODE	CYL.	DISPL. liters	cu. in.	Fuel System	HP
1986	0	4	1.8	112	TBI	84
	P	4	2.0	122	TBI	85
	R, U	4	2.5	151	TBI	92
	X	6	2.8	173	2V	112
	W	6	2.8	173	MFI	125
	L	6	3.0	181	MFI	125
	A	6	3.8	231	2V	110
	B	6	3.8	231	MFI	140
	3	6	3.8 HO	231 HO	MFI	150
	H	8	5.0	305	4V	155
	Y	8	5.0	307	4V	140
	9	8	5.0 HO	307 HO	4V	170
1985	0	4	1.8	112	TBI	84
	P	4	2.0	122	TBI	88
	R, U	4	2.5	151	TBI	92
	X	6	2.8	173	2V	112
	W	6	2.8	173	MFI	125
	E	6	3.0	181	2V	110
	L	6	3.0	181	MFI	125
	A	6	3.8	231	2V	110
	3	6	3.8	231	MFI	125
	T	6	4.3 D	262 D	MFI	85
	H	8	5.0	305	4V	155
	Y	8	5.0	307	4V	140, 150†
	9	8	5.0 HO	307 HO	4V	180
	N	8	5.7 D	350 D	MFI	105
1984	0	4	1.8	112	TBI	84
	P	4	2.0	122	TBI	86
	B	4	2.0	122	2V	88
	R	4	2.5	151	TBI	92
	X	6	2.8	173	2V	112
	Z	6	2.8 HO	173 HO	2V	135
	E	6	3.0	181	2V	110
	A	6	3.8	231	2V	110
	3	6	3.8	231	MFI	125
	4	6	4.1	252	4V	125
	T, V	6	4.3 D	262 D	MFI	85
	Y	8	5.0	307	4V	140
	9	8	5.0 HO	307 HO	4V	180
	N	8	5.7 D	350 D	MFI	105
1983	0	4	1.8	112	TBI	84
	P	4	2.0	122	TBI	86
	B	4	2.0	122	2V	88
	R	4	2.5	151	TBI	92
	5	4	2.5	151	2V	92
	X	6	2.8	173	2V	112
	Z	6	2.8 HO	173 HO	2V	135
	E	6	3.0	181	2V	110
	A	6	3.8	231	2V	110
	4	6	4.1	252	4V	125
	T, V	6	4.3 D	262 D	MFI	85
	Y	8	5.0	307	4V	140
	9	8	5.0 HO	307 HO	4V	180
	N	8	5.7 D	350 D	MFI	105

TBI — Throttle Body Injection. MFI — Multiport Fuel Injection.
2V — Two Venturi Carburetor. 4V — Four Venturi Carburetor.
D — Diesel. HO — High Output.
† Engine horsepower varies with model installation.

UNDERHOOD SERVICE SPECIFICATIONS

CYLINDER NUMBERING SEQUENCE

4-CYL. FIRING ORDER: 1 3 4 2

— Front of car —

1983-86 1.8L (112) FI, 1987-88 2.0L (122) OHC	1983-86 2.0L (122) ex. OHC	1987-89 2.0L (122)	1987-92 2.3L Code D, 1989-92 2.3L Code A, 1992 2.3L Code 3	1983-86 2.5L (151) FWD	1987-92 2.5L (151)

2.8L & 3.1L V6-CYL. FIRING ORDER 1 2 3 4 5 6

— Front of car —

1983-86 2.8L (173)	1987-89 2.8L (173), 1989-92 3.1L Code T, 1991-92 3.4L Code X	1983-85 3.0L (181) Code E 2V

All Other V6-CYL. FIRING ORDER: 1 6 5 4 3 2

Front of car 1989-92 3.3L code N	Front of car 1985-88 3.0L (181) FI, 1988 3.8L (231) FI Code 3 Some	Front of car 1986-87 3.8L (231) Code 3, 1988 3.8L (231) Code 3 Some

All Other V6-CYL. FIRING ORDER: 1 6 5 4 3 2

— Front of car —

1988-91 3.8L Code C, 1991-92 3.8L Code L Some	1983-87 3.8L (231) ex. FI, 4.1L (252)	1984-85 3.8L (231) FI	1991-92 3.8L Code L Some, 1992 3.8L Code 1

8-CYL. FIRING ORDER 1 8 4 3 6 5 7 2

 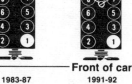

— Front of car —

1983-87 4.4L (267), 5.0L (305)	1991-92 5.0L Code E, 1992 5.7L Code 7	1983-90 5.0L (307)

— TIMING MARK —

 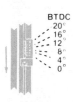 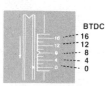

1983-86 1.8L (112) FI OHC	1983-86 2.0L (122)	1987-88 2.0L (122) OHC	1983-86 2.5L (151)	1983-86 2.8L (173)

   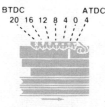 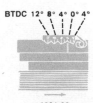

1983-85 3.0L (181) 2V, 1984-85 3.8L (231) FI	1983-87 3.8L (231) ex. FI, 4.1L (252)	1983-90 5.0L (307)	1983-87 4.4L (267), 5.0L (305)	1991-92 5.0L Code E, 1992 5.7L Code 7

ELECTRICAL AND IGNITION SYSTEMS

BATTERY

Engine	Year	STANDARD BCI Group No.	STANDARD Crank. Perf.	OPTIONAL BCI Group No.	OPTIONAL Crank. Perf.
1.8L (112) FI	1983-84	75	500	73	465
1.8L (112) FI	1985-86	75	630	—	—
2.0L (122)	1983	75	500	73	465
2.0L (122)	1984	71	390	75	500
2.0L (122)	1985-86	75	500	75	630
2.0L (122)	1987-88	75	525	75	630
2.3L	1988-91	75	630	—	—
2.5L (151)	1983	70	355	75	500
2.5L (151)	1984	71	390	75	500
2.5L (151)	1985-92	75	630	—	—
2.8L (173)	1983	70	315	75	500
2.8L (173)	1984	71	390	75	500
2.8L (173) 2V	1986	70	405	75	500
2.8L (173) FI	1985-86	75	500	75	630
2.8L (173): Ciera	1987-89	75	525	75	570
Firenza, Calais	1987-89	75	630	—	—
Cutlass	1988-89	75	525	—	—
3.0L (181)	1983	70	315	75	500
3.0L (181)	1984	75	500	75	630
3.0L (181) 2V 98	1985	75	630	75	770
3.0L (181) 2V Others	1985	75	500	75	630
3.0L (181) FI	1985-88	75	630	—	—
3.1L	1989-92	75	525	—	—
3.3L	1989-92	75	630	—	—
3.4L DOHC	1991-92	75	690	—	—
3.8L (231) 2V Delta 88	1983-84	71	390	78	550
3.8L (231) 2V Others	1983-84	70	315	75	500
3.8L (231) MFI	1984-85	75	630	78	770
3.8L (231) ex. Cutlass Supreme	1986	75	630	78	730
3.8L (231) Cutlass Supreme	1986	75	500	75	630
3.8L (231): Cutlass	1987	75	525	75	630
88, 98	1987-88	75	630	78	730
Ciera	1987-88	75	630	—	—
Toronado	1987-88	78	630	78	730
3.8L: 88, 98	1989-90	75	630	78	730
Toronado	1989-90	78	730	—	—
3.8L: 88	1991-92	75	630	78	770
98	1991-92	75	630	78	770
Toronado	1991-92	78	770	—	—
4.1L (252)	1983-84	71	390	78	500
4.3L (262) Diesel Ciera	1983	76	750	75	500
Ciera	1984-85	78	770	76	1075
Others	1983-84	75	500	78	550
4.3L	1991	75	525	—	—
4.3L	1992	78	630	—	—
5.0L (305) Canada	1983-85	71	390	78	550
5.0L (305) Canada	1986-87	75	525	75	570
5.0L (307) Toronado	1983-84	71	390	78	550
5.0L (307) All U.S. Models	1986	75	430	75	500
5.0L (307) Canada	1986	75	500	75	630
5.0L (307) Others	1983-84	71	390	75	500
5.0L (307) Cutlass	1987-88	75	430	75	525
5.0L (307) Custom Cruiser	1987-89	70	525	75	570
5.0L	1990	75	525	—	—
5.7L (350) Diesel	1983	75	500	78	550
5.7L (350) Diesel	1984-85	70	405	78	550

ALTERNATOR

See UNDERHOOD SERVICE INSTRUCTIONS at the beginning of this section for test/ adjustment diagrams.

Application	Rated Output (amps)	Test Output (amps)	Field Current Draw (amps @ 12V)
1983	42, 55, 63, 78, 85	†	4-5
1984	42, 55, 63, 66, 70, 78, 85, 94, 97	†	4-5

ALTERNATOR Continued

Application	Rated Output (amps)	Test Output (amps)	Field Current Draw (amps @ 12V)
1985	56, 63, 66, 78, 94, 97	†	4-5
1986	55, 56, 63, 66, 70, 78, 85	†	4-5
1986	97, 100, 108, 120	△	4-5
1987-88	78, 94	†	—
1988-92	74, 85, 100, 105, 108, 120, 124, 140	△	—

† Increase engine speed until maximum alternator output is obtained (approximately 2000 rpm); output must be within 10 amps of rated output.
△ Run engine at moderate speed; output must be within 15 amps of rated output.

REGULATOR

Application	Test Temp. (deg. F/C)	Voltage Setting
1983-85	Warm	12.5-15.4
1986-92	Warm	13.5-16.0

STARTER

Engine	Year	Cranking Voltage (min. volts)	Ampere Draw @ Cranking Speed
All	1983-92	9.0	—

SPARK PLUGS

Engine	Year	Gap (inches)	Gap (mm)	Torque (ft-lb)
1.8L (112) 2V & FI	1983-86	.035	.89	15
2.0L (122)	1983-87	.035	.89	15
2.0L (122) ex. OHC	1988	.035	.89	15
2.0L (122) OHC	1988	.060	1.52	15
2.3L	1989-91	.035	.89	17
2.3L	1992	.035	.89	11
2.5L (151)	1983-92	.060	1.52	15
2.8L (173)	1983-87	.045	1.14	7-15
3.0L (181)	1983-84	.080	2.03	15
3.0L (181) 2V	1985	.060	1.52	7-15
3.0L (181) FI	1985	.040	1.01	7-15
3.0L (181) FI	1986-88	.045	1.14	7-15
3.1L	1989-92	.045	1.14	11
3.3L	1989-92	.060	1.52	20
3.4L DOHC	1991-92	.045	1.14	11
3.8L (231) 2V	1983	.080	2.03	15
3.8L (231) 2V	1984-87	.060	1.52	7-15
3.8L (231) FI	1984-85	.080	2.03	7-15
3.8L (231) FI Code 3	1986-87	.045	1.14	7-15
3.8L Code C, L	1988-92	.060	1.52	11
4.1L (252)	1983-84	.080	2.03	15
4.3L	1991-92	.035	.89	11
5.0L (305)	1983-85	.045	1.14	15
5.0L (305)	1986-87	.035	.89	15
5.0L, 5.7L	1991-92	.035	.89	11
5.0L (307)	1983-84	.080	2.03	25
Canada	1984	.060	1.52	25
5.0L (307)	1985-90	.060	1.52	25

IGNITION COIL

See UNDERHOOD SERVICE INSTRUCTIONS at the beginning of this section for test/ adjustment diagrams.

Application	Year	Resistance (ohms) Primary●	Resistance (ohms) Secondary■
All w/distributor	1983-92	0-2	6,000-30,000
3.3L	1989-92	.5-.9	5,000-8,000
3.0L, 3.8L: Type I coils*	1985-91	.5-.9	10,000-13,000
Type II coils*	1986-88	—	5,000-10,000
Type II coils*	1992	.3-.5	5,000-7,000
3.8L Code L	1991	.3-.5	5,000-7,000
2.0L, 2.5L, 2.8L	1987-90	—	5,000-10,000
2.3L	1987-91	—	20,000 max.

* Type I coils, 3 coil towers on each side of coil pack.
Type II coils, 6 coil towers on one side of coil pack.
● Without distributor, measured between the two coil primary power wires on each coil.
■ Without distributor, measured across each coils two towers with spark plug wires removed.

OLDSMOBILE
1983-92
All Models Except Bravada, Silhouette

DISTRIBUTOR PICKUP
See UNDERHOOD SERVICE INSTRUCTIONS at the beginning of this section for test/adjustment diagrams.

Application	Year	Resistance (ohms)	Air Gap (in./mm)
All	1983-92	500-1500	—

BASE TIMING
See UNDERHOOD SERVICE INSTRUCTIONS at the beginning of this section for test/adjustment diagrams.

Set timing at slow idle and Before Top Dead Center, unless otherwise specified. Disconnect and plug distributor vacuum line, as equipped, at distributor.

1983-86 1.8L (112) FI, 2.5L (151), 4.3L (260), 5.0L (307) engines, ground diagnostic connector.

1983-86 2.0L (122) FI, 2.8L (173) FI; 1991-92 3.1L TBI, 5.0L, 5.7L disconnect EST bypass connector (single connector, tan/black wire).

1982-90 all others w/carburetor, disconnect 4-wire connector at distributor.

Timing MUST be set to specifications on emission label, if different from setting listed. If "Check Engine" light comes on during procedure, remove ECM fuse to clear.

Engine	Year	Man. Trans. (degrees) @ RPM	Auto. Trans. (degrees) @ RPM
1.8L (112) FI	1983-86	8	8
2.0L (122)	1983	0	0
Canada	1983	0 @ 850	0 @ 850 P
w/decal DBB	1983	—	2 @ 850 P
2.0L (122)	1984-86	6	6
Canada	1984	4 @ 850	0 @ 850 D
2.5L (151)	1983-86	8	8
Canada	1983	10	8 @ 750 P
2.8L (173) ex. HO	1983	10	10
Canada	1983	6 @ 650	10 @ 750 P
2.8L (173) High Output	1983	10	10
2.8L (173) 2V	1985-86	—	10
Canada	1985-86	—	6 @ 750 P
2.8L (173) FI	1985-86	10	10
3.0L (181) 2V	1983-85	—	15 P
3.1L TBI	1990-92	—	10 D
3.8L (231) w/distr.	1983-87	—	15 D
4.1L (252)	1983-84	—	15 D
5.0L (305)	1983-87	4	4
5.0L, 5.7L	1991-92	—	0 @ 500 D
5.0L (307)	1983-90	—	20 @ 1100 P
Canada	1983-84	—	12 @ 1100 P
Canada	1985-86	—	8 @ 1100 P
Canada	1987	—	8 @ 1500 P

DISTRIBUTOR TIMING ADVANCE
Engine degrees at engine rpm, no load, in addition to basic timing setting.

Mechanical advance distributors only.

Engine	Trans-mission	Year	Distributor Number	Degrees @ 2500 RPM Total	Centrifugal
2.0L (122)	MT & AT	1983-84	1103535, 48, 92	32.9-40.9	10.9-14.9
2.5L (151)	MT	1983	1103471	30.5-40.5	8.5-14.5
2.5L (151)	AT	1983	1103528	32.9-40.9	10.9-14.9
2.8L (173)	MT	1983-84	1103525	35-43	17-21
2.8L (173)	AT	1983-84	1103523	34.9-42.9	12.9-16.9
2.8L (173)	AT	1984	1103586	35-43	17-21
2.8L (173)	AT	1985	1103618	41.9-49.9	12.9-16.9
2.8L (173)	AT	1985-86	1103619	35-43	17-21
3.8L (231)	AT	1983-84	1110766	31-37	9.0-11.8
3.8L (231)	AT	1985-86	1103612	20.3-28.3	2.3-6.3
5.0L (305)	MT & AT	1983-86	1103282	29.8-37.8	11.18-15.8
5.0L (307)	AT	1983-84	1103490	43.5-51.5	15.5-19.5
5.0L (307)	AT	1985-86	1103607	23-27	9-11
5.0L (307)	AT	1987	1103718	41.2-49.2	19.2-23.2

FUEL SYSTEM

FUEL SYSTEM PRESSURE
See UNDERHOOD SERVICE INSTRUCTIONS at the beginning of this section for test/adjustment diagrams.

Carburetted models, pinch off fuel return line.

All models with TBI, pressure measured at fuel inlet of TBI.

All models with MFI, pressure measured at fuel rail.

FUEL SYSTEM PRESSURE Continued

Engine	Year	PSI	RPM
Carburetted, TBI:			
1.8L (112) FI	1983-86	9.0-13.0	ign. on
2.0L (122) FI	1983-89	9.0-13.0	ign. on
	1987-89	13.0 min.*	ign. on
Canada	1983-84	6.5-8.0	idle
2.5L (151) 2V	1983	6.5-8.0	idle
2.5L (151) FI	1983-92	9.0-13.0	ign. on
	1987-92	13.0 min.*	ign. on
2.8L (173) 2V	1983-86	5.5-6.5	idle
3.0L (181) 2V	1983-85	5.5-6.5	idle
3.1L TBI	1990-92	9-13	ign. on
		13.0 min.*	ign. on
3.8L (231) 2V	1983-86	5.5-6.5	idle
4.1L (252)	1983-84	5.5-6.5	idle
4.3L (262) Diesel	1983-85	5.8-8.7	ign. on
5.0L (305)	1983-87	5.5-6.5	idle
5.0L, 5.7L	1991-92	9-13	idle
		13.0 min.*	idle
5.0L (307)	1983-90	5.5-6.5	idle
5.7L (350) Diesel	1983-85	5.5-6.5	idle

* Fuel pump pressure with return line briefly restricted.

Engine	Year	Pressure (PSI) Ign. On	Idle	Fuel Pump†
Fuel Injected (MFI):				
2.3L (138)	1987-92	40-47	30-44	47 min.
2.8L (173)	1985-89	40-47	30-44	60 min.
3.0L (181)	1985-86	37-43	31-40	75 min.
3.0L (181)	1987	34-43	29-34	75 min.
3.0L (181)	1988	40-47	31-42	75 min.
3.1L, 3.4L DOHC	1989-92	40-47	30-44	47 min.
3.3L	1989	40-44	32-36	50 min.
3.3L	1990-92	40-47	31-44	47 min.
3.8L (231)	1984-86	34-43	24-37	75 min.
3.8L (231) Code 3	1987-88	34-40	25-35	75 min.
3.8L (231) Code C	1988-91	40-47	31-43	75 min.
3.8L Code L	1991-92	40-47	30-44	47 min.

† With fuel return line briefly restricted.

IDLE SPEED W/O COMPUTER CONTROL

1983-85 Diesel Engines: Start engine and allow it to warm up to operating temperature. Connect tachometer following manufacturer's instructions. Adjust screw on injection pump to obtain specified slow idle.

Turn ignition off and then attach jumper wire across fast idle switch connector terminals. Turn ignition on and adjust idle solenoid (energized) to obtain specified fast idle.

1983-87 Gasoline Engines: Make all adjustments with engine at operating temperature, choke fully open, and electric cooling fan off (if equipped). Engines with idle speed control, idle adjustments not recommended during tune-up.

Engines with C-4 system, connect dwell meter to carburetor fuel valve lead and ground. Set meter to 6-cylinder scale. When needle begins to vary engine is in closed loop mode and is ready to adjust.

All engines, disconnect and plug canister purge vacuum hose.

Adjust idle solenoid screw, plunger fully extended, or carburetor idle speed screw to specification. If equipped with idle stop solenoid, disconnect the electrical or vacuum lead and adjust carburetor body screw to specification.

Engines equipped with speed-up solenoid, turn A/C on and disconnect compressor clutch wire or apply vacuum or battery voltage to solenoid. Adjust solenoid to specification with plunger fully extended.

To set fast idle, disconnect and plug EGR and distributor vacuum hoses (as equipped). Set choke cam on specified step and adjust engine speed to specification.

Engine	Year	SLOW Man. Trans.	Auto. Trans.	FAST Man. Trans.	Auto. Trans.	Step of Cam
2.0L (122) Canada	1983-84	900	900 D	2400	2600 P	High
shutdown idle	1983	850	850 N			
AC speed-up	1983	1150	1250 D			
w/decal DXD	1983	—	900 D	—	3000 P	High
shutdown idle	1983	—	850 N			
speed-up	1983	—	1250 D			
2.0L (122) Canada	1984	900	800 D	3000	3000 P	High
base idle	1984	850	750 N			
speed-up	1984	1150	1250 D			
w/AC	1984	—	900 D		3000 P	High
base idle	1984	—	850 N			
speed-up	1984	—	1250 D			

IDLE SPEED W/O COMPUTER CONTROL Continued

| | | SLOW | | FAST | | |
		Man. Trans.	Auto. Trans.	Man. Trans.	Auto. Trans.	Step of Cam
Engine	Year					
2.5L (151) Canada	1983	750	750 D	2600	2600 P	High
base idle	1983	700	700 D			
speed-up	1983	1000	900 D			
w/AC	1983	—	800 D	—	2600 P	High
base idle	1983	—	750 D			
speed-up	1983	—	900 D			
2.8L (173) ex. HO	1983	775	600 D	2500	2500 P	High
solenoid	1983	1100	750 D			
w/5-speed	1983	800	—	2600	—	High
solenoid	1983	1000				
Canada	1983	700	700 D	2000	2000 P	High
solenoid	1983	1050	900 D			
2.8L (173) HO	1983	800	725 D	2600	2700 P	High
solenoid	1983	1100	850 D			
2.8L (173) ex. HO	1984	800	600 D	2500	2500 P	High
solenoid	1984	1100	750 D			
Canada	1984	700	700 D	2000	2000 P	High
solenoid	1984	1050	900 D			
2.8L (173) HO	1984	800	725 D	2600	2700 P	High
solenoid	1984	1100	850 D			
2.8L (173) 2V	1985-86	—	600 D		2500 P	High
solenoid	1985-86	—	750 D			
Canada	1985-86	—	700 D	—	2700 P	High
solenoid	1985-86	—	900 D			
3.8L (231) Canada	1983-86	—	550 D	—	2000 N	High
solenoid	1983-85	—	670 D			
solenoid	1986	—	750 D			
3.8L (231) Canada	1987	—	550 D	—	2200 P	High
solenoid	1987	—	750 D			
4.3L (262) Diesel						
Ciera, 98	1983-85	—	675 D	—	775 D	—
Cutlass	1983-85	—	660 D	—	775 D	—
5.0L (305) 4V	1983-86	—	500 D	—	1850 P	High
solenoid	1983-85	—	600 D			
solenoid	1986-87	—	650 D			
5.0L (307)						
Canada	1983-85	—	550 D	—	750 D	Low
solenoid	1983-85	—	700 D			
Canada	1986-87	—	550 D	—	725 D	Low
solenoid	1986-87	—	650 D			
5.0L (307) HO	1983-85	—	550 D	—	700 D	Low
solenoid	1983-85	—	650 D			
5.0L (307) HO	1986-87	—	600 D	—	750 D	Low
solenoid	1986-87	—	650 D			
5.7L (350) Diesel	1983-85	—	600 D	—	750 D	—

IDLE SPEED W/COMPUTER CONTROL

See UNDERHOOD SERVICE INSTRUCTIONS at the beginning of this section for test/adjustment diagrams.

Midpoint of range given is the preferred setting speed.

Idle speed is adjustable only if specifications are shown in the ''Minimum Speed'' column.

1983-86 All w/TBI: Gain access to throttle stop screw. With engine at operating temperature, disconnect idle air controller and install special tool to seal idle air passage of throttle body. Turn throttle stop screw to specified minimum speed value.

1983-86 All w/FI except TBI; 1987-91 All w/FI & TBI (when specifications appear in ''Minimum Speed'' column): Ground diagnostic lead and turn ignition on for 30 seconds. Remove IAC electrical lead and remove ground from diagnostic connector. Start engine and set minimum speed to specified value.

All carburetted w/ISC: With engine at operating temperature, turn ignition off and disconnect harness from ISC. Apply 12 volts (+) to third from top of ISC (C), and ground the fourth terminal from top (D) only long enough to retract ISC plunger. With engine running, set minimum idle to specified value by adjusting carb base screw. Apply 12 volts (+) to fourth terminal from top of ISC (D) and ground the third terminal from top (C) only long enough to fully extend ISC plunger. Set maximum speed to specified value by turning ISC plunger head.

Never apply voltage to first two upper terminals (A & B) or damage to the unit will result.

All carburetted w/ILC: Disconnect and plug vacuum hoses at EGR and canister purge valves. With engine at operating temperature, remove vacuum hose from ILC and plug. Set maximum speed to specified value by holding hex nut and turning plunger shaft. Reconnect ILC vacuum hose and check that minimum speed is at specified value. To adjust, remove rubber and metal plugs from rear center outlet tube, insert a ³/₃₂″ Allen wrench. Remove ILC hose and plug. Connect a remote vacuum source and apply vacuum to the unit. Adjust carb base screw to obtain specified base value.

IDLE SPEED W/COMPUTER CONTROL Continued

ALL FUEL INJECTED

| | | Minimum Speed | | Checking Speed | |
		Man. Trans.	Auto. Trans.	Man. Trans.	Auto. Trans.
Engine	Year				
1.8L (112)	1983-84	775-825	675-725 N	—	—
1.8L (112)	1985	775-825	675-725 N	900-1000	675-775 D
1.8L (112)	1986	775-825	675-725 N	900-1000	775-875 D
2.0L (122)	1983-86	625-675	625-675 D	—	—
2.0L (122)	1988	450-650	450-650 N	—	—
2.0L (122) OHC	1987-88	450-600	450-600 N	800 max.	800 N max.
2.3L	1990-92	—	—	800	800 N
2.5L (151)	1983-84	750-800	475-525 N	—	—
2.5L (151)	1985	750-800	475-525 N	900-1000	675-775 D
2.5L (151)	1986	750-800	475-525 N	850-950	750-850 D
2.5L (151)	1987	550-650	550-650 N	750-850	750-850 D
2.5L (151)	1988-92	550-650	550-650 N	800 max.	800 N max.
2.8L (173)	1985-86	600-700	500-600 D	—	—
2.8L (173)†	1987	625-725	500-600 D	—	—
2.8L (173)††	1988-89	—	—	750-950	650-750 D
3.0L (181)	1985-88	—	450-550 D	—	—
3.1L TBI	1990-91	—	650-750 N	—	—
3.1L MFI	1989-91	—	—	750-950	650-750 D
3.1L MFI	1992	—	—	—	700-800 N
3.3L	1989	—	—	—	650-750 N
3.3L Calais	1990	—	—	—	675-750 N
Ciera	1990	—	—	—	650-750 N
3.3L	1991-92	—	—	—	650-750 N
3.4L DOHC	1991-92	—	—	600-700	600-700 D
3.8L (231) FI Code 3	1984-88	—	450-550 D	—	—
3.8L Code C	1988-89	—	—	—	650-750 N
3.8L Code C	1990-91	—	—	—	650-850 N
3.8L Code L	1991-92	—	—	—	650-750 N
5.0L	1991	—	—	—	500-600 D

† Mass airflow system.
†† Speed density system.

ALL CARBURETTED

Engine	Year	Trans.	Min. Speed	Max. Speed	Fast	Step of Cam
3.0L (181)	1983	AT	500 D	1300 P	2400 P	High
3.0L (181)	1984-85	AT	500 D	1350 P	2400 P	High
3.8L (231)	1983	AT	450 D	900 D	2200 P	High
3.8L (231)	1984-85	AT	450 D	1000 D	2200 P	High
3.8L (231)	1986-87	AT	450 D	900 D	2200 P	High
4.1L (252)	1983-84	AT	470 D	900 D	2200 P	High
w/decal BGC, BGD	1983	AT	450 D	900 D	2100 P	High
5.0L (307)	1983-84	AT	500 D	725 D	700 D	Low
base idle	1983-84	AT	500 D	—		
5.0L (307)	1985-90	AT	450 D	700 D	550 D	Low
base idle	1985-90	AT	450 D			

ENGINE MECHANICAL

TIGHTENING TORQUES
See UNDERHOOD SERVICE INSTRUCTIONS at the beginning of this section for test/adjustment diagrams.

Some fasteners are tightened in more than one step.

Some values are specified in inches.

| | | Torque Ft-lbs/Nm | | | | |
Engine	Year	Cylinder Head	Intake Manifold	Exhaust Manifold	Crankshaft Pulley	Water Pump
1.8L (112) OHC	1983-86	18/25, +60°, +60°, +60°, plus 30°-50° eng. warm	25/34	16/22	20/27	19/25
1.8L (112) 2V, 2.0L (122)	1983-84	65-75/ 88-107	20-25/ 27-34	22-28/ 30-38	66-85/ 90-115	12-21/ 16-28
2.0L (122)	1985-86	65-75/ 88-107	18-25/ 24-34	34-44/ 46-60	66-89/ 90-120	12-21/ 16-28

OLDSMOBILE
1983-92
All Models Except Bravada, Silhouette

TIGHTENING TORQUES Continued

Engine	Year	Cylinder Head	Intake Manifold	Exhaust Manifold	Crankshaft Pulley	Water Pump
2.0L (122) ex. OHC	1987-88	73-83/ 99-113⊙ 62-70/ 85-95♦	15-22/ 20-30	6-13/ 8-18	66-89/ 90-120	15-22/ 20-30
2.0L (122) OHC	1987-88	18/25, +60°, +60°, +60°, plus 30°-50° eng. warm	16/22	16/22	20/27	18/25
2.3L	1987-90	26/35, +90°	18/25	27/37	74/100, +90°	10/12, cover 19/26, others
2.3L	1991	26/35, +110°■	18/25	31/42, nuts 106"/12, studs	79/100, +90°	106"/12, cover 19/26, others
2.3L	1992	◇	18/25	31/42, nuts 106"/12, studs	79/100, +90°	106"/12, cover 19/26, others
2.5L (151)	1983	85/115	29/40	44/60	200/260	25/34
2.5L (151)	1984	92/125	29/40	44/60	200/260	25/34
2.5L (151)	1985-86	18/25, 22/30‡	25/34	25/43* 37-50**	162/220	25/34
2.5L	1987-92	18/25, 26/35●, +90°	25/34	25/43* 37-50**	162/220	25/34
2.8L (173) Ciera, Omega	1983-86	70/95	20-25/ 27-34	22-28/ 30-38	66-84/ 90-115	8/10, M6 15/22, M8 25/34, M10
2.8L (173) Firenza	1985-86	77/105	13-25/ 18-34	19-31/ 25-42	66-84/ 90-115	6-9/ 8-12
2.8L, 3.1L ex. Cutlass	1987-89	33/45, +90°	15/20 24/33	20-30/ 15-22	76/103	7/10, short 18/24, long
2.8L, 3.1L Cutlass	1987-92	33/45, +90°	16/22 23/32	19/25	77/105	84"/10
3.0L (181) 2V	1983-84	80/108, after 15 minutes, 80/108	45/61	25/34	225/306	7/10
3.0L (181) FI	1985-88	25/34, +90°, +90°†	32/44	37/50	200/270	8/11
3.1L Silhouette	1990-91	41/55, +90°	13/18, 19/26	24/33	75/102	89"/10
3.3L	1989-90	35/47, +130°□	88"/10	30/41	219/297	8/10, short 22/30, long
3.3L	1991-92	35/47, +130°□	88"/10	38/52	111/150, +76°	29/39
3.4L DOHC	1991-92	37/50, +90°	18/25	116"/13	37/50♦ 75/108⊙	88"/10
3.8L (231) 2V, 4.1L (252)	1983-84	80/108, after 15 minutes, 80/108	45/61	25/34	225/306	7/10
3.8L (231) 2V	1985	72/98	35/47	20/27	200/270	7/10
3.8L (231) 2V	1986	25/34, +90°, +90°†	45/66	20/27	200/270	19/26
3.8L (231) 2V	1987	25/34, +90°, +90°†	32/44	37/50	219/297	10/13
3.8L (231) FI	1984	80/108, after 15 minutes, 80/108	13/18	25/34	225/306	7/10
3.8L (231) Code B, 3	1985-88	25/34, +90°, +90°†	32/44	37/50	200/270	8/11
3.8L Code C	1988	25/34, +90°, +90°†	88"/10	41/55	219/297	8/10
3.8L Code C	1989-90	35/47, +130°□	88"/10	41/55	219/297	8/10

TIGHTENING TORQUES Continued

Engine	Year	Cylinder Head	Intake Manifold	Exhaust Manifold	Crankshaft Pulley	Water Pump
3.8L	1991-92	35/47, +130°□	88"/10, lower 22/30, upper	38/52	111/150, +76°	84"/10, short 29/39, long
4.3L (262) Diesel	1983-85	142/193 ★	41/55	28/39	200-350/ 275/475	13/18, short 21/28, long
4.3L	1991-92	65/90	35/48	26/36, ☆ 20/28, others	70/95	30/40
5.0L (305)	1983-84	65/88	30/40	20/27	60/81	30/40
5.0L (305)	1985-87	60-75/ 81-102	25-45/ 34-61	20-32/ 27-43* 14-26/ 19-35**	65-75/ 87-102	25-35/ 34-47
5.0L, 5.7L	1991-92	68/92	35/47	20/27, studs 26/35, bolts	70/95	30/41
5.0L (307)	1983-86	60/81, 125/169	40/54	25/34	200-310/ 270-400	13/18
5.0L (307)	1987-88	90/122, 130/176	40/54	25/34	200-310/ 270-400	7/10
5.0L (307)	1989-92	40/54, +95°, first and last bolts on exhaust manifold side +120°, all others	40/54	25/34	200-310/ 270-400	11/14
5.7L (350) Diesel	1983-85	100/136, 130/176	40/54	25/34	200-310/ 270-400	13/18

† To 60/81 maximum.
* Four outer bolts.
** Three inner bolts.
‡ Turn last bolt on left (number nine) to 29/40. Then turn all except number nine 120°, turn number nine 90°.
★ Eight center bolts, three upper and lower, 59/80.
☆ Center two.
⊙ Long bolts.
♦ Short bolts.
● Turn last bolt on left (number nine) to 18/25.
□ Tighten four center bolts an additonal 30°.
■ Turn two bolts at front of engine (outside of valve cover) 100°.
◇ Tighten six center bolts to 26/35. Tighten two bolts at front of head to 15/20. Tighten two bolts at rear of head to 22/30. Back off all bolts one turn and repeat procedure.

COMPRESSION PRESSURE
At cranking speed or specified rpm, engine temperature normalized, throttle open.

Engine	Year	PSI	Maximum Variation PSI
All gasoline	1983-92	100 min.	†
All Diesel	1983	275 min.	†
All Diesel	1984-85	300 min.	*

* Lowest cylinder must be more than 80% of highest cylinder pressure at 200 rpm min.
† Lowest cylinder pressure must be more than 70% of highest cylinder pressure.

BELT TENSION
All Except With Automatic Tensioner
Use a strand tension gauge. Measurements are in pounds.

1983, a belt in operation 15 minutes is considered a used belt.

1984-92, a belt in operation 3 minutes is considered a used belt.

Engine	Year	Alternator	Power Steering	Air Cond.	Air Pump
Used Belts					
1.8L	1983-86	75	100	75	—
2.0L	1983-86	75	70	100	—
2.0L OHC	1987	75	100	75	—
2.0L OHC	1988	—	—	80	—
2.3L	1987-91	—	110	—	—
2.5L Code R	1983-86	75	70	75	—
2.5L Code U	1985-87	90	110	90	—
2.5L Code U	1988-91	90	90	90	—
2.8L 2V	1983-86	70	70	70	45
2.8L FI	1985-86	150	150	100	—
3.0L, 3.8L FI	1983-85	70	90	90	45
3.8L 2V, 4.1L	1983-87	70	80	80	45

BELT TENSION Continued

Engine	Year	Alternator	Power Steering	Air Cond.	Air Pump
4.3L Diesel	1983-85	—	—	—	75
5.0L (307), 5.7L Diesel	1983-84	80	90	90	45●
Cogged or 3/8″ belt	1983-84	55	—	—	70
5.0L (307), 5.7L Diesel	1985-90	110	110	110	55
Cogged or 3/8″ belt	1985-90	90	—	—	90

New Belts

Engine	Year	Alternator	Power Steering	Air Cond.	Air Pump
1.8L	1983-86	145	165	155	—
2.0L	1983-86	145	165	165	—
2.0L OHC	1987	145	165	155	—
2.0L OHC	1988	—	—	155	—
2.3L	1987-91	—	110	—	—
2.5L Code R	1983-86	145	145	165	—
2.5L Code U	1985-91	165	180	165	—
2.8L 2V	1983-86	145	135	145	100
2.8L FI	1983-86	210	205	165	—
3.0L, 3.8L FI	1983-85	145	165	165	75
3.8L 2V, 4.1L	1983-87	125	135	135	80
4.3L Diesel	1983-85	—	—	—	45
5.0L (307), 5.7L Diesel	1983-88	160	170	170	80●
Cogged or 3/8″ belt	1983-88	145	—	—	145
5.0L (307)	1989-90	150	165	165	135
Cogged	1989-90	135	—	—	—

All With Automatic Tensioner

If index marks on tensioner are outside the range, replace the belt. If marks are within range and belt tension is below specified value, replace tensioner.

Engine	Year	Tension
2.3L	1987-91	50 min.
2.5L Ciera	1987-88	40 min.
2.5L Ciera	1989-91	50-70
2.8L	1987	70 min.
2.8L	1988-89	50-70
3.0L	1985-86	67 min.
3.0L	1987-88	79 min.
3.1L Cutlass	1989-92	50-70
3.1L Silhouette	1990-92	50-70
3.3L	1989-92	67 min.
3.8L Code C, B, 3	1986-90	67 min.
4.3L Diesel	1983-85	100-140
5.0L, 5.7L	1991-92	105-125

● Vacuum pump belt: used, 55; new, 125.

ENGINE COMPUTER SYSTEM

COMPUTER DIAGNOSTIC CODES

See UNDERHOOD SERVICE INSTRUCTIONS at the beginning of this section for test/adjustment diagrams.

All ex. 1988-92 Toronado with CRT

Connect a jumper between terminals A and B on under dash connector (identified by a slot between the terminals or is two upper right cavities on a two row connector). Turn ignition switch on. Code 12 will flash three times, then codes in memory will be displayed. Do not run engine with jumper connected.

Remove ECM fuse for a minimum of ten seconds to clear memory.

1988-90 Toronado, Troféo with CRT

To enter diagnostic mode, turn ignition switch on and push ''off'' and ''warm'' buttons simultaneously for three seconds and release. Any stored codes will be displayed.

To clear ECM code, press the ''HI'' switch after the ECM message is displayed. After accessing the ECM system, continually press the ''LO'' switch after each message until ''CLEAR CODES'' is displayed. Press the ''BI LEVEL'' button to exit diagnostics.

The computer system monitors other systems and functions besides the ECM trouble codes.

See Service Manual for details.

All ex. 1988-91 Toronado, Troféo

Code 12 No tach reference to ECM
Code 13 Oxygen sensor circuit
Code 14 Coolant sensor circuit (high temperature indicated)
Code 15 Coolant sensor circuit (low temperature indicated)
Code 16 System voltage high
Code 17 Spark reference circuit
Code 21 Throttle position sensor circuit (1983)
Code 21 Throttle position sensor (voltage high) (1984-91)
Code 22 Throttle position sensor (voltage low) (1984-91)
Code 23 Open or ground MC solenoid (carburetted)
Code 23 Manifold air temperature circuit (low temperature indicated)

COMPUTER DIAGNOSTIC CODES Continued

Code 24 Vehicle speed sensor circuit
Code 25 Manifold air temperature (high temperature indicated)
Code 26 Quad driver circuit
Code 27 Second gear switch circuit
Code 28 Third gear switch circuit
Code 29 Fourth gear switch circuit open
Code 31 Canister purge solenoid (carburetted)
Code 31 Park/Neutral switch, MFI; EGR circuit, TBI
Code 32 Barometric or altitude sensor (carburetted)
Code 32 EGR system failure (FI)
Code 33 MAP sensor voltage high (FI)
Code 34 MAF sensor (3.3L, 3.8L)
Code 34 MAP sensor voltage low (FI, others)
Code 34 MAP sensor voltage high or low (carburetted)
Code 35 Idle speed or idle air control circuit
Code 36 MAF burnoff circuit (1986-89)
Code 36 Transaxle shift control (1990-91)
Code 37 MAT sensor temperature too high (1983-86)
Code 38 MAT sensor temperature too low (1983-86)
Code 38 Brake switch circuit (1988-90)
Code 39 Torque converter clutch circuit
Code 40 Power steering pressure switch open
Code 41 No distributor reference pulses to ECM (1984-90 carburetted)
Code 41 Faulty MEMCAL (4.3L)
Code 41 Cam sensor circuit (3.3L, 3.8L Code 3, C, L)
Code 41 Cylinder select error (1987-91 ex. 3.3L, 3.8L, 4.3L)
Code 42 EST or EST bypass circuit grounded or open
Code 43 ESC retard signal too long
Code 44 Air/fuel mixture lean
Codes 44 & 45 Faulty oxygen sensor
Code 45 Air/fuel mixture rich
Code 46 Power steering pressure switch circuit
Code 47 AC clutch and cruise circuit
Code 48 Misfire
Code 51 Faulty PROM or installation, faulty Memcal or ECM
Code 52 CALPAK error
Code 53 EGR vacuum sensor vacuum incorrect (carburetted)
Code 53 Alternator voltage out of range (FI)
Code 54 Shorted MC solenoid or faulty ECM (carburetted)
Code 54 Fuel pump circuit (FI)
Code 55 Grounded V-REF, faulty oxygen sensor or ECM
Code 58 PASS key fuel enable circuit
Code 61 Degraded Oxygen sensor (ex. 3.8L Code L)
Code 61 Cruise vent solenoid (3.8L Code L)
Code 62 Transmission gear switch (ex. 3.8L Code L)
Code 62 Cruise VAC solenoid (3.8L Code L)
Code 65 Fuel injector circuit (ex. 3.8L Code L)
Code 65 Cruise servo position (3.8L Code L)
Code 66 A/C pressure sensor
Code 67 Cruise switches
Code 68 Cruise system problem
Code 69 AC head pressure switch

1988-90 Toronado, Troféo w/CRT

Code 013 Open Oxygen sensor circuit
Code 014 Coolant sensor circuit high temperature
Code 015 Coolant sensor circuit, low temperature
Code 016 System voltage out of range
Code 021 TPS circuit, signal voltage high
Code 022 TPS circuit, signal voltage low
Code 023 Manifold air temperature, low temperature indicated
Code 024 Vehicle speed sensor circuit
Code 025 Manifold air temperature, high temperature indicated
Code 026 Quad driver error
Code 027 Second gear switch circuit
Code 028 Third gear switch circuit
Code 029 Fourth gear switch circuit open
Code 031 Park/Neutral switch circuit
Code 034 Mass air flow sensor circuit
Code 038 Brake switch circuit
Code 039 Torque converter clutch circuit
Code 041 Cam sensor circuit
Code 042 EST or bypass circuit
Code 043 ESC system
Code 044 Lean exhaust
Code 045 Rich exhaust
Code 046 Power steering switch circuit (AC clutch)
Code 047 ECM-BCM communication error
Code 048 Misfire
Code 051 PROM error

OLDSMOBILE
1983-92
All Models Except Bravada, Silhouette

OETU7

UNDERHOOD SERVICE SPECIFICATIONS

OETU7

COMPUTER DIAGNOSTIC CODES Continued

Code 063 EGR flow problem, small
Code 064 EGR flow problem, medium
Code 065 EGR flow problem, large

SENSORS, INPUT
TEMPERATURE SENSORS

Engine	Year	Sensor	Resistance Ohms @ deg. F/C
All	1983-90	Coolant	13,500 @ 20/−7
	1983-92	Manifold Air*	7500 @ 40/4
			3400 @ 70/20
			1800 @ 100/38
			450 @ 160/70
			185 @ 210/100
All	1991-92	Coolant	28,700 @ −4/−20
			12,300 @ 23/−5
			7200 @ 41/5
			3500 @ 68/20
			1460 @ 104/40
			470 @ 158/70
			180 @ 210/100

* As equipped, not used on all engines.

MANIFOLD ABSOLUTE, VACUUM, AND BAROMETRIC PRESSURE SENSORS
See UNDERHOOD SERVICE INSTRUCTIONS at the beginning of this section for test/ adjustment diagrams.

Engines may use one, or a combination of these sensors. All sensors appear the same. Manifold Absolute Pressure sensors have vacuum line connected between the unit and manifold vacuum. On Barometric Pressure sensors, the line is not used and the connector is either open or has a filter installed over it. Pressure sensors also have a vacuum line between the sensor and intake manifold and only appear on carburetted models.

Barometric Pressure Sensors: Measure voltage with ignition on and engine off.

Manifold Absolute Pressure Sensors: Measure voltage with ignition on and engine off. Start engine and apply 10 in./250 mm Hg to unit, voltage should be 1.5 volts minimum less.

Pressure Sensors: Measure voltage as indicated.
5 volts reference.

Engine	Year	Sensor	Voltage @ Altitude/Condition
All, as equipped	1983-90	Barometric	3.8-5.5 @ 0-1000
			3.6-5.3 @ 1000-2000
			3.5-5.1 @ 2000-3000
			3.3-5.0 @ 3000-4000
			3.2-4.8 @ 4000-5000
			3.0-4.6 @ 5000-6000
			2.9-4.5 @ 6000-7000
			2.5-4.3 @ 7000-

Engine	Year	Sensor	Voltage @ Vacuum In Hg/kPa
All	1983-91	Manifold Absolute	1.0-1.5 @ idle
			4.5-4.8 @ WOT
All	1992	Manifold Absolute	4.9 @ 0″ Hg/0 kPa
			3.8 @ 6″ Hg/20 kPa
			2.7 @ 12″ Hg/40 kPa
			1.7 @ 18″ Hg/60 kPa
			0.6 @ 24″ Hg/80 kPa
			0.3 @ 30″ Hg/100 kPa

Engine	Year	Sensor	Voltage @ Altitude
2.5L 2V, 2.8L 2V, 4.3L (260), 5.0L	1983-91	Vacuum	.50-.64 @ ign. on 1.7-3.0*

* 10 in./250 mm applied to unit.

CRANKSHAFT SENSORS
Air gap is measured between crankshaft sensor and interrupter rings.
Resistance is measured at room temperature.

Engine	Year	Resistance (ohms)	Air Gap (in./mm)
2.0L ex. OHC	1987-92	900-1200	—
2.3L, 2.8L, 3.1L	1988-92	900-1200	—
2.5L	1987-92	800-900	—
3.0L, 3.3L, 3.8L w/C³I	1984-92	—	.025/.65

SENSORS, INPUT Continued
THROTTLE POSITION SENSOR (TPS)
See UNDERHOOD SERVICE INSTRUCTIONS at the beginning of this section for test/ adjustment diagrams.

Verify that minimum idle is at specified value.
Make all checks/adjustments with engine at operating temperature.

Carburetted Models: Remove aluminum plug covering the adjustment screw. Remove the screw and connect a digital voltmeter from the TPS black wire (−) and either of the two other colored wires (+). If voltage is approximately 5 volts, this is the reference voltage lead. Connect DVOM to other wire in this case. Apply thread locking compound to the screw and with ignition on and engine not running (as applies), quickly adjust screw to obtain specified voltage at indicated condition.

Fuel Injected Models: Disconnect harness connector from TPS. Using three six-inch jumper wires, reconnect harness to TPS. With ignition on and engine not running (as applies), connect a digital voltmeter to black wire (−) and either of the two other colored wires (+). If voltage is approximately 5 volts, this is the reference voltage lead. Connect DVOM to other wire in this case. Check reading against specified value. If TPS is adjustable, loosen the unit retaining screws and rotate the unit to reach specified value.

Engine	Year	TPS Voltage Idle†	TPS Voltage WOT (approx.)
1.8L (112)	1983-86	.20-1.25*	5.0
2.0L (122) FI	1983-84	.525	—
2.0L (122)	1985-86	.20-1.25*	5.0
2.0L	1987-89	.33-1.33*	5.0
2.3L	1988-89	.54	4.7 min.
2.3L	1990-92	.40-.90*	4.7 min.
2.5L (151)	1983-90	.20-1.25*	5.0
2.5L	1991-92	.35-1.33*	5.0
2.8L (173)	1983	.26△	—
2.8L (173)	1984	.30△	—
2.8L (173) 2V	1985-86	.27	—
2.8L (173) FI	1985-88	.55	—
2.8L	1989	.29-.98*	5.0
3.1L TBI	1990-92	.20-1.25*	5.0
3.1L MFI	1989-92	.29-.98*	4.8 min.
3.3L	1989-92	.40	4.5 min.
3.4L DOHC	1991-92	.29-.98*	4.8
3.0L (181)	1983	.51♦	—
3.0L (181)	1984	.65■♦	—
3.0L (181) 2V	1985	.60■♦	—
3.0L (181) FI	1985	.50	—
3.0L (181)	1985-88	.55	—
3.8L (231) 2V	1983	.86●	—
3.8L (231) 2V	1984-88	.46♦	—
3.8L (231) FI	1984-91	.40	5.1
4.1L (252)	1983	.97●	—
4.1L (252)	1984	.57♦	—
4.3L	1991-92	.40-1.25*	5.0
5.0L, 5.7L	1991-92	.20-.95*	5.0
5.0L (307)	1983	.46♦	—
5.0L (307)	1984-90	.41♦	5.0

● High step of fast idle cam.
♦ Idle Speed or Load Compensator (ISC, ILC) retracted.
† ±.10 carburetted engines. ±.05 fuel injected engines.
* Not adjustable.
△ With anti-diesel solenoid disconnected.
■ With 3-speed AT, .57.

ACTUATORS, OUTPUT
IDLE SPEED CONTROL
See UNDERHOOD SERVICE INSTRUCTIONS at the beginning of this section for test/ adjustment diagrams.
All engines with ISC.
Measured between terminals A & B and C & D.

Engine	Year	Resistance (ohms)
All carburetted	1983-87	10 min.
2.8L, 3.1L Ciera, Cutlass	1988-89	48-58
3.8L Code C	1988-89	48-58
All others, TBI & MFI	1983-89	20 min.
All ex. Toronado	1990-92	40-80
3.8L Toronado	1990-91	48-58

MIXTURE CONTROL SOLENOID-CARBURETTED ENGINES
On some engines, the ECM will be damaged if the resistance of the mixture control solenoid is less than specified.

Engine	Year	Resistance (ohms)
All	1983-90	10 min.

ENGINE IDENTIFICATION

To identify an engine by the manufacturer's code, follow the four steps designated by the numbered blocks.

V.I.N. PLATE LOCATION:

Driver's side top of instrument panel, visible through windshield.

1 MODEL YEAR IDENTIFICATION:

10th character of V.I.N.
1991 — M; 1990 — L; 1989 — K;
1988 — J; 1987 — H; 1986 — G;
1985 — F; 1984 — E; 1983 — D.

2 ENGINE CODE LOCATION:

1984-83 — 6th character of V.I.N.
All others — Prefix to engine number, stamped on driver's side of engine block.

4 ENGINE IDENTIFICATION

YEAR	3 ENGINE CODE	CYL.	DISPL. liters	cc	Fuel System	HP
1991	XU9J2	4	2.0	1905	M	100
	XU9J4	4	2.0	1905	M	100
	N9TEA	4	2.2 T	2155 T	LU	160
	ZDJL	4	2.2	2165	LU	120
1990	XU9J2	4	2.0	1905	M	110
	XU9J4	4	2.0	1905	M	150
	N9TEA	4	2.2 T	2155 T	LU	160
	ZDJL	4	2.2	2165	LU	120
1989	X49J2	4	2.0	1905	M	110
	X49J4	4	2.0	1905	M	150
	N9TEA	4	2.2 T	2155 T	LU	160, 180
	ZDJL	4	2.2	2165	LU	120
	ZN3J	6	2.8	2849	LH	145
1988	N9TE	4	2.2 T	2155 T	LU	150
	N9TEA	4	2.2 T	2155 T	LU	180
	ZDJL	4	2.2	2165	LU	120
	ZN3J	6	2.8	2849	LU	145
1987	XN6	4	2.0	1971	CIS	97
	N9TE	4	2.2 T	2155 T	LU	150

4 ENGINE IDENTIFICATION

YEAR	3 ENGINE CODE	CYL.	DISPL. liters	cc	Fuel System	HP
1987 Cont'd.	ZDJL	4	2.2	2165	LU	120
	XD3T	4	2.5 TD	2498 TD	VE	95
	ZN3J	6	2.8	2849	LU	145
1986	XN6	4	2.0	1971	CIS	97
	N9TE	4	2.2 T	2155 T	LU	142, 150
1985	XN6	4	2.0	1971	CIS	97
	N9T	4	2.2 T	2155 T	LU	142, 150
	XD2S	4	2.3 TD	2304 TD	VE	80
	XD3T	4	2.5 TD	2498 TD	VE	95
1984	2	4	2.0	1971	CIS	97
	4	4	2.3 TD	2304 TD	VE	80
1983	1	4	2.0	1971	CIS	97
	2	4	2.3 D	2304 D	VE	71
	4	4	2.3 TD	2304 TD	VE	80

D — Diesel. TD — Turbo Diesel. T — Turbo.
CIS — Continuous Injection System. LU — LU-Jetronic.
M — Motronic. VE — Diesel Injection.

UNDERHOOD SERVICE SPECIFICATIONS

PTITU1   PTITU1

CYLINDER NUMBERING SEQUENCE

4-CYL. FIRING ORDER: 1 3 4 2   **V6 FIRING ORDER: 1 6 3 5 2 4**

—— Front of car ——

| 1989-91 1905cc | 1983-87 1971cc FI, 1987-91 2165cc | 1985-91 2155cc Turbo | 1987-89 2849cc FI |

TIMING MARK

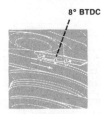

8° BTDC

1983-87
4-cyl. 1971cc

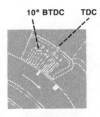

10° BTDC   TDC

1985-88
4-cyl. 2155cc Turbo

PEUGEOT
1983-91

ELECTRICAL AND IGNITION SYSTEMS

BATTERY

BCI equivalent shown, size may vary from original equipment. Check clearance and polarity before installing, holddown may need to be modified.

Model	Year	BCI Group No.	Crank. Perf.
405	1989-91	◆	495
504 Diesel	1983	†	450
505: Turbo	1987-91	48	660
4-cyl. Fl	1987-91	48	495
V6	1987-89	48	495
505 Diesel	1987	†	740
505 ex. Diesel	1983-86	24	300
505 Diesel	1983-85	†	450
604 Diesel	1983-84	†	450

† Special size: 12 volt 14¹⁵/₁₆″ × 6³/₄″ × 7³/₈″, no BCI equivalent.
◆ Special size: 12 volt 8¹/₄″ × 6³/₄″ × 7 ¹/₄″, no BCI equivalent.

ALTERNATOR

Application	Year	Rated Output (amps)	Test Output (amps @ rpm)
All	1983-87	83.3	—
505 ex. Turbo, V6	1988-91	83.3	—
Turbo, V6	1988-91	100	—
405	1989-91	83.3	—

REGULATOR

Application	Year	Test Temp. (deg. F/C)	Voltage Output Minimum	Voltage Output Maximum
504, 505	1983-91	63-81/17-27	12.8	14.8
405	1989-91	63-81/17-27	13.8	14.8

STARTER

Application	Year	Cranking Voltage (min. volts)
All	1983-85	9.6
All	1986-88	9.0

SPARK PLUGS

Engine	Year	Gap (inches)	Gap (mm)	Torque (ft-lb)
1905cc ex. DOHC	1989-91	.028-.036	.70-.80	16-24
DOHC	1989-91	.044-.052	1.1-1.3	16-24
1971cc	1983-85	.024	.60	16.5
1971cc	1986-87	.024-.028	.60-.70	16.5
2155cc	1985-91	.036-.040	.90-1.0	16.5
2165cc	1987-91	.024-.028	.60-.70	16.5
2849cc	1987-89	.024-.032	.60-.80	13

IGNITION COIL

Application	Year	Windings	Resistance (ohms)
1905cc	1989-91	Primary	0.7
		Secondary	6600
1971cc	1983-87	Primary	.48-.61
		Secondary	9000-11,000
2155cc	1985	Primary	.85
		Secondary	6000

IGNITION PICKUP

Engine	Year	Resistance (ohms)	Air Gap (in./mm)
1971cc	1983-86	900-1100	.012-.020/.30-.50

TIMING PROCEDURE

1. Connect timing light to No. 1 ignition lead (flywheel end).
2. Set idle speed to recommended rpm.
3. Rotate distributor housing to obtain specified timing.

BASE TIMING

Before top dead center, unless otherwise specified.

Engine	Year	Man. Trans. (degrees) @ RPM	Auto. Trans. (degrees) @ RPM
1971cc	1983-85	6-10 @ 800	6-10 @ 800
1971cc	1986-87	6-10 @ 900	6-10 @ 900
2155cc	1985	8-12 @ 910	8-12 @ 910
2155cc	1986-88	8-12 @ 900	8-12 @ 950
2165cc	1987-91	10 @ 900	10 @ 900

DISTRIBUTOR TIMING ADVANCE

Crankshaft degrees at engine rpm, no load, in addition to base timing.

Engine	Transmission	Year	Distributor Number	Degrees @ 2500 RPM Total	Degrees @ 2500 RPM Centrifugal
1971cc	MT & AT	1983-87	M118	23.3-31.3	11.3-15.3
2165cc	MT & AT	1987-91	M164E	17.5-29.5	5-10

FUEL SYSTEM

FUEL PRESSURE PROCEDURE

LH-, LU-Jetronic:
1. Connect appropriate pressure gauge between the fuel supply connector and the distribution pipe.
2. Start engine and run at idle. If engine will not start, energize fuel pump by bridging wires 20B and 76 of the tachymetric relay.
3. Disconnect the vacuum line from the fuel pressure regulator and read line pressure w/o vacuum.
4. Apply 14.8 in Hg of vacuum to pressure regulator and read line pressure w/vacuum.

CIS:
1. Connect appropriate pressure gauge in series between the control pressure regulator and the fuel distributor and bleed gauge assembly.
2. Start engine and run at idle. If engine will not start, energize fuel pump by jumping the tachymetric relay.
3. With pressure gauge valve in the closed position read line pressure.
4. With pressure gauge valve in the open position read control pressure.
5. Leave gauge valve open, stop engine and allow to sit for 20 minutes, read residual pressure.

FUEL PRESSURE; LH-, LU-JETRONIC, MOTRONIC

Engine	Year	Line Pressure w/o vacuum psi (bar)	Line Pressure w/vacuum psi (bar)
1905cc	1989-91	42.9 (3.0)	—
2155cc	1985	42-45 (2.9-3.1)	35-38 (2.4-2.6)
2155cc	1986-91	35-38 (2.4-2.6)	28-30 (1.9-2.1)
2165cc	1988-91	33-39 (2.3-2.7)	26-32 (1.8-2.2)
2849cc	1987-89	33-39 (2.3-2.7)	26-32 (1.8-2.2)

FUEL PRESSURE; CIS

Engine	Year	Line Pressure psi (bar)	Control Pressure† psi (bar)	Residual Pressure* psi (bar)
1971cc	1983-86	65-75 (4.5-5.2)	49-74 (3.4-5.1)	38 (2.6)

† With engine at normal operating temperature, varies with atmospheric pressure.
* After 20 minutes.

COLD CONTROL PRESSURE; CIS

Pressure Regulator Part Number	Pressure psi (bar) @ 50°F (10°C) Ambient Temp.	Pressure psi (bar) @ 68°F (20°C) Ambient Temp.	Pressure psi (bar) @ 86°F (30°C) Ambient Temp.
All	23-29 (1.6-2.0)	32-39 (2.2-2.7)	41-49 (2.8-3.4)

UNDERHOOD SERVICE SPECIFICATIONS

IDLE SPEED

Engine	Year	Manual Transmission	Automatic Transmission
Gasoline:			
1905cc ex. DOHC	1989-91	800-900	800-900 N
DOHC	1989-91	830-920†	830-920 N†
1971cc	1983	800	800 N
1971cc	1984-85	800-850	800-850 N
1971cc	1986-87	900-950	900-950 N
2155cc	1985-88	900-950	950-1000 N
2155cc	1989-91	850-950	900-1000 N
2165cc	1987-88	800-850	800-850 N
2165cc	1989-91	850-950	850-950 N
2849cc	1987-89	750-800†	750-800 N†
Diesel:			
2304cc ex. Turbo	1983	780-830	780-830 N
AC speed-up	1983	830-860	830-860 N
2304cc Turbo	1983-85	780-840	780-840 N
AC speed-up	1983-85	800-860	800-860 N
2498cc	1985-87	800-860	800-860 N

† Not adjustable, for reference only.

IDLE MIXTURE

Engine	Year	CO% Minimum	CO% Maximum
1905cc	1989	0.5	0.5
2155cc	1985-88	1.0★	1.6★
2849cc	1987-88	0.8★	1.5★

★ Measured before catalyst with oxygen sensor disconnected.

ENGINE MECHANICAL

TIGHTENING TORQUES

Engine	Year	Cylinder Head	Intake Manifold	Exhaust Manifold	Crankshaft Pulley	Water Pump
				Torque Ft-lbs/Nm		
DIESEL ENGINES						
4-cyl. 2.3L, 2.5L:						
W/o shoulder†	1983-87	22/30	—	—	40/55	—
2nd stage◆		47/65	—	—	+60°	—
Warm retorque●		47/65				
W/shoulder†	1983-87	22/30	—	—	40/55	—
2nd stage◆		51/70	—	—	+60°	—
3rd stage●		58/80				
GASOLINE ENGINES						
4-cyl. 2.0L	1983-85	36/50	—	—	123/170	—
2nd stage■		15/20				
3rd stage ★		+90°				
4-cyl. 2.0L	1986-87	36/50	—	—	123/170	—
2nd stage■		15/20				
3rd stage		+180°				
4th stage▲		+35°				
4-cyl. 2.2L:						
2155cc Turbo	1985-91	36/50	11/15	15/20	99/135	11/15
2nd stage		62/85				
2165cc	1987-91	36/50	—	—	94/130	—
2nd stage		58/80				
3rd stage⊙		69/95				
V6 2.8L	1987-89	44/60	—	—	—	—
2nd stage■		15/20				
3rd stage		+105°				
4th stage‡		+45°				

† Bolts w/o shoulder are class 10.9 and color coded yellow, shouldered bolts are class 12.9 and color coded black.

◆ Torque all bolts, back off one at a time and retorque to specification.

● Run engine at 3000 rpm for 10 minutes, allow to cool 3½ hours, back off bolts one at a time and retorque to specification. For bolts w/o shoulder, repeat procedure after 1000 miles of service.

■ Back off and bring to specification one bolt at a time.

★ Repeat stages 2 & 3 after running engine to operating temperature and allowing to cool for 6 hours, back off and tighten bolts one at a time.

TIGHTENING TORQUES Continued

▲ Run engine to operating temperature and allow to cool 6 hours before final torque.

⊙ Run engine at 2000 rpm for 12 minutes, allow to cool 2 hours, back off bolts one at a time and retorque to specification.

‡ Run engine at 2000 rpm for 12 minutes, allow to cool 2 hours and tighten to specification.

VALVE CLEARANCE

With cold engine, minimum cooling time of 6 hours.

Engine	Year	Intake (inches)	Intake (mm)	Exhaust (inches)	Exhaust (mm)
1905cc ex. DOHC	1989-91	.008	.20	.016	.40
1971cc	1983-87	.004	.10	.010	.25
2155cc	1985-91	.008	.20	.012	.30
2165cc	1987-91	.004	.10	.010	.25
2304cc ex. Turbo	1983	.010	.25	.010	.25
2304cc Turbo	1983-85	.006	.15	.010	.25
2498cc	1985-87	.005	.10	.010	.25
2849cc	1987-89	.004	.10	.010	.25

COMPRESSION PRESSURE

With engine at normal operating temperature.

Engine	Year	Normal Range PSI	Maximum Variation PSI
2304cc Diesel	1983-84	257★	72
2498cc Turbo Diesel	1985-87	257★	72

★ Minimum.

BELT TENSION

Model	Year	Alternator	Power Steering	Air Cond.	Vacuum Pump
STRAND TENSION:					
NEW BELTS					
1971cc	1983-85	90-100	65-90	100-120	—
2304cc	1983-85	88-110	88-110	88-110	44-66
USED BELTS					
1971cc	1983-85	65-90	65-90	65-90	—
2304cc	1983-85	31-44	31-44	31-44	33 max.

ENGINE COMPUTER SYSTEM

COMPUTER DIAGNOSTIC CODES

Run engine at idle and count number of flashes per cycle of the AUTODIAGNOSTIC LED located on the instrument cluster. Occasional or intermittent flashes indicates normal operation.

1987-91 4-cyl. 2155cc Turbo

Engine Flashes	Condition	Check
1	Running at maximum retard	Cooling system
		Base timing
		Turbo boost pressure
2	Low battery voltage	Battery
		Charging system
3	No detonation correction	Replace ignition ECU
4	Erroneous detonation signal	Detonation sensor
		Detonation sensor circuitry
5	High potentiometer voltage	Replace potentiometer
6	Loss of ECU signal	Check circuit continuity
		Replace ignition ECU
		Replace injection ECU

UNDERHOOD SERVICE SPECIFICATIONS

COMPUTER DIAGNOSTIC CODES Continued

1987-89 V6 2849cc

Engine Flashes	Condition	Check
2	No NTC temperature signal	Check circuitry
		Replace NTC temperature sensor
4	No detonation signal	Check circuitry
		Replace detonation sensor
		Replace ignition ECU
5	Erroneous load signal	Check circuitry
		Replace injection ECU
6	Erroneous TDC signal	Check circuitry
		Replace #1 cylinder sensor
Constant	Maximum retard	Cooling system
		Gasoline quality
		Ignition ECU

1989-91 4-cyl. 1905cc

Code	Application	Definition
11	End Sequence	All codes have been displayed
12	Begin Sequence	Memory accessed
13	Air Temperature Sensor	Defective sensor or circuit
14	Coolant Temperature Sensor	Defective sensor or circuit
15	Fuel Pump Relay	Defective relay or circuit
21	Throttle Switch	Defective switch or circuit, idle position
22	Idle Control Valve	Defective electrovalve or circuit
31	Mixture Control	Unmetered intake air leak
32	Mixture Control	Exhaust leakage
33	Air Flow Sensor	Defective sensor or circuit
34	Canister Purge	Defective solenoid or circuit
35	Throttle Switch	Defective switch or circuit, full load position
41	Engine RPM Sensor	Defective sensor or circuit
42	Fuel Injectors	Defective injectors or circuit
43	Detonation Control	System operating at maximum retard
44	Knock Sensor	Defective sensor or circuit
51	Mixture Control	Defective Oxygen Sensor or circuit
52	Mixture Control	Electronic Control Unit, internal defect
53	System Voltage	Charging system out of range
54	Control Unit	Defective Electronic Control Unit

SENSORS, INPUT

TEMPERATURE SENSORS

Engine	Year	Sensor	Resistance Ohms @ deg. F/C
4-cyl. 2.2L (2155cc) Turbo	1985-91	Coolant	8000-10,000 @ 14/−10
			2000-3000 @ 68/20
			500-650 @ 140/60
			100-250 @ 212/100
4-cyl. 2.2L (2165cc)	1987-91	Coolant	8000-10,000 @ 14/−10
			2000-3000 @ 68/20
			500-650 @ 140/60
			100-250 @ 212/100

AIRFLOW SENSOR

Engine	Year	Resistance Ohms @ Terminals
4-cyl. 2.2L (2155cc) Turbo	1985-91	340-450 @ 5 & 8
		160-300 @ 9 & 8
		60-1000 @ 5 & 7†
4-cyl. 2.2L (2165cc)	1987-91	340-450 @ 5 & 8
		160-300 @ 9 & 8
		60-1000 @ 5 & 7†

† Resistance varies with position of sensor plate.

ACTUATORS, OUTPUT

AUXILIARY AIR VALVE

Engine	Year	Resistance Ohms @ deg. F/C
4-cyl. 2.2L (2155cc) Turbo	1985-91	45-55 @ 68/20
4-cyl. 2.2L (2165cc)	1987-91	35-45 @ 68/20

COMPUTER TIMING ADVANCE

Crankshaft degrees at engine rpm, no load, including base timing.

Engine	Year	Trans-mission	Distributor Number	Speed Advance Degrees	Engine RPM
2155cc	1985-87	MT & AT	0237506004	23-28	1600-1900

ENGINE IDENTIFICATION

To identify any engine by the manufacturer's code, follow the four steps designated by the numbered blocks.

1 **MODEL YEAR IDENTIFICATION:** Refer to illustration of Vehicle Identification Number (V.I.N.). The year is indicated by a code letter.

2 **ENGINE CODE LOCATION:** Refer to V.I.N. plate illustration. The engine code is indicated as a letter or number.

3 **ENGINE CODE:** In the "CODE" column, find the engine code determined in Step 2.

4 **ENGINE IDENTIFICATION:** On the line where the engine code appears, read to the right to identify the engine.

V.I.N. PLATE LOCATION:

On top left side
of instrument panel

Model year of vehicle:
1992 — Model year is N.
1991 — Model year is M.
1990 — Model year is L.
1989 — Model year is K.
1988 — Model year is J.
1987 — Model year is H.
1986 — Model year is G.
1985 — Model year is F.
1984 — Model year is E.
1983 — Model year is D.

MODEL YEAR AND ENGINE IDENTIFICATION:

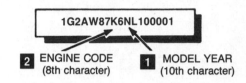

1G2AW87K6NL100001

2 ENGINE CODE
(8th character)

1 MODEL YEAR
(10th character)

4 ENGINE IDENTIFICATION

YEAR	3 ENGINE CODE	CYL.	DISPL. liters	cu. in.	Fuel System	HP
1992	6	4	1.6	97	TBI	74
	H	4	2.0	121	MFI	111
	3	4	2.3	138	MFI	120
	D	4	2.3	138	MFI	160
	A	4	2.3	138	MFI	180
	T	6	3.1	191	MFI	140
	N	6	3.3	204	MFI	160
	X	6	3.4	207	MFI	210
	L	6	3.8	231	MFI	170
	1	6	3.8	231	MFI	205
	E	8	5.0	305	MFI	170
	F	8	5.0	305	TBI	205
	8	8	5.7	350	MFI	240
1991	6	4	1.6	97	TBI	74
	K	4	2.0	121	TBI	96
	D	4	2.3	138	MFI	160
	A	4	2.3	138	MFI	180
	R, U	4	2.5	151	TBI	110
	T	6	3.1	191	MFI	140
	V	6	3.1 T	191 T	MFI	205
	X	6	3.4	207	MFI	200, 210†
	F	8	5.0	305	MFI	205, 225†
	E	8	5.0	305	TBI	170
	8	8	5.7	350	MFI	240
1990	6	4	1.6	97	TBI	74
	K	4	2.0	121	TBI	96
	M	4	2.0 T	121 T	MFI	165
	D	4	2.3	138	MFI	160
	A	4	2.3	138	MFI	180
	R, U	4	2.5	151	TBI	110
	T	6	3.1	191	MFI	135,140
	V	6	3.1 T	191 T	MFI	205
	D	6	3.1	191	TBI	120
	C	6	3.8	231	MFI	165
	E	8	5.0	305	TBI	170
	F	8	5.0	305	MFI	190, 225†
	Y	8	5.0	307	4V	140
	8	8	5.7	350	MFI	235
1989	6	4	1.6	97	TBI	74
	K	4	2.0	121	TBI	96
	M	4	2.0 T	121 T	MFI	165
	D	4	2.3	138	MFI	150
	R	4	2.5	151	TBI	98
	U	4	2.5	151	TBI	110
	W	6	2.8	173	MFI	125-130†
	S	6	2.8	173	MFI	135
	T	6	3.1	191	MFI	140
	C	6	3.8	231	MFI	165
	7	6	3.8	231	MFI	NA
	E	8	5.0	305	TBI	170
	F	8	5.0	305	MFI	195
	Y	8	5.0	307	4V	140
	8	8	5.7	350	MFI	225-235†

4 ENGINE IDENTIFICATION

YEAR	3 ENGINE CODE	CYL.	DISPL. liters	cu. in.	Fuel System	HP
1988	6	4	1.6	97	TBI	74
	K	4	2.0	122	TBI	96
	M	4	2.0 T	122 T	MFI	165
	D	4	2.3	140	MFI	150
	R, U	4	2.5	151	TBI	98
	W	6	2.8	173	MFI	125, 130†
	S	6	2.8	173	MFI	135
	9	6	2.8	173	MFI	135
	T	6	3.1	191	MFI	135
	3	6	3.8	231	MFI	150
	C	6	3.8 HO	231 HO	MFI	165
	E	8	5.0	305	TBI	170
	F	8	5.0	305	MFI	195-215†
	Y	8	5.0	307	4V	140
	8	8	5.7	350	MFI	225
1987	C	4	1.6	98	2V	65
	K	4	2.0	122	TBI	96
	M	4	2.0 T	122 T	MFI	165
	R, U	4	2.5	151	TBI	98
	W	6	2.8	173	MFI	125
	S	6	2.8	173	MFI	135
	9	6	2.8	173	MFI	135
	L	6	3.0	181	MFI	125
	A	6	3.8	231	2V	110
	3	6	3.8	231	MFI	150
	Z	6	4.3	262	TBI	140
	H	8	5.0	305	4V	150-165†
	F	8	5.0	305	MFI	205
	Y	8	5.0	307	4V	140
	8	8	5.7	350	MFI	225
1986	C	4	1.6	98	2V	65
	0	4	1.8	112	TBI	84
	J	4	1.8 T	112 T	MFI	150
	P	4	2.0	122	TBI	88
	R, U	4	2.5	151	TBI	92
	2	4	2.5	151	TBI	88
	X	6	2.8	173	2V	112
	W	6	2.8	173	MFI	125
	S	6	2.8	173	MFI	135
	9	6	2.8	173	MFI	140
	L	6	3.0	181	MFI	125
	A	6	3.8	231	2V	110
	Z	6	4.3	262	TBI	130
	H	8	5.0	305	4V	150, 165†
	G	8	5.0 HO	305 HO	4V	190
	F	8	5.0	305	MFI	210
	Y	8	5.0	307	4V	140
1985	C	4	1.6	98	2V	65
	D	4	1.8 D	111 D	MFI	51
	0	4	1.8	112	TBI	84
	J	4	1.8 T	112 T	MFI	150
	P	4	2.0	122	TBI	88
	R, U, 2	4	2.5	151	TBI	92

PONTIAC
1983-92 All Models Except Firefly, Sunburst, Trans Sport

ENGINE IDENTIFICATION Continued

4 ENGINE IDENTIFICATION

YEAR	CODE	CYL.	liters	cu. in.	Fuel System	HP
1985 Cont'd.	X	6	2.8	173	2V	112
	W	6	2.8	173	MFI	125
	S	6	2.8	173	MFI	135
	9	6	2.8	173	MFI	140
	L	6	3.0	181	MFI	125
	A	6	3.8	231	2V	110
	T	6	4.3 D	262 D	MFI	85
	Z	6	4.3	262	TBI	130
	H	8	5.0	305	4V	155, 165
	G	8	5.0 HO	305 HO	4V	190
	F	8	5.0	305	MFI	215
	N	8	5.7 D	350 D	MFI	105
	6	8	5.7	350	4V	165
1984	C	4	1.6	98	2V	65
	D	4	1.8 D	111 D	MFI	51
	0	4	1.8	112	TBI	84
	J	4	1.8 T	112 T	MFI	150
	P	4	2.0	122	TBI	86
	B	4	2.0	122	2V	N/A
	R, 2	4	2.5	151	TBI	92
	1	6	2.8	173	2V	107
	X	6	2.8	173	2V	112
	L	6	2.8 HO	173 HO	2V	125
	Z	6	2.8 HO	173 HO	2V	135
	A	6	3.8	231	2V	110
	T	6	4.3 D	262 D	MFI	85

4 ENGINE IDENTIFICATION

YEAR	CODE	CYL.	liters	cu. in.	Fuel System	HP
1984 Cont'd.	H	8	5.0	305	4V	145
	G	8	5.0 HO	305 HO	4V	190
	S	8	5.0	305	MFI	165
	N	8	5.7 D	350 D	MFI	105
1983	C	4	1.6	98	2V	65
	D	4	1.8 D	111 D	MFI	51
	0	4	1.8	112	TBI	84
	P	4	2.0	122	TBI	86
	B	4	2.0	122	2V	N/A
	R, 2	4	2.5	151	TBI	92
	5, F	4	2.5	151	2V	92
	1	6	2.8	173	2V	107
	X	6	2.8	173	2V	112
	L	6	2.8 HO	173 HO	2V	125
	Z	6	2.8 HO	173 HO	2V	135
	9	6	3.8	229	2V	110
	A	6	3.8	231	2V	110
	T	6	4.3 D	262 D	MFI	85
	H	8	5.0	305	4V	145
	7	8	5.0 HO	305 HO	4V	190
	S	8	5.0	305	TBI	165
	N	8	5.7 D	350 D	MFI	105

TBI — Throttle Body Injection. MFI — Multiport Fuel Injection.
2V — Two Venturi Carburetor. 4V — Four Venturi Carburetor.
D — Diesel. HO — High Output. T — Turbocharged.
† Engine horsepower varies with model installation.

UNDERHOOD SERVICE SPECIFICATIONS

PCTU1   PCTU1

CYLINDER NUMBERING SEQUENCE

4-CYL. FIRING ORDER: 1 3 4 2

Front of car

1988-92 1.6L LeMans | 1983-87 1.6L (98) | 1983-86 1.8L (112) OHC FI, 1987-91 2.0L (122) OHC | 1983-86 2.0L (122) ex. OHC | 1987-91 2.0L (122) ex. OHC, 2.2L Tempest Canada | 1992 2.0L Code H | 1988-92 2.3L Code D, 1989-92 2.3L Code A, 1992 2.3L Code 3

4-CYL. FIRING ORDER: 1 3 4 2

Front of car

1983-86 2.5L (151) FWD | 1987-91 2.5L (151) | 1983-86 Firebird 2.5L (151)

2.8L & 3.1L FIRING ORDER: 1 2 3 4 5 6

1987-89

1983-86 2.8L (173) ex. Firebird, 1985-89 2.8L (173) Fiero | 2.8L (173) ex. Firebird, Fiero, 1988-92 3.1L Code T FWD, 1990 3.1L Code V FWD, 1991-92 3.4L Code X | 1985-89 2.8L (173) Firebird, 1990-92 3.1L Code T Firebird

All Other V6 FIRING ORDER: 1 6 5 4 3 2

Front of car

 1985-88 3.0L (181) FI | 1992 3.3L Code N | 1983 3.8L (229) | 1983-87 3.8L (231) ex. FI | 1987-88 3.8L (231) FI Code C, 1992 3.8L Code L Some | 1988-90 3.8L (231) FI Code C, 1992 3.8L Code L Some | 1992 3.8L Code L Some, 3.8L Code 1 | 1985-87 4.3L (262) Gasoline

   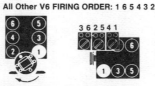

8-CYL. FIRING ORDER: 1 8 4 3 6 5 7 2

Front of car

1983-90 5.0L (307) | 1983-86 4.4L (267), 5.0L (305), 5.7L (350) Code L, 1987-91 5.7L Code 8 | 1987-92 5.0L (305) Codes E, F, 1992 5.7L (350) Code 8

UNDERHOOD SERVICE SPECIFICATIONS

PCTU2   **TIMING MARK**   PCTU2

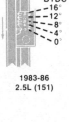
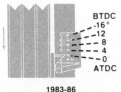
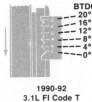
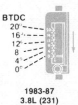
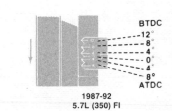

1983-87 1.6L (96)

1988-92 LeMans 1.6L Code 6

1983-86 1.8L (112) OHC

1983-86 2.0L (122), 1987 4.3L (262)

1987-91 2.0L (122) OHC

1992 2.0L Code H

1983-86 2.5L (151)

1983-86 2.8L (173) ex. Firebird, 1985-88 2.8L (173) Fiero

1983-89 2.8L (173) Firebird

1990-92 3.1L FI Code T RWD

1983-87 3.8L (231)

1985-86 4.3L (262), 1985-92 5.0L (305)

1983-84 3.8L (229), 4.4L (267), 5.0L (305)

1983-90 5.0L (307)

1987-92 5.7L (350) FI

ELECTRICAL AND IGNITION SYSTEMS

BATTERY

Engine	Year	STANDARD BCI Group No.	STANDARD Crank. Perf.	OPTIONAL BCI Group No.	OPTIONAL Crank. Perf.
1.6L (98) MT	1983-85	70	310	71	390
1.6L (98) AT	1983-85	70	355	71	390
1.6L (98) MT	1986	70	310	70	405
1.6L (98) AT	1986	70	355	70	405
1.6L (98) Canada	1986	70	405	—	—
1.6L (98) MT	1987	70	330	70	425
1.6L (98) AT	1987	70	385	70	425
1.6L LeMans	1988-91	85	550	—	—
1.8L (111) Diesel	1983-85	78	550	—	—
1.8L (112)	1983-85	75	500	73	465
2.0L (122)	1983-85	70	405	75	500
Canada	1983-85	75	500	—	—
2.0L (122) Sunbird	1986-91	75	630	—	—
Canada	1986	75	500	75	630
2.0L (122) Tempest: MT	1988-89	70	525	75	630
AT	1988-89	75	630	—	—
2.2L Tempest: MT	1990-91	75	525	75	570
AT	1990-91	75	570	—	—
2.3L (138)	1988-92	75	630	—	—
2.5L (151)	1983-85	70	405	75	630
Grand Am	1985	75	630	—	—
2.5L (151)	1986-91	75	630	—	—
2.8L (173) 2V	1983-85	70	315	75	500
2.8L (173) FI	1985	75	500	75	630
2.8L (173) 2V	1986	70	405	75	500
Canada	1986	75	630	—	—
2.8L (173)					
FI ex. Firebird	1986	75	500	75	630
FI Firebird	1986	70	525	75	570
2.8L (173)	1987	75	525	75	570

BATTERY Continued

Engine	Year	STANDARD BCI Group No.	STANDARD Crank. Perf.	OPTIONAL BCI Group No.	OPTIONAL Crank. Perf.
2.8L (173) 6000	1988-89	75	525	75	570
Fiero, Tempest	1988-89	75	525	75	630
Grand Prix	1988-89	75	525	—	—
Canada	1988-89	75	630	—	—
3.0L (181)	1985-87	75	630	—	—
3.1L Grand Prix	1991-92	75	525	—	—
Firebird	1991-92	75	525	—	—
Tempest	1991	75	525	75	630
6000	1991	75	525	75	570
3.3L	1992	75	630	—	—
3.4L DOHC	1991-92	75	630	—	—
3.8L (231) Others	1983-84	70	315	78	550
3.8L (231) Parisienne	1984	70	355	75	500
3.8L (231)	1985	71	390	75	500
3.8L (231)	1986	75	500	75	630
3.8L (231) Bonneville	1987	75	630	78	730
Grand Prix, 6000	1987	75	525	75	630
3.8L (231)	1988-92	75	630	78	730
4.3L (262) Gasoline	1985-87	75	630	—	—
4.3L (262) Diesel	1983	75	500	—	—
4.3L (262) Diesel	1984-85	78	770	76	1075
5.0L (305) Firebird	1983	70	405	75	500
5.0L (305) Others	1983	70	355	78	550
5.0L (305) Firebird	1984	75	500	75	630
5.0L (305) Others	1984	75	500	78	550
5.0L (305)	1985	75	500	75	630
5.0L (305)	1986	70	525	75	570
5.0L (305)	1987-89	70	525	75	570
5.0L: MT	1990-91	75	525	75	570
AT	1990-91	75	570	—	—
5.0L	1992	75	525	75	570
5.0L (307)	1986-89	70	525	75	570
5.7L (350) Diesel	1983	78	550	—	—

UNDERHOOD SERVICE SPECIFICATIONS

BATTERY Continued

Engine	Year	STANDARD BCI Group No.	STANDARD Crank. Perf.	OPTIONAL BCI Group No.	OPTIONAL Crank. Perf.
5.7L (350) Diesel Parisienne	1984-85	70	405	78	550
5.7L (350) Others	1984	78	550	—	—
5.7L (350)	1987-92	75	630	—	—

ALTERNATOR

See UNDERHOOD SERVICE INSTRUCTIONS at the beginning of this section for test/adjustment diagrams.

Application	Rated Output (amps)	Test Output (amps)	Field Current Draw (amps)
1983	42, 55, 56, 63, 78, 85	†	4-5
1984	42, 56, 66, 70, 78, 85, 94, 97	†	4-5
1985	42, 56, 66, 78, 94, 97, 108, 120	†	4-5
1986-87	56, 66, 78, 94, 97	†	4-5
1986-87	85, 105, 108, 120	△	5.5-7.0
1988	78, 94	†	4-5
1988-92	74, 80, 85, 100, 105, 108, 120	△	—

† Increase engine speed until maximum alternator output is obtained (approximately 2000 rpm); output must be within 10 amps of rated output.
△ Output at 2000 rpm must be within 15 amps of rated output.

REGULATOR

Application	Test Temp. (deg. F/C)	Voltage Setting
1983-84	Warm	12.5-15.4
1985-92	Warm	13.5-16.0

STARTER

Engine	Year	Cranking Speed† (min. volts)	Ampere Draw @ Cranking Speed
All	1983-90	9.0	—

† At 70°F (24°C) or higher.

SPARK PLUGS

Engine	Year	Gap (inches)	Gap (mm)	Torque (ft-lb)
4-cyl.				
1.6L (98) LeMans	1988-89	.060*	1.52*	7-15
1.6L LeMans	1990-92	.045	1.14	7-15
2.0L OHC ex. Turbo	1988	.060	1.52	7-15
2.0L OHC ex. Turbo	1989-92	.045	1.14	7-15
2.3L	1988-92	.035	.89	17
2.5L (151)	1983-91	.060	1.52	7-15
All Others	1983-90	.035	.89	7-15
6-cyl.				
2.8L (173)	1983-89	.045	1.14	7-15
3.0L (181)	1985	.040	1.02	20
3.0L (181)	1986-87	.045	1.14	20
3.1L, 3.4L	1988-92	.045	1.14	11
3.3L	1992	.060	1.52	11
3.8L (231)	1983	.080	2.03	7-15
3.8L (231) 2V	1984-88	.060	1.52	7-15
3.8L (231) FI Code 3	1987-88	.045	1.14	20
3.8L (231) Code C, L	1988-91	.060	1.52	20
3.8L	1992	.060	1.52	11
4.3L (262)	1985-87	.035	.89	7-15
8-cyl.				
5.0L (305)	1983	.045	1.14	7-15
5.0L (305)	1984-85	.045	1.14	7-15
HO or FI	1984-85	.035	.89	7-15
Canada	1984-85	.045	1.14	7-15
5.0L (305)	1986-91	.035	.89	22
5.0L	1992	.035	.89	11
5.0L (307)	1986-89	.060	1.52	20

SPARK PLUGS Continued

Engine	Year	Gap (inches)	Gap (mm)	Torque (ft-lb)
5.7L (350)	1987-91	.035	.89	20
5.7L	1992	.035	.89	11

* When AC R45XLS or equivalent plugs are used, .045 inch (1.14 mm).

IGNITION COIL

See UNDERHOOD SERVICE INSTRUCTIONS at the beginning of this section for test/adjustment diagrams.

Application	Year	Resistance (ohms) Primary●	Resistance (ohms) Secondary■
All w/distributor	1983-91	0-2	6,000-30,000
3.0L, 3.8L: Type I coils*	1986-92	.5-1.0	10,000-13,000
Type II coils*	1986-88	—	5,000-10,000
Type II coils*	1992	.3-.5	5,000-7,000
3.3L	1992	.5-.9	5,000-8,000
2.0L, 2.5L, 2.8L, 3.1L	1987-90	—	5,000-10,000
2.3L	1988-92	—	20,000 max.

* Type I coils, 3 coil towers on each side of coil pack.
Type II coils, 6 coil towers on one side of coil pack.
● Without distributor, measured between the two coil primary power wires on each coil.
■ Without distributor, measured across each coils two towers with spark plug wires removed.

DISTRIBUTOR PICKUP

See UNDERHOOD SERVICE INSTRUCTIONS at the beginning of this section for test/adjustment diagrams.

Engine	Year	Resistance (ohms)	Air Gap (in./mm)
All w/distributor	1983-92	500-1500	—

BASE TIMING

See UNDERHOOD SERVICE INSTRUCTIONS at the beginning of this section for test/adjustment diagrams.

Set timing at slow idle and Before Top Dead Center, unless otherwise specified.

Disconnect and plug distributor vacuum hose at distributor.

1983-88 1.8L (112) FI, 2.0L (122) OHC, 2.5L (151) FI, 3.8L (229), ground diagnostic test terminal under dash.

1983-86 2.0L (122) FI, 2.8L (173) FI, 5.0L (305) CFI, disconnect bypass connector (tan/black wire).

1987-92 All FI w/distributors, disconnect timing bypass connector, single lead in every harness between distributor and ECM.

1983-89 Others, carburetted, disconnect 4-wire connector at distributor.

Timing MUST be set to specifications on emission label if different from setting listed. If "Check Engine" light comes on during procedure, remove ECM fuse to clear.

Engine	Year	Man. Trans. (degrees) @ RPM	Auto. Trans. (degrees) @ RPM
1.6L (98)	1983	6	6
5-speed	1983	8	—
Canada	1983	6	10
1.6L (98)	1984-87	8	8
Canada	1984-87	8	12
w/leaded fuel	1984-86	4	—
1.6L LeMans	1988-90	10	10 N
1.8L (112)	1983-85	8	8 D
2.0L (122)	1983	0	0
Canada	1983	0 @ 850	0 @ 850 P
w/decal DBB	1983	—	2 @ 850 P
2.0L (122)	1984-86	6	6 D
Canada	1984	4 @ 850	0 @ 850 P
2.0L (121) OHC	1987-89	8	8 D
2.5L (151)	1983-86	8	8 D
Canada, all	1983	10	8 @ 750 D
2.8L (173) 2V & FI	1983-86	10	10 D
High Output 2V	1983-84	10	10
Canada Firebird	1983	10	16
Canada	1983-84	6 @ 650	10 @ 750 P
Wagons	1984	—	6 @ 750 P
Canada	1985-86	6 @ 650	6 @ 750 P
4-speed AT	1985-86	—	10 @ 750 P

UNDERHOOD SERVICE SPECIFICATIONS

PCTU4   PCTU4

BASE TIMING Continued

Engine	Year	Man. Trans. (degrees) @ RPM	Auto. Trans. (degrees) @ RPM
2.8L (173) Firebird, Fiero	1987-89	10	10 D
3.1L Firebird	1990-92	10	10 D
3.8L (231)	1983-86	—	15 D
3.8L (229)	1983	—	0 @ 1200 P
4.3L (262) Gasoline	1985-87	—	0 D
5.0L (305)	1983-84	6	6
5.0L (305)	1985-87	0	0
High Output & FI	1985-87	6	6
Canada	1983-87	4 @ 500	4 @ 500 D
5.0L TBI	1988-92	0	0 D
5.0L MFI	1988-92	6	6 D
5.0L (307)	1986-89	—	20 @ 1100 P
Canada	1987	—	8 @ 1500 P
5.7L (350) Police	1985	—	6
5.7L (350)	1987-92	—	6 D

DISTRIBUTOR TIMING ADVANCE

Engine degrees at engine rpm, no load, in addition to basic timing setting.
Mechanical advance distributors only.

Engine	Trans-mission	Year	Distributor Number	Degrees @ 2500 RPM Total	Degrees @ 2500 RPM Centrifugal
1.6L (98)	MT & AT	1983-84	1103504	24.3-32.3	6.3-10.3
1.6L (98)	MT & AT	1983-84	1103510, 65, 66	24.3-32.3	2.3-6.3
1.6L (98)	MT & AT	1983-84	1103511	24.3-32.3	6.3-10.3
1.6L (98)	MT & AT	1985-87	1103615, 16	24.3-32.3	6.3-10.3
1.6L (98)	MT	1985-87	1103613	24.2-36.2	6.2-10.2
1.6L (98)	MT	1985-87	1103614	25.3-33.3	2.3-6.3
2.0L (122)	MT & AT	1983-84	1103535, 48, 92	32.9-40.9	10.9-14.9
2.5L (151)	MT	1983	1103471	30.5-40.5	8.5-14.5
2.5L (151)	AT	1983	1103528	27.8-35.8	9.8-13.8
2.5L (151)	AT	1983	1103545	22.8-30.8	4.8-8.8
2.8L (173)	MT & AT	1983-84	1103523	34.9-42.9	12.9-16.9
2.8L (173)	AT	1983	1103522	27.2-35.2	5.2-9.2
2.8L (173)	MT	1983-84	1103525	35-43	17-21
2.8L (173)	AT	1984	1103586	25-33	17-21
2.8L (173)	MT	1985	1103617	45-53	17-21
2.8L (173)	AT	1985-86	1103618	41.9-49.9	12.9-16.9
2.8L (173)	AT	1985-86	1103619	35-43	17-21
3.8L (231)	AT	1983-84	1110766	31.0-37.8	9.0-11.8
3.8L (231)	AT	1985-87	1103612	20.3-28.3	2.3-6.3
5.0L (305)	MT & AT	1983-87	1103282	29.8-37.8	11.8-15.8
5.0L (307)	AT	1986	1103602	23-27	9-11
5.0L (307)	AT	1987	1103718	41.2-49.2	19.2-23.2

FUEL SYSTEM

FUEL SYSTEM PRESSURE

See UNDERHOOD SERVICE INSTRUCTIONS at the beginning of this section for test/adjustment diagrams.

Carburetted models, pinch off fuel return hose.

All models with TBI, pressure measured at fuel inlet of TBI unit.

All models with MFI, pressure measured at fuel rail.

All ex. Gasoline MFI

Engine	Year	PSI	RPM
4-cyl.			
1.6L (98)	1983-84	2.5-6.5	idle
1.6L (98)	1985-87	5.5-6.5	idle
1.6L (98)	1988-92	9.0-13	idle
		13 min.†	idle
1.8L (112) 2V, 2.0L (122) 2V	1983-84	4.5 min.	idle
1.8L (112) FI	1983-86	9.0-13.0	ign. on
2.0L (122) FI	1983-89	9.0-13.0	ign. on
		13 min †	idle
2.5L (151) 2V	1983	6.5-8.0	idle
2.5L (151) FI	1983-91	9.0-13.0	idle
		13 min.†	idle

FUEL SYSTEM PRESSURE Continued

All ex. Gasoline MFI

Engine	Year	PSI	RPM
6-cyl.			
2.8L (173)	1983	6.0-7.5	idle
2.8L (173) 2V	1984-86	5.5-6.5	idle
3.8L (231) 2V, 4.1L (252)	1983-87	5.5-6.5	idle
4.3L (262) Gas	1985-87	9.0-13.0	idle
4.3L (262) Diesel	1983-85	5.5-6.5	idle
8-cyl.			
4.3L (262) Diesel	1983-84	5.8-8.7	idle
5.0L (305) 4V	1983-87	5.5-6.5	idle
5.0L (305) FI	1983-84	9.0-13.0	idle
5.0L (305) TBI	1988-92	9.0-13.0	idle
		13 min.†	idle
5.0L (307)	1986-89	5.5-6.5	idle
5.7L (350) Diesel	1983-85	5.5-6.5	idle

Gasoline MFI

Engine	Year	Pressure (PSI) Ign. On	Pressure (PSI) Idle	Fuel Pump†
1.8L (112) Turbo	1984-86	30-40	24-37	60 min.
2.0L	1992	40-47	31-44	47 min.
2.0L (122) Turbo	1987-90	35-38	25-30	65 min.
2.3L (138)	1988-92	40.5-47	30.5-44	47 min.
2.8L (173), 3.1L	1985-91	40.5-47	30.5-44	47 min.
3.0L (181)	1985-86	37-43	31-40	75 min.
3.0L (181)	1987	34-43	29-34	75 min.
3.1L, 3.4L	1989-92	40-47	31-44	47 min.
3.3L	1992	40-47	31-44	47 min.
3.8L (231)	1986	34-43	24-37	75 min.
3.8L (231)	1987	34-43	29-34	75 min.
3.8L (231) Code 3	1988	34-40	25-35	75 min.
3.8L (231) Code C	1988-89	40-47	37-43	75 min.
3.8L	1990-92	40-47	31-44	47 min.
5.0L (305), 5.7L (350)	1985-92	40.5-47	30.5-44	47 min.

† With fuel return line briefly restricted.

IDLE SPEED W/O COMPUTER CONTROL

1983-85 Diesel Engine: Start engine and allow it to warm up to operating temperature. Connect tachometer following manufacturer's instructions. Adjust screw on injection pump to obtain specified low idle.

1.8L (111) Engine: Apply vacuum to fast idle actuator and adjust knurled nut to specification.

5.7L (350) Engine: Turn ignition off and then attach jumper wire across fast idle switch connector terminals. Turn ignition on and adjust idle solenoid (energized) to obtain specified fast idle.

All others: Make all adjustments with engine at operating temperature, choke fully open, and electric cooling fan off (if equipped). Engines with idle speed control, idle adjustments not recommended during tune-up.

Engines with C-4 system, connect dwell meter to carburetor fuel valve lead and ground. Set meter to 6-cylinder scale. When needle begins to vary engine is in closed loop mode and is ready to adjust.

All engines, disconnect and plug canister purge vacuum hose.

Adjust idle solenoid screw, plunger fully extended, or carburetor idle speed screw to specification. If equipped with idle stop solenoid, disconnect the electrical or vacuum lead and adjust carburetor body screw to specification.

Engines equipped with speed-up solenoid, turn A/C on and disconnect compressor clutch wire or apply battery voltage to solenoid. Adjust solenoid to specification with plunger fully extended.

To set fast idle, disconnect and plug EGR and distributor vacuum hoses (as equipped). Set choke cam on specified step and adjust engine speed to specification.

Engine	Year	SLOW Man. Trans.	SLOW Auto. Trans.	FAST Man. Trans.	FAST Auto. Trans.	Step of Cam
1.6L (98)	1983	800	700 D	2500	2500 P	High
solenoid	1983	1150	875 D			
5-speed	1983	950	—	2500	—	High
solenoid	1983	1150				
Canada	1983	700	700 D	2500	2500 P	High
1.6L (98) ex. 5-speed	1984-87	800	700 D	2500	2500 P	High
solenoid	1984-87	1250	875 D			
Canada	1984-87	700	700 D	2700	2800 P	High
w/leaded fuel	1984-85	850	—	2300		High

PONTIAC
1983-92 All Models Except Firefly, Sunburst, Trans Sport

UNDERHOOD SERVICE SPECIFICATIONS

IDLE SPEED W/O COMPUTER CONTROL Continued

Engine	Year	SLOW Man. Trans.	SLOW Auto. Trans.	FAST Man. Trans.	FAST Auto. Trans.	Step of Cam
1.6L (98) 5-speed	1984-85	1000	—	2500	—	High
solenoid	1984-85	1250	—			
Canada	1984-85	1000	—	2500	—	High
solenoid	1984-85	1000	—			
1.6L (98) 5-speed	1986-87	900	—	2500	—	High
solenoid	1986-87	1250	—			
Canada	1986-87	900	—	2700	—	High
solenoid	1986-87	1000	—			
1.8L (111) Diesel	1983-86	625	725 N	950	950 P	
2.0L (122) Canada	1983	900	900 D	2400	2600 P	High
base idle	1983	850	800 N			
speed-up	1983	1150	1250 D			
w/decal DXD	1983	—	900 D	—	3000 P	High
base idle	1983	—	850 N			
speed-up	1983	—	1250 D			
2.0L (112) Canada	1984	900	800 D	3000	3000 P	High
base idle	1984	850	750 N			
speed-up	1984	1150	1250 D			
w/AC	1984	—	900 D			
base idle	1984	—	850 N			
speed-up	1984	—	1250 D			
2.5L (151) Canada	1983	750	750 D	2600	2600 P	High
base idle	1983	700	700 D			
speed-up	1983	1000	900 D			
w/AC	1983	—	800 D	—	2600 P	High
base idle	1983	—	750 D			
speed-up	1983	—	900 D			
2.8L (173) Phoenix, 6000						
U.S. ex. 5-speed	1983	775	600 D	2500	2500 P	High
solenoid	1983	1100	750 D			
5-speed	1983	800	—	2600	—	High
solenoid	1983	1000	—			
Canada	1983	700	700 D	2000	2000 P	High
solenoid	1983	1050	900 D			
2.8L (173) Firebird	1983	800	600 D	2600	2600 P	High
solenoid	1983	1000	750 D			
Canada	1983	700	700 D	2000	2000 P	High
solenoid	1983	1200	950 D			
2.8L (173) HO	1983	800	725 D	2600	2700 P	High
solenoid	1983	1100	850 D			
2.8L (173) Phoenix, 6000						
U.S.	1984	800	600 D	2500	2500 P	High
solenoid	1984	1100	750 D			
Canada	1984	700	700 D	2000	2000 P	High
solenoid	1984	1200	900 D			
2.8L (173) Firebird	1984	800	600 D	2600	2500 P	High
solenoid	1984	1100	750 D			
Canada	1984	700	700 D	2000	2000 P	High
solenoid	1984	1200	920 D			
2.8L (173) HO	1984	800	725 D	2600	2700 P	High
solenoid	1984	1100	850 P			
2.8L (173) 2V U.S.	1985-86	—	600 D	—	2500 P	High
solenoid	1985-86	—	750 D			
Canada	1985-86	—	700 D	—	2700 P	High
solenoid	1985-86	—	900 D			
3.8L (231) Canada	1983-86	—	550 D	—	2000 P	High
solenoid	1983-85	—	670 D			
	1986	—	750 D			
3.8L (231) 2V Canada	1987	—	550 D	—	2200 P	High
solenoid	1987	—	750 D			
4.3L (262) Diesel	1983-85	—	675 D	—	775 D	—
5.0L (305) 4V ex. HO	1983-87	700	500 D	1800	2200 P	High
	1983-87	800	650 D			
Canada ex. Firebird	1983-87	—	500 D	—	1850 P	High
solenoid	1983-84	—	600 D			
solenoid	1985-87	—	650 D			
Canada Firebird	1983-87	650	550 D	1500	1850 P	High
solenoid	1983-87	750	650 D			
5.0L (305) 4V HO	1983-86	700	600 D	1800	2200 P	High
	1983-86	800	650 D			
5.7L (350) Diesel	1983-85	—	600 D	—	750 D	—
5.7L (350) Police	1985	—	500 D	—	2200 P	High
solenoid	1985	—	650 D			
Canada	1985	—	600 D	—	1850 P	High
solenoid	1985	—	650 D			

IDLE SPEED W/COMPUTER CONTROL

See UNDERHOOD SERVICE INSTRUCTIONS at the beginning of this section for test/adjustment diagrams.

Midpoint of range given is the preferred setting speed.

If no specifications are listed under "Minimum Speed", the idle is not adjustable.

1983-86 All w/single TBI: Gain access to throttle stop screw. With engine at operating temperature, disconnect idle air controller and install special tool to seal idle air passage of throttle body. Turn throttle stop screw to specified minimum speed value.

All w/dual TBI: Disconnect IAC electrical lead. Start engine and let idle speed stabilize. Remove cap on rear TBI unit and connect a water manometer. Adjust minimum speed to achieve 6″ of water on scale in drive. Reinstall cap on rear unit and remove cap on front TBI unit. If reading is not 6″ of water, adjust balance screw on linkage. Disconnect manometer and set minimum speed on rear TBI unit to specified value.

1983-86 All w/FI except TBI; 1987-92 All w/FI & TBI when specifications are listed in Minimum Speed column: 1.8L (112) Turbo, disconnect PCV valve hose and allow engine to draw air for two minutes. Disconnect IAC electrical lead and set minimum speed to specifications. All others, ground diagnostic lead and turn ignition on for 30 seconds. Remove IAC lead and remove ground from diagnostic connector. Start engine and set minimum speed to specified value.

All carburetted w/ISC: With engine at operating temperature, turn ignition off and disconnect harness from ISC. Apply 12 volts (+) to third terminal from top of ISC (C), and ground the fourth terminal from top (D) only long enough to retract ISC plunger. With engine running, set minimum idle to specifications by adjusting carb base screw. Apply 12 volts (+) to fourth terminal from top of ISC (D) and ground the third terminal from the top (C) only long enough to fully extend the ISC plunger. Set maximum speed to specifications by turning ISC plunger head.

NOTE: Never apply voltage to first two upper terminals (A & B) or damage to the unit will result.

All carburetted w/ILC: Disconnect and plug vacuum hoses at EGR and canister purge valves. With engine at operating temperature, remove vacuum hose from ILC and plug. Set maximum speed to specifications by holding hex nut and turning plunger shaft. Reconnect ILC vacuum hose and check that minimum speed is correct. To adjust, remove rubber and metal plugs from rear center outlet tube, insert a $3/32″$ Allen wrench. Remove ILC hose and plug. Connect a remote vacuum source and apply vacuum to the unit. Adjust carb base screw to obtain minimum speed.

ALL FUEL INJECTED

Engine	Year	Minimum Speed Man. Trans.	Minimum Speed Auto. Trans.	Checking Speed Man. Trans.	Checking Speed Auto. Trans.
1.6L (98)	1988-92	550-650	450-550 N	900 max.	900 N max.
1.8L (112) incl. Turbo	1983-84	775-825	675-725 N	—	—
1.8L (112) incl. Turbo	1985	775-825	675-725 N	900-1000	675-775 D
1.8L (112) incl. Turbo	1986	775-825	675-725 N	900-1000	775-875 D
2.0L (122) ex. OHC	1983-86	625-675	625-675 D	—	—
2.0L (122) ex. OHC	1988-89	450-650	450-650 N	—	—
2.0L (122) OHC	1987-90	450-600	450-600 N	800 max.	800 N max.
2.0L (122) OHC Turbo	1987-90	550-650	550-650 N	—	—
2.0L	1992	—	—	800-950	775-925 N
2.2L	1990-91	450-650	450-650 N	—	—
2.5L (151)	1983-84	750-800	475-525 N	—	—
2.5L (151)	1985	750-800	475-525 N	900-1000	675-775 D
2.5L (151)	1986	750-800	475-525 N	850-950	750-850 D
2.5L (151)	1987-91	550-650	550-650 N	750-850	750-850 N
2.8L (173)	1985-86	600-700	500-600 D	—	—
2.8L (173) Fiero	1985-86	600-700	500-600 D	860-940	760-840 D
2.8L (173)†	1987	625-725	500-600 D	—	—
Firebird	1987	600-700	500-600 D	—	—
2.8L (173), 3.1L††	1987-89	—	—	750-950	650-750 D
Firebird	1988-89	600-700	500-600 D	—	—
3.0L (181), 3.8L (231) Code 3	1985-88	—	450-550 D	—	—
3.1L MFI	1990-91	—	—	800 max.	800 N max.
3.1L MFI FWD	1992	—	—	800-900	700-800 N
3.1L Firebird	1992	—	—	800 max.	800 N max.
3.3L	1992	—	—	—	650-750 N
3.4L	1991-92	—	—	600-700	600-700 D
3.8L Code C	1988-89	—	—	—	650-750 N
3.8L	1990-91	—	—	—	650-850 N
3.8L	1992	—	—	—	600-750 N
4.3L (262)	1985-86	—	500-600 D	—	—
5.0L (305)	1983-84	—	475 D	—	—
5.0L (305)	1985	—	450-550 D	—	—
5.0L (305) MFI	1986	—	400 D	—	—
5.0L (305) MFI	1987-88	400	400 N	—	—
5.0L MFI	1989	400-450	400-450 N	—	—
5.0L MFI	1990-92	—	—	600-800	600-800 N

UNDERHOOD SERVICE SPECIFICATIONS

PCTU6   PCTU6

IDLE SPEED W/COMPUTER CONTROL Continued

ALL FUEL INJECTED

Engine	Year	Minimum Speed Man. Trans.	Minimum Speed Auto. Trans.	Checking Speed Man. Trans.	Checking Speed Auto. Trans.
5.0L (305) TBI	1988-89	400-450	400-450 N	—	—
5.0L TBI	1990-92	—	—	550-750	500-600 D
5.7L (350)	1987-88	—	450 N	—	—
5.7L	1989	—	400-450 N	—	—
5.7L	1990-92	—	—	—	600-800 N

† Mass airflow system.
†† Speed density system.

ALL CARBURETTED

Engine	Year	Trans.	Min. Speed	Max. Speed	Fast	Step of Cam
3.8L (229)	1983	AT	475 D	750 D	2200 P	High
w/AC	1983	AT	475 D	800 D	2200 P	High
3.8L (231)	1983	AT	450 D	900 D	2200 P	High
3.8L (231)	1984-86	AT	450 D	1000 D	2200 P	High
5.0L (307)	1986-89	AT	450 D	700 D	550 D	Low
base idle	1986-89	AT	450 D			

ENGINE MECHANICAL

TIGHTENING TORQUES

See UNDERHOOD SERVICE INSTRUCTIONS at the beginning of this section for test/adjustment diagrams.

Some fasteners are tightened in more than one step.

Some values are specified in inches.

Engine	Year	Cylinder Head	Intake Manifold	Exhaust Manifold	Crankshaft Pulley	Water Pump
1.6L (98)	1983-87	75/100	18/24	18/24	100/135	15/20
1.6L LeMans	1988-91	18/25, +60°, +60°, +60°, plus 30°-50° eng. warm	16/22	10/13	40/55	6/8
1.8L (111) Diesel	1983-86	21-36/ 28-48, 90-105/ 122-142	30/40	—	—	15/20
1.8L (112) OHC	1983-86	18/25, +60°, +60°, +60°, plus 30°-50° eng. warm	25/34	16/22	20/27	19/25
1.8L (112) 2V, 2.0L (122)	1983-84	65-75/ 88-107	20-25/ 27-34	22-28/ 30-38	66-85/ 90-115	12-21/ 16-28
2.0L (122)	1985-86	65-75/ 88-107	18-25/ 24-34	34-44/ 46-60	66-89/ 90-120	12-21/ 16-28
2.0L (122) ex. OHC	1987-89	73-83/ 99-113⊙ 62-70/ 85-95◆	15-22/ 20-30	6-13/ 8-18	66-89/ 90-120	15-22/ 20-30
2.0L (122) OHC ex. LeMans	1987-92	18/25, +60°, +60°, +60°, plus 30°-50° eng. warm	16/22	16/22	20/27	18/25
2.0L LeMans	1988-90	18/25, +60°, +60°, +60°, plus 30°-50° eng. warm	16/22	16/22	20/27	18/25
2.2L	1990-91	41/55, +45°, +45°, +20°⊙; +10°◆	18/25	88″/13, studs 10/13, nuts	85/115	18/25
2.3L	1987-91	26/35, +90°	18/25	27/37	74/100, +90°	10/12, cover 19/26, others

TIGHTENING TORQUES Continued

Engine	Year	Cylinder Head	Intake Manifold	Exhaust Manifold	Crankshaft Pulley	Water Pump
2.3L	1992	▄▄	18/25	31/42	74/100, +90°	10/12, cover 19/26, others
2.5L (151)	1983	85/115	29/40	44/60	200/260	25/34
2.5L (151)	1984	92/125	29/40	44/60	200/260	25/34
2.5L (151)	1985-86	18/25, 22/30‡	25/34	25/43* 37-50**	162/220	25/34
2.5L	1987-91	18/25, 26/35•, +90°	25/34	25/43* 37-50**	162/220	25/34
2.8L (173)	1983-86	70/95	20-25/ 27-34	22-28/ 30-38	66-84/ 90-115	8/10, M6 15/22, M8 25/34, M10
2.8L, 3.1L MFI ex. Firebird	1987-92	33/45, +90°	15/20, 24/33	15-22/ 20-30	76/103	7/10, short 18/24, long
2.8L, 3.1L Firebird	1987-89	33/45, +90°	13-18/ 18-24	25/34	66-84/ 90-115	15/21, short 27/37, long
3.1L Firebird	1990-92	40/55, +90°	15/21■ 19/26□	25/34	70/95	88″/10, small 15/21, med. 25/34, large
3.0L (181) FI	1985-88	25/34, +90°, +90°†	32/44	37/50	200/270	8/11
3.3L	1992	35/47, +130°☆	88″/10, upper 22/30, lower	38/52	110/150, +76°	90″/19, short 22/30, long
3.8L (229)	1983	65/88	30/40	20/27	60/81	30/40
3.8L (231), 4.1L (252)	1983-84	80/108, after 15 minutes, 80/108	45/61	25/34	225/306	7/10
3.8L (231)	1985	72/98	35/47	20/27	200/270	7/10
3.8L (231) 2V	1986	25/34, +90°, +90°†	45/66	20/27	200/270	19/26
3.8L (231) 2V	1987	25/34, +90°, +90°†	32/44	37/50	219/297	10/13
3.8L (231) Code B.3	1988	25/34, +90°, +90°†	32/44	37/50	200/270	8/11
3.8L (231) Code C	1988	25/34, +90°, +90°†	88″/10	41/55	219/297	84″/10
3.8L	1989-92	35/47, +130°☆	88″/10, lower 19/26, upper	41/55	219/297††	84″/10◆ 29/39⊙
4.3L (262), 5.0L (305), 5.7L (350)	1985-88	60-75/ 81-102	25-45/ 34-61	20-32/ 27-43*, 14-26/ 19-35**	65-75/ 87-102	25-35/ 34-47
4.3L, 5.0L, 5.7L	1989-92	68/93	35/47	20/27* 26/35**	70/95	30/40
4.3L (262) Diesel	1983-85	142/193★	41/55	28/39	200-350/ 275-475	13/18, short 21/28, long
5.0L (305), 5.7L (350)	1983-84	65/88	30/40	20/27	60/81	30/40
5.0L (307)	1983-86	60/81, 125/169	40/54	25/34	200-310/ 270-400	13/18
5.0L (307)	1987-88	90/122, 130/176	40/54	25/34	200-310/ 270-400	7/10
5.0L (307)	1989	40/54, +95°, first and last bolts on exhaust manifold side +120°, all others	40/54	25/34	200-310/ 270-400	11/14
5.7L (350) Diesel	1983-85	100/136, 130/176	40/54	25/34	200-310/ 270-400	13/18

UNDERHOOD SERVICE SPECIFICATIONS

PCTU7   PCTU7

TIGHTENING TORQUES Continued

† To 60/81 maximum.
†† 1991-92, 110/150 +76°.
* Four outer bolts.
** Three inner bolts.
‡ Turn last bolt on left (number nine) to 29/40. Then turn all except number nine 120°, turn number nine 90°.
★ Eight central bolts, three upper and lower, 59/80.
☆ Turn four inner bolts an additional 30°.
⊙ Long bolts.
♦ Short bolts.
● Turn last bolt on left (number nine) to 18/25.
■ Center two.
■■ Tighten six center bolts to 26/35. Tighten two bolts at front of head to 15/20. Tighten two bolts at rear of head to 22/30. Turn all bolts 90°. Back off all bolts one turn and repeat procedure.
□ Others.

VALVE CLEARANCE
Engine cold unless otherwise specified.

Engine	Year	Intake (inches)	Intake (mm)	Exhaust (inches)	Exhaust (mm)
1.8L (111) Diesel	1983-86	.010	.25	.014	.35

COMPRESSION PRESSURE
At cranking speed or specified rpm, engine temperature normalized, throttle open.

Engine	Year	PSI	Maximum Variation PSI
1.8L (111) Diesel	1983-86	370-441 @ 200 rpm	—
6-cyl., V8 Diesel	1983	275 min.	†
6-cyl., V8 Diesel	1984-85	300 min.	*
All Gasoline	1983-92	100 min.	†

† Lowest cylinder pressure must be more than 70% of highest cylinder pressure.
* Lowest cylinder pressure must be 80% of highest cylinder pressure at 200 rpm min.

BELT TENSION
All Except With Automatic Tensioner

A belt is considered used after one engine revolution.
Use a strand tension gauge. Measurements are in pounds.

Engine	Year	Alternator	Power Steering	Air Cond.	Air Pump
Used Belts					
1.6L	1983-87	70	70	90	—
1.6L	1988-90	77	—	80	—
1.6L	1991-92	71	—	80-100	—
1.8L	1983-86	75	100	75	—
1.8L Turbo	1984-86	100	100	80	—
2.0L	1983-86	75	70	100	—
2.0L OHC	1987	75	100	75	—
2.0L OHC	1988-89	—	—	80	—
2.0L OHC Turbo	1987-89	—	—	115	—
2.0L OHC	1990-92	—	—	112-124	—
2.3L	1988-91	—	110	—	—
2.5L Code R	1983-86	75	70	75	—
2.5L Code U	1985-87	90	110	90	—
2.5L Code U	1988-91	90	90	90	—
2.8L 2V	1983-86	70	70	70	45
2.8L FI	1985-86	210	205	165	—
2.8L FI Fiero	1987-88	70	70	70	50
3.8L 2V	1983-87	70	80	80	45
4.3L Diesel	1983-85	—	—	—	45
4.3L Gas	1985-87	70	70	70	90
5.0L (305) 4V	1983-87	70	70	90	70
5.0L (305) FI	1985-87	90	70	90	70
5.0L (307), 5.7L Diesel	1985-88	80	90	90	45
Cogged or 3/8″ belt	1985-88	55	—	—	70
5.7L Diesel	1983-84	80	90	90	45
Cogged belt	1983-84	55	—	—	—
New Belts					
1.6L	1983-87	145	145	165	—
1.6L	1988-90	90	—	155	—
1.6L	1991-92	90	—	80-100	—
1.8L	1983-86	145	165	155	—

BELT TENSION Continued

Engine	Year	Alternator	Power Steering	Air Cond.	Air Pump
1.8L Turbo	1984-86	165	165	155	—
2.0L	1983-86	145	145	165	—
2.0L OHC	1987	145	165	155	—
2.0L OHC	1988-89	—	—	155	—
2.0L OHC Turbo	1987-89	—	—	225	—
2.0L OHC	1990-92	—	—	225-236	—
2.3L	1988-91	—	110	—	—
2.5L Code R	1983-86	145	145	165	—
2.5L Code U	1985-91	165	180	165	—
2.8L 2V	1983-86	145	135	145	100
2.8L FI	1985-86	150	150	110	—
2.8L FI Fiero	1987-88	145	135	145	100
3.8L 2V	1983-87	125	135	135	80
4.3L Diesel	1983-85	—	—	—	75
4.3L Gas	1985-87	145	145	165	145
5.0L (305) 4V	1983-87	145	145	165	145
5.0L (305) FI	1985-87	135	145	165	145
5.0L (307), 5.7L Diesel	1985-88	160	170	170	80
Cogged or 3/8″ belt	1985-88	145	—	—	145
5.7L Diesel	1983-84	160	170	170	80
Cogged belt	1983-84	145	—	—	—

All With Automatic Tensioner

If index marks on tensioner are outside the range, replace the belt. If marks are within range and belt tension is below specified value, replace tensioner.

Engine	Year	Tension
2.0L OHC	1989-92	36-44
2.3L	1987-91	50 min.
2.5L 6000	1987-88	40 min.
2.5L 6000	1989-91	50-70
2.8L	1987	70 min.
2.8L FWD	1988-89	50-70
2.8L Firebird	1989	116-142
w/AC	1989	103-127
3.0L	1985-86	67 min.
3.0L	1987-88	79 min.
3.1L FWD	1989-92	50-70
3.1L Firebird	1990	116-142
w/AC	1990	103-127
3.1L Firebird	1991-92	95-140
w/AC	1991-92	85-110
3.3L	1992	67 min.
3.8L FWD	1987-90	67 min.
5.0L, 5.7L Firebird	1988-92	99-121

ENGINE COMPUTER SYSTEM

COMPUTER DIAGNOSTIC CODES
See UNDERHOOD SERVICE INSTRUCTIONS at the beginning of this section for test/adjustment diagrams.

Connect a jumper between A and B terminals on under dash connector (identified by a slot between the terminals or is two upper right-hand cavities of the two row connector). Turn ignition on. Code 12 will flash three times, then codes in memory will be displayed. Do not run engine with jumper connected.

Code 12 No tach reference to ECM
Code 13 Oxygen sensor circuit
Code 14 Coolant sensor circuit (high temperature indicated)
Code 15 Coolant sensor circuit (low temperature indicated)
Code 16 Missing 2X reference circuit (1992 2.3L)
Code 16 System over voltage (others)
Code 17 Spark reference circuit
Code 19 Crankshaft position sensor
Code 21 Throttle position sensor circuit (1983)
Code 21 Throttle position sensor voltage high (1984-86)
Code 22 Throttle position sensor voltage low
Code 23 Open or grounded MC solenoid (carburetted)
Code 23 Manifold air temperature circuit (low temperature indicated) (FI)
Code 24 Vehicle speed sensor circuit
Code 25 Manifold air temperature (MAT) circuit (high temperature indicated)
Code 26 Quad driver error
Codes 27, 28, 29 Transaxle gear switches

UNDERHOOD SERVICE SPECIFICATIONS

COMPUTER DIAGNOSTIC CODES Continued

Code 31 Wastegate solenoid (FI Turbo)
Code 31 Canister purge solenoid (carburetted)
Code 31 Park/Neutral switch (FI)
Code 32 Barometric or altitude sensor (carburetted)
Code 32 EGR system fault (FI)
Code 33 MAP, MAF sensor circuit (voltage high) (FI)
Code 34 MAP, MAF sensor circuit (voltage low) (FI)
Code 34 Vacuum sensor circuit (carburetted)
Code 35 Idle speed or idle air control circuit shorted
Code 36 MAF burn off circuit (1987-90)
Code 36 Transaxle shift control problem (1992)
Code 38 Brake switch
Code 39 Torque converter clutch
Code 41 No distributor reference pulses to ECM (1984-87 & carburetted)
Code 41 Cam sensor circuit (3.8L Code 3, C)
Code 41 Cylinder select error (others)
Code 42 EST or EST bypass circuit grounded or open
Code 43 ESC signal
Code 44 Air/fuel mixture too lean
Codes 44 & 45 Faulty oxygen sensor
Code 45 Air/fuel mixture rich
Code 46 Vehicle anti-theft system (Firebird)
Code 46 Power steering pressure switch (others)
Code 48 Misfire
Code 51 Faulty PROM, MEM-CAL, ECM or installation
Code 52 Fuel CALPAK
Code 53 EGR vacuum sensor incorrect (carburetted)
Code 53 Vehicle anti-theft system (5.0L TBI)
Code 53 System over voltage (FI, others)
Code 54 Shorted MC solenoid or faulty ECM (carburetted)
Code 54 Fuel pump circuit voltage low (FI)
Code 55 Grounded V-REF, faulty oxygen sensor or ECM
Code 58 PASS fuel enable circuit
Code 61 Cruise vent solenoid circuit (1992 3.8L)
Code 61 Degraded oxygen sensor (others)
Code 62 Transmission gear switch signal (others)
Code 62 Cruise vac circuit (3.8L)
Code 63 MAP sensor voltage high (3.8L)
Code 64 MAP sensor voltage low (3.8L)
Codes 63, 64 EGR flow problem (3.8L)
Code 65 EGR flow problem (1987-91 3.8L)
Code 65 Cruise servo position sensor (1992 3.8L)
Code 65 Fuel injector circuit (ex. 3.8L)
Code 66 AC pressure switch
Code 67 Cruise switch circuit
Code 68 Cruise system problem
Code 69 AC head pressure switch circuit

SENSORS, INPUT

TEMPERATURE SENSORS

Engine	Year	Sensor	Resistance Ohms @ deg. F/C
All	1983-90	Coolant,	13,500 @ 20/-7
	1983-92	Manifold Air*	7500 @ 40/4
			3400 @ 70/20
			1800 @ 100/38
			450 @ 160/70
			185 @ 210/100
All	1991-92	Coolant	28,700 @ 4/-20
			12,300 @ 23/-5
			7280 @ 41/-5
			3500 @ 68/20
			1460 @ 104/40
			470 @ 160/70
			1800 @ 210/100

* As equipped, not used on all engines.

MANIFOLD ABSOLUTE, VACUUM, AND BAROMETRIC PRESSURE SENSORS
See UNDERHOOD SERVICE INSTRUCTIONS at the beginning of this section for test/adjustment diagrams.

Engines may use one, or a combination of these sensors. All sensors appear the same. Manifold Absolute Pressure sensors have a vacuum line connected between the unit and manifold vacuum. On Barometric Pressure sensors, the line is not used and the connector is either open or has a filter installed over it. Pressure sensors also have a vacuum line between the sensor and intake manifold and only appear on carburetted models.

SENSORS, INPUT Continued

MANIFLOLD ABSOLUTE, VACUUM, AND BAROMETRIC PRESSURE SENSORS Continued

Barometric Pressure Sensors: Measure voltage with ignition on and engine off.
Manifold Absolute Pressure Sensors: Measure voltage with ignition on and engine off. Start engine and apply 10 in./250 mm Hg to unit, voltage should be 1.5 volts minimum less.
Pressure Sensors: Measure voltage as indicated.
5 volts reference.

Engine	Year	Sensor	Voltage @ Altitude
All, as equipped	1983-90	Barometric	3.8-5.5 @ 0-1000
			3.6-5.3 @ 1000-2000
			3.5-5.1 @ 2000-3000
			3.3-5.0 @ 3000-4000
			3.2-4.8 @ 4000-5000
			3.0-4.6 @ 5000-6000
			2.9-4.5 @ 6000-7000
			2.5-4.3 @ 7000-

Engine	Year	Sensor	Voltage @ Vacuum In Hg/kPa
All	1983-91	Manifold Absolute	1.0-1.5 @ idle
			4.5-4.8 @ idle
All	1992	Manifold Absolute	4.9 @ 0/0
			3.8 @ 6/20
			2.7 @ 12/40
			1.7 @ 18/60
			0.6 @ 24/80
			0.3 @ 30/100

Engine	Year	Sensor	Voltage @ Altitude
2.5L 2V, 2.8L 2V, 5.0L 4V, 5.7L 4V	1983-88	Vacuum	.50-.64 @ ign. on 1.7-3.0*

* 10 in./250 mm applied to unit.

CRANKSHAFT SENSORS
Resistance is measured at room temperature.

Engine	Year	Resistance (ohms)	Air Gap in./mm
2.0L	1987-91	900-1200	—
2.0L	1992	480-680	—
2.3L	1988-90	900-1200	—
2.3L	1991-92	500-900	—
2.5L	1987-91	800-900	—
2.8L, 3.1L, 3.4L	1987-91	900-1200	—
3.0L, 3.3L, 3.8L FI	1985-92	—	.035/.65

THROTTLE POSITION SENSOR (TPS)
See UNDERHOOD SERVICE INSTRUCTIONS at the beginning of this section for test/adjustment diagrams.

Verify that minimum idle is at specified value.

Make all checks/adjustments with engine at operating temperature.

Carburetted Models: Remove aluminum plug covering the adjustment screw. Remove the screw and connect a digital voltmeter to black wire (–) and either of the two other colored wires (+). If voltage is approximately 5 volts, this is the reference voltage lead. Connect DVOM to other wire in this case. Apply thread locking compound to the screw and with ignition on and engine not running (as applies), quickly adjust screw to obtain specified voltage at indicated condition.

Fuel Injected Models: Disconnect harness connector from TPS. Using three six-inch jumper wires, reconnect harness to TPS. With ignition on and engine not running (as applies), connect a digital voltmeter to black wire (–) and either of the two other colored wires (+). If voltage is approximtely 5 volts, this is the reference voltage lead. Connect DVOM to other wire in this case. Check reading against specified value. If TPS is adjustable, loosen the unit retaining screws and rotate the unit to reach specified value.

UNDERHOOD SERVICE SPECIFICATIONS

SENSORS, INPUT Continued

THROTTLE POSITION SENSOR (TPS) Continued

Model	Year	TPS Voltage† Idle	WOT (approx.)
1.6L (98)	1983-87	.92•	—
1.6L (98)	1988-90	.20-1.25*	—
1.6L	1991-92	.40-1.25*	4.5
1.8L (112)	1983-86	.20-1.25*	—
2.0L (122) FI	1983-84	.525	—
2.0L (122)	1985-86	.20-1.25*	—
2.0L	1987-89	.33-1.33*	5.0
2.0L	1990-91	.35-1.28*	4.5
2.0L	1992	.33-1.33*	4.5
2.2L	1990-91	.33-1.33*	4.5
2.3L (138)	1988-89	.54	—
2.3L	1990-92	.40-.90*	4.9
2.5L (151)	1983-89	.20-1.25*	4.5
2.5L	1990-91	.33-1.33*	4.8
2.8L (173)	1983	.26△	—
2.8L (173)	1984	.30△	—
2.8L (173) 2V	1985-86	.27	—
2.8L (173) FI	1985-88	.55	—
2.8L Tempest, 6000	1989	.29-.98*	—
2.8L Firebird	1989	.55	—
3.0L (181)	1985-87	.50	—
3.1L, 3.4L	1988-92	.29-.98*	4.8
3.3L	1992	.40	4.0 min.
3.8L (231)	1983	.86•	—
3.8L (231) 2V	1984-87	.46♦	—
3.8L (231) FI	1986-92	.40	4.0 min.
4.3L (262)	1985-87	.525	—
5.0L (305)	1983	.51	—
5.0L (305) 4V	1984-87	.48	—
5.0L (305) MFI, 5.7L	1985-89	.54	—
5.0L MFI, 5.7L	1990-91	.36-.96* max.*	5.0
5.0L MFI, 5.7L	1992	.36-.62*	4.0 min.
5.0L (305) TBI	1988-90	.20-1.25*	5.0
5.0L TBI	1991	.45-1.25*	5.0

SENSORS, INPUT Continued

THROTTLE POSITION SENSOR (TPS) Continued

Model	Year	TPS Voltage† Idle	WOT (approx.)
5.0L TBI	1992	.20-.95	5.0
5.0L (307)	1986-88	.41♦	—

- • High step of fast idle cam.
- ♦ Idle Speed Compensator (ISC) or Load Compensator (ILC) retracted.
- † ±.10, carburetted engines; ±.05 FI engines.
- △ With idle solenoid disconnected.
- * Not adjustable.

ACTUATORS, OUTPUT

IDLE SPEED CONTROL
See UNDERHOOD SERVICE INSTRUCTIONS at the beginning of this section for test/adjustment diagrams.

All engines with ISC.

Measured between terminals A & B and C & D.

Engine	Year	Resistance (ohms)
2.8L, 3.1L Grand Prix, 6000	1988-89	48-58
All Other TBI & MFI	1983-89	20 min.
All carburetted	1983-89	10 min.
LeMans	1990-91	20 min.
All Others	1990-91	40-80

MIXTURE CONTROL SOLENOID-CARBURETTED ENGINES
On some engines, the ECM will be damaged if the resistance of the mixture control solenoid is less than specified.

Engine	Year	Resistance (ohms)
All	1983-89	10 min.

PORSCHE
1983-92

ENGINE IDENTIFICATION

To identify an engine by the manufacturer's code, follow the four steps designated by the numbered blocks.

V.I.N. PLATE LOCATION:
Driver's side windshield pillar, visible through windshield.

1 MODEL YEAR IDENTIFICATION:
10th character of V.I.N.
1992 — N; 1991 — M; 1990 — L;
1989 — K; 1988 — J; 1987 — H;
1986 — G; 1985 — F; 1984 — E;
1983 — D.

2 ENGINE CODE LOCATION:
Prefix to engine number.
4-cyl. — 1988-92: Passenger's side of engine block, next to clutch housing. 1983-87: Driver's side of crankcase, next to clutch housing.
6-cyl. — Passenger's side of crankcase, next to fan housing.
8-cyl. — Top of front crankcase reinforcing rib.

4 ENGINE IDENTIFICATION

YEAR	3 ENGINE CODE	CYL.	DISPL. liters	cc	Fuel System	HP
1992	42N	4	3.0	2990	DME	236
	68N	6	3.3 T	3299 T	CIS	315
	62N	6	3.6	3600	DME	247
	81N	8	5.0	4957	LH	315
	85N	8	5.0	4957	LH	326
1991	42M	4	3.0	2990	DME	208
	68M	6	3.3 T	3299 T	CIS	315
	62M	6	3.6	3600	DME	247
	81M	8	5.0	4957	LH	315
	85M	8	5.0	4957	LH	326
1990	42L	4	3.0	2990	DME	208
	62L	6	3.6	3600	DME	247
	81L	8	5.0	4957	LH	316
	85L	8	5.0	4957	LH	326
1989	47K	4	2.5 T	2479 T	DME	247
	46K	4	2.7	2681	DME	162
	42K	4	3.0	2990	DME	208
	64K	6	3.2	3164	LH	214
	68K	6	3.3 T	3299 T	CIS	282
	62K	6	3.6	3600	DME	247
	81K	8	5.0	4957	LH	309
1988	46J	4	2.5	2479	LH	158
	42J	4	2.5	2479	LH	188
	45J	4	2.5 T	2479 T	LH	217
	64J	6	3.2	3164	LH	214
	68J	6	3.3 T	3299 T	CIS	282
	81J	8	5.0	4957	LH	316

4 ENGINE IDENTIFICATION

YEAR	3 ENGINE CODE	CYL.	DISPL. liters	cc	Fuel System	HP
1987	43H	4	2.5	2479	LH	150
	42H	4	2.5	2479	LH	188
	45H	4	2.5 T	2479 T	LH	220
	64H	6	3.2	3164	LH	217
	68H	6	3.3 T	3299 T	CIS	282
	67H	6	3.3 T	3299 T	CIS	300
	81H	8	5.0	4957	LH	320
1986	43G	4	2.5	2479	LH	150
	45G	4	2.5 T	2479 T	LH	220
	64G	6	3.2	3164	LH	207
	68G	6	3.3 T	3299 T	CIS	282
	67G	6	3.3 T	3299 T	CIS	300
	81G	8	5.0	4957	LH	292
1985	43F	4	2.5	2479	LH	143
	64F	6	3.2	3164	LH	231
	67F	6	3.3 T	3299 T	CIS	300
	81F	8	5.0	4957	LH	288
1984	43E	4	2.5	2479	LH	143
	64E	6	3.2	3164	LH	198
	67E	6	3.3 T	3299 T	CIS	300
	81E	8	4.7	4664	L	234
1983	43D	4	2.5	2479	LH	143
	64D	6	3.0	2994	CIS	172
	67D	6	3.3 T	3299 T	CIS	300
	81D	8	4.7	4664	L	234

T — Turbo. CIS — Continuous Injection System.
L — L-Jetronic. LH — LH-Jetronic.
DME — Digital Motor Electronics

UNDERHOOD SERVICE SPECIFICATIONS

PEITU1   PEITU1

CYLINDER NUMBERING SEQUENCE

4-CYL. FIRING ORDER: 1 3 4 2

6-CYL. FIRING ORDER: 1 6 2 4 3 5

8-CYL. FIRING ORDER: 1 3 7 2 6 5 4 8

1983-84
2479cc

1985-88
2479cc;
1989
2681cc;
1990-92
2990cc

1983-88
2994cc, 3164cc,
3299cc

1983-84
4474cc, 4664cc

1985-92
4957cc

TIMING MARK

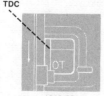
TDC

1983-88
4-cyl. 2479cc;
1989 4-cyl. 2681cc;
1990-92 4-cyl. 2990cc

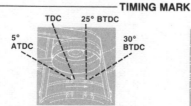
TDC   25° BTDC
5° ATDC   30° BTDC

1983-92
6-cyl. 2994cc, 3164cc,
3600cc, 3299cc Turbo

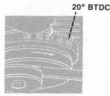
20° BTDC

1983-84
V8 4664cc

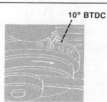
10° BTDC

1985-92
4957cc

ELECTRICAL AND IGNITION SYSTEMS

BATTERY

BCI equivalent shown, size may vary from original equipment. Check clearance and polarity before installing, holddown may need to be modified. Battery may be vented to outside of vehicle.

Model	Year	BCI Group No.	Crank. Perf.
911, 911 Turbo	1983-89	49	650
911 Carrera 4	1990-92	48	695
911 Carrera 2, Turbo Carrera	1991-92	48	695
924S	1987-88	41	500
944, 944 Turbo	1983-89	41	500
944 S2	1990-91	41	500
928, 928S	1983-86	49	650
928 S/4	1987-89	49	730
928 S/4, 928 GT	1990-92	48	695
968	1992	41	500

ALTERNATOR

Engine	Year	Rated Output (amps)	Test Output (amps @ rpm)
2479cc	1983-84	90	74 @ 3000
2479cc	1985-89	115	98 @ 3000
2681cc	1989	115	98 @ 3000
2990cc	1989-92	115	98 @ 3000
2994cc, 3299cc	1983	75	68 @ 3000
3164cc, 3299cc	1984-89	90	74 @ 3000
3600cc	1989-92	115	98 @ 3000
4664cc	1983-84	90	74 @ 3000
4957cc	1985-88	90	74 @ 3000
4957cc	1989-92	115	98 @ 3000

REGULATOR

Engine	Year	Voltage Output Min.	Voltage Output Max.
2994cc	1983	13.5	14.5
4664cc	1983	13.5	14.8

STARTER

Engine	Year	Cranking Voltage (min. volts)	Ampere Draw @ RPM
2994cc	1983	7.5	—
4664cc	1983-84	8.0	—
All	1985-92	8.0	—

SPARK PLUGS

Lubricate threads with anti-sieze compound.

Engine	Year	Gap (inches)	Gap (mm)	Torque (ft-lb)
2479cc	1983-88	.024-.032	.60-.80	22
2479cc Turbo	1989	.028-.032	.70-.80	22
2681cc	1989	.028-.032	.70-.80	22
2990cc	1989-92	.028	0.7	22
2994cc	1983	.024-.032	.60-.80	22
3164cc	1984-89	.024-.032	.60-.80	22
3299cc	1983-89	.024-.032	.60-.80	22
3299cc	1991-92	.024-.032	.60-.80	22
3600cc	1989-92	.031	0.8	22
4664cc	1983-84	.024-.032	.60-.80	22
4957cc	1985-92	.024-.032	.60-.80	22

IGNITION COIL

Engine	Year	Windings	Resistance (ohms)
2479cc	1983-86	Primary	0.4-0.6
		Secondary	5000-7000
4664cc	1983-84	Primary	0.4-0.7
		Secondary	5000-8700
4957cc	1985-92	Primary	0.4-0.7
		Secondary	5000-8700

BASE TIMING

Before top dead center, unless otherwise specified.

Engine	Year	Man. Trans. (degrees) @ RPM	Auto. Trans. (degrees) @ RPM
2479cc ex. Turbo	1983-84	3-7 @ 850-950†	2-8 @ 850-950†
2479cc Turbo	1985	3-7 @ 800-880†	3-7 @ 800-880†
2479cc ex. Turbo, DOHC	1986-88	2-8 @ 800-880†	2-8 @ 800-880†
2479cc Turbo	1986-89	2-8 @ 850-950†	—
2479cc DOHC	1987-88	7-13 @ 800-880†	7-13 @ 800-880†
2681cc	1989	2-8 @ 800-880†	2-8 @ 800-880†
2990cc	1989-92	10 ±3 @ 800-880	10 ±3 @ 840-920
2994cc	1983	3-7 @ 900-1000*	—
3164cc to 9-19-86	1984-87	0-6 ATDC @ 780-820†	—
3164cc from 9-19-86	1987-89	0-6 @ 860-900	—
3299cc Canada	1983-86	28-30 @ 4000*	—
3299cc ex. Canada	1986	25-27 @ 4000*	—
3299cc	1987-89	25-27 @ 4000*	—
3299cc	1991-92	25-27 @ 4000*	—
4664cc	1983-84	20 @ 3000*	20 @ 3000*
4957cc	1985-92	8-12 @ 650-700*	8-12 @ 650-700*

† Reference figure only, timing is not adjustable.
* Distributor vacuum hoses disconnected and plugged.

DISTRIBUTOR TIMING ADVANCE

Crankshaft degrees at engine rpm, no load, in addition to base timing.

Engine	Trans- mission	Year	Distributor Number	Degrees @ 2500 RPM Total	Degrees @ 2500 RPM Centrifugal
2994cc	MT	1983	0237304016	13.8-22.0	10.8-15.0
3299cc	MT	1983-86	0237302034	25-34	22-27
4664cc	MT & AT	1983-84	0237401019	25-33	12-16
4957cc	MT & AT	1985-86	0237404013	25-33	12-16

FUEL SYSTEM

FUEL INJECTION SYSTEM PRESSURE PROCEDURE

CIS System:
1. Connect appropriate fuel pressure gauge between the control pressure line of the fuel distributor and the outlet line of the warm-up regulator.
2. Energize fuel pump with jumper wire.
3. Bleed pressure gauge and set valve to open position, read control pressure.
4. Set valve to closed position, read line pressure.

DME System:
1. Connect pressure tester to fuel pipe.
2. Start engine and read pressure at idle.

L-Jetronic:
1. Connect appropriate fuel pressure gauge to inlet of fuel injection manifold.
2. Energize fuel pump by removing fuel pump relay and bridge cavities 30 & 87.

LH-Jetronic System:
1. Connect appropriate fuel pressure gauge to inlet of fuel injection manifold.
2. Energize fuel pump: 944: remove DME relay and bridge cavities 30 & 87b, 911: connect fuses 16 & 17 with a jumper wire, 928: remove fuel pump relay and bridge cavities 30 & 87b.
3. Read line pressure.
4. Disconnect jumper wire, pressure should immediately drop to residual specification and maintain pressure for 20 minutes.

FUEL PRESSURE: DME, L-, LH-JETRONIC

Engine	Year	System Pressure Not Running PSI (bar)	System Pressure At Idle PSI (bar)	Residual Pressure PSI (bar)
2479cc ex. DOHC	1983-88	33-39 (2.3-2.7)	29 (2.0)	15 (1.0)
2479cc DOHC	1987-88	52-55 (3.6-3.8)	48 (3.3)	44 (3.0)
2479cc Turbo	1985-89	33-39 (2.3-2.7)	29 (2.0)	15 (1.0)
2681cc	1989	52-58 (3.6-4.0)	48 (3.3)	44 (3.0)
2990cc	1989-92	52-58 (3.6-4.0)	46-51 (3.1-3.5)	44 (3.0)
3164cc	1984-89	33-39 (2.3-2.7)	29 (2.0)	29 (2.0)
3600cc	1989-92	52-58 (3.6-4.0)	46-51 (3.1-3.5)	39 (2.7)
4664cc	1983-84	33-39 (2.3-2.7)	29 (2.0)	15 (1.0)
4957cc	1985-86	33-39 (2.3-2.7)	29 (2.0)	15 (1.0)
4957cc	1987-92	52-58 (3.6-4.0)	48 (3.3)	44 (3.0)

UNDERHOOD SERVICE SPECIFICATIONS

PEITU3

FUEL INJECTION SYSTEM PRESSURE PROCEDURE
Continued

FUEL PRESSURE: CIS

Engine	Year	Control Pressure† PSI (bar)	Line Pressure PSI (bar)	Residual Pressure* PSI (bar)
2994cc	1983	51-57 (3.5-3.9)	65-75 (4.5-5.2)	22 (1.5)
3299cc	1983-89	51-57 (3.5-3.9)	87-97 (6.0-6.7)	22 (1.5)
3299cc	1991-92	51-57 (3.5-3.9)	87-97 (6.0-6.7)	22 (1.5)

† With engine running at normal operating temperature.
* Minimum pressure after 20 minutes.

COLD CONTROL PRESSURE: CIS

Model & Warm-up Regulator Part Number	Pressure† PSI (bar) @ 50°F (10°C) Ambient Temp.	Pressure† PSI (bar) @ 68°F (20°C) Ambient Temp.	Pressure† PSI (bar) @ 86°F (30°C) Ambient Temp.
911:			
0438140045	23-29 (1.6-2.0)	29-35 (2.0-2.4)	35-40 (2.4-2.8)
0438140069	17-23 (1.2-1.6)	26-32 (1.8-2.2)	35-40 (2.4-2.8)
0438140072	22-29 (1.5-2.0)	30-38 (2.1-2.6)	39-46 (2.7-3.2)
0438140090	20-26 (1.4-1.8)	29-35 (2.0-2.4)	38-45 (2.6-3.1)
911 Turbo:			
0438140016, 022	6-12 (0.4-0.8)	15-20 (1.0-1.4)	25-30 (1.7-2.1)
0438140054	15-22 (1.0-1.5)	23-30 (1.6-2.1)	33-39 (2.3-2.7)
0438140112	9-17 (0.6-1.2)	17-23 (1.2-1.6)	23-29 (1.6-2.0)
0438140153	13-23 (0.9-1.6)	22-26 (1.5-1.8)	32-36 (2.2-2.5)

† With vacuum applied.

IDLE SPEED

Engine	Year	Man. Trans.	Auto. Trans.
2479cc	1983-84	850-950	850-950 N
2479cc	1985-89	800-880	800-880 N
2681cc	1989	800-880	800-880 N
2900cc	1989-92	800-880	840-920 N
2994cc	1983	850-950	—
3164cc to 9-19-86	1984-87	780-820	—
3164cc from 9-19-86	1987-89	860-900	—
3299cc	1983-89	850-950	—
3299cc	1991-92	850-950	—
3600cc	1989-92	800-880	840-920 N
4664cc	1983-84	600-700	600-700 N
4957cc	1985-87	640-720	650-700 N
4957cc	1988-92	650-700	650-700 N

IDLE MIXTURE
Measured upstream of the catalytic converter, disconnect oxygen sensor and/or secondary air supply where applicable.

Engine	Year	CO% Low	High
2479cc ex. DOHC	1983-89	0.4	0.8
2479cc DOHC	1987-88	0.4	1.2
2681cc	1989	0.4	0.8
2990cc	1989-92	0.4	0.8
2994cc	1983	0.4	0.8
3164cc	1984-87	0.6	1.0
3164cc	1988-89	0.4	0.8
3299cc Canada	1983-87	1.5*	2.5*
3299cc ex. Canada	1986-87	0.4	0.8
3299cc	1988-89	0.4	0.8
3600cc	1989-92	0.4	1.2
4664cc	1983-84	0.4	0.8
4957cc	1985-86	0.4	0.8
4957cc	1987-92	0.4	1.2

* Measured at tailpipe with air pump hose disconnected & plugged.

ENGINE MECHANICAL

TIGHTENING TORQUES

Engine	Year	Torque Ft-lbs/Nm Cylinder Head	Intake Manifold	Exhaust Manifold	Crankshaft Pulley	Water Pump
4-cyl. 2.5L	1983-89	14/20	14/20	14/20	—	6/8†
2nd stage		36/50				
3rd stage		65/90				
4-cyl. 3.0L	1989-90	14/20	—	—	—	—
2nd stage		+60°				
3rd stage		+90°				
6-cyl. 3.0L	1983	24/33	—	—	58/80	—
6-cyl. 3.2L	1984-89	11/15	—	—	58/80	—
2nd stage		+90°				
6-cyl. 3.3L Turbo	1983-89	24/33	18/25	14/20	58/80	—
6-cyl. 3.6L	1989-92	11/15	—	17/23	173/235	—
2nd stage		+90°				
V8 4.7L	1984-83	14/20	—	—	—	—
2nd stage		36/50				
3rd stage		65/90				
V8 5.0L:						
W/studs	1985-92	14/20	11/15	—	218/195	—
2nd stage		90°, +90°, +90°				
W/bolts	1985-92	14/20	11/15	—	218/195	—
2nd stage		90°, +90°				

† Threads sealed with Loctite 270 or equivalent.
♦ Tighten to specification, allow to settle 30 minutes, back off and retorque one bolt at a time.

VALVE CLEARANCE

Engine	Year	Intake (inches)	Intake (mm)	Exhaust (inches)	Exhaust (mm)
Cold Setting:					
2994cc	1983	.004	.10	.004	.10
3164cc	1984-89	.004	.10	.004	.10
3299cc	1983-89	.004	.10	.004	.10
3299cc	1991-92	.004	.10	.004	.10
3600cc	1989-92	.004	.10	.004	.10

COMPRESSION PRESSURE

Engine	Year	Normal Range PSI	Maximum Variation PSI
2994cc	1983	142-184	22

BELT TENSION

Model	Year	Alternator	Power Steering	Air Cond.
All ex. serpentine (inches)	1983-89	3/8	3/16	3/16
(mm)	1983-89	10	5	5
Serpentine belt	1983-89	9.2-9.8†	—	—

† Porsche special tool No. 9201 required.

ENGINE COMPUTER SYSTEM

COMPUTER DIAGNOSTIC CODES
911 Carrera 4:
1. Connect Porsche Tester No. 9288 or 9268 using adapter No. 9268/2 to diagnostic connector in passenger footwell.
2. Read codes on tester. The second digit of a code may be displayed as a "2". This indicates the code was stored prior to the last operation of the vehicle.

944 S2:
1. Connect Porsche Tester to diagnostic connector.
2. Read codes on tester. The second digit of a code may be displayed as a "2". This indicates the code was set by a sporadic fault.

UNDERHOOD SERVICE SPECIFICATIONS

PEITU4   PEITU4

COMPUTER DIAGNOSTIC CODES Continued

Code	Fault
1000	End of output
1111	System voltage out of range
1112	Idle switch contact grounded
1113	Full load switch contact grounded
1114	Engine temperature sensor circuit
1121	Air flow sensor signal
1122	Idle control circuit
1123	Oxygen sensor signal out of range
1124	Oxygen sensor circuit
1125	Intake air temperature sensor circuit
1131	Knock sensor No. 1 signal
1132	Knock sensor No. 2 signal
1133	Knock control regulation circuit
1134	Hall sender signal
1141	DME control unit
1142	Fuel pump relay circuit
1143	Tank venting valve circuit
1151	Fuel injector No. 1 circuit
1152	Fuel injector No. 2 circuit
1153	Fuel injector No. 3 circuit
1154	Fuel injector No. 4 circuit
1155	Fuel injector No. 5 circuit
1156	Fuel injector No. 6 circuit
1500	No faults in memory

928 S/4:
1. Connect Porsche Tester No. 9268 to diagnostic connector.
2. Switch ignition on and activate tester to access codes.

EZK Code	LH Code	Fault
2000	1000	End of output
—	1111	System voltage out of range
2112	1112	Idle switch contact grounded
2113	1113	Full load switch contact grounded
2114	1114	Engine temperature sensor circuit
2115	—	Throttle position signal
—	1121	Air flow sensor signal
2121	—	Control unit signal
—	1122	Idle control circuit
—	1123	Oxygen sensor signal rich
—	1124	Oxygen sensor signal lean
—	1125	Lambda probe
2126	—	Transmission switch circuit
2131	—	Knock sensor No. 1 signal
2132	—	Knock sensor No. 2 signal
2133	—	Knock control regulation circuit
2134	—	Hall sender signal
2141	—	Control unit
2500	1500	No faults in memory

SENSORS, INPUT

TEMPERATURE SENSORS

Engine	Year	Sensor	Resistance Ohms @ deg. F/C
4-cyl. 2.5L	1983-88	Coolant	3300-4100 @ 50/10
			2200-2800 @ 68/20
			1000-1300 @ 104/40
			290-350 @ 176/80
			160-210 @ 212/100
		Intake Air	500-6200 @ 32/0
			2200-2800 @ 68/20
			1500-1900 @ 86/30
6-cyl. 3.2L	1984-89	Cylinder Head	3300-4100 @ 50/10
			2200-2800 @ 68/20
			1000-1300 @ 104/40
			250-390 @ 176/80
			160-200 @ 212/100
		Intake Air†	4400-6800 @ 32/0
			1400-3600 @ 59-86/15-30
			900-1300 @ 104/40

SENSORS, INPUT Continued

TEMPERATURE SENSORS Continued

Engine	Year	Sensor	Resistance Ohms @ deg. F/C
V8 4.7L	1983-84	Coolant	7000-12,000 @ 32/0
			2000-3000 @ 68/20
			250-400 @ 176/80
		Intake Air Thermo-Time	4000-6000 @ 68/20
			25-40 @ below 86/20
			50-80 @ above 104/40
V8 5.0L	1985-92	Coolant	4400-6800 @ 32/0
			1400-3600 @ 59-86/15-30
			900-1300 @ 104/40
			480-720 @ 140/60
			250-390 @ 176/80

† Measured at terminals 1 & 4 of the Airflow Meter.

AIRFLOW SENSOR

Engine	Year	Resistance (ohms) @ Terminal	Voltage @ Terminal
4-cyl. 2.5L	1983-88	—	less than 8V @ 9
			150-250mV @ 7 ★
			more than 8V @ 7♦
6-cyl. 3.2L	1984-89	—	4.5-5.5V @ 3
			260mV @ 2 ★
			4.6V @ 2♦
V8 4.7L●	1983-84	80-600 @ 6 & 7	—
		160-520 @ 6 & 8	
		400-800 @ 6 & 9	
		200-1000 @ 7 & 8	
		140-280 @ 8 & 9	
V8 5.0L	1985-92	0-1000 @ 3 & 6	4.5-5.5V @ 3
		3600-4100 @ 3 & 5	260mV @ 2 ★
			4.6V @ 2♦

★ With sensor plate in the closed position.
♦ With sensor plate in the open position.
● Only units with "024" stamped on the housing.

SPEED & REFERENCE SENSORS

Engine	Year	Resistance (ohms)
6-cyl. 3.2L	1984-89	600-1600

ACTUATORS, OUTPUT

AUXILIARY AIR VALVE

Engine	Year	Resistance (ohms)
6-cyl. 3.0L	1983	33
V8 4.7L	1983-84	40-75

FREQUENCY VALVE

Engine	Year	Resistance (ohms)
6-cyl. 3.0L	1983	2-3

THROTTLE BY-PASS VALVE

Engine	Year	Resistance (ohms)
4-cyl. 2.5L	1983-88	20-55

ENGINE IDENTIFICATION

To identify an engine by the manufacturer's code, follow the four steps designated by the numbered blocks.

V.I.N. PLATE LOCATION:

Driver's side of instrument panel, visible through windshield.

1 MODEL YEAR IDENTIFICATION:

10th character of V.I.N.

1992 — N; 1991 — M; 1990 — L;
1989 — K; 1988 — J; 1987 — H;
1986 — G; 1985 — F; 1984 — E;
1983 — D.

2 ENGINE CODE LOCATION:

1984-92 — 8th character of V.I.N.
1983 — 7th character of V.I.N.

4 ENGINE IDENTIFICATION

YEAR	3 ENGINE CODE	CYL.	DISPL. liters	cc	Fuel System	HP
1992	L	4	2.0 T	1985 T	LH	160
	E	4	2.1	2119	LH	140
	B	4	2.3	2290	LH	150
	M	4	2.3 T	2290 T	LH	200
1991	L	4	2.0 T	1985 T	LH	175
	E	4	2.1	2119	LH	140
	B	4	2.3	2290	LH	150
	M	4	2.3 T	2290 T	LH	200
1990	D	4	2.0	1985	LH	128, 130†
	L	4	2.0 T	1985 T	LH	160, 175†
	B	4	2.3	2290	LH	200
1989	D	4	2.0	1985	LH	128, 130†
	L	4	2.0 T	1985	LH	160, 165†
1988	I	4	2.0	1985	CIS	110
	D	4	2.0	1985	LH	125
	L	4	2.0 T	1985 T	LH	160, 165†

4 ENGINE IDENTIFICATION

YEAR	3 ENGINE CODE	CYL.	DISPL. liters	cc	Fuel System	HP
1987	J	4	2.0	1985	CIS	110
	D	4	2.0	1985	LH	125
	L	4	2.0 T	1985 T	LH	160, 165†
1986	J	4	2.0	1985	CIS	110
	D	4	2.0	1985	LH	125
	L	4	2.0 T	1985 T	LH	160
1985	I	4	2.0	1985	CIS	110
	L	4	2.0 T	1985 T	LH	160
1984	I	4	2.0	1985	CIS	110
	S	4	2.0 T	1985 T	CIS	135
1983	3	4	2.0	1985	CIS	110
	4	4	2.0 T	1985 T	CIS	135

† Engine horsepower varies with model installation and emissions equipment.   T — Turbo.   LH — LH-Jetronic.
CIS — Continuous Injection System.

UNDERHOOD SERVICE SPECIFICATIONS

SBITU1

CYLINDER NUMBERING SEQUENCE

FIRING ORDER: 1 3 4 2

Front of car

1983-88	1985-92	1986-90
1985cc 8 Valve	1985cc 16 Valve 900	1985cc 16 Valve 9000

SBITU1

TIMING MARK

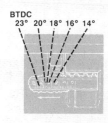

BTDC
23° 20° 18° 16° 14°

1983-90
1985cc

ELECTRICAL AND IGNITION SYSTEMS

BATTERY

Manufacturer's recommended BCI replacement shown, may vary from original equipment battery. Check clearance and polarity before installing, holddown may need to be modified.

Model	Year	BCI Group No.	Crank. Perf.
900	1983-92	26	530
9000	1986-92	47	450

ALTERNATOR

Application	Manufacturer	Year	Rated Output (amps)	Test Output (amps @ rpm)
900	Bosch	1983	70	46 @ 2000
900	Motorola	1983	70	48 @ 2000
All	Bosch	1984-88	80	54 @ 1900
900	Bosch	1989-92	80	54 @ 1900
9000 MT	Bosch	1989-92	80	54 @ 1900
9000 AT	Bosch	1989-92	115	—

REGULATOR

Integrated type, not adjustable.

Application	Year	Brush Wear Limit in. (mm)	Voltage Output Max.
All	1983-92	3/16 (5)	14.0

STARTER

Application	Year	Condition	Cranking Voltage (min. volts)	Ampere Draw @ RPM
All	1983-84	No load	11.5	35-55 @ 6500-8500
		Loaded	9.0	205-235 @ 1000-1300
		Locked stator	6.0	450-555 @ 0
All	1985-90	No load	12.0	70 @ 3000
		Loaded	9.0	315 @ 1700
		Locked stator	4.0	650-750 @ 0

SPARK PLUGS

Engine	Year	Gap (inches)	Gap (mm)	Torque (ft-lb)
All	1983-89	.024-.028	.60-.70	18.5-21.5
Turbo w/Direct Ignition	1990	.028-.035	.70-.90	18.5-21.5
All others	1990	.024-.028	.60-.70	18.5-21.5
1985cc Turbo	1991-92	.024-.028	.60-.70	18.5-21.5
2100cc	1991-92	.024-.028	.60-.70	18.5-21.5
2290cc, 2290cc Turbo	1991-92	.039-.046	1.0-1.2	18.5-21.5

IGNITION COIL

Application	Year	Windings	Resistance (ohms)
Canada ex. Turbo	1983	Primary	2.6-3.1
		Secondary	8000-11,000

SAAB
1983-92

IGNITION COIL Continued

Engine	Year	Windings	Resistance (ohms)
All ex. Canada	1983	Primary	.52-.76
		Secondary	7200-8200
Canada Turbo	1983	Primary	.52-.76
		Secondary	7200-8200
All	1984-90	Primary	.52-.76
		Secondary	7200-8200
9000 w/Direct Ignition	1991-92	Primary	0.3
		Secondary	800-900

TIMING PROCEDURE

Disconnect and plug distributor vacuum hose.

BASE TIMING

Before Top Dead Center, unless otherwise specified.

Engine	Year	Man. Trans. (degrees) @ RPM	Auto. Trans. (degrees) @ RPM
Canada Turbo	1983-84	20 @ 2000	20 @ 2000
8-Valve, ex. Canada	1983-83	20 @ 2000	20 @ 2000
Canada Non-Turbo	1983	18 @ 2000	18 @ 2000
Canada 8-Valve Non-Turbo	1984-87	20 @ 2000	20 @ 2000
16-Valve Turbo	1985-90	16 @ 850	16 @ 850
16-Valve Non-Turbo	1986-90	14 @ 850	14 @ 850
1985cc Turbo	1991-92	16 @ 850	16 @ 850
2119cc	1991-92	14 @ 850	14 @ 850

DISTRIBUTOR TIMING ADVANCE

Crankshaft degrees at engine rpm, no load, in addition to base timing.

Engine	Trans-mission	Year	Distributor Number	Degrees @ 2500 RPM Total	Degrees @ 2500 RPM Centrifugal
Canada ex. Turbo	MT & AT	1983	0231186032	28-36	10-14
Turbo w/APC	MT & AT	1983	0237026003	20-29	4-9
8-Valve ex. Turbo	MT & AT	1983-87	0231021014	21-29	8-12
Turbo	MT & AT	1984	0237026006	19-28	3-8

FUEL SYSTEM

FUEL SYSTEM PRESSURE

FUEL PRESSURE PROCEDURE

LH — Jetronic System:
1. Connect appropriate fuel pressure gauge to inlet of fuel injection manifold.
2. Energize fuel pump by connecting jumper wire from fuse #14 to fuse #22.
3. Read system pressure.
4. Disconnect jump wire, pressure should immediately drop to residual specification and maintain pressure for 10 minutes.

CIS System:
1. Connect appropriate fuel pressure gauge between the control pressure line of the fuel distributor and the outlet line of the warm-up regulator.
2. Remove fuel pump relay and energize pump by bridging cavities 30 & 87.
3. Bleed pressure gauge and set valve to open position, read control pressure.
4. Set valve to closed position, read line pressure.

FUEL PRESSURE; LH-JETRONIC

Engine	Year	System Pressure PSI (bar)	Residual Pressure PSI (bar)
1985cc Turbo	1985-86	35.5-36.9 (2.45-2.55)	33 (2.3)
1985cc Non-Turbo	1986-90	43.0 (3.06)	39 (2.8)
1985cc Turbo	1987	39.8-41.3 (2.75-2.85)	33 (2.3)
1985cc Turbo	1988-92	36.0 (2.5)	33 (2.3)
2119cc	1991-92	43 (3.0)	39 (2.8)
2290cc	1991-92	43 (3.0)	—

FUEL PRESSURE; CIS

Engine	Year	Control Pressure† PSI (bar)	Line Pressure PSI (bar)	Residual Pressure* PSI (bar)
8-Valve Turbo	1983-84	46-55 (3.4-3.8)	74-84 (5.1-5.8)	22 (1.5)
8-Valve Non-Turbo	1983-88	46-55 (3.4-3.8)	65-75 (4.5-5.2)	22 (1.5)

† With engine at operating temperature.
* Minimum pressure after 20 minutes.

FUEL SYSTEM PRESSURE Continued

COLD CONTROL PRESSURE; CIS

Pressure Regulator Part Number	Pressure PSI (bar) @ 50°F (10°C) Ambient Temp.	Pressure PSI (bar) @ 68°F (20°C) Ambient Temp.	Pressure PSI (bar) @ 86°F (30°C) Ambient Temp.	Pressure PSI (bar) @ 104°F (40°C) Ambient Temp.
0483140084†	21-29 (1.4-2.0)	29-35 (2.0-2.4)	38-44 (2.6-3.0)	44-51 (3.0-3.5)
0438140136, 084*	16-22 (1.1-1.5)	24-30 (1.6-2.1)	36-42 (2.5-2.9)	44-51 (3.0-3.5)
0438140020, 085, 070, 102, 111	8-21 (0.6-1.4)	21-24 (1.4-1.6)	24-30 (1.6-2.1)	30-36 (2.1-2.5)

† Up to 1984 model year, no green color coding.
* Early 1984 with green color coding.

IDLE SPEED

Engine	Year	Manual Trans.	Auto. Trans.
900 ex. Canada	1983	800-950	800-950 N
Canada	1983	800-900	800-900 N
900 8-Valve, all	1984-88	800-950	800-950 N
900 16-Valve Turbo	1985-89	775-925	775-925 N
900 16-Valve w/o Turbo	1986-89	775-925	775-925 N
900, all	1990-92	800-900	800-900 N
9000	1986-92	800-900	800-900 N

ENGINE MECHANICAL

TIGHTENING TORQUES

Engine	Year	Torque Ft-lbs/Nm Cylinder Head	Intake Manifold	Exhaust Manifold	Crankshaft Pulley	Water Pump
4-cyl. 2.0L	1983-87	—	14/18	15/20†	140/190	15/20
15mm bolts		44/60				
2nd stage♦		59/80				
3rd stage		+90°				
17mm bolts		44/60				
2nd stage♦		70/95				
4-cyl. 2.0L	1988-92	44/60	14/18	19/25	140/190	15/20
2nd stage		59/80				
3rd stage		+90°				

† Turbo models; 19 ft-lbs, 25 Nm.
♦ Tighten to specification, run engine to operating temperature and allow to cool 30 minutes, back off and retorque one bolt at a time.

VALVE CLEARANCE

Run engine to operating temperature, allow to cool 30 minutes before checking.

Engine	Year	Intake (inches)	Intake (mm)	Exhaust (inches)	Exhaust (mm)
8-Valve Turbo:					
Checking	1983-84	.006-.012	.15-.30	.016-.020	.40-.50
Adjusting	1983-84	.008-.010	.20-.25	.018-.020	.45-.50
8-Valve Non-Turbo:					
Checking	1983-88	.006-.012	.15-.30	.014-.020	.35-.50
Adjusting	1983-88	.008-.010	.20-.25	.016-.018	.40-.45

COMPRESSION PRESSURE

All models — Lowest cylinder must be within 10% of highest cylinder.

BELT TENSION

Model	Year	Alternator	Power Steering	Air Cond.
USED BELTS				
Strand Tension method				
9000 w/serpentine	1986-92	110-130	—	75-85
900 w/single belt	1991-92	65-75	65-75	75-85
w/double belt	1991-92	140-150	—	—
Deflection method				
900 (inches)	1983-90	3/16†	3/16♦	3/16†
(mm)	1983-90	5†	5♦	5†

† With 10 lb. of force at midpoint between pulleys.
♦ With 15 lb. of force at midpoint between pulleys.

UNDERHOOD SERVICE SPECIFICATIONS

SBITU3   SBITU3

ENGINE COMPUTER SYSTEM

COMPUTER DIAGNOSTIC CODES

1988 16-Valve Non-Turbo Engines, 1989-90 All engines:
1. 900 models: Connect switched jumper lead (Part No. 83 93 886) in line between the pin No. 3 of the test socket on the passenger's side of engine compartment and ground. 9000 models: Connect switched jumper lead (Part No. 83 93 886) in line between the test socket on the driver's side of engine compartment and negative battery terminal.
2. Switch on ignition, CHECK ENGINE light will come on, turn jumper switch on and light will go out.
3. When CHECK ENGINE light flashes immediately turn jumper switch off.
4. The primary error code will now be displayed by the CHECK ENGINE light as a series of short flashes. A long flash of the light will start and end each code, these are not part of the code.
5. To display additional codes, turn jumper switch on, after a brief flash of the light immediately turn switch off. Second code will now be displayed, repeat procedure for third code, 9 series of long flashes indicates no additional codes.
6. To erase memory, turn jumper switch on, after three short flashes of light turn switch off. Memory erased code will be displayed.

Code	Light♦	Fault
00000	—	No more faults
12111	off	Lambda adaptation, air-fuel mixture, throttle open
12112	off	Lambda adaptation, air-fuel mixture, throttle closed
12113	off	Idle control adaptation, pulse ratio low
12114	off	Idle control adaptation, pulse ratio high
12211	off	Incorrect battery voltage (engine running)
12212	off	Throttle position sensor, idling contacts
12213	off	Throttle position sensor, full throttle contacts
12214	on	Temperature sensor signal out of range
12221	on	Air mass meter signal absent, system in limp-home mode
12222	off	Idling control (AIC), no pulse switching, defective ECU
12223	on	Lean fuel mixture
12224	on	Rich fuel mixture
12225	on	Oxygen sensor signal, engine in limp home mode
12231	off	No RPM signal*
12232	off	Open memory circuit to ECU
12233	off	Auto diagnostic program error
12444	—	Memory erased

* If displayed as first fault with engine off, hold ignition key in start position until CHECK ENGINE light flashes, additional codes can now be accessed.

♦ Indicates condition while operating vehicle prior to testing.

1991-92 All engines: Special test equipment required. Connect tester according to manufacturer's instructions. Faults will be displayed as a five digit code. Intermittent faults are indicated by a first digit ''2'' or ''3''; permanent faults are indicated by a ''4'', ''5'', or ''6'' first digit. Read remaining four digits from table.

Code	Application	Definition
2241	Control Unit	Signal to unit over 16 volts
2251	Control Unit	Signal to pin ''4'' below 1 volt
2252	Control Unit	Signal to unit below 10 volts
2291	System Voltage	Battery voltage out of range
2440	Fuel Mixture	System rich, no oxygen sensor control
2441	Fuel Mixture	System rich at idle
2442	Fuel Mixture	System rich at speed
2450	Fuel Mixture	System lean, no oxygen sensor control
2451	Fuel Mixture	System lean at idle
2452	Fuel Mixture	System lean at speed
2460	Oxygen Sensor	Faulty sensor signal
2491	Fuel Mixture	Out of range at idle
2492	Fuel Mixture	Out of range at speed
4221	Speed Sensor	No speed signal recorded
4261	Speed Sensor	Faulty signal from road speed sensor
5641	Air Mass Meter	Reference signal too high
5651	Air Mass Meter	Reference signal too low
5691	Air Mass Meter	Reference signal out of range
5723	Drive Signal	Faulty transmission signal
5771	Throttle Signal	Potentiometer signal shorted
5772	Throttle Signal	Potentiometer signal open
6221	Temperature Sensor	Coolant sensor circuit open
6271	Temperature Sensor	Coolant sensor circuit shorted
6391	EGR System	Function faulty, temperature low
8121	Air Mass Meter	Burn-off not functioning
8321	Idle Control	Air control valve malfunction
8322	Canister Valve	Purge valve malfunction
8371	Fuel Injector	Faulty fuel signal
8372	Canister Valve	Purge valve circuit malfunction
8382	Canister Valve	Purge valve circuit shorted
7192	Control Unit	Internal defect

SENSORS, INPUT

COOLANT TEMPERATURE SENSOR

Engine	Year	Resistance Ohms @ deg. F/C
All	1983-92	14000 @ −4/−20
		5800 @ 32/0
		2600 @ 68/20
		320 @ 176/80

THROTTLE POTENTIOMETER

Engine	Year	Resistance Ohms @ Terminal	Throttle Position
2119cc, 2290cc	1991-92	1100-1500 @ 1 & 3	open
		2600-3000 @ 1 & 3	closed

ACTUATORS, OUTPUT

AUXILIARY AIR VALVE

Engine	Year	Resistance (ohms)
4-cyl. 2.0L	1983-85	40-60

IDLE CONTROLLER

Engine	Fuel System	Year	Resistance (ohms)
4-cyl. 2.0L	CIS	1986-87	36-44
	LH-Jetronic	1986-92	18-22 ★
4-cyl. 2.1L	LH-Jetronic	1991-92	10-15♦
4-cyl. 2.3L	LH-Jetronic	1990-92	10-15♦

★ Measured between terminals 3 & 4 and 4 & 5.
♦ Measured between terminals 1 & 2 and 2 & 3.

COMPUTER TIMING ADVANCE

Crankshaft degrees at engine rpm, no load, in addition to base timing.

Engine	Year	Transmission	Distributor Number	Speed Advance	Vacuum Retard Degrees @ in. Hg	Advance Degrees @ in. Hg
16-Valve Turbo	1985	MT & AT	0237507001	†	−8 @ 1.03	12 @ 10.3
16-Valve Turbo	1986-88	MT & AT	0237507007	†	−8 @ 7.4	12 @ 8.3

† Speed advance specifications not available.

COMPONENT AND SIGNAL TEST

1989-90 All engines:
1. Connect switched jumper lead between diagnostic socket and ground.
2. Set jumper switch to ''ON'' and switch ignition to run position, after a short flash of the ''check engine'' light, immediately set jumper switch to ''off''.
3. Listen for fuel pump to run as ''check engine'' begins to flash (no code).
4. Set jumper switch to ''on'' after a short flash of the ''check engine'' light, move switch to ''off'' position.
5. Read code displayed by ''check engine'' light and take action indicated below.
6. Repeat steps 4 & 5 until all components have been tested.

Code	Component	Action
None	Fuel pump	Listen, pump runs for less than 1 second
12411	Injection valves	Listen for operation
12412	Idle air control valve	Listen, valve switches once per second
12413	Cannister purge valve	Listen, valve switches once per second
12421	Drive signal, AT	Shift from D to N, flashing should stop
12424	Throttle position sensor (idle signal)	Depress accelerator, flashing should stop
12424	Throttle position sensor (full throttle signal)	Floor accelerator, flashing should stop

SATURN
1991-92

ENGINE IDENTIFICATION

To identify any engine by the manufacturer's code, follow the four steps designated by the numbered blocks.

1 MODEL YEAR IDENTIFICATION: Refer to illustration of the Vehicle Identification Number (V.I.N.). The year is indicated by a code letter which is the 10th character of the V.I.N.

2 ENGINE CODE LOCATION: Refer to illustration of V.I.N. plate for location of engine code.

3 ENGINE CODE: In the "CODE" column, find the engine code determined in Step 2.

4 ENGINE IDENTIFICATION: On the line where the engine code appears, read to the right to identify the engine.

MODEL YEAR AND ENGINE IDENTIFICATION:

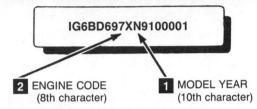

IG6BD697XN9100001

2 ENGINE CODE (8th character)
1 MODEL YEAR (10th character)

V.I.N. PLATE LOCATION:

On top left side of instrument panel

Model year of vehicle:
1992 — Model year is N.
1991 — Model year is M.

4 ENGINE IDENTIFICATION

YEAR	3 ENGINE CODE	CYL.	DISPL. liters	DISPL. cu. in.	Fuel System	HP
1992	9	4	1.9	116	TBI	85
	7	4	1.9	116	MFI	123
1991	9	4	1.9	116	TBI	85
	7	4	1.9	116	MFI	123

TBI — Throttle Body Injection.   **MFI — Multiport Fuel Injection.**

UNDERHOOD SERVICE SPECIFICATIONS

SNTU1   SNTU1

CYLINDER NUMBERING SEQUENCE

4-CYL FIRING ORDER: 1 3 4 2

1 2 3 4

4 1 2 3

1.9L

ELECTRICAL AND IGNITION SYSTEMS

BATTERY

Model	Year	BCI Group No.	Crank. Perf.
All	1991	—	525

SPARK PLUGS

Engine	Year	Gap (inches)	Gap (mm)	Torque (ft-lb)
All	1991	.039-.043	1.0-1.1	20

IGNITION COIL

Secondary resistance measured at each coil's high voltage terminals with spark plug wires removed.

Application	Year	Windings	Resistance (ohms)
1.9L	1991	Primary	—
		Secondary	7000-10,000

FUEL SYSTEM

FUEL PRESSURE

Engine	Year	Pressure PSI	Condition
1.9L SOHC	1991	38-44	ign. on
		26-31	idle
1.9L DOHC	1991	38-44	ign. on
		31-36	idle

ENGINE MECHANICAL

TIGHTENING TORQUES

Engine	Year	Cylinder Head	Intake Manifold	Exhaust Manifold	Crankshaft Pulley	Water Pump
1.9L SOHC	1991	22/30, 33/45, +90°	22/30	16/22	159/215	22/30
1.9L DOHC	1991	22/30, 37/50, +90°	22/30	23/31	159/215	22/30

Torque Ft-lbs/Nm

COMPRESSION PRESSURE

With engine at normal operating temperature.

Engine	Year	Normal Range PSI	Maximum Variation PSI
1.9L	1991	180 @ 250	—

ENGINE COMPUTER SYSTEM

Data not available at this time.

ENGINE IDENTIFICATION

To identify an engine by the manufacturer's code, follow the four steps designated by the numbered blocks.

V.I.N. PLATE LOCATION:

Left side of instrument panel, visible through windshield; also under hood on engine bulkhead.

1 MODEL YEAR IDENTIFICATION:

10th character of V.I.N.
1992 — N; 1991 — M; 1990 — L;
1989 — K; 1988 — J; 1987 — H;
1986 — G; 1985 — F; 1984 — E;
1983 — D.

2 ENGINE CODE LOCATION:

3-cyl.: On top of crankcase, flywheel end.
4-cyl. & 6-cyl.: On right side of crankcase, front of vehicle.

4 ENGINE IDENTIFICATION

YEAR	3 ENGINE CODE	CYL.	DISPL. liters	cc	Fuel System	HP
1992	EA12	3	1.2	1189	2V	66
	EA12	3	1.2	1189	MPFI	73
	EA82	4	1.8	1781	SPFI	90
	EJ22	4	2.2	2212	MPFI	130
	EJ22	4	2.2 T	2212 T	MPFI	160
	EG33	6	3.3	3318	MPFI	230
1991	EA12	3	1.2	1189	2V	66
	EA12	3	1.2	1189	MPFI	73
	EA82	4	1.8	1781	SPFI	90
	EJ22	4	2.2	2212	MPFI	130
	EJ22	4	2.2 T	2212 T	MPFI	160
	ER27	6	2.7	2672	MPFI	145
1990	EA12	3	1.2	1189	2V	66
	EA12	3	1.2	1189	MPFI	73
	EA82	4	1.8	1781	SPFI	90
	EA82	4	1.8 T	1781 T	MPFI	115
	EJ22	4	2.2	2212	MPFI	130
1989	EA12	3	1.2	1189	2 V	66
	EA81	4	1.8	1781	2 V	73
	EA82	4	1.8	1781	SPFI	90
	EA82	4	1.8	1781	MPFI	97
	EA82	4	1.8 T	1781 T	MPFI	115
	ER27	6	2.7	2672	MPFI	145
1988	EA12	3	1.2	1189	2 V	66
	EA81	4	1.8	1781	2 V	73
	EA82	4	1.8	1781	SPFI	90
	EA82	4	1.8	1781	MPFI	97
	EA82	4	1.8 T	1781 T	MPFI	115
	ER27	6	2.7	2672	MPFI	145

4 ENGINE IDENTIFICATION

YEAR	3 ENGINE CODE	CYL.	DISPL. liters	cc	Fuel System	HP
1987	EA71	4	1.6	1595	2 V	69
	EA81	4	1.8	1781	2 V	73
	EA82	4	1.8	1781	2 V	84
	EA82	4	1.8	1781	SPFI	90
	EA82	4	1.8	1781	MPFI	97
	EA82	4	1.8 T	1781 T	MPFI	115
1986	EA71	4	1.6	1595	2 V	69
	EA81	4	1.8	1781	2 V	73
	EA82	4	1.8	1781	2 V	84
	EA82	4	1.8	1781	SPFI	90
	EA82	4	1.8	1781	MPFI	94
	EA82	4	1.8 T	1781 T	MPFI	111
1985	EA71	4	1.6	1595	2 V	69
	EA81	4	1.8	1781	2 V	73
	EA82	4	1.8	1781	2 V	82
	EA82	4	1.8	1781	MPFI	94
	EA82	4	1.8 T	1781 T	MPFI	111
1984	EA71	4	1.6	1595	2 V	69
	EA81	4	1.8	1781	1 V	73
	EA81	4	1.8	1781	2 V	73
	EA81	4	1.8 T	1781 T	MPFI	95
1983	EA71	4	1.6	1595	2 V	69
	EA81	4	1.8	1781	1 V	73
	EA81	4	1.8	1781	2 V	73
	EA81	4	1.8 T	1781 T	MPFI	95

MPFI — Multi Point Fuel Injection.
SPFI — Single Point Fuel Injection.
T — Turbocharged.   V — Venturi.

UNDERHOOD SERVICE SPECIFICATIONS

SUITU1   SUITU1

CYLINDER NUMBERING SEQUENCE

3-CYL. FIRING ORDER: 1 3 2

4-CYL. FIRING ORDER: 1 3 4 2

6-CYL. FIRING ORDER: 1 6 3 2 5 4

— Front of car —

| 1988-91 3-cyl. 1189cc 2V | 1990-92 3-cyl. 1189cc FI | 1983-87 4-cyl. 1595cc, 1983-89 4-cyl. 1781cc OHV | 1985-92 4-cyl. 1781cc OHC | 1990-92 4-cyl. 2212cc | 1988-91 6-cyl. 2672cc |

TIMING MARK

1987-92
3-cyl. 1189cc

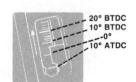

1983-84
4-cyl. 1781cc ex. Turbo,
1983-87
4-cyl. 1595cc,
1985-92
4-cyl. 1781cc

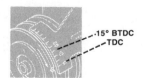

1983-84
4-cyl. 1781cc Turbo

1988-91
6-cyl. 2672cc,
1990-92
4-cyl. 2212cc

SUBARU
1983-92

ELECTRICAL AND IGNITION SYSTEMS

BATTERY

BCI equivalent shown, size may vary from original equipment. Check clearance before replacing, holddown may need to be modified.

Engine	Year	STANDARD BCI Group No.	STANDARD Crank. Perf.	OPTIONAL BCI Group No.	OPTIONAL Crank. Perf.
All MT	1983	24	310	24	450
All AT	1983	24	370	24	450
All MT	1984	24	270	—	—
All AT	1984	24	370	—	—
All MT ex. Turbo	1985	24	270	—	—
All AT ex. Turbo	1985	24	370	—	—
All Turbo	1985	24	450	—	—
All MT ex. Turbo	1986-87	25	306	—	—
All AT ex. Turbo	1986-87	25	420	—	—
6-cyl. MT	1988-91	25	350	—	—
6-cyl. AT	1988-91	24	490	—	—
3-cyl.	1987-92	35	405	—	—
4-cyl. 1.8L MT	1988-92	21	310	—	—
4-cyl. 1.8L AT ex. Turbo	1988-92	25	420	—	—
Turbo	1988-90	24	490	—	—
4-cyl. 2.2L MT	1990-92	85	430	—	—
4-cyl. 2.2L AT	1990-92	35	490	—	—
6-cyl. 3.3L	1992	24	585	—	—

ALTERNATOR

Application	Year	Rated Output (amps)	Test Output (amps @ rpm)
All ex. OHC	1983-89	55	55 @ 5000
All OHC	1985	60	58 @ 5000
XT Coupe 4-cyl.	1986-91	65	53 @ 3000
4-cyl. 1781cc OHC ex. XT Coupe	1986-92	60	49 @ 2500
3-cyl. 1189cc	1987-92	55	30 @ 2500
6-cyl. 2672cc	1988-91	90	62 @ 3000
4-cyl. 2212cc	1990	85	66 @ 3000
4-cyl. 2212cc	1991-92	70	60 @ 3000
6-cyl. 3318cc	1992	95	73 @ 2500

REGULATOR

Year	Test Temp. (deg. F/C)	Voltage Setting
1983-92	68/20	14.1-14.8

STARTER

Engine	Year	Cranking Voltage (min. volts)	Ampere Draw @ Cranking Speed
1595cc MT	1983-85	9.5	270
1781cc MT	1983-85	8.0	230
1781cc AT	1983-84	8.5	350
1781cc AT	1985	8.0	370
All 4-cyl.	1986-87	8.0	370
All 3-cyl.	1987-92	8.0	200
6-cyl. MT	1988-89	8.0	280
6-cyl. AT	1988-89	8.0	370
4-cyl. MT	1988-92	8.0	280
4-cyl. AT	1988-92	8.0	370
6-cyl.	1992	8.0	300

SPARK PLUGS

Engine	Year	Gap (inches)	Gap (mm)	Torque◆ (ft-lb)
All	1983-92	.039-.043	1.0-1.1	13-17

◆ With dry threads.

IGNITION COIL

Engine	Year	Windings	Resistance (ohms)
All 4WD	1983	Primary	1.04-1.27
		Secondary	7360-11,040

IGNITION COIL Continued

Engine	Year	Windings	Resistance (ohms)
All 2WD	1983	Primary	1.13-1.38
		Secondary	10,795-14,605
California MT	1984-85	Primary	1.13-1.38
		Secondary	10,795-14,605
Turbo	1984-85	Primary	0.84-1.02
		Secondary	8000-12,000
All Others	1984-85	Primary	1.04-1.27
		Secondary	7360-11,040
2V Hitachi	1986-87	Primary	1.04-1.27
		Secondary	7360-11,040
2V Nippondenso	1986-87	Primary	1.13-1.38
		Secondary	10,795-14,605
All TBI	1986-87	Primary	0.84-1.02
		Secondary	8000-12,000
All MPFI ex. Turbo	1986-87	Primary	1.13-1.38
		Secondary	10,795-14,605
Turbo	1986-87	Primary	0.93-1.02
		Secondary	8000-12,000
3-cyl. 1189cc	1987-92	Primary	0.84-1.02
		Secondary	8500-11,500
1781cc, 2672cc, all	1988-90	Primary	0.84-1.02
		Secondary	8000-12,000
1781cc	1991-92	Primary	0.1-1.0
		Secondary	8000-12,000
2212cc w/MT	1990-92	Primary	0.62-0.76
		Secondary	17,900-24,500
2212cc w/AT	1990-92	Primary	0.63-0.77
		Secondary	10,400-15,600
3318cc	1992	Primary	0.68-0.83

IGNITION PICKUP

Application	Year	Resistance (ohms)	Air Gap (in./mm)
All 4WD	1983-84	720	.012-.020/.3-.5
Nippondenso distr.	1985-87	130-190	.008-.016/.2-.4
Hitachi distr.	1985-87	—	.012-.020/.3-.5
3-cyl. 1189cc	1988-89	—	.012-.016/.3-.4

TIMING PROCEDURE

1. Disconnect and plug distributor vacuum hose(s). On turbocharged vehicles, disconnect black connector (2-pole) between distributor and knock control unit.
2. Connect timing light to No. 1 spark plug wire.
3. With engine at idle, check timing.
4. Rotate distributor to obtain recommended setting.

BASE TIMING

Set timing at Before Top Dead Center, unless otherwise specified. Disconnect and plug vacuum hose(s).

Engine	Year	Man. Trans. (degrees)	Auto. Trans. (degrees)
1189cc	1987-92	5 ±2	5 ±2
1595cc, 1781cc 2V	1983-89	8 ±2	8 ±2
1781cc Turbo	1984	—	15
1781cc Turbo	1985-86	25	25
1781cc MPFI	1985-86	6	6
1781cc SPFI	1986	—	20 ±2
1781cc	1987-92	20 ±2	20 ±2
2212cc ex. Turbo	1990-91	20 ±2	20 ±8
2212cc Turbo	1991	15 ±2	15 ±2
2212cc ex. Turbo	1992	20 ±8	20 ±8
2212cc Turbo	1992	15 ±8	15 ±8
2672cc	1988-91	20 ±2	20 ±2
3318cc	1992	—	20 ±8

DISTRIBUTOR TIMING ADVANCE

Engine degrees at engine rpm, no load, in addition to base timing setting.

Engine	Transmission	Year	Distributor Number	Degrees @ 2500 RPM* Total	Degrees @ 2500 RPM* Centrifugal
1189cc	MT	1987-89	100291-A080	39-47	11-15
1595cc	MT	1983	—	32-40	10-14
1595cc	MT	1984-87	0300	26.5-37.0	6.5-11.0

DISTRIBUTOR TIMING ADVANCE Continued

Engine	Trans-mission	Year	Distributor Number	Degrees @ 2500 RPM* Total	Degrees @ 2500 RPM* Centrifugal
1781cc	MT & AT	1983	7220	32-40	10-14
1781cc	MT	1984-85	D4R83-12	26.5-37.0	6.5-11.0
1781cc	AT	1984-85	D4R83-13	25-35	7-11
1781cc	AT	1984-85	D4R83-03	16-32	2-6
1781cc	MT	1985	0890	31-41	17-22
1781cc	AT	1985	0900	30-39	16-20
1781cc	MT	1985	0920	31-39	18-22
1781cc	MT & AT	1985	D4R84-16	37-45	28-32
1781cc	MT & AT	1985	0880	32.4-40.8	12-16
1781cc	MT & AT	1985	D4R84-20	27-36	19-24
1781cc	AT	1986-87	1430	28.3-36.3	12.3-16.3
1781cc	MT & AT	1986	1420	25-33	9-13
1781cc	MT & AT	1986-87	1500	21-29	15.5-19.5
1781cc	MT & AT	1985-87	D4R83-12	26.5-37	6.5-11
1781cc	MT & AT	1985-87	D4R83-13	25-35	7-11
1781cc	MT & AT	1986-87	D4R83-51, 52	28.8-36.8	9.8-13.8

* Does not include sub-advance.

FUEL SYSTEM

FUEL PUMP

Engine	Year	Pressure PSI	Pressure RPM
1189cc 2V	1987-91	1.25-2.0	idle
1595cc, 1781cc 2V	1983-85	1.3-2.1	—
1781cc MPFI	1984	43.4	—
1781cc MPFI	1985	61-71	—
1781cc 2V	1986-89	2.6-3.3	idle
1781cc SPFI	1986-91	20-24	idle
1781cc MPFI	1986-90	26-30	idle
2212cc	1990	26-30	idle
2672cc	1988-89	26-30	idle
3318cc	1992	36.3	idle

CARBURETOR CHOKE

Engine	Year	Make	Choke (notches) Man. Trans.	Choke (notches) Auto. Trans.
All	1984	Carter-Weber	1 rich	
All	1983-85	Hitachi	1 rich	1 rich
3-cyl. 1189cc	1987-89	Hitachi DFC328	high	high

IDLE SPEED W/O COMPUTER CONTROL

Disconnect and plug cannister purge hose at carburetor or throttle body.
With FI, ensure that auxiliary air valve is closed.

Engine	Year	Manual* Trans.	Auto.* Trans.
All	1983	600-800	700-900 N
All 1595cc	1984-89	600-800	—
All 1781cc	1984-91	600-800	700-900 N
AC speed-up, 2V	1984-89	900-1000	900-1000 N
AC speed-up, FI	1984-89	800-900	800-900 N
3-cyl. 1189cc 2V	1987-92	750-850	—
Speed-up	1987-92	850-950	—

* Preferred setting is mid-point of range given.

IDLE SPEED W/COMPUTER CONTROL

Disconnect air valve control connector and set to specified setting speed.

Engine	Year	Setting Speed	Checking Speed	Speed-up
1189cc	1990-92	—	650-750	—
1781cc SPFI	1986-87	550-650 N	600-800 N	800-900 N
1781cc SPFI	1988-90	500-600	600-800	800-900
2212cc	1990-92	—	600-700 N	800-900 N
2627cc	1988-91	—	650-850	800-900
3318cc	1992	—	510-710	750-850 N

IDLE MIXTURE

Engine	Year	CO%◆	CO%
All MT	1983-84	1-3	0-0.4
AT ex. Turbo	1983-84	0.5-2.5	0-0.4
Turbo, FI	1983-87	0.1	0.1
All 2V	1986-87	1.0-2.0	0-0.4

◆ Air injection disconnected.

ENGINE MECHANICAL

TIGHTENING TORQUES

Engine	Year	Torque Ft-lbs/Nm Cylinder Head	Intake Manifold	Exhaust Manifold	Crankshaft Pulley	Water Pump
3-cyl. 1.2L:	1987-88	29/39	14-22/	14-22/	47-54/	6.9-7.3/
2nd stage		43/59	20-29	20-29	64-74	9.3-10.3
3rd stage		51/69				
3-cyl. 1.2L:	1989	29/39	14-22/	14-22/	58-72/	6.9-7.3/
2nd stage		54/73	20-29	20-29	78-98	9.3-10.3
3rd stage†		57/77				
4-cyl. 1.6L	1983-87	22/30	13-16/	19-22/	47-54/	—
2nd stage		43/60	18-22	25-29	65-75	
3rd stage		47/65				
4-cyl. 1.8L OHV:	1983-84	22/30	13-16/	19-22/	47-54/	—
2nd stage		43/60	18-22	25-29	65-75	
3rd stage		47/65				
4-cyl. 1.8L OHV:	1985-88	22/30	17-20/	19-22/	47-54/	—
2nd stage		43/60	23-27	25-29	65-75	
3rd stage		47/65				
4-cyl. 1.8L OHC:	1985-91	22/30	13-16/	19-22/	66-79/	—
2nd stage		43/60	18-22	25-29	89-107	
3rd stage◆		47/65				
4-cyl. 2.2L DOHC	1990-91	51/69	—	19-26/	66-79/	6.5-8.0/
2nd stage●;				25-35	86-107	9-11
center 2		25/34				
outer 4		14/20				
3rd stage		+90°				
4th stage		+90°				
6-cyl. 2.7L	1988-91	22/30	13-16/	19-22/	66-79/	—
2nd stage		47/64	18-22	25-29	89-107	
3rd stage†		50/68				

† Back off 90° before bringing to final torque.
◆ Tighten to specification, run engine to operating temperature and allow to cool, back off and retorque one bolt at a time.
● Back off 180° before bringing to 2nd stage torque.

VALVE CLEARANCE

Engine cold.

Engine	Year	Intake (inches)	Intake (mm)	Exhaust (inches)	Exhaust (mm)
All	1983-84	.009-.011	.23-.28	.013-.015	.33-.38
4-cyl. ex. OHC	1985-89	.010	.25	.014	.35
3-cyl.	1987-92	.005-.007	.13-.17	.009-.011	.23-.27

COMPRESSION PRESSURE

At cranking speed, engine warm, throttle open.

Engine	Year	PSI	Maximum Variation PSI
All	1983	121-156	28
1595cc	1984	175	28
1781cc ex. Turbo	1984	171	28
1781cc Turbo	1984	156	28
1781cc 2V	1985-89	132-161	28
1781cc SPFI	1985-91	139-168	28
1781cc Turbo	1985-91	117-145	28
1190cc 3-cyl.	1987-91	135-156	14
2672cc 6-cyl.	1988-91	139-168	28
2212cc 4-cyl.	1990-91	156-185	28
3318cc 6-cyl.	1992	171-206	28

UNDERHOOD SERVICE SPECIFICATIONS

BELT TENSION
Deflection method: Table lists deflection at midpoint of longest belt segment under a 22 pound load.

Model	Year	Alternator	Power Steering	Air Cond.	Air Pump
USED BELTS:					
All (inches)	1983	1/2-9/16	9/16-3/4	—	1/2-9/16
(mm)	1983	31-14	15-20	—	13-14
All (inches)	1984	1/2-9/16	1/2-9/16	—	1/2-9/16
(mm)	1984	13-14	13-14	—	13-14
Brat, Hatchback (inches)	1985-86	1/2-9/16	5/16-3/8	7/16-1/2	1/2-9/16
(mm)	1985-86	13-14	8-9	11-12	13-14
Sedan, Wagon (inches)	1985-86	7/16-9/16	5/16-3/8	7/16-1/2	3/8-7/16
(mm)	1985-86	11-14	8-9	11-13	9-11
Ex. Justy (inches)	1987	1/2-9/16	3/8-7/16	7/16-1/2*	—
(mm)	1987	13-15	9-11	11-13*	—
Justy (inches)	1987-92	5/16-3/8	—	7/16-1/2	—
(mm)	1987-92	9-10	—	11-12	—
Ex. Justy (inches)	1988-89	3/8-7/16	1/4-3/8	3/8-1/2*	—
(mm)	1988-89	9-11	7-9	10-12*	—
Loyale (inches)	1990-92	1/2-9/16	3/8-7/16	7/16-1/2	—
(mm)	1990-92	13-15	9-11	11-12*	—
Legacy (inches)	1990-92	3/8-7/16	3/8-7/16	3/8-7/16	—
(mm)	1990-92	9-11	9-11	9-10	—
XT (inches)	1990-91	3/8-7/16	5/16-7/16	5/16-7/16	—
(mm)	1990-91	9-11	7-9	7-9	—
SVX	1992	3/16-1/4	3/16-1/4	9/32-5/16	—
		5-6	5-6	7-8	—

* With both AC & PS; inches—5/16-11/32, mm—7.5-8.5.

ENGINE COMPUTER SYSTEM

COMPUTER DIAGNOSTIC CODES
To activate codes, connect male and female connectors under steering wheel to left of module. Turn ignition on but do not start car. Codes will be displayed as pulses on LED mounted on module. Long pulses indicate tens, short pulses indicate ones.

1983 2V
Codes 11, 12, 21, 22 Ignition pulse system
Codes 14, 24, 41, 42 Vacuum switches remain on or off
Codes 15, 51, 52 Solenoid valve remains on or off
Code 23 Oxygen sensor
Code 32 Coolant temperature sensor
Code 33 Main system in feedback
Codes 34, 43 Choke power remains on or off
Code 42 Clutch switch

1984 2V
Codes 11, 18 Ignition pulse system
Code 22 Speed sensor
Code 23 Oxygen sensor
Codes 24, 25 Coolant temperature sensor
Codes 31, 32 Duty solenoid valve
Code 33 Main system in feedback
Codes 34, 35 Back up system
Codes 42, 45 Vacuum switch remains on or off
Codes 52, 53 Solenoid valve control system
Codes 54, 55 Choke control system
Code 62 EGR solenoid valve control
Codes 63, 64 Canister solenoid valve control
Codes 73, 77 Ignition pulse system

1985-86 2V
Code 11 Ignition pulse system
Code 22 Speed sensor
Code 23 Oxygen sensor
Code 24 Coolant temperature sensor
Code 25 Manifold vacuum sensor
Code 32 Duty solenoid valve

COMPUTER DIAGNOSTIC CODES Continued
Code 33 Main system in feedback
Code 34 Back up system
Code 42 Clutch switch
Code 52 Solenoid valve control system
Code 53 Fuel pump control system
Code 54 Choke control system
Code 55 Shift up control
Code 62 EGR solenoid valve control
Code 63 Canister solenoid valve control
Code 64 Vacuum line control valve
Code 65 Float chamber vent control valve
Codes 71, 73, 74 Ignition pulse system

1983-85 FI
Code 11 Ignition pulse
Code 12 Starter switch off
Code 13 Starter switch on
Code 14 Air flow meter
Code 21 Seized air flow meter flap
Code 22 Pressure or vacuum switches fixed
Code 23 Idle switch fixed
Code 24 Wide open throttle switch fixed
Code 32 Oxygen sensor
Code 33 Coolant sensor
Code 35 Air flow meter or EGR solenoid switch
Codes 31, 41 Atmosphere air sensor
Code 42 Fuel injector fixed

1986 FI
Code 11 Ignition pulse
Code 12 Starter switch off
Code 13 Starter switch on
Code 14 Air flow meter
Code 15 Pressure switch fixed
Code 16 Crank angle sensor
Code 17 Starter switch
Code 21 Seized air flow meter flap
Code 22 Pressure or vacuum switches fixed
Code 23 Idle switch fixed
Code 24 Wide open throttle switch fixed
Code 25 Throttle sensor idle switch
Code 31 Speed sensor
Code 32 Oxygen sensor
Code 33 Coolant sensor
Code 35 Air flow meter or EGR solenoid switch
Code 41 Atmosphere pressure sensor
Code 42 Fuel injector fixed
Codes 43, 55 KDLH control system
Code 46 Neutral or parking switch
Code 47 Fuel injector
Code 53 Fuel pump
Code 57 Canister control system
Code 58 Air control system
Code 62 EGR control system
Code 88 TBI control unit

1987 All TBI & MFI
Code 11 Ignition pulse
Code 12 Starter switch
Code 13 Crank angle sensor
Code 14 Injectors 1 & 2
Code 15 Injectors 3 & 4
Code 21 Coolant temperature sensor
Code 22 Knock sensor
Code 23 Air flow meter
Code 24 Air control valve
Code 31 Throttle sensor
Code 32 Oxygen sensor
Code 33 Vehicle speed sensor
Code 35 Purge control solenoid
Code 41 Lean fuel mixture
Code 42 Idle switch
Code 45 Kick-down relay
Code 51 Neutral switch
Code 61 Parking switch

1988-91 3-cyl. 1189cc Justy
Code 14 Duty solenoid valve control
Code 15 Coasting fuel cut system
Code 21 Coolant temperature sensor
Code 22 Vacuum line charging solenoid control
Code 23 Pressure sensor system
Code 24 Idle-up solenoid control

UNDERHOOD SERVICE SPECIFICATIONS

COMPUTER DIAGNOSTIC CODES Continued

Code 25 Fuel chamber vent solenoid control
Code 32 Oxygen sensor
Code 33 Vehicle speed sensor
Code 35 Purge control solenoid control
Code 52 Clutch switch
Code 62 Idle-up system
Code 63 Idle-up system

1988-91 All 4-cyl. 1781cc, 1988-91 6-cyl. 2672cc
Code 11 Crank angle sensor
Code 12 Starter switch
Code 13 Crank angle sensor
Code 14 Injectors 1 & 2
Code 15 Injectors 3 & 4
Code 21 Coolant temperature sensor
Code 22 Knock sensor
Code 23 Air flow meter
Code 24 Air control valve
Code 31 Throttle sensor
Code 32 Oxygen sensor
Code 33 Vehicle speed sensor
Code 34 EGR solenoid
Code 35 Purge control solenoid
Code 41 Lean fuel mixture
Code 42 Idle switch
Code 44 Duty solenoid valve (waste gate control)
Code 45 Kick-down control relay
Code 51 Neutral switch continuously in on position
Code 54 Neutral switch
Code 55 EGR temperature sensor
Code 61 Parking switch

1990-91 4-cyl. 2212cc
Code 11 Crankshafft angle sensor
Code 12 Starter switch
Code 13 Camshaft angle sensor
Code 14 Injector, cylinder 1
Code 15 Injector, cylinder 2
Code 16 Injector, cylinder 3
Code 17 Injector, cylinder 4
Code 21 Coolant temperature sensor
Code 22 Knock sensor
Code 23 Knock sensor
Code 24 Air control valve
Code 31 Throttle position sensor
Code 32 Oxygen sensor
Code 33 Vehicle speed sensor
Code 35 Canister purge solenoid
Code 41 Air/fuel adaptive control
Code 42 Idle switch
Code 45 Atmospheric pressure sensor
Code 51 Neutral switch (MT), inhibitor switch (AT)
Code 52 Parking switch

1992 6-cyl. 3318cc
Code 11 Crankshaft angle sensor
Code 12 Starter switch
Code 13 Camshaft angle sensor
Code 14 Injector, cylinder 1
Code 15 Injector, cylinder 2
Code 16 Injector, cylinder 3
Code 17 Injector, cylinder 4
Code 18 Injector, cylinder 5
Code 19 Injector, cylinder 6
Code 21 Coolant temperature sensor
Code 22 Knock sensor, right side
Code 23 Air flow sensor
Code 24 By-pass air valve
Code 28 Knock sensor, left side
Code 29 Crankshaft angle sensor
Code 31 Throttle position sensor
Code 32 Oxygen sensor, right side
Code 33 Vehicle speed sensor
Code 34 EGR solenoid valve
Code 35 Canister purge valve
Code 37 Oxygen sensor, left side
Code 38 No engine to transmission
Code 41 Air fuel ratio control
Code 45 Atmospheric pressure sensor
Code 51 Neutral switch
Code 52 Parking switch
Code 55 EGR temperature sensor
Code 56 EGR system

SENSORS, INPUT

TEMPERATURE SENSORS

Engine	Year	Sensor	Resistance Ohms @ deg. F/C
3-cyl. 1.2L	1987-89	Coolant	134-179 @ 122/50
			47-57 @ 176/80
			26-29 @ 212/100
			15-17 @ 248/120
4-cyl. 1.8L	1984-91	Coolant	7000-11,500 @ 14/–10
			2000-3000 @ 68/20
			700-1000 @ 122/50
4-cyl. 1.8L Turbo	1987-90	Coolant	7000-11,500 @ 14/–10
			2000-3000 @ 68/20
			700-1000 @ 122/50
		Wastegate	17-21 @ 68/20
6-cyl. 2.7L	1988-91	Coolant	7000-11,500 @ 14/–10
			2000-3000 @ 68/20
			700-1000 @ 122/50
4-cyl. 2.2L	1990-92	Coolant	2500 @ 68/20
			400 @ 176/80
6-cyl. 3.3L	1992	Coolant	2500 @ 68/20
			400 @ 176/80

AIRFLOW SENSOR

Engine	Year	Resistance Ohms @ Terminal	Voltage @ Terminal
4-cyl. 1.8L SPFI	1987-90	10 max. @ B & ground	10 min. @ R
			0.1-0.5 @ W & B
4-cyl. 1.8L Turbo	1987-90	10 max. @ B & BR	10 min. @ SA
			1-2 @ SA & BR
6-cyl. 2.7L	1987-91	10 max. @ B & BR	10 min. @ SA
			1-2 @ SA & BR

ATMOSPHERIC PRESSURE SENSOR

Engine	Year	Resistance (ohms)
3-cyl. 1.2L	1987-89	32.7-39.9

THROTTLE POSITION SENSOR

Engine	Year	Resistance Ohms @ Terminal
4-cyl. 1.8L SPFI	1984-90	3500-6500 @ B & D
		1000 max. @ B & C ★
		2400 min. @ B & C●
4-cyl. 1.8L Turbo	1987-90	6-18 @ 1 & 3
		5.8-17.8 @ 1 & 2★
		1.5-5.1 @ 1 & 2●
6-cyl. 2.7L	1988-91	3-7 @ 1 & 4
		100-11,000 @ 2 & 4★
		4200-15,000 @ 2 & 4●
4-cyl. 2.2L	1990-91	12,000 @ 2 & 3
		4300 @ 2 & 4★
		1000 @ 2 & 4●
6-cyl. 3.3L	1992	5000 @ 1 & 3
		12,000 @ 2 & 3●
		5000 @ 2 & 3★

★ With throttle plate open.
● With throttle plate closed.

ACTUATORS, OUTPUT

AIR CONTROL VALVE

Engine	Year	Resistance (ohms)
4-cyl. 1.8L SPFI	1984-86	8.6-10.6
4-cyl. 1.8L SPFI	1987-90	7.3-13
4-cyl. 2.2L w/MT	1990	9.6
4-cyl. 2.2L w/AT	1990	9.0

BY-PASS AIR CONTROLLER

Engine	Year	Resistance Ohms @ Terminal
6-cyl. 2.7L	1988-91	9500-11,500 @ 1 & 2
		8500-10,500 @ 2 & 3

IDLE UP SOLENOID

Engine	Year	Resistance (ohms)
All	1984-89	32.7-39.9

ENGINE IDENTIFICATION

To identify an engine by the manufacturer's code, follow the four steps designated by the numbered blocks.

V.I.N. PLATE LOCATION:

1983 Pickup — Attached to driver's door pillar.

1987-83 Land Cruiser — Under hood.

All Others — Attached to top of instrument panel visible through windshield.

1 MODEL YEAR IDENTIFICATION:

10th character of V.I.N.
1992 — N; 1991 — M; 1990 — L;
1989 — K; 1988 — J; 1987 — H;
1986 — G; 1985 — F; 1984 — E;
1983 — D.

2 ENGINE CODE LOCATION:

4230cc eng. — Prefix to engine number on right side of engine block.

All other engines — Prefix to engine number on side of engine block.

4 ENGINE IDENTIFICATION

YEAR	CODE	CYL.	liters	cc	Fuel System	HP
1992	3E-E	4	1.5	1456	MFI	82
	5E-FE	4	1.5	1456	MFI	100
	4A-FE	4	1.6	1587	MFI	102, 103†
	3S-GTE	4	2.0 T	1998 T	MFI	200
	5S-FE	4	2.2	2164	MFI	130, 135†
	22R-E	4	2.4	2366	MFI	116
	2TZ-FF	4	2.4	2438	MFI	138
	7M-GE	6	3.0	2954	MFI	190, 200†
	7M-GET	6	3.0 T	2954 T	MFI	232
	3VZ-E	6	3.0	2958	MFI	150, 185†
	3F-E	6	4.0	3955	MFI	155
1991	3E-E	4	1.5	1456	MFI	82
	4A-FE	4	1.6	1587	MFI	102, 103†
	4A-GE	4	1.6	1587	MFI	130
	3S-FE	4	2.0	1998	MFI	115
	3S-GTE	4	2.0 T	1998 T	MFI	200
	5S-FE	4	2.2	2164	MFI	130, 135†
	22R-E	4	2.4	2366	MFI	116
	2TZ-FE	4	2.4	2438	MFI	138
	2V-ZE	4	2.5	2507	MFI	156
	7M-GE	6	3.0	2954	MFI	190, 200†
	7M-GET	6	3.0 T	2954 T	MFI	232
	3V-ZE	6	3.0	2958	MFI	150
	3F-E	6	4.0	3955	MFI	155
1990	3E	4	1.5	1456	2V	78
	3E-E	4	1.5	1456	MFI	82
	4A-FE	4	1.6	1587	MFI	101, 103†
	4A-GE	4	1.6	1587	MFI	130
	3S-FE	4	2.0	1998	MFI	115
	3S-GTE	4	2.0 T	1998 T	MFI	200
	5S-FE	4	2.2	2164	MFI	130
	22R	4	2.4	2366	2V	102
	22R-E	4	2.4	2366	MFI	116
	2VZ-FE	6	2.5	2507	MFI	156
	7M-GE	6	3.0	2954	MFI	190, 200†
	7M-GET	6	3.0 T	2954 T	MFI	232
	3V-ZE	6	3.0	2958	MFI	150
	3F-E	6	4.0	3955	MFI	155
1989	3E	4	1.5	1546	2V	78
	4A-F	4	1.6	1587	2V	90
	4A-FE	4	1.6	1587	MFI	100
	4A-GE	4	1.6	1587	MFI	115
	4A-GELC	4	1.6	1587	MFI	115
	4A-GZE	4	1.6 S	1587 S	MFI	145
	3S-FE	4	2.0	1998	MFI	115
	3S-GE	4	2.0	1998	MFI	135
	3S-GTE	4	2.0 T	1998 T	MFI	190
	4Y-EC	4	2.2	2237	MFI	101
	22R	4	2.4	2366	2V	103
	22R-E	4	2.4	2366	MFI	116
	2V-ZE	6	2.5	2507	MFI	153
	7M-GE	6	3.0	2954	MFI	190, 200†
	7M-GET	6	3.0 T	2954 T	MFI	230
	3V-ZE	6	3.0	2958	MFI	150
	3F-E	6	4.0	3955	MFI	155
1988	3A-C	4	1.5	1452	2V	62
	3E	4	1.5	1456	2V	78
	4A-F	4	1.6	1587	2V	90
	4A-LC	4	1.6	1587	2V	74
	4A-GE	4	1.6	1587	MFI	110
	4A-GELC	4	1.6	1587	MFI	110, 115†
	4A-GZE	4	1.6 S	1587 S	MFI	145
	3S-FE	4	2.0	1998	MFI	115
	3S-GE	4	2.0	1998	MFI	135
	4Y-EC	4	2.2	2237	MFI	101
	22R	4	2.4	2366	2V	103
	22R-E	4	2.4	2366	MFI	116
	22R-TE	4	2.4 T	2366 T	MFI	135
	5M-GE	6	2.8	2759	MFI	156
	7M-GE	6	3.0	2954	MFI	200
	7M-GTE	6	3.0 T	2954 T	MFI	230
	3F-E	6	4.0	3955	MFI	154

4 ENGINE IDENTIFICATION

YEAR	CODE	CYL.	liters	cc	Fuel System	HP
1987	3A	4	1.5	1452	2V	N/A
	3A-C	4	1.5	1452	2V	60, 62†
	3E	4	1.5	1456	2V	78
	4A-C	4	1.6	1587	2V	70
	4A-LC	4	1.6	1587	2V	74
	4A-GEC	4	1.6	1587	MFI	112
	4A-GELC	4	1.6	1587	MFI	108, 112†
	3S-FE	4	2.0	1998	MFI	115
	3S-GE	4	2.0	1998	MFI	135
	4Y-EC	4	2.2	2237	MFI	101
	22R	4	2.4	2366	2V	103
	22R-E	4	2.4	2366	MFI	116
	22R-ET	4	2.4 T	2366 T	MFI	140
	5M-GE	6	2.8	2759	MFI	156
	7M-GE	6	3.0	2954	MFI	200
	7M-GET	6	3.0 T	2954 T	MFI	230
	2F	6	4.2	4230	2V	125
1986	3A	4	1.5	1452	2V	N/A
	3A-C	4	1.5	1452	2V	59, 62†
	4A-C	4	1.6	1587	2V	70
	4A-GEC	4	1.6	1587	MFI	112
	2C-T	4	2.0 D	1974 D	MFI	79
	2S-E	4	2.0	1995	MFI	95, 97†
	3S-GE	4	2.0	1998	MFI	135
	4Y-EC	4	2.2	2237	MFI	105
	22R	4	2.4	2366	2V	103
	22R-E	4	2.4	2366	MFI	116
	22R-ET	4	2.4 T	2366 T	MFI	135
	2L-T	4	2.4 D	2446 D	MFI	84
	5M-GE	6	2.8	2759	MFI	156
	7M-GE	6	3.0	2954	MFI	200
	2F	6	4.2	4230	2V	125
1985	3A	4	1.5	1452	2V	N/A
	3A-C	4	1.5	1452	2V	59, 62†
	4A-C	4	1.6	1587	2V	70
	4A-GEC	4	1.6	1587	2V	112
	1C	4	1.8 D	1839 D	MFI	56
	1C-T	4	1.8 TD	1839 TD	MFI	73
	2S-E	4	2.0	1995	MFI	92
	3Y-EC	4	2.0	1998	MFI	90
	22R	4	2.4	2366	2V	103
	22R-E	4	2.4	2366	MFI	116
	2L	4	2.4 D	2466 D	MFI	75
	2LT	4	2.4 TD	2466 TD	MFI	84
	5M-GE	6	2.8	2759	MFI	156, 161†
	2F	6	4.2	4230	2V	125
1984	4K-E	4	1.3	1290	MFI	58
	3A	4	1.5	1452	2V	N/A
	3A-C	4	1.5	1452	2V	59, 62†
	4A-C	4	1.6	1587	2V	70
	1C	4	1.8 D	1839 D	MFI	56
	1C-T	4	1.8 TD	1839 TD	MFI	72
	2S-E	4	2.0	1995	MFI	93
	3Y-EC	4	2.0	1998	MFI	90
	2L	4	2.5 D	2466 D	MFI	70, 75†
	22R	4	2.4	2366	2V	100
	22R-E	4	2.4	2366	MFI	105
	5M-GE	6	2.8	2759	MFI	143, 150†
	2F	6	4.2	4230	2V	125
1983	4K-E	4	1.3	1290	MFI	58
	3A	4	1.5	1452	2V	N/A
	3A-C	4	1.5	1452	2V	59, 62†
	4A-C	4	1.6	1587	2V	70
	2S-E	4	2.0	1995	MFI	93
	L	4	2.2 D	2188 D	MFI	62
	22R	4	2.4	2366	2V	96
	22R-E	4	2.4	2366	MFI	105
	5M-GE	6	2.8	2759	MFI	145
	2F	6	4.2	4230	2V	125

† Engine horsepower varies with model installation.
D — Diesel.   T — Turbocharged   TD — Turbo Diesel.
S — Supercharged.   MFI — Multiport Fuel Injection.
2V — Two Venturi Carburetor.

UNDERHOOD SERVICE SPECIFICATIONS

CYLINDER NUMBERING SEQUENCE
4-CYL. FIRING ORDER: 1 3 4 2

Front of car

| 1987-90 Tercel 1456cc 2V | 1990-92 Tercel 1456cc FI | 1992 Paseo 1456cc FI | 1984-89 MR2 1587cc FI, 1987-88 FX16 1587cc DOHC, 1986-87 Corolla FWD 1587cc DOHC | 1983-87 Corolla 1587cc 2V FWD | 1988-92 Corolla, Celica 1587cc 4AF, FE |

Front of car

| 1983-84 Starlet 1290cc | 1983-88 Tercel 1452cc, 1983-87 Corolla 1587cc 2V RWD |

Front of car

| 1988-91 Corolla 1587cc 4 AGE | 1985-87 Corolla GTS 1587cc FI | 1983-86 Camry, 1986 Celica ex. DOHC | 1986-92 Celica, Camry, MR2 1998cc DOHC ex. Turbo, 2164cc DOHC | 1988-92 Celica 1998cc Turbo | 1991-92 MR2 1998cc Turbo | 1984-90 Van 1998cc, 2237cc | 1983-91 Pickup, Corona, Celica 2189cc; 2366cc |

Front of car

6-CYL. FIRING ORDER: 1 5 3 6 2 4

V6 FIRING ORDER: 1 2 3 4 5 6

Front of car

| 1988-91 Camry 2507cc | 1983-88 Cressida, Supra 2759cc DOHC | 1986-91 Supra 2954cc | 1988-91 Pickup 2958cc | 1983-89 Land Cruiser 4230cc |

TIMING MARK

 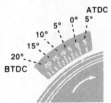 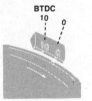 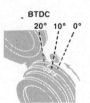 

| 1983-84 Starlet 1290cc | 1983-87 1452cc; 1983-87 1587cc RWD; 1987-88 FX16 DOHC 1587cc | 1987-92 Paseo, Tercel 1456cc | 1985-89 MR2 1587cc | 1983-92 Corolla, Celica 1587cc FWD, 1987-88 FX16 ex. DOHC 1587cc |

| 1983-92 Camry, Celica, MR2 1995cc, 1998cc 3S-FE, 2164cc | 1986-92 Celica, MR2 1998cc 3S-GE, 1998cc Turbo | 1985-90 Van 1998cc, 2237cc | 1983 85 Pickup, Corona 2366cc | 1986-92 Pickup 2366cc |

 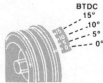

| 1991-92 Previa 2438cc | 1983-91 Supra, Cressida 2563cc; 2759cc; 2954cc | 1988-92 Camry 2507cc, 2958cc; 1989-92 Pickup 2958cc | 1983-91 Land Cruiser 4320cc |

ELECTRICAL AND IGNITION SYSTEMS

BATTERY

BCI equivalent shown, size may vary from original equipment. Check clearance before replacing, holddown may need to be modified.

Engine/Model	Year	STANDARD BCI Group No.	STANDARD Crank. Perf.	OPTIONAL BCI Group No.	OPTIONAL Crank. Perf.
1290cc Starlet	1983-84	21	320	—	—
1452cc Tercel	1983-88	21	320	25	350
1456cc Tercel: MT	1987-89	21R	320	—	—
AT & Canada	1987-89	35	350	—	—
1456cc	1990	35	350	—	—
1456cc	1991	21	310	—	—
1587cc Corolla	1983-89	21R	320	35	350
Canada	1983-89	35	350	—	—
1587cc MR2	1985-89	35	350	—	—
1587cc Celica	1990-91	35	350	—	—
1839cc Diesel	1984-86	27F	655	—	—
1995cc Camry	1983-87	21R	320	—	—
1995cc, 1998cc Celica	1986-91	35	350	—	—
1998cc Van	1984-85	21	320	25	380
1998cc Camry	1988-89	21R	320	35	380
Canada	1988-89	35	380	—	—
1998cc Camry:					
U.S. Prod.	1990-91	21R	330	—	—
Japan Prod.	1990-91	35	350	—	—
2164cc	1990-91	35	350	—	—
2188cc Diesel Pickup	1983	24, 24F	380	—	—
2237cc	1986-89	25	380	—	—
2366cc:					
Celica 2V	1983-85	24	365	—	—
Celica FI	1983-85	24F	365	—	—
Pickup, 4-Runner	1987-90	21	320	25	350
2366cc	1991	25	350	24	585
Canada	1991	24	585	—	—
2446cc Diesel Pickup	1984-85	24, 24F	380	25	380
2507cc Camry	1988-89	21R	320	35	350
Canada	1988-89	35	350	—	—
2507cc Camry:					
U.S. Prod.	1990-91	21R	330	—	—
Japan Prod.	1990-91	35	350	—	—
2759cc DOHC	1983-85	24F	375	27F	470
Canada	1983-85	27F	470	—	—
2759cc	1986-88	27F	560	—	—
2954cc	1986-91	27F	450	—	—
2958cc Pickup, 4-Runner	1988-89	25	380	—	—
4WD	1988-89	24	610	—	—
2958cc Pickup, 4-Runner	1989-91	24	585	—	—
3956cc Land Cruiser	1988-91	27	450	—	—
4230cc Land Cruiser	1983-87	27	450	—	—

ALTERNATOR

See UNDERHOOD SERVICE INSTRUCTIONS at the beginning of this section for test/adjustment diagrams.

Application	Rated Output (amps)	Test Output (amps @ rpm)
1983-85	40, 45, 50, 55, 60, 65, 70	30 min. @ 2000
1986-88	45, 50, 55, 60, 70	30 min. @ 2000
1989-92	50, 55, 60, 70, 80, 100	30 min. @ 2000

REGULATOR

Application	Year	Test Temp. (deg. F/C)	Voltage Setting
Camry	1983	77/25	13.5-14.3
All ex. Camry	1983	77/25	13.8-14.8
1452cc	1984-88	77/25	13.8-14.8
w/int. reg.	1986-88	77/25	13.9-15.1
1587cc, 1839cc	1984-85	77/25	13.5-15.1
1995cc	1984-85	77/25	13.8-14.4
2366cc, 2446cc	1984-85	77/25	13.5-15.1
2759cc	1984-88	77/25	13.9-15.1
4230cc	1984-85	77/25	13.8-14.8
1456cc	1987-88	77/25	13.9-15.1

REGULATOR Continued

Application	Year	Test Temp. (deg. F/C)	Voltage Setting
1587cc 2V FWD	1986-88	77/25	13.9-15.1
1587cc 2V RWD	1986-87	77/25	13.5-14.3
1587cc FI	1986-88	77/25	13.9-15.1
1995cc, 1998cc, 2237cc, 2366cc	1986-88	77/25	13.9-15.1
2954cc	1986-88	77/25	13.9-15.1
1587cc Supercharged	1989	77/25	13.7-14.8
3956cc	1989-92	77/25	13.8-14.4
All others	1989-92	77/25	13.9-15.1
		239/115	13.5-14.3

STARTER

Engine	Year	Cranking Voltage (min. volts)	Ampere Draw @ Cranking Speed
All gasoline	1983-85	10.0	200 max.

SPARK PLUGS

Engine	Year	Gap (inches)	Gap (mm)	Torque (ft-lb)
1290cc	1983-84	.043	1.1	11-15
1452cc (code 3AC) U.S.	1983-88	.043	1.1	11-15
Others	1983-88	.031	.80	11-15
1456cc	1987-92	.043	1.1	11-15
1587cc U.S.	1983-87	.043	1.1	11-15
Canada	1983-87	.031	.80	11-15
1587cc 2WD	1988-89	.043	1.1	11-15
Others	1988-89	.031	.80	11-15
1587cc GTS	1990	.043	1.1	11-15
Others	1990	.031	.80	11-15
1587cc	1991-92	.031	.80	11-15
1995cc, 1998cc ex. Turbo, 2164cc, 2237cc	1983-92	.043	1.1	11-15
1998cc Turbo	1989-92	.031	.80	11-15
2366cc Trucks	1989-92	.031	.80	11-15
2438cc	1991-92	.043	1.1	18
2507cc	1989-91	.043	1.1	18
2759cc	1983-88	.055	1.4	11-15
2954cc ex. Turbo	1986-92	.043	1.1	11-15
Turbo	1983-90	.031	.80	11-15
2958cc Trucks	1989-92	.031	.80	18
2958cc Camry	1992	.043	1.1	18
3956cc	1988-91	.031	.80	11-15
3956cc	1992	.043	1.1	18

IGNITION COIL

See UNDERHOOD SERVICE INSTRUCTIONS at the beginning of this section for test/adjustment diagrams.

Engine	Year	Windings	Resistance (ohms)
1290cc	1983-84	Primary	1.3-1.7
		Secondary	10,000-15,000
1452cc ex. Canada Wagon w/MT	1983-88	Primary	0.4-0.5
		Secondary	7700-10,400
1452cc Canada Wagon w/MT	1983-87	Primary	1.2-1.5
		Secondary	7700-10,400
1456cc U.S.	1987-89	Primary	1.3-1.5
		Secondary	10,200-13,800
Canada	1988-89	Primary	0.4-0.5
		Secondary	10,200-13,800
1456cc	1990-91	Primary	0.4-0.5
		Secondary	10,200-13,800
1456cc Tercel	1992	Primary	0.3-0.6
		Secondary	9000-15,000
1456cc Paseo	1992	Primary	0.4-0.5
		Secondary	10,000-14,000
1587cc 2V U.S.	1983-87	Primary	0.4-0.5
		Secondary	7700-10,400
1587cc 2V Canada	1983-86	Primary	1.2-1.5
		Secondary	7700-10,400

UNDERHOOD SERVICE SPECIFICATIONS

IGNITION COIL Continued

Engine	Year	Windings	Resistance (ohms)
1587cc 2V Canada	1987	Primary	1.3-1.5
		Secondary	10,200-13,800
1587cc 2V	1988-89	Primary	1.3-1.5
		Secondary	10,200-13,800
1587cc FI	1985-87	Primary	0.5-0.7
		Secondary	11,000-16,000
1587cc FI 2WD:			
Corolla, FX	1988-89	Primary	0.4-0.5
		Secondary	10,200-13,800
Corolla 4WD	1989	Primary	0.3-0.5
		Secondary	7700-10,400
MR2	1988-89	Primary	0.5-0.7
		Secondary	11,000-16,000
1587cc (4A-FE)	1990-91	Primary	1.28-1.56
		Secondary	10,400-14,000
1587cc (4A-GE)	1990-91	Primary	0.4-0.5
		Secondary	10,200-13,800
1587cc	1992	Primary	1.1-1.7
		Secondary	9000-15,000
1995cc Camry, Celica; 1998cc Van	1983-86	Primary	0.3-0.5
		Secondary	7500-10,400
1998cc Celica	1986	Primary	0.4-0.5
		Secondary	10,200-13,800
1998cc (3S-FE)	1987-91	Primary	0.4-0.5
		Secondary	7700-10,400
1998cc (3S-GE, GTE)	1987-91	Primary	0.4-0.5
		Secondary	10,000-14,000
1998cc	1992	Primary	0.3-0.6
		Secondary	9000-15,000
2164cc	1990-91	Primary	0.4-0.5
		Secondary	10,000-14,000
2164cc Camry	1992	Primary	0.4-0.5
		Secondary	10,200-14,300
Others	1992	Primary	0.3-0.6
		Secondary	9000-15,000
2237cc	1986-89	Primary	1.2-1.5
		Secondary	7700-10,400
2366cc Type III	1983-84	Primary	0.4-0.5
		Secondary	8000-11,000
2366cc Type IV	1983-85	Primary	0.9-1.1
		Secondary	10,700-14,500
2366cc 2V	1986-90	Primary	0.4-0.5
		Secondary	8500-11,500
2366cc FI & Turbo	1986-91	Primary	0.5-0.7
		Secondary	11,400-15,600
2366cc	1992	Primary	0.40-0.69
		Secondary	10,100-16,700
2438cc	1991	Primary	0.4-0.5
		Secondary	10,000-14,000
2438cc	1992	Primary	0.3-0.6
		Secondary	9000-15,000
2507cc	1988-91	Primary	0.4-0.5
		Secondary	10,200-13,800
2759cc	1983-86	Primary	0.4-0.5
		Secondary	8500-11,500
2759cc	1987-88	Primary	0.2-0.3
		Secondary	9000-12,500
2954cc	1986-92	Primary	0.2-0.3
		Secondary	9000-12,500
Turbo	1987-92	Primary	0.3-0.6
		Secondary	—
2958cc	1988-91	Primary	0.4-0.5
		Secondary	10,200-13,800
2958cc Camry	1992	Primary	0.21-0.32
		Secondary	6400-10,700
2958cc Trucks	1992	Primary	0.3-0.6
		Secondary	9000-15,000
3956cc	1988-90	Primary	.52-.64
		Secondary	11,500-15,500
3956cc	1991	Primary	0.4-0.5
		Secondary	10,200-13,800
3956cc	1992	Primary	0.3-0.6
		Secondary	9000-15,000
4230cc	1983-87	Primary	0.5-0.6
		Secondary	11,500-15,500
4230cc Canada	1983-87	Primary	1.3-1.6
		Secondary	11,900-16,100

DISTRIBUTOR PICKUP

See **UNDERHOOD SERVICE INSTRUCTIONS** at the beginning of this section for test/adjustment diagrams.

Application	Year	Resistance (ohms)	Air Gap (in./mm)
All	1983-90	130-190	.008-.016/.20-.40
1456cc	1991	410-510	.008-.016/.20-.40
1456cc Paseo	1992	185-265	.008-.016/.20-.40
NE Pickup	1992	155-240	.008-.016/.20-.40
1456cc Tercel	1992	370-530	.008-.016/.20-.40
1587cc, 1998cc	1991	205-255	.008-.016/.20-.40
Turbo	1991	140-180	.008-.016/.20-.40
1587cc	1992	185-265	.008-.016/.20-.40
1998cc Turbo	1992	125-190	.008-.016/.20-.40
NE Pickup	1992	155-240	.008-.016/.20-.40
2164cc	1990-91	140-180	.008-.016/.20-.40
NE Pickup	1990-91	180-220	.008-.016/.20-.40
2164cc Celica, Camry	1992	185-265	.008-.016/.20-.40
NE Pickup	1992	370-530	.008-.016/.20-.40
2164cc MR2	1992	150-230	.008-.016/.20-.40
2366cc, 2958cc	1991	205-255	.008-.016/.20-.40
2507cc, 2954cc	1991	140-180	.008-.016/.20-.40
NE Pickup	1991	180-220	.008-.016/.20-.40
Turbo	1991	205-255	.008-.016/.20-.40
2954cc	1992	125-190	.008-.016/.20-.40
NE Pickup	1992	155-240	.008-.016/.20-.40
2958cc	1990-91	205-255	.008-.016/.20-.40
2958cc	1992	125-190	.008-.016/.20-.40
NE Pickup	1992	155-240	.008-.016/.20-.40
3956cc	1988-91	140-180	.008-.016/.20-.40
3956cc	1992	185-265	.008-.016/.20-.40

TIMING PROCEDURE

See **UNDERHOOD SERVICE INSTRUCTIONS** at the beginning of this section for test/adjustment diagrams.

1983-87 1452cc, 1587cc 2V: Disconnect and plug distributor vacuum advance inner diaphragm vacuum hose only.

1983-90 2366cc 2V: Leave all hoses connected.

1983-92 All w/EST: EST can be identified by the absence of a vacuum advance unit on the distributor. Place a jumper wire between the check connector cavities T & E1 (1983-88) or TE1 & E1 (1989-92).

With jumper removed, timing should advance to Check specification.

All Others: Disconnect and plug vacuum advance hose(s) at the distributor.

BASE TIMING

Set at slow idle and Before Top Dead Center, unless otherwise specified.

Engine	Year	Man. Trans. (degrees) @ 950 max.	Auto. Trans. (degrees) @ 950 max.
1290cc	1983-84	5	—
1452cc	1983-88	5	5
1456cc 2V	1987-90	3	3
1456cc FI	1990-92	10	10
Check	1991-92	7-17	7-17
1587cc 2V	1983-89	5	5
1587cc FI	1985-92	10	10
Check, 4A-FE	1989	10 min.	10 min.
Check, 4A-FE	1990	5-15	5-15
Check, 4A-FE	1991-92	0-20	0-20
Check, 4A-GE: MT	1985-91	16 min.	16 min.
AT	1985-89	12 min.	12 min.
1995cc	1983-85	5	5
Check	1983-85	16 approx.	16 approx.
1995cc	1986	10	10
Check	1986	16 approx.	16 approx.
1998cc Van	1984-85	8	
Check	1984-85	20 approx.	20 approx.
1998cc	1986-92	10	10
Check, 3S-FE	1987-91	13-22	13-22
Check, 3S-GE	1986-89	14-19	14-19
Check, Turbo	1989	14-19	14-19
Check, Turbo	1990-92	12-21	12-21
2164cc	1990-92	10	10
Check	1990-92	13-22	13-22
2237cc	1986-89	12	12
2366cc	1983-84	5	5
2366cc 2V	1985-90	0	0

BASE TIMING Continued

Engine	Year	Man. Trans. (degrees) @ 950 max.	Auto. Trans. (degrees) @ 950 max.
2366cc FI & Turbo	1985-92	5	5
Check	1987-91	10-14	10-14
2438cc	1991-92	5	5
Check	1991-92	12 approx.	12 approx.
2507cc	1988-91	10	10
Check	1989-92	13-27	13-27
2759cc	1983-88	10	10
2954cc	1986-92	10	10
Check	1986-90	10-13	10-13
Check	1991-92	9-11	9-11
Check, Turbo	1987-92	12 min.	12 min.
2958cc	1988-92	10	10
Check	1989-92	8 approx.	8 approx.
3956cc	1989-92	—	7
4230cc	1983-87	7	—

DISTRIBUTOR TIMING ADVANCE

Engine degrees at engine rpm, no load, in addition to base timing setting.
Mechanical advance distributors only.

Engine	Transmission	Year	Distributor Number	Degrees @ 2500 RPM Total	Degrees @ 2500 RPM Centrifugal
1290cc	MT	1983-84	13030	22.7-30.7	8.7-12.7
1290cc	MT	1983-84	13300	21.8-29.8	7.8-11.8
1452cc	MT & AT	1983-88	15060, 70	34.4-41.4	7.4-11.4
1452cc	MT & AT	1983-87	15020, 40	32.2-40.2	8.2-12.2
1452cc	MT & AT	1983-86	15030	19.2-27.2	8.2-12.2
1456cc	MT & AT	1987-90	11010	35.1-43.1	7.1-11.1
1587cc 2V	MT & AT	1983-85	16010, 20, 70	34.5-42.5	8.5-12.5
1587cc 2V	MT & AT	1984-85	16050	32.5-42.5	8.5-12.5
1587cc 2V FWD	MT & AT	1986	16081, 90	33.9-41.9	7.9-11.9
1587cc 2V RWD	MT & AT	1986-88	16101, 10	33.9-41.9	7.9-11.9
1587cc 2V	MT & AT	1988-89	16120	24.5-32.5	2.5-6.5
1995cc	MT & AT	1983-85	74020	39-47	11-15
1998cc	MT & AT	1984-85	73020	10.1-16.1	1.1-5.1
2366cc FI	MT & AT	1983-84	35120	27-35	7-11
2366cc	MT & AT	1983-84	35130	26.3-34.3	6.3-10.3
2366cc	MT & AT	1985-90	35140	25.2-33.2	7.2-11.2
2366cc	MT & AT	1985-88	35150	30.2-38.2	7.2-11.2
4230cc	MT	1983-85	61092	16.3-24.3	9.8-13.8
4230cc	MT	1983-85	61102	12.3-20.3	4.3-8.3

FUEL SYSTEM

FUEL SYSTEM PRESSURE

See UNDERHOOD SERVICE INSTRUCTIONS at the beginning of this section for test/adjustment diagrams.

Engine	Year	Pressure PSI	Pressure RPM
Carburetted:			
1452cc	1983-88	2.6-3.5	idle
1456cc	1987-90	3.0	idle
1587cc	1983-89	2.5-3.5	idle
2366cc	1983-90	2.8-4.3	idle

Engine	Year	Pressure PSI*	Pressure PSI†
Fuel Injection:			
1290cc	1983-84	36-38	28 approx.
1456cc	1990-91	41-42	33-37
1587cc	1985-87	33-40	24-31
1587cc 2WD	1988-89	38-44	30-33
1587cc 4WD	1989	33-40	23-30
1587cc Supercharged	1988-89	33-40	20-27
1587cc	1990-91	38-44	30-37
1995cc, 1998cc	1983-86	33-38	27-31
1998cc, 2164cc, Celica	1988-91	38-44	33-37
1998cc, 2164cc MR2	1991	33-38	27-31

FUEL SYSTEM PRESSURE Continued

Engine	Year	Pressure PSI*	Pressure PSI†
2237cc	1986-87	33-38	27-31
2237cc	1988-89	38-44	30-33
2366cc	1983-84	36-38	28 approx.
2366cc	1985-88	33-38	27-31
2366cc FI	1989-91	38-44	33-37
2438cc	1991	38-44	30-37
2507cc	1988-91	38-44	33-37
2759cc	1983-84	36-38	28 approx.
2759cc	1985-88	33-38	27-31
2954cc	1986-88	33-40	23-30
2954cc	1989-91	38-44	33-37
Turbo	1989-91	33-40	23-30
2958cc	1988-89	38-44	33-37

* Measured at cold start injector with pressure regulator vacuum disconnected.
† Measured at cold start injector with pressure regulator vacuum connected.

IDLE SPEED W/O COMPUTER CONTROL

1983-90: 1290cc, 1995cc, 1998cc, 2237cc, 2366cc FI, with cooling fan off and air cleaner installed, race engine for two minutes and set idle to specified rpm. Turn AC on and verify that idle increases to speed-up speed. Speed-up can be adjusted if adjustment screw is found on idle up device.

1452cc, 1456cc, 1587cc, with cooling fan off and air cleaner installed, set idle to specified rpm.

2366cc 2V, disconnect and plug hoses for HAI, MC, EGR, and choke opener. Adjust idle to specified rpm.

1991-92: Set idle speed to specified value. Turn AC on and verify that speed increases to specified speed-up value.

Fast idle adjustment:
1452cc, 1587cc, disconnect and plug vacuum hoses for AS and HIC systems. Remove air cleaner, disconnect vacuum hose from TVSV "M" port, and plug port. Set cam to specified step and adjust to specified rpm.

1456cc, 2366cc, disconnect and plug EGR vacuum hose(s) and adjust speed with cooling fan off.

THROTTLE POSITIONER: All years, disconnect and plug vacuum hose on end of unit. Allow step to move into position and adjust linkage screw.

Engine	Year	SLOW Man. Trans.	SLOW Auto. Trans.	FAST Man. Trans.	FAST Auto. Trans.	Step of Cam
1290cc	1983-84	700	—	—	—	—
AC speed-up	1983-84	900-950				
1452cc	1983-87	550	800 N	3000	3000 N	High
Thrtl. pos. 3A eng.	1983-87	1700	1400 N			
Thrtl. pos. Others	1983-87	1400	1400 N			
w/5-speed	1983-88	650	—	3000	—	High
Thrtl. pos. 3A eng.	1983-87	1700	—			
Thrtl. pos. Others	1983-88	1400	—			
w/Pwr. Str.	1983-88	800	900 N	3000	3000 N	High
Thrtl. pos. 3A eng.	1983-87	1700	1400 N			
Thrtl. pos. Others	1983-88	1400	1400 N			
1456cc 2V	1987-90	700	900 N	3000	3000 N	High
Throttle positioner	1987-90	1100●	1100 N●			
AC speed-up	1987-90	900-1000	900-1000 N			
1456cc FI Tercel	1990-92	750	800 N	—	—	—
AC speed-up	1990-92	900-1000	900-1000 N			
1587cc RWD	1983	650	800 N	3000	3000 N	High
Throttle positioner	1983	1400	1400 N			
w/Pwr. Str.	1983	800	900 N	3000	3000 N	High
Throttle positioner	1983	1400	1400 N			
1587cc 2V RWD	1984-86	700	800 N	3000	3000 N	High
Throttle positioner	1984-86	1400	1400 N			
w/Pwr. Str.	1984-85	800	900 N	3000	3000 N	High
Throttle positioner	1984-85	1400	1400 N			
w/Pwr. Str.	1986	750	850 N	3000	3000 N	High
Throttle positioner	1986	1400	1400 N			
1587cc 2V FWD	1984-85	650	800 N	3000	3000 N	High
Throttle positioner	1984-85	800	900 N			
1587cc 2V	1987	700	800 N	3000	3000 N	High
Throttle positioner	1987	1400	1400 N			
w/Pwr. Str.	1987	750	850 N			
Throttle positioner	1987	1400	1400 N			

IDLE SPEED W/O COMPUTER CONTROL Continued

Engine	Year	SLOW Man. Trans.	SLOW Auto. Trans.	FAST Man. Trans.	FAST Auto. Trans.	Step of Cam
1587cc 2V	1988-89	650	750 N	3000	3000 N	High
Thrtl. pos., Corolla	1988-89	900	900 N			
Thrtl. pos., FX	1988-89	800	800 N			
AC speed-up	1988-89	900-1000	900-1000 N			
1587cc FI	1985-89	800	800 N	—	—	—
AC speed-up	1985-89	900-1000	900-1000 N			
1587cc: 2WD	1990-92	700	700 N	—	—	—
California	1991-92	800	800 N	—	—	—
4WD, GTS	1990-92	800	800 N			
AC speed-up	1990-92	900-1000	900-1000 N			
1839cc Diesel	1984-85	700	750 N	—	—	—
Maximum speed	1984-85	5100	5100	—	—	—
1839cc Turbo Diesel	1985	700	—	—	—	—
Maximum speed	1985	5100	—	—	—	—
1974cc Diesel	1986	750	—	—	—	—
Maximum speed	1986	5200	—	—	—	—
1995cc, 1998cc	1983-85	700	750 N	—	—	—
AC speed-up	1983-85	900-1000	900-1000 N			
1995cc	1986	700	700 N	—	—	—
AC speed-up	1986	900-1000	900-1000 N			
1998cc (3S-GE)	1986	750	750 N	—	—	—
AC speed-up	1986	900-1000	900-1000 N			
1998cc (3S-FE)	1987-88	650-750	750 N			
AC speed-up	1987	900-1000	900-1000 N			
1998cc (3S-GE)	1987-89	750	750 N	—	—	—
2164cc	1990	800	800 N	—	—	—
2188cc Diesel	1983	700	—	—	—	—
2237cc	1986-89	700	750 N	—	—	—
AC speed-up	1986-89	900-1000	900-1000 N			
2366cc 2V	1983-87	700	750 N	2600	2600 N	High
2366cc 2V	1988-90	700	700 N	3000	3000 N	High
AC speed-up	1988-90	900-1000	900-1000 N			
2366cc FI	1983	650	650 N	—	—	—
2366cc FI	1984-88	750	750 N	—	—	—
AC speed-up	1984-88	900-1000	900-1000 N			
2366cc Turbo	1986-88	800	800 N	—	—	—
AC speed-up	1986-88	900-1000	900-1000 N			
2366cc FI: 2WD	1989-92	750	750 N	—	—	—
4WD	1989-92	750	800 N			
AC speed-up, all	1989-92	900-1000	900-1000 N			
2446cc Diesel	1984-85	700	—	—	—	—
Maximum speed	1984-85	4900	—	—	—	—
2958cc	1988-92	800	800 N	—	—	—
AC speed-up	1988-92	900-1000	900-1000 N			
4230cc	1983-87	650	—	1800	—	High

● Inner diaphragm; outer diaphragm, 1800-2200 (N).

IDLE SPEED W/COMPUTER CONTROL

See UNDERHOOD SERVICE INSTRUCTIONS at the beginning of this section for test/ adjustment diagrams.

When idle speed is adjustable, jumper terminals T and E1 (1983-88) or TE1 and E1 (1989-92) of check connector under hood. Race engine at 1000-1300 rpm for five seconds and set idle to specified value. After setting idle, turn AC on and verify that speed increases to Speed-up value.

IDLE SPEED W/COMPUTER CONTROL Continued

Engine	Year	Transmission	Checking Speed	Setting Speed	Speed-up
1456cc Paseo	1992	MT	—	750	900-1000
		AT	—	750 N	900-1000 N
1587cc Supercharged	1988-89	MT	800	800	850-950
		AT	800 N	800 N	850-950 N
1998cc (3S-FE)	1989-91	MT	650-750	600-700	900-1000
	1989-91	AT	650-750	600-700 N	900-1000 N
Turbo	1988-90	MT	700-800	—	900-1000
Turbo	1991-92	MT	750-850	—	900-1000
2164cc Celica: U.S.	1990-91	MT	650-750	600-700	900-1000
		AT	650-750 N	600-700 N	900-1000 N
2164cc Canada	1990-91	MT	750-850	600-700	900-1000
		AT	700-800 N	600-700 N	900-1000 N
2164cc MR2: U.S.	1991-92	MT	700-800	650 min.	900-1000
		AT	650-750 N	650 N min.	900-1000 N
Canada	1991-92	MT	800-900	650 min.	900-1000
		AT	700-800 N	650 N min.	900-1000 N
2164cc Camry	1992	MT	700-800	—	850
		AT	700-800 N	—	850 N
2164cc Celica: U.S.	1992	MT	650-750	—	900-1000
		AT	650-750 N	—	900-1000 N
Canada	1992	MT	700-800	—	900-1000
		AT	700-800 N	—	900-1000 N
2438cc	1991-92	MT	650-750	—	900-1000
		AT	700-800 N	—	900-1000 N
2507cc	1988-90	MT	650-750	650 min.	780-820
		AT	650-750 N	650 N min.	780-820 N*
2507cc	1991	MT	700	—	780-820
		AT	700 N	—	780-820 N
2759cc	1983-88	MT	650	—	900
	1983-85	AT	650 D	—	750 D
	1986-88	AT	600	—	750 D
2954cc	1986-88	MT	700	—	900-1000
		AT	700 N	—	900-1000 N
2954cc	1989-92	MT	700	—	900
		AT	700 N	—	650 D
2954cc Turbo	1987-88	MT	650	—	900-1000
		AT	650 N	—	900-1000 N
2954cc Turbo	1989-92	MT	650	—	900
		AT	650 N	—	700 D
2958cc Camry	1992	AT	650-750 N	—	700 N
3956	1988-92	AT	650	—	900-1000 N

* With T-top, 950-1050 N.

ENGINE MECHANICAL

TIGHTENING TORQUES

See UNDERHOOD SERVICE INSTRUCTIONS at the beginning of this section for test/ adjustment diagrams.

Some fasteners are tightened in more than one step.

Some values are specified in inches.

Engine	Year	Torque Ft-lbs/Nm Cylinder Head	Intake Manifold	Exhaust Manifold	Crankshaft Pulley	Water Pump
1290cc	1983-84	40-47/ 53-64	15-21/ 20-39	15-21/ 20-39	55-75/ 74-102	11-18/ 14-24
1452cc	1983-88	43/59	18/25	18/25	87/118	11/15
1456cc Tercel	1987-92	22/29, 36/49, +90°	14/19	38/51	112/152	13/17
1456cc Paseo	1992	33/44, +90°	14/19	35/47	112/157	13/17
1587cc (4A-C)	1983-87	43/59	18/25	18/25	87/118	11/15
1587cc (4A-GE)	1985-87	43/59	20/27	18/25	105/142	11/15
1587cc (4A-GE)	1988-91	22/29, +90°, +90°	20/27	29/39	101/137	11/15
1587cc (4A-F, FE)	1988-92	44/60	14/19	18/25	87/118	11/15

UNDERHOOD SERVICE SPECIFICATIONS

TAITU6   TAITU6

TIGHTENING TORQUES Continued

Engine	Year	Cylinder Head	Intake Manifold	Exhaust Manifold	Crankshaft Pulley	Water Pump
			Torque Ft-lbs/Nm			
1839cc Diesel	1984-85	62/84	13/18	34/47	72/98	13/18
1995cc	1983-86	47/64	31/42	31/42	80/108	82″/9
1998cc, 2237cc	1984-85	65/88*	36/49	36/49	116/157	13/18
1998cc	1986-89	47/64	14/19	31/42	80/108	11/15
1998cc	1990-92	36/49, +90°	14/19	38/52	80/108	82″/9
2164cc	1990-92	36/49, +90°	14/19	36/49	80/108	82″/9
2366cc	1983-92	58/78	14/19	33/44	116/157	14/20
2438cc	1991-92	29/39, +90°, +90°	15/21	36/49	192/260	21/28*
2507cc	1988-91	25/34, +90°, +90°	13/18	29/39	181/145	73″/8
2759cc, 2954cc	1983-89	58/78	13/18	29/39	195/265	78″/9
2954cc	1990-92	58/78	13/18	29/39	195/265	78″/9, 10 mm 14/20, 12 mm
2958cc Truck	1988-92	33/44, +90°, +90°	13/18	29/39	181/145	13/18
2958cc Camry	1992	25/34, +90°, +90°	13/18	29/39	181/145	14/20
3956cc Camry	1988-92	90/123	†	†	253/343	23/37

* Small bolts, 14/17.

† 14 mm bolt, 37/50; 17 mm bolt, 51/69; nut, 41/56.

VALVE CLEARANCE

1985-90 1587cc FI, 1988-90 1587cc, 1998cc, 2507cc, 2958cc, engine cold. All others, engine hot.

1991-92 1456cc Tercel, 2366cc, engine hot. All others, engine cold.

Engine	Year	Intake (inches)	Intake (mm)	Exhaust (inches)	Exhaust (mm)
1452cc, 1587cc 2V	1983-88	.008	.20	.012	.30
1456cc Tercel	1987-92	.008	.20	.008	.20
1456cc Paseo	1992	.006-.010	.15-.25	.012-.016	.30-.40
1587cc FI	1985-92	.006-.010	.15-.25	.008-.012	.20-.30
1839cc, 1974cc Diesel	1984-86	.008-.012	.20-.30	.010-.014	.25-.36
1998cc (3S-GE, GET)	1986-91	.006-.010	.15-.25	.008-.012	.20-.30
1998cc Turbo Celica	1992	.006-.010	.15-.25	.011-.015	.28-.38
1998cc Turbo MR2	1992	.006-.010	.15-.25	.008-.012	.20-.30
1998cc (3S-FE)	1987-91	.007-.011	.19-.29	.011-.015	.28-.38
2164cc	1990-92	.007-.011	.19-.29	.011-.015	.28-.38
2366cc	1983-92	.008	.20	.012	.30
2438cc	1991-92	.006-.010	.15-.25	.010-.014	.25-.35
2446cc	1983-85	.010	.25	.014	.36
2507cc	1988-91	.005-.009	.13-.23	.011-.015	.27-.37
2954cc	1986-92	.006-.010	.15-.25	.008-.012	.20-.30
2958cc Truck	1988-92	.007-.011	.18-.28	.009-.013	.22-.32
2958cc Camry	1992	.005-.009	.13-.23	.011-.015	.28-.38
3431cc, 4230cc	1983-87	.008	.20	.014	.36
3956cc	1988-92	.008	.20	.014	.35

COMPRESSION PRESSURE

At cranking speed, engine temperature normalized, throttle open.

Engine	Year	PSI	Maximum Variation PSI
1290cc	1983-84	142-185	14
1452cc	1983-88	128-178	14
1456cc	1987-92	142-184	14
1587cc	1983-87	128-178	14
1587cc:			
2V ex. FX	1988	142-191	14
FI ex. FX	1988	142-179	14
Supercharged	1988	121-156	14
FX16	1988	128-179	14
1587cc (4A-F, FE)	1989-92	142-191	14
1587cc (4A-GE)	1989-91	142-179	14
1587cc Supercharged	1988-89	121-156	14
1839cc, 1974cc Diesel	1984-86	356-427	71

COMPRESSION PRESSURE Continued

Engine	Year	PSI	Maximum Variation PSI
1995cc, 1998cc	1983-85	142-171	14
1995cc	1986-87	126-171	14
1998cc	1986-91	142-178	14
1998cc Turbo	1988-92	128-178	14
2237cc	1986-89	128-178	14
2366cc	1983-92	142-171	14
Turbo	1985-88	120-149	14
2438cc	1991-92	128-178	14
2446cc Diesel	1983-86	284-427	71
2507cc	1988-91	142-178	14
2759cc	1983-88	128-164	14
2954cc ex. Turbo	1986-90	128-156	14
Turbo	1987-90	128-142	14
2958cc Truck	1988-92	142-171	14
2958cc Camry	1992	142-178	144
3956cc	1988-92	114-149	14
4230cc	1983-87	114-149	14

BELT TENSION

A belt in operation for 20 minutes is considered a used belt.

Deflection method: Measured with an applied load of 22-pounds at the midpoint of the longest segment.

Strand Tension method: Use belt tension gauge. Measurements are in pounds.

Engine	Year	Alternator	Power Steering	Air Cond.	Air Pump
USED BELTS					
Strand Tension Method					
4230cc	1983	80-120	80-120	60-100	80-120
All Others	1983	60-100	60-100	60-100	60-100
1290cc, 1452cc, 1587cc RWD, 2366cc, 2446cc	1984-92	60-100	60-100	60-100	60-100
1587cc 2V FWD	1984-89	110-150	60-100	60-100	110-150
1839cc	1984-85	70-100	80-120	95-135	—
1995cc	1984-85	75-115	60-100	140-150	75-115
1998cc	1984-85	95-135	60-100	60-100	95-135
2759cc	1984-86	105-155	105-155	105-155	—
1839cc Turbo	1985	70-110	70-110	70-110	—
2759cc	1985-88	105-155	60-100	60-100	—
1587cc FI	1986-87	95-135	95-135	95-135	—
1974cc FI	1986	60-100	80-120	80-120	—
1995cc, 1998cc (3S-GE)	1986-90	75-115	120-140	60-100	—
2237cc	1986-89	95-135	60-100	60-100	—
2954cc	1986-89	95-135	90-120	80-100	—
1456cc	1987-92	80-120	90-130	90-130	—
1998cc (3S-FE)	1987-91	75-115	120-140	60-100	—
1452cc	1988	60-100	60-100	60-100	60-100
1587cc 2V	1988	170-180	170-180	170-180	—
1587cc FI	1988-92	110-150	60-100	110-150	—
1587cc MR2	1988-89	95-135	95-135	95-135	—
Supercharged	1988-89	95-135	95-135	95-135	—
1998cc, 2164cc MR2	1991	85-125	85-125	80-120	—
2164cc Celica	1990-91	75-115	75-115	120-140	—
w/AC	1990-91	120-140	120-140	170-180	—
2366cc	1988-91	60-100	60-100	80-120	—
2438cc	1991-92	115-135	115-135	100-140	—
2958cc Truck	1988-92	80-120	60-100	60-100	—
2958cc Camry	1992	95-135	95-135	95-135	—
3956cc	1988-92	80-120	80-120	60-100	—
NEW BELTS					
Strand Tension Method					
4230cc	1983	120-170	120-170	100-150	120-170
All Others	1983	100-150	100-150	100-150	100-150
1290cc, 1452cc, 1587cc RWD, 2366cc, 2446cc	1984-92	100-150	100-150	100-150	100-150
1587cc 2V FWD	1984-89	140-180	100-150	100-150	140-180
1839cc	1984-85	75-125	140-180	170-180	—
1995cc	1984-85	75-115	100-150	170-180	75-115
1998cc	1984-85	170-180	100-150	100-150	170-180
2759cc	1984	160-180	160-180	160-180	—
1839cc Turbo	1985	75-125	75-125	75-125	—
2759cc	1985-88	160-180	100-150	100-150	—
1587cc FI	1986-87	170-180	140-180	140-180	—
1934cc	1986	60-100	80-120	80-120	—

BELT TENSION Continued

Engine	Year	Alternator	Power Steering	Air Cond.	Air Pump
1995cc, 1998cc (3S-GE)	1986-90	100-150	170-180	100-150	—
2237cc	1986-89	170-180	100-150	100-150	—
2954cc	1986-89	170-180	135-190	120-140	—
1456cc	1987-92	140-180	150-180	150-180	—
1998cc (3S-FE)	1987-92	100-150	170-180	115-135	—
1452cc	1988	100-150	100-150	100-150	100-150
1587cc 2V	1988	95-135	95-135	95-135	—
1587cc FI	1988-92	140-180	100-150	140-180	—
1587cc MR2	1988-89	170-180	170-180	140-180	—
Supercharged	1988-89	170-180	170-180	170-180	—
1998cc, 2164cc MR2	1991	100-140	100-140	135-185	—
2164cc Celica	1990-91	100-150	100-150	—	—
w/AC	1990-91	170-180	170-180	115-135	—
2366cc	1988-91	100-150	100-150	140-180	—
2438cc	1991-92	160-180	160-180	120-160	—
2958cc Truck	1988-92	135-185	100-150	100-150	—
2958cc	1992	170-180	170-180	150-185	—
3956cc	1988-92	120-170	120-170	100-150	—

ENGINE COMPUTER SYSTEM

COMPUTER DIAGNOSTIC CODES
See UNDERHOOD SERVICE INSTRUCTIONS at the beginning of this section for test/ adjustment diagrams.

1989-91 All ex. Van
1987-88 Pickup w/FI
1986-88 Celica, Corolla w/FI, Supra 3.0L w/o Super Monitor
1985-87 Camry, MR2, Cressida w/o Super Monitor
With engine at operating temperature, turn ignition switch on and place a jumper between cavities T and E1 (1985-88) or TE1 and E1 (1989-92) on the Check Engine connector located by the air flow meter or the strut tower. "Check Engine" light will flash codes.

1987-88 FX16
1985-89 Van
1985-86 Pickup w/FI, Supra 2.8L
1985 Celica, Corolla GTS
1983-84 Camry
With engine at operating temperature, turn ignition on and jumper the cavities on the two wire yellow connector in the engine compartment. "Check Engine" light will flash codes.

1985-88 Cressida, Supra w/Super Monitor
Turn ignition on and push "Select" & "Input" buttons simultaneously and hold for 3 seconds. Pause, then hold "Set" button for 3 seconds. Codes will appear on screen if any are stored.

1983-84 Cressida, Supra
With the engine at operating temperature, turn the ignition switch on and place a jumper between the cavities of the Check Engine connector located by the distributor. Connect an analog VOM to the EFI service connector located by the air intake pickup hose at right side of radiator. Connect plus (+) to upper cavity and minus (–) to lower left cavity. Needle on voltmeter will pulse between 2.5 & 5 volts if no codes are stored. Codes that are stored will be displayed as pulses on the meter.

All models
To clear memory, remove STOP or EFI fuse from fuseblock for 30 seconds.

1983-85 Camry, Van
1986 Camry Canada, Van
  Code 1 System OK
  Codes 2, 3 Airflow meter signal
  Code 4 Engine temperature sensor circuit
  Code 5 Oxygen sensor
  Code 6 Ignition signal circuit
  Code 7 Throttle position circuit

1988 Pickup Turbo
1987 Van
1985-87 MR2, Pickup w/FI, Corolla GTS
1986 Camry U.S., Celica 2S eng.
  Code 1 System OK
  Code 2 Airflow meter signal
  Code 3 Ignition signal
  Code 4 Engine temperature sensor circuit
  Code 5 Oxygen sensor
  Code 6 RPM circuit
  Code 7 Throttle position circuit

COMPUTER DIAGNOSTIC CODES Continued

  Code 8 Intake air temperature circuit
  Code 10 Starter signal
  Code 11 AC switch
  Code 12 Knock sensor
  Code 13 Turbocharger pressure

1989-92 All
1988 Corolla, MR2, FX, Van, Pickup ex. Turbo
1987-88 Camry
1986-88 Celica 3S eng.
1983-88 Supra, Cressida
  Code — System OK
  Code 11 ECU circuit
  Codes 12, 13 RPM signal circuit
  Code 14 Ignition signal
  Code 16 Transmission electronic control
  Code 21 Oxygen sensor circuit (left side, 2958cc)
  Code 22 Engine temperature sensor circuit
  Codes 23 & 24 Intake air temperature circuit
  Code 25 Air/fuel ratio lean
  Code 26 Air/fuel ratio rich
  Codes 28 Oxygen sensor circuit (right side, 2958cc)
  Code 31 Vacuum switches (1988-89 1.6L 2V Calif.)
  Code 31 Vacuum sensor (1989-92 1.5L FI, 1.6L FI, 2.2L)
  Codes 31, 32 Airflow meter circuit (others)
  Code 34 Turbocharger pressure signal
  Code 35 Turbocharger pressure sensor signal
  Code 35 AAC sensor signal (ex. Turbo)
  Code 41 Throttle position sensor circuit
  Code 42 Vehicle speed sensor circuit
  Code 43 Starter signal
  Code 51 Neutral start or AC switch
  Code 52 Knock sensor circuit
  Code 53 Knock sensor circuit in ECU
  Code 71 EGR
  Code 72 Fuel cut solenoid

SENSORS, INPUT

TEMPERATURE SENSORS
See UNDERHOOD SERVICE INSTRUCTIONS at the beginning of this section for test/ adjustment diagrams.

All FI: Manifold air temperature sensor when mounted in airflow meter is measured between terminals E2 & THA (first and last) of airflow meter electrical connector.

Engine	Year	Sensor	Resistance Ohms @ deg. F/C
All FI	1983-92	Coolant, Manifold Air	10,000-20,000 @ −4/−20
			4000-7000 @ 32/0
			200-3000 @ 68/20
			900-1300 @ 104/40
			400-700 @ 212/100
All, as equipped	1990-92	EGR	69,000-89,000 @ 122/50
			11,000-15,000 @ 212/100
			2000-4000 @ 302/150

MANIFOLD ABSOLUTE PRESSURE SENSOR
Measure output voltage with vacuum hose disconnected. Apply vacuum to unit and compare voltage drop with those listed.

Engine	Year	Volts @ in./mm Hg
1456cc FI, 1587cc (4A-FE), 2164cc	1988-92	0.3-0.5 @ 4/100
		0.7-0.9 @ 8/200
		1.1-1.3 @ 12/300
		1.5-1.7 @ 16/400
		1.9-2.1 @ 20/500
1998cc Turbo	1988-92	.15-.35 @ 4/100
		0.4-0.6 @ 8/200
		65-.85 @ 12/300
		0.9-1.1 @ 16/400
		1.15-1.35 @ 20/500

UNDERHOOD SERVICE SPECIFICATIONS

SENSORS, INPUT Continued

THROTTLE POSITION SENSOR
See UNDERHOOD SERVICE INSTRUCTIONS at the beginning of this section for test/adjustment diagrams.
Resistance measured between terminals E2 & VTA (first and third) of TPS.

Engine	Year	Resistance (ohms)	
		Idle	WOT
1456cc Tercel	1992	200-800	3300-10,000
1456cc Paseo	1992	200-6000	2000-10,000
1587cc (4A-GE, GZE)	1985-91	200-800	3300-10,000
1998cc (3S-GE, GET)	1986-91	200-800	3300-10,000
1998cc Celica	1992	470-610	3100-12,100
1998cc MR2	1992	200-600	2000-10,200
2156cc Camry, Celica	1990-92	200-600	2000-10,000
2156cc MR2 w/AT	1991-92	200-800	3300-10,000
2366cc (22R-E, RET)	1983-92	200-800	3300-10,000
2438cc	1991-92	300-6300	3500-10,300
2507cc	1988-91	300-6300	3500-10,300
2759cc (5M-GE)	1983-88	200-800	3300-10,000
2954cc (7M-GE, GET)	1986-92	200-1200	3500-10,300
2958cc Truck	1988-92	200-800	3300-10,000
2958cc Camry	1992	280-640	2000-11,600
3956cc	1989-92	300-6300	3500-10,300

AIRFLOW METER
See UNDERHOOD SERVICE INSTRUCTIONS at the beginning of this section for test/adjustment diagrams.
Resistance measured between terminals E2 & VS of airflow meter while moving measuring plate.

Engine	Year	Resistance (ohms)	
		Closed	Open
1290cc	1983-84	20-400	20-1200
1587cc (4A-GE)	1985-91	20-400	20-3000
1587cc (4A-GZE)	1988-89	20-600	20-1200
1995cc	1983-86	20-400	20-1200
1998cc (3S-FE, GE, GET)	1987-92	20-600	20-1200
2366cc (22RE, RET)	1983-92	20-400	20-1200

SENSORS, INPUT Continued

AIRFLOW METER Continued

Engine	Year	Resistance (ohms)	
		Closed	Open
2438cc, 2507cc	1988-92	20-600	20-1200
2759cc	1983-89	20-400	20-1200
2954cc, 2958cc, 3956cc	1988-92	20-600	20-1200

ACTUATORS, OUTPUT

IDLE SPEED CONTROL
See UNDERHOOD SERVICE INSTRUCTIONS at the beginning of this section for test/adjustment diagrams.
With three-terminal connector, measured between either left or right terminals and center terminal.

Engine	Year	Resistance (ohms)
1456cc Paseo	1992	30-33
1587cc (4A-GZE)	1988-89	16-17
1587cc Celica	1990-92	27-37
1998cc (3S-GE, GET)	1986-91	16-17
1998cc	1991-92	19-23
Turbo	1991-92	18-24
2164cc	1990-92	19-23
2438cc	1991-92	19-23
2507cc	1988-91	10-30
2759cc, 2954cc, 3956cc	1983-92	10-30

AIR VALVE
Provides high idle speed at cold start.
Measured with engine at operating temperature and air valve closed.

Engine	Year	Resistance (ohms)
1290cc	1983-84	40-60
1995cc	1983-86	40-60
1998cc 3Y, 2237cc 4Y	1984-89	40-60
1998cc (3S-FE)	1987-91	40-60
2366cc FI	1983-92	40-60

ENGINE IDENTIFICATION

To identify an engine by the manufacturer's code, follow the four steps designated by the numbered blocks.

V.I.N. PLATE LOCATION:

Left side of instrument panel visible through windshield.

1 MODEL YEAR IDENTIFICATION:

10th character of V.I.N.

1992 — N; 1991 — M; 1990 — L;
1989 — K; 1988 — J; 1987 — H;
1986 — G; 1985 — F; 1984 — E;
1983 — D.

NOTE: Air cooled vehicle type is first digit of chassis number.

2 ENGINE CODE LOCATION:

Prefix to engine number:

Vanagon — Stamped on crankcase below crankcase breather.

All Other Engines — Stamped on side of engine block below number 2 and 3 spark/glow plugs.

4 ENGINE IDENTIFICATION

YEAR	3 ENGINE CODE	CYL.	DISPL. liters	cc	Fuel System	HP
1992	1V	4	1.6 D	1590 D	VE	59
	JN	4	1.8	1780	DF	94
	2H	4	1.8	1780	DF	81
	RV	4	1.8	1780	DF	100
	PF	4	1.8	1780	DF	105
	PG	4	1.8 S	1780 S	DF	158
	9A	4	2.0	1984	CIS-E	134
	—	5	2.5	2459	DF	109
	VR	6	2.8	2792	CIS-E	172
1991	ME	4	1.6 D	1588 D	VE	52
	2H	4	1.8	1780	CIS	93
	JN	4	1.8	1780	CIS-E	81
	RV	4	1.8	1780	DF	100
	PF	4	1.8	1780	DF	105
	PG	4	1.8 S	1780 S	DF	158
	9A	4	2.0	1984	CIS-E	134
	MV	4	2.1	2109	DF	90
1990	ME	4	1.6 D	1588 D	VE	52
	JH	4	1.8	1780	CIS	93
	JN	4	1.8	1780	CIS-E	81
	RV	4	1.8	1780	DF	100
	PF	4	1.8	1780	DF	105
	PG	4	1.8 S	1780 S	DF	158
	9A	4	2.0	1984	CIS-E	134
	MV	4	2.1	2109	DF	90
1989	JN	4	1.8	1780	CIS-E	81
	JH	4	1.8	1780	CIS	90
	RV	4	1.8	1780	DF	100
	PF	4	1.8	1780	DF	105
	PL	4	1.8	1780	CIS-E	123
	PG	4	1.8 S	1780 S	DF	145
	MV	4	2.1	2109	DF	95
1988	ME	4	1.6 D	1588 D	VE	52
	MF	4	1.6 TD	1588 TD	VE	68
	JN	4	1.8	1780	CIS-E	81
	JH	4	1.8	1780	CIS	95
	RV	4	1.8	1780	DF	100
	PF	4	1.8	1780	DF	105
	PL	4	1.8	1780	CIS-E	123
	MV	4	2.1	2109	DF	95
	JT	5	2.2	2226	CIS-E	115
	KX	5	2.2	2226	CIS-E	130
1987	ME	4	1.6 D	1588 D	VE	52
	MF	4	1.6 TD	1588 TD	VE	68
	UM	4	1.8	1780	CIS	81
	GX	4	1.8	1780	CIS-E	85

4 ENGINE IDENTIFICATION

YEAR	3 ENGINE CODE	CYL.	DISPL. liters	cc	Fuel System	HP
1987 Cont'd.	JH, MZ	4	1.8	1780	CIS	90
	RD	4	1.8	1780	CIS-E	102
	PL	4	1.8	1780	CIS-E	123
	MV	4	2.1	2109	DF	95
	KX	5	2.2	2226	CIS-E	110
	JT	5	2.2	2226	CIS-E	115
1986	ME	4	1.6 D	1588 D	VE	52
	MF	4	1.6 TD	1588 TD	VE	68
	GX	4	1.8	1780	CIS-E	85
	JH, MZ	4	1.8	1780	CIS	90
	JN	4	1.8	1780	CIS-E	90
	RD	4	1.8	1780	CIS-E	102
	PL	4	1.8	1780	CIS-E	125
	MV	4	2.1	2109	DF	95
	KX	5	2.2	2226	CIS-E	110
	JT	5	2.2	2226	CIS-E	115
1985	JD, ME	4	1.6 D	1588 D	VE	52, 55†
	JR, MF, MD	4	1.6 TD	1588 TD	VE	68, 70†
	GX	4	1.8	1781	CIS-E	85
	MZ, JH	4	1.8	1781	CIS	90
	JN	4	1.8	1781	CIS-E	88
	HT	4	1.8	1781	CIS-E	100
	DH	4	1.9	1915	DJ	82
	KX	5	2.2	2226	CIS-E	110
1984	JK	4	1.6 D	1588 D	VE	52
	CY	4	1.6 TD	1588 TD	VE	68
	FX	4	1.7	1715	1V	65
	EN, WT	4	1.7	1715	CIS	74
	JH	4	1.8	1780	CIS	90, 88†
	DH	4	1.9	1915	DJ	82
	KM, WE	5	2.2	2144	CIS	100
1983	CS	4	1.6 D	1588 D	VE	48
	JK	4	1.6 D	1588 D	VE	52
	CY	4	1.6 TD	1588 TD	VE	68
	FX	4	1.7	1715	1V	65
	EN, WT	4	1.7	1715	CIS	74, 76, 78†
	JH	4	1.8	1780	CIS	90
	DH	4	1.9	1915	DJ	82
	CV	4	2.0	1970	AFC	67
	KM	5	2.2	2144	CIS	100

AFC — Air Flow Control. CIS — Continuous Injection System.
CIS-E — CIS Electronic. D — Diesel. DF — Digifont.
DJ — Digijet. S — Supercharged. TD — Turbo Diesel.
V — One Venturi Carburetor. VE — Diesel Injection.
† Engine horsepower varies with model installation.

UNDERHOOD SERVICE SPECIFICATIONS

VNITU1   VNITU1

CYLINDER NUMBERING SEQUENCE

Vanagon
FIRING ORDER: 1 4 3 2

All Other 4-Cyl. Models
FIRING ORDER: 1 3 4 2

5-Cyl. FIRING ORDER:
1 2 4 5 3

— Front of car —

| 1915cc, 1970cc, 2109cc Vanagon | 1983-88 1715cc, 1780cc Cabriolet, Golt, GTI, Jetta, Rabbit, Scirocco | 1987-91 1780cc Fox | 1989-91 1780cc Cabriolet, Corrado, Golf, GTI, Jetta | 1990-91 1780cc 1984cc Passat | 1983-88 2144cc, 2226cc Quantum |

VOLKSWAGEN
1983-92

UNDERHOOD SERVICE SPECIFICATIONS

TIMING MARK

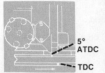

5° ATDC
TDC

1915cc, 2109cc
Vanagon

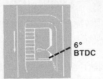

6° BTDC

1715cc
Quantum w/MT,
1780cc
Fox, Quantum

3° ATDC

1715cc
Quantum w/AT

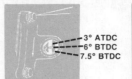

3° ATDC
6° BTDC
7.5° BTDC

1715cc, 1780cc
All models with
transverse engine

6° BTDC

1984cc
Passat

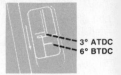

3° ATDC
6° BTDC

2144cc, 2226cc
Quantum

ELECTRICAL AND IGNITION SYSTEMS

BATTERY
BCI equivalent shown, size may vary from original equipment. Check clearance before replacing, holddown may need to be modified.

Engine	Year	STANDARD BCI Group	STANDARD Crank. Perf.	OPTIONAL BCI Group	OPTIONAL Crank. Perf.
1588cc Diesel	1983-91	41	650	—	—
1715cc All w/carb	1983-84	42	365	41	435
FI ex. Canada	1983-84	41	435	—	—
FI Canada	1983-84	41	650	—	—
1780cc ex. Canada	1984-86	41	435	41	450
Canada	1984-86	41	650	—	—
1780cc					
Jetta w/o AC	1987	42	350	41	500
Jetta w/AC	1987	41	450	41	500
Fox	1987	41	435	—	—
All others	1987	41	450	41	500
All models	1988-89	41	435	41	500
All models	1990-91	41	575	—	—
1915cc ex. Canada	1983-85	41	435	—	—
Canada	1983-85	41	650	—	—
1970cc ex. Canada	1983	41	435	—	—
Canada	1983	41	650	—	—
1984cc All models	1990-91	41	575	—	—
2109cc Vanagon	1986-87	41	450	41	500
	1988-89	41	500	—	—
	1990-91	41	575	—	—
2144cc Quantum	1983-84	41	435	—	—
2226cc ex. Canada	1985-87	41	435	—	—
Canada	1985-87	41	650	—	—
All models	1988	41	500	—	—

ALTERNATOR
See UNDERHOOD SERVICE INSTRUCTIONS at the beginning of this section for test/adjustment diagrams.

Application	Rated Output (amps @ eng. rpm)	Test Output (amps @ eng. rpm)
1983-84 4-cyl.	65	49 @ 3000
5-cyl.	75	—
1985-91 1588cc w/o AC	65	49 @ 3000
W/AC	90	74 @ 3000
1992 1590cc w/o AC	65	49 @ 3000
W/AC	90	74 @ 3000
1985-92 1780cc w/o AC	65	49 @ 3000
W/AC	90	74 @ 3000
1990-92 1984cc	90	74 @ 3000
1986-91 2109cc	90	74 @ 3000
1985-88 2226cc	90	74 @ 3000
1992-93 2459cc	90	74 @ 3000

REGULATOR

Application	Test Temp. (deg. F/C)	Voltage Setting
All	68/20	13.5-14.5

STARTER

Engine	Cranking Voltage (min. volts)	Ampere Draw @ Cranking Speed
All	8.0	260

SPARK PLUGS

Engine	Year	Gap (inches)	Gap (mm)	Torque (ft-lb)
1715cc: Code EN	1983-84	.024-.032	.60-.80	15
Code FX, WT	1983-84	.024-.032	.60-.80	15
1780cc: Code JH	1983-89	.024-.032	.60-.80	15
Code HT	1985	.028-.036	.70-.90	15
Code JN, Quantum	1985-86	.024-.032	.60-.80	15
Code GX, MZ	1985-87	.024-.032	.60-.80	15
Code RD	1986-87	.028-.036	.70-.90	15
Code PL	1986-89	.028-.036	.70-.90	15
Code UM	1987	.024-.032	.60-.80	17
Code JN, Fox	1988-92	.024-.032	.60-.80	17
Code PF	1988-92	.024-.032	.60-.80	15
Code RV	1988-92	.024-.032	.60-.80	15
Code PG	1989-92	.028-.032	.70-.80	15
Code 2H	1991-92	.028-.035	.70-.90	15
1915cc Code DH	1983-85	.024-.032	.60-.80	15
1970cc Code CV	1983	.024-.028	.60-.70	22
1984cc Code 9A	1990-91	.028-.032	.70-.80	15
2109cc Code MV	1986-91	.024-.032	.60-.80	15
2144cc: Code KM				
Ex. Canada	1983-84	.024-.032	.60-.80	15
Canada	1983-84	.028-.036	.70-.90	15
Code WE: U.S.	1984	.024-.032	.60-.80	15
Canada	1984	.032-.036	.80-.90	15
2226cc: Code KX	1984	.028-.032	.70-.80	15
	1985-86	.032-.036	.80-.90	15
Code JT	1986-88	.028-.032	.70-.80	15

IGNITION COIL
See UNDERHOOD SERVICE INSTRUCTIONS at the beginning of this section for test/adjustment diagrams.

Engine	Year	Windings	Resistance (ohms @ 68°F or 20°C)
1715cc	1983-84	Primary	.52-.76
		Secondary	2400-3500
1780cc Code JH	1983-90	Primary	.52-.76
		Secondary	2400-3500
Code HT	1985	Primary	.65-.79
		Secondary	6900-8500
Code JN	1985-86	Primary	.52-.76
		Secondary	2400-3500
Code GX	1985-87	Primary	.65-.79
		Secondary	6900-8500
Code MZ	1985-87	Primary	.52-.76
		Secondary	2400-3500
Code RD	1986-87	Primary	.65-.79
		Secondary	6900-8500
Code PL	1986-89	Primary	.65-.79
		Secondary	6900-8500
Code UM	1987	Primary	.52-.76
		Secondary	2400-3500
Code JN	1988-91	Primary	.52-.76
		Secondary	2400-3500
Code PF, RV	1988-92	Primary	.65-.79
		Secondary	6900-8500
Code PG	1989-92	Primary	.60-.80
		Secondary	2400-3500
1915cc	1983-85	Primary	.42-.76
		Secondary	2400-3500
1970cc ex. California	1983	Primary	2.6-3.1
		Secondary	6000-12,000
California	1983	Primary	.52-.76
		Secondary	2400-3500

UNDERHOOD SERVICE SPECIFICATIONS

VNITU3   VNITU3

IGNITION COIL Continued

Engine	Year	Windings	Resistance (ohms @ 68°F or 20°C)
1984cc	1990-92	Primary	.60-.80
		Secondary	2400-3500
2109cc	1986-91	Primary	.50-.80
		Secondary	2400-3500
2144cc	1983-84	Primary	.52-.76
		Secondary	2400-3500
2226cc	1985-88	Primary	.50-1.50
		Secondary	6000-9000

IGNITION RESISTOR

Engine	Year	Type	Resistance (ohms)	Temperature (deg. F/C)
1715cc, 1780cc	1983-85	Wire	.85-.95	68/20

BASE TIMING

See UNDERHOOD SERVICE INSTRUCTIONS at the beginning of this section for test/adjustment diagrams.

Set at slow idle and Before Top Dead Center, unless otherwise specified.

Set to specifications shown on emission label if different from setting listed.

All Engines: Connect tachometer and timing light; check idle speed, observe timing mark.

1983-84 Engines w/ISS (Integrated Idle Stabilizer): Disconnect plugs from stabilizer and connect them together.

1986-90 Engines w/Digifont: Disconnect coolant temperature sensor, check at 2000-2500 rpm.

All ex. Vanagon: Align mark on flywheel with pointer on bellhousing. Some models, remove TDC sensor to access mark.

Vanagon: Align notch on pulley with split in degree markings.

Engine	Year	Man. Trans. (degrees)	Auto. Trans. (degrees)
1715cc 1V	1983-84	7.5 ±1	—
1715cc FI	1983-84	6 ±2	3 ±2 ATDC
1780cc	1983-92	6 ±2	6 ±2
1915cc	1983-84	5 ±2 ATDC	5 ±2 ATDC
1970cc	1983	7.5	7.5
California	1983	5 ATDC	5 ATDC
1984cc	1990-92	6 ±2	6 ±2
2109cc	1986-91	5 ±2	5 ±2
2144cc	1983-84	6 ±2	6 ±2
Canada	1983-84	3 ±2 ATDC	3 ±2 ATDC
2226cc	1985-88	6 ±2	6 ±2

DISTRIBUTOR TIMING ADVANCE

Engine degrees at engine rpm, no load, in addition to base timing.

Engine	Trans-mission	Year	Distributor Number	Degrees @ 2500 RPM Total	Degrees @ 2500 RPM Centrifugal
1715cc 1V	MT	1983-84	055905205AA	24-30	15-19
1715cc FI	MT	1983-84	049905206B	26-33	16-21
1715cc FI	AT	1983-84	049905205Q	26-33	16-21
1780cc	MT & AT	1983-90	026905205B	24-33	14-19
1780cc	MT & AT	1985-87	027905205F	24-30	14-16
1915cc	MT & AT	1983-85	025905205D	29-37	17-21
1970cc	MT & AT	1983	022905205S	23-32	15-20
California	MT & AT	1983	039905205C	24-30	12-18
2144cc Code KM	MT & AT	1983-84	035905205AM	25-36	16-21
Canada	MT & AT	1983-84	035905205AE	26-37	15-22
2144cc Code WE	AT	1984	035905206A	25-36	16-21
2226cc	MT & AT	1985-88	035905205AM	25-36	16-21

FUEL SYSTEM

FUEL PRESSURE PROCEDURE

See UNDERHOOD SERVICE INSTRUCTIONS at the beginning of this section for test/adjustment diagrams.

CIS Systems:
1. With engine at operating temperature, connect appropriate pressure gauge between fuel distributor and warm-up regulator.
2. Set gauge valve to open position, start engine and run at idle, allow pressure to stabilize, read control pressure.

FUEL PRESSURE PROCEDURE Continued

3. Set gauge valve to closed position, allow pressure to stabilize, read system pressure.
4. Set gauge to open position, switch off ignition, after 10 minutes read residual pressure.

CIS-E Systems:
1. With engine at operating temperature, connect appropriate pressure gauge between cold start line and lower chamber test fittings of the fuel distributor.
2. Disconnect electrical connector from the differential pressure regulator.
3. Set gauge valve to open position, remove fuel pump relay and bridge terminals to energize pump, allow pressure to stabilize, read system pressure.
4. Set gauge valve to closed position, energize fuel pump, read differential pressure.
5. Set gauge valve to open position, energize fuel pump for 30 seconds, after 10 minutes read residual pressure.

AFC, Digijet, Digifont Systems:
1. Connect appropriate pressure gauge to test port of fuel rail.
2. Disconnect vacuum hose from pressure regulator, start engine and run at idle, allow pressure to stabilize and take reading.
3. Reconnect vacuum to pressure regulator and check gauge reading.
4. Digijet and Digifont only, switch ignition off, after 10 minutes read residual pressure.

FUEL PRESSURE: CIS, CIS-E

Engine	System	Year	System PSI	Control PSI	Differential PSI	Residual PSI
1715cc	CIS	1983-84	68-78	49-55	—	37
1780cc	CIS	1983-91	68-78	49-55	—	35-38
1780cc	CIS-E	1985-91	75-82	—	68-79	38
1984cc	CIS-E	1990-92	88-96	—	81-91	48
2144cc	CIS	1983-84	68-78	49-55	—	35-38
2226cc	CIS-E	1985-88	75-82	—	68-79	38

FUEL PRESSURE: AFC, Digijet, Digifont

Engine	Year	System Pressure W/O Vacuum PSI	System Pressure W/Vacuum PSI	Residual Pressure PSI
1780cc	1988-92	44	36	29
1915cc	1983-85	36	29	29
1970cc	1983	36	29	—
2109cc	1986-91	36	33	29

IDLE SPEED W/O COMPUTER CONTROL

All engines: Must be at operating temperature, all electrical equipment switched off, cooling fan not running. If equipped with ISS (idle speed stabilizer), disconnect both electrical plugs and connect them together.

1983 1970cc: Disconnect and plug canister vent hose at air filter.

1983-84 1715cc: Disconnect crankcase breather hoses from valve cover and intake air boot, position hoses to draw in fresh air. Disconnect canister vent hose at intake air boot.

1983-84 2144cc: Disconnect crankcase breather hoses, plug outlets but leave hoses open. Remove plug from canister vent pipe at intake boot.

Engine	Year	SLOW Man. Trans.	SLOW Auto. Trans.	FAST Man. Trans.	FAST Auto. Trans.	Step of Cam
1588cc Diesel	1983-85	810-950	—	5300-5400◆	—	—
1588cc Turbo Diesel	1983-85	810-950	810-950 N	5050-5150◆	5050-5150◆	—
1588cc Turbo Diesel	1986-88	920-980	920-980 N	5050-5150◆	5050-5150◆	—
1588cc Diesel	1986-91	920-980	—	5300-5400◆	—	—
1715cc 1V	1983-84	800-1000	—	2800-3200	—	2
1715cc FI	1983-84	850-1000	850-1000 N	—	—	—
1970cc	1983	850-950	850-1000 N	—	—	—
2144cc	1983-84	770-870	770-870 N	—	—	—

◆ Maximum speed.

IDLE SPEED W/COMPUTER CONTROL

See UNDERHOOD SERVICE INSTRUCTIONS at the beginning of this section for test/adjustment diagrams.

All engines: Must be at operating temperature, all electrical equipment switched off, cooling fan not running.

IDLE SPEED W/COMPUTER CONTROL Continued

1983-91 1780cc w/CIS: Disconnect crankcase breather hoses from valve cover and intake air boot, position hoses to draw in fresh air. Disconnect canister vent hose at intake air boot. Clamp off hose to idle speed boost valve.

1983-85 1915cc: Disconnect both electrical plugs from ISS (idle speed stabilizer) unit, and connect them together.

1985-88 1780cc w/CIS-E Quantum: Disconnect crankcase breather hoses from valve cover and intake air boot, position hoses to draw in fresh air. Remove plug from canister vent pipe at intake boot. Clamp off hose to idle speed boost valve.

1985-88 2226cc: Disconnect crankcase breather hoses, plug outlets but leave hoses open. Remove plug from canister vent pipe at intake boot. Clamp off hose to idle speed boost valve.

1985-91 1780cc w/CIS-E ex. Quantum: Disconnect crankcase breather hoses from valve cover and intake air boot, position hoses to draw in fresh air. Remove "T" fitting for canister from intake air boot, rotate fitting 90 degrees and install restricted end into boot. Clamp off hose to idle speed boost valve.

1988-91 1780cc w/Digifont: Disconnect crankcase breather hoses. Run engine at idle for one minute, disconnect coolant temperature sensor. Rev engine to 3000 rpm several times, allow idle to stabilize before adjusting.

1990-91 1984cc: Disconnect crankcase breather hose, disconnect canister vent hose at purge valve.

Engine	Code	Year	Checking Speed	Adjusting Speed
1780cc	JH	1983-89	850-1000	—
	HT	1985	800-1000	870-930
	JN	1985-86	850-1000	—
	GX, MZ	1985-87	800-1000	870-930
	RD	1986-87	800-900	870-930
	PL	1986-89	800-900	900-920
	UM	1987	800-1000	—
	JN	1988-91	800-1000	900-920
	PF, RV	1988-92	750-850	950-1000
	PG	1989-92	750-850	770-830
1915cc	DH	1983-85	800-900	—
1984cc	9A	1990-92	700-900	—
2109cc	MV	1986-91	830-930	—
2226cc	KX, JT	1985-88	750-850	780-820

ENGINE MECHANICAL

TIGHTENING TORQUES
See UNDERHOOD SERVICE INSTRUCTIONS at the beginning of this section for test/adjustment diagrams.

Engine	Year	Cylinder Head	Intake Manifold	Exhaust Manifold	Crankshaft Pulley	Water Pump
DIESEL ENGINES						
4-cyl. 1.6L						
12-point bolt	1983-84	30/40	18/25	18/25	15/20	7/10
2nd stage		44/60				
Warm retorque		+180°				
4-cyl. 1.6L	1985-91	30/40	18/25	18/25	15/20	7/10
2nd stage		44/60				
3rd stage		+180°				
Warm retorque		+90°				
GASOLINE ENGINES						
4-cyl. 1.7L	1983-84	30/40	18/25	18/25	15/20	7/10
2nd stage		44/60				
3rd stage ★		+180°				
4-cyl. 1.8L						
SOHC						
Ex. supercharged	1985-92	30/40	18/25	18/25	15/20	7/10
2nd stage		44/60				
3rd stage ★		+180°				
Supercharged	1990-92	30/40	11/15	18/25	18/25	7/10
2nd stage		44/60				
3rd stage ★		+180°				
4-cyl. 1.8L						
DOHC	1986-92	30/40	15/20	18/25	15/20	7/10
2nd stage		44/60				
3rd stage ★		+180°				

TIGHTENING TORQUES Continued

		Torque Ft-lbs/Nm				
Engine	Year	Cylinder Head	Intake Manifold	Exhaust Manifold	Crankshaft Pulley	Water Pump
4-cyl. 1.9L	1983-85	37/50	15/20	15/20	43/60	15/20
4-cyl. 2.0L	1983	22/30	11/15	15/20	22/30	—
4-cyl. 2.0L	1990-92	30/40	15/20	18/25	18/25	7/10
2nd stage		44/60				
3rd stage ★		+180°				
4-cyl. 2.1L	1986-91	37/50	15/20	18/25	43/60	15/20
5-cyl. 2.2L	1983-88	30/40	—	—	258/350/	15/20
2nd stage		44/60				
3rd stage ★		+180°				

† With engine at operating temperature, repeat after 1000 miles of service.
★ Two at 90° is permissible, must be in one even motion.
● Valid only when using special extension, Volkswagen Part No. 2079.

VALVE CLEARANCE
Engine at operating temperature.

Engine/Model	Year	Intake (inches)	Intake (mm)	Exhaust (inches)	Exhaust (mm)
1715cc	1983-84	.008-.012	.20-.30	.016-.020	.40-.50
1588cc	1983-86	.008-.012	.20-.30	.016-.020	.40-.50
1780cc	1983-85	.008-.012	.20-.30	.016-.020	.40-.50

COMPRESSION PRESSURE
At cranking speed, throttle open, engine at operating temperature.

Engine	Year	PSI	Maximum Variation PSI
1588cc Turbo Diesel	1983-88	406-493	73
1588cc Diesel	1983-91	406-493	73
1590cc Diesel	1992	406-493	73
1715cc	1983-84	131-174	44
1780cc SOHC	1983-92	131-174	44
Supercharged	1990-92	116-174	44
1780cc DOHC	1987-92	145-189	44
1915cc	1983-85	145-190	44
1970cc	1983	85-135	42
1984cc	1990-91	145-189	44
2109cc	1986-91	145-189	44
2144cc	1983-84	145-174	44
2226cc	1985-88	131-174	44

BELT TENSION
A belt in operation 20 minutes is considered a used belt.

Engine	Year	Alternator	Power Steering	Air Cond.
USED BELTS				
1715cc, 2144cc (inches)	1983-84	3/16	3/8	3/8
1715cc, 2144cc (mm)	1983-84	5	10	10
1780cc (inches)	1983-92	3/16	3/8	3/8
1780cc (mm)	1983-92	5	10	10
1984cc (inches)	1990-92	3/16	3/8	3/8
1984cc (mm)	1990-92	5	10	10
2109cc (inches)	1986-91	3/16	—	3/8
2109cc (mm)	1986-91	5	—	10
2226cc (inches)	1986-88	3/16	3/8	3/8
2226cc (mm)	1986-88	5	10	10
NEW BELTS				
1715cc, 2144cc (inches)	1983-84	5/64	3/8	3/8
1715cc, 2144cc (mm)	1983-84	2	10	10
1780cc (inches)	1983-92	5/64	3/8	3/8
1780cc (mm)	1983-92	2	10	10
1915cc (inches)	1984-85	3/8-9/16	—	3/8-9/16
1915cc (mm)	1984-85	10-14	—	10-14
1984cc (inches)	1990-92	5/64	3/8	3/8
1984cc (mm)	1990-92	2	10	10
2109cc (inches)	1986-91	5/64	—	3/8
2109cc (mm)	1986-91	2	—	10
2226cc (inches)	1986-88	5/64	3/8	3/8
2226cc (mm)	1986-88	2	10	10

ENGINE COMPUTER SYSTEM

COMPUTER DIAGNOSTIC CODES
Using On-Board Diagnostic System
1988-92 1780cc Golf, GTI, Jetta:
To activate: Turn ignition on but do not start engine, press and hold "CHECK" light rocker switch for at least 4 seconds. Codes will be displayed by light as a series of four digit codes with a 2.5 second pause between digits. Depress and hold switch for 4 seconds to access additional codes. When all codes have been displayed, code 0000 will flash, light on 2.5 seconds, light off 2.5 seconds.

To clear memory: Turn ignition switch off. Depress and hold rocker switch, turn ignition switch to on position, continue to hold rocker switch for at least 5 seconds, turn ignition off and release rocker switch.

Code	Application	Definition
2142	Knock Sensor	Defective sensor or circuit
2232	Air Flow Sensor Potentiometer	Defective potentiometer or circuit
2312	Coolant Temperature Sensor	Defective sensor or circuit
2322	Intake Air Temperature Sensor	Defective sensor or circuit
2342	Oxygen Sensor	Defective sensor or circuit
4444	No Faults	Memory clear
0000	End of Sequence	All fault codes have been displayed

Using External Diagnostic Tester
1988-92 1780cc Code RV, 1989-92 1780cc Code PG, 1990-91 1984cc:
Special tool required. Connect tester, VW Part No. VAG1551, and access codes.

Code	Application	Definition
1111	Control Unit	Defective, internal
1231	Speed Sensor	No automatic transmission signal
2112	Reference Sensor	No signal, out of range signal
2113	Hall Sender	No signal, out of range signal
2121	Idle Switch	Defective switch or circuit
2141	Knock Sensor I	Excessive detonation detected
2142	Knock Sensor I	Defective sensor or circuit
2144	Knock Sensor II	Defective sensor or circuit
2212	Throttle Potentiometer	Defective unit, open or short circuit
2222	Manifold Vacuum Sensor	Defective control unit, no vacuum supply
2231	Idle Control	Idle out of regulation limit
2232	Air Flow Sensor	Defective sensor or circuit
2242	CO Potentiometer	Defective potentiometer, open circuit
2312	Coolant Temperature Sensor	Defective sensor or circuit
2322	Intake Temperature Sensor	Defective potentiometer, open or short circuit
2323	Air Flow Potentiometer	Defective potentiometer, open circuit
2341	Oxygen Sensor	Control limit exceeded
2342	Oxygen Sensor	No signal, out of range signal
2411	EGR	No signal, system restricted
4411	Fuel Injector	Defective injector, open circuit
4431	Idle Stabilizer	No signal, out of range signal
4444	No Faults	Memory clear

SENSORS, INPUT
TEMPERATURE SENSORS

Engine	Year	Sensor	Resistance Ohms @ deg. F/C
1780cc	1985-92	Coolant, Intake Air	5000-6500 @ 32/0
			1500-2000 @ 86/30
			500-650 @ 140/60
			200-300 @ 194/90
1915cc	1983-85	Coolant	5000-6500 @ 32/0
			1500-2000 @ 86/30
			500-650 @ 140/60
			200-300 @ 194/90
1970cc	1983	Engine	5000-6500 @ 32/0
			1500-2000 @ 86/30
			500-650 @ 140/60
			200-300 @ 194/90
		Intake Air	2300-2700 @ 68/20

SENSORS, INPUT Continued
TEMPERATURE SENSORS Continued

Engine	Year	Sensor	Resistance Ohms @ deg. F/C
1984cc	1990-92	Coolant	5000-6500 @ 32/0
			1500-2000 @ 86/30
			500-650 @ 140/60
			200-300 @ 194/90
2109	1986-91	Intake Air	2300-2700 @ 68/20

† Measured at terminals 1 & 4 of the Airflow meter.

AIRFLOW SENSOR
See UNDERHOOD SERVICE INSTRUCTIONS at the beginning of this section for test/adjustment diagrams.

Engine	Year	Resistance Ohms @ Terminal
1780cc	1985-87	4 min. @ 1 & 2
		1 max. @ 2 & 3
Code PF, RV	1988-92	500-1000 @ 3 & 4
Code PG	1990-91	0-2000 @ 1 & 3
1915cc	1983-85	500-1000 @ 3 & 4
		500-1000 @ 6 & 9
1970cc	1983	560 @ 3 & 4
		560 @ 6 & 9
		2300-2700 @ 1 & 4
2109cc	1986-91	500-1000 @ 3 & 4
		500-1000 @ 6 & 9
		2300-2700 @ 1 & 4

ACTUATORS, OUTPUT
CONTROL PRESSURE REGULATOR

Engine	Year	Resistance (ohms)
1780cc w/CIS	1985-87	20-26
Canada code UN, JN	1988-89	16-22

DIFFERENTIAL PRESSURE REGULATOR
See UNDERHOOD SERVICE INSTRUCTIONS at the beginning of this section for test/adjustment diagrams.

Engine	Year	Resistance (ohms)
1780cc w/CIS-E	1985-90	17.5-21.5

FREQUENCY VALVE
See UNDERHOOD SERVICE INSTRUCTIONS at the beginning of this section for test/adjustment diagrams.

Engine	Year	Resistance (ohms)
All w/CIS	1983-89	2-3

COMPUTER TIMING ADVANCE
1780cc Engine: With engine at operating temperature, remove vacuum hose from control unit. Increase engine speed to specified rpm and compare to specified value.

2109cc Engine: With engine at operating temperature, disconnect Temperature Sensor II. Increase engine speed to 2000-2500 rpm and record timing. Reconnect Temperature Sensor II and increase engine speed to 3000 rpm, read timing and subtract previously recorded value. Compare with specified value.

Values given are in addition to base timing.

Engine/Model	Year	Engine Code	Timing Advance Degrees @ RPM
1780cc:			
GTI, Jetta GLI	1985-87	HT, RD	14 @ 4300
			16 @ 3000
Scirocco 16-valve	1986-89	PL	13 @ 2500
Golf, Jetta	1988-92	RV, PF	30 ±3 @ 2300
Corrado	1990-92	PG	25 ±5 @ 2500
2109cc Vanagon	1986-90	MV	35 ±3 @ 3000

ENGINE IDENTIFICATION

To identify an engine by the manufacturer's code, follow the four steps designated by the numbered blocks.

V.I.N.
PLATE LOCATION:

Top of instrument panel or left windshield post visible through windshield.

1 **MODEL YEAR IDENTIFICATION:**

10th character of V.I.N.
1992 — N; 1991 — M; 1990 — L;
1989 — K; 1988 — J; 1987 — H;
1986 — G; 1985 — F; 1984 — E;
1983 — D.

2 **ENGINE CODE LOCATIONS:**

6th and 7th characters of V.I.N.

4 **ENGINE IDENTIFICATION**

YEAR	**3** ENGINE CODE	CYL.	DISPL. liters	cc	Fuel System	HP
1992	82 (B230F)	4	2.3	2316	LH	114
	88 (B230F)	4	2.3	2316	LH	114
	88 (B230F)	4	2.3	2316	R	114
	87 (B230FT)	4	2.3 T	2316 T	LH	162
	89 (B234F)	4	2.3	2316	LH	153
	95 (B6304)	6	2.9	2922	M	204
1991	88 (B230F)	4	2.3	2316	LH	114
	88 (B230F)	4	2.3	2316	R	114
	87 (B230FT)	4	2.3 T	2316 T	LH	162, 188†
	89 (B234F)	4	2.3	2316	LH	153
1990	88 (B230F)	4	2.3	2316	LH	114
	88 (B230F)	4	2.3	2316	R	114
	89 (B234F)	4	2.3	2316	LH	153
	87 (B230FT)	4	2.3 T	2316 T	LH	162, 188†
	69 (B280F)	6	2.8	2849	LH	145
1989	88 (B230F)	4	2.3	2316	LH	114
	88 (B230F)	4	2.3	2316	R	114
	89 (B234F)	4	2.3	2316	LH	153
	87 (B230FT)	4	2.3 T	2316 T	LH	160, 175†
	69 (B280F)	6	2.8	2849	LH	144
1988	88 (B230F)	4	2.3	2316	LH	114
	87 (B230FT)	4	2.3 T	2316 T	LH	160
	69 (B280F)	6	2.8	2849	LH	145
1987	88 (B230F)	4	2.3	2316	LH	114
	87 (B230FT)	4	2.3 T	2316 T	LH	160
	69 (B280F)	6	2.8	2849	LH	145

4 **ENGINE IDENTIFICATION**

YEAR	**3** ENGINE CODE	CYL.	DISPL. liters	cc	Fuel System	HP
1986	88 (B230F)	4	2.3	2316	LH	114
	87 (B230FT)	4	2.3 T	2316 T	LH	160
	76 (D24T)	6	2.4 TD	2383 TD	VE	106
	69 (B28F)	6	2.8	2849	CIS	136
1985	41 (B21A)	4	2.1	2127	1V	100
	47 (B21FT)	4	2.1 T	2127 T	CIS	162
	88 (B230F)	4	2.3	2316	LH	114
	87 (B230FT)	4	2.3 T	2316 T	LH	160
	76 (D24T)	6	2.4 TD	2383 TD	VE	106
	69 (B28F)	6	2.8	2849	CIS	134
1984	41 (B21A)	4	2.1	2127	1V	100
	47 (B21FT)	4	2.1 T	2127 T	CIS	131
	88 (B23F)	4	2.3	2316	LH	111
	77 (D24)	6	2.4 D	2383 D	VE	80
	76 (D24T)	6	2.4 TD	2383 TD	VE	106
	69 (B28F)	6	2.8	2849	CIS	134
1983	41 (B21A)	4	2.1	2127	1V	102
	47 (B21FT)	4	2.1 T	2127 T	CIS	127
	84 (B23E)	4	2.3	2316	CIS	115
	88 (B23F)	4	2.3	2316	LH	107
	77 (D24)	6	2.4 D	2383 D	VE	78
	69 (B28F)	6	2.8	2849	CIS	130

† Engine horsepower varies with model installation.
1V — 1 barrel carb.   CIS — Continuous Injection System.
D — Diesel.   LH — LH-Jetronic.   M — Motronic
R — Regina Bendix Injection.   T — Turbo.
TD — Turbo Diesel.   VE — Diesel Injection.

UNDERHOOD SERVICE SPECIFICATIONS

VOITU1   VOITU1

CYLINDER NUMBERING SEQUENCE

4-CYL. FIRING ORDER:
1 3 4 2

V6-CYL. FIRING ORDER:
1 6 3 5 2 4

———————— Front of car ————————

1983-92	1983-92	1989-92	1983-86	1987-90
2127cc,	2316cc	2316cc	2849cc	2849cc
2316cc	700-Series	700-Series		
200-Series	SOHC	DOHC		

—————— TIMING MARK ——————

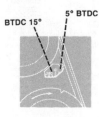

1983-85
2127cc

1983-92
2316cc

2894cc

UNDERHOOD SERVICE SPECIFICATIONS

VOITU2   VOITU2

ELECTRICAL AND IGNITION SYSTEMS

BATTERY

BCI equivalent shown, size may vary from original equipment. Check clearance before replacing, holddown may need to be modified.

Engine	Year	BCI Group No.	Crank. Perf.
4-cyl. 2316cc	1983-84	46	360
V6 2849cc	1983-84	46	450
4-cyl. 2127cc ex. Turbo	1983-85	46	360
Turbo	1983-85	46	450
6-cyl. 2383cc Diesel	1983-86	49	600
4-cyl. 2316cc ex. Turbo	1985-87	47	450
Turbo	1985-87	48	500
V6 2849cc	1985-87	48	500
4-cyl. 2316cc, all	1988	47	450
V6 2849cc: 760	1988	47	450
780	1988	48	500
4-cyl. 2316cc: 240	1989	47	450
740 ex. DOHC	1989	47	450
DOHC	1989	48	500
760 Turbo	1989	47	450
780 Turbo	1989	48	500
V6 2849cc	1989-90	48	500
4-cyl. 2316cc:			
Ex. DOHC, Turbo	1990	47	450
DOHC, Turbo	1990	48	500

ALTERNATOR

Application	Year	Rated Output (amps)	Test Output (amps @ eng. rpm)
2127cc	1983-85	70	46 @ 2000
Turbo	1983-85	55	36 @ 2000
2316cc ex. Turbo	1983-85	55	36 @ 2000
Turbo	1983-85	70	46 @ 2000
2316cc: 240	1986-88	70	46 @ 2000
740 ex. Turbo	1986-88	70	46 @ 2000
Turbo	1986-88	90	34 @ 1500
2316cc ex. Turbo	1989-92	80	46 @ 2000
Turbo	1989-92	100	34 @ 1500
2383cc	1983-85	55	48 @ 1500
2849cc	1983-85	70	46 @ 2000
2849cc	1985-86	90	90 @ 6000
2849cc	1987-90	100	34 @ 1500
2922cc	1992	120	60 @ 1800

REGULATOR

Voltage measured at battery terminals.

Application	Year	Test Temp. (deg. F/C)	Voltage Setting
All	1983-84	68/20	13.2-14.2
240 Series	1985	68/20	13.2-14.2
700 Series	1985	77/25	13.8-14.6
All	1986-92	77/25	13.8-14.6

STARTER

Manufacturer	Year	Cranking Voltage (min. volts)	Ampere Draw @ Cranking Speed
Bosch: 1.1 kW	1983-90	7.4	480-560
1.4, 2.0 kW	1983-92	9.0	185-220
Hitachi: Gas	1983-92	10.3	200
Diesel	1983-86	8.8	300

SPARK PLUGS

Engine	Year	Gap (inches)	Gap (mm)	Torque (ft-lb)
2127cc	1983-85	.028-.032	.70-.80	15-22
2316cc	1983-92	.028-.032	.70-.80	15-22
2849cc	1983-90	.024-.028	.60-.70	7-11
2922cc	1992	.024-.028	.60-.70	17-20

IGNITION COIL

Resistance (ohms @ 68°F or 20°C)

Engine	Year	Windings	Resistance (ohms)
2127cc, 2316cc	1983-85	Primary	1.1-1.3
Essex		Secondary	9600-11,600
Bosch		Secondary	7700-9300
2316cc	1986-88	Primary	0.6-0.9
		Secondary	6500-9000
2316cc w/Bendix injection	1989-92	Primary	0.5
		Secondary	5000
2316cc w/Bosch injection	1989-92	Primary	0.6-0.8
		Secondary	6900-8500
2849cc	1983-86	Primary	0.4-0.6
		Secondary	8000-11,000
2849cc	1987-90	Primary	0.6-0.9
		Secondary	6500-9000
2922cc	1992	Primary	0.5

IGNITION PICKUP

Engine	Year	Resistance (ohms)	Air Gap (in./mm)
2127, 2316cc w/o Hall effect	1983-85	0.95-1.25	0.10/.25
2849cc	1983-86	540-660	0.12/.30

IGNITION POINTS

Engine	Year	Gap (inches)	Gap (mm)	Dwell (degrees)	Spring Tension (ounces)
B21A Canada	1983-85	0.16	.40	59-65	14-18

IGNITION RESISTOR

Engine	Year	Resistance (ohms)
2127cc 1V	1983-85	1.2-1.4
2127cc FI w/o EST	1983-85	0.8-1.0
2316cc w/o EST	1983-85	0.8-1.0
2849cc	1983-86	0.9-1.1

TIMING PROCEDURE

1. Connect tachometer.
2. Connect timing light to No. 1 spark plug lead.
3. Disconnect and plug distributor vacuum hoses. Disconnect air injection on 1982 models, AC must be off.
4. With engine at specified rpm, observe timing marks and rotate distributor to obtain recommended setting.

BASE TIMING

Before Top Dead Center, unless otherwise specified.

Engine	Year	Man. Trans. (degrees) @ Idle	Auto. Trans. (degrees) @ Idle
2127cc 1V Canada	1983-85	7 ±2	7 ±2
2127cc Turbo	1983-85	12 ±2	12 ±2
2316cc	1983-84	12 ±1	12 ±1
Canada	1983-84	10 ±1	10 ±1
2316cc SOHC:			
Bendix injection	1989-92	10 ±2†	10 ±2†
Bosch injection	1985-92	12 ±2†	12 ±2†
2316cc DOHC	1989-92	15 ±2†	15 ±2†
2849cc	1983-86	—	23 ±1*
2849cc	1987-90	—	16†
2922cc	1992	—	5†

† For reference only, timing not adjustable.
* At 2500 rpm.

UNDERHOOD SERVICE SPECIFICATIONS

DISTRIBUTOR TIMING ADVANCE
Engine degrees at engine rpm, no load, in addition to base timing.

Engine	Trans- mission	Year	Distributor Number	Degrees @ 2500 RPM Total	Degrees @ 2500 RPM Centrifugal
2127cc Turbo	MT & AT	1983-85	0237003024	25.5-34	12.5-17
2127cc 1V Canada	MT & AT	1983-85	0231170284	29.5-38.5	16.5-21.5
2316cc Canada	MT & AT	1983	0237002039	27.5-35.5	14.5-18.5
2849cc	MT & AT	1983-85	0237402017	28-36	10-14

FUEL SYSTEM

FUEL PRESSURE
With engine warm and running at idle.

Engine	Fuel System	Year	Control Pressure PSI	Line Pressure PSI	Residual Pressure PSI
2127cc	1V	1983-85	—	2.1-3.8 @ 3000	—
2127cc	LH	1983	36	43	—
2127cc Turbo	CIS	1983-84	49-56	75-84	35-46
2127cc Turbo	LH	1985	36	43	—
2316cc	CIS	1983	50-55	65-77	22-35
2316cc	LH	1984-92	36	43	28-43
2849cc	CIS	1983-86	49-56†	64-75	24 min.
2849cc	LH	1987-90	36	43	—

† With vacuum, 44-50 psi with vacuum line disconnected.

COLD CONTROL PRESSURE: CIS

Pressure Regulator Part Number	Pressure PSI (bar) @ 50°F (10°C) Ambient Temp.	Pressure PSI (bar) @ 68°F (20°C) Ambient Temp.	Pressure PSI (bar) @ 86°F (30°C) Ambient Temp.	Pressure PSI (bar) @ 104°F (40°C) Ambient Temp.
0438140004	15-19 (1.0-1.3)	20-25 (1.4-1.7)	28-32 (1.9-2.2)	33-38 (2.2-2.6)
0438140079	17-22 (1.2-1.5)	26-31 (1.8-2.1)	36-41 (2.5-2.8)	45-49 (3.1-3.4)
0438140082	15-19 (1.0-1.3)	20-25 (1.4-1.7)	28-32 (1.9-2.2)	33-38 (2.2-2.6)
0438140099	22-26 (1.5-1.8)	28-32 (1.9-2.2)	33-38 (2.3-2.6)	39-44 (2.7-3.0)
0438140128†	23-26 (1.6-1.8)	29-36 (2.0-2.5)	35-45 (2.4-3.1)	41-54 (2.8-3.7)

† With vacuum applied.

IDLE SPEED W/O COMPUTER CONTROL
Midpoint of range given is the preferred setting speed.

Engine	Year	SLOW Man. Trans.	SLOW Auto. Trans.	FAST Man. Trans.	FAST Auto. Trans.
2127cc 1V	1983-85	850-950	850-950 N	1250-1350	1250-1350 N
2316cc Canada	1983	850-950	850-950 N	—	—
2383cc Diesel	1983-84	700-800	700-800 N	—	—
Maximum speed	1983-84	5200	5200 N	—	—
2383cc Turbo Diesel	1983-84	750	750 N	—	—
Maximum speed	1983-84	5400	5400 N	—	—
2383cc Turbo Diesel	1985-86	830	830 N	—	—
Maximum speed	1985-86	5400	5400 N	—	—

IDLE SPEED W/COMPUTER CONTROL
Midpoint of range given is the preferred setting speed.

Models with CIS: Idle speed is not adjustable.

Models with LH-Jetronic: Ground test point (blue/white wire) and adjust idle to specified setting value. Adjust throttle valve switch if setting value cannot be obtained. To adjust, loosen holddown screws and rotate unit clockwise, slowly rotate unit counter-clockwise to engage contact stop without opening throttle valve. Tighten holddown screws and check function by removing test point ground. Idle should increase to specified checking value.

Turn on AC to verify specified AC speed-up.

Disconnect fuel system temperature sensor and verify specified cold idle speed.

Engine	Year	Checking Speed	Setting Speed	Cold Idle	AC Speed-up
2127cc Turbo	1983-85	850-950 N	—	—	—
2316cc U.S.	1983-84	730-770 N	720 N	1600-2500 N	900 N

IDLE SPEED W/COMPUTER CONTROL Continued

Engine	Year	Checking Speed	Setting Speed	Cold Idle	AC Speed-up
2316cc	1985-87	730-770 N	720 N	1600-2500 N	900 N
2316cc	1988	730-770 N	750 N	1600-2500 N	900 N
2316cc SOHC ex. Turbo	1989-92	725-825 N	775 N	—	—
2316cc Turbo	1989-92	730-770 N	750 N	—	—
2316cc DOHC	1989-92	800-900 N	850 N	—	—
2849cc	1983-86	880-920 N	—	—	—
2849cc	1987-90	730-770 N	—	—	—
2922cc	1992	700-800 N	750	—	—

IDLE MIXTURE
Measured at slow idle with air pump or oxygen sensor disconnected. Take sample from access port upstream of catalytic converter.

Engine	Year	CO% Minimum	CO% Maximum
2127cc ex. LH, Canada	1983-85	0.7	1.3
Canada	1983-85	2.5	4.0
2127cc LH	1983	0.4	0.8
2316cc	1983	0.5	2.0
2316cc ex. DOHC	1984-90	0.4	0.8
DOHC	1989-90	0.2	1.0
2316cc ex. Turbo	1991-92	0.4	0.8
Turbo	1991-92	0.2	0.1
2849cc	1983-86	0.7	1.3
2849cc	1987-89	0.2	1.0
2922cc	1992	0.4	0.8

ENGINE MECHANICAL

TIGHTENING TORQUES

Engine	Year	Torque Ft-lbs/Nm Cylinder Head	Torque Ft-lbs/Nm Intake Manifold	Torque Ft-lbs/Nm Exhaust Manifold	Torque Ft-lbs/Nm Crankshaft Pulley	Torque Ft-lbs/Nm Water Pump
4-cyl. 2.1L	1983	15/20	15/20	15/20	120/165	—
2nd stage		44/60				
3rd stage		+90°				
4-cyl. 2.3L SOHC	1983-92	15/20	15/20	15/20	120/165	—
2nd stage		44/60				
3rd stage		+90°				
4-cyl. 2.3L DOHC	1989-92	15/20	15/20	15/20	120/165	—
2nd stage		30/40				
3rd stage		+115°				
6-cyl. 2.4L Diesel	1983-86	30/40	18/25	18/25	332/450	—
2nd stage		44/60				
3rd stage		55-75				
4th stage		+180°				
Warm retorque†		+90°				
V6 2.8L	1983-86	43/60	7-11/ 10-15	7-11/ 10-15	177-206/ 240-280	—
2nd stage◆		15/20, +106°				
Warm retorque†		+45°				
V6 2.8L	1987-89	43/60	—	—	177-206/ 240-280	—
2nd stage◆		15/20, +106°				
Warm retorque†		+45°				
V6 2.8L	1990	43/60	—	—	177-206/ 240-280	—
2nd stage◆		30/40				
3rd stage		+180°				

TIGHTENING TORQUES Continued

Engine	Year	Cylinder Head	Intake Manifold	Exhaust Manifold	Crankshaft Pulley	Water Pump
6-cyl. 2.9L	1992	14/20	15/20	18/25	220/300●	15/20
2nd stage		43/60			26/35	
3rd stage		+130°			+60° ★	

Torque Ft-lbs/Nm

† Run engine to operating temperature and allow to cool 2 hours before bringing to torque, repeat procedure after 1000 miles of service.
♦ Back off and torque to specification one bolt at a time.
● Center bolt.
★ Flange bolts.

VALVE CLEARANCE

Engine	Year	Intake (inches)	Intake (mm)	Exhaust (inches)	Exhaust (mm)
2127cc:					
Cold	1983-85	.012-.016	.30-.40	.012-.016	.30-.40
Hot	1983-85	.014-.018	.35-.45	.014-.018	.35-.45
2316cc SOHC:					
Cold	1985-92	.012-.016	.30-.40	.014-.016	.35-.40
Hot	1985-92	.014-.018	.35-.45	.016-.018	.40-.45
2383cc Cold	1983-84	.006-.010	.15-.25	.014-.018	.36-.46
2383cc Hot	1985-86	.008-.012	.20-.30	.016-.020	.40-.50
2849cc:					
Cold	1983-90	.004-.006	.10-.15	.010-.012	.25-.30
Hot	1983-90	.006-.008	.15-.20	.012-.014	.30-.35

COMPRESSION PRESSURE
At cranking speed, engine at operating temperature, throttle open.

Engine	Year	PSI @ RPM	Maximum Variation PSI
2316cc	1985-92	128-156	28
2383cc Diesel	1983-84	340-455	115
2849cc	1983-90	114-156	28
2922cc	1992	184-213	—

BELT TENSION
A belt in operation for 20 minutes is considered a used belt.

Deflection method: Models without automatic tensioner, applied pressure of 15-20 lbs. at midpoint of longest belt segment.

Engine	Year	Alternator	Power Steering	Air Cond.
All (inches)	1983-92	3/16-5/16	3/16-5/16	3/16-5/16
All (mm)	1983-92	5-10	5-10	5-10

ENGINE COMPUTER SYSTEM

COMPUTER DIAGNOSTIC CODES
1989-92 4-cyl. engines:
Remove cover from diagnostic unit, located behind the left front strut tower. Insert test probe into socket #2 to access injection codes, socket #6 for ignition codes. Depress button and read codes.

Code	Indicated Fault
1-1-1	No faults
1-1-2	Control unit
1-1-3	Faulty fuel injector or wiring, fuel mixture rich
1-2-1	Air mass meter signal absent
1-2-3	Coolant temperature sensor signal absent
1-3-1	Engine speed signal absent
1-3-2	Battery voltage out of range
1-3-3	Throttle switch, idle position
2-1-2	Oxygen sensor signal absent
2-1-3	Throttle switch, full load position
2-2-1	Emission control system malfunction, fuel compensation out of range
2-2-3	Idle valve signal absent
2-3-1	Adaptive emission control malfunction at speed
2-3-2	Adaptive emission control malfunction at idle
2-3-3	Closed idle valve or unmetered air leakage
2-4-1	EGR system malfunction
3-1-1	Speedometer signal absent
3-1-2	Knock enrichment signal absent

COMPUTER DIAGNOSTIC CODES Continued

3-2-1	Cold start valve signal absent
3-2-2	No air mass meter hot wire burn-off
4-3-1	EGR temperature sender

SENSORS, INPUT
COOLANT TEMPERATURE SENSOR

Engine	Year	Resistance Ohms @ deg. F/C
All 4-cyl.	1983-92	8100-10,800 @ 14/–10
		2300-2700 @ 68/20
		290-364 @ 176/80
V6 2.8L	1983-90	8100-10,800 @ 14/–10
		2300-2700 @ 68/20
		290-364 @ 176/80
6-cyl. 2.9L	1992	7300 @ 32/0
		1200 @ 104/40
		150 @ 212/100

AIRMASS METER

Engine	Fuel System	Year	Resistance Ohms @ Terminal
4-cyl. 2.3L	LH-2.2	1983-88	2.5-4.0 @ 2 & 3
			0-1000 @ 2 & 6
4-cyl. 2.3L SOHC	LH-2.4	1989-92	3.5-4.0 @ 2 & 3
			0-1000 @ 2 & 6
4-cyl. 2.3L DOHC	LH-2.4	1989-92	2.5-4.0 @ 2 & 3
			0-1000 @ 2 & 6
V6 2.8L	LH-2.2	1987-90	2.5-4.0 @ 2 & 3
			0-1000 @ 2 & 6
6-cyl. 2.9L	M-1.8	1992	2.5-4.0 @ 2 & 3

ACTUATORS, OUTPUT
AIR CONTROL VALVE

Engine	Fuel System	Year	Resistance Ohms @ Terminal
4-cyl. 2.3L	LH-2.2	1983-88	20 @ 3 & 4
			8 @ 4 & 5
4-cyl. 2.3L	Bendix	1989-92	4
4-cyl. 2.3L	LH-2.4	1989-92	8
V6 2.8L	LH-2.2	1987-90	20 @ 3 & 4
			20 @ 4 & 5
6-cyl. 2.9L	M-1.8	1992	25 @ 1 & 3

AUXILIARY AIR VALVE

Engine	Fuel System	Year	Resistance (ohms)
4-cyl. 2.1L, 2.3L	CIS	1983	40-60
V6 2.8L	CIS	1983-86	40-60

CONTROL PRESSURE REGULATOR

Engine	Fuel System	Year	Resistance (ohms)
4-cyl. 2.1L, 2.3L	CIS	1983	40-60
V6 2.8L:			
Regulator No. 038	CIS	1983-86	20-24
Regulator No. 099	CIS	1983-86	
Above 64°F (18°C)			12.6-15.4
Below 53°F (12°C)			31.5-38.5
Regulator No. 128	CIS	1983-86	
Above 64°F (18°C)			9.8-11.0
Below 53°F (12°C)			19.5-21.7

COMPUTER TIMING ADVANCE

Engine	Year	Transmission	Computer Number	Advance Vacuum Hose Disconnected	W/16 in. Hg Vacuum Applied
2316cc U.S.	1983	MT	499890	6-10	22-40
2316cc U.S.	1983	MT & AT	499802	6-10	30-46
2316cc	1984	MT & AT	—	6-10	22-40
2316cc ex. Turbo	1985	MT & AT	—	6-10	30-40
2316cc LH-FI ex. Turbo	1986-89	MT & AT	—	22-24	48-54

1992

JANUARY

SUN	MON	TUE	WED	THU	FRI	SAT
			1	2	3	4
5	6	7	8	9	10	11
12	13	14	15	16	17	18
19	20	21	22	23	24	25
26	27	28	29	30	31	

FEBRUARY

SUN	MON	TUE	WED	THU	FRI	SAT
						1
2	3	4	5	6	7	8
9	10	11	12	13	14	15
16	17	18	19	20	21	22
22	24	25	26	27	28	29

MARCH

SUN	MON	TUE	WED	THU	FRI	SAT
1	2	3	4	5	6	7
8	9	10	11	12	13	14
15	16	17	18	19	20	21
22	23	24	25	26	27	28
29	30	31				

APRIL

SUN	MON	TUE	WED	THU	FRI	SAT
			1	2	3	4
5	6	7	8	9	10	11
12	13	14	15	16	17	18
19	20	21	22	23	24	25
26	27	28	29	30		

MAY

SUN	MON	TUE	WED	THU	FRI	SAT
					1	2
3	4	5	6	7	8	9
10	11	12	13	14	15	16
17	18	19	20	21	22	23
24/31	25	26	27	28	29	30

JUNE

SUN	MON	TUE	WED	THU	FRI	SAT
	1	2	3	4	5	6
7	8	9	10	11	12	13
14	15	16	17	18	19	20
21	22	23	24	25	26	27
28	29	30				

1992

JULY

SUN	MON	TUE	WED	THU	FRI	SAT
			1	2	3	4
5	6	7	8	9	10	11
12	13	14	15	16	17	18
19	20	21	22	23	24	25
26	27	28	29	30	31	

OCTOBER

SUN	MON	TUE	WED	THU	FRI	SAT
				1	2	3
4	5	6	7	8	9	10
11	12	13	14	15	16	17
18	19	20	21	22	23	24
25	26	27	28	29	30	31

AUGUST

SUN	MON	TUE	WED	THU	FRI	SAT
						1
2	3	4	5	6	7	8
9	10	11	12	13	14	15
16	17	18	19	20	21	22
23/30	24/31	25	26	27	28	29

NOVEMBER

SUN	MON	TUE	WED	THU	FRI	SAT
1	2	3	4	5	6	7
8	9	10	11	12	13	14
15	16	17	18	19	20	21
22	23	24	25	26	27	28
29	30					

SEPTEMBER

SUN	MON	TUE	WED	THU	FRI	SAT
		1	2	3	4	5
6	7	8	9	10	11	12
13	14	15	16	17	18	19
20	21	22	23	24	25	26
27	28	29	30			

DECEMBER

SUN	MON	TUE	WED	THU	FRI	SAT
		1	2	3	4	5
6	7	8	9	10	11	12
13	14	15	16	17	18	19
20	21	22	23	24	25	26
27	28	29	30	31		

Grand Island Public Library